RESEARCH IN PSYCHOLOGY

Readings for the Introductory Course

RESEARCH IN PSYCHOLOGY

Readings for the Introductory Course

Edited by

B. L. Kintz
Western Washington State College

James L. Bruning
Ohio University

Scott, Foresman and Company

Preface

The study of behavior has traditionally been the special domain of the psychologist. Such is not the case today. Chemists and physiologists are turning their attention to the study of learning, memory, and motivation. Biologists and zoologists are investigating a wide range of social behaviors such as aggression, territoriality, and mating. Mathematicians are attempting to simulate thinking, problem solving, and decision making on the computer.

The diversity of this recent interest and the wide variety of data being collected suggests that the world of behavior may soon be incorporated into nearly all of the natural, as well as the social, sciences. And, in turn, new ideas and new findings from other sciences are taking their place beside the traditional concerns of the psychologist. In this context the study of behavior by psychologists takes on exciting new dimensions.

The articles in this book illustrate the various ways in which contemporary psychologists are studying behavior. The collection of readings is divided into eight sections, each representing a major subject area as presented in a typical introductory psychology course. The articles in each section have been selected and presented with the following goals in mind: to familiarize students with research methods appropriate for different areas of psychology; to give students a firsthand acquaintance with primary source materials, both historical and current; to trace the evolution of important concepts in psychology; to raise questions, provoke thought, and encourage critical reading; to accustom students to digging beneath the surface and looking for theoretical implications; to show what is going on at the current growing edges of psychology.

A number of the papers in this book are "classics." These are intended to represent a major beginning for a particular area and to serve as a model of the early work that generated the interest and research that followed. Articles that are representative of more recent research make up the major portion of the book. In cases where a selection represents a major point of view that has proved controversial, papers presenting the opposing points of view have been included. Selections dealing with the traditional areas of "physiological psychology" and "sensory psychology" have been placed in the sections where they seemed most meaningful and relevant, instead of being relegated to a separate section.

Many of the readings have been shortened by deleting some of the more difficult statistical discussions. This has been accomplished without changing the overall tenor of the article or making the result so elementary as to miss the major thrust of the original article. In a few cases complex issues that seem to lead away from the main idea presented in the article have been removed. We hope that in reading these papers, students will catch the flavor of the excitement that is involved in doing original research and following up its implications.

The section introductions are designed to show the relationships between the selected articles. It is hoped that as the student progresses through the studies in each section he will come to see the similarities that tie them together into one coherent whole. Headnotes to the individual selections point out the major thrust of each article and try to clarify any points that we believe might be particularly difficult for beginning students.

An original essay appears at the end of each section, to help students gain a fuller perspective on each of the eight areas, after they have had a chance to read the specific studies. The authors of these essays, each engaged in research in the particular area he is writing about, present some of the major research activities going on in these areas today and suggest what they consider to be important areas for future research. We believe that these original papers represent a unique and valuable feature of the book.

Any book of readings such as this owes most of its value to the authors of the papers that are contained in it. We wish to express our gratitude to the publishers and especially to the authors of the papers that we have included. Each of these authors has taken time to look over our changes, and several have made comments that have aided us in rounding out the complete list.

To the authors of the original essays in this book go our special thanks. We recognize that they have spent a great deal of their time trying to find out just what we had in mind, then much more time writing the essay, and we are grateful for their efforts.

Finally, we would like to express our appreciation to Louise Howe, Marguerite Clark, and Anna Lei for their persistent and welcome suggestions with reference to the choice of the articles for each section, for their help in obtaining permission to use the selected articles, and for their fine editing work that made readable copy out of our sometimes jumbled efforts.

Contents

Part Seven   Personality, Adjustment, and Mental Health   408

Part Eight   Social Behavior   464

RESEARCH IN PSYCHOLOGY

Readings for the Introductory Course

Part One

Psychology as a Science

A most significant event in the history of man's thinking about himself was modern psychologists' proposal that mental affairs can be studied scientifically. Traditionally, mental activity was considered somewhat ephemeral, slightly mystical, very individual, and definitely outside the realm of objective observation. Philosophers had even argued about the location of mind. Aristotle argued that mentation takes place in the most important part of the body—the heart—while Plato believed that the mind resides in the brain.

Modern psychologists have accepted the anatomical evidence that the brain is the main repository of higher central nervous system activity. The physiological behavior of the brain is considered to provide the basis for mental acts and thus for mind. We agree that physical, chemical, and general biological activity of the brain is somehow translated as personality, thinking, character, intelligence, and all the many complex characteristics of the fantastic constellation of organs that make up the human being.

The trend of modern psychological research is toward scientific investigation of how the physical, biological, human organism can be so dynamic as to have such a variety of personal characteristics. How can people who look reasonably similar—who have two arms, two legs, two eyes; who are symmetrical in form—behave so very differently? How can persons from even the same families behave so differently? What aspects of being born, of being raised and educated, of becoming an adult, produce the amazing variability seen among people?

Scientific procedures are essentially skeptical and inquisitive. The scientist is not willing to accept statements and beliefs of others, regardless of their positions of authority and prestige, unless he can test the logic of the statements and prove for himself that the "truths" are really true. Statements of various leaders and other eminent persons as to why people act as they do are not sufficient. The psychologist engages in research in the hope that he can find answers to these questions, answers that will provide insight into the mysteries of mind and of human behavior.

All investigations into the psychological activities of people are concerned with two sides of the psychological coin: (a) the hereditary beginnings of each human being—his genetic heritage that is passed along in the form of physical material, having as its medium the DNA molecule; and (b) the relationships that occur after birth, leading one person to learn to act differently from another. Environmental influences such as family members, friends, national culture and traditions, politics, religion, and the many teachers that an individual has all exert strong pressures on the person and result in major modifications of his behavior.

How then does the field of psychology differ from other scientific areas such as biology, chemistry, and sociology? Psychology descended from philosophy, as did all other major academic fields. The distinction between philosophy and her offspring, the sciences, is most clearly shown by the great dependence of philosophy upon logic and argument to prove her points. Many are the tragic examples of falsehoods being shown to be "logically true." Indeed, this is the major problem with the argumentative approach. A good strong logical argument can "prove" that untruths are true.

The scientists, on the other hand, insist that what they call truths be clearly visible to anyone who cares to look. Observation and confirmation take the place of argumentation. This does not mean that scientists do not indulge in occasional bouts of steamy rhetoric. Most scientists are philosophers too, and they delight in using clouds of words to discuss their particular pet projects. However—and here is the important point—scientists are not satisfied with such arguments until the observable facts are arrayed in plain sight for all to see. Far more than replacing philosophy as a superior method, science is built upon the firm foundation of philosophy and is superior in many ways because it adds its strengths to those of the older philosophy.

The articles in the first section of this book clarify the methods that are called scientific, methods that have come to be widely used by modern psychologists.

Historical and Modern Conceptions of Psychology

Kenneth W. Spence

Throughout the history of scientific psychology runs a recurrent question asking why psychology hasn't achieved the status of other branches of science. Why is it that we do not have precisely stated laws of the kind that were developed by physicists hundreds of years ago? Why cannot we state psychological reactions in the same manner that chemists are able to state the reactions of chemicals when mixed and intermingled?

Kenneth Spence wanted the scientific community to recognize that the methods of science could be applied to psychological phenomena with rewarding results. He was interested in trying to continue the laboratory tradition begun by the German psychologists such as Wundt, Fechner, Helmholtz, and Ebbinghaus. He also wanted to develop certain approaches to the study of psychological phenomena that would bring about tangible results in the form of laws. The dual goals of arguing that the methods of science could and should be applied to psychology and that lawful kinds of behavior would perforce result from such endeavors, were to occupy most of Spence's professional life.

In this paper Spence points out several historical antecedents of modern psychology. He lists and describes four different kinds of laws that psychologists should try to state. Then he makes a strong plea for patience on the part of those who demand quick and large-scale practical results from the scientific laboratory study of psychological phenomena. It will take a long time and great deal of effort before the current approaches to investigations of mind and behavior can be expected to bring such complex topics to a level of understanding that permits the development of precisely stated laws. Success will come as a direct result of patience, diligence, and the acquisition of adequate research funds and other assistance.

Psychology as Science

Writing in a textbook in 1892, William James expressed himself as follows concerning the status of psychology as a natural science:

A string of raw facts; a little gossip and wrangle about opinions; a little classification and generalization on the mere descriptive level; a strong prejudice that we have states of mind, and that our brain conditions them: but not a single law in the sense in which physics shows us laws, not a single proposition from which any consequence can causally be deduced. We don't even know the terms between which the elementary laws would obtain if we had them. This is no science, it is only the hope of a science (1892, p. 468).

One suspects that the more optimistic psychologists of the period shrugged off this none too complimentary evaluation of their field with a variety of excuses such as, for example, that psychology was, as an experimental endeavor, still very much in its infancy. Indeed, if one measured from the time of founding of the first psychological laboratories in Germany during the seventies, psychology was less than twenty-five years old. Or, possibly, the defense was based on an appeal to the complexity of the phenomena psychologists sought to investigate and to their relative inaccessibility to observation.

At the time the claim that not much could be expected of as young a science as psychology was a reasonable one. After all there must be a period of purely empirical fact-finding in order to provide a sufficiently comprehensive set of low-order laws before the more abstract, integrative aspects

Excerpts from Chapter I, "Historical and Modern Conceptions of Psychology," of Behavior Theory and Conditioning, *by Kenneth W. Spence. Copyright © 1956 by Yale University Press. Reprinted by permission of Yale University Press.*

of science can be expected to appear. A quarter of a century was, perhaps, too short a period to develop much in the way of a widely accepted systematic body of generalizations of any scope.

But what about now, . . . some sixty-odd years later and after almost a century of experimental study of psychological phenomena? Does psychology qualify as a natural science today? While it is probably safe to say that some areas of psychology have attained a respectable level of scientific development, it would nevertheless have to be admitted that much of the field does not qualify. . . .

That the progress of psychology toward the goal of being a natural science has been slow and, even to some psychologists, disappointing is readily apparent. It is reflected, for example, in a comment that E. G. Boring of Harvard University made in the opening paragraph of his book, *The Physical Dimensions of Consciousness*. After calling attention to the fact that Descartes's dichotomy between body and mind occurred just at the time that science was beginning the development that was to make it the dominating influence in modern civilization, Boring wrote as follows:

We all know how successful the physical sciences have been and we can also see that biology has prospered in abandoning a vitalism and identifying itself with the physical side of the Cartesian dichotomy. If Descartes was right, if there are these two worlds, then the success of science in attacking the one forms a challenge for the creation of a science of the other. . . . Yet, if psychology is coordinate with physics and if the scientific method is applicable to both, then it seems strange that psychology has come such a little way when physics has ramified into many fields and has come so far (1933, p. 3).

While not a historian or methodologist and hence not in a position to base my beliefs on careful comparative study of the developments in psychology during its first hundred years with those in other sciences during a comparable period, I nevertheless share this view that the development of psychology as a natural science has been much slower than might have been expected. Especially does this seem to me to be the case when we consider some of the advantages that a science beginning in the late nineteenth century would have as compared with physics, which, as an experimental science, began some three hundred years earlier.

*   *   *

In addition to starting out in an atmosphere highly supportive of its endeavors, psychology also had the benefit of all that had been learned about the methodology of science in three hundred years. Thus it had available many examples of the problems faced by scientists at various stages of development of their field and the manner in which they were approached and solved. The role of measurement and experimental control, the place of concepts and laws, and the functions that theories play in the ordering of knowledge had all been revealed many times over. Many of these scientific tools, particularly techniques of measurements and experimentation, were directly applicable to the problems of psychology and could be and were taken over and used. Moreover, the psychologist has recently had the advantage of the analysis of these methods by the philosophers of science, whose writings have helped greatly to clarify not only the relations among the different kinds of concepts employed in science but also the relation of the language of science to its empirical basis—the events in the consciousness or sense experience of the individual scientist.

Undoubtedly there are other advantages that psychology has had as a consequence of its late start, not the least of which would be the relatively greater support, financial and otherwise, that all scientific endeavors have received from our society in recent years. But enough has been cited, I believe, to indicate the basis of the great expectations that one might legitimately have held and the consequent disappointment that many have felt in the progress of psychology as a natural science.

*   *   *

Classical Psychology

Scientific experimental psychology as an independent discipline had its beginning in the work of men whose original training was in the biological sciences, particularly physiology. Thus the immediate forerunners were such well-known physiologists as Johannes Mueller, Fechner, and Helmholtz, while the first acknowledged experimental psychologist, Wilhelm Wundt, obtained a medical degree and taught physiology at Heidelberg for some years prior to turning, in 1870, more specifically to what he regarded as the study of psychological phenomena. While the interests of Wundt and his co-workers were, in part, concerned with the mediating neural processes underlying psychological or mental phenomena, particularly the sensory mechanisms, they considered that a portion of their work called for a uniquely new and independent science, psychology. This aspect of their work, which had to do with the mind or consciousness per se, was dominated by ideas and concepts that had their origins in the writings of such philosophers as Descartes and the early British empiricists, Locke, Berkeley, and Hume, and the later ideas of the British associationists. As Boring (1933) has pointed out, the establishment of the dichotomy between mind and body by Descartes provided the raison d'être of an independent science of psychology. Descartes introduced in his method of contemplative "meditation" the basic method of studying the mind, and he himself employed this earliest form of introspection to study the higher forms of cognition and the more complex emotional states. Interest shifted in the subsequent writings of the English empiricists from these central states to the peripherally aroused, simpler mental states known as sensations.

Between the psychological writings of these early philosophers and the beginning of experimental psychology a period of approximately 150 years elapsed, during which there was great interest in the mind and considerable writing and speculation concerning its nature. It was in this period that the conception subsequently known as classical psychology arose. Stemming from the writings of the English empiricists, classical psychology had its beginning in the speculative writings on the human mind of the English physician-philosopher Hartley and the Scottish philosopher Thomas Brown. Its pre-experimental culmination is to be found in the sensationistic-associationistic psychologies of the British associationists James Mill, his son John Stuart Mill, and Alexander Bain.

Wundt's new experimental psychology was essentially one with this early speculative classical psychology. The main differences were that more precise experimental procedures were introduced and considerable attention was given to the laws connecting the mental phenomena with the environment on the one hand and with their physiological correlates on the other. As such the work of Wundt and his successors in the German laboratories essentially constituted the final, experimental phase of classical psychology. This period came to an end in the first decade of the present century with the rise of functional psychology and behaviorism.

* * *

Structuralism and Phenomenalism

In its later phases, classical experimental psychology became subdivided into two main branches, structuralism and phenomenalism. Structuralism represented a later development of the elementarism of Wundt. In its final stages, as represented by the work of Titchener in this country, structuralism belatedly came to the realization that the concept of sensation is a logical, systematic construct and not a raw datum. In its place the structuralist substituted as the end product of introspective analysis, first, the attributes of sensations and, subsequently, the so-called dimensions of consciousness: quality, intensity, extensity, and protensity. The final form of this reconstructed structuralism, as exemplified by Boring (1933), considered its main task to be that of understanding the physiology of these dimensions of consciousness.

The second branch, phenomenalism, or as it has also been called, phenomenology, had its origins in the work of Brentano, one of Wundt's chief rivals. Brentano rejected sensory contents as the materials of psychology and instead proposed that psychical acts such as perceiving, judging, relating, recalling, and so forth were what was revealed by introspection. In his formulation the focus of attention shifted from the peripheral events back to the central regions of the mind. Subsequently the work of the Würzburg group on thinking and the Gestalt psychologists on perception brought out further objections to the type of analytical introspection employed by the Wundtians and the later structuralists.

The Würzburg psychologists were unable, under the particular set their observers employed, to reduce the experiences occurring during thinking to sensory materials as had the Wundtians. Indeed they found it difficult to establish descriptive categories in this area since our vocabulary is woefully inadequate to describe and communicate the contents of experience or processes occurring during such activities. The Gestalt psychologists also attacked the classical notion of perceptual experience as being compounded of sensations and criticized this conception as resulting from the suggestive influence of the knowledge from physiological psychology concerning the structure of the sensory mechanisms. The sensationistic interpretation of perception was suggested, they claimed, by the knowledge of the mosaic structure of the sensory surfaces and the afferent nerves with their bundles of fibers. The Gestaltists pleaded for an unbiased description of immediate experience, one that was free from any systematic preconceptions such as those held by the sensationists. Phenomenological introspection aimed to provide such an initial description of consciousness. It employed terms from everyday language, even slang words. While such pure description has its virtues, especially in a young science, sooner or later some kind of generalization of the initial descriptions must be attempted if the systematic kind of knowledge science seeks is to be obtained. Whereas structuralism tried and failed to formulate a system of constructs and laws of mental analysis and synthesis that gained general acceptance, phenomenalism never succeeded in providing any degree of integration of its observations.

* * *

Functionalism

Not only was a goodly portion of the first thirty years of work thus lost but still another twenty years of polemics were required before psychologists could concentrate their full energies on the task of building an objective science of behavior. The period 1900 to 1920 witnessed the rebellion against the classical orthodoxy. On the Continent the Würzburg group took the lead, questioning the adequacy of the classical type of introspection, while in this country the group of psychologists known as the functionalists was in the vanguard. If this were primarily a book about the history of psychology, which it is not, it would be appropriate at this point to trace the antecedents of functionalism to such influences as the biological theory of evolution, the writings of the early American psychologists, particularly William James, and last but by no means least, the pragmatic temper of America with its interest in success and the practical application of knowledge as a means of assuring it.

Functional psychology, as a formal school, had its birth at the University of Chicago under the guidance of John Dewey and James Rowland Angell. One of the leaders of functionalism, indeed its most effective spokesman, Angell was extremely influential both in his capacity as director of the psychological laboratory at Chicago for twenty-six years and in his writings. It was in his laboratory that Watson, his student, began his animal studies and developed the ideas that led eventually to behaviorism. Behaviorism is itself, of course, a functional psychology but one that, as we shall see, went beyond the functionalism of Dewey and Angell.

Objecting to the classical psychologist's preoccupation with the structural composition of consciousness, that is, with the question of *what* consciousness *is,* Angell and his group proposed to shift the focus of attention to the problems of how consciousness operates and what uses or functions it serves. The point of view they adopted was a Darwinian one in which the different operations of consciousness, sense perception, imagination, and emotion, were all regarded as different instances of organic adaptation to the environment. Interest was thus directed to the overt behavior of the organism in relation to its environment as well as to the functioning of the mind. However, the functionalists did not propose to neglect consciousness, and they continued to regard introspection, the direct examination of one's own mental processes, as the fundamental method of psychology.

This new functional orientation led to a rapid expansion of the kinds of phenomena that psychologists sought to investigate. Being concerned with the problem of the adjustment of the organism they became interested in the adaptive capacities of the individual and methods of measuring them. Thus was set in motion the development of mental tests and their subsequent use in a variety of situations, particularly in education. Interest in adaptive functions also led to a stressing of research on the genetic and developmental aspects of behavior both in the individual and in the species. Studies of the behavior of children were instituted, and laboratory experimentation with animals, which had just started with Thorndike's researches on cats and dogs in puzzle boxes at Columbia, was taken up with great enthusiasm at Chicago. Watson established an animal laboratory there and began the series of studies of animal behavior that led him eventually to his behavioristic position.

Behaviorism

Watson came to his behavioristic position primarily from his interest in animal research. There he had found that he could pursue quite successfully the study of behavior, even the traditional problems of sensory discrimination, without having to bring in conscious material. He simply proposed to extend the same objective behavioral methods of observation to the study of human behavior.

Watson's declaration of independence from the consciousness-dominated psychology of the period provoked a stormy period of polemical activity, which, as it continued, was marked by more and more extreme statements on both sides. If one goes back to Watson's initial formulation, the 1913 *Psychological Review* article entitled "Psychology as the Behaviorist Views It," it may be seen that he did not deny the existence of consciousness, as has sometimes been represented, but simply proposed to use it in the same way that other scientists do. His statement is so clear I should like to quote portions of it:

Psychology, as the behaviorist views it, is a purely objective, experimental branch of natural science which needs introspection as little as do the sciences of chemistry and physics. . . . It can dispense with consciousness in a psychological sense. The separate observation of "states of consciousness" is, on this assumption, no more a part of the task of the psychologist than of the physicist. We might call this the return to a nonreflective and naive use of consciousness. In this sense consciousness may be said to be the instrument or tool with which all scientists work (1913, p. 176).

In other words Watson was arguing that, contrary to the belief of the introspective psychologists, psychology does not, or at least should not, have a unique subject matter, mental or conscious events as contrasted with matter or physical events. Rather, he insisted, the data of the psychologist are of exactly the same kind as those of the physical scientist. That is to say, immediate experience, the initial matrix out of which all sciences develop, is no longer to be conceived as the special province of psychology. The psychologist, like other natural scientists, simply must take consciousness for granted and proceed to his task of describing certain happenings occurring in it and discovering and formulating the nature of the relationships holding among them. The subject matter of psychology is exactly the same *in kind* then as all other sciences; any differentiation among the sciences is merely a matter of convenience, a division of scientific labor resorted to as the amount of detailed knowledge increases beyond the capacity of a single person's grasp.

* * *

Modern Objective Psychology

I should like to turn now to an analysis of the general conception of their science that the majority of psychologists in this country hold today. While behavioristic in outlook, this conception is probably better described as objective psychology. As such it does not require adherence to the orthodox doctrines of Watson. Moreover, it provides within its framework not only for alternative theoretical formulations but also for a purely em-

pirical approach such as that espoused by most of the psychologists interested primarily in applied problems. Focusing attention as it does on the behavior of the organism in relation to two other classes of events, the environmental surroundings and the organic conditions of the organism, the concepts or variables of this modern conception fall into three groups or classes: (1) Response (R) variables: qualitative descriptions or measurements of the behavior properties of living organisms. (2) Stimulus (S) variables: qualitative descriptions or measurements of events or properties of the physical and social environment in which the organism behaves. (3) Organic (O) variables: qualitative descriptions or measurements of the anatomical and physiological properties of organisms.

Like every other scientist, the psychologist is interested in discovering and formulating the relations or laws holding among these different classes of variables. The several types of laws with which psychologists have been concerned are as follows: (I) $R = f(R)$; (II) $R = f(S)$; (III) $O = f(S)$; (IV) $R = f(O)$.

The first class, $R = f(R)$ laws, describes relations between different attributes or properties of behavior; they tell us which behavior traits are associated. This type of law is investigated extensively in the fields of intelligence and personality testing, and the laws that have been discovered have formed the basis of much of our technology in the areas of guidance, counseling, and clinical diagnosis. These empirical R-R relations also form the starting point for the theoretical constructs of the factor analysts. Beginning with the intercorrelations among a large number of test (response) scores these theorists have attempted by means of their mathematical methods to discover a minimum set of hypothetical factors that could account for the variance in the behavioral measures. The so-called field theory of Lewin (1935) was also concerned primarily with this R-R type of law, his theoretical concepts being introduced in terms of response variables and eventually returning to other response variables.

The second class of laws, $R = f(S)$, relates response measures as the dependent variable to the determining environmental conditions. There are really two subclasses of laws here, one relating to the environmental events of the present and the second to events of the past. The first subclass includes the traditional laws of psychophysics, perception, reaction time, and emotions. These laws describe how behavior varies with changes in the present physical stimulus. The theories that have been investigated by this kind of law are primarily of the reductionistic type, involving hypotheses as to the nature of the underlying neurophysiological-mediating mechanisms.

Insofar as the behavior at any moment is a function of environmental events that occurred prior to the time of observation one is dealing with laws of the second subclass. The most familiar instance of this kind of relation is represented by the so-called learning curve, which relates the response variable to previous environmental events of a specified character. Laws of primary and secondary motivation are other examples that fall in this group. These laws have provided the starting point of most theories of learning, although some learning theories have been initiated on the basis of neurophysiological laws.

*   *   *

. . . Whereas the term "theory" in modern physics refers to a system of constructs that serves to interrelate sets of already established laws, in psychology the term typically is applied to a device employed to aid in the formulation of the empirical laws describing a realm of observable phenomena.

*   *   *

Overemphasis of Practical and Real Problems

*   *   *

This brings me to the present-day scene in psychology. Early in the chapter I stated that an analysis of the contemporary factors retarding the development of psychology as a natural science required a degree of diplomacy far beyond my limited skill in such matters. And yet I feel I would be remiss if I did not, at least, call attention to what appear to be at present two major deterrents to progress toward the establishment of a scientific body of psychological knowledge. The first of these retarding influences is reflected in certain attitudes that are exhibited in the area of psychological theorizing, namely the tendency to criticize theoretical concepts in this field as being too elementaristic, too mechanistic, and as failing to portray the real essence or true nature of man's behavior. In particular, these critics have complained about the artificiality of the objective types of concepts such as those offered by the behavioristic psychologist. Thus they talk about such things as the impoverishment of the mind

and object to what is described as a lack of warmth and glowing particulars in the behaviorist's account of psychological events.

To the writer such criticisms reflect essentially a lack of appreciation as to the difference between *scientific knowledge* of an event and other kinds of knowledge, e.g., the kinds of knowledge the novelist and poet portray. Either by reason of their training or because of their basically nonscientific interests these critics have apparently never really understood the *abstract* character of the scientific account of any phenomenon. The only reply that can be made to such a critic is to point out that the scientist's interests just happen to be different from his. There are, of course, other perfectly legitimate interpretations of nature and man than the scientific one, and each has its right to be pursued. The science-oriented psychologist merely asks that he be given the same opportunity to develop a scientific account of his phenomena that his colleagues in the physical and biological fields have had. If there are aspects of human behavior for which such an account cannot ever be developed, there are not, so far as I know, any means of finding this out without a try. Unfortunately, the attitudes of too many psychologists with regard to this matter are not such as are likely to lead them to the discovery of such knowledge. The difficulty, in part, is that too many individuals whose interests are not those of the scientist have become psychologists. If these persons were aware of their different interests and were appreciative of what the behavior scientist is attempting to do, the kinds of knowledge he is attempting to build, much needless controversy would be eliminated.

The second factor in the current scene that I believe is somewhat unfortunate is the tendency of the great majority of persons working in the field to evaluate the significance of psychological concepts and research in terms of the degree to which they are applicable to some immediate practical or technological problem rather than the extent to which they enter into or contribute toward the development of a body of lawful relations of whatever degree of abstractness.

It is easy, of course, to understand why this predilection exists. The psychologist is under very pressing demands to help solve serious and important technological problems, particularly in the case of behavior disorders with all of the human suffering they cause. But, unfortunately, psychological phenomena are extremely complex. The behavior of living organisms, especially that of man, involves such a great variety of determining conditions and exhibits such a multiplicity of forms as to defy easy analysis and hence the discovery of lawful relations. As a consequence we find the psychologist being asked to cope with problems of immediate practical import, such as mental illness and juvenile delinquency, long before he has the adequate means, i.e., the laws, with which to do so.

The unfortunate situation in which the psychologist finds himself may perhaps be more vividly portrayed by the following imaginary happening. Suppose by some very strange set of circumstances that Galileo and his co-workers were somehow brought back to life in our modern world and were confronted with the wondrous array of machinery, electronic and otherwise, that exists today. Further, let us suppose that all the knowledge of the physical sciences that had been gained in the meantime had somehow been lost and that there were no engineers or technicians around to appeal to for aid. Consider now the plight Galileo and his colleagues would be in if, as physicists, they were called upon to help keep these devices in good working order. It is not difficult to imagine that the degree of chaos and disorder would soon outstrip even that currently exhibited by human beings, and that repair shops or institutes for the mechanically defective would in a very short time be overflowing with devices exhibiting serious forms of maladjustment.

In this predicament two courses of action would be open to our primitive physicists. They could, on the one hand, concentrate on the practical problems and attempt by trial-and-error methods to work out superficially understood recipes or rules of thumb for manipulating the various parts of the gadgets in an effort to keep them performing after a fashion. Or they could direct their main energies to the task of discovering the basic laws governing the behavior of the devices. But the latter undoubtedly would require a turning away from these complex devices to the investigation of simpler phenomena that would appear to have little or no obvious connection with the more complex. It is not difficult for the psychologist with similar interests to imagine the attitudes that the reincarnated Galileo would elicit in society and in his more repair-conscious colleagues if he were to insist on turning his back on the complex machines and start measuring the time it took little balls to roll down an inclined plane. In place of the scoffings of the scholastics who,

because of a frame of reference that evaluated everything in relation to some grand rational synthesis, couldn't understand the significance of the empirical laws of motion, Galileo would find himself confronted with the criticism that his activities had little or no significance for the *really* important problems of life, such as, for example, keeping the television and radio sets in good working order.

While fully recognizing that my imaginary example is probably overdrawn and that it could be the source of some quite erroneous implications, I nevertheless believe that it does point up an unfortunate overemphasis in psychology today. This is that far too many psychologists, under the pressures of the immediate practical problems and also, I fear, driven by an overzealous and self-conscious sense of professionalism, have adopted as the criterion of what is significant in their endeavors only that which gives the appearance of being immediately useful rather than the scientific criterion of whether the ideas or activities lead to the discovery of laws and the formulation of systematic theories of a comprehensive nature. Or, to put it another way, too much of the time and energy of too many psychologists is currently being spent on engineering rather than basic, scientific problems. Moreover, this is being done in spite of the fact that the history of other sciences has repeatedly shown that the range and adequacy of any engineering program rests upon the degree of development of a basic system of laws.

In concluding the discussion of this topic, I should like to be especially careful to make clear that I do not wish to imply that significant research in the scientific sense cannot be carried out in applied situations, e.g., in the factory or in the classroom. If the investigation is properly oriented many instances of the lower order types of laws, at least, can be formulated on the basis of research conducted under such conditions. . . .

* * *

REFERENCES

Boring, E. G. *The physical dimensions of consciousness.* New York: Appleton-Century-Crofts, 1933.

James, W. *Textbook of psychology: Briefer course.* New York: Holt, Rinehart & Winston, 1892.

Watson, J. B. Psychology as the behaviorist views it. *Psychological Review,* 1913, **20,** 158–177.

2

E. L. Thorndike:
The Psychologist as Professional Man of Science

Geraldine Jonçich

If any man can be described as the father of American scientific psychology, it is E. L. Thorndike. He formulated the basic ideas underlying the work that later psychologists such as Hull, Skinner, and Spence expanded into the major framework of scientific psychology. The early years of this century were exciting: Freud was developing his psychoanalytic theories, and the great German laboratories, under the direction of Wundt and Müller, were full of activity. Drawing on this strong European background, Thorndike began to build the structure of modern American psychology.

This article presents a portrait of this outstanding psychologist and of the era in which he was a central figure. The glimpses into his family background, early training, and especially his tremendous zeal and enthusiasm regarding his research and writing indicate some of the excitement involved in the creative work of the researcher.

During the celebration of Thorndike's twenty-fifth year at Teachers College, Columbia psychologist James McKeen Cattell quoted William James to the effect that E. L. Thorndike, more than anyone else he knew, had that objectivity essential to scientific work. And the introduction that James wrote for Thorndike's *The Elements of Psychology* seemed to Cornell psychologist E. B. Titchener to be so extreme in its "unstinted praise" that he even questioned its tastefulness in his review of the book that was written for the prestigious British journal, *Mind*—a review so sarcastic that Cattell protested to the editors of *Mind*. Titchener apparently shared fellow-psychologist James Mark Baldwin's view that if William James had a fault, it was his generous overestimation of others, or the view of American writer John Jay Chapman, who fondly noted of James' judgments that the last book he had read was always a great work and the last person he had seen a wonderful man. Whether or not James' assessment is overly generous and uncritical, in Thorndike's case, remains an open question. What appears a clear and indisputable fact is that James was expressing a judgment of Thorndike—one focusing upon his taste and temperament for scientific work—that precisely matched Thorndike's own self-image. Over his entire career Thorndike tried to guide his behavior by the "scientist" model because this

was what he wanted most to be, this was what he was convinced he could be, and this was what he thought he was.

As a professional man, Thorndike can be said to have occupied two other chairs: One is, of course, the psychologist's; he was also the educationist, concerned with professionalizing teaching and school management. Nevertheless, his position as professional scientist was the more important one to him. It overrode the others because it incorporated both while connecting him with a whole system of scientific expertise and its high prestige. There are innumerable indications of Thorndike's preference, but only one will be indicated here. Note the character of Thorndike's response to Titchener's attack upon *The Elements of Psychology*. To Titchener's warning that his book would receive harsh words, Thorndike replied in July 1905:

I do, of course, regret if I have fallen in your estimation with respect to accuracy of scholarship. However I cherish hopes of rising again if you will read my "Measurements of Twins" (to be out

From American Psychologist, *Vol. 23 (1968), 434–446. Copyright 1968 by the American Psychological Association, and reproduced by permission.*

soon) which is 75 pages of solid accuracy and of which there were 40 pages more accurate still but too expensive to print. I confess to two points of view—practical expediency in books for beginners and the limit of exactitude in contributions to my equals and superiors.

* * *

Titchener's reply failed to assure Thorndike's hurt from an attack that he interpreted as impugning his scientific integrity. He wrote a final time, opening with a deceptively offhand reference to his scientific enterprise and closing with a pious withdrawal to the scientific ethic of impersonality:

I must apologize for not answering your letter promptly, but I have been simply absorbed in justifying by empirical trials a new measure of correlation which I hope is an improvement on the Pearson coefficient, and have hardly thought of anything else.

I confess that you puzzle me still and that to all appearances you seem to have tried to lead English readers into the belief that I am prominent among psychologists for commercialism and carelessness. . . .

I would rather make a million errors in names, dates, references and the like than make such insinuations as you made unless I knew absolutely that the impression they would leave was in exact accord with the fact. Nor would I make them unless there was some clear benefit to the science.

However in my view of life it is all a small matter. The best thing about scientific work is that it may be impersonal. I do the best I can and if you think I misuse my time and effort so much the worse for me if you are right, and for you, if you are wrong. . . .

Of course I shall not write to Mind, either attacking you or defending the "Elements" I never used a scientific journal for the defense of my own or [for] an attack upon another man's personal judgments.

> *Yours truly*
> *Edward L. Thorndike*

Obviously, science is not an impersonal activity; what Thorndike was expressing was an ethic and ideology enjoying wide acceptance among his professional associates. It is inconceivable, then, that a Thorndike would ever echo Freud's self-description: "I am not really a man of science, not an observer, not an experimenter, and not a thinker. I am nothing but by temperament a conquistador —an adventurer."

* * *

To recapitulate, there is in Thorndike that certainty that he (like any trained investigator of human behavior) has as his major professional identification that of scientist *sui generis,* and that his primary reference group is the whole community of science. The explanation of this certainty inheres, it seems, in the greater (and, by today's standards, remarkable) cohesiveness of the scientific community in the late nineteenth century— when Thorndike left Wesleyan University a graduate in the classics and opted for science by selecting psychology at Harvard and Columbia. To sketch out an account that will explain this communality of science—using Thorndike for illustration—is the aim of the rest of this article. The responsible factors, in ascending order of importance, are (*a*) personalistic and sociological characteristics held in common by Thorndike's generation of scientists; (*b*) the recency and incompleteness of American science's attempts to professionalize itself; (*c*) the dominance of positivism; and (*d*) the messianic zeal of the "sciences of human nature" and especially of psychology.

Personal and Background Characteristics

In 1927, E. K. Strong asked Thorndike to take his Strong Vocational Interest Blank. His profile of scores showed a marked interest in the quantitative, a manipulative interest in ideas, a rather small interest in people, and a very low concern with objects. He shared most of the characteristics which Strong and later testers found associated with careers in mathematics and accounting, science and engineering. Had personality inventories been more widely applied to his generation, it seems more than likely that such a temperamental characteristic as Thorndike's preference for solitary work would have been found to have marked the whole scientific community then, as it does today. Lacking the evidence, however, we turn to factors of background—to find that psychologists typically shared common origins and a body of common experiences with the generality of other scientists.

Thorndike's may be called the "transitional generation" of men of science; they were the accommodation group, forced to adjust to an America in flux and tending to make similar decisions along similar career lines. They contrast significantly with scientists born before 1865 or so, men whose backgrounds and range of choices better describe them as the "security generation."

*   *   *

In 1884, Reverend Thorndike moved his family, including ten-year-old Edward, to Lowell, Massachusetts. For a community of 60,000 people, there were 30 churches, but it was the factory chimney, not the steeple, that dominated the Lowell skyline. Most scientists of Thorndike's generation still came from northeastern America, but their boyhoods were spent in similar mill-town surroundings, for when Thorndike entered college, New England alone led every country in the world in the per capita value of its manufactures. Like his fellows in science, Thorndike was of Yankee stock, but the decline of the "old-English" strain was obvious, for the cities and mill towns attracted huge numbers of immigrants. In 1800, Everett's population was 90 per cent of English ancestry; by Thorndike's time 25 per cent were immigrants and another 25 per cent were the children of immigrants.

Such population diversity, plus the secularizing influence of an urbanizing, industrializing economy, meant a less fundamentalistic, less secure Protestantism. This consequence was directly pertinent to our population of scientists, for the striking fact is that a clergyman's household, combined with a New England setting, was the best predictor of a future career in science. Indeed, among Americans born around 1870, as was Thorndike, the proportion which became notable and who were sons of clergymen was twice as large as the combined total coming from all the other professions.

Thorndike's was a day when organized religion was nonetheless steadily losing stature in the nation's social and intellectual life, when theology (like medicine) was becoming a specialized study and not a part of general education, when science was usurping its place in academic disputations and attracting college graduates away from ministerial careers. This was not, however, a day of atheism; most academic scientists of Thorndike's generation—while rejecting their father's careers and liberalizing their own confessional associations —were apparently quite sincere in professing Christianity *and* the new biology, geology, physics, psychology. Thorndike was atypical here because his conversion to science was preceded by his adopting an exclusively naturalistic view of man; he once called agnostics, like himself, "conscientious objec-

tors to immortality." Yet, like certain other wayward sons of the clergy, he (guiltily perhaps) infused his work with messianic fervor, so that science itself took on a crusadelike character. Moreover, in contending that agnostic scientists usually rate very highly for their private and public virtues, Thorndike was expressing the common tendency of nineteenth-century science to moralize about its advancement. Indeed, there has been a pronounced tendency in America to moralize all activities, all knowledge! "The proper study of nature begets devout affection [and] a true naturalist cannot be a bad man," one reads in *Knickerbocker* magazine in 1845. Similarly, General Francis A. Walker, President of M.I.T., told a gathering in 1893 that the scientific men of America were surpassed, if indeed approached, by no other group in their "sincerity, simplicity, fidelity and generosity of character, in nobility of aims and earnestness of effort."

*   *   *

The Professionalization of Science

A common characteristic of turn-of-the-century science in America was its heavy academic involvement. Government science was small, and industrial laboratories were still in the future. Full-time research was more rare in the United States than in Europe; Germany, in 1913, had six times as many research men in proportion to population as did the United States. In 1910, Cattell calculated that barely 1000 Americans were occupied with serious research, and then, on the average, for only half-time. Only one of the 38 physicists founding the American Physical Society in 1899 was not an academician, and every one of the psychologists selected for eminence in Cattell's first ranking in 1904 did some teaching.

Academe was, moreover, a setting where generalists and generalism had long reigned, where the standard of the broadly learned scholar hung on into the modern age of specialism. Since the typical college remained small—about 150 students— the philosopher-generalist had an employment advantage over the psychologist-specialist. For example, he would teach more subjects and rarely hounded the president for research time, laboratory space, and costly equipment. Small wonder that in 1898, Thorndike contemplated medical studies, or even a second doctorate in psychology. For months his only offer of employment was from the Oshkosh (Wisconsin) State Normal School, and

Teachers College would not even accept his offer to teach there at half pay!

*   *   *

In 1900, Thorndike was assisting Cattell in the editorship of *Popular Science Monthly* and *Science* when he met biologist Jacques Loeb at the Marine Biological Laboratory at Woods Hole. As Thorndike recorded it, "Loeb . . . told me I was a damned fool, that I was spoiling myself and ought to be shut up and kept at research work." He decided that Loeb was "largely right," and dropped this sideline; nevertheless, even this brief editorial experience only reinforced Thorndike's sense of familiarity with, and participation in, the totality of American science.

Thorndike was much less the committee man, the organizational figure, than was Cattell; despite this, he also became conspicuous in scientific circles. He was the first of the younger experimental psychologists to be elected (in 1917) to the National Academy of Sciences and attended its sessions fairly often. Like the Academy's membership, the leadership of AAAS has been dominated by chemistry, physics, astronomy, and geology; half of its presidents to date have come from these fields. Still, in 1934 Thorndike was chosen President of AAAS; except for economist W. C. Mitchell in 1938, no other social scientist headed this professional organization for the whole body of scientists since Thorndike's tenure until 1966, when Don Price became President.

Positivism—A Common Mental Set

In common with every working scientist, Thorndike constructed his experimental situations according to his own theoretical postulates; when possessed of even a rudimentary theory, he tried to test the predictions emanating from that theory. It is such choices of experimental situation that decrease the probability that one theorist will directly test the major premises of another's theory. The collecting and interpreting enterprise itself, however, must conform to certain expectations held in common with other scientists, for science is in part an attitude of mind shared by all its practitioners—even when they are ill-put or loath to articulate it.

Speaking of their college days together, Thorndike's long-time friend and associate, Robert S. Woodworth, said of him, "His sane positivism was a very salutary influence for a somewhat speculative individual like myself. . . ." The modifier "sane," conforms to Thorndike's own self-perception of his moderate, "common-sensical" intellectual approach in the quest for natural laws. In 1941, in recommending Thorndike for the William James Lectureship, Edwin G. Boring was impressed with his continued mental vigor and described Thorndike's latest research as "a very elementary positivism but a very interesting approach in the way it works out." The modifier here, "elementary," undoubtedly reflects the progress of philosophical sophistication about scientific method over the intervening 45 years.

Even before his conversion to psychology, Thorndike was victim of the optimistic and widespread assumptions of nineteenth century positivism. Even his college literary exercises revealed a hard tone, a disdain for the sentimental, a total confidence in dispassionate analysis ("the emotionally indifferent attitude of the scientific observer," he called it), the surety of the existence of "truth" and its ineluctable serviceability. Nature is above all, he wrote in his first article addressed to teachers, *"a thing to study, to know about, to see through."* He abhorred vagueness, and for indeterminacy he substituted positivism: Things do not happen by mere chance in human life any more than in the fall of an apple or an eclipse of the moon; behind the seemingly endless variety of human affairs there are invariably acting laws which make possible the advance of human control by reason.

That knowledge is power, that truth can be known, that facts can be trusted—these approached copybook maxims in Thorndike's youth, and such ideas . . . [were accepted by others who were] inducted into science in its perhaps most optimistic age. Facts were considered prepotent, and fact finding the essence of all scientific endeavors. This applied as well to the social sciences. "The husks of human opinion that have been growing for generations about the facts of society must be stripped off and the facts laid bare," entoned University of Chicago botanist John M. Coulter. In a college essay on the moral force of the realist school of fiction writing, Thorndike opined that, "Truth is only truth, I think, [and] knowledge of any fact, no matter how vile, cannot but be morally helpful if it is true in the perspective and import given to it." "Look and see" was his advice to all other investigators of animal intelligence. While he considered that school visitations (for the purpose of marrying theory to practice or for the demonstration of already known psychological principles) were a tedious, inefficient, and unnecessary expenditure of the time of an educational psychologist, he was willing even to go into a schoolroom if the purpose was collecting facts for science. His positivistic empiricism caused Abraham Maslow once to describe Thorndike's view of science as a kind of coral reef built up little bit, by little bit, by little bit; in this way science grows, and nature is conquered and put into servitude to man.

Academic circles in the late nineteenth century were strangers to scientific relativism. Instead, knowledge was considered something firm, and in all the disciplines the emphasis was upon the never again to be repeated, upon the definitive study. It is *not* that Thorndike craved certainty, as did Yale's Professor Taylor, who said of the mathematical physicist, Willard Gibbs, "I would rather have ten settled opinions and nine of them wrong than be like my brother Gibbs with none of the ten settled." . . .

* * *

The Messianic Character of the "New Psychology"

In his presidential address to the American Psychological Association in 1937, California's E. C. Tolman declared that—given psychology's inability even to predict the direction a rat would turn in a maze—he considered his science unready to furnish guidelines for human behavior. Thorndike's perceptions of both the possibilities and the actual achievements of psychology were considerably more immodest than Tolman's; he never lost much of that optimism, buoyancy, and sense of mission evident in the "new psychology" of the 1890's.

Fully accepting Karl Pearson's proposition in *The Grammar of Science* that science, rightly understood, is competent to solve all problems, Thorndike was understandably impatient with the backwardness of psychological knowledge, although not with its new aims. In a graduate seminar paper Thorndike noted with indignation:

[Descartes'] physiological theories have all been sloughed off by science long ago. No one ever quotes him as an authority in morphology or physiology. . . . Yet his theory of the nature of the mind is still upheld by not a few, and the differences between his doctrines of imagination, memory, and of the emotions, and those of many present-day psychology books are comparatively unimportant.

Not that this deplorable situation was all grim, however: A good opportunity for iconoclasm was made available, and Thorndike got much sheer delight from it in his early, "assertive years." Of his thesis he wrote to his future wife, "It is fun to write all the stuff up and smite all the hoary scientists hip and thigh. I shall be jumped on unmercifully when the thing gets printed, if I ever raise the cash to print it." And, a little later, "My thesis is a beauty. . . . I've got some theories which knock the old authorities into a grease spot." After one of those "old authorities," McGill University's Wesley Mills, attacked "Animal Intelligence" before the American Psychological Association in 1898, Thorndike reported that "New York wasn't much fun except that an oaf read a long paper soaking my book and me right and left. I said a few modest words in reply which made a good impression, and rather enjoyed the free advertising."

* * *

As an educator once reminded a normal school conference, however, sciences are built by research and not by proclamation. Mindful of this, the number of psychological laboratories was increased rapidly. Fifty-four were established in North America between 1874 and 1904. Even Titchener's group, espousing the unpopular method of introspection as a unique psychological tool, and in self-imposed, structuralist isolation from the main body of American psychologists, counted itself within the new psychology for its devotion to the laboratory. Cornell offered probably the nation's most stringent training, cultivating a highly technical vocabulary and conducting elaborately controlled investigations. Such among Titchener's students as Carl Seashore thought Titchener's four-volume *Experimental Psychology* "the highest embodiment of the idea of intensive, fundamental drill exercises" and lamented when such stylized training and laboratory formalism fell away.

The new psychology had its skeptics, of course, including William James, America's best known philosopher and psychologist. Dispatching a copy of his *Measurements* to James, Thorndike warned him:

I am sending you a dreadful book which I have written, which is no end scientific but devoid of any spark of human interest. You must make all your research men read it, but never look within its covers yourself. The figures and curves and formulae would drive you mad.

James' response was cordial, tactful, affectionate:

I open your new book with full feelings of awe and admiration for your unexampled energy. It was just the thing I hoped for when I was teaching psychology and wondered why no one wrote it. And now you are the man to have done it. I should think it would immediately be translated.

I am glad I have graduated from the necessity of using that kind of thing any longer. I shall stick to "qualitative" work as more congruous with old age. Nothing like metaphysics for people in their dotage.

Thorndike well knew that this teacher thought America already oversupplied with psychological laboratories, and that James doubted even the credibility of the "exact" sciences. James preferred, instead, "nonsystems"—in an eternally pluralistic, liberal, permissive, open universe. Thorndike revered him above all other men, but the younger psychologists were so anxious to give scientific status to their work that James seemed an "irritating impressionist." Lightner Witmer spoke for their professional aspirations when he accused James of encouraging a variety of "mystical and charlatan" incursions into legitimate psychology. Thorndike's own tolerance of James did not extend to G. Stanley Hall, however, and he never criticized or satirized anyone as severely as he did Hall. The possibility that the pseudo-scientific pretensions of the child-study movement might be mistaken for educational psychology was too horrible to contemplate.

*   *   *

3

Determinism-Freedom in Contemporary Psychology: An Ancient Problem Revisited

Ludwig Immergluck

Are you reading these words because you choose to, without any direction or guidance from other persons or events? Did you choose this article at this time, in this book, because you alone decided that you would like to read it? Or are you reading this as part of an assignment by your instructor (or, if you are the instructor, because you are looking for something to assign to your students)? If you are reading this for absolutely no reason other than that you "want to" or "feel like it," then it might be said that you are reading it "of your own free will." If you are reading it for any other reason or reasons, then it must be said that certain determinants (producers of action outside your own personal will) are inducing you to read.

The example above points out the problem that Immergluck is dealing with in this article. Common sense, tempered by certain historical and cultural traditions, suggests that we all have free will and that we exercise it frequently. Scientific explanation, on the other hand, is based upon the premise that all behavior to be explained is determined. That is, if the behavior can be explained, then there are specifiable causes for the behavior. Whether or not *all* human activity is caused by persons or events outside the individual is a problem that arouses the interest of most psychologists as well as of most other thinking persons.

When both classical and eighteenth-century vitalism and voluntarism gave way to a broad acceptance of philosophic determinism, the road

From American Psychologist, *Vol. 19 (1964), 270–281. Copyright 1964 by the American Psychological Association, and reproduced by permission.*

seemed cleared to establish psychology unambiguously as a science of behavior. The notion that *behavior,* as indeed all other events in nature, is lawfully related to antecedent and attendant events, and that such relationships may be quantitatively described, has been indispensable in at once liberating psychology from its metaphysical ancestry and bringing it into the fold of natural science. The road from ancient vitalism to modern determinism, however, has been neither smooth nor straight. Many curves, detours, and even backward turns have marked its course. In part, these delays in accepting a fully deterministic conception of behavior are probably due to an understandable reluctance to relinquish venerated and cherished philosophies of human nature. The notion that man in his barest essence is a free agent propelled by self-initiated inner forces that defy, by their very nature, prediction or the scientifically ordered description customarily applied to inanimate events, is deeply engraved not only in the thoughts and values of Western civilization but, to some extent at least, in man's self-conceptualizations throughout the history of all human societies.

Indeed, the emergence of a science of behavior has eroded not only the foundations of early animistic and metaphysical views regarding the nature of man, but it has also had a disquieting effect upon modern humanistic and, broadly speaking, liberally ethical approaches to human conduct and values. Scientific formulations, some hold, with their implicit determinism and cut-and-dried cause-and-effect relationships couched in quantitative terms, are bound to result in conceptualizations of man that will rob him of human dignity if not of his very essence.

Underneath these protestations lies, of course, often a tacit defense of the existence of at least some measure of an inner "free will," and the fear that complete lawfulness, when applied too rigorously, will render any notion of inner, personal freedom obtuse. As a matter of fact, perhaps no other issue than the by now all too familiar determinism–free-will dichotomy brings the antinomy between rigorous scientific formulations and other approaches to the theory of behavior into sharper focus. Indeed, this issue separates not only psychologists from nonpsychologists, but there is ample evidence that it is driving a divisive wedge also among present-day psychological theorizers.

A Philosophic Paradox

While most psychologists have come to accept, at least implicitly, determinism as a valid working model, an increasing number are growing greatly concerned about the emergence of an apparent paradox: There is, on the one hand, modern psychology's commitment to the scientific method, which has paid off not only in an impressive accruement of knowledge but which has also put on firm basis the causal and deterministic nexus of behavior; while on the other hand there remains the nagging conviction that man must somehow also be personally free. How to resolve this antinomy?

To some this ancient dichotomy seems resolvable by simply accepting the existence of a paradox and allowing for a kind of philosophic coexistence; others hope for the emergence of some future (and perhaps as yet unimaginable) conceptual scheme that might serve as that grand philosophical umbrella covering this antinomy. Concerns and preoccupations with these issues are witnessed in much of the current pertinent literature. In a recent symposium, for example, Carl Rogers (1961) takes full cognizance of this paradox but professes to see no resolution to it, at least for the present. While admitting that in our work as scientists we must assume that everything takes place in a strict cause-and-effect sequence and "that nothing occurs outside of that," he insists that we cannot, at the same time, hold on to this view in our lives as human beings, and he resigns himself to accept this inconsistency as a "genuine paradox" (p. 575). In the same symposium A. H. Maslow (1961) implies that while strict determinism may be valid, it is too narrow and not inclusive enough an approach. E. G. Boring (1957) expresses similar concern with regard to the free-will–determinism issue and proposes a formulation in which strict causality is seen as a kind of "truncated model" to which freedom may be added. And recently S. Koch (1961), in a lead article in the *American Psychologist,* goes as far as to speak approvingly of the "relegitimation of metaphysics," which he apparently sees as taking place in some currents of modern psychology.

But is the recently hard-won battle for strict determinism in psychology to be relinquished so soon? Certainly there should be no quarrel with those who might be deeply dissatisfied with perhaps overly simplistic early behavioral models, or possibly with the fact that laboratory and segmentally derived behavioral laws are as yet not readily applicable to the richness of the human condition *in vivo.* But, we might continue to ask, do the data of modern psychology really justify a return to an earlier metaphysics and a resurrection of a free-will ghost, albeit in more compact size than before, and now a cuddling up against a solidly established and much alive deterministic sibling?

While this is a complex question, and one that involves many philosophic and historical intricacies, I firmly believe that it would serve conceptual clarity if we regarded determinism and free will as representing two basically different and divergent views in modern psychology which simply cannot be dealt with through the fiat notion that "both are somehow right" within their own limited frameworks, or that they really complement one another in jointly reflecting the total realities of psychological life. Indeed, closer philosophic scrutiny of this admittedly tempting "bridge-gap" resolution of the dilemma uncovers some serious flaws. First, it fails to take into account the general, the unified nature of theory- and system-construction in science. Ideally, a *general theory*, in the sense of constituting a circumspect explanatory framework, should be inclusive and all encompassing, i.e., it should be capable of accounting for *all* observed, and also as yet unspecified, data falling under its purview. While philosophers of science may disagree with respect to the attainability of this ideal, it is nevertheless a very worthwhile conceptual objective to aim at, and one that should not be abandoned lightly.

Second, and apart from the question of whether the time is really ripe—both on philosophic and scientific grounds—to abandon an encompassing deterministic framework in psychology, it may be pertinent to point out that any attempts to mold both determinism and free will into some kind of unitary conceptual schema may likely serve to benefit only the free-will half of the dichotomy, and might in effect constitute a philosophic recommitment to psychological vitalism. It takes but one honest-to-goodness spook to prove the existence of ghosts, only one unnatural event to establish the existence of a supernature, and only one free-will act to contradict determinism. The implications of this point are well illustrated by the philosopher-physicist Charles Peirce (1935), who attempted to revive the Epicurean notion of acausality and spontaneity of atoms, and who also committed himself, primarily through his acausal conceptualizations in physics, to a strong belief in human free will. He states:

By supposing the rigid exactitude of causation to yield, I care not how little—be it but by a strictly infinitesimal amount—we gain room to insert mind into our scheme, and put it into the place where it is needed, into the position which, as the sole and self-intelligible thing, it is entitled to occupy, that of the fountain of existence; and in so doing we resolve the problem of the connection of soul and body (p. 112).

"Acausality" in Physics

The issue of the apparent indeterminism in the newer conceptualizations of modern physics lies of course at the bottom of many polemics and serious concerns with regard to their implications for the behavioral sciences in general and for the concept of human freedom in particular. In fact, it has become quite fashionable among many to point to the alleged revolt against strict causality in physics, and more particularly to Heisenberg's principle of uncertainty, as a "proof" for the existence of at least some measure of free will in man, or, at a minimum, for casting grave doubts upon the advisability of erecting too tight a deterministic model for the behavioral sciences. Psychology, the argument goes, has been attempting to emulate a system which is now outmoded in physics.

Let us take a closer look at this contention. Unfortunately, this type of reasoning is often the result of some misconstruing of both the factual and conceptual reorientation in modern physics. A penetrating analysis of current quantum theory applied to the physics of subatomic particles, and particularly of Heisenberg's so-called principle of uncertainty, would go a long way in underscoring the perfunctory, or in any case the one-sided, nature of the argument. Suffice it to state here that many theoretical physicists and certainly philosophers of science have been somewhat less enthusiastic in propagating post-Newtonian physics as irrefutable proof for the existence of free will in man, or indeed even for the nondeterministic nature of physical events themselves, than is popularly assumed.

Any kind of comprehensive evaluation of the nature and conceptual implications of modern quantum theory is of course out of place here, but even a cursory glance at some of the salient features of the conceptual framework of contemporary physics should prove useful in showing at least some of the serious problems one meets when attempting to apply such a framework uncritically to human events and to utilize it as an intransigent argument for the existence of personal freedom in man.

A meaningful evaluation of the conceptual reorientation in physics that has been taking place since about the turn of the century has to be predicated upon a clear distinction between factual data on the one hand and their theoretical interpretations on the other. It is precisely the failure to make this distinction that has resulted in much of the misunderstandings and confusions attendant upon the determinism-freedom issue.

To begin with, it is generally accepted that the type of comprehensive system of causality which stood at the heart of the development of modern science, reaching its pinnacle in the ubiquitous, mechanistic conceptualizations of the universe, had to be altered, or, putting it perhaps more correctly, "rephrased," as physics moved with progressive refinement from the macroscopic world of Newton into the microscopic world of ever smaller particles. The need for this rephrasing deprived primarily from two sources: (a) technological difficulties inherent in the manipulation, description, and measurement of these particles, and (b) encountering processes and events in the newly discovered microscopic world that *appear* to be qualitatively different from those encountered in the familiar daily world of large objects.

The first point refers, of course, to the by now very familiar discovery that it is, practically speaking, impossible in subatomic processes to ascertain *simultaneously* both the position and momentum of any given particle. The "uncertainty principle," first formulated by Heisenberg and further elaborated by Niels Bohr, proclaims essentially a limit of accuracy with which the motion (position *and* momentum) of a microscopic object can be ascertained, primarily because the process of measurement and observation itself is bound to interfere with the observed particle. Theoretically, an observer could locate, with the aid of a microscope, the position of a subatomic object with as great an accuracy as he wished to, but in so doing, he would have to expose the particle to a collision with a quantum of light necessary for the observation that would alter the velocity (momentum) of the particle by an unknown amount. Conversely, a highly accurate assessment of the velocity of a given particle would, again by necessity, involve such a disturbance of its momentum and direction as to render its subsequent position highly uncertain.

It should be noted that, in principle, this situation differs in no way from that pertaining to macroscopic objects where observations, measurements, and assessments also constitute "interfering" forces. These disturbances, however, are, relatively speaking, of virtually no consequence and, at any rate, the amount of the perturbance can often be calculated and incorporated into the parameters of the measurement.

The second point, however, refers to attributes of the microscopic world which appear to be truly novel, which are not encountered in the world of daily objects, and which in fact have driven physicists into philosophic speculation. Briefly, the major point here is that it has been recognized, semantically and conceptually, that a microscopic particle is not merely "an extension downward" of the familiar attributes characterizing objects in the world of our direct experience, but, indeed, that subatomic events are of such a nature as to render the very concept of "particle" ambiguous, if not obtuse. In the first place, pertinent experimental data compel the conclusion that subatomic elements possess what has been referred to as a "dual nature"; In some situations such elements behave like particles while in other instances they exhibit properties that fit most closely those of waves.

And then there are problems of a definitional and logical nature. Visualize, if you will, a progression of "infinite" division of an object into its component parts, moving downwards from its macroscopic state to its ever more minute constituents. Ultimately, a point must be reached where the component building blocks at the very bottom of matter can no longer be thought of as "particles," in the customary sense of the term, since "particle" can only designate a spatial entity which, as such, must, at least logically, be capable of being further divided into component parts. In other words, in the process of turning infinity inward, so to speak, we are forced to renounce either our system of deductive reasoning or else our customary spatiotemporal conceptualizations which have been an integral part both of our daily world of objects and of classical physics.

This logical impasse has in fact been recognized as early as the middle of the eighteenth century by Roger Joseph Boscovich (Whyte, 1961), who proposed the concept of "point atoms" as juxtaposed to the traditional definition of atoms in terms of minute "particles," and who anticipated, albeit crudely, many of the important newer formulations of modern subatomic physics. And modern physicists, from Einstein's "mass-energy" concept to Schrodinger's "wave" formulations, have been preferring, of course, to think in terms of subatomic "processes" or "events" rather than the customary "particles."

So much, then, for a necessarily very cursory

glance at some of the pertinent facts which characterize the conceptual reorientation of modern physics. There are essentially no polemics among competent scientists on this level. Disputes and wide philosophic divergences derive only from inferences and implications based upon this reorientation.

Some Implications of Modern Physics

One such inference has, of course, been the contention that physics' newer concepts have reestablished once again, as it were, "freedom" in man. But scientists and philosophers of science have counseled great caution against precisely this type of reasoning. Heisenberg's formulation, many remind us, describes at most a principle of "uncertainty" and not necessarily "indeterminism."

* * *

There is yet another issue deserving consideration. The strict lawfulness ascribed to physical objects by Newton's determinism is so much in accord with our everyday experience of material objects around us, that very few would deny the existence of such tight regularity. Water—all conditions being equal—*always* boils or freezes at a specific temperature. The milk will spill every time the glass is knocked over. And the high school student observes in his science class—again under controlled conditions—that bodies fall in a fixed ratio of acceleration, every single time the experiment is performed.

Does the "revolution" in modern physics with its quantum mechanics really imply that while the path of a Ping-Pong ball may be strictly determined, its component particles are not, that they are "free" and operate at a true random? If so, we are brought again to a logical impasse at which we are left to explain the precise point at which randomness changes into the observed lawfulness. But doesn't parsimony, if not logic alone, many ask, mitigate against such an assumption, and is it not therefore more advisable, and adhering to a unified theoretical framework, to view all events, micro- and macroscopic, within a lawful and deterministic nexus?

De Broglie (1939), in referring to the assumed statistical nature of subatomic processes, intimates that this theoretical indeterminacy is the result of experimental error, and that "in practice and also in experiment, everything happens as though . . . there were a strict Determinism." And again

Nagel (1961) more recently implies clearly and emphatically that we can draw no conclusions regarding human freedom from any alleged "acausal" or "indeterministic" properties of subatomic processes (p. 316).

* * *

We cannot draw on contemporary physics, then, for scientific or philosophic "proof" for the existence of free will in man, and at this stage of our scientific conceptualizations, be they modern or classical, it might at best perhaps be most prudent to state that the scientific model of the universe neither proves nor disproves the existence of nondeterministic forces.

Determinism in Modern Psychology

The question that now confronts us is, where does determinism, not only as a methodological principle but also as a philosophic framework, fit into present-day psychology? First, I think it is important to realize that psychology, in its broadest sense, represents a very natural last outpost for vitalistic and antideterministic viewpoints. Traditionally, both the lay person and men of learning have always been quick to draw a sharp distinction between material things and objects on the one hand and living organisms on the other, in formulating conceptual frameworks pertaining to these respective sets of events. It has been relatively easy to live with the notion that inanimate processes are lawfully anchored in causal chains to antecedent conditions, that such events are quantifiable and predictable, and that knowledge of these natural laws can lead to a type of control and mastery of these events as is impressively shown by our staggering advances in physical technology. But typically serious doubt is cast on even the possibility of life processes and indeed "psychological" events being governed by such strict lawfulness, that is quantifiable, and that may lead, at least potentially, to a similar degree of predictability.

* * *

Not only are such admonitions often transparent apologies for a dualism allegedly long abandoned, but they also seem to misconstrue the very nature of scientific methodology. It might be helpful to remind ourselves that science is not a given field of inquiry or a circumscribed body of knowledge, but that it represents rather an arduously developed *method* of inquiry which constitutes in its barest essence a culmination of man's attempts to discover and shape a means of inquiry that is designed to lead to a more penetrating and valid understanding of nature (and of human nature as well!) than has been yielded by other methods, including metaphysical speculation. . . .

*   *   *

The fact that the dualistic position is old and that it antedates the emergence of scientific thinking is, of course, alone no valid argument against it. Nor is its kinship to present-day popular thinking about the nature of the human mind. But, both in the light of factual data pertaining to human behavior and accepted tenets of modern theory construction, we do have the right to question the necessity for such dualism.

Psychologists Divided

It is quite clear that the definition of psychology as a science of behavior, with the implied presumption of strict and encompassing lawfulness, is by no means unequivocally embraced by all psychologists. There are multifarious banners under which psychologists cluster, and the gap between the conditioned-response-oriented dissectionist at one end of the psychological spectrum and the existential therapist at the other, is wide indeed. . . .

*   *   *

The effects of the wedge which the determinism-freedom issue has driven into the camp of modern psychology should, however, not be misconstrued into a belief that large segments of psychologists have abandoned any notions of lawfulness altogether or returned to some prescientific mentalism. This is certainly not the case, and when considering the matter logically, it would be inconceivable to think of a science of behavior without a systematic deterministic position. The research-oriented clinician, too, recognizes this as does, of course, the personality psychologist. As a matter of fact, the incessant search for *causes* of schizophrenia, of feeblemindedness, of anxiety, of aggression, of passivity and conformity, and of an ever widening range of specific personality attributes, betrays clearly an at least implicit deterministic assumption. It is only when some investigators are not willing to go all the way, when they are, as it were, merely willing to concede determinism "up to a point," the existence

of lawfulness—"but," that conceptual confusion arises.

*   *   *

Probability and Determinism

Many regard the probabilistic or statistical character of behavioral laws as still another signpost pointing away from strict determinism. Certainly the notions of determinism and *predictability* are closely interconnected and the fact that complex behavior can be predicted at best only along some probabilistic formulations has often appeared to lend scientific support to the popular view that human behavior is "unpredictable," providing another argument against strict determinism.

There is no need here to elaborate the various mathematical meanings of the term probability nor the philosophical implications adjoining the differences between mathematical and statistical laws. It is imperative, however, for the discussion at hand, to point to the common failure to distinguish between predictability in principle and predictability in fact as a major source of confusion. No physical scientist, for example, would deny the *practical* impossibility to predict precisely all physical events in nature. It would be impossible, practically speaking, to calculate the precise course and time span involved in, say, the descent of an autumn leaf from the top of a particular tree to the ground. Obviously, the large number of unknown determining variables would make such calculation impossible, in any precise mathematical sense. At the same time, however, no one would doubt for a moment the intrinsic operation of strict lawfulness pertaining to this event, nor would anybody, because of the practical unpredictability and uncertainty, imbue the leaf with any kind of "free-will" attribute.

The analogy for psychology is quite obvious: Our inability to predict with any great precision specific behavior patterns of any given individual, locomoting literally in an ocean of unknown variables, does not, of course, preclude the potential existence of precise behavioral laws. The statistical nature of observed regularities, then, does really not illuminate the issue of indeterminism versus lawfulness.

There are now, however, some important attributes of behavior facing us which, by definition alone, are alleged to stand in direct contradiction to a wholly deterministic view of man. How can we speak, for example, of "response alternatives," "behavior variability," or indeed "choice or selective behavior" without allowing for at least a crack in the deterministic enclosure?

Choice, Freedom, and Response Variability

To a greater extent than is the case in any other science, the language of psychology has borrowed heavily from daily life terminology, and the technical meaning of a given term often has a totally different connotation from the one in common usage, a situation which unfortunately has added considerably to the lack of conceptual clarity in many areas. *Choice* as an assumed behavioral attribute, especially of higher organisms, represents one such term; and since as a concept it is of immediate pertinence to any discussion of the determinism-freedom issue, it merits closer attention. In fact, much of the definitional vagueness enveloping terms such as "choice" and, concomitantly, "personal freedom" is, as Gustav Bergmann (1957) implies, directly related to a notable absence of proper analysis (both logical and psychological) of the concept of freedom.

Without attempting here to undertake such analysis, let us at least look at the connotative difference of the term "choice" as it is popularly understood and as the experimental psychologist, for example, uses it. Commonly used, the concept of "choice" implies the notion that an organism, when confronted with a variety of stimulus conditions, is capable of making *alternate* responses, with the attendant hidden connotation that true response alternatives must be predicated upon at least some measure of inner freedom. Defined in this manner, "choice," then, can derive only from inner freedom.

The experimental psychologist also speaks of "choice points" in a rat maze, but to him that term connotates an entirely different meaning. He knows that whether any given rat will turn this way or that, will depend directly on the preceding experimental conditions and upon the organism's past experience, his physiological states, and the pushing and pulling forces in his present environment. If a painful electric shock has been associated with, say, a left turn and/or food with a right, the organism really has no choice and will be "determined" to turn right. Such behavior is quite predictable and subject to calculation. We are tempted, on the other hand, to label the behavior of the rat as "random" (or else "choice" in the common usage sense) when no experimental conditioning has taken place and

when the antecedent conditions and variables operating upon the organism are largely unknown. The behavior of the rat is then likely to appear to be quite variable and at the same time highly unpredictable. The point is obvious, of course, that in both instances the behavior of the rat is *in principle* precisely determined and predictable; and the descriptive label "randomness" implies essentially ignorance of the pertinent variables. We might even be permitted to assume that in both instances the rat would, if he could only talk, reply to the question "Why did you turn the way you did?" with an emphatic "Because I wanted to!" It is contended that in this sense the term "choice" represents an artifact, a convenient term borrowed from everyday language, and one that reflects neither philosophic tenacity nor psychological reality.

* * *

On the human level the determinism-freedom issue is still further blurred by the common practice of equating any absence of freedom with *external* constraints only. This assumes particular relevance in the minds of those who view determinism as being irreconcilable with any notion of social and political freedom. Let us take a brief look at this position. A feudal society, where marriages might be typically prearranged, does not offer the serf the freedom to select a wife of his own choosing. Such selection is determined for him by external authority. But is not a present-day Western man who declares "I chose my wife because I wanted to," like our rat at the choice point, simply unaware of the complex mosaic of antecedent causes, the multitude of interlocking events and experiences which define his personal history, including in his case perhaps such factors as unresolved (and unconscious) conflicts, all of which have funneled into the really unavoidable determination of his particular marital choice? And should all these factors not properly be regarded as *internal* constraints or determiners of action?

In this sense, in both a totalitarian and democratic setting the individual is not really free, in the basic philosophical meaning of that term, but his behavior may be regarded as being determined to varying degrees by two different sets of factors: external in one instance and internal in the other.

The relationship between political freedom and the philosophic notion of personal free will merits more perspicacious discussion than can be afforded here, but suffice it to state that determinism, with its intrinsic lack of freedom, need not alarm those of us who are ideologically committed to a democratic way of life. Indeed, it follows that the severe external constraints inherent in totalitarian settings merely serve to narrow and constrict the potential pool of behavioral determiners and thus stifle individual variability, the very attribute of higher organisms!

There need be no contradiction between political freedom and philosophic determinism; such contradiction exists only if we insist on basing our notions of political and social freedom on free-will metaphysics.

Freedom: Levels of Perceiving

Throughout this discussion there has been an implicit underscoring of the contention that the scientific model of man, with its concomitant deterministic image, does not at all accord with our subjective experience. And after all philosophic and scientific polemics have been brushed aside, the cogency of the individual's own perception of his personal freedom still emerges as perhaps the most potent argument against determinism. We are faced with a dilemma: Scientific observation leads to one conclusion, self-perception to another. How can we reconcile these contradictions?

I believe we can cut the Gordian knot by regarding the act of perceiving as being capable of taking place on different levels, and that these diverse levels in turn are capable of conveying different information concerning the observed data. We may then visualize the difference between subjective experience on the one hand and scientific description on the other primarily as a distinction between two levels of perceptual analysis: *experiential* and *experimental*. One implies a direct, unanalyzed, and global percept, while the other refers to a very special, almost endlessly detailed, contrived, and admittedly artificial observational procedure, if by "artificial" we mean a procedure by which certain data can be yielded only when special conditions are established which typically do not prevail in ordinary daily life encounters.

This point is well illustrated by the commonly known visual illusion phenomena. The same strip of neutral gray is perceived as almost black when held against a white background, while it appears to be grayish white when a black background is substituted. While this illusory effect may be an unavoidable and "natural" attribute of perceiving, the scientist is perfectly justified in probing beyond this surface appearance and in regard-

ing these two gray strips as being *really* identical. We might even add, that *unless* he probed beyond phenomenologic appearance, his image of reality would be in error. Indeed, in this particular instance he could not begin to formulate comprehensive scientific conceptualizations about color if he restricted his data solely to surface perceptual experience.

*   *   *

Without elaborating further the psychological issues inhering in the objective-reality–perceptual-reality distinction (for such distinction really goes to the heart of the nature of perceiving itself), we need be concerned here only with the recognition that subjective experience is often, if not typically, at odds with objective reality. And while it may also be argued that, borrowing a solipsistic aphorism, objective reality is always withheld from us, in the sense that no sensory-derived knowledge is really exempt from perceptual distortion (after all, the most controlled and punctilious scientific analysis still involves in the end human perceiving and, therefore, at least in some sense "subjective experience"), the fact still remains that scientific probing, and especially experimental analysis, has given us an image of objects and events that is often radically different from that obtained through global daily life experience.

It might be important to interject at this point that the propounded dual-level character of perceiving, experiential and experimental, need not imply that ordinary perceiving is completely illusory and totally divorced from objective reality. Obviously we could have survived neither as species nor as individuals if our senses were in fact so alienated from objects and events around us. Yet of basic concern, both for philosopher and psychologist, is the issue of how physical reality itself participates in the shaping of the perceptual process. If there is any single lesson which the entire history of scientific analysis has taught us, it is surely the recognition that common sense perception is at best incomplete and often leads to quite distorted images of object and event reality.

A Necessary Illusion

So much, then, for the experience of inner freedom as a distorted percept. But does this alone provide sufficient explanation for the universal presence of this aspect of self-awareness? I think not. The free-will character of our action is an illusion, but it may well turn out to be a *necessary* illusion. We may have cleansed biology of all vitalistic and teleological remnants and are willing now to accept a broadly deterministic framework when viewing the behavior of animals.[1] However, on the human level we have come to accept determinism at most, and practically speaking, only in some vague and restricted way, perhaps as an abstraction that need not be taken too literally. It is true, we often derive genuine satisfaction, if not clandestine pleasure, out of being able to "explain" or understand the behavior of others in terms of complex but nonetheless clearly seen determining factors. We identify economic motives, a slum environment, the background of a broken home, the presence of intellectual stimulation in early childhood, neurotic conflicts, an intolerable present environment, and a host of other variables, both general and specific, as sufficient determining conditions that enable us to understand quite fully a given person's particular behavior patterns. We may be willing, then, to concede the presence of even strict determinism also on the human level, but really only in *others*.

The last comment is not intended as a facetious aside. I am, in fact, raising serious doubt as to the psychological feasibility of an individual, at least within our particular cultural fabric, being able to regard his *own* thoughts and actions as being totally determined. Our self-image, such as it is, and such as it has possibly evolved in all human cultures, appears to demand at least some feeling of inner spontaneity, a psychological conviction that one is not helplessly entrapped by circumstances, past and present, and that one can, after all is said and done, transcend one's own determining confines. The immediacy of the feeling to be able to *will* action (even though we are at times and under special conditions quite capable of spelling out specific antecedents that have shaped even our own "spontaneous" acts) appears to have developed somehow as a necessary attribute of our self-image, and it is virtually inconceivable to be able to interact with oneself on any other terms, unless one can conceive of a development of human consciousness so radically different from our own that only an almost completely novel cultural matrix, with totally different language, thinking, and conceptual habits, could account for it. These factors have probably contributed immensely to the conceptual difficulties and polemics centering around the determinism–free-will issue and to the philosophic "paradox" so keenly felt by many contemporary psychologists.

It might be added, parenthetically, that the physical scientist, likewise, perceives and interacts with his daily life environment on a basis that is often much at variance with his scientifically derived knowledge. It is probably quite impossible for an astronomer to see the sun other than circling the earth, as he gazes out of his livingroom window; or for the physicist to regard the chair he is sitting on not as a solid, stable object, but as a swirling and ever changing hive of atomic and subatomic particles.

The contention is, then, that free-will possesses a "surface validity" which is predicated upon a complex intertwining of perceptual-process attributes and deeply entrenched cultural conditioning. This conditioning has profoundly shaped our values, our beliefs, our customs, our laws, our notions of personal responsibility, finally also our self-perceptions, all of which are very difficult to reconcile with a strict deterministic framework of human actions. I propose that even in the event that such encompassing determinism should ever become unambiguously and universally accepted, we will (must?) still persist to behave *as if* inner freedom were a fact, if not for those around us, then at least for ourselves.

Having stated this, however, we must realize that the widely held contention that ubiquitous determinism destroys any notion of the dignity, morality, and personal responsibility of man, is alone really no valid argument against the deterministic view, and when used as such it is destined to turn into an ill-fated tautology. Inner freedom may be a necessary language symbol and, more than that, a necessary human percept. If it turns out to be a culturally and psychologically unavoidable illusion, so be it! But are we thereby compelled to build a science of behavior predicated upon illusion?

Does, however, determinism in fact corrode the concept of human dignity? Perhaps only if we have chosen, in an a priori manner, to equate dignity with free will. On the other hand, should a deterministic framework propel us to search ceaselessly for specific and general behavioral laws, we might, some day, understand not only the variables that lead to neurosis, feeble-mindedness, mental illness, and delinquency, but perhaps also the richness and complexity of the specific events

---

[1] Johannes Muller, possibly the most outstanding biologist of the last century, was one of the first modern scientists to present us with a rigorous mechanical account of animal behavior. But he stopped short of man, whom he still imbued with a vitalistic core. He might well be regarded, in contemporary terminology, as a "behaviorist" who exempted man.

and factors which lawfully shape intelligence, problem-solving skills, behavioral integration, and creativity. We might even be able to use such knowledge to advantage. And would this alone not constitute eloquent testimony to the dignity of man?

Epilogue

Only a few decades have intervened since the establishment of the first psychological laboratory. The notion of strict lawfulness is still novel in the realm of behavior, and we can as yet not boast of many low-order laws of a kind characteristically found in the older sciences. But we are beginning to uncover some of the more elemental factors that are systematically associated with simpler slices of behavior, and there is every reason to believe that eventually we should be able to spell out the inevitably complex lawful nexus of higher-order behavior patterns. We might even close the gap between experience and experiment. In the meanwhile, it is incumbent that we remain receptive not only to new incoming data, but also to fresh conceptualizations.

The scientific enterprise has over the years altered radically our image of the physical universe. We should, therefore, not be surprised that this same enterprise, when directed to the study of human behavior, may likewise yield a radically altered view of the nature of man. Indeed, it should be surprising if this were not the case.

REFERENCES

Bergmann, G. Philosophy of science. Madison: University of Wisconsin Press, 1957.

Boring, E. G. When is human behavior predetermined? Scientific Monthly, 1957, **84**, 189–196.

De Broglie, L. Matter and light. New York: Norton, 1939.

Koch, S. Psychological science versus the science-humanism antinomy: Intimations of a significant science of man. American Psychologist, 1961, **16**, 629–639.

Maslow, A. H. Cultural evolution as viewed by psychologists. Daedalus, 1961, **90**, 572–573.

Nagel, E. The structure of science. New York: Harcourt, Brace & World, 1961.

Peirce, C. S. Collected papers. Cambridge: Harvard University Press, 1935.

Rogers, C. Cultural evolution as viewed by psychologists. Daedalus, 1961, **90**, 574–575.

Whyte, L. L. (Ed.) Roger Joseph Boscovich. London: Allen & Unwin, 1961.

4

An Overview of Experimentation

F. J. McGuigan

Increased technological ability through scientific research is often given as a major reason for the dramatic increase in the standard of living in the Western world. Machines whiz us from place to place quickly and comfortably, a visit to any supermarket will assure everyone that food is almost embarrassingly plentiful, and there is an enormous selection of stylish clothing with which to colorfully adorn ourselves.

Why, then, is there strife and ferment in the world? Why are there discontented people amid all this luxury? These questions lie within the realm of the social scientist, including the psychologist. They attempt to discover the answers through research, which, for example, tries to understand why supposedly sophisticated men act in a warlike and aggressive manner toward other men, or examines the ways in which children learn the attitudes and emotions that guide their behavior when they become adults. This article presents a discussion of some of the research tactics currently being used by psychologists as they try to find answers to these troubling questions.

The Nature of Science

One of the main differences between humans and the lower animals is man's ability to engage in

F. J. McGuigan, Experimental Psychology: A Methodological Approach, 2nd ed., © 1968. Reprinted by permission of Prentice-Hall, Inc., Englewood Cliffs, New Jersey.

abstract thinking. For instance, man is much more able to survey a number of diverse items and abstract certain characteristics that they have in common. In attempting to arrive at a general definition of science we might well proceed in such a manner. That is, we might consider the various sciences as a group and abstract the salient characteristics that distinguish them from other disciplines. Figure 1 is a schematic representation of the disciplines which man studies, rather crudely categorized into three groups (excluding the formal disciplines, mathematics and logic). Within the inner circle we have represented what are commonly called the sciences. The next circle embraces various disciplines that are not usually thought of as sciences, such as the arts and some of the humanities. Outside of that circle are yet other disciplines which, for lack of a better term, are designated as metaphysical disciplines.

The sciences in the inner circle certainly differ among themselves in a number of ways. But in what important ways are they similar to each other? Likewise, what are the similarities among the disciplines in the outer circle? What do the metaphysical disciplines outside the circle have in common? Furthermore, in what important ways do each of these three groups differ from each other? Answers to these questions should enable us to arrive at an approximation to a general definition of "science."

One common characteristic of the sciences is that they all use the same general approach in solving problems—"the scientific method." The "scientific method" is a serial process by which all the sciences obtain answers to their problems. Neither of the other two groups explicitly uses this method.

We may also note that the disciplines within the two inner circles differ from the metaphysical disciplines in type of problem studied. Those disciplines within the two circles attempt to study "meaningful" problems, while those outside of the circle generally study "meaningless" problems. Briefly, a meaningful problem is one that can be answered with the use of man's normal capacities. A meaningless problem is one that is essentially unanswerable. Such meaningless problems usually concern supernatural phenomena or questions about *ultimate* causes. For example, the question of what caused the universe is meaningless and typical of studies in religion, classical philosophy, etc.[1] . . .

---

[1] Crude categorizations are dangerous. We want to point out *general* differences among the various dis-

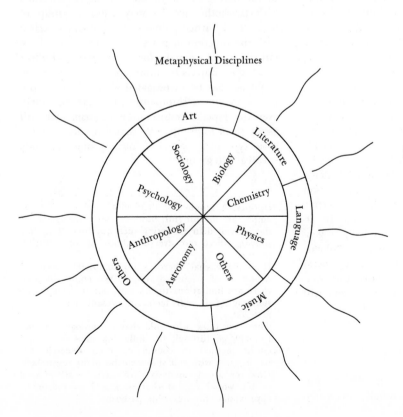

FIGURE 1 *Three groups of disciplines which man studies. Within the inner circle are the sciences. The second circle contains the arts and some types of the humanities, while the metaphysical disciplines fall outside the circles.*

"Meaningful" and "meaningless" are technical terms and certain vernacular meanings should not be read into them. It is not meant, for instance, to establish a hierarchy of values among the various disciplines by classifying them according to the type of problem they study. We are not necessarily saying, for example, that the problems of science are "better" than the problems of religion. The distinction is that meaningful problems are capable of being solved, but meaningless ones are not. The problems of the metaphysical disciplines are in no sense of any lesser importance—in fact, many intelligent men would argue that they are more important. Those who stay within the two circles simply believe they must limit their study to problems that they are capable of solving. Of course, many scientists also devote part of their lives to the consideration of supernatural phenomena. But it is important to realize that when they do, they have "left their circle" and are, for that time, no longer behaving as scientists.

In summary, first, the sciences use the scientific method, and they study meaningful problems. Second, the disciplines in the outer circle do not use the scientific method, but they do study meaningful problems. And third, the disciplines outside of the circles neither use the scientific method nor study meaningful problems. These considerations lead to the following definition—*"Science" is the application of the scientific method to meaningful problems.* Generally, neither of the other two groups of disciplines have *both* these features in common.[2]

With this general definition in hand let us consider the scientific method, primarily as it is applied in psychology. And since the most powerful application of the scientific method is experimentation, we shall focus primarily on how experiments are conducted. The problems with which psychologists are concerned are among the most challenging and complex that man faces. For this reason it is necessary to bring to bear the most effective methods that science can make available in attempting to solve them. . . . By studying a general picture of how the experimental psychologist proceeds, you should be able to obtain a general orientation to experimentation. Because this overview is so brief, however, complex matters will necessarily be oversimplified. . . .

Psychological experimentation— An application of the scientific method[3]

A psychological experiment starts with the formulation of a problem which is usually best stated in the form of a question. The only requirement that the problem must meet is that it be meaningful—it must be answerable with the tools that are available to the psychologist. Beyond this, the problem may be concerned with any aspect of behavior, whether it is judged to be important or trivial. One lesson of history is that we must not be hasty in judging the importance of the problem on which a scientist works, for many times what was discarded as being of little importance contributed sizeably to later scientific advances.

The experimenter generally expresses a tentative solution to the problem. This tentative solution is called a *hypothesis,* and it may be a reasoned potential solution or it may be only a vague guess. . . . Following the statement of his hypothesis, the experimenter seeks to determine whether the hypothesis is probably true or probably false, i.e., does it answer the problem he has set for himself? To answer this question, he must collect data, for a set of data is his only criterion. Various techniques are available for data collection, but we are mainly concerned with the use of experimentation for this purpose.

One of the first steps that the experimenter will take in actually collecting his data is to select a group of subjects with which to work. The type of subject he studies will be determined in part by the nature of the problem. If he is concerned with psychotherapy, he may select a group of mentally disturbed patients. A problem concerned with the function of parts of the brain would entail the use of animals (for few humans volunteer to serve as subjects for brain operations). Learning problems may be investigated with the use of college sophomores, chimpanzees, rats, etc. But whatever the type of subject, the experimenter will assign them to groups. We shall consider here the basic type of experiment, namely one that only involves two groups.

---

ciplines. A number of theological problems, for example, are meaningful; however most theologians are not interested in answering such questions (e.g., does praying affect our everyday life?) in an empirical manner.

[2] It is likely that there is no completely adequate definition of science available. We emphasize that there are limitations to this one, but that an understanding of it will facilitate presentation of later material.

[3] There are those who hold that psychologists do not formally go through the following steps of the scientific method in conducting their research. We would agree with this statement for many researchers. However, a close analysis of the actual work of such people would suggest that they at least informally approximate the following pattern.

0″ 1″ 2″ 3″ 4″ 5″ 6″ 7″ 8″ 9″ 10″ 11″ 12″ 13″ 14″ . . . . ∞

Speed of Running a Maze ⎯⎯⎯⎯⎯⎯→

FIGURE 2 *Diagrammatic representation of a continuous variable*

The assignment of subjects to groups must be made in such a way that the groups will be approximately equivalent at the start of the experiment. The experimenter next typically administers an experimental treatment to one of the groups. The experimental treatment is what he wishes to evaluate, and it is administered to the *experimental group*. The other group, called the *control group,* usually receives a normal or standard treatment. It is important, here, to understand clearly just what the terms "experimental" and "normal" or "standard treatment" mean.

In his study of behavior, the psychologist generally seeks to establish empirical relationships between aspects of the environment, broadly conceived, and aspects of behavior. These relationships are known by a variety of names, such as hypotheses, theories, or laws. Such relationships in psychology essentially state that if a certain environmental characteristic is changed, behavior of a certain type also changes.[4]

The aspect of the environment which is experimentally studied is called the *independent variable;* the resulting change in behavior is called the *dependent variable.* Essentially, a variable is anything that changes in value. It is a quality that can exhibit differences in value, usually in magnitude or strength. Thus it may be said that a variable generally is anything that may assume different numerical values. Psychological variables change in value from time to time for any given organism, between organisms, and according to various environmental conditions. Some examples of variables are the height of men, the weight of men, the speed with which a rat runs a maze, the number of trials required to learn a poem, the brightness of a light, the number of words a patient says in a psychotherapeutic interview, and the amount of pay a worker receives for performing a given task.

Figure 2 schematically represents one of these examples, "the speed with which a rat runs a maze." It can be seen that this variable can take on any of a large number of magnitudes, or more specifically, it can exhibit any of a large number of time values. In fact, it may "theoretically" assume any of an infinite number of such values, the least being zero seconds, and the greatest being an infinitely large amount of time. In actual

situations, however, we would expect it to exhibit a value of a number of seconds, or at the most, several minutes. But the point is that there is no limit to the specific time value that it may assume, for this variable may be expressed in terms of any number of seconds, minutes, hours, etc., including any fraction of these units.

For example, we may find that a rat ran a maze in 24 seconds, in 12.5 seconds, or in 2 minutes, 19.3 seconds. Since this variable may assume any fraction of a value (it may be represented by any point along the line in Figure 2), it is called a *continuous* variable. A continuous variable is one that is capable of changing by any amount, even an infinitesimally small one. A variable that is not continuous is called a *discontinuous* or *discrete* variable. A discrete variable can assume only numerical values that differ by clearly defined steps with no intermittent values possible. For example, the number of people in a theatre would be a discrete variable, for, barring an unusually messy affair, one would not expect to find a part of a person in such surroundings. Thus, one might find 1, 15, 299 or 302 people in a theatre, but not 1.6 or 14.8 people. Similarly, sex (male or female) eye color (brown, blue, etc.) are frequently cited as examples of discrete variables.[5]

---

[4] By saying that the psychologist seeks to establish relationships between environmental characteristics and aspects of behavior, we are being unduly narrow. Actually he is also concerned with unobservable processes (variously called logical constructs, intervening variables, hypothetical constructs, etc.). Since, however, it is unlikely that your elementary work will involve hypotheses of such an abstract nature, they will not be further discussed. The highly arbitrary character of defining and differentiating among the various kinds of relationships should be emphasized— frequently the grossly empirical kind of relationship that we are considering under the label "hypothesis," once it is confirmed, is referred to as an empirical or observational law, or before it is tested merely as "hunch" or "guess."

[5] A more advanced consideration of discrete variables cannot be offered here. We may simply note that some scientists question whether there are actually any discrete variables in nature. They suggest that we simply "force" nature into "artificial" categories. Color, for example, may more properly be conceived of as a continuous variable—there are many gradations of brown, blue, etc. Nevertheless, scientists find

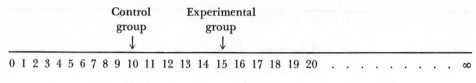

FIGURE 3 *Diagrammatic representation of an independent variable as a continuum. The value of the independent variable assigned to the control group is 10 trials; that assigned to the experimental group, 15 trials.*

We have said that the psychologist seeks to find relationships between independent and dependent variables. There are an infinite (or at least indefinitely large) number of independent variables available in nature for the psychologist to examine. But he is interested in discovering those *relatively* few ones that affect a given kind of behavior. In short, we may say that an independent variable is any variable that is investigated for the purpose of determining whether it influences behavior. Some independent variables that have been investigated in experiments are age, hereditary factors, endocrine secretions, brain lesions, drugs, race, and home environments.

To determine whether a given independent variable affects behavior the experimenter administers one value of it to his experimental group and a second value of it to his control group. The value administered to the experimental group is as we have said, the "experimental treatment," while the control group is usually given the "normal treatment." Thus, the essential difference between the "experimental" and "normal" treatment is the specific value of the independent variable that is assigned to each group. For example, the independent variable may be the intensity of a light (a continuous variable). The experimenter may subject the experimental group to a high intensity, and the control group to a zero intensity.

For a better understanding of the nature of an independent variable, let us consider another example of how one might be used in an experiment. Visualize a continuum similar to Figure 2, composed of an infinite number of possible values that the independent variable may take. If, for example, we are interested in determining how well a task is retained as a result of the number of times it is practiced, our continuum would start with zero trials and continue with one, two, three, etc. trials (this would be a discrete variable).

Let us suppose that in a certain industry workers are trained by performing an assembly line task ten times before being put to work. After a time, however, it is found that the workers are not assembling their product adequately and it is judged that they have not learned their task sufficiently well. Some corrective action is indicated and the foreman suggests that the workers would learn the task better if they were able to practice it fifteen times instead of ten. Here we have the makings of an experiment of the simplest sort.

We may think of our independent variable as the "number of times that the task is performed in training," and will assign it two of the possibly infinite number of values that it may assume—ten trials and fifteen trials. (See Figure 3.) Of course, we could have selected any number of other values, one trial, five trials, or five thousand trials, but because of the nature of the problem with which we are concerned ten and fifteen seem the best values to study. We will have the experimental group practice the task fifteen times, the control group ten times. Thus, the control group receives the normal treatment (ten trials), and the experimental group is assigned the experimental or new treatment (fifteen trials). In many cases, of course, it is arbitrary which group is labeled the control group and which is called the experimental group. Sometimes both treatments are novel ones, in which case it is impossible to label the groups in this manner—they might simply be called "Group 1" and "Group 2." In another instance, if one group is administered a "zero" value of the independent variable, and a second group is given some positive amount of that variable, then the zero treatment group would be called the "control group" while the other would be the "experimental group."

The *dependent* variable is usually some well defined aspect of behavior (a response) which the experimenter measures in his experiment. It may

---

it useful to categorize variables into classes as discrete variables, and to view such categorization as an approximation.

be the number of times the subject says a certain word, the rapidity with which a subject learns a given task, the number of items a worker on a production line can turn out in an hour, and so on. The value obtained for the dependent variable is the criterion of whether or not the independent variable is effective. It is in this sense that it is called a *dependent* variable—the value that it assumes is expected to be dependent on the value assigned to the independent variable.[6] Thus, an experimenter will vary the independent variable and note whether the dependent variable changes. If the dependent variable changes in value as the independent variable is manipulated, then it may be asserted that there is a relationship between the two. If the dependent variable does not change, however, it may be asserted that there is a lack of relationship between them. For example, let us assume that a light of high intensity is flashed into the eyes of each subject of the experimental group, while those of the control group are not subjected to any light. The dependent variable might be the amount of contraction of the iris diaphragm (the pupil) of the eye which, it may be noted, is an aspect of behavior—a response. If we find that the average contraction of the pupil of the experimental subjects exceeds that of those in the control group, we may conclude that intensity of light is an effective independent variable. We can assert the following relation: The greater the intensity of a light that is flashed into a subject's eyes, the greater the contraction of the pupil. If, on the other hand, we find no difference in the amount of contraction of the pupil between the two groups, we would assert that there is a lack of relationship between these two variables.

Perhaps the most important principle of experimentation, stated in an ideal form, is that the experimenter must hold constant all of the variables that may affect his dependent variable, except the independent variable(s) that he is attempting to evaluate. Obviously, there are a number of variables that may affect the dependent variable, but the experimenter is not immediately interested in these. He is, for the moment, interested in only one thing—the relationship, or lack of it, between his independent and his dependent variable. If the experimenter allows a number of other variables to operate in the experimental situation (call them *extraneous* variables) his experiment is going to be contaminated. For this reason he must *control* the important extraneous variables in his experiment. There are various techniques available for controlling extraneous variables. . . .

A simple illustration of how an extraneous variable might contaminate an experiment and thus make the findings unacceptable might be made using the last example. Suppose that the intensity of light is varied on subjects who have just received a vaccination. But the serum contains a substance that affects the contraction of the pupil of the eye. The data obtained will probably be useless. If the effect was such as to cause the pupil not to contract, the experimental subjects would show about the same amount of contraction (or rather, lack of contraction) as the control subjects. We would thus conclude that the independent variable did not affect the response being studied. Our findings would assert that these two variables of light and pupil contraction are not related, when in fact they are.

With this discussion of independent and dependent variables behind us let us return to our general discussion of the scientific method as applied to experimentation. We have said that a scientist starts his investigation with the statement of a problem, after which he advances a hypothesis as a tentative solution to that problem. He may then conduct an experiment to collect data, data which should indicate the probability that his hypothesis is true or false. He may find it advantageous to use certain types of apparatus and equipment in his experiment. The particular type of apparatus used will naturally depend on the nature of the problem. In general, apparatus is used in an experiment for two main reasons. First, to administer the experimental treatment, and second, to allow, or to facilitate, the collection of data.

The hypothesis that is being tested will predict the way in which the data should point. It may be that the hypothesis will predict that the experimental group will perform better than the control group. By confronting the hypothesis with the dependent variable scores of the two groups the experimenter can determine if this is so. But it is difficult to tell whether the (dependent variable) scores for one group are higher or lower than the scores for the second group simply by looking at a number of unorganized data for the two groups of subjects. Therefore, the experimenter must reduce all of the data with which he is dealing to numbers that can be reasonably handled, numbers

---

6 Assuming, of course, that the independent variable is effective. It may be added that the dependent variable is also dependent on some of the extraneous variables, discussed later, that are present in the experiment.

that will provide him with an answer—For this reason, he must resort to statistics.

For example, he may compute an average (mean) score for both the experimental group and the control group. He might find that the experimental group has a higher mean score (say, 100) than the control group (say, 99). While we note that the experimental group has a higher mean score, we also note that the difference between the two groups is very small. Is this difference, then, a "real" difference, or is it only a chance difference? What are the odds that if we conducted the experiment again we would obtain the same results? If the difference is a "real," reliable difference, then the experimental group should obtain a higher mean score than the control group almost every time the experiment is repeated. But if there is no "real" difference between the two groups we would expect to find the experimental group receiving the higher score half of the time, and the control group being superior the other half of the time. To tell whether the results of one experiment are "real," rather than simply due to chance, the experimenter resorts to any of a variety of statistical tests. The particular statistical test(s) that he uses will be determined by the type of data obtained and the general design of the experiment. But the point is that, on the basis of such tests, it can be determined whether the difference between the two groups is "real" and reliable or merely "accidental." More appropriately, the tests indicate whether or not the difference is statistically *significant,* for this is what is meant by "real" and "reliable" differences. If the difference between the dependent variable scores of the groups is significant, it may be assumed that this is not due to chance and that the independent variable is effective.

Thus, by starting with two equivalent groups, administering the experimental treatment to one but not to the other, and collecting and analyzing the data thus obtained, suppose we find a significant difference between the two groups. We may legitimately assume that the two groups eventually differed because of the experimental treatment. Since this is the result that was predicted by our hypothesis, the hypothesis is supported, or confirmed. In other words, when a hypothesis is supported by experimental data, the hypothesis is probably true. On the other hand, if, in the above example, the control group is found to be equal or superior to the experimental group, the hypothesis is not supported by the data and we may conclude that it is probably false. Naturally, this step of the scientific method in which the hypothe-

sis is tested is considerably oversimplified in our brief presentation. . . .

Closely allied with testing of the hypothesis is an additional step of the scientific method, "generalization." After completing the phases outlined above, the experimenter may feel quite confident that the hypothesis is true for the specific conditions under which he tested it. He must underline *specific* conditions, however, and not lose sight of how specific they are in any given experiment. But the work of the scientist *qua* scientist is not concerned with truth under any *specific* set of conditions. Rather, he usually wants to make as *general* a statement as he possibly can about nature. And herein lies much of his joy and grief, for the more he generalizes his findings, the greater are the chances for error. Suppose that he has used college students as the subjects for his experiment. This selection does not mean that he is interested *only* in the behavior of college students. Rather, he is probably interested in the behavior of *all* human beings, and perhaps even of *all* organisms. Because he has found his hypothesis to be probably true for his particular group of subjects, can he now say that it is probably true for all humans? Or must he simply restrict his results to college students? Or must he narrow the focus even further, limiting it to those students attending the college at which he conducted his experiment? This, essentially, is the question of generalization— how widely can the experimenter generalize his results? He wants to generalize as widely as possible, yet not so widely that the hypothesis "breaks down." . . . The broad principle to remember is that he should state that his hypothesis is applicable to as wide a set of conditions (e.g., to as many classes of subjects) as the nature of his experiment warrants.

The next step in the scientific method, closely related to the preceding ones, concerns making predictions on the basis of the hypothesis. By this we mean that a hypothesis may be used to predict certain events in new situations—to predict for example, that a different group of subjects will act in the same way as a group studied in an earlier experiment.[7] We can add a final step in the scientific method, *replication.* In *replication* the experimenter conducts an additional experiment. He uses the confirmed hypothesis as the basis for predicting that a new sample of subjects will behave as did the original sample. If the prediction made

---

[7] A case can be made for not including prediction as a part of the scientific method, at least in some sciences (cf. Scriven, 1959).

by the use of the previously confirmed hypothesis is found to hold in the new situation, the probability that the hypothesis is true is tremendously increased.

In summary let us set down the various steps in the scientific method. (Be advised, however, that there are no rigid rules to follow in doing this. In any process that one seeks to classify into a number of arbitrary categories, some distortion is inevitable. Another source might offer a different classification, while still another one might refuse, quite legitimately, to attempt such an endeavor.)

First, the scientist states a problem that he wishes to investigate. Next, he formulates the hypothesis, a tentative solution to that problem. Third, he collects data relevant to the hypothesis. Following this, he tests the hypothesis by confronting it with the data and makes the appropriate inferences—he organizes the data through statistical means and determines whether the data support or refute the hypothesis. Fifth, assuming that the hypothesis is supported, he may wish to generalize to all things with which the hypothesis is legitimately concerned, in which case he should explicitly state the generality with which he wishes to advance his hypothesis. Sixth, he may wish to make a prediction to new situations, to events not studied in the original experiment. And finally, he may wish to test the hypothesis anew in the novel situation; that is, he might replicate (conduct a new experiment) to attempt to increase the probability of his hypothesis.

An example of a psychological experiment

To make the preceding discussion more concrete, consider an example of how an experiment might be conducted from its inception to its conclusion. Let us assume that a psychotherapist has some serious questions about how best to proceed with his clients in order to effect a "cure" as efficiently as possible. It usually happens that psychotherapists become aware of the basic ("real") problems of their clients before the clients themselves do. Thus, they are generally in a position to offer advice to the clients. In our example, however, the psychotherapist is not sure whether offering direct advice is a good procedure to follow. Not only may the client ignore the advice, but he may even react violently against it, thus retarding the therapeutic process. The problem may be stated as follows: Should a psychotherapist authoritatively advise his clients what their problems are and what they should do about them, or should he just

sit back and let the clients arrive at their own assessment of the problem and determine for themselves the best course to take? Assume that the psychotherapist believes the latter to be the better procedure. The reasons for or against his opinion need not detain us here. We simply note his hypothesis: If a client undergoing psychotherapy is allowed to arrive at the determination of his problem and its proposed solution by himself, then his recovery will be more efficient than if the psychotherapist gives him this information in an authoritative manner. We might identify the independent variable as "the amount of guidance furnished to the clients," and assign two values to it: first, a maximal amount of guidance, and second, a zero (or at least minimal) amount of guidance.[8]

Suppose that the psychotherapist has ten clients, and that he assigns them to two groups of five each. A great deal of guidance will then be given to one of the groups, while a minimum amount will be administered to the second group. The group that receives a minimum amount of guidance will be called the control group; the group that receives the maximum amount of guidance will be called the experimental group.

Throughout the course of therapy, then, the psychotherapist administers the two different treatments to the experimental and control groups. During this time he prevents the important extraneous variables from acting differently on the two groups. For example, he would want the clients from both groups to undergo therapy in the same place (his office, for instance) to eliminate the possibility that the progress of one group might differ from that of the other group because of the immediate surroundings in which the therapy takes place.

The dependent variable here may be specified as the progress toward recovery. Such a variable is obviously rather difficult to measure, but for illustrative purposes we might use a time measure. Thus, we might assume that the earlier the client is discharged by the therapist, the greater is his progress toward recovery. Assuming that the extraneous variables have been adequately controlled, the progress toward recovery (the dependent variable) depends on the particular values of the independent variable used, and on nothing else.

---

[8] This example well illustrates that *frequently* it is not appropriate to say that a zero amount of the independent variable can be administered to a control group.

As therapy progresses the psychotherapist collects his data. Specifically, he determines the amount of time each client spends in therapy before he is discharged. After all of the clients are discharged, the therapist compares the times for the experimental group against those for the control group. Let us assume that he finds that the mean amount of time in therapy of the experimental group is higher than that of the control group, and further, that a statistical test indicates that the difference is significant. That is, the group that received minimum guidance had a significantly lower time-in-therapy (the dependent variable) than did the group that received maximal guidance. It will be recalled that this is precisely what the therapist's hypothesis predicted. Since the results of the experiment are in accord with the hypothesis, we may conclude that the hypothesis is confirmed.

Now the psychotherapist is happy, since he has solved his problem and now knows which of the two methods of psychotherapy is better. But has he found "truth" only for himself, or is what he has found applicable to other situations—can other therapists also benefit by his results? Can his findings be extended, or generalized, to all therapeutic situations of the nature that he has studied? After serious consideration, he decides to assert that his findings are applicable to the psychotherapy conducted by other psychologists and publishes his findings in a scientific journal.

Inherent in the process of generalization is that of prediction (although there can be generalizations that are not used to make predictions). Here, in effect, what the therapist is doing when he generalizes, is predicting—predicting that the same results would be obtained if a new situation were studied. In this simple case the therapist is essentially saying that for other subjects, offering minimal guidance would result in more rapid recovery than if maximal guidance is offered them. To test this prediction, another psychotherapist conducts an experiment as outlined above (the experiment is replicated). His findings prove to be the same, and the hypothesis is again supported by the data. With this independent confirmation of the hypothesis as an added factor, it may be concluded that the probability of the hypothesis is increased. That is, our confidence that the hypothesis is true is considerably greater than before.[9]

REFERENCE
Scriven, M. Explanation and prediction in evolutionary theory, *Science*, 1959, **130**, 477–482.

[9] The oversimplication of several topics in this chapter is especially apparent in this fictitious experiment. For instance, the important extraneous variable of the therapist's own confidence in one method of psychotherapy is undoubtedly going to affect the results, and we have left this variable uncontrolled.

5

Dermo-optical Perception: A Peek Down the Nose

Martin Gardner

Those of us who are interested in the workings of the mind are constantly bombarded with accounts of all manner of spooky and ghostlike phenomena that remind us graphically of our very recent ignorance concerning the ways in which nature operates. Primitive man sought to explain what he didn't understand. Using his own experience and knowledge, he frequently arrived at a meaningful answer that enabled him to adapt his behavior to environmental conditions so that he and his family could survive. But there were also powerful and frightening happenings such as flashing lightning, crashing thunder, and howling winds that were beyond his comprehension. In order to rationalize such impor-

From Science, *Vol. 151, No. 11 (February 1966), 654–657. Copyright 1966 by the American Association for the Advancement of Science.*

tant experiences and to be able to talk about them, and in the hope that some sort of control could be exerted upon them, supernatural explanations were advanced. Throughout his early history, and indeed even into such highly organized and intellectual periods as the age of classical Greece, man "explained" natural phenomena as being the actions of certain gods or spirits.

Today we are still ignorant of many of the mysterious ways of nature. Even as our ancestors invented spirits and ghosts to try to explain and understand nature's ways, modern man, in attempting to explain what he doesn't understand, reverts to such primitive intermediaries between knowledge and the unknown as spirits and spiritualism.

Belief in extrasensory perception (ESP) is related to this. We know that we become aware of the world through our senses. We have long known that the very important senses of sight and hearing are augmented by the lesser-used sense of smell and by the rather poorly developed senses of touch and taste. We are not quite so aware of probably the most important sense of proprioception whereby we are enabled to move about and to be aware of just which part of our body is moving and in what way. We know about our environment and about ourselves, then, because we have senses that feed such information into our central nervous system where it becomes conscious.

But it often seems to us that we become aware of many things for which we can offer no sensible sensory explanation. How is it that a mother who is thousands of miles away from a child wakes in the night and "knows" that the child is ill or in some danger? Believers in extrasensory perception assert that such awareness comes to us through means outside our normal sensory channels.

Probably a large majority of psychologists remains skeptical of a method of information input that hasn't yet been discovered. In other words, we just do not believe that there is some "extra" sense that transmits and receives messages over miles of space and often over long periods of time. We believe that there are other explanations. Suppose that twenty-thousand mothers are miles away from their children and that they worry about their children as mothers are apt to do. If three or four of the children are really in danger, can we say that their mothers have extrasensory perception? What about all the mothers who are wrong? Most, if not quite all, of such seeemingly extrasensory experiences can probably be accounted for in such terms. Being dedicated to the scientific method, however, we recognize that the only way to prove or disprove the existence of such phenomena is to subject them to objective investigation.

An extrasensory phenomenon that has received a great deal of attention lately is dermo-optical perception (DOP), the supposed ability to "see" with one's fingers, toes, forehead, etc. In this selection, Gardner provides a particularly lucid account of the scientific study of such phenomena.

Science reporting in United States newspapers and mass-circulation magazines is more accurate and freer of sensationalism than ever before, with pseudoscience confined largely to books. A reverse situation holds in the Soviet Union. Except for the books that defended Lysenko's theories, Soviet books are singularly free of pseudoscience, and now that Lysenko is out of power, Western genetics is rapidly entering the new Russian biology textbooks. Meanwhile, Russian newspapers and popular magazines are sensationalizing science much as our Sunday supplements did in the 1920's. The Soviet citizen has recently been presented with accounts of fish brought back to life after having been frozen five thousand years, of deep-sea monsters that leave giant tracks across the ocean floor, of absurd perpetual-motion devices, of extraterrestrial scientists who have used a laser beam to blast an enormous crater in Siberia, and scores of similar stories.

By and large, the press in the United States has not taken this genre of Soviet science writing seriously. But in 1963 and 1964 it gave serious attention to a sudden revival, in Russia's popular press, of ancient claims that certain persons are gifted with the ability to "see" with their fingers.

The revival began with a report, in the summer of 1962, in the Sverdlovsk newspaper *Uralsky Rabochy*. Isaac Goldberg, of First City Hospital in Lower Tagil, had discovered that an epileptic patient, a twenty-two-year-old girl named Rosa Kuleshova, could read print simply by moving a fingertip over the lines. Rosa went to Moscow for more testing, and sensational articles about her abilities appeared in *Izvestia* and other newspapers and popular magazines. The first report in the United States was in *Time,* January 25, 1963.

When I first saw *Time's* photograph of Goldberg watching Rosa, who was blindfolded, glide her middle finger over a newspaper page, I broke into a loud guffaw. To explain that laugh, I must back up a bit. For thirty years my principal hobby has been magic. I contribute to conjuring journals, write treatises on card manipulation, invent tricks, and, in brief, am conversant with all branches of this curious art of deception, including a branch called "mentalism."

For half a century professional mentalists—performers, such as Joseph Dunninger, who claim unusual mental powers—have been entertaining audiences with "eyeless vision" acts. Usually the mentalist first has a committee from the audience seal his eyes shut with adhesive tape. Over each eye is taped something opaque, such as a powder puff or a silver dollar. Then a large black cloth is pulled around the eyes to form a tight blindfold. Kuda Bux, a Mohammedan who comes from Kashmir, is perhaps the best known of today's entertainers who feature such an act. He has both eyes covered with large globs of dough, then many yards of cloth are wound like a turban to cover his entire face from the top of his forehead to the tip of his chin. Yet Kuda Bux is able to read books, solve mathematical problems on a blackboard, and describe objects held in front of him.

The Nose Peek

Now I do not wish to endanger my standing in the magic fraternity by revealing too much, but let me say that Kuda Bux and other mentalists who feature eyeless vision do obtain, by trickery, a way of seeing. Many ingenious methods have been devised, but the oldest and simplest, surprisingly little understood except by magicians, is known in the trade as the "nose peek." If the reader will pause at this point and ask someone to blindfold him, he may be surprised to discover that it is impossible, without injury to his eyes, to prepare a blindfold that does not permit a tiny aperture, on each side of the nose, through which light can enter each eye. By turning the eyes downward one can see, with either eye, a small area beneath the nose and extending forward at an angle of 30 to 40 degrees from the vertical. A sleep-mask blindfold is no better; it does not fit

snugly enough around the nose. Besides, slight pressure on the top of the mask, under the pretense of rubbing the forehead, levers out the lower edge to permit even wider peeks. The great French magician Robert-Houdin (from whom Houdini took his name), in his memoirs (Robert-Houdin, 1958), tells of watching another conjuror perform a certain card trick while blindfolded. The blindfold, Robert-Houdin writes,

was a useless precaution . . . for whatever care may be taken to deprive a person of sight in this way, the projection of the nose always leaves a vacuum sufficient to see clearly.

Pushing wads of cotton or cloth into the two apertures accomplishes nothing. One can always, while pretending to adjust the blindfold, secretly insert his thumb and form a tiny space under the wadding. The wadding can actually be an asset in maintaining a wider aperture than there would be without it. I will not go into more subtle methods currently used by mentalists for overcoming such apparent obstacles as adhesive tape crisscrossed over the eyelids, balls of dough, and so on.

If the mentalist is obtaining information by a nose peek (there are other methods), he must carefully guard against what has been called the "sniff" posture. When the head of a blindfolded person is in a normal position, the view down the nose covers anything placed on the near edge of a table at which the person is seated. But to extend the peek farther forward it is necessary to raise the nose slightly, as though one is sniffing. Practiced performers avoid the sniff posture by tilting the head slightly under cover of some gesture, such as nodding in reply to a question, scratching the neck, and other common gestures.

One of the great secrets of successful blindfold work is to obtain a peek in advance, covered by a gesture, quickly memorize whatever information is in view, then later—perhaps many minutes later —to exploit this information under the pretense that it is just then being obtained. Who could expect observers to remember exactly what happened five minutes earlier? Indeed, only a trained mentalist, serving as an observer, would know exactly what to look for.

Concealing the "sniff" demands much cleverness and experience. In 1964, on a television show in the United States, a girl who claimed powers of eyeless vision was asked to describe, while blindfolded, the appearance of a stranger standing before her. She began with his shoes, then went on to his trousers, shirt, and necktie. As her description moved upward, so did her nose. The photograph in *Time* showed Rosa wearing a conventional blindfold. She is seated, one hand on a newspaper, and sniffing. The entire newspaper page is comfortably within the range of a simple nose peek.

Other DOP Claimants

After the publicity about Rosa, Russian women of all sorts turned up, performing even more sensational feats of eyeless vision. The most publicized of these was Ninel Sergyeyevna Kulagina. The Leningrad newspaper *Smena*, January 16, 1964, reported on her remarkable platform demonstration at the Psychoneurological Department of the Lenin-Kirovsk District. The committee who examined Ninel's blindfold included S. G. Fajnberg (Ninel's discoverer), A. T. Alexandrov, rector of the University of Leningrad, and Leonid Vasiliev, whose laboratory at the University is the center of parapsychology research in Russia. No magicians were present, of course. While "securely blindfolded," Ninel read from a magazine and performed other sensational feats. Vasiliev was reported as having described her demonstration as "a great scientific event."

There were dozens of other DOP claimants. The magazine *USSR* (now *Soviet Life*), published here in English, devoted four pages to some of them in its February 1964 issue (*USSR*, 1964). Experiments on Rosa, this article said, made it unmistakably clear that her fingers were reacting to ordinary light and not to infrared heat rays. Filters were used which could block either light or heat. Rosa was unable to "see" when the light (but not heat) was blocked off. She "saw" clearly when the heat rays (but not light) were blocked off. "The fingers have a retina," biophysicist Mikhail Smirnov is quoted as saying, "The fingers 'see' light."

Accounts of the women also appeared in scientific publications. Goldberg contributed a report on his work with Rosa to *Voprossy Psikhologii* in 1963.[1] Biophysicist N. D. Nyuberg wrote an article about Rosa for *Priroda*, May 1963.[2] Nyuberg reports that Rosa's fingers, just like the human eye, are sensitive to three color modes, and that, after special training at the neurological institute, she "succeeded in training her toes to distinguish between black and white." Other discussions of Rosa's exploits appeared in Soviet journals of philosophy and psychology.

Not only did Rosa read print with her fingers, she also described pictures in magazines, on cigarette packages, and on postage stamps. A *Life* correspondent reported that she read his business card by touching it with her elbow. She read print placed under glass and cellophane. In one test, when she was "securely blindfolded," scientists placed a green book in front of her, then flooded it with red light. Exclaimed Rosa: "The book has changed color!" The professors were dumbfounded. Rosa's appearance on a TV program called "Relay" flushed out new rivals. *Nedelya*, the supplement of *Izvestia*, found a nine-year-old Kharkov girl, Lena Bliznova, who staggered a group of scientists by reading print ("securely blindfolded") with fingers held a few inches *off* the page. Moreover, Lena read print just as easily with her toes and shoulders. She separated the black from the white chess pieces without a single error. She described a picture covered by a thick stack of books (see my remarks above about exploiting previously memorized information).

In the United States, *Life* (June 12, 1964) published a long uncritical article by Albert Rosenfeld (1964), the writer whose card Rosa had read with her elbow. The Russian work is summarized and hailed as a major scientific breakthrough. Colored symbols are printed on one page so the reader can give himself a DOP test. Gregory Razran, who heads the psychology department at Queens College, New York, is quoted as saying that perhaps "some entirely new kind of force or radiation" has been detected. Razran expected to see "an explosive outburst of research in this field. . . . To see without the eyes—imagine what that can mean to a blind man!"

Let us hope that Razran, in his research, will seek the aid of knowledgeable mentalists. In a photograph of one of his DOP tests, shown in the *Life* article, the subject wears a conventional sleepmask, with the usual apertures. She is reaching through a cloth hole in the center of an opaque partition to feel one of two differently colored plates. But there is nothing to prevent her from reaching out with her other hand, opening the cloth a bit around her wrist, then taking a nose peek through the opening.

The most amusing thing about such experimental designs is that there is a simple, but never

---

[1] For English translation, see I. Goldberg, *Soviet Psychology and Psychiatry*, 1963, **2**, 19.

[2] For English translation, see N. D. Nyuberg, *Federation Proceedings*, 1964, **22**, T701.

used, way to make sure all visual clues are eliminated. A blindfold, in any form, is totally useless, but one can build a light-weight aluminum box that fits over the subject's head and rests on padded shoulders. It can have holes at the top and back for breathing, but the solid metal must cover the face and sides, and go completely under the chin to fit snugly around the front of the neck. Such a box eliminates at one stroke the need for a blindfold, the cumbersome screen with arm holes, various bib devices that go under the chin, and other clumsy pieces of apparatus designed by psychologists unfamiliar with the methods of mentalism. No test made without such a box over the head is worth taking seriously. It is the only way known to me by which all visual clues can be ruled out. There remain, of course, other methods of cheating, but they are more complicated and not likely to be known outside the circles of professional mentalism.

In its 1964 story *Life* did not remind its readers of the three pages it had devoted in 1937, to Pat Marquis, "the boy with the X-ray eyes" (*Life,* 1937). Pat was then thirteen and living in Glendale, California. A local physician, Cecil Reynolds, discovered that Pat could "see" after his eyes had been taped shut and covered with a blindfold. Pat was carefully tested by reporters and professors, said *Life,* who could find no trickery. There are photographs of Pat, "securely blindfolded," playing Ping-Pong, pool, and performing similar feats. Naturally he could read. Reynolds is quoted as saying that he believed that the boy "saw" with light receptors in his forehead. Pat's powers were widely publicized at the time by other magazines and by the wire services. He finally agreed to being tested by J. B. Rhine (1963), of Duke University, who caught him nose peeking.

The truth is that claims of eyeless vision turn up with about the same regularity as tales of sea serpents. In 1898 A. N. Khovrin (1898), a Russian psychiatrist, published a paper on "A rare form of hyperaesthesia of the higher sense organs," in which he described the DOP feats of a Russian woman named Sophia. There are many earlier reports of blind persons who could tell colors with their fingers, but "blindness" is a relative term, and there is no way now to be sure how blind those claimants really were. It is significant that there are no recent cases of persons known to be totally blind who claim the power to read ordinary print, or even to detect colors, with their fingers, although it would seem that the blind would be the first to discover and develop such talents if they were possible.

Jules Romains' Work

Shortly after World War I the French novelist Jules Romains (1919), interested in what he called "paroptic vision," made an extensive series of tests with French women who could read while blindfolded. His book, *Vision Extra-Rétinienne* should be read carefully by every psychologist tempted to take the Russian claims seriously, for it describes test after test exactly like those that have been given to today's Russians. There are the same lack of controls, the same ignorance of the methods of mentalism, the same speculations about the opening of new scientific frontiers, the same unguarded predictions about how the blind may someday learn to "see," the same scorn for those who remain skeptical. Romains found that DOP was strongest in the fingers, but also present in the skin at any part of the body. Like today's Russian defenders of DOP, Romains is convinced that the human skin contains organs sensitive to ordinary light. His subjects performed poorly in dim light and could not see at all in total darkness. Romains thought that the mucous lining of the nose is especially sensitive to colors, because in dim light, when colors were hard to see, his subjects had a marked tendency to "sniff spontaneously."

The blindfolding techniques Romains used are similar to those used by the more recent investigators. Adhesive tape is crossed over the closed eyes, then folded rectangles of black silk, then the blindfold. At times cotton wool is pushed into the space alongside the nose, at times a projecting bib is placed under the chin. (Never a box over the head.) Anatole France witnessed and commented favorably on some of Romain's work. One can sympathize with the novelist when he complained to a U.S. reporter (Davy, 1964) that both Russian and American psychologists had ignored his findings and had simply "repeated one-twentieth of the discoveries I made and reported."

It was Romains' book that probably aroused magicians in the United States to devise acts of eyeless vision. Harlan Tarbell, of Chicago, worked out a remarkable act of this type which he performed frequently.[3] Stanley Jaks, a professional

---

[3] See H. Tarbell, "X-ray Eyes and Blindfold Effects." *The Tarbell Course in Magic* (New York: Tannen, 1954) **6,** 251–261. Tarbell speaks of his own work in this field as a direct result of his interest in Romains' work, and briefly describes an eyeless vision act by a woman who performed under the stage name of Shireen in the early 1920's.

mentalist from Switzerland, later developed his method of copying a stranger's signature, upside down and backward, after powder puffs had been taped over his eyes and a blindfold added (Gardner, 1949). Kuda Bux uses still other techniques.[4] At the moment, amateurs everywhere are capitalizing on the new wave of interest in DOP. In my files is a report on Ronald Coyne, an Oklahoma boy who lost his right eye in an accident at the age of seven. When his left eye is "securely blindfolded," his empty right eye socket reads print without hesitation. Young Coyne has been appearing at revival meetings to demonstrate his miraculous power. "For thirteen years he has had continuous vision where there is no eye," reads an advertisement in a Miami newspaper for an Assembly of God meeting. "Truly you must say 'Mine eyes have seen the glory of God.' "[5]

Tests in the United States

The most publicized DOP claimant in the United States is Patricia Stanley. Richard P. Youtz, of the psychology department at Barnard College, was discussing the Soviet DOP work at a faculty lunch one day. Someone who had taught high school in Owensboro, Kentucky, recalled that Patricia, then a student, had astounded everyone by her ability to identify objects and colors while blindfolded. Youtz traced Patricia to Flint, Michigan, and in 1963 he made several visits to Flint, tested her for about sixty hours, and obtained sensational results. These results were widely reported by the press and by such magazines of the occult as *Fate* (Saltzman, 1964). The soberest account, by science writer Robert K. Plumb (1964), appeared in the *New York Times*. Mrs. Stanley did not read print, but she seemed able to identify the colors of test cards and pieces of cloth by rubbing them with her fingers. Youtz's work, together with the Russian, provided the springboard for Leonard Wallace Robinson's article "We have more than five senses" in the *New York Times Magazine,* Sunday, March 15.

Youtz's first round of tests, in my opinion, were so poorly designed to eliminate visual clues that they cannot be taken seriously. Mrs. Stanley wore a conventional sleep-mask. No attempt was made to plug the inevitable apertures. Her hands were placed through black velvet sleeves, with elastic around the wrists, into a lightproof box constructed of plywood and painted black. The box could be opened at the other side to permit test material to be inserted. There was nothing to prevent Mrs. Stanley from picking up a test card or piece of colored cloth, pushing a corner under the elastic of one sleeve, and viewing the exposed corner with a simple nose peek. Youtz (1963) did have a double sleeve arrangement that might have made this difficult, but his account of his first round of tests, on which Mrs. Stanley performed best, indicate that it was attached only on the rare occasions when a photomultiplier tube was used. Such precautions as the double sleeve, or continuous and careful observation from behind, seemed unnecessary because Mrs. Stanley was securely blindfolded. Moreover, there was nothing to prevent Mrs. Stanley from observing, by nose peeks, the test material as it was being placed into the light-tight box.

Here is a description of Mrs. Stanley's performance by the *New York Times* reporter who observed her:

Mrs. Stanley concentrates hard during the experiments. . . . Sometimes she takes three minutes to make up her mind. . . . She rests her forehead under the blindfold against the black box as though she were studying intently. Her jaw muscles work as she concentrates (New York Times, 1964).

While concentrating, she keeps up a steady flow of conversation with the observers, asking for hints on how she is doing.

Youtz returned to Flint in late January 1964 for a second round of tests, armed with more knowledge of how blindfolds can be evaded (we exchanged several letters about it[6]) and plans for tighter controls. I had been unsuccessful in persuading him to adopt a box over the head, but even without this precaution, results of the second round were not above chance expectation. These negative results were reported by the *New York Times* (1964), but not by any other newspaper or news magazine that had publicized the positive results of the first round of tests. Youtz (1964) was disappointed, but he attributed the failure to cold weather.

---

[4] A description of an early eyeless vision act by Kuda Bux will be found in H. Price, *Confessions of a Ghost-hunter* (New York: Putnam, 1936), chap. 19.

[5] For the story of Ronald Coyne, who was born in 1943 at Chouteau, Oklahoma, see Mrs. R. R. Coyne, *When God Smiled on Ronald Coyne,* rev. ed. (Tulsa, Okla.: Ronald Coyne Revivals, P.O. Box 1265, 1965), 77 pp.

[6] For an exchange of published letters, see M. Gardner, *New York Times Magazine,* April 5, 1964; and R. P. Youtz, *Ibid.,* April 26, 1964.

A third series of tests was made on April 20, for an observing committee of four scientists. Results were again negative. In the warm weather of June, Youtz tested Mrs. Stanley a fourth time, over a three-day period. Again, performance was at chance level. Youtz (1964) attributes this last failure to Mrs. Stanley's fatigue. He remains convinced that she does have the ability to detect colors with her fingers and suspects that she does this by sensing delicate differences in temperature (Youtz, 1965). Although Russian investigators had eliminated this as an explanation of Rosa's powers, Youtz believes that his work with Mrs. Stanley, and later with less skillful Barnard students, will eventually confirm this hypothesis. He strongly objects to calling the phenomenon "vision." None of his subjects has displayed the slightest ability to read with the fingers.

Ninel Is Caught Cheating

In Russia, better-controlled testing of Rosa has strongly indicated nose peeking. Several articles have suggested this, notably those by L. Teplov, author of a well-known book on cybernetics, in the March 1-7, 1964 issue of *Nedelya,* and in the May 25 issue of the Moscow *Literaturnaya Gazeta.* Ninel Kulagina, Rosa's chief rival was carefully tested at the Bekhterev Psychoneurological Scientific Research Institute in Leningrad. B. Lebedev (1964), the institute's head, and his associates summarize their findings as follows:

In essence, Kulagina was given the same tasks as before, but under conditions of stricter control and in accordance with a plan prepared beforehand. And this was the plan: to alternate experiments in which the woman could possibly peek and eavesdrop with experiments where peeking would be impossible. The woman of course did not know this. As was to be expected, phenomenal ability was shown in the first instance only. In the second instance [under controls] Kulagina could distinguish neither the color nor the form. . . .
Thus the careful checking fully exposed the sensational "miracle." There were no miracles whatever. There was ordinary hoax.

In a letter to *Science,* Joseph Zubin (1965), a biometrics researcher at the New York State Department of Mental Hygiene, reported the negative results of his testing of an adolescent who "read fluently" after blindfolds had been secured around the edges with adhesive tape. Previous testing by several scientists had shown no evidence of visual clues. It became apparent, however, that the subject tensed muscles in the blindfolded area until "a very tiny, inconspicuous chink appeared at the edge. Placing an opaque disk in front of the chink prevented reading, but not immediately. The subject had excellent memory and usually continued for a sentence or two after blocking of the reading material." Applying zinc ointment to the edges of the adhesive proved only temporarily effective, because muscle tensing produced new chinks (made easier to detect by the white ointment). A professional magician, James Randi, participated in the investigations.

The majority of psychologists, both here and in the Soviet Union, have remained unimpressed by the latest revival of interest in DOP. In view of the failures of subjects to demonstrate DOP when careful precautions were taken to rule out peeks through minute apertures, and in view of the lack of adequate precautions in tests that yielded positive results, this prevailing scepticism appears to be strongly justified.

REFERENCES

Davy, J. *Observer,* February 2, 1964.
Gardner, M. *Sphinx,* February 1949, **12,** 334–337; *Linking Ring,* October 1954, **34,** 23–25. Also, G. Groth, He writes with your hand. *Fate,* October 1952, **5,** 39–43.
Khovrin, A. N. In *Contributions to neuropsychic medicine.* Moscow, 1898.
Lebedev, B. *Leningradskaya Pravda,* March 15, 1964. Translated for me by Albert Parry, department of Russian studies, Colgate University.
Life, Pat Marquis of California can see without his eyes. April 19, 1937, 57–59.
New York Times, Housewife is unable to repeat color "readings" with fingers. February 2, 1964.
Plumb, R. K. Woman who tells color by touch mystifies psychologist. *New York Times,* January 8, 1964. See also Plumb's follow-up article, Sixth sense is hinted in ability to "see" with fingers. *Ibid.,* January 26, 1964. The *New York Times* also published an editorial, Can fingers "see"? February 6, 1964.
Rhine, J. B. *Parapsychology Bulletin,* August 1963, **66,** 2–4.
Robert-Houdin, J. E. *Confidences d'un prestidigitateur.* Blois, 1858. Chap. 5. English translation, *Memoirs of Robert-Houdin: Ambassador, author, and conjuror.* London, 1859. Reprinted as *Memoirs of Robert-Houdin: King of the conjurers.* New York: Dover, 1964.
Romains, J. *Vision extra-rétinienne.* Paris, 1919. English translation by C. K. Ogden, *Eyeless vision.* New York: Putnam, 1924.
Rosenfeld, A. Seeing color with the fingers. *Life,* June 12, 1964, 102–113.
Saltzman, P. *Fate,* May 1964, **17,** 38–48.
USSR, 1964, **89,** 32.

Youtz, R. P. Aphotic digital color sensing. A case under study. Photocopied for the Bryn Mawr meeting of the Psychonomic Society, August 29, 1963.

Youtz, R. P. The case for skin sensitivity to color; with a testable explanatory hypothesis. Photocopied

for the Psychonomic Society, Niagara Falls, Ontario, October 9, 1964.

Youtz, R. P. Letter. *Scientific American,* June 1965, **212,** 8–10.

Zubin, J. *Science,* 1965, **147,** 985.

6

The Measurement of Psychological Entities

William L. Hays

Probably the most easily overlooked requirement for good work in science and scientific psychology is that of accurate measurement. Imagine the difficulty that road builders would have if they used a stretchy rubber ruler to measure the width, thickness, and length of their roads. Depending upon how much they stretched the rubber ruler, the road would widen and narrow, twist and meander, much as a cow path in a pasture. Fortunately, the wood and metal measuring instruments that are used vary only slightly in length from time to time and from place to place.

Unfortunately, the psychologist often finds himself in the position of the man who is using a rubber ruler. He is interested in measuring such characteristics as motivation, knowledge, attitude, and intelligence. The measuring instruments he uses are tests, and scores on a given test may vary from one administration to another. Test results depend to some extent upon how much the individuals giving and scoring the test stretch and twist their rubber ruler. This article points out several problems and some solutions in the area of measurement.

Measurement in Science

A hallmark of the slow but steady growth of psychology from a branch of speculative philosophy to a scientific discipline is its increasing concern with quantification. It is generally agreed that science has as its ultimate goal the statement of relationships in precise and easily communicated form. The greatest precision and succinctness of communication is achieved by a numerical or quantitative statement of relationships. That is, certain properties of the things studied by the scientist are measured, or given numerical values; and at their simplest, the general principles or laws of the science are statements about the connection between the numerical value of one phenomenon and that of another. An example in physics is Boyle's Law, which states the relationship between temperature and pressure exerted by an enclosed gas. An example in chemistry is the weight relations in chemical reactions as given by the molecular weights of the compounds involved. Modern physics and chemistry are filled with such

highly precise statements of numerical relationships, which summarize and communicate results that can be checked in the laboratory.

Naturally, quantitative principles from physics and chemistry represent some of the most highly developed parts of modern science, and principles of similar exactitude and elegance are not so common in other newer, and less well-developed sciences. Only in modern times have the biological sciences, for example, established quantitative principles that are on a par with those established in chemistry and physics. The behavioral sciences (psychology, as well as economics, sociology, political science, and anthropology) still lag behind even biology in this respect.

However, a given discipline that does not possess a large body of established quantitative laws is not necessarily less "good," or less "scientific,"

From Quantification in Psychology *by William L. Hayes.* © *1967 by Wadsworth Publishing Company, Inc. Belmont, California. Reprinted by permission of publisher, Brooks/Cole Publishing Company.*

than the physical sciences. Science is, after all, properly thought of as *a method for gaining systematic knowledge,* rather than the finished products of that method. Scientific method consists of the application of careful, controlled observation, under conditions that are public and repeatable, followed by communication and attempts at coordination of results. Any pursuit of knowledge that adheres to the ideal of open, careful, and controlled observation, and attempts to arrive at systematic accounts of what was observed and why, is scientific. It is scientific irrespective of the area studied or the details of the methods used. Systematic dating of cultures by potsherds is as scientific as any method used in high-energy physics, although the concerns and methods of scientists working in these two fields are understandably different.

*   *   *

Measurement and Human Values

For centuries, while man was already applying careful empirical observations·to the world about him and developing the foundations for physics, chemistry, biology, and astronomy, with all of their various branches, the serious study of man *himself* was left largely to the poets, priests, politicians, and philosophers of the world. Man as an ethical and religious being, man as a social animal, man as the object or wielder of power, man's place in the universe—all of these questions have been the subjects of inquiry since the dawn of time. "What and who is man?" the finest intellects of the ages have asked, and their answers still move us by their beauty and their profundity. But these are the answers given by informal observation, by intuition, by speculation, by unaided reason, and by revelation. And there are as many answers to this question as there are askers. These answers move us, indeed, but not because they are true or testable in the wide and concrete sense of a physical law. When we read Aristotle, St. Thomas Aquinas, Machiavelli, or Shakespeare, we may exclaim, "Yes, that is exactly what people are like!" But we do so because the author touches our emotions and our private experience, and not because he draws upon the recorded results of a large body of careful, precise, and controlled observation.

There is great confusion over this point; but perhaps the author can at least make his own position clear: The study of man by the poet and the philosopher has always been and will always

be necessary to point out the meanings and the values of human existence and the proper role of man in the scheme of things. A scientist acting *as scientist* does not aspire to answer such questions. Psychology properly is concerned with *how* man behaves—as an organism, as a personality, and as a social being, and not with the ultimate values and goals of human life, important as these may be. Viewed in this way, man is as appropriate an object of scientific study as a physical element, a stone, or a tree. The serious psychologist realizes that by treating man as an object of systematic study he by no means answers questions of the meaning of man's existence or obviates such questions. Questions of *how* and of the *ultimate why* are very different indeed, and the true scientist knows his limitations.

*   *   *

Observation and Measurement

Granted, then, that the proper concern of psychology is the objective study of behavior, its mechanisms, and its underlying psychological foundations, how does one go about objectifying the behavior under study? The first principle of a scientific study is that *the investigator must describe appropriately and unambiguously and communicate explicitly what he observes.* The psychologist, like any other scientist, is under an obligation to report not only what he observes but also the circumstances and methods by which he made his observations. Only if this is done will the observations be scientific, in the sense that other scientists can repeat the circumstances of the observations (at least in principle) and question, accept, or reject their validity. The report of the conditions under which data were collected, in sufficient detail that these observations may be repeated, is an essential ingredient of the scientific enterprise. Indeed, as we shall see, the specification of the conditions of observation is the first step in the *measurement* of a given phenomenon, such as a behavior.

When one can specify the conditions under which something occurred, the next problem is to specify *what* occurred. This must be ·done in such a way that any other sufficiently trained observer will be able to say "Yes, that is what is happening," or "No, that did not occur," when he repeats the procedure. What is required of the original investigator is an explicit statement of the procedure he followed while observing and categorizing events as they occurred.

A systematic rule of procedure that permits one to identify each possible event that might occur in the given observational situation with one of a set of different categories or symbols is called a measurement operation or measurement rule. In order to measure something, the observer must follow a procedure by which each observed event can be classified unambiguously into a category represented by a label, a number, or some other symbol. The words *operation* and *rule* in the definition given above are not to be taken too literally. Sometimes the measurement operation requires the use of a mechanical device such as a thermometer: Application of the thermometer is a standardized mechanism or procedure which, when carried out on a given object, gives a number, its temperature. Sometimes the measurement operation may make use of a physical, though nonmechanical, component or stimulus. An example is the use of the intelligence quotient (IQ). A person in this case is presented with a test. After he has responded and his score is computed, he is assigned a number—his IQ score. . . .

*   *   *

So far, then, we have seen that measurement involves (1) an object of measurement, (2) a specified standard situation, (3) a measurement operation in which a rule of procedure is followed, and (4) an assignment of the object in question to a category, number, or symbolic class. An essential requirement of a measurement operation is that it must enable one to say exactly *how* the category, number, or symbol assigned to an object was actually found. The measurement operation must be specifiable.

Categorical Measurement

Ordinarily, we think of measurement as the assignment of a *number* to an object, as when weight is measured in pounds, when length is measured in inches, or when a test is scored by the number of questions answered correctly. However, no one would be satisfied with a measurement procedure that simply gave numbers if these numbers had no meaning. For instance, if someone drew a card from a playing deck and assigned *you* the number of the card drawn, would the number mean anything? Would it tell anything about *you?* Note that this procedure could be elaborated into a perfectly good measurement *operation* under certain circumstances. The trouble is that the numbers obtained mean absolutely

nothing. At least they mean nothing as applied to the person to whom they are assigned, thus, the two questions that must be raised next: What roles do numbers play in measurement? How does one discuss the meaning of the results of a measurement operation?

As has already been pointed out, before a scientist can record and communicate the *different* events he observes, he must have some scheme for grouping differing events into different categories or types. At the very least he must have some *classification scheme.* The measurement rule tells him how to go about putting each event into the proper category of his scheme. In everyday life we classify constantly. For example, the common and proper nouns in our language form a large and complex classifying scheme. When we wish to record and communicate what we experience, we place our experience into a particular category by giving it a name. Our training in the language has taught us this measurement procedure. Its formal rules are given in dictionaries and lexicons, which tell us when a particular object of our experience should be called a "teapot" and when an "elephant." Science, too, has its own vocabularies or schemes of categories and labels for the things it studies. In biology, for instance, objects of study are classified as plant and animal. Elaborate rules have been evolved so that any living object can be classified as one or the other with high consensus among biologists. Modern physics has classified elementary particles of matter into such categories as proton, neutron, electron, and positron. The measurement operation for the classification of a particular occurrence of a particle includes, among other things, its observed path on a photographic plate or in a bubble chamber. Medical diagnosis uses a classification scheme that is based partly on the history and symptoms the patient shows and partly on the apparent source of the disease. The skilled diagnostician knows the conventional measurement rules and applies them when he assigns a particular patient to a particular category. All branches of science, in fact, make use of sets of qualitative labels or categories, along with the measurement rules or operations specifying how to assign an observed phenomenon to a given category.

The assignment of objects of observation to categories according to some classifying scheme and following some specified rules of procedure is measurement at its simplest and most primitive level. In psychology this has come to be called *categorical* or *nominal measurement.* . . .

*   *   *

Numerical Measurement

Although any measurement operation can be thought of as involving a set of mutually exclusive and exhaustive categories into which objects of observation are assigned, "measurement" commonly means the assignment of a number to each object measured. For this reason one must inquire into the kinds of numbers that are frequently the end products of measurement operations.

In the first place, numbers may be used simply as arbitrary *names* for the categories into which objects are mapped. In recent years the United States has been divided into service areas, and each has been given a number by the telephone company. These are the familiar area-code numbers. Thus, any telephone subscriber in the New York City area currently is given the number 212, in the Chicago area the number 312, and so forth. The rule for this assignment is provided by a table in the front portion of a telephone directory. If one wishes to know the area code number for a person living in Oshkosh, Nebraska, for example, he simply consults the table. Note that these numbers are only names or arbitrary symbols to denote residence in a particular area. No one would assert that because person X living in Chicago has area code 312 and person Y living in New York has area code 212, that X somehow has 100 units more of something than does person Y. One must always remember that numbers *can* serve merely as names or category labels. Such labels represent *qualitative* differences though not necessarily quantitative differences.

On the other hand, some measurement operations produce *ordinal numbers.* Such numbers simply show the *place in order,* according to some characteristic, each object achieved under observation. For example, in a footrace the runner who breaks the tape is given first place or is assigned the number 1. The runner who comes in second is assigned the number 2, and so on for the other runners. Thus, the race itself can be thought of as a procedure for measuring the speed of each runner according to an earned *ordinal* position. It really makes no difference whether X beats Y by .001 second or by 100 seconds. X is still assigned the number 1 (or first place) and Y the number 2 (or second place) if the relative position of each runner at the finish is all that counts. Ordinal numbers always have the characteristic that they symbolize *relative position* or *relative amount* according to some characteristic. However, *differences in ordinal numbers do not necessarily tell anything at all about the differences in amount of*

the characteristic the objects actually possess. Thus, although X comes in first in the race, Y second, and Z third and although $2 - 1 = 1$ and $3 - 2 = 1$ in arithmetic, one cannot say that the difference in speed between Y and Z is the same as the difference in speed between X and Y. From ordinal information alone, all one can say is that X was faster than either Y or Z and that Y was faster than Z in the particular race. A very large variety of measurement operations in psychology yield ordinal numbers. They show only that X was *more something* than Y, and give no information at all about the true amount or quantity of difference between X and Y.

* * *

Particularly in the physical sciences, certain measurement operations give numbers for which not only the order but also the arithmetic differences between numbers are meaningful. This is called *interval scaling.* The thermometer is used as a mechanical part of a procedure for assigning a number, temperature, to any given object. Two objects measured with a Fahrenheit thermometer may give readings of perhaps 98° and 112°. Here one can say not only that the second object shows a higher temperature than the first but that the second object has $112° - 98° = 14°$ *more* temperature than the first. The differences between numerical values can be interpreted directly as differences in amount of the characteristic measured. In interval scaling, when two pairs of numbers differ by the same arithmetic amount, one can be certain that the objects assigned those numbers differ by the same true amount of the characteristic measured. Furthermore, in interval scaling, the numbers assigned to objects may be multiplied by any positive constant number and have any constant number added to them and the result will still be an interval scale (though with a different unit and zero point from the original). This principle is illustrated by the Fahrenheit and Centigrade thermometers. Temperature read on a Centigrade thermometer can always be transformed into Fahrenheit temperature, and vice versa, by multiplying by the appropriate constant and adding a constant. (Fahrenheit temperature $= 9/5$ Centigrade $+ 32$.)

* * *

Certain physical measurement operations also produce *ratio scales.* The measurement of length is a good example. When object X has a length of 25 feet and object Y a length of 50 feet, it is meaningful to say not only that Y is 25 feet longer than

X but also that Y has *twice as much length* as X. Note that this statement is not meaningful when applied to two objects showing temperatures of 25° and 50° Fahrenheit. One does not say that the second object has twice as much temperature as the first. Notice also that the readings of temperature of these same objects taken on a Centigrade thermometer would give a different ratio. In ratio-scale measurement, ratios of values are *directly* interpretable as ratios of amounts of the property being measured. An object with no length at all must get the value 0 length. There is nothing arbitrary about the phenomenon assigned value 0 in a ratio scale—unlike the situation of temperature measurement, in which one can have negative values and the assignment of 0 can be changed about at will. Only the unit of measurement for length is arbitrary. One can quite arbitrarily convert feet into inches, into miles, into meters, or into other units by multiplying by the proper positive constants. Any ratio scale, such as that for length, can be altered by multiplication by a positive constant, and the resulting numbers will still be a ratio scale.

*   *   *

Different measurement operations in psychology are based on a wide variety of theoretical and empirical underpinnings. Some measurement operations yield, at best, only nominal or categorical measurement. Often measurement in psychology is based only on the most informal and ad hoc rules of procedure. On the other hand, rather elaborate theoretical justification exists for some of the operations used by psychologists to measure psychological events. Such theoretically supported procedures can often be regarded as yielding at least interval-scale values to the objects measured. However, before the psychologist can claim that the properties he measures are indeed represented at the interval-scale level—so that differences between numerical values can be interpreted as differences in amount of the property under study—he *must* be able to provide both a theoretical and an empirical justification for his procedure. For a science as undeveloped as psychology in many of its branches, this is not always possible, of course. But unless such a rationale is available, one has a right to question any interpretation of numerical measurements that treats the numbers as more than labels or indicators of order. On the other hand, even such labeling numbers or ordinal numbers can be very useful to the scientist in his search for valid and predictive relationships, even though such numbers may not give the scientist the ability

to state and to use the relationships he finds as precisely and simply as he would be able to do if the numbers were more adequate reflections of amount.

*   *   *

How does one go about measuring some property of an animal or human? Where does one start? Clearly the psychologist must have some idea of the characteristic he wishes to measure. Even before he faces the problem of how to measure, he must have singled out the property or properties that he feels it important to observe in order to answer his particular research question. Granted that this decision has been made, and he knows that he wants to measure the degree of some property that each of a group of human beings shows, he then must face the question of how to proceed. How will this property be reflected in his observations? What relation exists between the behaviors he can actually observe and the amounts of the property in question? Perhaps this is a property that can be observed directly, and perhaps the individuals to be measured can even be compared directly with a standard. For example, if the scientist wishes to describe the weight of each of a group of boys, his problem is relatively simple. Very routine procedures exist for comparing each boy with a set of standard weights and arriving at a "weight number" for each. On the other hand, suppose that the scientist is interested in the mechanical ability each boy possesses. Here, the problem is more complex, since mechanical ability is hardly a directly observable physical property, and there is no simple standard against which he can judge each boy. Ordinarily, the psychologist would then use a test or a situation designed to elicit evidence of mechanical ability from each subject. Each boy is made to behave in a way that should give evidence of mechanical ability. Then the psychologist has some overt behaviors which can be compared from boy to boy, so that at least some relative standing on this characteristic may be assigned to each subject.

Suppose, however, that the psychologist is interested in a characteristic such as the masculinity of each boy. This is a much more difficult characteristic to define or to elicit as behavior. Certainly there is no obvious standard against which each boy might be compared to measure his degree of this characteristic. The degree of masculinity would probably have to be inferred indirectly from a variety of behavioral responses. Many of the behavioral or physical indicators the psychologist would eventually use in arriving at an index of masculinity might have little or no obvious connection with the trait he hopes to measure. Rather, the psychologist must construct his own measurement operation. It would be based on theory or other empirical studies about the connections, often quite indirect, between responses to situations and masculinity. The measurement of the trait itself may not be at all possible in any direct and obvious way. This raises a point that it is important to bear in mind in any discussion of measurement and, in particular, of the differences in measurement procedures among the various sciences.

Fundamental and Derived Measurement Operations

In the physical world there are a few properties of objects that are so obvious and all-pervasive in our experience that they were long ago singled out as "fundamental" physical characteristics. One such property is *length,* or *linear extent,* which—as height, breadth, distance, etc.—can be applied to an enormous number of the objects of our experience. Length is a property that almost all objects of our experience possess to some degree. Weight is another very compelling physical property of objects: We think of virtually everything in the field of our everyday experience as having weight. Furthermore, both length and weight can be measured directly by comparisons with standards. We can express the length of an object by comparing it with the length of a standard object such as a ruler. We can determine the weight of an object by achieving a state of balance between it and one or more objects of standard weight. Such measurement operations, in which an amount of the property possessed by an object is determined by a simple and direct comparison with an object showing a standard amount of that property, are called *fundamental measurement operations.* The characteristics of objects that are measurable by fundamental operations are often called *extensive* properties. One need not define length by reference to other quantities. Length is measured *in terms* of length. Similarly, weight is measured in terms of other weights and the principle of a balance. In this sense these properties are truly fundamental.

On the other hand, as the physical sciences developed, scientists turned their attention to other and less obvious properties of objects, which could not be measured by a simple comparison of objects with standards. Rather, the operations for measuring these other, *intensive,* properties had to be *derived* from the known or presumed connections between amounts of the intensive property and amounts of one of the more fundamental characteristics. As an example of such *derived measurement* consider temperature measurement once again. The temperature of an object is not measured by the direct comparison of an object with another object of standard temperature. Instead, the known relationship of increasing temperature to the increasing volume of a fluid in a tube is used. The warmer an object is, the higher will the mercury in an adjacent thermometer rise. What one actually observes when he reads a thermometer is *not* the temperature. It is the height (i.e., cylindrical volume calibrated as length) of a column of mercury. The relationship of this height of the column of mercury to the temperature of the object is derived from what we know about heat and expansion. This known relationship gives us the ability to talk about the height of the column of mercury as though it stood directly for amount of temperature. In this way temperature measurement via thermometer is derived rather than fundamental. . . .

The situation of the psychologist is identical to that of the physical scientist so long as he deals with the physical aspects of his subjects or with the physical characteristics of their behaviors. As physical objects, humans or animals can be measured in physical ways. Behaviors can be measured in the same ways that any other observable physical events can be measured. For many of the psychologists' purposes such measurements are sufficient. On the other hand, the psychologist often wishes to go beyond directly observable behaviors and to measure psychological states or characteristics, which can be inferred only indirectly from observable behaviors. Then, like the physical scientist, he must depend upon measurement operations that are derived from known or theorized connections between the psychological situation of the subject and his behaviors in a given stimulus situation.

*   *   *

Measurement and Arithmetic

In the case of a fundamental measurement of a property such as length each arithmetic operation on numbers is paralleled by the possibility of a physical operation in terms of length. For example, the addition of numerical length A to numerical length B is paralleled by the physical operation of placing two straight rods end to end, one with length A and the other with length B.

When the ends of the two rods are joined, the result is a single rod with $A + B$ amount of length. Thus, the mathematical operation of addition of the two numbers, A and B, is an exact parallel of the *physical addition,* or concatenation, of two amounts of the property being measured. Similarly, laying ten rods of standard length A in series end to end produces a rod with length $10A$ just as arithmetically as A multiplied by the number 10 yields the number $10A$. If a rod of length A is sawed into three rods of equal length, each will be found to have length $A/3$ just as the rules of arithmetic lead us to expect.

* * *

As yet, the social and behavioral sciences lack clear agreement about those properties of man and his behavior that might be identified as fundamental *psychological* properties. Thus, for psychological measurement there exists no clear-cut parallel between such mathematical operations as addition and experimental psychological procedures. What exactly should one mean by psychological or behavioral addition? This problem may be solved someday; but at the present time only very primitive attempts have been made. It is safe to say that until the day comes and until psychologists and other behavioral scientists isolate and agree upon the fundamental measurement operations from which other measurement procedures will be derived and justified, the theory of measurement of psychological entities will be more incomplete and disorganized than measurement theory in the physical sciences.

Psychological and Physical Measurement

It was discovered long ago that the really obvious physical properties of a person or his behavior need have little or nothing to do with psychological properties such as intelligence, or the amount of fear a person is experiencing at a given moment, or what he perceives some stimulus to be. Certainly there seem to be no fundamental or extensive psychological properties that one may measure by simple ruler-like comparisons with a standard, as is possible in the physical sciences. It is true that certain behaviors, like simple choice responses, can be merely counted, whereas other activities of the living organism, such as galvanic skin response, heartbeat, and blood pressure, can be given quite precise physical representation. However, no easily quantified physical aspect of a living being has yet been found sufficiently useful to serve as a fundamental yardstick for searching out psychological relationships. Since psychologists and other behavioral scientists are not at all in agreement about what aspects of psychological life they should identify as the most basic, they cannot be expected to agree on a basic set of properties that ought to be measured in order to provide a standard from which other, derived, measurement operations might be established.

A great many measurement operations in psychology are derived from theoretical postulates. The postulates show how magnitudes of some psychological property *ought* to be reflected in occurrences of particular behaviors. In a great many instances, however, these theoretical rationalizations for measuring in a particular way remain purely theoretical, since they are not yet supported by a solid experimental underpinning. It is, of course, quite true that some physical measurement operations appeal ultimately to theory —theory that has not been, or that cannot be, verified. On the other hand, virtually all of the measurement procedures used in the physical sciences rest both on theory and on a great deal of supporting empirical evidence. This evidence shows not only that the assumed physical relationships on which the measurement procedure rests are tenable but also that the derived measurements are *predictively valid* and actually do the work they were designed to do by giving useful relationships in their own right. Although psychologists and other behavioral scientists are aware of the need to establish the *validity* of a particular measurement operation, in most instances they do not have enough evidence either to support the theoretical foundations of the procedure or to establish its predictive usefulness.

The foregoing should not be taken to mean that the problems of psychological measurement are somehow essentially different from measurement problems in the physical sciences. Neither does it mean that psychologists have been remiss in their responsibility to support their measurement operations with theoretical and empirical backing. On the contrary, psychologists are acutely aware of the difficulty of this problem and give a great deal of effort and attention to the establishment of theoretically and empirically valid measurement operations. The problem is exceedingly complex, however, and it is unfair to compare the accomplishments of only a few generations of psychologists with the accomplishments of a line of physical scientists that extends into the distant past. Much remains to be done, and it is significant that research into problems of measurement occupies a great deal of the attention of psychologists today.

7

Will Psychologists Study Human Problems?

Nevitt Sanford

In the first article in this section Spence argues against a premature attempt by psychologists to answer practical problems. Contrasting this approach, Sanford here argues the urgent necessity of making a start on the global, significant human problems of today. He challenges the widely accepted assumption that the building blocks established by studying simple variables in very simple situations will someday add up to an understanding of the complexities of real life.

Immergluck, in another article in this section, shows that it can be logically inferred that personal, psychological, and social behavior all fit into a deterministic framework. This implies that important research can be undertaken at any level of complexity with good expectations that useful scientific data will result.

* * *

We have produced a whole generation of research psychologists who never had occasion to look closely at any one person, let alone themselves, who have never imagined what it might be like to be a subject in one of their experiments, who, indeed, have long since lost sight of the fact that their experimental subjects are, after all, people. (Let us leave the rats out of it for the moment.) They can define variables, state hypotheses, design experiments, manipulate data statistically, get publishable results—and miss the whole point of the thing. Reading their papers you get a strange sense of the unreality of it all; the authors' conceptions of variables and processes seem a bit off; and then you realize that the authors have never looked at human experience; they went straight from the textbook or journal to the laboratory and thence into print—and thence into the business of getting research grants.

The plain fact is that our young psychological researchers do not know what goes on in human beings, and their work shows it. Not only is it dull, which psychology should never be, but it is often wrong, for that context of processes-in-the-person, which they have been trained to ignore, is usually doing more to determine what happens in the situation under study than the variables that have been "isolated experimentally."

What has happened is that the revolution in psychology that occurred during World War II and in the five years thereafter has been over for

some time and we are in the midst of the reaction. Or perhaps one might better say that normal operating procedures have been restored, that it is only in times of crisis that the academic disciplines are brought into contact with real life and shaken out of their professional preoccupations.

The revolution reached its high water mark in 1949 when Erik Erikson was appointed professor at Berkeley. Two years later this would not have been possible, nor has such a thing since been possible in any psychology department in the country. (The appointments at Harvard are special and do not really count. Harvard is special, too, in that it is the only place that can afford to make mistakes.)

The critique is not of the experimental approach in psychology or of general psychology as a discipline; it is of a state of affairs in which the advocates of a particular kind of psychology—psychology-without-a-person—have been able to gain and maintain power through putting across the idea that they are the representatives in psychology of *true science*.

It is quite possible that nothing can be done about the state of affairs I describe. Maybe we are just playthings of social forces that no one can control. The issues underlying the situation are

From American Psychologist, *Vol. 20 (1965), 192–202. Copyright 1965 by the American Psychological Association, and reproduced by permission.*

ones that have divided psychologists for a long time. I believe, however, that there is a constructive alternative to the prevailing orientation, one that might be called a "human-problems" approach. It is an approach that has a highly respectable past, but today it is staunchly opposed and falls outside the main current of contemporary work in psychology. It has many silent supporters, but few spokesmen.

The Kind of Approach Needed

Psychology and social science have, of course, always been oriented to action, in the sense that they have proceeded on the assumption that their theories and empirical knowledge would eventually be applied. Psychology, when it has thought seriously about itself, has included among its aims "to promote human welfare." Sociology, traditionally, has been concerned with the solution of social problems and with "building a better society." The National Institute of Mental Health, which has supported so much research in biology, psychology, and the newer social sciences, has been guided by the principle that such research should be "mental-health relevant," but in practice any fundamental work in these fields has been considered to have this characteristic.

Yet there is no denying that at the present time there exists a wide gap between research and practice. Psychology participates fully in the trend toward specialization and disciplinary professionalism that dominates in the universities today. The discipline is still much concerned to establish itself as a science, but the psychologists' naive conception of science has led them to adopt the more superficial characteristics of the physical sciences. This has made it difficult for them to study genuine human problems, since quantification, precision of measurement, elegance of experimental design, and general laws are so much more difficult to achieve once one goes beyond simple, part processes.

There is, of course, a rationale for all this. It is not without some reason that the National Institute of Mental Health regards the so-called "pure science" of these disciplines as relevant to mental health. Science has always made progress through specialization. It can be argued, and it is argued, that findings concerning simple and isolated processes will eventually add up to systematic knowledge that can then be applied to human problems.

There are two things to be said about this. One is that the "adding up" function is rather neglected today, and the other is that many of these findings just do not add up. Concerning the first, the accent today is on the production of knowledge rather than on its organization. There are few attempts at systematization of the sort that would put particular facts in perspective and show their significance. More than that, there seem to be few attempts to organize knowledge in such a way that its relevance to practice or to policy becomes apparent. A college president might examine a large number of issues of educational or psychological journals without coming across anything that struck him as relevant to his purposes or helpful in the solution of his problems. It is not that all this material is irrelevant, but rather that the task of organizing and interpreting it so that it might be useful is so largely neglected. Scientists write for each other; and when they are looking for a problem to investigate, they turn to their professional journals rather than ask such questions as what might be troubling the college presidents.

When I say that the study of simple, isolated processes does not add up to an understanding of more complex ones, I am assuming that human and social processes are organized on different levels, and that processes on higher (more complex) levels have a character of their own, are just as "real" as processes on lower levels, and must be studied directly. It is just as "scientific" to study, say, self-esteem in it relations to other factors of equal complexity as it is to study the manifold, conditioned responses into which self-esteem might be analyzed; it is just as scientific to study conditioned responses as it is to study by physiological methods the nerve processes that underlie them. . . .

* * *

Personality-social aspects

It seems clear enough that for an effective approach to human problems we must have an integration of personality theory and social theory. This is not as easy as might first appear. Most sociologists seem to get along quite well without giving much attention to the individual personality, and probably the great majority of clinical practitioners rely on an "individual-psychodynamic" approach that gives little attention to social and cultural factors. There is even a certain amount of interdisciplinary rivalry here: In discussions of problems such as prejudice or delinquency there is a tendency to oppose personality factors and social factors and argue about which is more important. But progress toward integration is being made. Certainly personality theory is far more "social" today than it was twenty-five years ago, and there is evidence, I think, that when sociologists note signs that their psychological colleagues are seeing the light, they are willing to go halfway toward rapprochement. . . .

Consider authoritarianism and how it might be changed. I assume that there are social organizations that can bring out the authoritarianism in almost anybody; but I would also assume that when it came to changing a particular organization, the difficulty—and the strategy—would depend on how much authoritarianism in personality was found in people who occupied the key positions. To put this idea in more general terms: In order to induce change in personality it may sometimes be necessary first to change the role structure in the organization in which the individual lives or works. By the same token, since we deal with a dynamic interaction between personality and social system, it may sometimes be necessary to change certain personalities in order to change the social system. Individuals use their social roles for the expression of their personality needs, hence a change in organizational role structure will be resisted by individuals in the same way that they resist change in internal adaptive devices that have been found to be more or less satisfying. Thus a practicing social scientist needs to be familiar with personality dynamics.

Dynamic aspects

A personality, or an organized social group, seems best conceived as a system of interacting forces, a going concern in which energy is distributed among constituent parts and between the system (or its subsystems) and its environment. Dynamic organization refers to the way in which these forces or units of energy interact. Personalities and social systems also exhibit formal organization. They may be examined with attention to such overall features as number of different parts or the connectedness of parts, or with attention to such formal relationships among parts as similarity, proximity, or inclusion. In general, the analysis of systems into states, conditions, or arrangements prepares the way for explanation in terms of dynamic theory.

Dynamic theory is essential when it comes to consideration of how a system might be changed. The question here, typically, is how to bring force to bear upon a particular subsystem that one

wishes to modify. One might think first of bringing to bear upon the subsystem in question a potent set of environmental stimuli, and this might indeed be effective sometimes. It usually turns out, however, that the particular subsystem is really being determined by other subsystems and by processes of the whole system. The problem, then, is to find out what within the larger system determines what, and then to get a purchase on the master processes. . . .

*   *   *

Holism

The essential idea was introduced above in our discussion of the neglect of complex processes: particular phenomena such as a "perception" or a "conditioned response" are almost always in part determined by—their very nature depends upon— the larger organismic patterns and purposes within which they have a place.

The implications of this are great, and I would like to carry my argument further.

The first point to be made is that few psychologists care to deny, on principle, the holistic premise. It seems to be almost universally understood and agreed that how a stimulus is perceived depends on the context in which it exists at the moment, that whether or not an idea will be assimilated by a cognitive system depends on the degree of that idea's consistency with ideas that are already present there, and that the meaning of a particular act depends on its place in a larger pattern of striving. It can be said with perfect safety that all personality theories are holistic in the sense that they are concerned with the relations of particular processes to larger personality functions.

What, then, is the argument about? It is not so much about high theory as it is about what is the best strategy for research. The basic complaint against holistic theory is that it does not lend itself to testing by empirical methods. The very term "whole" suggests something that cannot be analyzed, and American psychologists have been taught to be wary of anything "global." This argument would have force—complete force—if it were true that the study of part-whole relationships were impossible. . . .

*   *   *

One can sometimes carry over into a life situation all the conditions that obtain in the laboratory and show that the general laws still hold. This has been done, for example, in the case of the teaching machine, which enables a student to learn material in just the way that laboratory subjects do. But this involves the dangers suggested above. Unless the educators, and their consultants, are very much aware of the limited role of content learning in education, of its embeddedness in a large context of other processes, the tendency is to transform life into a laboratory experiment. B. F. Skinner, the leading pioneer in the development of teaching machines, is himself fully aware of this danger—unlike many educators and many of his disciples. And yet he is deeply concerned with practice and cannot resist becoming involved with it. He says that his strategy of research is the slow but sure building up of a science from simple beginnings, and that so far he and his colleagues have attacked only the simple problems; but this does not prevent him from remaking schoolrooms and designing new cultures.

*   *   *

I have put the case for holism as strongly as I can; yet I do not see how we can do without the intensive study of abstracted part-functions. The student of personality, after all, engages in this activity when he undertakes to explain the functioning of social groups. Here he might well be inclined to favor analysis in terms of the personality types of the group's members, but if he is a holist he would not be surprised or put off if a social theorist reminded him that there are things about personality that do not become apparent until the individual is seen in the context of the social group.

At a time when the holistic orientation seems rather neglected in psychology and social science, it seems proper to accent it as is done here. If we must abstract parts from wholes let us be fully aware of the fact that we *are abstracting,* and let us devote as much energy to finding out how special bits of knowledge fit into the larger picture as we do to analyzing wholes in the conventional, scientific way.

Comprehensiveness

The holistic orientation requires that we consider in what respects living systems function as units. It says nothing about the size or complexity of the unit. Such a unit might be the context of a perception, a pattern of striving that organizes particular acts, or the self that is expressed in numerous personality characteristics. The argu-

ment here is for bigger units; we must examine large areas of the person and of society, and long sections of behavior; and we must have theoretical models that permit us to do this.

The whole that helps to determine a particular personality characteristic may be the whole personality, and not merely the whole self or ego; hence, we need a theoretical model of the personality that permits us to deal with the relations of self to ego, and of these relatively large structures to others of like kind. Similarly for social structures. One may study, holistically, a department of an industrial organization or a classroom in a school, but for full understanding he would have to see the department or classroom in relation to the whole institution, and the institution in relation to the whole society.

*   *   *

Level of Abstraction

When men are confronted with practical problems, their natural tendency is to focus on the concrete and particular. The psychotherapist, faced with the task of taking action on short notice, has to deal with what is happening to a particular patient in the situation of the moment; he cannot stop to translate his thoughts into the terms of a general theoretical system. The test specialist who wishes to develop an instrument for predicting some practical and important pattern of overt behavior does not need abstract concepts to stand for general dispositions of personality; he can go far with a set of concrete test items that correlate with the behavior in which he is interested. And the business man or the administrator of an organization is likely to see his problems as particular, local, and pressing; he seeks solutions through manipulating plainly observable features of the immediate situation.

This kind of orientation to practical problems is a far cry from the most characteristic work of the scientist. The scientist interested in psychopathology must use terms for describing a patient that are sufficiently abstract so that one patient may be compared with others and with nonpatients. The myriad specific acts of patients must be ordered to a conceptual scheme, so that future observations may be systematic, and general relationships among patients' processes may be established. As for organizations, one might say that we have hardly begun the scientific study of them until we have derived a set of abstract concepts—such as role, communication, power—that apply to organizations generally, so that we can carry over what we learn from one organization to the study of others.

*   *   *

Choice of Problems

A human-problems approach not only calls for a different theoretical orientation, it implies a different basis for choosing problems. I would like to see the new Institute include something of the following in its program:

1. Accent problems defined in terms of their human significance rather than in the terms of particular scientific disciplines. Study of these will require interdisciplinary theory and multidisciplinary research teams. It may work if the starting point is a human problem and not a disciplinary question or issue. And let us get away for the moment from the familiar psychiatric categories. I have in mind such problem areas as transitional stages, developmental crises, commitment (premature or delayed), institutional dependence, pleasure and play, problem drinking, and aging.

2. Look at these problems in the perspective of long-range goals for the individual. If we want people to give up or get over some sort of problematic behavior we have to think of suitable alternatives to that behavior. Think about this for a while and we are bound to come to considerations of what is good for people and of what they might well become. Why not? There are good philosophical as well as practical reasons for this.

3. To think about long-range goals and how they might be reached, we have to use a developmental perspective. We have to consider present events with attention to their future consequences. Otherwise, we can have no part in the planning of institutional arrangements for the development of young people. Nor can we have anything sensible to say about when is the best time to introduce young people to particular ideas or experiences.

4. If we adopt a developmental perspective, there is no way to avoid attention to the whole life cycle. We cannot leave this whole area to Erik Erikson—and Charlotte Buhler. We have to have longitudinal studies, or suitable substitutes for them. At the least we must have studies of lives.

5. But study the conditions and processes of developmental change—in general, at any age. Assume that such changes can occur at any age. It is a matter of the right conditions being present. I say development in general—so I am interested in general laws. I mean organismic laws, which state relationships between part-processes and the larger personal contexts in which they are imbedded.

6. This means study the general psychology of personality—particularly the general psychology of personality development. We have to conceive of structures in the person and we have to have theory to explain how these structures are modified through experience. Studies of structures—experimental studies or others—may of course be appropriately investigated in isolation, but there should be awareness of the fact that they *are* being studied in isolation and must eventually be related to persons.

7. Look at various kinds of social settings in which developmental changes occur, particularly settings that have been designed to modify people in some desired way: schools, training programs, correctional institutions, hospitals, psychotherapeutic programs, summer camps, etc. Or, look at development in unnatural environments, forms of rigid institutionalization, for example, which result in regressive changes or fixations. Let all these settings be described and analyzed in sociological terms, but keep the focus of attention upon developmental change in individuals.

8. Give special attention to youth, but be flexible in defining its boundaries, and of course do not neglect its relation to earlier and later periods. Youth is a neglected area as compared with childhood and old age. It is not so much behavior of youth as development in youth that has been neglected. The theoretical bias has been that little or no development occurs during this period.

The study of development in youth is bound to force a confrontation of theoretical issues. It should lead to the production of new theory concerning the interaction of social and personality variables. If we assume that personality goes on developing, after the age of, say, sixteen, after the young person has been brought very much under the influence of factors outside the home, then we have to formulate such factors and conceive the ways in which they do their work. Classical personality theory has little to say on this subject—but it can be appropriately modified.

*   *   *

8

Social Engineering and the Future Environment

Donald N. Michael

Everyone understands what the word "engineering" implies. It suggests using knowledge in certain precise ways to produce a specific product or effect. Mechanical engineers design machinery to produce the necessities and luxuries of modern living. Civil engineers design roads and bridges to expedite the flow of transportation and trade. The increasingly troublesome problems that have arisen as a result of growing societies must also be dealt with in sensible, planned ways. The term "social engineer" has been applied to those who use the knowledge provided by biological and social scientists in an attempt to alleviate such problems.

Michael, in testifying before a congressional committee that was meeting to investigate ways in which social scientists can contribute to governmental operations, suggests that social engineers will eventually be able to use their accumulating knowledge to produce specific answers to society's problems. The art of social engineering is in a primitive state at present, but in the future we can look forward to an overwhelming increase in the emphasis upon social research and a resulting increase in knowledge.

Mr. Chairman and members of the Subcommittee, it is a privilege indeed to have this opportunity to testify before you with regard to Senate Resolution 68, providing for the establishment of a Select Committee of the Senate on Technology and the Human Environment. That my endorsement of your resolution is enthusiastic is evidenced by my own writing and speaking efforts to draw attention to this critical area. After reviewing the previous testimony in response to the proposed legislation, and after reviewing the resolution itself, I think I can be most useful this morning by emphasizing two aspects of the impact of technology on the human environment that have been mentioned in passing by those who have previously testified, though recognition of these [aspects is] implicit in Senate Resolution 68 of the Ninetieth Congress. I refer, specifically, to the impact of social technology or social engineering. I would like to talk about its significance over the next fifty years. And I would also like to share with you some speculations about the relationship of the present state of social engineering to the important studies you are proposing the Select Congressional Committee undertake in the next three years.

Let me begin my remarks by allying myself with the hopes and fears of those who have preceded me in testifying with regard to Senate Resolution 68. Let me say, too, at the beginning of my remarks, that I feel that there is no way we can deal with the social impacts of the new technologies, or the consequences of those technologies that have already had a substantial impact, without using more technology—both physical technology and social technology. I do not believe, however, that physical technologies by themselves can take advantage of the opportunities present and future technologies may offer or avoid the problems they hold. If we are to cope with the impact of technology, we must have major social inventions as well as hardware inventions, and the social inventions will, I believe, alter the very core of our way of life, values, beliefs, and aspirations over a fifty-year perspective. We face the challenge of inventing a social as well as a physical world which will be humane and dignifying of the individual. For the overriding characteristic of the new technologies is their enormous, simultaneous potential for

From American Psychologist, *Vol. 23 (1967), 888–892. Copyright 1967 by the American Psychological Association, and reproduced by permission.*
Statement of the author at **Hearings on S. 68 before the Senate Subcommittee on Intergovernmental Relations, Committee on Governmental Operations, 90th Congress, 1st Session (1967).**

enhancing or degrading man's environment, [and] man himself. This, as I shall try to show, will also hold true for social technology, perhaps even more so. Social technology is today less advanced than hardware technology, but the need for it and future potency of it mean that its implications merit just as intense [an] examination as do the implications, good and bad, of the physical technologies.

The Technology of Social Engineering

By social technology or social engineering, I mean the deliberate application of systematically accumulated knowledge and theory about the nature of man and his institutions for the purpose of influencing the behavior of man and his institutions. This area of technology is already with us in its early and relatively primitive forms. Examples would include the human engineering of weapon systems, the use of systems analysis, and program budgeting and planning systems in the development of long-range economic planning; Keynesian-type economic interventions; the application of behavioral science knowledge to urban design; the research leading to and the evaluation of Operation Head Start; the extensive work in new managerial theory and application, especially as applied to industry. In addition to the extension and refinement of these ongoing applications, other developments are in the laboratory stage, so to speak. For instance, we are beginning to think seriously of collecting data which will give us "social accounts" that provide us a kind of social understanding analogous to that provided by our present economic data. There is work under way in the overlapping areas of biology and psychology that is rapidly enlarging our understanding of and ability to manipulate intellectual and emotional states. We are familiar with the research and in some cases preliminary applications of computer-assisted instruction for education.

Future Growth of Social Technology

In addition to these developments, there are two other circumstances that practically insure an ever accelerating accumulation of behavioral science knowledge for social engineering purposes.

In the first place, if we are to have highly effective programs for the elimination of poverty, [for] the enhancement of education, [for] the improvement of old age services, and in other areas where we are trying to improve the social and material welfare of our people, or those anywhere in the world, we must have a great deal of research on what produces and what can change the inadequate circumstances being attacked. That the government increasingly realizes this is evidenced by the research funds associated with each of these programs. In order to use our scarce, highly skilled manpower efficiently and in order to allocate our financial and material resources effectively, we will have to do more social research and apply more of the findings.

In the second place, the computer provides the social scientist with two conditions he has always needed and never had in order to develop a deep understanding of and technology for the manipulation of such social processes. The computer provides him with the means for combining in complex models as many variables as he needs in order to simulate the behavior of men and institutions. Previously the behavioral scientist simply could not deal with as many important variables as are needed to understand and predict human behavior. From now on he will increasingly be able to do so. (Please understand that I am not asserting that everything that is important about human beings can be so formulated. However, much that is important can be put in these terms, certainly enough to bring about substantial improvements in our ability to understand and predict and, hence, control behavior.)

In addition to the capacity to build enormously complex models which simulate the real life behavior of men and institutions, the social scientist can for the first time test these models against conditions representing "real life." For the computer, through its enormous capacity for collecting and processing data, can tell us what is happening to the society *today*, not as has usually been the case with our data about society: what was happening five or ten years ago. Thus, the social engineer not only can know the state of society now as represented by these data, but he can use them to test and refine his theoretical models in ways analogous to those used in the development of simulation models for describing the behavior of rockets, aircraft, etc.

The convergence of government programs, government funds, social incentives, and the computer is of critical importance for the impact of social technology. It will result in an increased number of studies of individual and institutional change as these alter under the impact of other changes in the social and physical environment acting over long periods of time. Such knowledge about the cumulative impact of changes is relatively nonexistent. As we acquire this kind of knowledge, we will inevitably increase our ability to effect social change. And given the convergence of the powerful physical technologies and social technologies, and given our already enormously complex and huge society, it would seem that deliberate social manipulation will be necessary if we are to introduce appropriate changes in society at the appropriate time. The overriding questions, of course, will be *who* is to decide *whom* is to be manipulated and for *what* ends. It is in the resolution of these questions, I believe, that we will have to invent social institutions, values, and aspirations just as we invent hardware to meet other of our social needs.

Just as applications of physical technology have accelerated, as knowledge and experience gained in earlier technologies multiply the capability to produce newer and more powerful physical technologies, so too, we can expect the same effect in the social engineering areas. If we add to the increasing potential capability of social engineering the increasing needs to apply it, I think it is clear that the chances are that the social impact of social engineering will be formidable indeed over the next fifty years.

Coming Pressures to Apply Social Technology

All evidence indicates that certainly for the next couple of decades we shall be extremely shorthanded in the areas of great professional and managerial skill. By "skill" I mean both what we conventionally think of as occupational skill and what we vaguely but significantly call wisdom and compassion about the human condition. We will be short of these people because we do not turn out very many highly skilled people now, because we do not know how to, and because the combined impacts of the new technology, urban growth, population growth, social service demands, and the associated changes in life ways all mean that we will need relatively more highly skilled people than we do now. [Furthermore], in most societally important areas, we shall need more time than is easily available to deal with the problems and take advantage of the opportunities facing us in the future or facing us today. We should have started two decades ago to produce the educational system we need for today. We are desperately behind in producing the educational system we need for tomorrow's citizens. We are all familiar with the terrible backlog of almost insuper-

able—some observers feel they are insuperable—problems of urban areas. Air pollution cannot be cured overnight. A solution to the growing shortage of water cannot be developed overnight. Mass transit cannot be provided overnight, and so on. This means that, because of the skill shortages and time shortages, we shall have to assign priorities to our social tasks and we shall have to carry through on them carefully and consistently over long time periods. Assigning priorities obviously will involve much more than the economic cost and benefits, and carrying out a program over long time periods will involve the most astute and advanced social engineering context we can imagine.

Thus, we can expect social engineering will be increasingly used to *analyze* the implications of other technologies. That is, social technology will increasingly influence the nature of plans for the implementation and application of other technologies. And social engineering will be increasingly used to *carry out* the application of other technologies. In addition, of course, social engineering will be used to apply social engineering.

If I am at all right, the application of social engineering confronts us with formidable challenges and dilemmas over what we want, what we believe in, and how we obtain what we want in terms of what we believe in. We have *already* seen social institutions destroyed, threatened, or radically altered by existing technologies. For example, slavery was destroyed by machine power, and now the concept and the purposes of the nation-state are threatened by the power of nuclear weapons and, eventually, biological weapons.

On the Problems of Forecasting Studies

This is an appropriate transition point to move from speculations about the need to include examination of the implications of future social technology along with those of hardware technologies to some observations on the challenges for present-day social engineering contained in the proposed studies.

Let me begin by suggesting that all studies aimed at forecasting the future inherently contain a substantial political component. I do not mean political in a partisan sense, rather, I mean it in the broad sense of having influence or being perceived as having influence on preferences for action. That is to say, one is concerned about the future in order to do something about it in the present. Any study attempting to speculate on future social implications thereby is also making observations on the present effects of technology. Or putting it another way, to some substantial degree, observations about future impacts will be accepted or rejected to the degree they are compatable with preferred views about and vested interest in the present and how it got that way and what it is. One tends to accept a view of the direction of the future that is compatable with views about the nature of the present and with what one's interests are in preserving or changing the present.

It is in this light that I respectfully suggest that the kind of study you propose to undertake may very well turn around and "bite the hand that feeds it." For over the next fifty years, particularly under the impact of technology, many of our premises and cherished values may very well become outmoded and transformed. Such concepts as private investment, the nation-state, privacy, federal, state, and local prerogatives, free enterprise, freedom of science, these and other terms which carry with them a variety of deep beliefs and needs, may be so transformed as to be unrecognizable or disappear altogether. It is not at all clear that the options before us can be realized within the conventional social and institutional forms we have used so far.

Let me suggest a few examples of the kind of technologically related social impacts that merit candid recognition and exploration:

1. With the development of computer-assisted teaching and increased understanding of learning, it is likely that economic and scientific considerations will lead at least to regional-size educational systems that use the same materials and teaching methods. What then happens to our cherished belief in and practice of local school district autonomy?

2. We will need increasing amounts of information about people and their activities in order to better plan for their growth and development. Obtaining such knowledge is bound to confront us with invasion of privacy issues. What will be the balance between future social planning needs and traditional values and expressions of individual privacy?

3. Long-range planning and assignment of social priorities will necessarily conflict with some meanings of the idea of private and business freedom. What is to be the basis for trade-offs between these needs?

4. Accumulating evidence from research about management technology indicates that open and free exchange of information throughout the organization is necessary for high production and morale. Power in industrial, university, and government bureaucracies has in part been determined by who has privileged access to information. Certainly this cannot be the case in the future as information becomes more critical to the conduct of society. What is to be the resolution in view of conventional political and bureaucratic processes?

The Place of Social Technology in the Conduct of the Proposed Studies

This brings us then to the question of the role of social technology, of social science knowledge, in forecasting social impacts in the light of interpretations of present social conditions and their change over the years ahead. And this brings us up against a very unhappy fact. The fact is that in general we do not have enough detailed data about society to know what is happening to us, much less what will happen to us, as a function of technology. This is even true in the much argued, much written about, area of the present impact of automation on the work force. In spite of many books arguing the matter learnedly and statistically to one decimal point, the fact is that there are today no adequate sources of economic and work-force data for decisively answering the questions with the subtlety required, even though so many figures are thrown around so authoritatively in and out of government on one side or the other.

The data are even less clear when it comes to documenting the specific impacts of technology on poverty, or [on] the conditions for effective learning, or on the use and amount of leisure, or on the effects of urban crowding, and so on through the whole set of social consequences that we *believe*—but do not know for sure—are, in important part, the result of technological developments. This means that the studies the Select Committee might undertake must be highly tentative in their findings.

You will, of course, use experts and the best available predictive models, but we do not know what it really means to be expert about the future or whether we have models that predict the future well. After all, until very recently, we did not even try to do these things, and as a result we have no accumulated knowledge about the validity and reliability of experts or predictions.

Now I am *not* saying that in its present state, social engineering has nothing to offer. On the contrary, as I described earlier, it has a great deal to offer, judging from what is under way now. What I am saying is that, as of now, social science is "data poor" with regard to what it can say definitively about present and future impacts of technology on the human environment. But, and this is of utmost importance, it seems to me that the physical technologists are much poorer comparatively when it comes to predicting the social consequences of their hardware. For, while social scientists may disagree about the meaning of data we do have, and while some may stretch data too far to make a point, still there is an enormous repository of laboratory and real life data and theory that the social scientist can usefully bring to these problems. These data and theory the physical technologist is untrained to bring to these issues—though too often he is not at all reluctant to set forth his "common sense" and preferred mythology about men and institutions as if they were the best there is available.

I would respectfully suggest, then, that one of the most important outcomes of the studies the Select Committee undertakes would be a set of strong recommendations as to what kinds of data need to be collected systematically in the years ahead if the vision inherent in the work of this Committee is to be realized. Since these studies will necessarily raise questions about present value preferences and since such studies inevitably are perceived as "influential," the task you propose to undertake is truly formidable—itself a social consequence of technology. Indeed, I believe that it will take the prestige of such a Select Committee to legitimize recognition of the issues described here and of the need for data in order to understand them, so that others will then face and deal with them imaginatively and courageously. I have high hopes that your reports will thereby influence the present, and therefore, in the words of Dennis Gabor, they will help us all to "invent the future."

Thank you for this opportunity to share these concerns and hopes with you.

9

Psychology as a Profession

American Psychological Association

In 1954 the American Psychological Association, with the consent of the Council of Representatives, published a policy statement entitled *Psychology and Its Relations with Other Professions.* Fourteen years have passed since the adoption and publication of this statement, and many changes have taken place in the interim. The present article represents a revision, updating, and retitling of the former statement in order to reflect the development and the growth of the profession. The Board of Professional Affairs was given the responsibility for preparing this statement subject to the review and approval of the Board of Directors and other governing bodies of the Association. This new document was approved by the Council of Representatives on September 5, 1967, as an official policy statement of the Association and replaces the previous booklet.

ARTHUR H. BRAYFIELD
Executive Officer
American Psychological Association

Like other professions, American psychology is a social entity operating in a supporting society. As a relative newcomer among the sciences and professions, psychology is not widely known or fully understood by the public at large. This article, prepared by the American Psychological Association, provides information about this emerging science and profession and describes some of the

From *American Psychologist, Vol. 23 (1968), 195–200.
Copyright 1968 by the American Psychological Association, and reproduced by permission.*

values that guide its members as they seek to move psychology toward greater maturity, responsibility, and public usefulness.

Psychology has three major purposes: to increase the body of knowledge in its content area, to communicate this knowledge, and to apply it in a socially useful and responsible manner. Within this threefold mission, however, one encounters marked diversity in the work of people who are called psychologists.

Psychologists engage in research, teaching, psychological services to individuals and groups, consultation, and administration. Individual psychologists generally devote themselves to more than one of these activities. For example, most research psychologists also teach, many teachers also engage in some applied or service functions, some practitioners also do research. Psychologists also differ from one another in their type and amount of training, in their areas of subsequent professional specialization, and in their work settings. The settings for their work vary from laboratory to factory, from classroom to hospital ward, from nursery school to university, from school of education to school of medicine, from outpatient clinic to private consulting room, and [from] large governmental or military agency to local community project.

The great majority of American psychologists are members of the American Psychological Asso-

TABLE 1   *Division Membership for 1967*

Division	Fellows	Members	Associates	Total members
1. General psychology	165	748	337	1,250
2. Teaching of psychology	319	1,424	509	2,252
3. Experimental psychology	405	656	—	1,061
5. Evaluation and measurement	216	598	—	814
6. Physiological and comparative psychology	82	413	—	495
7. Developmental psychology	244	583	26	853
8. Personality and social psychology	353	2,661	885	3,899
9. The society for the psychological study of social issues—A division of the APA	285	1,076	188	1,549
10. Psychology and the arts	44	161	47	252
12. Clinical psychology	771	2,467	—	3,238
13. Consulting psychology	278	332	—	610
14. Industrial psychology	248	660	111	1,019
15. Educational psychology	366	1,632	593	2,691
16. School psychologists	134	700	276	1,110
17. Counseling psychology	228	1,226	210	1,664
18. Psychologists in public service	55	459	135	649
19. Military psychology	156	213	20	389
20. Maturity and old age	107	180	11	298
21. The society of engineering psychologists—A division of the APA	66	293	43	402
22. Psychological aspects of disability	70	814	171	1,055
23. Consumer psychology	26	220	—	246
24. Philosophical psychology	97	370	61	528
25. Experimental analysis of behavior	54	435	—	489
26. History of psychology	93	200	—	293
27. Community psychology	86	550	—	636
28. Psychopharmacology	74	254	—	328
29. Psychotherapy	—	—	—	—

Note.—There are no figures available for Division 29.

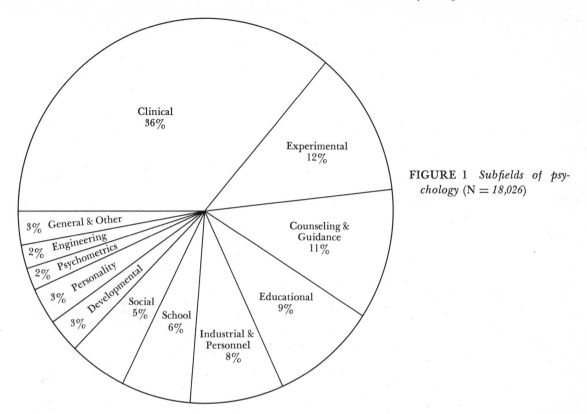

FIGURE 1 *Subfields of psychology* (N = *18,026*)

ciation; in 1967 the APA had 25,800 members.[1] Basic information about the membership of this national organization should indicate the complex nature of psychology and the heterogeneity among those who constitute the profession. Many of the Association's activities are organized around divisions, presently twenty-seven in number, which represent different areas of specialized interest in psychology; however, some members join more than one division. Divisional titles and membership totals are presented in Table 1.

State psychological associations represent American psychologists in their geographical areas. Psychological associations in all but one of the fifty states (Alaska), in the District of Columbia, in Puerto Rico, and in the province of Ontario in Canada are affiliates of APA. In recent years there has also been a rapid expansion of local professional groups—estimates based on a recent survey indicate approximately 125 local groups—which represent further geographical subunits.

The diverse activities of American psychologists are graphically portrayed in their responses to a recent questionnaire. The questionnaire covered (*a*) their stated area of specialization (or subfield), (*b*) their major employment, and (*c*) their primary work activities.[2] (Data for Figures 1, 2, and 3 are

based on information obtained from the National Science Foundation's National Register of Scientific and Technical Personnel in the Field of Psychological Science Questionnaire, 1966.)

Psychology and Its Relations with Other Professions

Psychology today finds itself involved in intricate relations with many other fields. Historically rooted in both philosophy and the natural sciences, some of the content of psychology overlaps

1 The Association presently recognizes three major types of membership—Member, Associate, and Fellow. Qualifications for *Member* include a doctoral degree based in part upon a psychological dissertation and conferred by a graduate school of recognized standing. *Associate* (nonvoting) membership requires a master's degree in psychology from a recognized school plus a year of acceptable experience, or two years of graduate work in psychology in a recognized graduate school. *Fellow* status may be conferred upon members for whom sponsoring divisions present evidence of unusual and outstanding contribution or performance in psychology.

2 Primary work activity is defined in terms of working time devoted to that activity. (*N* = 17,707)

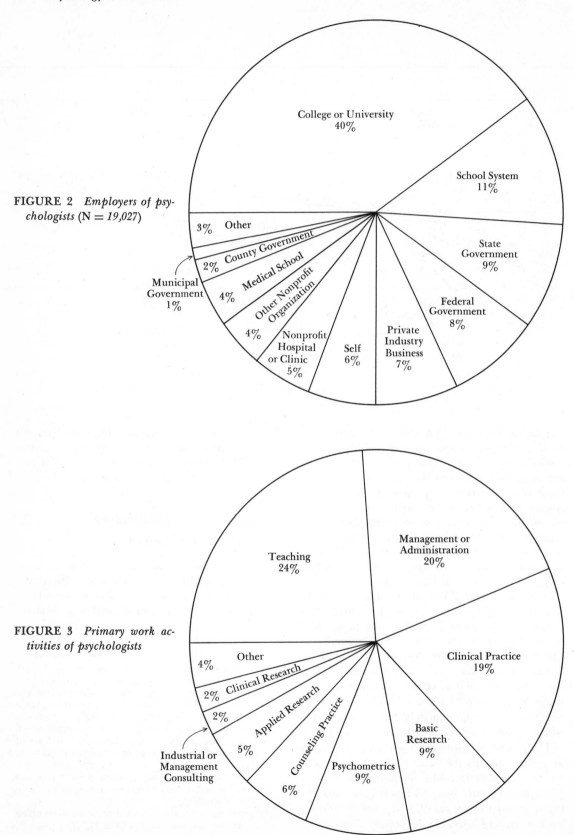

FIGURE 2 *Employers of psychologists* (N = *19,027*)

FIGURE 3 *Primary work activities of psychologists*

that of other academic and professional disciplines. Many applications of psychology occur in settings where other professions are also involved. Thus, psychologists apply their techniques and insights to problems of concern to clergymen, lawyers, social workers, educators, administrators, politicians, physicians, engineers, and other professionals. This state of affairs is not unusual. Almost every emerging profession brings new viewpoints and methods to old problems. By joining with other professions having related concerns for human welfare, psychology has contributed new techniques and distinctive theoretical approaches for understanding and modifying behavior.

To a marked extent, professions supplement one another in their interrelations, each bringing some unique and desirable contribution. They also overlap; many problems can be appropriately and effectively met by two or more professions. When a psychologist's contribution is supplementary and distinctive, he is usually welcomed; when it overlaps with the contributions of other professions, misunderstandings may arise. The effectiveness of a psychologist's contribution, and occasionally even his opportunity to make it, are determined in part by the relations he establishes with the other disciplines and professions that share his interests and concerns.

Professional persons have an obligation to know and take into account the traditions and practices of other professional groups with whom they work and to cooperate fully with members of such groups with whom research, service, and other functions are shared.

Principles Underlying the Roles of Psychologists

The American Psychological Association, as the official national organization of psychologists functioning in all of their specialties, accepts responsibility for coordinating the development and functioning of psychology as a profession. In this role the Association is guided primarily by general criteria of human welfare. For psychologists the Association provides a national voice in the pursuit of their work, be it teaching, research, service functions, consultation, or administration.

The Association has among its purposes responsibility for:

1. Advancing basic knowledge concerning behavior

2. Setting standards for training qualified aspirants to professional competence

3. Cooperating with state associations and with governmental bodies in establishing and maintaining standards of professional competence

4. Developing and enforcing a code of ethics.

The sections that follow identify certain principles which underlie psychologists' activities in their roles as researcher, teacher, practitioner, and administrator.

Research

Psychologists are concerned with the application of the methods of science to the study of the behavior of living organisms. The profession assumes the responsibility for encouraging research and facilitating the communication of research findings. This includes:

1. Encouraging research by emphasizing its importance during the preparation of students for careers in psychology

2. Identifying and developing sources of support for behavioral research

3. Sponsoring journals, professional meetings, and other means for the dissemination of research findings

4. Protecting freedom of investigation and fostering a climate favorable to scientific inquiry

5. Fostering high ethical standards in the conduct of research

6. Encouraging cooperation with other scholarly disciplines in the development of new knowledge about behavior.

Teaching

As teachers, psychologists accept and share the ethics and ideals of the teaching profession. These include:

1. According freedom to teach and freedom to learn to all participants in the educational process set forth in the AAUP Statement on Academic Freedom, which the APA formally endorses

2. Limiting one's teaching activities to the boundaries of one's own skill, knowledge, and competence

3. Being willing to teach all that one knows to all qualified persons who seek to learn

4. Contributing to the maximum attainment of potential of students in their area of instruction.

Service

As appliers of their knowledge, skills, and techniques, psychologists accept and share the values and guiding principles of those professions which deal with human welfare. Psychologists accept the responsibilities for:

1. Demanding for themselves and their colleagues the highest quality account of their abilities in utilizing psychological knowledge consonant with the state of the art and science

2. Engendering in aspirant members of the profession and displaying in their own practice a keen sense of social responsibility

3. Employing available psychological knowledge for the enhancement of human effectiveness and the betterment of human welfare

4. Making the services of psychologists available to all persons who seek and may benefit from such services

5. Sharing with related professions knowledge of research methods and findings, training techniques, and skills in the application of psychological knowledge.

Administration

As administrators of the professional activities of psychologists and other persons, psychologists share the responsibilities and accept the values of persons serving in such capacities. These include:

1. Accepting a primary loyalty to the overall purposes of the organization in which he has administrative responsibilities rather than to special interests within the organization

2. Willingness to utilize to the maximum the professional competence of all staff members in achieving the goals of the organization

3. Protecting the maximal freedom of behavior of staff members consonant with the effective functioning of the organization.

Standards of Practice

The national Association accepts responsibility for (a) encouraging the establishment of meaningful standards of professional competence through statutory enactment and administrative policy particularly at the state level and by other means, (b) effectively informing the public concerning the meaning of the established standards of competence,

and (c) designating to the public those members of the profession who have met these standards. In performing their applied functions, either alone or in association with other professions, psychologists accept the responsibility for taking appropriate steps to protect the public from the incompetent or unwise application of psychological knowledge and techniques and to establish and maintain high standards of professional competence and practice in all settings.

The public interest is advanced by the competent performance of socially useful services by a number of professions. The American Psychological Association believes it is undesirable to attempt to control the practice of all psychological functions by restricting them to members of any single profession except insofar as it can be clearly demonstrated that such restriction is necessary for the protection of the public. The Association's policy, therefore, is to oppose narrowly restrictive legislation or administrative policies which provide that only psychologists (or teachers, or physicians, or any other designated professional group) may engage in applications of certain knowledge and techniques of their field.

For example, the psychologist may engage in psychotherapy, other forms of behavior modification, and psychodiagnosis when his training and experience qualify him for such pursuits. In his practice he is responsible for assisting his client in obtaining professional help for problems that fall outside the boundaries of good psychological practice. The psychologist makes referrals to or seeks consultation with other specialists as needed. It is recognized that other professions are by virtue of their training and experience also qualified to render such services.

In the interest of both the public and the client and in accordance with the requirements of good professional practice, the profession of psychology seeks recognition of the privileged nature of confidential communications with clients preferably through statutory enactment or by administrative policy where more appropriate.

The APA has formulated a code of ethics to protect the public and has accepted responsibility for enforcing this code among its members (APA, 1967).

Independent practice

Independent practice is one form of activity for qualified members of the profession. Good professional practice is usually facilitated by the maintenance of ongoing and meaningful working relationships with one's professional colleagues, and this principle applies with equal relevance to all forms of activity including independent or private practice.

Psychologists regarded as qualified for independent practice are those who (a) have been awarded a diploma by the American Board of Examiners in Professional Psychology, or (b) have been licensed or certified by state examining boards, or (c) have been certified by voluntary boards established by state psychological associations.

Psychologists who do not yet meet the qualifications recognized for independent practice should gain experience under qualified supervision. The Association strongly supports efforts in state legislation regulating the practice of psychology for a fee, which move toward a requirement of a doctoral degree and two years of acceptable experience.

Rights and Responsibilities of a Profession

As a profession, psychology in America is sensitive to its rights and responsibilities. In this concluding section, some principles and statements are presented which describe the Association's policies and points of view.

The question of rights

As a member of an autonomous profession, a psychologist rejects limitations upon his freedom of thought and action other than those imposed by his moral, legal, and social responsibilities. The Association is always prepared to provide appropriate assistance to any responsible member who becomes subjected to unreasonable limitations upon his opportunity to function as a practitioner, teacher, researcher, administrator, or consultant. The Association is always prepared to cooperate with any responsible professional organization in opposing any unreasonable limitations on the professional functions of the members of that organization.

This insistence upon professional autonomy has been upheld over the years by the affirmative actions of the courts and other public and private bodies in support of the right of the psychologist—and other professionals—to pursue those functions for which he is trained and qualified to perform.

Some criteria for psychology as a profession

Psychologists share enough common values which yield a description of what they regard as criteria for a good profession. A combination of values which psychologists share and strive to protect is a respect for evidence combined with a recognition of the dignity of the human being. These give rise to the following characteristics of a good profession to which psychologists subscribe and aspire. As members of a good profession, psychologists:

1. Guide their practice and policies by a sense of social responsibility
2. Devote more of their energies to serving the public interest than to "guild" functions and to building ingroup strength
3. Represent accurately to the public their demonstrable competence
4. Develop and enforce a code of ethics primarily to protect the client and only secondarily to protect themselves
5. Identify their unique pattern of competencies and focus their efforts to carrying out those functions for which they are best equipped
6. Engage in cooperative relations with other professions having related or overlapping competencies and common purposes
7 Seek an adaptive balance among efforts devoted to research, teaching, and application
8. Maintain open channels of communication among "discoverers," teachers, and appliers of knowledge
9. Avoid nonfunctional entrance requirements into the profession, such as those based on race, nationality, creed, or arbitrary personality considerations
10. Insure that their training is meaningfully related to the subsequent functions of the members of the profession
11. Guard against premature espousal of any technique or theory as a final solution to substantive problems
12. Strive to make their services accessible to all persons seeking such services, regardless of social and financial considerations.

REFERENCE
American Psychological Association. *Casebook on ethical standards of psychologists.* Washington, D.C.: APA, 1967.

Psychology as a Science:
A Contemporary Perspective

Richard W. Thompson
Western Washington State College

Centerville—John Smith, son of local merchant Fred Smith, was arrested by police last night on charges of stealing a car and wrecking it. At the same time Bill Smith, John's twin brother, was receiving the Mayor's award for distinguished service to the community. Mr. Smith, who was interviewed in the county jail where he was being held on charges of being drunk and disorderly, could give no explanation of either boy's behavior.

This fictitious news story highlights the problem of psychology: Why do people behave the way they do? The goal of psychology is an understanding of the behavior of organisms: What caused John to steal a car? Why was Bill so active in civic work? What events resulted in Mr. Smith being arrested for being drunk and disorderly? These questions might be answered by examining the Smiths' motivations, but a careful analysis of their behavior would reveal that motivation alone is an insufficient "explanation." Only when we know the circumstances that led up to an event will we be able to understand that event. There almost certainly will be references to the motivation involved in a particular behavior, but the explanation of the behavior includes more than statements about motives.

Scientific explanation, the formal procedure by which an event is explained, is used by all sciences, physical and social alike. The formal structure and the logic of scientific explanation has been clearly described by Hempel and Oppenheim (1948). In attempting to account for behavioral events, scientific psychology also uses this procedure. Psychologists must understand it to be able to distinguish scientific explanations from pseudo-explanations of behavior. Perhaps the easiest way to see what is meant by scientific explanation is to look at an example.

Some years ago, I was on a fishing trip in the mountains of Montana during the last part of September. The weather turned unseasonably cold one night, and the next day when my fishing companion, a physicist, and I stepped outside to drive to town for more supplies, we discovered a disgusting puddle of rust-colored water beneath the front end of my car.

It is not hard to guess what had happened. The water in my car's radiator and block had frozen during the night, cracking the block. Then, as the temperature increased, the ice had melted and dripped out through the newly created crack. Walking the ten miles to the nearest phone, I asked my friend to give me an explanation, a scientific explanation, of this event—a cracked block—and this is how the discussion proceeded.

"First," he said, "we must establish what the conditions were preceeding the event in question. Last night, the temperature dropped to below 0° C. and stayed there for some hours. You had water in your car's radiator and block, and the water was relatively pure, that is, you had no alcohol in it. The water in the radiator and block was in a closed container. The radiator and block are made of iron. Iron has a tensile strength (breaking strength) of a particular value. There were many other conditions present, but these are the ones essential to the explanation of the event in question.

"Secondly, we must state the general laws which relate these antecedent conditions to each other and to the event to be explained. A general law is a universal generalization of the 'If A, then B' type. In this particular case we know the following general laws:

1. If water is reduced to 0° C., then it will freeze and expand.
2. If iron is reduced to 0° C., then it will contract.
3. If the stress on a piece of metal exceeds its tensile strength, then it will break.

"As you can see, the general laws we have just stated relate the described antecedent conditions to each other and to the event to be explained.

"Last night, the water in your car's radiator and block froze and expanded, and since the radiator and block were a closed container, there was no place for the expanded water to go. This produced pressure on the sides of the radiator and block, which were contracting while the water was expanding. The pressure was great enough to exceed the tensile strength of the iron, thus producing a fracture in the metal. In the morning, as the air warmed, the ice melted and the water began to flow out through this crack. This, then, is a full scientific explanation of the event of interest."

As you can see, a scientific explanation is really quite simple. It is a complete description of the relevant conditions preceding the event to be explained, together with a statement of the general laws that relate these conditions to each other and to the event to be explained. The antecedent conditions ($C_1 \ldots C_N$) and general laws ($L_1 \ldots L_N$) are given a special name, the *explanans,* and the event to be explained is called the *explanandum* (*E*). The form of the explanation is that of a deductive argument with the conclusion being the event to be explained. The schematic form is:

$$
\left.
\begin{array}{ll}
\text{Antecedent conditions} & C_1 \ldots C_N \\
\text{General laws} & L_1 \ldots L_N
\end{array}
\right\} \quad (Explanans)
$$

$$
\text{Event to be explained} \qquad E \qquad (Explanandum)
$$

Two conditions must be satisfied for such an explanation to hold true. First, the event to be explained must be deducible from the *explanans.* Second, the *explanans* must be true or, at least, highly confirmed.

Note that not all the antecedent conditions that existed prior to the occurrence of the event are necessary for its explanation. For example, the facts that my car was painted chartreuse and that the moon was full are not necessary for the explanation of the event, although they were true. Nor is the general law, "If a body is freely falling at or near the earth's surface, then it will fall with an acceleration of 32 feet per second per second," required for the explanation of the cracked block, although the law is also true. Only *relevant* antecedent conditions and their related general laws are required for the explanation of an event. These must be included and all others excluded.

It may be obvious that if an event can be *explained* using this deductive argument, then it can also be *predicted.* That is, had I known that the temperature was going to drop to 0° C. and stay at that level for some time and that I had only water in the radiator and block of my car, then I could have predicted the unfortunate damage to the block and radiator. The only difference between scientific prediction and scientific explanation is whether the event has occurred or not; given the same antecedent conditions and the required general laws, an event may be predicted or explained, there being no greater risk of error in one case over the other.

It should also be apparent that the capability of explaining or predicting an event brings with it, in many cases, the opportunity for *control* of the event. For example, had I known the temperature was to drop to 0° C. and stay there for some time, I could have protected the block and radiator of my car by filling it with the contents of the several bottles of very good Scotch that I always take on my fishing trips to use in case of snake bite. By adding the alcohol to the water I would have modified the antecedent conditions and thus prevented the event from occurring. Or, if I had wrapped the motor with an electric blanket and prevented the water from reaching 0° C., this would have prevented the fracture. In both cases the antecedent conditions are modified so that they are no longer in a state to which the general laws can apply.

A general law is true only for a specified set of conditions. The more widely these conditions can vary, the more general is the law. We can't modify the laws which specify the relationships between variables, but often, as in the example just given, we can modify the conditions which precede an event.

However, in some cases, even though the event can be predicted and explained, there is little practical capability of control. For example, an eclipse of the moon is an event that can be predicted with a high degree of accuracy, but at this time it seems unlikely that we will be able to control its occurrence because we have no way of modifying the antecedent conditions.

This description of scientific explanation and prediction is all well and good for physical events, but can it be applied to psychology and the behavior of man? Again I believe the answer to the question can best be provided by an example.

While I was a student, a friend and I took a laboratory course in sensory physiology. We were studying the vestibular sense (this is the sense modality which provides information concerning our head position and whether we are accelerating in a straight line or radially), and our lab experiment involved the use of a chicken. We were to spin the chicken and then observe the resulting head movements. My friend, a student named Lush, who had not read the experiment for the day, came in and opened the box containing the chicken. He took one look, blanched visibly, and fled from the lab not to return for several days. The next time I saw Lush I questioned him about his strange behavior. He told me that he didn't like chickens, wouldn't eat chicken no matter how prepared if he could help it, and wasn't even very fond of birds. With continued questioning the following story was told:

As a child of three or four Lush had gone with his parents to visit some friends who lived on a farm. The family had all gone into the house and had left Lush to explore the farmyard. In the yard was a flock of chickens, and Lush amused himself for a while by throwing rocks at them. Suddenly, Lush was attacked by an extremely pugnacious Bantam rooster. The rooster pecked Lush's legs and even drew blood. The painful attack frightened Lush, and he ran screaming for the farmhouse and tried to open the back door, but it was latched. Lush abandoned the back door, still screaming from fear and pain and still being attacked, and ran for the front door, with the Bantam rooster right behind. By this time the adults, having heard the commotion out back, had rushed to the back door to see what was wrong. When Lush arrived at the front door he found that it, too, was latched and that everyone was out back, so off he went for the back door, the aggressive rooster hard on his heels. In the meantime everyone had now rushed to the front door. This sequence of events continued for several more rounds until someone thought to stay at the back door and Lush was finally saved from the now bloody and triumphant rooster. Lush has feared and avoided chickens ever since.

Can we explain this chicken phobia (a phobia is an irrational fear) in the same framework we used to explain the cracked radiator and block? To do so, we must state the antecedent conditions and the general laws that relate these antecedent conditions to the event to be explained.

In this story of Lush's traumatic experience with the rooster and his subsequent behavior, the antecedent conditions were presented. Just which of these conditions are necessary for the explanation of Lush's behavior will be apparent from our discussion of the general laws.

1. If a neutral stimulus is paired with a stimulus that elicits pain and fear, then that neutral stimulus will come to elicit fear when presented without the pain-eliciting stimulus. This is the Law of Classical Conditioning, first demonstrated by Ivan Pavlov with the salivary response in dogs. When a neutral stimulus (the conditioned stimulus or CS) is consistently paired with another stimulus (the unconditioned stimulus or US) that consistently elicits a particular response (the unconditioned response or UR), then the CS will come to elicit a similar response (the conditioned response or CR). In the case of Lush the conditioned stimulus was the chicken, the unconditioned stimulus was the pecking of his legs, eliciting pain and fear, and the conditioned response was fear. Lush had been conditioned to fear chickens.

2. If a response is followed by escape from a conditioned fear stimulus, then the probability of that response will be increased. This is the Law of Active Avoidance Conditioning (see Mowrer, 1960). Lush, by escaping into the farmhouse and by preventing anxiety through avoiding chickens over the years, had learned a very effective active avoidance response, his abrupt departure from the lab being an example.

3. If a response has been conditioned to a stimulus, then other stimuli similar to that stimulus will elicit the conditioned response to some degree. The more similar the stimulus is to the conditioned stimulus, the greater the magnitude of the conditioned response will be. This is the Law of Stimulus Generalization, which accounts for the fact that Lush feared not only the Bantam rooster that actually attacked him but other chickens and even birds in general.

Given these general behavioral laws and the antecedent conditions described in Lush's story, i.e., being pecked by the chicken, finally escaping, and avoiding chickens thereafter, it can be seen that Lush's behavior in the laboratory exactly fits the paradigm presented for the explanation of the cracked radiator and block. The event to be explained is deducible from the general laws and antecedent conditions.

We have seen that with physical events, explanation is symmetrical with prediction, the only difference between the two being the temporal vantage point. Does this symmetry hold for behavioral events? Could we have predicted Lush's phobia? We could repeat the experiment using another child and another chicken, but ethical considerations preclude that approach. (See, however, Watson and Rayner, 1920, who demonstrated fear conditioning and extinction in a child named Albert.) Similar fear conditioning and active avoidance learning experiments have been conducted with rats, cats, dogs, and monkeys with the results exactly as predicted.

We have also seen that with prediction and explanation of some physical events also comes the possibility of control of those events. By appropriately manipulating the antecedent conditions, an event can be brought about or prevented. Again the question is, can behavior and psychological events be controlled in the same way? To answer this question, let us return to the drama of Lush and the chicken.

After hearing Lush's story I decided that for a grown man (6 feet, 2 inches; 220 pounds) to be irrationally afraid of chickens was unfortunate and that some attempt should be made to "cure" him of his phobia. I was going to predict an event and control some behavior. As we know, to predict and control an event requires general laws and the possibility of manipulating the antecedent conditions which are related to the general laws and the event to be predicted. I wanted to change Lush's fear response to chickens to some other response, preferably some relaxed, pleasant response. The event predicted, then, is relaxation when presented with the stimulus, chicken. The general laws required in this case are those dealing with the extinction of conditioned responses. Extinction of a conditioned response is the process by which a conditioned stimulus loses its power to elicit a conditioned response. One law governing this process is: *If a conditioned stimulus is consistently paired with a stimulus which elicits a response antagonistic to the conditioned response, then the conditioned response will be reduced and the antagonistic response will become conditioned to the conditioned stimulus.* This is a counterconditioning procedure. A necessary condition, not stated in this law, is that the stimulus which elicits the antagonistic response must elicit the antagonistic response to a greater degree than the conditioned stimulus elicits the conditioned response. To assure that this occurs, we can take advantage of the law of stimulus generalization; that is, instead of using a chicken we will use a stimulus similar to the conditioned stimulus. It will elicit the conditioned response but to a lesser degree than the original conditioned stimulus. Since in this form of extinction we are actually dealing with counterconditioning, we can expect that the new counterconditioned response will generalize to the original conditioned stimulus.

Now considering these general laws, what must be done to achieve the desired end? First, a stimulus must be found that elicits a response antagonistic to the fear response. In this case, the most antagonistic response to fear is relaxation. Knowing Lush as I did, I knew the stimulus that consistently elicited a relaxational response in him was a tall, cool, glass of beer. By consistently pairing beer drinking with chickens, I could counter-condition the fear. However, it was important not to elicit too much fear in the presence of beer, otherwise beer could come to be a conditioned stimulus for fear (this would be predicted by the Law of Higher-Order Conditioning).

My plan was to meet with Lush a couple of times each week for a beer—this he was willing to do since I was buying—and gradually introduce the fear stimulus. On the first day of "therapy," after we had had a beer or two, I presented Lush with an imitation baby chick (the kind used for decorating Easter baskets). Lush didn't like it; there were some signs of fear, but with continued coaxing he tolerated the toy chicken, and by the time he had consumed several more beers, there was no evidence of fear.

The next session I brought a live baby chick and kept it in a box under the table. When I told Lush what was in the box he almost bolted from the room, but with coaxing and the promise of more beer he was persuaded to stay, and by the end of the session he was capable of holding the chick without evidence of fear.

The sessions continued in this fashion, each session the chicken being bigger and closer until one week I brought a Bantam rooster to walk around on the table (much to the barkeep's displeasure). At first Lush evidenced fear, but again by the end of the hour he was relaxed and could pet the rooster with no signs of fear. The therapy had been successful; Lush showed no signs of fear at the sight of chickens and loved barbecued chicken for Sunday dinner. In fact, now every time Lush sees a chicken he says, "Let's have a beer."

As you can see by this example, not only is it possible to predict the occurrence of a certain behavior, but also it is possible to control it. Many of our responses, both negative and positive, can be predicted, explained, and controlled in just this way. (See Wolpe, 1958, for further discussion of this therapy technique.)

It is obvious from this discussion that behavior can be controlled. All events in the universe, including the behavior of man, are determined. The idea that the behavior of others is determined is easy to accept, but not so easy to accept is the fact that our own behavior is equally determined and ultimately predictable. (A discussion of the free-will–determinism question is beyond the scope of this paper, but the interested reader may refer to Immergluck (1964) for further discussion.) The fact that behavior can be controlled should not conjure up visions of Huxley's *Brave New World* or Orwell's *1984*—although their warning should be heeded—but should evoke a feeling of hope. It is only through control of behavior that psychotherapy can be successful, education fruitful, or the hope of overcoming prejudice realized. All behavior is a result of causes, and it is only by knowing the nature of these causes that it will be possible for us in any way to be free.

At the present time psychology is still a young science and yet it deals with the most complicated events in the universe. Psychology has few laws of the stature of the Law of Gravity as yet. Many psychologists would say that even the laws of conditioning used in the example just given are not the same kind as found in physical science, but rather are of a statistical nature. For example, our law of conditioning might have read: *If a neutral stimulus is consistently paired with another stimulus that consistently elicits a particular response,* then there is a high probability that *the neutral stimulus will come to elicit that response.* The form of the explanation or prediction of an event using such probabilistic or statistical laws is exactly the same as that for general laws, the difference being that the event to be explained is probable rather than certain. The paradigm would look like this:

$$
\left.
\begin{array}{ll}
\text{General laws} & L_1 \ldots L_N \\
\text{Antecedent conditions} & C_1 \ldots C_N
\end{array}
\right\} \quad (Explanans)
$$

$$
\frac{}{E} \qquad \begin{array}{l} \text{(makes highly probable)} \\ (Explanandum) \end{array}
$$

As our knowledge continues to grow in psychology, sociology, and physiology, we will find that many, if not all, of these probabilistic explanations will become full explanations as described in this paper. It is lack of knowledge that makes these laws probabilistic. (See Rudner, 1966, and Hempel, 1966.)

The job of science is to establish the general laws with which to explain and predict events. These general laws are the results of long and painstaking empirical investigation. Even after the relationship between two variables, such as the conditioned stimulus and the unconditioned stimulus, has been observed, there is still the matter of establishing the conditions under which the relationship holds. The broader the conditions under which the relationship holds, the broader the general law. General laws become part of scientific theories, and often scientific theories suggest general laws. In this way theories can predict and explain events. A discussion of theory and theory construction is beyond the scope of this paper; for a full discussion, the interested reader is referred to Rudner (1966) and Hempel (1966).

REFERENCES

Hempel, C. G. *Philosophy of natural science.* Englewood Cliffs, N.J.: Prentice-Hall, 1966.

Hempel, C. G., & Oppenheim, P. Studies in the logic of explanation. *Philosophy of Science,* 1948, **15.**

Immergluck, L. Determinism-freedom in contemporary psychology: An ancient problem revisited. *American Psychologist,* 1964, **19,** 270–281.

Mowrer, O. H. *Learning theory and behavior.* New York: Wiley, 1960.

Rudner, R. S. *Philosophy of social science.* Englewood Cliffs, N.J.: Prentice-Hall, 1966.

Watson, J. B., & Rayner, R. Conditioned emotional reaction. *Journal of Experimental Psychology,* 1920, **3,** 1–14.

Wolpe, J. *Psychotherapy by reciprocal inhibition.* Stanford: Stanford University Press, 1958.

Part Two

Heredity,
Environment,
and Development

Every human being ever born developed from a fertilized ovum, passed through the nine-month gestation period culminating in birth, and, by a very long process through the periods of infancy, childhood, and the teens, finally reached adulthood. It might seem that such a universally experienced process would be rather thoroughly understood. Such is not the case. Although many psychologists and other behavioral and social scientists have devoted themselves to gathering data and studying what takes place during the development of a human being, our present knowledge is only just enough to stimulate most persons to want much more.

One of the earliest questions about human development was "Are a person's personality and his essential intellectual characteristics already determined at the time of birth, or do these depend upon the training and experiences he undergoes?" That question was broadened into the heredity-environment issue, which once assumed the proportions of a major tempest but has recently abated until only occasional flares of excitement erupt.

It seems that most current thinkers on the developmental scene have chosen to follow a somewhat eclectic route. The extreme importance of genetic characteristics is acknowledged. The flexibility of human organisms, given a particular hereditary framework, is also recognized. The emphasis now centers around the interaction of specific hereditary endowment with a specific series of environmental influences. Short people, tall people, smart people, dumb people, rich people, poor people—all can achieve nearly equal positions in life if they receive the proper environmental influences. By the same token, if identical twins, who of course have identical genetic characteristics, are subjected to different environmental influences, they can reach very different stations in later life. Thus, the combination of heredity and environment is probably more important in understanding the development of an individual than is either his heredity or his environment alone.

Recently, some attempts have been made to carry out specific environmental changes and to observe their effect upon developing young organisms of several different species. The work of behavioral biologists who have been influenced by the writings of Darwin and by an interest in genetics has led the way. The emphasis that B. F. Skinner and his followers have placed upon the shaping of behavior has also led to the stimulation of new kinds of research.

Many observers of current social problems are beginning to formulate exciting goals for the future. As we already know how to produce rather dramatic changes in populations of organisms and in their patterns of behavior, some of these modern thinkers say, let us then set out upon a reasoned program of change that will enable us to get rid of some of our most troublesome social ills. Since all human beings go through a very similar process of development, albeit in quite different home and school environments, the starting point and major emphasis of such a program would involve the early development of the child. The child's formative years provide unparalleled opportunity for parents and teachers to teach social goals and behaviors that will make the world of the future a better place to live in.

10

Heredity Versus Environment

J. McV. Hunt

Does every newborn infant come into the world with a fixed amount of intelligence, or is it possible to increase or decrease an individual's intelligence through certain programs of training? This question, much debated by psychologists over the years, is often referred to as the "heredity-environment" issue, or in more popular terms as the "nature-nurture" issue.

If the answer to the question is that genetic characteristics account for all of a person's intelligence, then it would follow that no amount of education or training could possibly have an effect upon intelligence. If, on the other hand, only some specifiable part of intelligence depends upon genetic factors, and some other specifiable part depends upon environmental factors, then we can try to arrange training situations that will maximize the effect of education upon intelligence. In this paper Hunt discusses various attempts that have been made in trying to discover whether some part of intelligence is to be attributable to environment, and if so, how much.

To early investigators, one approach to answering the question seemed obvious: Take several sets of identical twins, who necessarily have the same heredity, subject them to different environmental influences, and observe whether the different environments produce different amounts of intelligence. This rather clear-cut experimental approach has foundered upon the problem of adequately defining and measuring intelligence itself. In order to discover whether intelligence changes, one must first be able to measure the amount of intelligence that exists both before and after the environment has been allowed to exert its influence. (We shall examine the topics of measurement and intelligence testing in Part Three.)

You will meet one technical term in this and other readings that must be clearly understood. That term is "correlation," which is often represented by the symbol r. A correlation shows how closely two variables are related. If r is zero, there is no relationship between the variables. If r is some positive value, e.g., $+.76$, this means that the values of the two variables tend to increase and decrease together. An example of a positive r would be that as age increases from 0 to 10 years, height also increases. If r is some negative value, e.g., $-.43$, this means that as the value of one variable increases, the value of the other decreases. An example of a negative r would be that as men's ages increase beyond age 20, the amount of hair on their heads tends to decrease. A perfect positive correlation would be $+1.00$ and a perfect negative correlation -1.00, but such perfection is rarely found.

* * *

Ever since Francis Galton pioneered with the use of twins to compare the relative influence of heredity and environment in the causation of various traits, efforts have been directed chiefly toward assessing the proportional importance of each. Thorndike attempted to answer this question with respect to intelligence in his classical application of correlational methods to the study of the differences in the intellectual achievement of twins.

In 1913, moreover, he indicated that, while in one sense, nothing in human nature is due either to heredity or to environment, "in another sense, the most fundamental question of human education asks precisely that we assign separate shares in the causation of human behavior to man's original nature on the one hand and his environment on the other." Some twenty years later, Shuttleworth saw the problem of selecting methods of improving the health, intelligence, and general welfare of mankind to be dependent upon an answer to this proportion question. Woodworth echoed the same view in the introduction to his critical survey of the studies of twins and foster children. Very recently, Cattell and his collaborators have expressed this view again. Without doubting that both the genes and the series of encounters with the environment during development influence individual differences in tested intelligence, one can have grave doubts about both the method by which answers have been sought to this proportion question, about the answerability of the question, and about the strategy of asking this particular question.

Samplings of the Traditional View

In a competent review of the studies which have attempted to answer this proportion question, Jane Loevinger (1943) has credited Fisher (1918) with introducing the statistical model and technique for answering the proportion question. Using the correlations between relatives (identical twins, siblings, foster children, etc.), he assumed additive Mendelian factors as the hereditary causes of the physical traits in which he happened to be interested, and he assumed that the effects of the environment would be added to the effects of heredity. Fisher, moreover, used the ratio of variances, now familiar as F, to assess the proportional contributions. The proportion of variance attributable to heredity, for instance, is the ratio of the variance contributed by indicators of the hereditary factor to the variance in the trait concerned; here the trait is some measure of intelligence. . . . In some instances, moreover, the square of the coefficient of correlation, which states the variance common to the correlated variables, has been used to assess the variance attributed to the special factor the two have in common.

In one approach, which has yielded two of the most widely quoted answers to the proportion question, Burks (1928) and Leahy (1935) compared the correlations obtained from foster children and from biological children with various indicators of the interfamilial differences in the intellectual value of their homes. Using father's IQ, mother's IQ, material advantages of the home, cultural advantages of the home, and income (i.e., of foster parents for foster children, and of biological par-

ents for their children), Burks got multiple correlations of $+.42$ for the foster children and $+.61$ for the biological children. She wrote, "the *square* of this [former] multiple (.17) represents the variance of children in ordinary communities that is due to home environment." Squaring the latter coefficient, she got .37 as the proportion of the variance which "represents the combined effect of home environment and parental mental level . . ." This latter proportion leaves 63 per cent of the variance not accounted for. Inasmuch as only one-half of the chromosomes of each parent are present in a child, however, Burks inferred that the correlation between the IQs of children and their parents would underestimate the true correlation between intelligence and heredity. She therefore considered that the major share of this residual variance would be due to genetic constitution, and so concluded that "close to 75 or 80 per cent of the IQ variance is due to innate and heritable causes." Leahy did not use multiple correlation, and the corresponding coefficients that she obtained were $+.23$ (foster children with foster parents and homes) and $+.53$. The same procedure yields estimates of 5 per cent of variance in IQ attributable to environment and over 90 per cent to heredity.

In a second approach, Wright (1921) devised the method of "path coefficients" for this same purpose. His approach assumed that the variance in an effect variable is equal to the weighted sum of the variances in a set of causal variables. From the correlations between the effect variable and measures of several related factors, he computed the weights that he called "path coefficients." The squares of these weights were then taken as the proportional contributions of the cause of the variance in the effect variable. After finding fault with Burks' analysis, Wright suggested as an alternative a procedure based on the fact that parents' intelligence is a variable correlated with the other variables in Burks' biological families but uncorrelated with heredity in the foster group. Using the two sets of correlations between child IQ and parent IQ to solve for the unknown correlations with the postulated "heredity factor," Wright developed "path coefficients" from which he concluded that home environment contributed approximately only 9 per cent of the variance in IQ, and he assumed that the residual 91 per cent should be attributed to error and to heredity, with error getting but a very minor share.

In a third widely quoted approach, Newman, Freeman, and Holzinger (1937) explicitly limited their answer to the proportion question to fraternal twins reared together. Because the gene patterns of identical twins are identical, they assumed that any differences between the pairs must be attributed to environment. In essence they developed from the formula relating variance to correlation a method of subtracting the variance of the differences attributable to environment, between pairs of identical twins, from the variance of the differences between fraternal twins, and then determining the proportion that the remaining variance of the differences between pairs of fraternal twins was of the total variance among their sample of fraternal twins. This was achieved in their formula for h^2 [$h^2 = (_i r - _f r) / (1 - _f r)$, where $_i r$ is the coefficient of correlation between identical twins, and where $_f r$ is the correlation between fraternal twins]. For their sample, the proportions of variance thus attributed to heredity in fraternal twins reared together ranged from .65 for Binet mental age to .80 for Otis IQ.

From such types of evidence come the commonly quoted statement that 80 per cent of the variance in tested intelligence can be attributed to heredity, only 20 per cent to the environment.

Recently efforts have been made to refine the analysis-of-variance model for answering the proportion quesiton. Cattell (1958) designates four sources of individual differences: (1) between-family environmental differences, (2) between-family hereditary differences, (3) within-family environmental differences, and (4) within-family hereditary differences. He contends that it is these variances and their interactions that need to be taken into account in the predictions that the clinician and the educator must make.

Existing Conditions Versus Potential Conditions and the Proportion Question

So long as the goal is obtaining a general answer to the proportion question, efforts to refine the statistical model are irrelevant to the contention that various classes of hereditary and environmental variance are what need to be taken into account by the clinician and the educator. There is no general answer to the proportion question, and any educational or welfare policies formed on the basis of any given answer purporting to be general are likely to have unhappy consequences.

Although geneticists . . . and investigators of the genetic factor in human intelligence . . . have warned against seeking a general answer to the proportion question, the effort to find one seems never to die, and those answers available get implications attributed to them which they do not have. Although Woodworth (1941) made several still highly pertinent and useful suggestions for future research on the roles of heredity and environment, he, for instance, also included among the conclusions of his review of attempts to answer the proportion question from the studies of twins and foster children the statement that "not over a fifth, apparently, of the variance of intelligence in the general population can be attributed to differences in homes and neighborhoods acting as environmental factors" (p. 85). Following the assumptions underlying the sort of contentions about what needs to be taken into account by clinicians and educators attributed above to Cattell, this statement has been used to justify the estimate that no matter what might be done in the way of manipulating a child's encounters with the environment during the course of his development, one could not expect to modify his IQ appreciably, and certainly not by more than about 20 per cent of the variance in IQ to be found in the population. The available data provide no justification for such an estimate. Leaving aside the appropriateness of the analysis-of-variance model, so long as samplings are based on any given set of existing conditions, the answer to the proportion question obtained from them says nothing about what answer might be obtained from another set of conditions.

Inferring from existing answers to the proportion question to clinical or educational policy assumes that samples of the existing variation in the conditions of heredity and environment are statistically representative. They are probably not representative for heredity, and they definitely cannot be representative for the environment. The fact is that between-family and within-family variations in environment within the full range of the social classes in the culture of America constitute but a small part of the variation that has existed historically on the face of this earth. Moreover, if the assumptions that intelligence is largely fixed and that development is largely predetermined are discarded, and if behavior scientists devote themselves to the task of manipulating the encounters of children with their environments to maximize their potential for happy intellectual growth, who knows what the limits are? It is inconceivable that they are to be fixed by any given set of existing conditions.

In order to simplify this point, consider the potentialities for variance in Binet IQ attributable to environmental conditions in the case of identical twins, where heredity is held constant. From the work of Newman, Freeman, and Holzinger, one finds the correlation between the IQs of identical twins reared together to be $+.88$. According to the formula for relating variance ratio to correlation . . . , the proportion of variance attributable to environment would be 24 per cent. From the same study, when the IQs of identical twins reared apart were correlated, the resulting coefficient was $+.67$, and the variance attributable to environment became, by the same logic, 66 per cent. Now, suppose that one obtains a sample of identical twins in which one of each pair is reared in a family while the other is reared in an orphanage like the one Dennis (1960) found in Teheran, what will the proportion attributable to environment become? Any answer would be pure conjecture, but it could be expected to drop further. If the interaction between heredity and environment, a factor assumed to be omitted by the analysis-of-variance model, is not great across such a contrast in environments, considerable correlation might continue to be evident, and the main evidence of effect might show in the difference between the pairs. But if the interaction is considerable, the correlation between the pairs would drop considerably. Now again, suppose that one obtains yet another sample of identical twins in which one is reared in such an orphanage while the other is given an enriched program of encounters with the environment. . . . What will the correlation between the IQs of these twins be?

It is obvious from such considerations that the answer to the proportion question depends upon the environmental conditions sampled, and that the potential range of variation in environmental conditions is limited only by the inventive genius of behavior scientists. Since such genius grows as it feeds upon the results of its efforts, the potential range is not specifiable. On these grounds alone, there is thus no general answer to the proportion question.

It is obvious also from such considerations that any policies concerning division of effort in the clinic or the classroom based on the commonly quoted answer of a 20/80 percentage split between environment and heredity would be quite wrong. Even if the figure has the meaning for the general population that Woodworth attributed to it, this does not mean that intellectual development is predetermined by the genes, but rather, given the existing culture of the subjects used in the studies of twins and foster children, children's encounters with the environment during their development is

sufficiently similar in its growth-evoking capacity to yield this figure. On the side of reducing the variation of stimulation, it is clear from Dennis' observations of children in the orphanage in Teheran that the appearance of the walking schema can be delayed by at least from age two to age four, a DQ shift of 50 points. On the side of manipulating children's counters with the environment from birth on to maximize intellectual growth, who knows what might be done? Various bits of evidence reviewed here indicate that substantial increases in intelligence as now measured may be possible. The important question for educational policy, the important question for the welfare of man now living in technological cultures that demand a higher and higher proportion of people with high capacity for the manipulation of symbols in problem solving, is to determine what the potential for increasing intellectual capacity may be. Answers to the proportion question based on an analysis of the variance within any sampling from the status quo have no bearing on this potential.

*   *   *

More Appropriate Questions

It appears that Thorndike's (1913) question about the proportionate shares of heredity and environment in the causation of intelligence is an unfortunate one. A more sensible strategy is to ask specific questions which are of significance either for programs of education, child rearing, and human welfare in general, or for specific issues in the theory of human development and human nature.

To questions significant for educational planning and human welfare belongs the one about how much the intelligence of the feebleminded children can be elevated by such special programs of environmental encounters as come in nursery school experience. Kirk (1958) has asked this question and obtained one answer in a carefully conducted study. This one answer, of course, is a function of the particular nursery school experiences supplied. Some 81 retarded children, aged between three and six and with IQs between 45 and 80, were identified and studied over a period of years. A group of 28 attended a special nursery school in the community and were followed up with tests and observations from three to five years after leaving school. A second group of 15 children, all of whom had been committed earlier to an institution for mental defectives, were enrolled in an institutional nursery school, and these were followed up after discharge from the school either to the institutional primary school or to the community. A third group of 26 children, similar in age, IQ, and social status to those in the community group, remained in their community environments without attending nursery school. A fourth group of 12 children, already committed to a second institution for mental defectives, remained in their institutional environment without attending nursery school. Both of these latter two groups were tested at the same intervals as were those children who got the special nursery schooling, and they were also followed up after they entered primary schools at the age of six. The evidence was processed both as case studies of the various experimental children and in terms of statistical comparisons of the two groups that got nursery schooling with the two contrast-groups that got none. The overall effects of the nursery schooling on these retarded children were positive. Of the 43 retarded children who received the nursery school experience 30 (70 per cent) showed an acceleration in rates of intellectual growth ranging from 10 to 30 points in IQ. The overall average increase in IQ for the experimental groups was greater than that for the contrast groups (p < .05). Moreover, and this is an important item, the children retained the accelerated rates of growth established during the nursery school experience during the follow-up period of from three to five years. Such findings indicate that society would not be wasting its time to supply nursery school experience for retarded youngsters of the preschool age. For instance, six of the 15 children in the institutional nursery school gained enough to permit them to be placed in foster homes in the community with apparently good adjustments, whereas not one of the 12 contrast children could be placed. Inasmuch as the United States Public Health Service has estimated that committing a child to an institution for the retarded at an early age and keeping him there for life costs the state approximately $50,000, an institution could apparently save a state money simply by employing one nursery school teacher for each five such children, even if only one instead of two out of five were placed after nursery school experience of two or three years. But this experiment also has some theoretical significance. It adds, for instance, another item of evidence against the notion that rates of growth are irrevocably fixed by inheritance or by the conditions of the organism at the time of testing. On the other hand, 30 per cent of the children failed to gain from the nursery school experience. Would other

approaches in nursery school affect them? How are they limited?

Especially important for both educational practice and theory of human development and nature are questions, as Anastasi (1958) has pointed out, about *how* both the genotype and the environment operate to produce such phenotypical characteristics as intelligence. At the present stage of behavior science in this area, strategy still concerns what kinds of factors make a difference. Thus, on the environmental side, it is important that Pasamanick, Knobloch, and Lilienfeld (1956) have found that various deficiencies of maternal diet associated with socio-economic level can produce complications of both pregnancy and parturition which result in intellectual retardation and behavioral disorders in offspring. It is important that Harrell, Woodyard, and Gates (1955) have found evidence that supplements for maternal nutrition in women whose diets were known to be deficient resulted in significantly higher IQs in their offspring at ages three and four than were found in the offspring of control mothers not given the supplement. It is important that Milner (1951) has found reading readiness in the first grade to be a function of opportunities for verbalization at home. On the genetic side, it is important that Jervis (1939) has traced some of the mechanisms whereby the gene that controls the enzyme which disposes of phenylpyruvic acid in cerebral metabolism causes feeblemindedness. It is important to look for the kinds of genetic factors that indirectly, as Dobzhansky (1950) puts it, set the "norm" or, in the terminology of psychological statistics, the "range of variation" within which environmental circumstances determine the eventual outcome. Hebb's A/S ratio may be one of these factors. Another may reside in biochemical conditions which limit the readiness with which cerebral firing-systems can be established and modified.

Much of the evidence reviewed in this work is concerned with showing that experience, and especially early experience, is of importance. In spite of all the information psychologists have gathered about learning, much of the conceptualizing is unfruitful, and so much remains to be learned about how encounters with the environment influence the rate of development that one can say only that beginnings of essential knowledge are available.

In asking *how* experience influences development, moreover, knowledge of *how much* comes inevitably, because amounts of change in such variables as tested intelligence or the age at which landmarks of intellectual development appear become the criteria by which answers to the question of *how* are to be recognized. For instance, Dennis' finding that the conditions of development prevailing in a Teheran orphanage increase the age at which nearly all children learn to walk from a little less than two years to more than four years, a reduction in DQ of over 50 points, does not by itself say *how* the orphanage experience works, but a hint comes from the fact that Dennis and Dennis (1940) found no delay in the age at which the walking schema appeared in Hopi children reared for the first year on cradle boards, even though the boards greatly hampered their use of their legs. It should be noted, in connection with the question *how*, that these Hopi children got a rich variety of visual and auditory experience while being carried about on the backs of their mothers. One may hypothesize, for the purpose of future testing, that it is relatively unimportant that the firing-systems established in those regions of the brain not immediately involved with either receptor inputs or motor outputs be based on use of legs. Hebb (1949) may be essentially correct in his emphasis on perceptual experience in primary learning. On the other hand, he may be missing the fact that both looking and listening involve motor outputs as well as receptor inputs, i.e., the fact that they are, as Piaget (1936) calls them, sensorimotor schemata. Perhaps it is true, nevertheless, that the visual and auditory schemata are of essential importance during the early months while the use of the limbs is not. Perhaps it is only later after these early cerebral firing-systems have been established and such schemata as walking are already established that motor activities become important for future development. But this is not the place to go into detail. The point to be made here concerns the fact that it is by determining *how much* rates of growth and the ages at which various behavioral landmarks appear are displaced by various programs of encounters with the environment that one learns *how* experience operates. Such questions, emerging from the view of development as continuous organism-environment interaction, are markedly different from the traditional proportion question, and they promise to be much more fruitful. The answers should supply the basis for an educational psychology of infancy which should bring the race to a new level of adaptability.

REFERENCES

Anastasi, A. Heredity, environment, and the question "How?" *Psychological Review*, 1958, **65**, 197–208.

Burks, B. S. The relative influence of nature and nurture upon mental development: A comparative study of foster parent—foster child resemblance and true parent—true child resemblance. *Yearbook of the National Society for the Study of Education*, 1928, **27** (I), 219–316.

Cattell, R. B. Variance analysis equations and solutions for nature-nurture research. *Psychological Review*, 1958, **67**, 353–372.

Dennis, W. Causes of retardation among institutional children. *Journal of Genetic Psychology*, 1960, **96**, 47–59.

Dennis, W., & Dennis, M. G. The effect of cradling practice upon the onset of walking in Hopi children. *Journal of Genetic Psychology*, 1940, **56**, 77–86.

Dobzhansky, T. Heredity, environment, and evolution. *Science*, 1950, 111, 161–166.

Fisher, R. A. The correlation between relatives on the supposition of Mendelian inheritance. *Transactions of the Royal Society, Edinburgh*, 1918, **52**, 399–433.

Harrell, R. F., Woodyard, E., & Gates, A. I. *The effect of mothers' diets on the intelligence of the offspring.* New York: Bureau of Publications, Teachers College, Columbia University, 1955.

Hebb, D. O. *The organization of behavior.* New York: Wiley, 1949.

Jervis, G. A. A contribution to the study of the influence of heredity on mental deficiency. The genetics of phenylpyruvic oligophrenia. *Proceedings of the American Association for the Study of Mental Deficiency*, 1939, **44**, 13–24.

Leahy, A. M. Nature-nurture and intelligence. *Genetic Psychology Monographs*, 1935, **17**, 235–308.

Loevinger, J. On the proportional contributions of differences in nature and nurture to differences in intelligence. *Psychological Bulletin*, 1943, **40**, 725–756.

Milner, E. A. A study of the relationships between reading readiness in grade-one school children and patterns of parent-child interaction. *Child Development*, 1951, **22**, 95–112.

Newman, H. H., Freeman, F. N., & Holzinger, K. J. *Twins: A study of heredity and environment.* Chicago: University of Chicago Press, 1937.

Pasamanick, B., Knobloch, H., & Lilienfeld, A. M. Socio-economic status and some precursors of neuropsychiatric disorder. *American Journal of Orthopsychiatry*, 1956, **26**, 594–601.

Piaget, J. *The origins of intelligence in children.* 1936. Translated by Margaret Cook. New York: International Universities Press, 1952.

Thorndike, E. L. *The original nature of man.* New York: Columbia University Press, 1913.

Woodworth, R. S. Heredity and environment: A critical survey of recently published material on twins and foster children. *Social Science Research Council Bulletin*, 1941, No. 47.

Wright, S. Systems of mating. I. The biometric relations between parent and offspring. *Genetics*, 1921, **6**, 111–123.

11

Selection and Test of Response Measures in the Study of the Human Newborn

William Kessen, E. Jane Williams, and Joanna P. Williams

Most investigators agree that if we wish to obtain accurate information about the course of development in infancy, the way to get it is to make careful observations of a group of infants as they grow. But a bit of reflection will show that in order to observe large numbers of infants for the first several years of their lives, keeping careful records of all their activities, one would require a vast research establishment. Thus we are faced with the problem of wanting that which we cannot easily, or perhaps even reasonably, expect to get.

The next-best way to get accurate information is to study a small group of infants intensively for a brief period of time. Since it would still be difficult or impossible to record all activity, and subsequently to make sense of so much data, it is necessary to select a few specific activities and to measure only these.

In the series of observations on newborn infants reported in this article, four specific activities were measured: (1) gross movement, (2) hand-mouth contacting, (3) mouthing movements, and (4) crying. These measures were made at specific times during the first five days of the infants' lives, and changes in each kind of activity were noted.

Thirty years ago, Weiss (1929) stated the problems of response selection in studies of the human newborn:

. . . There is a very little coordination of the different movements. . . . The assumption that no movement is ever repeated exactly becomes a very obvious fact. It seems at first futile to speak of classifying the behavior. While this is true theoretically, as a matter of fact we do group together certain types of movements according to their resemblances (p. 454).

Unfortunately, Weiss' criterion of classification—the occurrence of "resemblances"—does not provide an unambiguous rule for ordering the behavior of newborns. Should we attend to resemblances in anatomical topography, or speed, or temporal overlap, or effect on the environment, or relation to antecedent stimulation? In fact, all of these criteria for classification have been used by students of neonatal behavior, with little evidence that a simple general rule for response definition is emerging. The problem of response definition is by no means confined to research with infants—it has long been an issue in general psychology—but

the newborn presents special difficulties in answering this most basic of research questions: What are the effective response classes?

In the observation of animals and older human beings, psychologists of all theoretical commitments depend on *movement in relation to the environment* and on *speech* to provide the most elemental definition of response categories. Whether in the study of maze learning or of psychotherapy, the psychologist of mature behavior can make use of the fact that his subjects move through space or speak; the student of newborns can claim no such advantage. This difference turns out to be quite important in the first stages of the search for meaningful response categories. . . .

When the psychologist sets out on his systematic study, he almost invariably adapts his observation to these everyday classificatory rules. Such a strategy is reasonably successful when used with mature human beings and even with animals, but in most cases of newborn behavior the "natural" rules are

From Child Development, *Vol. 32 (1961), 7–24. Copyright 1961 by the Society for Research in Child Development, Inc.*

inapplicable. It is largely for this reason that the behavior of newborns is seen as meaningless; we are unable to organize the neonate's behavior with the rules of classification natural for older organisms.

*   *   *

. . . Dennis' (1934) survey of the response repertory of the human infant lists the response classes which resulted from pioneer work on neonatal reflexology, and his summary is convincing demonstration that a relatively large number of response categories for neonatal behavior can be described under the criterion of close temporal relation to external stimulation.

In the course of early research on newborn behavior, there was developed a response class very different from the simple "reflexive" activities which dominate Dennis' list. Called variously "mass activity" or "general activity," this response category was the antithesis of the stimulus-response descriptions and had as its criterion of inclusion *any* detectable movement of the newborn. Several techniques were used to determine measures for this response class, but in general they aimed at representing all movements of the infant, whether these movements, collected in smaller subclasses, could be reliably related to external stimulation or not. For example, a response class defined in this way was the chief tool in Irwin's (1930) fundamental work describing the effect of several antecedent manipulations on neonatal activity. There was promise, during the thirties, that "general activity" would serve for the study of newborn behavior the same broad function that "pressing a bar" or "running a maze" had served for other psychological problems. Perhaps because the specific measures devised for neonatal activity were not sensitive enough to detect response changes of brief duration, this promise was not fulfilled.

The study of the newborn as species, directed more by interest in reliable description than by commitment to elaborated theoretical issues, produced a natural history of neonatal behavior which was fundamental to later study and developed a response class—general activity—which was shown to be responsive to manipulation.

Running alongside research interest in newborns as behavioral variants, and never independent of it, has been the study of neonatal behavior as the precursor of later behavior. In this view, the newborn is seen as part of a long development toward adult human functioning, and response classes have been sought which will show continuity of this development over time. . . .

Gesell's work has had by far the widest research impact, leading to a line of studies on the normative development of the human being, particularly with regard to relatively simple motor behavior. Piaget's interest has been in aspects of neonatal behavior which show the operation of what he considers general intellective functions, and his observations have as a theme the infant's development of increasingly effective ways of dealing with the environment. To date, no systematic study has been made of newborn behavior with Piaget's postulations as guide. The developmental theory outlined by Freud, which emphasized the early expression and control of impulse, has produced a great deal of commentary and some provocative research. Its implications for the study of neonatal behavior have been treated in detail by Lustman (1956), who also discusses the data on newborn behavior relevant to psychoanalytic theory.

Whatever theoretical position is taken, the study of the immature organism as precursor of the mature organism involves two interrelated problems: the establishment of developmental sequences common to all human beings (e.g., changes in prone progression, psychosexual development) and the determination of parameters which permit the description of individual differences (e.g., accelerated development, regression rate). In the specific instance of the newborn, one may ask: What behavior or change in behavior is common to all infants (e.g., occurrence of sucking movements when orally stimulated)? Or one may ask: What behavior or change in behavior is characteristic of one child or of a limited group of children (e.g., variations in intensity of sucking movements)? Although the first kind of normative question receives continuing examination, research interest in the study of newborns has shifted in recent years to the second. The investigations of Fries (1944, 1947) on activity, of Balint (1948) on sucking style, of Lustman (1956) on response to tactile stimulation, and of Graham *et al.* (1956) on sensitivity, among others, reflect an increasing interest in the dimensions of variations among human newborns.

In short, the consideration of the newborn as a precursor brings to the problem of response selection two points of emphasis: the relevance of neonatal behavior to later behavior and the detection of individual differences. Attention to these aspects of the problem also makes clear that the lack of obvious and common-sense continuities between neonatal and later behavior requires that the selection of response classes be directed in the first instance by hunch or preconception or theory.

*   *   *

The research to be reported in part here grew from an interest in the early history of tension and tension-control. As Wolf has pointed out, the history of the child can be seen as the history of his responses to developmental "problems," and "the earliest behavioral manifestations of problem solving are the baby's modes of tension reduction." A closely related concern with tension or disequilibrium as important in the understanding of behavior is reflected in the notions of "drive" in contemporary learning theory and of "instinct" in psychoanalytic theory. In the apparent chaos of neonatal behavior, two primitive generalizations related to these theoretical notions seem to be warranted. First, there are changes from occasion to occasion in the tension or disturbance or disequilibrium of the human newborn. He may be quietly asleep and the next moment [be] awake and screaming; he may be slowly moving his arms and legs and then suddenly startle; he may produce sighs of contentment [for] the observer or twitches of distress. The second generalization about which we can be relatively certain is that these early variations in tension come to be more and more closely related to environmental events. In fact, to the degree that one is able to set up a stable relation between some aspect of the environment and changes in the infant's level of tension, to that degree will his behavior become meaningful. The infant may become quiet when lifted to the feeding position, for example, or begin to cry "for food" at regular temporal intervals. . . .

*   *   *

The selection of oral behaviors as possibly relevant to tension-control was dictated by both observation and theory. Whatever other disagreements may separate theorists of early development, all agree that mouthing and sucking are fundamentally important responses in the newborn. Moreover, preliminary observation had suggested that two oral responses—hand-mouth contacting and mouthing—could be reliably observed and might reflect systematic individual differences.

*   *   *

Method

Subjects

The subjects of the research were mature, normal infants in the maternity service of Grace–New Haven Community Hospital. Each subject was seen several times during his hospital stay; most

subjects were observed at least once each day (*see* below, *Schedule of Observations*). In order to eliminate systematic bias in the selection of subjects, the following criterion was established for inclusion in the sample: that, whenever we began an observation series, the subject chosen be the youngest newborn in the nursery who had not yet been fed. Thus, the age of subjects at the time of their first observation ranged from 1½ hours to 13½ hours, with the median age at 8½ hours. This criterion of selection had the further advantage of permitting the comparison of neonatal behavior before and after the first feeding.

The present report is based on the repeated observation of fifty newborns. The specific observational procedures used were changed as the research became more focused and detailed, with the subjects falling into two main groups: Group I ($N = 34$), where our chief interest centered on the observation of hand-mouth contacting; and Group II ($N = 16$), where a detailed examination was made of mouthing, crying, contacting, and movement. Each of these groups was subdivided to provide information on special problems (*see* below, *Schedule of observations*).

Schedule of observations

Typically, each infant was observed on each of the five days of his hospital stay. Shortly before noon, the infant was brought from nursery to the observation room, which was an unoccupied nursery on the same floor of the hospital. Blankets and other wrappings were removed, and the newborn (dressed in hospital shirt and diaper) was placed supine on the observation pad. If the child was crying, he was held or rocked in arms until he quieted. Once the observation was begun, however, the child was not handled except in cases of acute distress, when a nurse was called to tend to him. The observation period covered from 10 to 30 minutes, depending on the group to which the child was assigned, after which the child was returned to nursery. The schedule of observations for each group of subjects was as follows:

Group Ia ($N = 25$): General observation, followed by five-minute observation (checklist) by at least two observers of hand-mouth contacting. This procedure was repeated, when possible, on days 1, 2, 3, 4, and 5. For 10 subjects in this group, a pilot run of motion photography (30 seconds in duration) was made on three successive days.

Group Ib ($N = 9$): General observation, followed by five-minute observation (checklist) by at least two observers of hand-mouth contacting. This procedure was repeated, when possible, three times each day (at 8–9 A.M., at 11–12 A.M., and at 5–6 P.M.) on days 1, 2, 3, 4, and 5.

Group IIa ($N = 11$): General observation, followed by five-minute observation (key-depression with record made on an Esterline-Angus operations recorder) of crying, mouthing, and hand-mouth contacting. After this observation, the same measures were taken over five one-minute observation periods, each separated from the next by one minute of no recorded observations. During each of the one-minute observation periods, a 30-second sample of motion photography was obtained. For 10 to 15 seconds of minute-observations 8 and 12, the observer inserted his shielded index finger into the baby's mouth. The procedure was repeated on days 1, 2, 3, 4, and 5.

Group IIb ($N = 5$): Procedure was exactly the same as that for group IIa, except that no oral stimulation was applied and observations were not made during minutes 8, 10, 12.

Response measures

HAND-MOUTH CONTACTING. The newborn's response of bringing his fingers or hands to his mouth was recorded in two ways. The first, used with Group I, involved placing a check-mark on a mimeographed sheet whenever a contact occurred, recording thereby the finger which made contact and the *frequency* of contacts over a predetermined period of time. For Group II, the depression of one of two telegraph keys marked a line on an Esterline-Angus operations recorder (Recorder), indicating which had made contact, the *frequency* of contacts over a predetermined period, and the *duration* of hand-mouth contacting.

MOUTHING. In addition to the movements of the newborn's mouth which can be observed in the feeding situation and which frequently accompany hand-mouth contacting, mouthing movements occur in the newborn in the absence of external stimulation. For Group II, a telegraph key was depressed, marking a line on the Recorder whenever the infant's lips moved in a characteristic sucking pattern, either in the presence or absence of external stimulation. In the analysis presented below, the *duration* of mouthing is the measure of this activity.

CRYING. For Group II, a telegraph key was depressed, marking a line on the Recorder whenever the infant made an audible cry. In order to avoid

observer anticipation of crying, the recording key was depressed only on the exhalation part of the crying cycle. As in the case of mouthing, *duration* of crying is the measure used for analysis.

For all duration measures, the Recorder tape was scored by seconds of observation, and a score of 1 was assigned for each second in which hand-mouth contacting, mouthing, or crying was recorded. Thus, for all three duration measures, an infant's score could vary from zero to whatever number of seconds elapsed during the observation. For comparability among observations of different lengths, all scores were reduced to a "per 30-seconds" base. Therefore, for any observation, an infant's crying, mouthing, or hand-mouth contacting duration score varied in a range from zero to 30.

GENERAL MOVEMENT. Each child in Group II and 10 children in Group I were photographed by a fixed position, overhead camera for one or more runs of 30-seconds duration on several days of the lying-in period. The whir of the camera's spring drive did not, by and large, alter the infant's behavior. No artificial illumination was used other than the overhead lights permanently installed in the nursery. These filmstrips were analyzed to provide a measure of the horizontal displacement of hands and feet over five-second intervals. The details of the technique are described elsewhere (Kessen *et al.*, 1961); although the technique is tedious and time consuming (requiring the examination and measured comparison of 50 film-frames per child per observation), it provides a reproducible and permanent record of the infant's movements.

Results

Reliability of measures

[The observers agreed very well in recording the number of each kind of response that the babies made.]

* * *

Individual stability of measures

Being assured that reliable protocols can be established for movement, crying, hand-mouth contacting, and mouthing, we put this next question to the data: Are these measures stable from infant to infant over the lying-in period; that is, is there evidence of consistent individual variation among newborns for these response categories?

HAND-MOUTH CONTACTING. Hand-mouth contacting is by no means an infrequent response in the human newborn. Without exception, every infant seen in pretest series and in the research proper was observed to bring his hand to his mouth at least once during the five-minute observation periods. Moreover, the variation in frequency of the response is great; among the 32 subjects who were observed on each of the five days of hospital stay, the average number of hand-mouth contacts during five minutes ranged from 3 to above 30, with two subjects making contact 60 times in a single observation period.

[For both Group I (checklist) and Group II (Recorder) analysis of the data showed that the infants who tended to put their hands to their mouths frequently one day, also tended to do it frequently on other days. Also, those infants who only infrequently put their hands to their mouths one day, tended to do so only infrequently on other days.]

* * *

In evaluating these findings, it must be remembered that they are based on a relatively brief sample of the infant's total stay in the hospital (about 0.5 per cent) and under circumstances (e.g., variation in maternal handling) which introduce considerable unsystematic variation. Therefore, the stability demonstrated here is almost certainly an underestimate of the stability to be expected from a longer time sample or in an artificially controlled setting.

It is interesting to note that the data from Group II provided no evidence of significant individual stability for *total duration* of hand-mouth contacting nor for *mean duration per contact*. This result suggests that getting the hand to the mouth may be under the control of variables different from those which control the maintenance of a contact once made.

MOUTHING. Some activity of the mouth, whether responsive to external stimulation or not, is a strongly prepotent response in the human newborn. . . . For the conditions of observations obtaining in the present study, mouthing is apparently not as sensitive a measure of stable individual variation as is hand-mouth contacting.

CRYING. For the 16 subjects in Group II, the crying measure showed wide variation. . . . The distribution of crying durations was irregular in shape, with 27 of 80 observations showing no crying at all. No significant individual differences were found on the crying measure. General observation of the infants suggested that this response is both too infrequent and too much under the

control of fluctuating external stimulation (e.g., wet diapers) to be a convincing index of individual variation.

MOVEMENT. The 30-second filmstrips run for each subject in Group II on each day of his hospital stay provided a measure of neonatal movement. The sum of displacements over five-second intervals of right and left palm and right and left ankle was the primary score submitted to analysis. For 10 subjects in Group IIa, this score was computed for five daily observations and these scores combined to provide a single daily value of movement for each infant. . . .

[These measures of movement showed that individual infants tended to be either "movers" or "nonmovers." This stability in movement from infant to infant can also be seen in the scores of Groups IIa and IIb for the *first* 30-second observation each day. The measures were so stable that these 30-second samples taken on each day reliably show that movers tend to move and nonmovers tend to lie quietly.]

* * *

In assessing the four measures under examination in the present study for their sensitivity in showing stable individual variation, we may conclude that hand-mouth contacting and general movement vary . . . from child to child, that mouthing is a marginally sensitive measure of individual variation, and that crying as measured in the present setting does not provide a reliable index of individual variation.

Relatedness of measures

DAY-TO-DAY EFFECTS. During the first five postnatal days, the newborn does not merely age; he is trained to a new feeding technique, he is extensively handled, if he is a male he undergoes minor surgery, and so on. It is therefore difficult to assign sources of variation in day-to-day effects. However, several meaningful questions may be asked. Does the behavior show regular and systematic change over days? Are there significant differences between Day 1 (when, for our sample, no feeding had occurred) and later days? Do relationships among variables change over time? There are 15 subjects in Group II on whom complete data are available which can be used to answer these questions. [The amount of crying does not change between Day 1 and Day 4, nor does hand-mouth contacting.] Mouthing is [not] different from Day 1 to later days. It might have been anticipated that feeding experience would affect mouthing, either

FIGURE 1 *Changes in neonatal movement over the first five days of life*

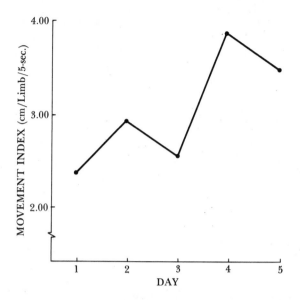

increasing it as a function of the reinforcement operation of feeding or decreasing it as a function of the increasing frustration of nonnutritive mouthing. Neither [appears to have happened]. . . .

* * *

The day-to-day . . . movement for Group IIa subjects . . . is relatively free of ambiguity. There is a systematic . . . increase in neonatal movement during the early days of postnatal life. This finding, beyond confirming the observations of other investigators, adds to our confidence that the movement measure used in the present research is a sound measure of individual and situational variation.

* * *

The effects of stimulation

On two observations each day, the infants in Group IIa were given an opportunity to suck on the observer's shielded index finger for 10 to 15 seconds. Under the conditions of the present study, no stable immediate effect on neonatal movement could be detected; although the infants seemed to quiet somewhat when the stimulation was present, this general observation was not confirmed by an examination of the filmstrips.

SEX DIFFERENCES. Some variation between the behavior of males and the behavior of females was noted in each group but no [overall] sex differences were found. . . .

Discussion

Two of the measures of newborn behavior under study, movement and hand-mouth contacting, met reasonable demands for reliability of observation and for sensitivity to individual variation. The other measures, mouthing and crying, can be observed in the neonate with satisfactory precision, but did not show in the setting described here significant sensitivity to individual differences. Of the four, movement showed systematic changes over the lying-in period.

The finding of stable individual differences in movement and hand-mouth contacting among human newborns confirms the often stated but infrequently demonstrated proposition that human beings show substantial variations one from another aboriginally. Even for the relatively homogeneous group of children observed for this research, wide and stable differences were shown. Knowing this, it is important to turn to two further questions. Do these early differences make any difference later? Does it make good sense to consider these variations, whether from time to time or from baby to baby, as representing differences in tensions? The first of these questions requires longitudinal study; the second demands an examination in some detail of the relation between activity and contacting on one hand and environmental events and other neonatal responses on the other. If neonatal movement is to serve as an index or partial interpretation of the term "tension," then it should be possible to demonstrate systematic relations to privation, to noxious external stimulation, and to the environmental operations used by parents and clinical practitioners to reduce distress in infants. On the basis of the present study, we can proceed to an attack on these next empirical questions with some confidence in the precision and the stability of measures for hand-mouth contacting and infant movement.

* * *

REFERENCES

Balint, M. Individual differences of behavior in early infancy and an objective method for recording them. *Journal of Genetic Psychology,* 1948, **73,** 57–59; 81–117.

Dennis, W. A description and classification of the responses of the newborn infant. *Psychological Bulletin,* 1934, **31,** 5–22.

Fries, M. E. Psychosomatic relationships between

mother and infant. *Psychosomatic Medicine*, 1944, **6**, 159–162.

Fries, M. E. Diagnosing the child's adjustment through age-level tests. *Psychoanalytic Review*, 1947, **34**, 1–31.

Graham, F. K., Matarazzo, R. G., & Caldwell, B. M. Behavioral differences between normal and traumatized newborns. *Psychological Monographs*, 1956, **70** (20, 21).

Irwin, O. C. The amount and nature of activities of new-born infants under constant external stimulat-

ing conditions during the first ten days of life. *Genetic Psychology Monographs*, 1930, **8**, 1–92.

Kessen, W., Hendry, A. L. S., & Leutzendorff, A. M. Measurement of movement in the human newborn: A new technique. *Child Development*, 1961, **32**, 95–105.

Lustman, S. L. Rudiments of the ego. *Psychoanalytic Study of the Child*, 1956, **11**, 89–98.

Weiss, A. P. The measurement of infant behavior. *Psychological Review*, 1929, **36**, 453–471.

12

Ontogenetic Development of the Human Sleep-Dream Cycle

Howard P. Roffwarg, Joseph N. Muzio, and William C. Dement

Long before the magnificent Greek philosophers and playwrights emphasized the importance of dreams in the conscious lives of men, it was known that man is a dreaming creature. Freud pushed the analysis of dreams and their apparent importance to man's mental well-being further than ever. Today, as we are aware that dreams occur and that they are evidently very important in the development of normal mental activity, we would like to know more about the function of dreams and the physiological characteristics that accompany the state of dreaming.

This paper discusses the history of modern laboratory dream research, which uses the techniques of the electronic age. With the help of the electronics engineer, the laboratory animal, and ingenious research projects we are beginning to gain a clear insight into the ways in which dreaming occurs and the functions that dreaming serves in the course of development as well as in adult life.

You will find that the acronyms REM and NREM are used frequently in this article. They stand for "rapid eye movement" and "nonrapid eye movement," respectively. It appears that during sleep there are periods when the eyes are moving rapidly back and forth. These rapid eye movements have been found to accompany dreaming, and it is assumed that when we dream about seeing and looking we move our eyes, the better to see and look. All this takes place despite the fact that our eyes are closed. Between periods of REM sleep, the rapid eye movements cease and a period of NREM sleep occurs. The apparent explanation is that when we have finished one dream journey, we wait a bit before embarking upon another.

A major reason for the present interest in dreaming is that it seems fairly likely that the neural activity that takes place while we are dreaming is deeply involved in learning and remembering and the conduct of day-to-day living. If indeed dreams are so deeply wrapped up in our daily affairs and whether they run smoothly or not, then it is important that we reach a better level of understanding of the process of dreaming.

The mystery of just how an infant changes in the first few months of life from a very nearly vegetative creature into a perceiving human being is one of the more intriguing questions intimately tied up with the topic of dreams. If, as the authors of this article

From Science, *Vol. 152, No. 29 (April 1966), 604–619. Copyright 1966 by the American Association for the Advancement of Science.*

suggest, dreaming is related to development of the neural tissue of the cortex and is further involved in the development of that most human of all behaviors, language, then we must proceed with all speed to study dreaming and its relationship to human development.

Within the last decade new discoveries have forced extensive modification of traditional concepts of sleep. In the past there was always considerable interest in mechanisms of sleep (Kleitman, 1939; Foster, 1901), but its function was largely taken for granted. The view prevailed that the role of sleep is self-evidently allied to the need for restitution or, at least, for rest.

Since the demonstration that there are two distinct phases of sleep (Aserinsky and Kleitman, 1955; Dement and Kleitman, 1957a, 1957b) we realize that more than a simple parallelism between rest and sleep is required to elucidate the role of sleep in our biological economy. As a matter of fact, it is probably begging the question of function to discuss *sleep* as a totality at all. For the physiological characteristics of the alternating states within behavioral sleep are so different that it is questionable whether a single designation, purporting to apply meaningfully to the normal condition of the individual when not awake, is any longer adequate. Currently, a "dualistic" hypothesis about sleep mechanisms is widely, though not universally, accepted in which the two major types of sleep are viewed as qualitatively distinct states. It is likely that a dichotomy will and should apply to the question of function as well.

Owing to its singular properties and recent discovery, the sleep stage accompanied by rapid eye movements (REM sleep) has received a greater share of investigative attention (Aserinsky and Kleitman, 1955; Dement and Kleitman, 1957a, 1957b) than the nonrapid eye movement stages (NREM sleep). Most studies have been concerned with the physiological attributes of REM sleep or with the factors that influence its percentage of total sleep. In an attempt to assess the factor of age we began a series of observations on the proportions of REM and NREM sleep in various age groups. Another reason for our interest in the REM sleep process in preadult groups was the wish to determine the onset of dreaming. Since Aserinsky and Kleitman (1955), and Dement and Kleitman (1957b) first demonstrated a relationship between REM sleep and dreaming, confirmations of the association have been numerous. We therefore thought it might be possible to designate when dreaming begins by determining the age when REM sleep first appears. Surprisingly, we found

that preschool children had a higher percentage of REM sleep than adults. We also observed REMs in apparently sleeping newborn infants. Such unexpected findings suggested the need for a thorough polygraphic investigation of sleep in human neonates.

In this article we shall attempt a new synthesis of current information about the REM state, dream phenomena, and the relationship between sleep pattern and maturation; present our findings in newborns which carry implications with regard to a "functional consequence" of REM sleep; and explore some of the data which lead us to suggest that REM sleep plays an important role in the ontogenetic development of the central nervous system.

Typical Pattern in Sleep

A normal adult, upon falling asleep, exhibits a typical succession of electroencephalographic (EEG) changes. After fragmentation and disappearance of alpha activity, the waves diminish slightly in frequency as their amplitudes grow (descending stage 1). High-voltage, notched slow waves, "K complexes," and characteristic trains of 14-cycle-per-second "sleep spindles" invade the background activity (stage 2). Tall "delta" waves (1 to 2 cycles per second) progressively fill the record (stage 3) and finally dominate it in virtually unbroken sequence (stage 4). The distinguishing criteria of these EEG "stages" are arbitrary but the stages are all considered phases of NREM sleep.

Approximately 50 to 70 minutes after onset of sleep, the initial REM period of the night begins. Appearing just before the first REMs are manifest, and persisting until the last terminate, the characteristic low-voltage, relatively fast, nonspindling EEG of stage 1 sleep resumes, encompassing an interval termed a stage-1–REM period, or REM sleep. Short trains of "sawtooth" waves (2 to 3 cycles per second) invade the stage-1–EEG, presaging or coinciding with the REM clusters. The periods recur every 80 to 90 minutes and comprise 20 to 25 per cent of the conventional night's sleep of young adults. Short early in the night and longer towards morning, they average 20 minutes in length. Spindle and high-voltage EEG patterns reappear between the REM periods.

Although the nocturnal sleep cycle of an individual on a consistent diurnal schedule tends to be fairly constant from night to night (Dement, 1957b), it may vary under conditions such as apprehension or anxiety (the "first night effect" in the laboratory), hypnotic suggestion, the effects of certain drugs and their withdrawal, compensation from experimental interruptions of REM sleep, and acute and chronic psychotic states. Age is also an important variable.

The state of the adult in REM sleep is singularly distinct from that in NREM sleep. Hence REM sleep has been classified as a "third" state alongside NREM sleep and waking. . . . We shall attempt here only to summarize the basic phenomena, focusing our attention on the events in the central nervous system.

Whereas respiratory rhythm, heart rate, and blood pressure tend to be basal in NREM sleep, they display greater activity and greater variability during REM phases (Aserinsky and Kleitman, 1955; Dement and Kleitman, 1957a, 1957b). The fine muscles of the face and extremities contract frequently, though there are few gross body displacements. In the absence of movement, however, muscle tone measured from the head and neck virtually disappears in REM periods. The extrinsic ocular muscles are an exception to this rule. Before and during shifts of eyeball position, tone may be sustained in uninvolved and antagonist muscles. Penile erections are specific to the REM periods, detumescence occurring as NREM sleep ensues. Basal skin resistance, which should fall with heightened arousal, has been reported to rise in REM sleep by some investigators but not by others. In view of the eye activity and oneiric phenomena during REM sleep, it is intriguing that the REM sleep EEG is remarkably similar to that of a subject awake under circumstances of visual imaging or stimulation, when alpha activity is blocked. Furthermore, cortical responses evoked during the waking state are extremely similar to those evoked in REM sleep.

An unexpected finding has been that motor-response and arousal thresholds are no higher in deep NREM sleep than in REM sleep (Dement and Kleitman, 1957a). This seems to fit with the finding in cats that during REM sleep there is a high response threshold in the mesencephalic reticular formation to auditory as well as to direct stimulation. In spite of the lowered responsiveness to stimulation, however, there is greater spontaneous activity in the reticular formation during REM sleep. (It is precisely this aspect of brain functioning in REM sleep which renders "depth of sleep" so difficult to designate.) Huttenlocher has speculated that in REM sleep, evoked responses may be *occluded* because of this high level of spontaneous activity. Recently, however, Adey, Kado, and Rhodes (1963) were not able to demonstrate higher response thresholds in the mesencephalic reticular formations of chimpanzees during REM sleep.

Studies in Animals

A dual neurophysiological organization of sleep is not specific to human beings. Every species of mammal so far studied exhibits rhythmically alternating periods of REM and NREM activity which are marked by vegetative alterations similar in most respects to those that are found in man.

Moreover, animal experimentation has greatly extended our knowledge of the active processes occurring in the central nervous system during the REM state, such as: increase in blood flow to the cortex, rise in brain temperature, elevation in frequency of spontaneous neuronal firing in the MRF [mesencephalic reticular formation], medial and descending vestibular nuclei, pyramidal tract, and occipital cortex; development of monophasic wave aggregates in the pons, lateral geniculate body, and other subcortical areas; continuous theta activity in the hippocampus (even more regular than during arousal); and evidence of facilitatory influences at the somatic afferent and visual afferent (lateral geniculate body) thalamic relays. During REM sleep, excitability as measured by the evoked-response technique in motor cortex is higher than, and in sensory cortex is at least as high as it is during, NREM sleep. In both regions, excitability is greater than it is in the waking state (Dement, 1957b). A shift in cortical and subcortical direct-current potentials toward the level in arousal and away from that during NREM sleep has also been demonstrated. In general, we find, surprisingly, that during REM sleep, thalamic and cortical neurons are more responsive than they are in the waking state. Many of the changes noted are most marked during actual REM bursts. Accordingly, there are both phasic and tonic components to REM-state activity.

Seemingly contrary to the direction of all these changes is a sharp attenuation of spinal reflexes and resting muscle tone in REM sleep, but these phenomena are probably due to an active inhibitory system. Therein lies the unique quality of REM sleep, that it is a time of considerable excitation within the brain which is largely blocked at the periphery. Perhaps it is this inhibition of motor and reflex activity that allows perpetuation of behavioral sleep when many areas of the brain are discharging at frequencies approximating those during alert wakefulness.

The exhaustive studies of M. Jouvet (1962) and his colleagues have provided some understanding of the mechanism of REM sleep. These investigators have demonstrated an indispensable region for REM sleep in the rostral pons (nucleus pontis caudalis) which appears to be crucial for the entire range of REM phenomena. A cat with this area ablated no longer exhibits REM phases or low-voltage fast EEG activity in sleep. It shows only two states, NREM sleep and wakefulness which may gradually progress to insomnia leading to death. Conversely, a decorticated cat shows no evidence of NREM sleep. The . . . EEG never deviates from the low-voltage, fast tracing. However, REMs, myoclonic twitches, respiratory irregularity, and diminished muscle tone continue to appear regularly, in precise periods associated with discharges in subcortical structures identical to the discharges in intact animals during REM sleep. In between the episodes of REM sleep, the decorticate animal appears for the most part awake. Accordingly, Jouvet suggests that the pontine mechanism is both necessary and sufficient for REM sleep, whereas NREM sleep requires the presence of cortical tissue. His studies in decorticate and decerebrate humans indicate that in man there is an analogous dependence of REM sleep upon brainstem and of NREM sleep upon cortex. Rossi, Minobe, and Candia (1963) have disagreed with Jouvet as to specific nuclei but have validated his basic finding of an essential area for REM sleep in the pons. There is still some doubt concerning the specific connecting pathways from the pontine center to the midbrain. More extensive studies are necessary before we can be certain that, in cats, the exact site of initiation of the REM state discharges is the mid- to rostral pontine reticular nuclei or that the mechanism is applicable in every detail to higher forms.

REM Sleep and Dreaming

It is now widely acknowledged that dreaming sleep and REM sleep are identical, though ideational material and poorly defined imagery can apparently persist through the entire range of sleep stages. Numerous associations between dream hallucinations and alterations in physiological systems have been observed in the REM state. Although such correspondences are by no means always demonstrable or precise, they may reach a high order of specificity in the visual system. For example, REMs in abundance are observed at times of frequent alterations of gaze in the dream, whereas the presence of few REMs, or a total absence of REMs (during dreaming sleep), is correlated either with staring at immobile objects or with breaks in the pictorial imagery. Roffwarg, Dement, Muzio, and Fisher (1962) have shown that the number and direction of REMs may be predicted with reasonable accuracy by treating the dream scene as a visual event that the dreamer has scanned as he would the same event when awake. The fact that sequences of REMs associated with visual dream events can be correctly predicted through reference to the REMs expected in replicated waking experience renders the old notion of the instantaneous dream extremely unlikely. Dement and Wolpert (1958) fixed particular points in the flow of time in dreams by provoking incorporations of identifiable stimuli into the dream sequence and demonstrated a close correspondence between actual time and the sense of time in dreams. Dream events evidently have a dimension in real time, though intermediary steps in an action may be skipped ("telescoping").

Additional psychophysiological relationships have been suggested by Wolpert's finding (1960) of a correlation between dreamed limb excursions and action potentials in wrist muscles. Moreover, when sleep talking takes place in REM sleep (it usually does not), it may relate to the situation in the dream. Hobson, Goldfrank, and Snyder (1965) have shown that major respiratory irregularities (such as periods of apnea) are frequently linked to concurrent dream experiences such as talking, laughing, or choking. And penile erections, though typically present in the REM state, show size fluctuations in association with specific dream content (such as sexual activity, anxiety, attack). A single experience in Snyder's laboratory dramatically highlights these correlations. In the middle of a REM period a subject's respirations and heartbeat began to race. When awakened a few minutes later, he recalled that he was dreaming of participating in sexual intercourse. He had experienced a nocturnal emission just prior to the arousal.

Other physiological "windows into the dream" may become available as new parameters are studied. The recently reported elevations of gastric hydrochloric acid in peptic-ulcer patients and the increases of adrenal corticoids in normal subjects during REM sleep may turn out to vary in magnitude in relation to simultaneous dream content. It has already proved possible to derive crude inferences about dream content from variations in physiological activity during the REM period. Additional indirect support for existence of a biological relationship between mind and body events during the REM state is contributed by the finding of heightened vividness of imagery at moments of greatest physiological variation. There can no longer be any doubt that a dream, far from being merely a diaphanous and elusive creature of mind, is the sensate expression of a fundamental and rhythmically repetitive and enormously active neurophysiological state. Hence dreaming, heretofore knowable only via subjective report and intuitive conjecture, is now accessible to more objective investigation.

Hallucinatory Activity

There is general agreement that, with the exception of certain delirious states, dream hallucinations are more encompassing than other hallucinatory events, most of which are merely superimposed on a background of uninterrupted sensory input from the environment. In the dream the total perceptual field is hallucinated. Though predominantly visual, the imagery may include realistic components from most if not all sensory systems simultaneously. It is common experience that every nuance of emotion as well as of perception— the full world of our experience—may be reduplicated in dreams. A substantial portion of the brain must be active during this state.

Dement has suggested that dream hallucinations may constitute the only "true" hallucinations because the sensory material in dreams does not depend upon external input at the time of dreaming (although concurrent stimulations may be incorporated into a dream in progress). During REM sleep, the brain appears to be "in business for itself." Blinded individuals continue to experience visual imagery in dreams. . . . During the REM state the optic tract of intact cats does not exhibit the sharp elevations in discharge frequency that are seen in the lateral geniculate body and occipital cortex, and firing in the geniculate body does not diminish as a result of acute enucleation of the eyeball. These findings suggest that visual "information" supplying the dream appears to originate within the brainstem and "feeds" into the visual afferent pathway at some intermediary point along its route. The fact that the spike discharges in the lateral geniculate body are synchronous with those in both the pontine reticular formation and visual cortex further supports this view.

Just as the dreamer, as an observer of the dream, is confronted by (hallucinated) sensory "percepts," he is also involved as a participant in the dream action in responding to them with (hallucinated) motor activity. The dreamer may experience the appearance and proprioceptive sense of his arm moving to brush away a bee that he hears in flight and sees alighting on his nose. Hence hallucinatory experiences occur not only of sensory objects but also of sensory components of motor performance "evoked" by the hallucinated object. As mentioned above, in REM sleep, upper motor-neuron activity is markedly increased, spikes in the extraocular muscles are coordinated with discharges in the visual afferent system, and phasic bursts of muscle potentials may accompany hallucinated movements. We may conjecture, therefore, that impulses are introduced from within the central nervous system into motor as well as sensory pathways, and that the recordable motor discharges may be correlated with hallucinated "percepts" of, or "intentions toward," movement.

Not only, then, is the brain highly activated during REM sleep from a physiological point of view, but as we have just speculated it seems to be "perceiving" and "reacting" to its percepts much as an awake brain does. If the dreaming brain is in any sense "awake," however, it seems attuned primarily to the compelling phenomena originating and being perceived within itself. On the other hand, under conditions such as direct suggestion (hypnotic or otherwise) or threat of negative reinforcement, subjects in REM sleep can increase their reactivity to exogenous stimuli to levels greater than during any other stage of sleep. Inattention, therefore, may to some extent explain the high arousal thresholds in REM sleep. When external events compete with internal events for significance, however, attention may be diverted from the latter.

Approaches to Function

Speculations concerning the role of the REM state have risen mainly from two previous lines of study: phylogenetic and deprivational. Because of the location of the pontine REM sleep mechanism, Jouvet first considered REM sleep to be a phylogenetically archaic state. The findings that in the newborn cat the behavioral and EEG characteristics of the REM state mature earlier than those of NREM sleep or waking, and that sustained periods of REM sleep appear directly after arousal without intermediary NREM sleep, initially seemed to confirm the more "primitive" quality of the REM state.

Correspondingly, Jouvet believed NREM sleep to be a state which depends on a functioning neocortex, acquired in the course of phylogenetic telencephalization. He therefore referred to it as "neo-sleep" (M. Jouvet, Michel, and Mounier, 1960). A corollary of this schema is that species having less neocortical tissue would be expected to manifest greater proportions of REM sleep. However, studies on the rat, opposum, sheep, goat, cat, and monkey have not shown a consistent trend in that direction. The most primitive vertebrates polygraphically demonstrated to have REM sleep are birds, in which the periods are exceedingly brief (0.3 per cent). Among the reptiles, the tortoise has been studied but the REM state has not been demonstrated. Therefore, only in the ontogenetic sense can REM sleep be considered a "primitive" state. More data are needed concerning the phylogeny of REM sleep, but if it is borne out that REM sleep developed later in evolution than NREM sleep, phylogenetic studies may still clarify two important questions: (i) What functional requirement was met by the development of REM sleep? (ii) Why did the rhombencephalon become the site of the REM sleep mechanism?

The attempt to study the function of REM sleep by experimentally eliminating it was first made by Dement. By awakening subjects at the commencement of each REM period he effectively reduced the amount of REM sleep. After a series of consecutive "deprivation" nights the subjects were allowed uninterrupted sleep, and almost all exhibited a dramatic rise in amount and percentage of the REM phase. This was regarded as evidence of a physiological "need" for REM sleep. Additional experiments in humans and animals have confirmed the tendency to compensate for lost REM sleep after artificial interruptions of sleep.

Suppression of REM sleep by experimental destruction of the nucleus pontis caudalis causes hyperirritability and hallucinating-like behavior in animals. These changes are reversible if only small amounts of REM sleep reappear, whereas cats who do not recover any capacity for REM sleep may progress to a state of insomnia and agitation and eventually die. These animals have brainstem lesions, and thus to implicate loss of REM sleep exclusively for these difficulties may not be warranted. In contrast, studies of *functional* deprivation of REM sleep in cats currently being pursued by D. Jouvet, Vimont, Dolorme, and M. Jouvet (1964) and Dement reveal surprisingly few overt behavioral changes in the animals even after lengthy periods of complete deprivation, though persistent tachycardia and a faster auditory-recovery cycle have been demonstrated during the deprivation. Hypersexuality is also a feature of the deprived cats, but when awake the animals may appear remarkably unaffected by the deprivation. Behavioral changes in humans have been observed only after the 15th day of continuous deprivation of REM sleep in recent studies. Therefore, it appears that the function of REM sleep in the intact adult organism is not so immediate that the consequences of REM sleep deprivation are soon apparent or necessarily fatal.

Evolution of Sleep Patterns

Because of the inconclusiveness of phylogenetic and deprivational approaches to the function of REM sleep, we and others have begun to examine its role in human ontogenetic development. These observations, as well as those in newborn and immature animals, reveal that REM sleep assumes a high proportion of total sleep in the first days of life and that its amount and ratio diminish as maturation proceeds (Figure 1). Earlier work in our laboratory with infants and children pointed to certain relationships among maturation, daily behavior, and evolving sleep patterns.

In infancy, when the proportion of time awake is smaller than in any other period of life, there is a large amount of REM activity. REM periods appear soon after sleep begins and are of random duration at any time of the night. Later, when the developing infant spends protracted intervals awake in increasingly active involvement with the environment (particularly when locomotive capacity is attained), the total amount as well as the percentage of REM sleep diminishes.

This evolution in the relative proportions of the sleep stages continues through the period when napping terminates. Long stretches of deep NREM sleep occupy the first hours. Correspondingly, the first REM period in children past the napping age appears much later and is shorter than in children who nap. REM periods become longer toward morning. We have considered it probable that the child's progressively closer approximation of a diural pattern of uninterrupted daytime wakefulness causes corresponding changes

FIGURE 1 *Graph showing changes (with age) in total amounts of daily sleep, daily REM sleep, and in percentage of REM sleep. Note sharp diminution of REM sleep in early years. REM sleep falls from 8 hours at birth to less than 1 hour in old age. The amount of NREM sleep throughout life remains more constant, falling from 8 hours to 5 hours. In contrast to the steep decline of REM sleep, the quantity of NREM sleep is undiminished for many years. Although total daily REM sleep falls steadily during life, the percentage rises slightly in adolescence and early adulthood. This rise does not reflect an increase in amount; it is due to the fact that REM sleep does not diminish as quickly as total sleep. Work in progress in several laboratories indicates that the percentage of REM sleep in the 50- to 85-year group may be somewhat higher than represented here. Data for the 33- to 45- and 70- to 85- year groups are taken from Strauch (1963) and Lairy, Cor-Mordret, Faure, and Ridjanovic (1962) respectively.*

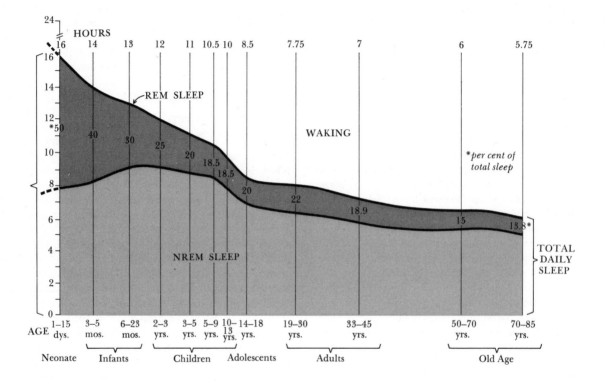

in the sleep-stage pattern. Post-nappers four and one-half to seven years) average 110 to 120 minutes of deep NREM sleep (stage four) in comparison to 75 to 80 minutes in the pubescent group. It is of course not yet clear whether these changes are a consequence of lengthening periods of sustained arousal, increased muscular activity, maturation of the central nervous system, or a combination of these factors.

The first REM period of the night usually appears 50 to 70 minutes after sleep commences, whereas in the four and one-half- to seven-year-old group, latency of REM onset is 3 to 4 hours. Latency continues to shorten as children mature but it does not assume the adult interval consistently until mid-adolescence. This phenomenon of a delayed or "missed" first REM period may reappear in adults under conditions of sleep loss. Moreover, nocturnal sleepers who nap in the afternoon have a shorter REM latency in their naps than those who nap in the evening. These findings suggest that a condition ("fatigue," for lack of a more exact term) develops under circumstances of prolonged arousal (and possibly intensive activity) which tips the normal balance between REM and NREM sleep mechanisms, augmenting temporarily the "need" for deep NREM sleep and antagonizing REM sleep processes. We speculate that the immature central nervous system is more vulnerable to "fatigue," though youngsters are unquestionably more active than adults.

REFERENCES

Adey, W. R., Kado, R. T., & Rhodes, J. M. *Science,* 1963, **141**, 932.

Aserinsky, E., & Kleitman, N. *Journal of Applied Physiology,* 1955, **8**, 1.

Dement, W. C., & Kleitman, N. *Electroencephalography and Clinical Neurophysiology,* 1957, **9**, 673. (a)

Dement, W. C., & Kleitman, N. *Journal of Experimental Psychology,* 1957, **53**, 339. (b)

Dement, W. C., & Wolpert, E. A. *Journal of Experimental Psychology,* 1958, **55**, 543.

Foster, H. H. *American Journal of Psychology,* 1901, **12**, 145.

Hobson, J. A., Goldfrank, F., & Snyder, F. *Journal of Psychiatric Research,* 1965, **3**, 79–90.

Jouvet, D., Vimont, P., Delorme, F., & Jouvet, M. *Comptes Rendes des Seances de la Societé de Biologie,* 1964, **158**, 756.

Jouvet, M. *Archives Italiennes Biologie,* 1962, **100**, 125.

Jouvet, M., Michel, F., & Mounier, D. *Revue Neurologique,* 1960, **103**, 189.

Kleitman, N. *Sleep and wakefulness.* (Rev. ed.) Chicago: University of Chicago Press, 1963.

Lairy, G. C., Cor-Mordret, M., Faure, R., & Ridjanovic, S. *Revue Neurologique,* 1962, **107**, 188.

Roffwarg, H. P., Dement, W. C., Muzio, J. N., & Fisher, C. *Archives of General Psychiatry,* 1962, **7**, 235.

Rossi, G. F., Minobe, K., & Candia, O. *Archives Italiennes Biologie,* 1963, **101**, 470.

Strauch, I. H. Paper presented to the Association for Psychological Study of Sleep, New York, March 1963.

Wolpert, E. A. *Archives of General Psychiatry,* 1960, **2**, 231.

13

Behavioral Correlates of Mental Growth: Birth to Thirty-Six Years

Nancy Bayley

This article reports on an extensive study of the relationships between intelligence, certain personality characteristics, and sex at various age levels. It gives a good picture of what is involved in planning and carrying out a longitudinal study of development, and in analyzing and interpreting the vast amounts of data obtained.

You will find that there are many figures that are loaded with data. Some comments here will help you understand the bulk of the material presented. Each figure should be studied carefully. Read the title of the figure and the labels on the vertical and horizontal axes. Pay particular attention to Figure 3, since all later figures will make reference to material contained therein.

As you come across such technical terms as "Q sort," "circumplex orientations," "cluster scores," and others, don't feel dismayed if you don't fully understand what they mean. These terms are important to persons involved in the technical aspects of doing research, but you will not miss anything if you read lightly over them.

The accumulated records of the Berkeley Growth Study have much to offer for explorations into the processes of growth. Their value is in part a function of the unusually complete set of longitudinal records, which cover a 36-year life span for the 54 cases who were seen at the most recent round of tests and interviews. Thus it is possible to trace the mental and physical trends of development in individuals with data observed and recorded at up to 56 scheduled testing sessions. Although the records include a variety of mental, motor, physical, and behavioral measures, this report is concerned with mental growth and the relation to it

From American Psychologist, *Vol. 23:1 (1968), 1–17. Copyright 1968 by the American Psychological Association, and reproduced by permission. This research was supported, in part, by Grant MH08135 from the National Institute of Mental Health, United States Public Health Service.*

of expressed emotions, attitudes, and characteristic reaction tendencies.

This sample was purposely selected for homogeneity, as full-term, healthy, hospital-born babies of white, English-speaking parents. The full sample of 74 babies remained in the study through 7 months, 63 remained through at least 3 years, and of these 48 were seen regularly throughout the first 18 years (at least 40 times). At the 36-year round, 61 of the 3-year-or-longer sample were located and 54 of them were tested.

Although the sample is not strictly representative of the Berkeley population, it has a wide socio-economic distribution which has remained essentially unchanged. This distribution is shown in Figure 1, which gives for the tested sample at each of three ages, birth, 3 years, and 36 years, the frequencies, by percentage of each sample, on a 19-point scale. This scale is a combination of their parents' education, occupation, income, and a rating of the home and neighborhood made at the start of the study (Bayley and Jones, 1937).

Our well-documented 36-year histories of this essentially healthy population, though for the most part limited to certain developmental aspects of their lives, have generated data of a very compelling nature. These data, from very early in the study, have indicated the need to make changes in many of our assumptions, theories, and hypotheses. Hence, from time to time, we have made relevant changes in the research design, both in the nature of the data which were collected at successive ages,

and in the procedures used in organizing and evaluating the data.

The first challenge to accepted theory which was suggested by the data was reported in a 1933 monograph on mental growth during the first 3 years (Bayley, 1933b). The scores on the mental tests had not conformed to the assumption, at that time widely held, that "the IQ is constant." The finding that in the first two or three years of life the children's rates of mental growth, and hence their IQs, were unstable led me to various analyses of the items and subgroups of the items, in an effort to understand the nature of the early mental processes, and to find a core of mental items in the First-Year scale (Bayley, 1933a) that *would* predict later intelligence.

In one form or another I have been continually preoccupied with this process of analysis of the mental test scores and their correlates ever since. During the first 20 years, with the exception of two studies on socio-economic correlates, one of which included some moderate correlations with optimal and attitude ratings (Bayley, 1940; Bayley and Jones, 1937), our analyses were concerned primarily with the nature of the intellective processes themselves. Reports have been made on the consistencies, labilities, and variabilities over time of scores on different aspects of mental function (Bayley, 1949, 1955).

These early studies, as I look back on them now, appear to have suffered from too much combining, both of population samples and of test scores. That is, almost invariably statistical analyses were made only on the total sample of approximately equal numbers of males and females. Furthermore, the emotional and attitudinal variables were selected and combined by armchair decisions as to which kinds of behaviors might enhance or depress the scores. Over time, it has become increasingly evident that the cognitive as well as the emotional processes of males and females must be treated separately in all statistical analyses. Also, recently, with the able help of colleagues (with both theoretical and statistical sophistication) and with the advantages of modern computer techniques, it has been possible to reanalyze both the test items and behavior ratings and to combine them, on the basis of their intercorrelations, into new meaningful clusters composed of related variables. When these new "factors" are used in correlational analyses they have revealed many intriguing patterns of interrelations.

Some 10 years ago Schaefer and Bell's development of a material behavior research instrument,

FIGURE 1   *Socio-economic distributions of Berkeley Growth Study Sample*

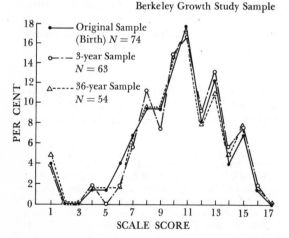

Distributions of Parents' Socio-Economic Scale Scores at Time of Birth

Berkeley Growth Study Sample

from notes and descriptive materials in the Berkeley Growth Study files (Schaefer, Bell, and Bayley, 1959), furnished a new tool and initiated a new approach to the analyses of the behavioral data. Out of the use of the maternal behavior scale and subsequent similar treatments of child behaviors, there grew a series of reports by Bayley and Schaefer, covering the first 18 years of records and exploring the interrelations among maternal and child behaviors and their relations to intelligence (Bayley and Schaefer, 1964; Schaefer and Bayley, 1963).

It has now become possible to extend these studies of both behavioral and mental variables through 36 years and to look into patterns of interrelations among various kinds of cognitive abilities as well as among a variety of behaviors expressing emotions and attitudes.

We can look at concurrent intercorrelations of behaviors and cognitive functions; we can select cognitive abilities at any one age level and note the manner in which they relate over time, forward or backward, to various behaviors, or we can start with certain behaviors at a given age and explore their relations to mental abilities over time. It will be possible here to explore only a sampling of these interrelations, and I have chosen to concentrate on a series of scores based on two sets of data, one at each end of the 36-year span. These are the Precocity factor scores of the First-Year Mental scale and concurrent infant behavior ratings at one end of the age span; and at the adult end, the Wechsler intelligence subscales and the circumplex-ordered personality variables of the Block *Q* set as rated from the 36-year interviews.

First-Year Mental Factors

First, let us review briefly the First-Year Mental precocity scores, which have, in part, been reported previously (Bayley, 1966; Cameron, Livson, and Bayley, 1967). Because the children were tested at monthly intervals from 1 through 15 months, it was possible to derive an age-at-first-passing score for each of the 115 items in this scale. With this range of scores, we were able to compute product-moment correlations for each item with each of the other 114, even though they might be at widely different levels of ability. A factor derived from this correlation matrix could, therefore, contain items from the scale's entire 15-month span of difficulty. Actually, the six factors which were derived by the Tryon cluster analysis did not follow any neat set of concom-

FIGURE 2 *First-year Vocalization precocity scores correlated with IQ through 36 years (From Bayley, 1966)*

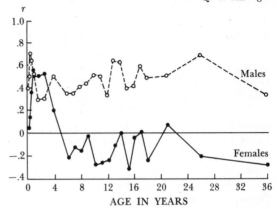

Correlations of Vocalization Factor Scores (8–13 mos.) with IQs at All Ages

itantly developing separate functions. Instead they tend to draw loadings from restricted age ranges. Thus the six factors can be arranged in a chronological sequence. They fall into order, from Visual Following at 2 to 3 months, through Social Responsiveness 3 to 7 months, Perceptual Interest at two levels, 1 to 2 and 15 to 17 months, Manual Dexterities 4 to 7 months, Vocalizations 5 to 14 months, and Object Relations 10 to 17 months. Of the six, only one factor, which we have called "Vocalizations," and whose items range, in their median age placement, from 5.6 to 13.5 months, shows any clear correlation with later intelligence. However, this relationship after 3 years of age is found only for the girls and not for the boys. Figure 2 shows the correlations between this factor, as it was first derived from the combined sample, and the boys' and girls' IQs at all ages through 36 years (Bayley, 1966). There is a striking sex difference in the correlations, and for the girls a striking consistency of the correlations into the adult years.

The Thirty-Six-Year Interview Q Sort

Before exploring further the various correlates of this infant Vocalization factor, let us now turn to the 36-year interview material, to present a new set of adult behavior variables for use in further comparisons.

For the most recent round of tests and measures on this sample, after each subject's customary mental and physical tests and measures, an appointment was made with him or her for an interview with a person who knew nothing of the early history or current status beyond a few items such as education, marital status, and possibly occupation. With two exceptions, the women were interviewed by an experienced woman (Katherine Thanas) with a master's degree in social welfare. Two women, of necessity, were interviewed in places far removed from California, one by D. Eichorn and one by N. Bayley. The men were interviewed by a clinical psychologist (William Smelser) who had previously interviewed for one of the other Institute studies. All interviews were tape-recorded and transcribed. Each interview was Q sorted by three persons, the interviewer (with the two exceptions noted above) and two clinical psychologists (drawn from a pool of 10 sorters), on the 100-item Block Q set (Block, 1961). The sorters listened to short segments of the tapes and then rated from the typescripts.

For each sex, the 70 Q-set items with the highest interrater agreement have been arrayed in a Guttman circumplex (Guttman, 1954), using the computer program developed by Lingoes (1965). The resulting order of behaviors is indicated diagrammatically in Figure 3. The circumplex for males follows, in a general way, the pattern of correlational "neighboring" that had been derived for their earlier behaviors in infancy, childhood, and adolescence. That is, if we section the circle by two orthogonal vectors, the behaviors on the upper half tend to be expressive or extraverted, those on the lower half internalized, withdrawn, or introverted. Behaviors in the upper right quadrant in this instance described men who are uncontrolled, impatient, tending toward maladjustment. Behaviors in the lower right quadrant are hostile, fearful, and distant. The lower left quadrant describes men who are problem-oriented, philosophical, with cognitive concerns and wide interests. As they move along the circle toward 270° they grow increasingly well-adjusted, and in the upper left quadrant, the behaviors include warmth, poise, social acceptance, and gregariousness.

The circumplex for the women, shown here on the right, is somewhat different, primarily in the upper right quadrant. In this quadrant, we find women's behaviors which are conventional, bland, and more controlled; in the lower right quadrant are the negative, hostile, and moody behaviors. The lower left quadrant, as for the males, contains behaviors which may be characterized as intellectual, insightful, thoughtful, with wide interests; while the upper left quadrant may be described in part by the adjectives cheerful, poised, gregarious.

The Relation of Thirty-Six-Year Q Set to Mental Scores

In Figure 4 we see, in their circumplex order, the pattern of correlations for the males of each of the 70 most reliable Q-set items, with the 36-

FIGURE 3   *General circumplex orientations of 70 Block Q-set items at 36 years*

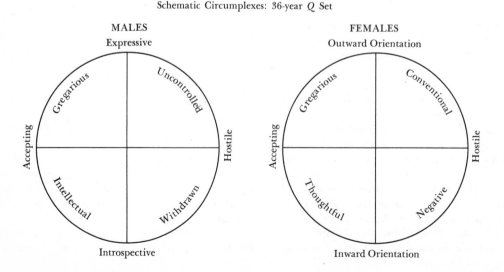

Schematic Circumplexes: 36-year Q Set

year WAIS Verbal and Performance IQs (Wechsler, 1958).

The 25 adult males for whom we have *Q* sorts from interviews at approximately 36 years show a clear pattern of correlations between IQs and these personality variables. The patterns of correlations are similar for both Verbal and Performance IQs but, at the extremes of both negative and positive relationships, the correlations are larger for the Verbal IQs.

From this pattern of correlations we see that the impatient men who are lacking in inner controls have low IQs. The strongest correlation, of —.68, is between Verbal IQ and the item, "various needs tend toward relatively direct and uncontrolled expression; unable to delay gratification." Other significant negative correlations are with more clearly maladjusted variables represented by the adjectives "negativistic," "self-pitying," "moody," and "hostile." As we move along through fearful and withdrawn to increasingly controlled behaviors, the correlations change from negative to zero with behaviors characterized as distant and avoiding. They then shift to correlations of positive sign with the attributes "fantasy" and "unusual thought processes." The correlations become strongly positive with such *Q*-set variables as "critical," at 185°, "introspective," and "concern with philosophical problems," "socially perceptive," "intellectual value," and "wide interests" (244°). The highest correlation with Verbal IQ, .84, is with the rating: "A high degree of intellectual capacity" (246°).

The correlations become much more modest in the extraverted, adjusted quadrant, where we find *r*s below .20 with "warm" (273°) and the neighboring items "calm" and "talkative," and a tendency toward negative *r*s with "gregarious" (333°) and "conservative values" (351°).

In general, according to this circumplex order of behaviors, the men in this sample with high intelligence are best characterized as introspective,

FIGURE 4   *Angular-placement-ordered Q set (70 items): Correlations with WAIS Verbal and Performance IQs at 36 years, males*

Circumplex-Ordered Correlations between 36-Year Block *Q*-set Scores and WAIS Verbal and Performance IQs at 36 Years, Males

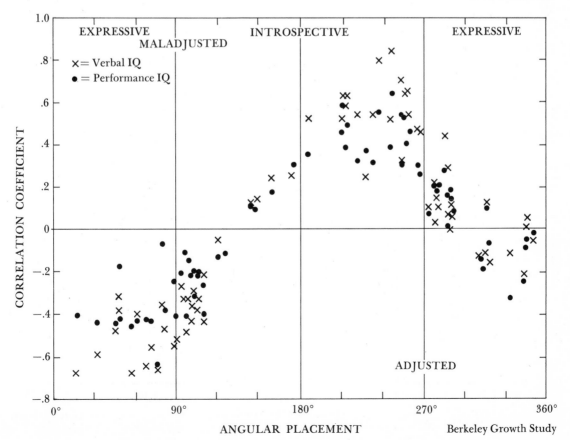

Berkeley Growth Study

thoughtful, and concerned with problems, meanings, and values; they are men who are perceptive and have a wide range of interests. The least intelligent are more often found to be impatient, prone to vent their hostilities and to project them onto others.

The women's correlations (for an N of 25) between behavior and intelligence test scores are much smaller than the men's. However, the pattern of positive and negative correlations is very similar.

The women's IQs correlate negatively with the conventional, bland, vulnerable, and anxious; positively with the thoughtful and insightful with wide interests; and very insignificantly with the cheerful, poised, and gregarious attributes. Again, in the areas where the women's correlations tend toward significance, they are larger with the Verbal than the Performance IQs.

The foregoing patterns of relations are with the two main subdivisions of the WAIS (the Verbal

and the Performance scales) and for the concurrent (36-year) data, both interview and mental test. We may extend the comparisons both by a look into selected subscales of the tests and by inquiry into the stabilities of these relations over time.

A Tryon cluster analysis was made on this sample by James Cameron for the Wechsler scores on tests at five ages—the 11 scales of W-B at 16, 18, 21, and 26 years and the WAIS at 36 (Bayley, 1968). I shall not at this time go into the details of this analysis. However, I have selected for comparisons on the Q sort, two scales which represent clearly different factors.

In Figure 5 we see the males' circumplex-ordered 36-year Q-set variables correlated with their scores on Information, at two ages, at 36 and at 16 years (Wechsler, 1944, 1958). The information test has the largest factor coefficients in the Information-Vocabulary dimension of the male cluster analysis. It is also, for these males, a highly stable test: The

FIGURE 5 *Male Q-set circumplex: Correlations with Information at 16 and 36 years*

Correlations: Circumplex-Ordered Q-set at 36 Years, with Information Scores at 16 and 36 Years, Males

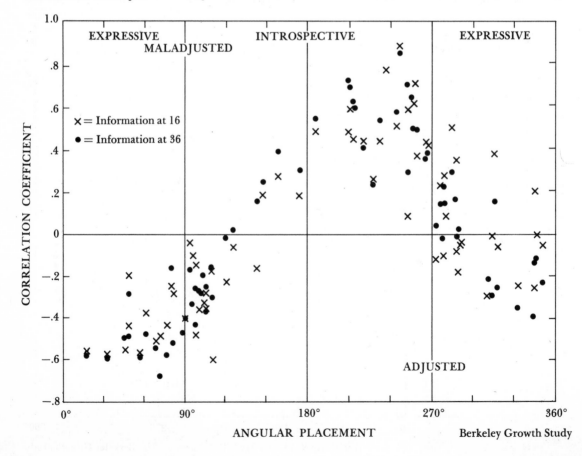

correlation between Information scores at 16 and 36 years is .79 (Bayley, 1966).

There is, here, marked stability in the patterns of behavioral-mental correlations over this 20-year interval. In some instances, notably in the "adjusted" half of the circumplex, the correlations with the 16-year Information scores are higher than with the 36-year scores. Again, the highest *r*s are with "intellectual capacity" .84 at 36 years and .88 at 16 years.

By contrast the women's correlations between personality variables and scores on Information are not only lower, but also unstable over time. Their 16- to 36-year retest correlation on the Information subscale is only .38. The pattern of the concurrent 36-year correlations tends to be in the same direction as for the males. However, at 16 years the correlations are reversed, with positive, though mostly low, correlations between scores and such attributes as "weak ego" and "thin-skinned," and negative correlations with the traits "ethically consistent" and "candid." The largest negative *r* (−.43) is with "interest in the opposite sex."

* * *

Mental Scores and Behaviors at Adolescence

Possibly, we may find some clues to the sex differences in these correlations if we move further backward, down the age scale to an earlier set of behaviors.

The adolescent behavior scores were developed by Schaefer (Schaefer and Bayley, 1963) from a set of notes written at the time of the tests for ages 13 to 18 years. Each child was rated on 96 adjectives which had been selected to represent Schaefer's theoretical personality circumplex. Cluster scores were then derived on the basis of intercorrelations of items; there are 12 behavior clusters for the males and 14 for the females. The ordinates of the circumplex-ordered variables have been called extraversion versus introversion and adjusted versus maladjusted. A set of correlations with mental scores on the 12 male behaviors, in their circumplex angular placements is shown in Figure 6. The mental scores presented here are of verbal scores at five ages; the 11-month Vocalization Precocity Score, the 8-year Stanford-Binet First Factor, which is primarily verbal (McNemar, 1942),

FIGURE 6 *Adolescent behaviors (male) in circumplex order correlated with Verbal scores at five ages*

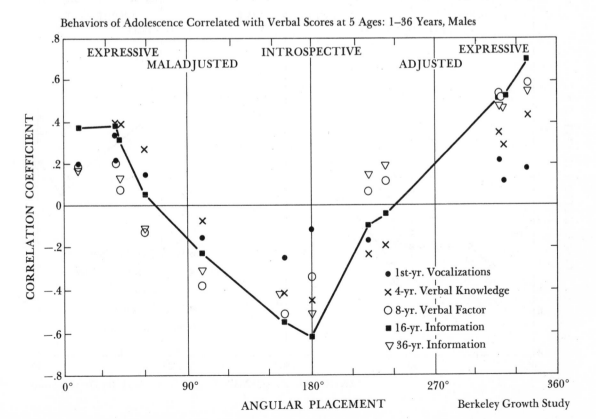

Behaviors of Adolescence Correlated with Verbal Scores at 5 Ages: 1–36 Years, Males

- • 1st-yr. Vocalizations
- × 4-yr. Verbal Knowledge
- ○ 8-yr. Verbal Factor
- ■ 16-yr. Information
- ▽ 36-yr. Information

CORRELATION COEFFICIENT

ANGULAR PLACEMENT   Berkeley Growth Study

and the Wechsler Information Scale at 16 and at 36 years. Verbal scales were selected as most likely to show persistent relations. A line is drawn through the 16-year points, to show the trend at the age concurrent with the behavior ratings. The solid dots represent the earliest test—the 11-month Vocalization factor, the open triangles, the 36-year *r*s. There is, for the males, a surprisingly consistent pattern of correlations over the 36-year span. Note that, although the 11-month Vocalization scales are not related to the boys' later IQs, they do relate in the same way to the personality variables.

Figure 7 shows the correlations of the same mental tests with the female adolescent behaviors. The positive correlations occur in the introverted-adjusted quadrant for 8-year and older tests. There is little or no pattern or consistency in these correlations. Even the concurrent 16-year Information test shows only a mild directional pattern of correlations with the behaviors. The female Verbal intelligence scores, again, are seen to be relatively independent of their behaviors. It may be that the

emotional turmoil of adolescence is more disruptive of the girls' than of the boys' cognitive processes. As we have already noted, for the 36-year *Q* sort the girls' correlations with the 16-year W-B scores are unlike those at later ages. However, at all of these ages their mental scores are correlated with 11-month Vocalization scores.

Mental Scores and Behaviors in Infancy

So far, we have been discussing the relations of intelligence to behaviors at mid-adulthood and at adolescence. Let us now look at behaviors in infancy, and their relations to later mental functioning.

For each of 13 ages, 10 through 36 months, when the babies were given a variety of mental and physical measures and tests, they were rated (on a 7-point scale) on a number of behaviors. Some of these behaviors have been utilized in our studies of maternal and child interrelations. In their cir-

FIGURE 7   *Adolescent behaviors (female) in circumplex order correlated with Verbal scores at five ages*

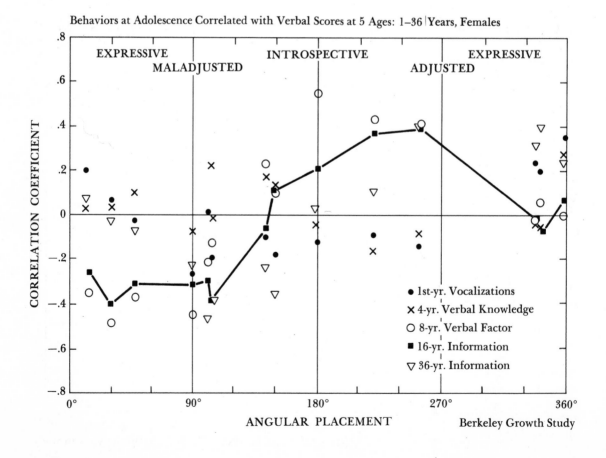

Berkeley Growth Study

cumplex order, they may be identified by the names: Active, Rapid, Responsive to Persons, Calm, Positive Behavior, Happy, and Not Shy.

Bayley and Schaefer (1964) have shown that there are complex, but internally consistent patterns of correlation over the first 18 years between these behaviors and Full Scale IQs. Briefly, boy babies who are active and rapid before 15 months earn high mental ability scores in infancy but low scores later; while if they are active and rapid at 18 to 36 months the reverse is true. Calm, happy, and positively responding boys, particularly at 27 to 36 months may earn low scores in infancy but are likely to have above-average IQs at 5 years and thereafter. In contrast, girl babies' scores were found to be correlated with concurrent measures, so that high scores were found for infant girls who tended to be responsive to persons, active, happy, positively responding, and calm, but after 3 years of age the correlations with IQ dropped to insignificant levels.

It has seemed possible, however, that there might be greater consistency in patterns of correlation between these behaviors and certain kinds of mental ability, that is, factor or subscale scores. To explore this possibility, again verbal scores have been selected because they seem to offer the greatest likelihood of long-term significant relations. Throughout our various comparisons with intelligence subscales, the verbal scores are most highly correlated with personality variables. Also, the verbal scores appear to be most stable. It is a Vocalization scale in the first year that, for the girls, shows significant correlations with their verbal scores over time; and in the 20-year adult span the males' verbal scales are most stable.

We have, therefore, explored the correlations of verbal scores at all ages with each of the seven infant behaviors.

* * *

In summarizing the patterns of correlation between behaviors in the first 3 years and verbal scores over the 36-year span, there are, for these samples, some persistent patterns of correlation. If we were to generalize from these patterns, we should expect high verbal scores for the boys who are calm, positively responding, and happy, and who are active after 15 months. What is more, these scores should remain high through 36 years. However, if we were to try to predict the girls' adult verbal scores from these behaviors, we could only make some tentative guesses that high scorers would have been shy between 10 and 24 months, and perhaps unhappy between 10 and 12 months.

Maternal Behaviors and IQs

An aspect of the children's early environment which also plays a part in their mental abilities is the maternal behaviors which these children experienced. Ratings of maternal behaviors in the first 3 years were shown by Schaefer and Bayley (1963) to be correlated with their children's behaviors, and also (Bayley and Schaefer, 1964) with the children's intelligence through 18 years. The correlations were greater for the boys than for the girls. Furthermore, the boys' scores, of both behaviors and intelligence, correlated throughout the 18-year span with maternal behaviors in the first 3 years. The girls' scores, on the other hand, showed persistent correlations primarily with indicators of parental *ability*. These sex differences in patterns of correlations led us to the suggestion that there are genetically determined sex differences in the extent to which the effects of early experiences (such as maternal love and hostility) persist. The girls appeared to be more resilient in returning to their own characteristic inherent response tendencies. Boys, on the other hand, were more permanently affected by the emotional climate in infancy whether it was one of warmth and understanding or of punitive rejection.

To bring this aspect of the study up to date, we show in Figure 8 the patterns of correlations between the early maternal behaviors and their children's IQs at 36 years. Although most of the correlations are small, again we find negative correlations as low as —.60 with maternal hostility and positive correlations as high as .49 with maternal love and understanding, with the stronger relations for the boys.

In general, these findings extend through the entire 36-year span the same patterns of correlations Bayley and Schaefer (1964) reported for the first 18 years. They reflect stability in a number of both personality variables and mental abilities. We have noted elsewhere (Bayley, 1966) that in this study the females' mental abilities stabilize at an earlier age, while the males exhibit greater stability later.

When one general type of mental function is involved, in this instance vocal-verbal ability, then the girls' scores at as young as 1 year, on the Vocalization Precocity score, are persistently correlated with later verbal scores. The relation reaches a high point with W-B Verbal IQ at 26 years, when the r is .80 for the girls, but only .26 for the boys. At 36 years, there is something of a drop, with correlations of .35 for the women and .06 for the men. A study of the personality cor-

FIGURE 8   *Correlations between maternal behaviors (0 to 3 years) and WAIS IQs at 36 years*

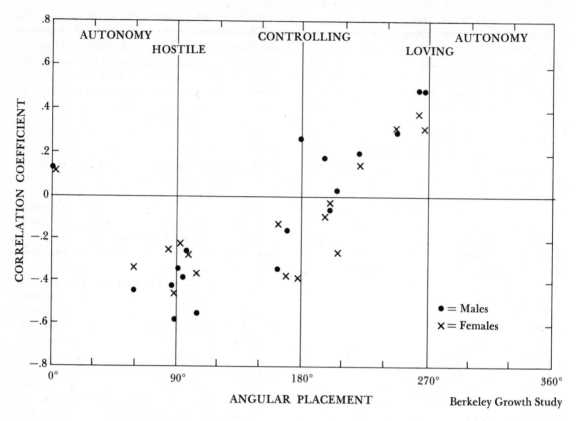

ANGULAR PLACEMENT   Berkeley Growth Study

relates of these intelligence scores repeatedly reveals considerable independence of the girls' intelligence from their personality variables. The only early behavior which shows even moderate relations with the females' later intelligence is shyness. Later, their correlations with both adolescent and adult attributes of personality are for the most part small and insignificant.

By contrast to the girls, the boys' test scores are far more bound to behavior variables which may be characterized as adjusted or introspective versus maladjusted or hostile. Their close tie between intelligence and introspective adjusted behaviors becomes established at or near 3 to 4 years of age. Their verbal test scores become stable only with the 4-year Verbal Knowledge Precocity score. There is, before this age, short-term consistency in the boys' First-Year Vocalization scores. Their correlations with total mental scores, at three age levels for tests at months 13 through 36 are .51, .51, and .53, but at the 48-month level the correlation drops suddenly to .20, and subsequent correlations remain low, varying between plus and minus .26 (see Figure 2). When this abrupt change in the boys' retest correlations between intelligence test scores

is compared with the increase at about the same age of correlations between their test scores and ratings of Positive Behavior and Happiness, it seems possible that this is a "critical period" for boys and that emotional factors operating at this time may serve permanently to depress or to enhance the abilities of many children, primarily boys.

Summary

This paper has been a factual and objective report on some behavioral correlates of mental growth. The nonspecialist, in reading it, may well suffer from data overload and understandably yearn for a good theory, or set of coherent theories, to explain the data and correlations presented. But on this occasion, at least, I must leave this needed theory construction to others. What I have tried to do, rather, is to give you an empirically warranted map which, though incomplete, has, I trust, helped to focus attention on some heretofore overlooked areas that appear to be well worth exploring. Much available information from other studies, using both similar and different research methods, is in accord with our findings (e.g., Drews, 1964; Honzik, 1967; Kagan and Moss, 1962; Terman and Oden, 1947). To this extent other researches tend to confirm the assumption that our Berkeley Growth Study sample is generally representative. When we have integrated, from this and other studies, the available information on the pattern of interrelations among cognitive processes and other behavior variables, together with their relative stability over time, for each sex separately, we shall have gained useful knowledge about the processes of mental growth. We can then see more clearly what new researches will be most fruitful. More specifically, we shall be better prepared to undertake scientific inquiries into sex-linked processes of interaction between the genes and their various environments in the growth of intelligence.

REFERENCES

Bayley, N. *The California first-year mental scale.* Berkeley: University of California Press, 1933. (a)

Bayley, N. Mental growth during the first three years: A developmental study of sixty-one children by repeated tests. *Genetic Psychology Monographs,* 1933, **14,** 1–92. (b)

Bayley, N. Factors influencing the growth of intelligence in young children. In G. M. Whipple (Ed.), *Intelligence: Its nature and nurture.* Part 2. *39th Yearbook of the National Society for the Study of Education.* Bloomington, Ill.: Public School Publishing, 1940. Pp. 49–79.

Bayley, N. Consistency and variability in the growth of intelligence from birth to eighteen years. *Journal of Genetic Psychology,* 1949, **75,** 165–196.

Bayley, N. On the growth of intelligence. *American Psychologist,* 1955, **10,** 805–818.

Bayley, N. Learning in adulthood: The role of intelligence. In H. J. Klausmeier and C. W. Harris (Eds.), *Analyses of concept learning.* New York: Academic Press, 1966. Pp. 117–138.

Bayley, N. Cognition and aging. In K. W. Schail (Ed.), *Theory and methods of research on aging.* Morgantown, W. Va.: West Virginia University, 1968. Pp. 97–119.

Bayley, N., & Jones, H. E. Environmental correlates of mental and motor development: A cumulative study from infancy to six years. *Child Development,* 1937, **8,** 329–341.

Bayley, N., & Schaefer, E. S. Correlations of maternal and child behaviors with the development of mental abilities: Data from the Berkeley Growth Study. *Monographs of the Society for Research in Child Development,* 1964, **29** (6, Whole No. 97).

Block, J. *The Q-sort method in personality assessment and psychiatric research.* Springfield, Ill.: Charles C Thomas, 1961.

Cameron, J., Livson, N., & Bayley, N. Infant vocalizations and their relationship to mature intelligence. *Science,* 1967, **157,** 331–333.

Drews, E. M. *The creative intellectual style in gifted adolescents: 1. Motivation to learn.* East Lansing: Michigan State University, 1964.

Guttman, L. A new approach to factor analysis: The radex. In P. F. Lazarsfeld (Ed.), *Mathematical thinking in the social sciences.* New York: Free Press, 1954. Pp. 258–348.

Honzik, M. P. Prediction of differential abilities at age 18 from the early family environment. In, *Proceedings 75th Annual Convention American Psychological Association: 1967.* Vol. 2. Washington, D.C.: American Psychological Association, 1967. Pp. 151–152.

Kagan, J., & Moss, H. A. *Birth to maturity: A study in psychological development.* New York: Wiley, 1962.

Lingoes, J. C. An IBM-7090 program for Guttman-Lingoes smallest space analysis-1. *Behavioral Sciences,* 1965, **10,** 183–184.

McNemar, Q. *The revision of the Stanford-Binet Scale: An analysis of the standardization data.* Boston: Houghton Mifflin, 1942.

Schaefer, E. S., & Bayley, N. Maternal behavior, child behavior and their intercorrelations from infancy through adolescence. *Monographs of the Society for Research in Child Development,* 1963, **28** (3, Whole No. 87).

Schaefer, E. S., Bell, R. Q., & Bayley, N. Development of a maternal behavior research instrument. *Journal of Genetic Psychology,* 1959, **95,** 83–104.

Terman, L. M., & Oden, M. H. *Genetic studies of genius.* Vol. 4. *The gifted child grows up.* Stanford: Stanford University Press, 1947.

Wechsler, D. *The measurement of adult intelligence.* Baltimore: Williams & Wilkins, 1944.

Wechsler, D. *The measurement and appraisal of adult intelligence.* (4th ed.) Baltimore: Williams & Wilkins, 1958.

14

Effects of Adult Social Reinforcement
on Child Behavior

Florence R. Harris, Montrose M. Wolf, and Donald M. Baer

Child behavior problems comprise one of the most promising areas in which psychologists have been able to put laboratory findings to practical use. The basic tenets of reinforcement theory are that if a particular action is followed by reinforcement, the organism will tend to repeat that action; if an action is not followed by reinforcement, the organism will tend not to repeat it. These simple principles are used to train animals in laboratories and in circuses to perform lengthy and complex chains of responses.

Children's behavioral problems that worry their parents and teachers fall generally into two categories: The child does things he shouldn't, or he doesn't do the things he should. He doesn't do his lessons or he throws things and pushes other children. This article presents information showing how the simple principles of reinforcement and nonreinforcement were used in a preschool setting to effectively modify undesirable behavior.

There is general agreement among educators that one of the primary functions of a nursery school is to foster in each child social behaviors that contribute toward more pleasant and productive living for all. However, there is no similar consensus as to precisely how this objective is to be attained. Many writers subscribe to practices based on a combination of psychoanalytic theory and client-centered therapy principles, usually referred to as a mental hygiene approach. Yet there is considerable variation and vagueness in procedures recommended, particularly those dealing with such problem behaviors as the child's hitting people, breaking valuable things, or withdrawing from both people and things. Read (1955), for example, recommends accepting the child's feelings, verbalizing them for him, and draining them off through vigorous activities. Landreth (1942) advises keeping adult contacts with the child at a minimum based on his needs, backing up verbal suggestions by an implicit assumption that the suggestion will be carried out, and, when in doubt, doing nothing unless the child's physical safety is involved. In addition to some of the above precepts, Taylor (1954) counsels parents and teachers to support both desirable and undesirable behaviors and to give nonemotional punishment. According to

Standing (1959), Montessori advocates that teachers pursue a process of nonintervention, following careful preparation of a specified environment aimed at "canalizing the energy" and developing "inner command." Nonintervention does not preclude the "minimum dose" of instruction and correction.

Using some combination of such guidance precepts, teachers have reported success in helping some nursery school children who showed problem behaviors, but sometimes adherence to the same teaching principles has not been helpful in modifying the behavior of concern. Indeed, it is usually not at all clear what conditions and principles may or may not have been operative. All of these precepts have in common the adult behaviors of

Reprinted with permission from Young Children, *Vol. XX, No. 1, October 1964 and* The Young Child: Reviews of Research. *Copyright © 1964, 1967, National Association for the Education of Young Children, 1629 21st St., N.W., Washington, D.C. 20009.*

These studies were supported in part by research grants from the National Institute of Mental Health (MH-02208-07) and the University of Washington Graduate School Research Fund (11-1873). The authors are also indebted to Sidney W. Bijou for his general counsel and assistance.

approaching and attending to a child. Therefore, it seemed to the staff of the Laboratory Preschool at the University of Washington that a first step in developing possible explicit criteria for judging when and when not to attend was to study the precise effects that adult attention can have on some problem behaviors.

This paper presents an account of the procedures and results of five such studies. Two groups of normal nursery school children provided the subjects studied. One group enrolled 12 three-year-olds and the other, 16 four-year-olds. The two teachers of the younger group and the three teachers of the older group conducted the studies as they carried out their regular teaching duties. The general methodology of these studies was developed in the course of dealing with a particularly pressing problem behavior shown by one child at the beginning of the school year. It is worth considering this case before describing the procedures which evolved from it.

The study dealt with a three-year-old girl who had regressed to an excessive amount of crawling (Harris, Johnston, Kelley, and Wolf, 1964). By "excessive" is meant that after three weeks of school she was spending most of her morning crawling or in a crouched position with her face hidden. The parents reported that for some months the behavior had been occurring whenever they took her to visit or when friends came to their home. The teachers had used the conventional techniques for building the child's "security."

Observations recorded in the third week at school showed, however, that more than 80 per cent of the child's time was spent in off-feet positions. The records also showed that the crawling behavior frequently drew the attention of teachers. On-feet behaviors, such as standing and walking, which occurred infrequently, seldom drew such notice.

A program was instituted in which the teachers no longer attended to the child whenever she was crawling or crouching, but gave her continuous warm attention as long as she was engaging in behavior in which she was standing, running, or walking. Initially the only upright behaviors that the teachers were able to attend to occurred when the child pulled herself almost to her feet in order to hang up or take down her coat from her locker and when she pulled herself up to wash her hands in the wash basin. Within a week of the initiation of the new attention-giving procedure, the child acquired a close-to-normal pattern of on-feet behavior.

In order to see whether the change from off- to on-feet behavior was related to the differential at-

tention given by the teachers, they reversed their procedure, making attention once again contingent only upon crawling and other off-feet behavior. They waited for occasions of such off-feet behavior to "reinforce" with attention, while not attending to any on-feet behavior. By the second day the child had reverted to her old pattern of play and locomotion. The observational records showed that the child was off her feet 80 per cent of the class session.

To see whether on-feet behavior could be reestablished, the teachers again reversed their procedure, giving attention to the child only when she was engaging in behaviors involving upright positions. On-feet behavior rose markedly during the first session. By the fourth day, the child again spent about 62 per cent of the time on her feet. Once the child was not spending the greater portion of her day crawling about, she quickly became a well-integrated member of the group. Evidently she already had well-developed social play skills. As a result of this demonstration that either walking or crawling could be maintained and that the child's responses depended largely upon the teachers' attending behaviors, the teachers began a series of further experimental analyses of the relationship between teacher attention and nursery school child behavior.

Procedures

A specified set of procedures common to the next studies was followed. First, a child showing problem behavior was selected and records were secured. An observer recorded all of the child's behavior, the environmental conditions under which it occurred, and its immediate consequences under conventional teacher guidance. This was done throughout the 2½-hour school session, daily, and for several days. The records gave detailed pictures of the behavior under study. In each case, it became apparent that the problem behavior almost always succeeded in attracting adult attention.

As soon as these records, technically termed "baseline" records, of the typical behavior of the child and teachers were obtained, teachers instituted a program of systematically giving differential attention to the child. When the undesired behavior occurred, they did not in any way attend to him but remained absorbed in one of the many necessary activities of teachers with other children or with equipment. If the behavior occurred while a teacher was attending to the child, she at once turned to another child or task in a matter-of-fact and nonrejecting manner. Concurrently, teachers gave immediate attention to other behaviors of the child which were considered to be more desirable than the problem behavior. The net effect of these procedures was that the child could gain a great deal of adult attention if he refrained from engaging in "problem behavior." If under this regime of differential attention the problem behavior diminished to a stable low level at which it was no longer considered a problem, a second procedure was inaugurated to check out the functional relationship between changes in the child's behavior, and the guidance procedures followed.

The second procedure was simply to reverse the first procedure. That is, when the problem behavior occurred, the teacher went immediately to the child and gave him her full, solicitous attention. If the behavior stopped, she turned to other children and tasks, remaining thus occupied until the behavior recurred. In effect, one sure way for the child to secure adult attention was to exhibit the problem behavior. This procedure was used to secure reasonably reliable information on whether the teachers' special program had indeed brought about the changes noted in the child's behavior. If adult attention was the critical factor in maintaining the behavior, the problem behavior should recur in stable form under these conditions. If it did so, this was evidence that adult attention was, technically speaking, a positive social reinforcer for the child's behavior.

The final stage of the study was, of course, to return to procedures in which attention was given at once and continuously for behaviors considered desirable. Concurrently, adult attention was again withheld or withdrawn as an immediate consequence of the problem behavior. As the problem disappeared and appropriate behaviors increased, the intense program of differential adult attention was gradually diminished until the child was receiving attention at times and in amounts normal for the teachers in the group. However, attention was given only on occasions of desirable behavior and never (or very seldom) for the undesirable behavior.

Crying and Whining

Following the above procedures, a study was conducted on a four-year-old boy who cried a great deal after mild frustrations (Hart, Allen, Buell, Harris, and Wolf, 1964). This child averaged about eight full-fledged crying episodes each school morn-

ing. The baseline observations showed that this crying behavior consistently brought attention from the teachers, in the form of going to him and showing solicitous concern. During the following days, this behavior was simply ignored. (The only exceptions to this were to have been incidents in which the child had hurt himself considerably and was judged to have genuine grounds for crying. Naturally, his hurts were to be attended to. Such incidents, however, did not occur.) Ten days of ignoring the outcries, but giving approving attention for verbal and self-help behaviors, produced a steady weakening of the crying response to a nearly zero level. In the final five days of the interval, only one crying response was recorded. The number of crying episodes on successive days is graphed in cumulative form in Figure 1.

During the next 10 days, crying was again reinforced whenever it occurred, the teachers attending to the boy on these occasions without fail. At first, it was necessary to give attention for mere grimaces that might follow a bump. The daily crying episodes quickly rose to a rate almost as high as formerly. A second 10-day period of ignoring the outcries again produced a quick weakening of the response to a near-zero level, as is apparent in the figure. Crying remained at this low level thereafter, according to the informal judgment of the teachers.

The same procedures were used in another study of "operant crying" of a four-year-old boy, with the same general results.

FIGURE 1 *Cumulative record of the daily number of crying episodes*

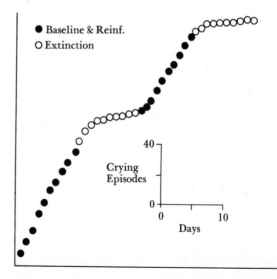

Isolate Play

Two studies involved children who exhibited markedly solitary play behavior. Extremely little of their morning at nursery school was spent in any interaction with other children. Instead, these children typically played alone in a quiet area of the school room or the play yard, or interacted only with the teachers. For present purposes, both of these response patterns will be called "isolate play." Systematic observation showed that isolate play usually attracted or maintained the attention of a teacher, whereas social play with other children did so comparatively seldom.

A plan was initiated in which the teacher was to attend regularly if the child approached other children and interacted with them. On the other hand, the teacher was not to attend to the child so long as he engaged in solitary play. To begin with, attention was given when the child merely stood nearby, watching other children; then, when he played beside another child; and finally, only when he interacted with the other child. Teachers had to take special precautions that their attending behaviors did not result in drawing the child away from children and into interaction solely with the teacher. Two techniques were found particularly effective. The teacher directed her looks and comments to the other child or children, including the subject only as a participant in the play project. For example, "That's a big building you three boys are making; Bill and Tom and Jim (subject) are all working hard." Accessory materials were also kept at hand so that the teacher could bring a relevant item for the subject to add to the play: "Here's another plate for your tea party, Ann." In both isolate cases this new routine for giving adult attention produced the desired result. Isolate play declined markedly in strength while social play increased two- or threefold.

After about a week of the above procedure, the consequences of nonisolate and isolate play were reversed. The teachers no longer attended to the child's interactions with other children, but instead gave continuous attention to the child when he was alone. Within a week, or less, isolate play became the dominant form of activity in both cases.

The former contingencies were then reinstated. The teachers attended to social interactions by the child and ignored isolate play as completely as they could. Again, isolate play declined sharply while social interaction increased as before. The results of one of these studies (Allen, Hart, Buell, Harris, and Wolf, 1964) are summarized in Figure 2.

Figure 2 shows the changes in behavior of a four and one-half-year-old girl under the different guidance conditions. The graph shows the percentage of play time that she spent in interaction with other children and the percentage of time spent with an adult. The remainder of her time was spent alone. It is apparent that only about 15 per cent of this child's play time was spent in social play as long as the teachers attended primarily to her solitary play. But interacting behaviors rose to about 60 per cent of total play time when the teachers attended only to her social play. At the same time, her interactions solely with teachers, not being reinforced, fell from their usual 40 per cent of the child's play time to about 20 per cent. These were considered reasonable percentages for this nursery school child. During Days 17–25, the schedule of adult reinforcement of social play was gradually reduced to the usual amount of attention, given at the usual irregular intervals. Nevertheless the social behavior maintained its strength, evidently becoming largely self-maintaining.

After Day 25, the teachers took care not to attend too often to the child when she was alone, but otherwise planned no special contingencies for attending. Four checks were made at later dates to see if the pattern of social behavior persisted. It is apparent (Figure 2, post-checks) that the change was durable, at least until Day 51. Further checks were not possible because of the termination of the school year.

A parallel study of a three-year-old isolate boy (Johnston, Kelley, Harris, Wolf, and Baer, 1964) yielded similar results showing the same pattern of rapid behavioral change in response to changing contingencies of adult attention. In the case of this boy, post-checks were made on three days during the early months of the school year following the summer vacation period. The data showed that on those days his interaction with children averaged 55 per cent of his play time. Apparently his social play was well established. Teachers reported that throughout the remainder of the year he continued to develop ease and skills in playing with his peers.

The immediate shifts in these children's play behavior may be partly due to the fact that they had already developed skills readily adapted to play with peers at school. Similar studies have shown that, for some children, development of

FIGURE 2   *Daily percentages of time spent in social interaction with adults and with children during approximately two hours of each morning session*

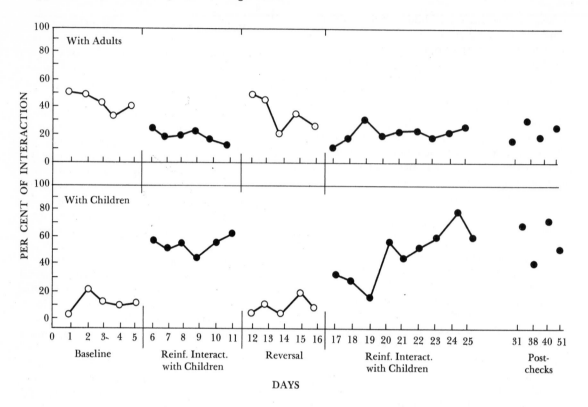

social play behaviors may require much longer periods of reinforcement.

Excessive Passivity

A fifth case (Johnston, Kelley, Harris, and Wolf, 1966) involved a boy noted for his thoroughgoing lack of any sort of vigorous play activity. The teachers reported that this child consistently stood quietly about the play yard while other children ran, rode tricycles, and climbed on special climbing frames, trees, fences, and playhouses. Teachers also reported that they frequently attempted to encourage him, through suggestions or invitations, to engage in the more vigorous forms of play available. Teachers expressed concern over his apparent lack of strength and motor skills. It was decided to select a particular form of active play to attempt to strengthen. A wooden frame with ladders and platforms, called a climbing frame, was chosen as the vehicle for establishing this activity. The teachers attended at first to the child's mere proximity to the frame. As he came closer, they progressed to attending only to his touching

it, climbing up a little, and finally to extensive climbing. Technically, this was reinforcement of successive approximations to climbing behavior. Figure 3 shows the results of nine days of this procedure, compared to a baseline of the preceding nine days. In this figure, black bars represent climbing on the climbing frame, and white bars represent climbing on any other equipment in the play yard. The height of the bars shows the percentage of the child's play time spent in such activities. It is clear that during the baseline period less than 10 per cent of the child's time was spent in any sort of climbing activity but that during the course of reinforcement with pleased adult attention for climbing on the frame, this behavior greatly increased, finally exceeding 50 per cent of the child's morning. (Climbing on other objects was not scored during this period.) There then followed five days during which the teachers ignored any climbing on the frame, but attended to all other appropriate activities. The rate of climbing on the frame promptly fell virtually to zero, though the child climbed on other apparatus and was consistently given attention for this. Another five days of reinforcement for use of the climbing

FIGURE 3   *Daily percentages of time spent in using a climbing-frame apparatus. Open bars indicate time spent in climbing on other equipment.*

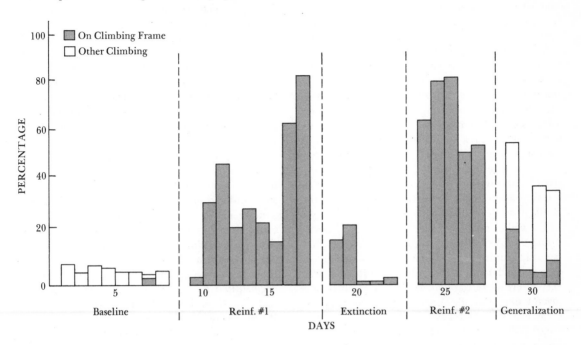

frame immediately restored the climbing-frame behavior to a high stable level, always in excess of 40 per cent of the boy's play time. After this, the teachers began an intermittent program of reinforcement for climbing on any other suitable objects, as well as vigorous active play of all sorts, in an effort to generalize the increased vigorous activity. Frame-climbing weakened considerably, being largely replaced by other climbing activities, which were now scored again as data. Activities such as tricycle-riding and running were not systematically recorded due to difficulties in reliably scoring them. It is clear from the data obtained, however, that climbing activities were thoroughly generalized by this final procedure. Checks made the following school year in another play yard indicated that vigorous climbing had become a stable part of his behavior repertory.

Summary and Discussion

The above studies systematically examined effects of adult attention on some problem behaviors of normal preschool children. The findings in each case clearly indicated that for these children adult attention was a strong positive reinforcer. That is, the behavior that was immediately followed by a teacher's giving the child attention

rose rapidly to a high rate, and the rate fell markedly when adult attention was withheld from that behavior and concurrently given to an incompatible behavior. While it seems reasonable that for most young children adult attention may be a positive reinforcer, it is also conceivable that for some children adult attention may be a negative reinforcer. That is, the rate of a behavior may decrease when it is immediately followed by the attention of an adult and rise again as soon as the adult withdraws. Actually, for a few children observed at the preschool, it has been thought that adult attention was a negative reinforcer. This seemed to be true, for instance, in the case of the climbing-frame child. Before the study was initiated, the teachers spent several weeks attempting to make themselves positively reinforcing to the child. This they did by staying at a little distance from him and avoiding attending directly to him until he came to them for something. At first, his approaches were only for routine help, such as buttoning his coat. On each of these occasions they took care to be smilingly friendly and helpful. In time, he began making approaches of other kinds, for instance, to show a toy. Finally, when a teacher approached him and commented with interest on what he was doing, he continued his play instead of stopping, hitting out, or running off. However, since his play remained lethargic and sedentary, it was decided that special measures were necessary to help him progress more rapidly. It was the use and effects of these special measures that constituted the study. Clearly, however, adult attention must be or become positively reinforcing to a child before it can be successfully used to help him achieve more desirably effective behaviors.

Studies such as those reported here seem to imply that teachers may help many children rapidly through systematic programming of their adult social reinforcements. However, further research in this area seems necessary. Some of our own studies now in progress suggest that guidance on the basis of reinforcement principles may perhaps bring rapidly into use only behaviors which are already available within the repertory of the child. If the desired behavior requires skills not yet in the child's repertory, then the process of developing those skills from such behaviors as the child has may require weeks or months. For example, a four-year-old child who could verbalize but who very rarely spoke was helped to speak freely within several days. On the other hand, a child of the same age who had never verbalized required a lengthy shaping process that involved reinforcing first any vocalization, then gradually more appropriate sounds and combinations of sounds. The latter study was still incomplete at the close of a year of work. The time required to develop social behaviors in isolate children has likewise varied considerably, presumably for the same reasons.

Although the teachers conducted these studies in the course of carrying out their regular teaching duties, personnel in excess of the usual number were necessary. The laboratory school was staffed with one teacher to no more than six children, making it possible to assign to one teacher the role of principal "reinforcer teacher" in a study. This teacher was responsible for giving the child immediate attention whenever he behaved in specified ways. In addition, observers were hired and trained to record the behavior of each child studied. Each observer kept a record in 10-second intervals of his subject's behavior throughout each morning at school. Only with such staffing could reinforcement contingencies be precisely and consistently administered and their effects recorded.

Unless the effects are recorded, it is easy to make incorrect judgments about them. Two instances illustrate such fallibility. A boy in the laboratory preschool frequently pinched adults. Attempts by the teachers to ignore the behavior proved ineffective, since the pinches were hard enough to produce at least an involuntary startle. Teachers next decided to try to develop a substitute behavior. They selected patting as a logical substitute. Whenever the child reached toward a teacher, she attempted to forestall a pinch by saying, "Pat, Davey," sometimes adding, "Not pinch," and then strongly approving his patting, when it occurred. Patting behavior increased rapidly to a high level. The teachers agreed that they had indeed succeeded in reducing the pinching behavior through substituting patting. Then they were shown the recorded data. It showed clearly that although patting behavior was indeed high, pinching behavior continued at the previous level. Apparently, the teachers were so focused on the rise in patting behavior that, without the objective data, they would have erroneously concluded that development of a substitute behavior was in this case a successful technique. A second example illustrates a different, but equally undesirable, kind of erroneous assumption. A preschool child who had to wear glasses (Wolf, Risley, and Mees, 1964) developed a pattern of throwing them two or three times per day. Since this proved expensive, it was decided that the attendants should put him in his room for 10 minutes following each glasses-throw. When the attendants were asked a few days later how the procedure was working, they said that the glasses-throwing had not diminished at all. A check of the records, however, showed that there was actually a marked decrease. The throwing dropped to zero within five days. Presumably, the additional effort involved in carrying out the procedure had given the attendants an exaggerated impression of the rate of the behavior. Recorded data, therefore, seem essential to accurate objective assessments of what has occurred.

The findings in the studies presented here accord generally with results of laboratory research on social development reviewed by Horowitz (1963). The importance of social reinforcement was also noted by Bandura (1963) in his investigations of imitation. Gallwey (1964) has replicated the study of an isolate child discussed here, with results "clearly confirmatory of the effectiveness of the technique." Further studies in school situations that can combine the function of research with that of service seem highly desirable.

REFERENCES

Allen, K. E., & Harris, F. R. Elimination of a child's excessive scratching by training the mother in reinforcement procedures. *Behavior Research Therapy,* 1966.

Allen, K. E., Henke, L. B., Harris, F. R., Baer, D. M., & Reynolds, N. J. Control of hyperactivity by social reinforcement of attending behavior. *Journal of Educational Psychology,* 1967, **58,** (4), 231–237.

Allen, K. E., Hart, B. M., Buell, J. S., Harris, F. R., & Wolf, M. M. Effects of social reinforcement on isolate behavior of a nursery school child. *Child Development*, 1964, **35**, 511–518.

Brawley, E. R., Harris, F. R., Peterson, R. F., Allen, K. E., & Fleming, R. E. Behavior modification of an autistic child. Unpublished manuscript, University of Washington, 1966.

Bandura, A. The role of imitation in personality development. *Journal of Nursing Education*, 1963, **18**, 207–215.

Gallwey, M. Personal communication, Pullman, Wash.: Washington State University, 1964.

Harris, F. R., Johnston, M. K., Kelley, C. S., & Wolf, M. M. Effects of positive reinforcement on regressed crawling of a nursery school child. *Journal of Educational Psychology*, 1964, **55**, 35–41.

Hart, B. M., Allen, K. E., Buell, J. S., Harris, F. R., & Wolf, M. M. Effects of social reinforcement on operant crying. *Journal of Experimental Child Psychology*, 1964, **1**, 145–153.

Horowitz, F. D. Social reinforcement effects on child behavior. *Journal of Nursing Education*, 1963, **18**, 276–284.

Johnston, M. K., Kelley, C. S., Harris, F. R., & Wolf, M. M. An application of reinforcement principles to development of motor skills of a young child. *Child Development*, 1966, **37**, 379–383.

Johnston, M. K., Kelley, C. S., Harris, F. R., Wolf, M. M., & Baer, D. M. Effects of positive social reinforcement on isolate behavior of a nursery school child. Unpublished manuscript, University of Washington, 1964.

Landreth, C. *Education of the young child.* New York: Wiley, 1942.

Read, K. H. *The nursery school.* (2nd ed.) Philadelphia: Saunders, 1955.

Standing, E. M. *Maria Montessori: Her life and work.* Fresno: American Library Guild, 1959.

Taylor, K. W. *Parent cooperative nursery schools.* New York: Teachers College, Columbia University, 1954.

Wolf, M. M., Risley, T. R., & Mees, H. L. Application of operant conditioning procedures to the behavior problems of an autistic child. *Behavior Research Therapy*, 1964, **1**, 305–312.

15

Some Thoughts on Communication with One's Children

S. I. Hayakawa

The point at which most of us come face to face with the subject of child development is in raising our own child. In spite of all the studies by all the experts that we have carefully digested, somehow nothing fully prepares us for the fact of his existence. There he is, a pint-sized human being with whom we must learn to communicate and whose future happiness depends on the wisdom with which we do so. In this article a noted semanticist discusses the problems that parents face when they try to use adult language to communicate with their children who are just learning to deal with the immense complexities of language. He also discusses another phase of the communications problem—the difficulties that new parents face when they try to comprehend the language used by experts on child rearing. The language used by professional counselors often becomes so filled with jargon and special references to previous cases and to theory that a beginning parent often feels, with good reason, that the advice is nearly impossible to follow.

I have decided to bring up to date an unpublished lecture I have given a few times before on the use and misuse of language in the bringing up of children. It has remained unpublished because the children are not yet grown up. By developing into social menaces or (perish the thought!) into Aristotelian philosophers, they may yet confute my best theories on how to bring up children. Hence the publication of this speech may be premature. I am uncomfortably reminded of a lady of my acquaintance who sold an article on success in marriage to a national magazine. By the time her article appeared in print, some six or seven months

Abridged by permission of the Publisher from "The Use and Misuse of Language: Some Thoughts on Communication with One's Children," by S. I. Hayakawa. In Richard E. Farson (Ed.), Science and Human Affairs. Palo Alto, California: Science and Behavior Books, Inc., 1965.

after acceptance, her marriage had already broken up. Perhaps I am rash to give this speech and to permit it to be published. So, nervously repeating Admiral Farragut's defiant "Damn the torpedoes! Go ahead!" I shall proceed.

General semantics is a general theory of how you can act a little more sanely because you talk to yourself a little more sanely. There are two facets to this question of general semantics and children. First of all, how do you teach general semantics to children? How do you get them to be semantically well-oriented and extensional and fact-minded? The second, however, is a much more important question: How do we teach ourselves to be semantically well-oriented and fact-minded and extensional towards our children? That is, what chance have our children to become extensional if we do not ourselves manifest extensional attitudes in our behavior towards them? So I shall start by addressing myself to this first question.

Whenever I say "extensional" you can use the term "fact-minded" instead; "extensional" is a term I am more used to because it's part of the vocabulary of general semantics. The extensional meaning of a word is *that which it refers to* in the nonverbal world. When I say "glass of water" it's not a verbal definition, this thing in my hand is *it*. So an extensional attitude tells you to look not for *verbal* definitions but for the *events,* the *situations in the outside world*—not words—which the words are all about.

We live in an age which is relatively extensional about children, at least in that section of our culture which is capable of being reached by new ideas. As we look back in our own culture, I think it is safe to say that previous ideas about the nature of children were highly doctrinaire and sometimes quite dogmatic. Let's take a few examples of beliefs about children which have had their currency at one time or another. First, there is the theological approach which tells us that babies come to us full of original sin: that is, they are inhabited by nature with devilish wills that have to be broken, and the task of bringing up a child is somehow or other to exorcise that original sin which is in it. We never quite succeed! Then there is a less theological approach, another kind of theory about children—that they are formless clay. They just aren't anything at all until we shape them in some way or other by the molding we give them—by wise counsel, and proper restraints and advice, and so on. And if you don't keep at it all the time, molding them, then they go out of shape. Under the impact of psychological behaviorism there arose still another notion that

the basic idea in bringing up children is conditioning—that the child should be favorably conditioned to good habits and conditioned against bad habits, and that the child will learn the right habits more readily if you start your conditioning very early. This body of doctrine led to the fashion which raged some twenty or thirty years ago of extremely early toilet training and rigid schedules. Babies would cry their hearts out, but if it wasn't time to feed them according to the schedule, you had to let them cry. The likes and dislikes which the child was to carry through life were fed into him as if a problem were being set up in an electronic computer.

All of these theories, and more, have had their currency at various times, and they are still held by various segments of the public. Each of them represents, shall I say, the effort of people to develop their children according to the models of human nature which they have inside their heads. But each of them can also be described as an activist theory, in the sense that the active doing *of* something *to* the child is felt to be necessary if the child is to grow up into an acceptable citizen and taxpayer. We are an activist culture; America is a fantastically energetic nation. Perhaps it is because of our very energetic character that it did not occur to anyone until quite recently to ask what would happen with children if you tried to leave them alone. From the point of view of activist theories, as you can imagine, leaving children alone represented quite a fearful idea. What anarchy you would have! What damage to personality! Surely they would all develop into little hoodlums and savages.

Nevertheless, within our time pioneers in the study of child development have tried in various ways to leave children alone, or at least to let them determine certain things for themselves. Many of you, for example, may remember the famous experiments which involved ignoring all ideas as to when babies should be fed and only feeding them when they expressed hunger; it was called "demand feeding." There were also experiments in which they put dishes in front of little children, fruit and sweets and ground meat and all sorts of things, and they let them choose for themselves without anyone trying to decide what was good for them. The investigators found that instead of anarchy and indigestion and autocratic infants, there resulted healthy happy babies with a surprisingly orderly pattern of needs and a kind of internal schedule of their own, a pattern that could be studied and described. They tried letting eight-month-old children choose their own diets, and they found that although on some days they would eat too much of some things, over a two-week period they would balance their own diets without any worrying on the part of adults.

Then the investigators went on to the neurology and physiology and behavior of infants and children in an extremely detailed way, asking questions like: When do they wake? When do they sleep? Eat? Cry? At what age do they sit up? At what age do they walk? When do they start piling up blocks, working puzzles? When do they start playing cooperatively with other children? And so on. Gradually a vast amount of information was built up. . . . Let me add, lest I be misunderstood, that when I say an attempt was made to see how children would develop if they were left alone, I do not mean to give the impression that anyone thinks a child can actually be left alone without parents, siblings, or society around him. This awareness of context is given in the title of Arnold Gesell and Frances Ilg's widely read book, *Infant and Child in the Culture of Today.* What I mean is that for a variety of reasons, among which can be scientific curiosity, there has been a trend away from what I call "activist" theories of child-rearing. It is only by knowing what children, in one area or another of their lives, will do when left alone that we discover what remains necessary to be done in addition.

Another manifestation of this trend away from activist theories of child rearing is to be found in the client-centered theories of Carl Rogers and his associates, and in other related theories that emerge from psychiatry, psychoanalysis, and clinical psychology. For generations it has been believed that the principal job of being a parent is to issue sufficient and proper directives. You say, "Do this" and "Don't do that" and "Stop that" and "Keep on doing this" and so on, and you keep this up all day long. If you direct them often enough, the theory is, they'll straighten out and fly right. My mother-in-law, whom I love very much, has this habit. She finds it very difficult to speak to my children, without in some way or other making a generalization for all time; that is, a directive that has to be good not only for now but has to be a lesson. She is very sweet and wonderful to them but I cannot help noticing this habit of talking to children always in an instructive kind of way. There's the fear that if you let them do something unmannerly or incorrect once, it will become a lifetime habit. Sometimes in a spirit of play I will violate ordinary good table manners. I amused my children very much once by taking a great mound of jello and bringing up

the plate and slurping it down in one gulp. The children were enormously impressed with father for being able to do this. But the example I was setting them worried my mother-in-law very much. She kept saying, "Suppose the children do this at the St. Francis Hotel!" I said, "Well, they're not likely to do that in the St. Francis Hotel." This idea that there's something permanent about what you say to children, that you always have to be setting an example and laying down a rule, is a very burdensome way of looking at communication with children.

* * *

Let me give another example from Wendell Johnson, the semanticist at the University of Iowa, whose specialty is the study of stuttering because he started out as a stutterer himself. In studying child development he discovered that all children, *all* children, when they begin to talk, repeat words and syllables the way a stutterer does. Sometimes they repeat these words and sounds and syllables eight or ten times before they get the word out. You've had this experience with your own children. A child comes into the house, a little child about two-and-a-half years old in great excitement, and says, "Mommy, I saw, I saw, I saw . . ." He is far too excited to be able to say it calmly. Now the mother's evaluation of this kind of utterance is of crucial importance. If she regards this repetitiousness as normal, she'll just relax and wait for the child to finish the sentence. And that's all there is to it. But if she expects the speech fluency of an older child in a child who is only two-and-a-half, then she may say, whether to herself or to the child, "What's wrong with the child? He's stuttering." Once she begins to *say* this, and *to react to what she has said,* she can make the child so self-conscious about his speech that he becomes a stutterer. This is Wendell Johnson's semantogenic theory of stuttering—that stutterers are not born, they're made. They are made by overconscientious mothers. This may very well be true, because very often stutterers are first children, not the second, third, or fourth—certainly never the fifth, because the mothers don't care by that time (Johnson, 1946).

Wendell Johnson's account of what he regards as the chief cause of stuttering—of course I've oversimplified the theory in stating it—suggests that many of our problems with our children are created not so much by the children as by our unrealistic expectations about them. Supposing little Howard wets his pants. Is it a problem or isn't it? Well, this depends on two things. It depends first on how old Howard is, and second, it depends on *what you expect* of a child of that age, whatever that age may be. Is the fact that Susan eats messily at table a problem? Again, it is or is not, depending on what your expectations are of a child of Susan's age. If you expect more of Howard or Susan than you have any right to expect at their developmental stage, you've really got a problem —you created it yourself!

The advantage of living in our times is that we have, on the whole, better information than any previous generation on how children develop. Today the parent of a firstborn child can start out with the wisdom and relaxation and predictability which he formerly had to have five children to acquire. That's the advantage of "time-binding," as general semanticists call it.

Of course, what we believe about children today may not be the last word; there will be changes and corrections. But the extensionality of the approach, I think, is likely to last because we live in an age in which there is some respect for the scientific gathering of data, especially about such matters as child development. And likely to last, too, I believe, is the realization that the child has certain needs and drives and a certain general pattern of development which are born in him. It is the job of the parent to understand these patterns and go along with them, and to create an atmosphere in which the human personality can unfold.

*   *   *

What is the bearing of general semantics on these matters? First of all it seems to me that training in general semantics gives a kind of readiness to receive and absorb and utilize the kind of information about children which scientific research has given us, because so much of what has been outlined here fits in perfectly with the principles of general semantics. I don't know if you have ever encountered the pediatrician who won't let mothers read baby books. The reason they forbid mothers to read is not that the books are bad, although some of them may be; it is that many mothers, unused to scientific ways of thinking, and perhaps overanxious too, often misread the books they read. Unaccustomed to distinguishing between levels of abstraction, they often confuse the general with the particular. To give an example, a woman wrote once in a letter to me: "If our baby wanted only two ounces of milk when the book said she should have eight, we used to waste an enormous amount of time and energy and emotion trying to coax her into taking what she didn't want." And the point about her comment is that

until the difference between the *statistical* baby who wants eight ounces per feeding on the average, and her *particular* baby who sometimes wanted two ounces and sometimes wanted twelve was pointed out to her, she *was* confusing the two and trying to give the baby eight ounces at each and every feeding.

*   *   *

Permissiveness is a very interesting idea. Permissiveness does not mean, and no one has ever meant it to mean, allowing children to break up the furniture or to pour hot soup on their little sisters. Permissiveness means permitting children to do what they want, up to the point of not creating disturbances for others, not hurting others. But a more important component of permissiveness is that children should feel free to *express* their deepest feelings. Whether they do anything about them or not, they should always feel free to express them. Very often the expression is verbal or symbolic. In Virginia Axline you read about children, for example, who are very jealous of a little brother, and then they pound the doll to pieces. This is a way of fully expressing feelings in order to understand them and master them. Therefore permissiveness means, among other things, symbolic or expressive permissiveness. Even in a therapy situation, however, actions are held within certain well-defined limits (Axline, 1947). But most people don't distinguish between words and actions very clearly. So even after you've described what you mean by permissiveness, people still sometimes ask, "But you can't let the kids break up the furniture!"

*   *   *

Those who still believe, after all the writing that semanticists have done, that semantics is a science of words, may be surprised to learn that semantics has had upon me, at least, and on many others, the effect of reducing rather than increasing one's preoccupation with words. Let me explain what I mean by this in connection with communication with our own children. First of all there's that vast area of nonverbal communication with children that we accomplish through holding, touching, rocking, caressing our children, putting food in their mouths, and all the little things that we do. These are all communication, and we do this for a long time before the children even start to talk.

Then, after they start to talk there is always the constant problem of interpretation. There is a sense in which small children are recent immigrants in our midst. They have trouble both in understanding and in using the language, and they often make errors. So many people (you can notice this in the supermarkets, especially with two- and three-year-old children) talk to their children and get angry at them because the children don't seem to mind, and anyone standing around can tell that the children just haven't understood what mother said, because the mother's vocabulary happened to be beyond them and the mother's intention was not clear to them. But mother feels, "Well, I said it, didn't I? What's wrong with the child that he doesn't understand. It's English, isn't it?" But, as I say, the child is a recent immigrant in our midst and there are things that the child doesn't understand.

There are curious instances. Once, when our little girl was three years old, she found the bath too hot and she said, "Make it warmer." It took me a moment to figure out that she meant, "Bring the water more nearly to the condition we call warm." It makes perfectly good sense if you look at it that way. Confronted with unusual formulations such as these which children constantly make, it seems to me that many of us react with incredible lack of imagination. Sometimes children are laughed at for making silly statements when it only requires looking at them—at their way of abstracting and their way of formulating their abstractions—to see that they are not silly at all.

Children are newcomers to the language: One thing that happens that people don't really understand well enough—and even linguists are only beginning to understand it—is that when you learn a language you don't just learn words; you learn the rules of the language at the same time as you're learning the words. How do you prove this? Very simply. Little children use a past tense like, "I runned all the way to the park and I swimmed in the pool." "Runned" and "swimmed" are words they did not hear. They made them up by analogy from other past tenses they had heard. This means that they not only learned the language, they learned the rule for making the past tense—except that the English language doesn't follow its own rules. And when the child proves himself to be more logical than the English language we take it out on the child. Which is nonsense. Therefore I think that children's language should be listened to with great attentiveness.

Again, when my child was a three-year-old— that's the little girl—I was pounding away at my typewriter in my study and she was drawing pictures on the floor, and she suddenly said, "I want to go see the popentole."

I kept typing.

Then I stopped and said, "What?!"

She said, "I want to see the popentole."

"Did you say *popentole?*"

Yes, she said popentole.

I just stopped. It was a puzzle to figure out, and I did. In a few seconds I said, "You mean like last Sunday, you want to go to Lincoln Park and see the totem-pole?"

She said "Yes."

And what was so warm about this, so wonderful about it, was that having got her point across she played for another twenty minutes singing to herself, very very happy that she had communicated. And I felt very proud of myself at the time for having understood. I didn't say to her, "Okay, I'll take you next Sunday to see the popentole." The mere fact that she'd made her point and got it registered was a source of intense satisfaction to her.

* * *

As a final comment I should like to remark that one of the terrible things about child psychologists of various schools is that they make the job of being a parent seem hopelessly complex. With vitamin deficiencies, Freudian theory, individual psychology theory, Jungian theory, conditioned reflex theory, and now general semantics theory to worry about, the problem of bringing up children seems just too much to contemplate without at least a Ph.D.! But I don't really think one needs to worry too much. So much of the literature about children is written on the basis of the study of disturbed children; hence the emphasis has been upon the *disorders* of psychological development. Some people, as you know, cannot read a medical book without feeling all the symptoms of every disease described in the book. Similarly, when we read of the psychological disorders of children, of extremely sick children, some of us cannot help projecting our own experiences and our own children into all the case histories. If you do this, you can make yourself extremely miserable.

But there is also a lot of literature which is worth reading on the study of children in general —normal children, not sick children—and the implication I have found in much of this literature is that children are amazingly hardy creatures. Hundreds of mistakes can be made in the handling of children and they survive. Instead of being damaged they just grow smarter. Given a reasonable amount of care and affection, especially in their tenderest years, they grow, they mature, they develop insight—sometimes, it seems, in spite of the best efforts of their parents to gum things up. Some of the finest young people I know were brought up by parents whom I would judge to be hopelessly incompetent. In one case I remember —the children are grown up and married now— but when the children were tiny, I used to worry because their mother was so hopelessly shiftless. The mother was so shiftless that the children learned to take care of themselves extremely well, so that they grew up to be the finest, most self-reliant young people you ever saw. Another set of parents were over-solicitous to the point of suffo-cating the child with attention and love, but the child managed to escape suffocation by finding enough associates outside the home, in friends' homes, to develop himself. In other words, there are many ways in which the child knows better than we do what he needs and what is good for him. So if we provide the child with the basic security of love and attempted understanding, there are many matters about which we can relax.

Finally, it is sharply to be emphasized that all books, articles, and lectures about child care, in-cluding everything I have said tonight, are at rela-tively high levels of abstraction—they are general-izations. But your child is not a generalization. He is a *particular* child who has *you* for parents, your house for a home, a particular school to go to, a particular teacher, and a particular set of play-mates on a particular street. What's right for him is not for any outsider to determine, not Gesell nor Spock nor Carl Rogers nor Brock Chisholm nor Lawrence Frank nor me nor anybody else. And often you will find yourself acting under the necessities of a particular situation without a sin-gle psychological theory or developmental chart to authorize you to do what you are doing. Under these conditions, if you can do what needs to be done firmly and without anxiety, because you know that no theory or body of theories can pre-dict and cover every eventuality, you are well on the way to becoming an adequate parent—and maybe a general semanticist too.

REFERENCES

Axline, V. *Play therapy*. Boston: Houghton Mifflin, 1947.

Johnson, W. *People in quandaries*. New York: Harper & Row, 1946. Especially Chapter XVII, The Indians have no word for it: The problem of stuttering.

16

Changing Man

Theodosius Dobzhansky

Since the Second World War, a modern miracle has been wrought by agricultural workers in our country. These creative geniuses have altered the hereditary patterns of plants ranging from corn and wheat to roses and rhododendrons. They have changed scrubby, slow maturing pigs and cattle into sleek, fat, fast-growing marvels. The nutritional needs of our people are so adequately supplied that we are all eating better than kings of only a few decades ago—and still have enough to provide for many of the needs of other countries that have not yet learned to use the technological methods of our time.

All these facts of hereditary change and selective breeding techniques have been brought about by the intelligent use of genetic knowledge. With considerable shock and surprise, however, a visitor from some other planet would find that while we readily apply our genetic knowledge in working with plants and farm animals, we have as yet completely failed to apply our voluminous knowledge and time-tested techniques to the highest and most important of animals: man himself.

From Science, *Vol. 155, No. 27 (January 1967), 409–415. Copyright 1967 by the American Associa-tion for the Advancement of Science.*
This article is the basis of a lecture presented December 26, 1966, at the Washington meeting of the American Association for the Advancement of Science.

We look about us and see babies by the thousands born with hereditary defects that could have been predicted from the time of conception, and probably were. We see these children born and raised to a lifetime of pain and sorrow because they were unfortunate enough to have genetic material that could have been eliminated almost entirely with simple techniques that the average farmer routinely uses with his chickens and his hogs. Dobzhansky discusses some of the ways in which it is possible for man to use his knowledge and his good sense to improve his own species. He also discusses the relationship of this question of genetics to the society that man has created for himself—a creation that has also changed many times and in many ways since the earliest men banded together.

Optimists believe that ours is the best of all possible worlds. And pessimists are those who fear that the optimists are right. This is a flippant, but valid, statement of a truth. Optimism is often a result of ignorance of cold and unwelcome realities. There is, however, another kind of optimism, which is pessimism surmounted. The world is far from perfect, but it is not unalterable. I am tempted to call this evolutionary optimism.

The clash of optimistic and pessimistic world views is nowhere more poignant than in the evaluation of the prospects of mankind. Human nature has flaws too evident to be shrugged off. What is the outlook for the future? Prophets of doom are not in short supply, and they receive strong support from some eminent biologists. It is alleged that the genetic endowment of the human species is deteriorating. The evolutionary future is consequently bleak. A catastrophe may be avoided only by drastic measures, applied without delay. Regardless of whether they may be effective biologically, these measures are not likely to gain rapid acceptance psychologically and sociologically.

Mankind is exposed to some biological dangers. Ways to avoid them, or to minimize their effects, must be found. Yet cogent arguments may be adduced in favor of the view that man's evolution is still ascending, rather than going downhill. Rapid advances of the biological sciences, though not in themselves sufficient to solve all problems, may make evolutionary progress easier to achieve.

Darwin Versus Copernicus

Two crucial discoveries were decisive in shaping modern man's image of himself. The names of Copernicus and Darwin stand as symbols of these discoveries, although others anticipated them or contributed to their validation. It is often held that the Copernican and Darwinian ideas make a pessimistic world view compelling. I wish to argue that this is a mistaken judgment. The post-Copernican and post-Darwinian man would not like to find himself back in the childhood of the pre-Darwinian and pre-Copernican world. Childhood memories may be pleasing indeed, but we have simply outgrown them.

Man is not the center of a snug little world created expressly to serve as his abode. Our earth is a second-rate planet, and our sun is only one among myriads of suns in the universe. This universe runs according to precise and inexorable laws; the more comprehensible of these were discovered by Newton, while Einstein and other modern physicists and cosmologists added some less comprehensible ones. And finally, man himself is very much a newcomer; he inhabits a vanishingly small bit of the cosmic scene, for at most two million years, while the scene itself is somewhere between five and ten billion years old.

Man's smallness and recency are undeniable. Are these valid grounds for regarding him as no more than a bit of slime with a capacity for self-deception? This seems to be the opinion of some avant-garde writers, painters, and musicians. Even a theologian has recently published a book entitled *The Lord of the Absurd*. What these sages overlook can be summed up in a single word: evolution.

An evolutionist need not be a Pangloss or a Pollyanna; he may recognize that the absurd is widespread. Evolution is not predestined to promote always the good and the beautiful. Nevertheless, evolution is a process which has produced life from nonlife, which has brought forth man from an animal, and which may conceivably continue doing remarkable things in the future. In giving rise to man, the evolutionary process has, apparently for the first and only time in the history of the Cosmos, become conscious of itself. This opens at least a possibility that evolution may some day be directed by man, and that the prevalence of the absurd may be cut down.

Evolution comprises all the stages of the development of the universe: the cosmic, biological, and human or cultural developments. Attempts to restrict the concept of evolution to biology are gratuitous. Life is a product of the evolution of inorganic nature, and man is a product of the evolution of life. In a sense, the discovery of evolution reinstates man in the station from which he was demoted by Copernicus: Man is again the center of the stage—at least of the planetary, and quite possibly of the cosmic, one. Most important of all, the stage and the actor not only have evolved but are evolving.

Man Continues to Evolve

Mankind evolves. For perhaps as long as 100,-000 years the most rapid and radical changes have been cultural ones. Man is a product of his cultural development as well as of his biological nature. The preponderance of cultural over biological evolution will continue or increase in the foreseeable future. We would not wish this to be otherwise; adaptation to the environment by culture is more rapid and efficient than biological adaptation. Moreover, control of the cultural evolution is achievable probably more easily than control of the biological evolution.

And yet mankind has not ceased to evolve biologically. Cultural evolution is superimposed on, it has not supplanted, biological evolution. The claim that something called "man's intrinsic intelligence" has remained constant at least since Paleolithic times is most likely erroneous, although a proof one way or the other is difficult to come by. The cranial capacity of the Neanderthal race of *Homo sapiens* was, on the average, equal to or even greater than that in modern man. Cranial capacity and brain size are, however, not reliable criteria of "intelligence" or intellectual abilities of any kind. The painters of the Altamira and Lascaux caves may have been no less talented than Picasso, and the intellectual powers of Aristotle were at least equal to those of the Nobel prize winners. But it does not follow that all the contemporaries of Aristotle were his intellectual equals, or that all inhabitants of Altamira could paint equally well.

The argument in favor of the view that mankind continues to evolve biologically is deductive and inferential, but it seems strong enough nevertheless. There are but two necessary and sufficient conditions for the occurrence of evolutionary change. First, there must be available genetic variance affecting different traits, and, second, this variance must be relevant to Darwinian fitness in different available environments which change in time and in space. Both conditions are fulfilled: Many human traits, including intellectual and behavioral ones, are genetically variable; at least some of these variations affect the chances of survival and of reproductive success; and human environments, most of all cultural environments, are changing constantly and rapidly. Cultural and biological evolution are linked by feedback relationships (Dobzhansky, 1962).

If, then, mankind changes biologically, are the changes beneficial or detrimental? Cassandras prophesying doom attract public attention more easily than do those who hold the unspectacular view that a disaster is not around the corner, and not even inevitable. The alarmist argument is by now so well known that a brief summary will suffice here. Mankind's distinctive attributes and capacities arose in evolution under the control of natural selection. Natural selection makes the evolutionary changes usually adaptive in the environments in which the species lives. It fosters the gene patterns which enable their carriers to survive and to reproduce, and it fails to perpetuate the patterns less well attuned to the demands of the environments. Genetic variants of low fitness constantly arise in all living species, owing to the pressure of mutation. Some generations may elapse between the origin of a harmful mutant by mutation and its elimination by selection; therefore, the populations of every living species carry genetic loads of relatively unfit or downright inviable or sterile variants.

Mankind, like any other biological species, has carried a genetic load since the dawn of time. It is claimed, however, that man's genetic load grows rapidly heavier. Civilized living, technology, medicine, help to the handicapped, protection of the weak—all these factors are blamed for the relaxation of natural selection. Pessimists go even further and declare that natural selection and civilization are incompatible. On the other hand, the mutation rates have, if anything, increased, owing to radiation exposure and to chemical mutagens. A vision is thus conjured of mankind's degenerating rather than improving biologically, of his sliding downhill rather than rising upward.

Negative Eugenics

If, in developing culture and civilization, mankind has somehow managed to imperil its genetic endowment, the situation can be corrected only by more and better civilization. Even if one does not accept the pessimist rendering of the situation as accurate, one may well ponder the ways and means for possible control of the evolution of the human species. Any deliberate measures to improve genetic endowment belong to the province of eugenics. Euthenics and "euphenics" (Lederberg, 1963, 1966) are concerned with amelioration of the manifestation of existing genetic endowments. Eugenics, euthenics, and euphenics are complementary rather than alternative. It is in the highest degree unlikely that an "optimal" genotype will be found that could produce excellent physical and mental health and vigor in all environments, and equally unlikely that environments could be devised to elicit satisfactory products from any and all genotypes. Environmental engineering, education, and social betterment are not made any less necessary by eugenics; the converse is also true, at least in the long run.

There is no agreement as to which eugenical measures may be effective and, at the same time, in good taste and ethically acceptable. The measures proposed are roughly classifiable into negative and positive, and range from persuasion to coercion. Nobody (outside Hitler's Germany) advocates killing the weak and the defective. Sterilization, optional or mandatory, is legal in some states. There is nothing cruel about eugenic sterilization, and, hedged with proper medical and legal guarantees, it may be acceptable in some circumstances. Its overall effectiveness in reducing the load of major genetic defects in the human species is, however, inadequate. Recessive defects are carried mainly in heterozygotes and escape detection, while the dominant ones are due mostly to new mutations.

I am inclined to favor a more tender-minded form of negative eugenics, which is the spread of elementary knowledge of genetics and of genetic counseling. The carriers of genetic defects must be assured that their condition is not their fault or sin or shame. They may also be informed of the probable consequences of their begetting children. It is perhaps not silly optimism to hope that some of such prospective parents would draw the proper conclusions from the information made available to them. Nobody is more competent than the carrier of a genetic defect to decide whether he wants to pass it on to descendants.

Positive Eugenics

Some eugenists are skeptical about the good judgment of their fellow men. Indeed, the carriers of certain genetic defects are patently incapable of exercising such judgment. One may also feel that negative eugenics is not enough. In addition to keeping down the incidence of major genetic defects, one may aspire to attain a vastly more ambitious goal—no less a goal than to reform the genetic endowment of the human species and to engineer the genetic foundation of a New Man. This is positive eugenics. The difficulty of this enterprise should be obvious. There is, unfortunately, more than a grain of truth in Lederberg's remark (1966) that "positive eugenic programs can be defended roughly in proportion to their ineffectiveness."

Perhaps the boldest of all such programs, one which certainly would be effective if it were put into operation, has been outlined in numerous popular and technical writings of H. J. Muller and Sir Julian Huxley (see, for example, Muller, 1959, 1961). We shall restrict our consideration here to the first stage of the Muller-Huxley program, which is relatively "modest" and would seem to be technically feasible at present.

This first stage relies on a "germinal choice" of the male parents. Semen of selected donors (or of all healthy males) is to be collected and stored at low temperatures in "sperm banks." After a time sufficient for reaching a dispassionate judgment concerning the biological and other virtues of the donors, the sperm will be withdrawn from the banks, unfrozen, and utilized for artificial insemination of as many women as the supply permits, or of as many as may wish to have it. The application of germinal choice may, however, start on a relatively less ambitious scale immediately. Artificial insemination of women whose husbands produce no functional sperm is practiced at present, the donors not being selected with genetic considerations in view and remaining unknown to the prospective mothers. Muller gives 10,000 per year as an estimate of the number of artificial inseminations in the United States. Make the selection eugenically motivated and you have an entering wedge for the more ambitious schemes.

Many objections can be made to Muller-Huxley eugenical schemes. Not all the objections are, of course, equally serious. The recommended techniques will be branded by some as "unnatural," with as much or as little justification as in the case of family planning. In my opinion there is nothing wrong in this "unnaturalness" or in letting women who must or who wish to produce children by artificial insemination have a choice of sperm donors and thus of the biological father of their offspring. Keeping human semen for long periods in deep-frozen state is not to be accepted so lightly, since there is no evidence to rule out the possibility that such treatment may cause mutational changes and thus increase rather than decrease man's genetic load.

What Should the Selection Select?

Even if we had safe and dependable *means* of selection, very difficult questions would arise regarding the *ends*. As with other ambitious schemes of positive eugenics, that of Muller and Huxley is likely to be shipwrecked on attempts to decide what sort of man is the ideal to be striven for. Does anyone know what will be best for mankind centuries or millennia hence? Muller wants man to be intelligent, compassionate, altruistic. This is unexceptionable, but shall we endeavor to breed a race of brawny athletes, or brainy intellectuals, or sensitive esthetics, or some combination of these qualities, or a population containing certain proportions of each kind? Negative eugenics meets fewer difficulties in this regard. It is easier to reach a consensus on which defects man would be better off without than on which traits and abilities he should possess.

In general, dominant defects give rise to the fewest doubts. One can hardly imagine circumstances in which such disorders as dominant muscular dystrophy, aniridia, epiloia, multiple polyposis of the colon, fragile bones, and neurofibromatosis may be useful. However, these conditions lower the fitness of their carriers so greatly that almost the only measure to be considered for their control is minimization of the rates of their origin by mutation. With recessive defects the thorny question has to be faced of whether they are maintained in populations only by the mutation pressure or also by increased fitness of the heterozygous carriers—that is, by hybrid vigor, or heterosis.

The classic example of this sort is, of course, the sickle-cell condition, which is almost completely lethal when homozygous but which confers some protection against falciparum malaria when heterozygous. Increased Darwinian fitness of heterozygotes appears, however, in most unexpected places; Myrianthopoulos and Aronson (1966) have published fairly convincing evidence that the heterozygous carriers of the Tay-Sachs disease (infantile amaurotic idiocy) may show a reproductive advantage of about 6 per cent in Ashkenazic Jewish populations. How widespread such situations are in human, or for that matter in *Drosophila*, populations is one of the outstanding still-unsolved problems of population genetics. Some authorities have declared them to be negligibly rare, but this only shows a cavalier disregard of increasingly substantial evidence to the contrary.

The average and above-average fitness and vigor in populations of sexually reproducing organisms, including man, are quite possibly the result of multiple heterozygosis for many genetic variants which decrease the fitness in homozygous condition. This does not quite mean that we should perpetuate recessive hereditary diseases in human populations, even if they do have heterozygous heterotic effects. It means that the problem is too complex for a simpleminded approach. The ideal of mankind free of all forms of genetic loads may be not only unattainable but also unacceptable, owing to the adaptively ambivalent effects of some of these load forms. Such a load-free mankind may turn out to be a dull stereotype, with no particular physical or mental vigor. At present we simply do not know enough to be sure either way, and more research, both in man and with animals, is needed.

Possible Antagonisms
of Old and New Adaptations

Civilization has often been blamed for diverting human biological evolution from its "natural" and beneficial to its present and allegedly pernicious course. Pampered by civilization, medicine, technology, and growing security, the human species, or at least the pampered part of it, is losing its physical and mental stamina and its resistance to environmental shocks of various kinds. It is becoming flabby and vulnerable. It is indeed possible, though not proved, that even if we were brought up to lead the life of our Paleolithic ancestors we would be less efficient in their environments than they were.

Is this, however, a terrible loss? Except for "roughing it" during summer vacations, most of mankind, or at least the inhabitants of technologically advanced countries, rarely face these ancient environments; nor, barring a breakdown of civilization, are our descendants likely to face them. What is needed is, rather, the strength and energy to face the ever more complex, and chiefly psychological, problems with which our industrial civilization is confronting us. If this strength and the primitive ruggedness were genetically one and the same, or if they were compatible, we would of course like to have them both. The process of adaptation by natural selection frequently works out, however, in such ways that a high adaptedness in some respects has to be paid for by a lesser development of other adaptive traits, or even by toleration of some downright harmful features. This is a part of what is sometimes referred to as the opportunism of natural selection. The Darwinian fitness is a property of a genotype as a whole, in relation to its environment, and not of this or that genetic factor in isolation. Now, if forced to make a choice, we must certainly prefer an adaptedness to the present environments, not to those long defunct.

The choice may be clearest in the case of resistance to certain diseases. As pointed out first, apparently, by Haldane (1949), until very recent times, selection for resistances to multifarious infectious diseases was probably one of the major factors in the biological evolution of man. With the infections more and more under control, this selection is relaxed and possibly reversed. Genetic resistance to a disease may have to be paid for by disadvantages in other respects. The sickle-cell condition mentioned above is a paradigm: A resistance of the population to falciparum malaria is bought by the death of the anemic homozygotes, and possibly by a slight anemia in the heterozygotes as well. When a population learns to combat malaria by mosquito control or by chemotherapy, must it strive at all costs to retain the genetic resistance as well? The answer evidently depends on one's confidence that our civilization is here to stay. Although Dubos (1965) has, with good reason, warned against overconfidence in this matter, it is a fact that an increasingly large part of mankind now lives in environments in which infectious diseases and old environmental hazards are being gradually brought under control. For this part of mankind, a source of genetic improvement may be, paradoxical as this may sound, a weakening or elimination of resistances to environmental hazards, resistances which were indispensable to our not-so-remote ancestors.

Euthenics, Euphenics, and Algeny

There is considerable distrust of eugenics, especially among some social scientists. The reason is that the name, though of course not the substance, of eugenics has often been exploited by those who want to obstruct social change. They claim that social ills stem from bad heredity and cannot be corrected by anything in the environment (Haller, 1963). The fallacy is evident. No heredity is "good" regardless of the environment. Genetic improvements are worthless if the improved genotypes have no access to environments which elicit their strong and inhibit their weak qualities. Man adapts his environments to his genes more often than he adapts his genes to his environments. Euthenics— environmental engineering, ranging all the way from control of infectious diseases to education and to social and political reforms—is not an alternative but is an indispensable partner of eugenics. Osborn (1951) has pointed out not only the need of this partnership but also the possibility that positive eugenics—selection of superior genetic endowments—may result from properly directed social change. I return to this idea below.

Lederberg (1963) has suggested "euphenics" as a designation for that part of euthenics concerned particularly with "the engineering of human development." Euphenics can compensate for, or redeem, certain genetic defects. The simplest example is the provision of eyeglasses to those with weak eyesight. Some forms of weak eyesight are genetically conditioned. There exist treatments to relieve the symptoms of, and in this sense to "cure," certain genetic defects. Among these defects are some otherwise fatal, or at any rate crippling, hereditary diseases. Galactosemia is an example. Children homozygous for a certain recessive gene lack an enzyme that converts the milk sugar galactose into glucose; if the condition is discovered sufficiently early, galactose-free diets permit fairly normal development; otherwise the homozygotes suffer severe liver damage and mental retardation. There is every reason to hope that treatments will be discovered for many other genetic defects.

Spectacular achievements of molecular biology have raised the hopes for euphenics very high. According to Lederberg (1963), we are witnessing a "medical revolution" which may lead to the invention of such new techniques as construction of artificial organs; synthesis of hormones, enzymes, antigens, and structural proteins; and breeding of suitable laboratory animals to serve as donors of organs or tissues that could be transplanted to human bodies. Finally, he thinks, we may come to "more confidently design genotypically programmed reactions, in place of evolutionary pressures, and search for further innovations."

Distant vistas equally alluring seem to be opened by the discovery that the functioning of genes or gene groups in the development of the individual is subject to repression or to stimulation at the intracellular level. If one learns the art of "switching" on or off at will the action of desirable and undesirable genes at specified periods of development, the possibilities of controlling realization of the heredity in the treated individuals would be impressive indeed.[1]

Still another array of conceivable techniques are called genetic engineering by Tatum (1965), genetic surgery by Muller (1959), and "algeny" by Lederberg (1966). This concept is the altering of genes in the body cells or in germinal tissues, or the introduction of desired genes from outside. In Luria's words (1965), "If the code sequence of a given gene can be deciphered, it might then be feasible to synthesize in vitro a segment of DNA with a desired 'improved' sequence, but with enough similarity to the recognized sequence of the gene in question to be able to replace it in the genetic apparatus." These techniques would, then, straddle the dividing line between euphenics and eugenics and would represent an instrument of scarcely imaginable power for guidance of the evolution of the human species.

Is this "Brave New World" of algeny more than a daydream? Some biologists talk and write about it as though all the wonderful techniques are as good as ready to be applied tomorrow. It would be very unwise for a scientist to maintain that some inventions (short of *perpetuum mobile*) will never be made. Such claims have too often been belied by subsequent discoveries. It is permissible, however, to doubt that genetic surgery would easily solve all problems. I am forced to agree with Muller (1950) that, even if the needed techniques were available, "it would be a task of transcendent magnitude, intricacy, and reconditeness to do all this by genetic surgery for any one individual. Moreover, every individual to be operated on would present his own unique complex of labyrinthine problems. . . ."

Translation of the existing genetic knowledge into social practice may give man considerable powers to make Man. New discoveries will doubtless enhance these powers incalculably. This obviously raises many thorny questions which cannot be dealt with here. A biologist should have the humility to recognize that these questions are more sociological than biological. Are we to have, in place of Plato's philosopher-king, a geneticist-king? And who will be the president of the National Sperm Bank and of the National DNA Bank? What checks and balances are to be imposed on the genetic legislative and the genetic executive powers? Who will guard the guardians?

Genetic Consequences of Equality of Opportunity

While eugenic and euphenic projects are being framed, evolutionary changes, cultural and biological, are going on. On the biological side, insufficient attention has been given to these changes. They are discussed mostly from the point of view of the alleged relaxation or stoppage of natural selection, which is at most a half-truth. Natural selection is operating, although in modern man it does not always select the same gene patterns which it selected in the past. Its operation is conditioned by the tremendous social changes which are taking place throughout the world. We may consider here briefly the genetic effects of social mobility and of equality versus inequality of opportunity, a topic which I discussed in *Science* earlier from a different point of view (Dobzhansky, 1957).

None other than President Dwight D. Eisenhower proclaimed that "humanity shall one day achieve the unity of freedom to which all men have aspired from the dawn of time." Herbert J. Muller, the historian, comments (1966) that this idea

truly reflects the history of Western civilization, especially in recent centuries. It points to a significant change in the basic mentality of ordinary men, or to some extent [in] their "nature." Today it reflects the extraordinary stir all over the world, as "backward" peoples are beginning to realize possibilities and demand opportunities that through ages they scarcely dreamed of. With this stir the revolutionary doctrine of the Rights of Man . . . has swept the world as has no other idea or religion. If it is still widely violated in practice, it is now universally accepted in theory as the bill of "human rights" affirmed by the United Nations.

In caste and rigid class societies the ascription of status and the assignment of occupation is made according to the social position of the parents. In-group marriage maintains the genetic as well as the social stratification. The explicit, or more often implied, justification is the belief that the different estates concentrate genes for different aptitudes. The truth of this is questionable. What is, however, undeniable is the fact that individual differences within each class have remained greater than

[1] I am obliged to Professor A. E. Mirsky for pointing out some of these possibilities to me.

any possible average differences between the classes. This is true even of the most rigorous and most enduring caste system, that of India.

The transition, taking place at different rates in different countries, from closed to open class systems increases the social mobility and the consequent gene exchange. As equality of opportunity is approached, will the significance of the genetic differences among men be reduced to naught? The truth is the exact opposite. Equality of opportunity should not be confused with genetic identity. More than one eminent biologist has been hailed in the popular press for having discovered that "men are not equal," when all he wanted to say was that men are not genetically alike. Equality and inequality are social, identity and diversity are biological, phenomena. Equality may be bestowed upon diverse people, and identical twins may have unequal opportunities.

Social mobility does not lead to genetic uniformity. Neither does interracial marriage. The genetic differences between populations are transmuted into genetic variability of individuals. The variety of genetic constitutions increases. The greater the diversity of environments—of social, economic, and educational opportunities—the fewer the genetic differences manifested in the observable variety of personalities and abilities. In exactly uniform environments all differences would be genetically determined. Environmental uniformity is a theoretically thinkable condition not realized anywhere. The existing societal arrangements form a spectrum, ranging from very restricted to relatively free social mobility and from inequality to equality of opportunity. The trend is, however, toward the equality side; this is acknowledged by those who welcome this trend and by those who oppose it.

If all humans had the same genetic endowment, if man were born a *tabula rasa,* if every individual had the same potentialities for intelligence, for special abilities, and for all other socially significant traits, then the differences between most rigid caste societies and societies providing equality for their members would be inconsequential. With "equality," different occupations could be distributed by lot, or according to the day of the week on which one was born. Equality is invaluable because it enables people to be different and to follow their diverse inclinations.

The genetic variety of capacities and aptitudes is partly concealed and smothered under rigid caste and class systems. A son of a peasant, of an artisan, or of a musician is encouraged, and sometimes even pressured or forced, to become a peasant,

an artisan, or a musician, as the case may be. If his tastes or abilities, no matter whether genetically conditioned or otherwise, make him attracted to or suited for a social role or a profession different from that of his parents, he may encounter a resistance severe enough to frustrate his plans. The situation would be equally unpropitious for individual self-actualization in a society so compulsively egalitarian that it would insist on reducing the diversity of abilities to a uniform level by differential treatment and education. It is in open class societies that genetic diversity can be most fully utilized for social good.

According to Gardner (1960),

our devotion to equality does not ignore the fact that individuals differ greatly in their talents and motivations. It simply asserts that each should be enabled to develop to the full, in his own style and to his own limit. Each is worthy of respect as a human being. This means that there must be diverse programs within the educational system to take care of the diversity of individuals; and that each of these programs should be accorded respect and stature.

I believe that Gardner gives here what amounts to a concise statement of a program of both positive eugenics and euthenics.

Assortative Mating

Equality of opportunity and social mobility are not unidimensional but are pluridimensional. They should not be envisaged solely in terms of individuals becoming members of wealthier classes or of less privileged groups. The diversity of human abilities cannot be accommodated in so simple a model. What is significant to a biologist is the fact that people not only rise upward or fall downward on a scale of social status and emoluments but also choose among a great variety of occupations. Man's outstanding evolutionary adaptation is his trainability and behavioral plasticity; most people can become competent in any one of many vocations and employments. This does not preclude the existence of genetically conditioned aptitudes, preferences, and special abilities. And it is a reasonable generalization to say that people do best in what they find congenial and where they feel they are most likely to pass muster. A practical recognition of the diversity of abilities can be seen in the fact that between 150 and 250 million standardized aptitude tests of various types are now administered per year in the United States (Goslin, 1963). Although the usefulness of these tests has been questioned, they are apparently here to stay. The Russian poet Voznesensky has been quoted as follows: "Talent cannot be grown like potatoes. It is a national resource, like radium deposits, healing springs, or autumn in Sigulda [a resort]."

Given something close to freedom of social mobility, the most significant genetic consequence of the occupational diversity is the fact that it almost necessarily leads to assortative mating. An old saying has it that "birds of a feather flock together." A mathematician may marry a ballerina, and a boxer a philosopher. Yet mathematicians meet mathematicians and members of their families on the average more often than they meet ballerinas, and boxers do not as a rule spend their leisure time in the company of philosophers. Positive assortative mating, marriage of persons with similar genetic abilities and preferences, has greater freedom to operate in open class societies than in societies with rigid class boundaries. This is a matter of probability, not an inflexible rule. Assortative mating operates more freely among people of higher than of lower educational levels, and more freely in urban than in rural communities.

The genetic consequences of assortative mating in man have not been adequately studied [Spuhler (1962) is one of the pioneers in this field]. It does not of itself change the gene frequencies in the populations in which it occurs. It may nevertheless be a genetic and evolutionary agent of appreciable importance. Spassky and I (Dobzhansky and Spassky, 1967) made experiments, with *Drosophila* flies, which may simulate the processes of assortative mating in human societies. The experimental results show that genetically different moieties may differentiate out of a formerly random breeding, but, of course, genetically variable, population. In these experiments the gene exchange between the moieties in a measure simulates the social mobility in human populations. Without going into technical details, one may state that the assortative mating, although it created no new genes, permitted the formation of gene combinations which would have been unlikely to arise in a randomly breeding population.

Equality of opportunity and assortative mating are not alternatives to other eugenics programs. As pointed out particularly by Osborn (1951), they are, rather, necessary conditions for the success of such programs. Equality of opportunity promotes formation of professional and occupational aggregations of people; the genes which predispose for, or enhance the chances of, success in certain lines of endeavor may be concentrated in such aggregations. And yet such aggregations have, in at least their biological aspects, no resemblance to traditional class societies. They promote, rather than impede, social mobility and make it genetically meaningful. They further positive assortative mating and thus increase the likelihood that gene combinations propitious for particular kinds of achievement will appear.

Conclusions

The human condition is changing both culturally and biologically. Although the cultural evolution overshadows the biological, the two are connected by feedback relationships; culture has a biological foundation. Natural selection continues to operate in modern mankind, but its action ought to be supplemented by artificial selection. The problems of the management of human evolution are, however, as much sociological as they are biological. The success of any eugenical program depends on the creation of favorable conditions for human development and self-actualization. In particular, the urgency of the problem of uncontrolled overpopulation exceeds at present that of genetic improvement. Contrary to the alarmist views of some biologists, the evolutionary perspectives for the human species may be regarded as favorable, although, of course, subject to improvement. Man should be the maker of his history, including his evolutionary history. The trend toward increasing social mobility and equality of opportunity may have desirable genetic effects because of the positive assortative mating which it encourages. It makes possible the realization of many hitherto concealed genetically conditioned talents and aptitudes. Rapid progress of both molecular and organismic, Cartesian and Darwinian, biology gives hope of development of new and powerful methods of genetic engineering, control of gene action, betterment of the environment, and improved understanding of the evolutionary processes in the living world, including man.

REFERENCES

Dobzhansky, T. *Science*, 1957, **126**, 191. *Science*, 1962, **137**, 112.

Dobzhansky, T. *Mankind evolving.* New Haven, Conn.: Yale University Press, 1962.

Dobzhansky, T., & Spassky, B. Proceedings of the Royal Society of London, Series B, 1967, **168**, 27–47.

Dubos, R. *Man adapting.* New Haven, Conn.: Yale

University Press, 1965.

Gardner, J. W. In *Goals for Americans*. Englewood Cliffs, N.J.: Prentice-Hall, 1960. P. 81.

Goslin, D. A. *The search for ability*. New York: Russell Sage Foundation, 1963.

Haldane, J. B. S. *Ricerca scientifica. Supplemento*, 1949, **19**, 68.

Haller, M. H. *Eugenics: Hereditarian attitudes in American thought*. New Brunswick, N.J.: Rutgers University Press, 1963.

Lederberg, J. *American Naturalist*, 1966, **100**, 519.

Lederberg, J. In G. Wolstenholme (Ed.), *Man and his future*. Boston: Little, Brown, 1963.

Luria, S. E. In T. M. Sonneborn (Ed.), *The control of human heredity and evolution*. New York: Macmillan, 1965.

Muller, H. J. *American Journal of Human Genetics*, 1950, **2**, 111. *Perspectives in Biology & Medicine*, 1959, **3**, 1. In G. Wolstenholme (Ed.), *Man and his future*. Boston: Little, Brown, 1963. In T. M. Sonne-born (Ed.), *The control of human heredity and evolution*. New York: Macmillan, 1965.

Muller, H. J. An address given at the 3rd International Congress on Human Genetics. Huxley, J. *The humanist frame*. London: Allen & Unwin, 1961. *Eugenics in evolutionary perspective*. London: Eugenics Society, 1962. *Essays of a humanist*. New York: Harper & Row, 1964.

Muller, H. J. *Freedom in the modern world*. New York: Harper & Row, 1966.

Myrianthopoulos, N. C., & Aronson, S. M. *American Journal of Human Genetics*, 1966, **18**, 313.

Osborn, F. *Preface to eugenics*. New York: Harper & Row, 1951.

Spuhler, J. N. In *The use of vital and health statistics for genetic and radiation studies*. New York: United Nations, 1962. P. 241.

Tatum, E. L. In T. M. Sonneborn (Ed.), *The control of human heredity and evolution*. New York: Macmillan, 1965.

Heredity, Environment, and Development:
A Contemporary Perspective

Charles D. Smock
University of Georgia

Science is a knowledge-acquisition process. As such, it is influenced by sets of implicit assumptions, hypotheses, and biases that vary from time to time depending upon the extent of accumulated knowledge, nonscientific but contemporaneous factors, and the impact of a few outstanding theorists. Superficial historical analysis might lead one to suspect that fads and foibles are primarily responsible for shifts in emphasis from time to time within a science. To some extent this is true, but a deeper analysis indicates also the importance of creative working hypotheses, reliable knowledge, innovative technology, and heuristic theories in bringing about the progress that is made. The papers in Part Two reflect the depth and breadth of the current impact on the behavioral sciences made by the greatest intellectual innovation of the nineteenth century: Darwin's theory of evolution.

During the early part of the twentieth century, the theory of evolution had a significant influence on both the biological and the behavioral sciences. G. Stanley Hall, second only to James Baldwin as the father of developmental psychology, proposed that "ontogeny recapitulates phylogeny"; i.e., the stages of human behavioral and psychological development follow the pattern of the Darwinian evolution of species. The human embryo, at various stages of development, does have many characteristics in common with organisms lower on the evolutionary scale, which at first seemed to lend some credibility to that hypothesis. Careful analysis of both physical and behavioral development, however, quickly discredited it and, as is often the case, directed attention away from other hypotheses that the general evolutionary perspective might have suggested. Instead, the development of intelligence tests and the child study movement led to an emphasis on environmental influences on mental development. Although developmental psychologists tried to examine critically the effects of deprived and enriched environments on the development of innate potentials, their methodology and theory proved inadequate to the task.

Only recently has a more sophisticated understanding of the elements involved in the relationship between heredity, environment, and human development held out the promise of some satisfactory answers. We now have available more evidence concerning early man, more detailed information on the nature and structure of the chromosomes, the mechanisms for genetic transmission of information. Our increased understanding of biochemical processes makes possible new conceptions in the behavioral sciences which are more congruent with those in biological science. The modern concept of development encompasses both the hereditary (genetic) *and* the environmental components as joint, continuously interacting influences on the characteristics of adult organisms.

To illustrate some of the ideas basic to this new approach, let us look at the problem of long-term "development" as the naturalist sees it. The naturalist accepts as commonplace the fact that various species of fauna and flora are well fitted to meet the environmental demands of their habitats and to exploit the resources of those habitats. The way adaptive structures have often developed from the most unlikely material is most intriguing, however. For example, our ears—those curiously shaped parts of our bodies that are so important in locating the direction of sounds—have evolved from the gill arches of fish! This is an ingenious redesigning of a structure whose original function has become obsolete. Can such adaptations be considered "intelligent" changes? And are similar adaptive mechanisms reflected in human development?

The complexity of patterned interrelationships among flora, fauna, and resources of a region is also obvious to the biologist. It is almost as though some sort of pressure were present for some species to develop the ability to make use of every possible environmental resource. A striking example is to be found in a comparison of the animal life of Australia and other continents. Australia has a large number of marsupials, such as opossums and kangaroos, who give birth to living young in a very immature stage and raise them in external pouches instead of internal utera. Many of the species of marsupials that have evolved in Australia are analogous to the sizes and types of other mammals found on other continents. For example, there are tiny marsupials that burrow like rats and mice and feed on similar food, herding marsupials of large size that live on grassy plains, wolf-like marsupials that exist on flesh, etc. Thus the question arises, are biological structures somehow stimulated into evolutionary changes to fill the various roles made possible by the overall environmental framework? And is it possible that adaptive changes in the development of an individual may be guided by comparable biochemical mechanisms?

Finally, within this adaptation process there are many balances and counterbalances, regulatory devices, and reactions to regulation. The supply of food roughly matches the supply of consumers; predators keep down the population that would overtax the food supply, etc. Such regulatory mechanisms for individual development have been postulated by most theorists.

A general theory of human development incorporating the evolutionary perspective and the facts of biology and psychology has been constructed by Jean Piaget, a Swiss epistemologist, biologist, and psychologist who is, without doubt, the most influential of current developmental theorists. Piaget's view of human development strongly resembles the above picture of living organisms as complex, mutually regulating systems in equilibrium. Two particular features of biological evolution are basic to his theories of the development of individuals. One is the continuous fitting of old structures into new functions and the development of new structures to carry out old functions under changed circumstances. Development is rooted in what already exists and displays a continuity with the past (thus, genetic psychology). At the same time, structures change to fit new demands. Secondly, these adaptive structures do not develop in isolation. All of them form a coherent pattern so that the totality of biological life is adapted to the environment. Although each species is adapted to its environment, the particular nature of its adaptation is a function not of its nature alone but of the total system.

Piaget tries to identify the behavioral and psychological characteristics of each age level, and then to show how they adapt to environmental demands and to one another and how they in turn modify what the environment demands. For example, when the child walks he is able to attain goals otherwise unattainable. At the same time, walking puts the child in a position to have goals that he would not otherwise have. The interrelatedness of the entire pattern is illustrated by the fact that, because people walk, our whole social environment is set up to require walking. Furthermore, walking and other behavior patterns are interrelated. The pattern of holding an object in the hand is modified when the child must hold it while walking, and the walking behavior changes depending upon what the child is carrying—a heavy box, a fishing pole, a brimful bowl of soup, etc.

The impact of Piaget's theory on our view of human development is difficult to estimate because of its recency. The current *generality* of its effect is, however, undeniable. He makes it clear that the evolutionary "selection" processes postulated by Darwin are as appropriate to ontogenetic as to phylogenetic study. For example, we can discuss the transmission of behavior patterns that have proven adaptive for a particular culture, and the "selection" of the individual organisms who are able to meet such cultural adaptive requirements.

Thus, today we find that developmental biologists, developmental psychologists, developmental sociologists, and others, are all working from the same grand theoretical position enunciated by Darwin over 100 years ago. Psychology, emerging from the strong environmentalistic position proposed by Watson, has recognized that development is a continuing process of interaction between organism and environment, and that the development of individuals is not under the control of *either* genetic or evironmental factors alone. The earlier all-or-none position generated much useful information and many heated controversies but proved inadequate to the challenge of providing a full understanding of development. Genetic controls are now seen as operating under constant environmental pressures that modify functional (psychological) characteristics. Although it is extremely difficult to identify any direct genetic control of complex organismic or behavioral processes, it is generally recognized that understanding human development on the basis of environmental factors alone (i.e., strict empiricism) is not possible.

Modification of genetic control through environmental influences and intervention may occur in at least three ways. First, and it is not wishful (or fearful!) thinking, the human organism is undergoing continuing change—whether evolutionary progression or regression depends on one's point of view. The descent of man has been accompanied by continual selection of organisms with more complex adaptive structures and the functional plasticity necessary for the adaptations required by our modern environments. The human organism appears to possess considerably more variability in the potential uses of complex structures (intelligence) than in the past. There is the distinct possibility that increasing knowledge and new experiences (e.g., space flight) may modify both behavioral characteristics and the genetic patterns underlying them, just as, at some time during evolution, the frontal lobes evolved. For example, living in a highly industrialized technical society may well induce the selection of individuals with particular adaptive characteristics that are more or less genetically determined (for example, resistance to air pollution effects, resistance to heart disease, and changes in temperamental characteristics).

Second, as our knowledge increases, it becomes possible to counteract more and more of the specific genetically controlled processes that are detrimental to normal development. One of the clearest examples is the ability to counteract *phenylketonuria,* a form of mental retardation that results from a genetic defect in the metabolic processes involved in brain development. Simple tests and corrective diets instituted within the first month of life and continued until the completion of brain growth are all that are required. A third possibility, not yet realized, is that microbiologists will discover sufficient information about the nature of genes to actually introduce change in the information contained therein.

Studies of early experience indicate that environmental stimulation is necessary for the maintenance of reflexes and the development of more complex adaptive structures. However, the limits, permanence, and long-range effects of these early environmental influences are not yet known. Evidence to date indicates that (*a*) the timing of the environmental stimulation, and (*b*) the patterning (structure) of the environmental influence are two critical factors. In the first case, we speak of the "critical-period hypothesis," which refers to the fact that environmental stimulation and activation of the adaptive mechanisms, occurring at periods of optimum "sensitivity," are crucial to later stages of development. In many, but not all, cases the earlier in life the stimulation is required, the greater the effect of occurrence or nonoccurrence. However, no general conclusions about early experiences are possible at this date, for two reasons: (*a*) the effects of early environmental stimulation on different processes varies considerably; and (*b*) there are a number of instances in which specific kinds of environmental influences during early life have no immediate effect but do have *delayed effects* at other stages of development, e.g., rearing of primates in isolation appears to result in atypical social-sexual behavior later on.

The second critical factor, the patterning (or structure) of environmental events during the most plastic stages of growth (i.e., infancy and early childhood), clearly is an important influence on the rate and patterning of many cognitive and behavioral acquisitions. For example, through use of experimentally controlled stimulation in the infant's crib, investigators have been able to modify the usual sequence of development of behavioral coordinations, e.g., hand-eye, hand-foot, eye-foot, etc. These findings, together with the discovery that the infant is not a "tabula rasa" at birth, have many important implications, both theoretical and practical, that add as much excitement to the study of development as the recent progress in genetics and molecular biology. Of special interest is the problem of how much psychological and behavioral plasticity is provided, and most especially the problem of to what extent acceleration of development is possible. Numerous investigators have demonstrated that it is possible to teach three-year-old children to read, and a "cognitive orientation" is replacing the "play and learn to work together" philosophy of many preschool programs. It is too early to determine the ultimate effect of these programs on later personality, social, and cognitive characteristics, but the issue is sufficiently important to have warranted considerable attention from both scientists and educators.

The fact that early experiences modify the typical rate of development of many characteristics does not lessen the possibility of strong hereditary contribution to the potential nature and limits of the effects. Although physical size or intellectual competence may be affected by variation of the environment (improved nutrition in the first case and "enrichment" programs in the second), a hereditary component provides constraints and limits of those effects. You can, perhaps, make *some* kind of a purse of a sow's ear, but it will be an unusual purse in many respects. And whether it will be functional (i.e., adaptive) or not remains to be seen.

Progress in understanding the relation of heredity and development has seemed to be great in recent years. And indeed it has been—but each step forward takes us to a higher level from which we can see further than before; ideas and problems continue to expand in number and scope. The task now involves learning more about early man and early infancy as well as studying the complex physiological and psychological changes that take place throughout the life cycle of individuals. Individual variations in development stimulate the central questions—why and how; as the articles in this section demonstrate, ideas, research strategies, and answers are, at this stage of knowledge, variable also.

Part Three

The Measurement
of Human Abilities

Undoubtedly the first measurements men made were by counting things, probably in a trade or barter situation. One man had two goats, another had a pile of edible berries—an ideal situation for a trade, if they could communicate and agree upon the conditions of the trade. The goat problem would be simple—by merely pointing at one of the animals, the owner could indicate that he wanted to make a trade. The man with the berries had a more difficult problem.

Today we could easily solve the problem by using the measure of weight to arrange the conditions of the trade. If goat is worth twenty cents a pound and berries are worth forty cents a pound, then one pound of berries for two pounds of goat would be a fair trade. In those days, however, the concept of weight had not yet been developed. So the man with the berries probably split his pile into two parts. When he believed that he had a pile of berries equivalent in value to one goat, he could make his offer. Most likely a bit of trade talk ensued, during which berries were moved from one pile to the other until either agreement was reached and the trade completed or it became apparent that no agreement was possible and the bargaining ended.

Thus *dichotomy*, or two-group categorizing, was probably the first kind of measurement ever done. As such social activity continued and as trading became an integral part of men's lives, the separation of things, or of piles or groups of things, into threes and fours was a logical step. Almost certainly, men used their own "private computer" to keep such single counts. This private computer is represented by the ten fingers of the hands. Two fingers extended would indicate how many piles of berries were required for the trade. Four fingers extended would show how many goats were being offered to a father for the hand of a comely daughter. Our use of the decimal system most likely stems from this early use of the ten fingers as the basic computing equipment.

Such simple counting served its purpose well for millenia. Certainly, even today, counting lies at the very center of our use of arithmetic and record keeping. However, it soon became apparent that something was missing when goods such as berries, grain, fish, etc., were arranged into piles. A sly dealer would make his piles very small, whereas a foolish trader would make his piles too large. To trade four fingers (piles) of berries for four fingers of grain was sensible only if there was some sort of standard size for the pile. Most likely, the earliest standards were provided by using naturally occurring containers. A palm leaf could be laid on the ground and berries piled upon it. One palm leaf piled high would contain nearly the same quantity as another palm leaf. Or perhaps a particular sea shell would be used as the standard measure. Five shells full of grain would be essentially equivalent to another five shells full of grain. Thus originated the next stage of measurement, indicated by the concept of size.

Long before Moses led his people, long before the great pharaohs ruled Egypt, and very long before the Greeks created their advanced civilization, these two levels of measurement were in use. And they form the very basis for all of technical, organized social living. They provide the essentials for the methods of science. The basic concepts of number and size, when modified, when made specific, and when extrapolated, provide us with all the varied kinds of measures of physical objects that are in use today.

The third kind of measurement that we use so widely and so easily today actually came much later than the other two. That other kind of measurement is *time*. Today we can buy, for a few dollars, a time-measuring device that is marvelously accurate. Indeed, we would find our lives very difficult to pursue without being able to "tell time." We would miss our classes, our appointments, our so regularly scheduled meals.

Certainly the ancients were aware of time intervals such as day and night. They were also aware of gradual changes such as seasons of the year. But the actual measurement of time was probably not made until regular astronomical observations had begun. The plotting of the changes that take place in the position of the sun, moon, and other heavenly bodies seems to be very well coordinated with the great growth of social organization. Societies need ordered temporal procedures in order to work effectively. Thus, techniques for the measurement of time seem to develop simultaneously with social progress.

With the discovery and understanding of time as one integral part of the natural course of events, man was on the threshold of the modern age. Our current scientific measures are but modifications of number, size, and time. Out of these basics Galileo and Newton fashioned their science of mechanical physics. Out of these basics modern nuclear physicists and chemists measure the size, energy components, life, and other aspects of their submicroscopic particles. But modern social scientists are faced with the problem of developing ways to measure things nobody ever thought of trying to measure before.

Psychologists ask how much intelligence a person has and attempt to measure it by using a test. Teachers ask how much knowledge of history a student has and attempt to measure it using a test. A police chief in a large city asks how much emotional stability a prospective rookie has and attempts to measure it using a test. The task of measuring human abilities, of trying to put them into piles that can be counted, much as the ancients put their grain and berries into piles, is the task that falls under the heading of "measurement problems" today. We have indeed come a long, long way.

The articles in this section deal with the kinds of instruments psychologists have developed for measuring intelligence and other human abilities and with some of the uses to which those instruments have been put.

17

What Is an "Objective" Test?

Ivan H. Scheier

A never ending problem facing high school principals and parents of teen-agers is that of the appropriate length for girls' skirts. Almost everyone has an opinion on the subject, ranging from "below the knee" to "somewhere below the waist." Thus, it is small wonder that a unanimous opinion is difficult to obtain.

The essential problem with trying to establish such a nebulous standard as "the appropriate skirt length" is that everybody has his own opinion. When each observer can permit his opinion to operate, we say that the decision is *subjective*. A characteristic of subjectivity is that subjectively determined standards tend to vary from one indvidual to another.

Some school officials do manage to come to a decision as to an "appropriate skirt length." A popular recent decision was that the skirt should be no more than three inches above the knee. Once the decision had been made the arguments tended to subside because now anyone could take a ruler and measure the distance from knee to hem. There was no longer room for personal opinion. The skirt either was or was not less than three inches above the knee.

One of the major measurement problems that psychologists have tried to solve is that of producing instruments for objective measurement. It is easy to measure length. The task of measuring unobservables such as emotional response, character, attitude, and intelligence is vastly more difficult.

One of the ways in which psychologists attempt to get around this problem is by measuring physiological responses which *are* observable. One such response that is frequently used as a measure of emotional reaction is the *psychogalvanic response* (PGR), which is a change in skin resistance to a weak electric current. The changes are produced by sweat gland activity—not the wetness of perspiration—as the glands open and close in response to emotional influences. But such a correlation between psychological and measurable physiological responses is not always possible. Less objective tests must often be relied upon by psychologists.

Introduction

* * *

There are many meanings [as well as] a tendency to use objectivity to mean anything desirable or necessary in psychological measurement. For example, at one point, Anastasi (1954) gives objectivity as part of the definition of the term "psychological test." If psychological usefulness is to be salvaged for the term, an intensive and organized effort must be made to define it explicitly and distinguish it from other concepts and modes of measurement. But, as soon as one tries to be explicit, psychologists are certain to disagree on the proper meaning of the concept. We have approached this problem in two ways. Firstly, in defining test objectivity we have tried to take into account the main criteria of objectivity stated or implied in the literature (see pp. 130–132). Thus, the reader will have an overview of what objectivity has meant or can mean, even if in many cases he disagrees with the assigned meaning. The reader is also urged to consider seriously the merits of a definition of objectivity proposed in the present paper. This definition, for which the writer assumes responsibility, attempts an intelligible integration of what is common to most previous con-

Reprinted with permission of the author and Psychological Reports, *1958,* **4,** *147–157.* © *Southern Universities Press, 1958.*

ceptions of objectivity but goes beyond them in having definite and explicit implications for psychometric method and analysis.

A Definition of Test Objectivity

Initial definition

Our basic definition holds that a test is objective only insofar as testing operations prevent distorting or obscuring processes from intervening between the tester and the events to be measured. More precisely, we mean that on an objective test, S cannot misrepresent himself on whatever behavior or characteristics are being measured by the test. Measurements of bodily dimensions such as height are objective because S cannot easily alter his score value from what it actually or naturally is. That is, testing operations and/or test-taking behavior are such that the relation between S and score is "determinate," in the sense that conscious conation or failure of memory cannot affect it.

Test objectivity as distinguished from test validity

Objectivity refers to a relation between S and score while validity is most intelligibly understood as based on or being an empirical relation between the test score and another measurement external to that test, e.g., another test score or performance, or predicted (vs. observed) performance on the test being validated. Though the two concepts are easily confused, there is no necessary relation between them. For example, given proper instrumentation and scoring technique, a measurement of "average size of PGR deflection to threat" will be objective, that is, S cannot misrepresent the natural size of his PGR. However, this measurement can still be *invalid* if uncorrelated with a validating criterion, e.g., "success as a 6th grade teacher." Similarly, a test can be valid though unobjective. As Meehl notes (1945), a self-rating may have interesting correlations with other measures (including validity in our sense) even though it is not an accurate indicator of the characteristic on which S is rating himself. For example, if, in attempting to measure frequency of crying we simply ask S how frequently he cries, the measurement is likely to be less than perfectly objective, for S's answer may reflect poor memory and deliberate faking as well as his actual frequency of crying. However, the score of this unobjective measurement can still be valid, i.e., highly correlated with the "teaching success" criterion, if it happens that tendency to forget or lie about crying is related to teaching success.

Advantages of test objectivity

Though the two are not necessarily related, test objectivity may often increase the probability of test validity, particularly as there is more *a priori* certainty that a given behavior, e.g., frequency of crying, is actually related to the validating criterion. The problem then becomes one of developing test operations to objectively measure frequency of crying, so we can be certain that the test score reflects *only* this, and not other behaviors or characteristics which we have no reason to believe are related to the criterion. To the extent that a test is not objective, we cannot know exactly what is contributing to the test score; hence any relation of this test to the validating criterion will be more or less a lucky coincidence, rather than the result of guidance by enlightened hypothesis.

Test objectivity also adds precision to interpretations of whatever relationships do emerge. Thus, interpretation is more rigorous if, to take a hypothetical example, we know that what correlates with teaching success is actually a tendency to cry frequently, not this plus other influences (such as a tendency to lie), the type and degree of which cannot be certainly known. A third advantage to be expected from objective measurement is a greater stability of data through differences in motivating conditions incidental to the measurement itself. Thus, if a measurement *can* be faked, i.e., is not objective, it probably *will* be faked by some Ss under certain conditions, for example, when the test is being used for job selection. Relationships (including validity coefficients) obtained under these conditions will differ from those obtained under conditions when S is less disposed to fake, e.g., when the test is being used for research purposes only, with all records confidential, etc. [However, the above does not mean that relationships among objective measurements will necessarily remain stable through *all* types of changes in type of population, administration conditions, cultural conditions, etc., as required for high test durability or immutability in Cattell's sense (1957).] The above are the major reasons why personality measurement (which starts with ratings and questionnaires) should aim ultimately at objective measurement.

We have stated a working definition of objectivity and compared it with the concept of validity. Let us now compare objective tests, as a medium of measurement, with the rating and questionnaire media. Our method will be to contrast the media on each of several attributes of measurement in general. These criteria deal primarily with testing and scoring operations, and test-taking behavior, and only indirectly with statistical operations and values (as in the definition of reliability or validity). As noted before, the criteria will be helpful in understanding possible ways measurements can differ from one another, even if one disagrees with the definitions offered of any one medium of measurement, or questions the overall value of the threefold classification that we aim to clarify.

Criteria for Distinguishing Between the Three Media of Observation

The nature of the task

Susceptibility to Misrepresentation

DELIBERATE MISREPRESENTATION OR FAKING. The first criterion applicable to the distinction between rating, questionnaire, and objective test media is: Does the test situation allow S deliberately to change his response from what it would ordinarily or naturally be, i.e., does it allow him to fake? We assume here, as a minimum in all tests, that the test instructions are clear, that S is not confused as regards the actual operations the tester wishes him to perform on the test. However, S may or may not have insight into what the tester wants to find out from his behavior in the test situation. Insightfully-directed faking may be more "effective" from S's point of view, but—and this is the important point for psychometricians—deliberately unnatural behavior, with or without insight, lowers measurement accuracy, confuses interpretation, and may even lower validity.

Obviously, S can deliberately behave unnaturally in most rating situations and deliberately answer "no" to a questionnaire item even when he knows that "yes" is the most natural or appropriate answer for him. Faking is also possible in many non-verbal tasks, as when S intentionally slows or speeds his tempo of leg circling. However, a measurement is objective only insofar as it approaches the ideal of unfakeability. The relatively few measurements of psychological interest that fully meet this condition are mainly physiological or measurements of personality-related bodily dimensions. In speaking of objective tests we are describing in general an ideal which is attained at present only rarely and with great difficulty.

UNINTENTIONAL DISTORTION—FAILURE TO REMEMBER. Should objective test operations prevent unintentional ("unconscious") as well as deliberate misrepresentation? As noted before, test objectivity is the absence of *any* distorting or obscuring processes between the observer and the events we intend to observe. The previously discussed stipulation that objective test operations must prohibit deliberate faking is one application of this general rule. A second application is that objective test operations must also prohibit or minimize the possibility of "unintentional" forgetting of the event which we wish to observe, whenever the measurement makes some person or persons responsible for recording that event. It is assumed that there is such a thing as "unintentional," dynamically-unrelated forgetting; that there is a recognizable, definable, and potentially measurable event being studied; and that this event is not the distorting process itself. In such cases, unintentional forgetting can stand between the observer and accurate representation of the event we wish to study; hence a test is more objective insofar as time relationships between observer and observed are such as to facilitate accurate recall of the event. Thus, if we aim to measure "rate of speaking when fifteen years of age," the following three measurements, all other things being equal, would be progressively less objective: (i) recording of S's speech under various conditions at fifteen years of age, (ii) S's statement made at seventeen years of age, about his rate of speech when fifteen years old, and (iii) S's statement made at forty years of age, about his rate of speech at fifteen years of age.

Evidently, unintentional forgetting can occur in questionnaires when S is asked to recall and comment upon events which may have taken place many years ago or throughout his life. Similarly, in rating situations lapses of memory in either the rater or S could conceivably obscure the events we actually wish to measure, but the applicability of the criterion is not so clear in this case.

MISPERCEPTIVE OR PROJECTIVE PROCESSES. Both unintentional forgetting and deliberate faking lower test objectivity because they can be distorting or obscuring processes between the observer and the events we wish to observe. What about unintentionally distorting processes other than simple forgetting, the so-called projective or misperceptive tendencies? Must such processes be removed before a test can be termed "objective"? Obviously not. In the first place, the above distinction between event and (distorting) process of observation does not easily apply to some projective tests, for when dynamically actuated misperceptive processes are assigned the role of "process of observation," it is often impossible to determine empirically or even define intelligibly the event or entity they are distorting, e.g., the "true" person, or the "real" self. But even where this classification is possible, for example, in measurements of tendency to misperceive (process of observation) the size of a coin (event), very often the misperceptive *process* itself is the event we wish to measure. Removing it as a distorting process will not make the measurement objective; it will remove the object of measurement, e.g., there will remain only an objective test of "ability to perceive coin size accurately," a measure of more interest to optometrists than to psychologists. On the other hand, if tendency to misperceive is understood as the event to be measured, objectivity lies mainly in S's inability to deliberately change his degree of misperception (over- or under-estimation of coin size) from what it is naturally. Thus, projective tests may or may not be objective, but their objectivity obviously does not depend on the degree to which perceptual distortions are removed from the measurement.

S's Insight into the Diagnostic Import of the Task

The question here is: Does S know what we are trying to find out about him via the testing situation? Consider these two verbal items: (a) "Do you worry a lot?" and (b) "The atomic bomb has been overrated. After all, it's just another more powerful weapon." In both cases, a "yes" response indicates a higher level of anxiety, but in (b) S is much less likely to "know what you're after." Campbell (1950) is referring to this principle of disguise in discussing "disguised-structured" tests, where S's attitudes are diagnosed from systematic biases in his performance on what looks like an achievement test. Nonverbal tasks tend to make good "hidden meaning" tests. Thus, slow natural tempo in rotary leg circling correlates positively with anxiety, but what unsophisticated S would guess this? Questionnaire items differ widely in the degree to which their diagnostic significance is hidden [see examples (a) and (b) above], and rating situations may or may not be disguised so that S is unaware of what he is being rated on (or even that he is being rated at all).

In the writer's view, "hidden meaning" is a necessary ingredient of objective tests only insofar as it reduces the probability of faking. Presumably, if S fails to perceive the diagnostic significance of a task, or even that it has any diagnostic significance at all, he is *less likely* to fake, even though it is physically possible to do so. But, as noted before, hidden meaning is not enough by itself, for deliberately controlled faking is just as damaging when undertaken in accordance with a misapprehension as to the significance of a task, or an otherwise undirected desire to fool the psychologist. Moreover, there are rare (at present) cases where measurements can be unfakeable, even though their meaning is *not* hidden, for example, in the "lie detector." The best conclusion at present is that hidden meaning never does any harm in an objective test and usually has positive value in reducing the probability of faking attempts. It is therefore to be looked for as a characteristic of objective tests.

Lifelikeness of the Task

The criterion here is: How similar to real life is the situation in which S is being tested? Our conception of "lifelike" parallels May and Hartshorne's (1925) conception of "natural," the naturalness of a situation being judged by the frequency with which it is likely to occur in the individual's ordinary run of experience. Technically, it is possible to rate S's behavior in narrow "laboratory" situations, but ratings are usually made in lifelike situations. This provides the richness of manifest content which makes rating measurements so useful in the initial identification of personality factors and in the generation of hypotheses concerning personality. Questionnaires usually ask S to comment on what he believes he does or would do in lifelike situations, but the testing situation itself is not lifelike, and there may be a difference between what S says he does and what he actually does. At the present time, objective tests tend to involve relatively narrow laboratory-type situations. Primarily, this is because an agreed-upon numerical scoring system, hidden meaning, and unfakeability are difficult to attain in a lifelike situation. But none of these difficulties are insuperable, and, as May and Hartshorne (1925) observe, E can exercise control over a test situation without destroying its naturalness. Lifelike objective tests are to be expected in the future.

Dependence on Verbal Material

In questionnaires, both question and response are in verbal terms. Rating assessments are usually expressed in terms of common verbal categories such as "cheerfulness," "cooperativeness," etc., with some indication of "how much" of each. The behavior which is rated may or may not be verbal.

For example, there will be a substantial verbal component if S is rated in an interview situation or when participating in group discussions, but the verbal element will be relatively unimportant when posture or expressive movements are rated. The tests which best meet objective test criteria tend to be nonverbal, e.g., physiological and physical measurements, but a test can be objective even though employing verbal material. Thus, "PGR deflection to threat" remains an objective test even though the threat stimulus is verbal, since the PGR *response* to threat is not easily subject to deliberate control. Even when the response itself is verbal, we can *approach* objectivity of measurement, if, as noted before, the nature of the task is well-hidden, e.g., with innocuous-appearing verbal questions or problems whose diagnostic significance is well-hidden. In this approximate sense, it is possible to have a verbal objective test, with verbal test material and/or verbally mediated responses.

Scoring

Agreement Among Observers

In both questionnaire and objective tests, all observers will agree on the score to be assigned S, once the test rationale has been formulated and a scoring key or system has been agreed upon. But raters are notoriously prone to disagree on their ratings of a given person in a given situation. In other words, conspect (inter-observer) reliability will be perfect in questionnaires and objective tests (within limits of clerical scoring errors), while disagreement among observers will produce less than perfect conspect reliabilities in rating measurements.

The Importance of the Observer

An observer is always *present,* in any type of measurement, if only to apply a scoring key to S's test results and record them. The question here is: When and how is the observer important, in the sense that the score obtained depends on who the observer is? Thus, the rating observer is important, as just noted, insofar as different observers disagree in their evaluations of a given person's behavior.

An observer can be important in another sense, as an *interpreter* of S's actual behavior. In ratings, the score is not what S actually does; it is an *interpretation* of what he does by an observer who

may not want or be able to see everything. Thus, he functions as a distortion between the actual event and accurate recording of the event. Clearly, this is a defect in ratings, over and above disagreement among observers, for even insofar as raters agree, it may be only on a systematically biased interpretation common to an entire group of raters. Thus, a certain school of clinicians may tend to agree in imputing to S characteristics which he does not actually possess, at least in the alleged degree.

It is perhaps not quite so clear that in questionnaires, too, the observer may be important as an interpreter. As Cattell explicitly recognizes, questionnaires are in this sense self-ratings, with the "observer-self" interpreting what the "observed-self" actually does in certain situations. S, as observed-self, may actually have cried frequently as a child, but he can be unintentionally or deliberately inaccurate in his observation of himself as a child and answer "no" to the question: "Did you cry frequently as a child?" Clearly, the self-observer in questionnaires is important as a potentially distorting interpreter of his own behavior.

Only in objective tests is the observer unimportant as an interpreter of S's behavior. Here the test yields the actual behavior or characteristics in which we are interested. S's score *is* this behavior, e.g., his PGR response or his bodily dimensions, which the observer has only to record. Obviously the above distinction does not apply to all types of interpretation. The psychometrician will always interpret S's response in trying to understand its relation to other aspects of S's personality or even in deciding the method of scoring or scoring key. *The point here is that in objective tests, as contrasted with ratings and questionnaires, there is no interpretation of the degree to which the behavior or event in which we are interested actually occurred.*

Presence of a Number Score

In questionnaires and objective tests, a numerical quantity is assigned as score. Evaluation of S's verbal responses by another person who does not use a scoring key is referred to more properly as a rating of verbal behavior. Rating evaluations almost always involve *some* recognition of amount, ranging from "presence or absence" and "more or less" to actual numerical values. However, numerical values are not a *necessary* characteristic of ratings and do not imply agreement among observers on the value to be assigned, as is the case in questionnaires and objective tests.

TABLE 1   *Summary of Relationships Among Rating, Questionnaire, and Objective Tests*

	Rating	Questionnaire	Objective test
Content of variables directly helpful in understanding their nature and in forming hypotheses about personality characteristics, factors, and relationships	Good	Good	Not so good by themselves
Results subject to deliberate distortion by S	Yes	Yes	No
Conditions permit unintentional forgetting of event, if it is being studied via S's report on it	Maybe	Maybe	No
S has insight into diagnostic import of task	Maybe	Maybe	Not usually. Desirable that he does not
Behavior studied is lifelike, *in situ*	Usually	Usually S comments on this type of behavior for himself	Not usually but is possible
Dependence on verbal material	Maybe	Always	Maybe in stimulus. If in responses, can only approach objectivity
Observer is present as scorer	Always	Always	Always
Observers agree on score to be assigned (once scoring method or key is decided upon)	No	Yes	Yes
Observer (other than S) can misrepresent actual behavior, characteristic, or event studied	Yes	No	No
Observer (as S himself) can misrepresent his own actual or typical behavior	Yes	Yes	No
Score is a number	Not necessarily, but usually some indication of quantity	Yes	Yes

Summarizing Definitions of the Three Modes of Measurement

Table 1 summarizes the relationships discussed between the three media of observation. These have been used to develop the definitions of each medium.

In a *rating (Life-Record)* S's behavior is observed and evaluated by others. The rated behavior may involve verbal or nonverbal components to any degree and is usually but not necessarily in a lifelike situation. Rating evaluations generally indicate the amount of a given, verbally defined characteristic, but the score is not necessarily a number, and there is less than perfect agreement among observers on its value. S may or may not understand the diagnostic significance of the rating situation but is usually capable of behaving unnaturally in it. Distortion in ratings may arise both from faking by the observed and from bias in the observer. However, rating measurements have the sort of obvious or "face valid" content which facilitates hypothesizing concerning the factors or mechanisms involved.

Like ratings, *questionnaire measurements (Self-Rating)* tend to have useful "face valid" content. S rates himself on what he does or would do in various situations (usually of a lifelike nature). Both questions and responses are verbally mediated. S can deliberately control his responses in order to fake and may misperceive or unintentionally forget the events on which he is asked to report. He may or may not be able to perceive the diagnostic significance of the questions asked. Once the scoring rationale has been decided upon, all observers will agree on the numerical score to be assigned.

The concept of test *objectivity* refers to *a relation between* S *and the resultant score,* as determined by the nature of testing operations and test-taking behavior. The concept of test *validity* refers to *a relation between one set of scores and another (criterion) set,* determined empirically and evaluated statistically. *Basically, the* objective test *aims at the elimination of distorting or obscuring processes between the final observer and the events he intends to study.* This requires minimization of the possibility of deliberate faking, and one way of doing this is to hide the diagnostic significance of the task from S. Objectivity further requires minimization of the possible unintentional forgetting of events which are the goal of measurement, via S's report on them. Dynamically-actuated misperceptive processes are almost always intelligibly considered not as a hindrance to objectivity, but as

themselves the goal of a measurement which on other grounds may or may not be objective.

Objective tests require agreement among observers on the numerical value assigned as score (an agreement which naturally would be expected in accurate perception of a real event). Physiological, physical, and other primarily nonverbal measurements best meet the criteria for objective tests, but such tests can involve verbal stimuli. Even when verbally mediated responses are used, a test can approach objectivity if the diagnostic significance of the task is well hidden. At present, objective test situations are usually not lifelike, but there is no reason why they might not eventually be so.

Most tests presently termed "objective" actually only approach the ideal as we have defined it, to a degree which can be assessed by application of the criteria discussed in this paper. For example, most projective tests can be deliberately faked, and even ability tests permit malingering. Almost any test involving verbal responses is not fully objective since S can control these responses and *choose* to give an answer which is not true or natural for him. Though rare at present, perfectly objective tests may be expected to appear in greater numbers as personality measurement progresses.

*   *   *

REFERENCES

Anastasi, A. *Psychological testing.* New York: Macmillan, 1954.

Campbell, D. T. The indirect assessment of social attitudes. *Psychological Bulletin,* 1950, **47,** 15–38.

Cattell, R. B. *Personality and motivation structure and measurement.* New York: World Book, 1957.

May, M. A., & Hartshorne, H. Objective methods of measuring character. *Pedagogical Seminar,* 1925, **32,** 45–67.

Meehl, P. E. The dynamics of "structured" personality tests. *Journal of Clinical Psychology,* 1945, **1,** 296–303.

18

The Use of Comprehensive Rationales
in Test Development

John C. Flanagan

People who produce and use tests talk a great deal about the concept of validity. Although there are many definitions of this term in current use, the most widely respected might be paraphrased as: The validity of a test is the degree to which the test does what you want it to do. For example, a test of knowledge should really measure knowledge. The people who get a high "knowledge" score should be those who really know a lot and are able to demonstrate it in other ways. The people who score poorly on a "social compatibility" test should be those who really are unsocial and who demonstrate it in other ways.

These "other ways" are usually given the single name *criterion*. A valid test is one that is highly related to the criterion. This relationship between validity and criterion looks simple, but actually the job of specifying a good criterion is terribly difficult. This article suggests one way to establish test criteria.

. . . Much of the recent test-development work has been at the level of the technician rather than at the level of the professional worker. Typically, someone has gotten an idea for a test and has written items which appeared to him to be suitable and, after giving the items a preliminary tryout to check their homogeneity and obtaining norms from a small and unrepresentative sample, has published the test for general use by the test-using public. On the whole, crude as this procedure is, its results have been mainly beneficial. Its use has, however, placed a strong emphasis on the obtaining of empirical validity coefficients. The textbooks and the instructors have cautioned the prospective user to be wary and to ask, "Where are the validity data?"

Empirical validity data are certainly a very desirable type of information to have. In quest of these data a lot of technical work has been done in administering tests, following up and collecting criterion data, then correlating these to obtain validity coefficients. Too often these validity coefficients have been disappointing, and frequently this has led the investigator to suggest that the criterion with which the test results were compared was not very good anyway.

Gradually this led to a frontal attack on the problem of the criterion. This attack seems to be bearing fruit, but that is another story. This follow-up work also led to a reexamination of the test-development process and to a more frequent raising of the question, "If this test isn't valid, why isn't it?"

Because of the informal and unsystematic way in which many tests were developed, and also because of the even less adequate way in which this developmental process was usually reported, other professional workers and the test-development personnel themselves have become increasingly dissatisfied with these early procedures.

To develop along professional lines, test-development work must place greater emphasis on clear and precise definitions of what is to be measured, and explicit inferences and hypotheses regarding the way in which valid tests can be prepared. There has been increasing attention given at professional meetings and in professional journals to the problem of validity. Some attempts (such as those in 1940 in connection with the *Cooperative Achievement Tests* and the *National Teacher Examinations*) have been made to develop and apply more systematic procedures. The present paper will report progress in the development of a

From Educational and Psychological Measurement, *Vol. 11 (1951), 151–155.*

method to be called *rationales* at the American Institute for Research during the past year.

The method of *rationales* begins with a list of behaviors to be sampled or predicted. The objective of the procedure is to develop a series of sets of specifications for writing items which will provide valid estimates of each of the behaviors on the list. If the behavior is of a type which can be tested directly, such as adding or multiplying, the problem is to define a standard sample of this behavior which will represent as validly as possible the behavior defined on the list. If the behavior cannot be tested directly but is something like succeeding or failing as a clinical psychologist or adjusting or not adjusting to a difficult social situation, the problem is one of specifying test items which will predict as accurately as possible this behavior.

Since most of the lists of behaviors for which tests are desired refer to specific practical situations, and since tests usually tend to be abstract and artificial in order to be efficient and precise, the problem referred to the test developer is, most often, one of prediction. It is very important that the list of behaviors to be predicted be a valid one. This is primarily a matter of job analysis, job definition, and the criterion, and will not be discussed here. However, it should be emphasized that a valid list of behaviors is not easily obtained and can only be expected to result from a systematic and comprehensive set of records of observations by competent personnel.

Assuming that a valid list of the behaviors to be sampled or predicted is available, the development of *rationales* regarding the measurement of these behaviors consists of three parts. These are: (1) Description of the Behavior, (2) Analysis of the Behavior, and (3) Formulation of Item Specifications.

1. Description of the Behavior involves the definition, delimitation, and illustration of the variety and scope of the actions included. Two examples of this procedure are given. These are taken from work on a project now being carried out under the immediate supervision of Dr. Ralph F. Wagner for the United States Air Force School of Aviation Medicine.

The first behavior is "Performed a series of simple computations without error." The Description of Behavior is as follows:

This behavior consists of doing a series of simple arithmetic problems with no errors. Calculations may be done either entirely "in one's head" or with the aid of paper and pencil. By "simple arith-

metic" is meant addition, subtraction, multiplication, division, percentage, and fractions. Speed is of little concern here—accuracy throughout an extended series of calculations is the important factor. In many instances, the individual has plenty of time to perform the necessary arithmetic computations which are a part of his job. In spite of this, however, some individuals make errors even though they are trying to be very careful. A flight engineer would be considered ineffective if his computation on gas consumption was erroneous because he said $43 - 11 = 22$. Effective behavior, on the other hand, would be illustrated by a navigator whose computations while making a round-the-world training flight were found both by himself and by others who checked his work periodically, to contain not a single error.

The second behavior is "Defining a difficult problem correctly and explicitly." The Description of the Behavior is as follows:

This behavior consists of identifying and defining the nature and extent of a problem. The fact that a problem exists has already been recognized, and the task is now one of defining the exact nature of the problem so that its solution can be directly and systematically attempted. Ineffective behavior in this respect is illustrated by an airplane commander who recognizes that the morale of his crew is bad and proceeds to institute new policies and take miscellaneous actions without determining first what the specific nature of the problem is. Effective behavior, on the other hand, is illustrated by a navigator who recognizes that he is not determining his positions accurately and sets out systematically to find where the difficulty lies so that he can take the necessary steps to correct the situation.

2. Analysis of the Behavior includes classifying it with respect to other behaviors and making inferences about its nature, culminating in the formulation of one or more hypotheses regarding its generality and predictability.

Examples of this step are given for the same two behaviors for which the Descriptions of Behavior were given:

The performing of simple computations is probably influenced by both basic aptitude and long-established training or habits. Individuals effective in this regard do not have to make a conscious effort to avoid errors; their computations are "just naturally" correct. Individuals lacking the funda-

mental characteristics may also turn in errorless work but their effectiveness is due to the fact that they very carefully checked and rechecked their work so that all errors were eliminated. Actually, it may be that the person who is given credit for possessing the fundamental ability has an "automatic" checking system of which he is not consciously aware and which operates simultaneously during the making of the actual computations. In any event, his computations come out accurately the first time without undue effort or concern on his part.

The basis of the behavior identified as defining a difficult problem seems to lie in the ability to crystallize and order a conglomeration of diverse factors. This includes recognizing the relationship among factors and evaluating their relative importance. It involves sorting out and organizing the relevant aspects in such a way that the most direct and efficient attack on the problem is clearly discernible. The characteristic might be termed "clear and orderly thinking" and is probably uniquely important in determining effectiveness in this category of behavior.

3. Formulation of Item Specifications carries the procedure on to describing a specific type of item which it appears should provide a valid estimation of the specified behavior. It consists mainly of deductions and practical suggestions.

The examples of this step for these same behaviors are given below:

For measuring computational behavior, the test should consist of a large number of relatively simple problems involving addition, subtraction, multiplication, division, fractions, and percentages. They should not include any particularly difficult or any "trick" problems. The examinee would be instructed to work at his own rate but not to spend more time on any problem than is necessary to get an answer.

For measuring the ability to define difficult problems a printed test would be used. The examinee would be presented with a paragraph, as brief as possible, containing a conglomeration of factors dealing with a problem situation. Some factors would be relevant and others irrelevant. The examinee would be required to select the statement which most concisely and directly summarizes the essential aspects of the problem.

Other examples might be cited from the work of Mrs. Mary Weislogel on projects regarding research personnel for the Human Resources Division of the Office of Naval Research and from the work of Mrs. Dorothy Berger on attitude-measurement projects. The preceding examples were selected as fairly representative of the materials recently developed by the staff.

The primary advantages to be gained by this method of explicit *rationales* are a more systematic consideration of the available information by the test constructor; the easy and efficient checking of his descriptions, analyses, inferences, and item specifications by editors and critics before the test items are prepared; and the availability of detailed hypotheses for testing against the findings obtained from the test items as prepared.

The use of comprehensive *rationales* based on systematic empirically developed definitions in terms of actual behavior of the functions to be measured and consisting of carefully formulated hypotheses regarding the specifications for items which can be expected to provide valid measures or predictions of the behaviors involved rather than merely test knowledge about the topics involved, should significantly improve the quality of many examinations.

19

The Discovery and Encouragement of Exceptional Talent

Lewis M. Terman

The most famous and widely used individual intelligence test is the revision of Binet's monumental work done mainly under the guidance of Lewis Terman at Stanford University. The Stanford-Binet test of intelligence represents only one aspect of Terman's interest in intelligence and talent, however. He became increasingly curious as to the characteristics of those individuals whose test scores showed them to be of superior intelligence. In this article he describes the ambitious series of studies through which he followed the lives and fortunes of a group of highly intelligent youngsters. In reading it you will have a taste of the enthusiasm and spirit of scientific inquiry which keeps such an investigator at his task.

The experience of awe and envy that association with an exceptionally talented person arouses is something that most of us have encountered. We marvel at the way in which certain individuals can learn quickly, can organize effectively, and can remember vividly. Beyond that, we are astounded at the ways in which they grasp the full scope of a topic while others struggle grimly with individual words and phrases.

Unquestionably, the rush of progress owes its greatest debt to those outstanding persons who have shown the way. Surely, we must direct ourselves to the task of learning more about such individuals so that we will be able to identify their successors at an early age. We permit talent to fade and die only at our peril.

I have often been asked how I happened to become interested in mental tests and gifted children. My first introduction to the scientific problems posed by intellectual differences occurred well over a half-century ago when I was a senior in psychology at Indiana University and was asked to prepare two reports for a seminar, one on mental deficiency and one on genius. Up to that time, despite the fact that I had graduated from a normal college as a Bachelor of Pedagogy and had taught school for five years, I had never so much as heard of a mental test. The reading for those two reports opened up a new world to me, the world of Galton, Binet, and their contemporaries. The following year my MA thesis on leadership among children (Terman, 1904) was based in part on tests used by Binet in his studies of suggestibility.

Then I entered Clark University, where I spent considerable time during the first year in reading on mental tests and precocious children. Child prodigies, I soon learned, were at that time in bad repute because of the prevailing belief that they were usually psychotic or otherwise abnormal and almost sure to burn themselves out quickly or to develop postadolescent stupidity. "Early ripe, early rot" was a slogan frequently encountered. By the time I reached my last graduate year, I decided to find out for myself how precocious children differ from the mentally backward and accordingly chose as my doctoral dissertation an experimental study of the intellectual processes of fourteen boys, seven of them picked as the brightest and seven as the dullest in a large city school (Terman, 1906). These subjects I put through a great variety of intelligence tests, some of them borrowed from Binet and others, many of them new. The tests were given individually and required a total of 40 or 50 hours for each subject. The experiment contributed little or nothing to science, but it contributed a lot to my future thinking. Besides "selling" me completely on the value of mental tests as a research method, it offered an ideal escape from the kinds of laboratory work which I disliked and in which I was more than ordinarily inept. (Edward Thorndike confessed to me once that *his* lack of mechanical skill was partly responsible for turning *him* to mental tests and to the kinds of experiments on learning that required no apparatus.)

However, it was not until I got to Stanford in 1910 that I was able to pick up with mental tests where I had left off at Clark University. By that time Binet's 1905 and 1908 scales had been published, and the first thing I undertook at Stanford was a tentative revision of his 1908 scale. This, after further revisions, was published in 1916. The standardization of the scale was based on tests of a thousand children whose IQs ranged from 60 to 145. The contrast in intellectual performance between the dullest and the brightest of a given age so intensified my earlier interest in the gifted that I decided to launch an ambitious study of such children at the earliest opportunity.

My dream was realized in the spring of 1921 when I obtained a generous grant from the Commonwealth Fund of New York City for the purpose of locating a thousand subjects of IQ 140 or higher. More than that number were selected by Stanford-Binet tests from the kindergarten through the eighth grade, and a group mental test given in ninety-five high schools provided nearly four hundred additional subjects. The latter, plus those I had located before 1921, brought the number close to 1500. The average IQ was approximately 150, and 80 were 170 or higher (Terman, 1925).

The twofold purpose of the project was, first of all, to find what traits characterize children of high IQ, and secondly, to follow them for as many years as possible to see what kind of adults they might become. This meant that it was necessary to select a group representative of high-testing children in general. With the help of four field assistants, we canvassed a school population of nearly a quarter-million in the urban and semi-urban areas of California. Two careful checks on the methods used showed that not more than 10 or 12 per cent of the children who could have qualified for the group in the schools canvassed were missed. A sample of close to 90 per cent insured that whatever traits were typical of these children would be typical of high-testing children in any comparable school population.

Time does not permit me to describe the physical measurements, medical examinations, achievement tests, character and interest tests, or the trait ratings and other supplementary information obtained from parents and teachers. Nor can I here describe the comparative data we obtained for control groups of unselected children. The more

important results, however, can be stated briefly: Children of IQ 140 or higher are, in general, appreciably superior to unselected children in physique, health, and social adjustment; markedly superior in moral attitudes as measured either by character tests or by trait ratings; and vastly superior in their mastery of school subjects as shown by a three-hour battery of achievement tests. In fact, the typical child of the group had mastered the school subjects to a point about two grades beyond the one in which he was enrolled, some of them three or four grades beyond. Moreover, his ability as evidenced by achievement in the different school subjects is so general as to refute completely the traditional belief that gifted children are usually one-sided. I take some pride in the fact that not one of the major conclusions we drew in the early 1920's regarding the traits that are typical of gifted children has been overthrown in the decades since then.

Results of thirty years' follow-up of these subjects by field studies in 1927–1928, 1939–1940, and 1951–1952, and by mail follow-up at other dates, show that the incidence of mortality, ill health, insanity, and alcoholism is in each case below that for the generality of corresponding age, that the great majority are still well adjusted socially, and that the delinquency rate is but a fraction of what it is in the general population. Two forms of our difficult Concept Mastery Test, devised especially to reach into the stratosphere of adult intelligence, have been administered to all members of the group who could be visited by the field assistants, including some 950 tested in 1939–1940 and more than 1000 in 1951–1952. On both tests they scored on the average about as far above the generality of adults as they had scored above the generality of children when we selected them. Moreover, as Dr. Bayley and Mrs. Oden have shown, in the twelve-year interval between the two tests, 90 per cent increased their intellectual stature as measured by this test. "Early ripe, early rot" simply does not hold for these subjects. So far, no one has developed postadolescent stupidity!

As for schooling, close to 90 per cent entered college and 70 per cent graduated. Of those graduating, 30 per cent were awarded honors and about two-thirds remained for graduate work. The educational record would have been still better but for the fact that a majority reached college age during the great depression. In their undergraduate years 40 per cent of the men and 20 per cent of the women earned half or more of their college expenses, and the total of undergraduate and graduate expenses earned amounted to $670,000, not counting stipends from scholarships and fellowships, which amounted to $350,000.

The cooperation of the subjects is indicated by the fact that we have been able to keep track of more than 98 per cent of the original group, thanks to the rapport fostered by the incomparable field and office assistants I have had from the beginning of the study to the present. I dislike to think how differently things could have gone with helpers even a little less competent.

The achievement of the group to midlife is best illustrated by the case histories of the 800 men, since only a minority of the women have gone out for professional careers (Terman, 1954). By 1950, when the men had an average age of 40 years, they had published 67 books (including 46 in the fields of science, arts, and the humanities, and 21 books of fiction). They had published more than 1400 scientific, technical, and professional articles; over 200 short stories, novelettes, and plays; and 236 miscellaneous articles on a great variety of subjects. They had also authored more than 150 patents. The figures on publications do not include the hundreds of publications by journalists that classify as news stories, editorials, or newspaper columns; nor do they include the hundreds if not thousands of radio and TV scripts.

The 800 men include 78 who have taken a Ph.D. degree or its equivalent, 48 with a medical degree, 85 with a law degree, 74 who are teaching or have taught in a four-year college or university, 51 who have done basic research in the physical sciences or engineering, and 104 who are engineers but have done only applied research or none. Of the scientists, 47 are listed in the 1949 edition of *American Men of Science*. Nearly all of these numbers are from 10 to 20 or 30 times as large as would be found for 800 men of corresponding age picked at random in the general population, and are sufficient answer to those who belittle the significance of IQ differences.

The follow-up of these gifted subjects has proved beyond question that tests of "general intelligence," given as early as six, eight, or ten years, tell a great deal about the ability to achieve either presently or thirty years hence. Such tests do not, however, enable us to predict what direction the achievement will take, and least of all do they tell us what personality factors or what accidents of fortune will affect the fruition of exceptional ability. Granting that both interest patterns and special aptitudes play important roles in the making of a gifted scientist, mathematician, mechanic, artist, poet, or musical composer, I am convinced that to achieve greatly in almost any field, the special talents have to be backed up by a lot of Spearman's *g*, by which is meant the kind of general intelligence that requires ability to form many sharply defined concepts, to manipulate them, and to perceive subtle relationships between them; in other words, the ability to engage in abstract thinking.

The study by Catharine Cox of the childhood traits of historical geniuses gives additional evidence regarding the role of general intelligence in exceptional achievement. That study was part of our original plan to investigate superior ability by two methods of approach: (*a*) by identifying and following living gifted subjects from childhood onward; and (*b*) by proceeding in the opposite direction and tracing the mature genius back to his childhood promise. With a second grant from the Commonwealth Fund, the latter approach got under way only a year later than the former and resulted in the magnum opus by Cox (1926) entitled *The Early Mental Traits of Three Hundred Geniuses*. Her subjects represented an unbiased selection from the top 510 in Cattell's objectively compiled list of the 1000 most eminent men of history. Cox and two able assistants then scanned some 3000 biographies in search of information that would throw light on the early mental development of these subjects. The information thus obtained filled more than 6000 typed pages. Next, three psychologists familiar with mental age norms read the documentary evidence on all the subjects and estimated for each the IQ that presumably would be necessary to account for the intellectual behavior recorded for given chronological ages. Average of the three IQ estimates was used as the index of intelligence. In fact two IQs were estimated for each subject, one based on the evidence to age 17, and the other on evidence to the mid-twenties. The recorded evidence on development to age 17 varied from very little to an amount that yielded about as valid an IQ as a good intelligence test would give. Examples of the latter are Goethe, John Stuart Mill, and Francis Galton. It was the documentary information on Galton, which I summarized and published in 1917 (Terman, 1917), that decided me to prepare plans for the kind of study that was carried out by Cox. The average of estimated IQs for her three hundred geniuses was 155, with many going as high as 175 and several as high as 200. Estimates below 120 occurred only when there was little biographical evidence about the early years.

It is easy to scoff at these post-mortem IQs, but as one of the three psychologists who examined the evidence and made the IQ ratings, I think the author's main conclusion is fully warranted; namely, that "the genius who achieves highest eminence is one whom intelligence tests would have identified as gifted in childhood."

Special attention was given the geniuses who had sometime or other been labeled as backward in childhood, and in every one of these cases the facts clearly contradicted the legend. One of them was Oliver Goldsmith, of whom his childhood teacher is said to have said "Never was so dull a boy." The fact is that little Oliver was writing clever verse at seven years and at eight was reading Ovid and Horace. Another was Sir Walter Scott, who at seven not only read widely in poetry but was using correctly in his written prose such words as "melancholy" and "exotic." Other alleged childhood dullards included a number who disliked the usual diet of Latin and Greek but had a natural talent for science. Among these were the celebrated German chemist Justus von Liebig, the great English anatomist John Hunter, and the naturalist Alexander von Humboldt, whose name is scattered so widely over the maps of the world.

In the cases just cited one notes a tendency for the direction of later achievement to be foreshadowed by the interests and preoccupations of childhood. I have tried to determine how frequently this was true of the one hundred subjects in Cox's group whose childhood was best documented. Very marked foreshadowing was noted in the case of more than half of the group, none at all in less than a fourth. Macaulay, for example, began his career as historian at the age of six with what he called a "Compendium of Universal History," filling a quire of paper before he lost interest in the project. Ben Franklin before the age of 17 had displayed nearly all the traits that characterized him in middle life: scientific curiosity, religious heterodoxy, wit and buffoonery, political and business shrewdness, and ability to write. At 11 Pascal was so interested in mathematics that his father thought it best to deprive him of books on this subject until he had first mastered Latin and Greek. Pascal secretly proceeded to construct a geometry of his own and covered the ground as far as the 32nd proposition of Euclid. His father then relented. At 14 Leibnitz was writing on logic and philosophy and composing what he called "An Alphabet of Human Thought." He relates that at this age he took a walk one afternoon to consider whether he should accept the "doctrine of substantial forms."

Similar foreshadowing is disclosed by the case histories of my gifted subjects. A recent study of the scientists and nonscientists among our 800

gifted men (Terman, 1954) showed many highly significant differences between the early interests and social attitudes of those who became physical scientists and those who majored in the social sciences, law, or the humanities. Those in medical or biological sciences usually rated on such variables somewhere between the physical scientists and the nonscientists.

What I especially want to emphasize, however, is that both the evidence on early mental development of historical geniuses and that obtained by follow-up of gifted subjects selected in childhood by mental tests point to the conclusion that capacity to achieve far beyond the average can be detected early in life by a well-constructed ability test that is heavily weighted with the *g* factor. It remains to be seen how much the prediction of future achievement can be made more specific as to field by getting, in addition, measures of ability factors that are largely independent of *g*. It would seem that a 20-year follow-up of the thousands of school children who have been given Thurstone's test of seven "primary mental abilities" would help to provide the answer. At present the factor analysts don't agree on how many "primary" mental abilities there are, nor exactly on what they are. The experts in this field are divided into two schools. The British school, represented by Thomson, Vernon, and Burt, usually stop with the identification of at most three or four group factors in addition to *g*, while some representing the American school feed the scores of 40 or 50 kinds of tests into a hopper and manage to extract from them what they believe to be a dozen or fifteen separate factors.[1] Members of the British school are as a rule very skeptical about the realities underlying the minor group factors. There are also American psychologists, highly skilled in psychometrics, who share this skepticism. It is to be hoped that further research will give us more information than we now have about the predictive value of the group factors. Until such information is available, the scores on group factors can contribute little to vocational guidance beyond what a good test of general intelligence will provide.

I have always stressed the importance of *early* discovery of exceptional abilities. Its importance is now highlighted by the facts Harvey Lehman (1953) has disclosed in his monumental studies of the relation between age and creative achievement. The striking thing about his age curves is how early in life the period of maximum creativity is

---

[1] [See the article in this section by J. P. Guilford, "Intelligence Has Three Facets," p. 153.]

reached. In nearly all fields of science, the best work is done between ages 25 and 35 and rarely later than 40. The peak productivity for works of lesser merit is usually reached 5 to 10 years later; this is true in some twenty fields of science, in philosophy, in most kinds of musical composition, in art, and in literature of many varieties. The lesson for us from Lehman's statistics is that the youth of high achievement potential should be well trained for his life work before too many of his most creative years have been passed.

This raises the issue of educational acceleration for the gifted. It seems that the schools are more opposed to acceleration now than they were thirty years ago. The lockstep seems to have become more and more the fashion, notwithstanding the fact that practically everyone who has investigated the subject is against it. Of my gifted group, 29 per cent managed to graduate from high school before the age of $16\frac{1}{2}$ years (62 of these before $15\frac{1}{2}$), but I doubt if so many would be allowed to do so now. The other 71 per cent graduated between $16\frac{1}{2}$ and $18\frac{1}{2}$. We have compared the accelerated with the nonaccelerated on numerous case-history variables. The two groups differed very little in childhood IQ, their health records are equally good, and as adults they are equally well adjusted socially. More of the accelerates graduated from college, and on the average nearly a year and a half earlier than the nonaccelerates; they averaged higher in college grades and more often remained for graduate work. Moreover, the accelerates on the average married .7 of a year earlier, have a trifle lower divorce rate, and score just a little higher on a test of marital happiness (Terman and Oden, 1947). So far as college records of accelerates and nonaccelerates are concerned, our data closely parallel those obtained by the late Noel Keys (1938) at the University of California and those by Pressey (1949) and his associates at Ohio State University.

The Ford Fund for the Advancement of Education has awarded annually since 1951 some 400 college scholarships to gifted students who are not over $16\frac{1}{2}$ years old, are a year or even two years short of high school graduation, but show good evidence of ability to do college work. Three-quarters of them are between $15\frac{1}{2}$ and $16\frac{1}{2}$ at the time of college entrance. A dozen colleges and universities accept these students and are keeping close track of their success. A summary of their records for the first year shows that they not only get higher grades than their classmates, who average about two years older, but that they are also equally well adjusted socially and participate in as many extracurricular activities (Fund for the Advancement of Education, 1953). The main problem the boys have is in finding girls to date who are not too old for them! Some of them have started a campaign to remedy the situation by urging that more of these scholarships be awarded to girls.

The facts I have given do not mean that all gifted children should be rushed through school just as rapidly as possible. If that were done, a majority with IQ of 140 could graduate from high school before the age of 15. I do believe, however, that such children should be promoted rapidly enough to permit college entrance by the age of 17 at latest, and that a majority would be better off to enter at 16. The exceptionally bright student who is kept with his age group finds little to challenge his intelligence and all too often develops habits of laziness that later wreck his college career. I could give you some choice examples of this in my gifted group. In the case of a college student who is preparing for a profession in science, medicine, law, or any field of advanced scholarship, graduation at 20 instead of the usual 22 means two years added to his professional career; or the two years saved could be used for additional training beyond the doctorate, if that were deemed preferable.

Learned and Wood (1938) have shown by objective achievement tests in some forty Pennsylvania colleges how little correlation there is between the student's knowledge and the number of months or years of his college attendance. They found some beginning sophomores who had acquired more knowledge than some seniors near their graduation. They found similarly low correlations between the number of course units a student had in a given field and the amount he knew in that field. Some with only one year of Latin had learned more than others with three years. And, believe it or not, they even found boys just graduating from high school who had more knowledge of science than some college seniors who had majored in science and were about to begin teaching science in high schools! The sensible thing to do, it seems, would be to quit crediting the individual high school or the individual college and begin crediting the individual student. That, essentially, is what the Ford Fund scholarships are intended to encourage.

*   *   *

. . . In closing I will tell you briefly about an attempt we made a dozen years ago to identify some of the nonintellectual factors that have influenced life success among the men in my gifted group. Three judges, working independently, examined the records (to 1940) of the 730 men who were then twenty-five years old or older, and rated each on life success. The criterion of "success" was the extent to which a subject had made use of his superior intellectual ability, little weight being given to earned income. The 150 men rated highest for success and the 150 rated lowest were then compared on some 200 items of information obtained from childhood onward (Terman and Oden, 1947). How did the two groups differ?

During the elementary school years, the *A*s and *C*s (as we call them) were almost equally successful. The average grades were about the same, and average scores on achievement tests were only a trifle higher for the *A*s. Early in high school the groups began to draw apart in scholarship, and by the end of high school the slump of the *C*s was quite marked. The slump could not be blamed on extracurricular activities, for these were almost twice as common among the *A*s. Nor was much of it due to difference in intelligence. Although the *A*s tested on the average a little higher than the *C*s both in 1922 and 1940, the average score made by the *C*s in 1940 was high enough to permit brilliant college work, in fact was equaled by only 15 per cent of our highly selected Stanford students. Of the *A*s, 97 per cent entered college and 90 per cent graduated; of the *C*s, 68 per cent entered but only 37 per cent graduated. Of those who graduated, 52 per cent of the *A*s but only 14 per cent of the *C*s graduated with honors. The *A*s were also more accelerated in school; on the average they were six months younger on completing the eighth grade, 10 months younger at high school graduation, and 15 months younger at graduation from college.

The differences between the educational histories of the *A*s and *C*s reflect to some degree the differences in their family backgrounds. Half of the *A* fathers but only 15 per cent of the *C* fathers were college graduates, and twice as many of *A* siblings as of *C* siblings graduated. The estimated number of books in the *A* homes was nearly 50 per cent greater than in the *C* homes. As of 1928, when the average age of the subjects was about 16 years, more than twice as many of the *C* parents as of *A* parents had been divorced.

Interesting differences between the groups were found in the childhood data on emotional stability, social adjustments, and various traits of personality. Of the 25 traits on which each child was rated by parent and teacher in 1922 (18 years before the *A* and *C* groups were made up), the only trait on which the *C*s averaged as high as the *A*s was general health. The superiority of the *A*s was especially marked in four volitional traits: prudence, self-confidence, perseverance, and desire to excel. The *A*s also rated significantly higher in 1922 on leadership, popularity, and sensitiveness to approval or disapproval. By 1940 the difference between the groups in social adjustment and all-round mental stability had greatly increased and showed itself in many ways. By that time four-fifths of the *A*s had married, but only two-thirds of the *C*s, and the divorce rate for those who had married was twice as high for the *C*s as for the *A*s. Moreover, the *A*s made better marriages; their wives on the average came from better homes, were better educated, and scored higher on intelligence tests.

But the most spectacular differences between the two groups came from three sets of ratings, made in 1940, on a dozen personality traits. Each man rated himself on all the traits, was rated on them by his wife if he had a wife, and by a parent if a parent was still living. Although the three sets of ratings were made independently, they agreed unanimously on the four traits in which the *A* and *C* groups differed most widely. These were "persistence in the accomplishment of ends," "integration towards goals, as contrasted with drifting," "self-confidence," and "freedom from inferiority feelings." For each trait three critical ratios were computed showing, respectively, the reliability of the *A*–*C* differences in average of self-ratings, ratings by wives, and ratings by parents. The average of the three critical ratios was 5.5 for perseverance, 5.6 for integration toward goals, 3.7 for self-confidence, and 3.1 for freedom from inferiority feelings. These closely parallel the traits that Cox found to be especially characteristic of the 100 leading geniuses in her group whom she rated on many aspects of personality; their three outstanding traits she defined as "persistence of motive and effort," "confidence in their abilities," and "strength or force of character."

There was one trait on which only the parents of our *A* and *C* men were asked to rate them; that trait was designated "common sense." As judged by parents, the *A*s are again reliably superior, the *A*–*C* difference in average rating having a critical ratio of 3.9. We are still wondering what self-ratings by the subjects and ratings of them by their wives on common sense would have shown if we had been impudent enough to ask for them!

Everything considered, there is nothing in which

our *A* and *C* groups present a greater contrast than in drive to achieve and in all-round mental and social adjustment. Our data do not support the theory of Lange-Eichbaum (1932) that great achievement usually stems from emotional tensions that border on the abnormal. In our gifted group, success is associated with stability rather than instability, with absence rather than with presence of disturbing conflicts—in short, with well-balanced temperament and with freedom from excessive frustrations. The Lange-Eichbaum theory may explain a Hitler but hardly a Churchill. . . .

At any rate, we have seen that intellect and achievement are far from perfectly correlated. To identify the internal and external factors that help or hinder the fruition of exceptional talent, and to measure the extent of their influences, are surely among the major problems of our time. These problems are not new; their existence has been recognized by countless men from Plato to Francis Galton. What is new is the general awareness of them caused by the manpower shortage of scientists, engineers, moral leaders, statesmen, scholars, and teachers that the country must have if it is to survive in a threatened world. These problems are now being investigated on a scale never before approached, and by a new generation of workers in several related fields. Within a couple of decades vastly more should be known than we know today about our resources of potential genius, the environmental circumstances that favor its expression, the emotional compulsions that give it dynamic quality, and the personality distortions that can make it dangerous.

REFERENCES

Cox, C. C. In L. M. Terman (Ed.), *Genetic studies of genius*. Vol. I. *The early mental traits of three hundred geniuses*. Stanford: Stanford University Press, 1926.

Fund for the Advancement of Education. *Bridging the gap between school and college*. New York: Author, 1953.

Keys, N. The underage student in high school and college. *University of California Publications in Education*, 1938, **7**, 145–272.

Lange-Eichbaum, W. *The problem of genius*. New York: Macmillan, 1932.

Learned, W. S., & Wood, B. D. The student and his knowledge. *Carnegie Foundation for the Advancement of Teaching Bulletin*, 1938, **29**.

Lehman, H. C. *Age and achievement*. Princeton: Princeton University Press, 1953.

Pressey, S. L. *Educational acceleration: Appraisals and basic problems*. Columbus: Ohio State University Press, 1949.

Terman, L. M. A preliminary study in the psychology and pedagogy of leadership. *Pedagogical Seminar*, 1904, **11**, 413–451.

Terman, L. M. Genius and stupidity: A study of some of the intellectual processes of seven "bright" and seven "dull" boys. *Pedagogical Seminar*, 1906, **13**, 307–373.

Terman, L. M. The intelligence quotient of Francis Galton in childhood. *American Journal of Psychology*, 1917, **28**, 209–215.

Terman, L. M., *et al.* (Eds.) In *Genetic studies of genius*. Vol. I. *Mental and physical traits of a thousand gifted children*. Stanford: Stanford University Press, 1925.

Terman, L. M., & Oden, M. H. In *Genetic studies of genius*. Vol. IV. *The gifted child grows up*. Stanford: Stanford University Press, 1947.

Terman, L. M. Scientists and nonscientists in a group of 800 gifted men. *Psychological Monographs*, 1954, **68** (7, Whole No. 378), 44p.

Witty, P. (Ed.) *The gifted child*. Boston: D. C. Heath, 1951.

20

Intelligence—Why It Grows, Why It Declines

John L. Horn

As we have studied and pondered the relationship between intelligence and human behavior, we have come to recognize that intelligence seems to refer to more than a single concept. Early investigators entered into dialogues that sometimes developed into life-long feuds over whether intelligence is a product of heredity or of environment. The importance of "nature" and of "nurture" became rallying points around which teams of supporters were organized.

More recently, calmer souls have predominated by suggesting that both are important contributing factors to the concept of intelligence. The author of this article carries the issue farther by postulating two types of intelligence, one (fluid intelligence) influenced primarily by hereditary factors and the other (crystallized intelligence) influenced primarily by environmental factors. He sees heredity and environment as acting together, with the passage of time, to govern the intelligence level of the individual.

You will want to compare this discussion of the components of intelligence with those presented by J. P. Guilford (p. 153) and Alexander Wesman (p. 160) in other articles in this section.

One of the oldest and most thoroughly studied concepts in psychology is the concept of intelligence. Yet the term "intelligence" still escapes precise definition. There are so many different kinds of behavior that are indicative of intelligence that identifying the essence of them all has seemed virtually impossible. However, some recent research indicates that much of the diversity seen in expressions of intelligence can be understood in terms of a relatively small number of concepts. What's more, this research has also given us insight into understanding where intelligence originates, how it develops, and why and when it increases or decreases.

Studies of the interrelationships among human abilities indicate that there are two basic types of intelligence: *fluid* intelligence and *crystallized* intelligence. Fluid intelligence is rather formless; it is relatively independent of education and experience; and it can "flow into" a wide variety of intellectual activities. Crystallized intelligence, on the other hand, is a precipitate out of experience. It results when fluid intelligence is "mixed" with what can be called "the intelligence of the culture." Crystallized intelligence increases with a person's experience, and with the education that provides new methods and perspectives for dealing with that experience.

These two major kinds of intelligence are composed of more elementary abilities, called "primary" mental abilities. The number of these primaries is small. Only about 30 can be accepted as really well established. But with just these 30 primaries, we can explain much of the person-to-person variation commonly observed in reasoning, thinking, problem-solving, inventing, and understanding. Since several thousand tests have been devised to measure various aspects of intelligence, this system of primaries represents a very considerable achievement in parsimony. In much the same way that the chemical elements are organized according to the Periodic Law, these primary mental abilities fall into the patterns labeled fluid and crystallized intelligence.

Fluid Intelligence

What follows are some examples of the kinds of abilities that define fluid intelligence—and some of the tests that measure this kind of intelligence.

Induction is the ability to discover a general rule from several particular incidents and then apply this rule to cover a new incident.

For example, if a person observes the characteristics of a number of people who are members of a particular club or lodge, he might discover the rule by which membership is determined (even when this rule is highly secret information). He might then apply this rule to obtain an invitation to membership!

Among the tests that measure induction ability is the letter series. Given some letters in a series like

ACFJO—

the task is to provide the next letter. Of course, the test can be used only with people who know the alphabet, and this rules out illiterates and most children. We can't eliminate the influence of accumulated learning from even the purest examples of fluid intelligence.

Figural Relations refers to the ability to notice changes of differences in shapes and use this awareness to identify or produce one element missing from a pattern.

An everyday example of intelligence in figural relations is the ability to navigate cloverleaf and expressway turnoff patterns—an ability that may mean as much for adequate adjustment today as skill in finding one's way through a virgin forest had in the days of Daniel Boone. This ability also has ready application in interior decorating and in jobs where maps (or aerial views) must be compared a good deal—as by cartographers, navigators, pilots, meteorologists, and tourists.

Span of Apprehension is the ability to recognize and retain awareness of the immediate environment. A simple test is memory span: Several digits or other symbols are presented briefly, and the

FIGURE 1   *What figure fits into the lower right?*
(Answer: A square with two dots.)

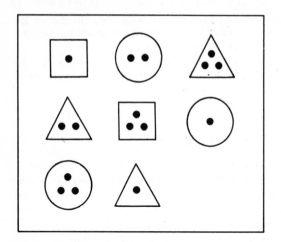

task is to reproduce them later, perhaps in reverse order. Without this ability, remembering a telephone number long enough to dial it would be impossible.

Other primary abilities that help define fluid intelligence include:

General Reasoning (example: estimating how long it would take to do several errands around town);

Semantic Relations (example: enjoying a pun on common words);

Deductive Reasoning, or the ability to reason from the general to the particular (example: noting that the wood of fallen trees rots and concluding that one should cover—for example, paint—wooden fence posts before inserting them into the ground);

Associative Memory, or the ability to aid memory by observing the relationships between separate items (example: remembering the way to grandmother's house by associating various landmarks en route, or remembering the traits of different people by association with their faces).

Crystallized Intelligence

Most of what we call intelligence—for example, the ability to make good use of language or to solve complex technical problems—is actually crystallized intelligence. Here are some of the primary abilities that demonstrate the nature of this kind of intelligence:

Verbal Comprehension. This could also be called general information, since it represents a broad slice of knowledge. Vocabulary tests, current-events tests, and reading-comprehension tests all measure verbal comprehension, as do other tests that require a person to recall information about his culture. The ability is rather fully exercised when one quickly reads an article like this one and grasps the essential ideas. Verbal comprehension is also called for when a person reads news items about foreign affairs, understands their implications, and relates them to one another and to their historical backgrounds.

Experiential Evaluation is often called "common sense" or "social intelligence." Experiential evaluation includes the ability to project oneself into situations, to feel as other people feel and thereby better understand interactions among people. Everyday examples include figuring out why a conscientious foreman is not getting good results from those under him, and why people disobey traffic laws more at some intersections than at others.

One test that measures experiential evaluation in married men is the following:

Your wife has just invested time, effort, and money in a new hairdo. But it doesn't help her appearance at all. She wants your opinion. You should:

1. Try to pretend that the hairdo is great;
2. state your opinion bluntly;
3. compliment her on her hairdo, but add minor qualifications; or,
4. refuse to comment.

Answer 3 is considered judged correct—on the grounds that husbands can't get away with answers 1 and 4, and answer 2 is likely to provoke undue strife.

Formal Reasoning is reasoning in ways that have become more or less formalized in Western cultures. An example is the syllogism, like this one:

No Gox box when in purple socks.
Jocks is a Gox wearing purple socks.
Therefore: Jocks does not now box.

The task is to determine whether or not the conclusion is warranted. (It is.)

An everyday example of formal reasoning might be to produce a well-reasoned analysis of the pros and cons of an issue presented to the United Nations. Formal reasoning, to a much greater extent than experiential evaluation or verbal comprehension, depends upon dealing with abstractions and symbols in highly structured ways.

Number Facility, the primary ability to do numerical calculations, also helps define crystallized intelligence, since to a considerable extent it reflects the quality of a person's education. In a somewhat less direct way, this quality is also represented in the primary abilities called mechanical knowledge, judgment, and associational fluency.

Semantic relations and *general reasoning,* listed as primary aspects of fluid intelligence, are also—when carrying a burden of learning and culture—aspects of crystallized intelligence. This points up the fact that, although fluid and crystallized intelligence represent distinct patterns of abilities, there is some overlap. This is what is known as *alternative mechanisms* in intellectual performance. In other words, a given kind of problem can sometimes be solved by exercise of different abilities.

Consider the general-reasoning primary, for example. In this, typical problems have a slightly mathematical flavor:

There are 100 patients in a hospital. Some (an even number) are one-legged, but wearing shoes. One-half of the remainder are barefooted. How many shoes are being worn?

We may solve this by using a formal algebraic equation. Set x equal to the number of one-legged patients, with $100 - x$ then being the number of two-legged patients, and $x + \frac{1}{2}(100 - x)2$ being the number of shoes worn. We don't have to invent the algebraic techniques used here. They have been passed down to us over centuries. As Keith Hayes very nicely puts it, "The culture relieves us of much of the burden of creativity by giving us access to the products of creative acts scattered thinly through the history of the species." The use of such products is an important part of crystallized intelligence.

But this problem can also be solved by a young boy who has never heard of algebra! He may reason that, if half the two-legged people are without shoes, and all the rest (an even number) are one-legged, then the shoes must average one per person, and the answer must be 100. This response, too, represents learning—but it is not so much a product of education, or of the accumulated wisdom passed from one generation to the next, as is the typical product of crystallized intelligence. Fluid intelligence is composed of such relatively untutored skills.

Thus the same problem can be solved by exercise of *either* fluid intelligence *or* crystallized intelligence. We can also see the operation of such alternative mechanisms in these two problems.

ZEUS—JUPITER: :ARTEMIS—?
   Answer: Phidias   Coria   <u>Diana</u>
HERE—NOW: :THERE—?
   Answer: Thus   Sometimes   <u>Then</u>

The first problem is no harder to solve than the second, *provided* you have acquired a rather sophisticated knowledge of mythology. The second problem requires learning too, but no more than simply learning the language—a fact that puts native-born whites and Negroes on a relatively equal footing in dealing with problems of this sort, but places Spanish-speaking Puerto Ricans or Mexican-Americans at a disadvantage. As measures of fluid intelligence, both items are about equally good. But the first involves, to a much greater extent, crystallized intelligence gleaned from formal education or leisure reading.

Because the use of alternative mechanisms is natural in the play of human intelligence, most intelligence tests provide mixed rather than pure measures of fluid or crystallized abilities. This only reflects the way in which we usually go about solving problems—by a combination of natural wit and acquired strategies. But tests can be devised in which one type of intelligence predominates. For example, efforts to devise "culture fair" intelligence tests that won't discriminate against people from deprived educational or cultural backgrounds usually focus on holding constant the effect of crystallized capabilities—so that fluid capabilities can be more fully represented.

Now that we have roughly defined what fluid and crystallized intelligence are, let us investigate how each of them develops over time.

The infant, whose reasoning powers extend little beyond the observation that a determined howl brings food, attention, or a dry diaper, becomes the man who can solve legal problems all day, execute complicated detours to avoid the five o'clock traffic on his way home, and deliver a rousing speech to his political club in the evening. But how? To understand the intertwined development of the fluid and crystallized abilities that such activities require, we need to consider three processes essential to the development of intelligence: *anlage function,* the *acquisition of aids,* and *concept formation.*

Anlage function, which includes the complex workings of the brain and other nervous tissue, provides the physical base for all of the infant's future mental growth. ("Anlage" is a German word meaning "rudiment.") The second two factors—the aids and concepts the child acquires as he grows up—represent the building blocks that, placed on the anlage base, form the structure of adult intelligence.

The anlage function depends crucially and directly upon physiology. Physiology, in turn, depends partly on heredity, but it can also be influenced by injury, disease, poisons, drugs, and severe shock. Such influences can occur very early in life—often even in the womb. Hence it is quite possible that an individual's anlage functioning may have only a remote relationship to his hereditary potential. All we can say for sure is that the anlage process *is* closely tied to a physiological base.

A good everyday measure of a person's anlage functioning is his memory span (provided we can rule out the effects of anxiety, fatigue, or mental disturbance). Given a series of letters or numbers, most adults can immediately reproduce only about six or seven of them in reverse order. Some people may be able to remember 11, others as few as four, but in no case is the capacity unlimited or even very great. Memory span increases through childhood—probably on account of the increasing size and complexity of the brain—but it is not much affected by learning. This is generally true of other examples of anlage functioning.

Short-cuts to Learning

Aids are techniques that enable us to go beyond the limitations imposed by anlage functioning. An aid can, for example, extend our memory span. For example, we break up a telephone or social-security number with dashes, transforming long numbers into short, more easily recalled sets, and this takes the strain off immediate memory.

Some aids, like the rules of algebra, are taught in school. But several psychologists (notably Jean Piaget) have demonstrated that infants and children also invent their own aids in their untutored explorations of the world. In development, this process probably continues for several years.

Concepts are categories we impose on the phenomena we experience. In forming concepts, we find that otherwise dissimilar things can be regarded as "the same" in some sense because they have common properties. For instance, children learn to distinguish the features associated with "bike"—two wheels, pedaling, riding outside, etc.—from those associated with "car." Very early in a child's development, these categories may be known and represented only in terms of his own internal symbols. In time, however, the child learns to associate his personal symbols with conventional signs—that is, he learns to use language to represent what he "knows" from direct experience. Also, increased proficiency in the use of language affords opportunities to see new relations and acquire *new* concepts.

The concepts we possess at any time are a residue of previous intellectual functioning. Tests that indicate the extent of this residue may, therefore, predict the level of a person's future intellectual development. A large vocabulary indicates a large storehouse of previously acquired concepts, so verbal ability itself is often taken as a good indication of ability to conceptualize. Many well-known tests of intelligence, especially of crystallized intelligence, are based on this rationale.

However, language is really only an indirect measure of concept awareness. Thus verbally-oriented tests can be misleading. What about the child raised in an environment where language is seldom used, but which is otherwise rich in opportunity to perceive relationships and acquire concepts (the backwoods of Illinois, or by a pond in Massachusetts)? At the extreme, what about a person who never hears the spoken word or sees the written word? He does not necessarily lack the awareness that we so glibly represent in language. Nor does he necessarily lack intelligence. A child who doesn't know the spoken or written word "key" surely understands the concept if he can distinguish a key from other small objects and use it to open a lock.

What is true of conventional language is also true of conventional aids. Lack of facility or familiarity with aids does not mean that a child has failed to develop intellectually, even though it may make him *appear* mentally slow on standard intelligence tests. Just as verbally-oriented tests penalize the child who has not had the formal schooling or proper environment to develop a large vocabulary, many tests of so-called mathematical aptitude rely heavily on the use of conventional aids taught in school—on algebraic formulas, for example. Someone who has learned few of these conventional aids will generally do poorly on such tests, but this does not mean that he lacks intelligence.

We cannot overlook the fact that an intelligent woodsman may be just as intelligent, in one sense of this term, as an intelligent college professor. The particular combination of primary abilities needed to perform well may differ in the two cases, but the basic wherewithal of intellectual competence can be the same—adequate anlage functioning, plus an awareness of the concepts and a facility with the aids relevant to dealing with the environment at hand. Daniel Boone surely needed as much intelligence to chart the unexplored forests of the frontier as today's professor needs to thread his way through the groves of academe.

Education and Intelligence

It is obvious, then, that formal education is not essential to the development of important aspects of intelligence. Barring disruption of anlage functioning by accident or illness, the child will form concepts and devise aids to progressively expand his mental grasp as he grows up, and this will occur whether he goes to school or not.

Where formal instruction *is* significant is in making such development easier—and in passing along the concepts and aids that many people have deposited into the intelligence of a culture. The schools give children awareness of concepts that they may not have had the opportunity to gain from first-hand experience—the ability to recognize an Australian platypus, for example, without ever having seen one, or a knowledge of how the caste system works in India. Aids, too, are taught in school. A child well armed with an array of mathematical formulas will likely be able to solve a problem faster and more accurately than one who must work it out completely on his own. Indeed, some problems simply cannot be solved without mathematical aids. Since the acquisition of both concepts and aids is cumulative, several years of formal education can put one child well ahead of another one, unschooled, who has roughly the same intellectual potential.

Education can thus play a powerful role in developing intelligence. Too often, however, it doesn't. Even in school, some children in perfectly good health and physical condition fail to develop, or develop slowly. Some even seem to be mentally stunted by their school experience. Why? What sorts of experiences can foster—or retard—the developmental processes of concept-formation and aid-formation in the school environment?

Even though we are only beginning to find answers in this area, it is already clear that learning can be speeded up, slowed down, or brought almost to a dead halt by a variety of school experiences. On the favorable side, abilities improve by *positive transfer.* Learning one skill makes it easier to learn a related one. A student who already knows Spanish, for example, will find it easier to learn Portuguese. And positive transfer also works in less obvious ways. There is even evidence to suggest that new learning is facilitated simply by having learned before—by a sort of learning how to learn.

But other factors too can affect the course of learning, and these factors are particularly prominent in the context of our formal educational system. For example, merely having the *opportunity* to learn may depend on both previous learning and previous opportunity to learn. Thus, even if his native potential and level of self-education are good, the person who has not had the opportunity to finish high school has a poor chance of going on to college.

Labeling operates in a similar way. If a person is labeled as lacking in ability, he may receive no further chance to develop. Kenneth B. Clark states this very well:

If a child scores low on an intelligence test because he cannot read and then is not taught to read because he has a low score, then such a child is being imprisoned in an iron circle and becomes the victim of an educational self-fulfilling prophecy.

Avoidance-learning is similar. This is learning not to learn. Punishment in a learning situation—being humiliated in school, for example—may make a child "turn off." Problem solving may become such a threat that he will avoid all suggestion of it. Since an active, inquiring curiosity is at the root of mental growth, avoidance-learning can very seriously retard intellectual development. Moreover, since a child typically expresses avoidance by aggression, lack of attention, sullenness, and other behavior unacceptable to educators and parents, they—being human—may react by shutting the child out of further learning situations, and thus create another kind of iron circle.

Labeling, lack of opportunity, and avoidance-learning affect the development of both fluid and crystallized intelligence. Both depend upon acculturational influences—the various factors that provide, or block, chances for learning. And both depend upon anlage function and thus upon physiological influences as well. However, fluid intelligence depends more on physiological factors, and crystallized intelligence more on acculturational ones. It is the interplay of these factors throughout a child's development that produces the fact that fluid and crystallized intelligence can be separated in adult intellectual performances. But how does this separation arise?

A Climate for Growth

In many respects, the opportunities to maintain good physiological health are the same for all in our society. The climate, air pollution, water, the chances of injury, and other hazards in the physical environment do not vary greatly. Even the social environments are similar in many ways.

We acquire similar language skills, go to schools that have similar curricula, have a similar choice of television programs, and so on. In this sense, the most advantaged and the most disadvantaged child have some of the same opportunities to develop anlage functioning, and to acquire concepts and aids.

Moreover, we should be careful about how we use the term "disadvantaged." We do not yet know what is superior in all respects, at every age level, for the development of all the abilities that go into intelligence. At one stage, what seems a "bad" home may give intelligence a greater impetus than an apparently "good" home. It may be, for instance, that in early childhood "lax" parents allow more scope for development. In later development, "stimulating" and "responsible" (but restrictive?) parents might be better. Some of the intellectual leaders of every period of history and of every culture have developed in environments that, according to many definitions, would have had to be classified as "disadvantaged."

It is clear, however, that favorable conditions for the development of intelligence are not the same for all. To avoid the iron circle, to gain opportunities to go on, children have to display the right abilities at the right times. To some extent, this depends on early and basic endowment. Intelligent parents may provide good heredity, good environmental conditions for learning, and good stimulation and encouragement. But the opportunities a child gets, and what he meets them with, can also be quite independent of his own characteristics. His opportunities depend on such haphazard factors as the neighborhood in which he lives, the kind of schooling available, his mother's interests and his father's income, the personality qualities of the teachers he happens to get, and the attitudes and actions of his playmates.

Thus, through a child's years of growth and education, societal influences can produce an effect that is largely independent of those produced by physiological influences. In an infant, cultural influences could not have accumulated independently of the physiological. But as children pass through preschool and school, their awareness of concepts and use of aids becomes more evident, and the influence of acculturation is felt and exhibited. The probable shape of future learning and opportunity becomes more clear. The child who has already moved ahead tends to be ready to move farther ahead, and to be accepted for such promotion. Crystallized intelligence feeds the growth of crystallized intelligence. By contrast, the child who has not moved ahead, for whatever reasons, tends

to be less ready and to be viewed as such. His acquisition of the lore of the culture proceeds at a decelerating rate. This is how two children with roughly the same hereditary potential can grow apart in their acquisition of crystallized intelligence. Among adults, then, we should expect to find great variation in the crystallized pattern of abilities—and we do!

The cultural influences that can produce this kind of inequality operate almost independently of physiological factors, however. Thus, the child who fails to progress rapidly in learning the ever-more-abstruse concepts and aids of crystallized intelligence may still acquire many concepts and aids of a more common type. And if he is lucky in avoiding accidents and maintaining good health, this kind of development can be quite impressive. His intellectual growth may even surpass that of a seemingly more favored child who is slowed down by illness or injury. Thus, two children with about the same hereditary makeup can grow apart in fluid intelligence, too. The result is a wide range of variation in adult fluid intelligence—a range even wider than we would expect to be produced by differences in heredity alone.

The Declining Years

Both fluid and crystallized intelligence, as we have just seen, develop with age. But intelligence also declines with age. This is especially true of the fluid kind. Looked at in terms of averages, fluid intelligence begins to decline before a person is out of his twenties. Crystallized intelligence fares better, however, and generally continues to increase throughout life. Because crystallized intelligence usually increases in this fashion, the decline in fluid abilities may not seriously undermine intellectual competence in people as they mature into middle age and even beyond. But let us look at these matters more analytically.

Figure 2 represents results from several studies, each involving several hundred people. Notice, first, that the curves representing fluid intelligence (*FI*) and crystallized intelligence (*CI*) are at first indistinguishable, but become separate as development proceeds. This represents the fact that both are products of development. It also illustrates the fact that it is easier to distinguish between fluid intelligence and crystallized intelligence in adults than in children.

The maturation curve (*M*) summarizes evidence that the physical structures and processes that support intellect (the brain, for instance) grow and

FIGURE 2 *Development of Fluid Intelligence (FI) and Crystallized Intelligence (CI) in relation to effects produced by Maturation (M), Acculturation (A), and loss of Physiological Base (PB) due to injury*

increase in complexity until the late teens or the early twenties. Development is rapid but decelerating. Since both fluid and crystallized intelligence depend on maturation, their curves more or less follow it.

But maturation accounts for only part of the change in the physical structures that support intelligence. They are also affected by injuries, such as birth complications, blows to the head, carbon-monoxide poisoning, intoxication, and high fever. Such injuries are irreversible and thus cumulative. In the short run, they are difficult to discern, and their effects are masked during childhood by the rising curves of learning and maturation. In the long run, however, injuries resulting from the exposures of living take their toll. The older the person, the greater the exposure. Thus, part of the physiological base for intellectual functioning will, on an average, decrease with age (curve *PB*).

The sum of the influences represented by *M* and *PB* form the physiological base for intellectual processes at any particular time. In the early years, the effects of one compensate for the effects of the other. But as the *M* curve levels off in young adulthood and the *PB* curve continues downward, the total physiological base drops. Those intellectual abilities that depend very directly upon physiology must then decline.

The effects of brain-tissue loss are variable, however. At the physiological level, an ability is a complex network of neurons that "fire" together to produce observable patterns of behavior. Such

networks are overdetermined—not all of the neurons in the network need to "fire" to produce the behavior. And some networks are much more overdetermined than others. This means that when a loss of brain tissue (that is, a loss of neurons) occurs, some networks, and hence some abilities, will be only minimally affected. Networks that are not highly overdetermined, though, will become completely inoperative when a critical number of neurons cease to fire.

The crystallized abilities apparently correspond to highly overdetermined neural networks. Such abilities will not be greatly affected by moderate loss of neurons. The fluid abilities, on the other hand, depend much more significantly upon anlage functions, which are represented by very elementary neural networks. These abilities will thus "fall off" with a loss of neurons.

Curve *A* in the graph shows how, potentially at least, the effects of acculturation and positive transfer may accumulate throughout a lifetime. On this basis alone, were it not for neural damage, we might expect intelligence to increase, not decline, in adulthood.

Whether intellectual decline occurs or not will depend upon the extent of neuron loss, and upon whether learning new aids and concepts can compensate for losing old skills. For example, the anlage capacity to keep six digits in immediate awareness may decline with loss of neurons. But the individual, sensing this loss, may develop new techniques to help him keep a number in mind.

Thus the overall effect may be no loss of ability. What the evidence does indicate, however, is that, with increasing age beyond the teens, there is a steady, if gentle, decline in fluid intelligence. This suggests that learning new aids and concepts of the fluid kind does not quite compensate for the loss of anlage function and the loss of previously learned aids and concepts.

On a happier note, and by way of contrast, the evidence also shows that crystallized intelligence *increases* throughout most of adulthood. Here alternative mechanisms come into play. Compensating for the loss of one ability with the surplus of another, the older person uses crystallized intelligence in place of fluid intelligence. He substitutes accumulated wisdom for brilliance, while the younger person does the opposite.

A word of caution about these results. They represent averages, and averages can be affected by a relatively few extreme cases. For example, if only a relatively few individuals experience brain damage, but the effect is rather pronounced in each case, this will show up in the averages. If such damage occurs more frequently with older people than with younger people, a corresponding decline of abilities with age will show up—even though such decline may not be an inevitable aspect of aging for everyone. But even though these cautions must be kept in mind, we should not lose track of the fact that the *FI* curve parallels the *PB* in adulthood.

Intelligence tests that measure mixtures of fluid and crystallized intelligence (and most popular ones do) show varying relationships between aging and intelligence in adulthood. If fluid tests predominate, decline is indicated. If crystallized intelligence is well represented, then there is no apparent decline.

Intellectual performance in important jobs in life will depend on both kinds of intelligence, and may be represented by a composite curve (*FI* and *CI* in Figure 3).

Notice that the peak of this curve occurs later than the peak of the *FI* curve below it. If fluid intelligence reaches its peak in the early twenties, intelligence in overall performance, influenced by

FIGURE 3 *Fluid intelligence, crystallized intelligence, and the effect of the two added together*

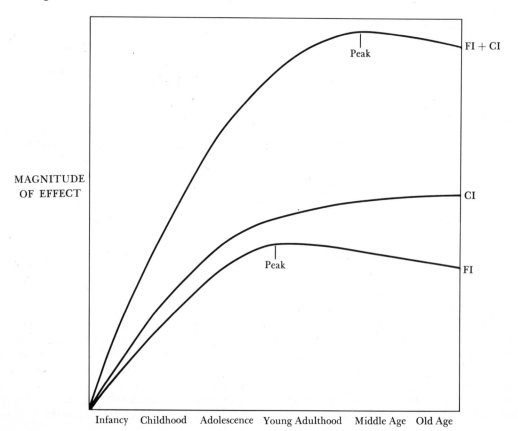

the cultural accretion, may peak in the thirties. The evidence indicates that the greatest intellectual *productivity* tends to occur in the thirties or early forties, although the most *creative* work often is accomplished earlier. For example, half of the 52 greatest discoveries in chemistry (as judged by chemists) were made before the innovator had reached age 29, and 62 per cent were made before he was 40. It would seem that creativity and productivity represent somewhat different combinations of fluid and crystallized intelligence, with productivity being relatively more affected by cultural factors.

The age at which the combined *FI* and *CI* function peaks varies from one person to another, depending on the development of new concepts and aids, the amount of brain damage, and other factors such as diet and general health.

Perhaps the most interesting result of all this recent work is the questions it provokes. What are the factors producing the apparent decline in fluid intelligence? Are they intrinsic to aging, or do they merely reflect the hazards of living? Are they associated with the hazards of different occupations? Do auto mechanics, for example, who are repeatedly exposed to carbon monoxide, show more decline in fluid intelligence than cement finishers, who work in the open air?

Most important of all, what experiences in infancy and childhood have favorable or unfavorable effects on the future growth of fluid intelligence? Of crystallized intelligence? Of both? Do experiences that affect fluid intelligence always affect crystallized intelligence, too? We are still far from finding firm and comprehensive answers to these questions, but they very clearly hold massive implications for our child-rearing practices, for our educational system, and for the whole complex of fields that bear on the development and management of human potential.

21

Intelligence Has Three Facets

J. P. Guilford

The word *intelligence* is used to express the idea that people (and other animals too) differ in their quickness to learn new information and to deal with old information. The differences, we say, are due to the presence of more or less intelligence. This sort of approach seems clear and simple; however, if we are to be able to use the idea of intelligence for any purposes other than discussion, we must understand it better.

As scientific procedures have been stunningly successful in providing knowledge about previously uncharted areas, it is, therefore, small wonder that they have been brought to bear upon the problem of determining the meaning of "intelligence." As we have seen, the starting point for scientific understanding is good measurement. Binet's test provided a good beginning for the attack on this phase of the problem.

At first, intelligence was treated as a single attribute, but as measuring instruments became more refined, it became possible, through the statistical technique known as *factor analysis*, to determine how many distinct abilities were being measured by a given battery of tests. Early factor analyses suggested that intelligence really consisted of about nine separate factors. This article reports on further analyses that have led the author to postulate a far greater number of basic factors in intelligence.

Many a layman who has taken a psychologist's intelligence test, especially if he did not do as well as he thought he should, has the conviction that a score, such as an IQ, does not tell the whole story regarding intelligence. In thinking so, he is absolutely right; traditional intelligence tests fall far short of indicating fully an individual's intellectual status. Just how far short and in what re-

From Science, *Vol. 160, No. 10 (May 1968), 615–620. Copyright 1968 by the American Association for the Advancement of Science.*

spects have not been well realized until very recent years during which the whole scope of human intelligence has been intensively investigated.

This is not to say that IQ tests are not useful, for they definitely are, as years of experience have demonstrated. Intelligence-quotient tests were originated more than sixty years ago for the purpose of determining which children could not learn at normal rates. This meant that the content of IQ tests weights heavily those intellectual abilities that are pertinent to school learning in the key subjects of reading and arithmetic, and other subjects that depend directly upon them or are of similar nature psychologically. IQ tests (and also academic-aptitude tests, which are essentially similar) predict less well at educational levels higher than the elementary grades, for at higher levels subject matter becomes more varied. Even at the elementary level, predictions of achievement have been poor in connection with the *initial* stages of learning to read, in spelling, and in the arts. The defender of the IQ test might say that intelligence is not involved in such subjects. But he would not only be wrong, he would also be dodging problems.

One Intelligence, or Many Abilities?

The father of IQ tests, Alfred Binet, believed firmly that intelligence is a very complex affair, comprising a number of different abilities, and he manifested this conviction by introducing tests of many kinds into his composite scale. He did not know what the component abilities are, although he suggested that there are several different kinds of memory, for example. He went along with the idea of using a single, overall score, since the immediate practical goal was to make a single administrative decision regarding each child.

Test makers following Binet were mostly unconcerned about having a basic psychological theory for intelligence tests, another example of technology running far in advance of theory. There was some concern about theory in England, however, where Charles Spearman (1904) developed a procedure of factor analysis by which it became possible to discover component abilities. Spearman was obsessed with a very restricting conception that there is a universal *g* factor that is common to all tests that have any claim to the label of "intelligence tests," where each test has its own unique kind of items or problems. His research, and that of others in his country, found, however, that correlations between tests could not be fully accounted for on the basis of a single common

factor.[1] They had to admit the existence of a number of "group" factors in addition to *g*. For example, sets of tests having verbal, numerical, or spatial material, respectively, correlated higher within sets than with tests in other sets. The extra correlation among tests within sets was attributed to additional abilities each of limited scope.

Factor analyses in the United States have followed almost exclusively the multiple-factor theory of Thurstone (1935), which is more general than Spearman's. In Thurstone's conception, a *g* factor is not necessary but analysis by his methods would be likely to find it if the intercorrelations warrant such a result. It is not necessary to know the mathematics basic to factor theory in order to follow the remaining content of this article. . . . To all readers it may be said that factor analysis is a sensitive procedure, which, when properly used, can answer the taxonomic questions of *what* intellectual abilities or functions exist and what their properties are.

* * *

Discovery of Multiple Abilities

Only a few events in discovering factors by the Thurstone approach will be mentioned. In Thurstone's first major study (1938) as many as nine common factors were thought to be sufficiently interpretable psychologically to justify calling them "primary mental abilities." A factor is interpreted intuitively in terms of the apparent human resource needed to do well in the set of tests loaded strongly together on the mathematical factor. A distinction between mathematical factors and psychological factors is important. Surface features of the tests in the set may differ, but examinees have to perform well in some unique way in all of them. For example, Thurstone designated some of the abilities as being visual-perceptual, inductive, deductive, numerical, spatial, and verbal. Two others dealt with rote memory and word fluency. Thurstone and his students followed his 1938 analysis with others that revealed a few additional kinds of abilities.

Another major source of identified intellectual abilities was the research of aviation psychologists in the U.S. Army Air Force during World War II

---

[1] For the benefit of the uninitiated, a (positive) correlation between any two tests means that if certain individuals make high (low) scores in one of them, they are likely also to make high (low) scores in the other.

(Guilford and Lacey, 1947). More important than the outcome of adding to the number of intellectual abilities that called for recognition was the fact that where Thurstone had found one spatial ability, there proved to be at least three, one of them being recognized as spatial orientation and another as spatial visualization. Where Thurstone had found an inductive ability, there were three reasoning abilities. Where Thurstone had found one memory ability, there were three, including visual memory. In some of these cases a Thurstone factor turned out to be a confounding of two or more separable abilities, separable when more representative tests for each factor were analyzed together and when allowance was made for a sufficient number of factors. In other cases, new varieties of tests were explored—new memory tests, space tests, and reasoning tests.

The third major event was in the form of a program of analyses conducted in the Aptitudes Research Project at the University of Southern California since 1949, in which attention was first concentrated on tests in the provisional categories of reasoning, creative thinking, planning, evaluation, and problem solving.[2] Nearly twenty years later, the number of separate intellectual abilities has increased to about 80, with at least 50 per cent more predicted by a comprehensive, unified theory. The remainder of this article is mainly concerned with that theory.

The Structure-of-Intellect Model

Two previous attempts to put the known intellectual abilities into logical schema had been made by Burt (1949) and Vernon (1950), with similar results. In both cases the models were of hierarchical form, reminiscent of the Linnaeus taxonomic model for the animal kingdom. Following the British tradition of emphasis upon *g*, which was placed at the apex of the system, there were broad subdivisions under *g* and under each subdivision some subsubcategories, on down to abilities that are regarded as being very narrow in scope.

My first attempts (Guilford, 1956) found that the hierarchical type of model had to be discarded for several reasons. First, there had to be a rejection of *g* itself, for reasons mentioned earlier. Furthermore, most factors seemed to be of somewhat comparable level of generality, where generality is operationally defined in terms of the number and variety of tests found to represent each ability. There did appear to be categories of abilities, some concerned with discovery or recognition of infor-

mation, memory for information, productive thinking, and evaluation, with a number of abilities in each category, but there are other ways of organizing categories of abilities. The most decisive observation was that there were a number of parallels between abilities, in terms of their common features.

Some examples of parallels in abilities will help. Two parallel abilities differ in only one respect. There was known to be an ability to see relations between perceived, visual figures, and a parallel ability to see relations between concepts. An example of a test item in the first case would be seeing that one figure is the lower-left half of another. An item in the second case might require seeing that the words "bird" and "fly" are related as object and its mode of locomotion. The ability to do the one kind of item is relatively independent of the ability to do the other, the only difference being that of kind of information—concrete or perceived in the one case and abstract or conceived in the other.

For a pair of abilities differing in another way, the kind of information is the same for both: One of the abilities pertains to *seeing* class ideas. Given the set of words *footstool, lamp, rocker, television,* can the examinee grasp the essence of the nature of the class, as shown by his naming the class, by putting another word or two into it, or by recognizing its name among four alternatives? The ability pertains to discovery or recognition of a class concept. In another kind of test we ask the examinee to *produce* classes by partitioning a list of words into mutually exclusive sets, each with a different class concept. These two abilities are relatively independent. The one involves a process of understanding and the other a process of production. These processes involve two psychologically different kinds of operation.

A third kind of parallel abilities has pairs that are alike in kind of information involved and in kind of operation. Suppose we give the examinee this kind of test item: "Name as many objects as you can that are both edible and white." Here we have given the specifications for a class and the examinee is to produce from his memory store some class members. The ability involved was at first called "ideational fluency." The more of ap-

[2] We are indebted to the Office of Naval Research, Personnel and Training Branch, for continued support, and to the U.S. Office of Education and the National Science Foundation, Biological and Medical Sciences Division, for additional support at various times.

propriate members the examinee can produce in a limited time, the better his score. In a test for a parallel ability, instead of producing single words the examinee is to produce a list of sentences. To standardize his task for testing purposes and to further control his efforts, we can give him the initial letters of four words that he is to give in each of a variety of sentences, for example: W——— c——— s——— d———. Without using any word twice, the examinee might say, "Why can't Susan dance?," "Workers could seldom deviate," or "Weary cats sense destruction." The ability was first called "expressional fluency." The kind of information in both these tests is conceptual, and the kind of operation is production.

But the kind of operation in the last test is different from that for the classifying test mentioned before. In the classifying test, the words given to the examinee are so selected that they form a unique set of classes and he is so told. The operation is called "convergent production." In the last two tests under discussion, there are many possible responses and the examinee produces alternatives. The operation is called "divergent production." It involves a broad searching or scanning process. Both operations depend upon retrieval of information from the examinee's memory store.

The difference between the two abilities illustrated by the last two tests is in the nature of the things produced. In the first case they are single words that stand for single objects or concepts. The thing produced, the "product," is a *unit* of information. In the second case, the product is an organized sequence of words, each word standing for a concept or unit. This kind of product is given the name of "system."

In order to take care of all such parallels (and the number increased as time went on and experience grew), a matrix type of model seemed called for in the manner of Mendeleev's table of chemical elements. The differences in the three ways indicated—operation (kind of processing of information), content (kind of information), and product (formal aspect of information)—called for a three-dimensional model. Such a model has been called "morphological" (Zwicky, 1957). The model as finally completed and presented in 1959 (Guilford, 1959) is illustrated in Figure 1. It has five categories of operation, four categories of content, and six categories of product.

FIGURE 1   *The structure-of-intellect model*

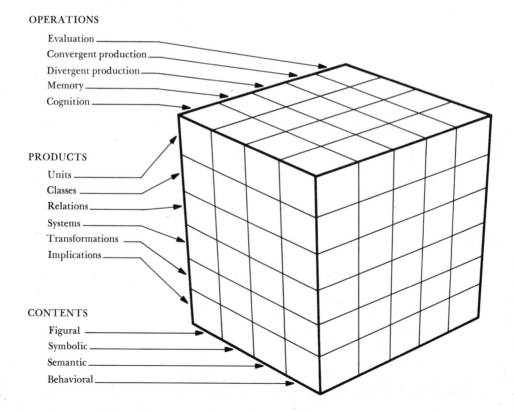

It is readily seen that the theory calls for $5 \times 4 \times 6$, or 120, cubical cells in the model, each one representing a unique ability, unique by virtue of its peculiar conjunction of operation, content, and product. The reader has already been introduced to three kinds of operation: cognition (discovery, recognition, comprehension), divergent production, and convergent production. The memory operation involves putting information into the memory store and must be distinguished from the memory store itself. The latter underlies all the operations; all the abilities depend upon it. This is the best logical basis for believing that the abilities increase with experience, depending upon the kinds of experience. The evaluation operation deals with assessment of information, cognized or produced, determining its goodness with respect to adopted (logical) criteria, such as identity and consistency.

The distinction between figural and semantic (conceptual) contents was mentioned earlier. The distinguishing of symbolic information from these two came later. Symbolic information is presented in tests in the form of letters or numbers, ordinarily, but other signs that have only "token" value or meaning can be used.

The category of behavioral information was added on the basis of a hunch; no abilities involving it were known to have been demonstrated when it was included. The basis was E. L. Thorndike's suggestion (1920) many years ago that there is a "social intelligence," distinct from what he called "concrete" and "abstract" intelligences. It was decided to distinguish "social intelligence" on the basis of kind of information, the kind that one person derives from observation of the behavior of another. Subsequent experience has demonstrated a full set of six behavioral-cognition abilities as predicted by the model, and a current analytical investigation is designed to test the part of the model that includes six behavioral-divergent-production abilities. In a test for cognition of behavioral systems, three parts of a four-part cartoon are given in each item, with four alternative parts that are potential completions. The examinee has to size up each situation, and the sequence of events, correctly in order to select the appropriate part. As a test for divergent production of behavioral systems, the examinee is given descriptions of three characters, for example, a jubilant man, an angry woman, and a sullen boy, for which he is to construct a number of alternative story plots involving the characters and their moods, all stories being different.

The reader has already encountered four kinds of products: units, classes, relations, and systems, with illustrations. The other two kinds of products are transformations and implications. Transformations include any kind of change: movement in space, rearrangement or regrouping of letters in words or factoring or simplifying an equation, redefining a concept or adapting an object or part of an object to a new use, revising one's interpretation of another person's action, or rearranging events in a story. In these examples the four kinds of content are involved, from figural to behavioral, illustrating the fact that all six kinds of products apply in every content category.

Implied information is suggested by other information. Foresight or prediction depends upon extrapolating from given information to some naturally following future condition or event. If I make this move in chess, my knight will be vulnerable. If I divide by X, I will have a simpler expression. If it rains tonight, my tent will leak. If I whistle at that girl, she will turn her head. The "If .'. . then" expression well describes an instance of implication, the implication actually being the thing implied.

Some Consequences of the Theory

The most immediate consequence of the theory and its model has been its heuristic value in suggesting where to look for still undemonstrated abilities. The modus operandi of the Aptitudes Research Project from the beginning has been to hypothesize certain kinds of abilities, to create new types of tests that should emphasize each hypothesized ability, then factor analyze to determine whether the hypothesis is well supported. With hypotheses generated by the model, the rate of demonstration of new abilities has been much accelerated.

At the time this article was written, of 24 hypothesized abilities in the category of cognition, 23 had been demonstrated. Of 24 expected memory abilities, 14 were recognized. In the other operation categories of divergent production, convergent production, and evaluation, 16, 13, and 13 abilities, respectively, were accounted for, and in all these categories 17 other hypotheses are under investigation. These studies should bring the number of demonstrated abilities close to the century mark. It is expected that the total will go beyond the 120 indicated by the model, for some cells in the figural and symbolic columns already have more than one ability each. These proliferations arise from the differences in kind of sensory input.

Most known abilities are represented by tests with visual input. A few have been found in tests with auditory input, and possibly one involving kinesthetic information. Each one can also be placed in the model in terms of its three sources of specification—operation, content, and product.

Having developed a comprehensive and systematic theory of intelligence, we have found that not the least of its benefits is an entirely new point of view in psychology generally, a view that has been called "operational-informational." I have elaborated a great deal upon this view elsewhere (Guilford, 1967). Information is defined for psychology as that which the organism discriminates. Without discrimination there is no information. This far, there is agreement with the conception of information as viewed by communication engineers, but beyond this point we part company. Psychological discriminations are most broadly and decisively along the lines of kinds of content and kinds of products, from which arise hiatuses between intellectual abilities. Further discriminations occur, of course, within the sphere of a single ability. I have proposed that the 4×6 intersections of the informational categories of the SI (structure of intellect) model provide a psychoepistemology, with 24 subcategories of basic information. I have also proposed that the six product categories—units, classes, relations, systems, transformations, and implications—provide the basis for a psycho-logic (Guilford, 1967, Ch. 10). Although most of these terms are also concepts in modern logic, a more complete representation appears in mathematics.

The operational-informational view regards the organism as a processor of information, for which the modern, high-speed computer is a good analogy. From this point of view, computer-simulation studies makes sense. In addition to trying to find out how the human mind works by having computers accomplish the same end results, however, it might be useful, also, to determine how the human mind accomplishes its ends, then to design the computer that performs the same operations. Although a psychology based upon the SI concepts is much more complicated than the stimulus-response model that became traditional, it is still parsimonious. It certainly has the chance of becoming more adequate. The structure of intellect, as such, is a taxonomic model; it provides fruitful concepts. For theory that accounts for behavior, we need operational models, and they can be based on SI concepts. For example, I have produced such a model for problem solving (Guilford, 1967, Ch. 14).

There is no one problem-solving ability. Many different SI abilities may be drawn upon in solving a problem, depending upon the nature of the problem. Almost always there are cognitive operations (in understanding the nature of the problem), productive operations (in generating steps toward solution), and evaluative operations (in checking upon both understanding and production). Memory operations enter in, to keep a record of information regarding previous steps, and the memory store underlies all.

There is something novel about producing solutions to problems, hence creative thinking is involved. Creative thinking depends most clearly upon divergent-production operations on the one hand, and on transformations on the other. Thus, these two categories have unique roles in creative problem solving. There is accordingly no one unique ability to account for creative potential. Creative production depends upon the area in which one works, whether it is in pictorial art, music, drama, mathematics, science, writing, or management. In view of the relative independence of the intellectual abilities, unevenness of status in the various abilities within the same person should be the rule rather than the exception. Some individuals can excel in more than one art form, but few excel in all, as witness the practice of having multiple creative contributors to a single motion picture.

The implications of all this for education are numerous. The doctrine that intelligence is a unitary something that is established for each person by heredity and that stays fixed through life should be summarily banished. There is abundant proof that greater intelligence is associated with increased education. One of education's major objectives should be to increase the stature of its recipients in intelligence, which should now mean stature in the various intellectual abilities. Knowing what those abilities are, we not only have more precise goals but also much better conceptions of how to achieve those goals.

For much too long, many educators have assumed, at least implicitly, that if we provide individuals with information they will also be able to use that information productively. Building up the memory store is a necessary condition for productive thinking, but it is not a sufficient condition, for productive abilities are relatively independent of cognitive abilities. There are some revealing findings on this point (Guilford and Hoepfner, 1966). In a sample of about 200 ninth-grade students, IQ measurements were available and also the scores on a large number of tests of various divergent-production (DP) abilities. Table 1 shows a scatter diagram with plots of DP scores

TABLE 1 *Scatterplot of Expressional Fluency (One Aspect of Divergent Production) Scores in Relation to CTMM (California Test of Mental Maturity) IQ.*

DP score	Intelligence quotient								
	60–69	70–79	80–89	90–99	100–109	110–119	120–129	130–139	140–149
50–59						1	3		1
40–49						2	4	1	
30–39			2	3	4	11	17	6	2
20–29			1	3	10	23	13	7	
10–19	1	5	3	9	11	19	7	3	1
0– 9	1	3	1	4	10	11	2		

as a function of IQ.[3] The striking feature of this diagram pertains to the large proportion of high-IQ students who had low, even some very low, DP scores. In general, IQ appears to set a kind of upper limit upon DP performance but not a lower limit. The same kind of result was true for most other DP tests.

On the basis of present information, it would be best to regard each intellectual ability of a person as a somewhat generalized skill that has developed through the circumstances of experience, within a certain culture, and that can be further developed by means of the right kind of exercise. There may be limits to abilities set by heredity, but it is probably safe to say that very rarely does an individual really test such limits. There is much experimental evidence, rough though it may be, that exercise devoted to certain skills involved in creative thinking is followed by increased capability (Guilford, 1967, p. 336). Although special exercises have their demonstrated value, it is probably better to have such exercises worked into teaching, whatever the subject, where there are opportunities. Informing individuals regarding the nature of their own intellectual resources, and how they enter into mental work, has also been found beneficial.

There is not space to mention many other problems related to intelligence—its growth and its decline, its relation to brain anatomy and brain functions, and its role in learning. All these problems take on new aspects, when viewed in terms of the proposed frame of reference. For too long, many investigators have been handicapped by using a single, highly ambiguous score to represent what is very complex but very comprehensible.

Without the multivariate approach of factor analysis, it is doubtful whether any comprehensive and detailed theory of the human intellect, such as the model in Figure 1, could have been achieved. Application of the method uncovers the building blocks, which are well obscured in the ongoing activities of daily life. Although much has already been done by other methods to show the relevance and fruitfulness of the concepts generated by the theory (Guilford, 1967), there is still a great amount of developmental work to be done to implement their full exploitation, particularly in education.

Summary

In this limited space I have attempted to convey information regarding progress in discovering the nature of human intelligence. By intensive factor-analytic investigation, mostly within the past twenty years, the multifactor picture of intelligence has grown far beyond the expectations of those who have been most concerned. A comprehensive, systematic theoretical model known as the "structure of intellect" has been developed to put rationality into the picture.

The model is a cubical affair, its three dimensions representing ways in which the abilities differ from one another. Represented are: five basic kinds of operation, four substantive kinds of information or "contents," and six formal kinds of information or "products," respectively. Each intellectual ability involves a unique conjunction of one kind of operation, one kind of content, and one kind of product, all abilities being relatively independent in a population, but with common joint involvement in intellectual activity.

This taxonomic model has led to the discovery of many abilities not suspected before. Although the number of abilities is large, the fifteen-category constructs provide much parsimony. They also provide a systematic basis for viewing mental operations in general, thus suggesting new general psychological theory.

---

[3] Expressional Fluency is the sentence-construction test illustrated earlier.

The implications for future intelligence testing and for education are numerous. Assessment of intellectual qualities should go much beyond present standard intelligence tests, which seriously neglect important abilities that contribute to problem solving and creative performance in general. Educational philosophy, curriculum building, teaching procedures, and examination methods should all be improved by giving attention to the structure of intellect as the basic frame of reference. There is much basis for expecting that various intellectual abilities can be improved in individuals, and the procedures needed for doing this should be clear.

REFERENCES

Burt, C. *British Journal of Educational Psychology,* 1949, **19**, 100, 176.

Guilford, J. P. *Psychological Bulletin,* 1956, **53**, 267.

Guilford, J. P. *American Psychologist,* 1959, **14**, 469.

Guilford, J. P. *The nature of human intelligence.* New York: McGraw-Hill, 1967.

Guilford, J. P., & Hoepfner, R. *Indian Journal of Psychology,* 1966, **41,** 7.

Guilford, J. P., & Lacey, J. I. (Eds.) *Printed classification tests.* Washington, D.C.: Government Printing Office, 1947.

Spearman C. *American Journal of Psychology,* 1904, **15**, 201.

Thorndike, E. L. *Harper's Magazine,* 1920, **140**, 227.

Thurstone, L. L. *Vectors of mind.* Chicago: University of Chicago Press, 1935.

Thurstone, L. L. Primary mental abilities. *Psychometric Monographs No. 1,* 1938.

Vernon, P. E. *The structure of human abilities.* New York: Wiley, 1950.

Zwicky, F. *Morphological analysis.* Berlin: Springer, 1957.

22

Intelligent Testing

Alexander G. Wesman

Two major theoretical positions concerning the nature of intelligence were presented by Horn and Guilford in the preceding articles. The author of this selection takes a different approach, somewhat more practical and less theoretical. He also presents a careful review of the purposes for which intelligence tests are used.

The nature of intelligence has been a favorite subject for contemplation and disputation for centuries—perhaps from the dawn of man as Homo sapiens. The topic is being studied and debated today by educators, sociologists, geneticists, neurophysiologists, and biochemists, and by psychologists specializing in various branches of the discipline. Despite this attention and effort, however—or perhaps *because* of it—there appears to be no more general agreement as to the nature of intelligence or the most valid means of measuring intelligence than was the case fifty years ago. Concepts of intelligence and the definitions constructed to enunciate these concepts abound by the dozens, if not indeed by the hundreds.

With so many diverse definitions of intelligence, it is perhaps not surprising that we cannot agree on how to measure intelligence. It is my conviction that much of the confusion which plagued us in the past, and continues to plague us today, is attributable to our ignoring two propositions which should be obvious:

1. Intelligence is an attribute, not an entity.
2. Intelligence is the summation of the learning experiences of the individual.

We have all too often behaved as though intelligence were a physical substance, like a house or an egg crate composed of rooms or cells; we might better remember that it is no more to be reified than attributes like beauty or speed or honesty. There are objects which are classifiable as beautiful; there are performances which may be characterized as speedy; there are behaviors which display honesty. Each of these is measurable, with greater or lesser objectivity. Because they can be measured, however, does not mean they are substances. We may agree with E. L. Thorndike that if something exists it can be measured; we need not accept the converse notion that if we can

From American Psychologist, *Vol. 23:4 (1968), 267–274. Copyright 1968 by the American Psychological Association, and reproduced by permission.*

measure something it has existence as a substance.

Intelligence as here defined is a summation of learning experiences. The instances in which intelligent behavior is observed may be classified in various ways that appear to be logical or homogeneous, but they are individual instances all the same. Each instance represents a response the organism has learned; each learned response in turn predisposes the organism for learning additional responses which permit the organism to display new acts of intelligent behavior.

For our present purposes, it matters little whether we are more comfortable with stimulus-response bonds, with experience-producing drives, with imprinting, or with neuropsychological explanations of *how* or *why* learning occurs; whatever the learning theory, the fundamental principle is universal. We start with an organism which is subject to modification by interaction with the environment; as a product of that interaction, the organism has been modified. Further interaction involves a changed organism—one which is ready to interact with its environment in a new way.

Organisms may differ from one another in their susceptibility to modification. One organism may need a more potent stimulus to trigger reaction to the environment than does another. A particular organism may respond to a given class of stimuli more readily than it does to other kinds of stimuli. Organisms may differ from one another in their readiness to respond to different classes of stimuli. There may be important differences in the ability of organisms to modify their behavior in effective ways as a result of experience.

We may develop and investigate hypotheses as to whether such differences in response as are displayed arise from variations in neurological endowment or in conducive environment. All that we can be sure of, at least as of now, is that what we are dealing with is a response-capable organism which has been exposed to environmental stimuli, has interacted in some way with those stimuli, and has been modified thereby.

The bits or modules which constitute intelligence may be information or may be skill; i.e., they may be content or process. Furthermore, they are multidimensional, and some modules may have more dimensions than do others. Each module is subject to essential change as the individual is exposed to further learning experiences. Each act of learning serves to create new modules, change the existing ones, or both. Modules are not independent; rather, they may overlap with several or many other modules; thus, they are complex both in their number of dimensions and in their interrelationships. Even early percepts are rarely if ever

simple. A toy ball when first seen has at least size, shape, and color; if it is touched, it has texture and hardness as well. Accordingly, few if any modules of learning are truly simple.

The whole of a person's intelligence at any given moment may well be thought of as an amorphous mass—not a regular geometric figure. Within this mass, modules may cluster with greater or lesser permanence, and may be organized along principles of relatedness. Thus, word knowledge may form a cluster—but the words of which one has knowledge will be components of other clusters as well. A pencil is an object one writes with; it has shape in common with other objects, it has function in common with pens and crayons, it produces color of varying intensity, it has a number property, it is usually associated with paper. The learned module "pencil" may thus be part of many clusters.

One need not posit that a learning module is permanent. It could, presumably, disappear entirely, although far more often we would expect it to undergo essential change by taking on a more complex character. This model does assume that higher learning depends so intimately and essentially on certain previous learnings that the more complex modules cannot exist without the antecedent modules from which they grew. For example, if the ability to subtract numbers should disappear, the ability to do long division could not remain unaffected. Thus, retention of learning is integral to the concept here proposed.

The simple-minded conceptualization outlined above may have horrified those of my colleagues who are even moderately sophisticated with respect to modern learning theories. To those colleagues I apologize, but I also beg their indulgence. Oversimplified as the conceptualization undoubtedly is, I believe it does no *essential* violence to any current theory; it has, I hope, the virtue of permitting a view of the organization of intelligence, and of the nature of the testing of intelligence, which may prove illuminating for several issues which confront us.

Issue I: The Classification of Ability Tests into Aptitude, Achievement, and Intelligence Measures

As soon as we have agreed that what we know and what we can do intellectually is learned, the artificiality of the above classification becomes self-evident. Historically, we have recognized that what achievement tests measure is what the examinee has learned. We have been less ready to accord similar recognition to intelligence tests. In their case, we have too often behaved as though what these tests measure is somehow independent of the learning phenomenon. We have played the role of Aladdin seeking a magical lamp, complete with a genie ready to spring forth with full power to accomplish all sorts of wondrous things. We have pondered wistfully on the number of critical issues that would be resolved if we could only somehow measure "intelligence" separately from "achievement."

We have been similarly unrealistic in treating the concept of "aptitude." Our textbooks enunciate the distinction that aptitude tests measure what the individual *can* learn, while achievement tests measure what he *has* learned. Some of our leading theorists aggravate the confusion by ignoring the implications of their special use of the term. "Aptitude" is typically used in laboratory learning experiments as a matching or otherwise controlling variable; it is employed to assure that groups to be compared start the experiment as equal in initial ability. One gets a strong impression that the aptitude instrument is perceived as measuring the innate potential of the individual as distinguished from what is to be achieved (i.e., learned) in the experimental process. If learning theorists recognize that what they are calling "aptitude" (or, for that matter, "intelligence") is "previously learned" (as, clearly, at least some of them do), the artificiality of the distinction between "aptitude" or "intelligence" and "achievement" should be eminently apparent.

I wish that at least a few of my psychometric colleagues would leave off searching for *the* structure of intelligence, and devote their wisdom and energy to learning more about the learning process, and to teaching learning theorists about testing. I am convinced that both specialties would profit immeasurably from the cooperative enterprise. It is my strong impression that the inattention of the psychometrician to the facts of learning is matched fully by the unsophisticated treatment accorded to testing by many learning theorists.

All ability tests—intelligence, aptitude, and achievement—measure what the individual *has* learned—and they often measure with similar content and similar process. Let us take, for example, an item[1] such as this: A square and a rectangle have the same perimeter. The square has an area of 10,000 square feet. The rectangle has an area of 9,324 square feet. What are the dimensions of the rectangle?

This item would clearly be deemed appropriate whether it appeared in an achievement test in high school mathematics, a test of aptitude for mathematics, or the numerical portion of an 'intelligence" test. I submit that a great many items can equally readily fit any of the three categories.

Such justification as we have for our labeling system resides entirely in the *purpose* for which the test is used, not in the test document itself. If our intent is to discover how much the examinee has learned in a particular area, such as a school course, we may select items which probe for the distinctive learnings the schooling was intended to stimulate. We label the test an "achievement" test. If our intent is to predict what success an individual is likely to attain in learning a new language, or a new job, we seek those specific previous learnings the possession of which bodes favorably for that future learning, and we label the test an "aptitude" test or a "special aptitude test." If our intent is to predict future acquisition of learning over broad areas of environmental exposure, we seek those previous learnings the possession of which will be relevant to as many, and as important, future learning situations as we can anticipate. This test we label an "intelligence" test. The selection of test items or sample tasks for the three purposes may or may not differ, but in each instance what is measured is what was previously learned. We are not measuring different abilities; we are merely attending to different criteria. It is the *relevance* of the learnings we select for investigation that largely determines how we name our test and whether we will succeed in our purpose.

Issue II: The Utility of Culture-Free and Culture-Fair Tests

The notion of relevance of previous learnings leads naturally to a consideration of some follies we have committed in the search for culture-free or culture-fair instruments. I do not wish to impugn the high social motives which stimulate the search for such devices; I do wish to question that such a search, in its usual setting, is sensible. A culture-free test would presumably probe learnings which had not been affected by environment; this is sheer nonsense. A culture-fair test attempts to select

---

[1] This item was proposed by G. K. Bennett in another context as an example of an arithmetic problem which might be correctly answered by any of several methods.

those learnings which are common to many cultures. In the search for experiences which are common to several different cultures or subcultures, the vital matter of relevance of the learning for our purpose is subordinated or ignored.

The implicit intent in the attempt to create culture-free or culture-fair tests is somehow to measure intelligence without permitting the effects of differential exposure to learning to influence scores. This contains the tacit assumption that "native intelligence" lies buried in pure form deep in the individual, and needs only to be uncovered by ingenious mining methods. If we recognize that intelligence comprises learning experiences, it becomes clear that our attempts are not ingenious, but ingenuous.

It is true that we can probe learnings that have occurred in nonverbal, nonnumerical domains. This means only that we can test selected aspects of intelligence. The question immediately arises of the relevance of these special domains to the kinds of learnings we will want to predict. The measurement purpose for which culture-fair tests are ordinarily developed is that of predicting academic or industrial performance. Most academic courses and most industrial jobs involve some use of verbal abilities. Since further learning is conditioned by relevant past learning, the individual who has developed more of the prerequisite ability inevitably has an advantage over the individual with less of the prerequisite ability. If we wish to predict whether an individual will profit appreciably from additional exposure to learning, our best predictor must be a measure which appraises what prerequisite learning he has acquired heretofore. Appropriate verbal abilities are more relevant to the largely verbal learning we usually wish to predict than other abilities are.

It has on occasion been suggested that tests be developed which sample the verbal skills or factual information which are peculiar to a given subculture. Such tests are proposed as a "fairer" measure of the "intelligence," or readiness to learn, of the members of that subculture. The response to this proposal is "readiness to learn *what?*" If our purpose is to distinguish members of that subculture from their peers with respect to how much of that special culture they have assimilated, such a test might well be useful. If, as is more likely the case, we wish to predict future learnings of the content of the more general culture (e.g., the so-called white, middle-class culture such as typifies what the majority of our schools are organized to transmit), tests designed for the subculture will be less relevant than those which sample from the general culture. This is not intended to imply that the members of the subculture *could* not learn what the schools as constituted are offering. It does emphasize that, at the moment at which we make our appraisal, what the individual has already learned from the general culture domain is the most significant information as to what he is then ready to learn. The less relevant the previous learnings we appraise, the more hazardous must be our predictions of future learnings.

As long as our educational system and our general culture are dependent on conventional verbal abilities, those who aspire to progress in that system and that culture will need to command those abilities. In a verbal society, verbal competence cannot sensibly be ignored.

Issue III: Is "Verbal Ability" Synonymous with "Intelligence"?

To say that we cannot afford to ignore learnings in relevant verbal areas when we are appraising "intelligence" does not imply that *only* the verbal domain is important. The development of tests of "general mental ability" which sample only the verbal domain implies that since verbal tests predict school criteria best, it is unnecessary to attend to other cognitive abilities the student has developed; in other words, that, in effect, "verbal ability" is synonymous with "intelligence." It would be most unfortunate if, consciously or unconsciously, we adopted this too narrow perspective.

That verbal tests are typically good predictors of grades in many academic courses is undeniable. *Why* this is the case warrants some thought. Is it because all, or even most, of what constitutes "intelligence" is represented by verbal ability? Certainly the chief symbol system of our society is verbal. Even when we deal with numerical, spatial, or figural problems we often transform them to verbal expressions. It is one thing, however, to recognize the involvement of verbal abilities in all kinds of learning experiences and quite another to grant them exclusive sovereignty over learning domains. Many domains require the possession of other abilities as well, but our appraisal methods are often inadequate to reveal that need. Because it is easier to employ verbal criteria, or more convenient—or because we have given insufficient thought to criterion validity—we predetermine the finding that verbal abilities dominate the scene.

A particularly revealing demonstration of this

phenomenon came to the attention of the authors of the Differential Aptitude Tests some years ago. Grades in an auto mechanics course were found to be better predicted by the Verbal Reasoning test of the DAT than by the Mechanical Reasoning test. We had the unusual good fortune of having access to further information about the course. We discovered that early in the course the teacher had been called from the room for almost a half-hour. In his absence, the students had disobeyed his instructions not to fool around with the automobile motors. To let the punishment fit the crime, he conducted the rest of the course almost entirely by lecturing, giving the students minimum opportunity for actually working with the engines. That grades in a course taught by lecture and evaluated by a written test should be best predicted by a verbal test is not too surprising!

An illustration such as the above should force us to stop and think. As we study tables replete with validity coefficients, how many of those coefficients represent similar instances? As we develop hypotheses as to the importance of particular aspects of intelligence, how well do we understand the *criteria* which gave rise to the coefficients on which our hypotheses are based? Would the use of more valid criteria in courses for which curricular goals transcend verbal skills, have produced similar data, or different? Would the admittedly broad pervasiveness of verbal skills seem quite so broad if more appropriate measures of learning were employed? If we remain complacent about criteria composed largely of behaviors from the verbal domain, we are unlikely to see the relevance of other abilities.

In his APA presidential address in 1964, Mc-Nemar paid flattering attention to the Differential Aptitude Tests; he quite accurately reported that the verbal tests were most frequently the best predictors of course grades. The data he cited certainly supported the point he was making: Verbal tests predict grades in many academic courses. What might well have been added was recognition that the nature of our educational criteria exaggerates the real importance of verbal skills. If (and it is hoped *when*) grades or other criterion statements become more content valid, the relevance of a number of other skills will be more demonstrable.

Industry has perforce learned this lesson. Few mechanical apprentices are selected solely, or even primarily, because they can describe a process, rather than perform it. The military has learned that the ability to diagnose a malfunctioning torpedo is poorly demonstrated by verbal exposition, but well demonstrated by a work sample requiring actual mechanical repairs. It is to be hoped that

education will increasingly become more realistic with respect to what *its* criteria *should* be.

Issue IV: The Growth and Decline of "Intelligence"

So preoccupied have we been with reifying intelligence as some mystical substance that we have too often neglected to take a common-sense look at what intelligence tests measure. We find ourselves distressed at our failure to predict with satisfactory accuracy the intelligence test scores of a teen-ager from his intelligence test scores as an infant. Why should this occasion surprise, let alone distress? If we look inside the tests, it should be obvious that the kinds of learnings we typically appraise at the earlier ages bear little resemblance, and may have little relevance, to the kinds of learnings we appraise later.

At the earlier age levels, we have typically tested for such characteristics as motor dexterity, perception, and similar features of physical development. When intellectual concepts become available for testing as baby grows to infant, to child, to teen-ager, we change the focus of our testing from the physical domains to the cognitive—we appraise knowledge, concept formation, and reasoning.

It is possible that future research will disclose that possession of certain physical abilities or tendencies is prerequisite to the development of concept formation, and that earlier possession of these characteristics will foretell the future intellectual development of the individual. Interesting and promising research now being conducted is directed toward this goal. It is my opinion that, because learning experiences vary so from one child to another, there is some practical limit beyond which we will be unable to predict, however penetrating our research. In any event, we would do well at this moment to recognize that since we are measuring in different ability domains at infant and school-age levels, we should not expect good prediction from one level to the other—and we should certainly not behave as though the data permitted confident prediction.

At the other end of the age spectrum we have, with similar lack of insight, proceeded to corollary errors. We have accepted the gloomy dictum that once we have passed the age of 18 or 25 or 35, we have passed our peak; from that age, our ability to learn declines. Our texts are peppered with charts showing that depressing downhill slide.

What is the basis for this widely accepted conclusion? The principal basis is that when we apply our conventional measures of intelligence to older people, we find that average scores decrease. We have implicitly accepted the idea that intelligence is defined by what is measured by these particular intelligence tests. If, however, we return to our previous formulation of intelligence as what we know in a wide variety of domains, and hence as a base for what we can learn at a given moment, our perspective changes. We then proceed to compare what the intelligence tests measure with the kinds of learning individuals have engaged in from age 30 or 40 on. The relevance of the tests, except perhaps as measures of retention, is seen as increasingly remote with each passing year. Most individuals have not failed to learn more with added years of life. Their learnings have occurred in areas (science, business, politics, psychology, psychometrics), often relatively specialized, which are not measured by conventional intelligence tests.

It is true that new learnings of adults occur in such a variety of endeavors that it would be virtually impossible to find a common core on which all could be examined. We should not, however, pretend we do not suffer this psychometric disability; we should not continue to use less relevant measures to support deceptive graphs and curves of the decline of "intelligence." We might better recognize the limitations of our measure, until such time as we can devise relevant measures of the significant learnings which do occur. For the present, we can conclude only that with each passing decade older people do less well on tests designed for younger adults.

Issue V: The Search for Purity

A discussion of the nature of intelligence, and of intelligent testing, should not ignore the topic of factor analysis. It is a method which has influenced test construction and test selection. It is a technique which has stimulated the promulgation of theories of the structure of intellect.

The history of psychometrics gives evidence that each new major technique has attained a heyday of popularity, during which unrealistic hopes led to unbridled use. In the 1920's and 1930's, Pearson product-moment coefficients held the stage; everybody seemed to be correlating everything with everything else with wild abandon. We appear, in more recent times, to have been engaging in factor analyses with almost equal frenzy. With so much activity going on, it is perhaps to be expected that

some studies, and some conclusions, would be characterized more by enthusiasm than by wisdom.

To criticize factor analysis as a procedure because individuals have misled themselves through its use would be very silly indeed. Among the benefits it has provided are the ability to summarize vast masses of data and to facilitate the organization of information in a way that inspires, and then leads to investigation of interesting and often fruitful research hypotheses. At the same time, we need not believe that the power of the tool assures the validity of the product. Some of the conclusions which have been drawn, some attitudes which have been adopted, and some theories which have occasionally been treated as though they were established fact might well be exposed to scrutiny.

There have been instances in which a test battery was chosen for practical use *because* it had its origins in a program of factorial research. Presumably, the rationale was that such a battery consists of relatively "pure" tests and would show near-zero intercorrelation among the tests; it would therefore be more efficient than a battery of similar measures not derived from factorial studies. If this rationale survived empirical study, it would still not of itself be adequate justification for selecting one set of tests rather than another. Efficiency is certainly desirable—but *validity* is *crucial*. How tests were constructed is interesting and even germane; how they *work* is the critical issue.

Let us return, however, to the rationale. Is the leap from "factorial origin" to "purity" defensible? The "pure" tests developed in psychometric laboratories often do correlate very little with one another. To some degree, at least, this low correlation is frequently ascribable to the unreliability of short, experimental tests, or to restriction in range of the various abilities of the subject, or both. For exploratory and research purposes, these conditions represent a reasonable situation. Practical test-use situations are something else again.

When batteries of reliable tests with factorial ancestry, and batteries testing in similar domains but not factor oriented, are given to the same students, the within-battery intercorrelation of scores is ordinarily of about the same order. For example, with one ninth-grade group of boys, the average inter-r among the Differential Aptitude Tests was .37; for the same group, the average inter-r of the Primary Mental Abilities Tests was .36. Similar results were obtained in a comparison of the DAT and the General Aptitude Test Battery scores for a twelfth-grade group. Thus, there was little evidence of greater "purity" in the factorially derived batteries than in the DAT, which were not so derived. (In the everyday world, it appears, "purity" is all too likely to be an illusion.) Accordingly, we would be well advised when choosing tests for practical use to concentrate on how they work, not on how they were built.

Let us now turn briefly to the role of factor analysis as a stimulator of hypotheses concerning the structure of intellect. Its influence has often seemed to be not so much mathematicodeductive as mathematico*seductive!* The power of the method as a way of manipulating great masses of data appears all too often to have led us astray. Even our more eminent protagonists of the technique have not always appeared immune. When expounding on the theory of factor analysis, experts almost invariably agree that factors are merely descriptive categories; they are not functional entities. But when engaged in interpreting the factors which have emerged from their studies, some analysts apparently succumb to the mystic charm of rotating axes and perceive entities which, they have told us, do not exist. The lure of the temptation to discover a psychological structure analogous to the periodic table of the elements is too powerful to resist. We then hear of "primary mental abilities" or are shown "the three faces of intellect." Though the authors of such creations have sometimes demonstrated in other writings that they well understand the difference between the reality of descriptive categories and the illusion of underlying entities, some of their disciples and many of their readers seem less clear in their perception.

If we accept the thesis that the modules or bits which constitute intelligence are themselves complex, a combination of such modules can hardly be expected to be simple or "pure." A six-year-old who assembles three alphabet blocks to spell out "cat" has employed, at a minimum, verbal and spatial skills; if he is aware that there are three blocks or letters, he has engaged in numerical perception as well. The ability to perform the task has required cognition, memory, convergent thinking, and evaluation. The product is figural, symbolic, and semantic. All this, and we have not yet taken into account such considerations as the motor-manipulative activity, the perception of color, the earlier learning experiences which enabled him to perform the task successfully, or the imagery which the concept "cat" induces in him. We, as analysts, may choose to attend to only a single aspect of the behavior—but the behavior itself remains multifaceted and complex. To assume that we can abstract from a host of such activities a pure and simple entity is to ignore the psychological meaning of intelligent behavior.

Let us continue to explore, by all means available to us (including factor analysis) the nature of man's abilities. Let us *not* assume that the results of research obtained under closely managed conditions in the laboratory will hold true as realities in day-to-day situations. Let us not unwittingly forget that the descriptive categories we adopt for convenience in communication do not have real existence as ultimate psychological entities.

Conclusion

To what view of a structure of intellect am I led by the ideas I have enunciated here? Essentially, I believe intelligence is *un*structured. I believe that it is differently comprised in every individual—the sum total of all the learning experiences he has uniquely had up to any moment in time. Such structure as we perceive is structure which we have imposed. We can so select samples of previous learnings to examine as to reveal a general factor, or group factors, or specifics. We can sample from domains that are relatively homogeneous and apply labels such as verbal, numerical, spatial; we can sample from a wider variety of learnings and apply labels such as "general mental ability" or, simply, "intelligence."

There are many bases on which we may choose which kinds of learnings we will sample. The most reasonable basis, I believe, is that of predictive purpose. Those previous learnings should be probed which are most relevant to the particular future learnings we wish to predict. In addition to criterion—or, more likely, *criteria*—relevance, the principles of band width and fidelity (as enunciated by Cronbach and Gleser) might well serve as guides. If we are interested in forecasting narrow-band criteria, selection of highly homogeneous, directly relevant behaviors is indicated. If we are interested in a wide range of criteria, we have at least two options: We may choose to select small samples from widely scattered domains—as in a Binet, a Wechsler, or a broader gauge instrument still to be devised—or examine more intensively with several narrower gauge tests, as in the Differential Aptitude Tests. The broader gauge instruments will offer economy but lesser fidelity for selected criteria. The narrower gauge instruments will be longer and more time consuming—but the possibility of more direct relevance to one or more particular criteria should permit higher fidelity.

The critical issue, then, is not which approach measures intelligence—each of them does, in its own fashion. No approach save sampling from every domain in which learnings have occurred—

an impossible task—fully measures intelligence. The question is rather which approach provides the most useful information for the various purposes we wish the test to serve. Recognition that what we are measuring is what the individual has learned, and composing our tests to appraise *relevant* previous learnings, will yield the most useful information. We, and those who utilize the results of our work—educators, personnel men, social planners— face problems for which intelligence test data are relevant, and sometimes crucial. We must remember, and we must teach, what our test scores really reflect. The measurement of intelligence is not, and has not been, a matter of concern only to psychology. It has always been, and continues to be, an influence on educational and social programs. If we are to avert uninformed pressures from government agencies, from school administrators, from the courts, and indeed from psychologist colleagues, we must understand and we must broadly communicate what these scores truly represent. Only then can we who build tests and they who use them properly claim that we are indeed engaged in intelligent testing.

23

Guidelines for Testing Minority Group Children

Martin Deutsch, Joshua A. Fishman, Leonard Kogan, Robert North, and Martin Whiteman

Imagine you have just arrived in a large American city from your former homeland in Europe. You are twelve years old and your parents wish to enroll you at the nearest school. However, since you have not gone through the same school system as the other youngsters your age, the principal decides to give you a battery of tests to determine your scholastic aptitude. Although you have always done well in school, your command of English is still fairly shaky and in several places you have trouble understanding what you are to do. Furthermore, the strangeness of the situation and your mother's anxiety that you do well make it difficult for you to concentrate. You do rather poorly on the test, and the principal decrees that you must be set back two years in order to compensate for your language deficiency. Did he make the right decision, or would you quickly catch up with your classmates if you were put in with students your own age?

This same kind of situation happens many thousands of times each year all over the country. Immigrants, Indians, and youngsters with widely varying cultural backgrounds are evaluated with tests that have been standardized on groups of white middle-class students. Some guidelines for sensible testing of such minority groups are given in this selection. A useful glossary of technical terms appears at the end of the article.

Introduction

American educators have long recognized that they can best guide the development of intellect and character of the children in their charge if they take the time to understand these children thoroughly and sympathetically. This is particularly true with respect to the socially and culturally disadvantaged child.

Educators must realize that they hold positions of considerable responsibility and power. If they apply their services and skills wisely they can help minority group children to overcome their early disadvantages, to live more constructively, and to contribute more fully to American society.

Educational and psychological tests may help in

From The Journal of Social Issues, *Supplement Vol. No. XX, No. 2, pp. 129–145. Reprinted with the permission of The Society for the Psychological Study of Social Issues and the author. Prepared by a Work Group of the Society for the Psychological Study of Social Issues (Division 9 of the American Psychological Association),* Martin Deutsch, Joshua A. Fishman, *Chairman,* Leonard Kogan, Robert North, *and* Martin Whiteman.

the attainment of these goals if they are used carefully and intelligently. Persons who have a genuine commitment to democratic processes and who have a deep respect for the individual, will certainly seek to use educational and psychological tests with minority group children in ways that will enable these children to attain the full promise that America holds out to all its children.

Educational and psychological tests are among the most widely used and most useful tools of teachers, educational supervisors, school administrators, guidance workers, and counselors. As is the case with many professional tools, however, special training and diagnostic sensitivity are required for the intelligent and responsible use of these instruments. That is why most colleges and universities offer courses in educational and psychological testing. It is also the reason for the growing number of books and brochures designed to acquaint educators and their associates with the principles and procedures of proper test selection, use, and interpretation.

Responsible educational authorities recognize that it is as unwise to put tests in the hands of untrained and unskilled personnel as it is to permit the automobile or any highly technical and powerful tool to be handled by individuals who are untrained in its use and unaware of the damage that it can cause if improperly used.

The necessity for caution is doubly merited when educational and psychological tests are administered to members of minority groups. Unfortunately, there is no single and readily available reference source to which test users can turn in order to become more fully acquainted with the requirements and cautions to be observed in such cases. The purpose of this committee's effort is to provide an introduction to the many considerations germane to selection, use, and interpretation of educational and psychological tests with minority group children, as well as to refer educators and their associates to other more technical discussions of various aspects of the same topic.

The term "minority group" as we are using it here is not primarily a quantitative designation. Rather it is a status designation referring to cultural or social disadvantage. Since many Negro, Indian, lower-class white, and immigrant children have not had most of the usual middle-class opportunities to grow up in home, neighborhood, and school environments that might enable them to utilize their ability and personality potentials fully, they are at a disadvantage in school, and in after-school and out-of-school situations as well. It is because of these disadvantages, reflecting environmental deprivations and experiential atypicalities,

that certain children may be referred to as minority group children.

The following discussion is based in part on some of the technical recommendations developed for various kinds of tests by committees of the American Psychological Association, the American Educational Research Association, and the National Council on Measurement in Education. Our contribution is directed toward specifying the particular considerations that must be kept in mind when professional educators and those who work with them use educational and psychological tests with minority group children.

Critical Issues in Testing Minority Groups

Standardized tests currently in use present three principal difficulties when they are used with disadvantaged minority groups: (1) they may not provide reliable differentiation in the range of the minority group's scores, (2) their predictive validity for minority groups may be quite different from that for the standardization and validation groups and, (3) the validity of their interpretation is strongly dependent upon an adequate understanding of the social and cultural background of the group in question.

I. Reliability of differentiation

In the literature of educational and psychological testing, relatively little attention has been given to the possible dependence of test reliability upon subcultural differences. It is considered essential for a test publisher to describe the reliability sample (the reference group upon which reliability statements are based) in terms of factors such as age, sex, and grade-level composition, and there is a growing tendency on the part of test publishers to report subgroup reliabilities. But to the best of our knowledge, none of the test manuals for the widely used tests give separate reliability data for specific minority groups. Institutions that use tests regularly and routinely for particular minority groups would do well to make their own reliability studies in order to determine whether the tests are reliable enough when used with these groups.

Reliability Affected by Spread of Scores

In addition to being dependent on test length and the specific procedure used for estimating reliability (e.g., split-half or retest), the reliability coefficient for a particular test is strongly affected by the spread of test scores in the group for which the reliability is established. In general, the greater the spread of scores in the reliability sample, the higher the reliability coefficient. Consequently, if the tester attempts to make differentiations within a group which is more homogeneous than the reference or norm group for which reliability is reported, the actual effectiveness of the test will tend to be lower than the reported reliability coefficient appears to promise. For many tests, there is abundant evidence that children from the lower socio-economic levels commonly associated with minority group status tend to have a smaller spread of scores than do children from middle-income families, and such restriction in the distribution of scores tends to lower reliability so far as differentiation of measurement with such groups is concerned.

Characteristics of Minority Group Children that Affect Test Performance

Most of the evidence relating to the contention that the majority of educational and psychological tests tend to be more unreliable, i.e., more characterized by what is technically called "error variance," for minority group children, is indirect, being based on studies of social class and socio-economic differences rather than on minority group performance per se. Nevertheless, the particular kinds of minority groups that we have in mind are closely associated with the lower levels of socio-economic status. . . .

For children who come from lower socio-economic levels, what characteristics may be expected to affect test performance in general, and the accuracy or precision of test results in particular? The list of reported characteristics is long, and it is not always consistent from one investigation to another. But at least it may be hypothesized that in contrast to the middle-class child the lower-class child will tend to be less verbal, more fearful of strangers, less self-confident, less motivated toward scholastic and academic achievement, less competitive in the intellectual realm, more "irritable," less conforming to middle-class norms of behavior and conduct, more apt to be bilingual, less exposed to intellectually stimulating materials in the home, less varied in recreational outlets, less knowledgeable about the world outside his immediate neighborhood, and more likely to attend inferior schools.

Some Examples

Can it be doubted that such characteristics—even if only some of them apply to each "de-prived" minority group—will indeed be reflected in test taking and test performance? Obviously, the primary effect will be shown in terms of test validity for such children. In many cases, however, the lowering of test validity may be indirectly a result of lowered test reliability. This would be particularly true if such characteristics interfere with the consistency of performance from test to retest for a single examiner, or for different examiners. Consider the following examples and probable results:

Example: A Negro child has had little contact with white adults other than as distant and punitive authority figures. *Probable Result:* Such a child might have difficulty in gaining rapport with a white examiner or reacting without emotional upset to his close presence. Even in an individual testing situation, he might not respond other than with monosyllables, failing to give adequate answers even when he knows them. The examiner, reacting in terms of his own stereotypes, might also lower the reliability and validity of the test results by assuming that the child's performance will naturally be inferior and by revealing this attitude to the child.

Example: Children from a particular minority group are given little reason to believe that doing well in the school situation will affect their chance for attaining better jobs and higher income later in life. *Probable Result:* Such children will see little purpose in schooling, dislike school, and will reject anything associated with school. In taking tests, their primary objective is to get through as rapidly as possible and escape from what for them might be an uncomfortable situation. Their test performance might, therefore, be characterized by a much greater amount of guessing, skipping, and random responses than is shown by the middle-class child who never doubts the importance of the test, wants to please his teacher and parents, and tries his best.

Special Norms Often Needed

When the national norms do not provide adequate differentiation at the lower end of the aptitude or ability scale, special norms, established locally, are often useful. For instance, if a substantial number of underprivileged or foreign-background pupils in a school or school district rank in the lowest 5 per cent on the national norms, local norms might serve to provide a special scale within this range. If the score distribution with the first few percentiles of the national norms is mainly a function of chance factors, however, a lower level of the test or an easier type of test is needed for accurate measurement of the low-scoring children.

Responsibilities of Test Users

The sensitive test user should be alert to reliability considerations in regard to the particular group involved and the intended use of the tests. In assessing reports on test reliability provided by test manuals and other sources, he will not be satisfied with high reliability coefficients alone. He will consider not only the size of the reliability samples, but also the nature and composition of the samples and the procedures used to estimate reliability. He will try to determine whether the standard error of measurement varies with score levels, and whether his testing conditions are similar to those of the reliability samples. He will ask whether the evidence on reliability is relevant to the persons and purposes with which he is concerned. He will know that high reliability does not guarantee validity of the measures for the purpose in hand, but he will realize that low reliability may destroy validity.

The examiner should be well aware that test results are characteristically influenced by cultural and subcultural differentials and that the performance of underprivileged minority group children is often handicapped by what should be test-extraneous preconditions and response patterns. He should not necessarily assume that the child from a minority group family will be as test-sophisticated and motivated to do his best as are the majority of environment-rich middle-class children.

If the examiner finds—and this will be typical—that the reliability sample does not provide him with information about the reliability of the test for the kind of children he is testing, he should urge that the test results not be taken at face value in connection with critical decisions concerning the children. Very often, careful examination of responses to individual test items will indicate to him that the apparent performance of the child is not adequately reflecting the child's actual competence or personality because of certain subcultural group factors.

II. Predictive validity

Of course, if an individual's test scores were to be used only to describe his relative standing with respect to a specified norm group, the fact that the individual had a minority group background would not be important. It is when an explanation of his standing is attempted, or when long-range predictions enter the picture (as they usually do), that background factors become important.

For example, no inequity is necessarily involved if a culturally disadvantaged child is simply reported to have an IQ of 84 and a percentile rank of 16 on the national norms for a certain intelligence test. However, if this is interpreted as meaning that the child ranks or will rank no higher in learning ability than does a middle-class, native-born American child of the same IQ, the interpretation might well be erroneous.

Factors Impairing Test Validity

Three kinds of factors may impair a test's predictive validity. First, there are test-related factors—factors or conditions that affect the test scores but which may have relatively little relation to the criterion. Such factors may include test-taking skills, anxiety, motivation, speed, understanding of test instructions, degree of item or format novelty, examiner-examinee rapport, and other general or specific abilities that underlie test performance but which are irrelevant to the criterion. Examples of the operation of such factors are found in the literature describing the problems of white examiners testing Negro children, of American Indian children taking unfamiliar, timed tests, and of children of certain disadvantaged groups being exposed for the first time to test-taking procedures.

It should be noted that some test-related factors may not be prejudicial to disadvantaged groups. For example, test-taking anxiety of a disruptive nature may be more prevalent in some middle-class groups than in lower-class groups. In general, however, the bias attributable to test-related factors accrues to the detriment of the culturally disadvantaged groups.

The problem of making valid predictions for minority group children is faced by the Boys' Club of New York in its Educational Program,[1] which is designed to give promising boys from tenement districts opportunities to overcome their environmental handicaps through scholarships to outstanding schools and colleges. Although the majority of the boys currently enrolled in this program had mediocre aptitude and achievement test scores up to the time they were given scholarships, practically all of the boys have achieved creditable academic success at challenging secondary boarding schools and colleges. In this program, normative scores on the Otis Quick-Scoring Mental Ability

[1] Information about this program is obtainable from The Boys' Club of New York, 287 East 10th Street, New York, N.Y.

Test and the Stanford Achievement Test are used for screening purposes, but they are regarded as minimal estimates of the boys' abilities. The Wechsler Intelligence Scale for Children (WISC) is frequently used in this program to supplement the group tests. The boys typically score 5 to 10 points higher on the WISC than on the Otis, probably because the WISC gives less weight to educational and language factors.

Interest and Personality Inventory Scores

When standardized interest inventories are used, special caution should be observed in making normative interpretations of the scores of culturally disadvantaged individuals. When a child has not had opportunities to gain satisfaction or rewards from certain pursuits, he is not likely to show interest in these areas. For example, adolescent children in a particular slum neighborhood might rank consistently low in scientific, literary, musical, and artistic interests on the Kuder Preference Record if their home and school environments fail to stimulate them in these areas. With improved cultural opportunities, these children might rapidly develop interests in vocations or avocations related to these areas.

Scores on personality inventories may also have very different significance for minority group members than for the population in general. Whenever the inventory items tap areas such as home or social adjustment, motivation, religious beliefs, or social customs, the appropriateness of the national norms for minority groups should be questioned. Local norms for the various minority groups involved might again be very much in order here.

Predicting Complex Criteria

A second class of factors contributing to low predictive validity is associated with the complexity of criteria. Criteria generally represent "real life" indices of adjustment or achievement and therefore they commonly sample more complex and more variegated behaviors than do the tests. An obvious example is the criterion of school grades. Grades are likely to reflect motivation, classroom behavior, personal appearance, and study habits, as well as intelligence and achievement. Even if a test measured scholastic aptitude sensitively and accurately, its validity for predicting school marks would be attenuated because of the contribution of many other factors to the criterion. It is important, therefore, to recognize the influence of other factors, not measured by the tests, which may contribute to criterion success. Since

disadvantaged groups tend to fare poorly on ability and achievement tests, there is particular merit in exploring the background, personality, and motivation of members of such groups for compensatory factors, untapped by the tests, which may be related to criterion performance.

In some instances, such as in making scholarship awards on a statewide or national basis, test scores are used rigidly for screening or cut-off purposes to satisfy demands for objectivity and "impartiality." The culturally disadvantaged child (quite possibly a "diamond-in-the-rough") is often the victim of this automatic and autocratic system. Recourse lies in providing opportunities where the hurdles are less standardized and where a more individualized evaluation of his qualifications for meeting the criterion may prove to be fairer for him.

For example, the following characteristics that may be typical of minority group children who have above-average ability or talent are among those cited by DeHaan and Kough (1956), who have been working with the North Central Association Project on Guidance and Motivation of Superior and Talented Secondary School Students.

> *They learn rapidly, but not necessarily those lessons assigned in school.*
> *They reason soundly, think clearly, recognize relationships, comprehend meanings, and may or may not come to conclusions expected by the teacher.*
> *They are able to influence others to work toward desirable or undesirable goals.*

Effects of Intervening Events on Predictions

A third set of contributors to low criterion validity is related to the nature of intervening events and contingencies. This class of conditions is particularly important when the criterion measure is obtained considerably later than the testing—when predictive rather than concurrent validity is at stake. If the time interval between the test administration and the criterial assessment is lengthy, a host of situational, motivational, and maturational changes may occur in the interim. An illness, an inspiring teacher, a shift in aspiration level or in direction of interest, remedial training, an economic misfortune, an emotional crisis, a growth spurt or retrogression in the abilities sampled by the test—any of these changes intervening between the testing and the point or points of criterion assessment may decrease the predictive power of the test.

One of the more consistent findings in research with disadvantaged children is the decline in academic aptitude and achievement test scores of such children with time. The decline is, of course, in relation to the performance of advantaged groups or of the general population. It is plausible to assume that this decline represents the cumulative effects of diminished opportunities and decreasing motivation for acquiring academic knowledge and skills. When such cumulative effects are not taken into consideration, the predictive power of academic aptitude and achievement tests is impaired. If it were known in advance that certain individuals or groups would be exposed to deleterious environmental conditions, and if allowances could be made for such contingencies in connection with predictions, the test's criterion validity could be improved.

Looking in another direction, the normative interpretation of the test results cannot reveal how much the status of underprivileged individuals might be changed if their environmental opportunities and incentives for learning and acquiring skills were to be improved significantly. In the case of the Boys' Club boys mentioned above, estimates of academic growth potential are made on the basis of knowledge of the educational and cultural limitations of the boys' home and neighborhood environment, observational appraisals of the boys' behavior in club activities, and knowledge of the enhanced educational and motivational opportunities that can be offered to the boys in selected college preparatory schools. With this information available, the normative interpretation of the boys' scores on standardized tests can be tempered with experienced judgment, and better estimates of the boys' academic potential can thus be made.

In situations where minority group members are likely to have to continue competing with others under much the same cultural handicaps that they have faced in the past, normative interpretation of their aptitude and achievement test scores will probably yield a fairly dependable basis for short-term predictive purposes. When special guidance or training is offered to help such individuals overcome their handicaps, however, achievement beyond the normative expectancies may well be obtained, and predictions should be based on expectancies derived specifically from the local situation. In this connection, it should be recognized that attempts to appraise human "potential" without defining the milieu in which it will be given an opportunity to materialize are as futile as attempts to specify the horsepower of an engine without knowing how it will be energized.

"Culture Fair" and "Unfair"
—in the Test and in Society

The fact that a test differentiates between culturally disadvantaged and advantaged groups does not necessarily mean that the test is invalid. "Culturally unfair" tests may be valid predictors of culturally unfair but nevertheless highly important criteria. Educational attainment, to the degree that it reflects social inequities rather than intrinsic merit, might be considered culturally unfair. However, a test must share this bias to qualify as a valid predictor. Making a test culture-fair may decrease its bias, but may also eliminate its criterion validity. The remedy may lie in the elimination of unequal learning opportunities, which may remove the bias in the criterion as well as in the test. This becomes more a matter of social policy and amelioration rather than a psychometric problem, however.

The situation is quite different for a test that differentiates between disadvantaged and advantaged groups even *more* sharply than does the criterion. The extreme case would be a test that discriminated between disadvantaged and advantaged groups but did not have any validity for the desired criterion. An example of this would be an academic aptitude test that called for the identification of objects, where this task would be particularly difficult for disadvantaged children but would not be a valid predictor of academic achievement. Here, one could justifiably speak of a true "test bias." The test would be spuriously responsive to factors associated with cultural disadvantage but unrelated to the criterion. Such a test would not only be useless for predicting academic achievement, but would be stigmatizing as well.

While certain aptitude and ability tests may have excellent criterion validity for some purposes, even the best of them are unlikely to reflect the true *capacity for development* of underprivileged children. For, to the extent that these tests measure factors that are related to academic success, they must tap abilities that have been molded by the cultural setting. Furthermore, the test content, the mode of communication involved in responding to test items, and the motivation needed for making the responses are intrinsically dependent upon the cultural context.

Elixir of "Culture-Fair" Tests

The elixir of the "culture-fair" or "culture-free" test has been pursued through attempts to minimize the educational loading of test content and to reduce the premium on speed of response. However, these efforts have usually resulted in tests that have low validities for academic prediction purposes and little power to uncover hidden potentialities of children who do poorly on the common run of academic aptitude and achievement tests.

In spite of their typical cultural bias, standardized tests should not be sold short as a means for making objective assessments of the traits of minority group children. Many bright, nonconforming pupils, with backgrounds different from those of their teachers, make favorable showings on achievement tests, in contrast to their low classroom marks. These are very often children whose cultural handicaps are most evident in their overt social and interpersonal behavior. Without the intervention of standardized tests, many such children would be stigmatized by the adverse subjective ratings of teachers who tend to reward conformist behavior of middle-class character.

III. The validity of test interpretation

The most important consideration of all is one that applies to the use of tests in general—namely, that test results should be interpreted by competently trained and knowledgeable persons wherever important issues or decisions are at stake. Here, an analogy may be drawn from medical case history information that is entered on a child's record. Certain features of this record, such as the contagious-disease history, constitute factual data that are easily understood by school staff members who have not had medical training. But other aspects of the medical record, as well as the constellation of factors that contribute to the child's general state of health, are not readily interpretable by persons outside the medical profession. Consequently, the judgment of a doctor is customarily sought when an overall evaluation of the child's physical condition is needed for important diagnostic or predictive purposes. So, too, the psychological and educational test records of children should be interpreted by competently trained professional personnel when the test results are to be used as a basis for decisions that are likely to have a major influence on the child's future.

There are several sources of error in test interpretation stemming from a lack of recognition of the special features of culturally disadvantaged groups. One of these may be called the "deviation error." By this is meant the tendency to infer maladjustment or personality difficulty from responses which are deviant from the viewpoint of a majority culture, but which may be typical of a minority group. The results of a test might accurately reflect a child's performance or quality of ideation, but still the results should be interpreted in the light of the child's particular circumstance in life and the range of his experiences. For example, a minister's son whose test responses indicate that he sees all women as prostitutes and a prostitute's son whose test responses give the same indication may both be accurately characterized in one sense by the test. The two boys may or may not be equally disturbed, however. Clinically, a safer inference might be that the minister's son is the one who is more likely to be seriously disturbed by fantasies involving sex and women.

There is evidence to indicate that members of a tribe that has experienced periodic famines would be likely to give an inordinate number of food responses on the Rorschach. So too might dieting Palm Beach matrons, but their underlying anxiety patterns would be quite different than those of the tribesmen. Or, to take still another example, the verbalized self-concept of the son of an unemployed immigrant might have to be interpreted very differently from that of a similar verbalization of a boy from a comfortable, middle-class, native-American home.

A performance IQ that is high in relation to the individual's verbal IQ on the Wechsler scales *may* signify psychopathic tendencies but it also may signify a poverty of educational experience. Perceiving drunken males beating up women on the Thematic Apperception Test may imply a projection of idiosyncratic fantasy or wish, but it may also imply a background of rather realistic observation and experience common to some minority group children.

For children in certain situations, test responses indicating a low degree of motivation or an oversubmissive self-image are realistic reflections of their life conditions. If these children were to give responses more typical of the general population, they might well be regarded as sub-group deviants. In short, whether test responses reflect secondary defenses against anxiety or are the direct result of a socialization process has profound diagnostic import so that knowledge of the social and cultural background of the individual becomes quite significant.

What Does the Test Really Measure

A second type of error, from the viewpoint of construct and content validity, might be called the "simple determinant error." The error consists in thinking of the test content as reflecting some absolute or pure trait, process, factor, or construct, irrespective of the conditions of measurement or of the population being studied. Thus, a fifth-grade achievement test may measure arithmetical knowledge in a middle-class neighborhood where most children are reading up to grade level, but the same test, with the same content, may be strongly affected by a reading comprehension factor in a lower-class school and therefore may be measuring something quite different than what appears to be indicated by the test scores.

Generally, the test-taking motivation present in a middle-class group allows the responses to test content to reflect the differences in intelligence, achievement, or whatever the test is designed to measure. On the other hand in a population where test success has much less reward-value and where degree of test-taking effort is much more variable from individual to individual, the test content may tap motivation as well as the trait purportedly being measured.

Caution and knowledge are necessary for understanding and taking into account testing conditions and test-taking behavior when test results are being interpreted for children from varying backgrounds. A child coming from a particular cultural subgroup might have very little motivation to do well in most test situations, but under certain conditions or with special kinds of materials he might have a relatively high level of motivation. As a result, considerable variability might be evident in his test scores from one situation to another, and his scores might be difficult to reconcile and interpret.

How a question is asked is undoubtedly another important factor to consider in interpreting test results. A child might be able to recognize an object, but not be able to name it. Or, he might be able to identify a geometric figure, but not be able to reproduce it. Thus, different results might be obtained in a test depending upon whether the child is asked to point to the triangle in a set of geometric figures or whether he is required to draw a triangle.

Response Sets May Affect Test Results

In attitude or personality questionnaires, response sets such as the tendency to agree indiscriminately with items, or to give socially desirable responses, may contribute error variance from the viewpoint of the content or behavior it is desired to sample. To the extent that such sets discriminate between socially advantaged and disadvantaged groups, the target content area may be confounded by specific test format. Thus, a scale of authoritarianism may be found to differentiate among social classes, but if the scale is so keyed that a high score on authoritarianism is obtained from agreement with items, the social class differences may be more reflective of an agreement set rather than an authoritarian tendency. If authoritarian content is logically distinct from agreement content, these two sources of test variance should be kept distinct either through statistical control, by a change in the item format, or by having more than one approach to measurement of the trait in question.

From the standpoint of content validity, there is a third type of error. This may be termed the "incompleteness of content coverage" error. This refers to a circumscribed sampling of the content areas in a particular domain. In the area of intelligence, for instance, Guilford has identified many factors besides the "primary mental abilities" of Thurstone and certainly more than is implied in the unitary concept of intelligence reflected by a single IQ score. Differences in intellectual functioning among various groups cannot be clearly defined or understood until all components of a particular content area have been systematically measured.

Familiarity with the cultural and social background of minority group children not only helps to avoid under-evaluating the test performance of some children, but also helps to prevent over-evaluating the performance of others. For example, children who have been trained in certain religious observances involving particular vocabularies and objects, or those who have been encouraged to develop particular skills because of their cultural orientations, might conceivably score "spuriously" high on some tests or on particular items. In other words, any special overlap between the subgroup value-system of the child and the performances tapped by the test is likely to be an important determinant of the outcome of the test.

Failure Barriers May Be Encountered

Failure-inducing barriers are often set up for the minority group child in a testing situation by requiring him to solve problems with unfamiliar tools, or by asking him to use tools in a manner that is too advanced for him. To draw an analogy, if a medical student were handed a scalpel to lance a wound, and if the student were to do the lancing properly but were to fail to sterilize the instrument first, how should he be scored for his accomplishment? If he had never heard of sterilization, should his skillful performance with the instrument nevertheless be given a "zero" score? Similarly, if a child from a disadvantaged social group shows a considerable degree of verbal facility in oral communication with his peers but does very poorly on tests that stress academic vocabulary, can he justifiably be ranked low in verbal aptitude?

In a broad sense, most intelligence test items tap abilities involving language and symbol systems, although opportunities for developing these abilities vary considerably from one social group to another. One might reasonably expect that a child living in a community that minimizes language skills—or a community that uses a language form that is highly concrete—will earn a score that has a meaning very different from that of the score of a child in a community where language skills are highly developed and replete with abstract symbolism. It is important, therefore, to interpret test results in relation to the range of situations and behaviors found in the environments of specific minority groups.

Some Suggested Remedies

While this analysis of the problems involved in the use and interpretation of tests for minority group children may lead to considerable uneasiness and skepticism about the value of the results for such children, it also points up potential ways of improving the situation. For example, one of these ways might consist of measuring separate skills first, gradually building up to more and more complex items and tests which require the exercise of more than one basic skill at a time. With enough effort and ingenuity, a sizable universe of items might be developed by this procedure. Special attention should also be given to the selection or development of items and tests that maximize critical differentiations and minimize irrelevant discriminations. If a test is likely to be biased against certain types of minority groups, or if its validity for minority groups has not been ascertained, a distinct caveat to that effect should appear in the manual for the test.

Furthermore, we should depart from too narrow a conception of the purpose and function of testing. We should reemphasize the concept of the test as an integral component of teaching and training whereby a floor of communication and understanding is established and *learning* capabilities are measured in repeated and cyclical fashion.

Finally, we should think in terms of making more use of everyday behavior as evidence of the coping abilities and competence of children who do not come from the cultural mainstream. Conventional tests may be fair predictors of academic success in a narrow sense, but when children are being selected for special aid programs or when academic prediction is not the primary concern, other kinds of behavioral evidence are commonly needed to modulate the results and implications of standardized tests.

Conclusion

Tests are among the most important evaluative and prognostic tools that educators have at their disposal. How unfortunate, then, that these tools are often used so routinely and mechanically that some educators have stopped *thinking* about their limitations and their benefits. Since the minority group child is so often handicapped in many ways his test scores may have meanings different from those of nonminority children, even when they are numerically the same. The task of the conscientious educator is to ponder what lies behind the test scores. Rather than accepting test scores as indicating fixed levels of either performance or potential, educators should plan remedial activities which will free the child from as many of his handicaps as possible. Good schools will employ well-qualified persons to use good tests as one means of accomplishing this task.

In testing the minority group child it is sometimes appropriate to compare his performance with that of advantaged children to determine the magnitude of the deprivation to be overcome. At other times it is appropriate to compare his test performance with that of other disadvantaged children—to determine his relative deprivation in comparison with others who have also been denied good homes, good neighbors, good diets, good schools, and good teachers. In most instances it is especially appropriate to compare the child's test performance with his previous test performance. Utilizing the individual child as his own control and using the test norms principally as "bench marks," we are best able to gauge the success of our efforts to move the minority group child forward on the long, hard road of overcoming the deficiencies which have been forced upon him. Many comparisons depend upon tests, but they also depend upon *our* intelligence, our good will, and our sense of responsibility to make the proper comparison at the proper time and to undertake proper remedial and compensatory action as a result. The misuse of tests with minority group children, or in any situation, is a serious breach of professional ethics. Their proper use is a sign of professional and personal maturity.

REFERENCE

DeHaan, R., & Kough, J. *Teacher's guidance hand-book: Identifying students with special needs* (Vol. I, Secondary School Edition). Chicago: Science Research Associates, 1956.

GLOSSARY

Criterion. A standard that provides a basis for evaluating the validity of a test.

Cultural bias. Propensity of a test to reflect favorable or unfavorable effects of certain types of cultural backgrounds.

Culture-fair test. A test yielding results that are not culturally biased.

Culture-free test. A test yielding results that are not

influenced in any way by cultural background factors.

Error variance. The portion of the variance of test scores that is related to the unreliability of the test.

Educational loading. Weighing of a test's content with factors specifically related to formal education.

Norms. Statistics that depict the test performance of specific groups. Grade, age, and percentile are the most common type of norms.

Normative scores. Scores derived from the test's norms.

Reliability. The degree of consistency, stability, or dependability of measurement afforded by a test.

Reliability coefficient. A correlation statistic reflecting a test's consistency or stability of measurement.

Standard deviation. A statistic used to depict the dispersion of a group of scores.

Standard error of measurement. An estimate of the standard deviation of a person's scores that would result from repeated testing with the same or a similar test, ruling out the effects of practice, learning, or fatigue.

Validity. The extent to which a test measures the trait for which it is designed, or for which it is being used, rather than some other trait.

24

A New Look at the Creativity-Intelligence Distinction

Michael A. Wallach and Nathan Kogan

Of all the many characteristics that people would choose to possess if they could—beauty, strength, poise, wealth, etc.—the one that would probably be most frequently chosen by educated persons is *creativity*. If it is possible to achieve some sort of immortality, it seems that the surest route is to create something of beauty or value. To those persons who create, the world will come a-worshipping—or at least this very often seems to be the case.

If creativity is so highly desirable, why haven't we studied it and understood it? Why aren't prospective college students required to take creativity tests or to otherwise demonstrate that they possess an adequate amount of this important quality? One reason seems to be that many people believe that creativity doesn't exist—that what we are really talking about is intelligence, or at least some subfactor of intelligence. Thus, the major thrust of effort has been directed at the topic of intelligence. This article suggests a different approach to determining the nature of creativity.

For several years we have been concerned with two modes of thinking in young children, which, it turns out, bear directly upon what has assumed the proportions of a controversy in recent psychological history. The nature of the controversy might be put somewhat as follows: Is there an aspect of cognitive functioning which can be appropriately labeled "creativity" that stands apart from the traditional concept of general intelligence? A close appraisal of the quantitative findings available on this subject led us to a pessimistic answer. We shall pass some of these findings

Adapted and reprinted from Chapter Eight from Modes of Thinking in Young Children: A Study of the Creativity-Intelligence Distinction, *by Michael A. Wallach and Nathan Kogan. Copyright © 1965 by Holt, Rinehart and Winston, Inc. Adapted and reprinted by permission of Holt, Rinehart and Winston, Inc.*

quickly in review. Our examination of this literature opened up to us, however, the possibility of a valid distinction between creativity and intelligence that had not, in our view, been sufficiently pursued and developed. The next step, therefore, was empirical research in terms of this distinction. Finally, if creativity and intelligence could be validly distinguished, we were interested in studying the possible psychological correlates that might distinguish individual differences on these two dimensions considered jointly. Specifically, we were concerned with correlates in such areas as the child's observed behavior in school and play settings, his aesthetic sensitivities, his categorizing and conceptualizing activities, and his test anxiety and defensiveness levels. We can, of course, give but an overview of this work.

We began with a simple question: Does the relevant psychological literature support the assumption of a unified dimension of individual differences describing more and less creative cognitive behavior? To put this question another way, can one demonstrate the existence of greater and lesser degrees of a cognitive capability that is like intelligence in regard to being a pervasive, broad dimension, but yet is independent of intelligence and which can appropriately be labeled "creativity"? It is clear that to talk of "creativity" is to imply a referent different from that of the general intelligence concept. If that is not intended, then the creativity label becomes quite superfluous. The typical evidence that we found on this issue led, however, to an opposite conclusion. Let us consider an example.

The volume by Getzels and Jackson (1962), *Creativity and Intelligence,* is perhaps the best known of recent efforts in the field. Five alleged tests of creativity were administered to large samples of students ranging in class from sixth grade through the end of high school. Four of the five creativity tests correlated significantly with IQ for the girls, and all five of these tests correlated significantly with IQ for the boys. Consider next the relationships among the instruments in the creativity battery—that is, the question of whether they define a unitary dimension of individual differences. The Getzels-Jackson results showed that the five creativity tasks are virtually no more strongly related among themselves than they are related with intelligence. . . . There is no evidence, in short, for arguing that the creativity instruments are any more strongly related to one another than they are related to general intelligence. The inevitable conclusion is that little warrant exists here for talking about creativity *and*

intelligence as if these terms refer to concepts at the same level of abstraction. The creativity indicators measure nothing in common that is distinct from general intelligence. Inspection of the creativity battery reveals a quite varied range of materials, including measures of the ability to devise mathematical problems, to compose endings for fables, to detect embedded geometric figures, to think up word definitions, and to imagine uses for an object.

Comparable examination of other research reports in the literature forced us to the same kind of conclusion. Our survey included the study of findings reported by [many investigators]. . . . Again and again, in reviewing the research in this area the evidence led to the conclusion that the various creativity measures utilized are almost as strongly, equally strongly, or even more strongly related to general intelligence than they are related to each other. The evidence in hand thus seemed not to permit the very type of conceptualization that Getzels and Jackson (1962) and other researchers were proposing: namely, that there exists a pervasive dimension of individual differences, appropriately labeled "creativity," that is quite distinct from general intelligence. We should note that this same critical point has been made by Thorndike in a recent article.

Appropriate wielding of Occam's razor at this juncture thus dictated the tough-minded conclusion that little of any generality was being measured here beyond differences in the traditional notion of intelligence. Let us pose two issues, however, that made it seem premature to let the matter go at that. First, a potpourri of abilities was being assessed in the good name of "creativity"; second, all of the work that we had seen failed to consider the implications of the social psychology of the assessment situation within which measurement of "creativity" was attempted. Consider each of these points in turn.

If we return to the introspections of highly creative artists and scientists, one major focus emerges. The majority of the available introspective accounts have in common a concern with associative freedom and uniqueness. These accounts consistently stress the ability to give birth to associative content that is abundant and original, yet relevant to the task at hand rather than bizarre. The writer's classical fear of "drying up" and never being able to produce another word, the composer's worry over not having another piece of music within him, the scientist's concern that he won't be able to think of another experiment to perform—these are but indications of how preoccupied creative individuals can become with the question of associative flow. Introspections about times of creative insight also seem to reflect a kind of task-centered, permissive, or playful set on the part of the person doing the associating. Einstein refers to "associative play" or "combinatory play." The person stands aside a bit as associative material is given freedom to reach the surface.

We would propose that the essentials of the creative process may be contained in the two elements just considered: first, the production of associative content that is abundant and that is unique; second, the presence in the associator of a playful, permissive task attitude. Given a task clear enough that bizarre associative products do not readily occur, and given a permissive context within which the person works, two variables should permit us to index individual differences in creativity: the number of associations that the person can generate in response to given tasks, and the relative uniqueness of the associations that he produces.

One implication of this view is that productivity and uniqueness of associates should be related variables. Defining uniqueness as a relative infrequency of a given associative response to the task at hand for a sample of Ss, we would then expect stereotyped associates to come earlier and unique associates to come later in a sequence of responses. Such an expectation would also be consistent with recent work by Mednick. If unique associates tend to come later in time, then it becomes clear also that an appropriate assessment context will require freedom from the pressure of short time limits, and perhaps freedom from any temporal pressure at all. The postulated need for a permissive, playful attitude also implies the desirability of freedom from time pressure. Such temporal freedom is one aspect of what a permissive situation would involve. Permissiveness further connotes a relative lessening of evaluational pressures—that is, a focus upon the task rather than upon the self, a relaxed entertaining of the possible rather than tense insistence upon an answer that must be correct if one is not to lose face. The Taoists have called such a relaxed attitude a state of "letting things happen." Clearly, we are describing a type of situation in which the individual does not feel that he is being tested, and hence does not feel that what he does will have a bearing upon his self-worth in the eyes of others.

The foregoing analysis of creativity hence suggests a concentration of assessment attempts in the area of associational processes, in contrast to the quite heterogeneous types of tasks that have received the "creativity" label in studies of the kind touched upon earlier. This theoretical analysis also suggests that the assessment context must be quite different from the kind utilized in the studies that we have reviewed; there should be freedom from time pressure and there should be a playful, game-like context rather than one implying that the person is under test. Interestingly enough, the kind of context present in the case of *all* of the studies on creativity that we reviewed earlier has borne strong connotations that a test or examination is at issue; the creativity procedures invariably have been referred to as "tests," they have been administered to large groups of students in a classroom, and temporal constraint has been present—either explicitly, through the use of relatively brief time limits, or implicitly, through the use of group administration procedures. In all of this work, there has been the evident assumption that a testing context, with its implication that the respondent is being evaluated in terms of some success-failure criterion, is quite appropriate for studying creativity. The associative approach to creativity that we have taken, however, with its emphasis upon an attitude of playful entertaining of possibilities in a task-centered rather than ego-centered environment, suggests otherwise.

At this point we were ready to begin some experimentation of our own. Following the prescriptions just stated, could one empirically define a dimension of individual differences that concerned the ability to produce many cognitive associates, and many that are unique? Would this dimension possess a substantial degree of generality across differences in types of tasks—for example, verbal vs. visual kinds of procedural formats? Such a contrast was of special interest since the general intelligence concept is defined with respect to a kind of ability that manifests itself in visual (performance) as well as verbal types of tasks, and we were presuming to assess a characteristic possessing approximately the same level of generality as conventional intelligence. Finally, and most important, would the foregoing dimension of associational ability be independent of individual differences in the traditional area of general intelligence? If research findings could provide affirmative answers to these questions, then, and only then, would one be in a position to talk about a kind of thinking ability appropriately labeled *creativity*, with the evident implication of a characteristic different from general intelligence but yet a characteristic which also possesses a substantial degree of generality across task variations.

Our work, conducted with 151 children comprising the entire fifth-grade population of a suburban public school system in a middle-class region, took great pains to establish a game-like, nonevaluational context for the administration of procedures. The *Es* [experimenters], two young women, were introduced as visitors interested in children's games, and spent two initial weeks with each class gaining rapport with the children. This initial period of familiarization also provided the basis for observations leading to ratings of the children's behavior on various dimensions, to be discussed later. Great effort was expended in communicating to the children that the presence of the *Es* did not concern examinations or tests. The teachers and principals, furthermore, did their utmost to dissociate the *Es* from any concern with intellectual evaluation. Finally, it was our view that the establishment of a game-like context required the *Es* to work individually with each of the 151 children. We sedulously avoided group administration with its academic testing implications.

Five procedures formed the basis for our exploration of creativity in these children. They concerned the generation of five kinds of associates. Two variables were measured in the case of each: uniqueness of associates and total number of associates. Some of the procedures were verbal, others were visual in nature. One verbal procedure, for example, requested the child to generate possible instances of a verbally specified class concept, such as "round things," or "things that move on wheels." Here and for every other creativity procedure, the child is given as much time on each item as he desires. Number of unique responses to an item is defined as the number of responses given by only one child in the sample of 151 to the item in question. Total number of responses offered to an item is, of course, self-defining. For "round things," for example, "life savers" is a unique response, while "buttons" is not. Another verbal procedure requests the child to think of possible uses for various objects presented orally, such as "shoe" or "cork." "To trap a mouse in," is a unique use suggested for "shoe," while "to throw at a noisy cat" is not. A third verbal procedure asks the child to propose possible similarities between two objects specified in verbal terms. For instance, one pair is "train and tractor," another is "milk and meat." A unique response to "milk and meat" was "they are government-inspected," while "they come from animals" was not unique. The visual procedures, in turn, request the child to think of pos-

sible interpretations or meanings for each of various abstract visual patterns and line forms.

These procedures obviously owe a debt to the Guilford group. They are administered, however, in a carefully constructed game-like context, with each child taken individually and encouraged to spend as much time as he wishes, in a relaxed atmosphere, on every item. These administration arrangements were very different from those employed by the Guilford group. It should be emphasized, furthermore, that the use of a game-like context did not lead to a violation of the task constraints present in the various items of the procedure. Bizarre or inappropriate responses were exceedingly rare.

To assess the traditionally demarcated area of general intelligence, ten indicators were utilized. These included verbal and performance subtests from the Wechsler Intelligence Scale for Children, the School and College Ability Tests, which provide measures of verbal and quantitative aptitude, and the Sequential Tests of Educational Progress, which provide yardsticks of achievement in various academic content areas.

The ten creativity indicators—a uniqueness and a productivity measure for each of five procedures—proved to be highly reliable, in terms of both split-half and item-sum correlations. The reliabilities of the ten intelligence instruments, in turn, are known to be quite high. We now were in a position, therefore, to study the dimensionality of the creativity and intelligence indexes. The findings were as follows. Whether examining results for the sample as a whole or separately for the 70 boys and the 81 girls, the ten creativity measures proved to be highly intercorrelated, the ten intelligence measures proved to be highly intercorrelated, and the correlation *between* the creativity and the intelligence measures proved to be extremely low. . . .

We may conclude, therefore, that a dimension of individual differences has been defined here which, on the one hand, possesses generality and pervasiveness, but which, on the other hand, nevertheless is quite independent of the traditional notion of general intelligence. This new dimension concerns a child's ability to generate unique and plentiful associates, in a generally task-appropriate manner and in a relatively playful context. It is a considerable surprise that such a dimension should prove to be quite independent of general intelligence, and it seems indeed appropriate to label this dimension "creativity." The independence of this dimension from general intelligence seems all the more intriguing for two reasons:

First, the creativity procedures almost inevitably call upon verbal facility in some degree, and verbal facility is a very basic element of the general intelligence concept; second, the independence in question is found for elementary school children, and one would expect young children to show less differentiation in modes of cognitive functioning than adults.

In a sense, all that has been described thus far constitutes a prelude. Having isolated a mode of thinking in children that is pervasive, independent of intelligence, and appropriately described as a dimension of individual differences in "creativity," we now wish to understand its psychological significance. The appropriate research strategy at this point seemed to require consideration of individual differences on the creativity and the intelligence dimensions taken *jointly*. That is, a child's location had to be defined with respect both to general intelligence and to creativity as we have conceived of it. It was necessary, in other words, to compose four groups of children within each sex: those high in both creativity and intelligence, those high in one and low in the other [and vice versa], and those low in both. In order to define these groups, a single creativity index score and a single intelligence index score were obtained for each child. These index scores were the summed standard scores of the ten measures in each respective domain. The distributions of creativity index scores and of intelligence index scores then were dichotomized at their respective medians, within sex, to yield the groups that exemplified the four possible combinations of creativity and intelligence levels. The two sexes, incidentally, were quite similar with regard to the distributions of these index scores. Since all cases were retained, rather than just the extremes, it is evident that the procedure used for composing creativity and intelligence combinations was a conservative one.

Consider now some of the psychological differences that we found to distinguish children who are both creative and intelligent, creative but not intelligent, intelligent but not creative, and neither creative nor intelligent.

To begin with, we turn to the behavior of these several groups of children in the school environment. The two *E*s made independent ratings of the children along specifically defined behavioral dimensions during an initial two weeks of observation in each class. This work was carried out prior to any further contact with the children, so that the ratings could not be influenced by the performances of the children on the various experimental procedures used in our research. Furthermore, no other possible sources of information about the children were made available to the raters during the observation period. In short, every effort was made to insure that the ratings would be unbiased.

It should also be mentioned that these rating dimensions possess high interrater reliability, a very important point that the use of two independent observers permitted us to establish. Without this kind of reliability, investigation of individual differences on these behavioral dimensions would have been fruitless.

The judges rated each child's status on a given dimension in terms of a nine-point scale. For example, one characteristic was defined in terms of the following question: "To what degree does this child seek attention in unsocialized ways, as evidenced by such behavior as speaking out of turn, continually raising his hand, or making unnecessary noises?" The first, third, fifth, seventh, and ninth points on the rating scale for this question were given the verbal labels "never," "seldom," "sometimes," "usually," and "always," respectively. Other questions rated in the same manner included: "To what degree does this child hesitate to express opinions, as evidenced by extreme caution, failure to contribute, or a subdued manner in a speaking situation?" "To what degree does this child show confidence and assurance in his actions toward his teachers and classmates, as indicated by such behavior as not being upset by criticism, or not being disturbed by rebuffs from classmates?" "To what degree is this child's companionship sought by his peers?" "To what degree does this child seek the companionship of his peers?"

The preceding questions were focused upon issues of social behavior. Several questions of an achievement-centered nature also were included. These inquired about such matters as the following: "How would you rate this child's attention span and degree of concentration for academic school work?" "How would you rate this child's interest in academic school work, as indicated by such behavior as looking forward to new kinds of academic work, or trying to delve more deeply into such work?" For these questions, the first, third, fifth, seventh, and ninth points of the rating scales were labeled "poor," "below average," "average," "good," and "superior," respectively.

Let us look in some detail at the results for the girls. Those high in both creativity and intelligence show the least doubt and hesitation of all the groups, show the highest level of self-confidence, and display the least tendency toward deprecation of oneself and one's work. Concerning companionship, these girls are sought out by their peers more eagerly than is any other group, and this high intelligence–high creativity group also seeks the companionship of others more actively than does any other group. There is reciprocity in social relationships for the members of this group. With regard to achievement, this group shows the highest levels of attention span, concentration, and interest in academic work. In all of these respects, the high-high group obviously is reflecting highly desirable modes of conduct in both the social and the achievement spheres. Interestingly enough, however, this group also is high in regard to disruptive, attention-seeking behavior. The high-high children may well be brimming over with eagerness to propose novel, divergent possibilities in the classroom, in the face of boredom with the customary classroom routines. Against the context of classroom programs that emphasize equal participation by class members and academic values that are likely to center around the traditional intelligence dimension, the cognitive behavior reflected in high creativity levels in the case of these girls may well possess a nuisance value and exert a rather disruptive effect in the classroom situation.

Consider next the group high in creativity but low in intelligence. In many respects it turns out that this group is at the greatest disadvantage of all in the classroom—and, indeed, under more of a disadvantage than the group which is low in both creativity and intelligence. Those of high creativity but low intelligence are the most cautious and hesitant of all the groups, the least confident and least self-assured, the least sought after by their peers as companions, and in addition are quite avoidant themselves of the companionship of others. There is a mutuality of social avoidance in the case of these girls. In the academic sphere, they are the most deprecatory of their own work and the least able to concentrate and maintain attention. In terms of the ratings for disruptive attention-seeking, however, these girls are high, and in this one respect similar to the high creativity–high intelligence group. Most likely, however, the attention-seeking of these two groups is quite different in quality, given the highly different contexts of other behaviors in the two cases. While the disruptive behaviors of the high-high group suggest enthusiasm and overeagerness, those of the high creative–low intelligent group suggest an incoherent protest against their plight.

It affords an interesting comparison to turn next to the group low in both intelligence and creativity. These girls actually seem to be better off than their high creativity–low intelligence peers. The low-low group possesses greater confidence and assurance, is less hesitant and subdued, and is considerably more outgoing toward peers in social relationships than is the high creative–low intelligent group. The low-low group members appear to compensate for their poor academic performances by activity in the social sphere, while the high creative–low intelligent individuals, possessing seemingly more delicate sensitivities, are more likely to cope with academic failure by social withdrawal and a retreat within themselves.

Finally, we turn to the group high in intelligence but low in creativity. As in the case of the high-high group, these girls show confidence and assurance. In terms of companionship patterns, however, an intriguing difference emerges. While sought quite strongly as a companion by others, the girl in this group tends not to seek companionship herself. She also is least likely to seek attention in disruptive ways and is reasonably hesitant about expressing opinions. Attention span and concentration for academic matters, in turn, are quite high. The impression that emerges, then, is of a girl who is strongly oriented toward academic achievement, is somewhat cool and aloof in her social behavior but liked by others anyway, and is unwilling to take the chance of overextending or overcommitting herself; there is a holding back, a basic reserve.

These results make it clear that one needs to know whether creativity in a child is present in the context of high or low intelligence, and one needs to know whether intelligence in a child is present in conjunction with high or low creativity. It is necessary to consider a child's joint standing on both dimensions. One must seriously question, therefore, the Getzels and Jackson (1962) procedure of defining a "high creative" group as children who are high in creativity *but* low in intelligence, and defining a "high intelligent" group as children who are high in intelligence *but* low in creativity. If one wishes to establish generalizations about the nature of creativity and of intelligence as distinct characteristics, one cannot afford to ignore those children who are high in both and who are low in both.

Let us consider now some evidence in a different area—that of conceptualizing activities. This evidence will cast light on differences among the groups of boys. In one of our procedures, the child was asked to group pictures of everyday physical objects and was requested to give the reason for his grouping in each case. Among the fifty objects pictured were, for example, a rake, a screwdriver, a telephone, a lamppost, a candle. The groupings were to be carried out in terms of putting together things that seem to belong together. When this phase was completed, reasons for grouping were obtained. These reasons later were content-analyzed—blindly, of course, with respect to the identities of the children—and the reliability of the content analysis system was evaluated by having all materials scored by two independent judges. Reliability was found to be quite high. Consider briefly now one of the content-analysis distinctions employed.

We were interested in contrasting relational or thematic reasons for grouping with reasons based upon abstracted similarities among the objects. In the latter type of reason, every object in the group is an independent instance of the label applied, whether the labels refer to shared physical properties or to shared conceptual properties. An example of the physical-descriptive type of category would be the label, "hard objects," for a group consisting of a lamppost, a door, and a hammer. An example of the conceptual-inferential type of category would be the label, "for eating," in the case of a group containing a fork, a spoon, a cup, and a glass. By a relational or thematic type of reason, on the other hand, we refer to a label deriving from the relationship among the objects in the group; no single object is an independent instance of the concept, but rather all of the objects in the grouping are required in order to define it. An example of a thematic category is the label, "getting ready to go out," for a group consisting of a comb, a lipstick, a watch, a pocketbook, and a door.

. . . Thematizing under such circumstances may represent a passive, global approach to the materials provided. In the procedure that we employed, however, a large number of stimuli—fifty in all—were present, and their nature as well as the instructional context were such as to reduce markedly the *Eindringlichkeit* or prominence of thematic relationships. The child was encouraged to group in terms of abstractions, since the instructions implied to him that similarity be used as the basis for sorting. In addition, the objects were commonplace physical things, and there were many of them. Under these circumstances, it might well be the case that relational or thematic grouping would constitute a free-wheeling, unconventional type of response to the given task, in contrast to the more customary practice of sorting the objects in terms of common elements, whether such elements be physical or conceptual. Constraints arising from the nature of the stimuli would be considerably stronger in the case of groupings based upon shared physical or conceptual properties. Groupings based on relationships or themas, on the other hand, would permit greater free play for the evolving of unique combinations of stimuli. With these considerations in mind, let us turn to some results.

The findings for males point to a particularly clear phenomenon. The group of high intelligence but low creativity stands out as avoiding the use of thematic or relational bases for grouping. Rather, they concentrate on conceptual common elements. For whatever reasons—and the reasons may differ in the case of different groups—the other three groups are more willing to indulge in thematic forms of conceptualizing. It is the high intelligence–low creativity group that shows a disproportionate avoidance of thematizing. Such a finding reinforces the hypothesis that thematic responding may, under the conditions of the present procedure, represent a more playful, imaginative approach to the grouping task than does strict common-element sorting.

To suggest that the low incidence of thematizing by the high intelligence–low creativity group is evidence for an avoidance reaction, however, is to imply a further distinction. In principle, a low incidence could reflect either an inability to thematize or an avoidance of it. In another experimental procedure, however, we assessed the ability of the children to integrate a set of words into a unified theme in story telling: that is, in this new task, thematizing was required of the child. Under such conditions, the high intelligence–low creativity group thematizes as well as the group high in both creativity and intelligence. It is when the option not to thematize is available that thematizing drops out of the behavior of the high intelligent–low creative group. Such evidence, then, suggests that we are dealing with a disinclination to thematize on the part of this group, not an inability to thematize.

It has typically been proposed in work on cognitive development that the most mature cognitive functioning involves inferential abstraction—the kind of organizing that would be reflected in terms of sorting objects on the basis of shared conceptual properties. Thematizing has been considered a developmentally primitive response. Our findings suggest, however, that a more critical consideration may be the relative balance between conceptual-inferential and thematizing tendencies. Consider the results for the various groups of boys on the sorting task in somewhat more detail. For both of the high creativity groups, the relative incidence of thematizing *and* inferential-conceptual grouping is fairly high. For the high intelligence–low creativity group, the relative incidence of thematizing is quite low, while the relative incidence of inferential-conceptual sorting is quite high Finally, for the low intelligence–low creativity group, the relationship is reversed; the incidence of thematizing is high, while the incidence of inferential-conceptual sorting is relatively low.

In sum, the creative boys seem able to switch rather flexibly between thematizing and inferential-conceptual bases for grouping; the high intelligence–low creativity boys seem rather inflexibly locked in inferential-conceptual categorizing and strongly avoidant of thematic-relational categorizing; finally, the low intelligence–low creativity boys tend to be locked within thematic modes of responding and relatively incapable of inferential-conceptual behavior. Parenthetically, it might be well to offer the reminder that the incidences of thematic and inferential-conceptual groupings both can be high since there also exists the third scoring category of grouping in terms of common physical elements.

When we consider some of our data concerning sensitivity to the expressive potential of visual materials, a result similar to the thematizing findings is obtained for the high intelligence–low creativity group of girls. With line drawings of stick figures in various postures as stimuli, various emotional states were proposed to the child as possibilities for one or another figure, and the child indicated a willingness or disinclination to entertain each possibility. Let us focus our attention upon two kinds of affective labels for each stick figure: a label constituting a highly likely, conventional suggestion, and a label representing a quite unlikely, unconventional possibility. Unconventional and likely emotional attributions for the various stick figures were defined with reference to the consensus of adult judges. Each of some twenty-four stick figures was offered to the child with one affective label upon each presentation. A different type of label would be proposed each time a given figure was presented, and a given figure was repeated only after all the others had been shown. More inappropriate and more appropriate kinds of labels for the various figures would be offered on a random schedule. Note that a choice is never forced between these two classes of emotional attributions. Each presentation involves one stick figure and one label, with the child requested to accept or reject the label as a descrip-

tive possibility. The child thus is free to accept appropriate and unconventional emotional attributions, to reject both kinds, or to accept one kind and reject the other.

The main results with this procedure for the girls were as follows. Although the four groups did not differ in regard to their acceptance of appropriate or likely affective attributions for the stick figures, they differed in a particular way regarding acceptance of the unconventional attributions—the group high in intelligence but low in creativity exhibited a conspicuously low level of such acceptance. Although the rate of acceptance of such attributions by the other three groups was generally quite low (about 5 per cent), the high intelligence–low creativity group accepted virtually none at all. The comparability among the groups regarding acceptance of appropriate attributions acts as a control, indicating that the differential acceptance behavior just described relates to the entertainment of unconventional attributions in particular, rather than simply to the acceptance of any kind of affective labels. Furthermore, there is no relationship between degree of acceptance of unconventional and of appropriate attributions. It is safe to conclude, therefore, that an acquiescence or "yea-saying" response set cannot account for the differential acceptance of unconventional attributions.

The implications of the present findings appear to be quite similar to the thematizing results considered before in the case of the boys. In both cases, the high intelligence–low creativity group is intolerant of unlikely, unconventional, types of hypothesizing about the world. This particular group appears conspicuously loath to "stick its neck out," as it were, and try something that is far out, unconventional, and hence possibly "wrong." It is of particular interest that the high intelligence–low creativity group of girls avoids entertaining the possibility of unconventional emotional attributions under the present experiment's conditions. Recall that the entertainment of such possibilities has no effect upon the availability for acceptance of the likely and highly appropriate possibilities; it is not an "either-or" situation. The high intelligence–low creativity girls seem to be so attuned to error that even where appropriate responses are not sacrificed, they refuse to deviate from a critical standard of "correctness."

Consider next some of the other findings in the domain of expressive sensitivity. Included in this domain were tasks requiring free descriptions of stimuli with implicit emotive significance. We content-analyzed these free descriptions in order to determine the extent to which a child would confine his descriptions to comments upon the physical and geometric characteristics of the various, as contrasted with the extent to which he would "go beyond" such physical categories and discuss the affective or expressive connotations of such materials. In the case of both sexes, the ability to range beyond the physical and into the realm of affective content tended to be maximal in the group high in both creativity and intelligence. That creativity and intelligence both could contribute to such physiognomic sensitivity—responsiveness to "inner" feeling states on the basis of perceivable externals—suggested that two processes could be jointly involved in the display of this sensitivity. On the one hand, the capacity to make inferential translations from one mode of experience to another seems to be reflective of the general intelligence concept; on the other hand, the associational freedom implied by the creativity concept evidently enhances the range of experience available for making inferential linkages.

Let us turn now to some evidence on how the children describe themselves with respect to general anxiety symptoms and to those symptoms experienced under the stress of tests or examinations. Consider the findings for the boys. . . . The level of anxiety is lowest for the group that is high in intelligence but low in creativity. Anxiety level is middling for the two groups that are high in creativity, regardless of intelligence level. Finally, anxiety level is highest for the group that is low in intelligence and low in creativity. . . . If anxiety is either too low or too high, then creativity is reduced. Just as interesting, however, are the particular conditions under which anxiety level is lowest. It is the group high in intelligence but low in creativity who, by self-report, are least anxious. At the other end of the dimension, with the highest anxiety scores, stands the group low in both intelligence and creativity.

What are the implications of these findings? First of all, they force us to question whether creativity should be conceptually associated with a state of maximal freedom from anxiety symptoms. It is not those children who are lowest in anxiety level, but those who report a moderate degree of anxiety, whom we find to be most creative in their thinking processes. Traditional conceptions of mental health place considerable emphasis upon anxiety as a debilitator of cognitive performance and as a signal of inappropriate or ineffective adjustment. This no doubt is true when anxiety reaches quite high levels. We need only

remember that the strongest degree of anxiety is found in the most cognitively deprived group of children—those who are low both in general intelligence and creativity. However, it may also be the case that a modicum of anxiety is reflecting more the presence of sensitivity to internal states than the presence of disturbance. This should not be construed, of course, as acceptance of the old saw that neuroticism breeds creativity. However, the data in hand do suggest that it is equally unrealistic to assume that the most creative children are the happiest children. There may well be elements of obsessiveness present in the kind of associative freedom that leads to high creativity status. A playful contemplation of the possible, but also an obsessive, task-centered reluctance to put a problem aside may be involved in the production of many associates and of a large number of unique associates. Creativity need not be all sweetness and light, therefore, but may well involve a tolerance for and understanding of sadness and pain. To think otherwise is to fall prey to the rather widespread American stereotype that suffering is always a bad thing and is to be avoided at all costs.

One possible cost of the avoidance of suffering is evident in the group whose levels of general anxiety and of test anxiety are lowest—the group high in intelligence but low in creativity. This result may well stem from the fact that the group in question is the most closely attuned to the demands of the classroom environment. In that environment, traditionally defined intelligence and its manifestations in the form of high academic achievement most likely are heavily rewarded, while creativity may well be viewed as more of a disruption than a boon. The mode of operation of the high intelligence–low creativity child, therefore, may be such as to minimize the sources of possible conflict between himself and the school environment and to maximize the sources of reward from that environment. It is not surprising that such a close fit between individual and social context would be reflected in a minimal level of anxiety.

From the kinds of results that have been passed in review, pictures begin to emerge concerning the psychological nature of the children in the four cognitive groupings: high creativity–high intelligence, high creativity–low intelligence, low creativity–high intelligence, and low creativity–low intelligence. In addition to our quantitative studies, clinical accounts describing various children in the sample also have been prepared, and these clinical materials have tended to reinforce the conclusions derived from the experimental work. The case studies can be summarized in terms of the generalizations presented below. These will also serve to underline the major points of congruence between the clinical and the experimental sources of information concerning the four creativity and intelligence groupings.

High creativity–high intelligence: These children can exercise within themselves both control and freedom, both adult-like and child-like kinds of behavior.

High creativity–low intelligence: These children are in angry conflict with themselves and with their school environment, and are beset by feelings of unworthiness and inadequacy. In a stress-free context, however, they can blossom forth cognitively.

Low creativity–high intelligence: These children can be described as "addicted" to school achievement. Academic failure would be perceived by them as catastrophic, so that they must continually strive for academic excellence in order to avoid the possibility of pain.

Low creativity–low intelligence: Basically bewildered, these children engage in various defensive maneuvers ranging from useful adaptations such as intensive social activity to regressions such as passivity or psychosomatic symptoms.

In conclusion, this presentation has traced in outline form the history of our research on two modes of thinking in young children, modes which constitute quite different, but yet quite pervasive, dimensions of individual differences. Our work progressed from the definition and operationalization of the cognitive types in question to an investigation of their correlates in such areas as observable social and achievement-relevant behaviors, ways of forming concepts, physiognomic sensitivities, and self-described levels of general anxiety and test anxiety. From the findings obtained, it seems fair to conclude that the present definition of creativity denotes a mode of cognitive functioning that matters a great deal in the life of the child. Most critical of all for advancing our understanding is a consideration of the child's *joint* status with regard to the conventional concept of general intelligence and creativity as here defined.

REFERENCE

Getzels, J. W., & Jackson, P. W. *Creativity and intelligence.* New York: Wiley, 1962.

25

How Is a Test Built?

Kenneth F. McLaughlin

Early in their careers, teachers discover that "knowledge" is an abstract idea as difficult to deal with as are other abstractions such as character, moral purity, intellectual curiosity, etc. Since psychologists have such an incredibly difficult time trying to measure intelligence and attitude (as just two examples), is it any wonder that teachers experience quaking traumas when required to measure knowledge?

If teachers, counselors, personnel directors, and other interested parties are to construct tests that do their measurement job well, they must have guidelines explaining how one constructs a good test. Then, the most essential ingredient is practice. To do anything well requires a good deal of intense practice aimed toward acquiring the skill.

The test, as a measuring instrument, can be constructed well only when the test builder is aware of exactly what he is trying to do. This article sets forth a "recipe" that will be helpful in constructing any kind of test.

From Interpretation of Test Results, *U.S. Department of Health, Education, and Welfare, Sections III and IV, 1964.*

Each of you is familiar with such daily tests as sampling a bowl of soup to see if it suits your taste or sighting down several long boards to determine which one is most suitable for a kitchen shelf. While a few tests in school are similar to the "work-sample" type just described, most of them are of the "paper-and-pencil" variety made by the teacher.

Daily or weekly teacher-made tests serve a definite purpose as indicators of pupil and class progress in specific subject matter. You may remember that many of the subject tests of your school days consisted of three or four essay questions written on the blackboard. As a pupil you spent part of the class period writing essays on the questions—being specific, if you knew the answer, or verbose, if you were not too sure of your subject.

While you may have been unhappy about the amount of writing required by a test, you were never much concerned that after regular school hours your teacher had to read all that you had written to try to evaluate it fairly. Your teacher may not have had a course in tests and measurements during her formal teacher training and consequently may not have known how to construct objective tests which cover more topics in less time and require minutes instead of hours to score.

Most published tests of the objective type are called standardized tests. They are available as single-subject tests or as a battery of several tests covering a number of subject areas. Some objective tests, however, are prepared to be used with certain textbooks and are not standardized.

A standardized test is one which samples the subject matter in a systematic way, is administered in a particular way, is scored objectively, and has meaningful norms for comparing the achievement of pupils.

There are a number of reasons for making standardized tests a part of the evaluation program of a school. First, in a given period of time, a large body of information can be covered. Second, test items or test questions are included which aid the teacher in distinguishing good pupils from poor ones. Third, they make it possible to compare the achievement of each pupil with the achievement of his class or with the pupils of another year, another city, or of the country as a whole.

Steps in Constructing

Described below are some of the procedures a test publisher must take in order to make available tests which will give a reasonably accurate measure of a person's aptitude for learning or the degree of his mastery of a specific subject area at a specified grade level—kindergarten through college. Most of these steps can also be used in constructing a classroom test—although it would not be completely standardized.

To illustrate, suppose a test publisher decides to build a measuring instrument in eighth-grade mathematics. The company's mathematics specialist would procure from many school systems, for grade eight, a number of recognized texts in mathematics and representative courses of study. He would analyze the content and amount of time scheduled for each major topic.

Further, he would seek the assistance of the best available curriculum specialists in mathematics in schools and universities. He might solicit advice of these experts individually or bring them together in a conference to consider the educational objectives to be measured and the topics to be included in the test.

Armed with information from the analysis of current textbooks and the suggestions of the experts, the company specialist would develop a table of specifications outlining the kinds of topics and subtopics to be covered by the projected test. Such a table would correspond to the shopping list a cook makes in planning a dinner or the materials list of a craftsman planning a coffee table.

In using any recipe for a dinner dish or a blueprint for making a table, you must know not only the kinds of materials in it but also the quantity of each. Similarly, to obtain a well-balanced test, the company specialist uses the textbook analyses and the opinions of the subject specialists in determining the relative importance of each topic and the proper proportion of the final test which should be devoted to it.

On some essay tests of your school days, you may recall, the teacher indicated the number of minutes you should spend on each topic or question, depending on its importance. With a standardized test, this time rationing is no longer necessary since the amount of time spent on any one topic is automatically controlled by the number of questions chosen for it.

Most tests are designed either to cover one complete class period of 40–50 minutes or to have one or more of the subsections completed within that time limit. Psychological tests, reading tests, and the like are generally long enough to keep all pupils busy during the complete testing time. In most subject-matter tests the time allotment is usually generous enough to permit most of the pupils to try all of the items.

Among the kinds of test items used in an objective test are true-false, matching, or multiple-choice. The type used most frequently is the four-choice or five-choice multiple choice item, although in certain subject areas other types may be more appropriate.

After the proportion of questions for each topic has been determined, a number of qualified mathematics teachers may be requested to write four or five multiple-choice test items on each specified section of the test. The publisher provides special instructions and sample items as guides. He encourages each item writer to use his ingenuity and skill in assembling questions that require the pupil to think or to apply principles based on the material of the course he has studied rather than merely to recall facts.

Item writing is hard work. It takes time to construct a good clear question with four or five choices. While only one choice may be correct, the other choices must appear plausible or reasonable to the pupil who has only partial information, misinformation, or who does not understand a fundamental principle. No test maker attempts to write complicated or trick questions, although for every test there are nearly always some pupils who insist that such questions are included.

The total number of items requested from item writers is generally four or five times the number actually needed. For example, for a 50-item test, at least 250 questions may be constructed. If there are enough usable items, it may be possible for the publisher to make two comparable forms—that is, two similar tests with questions covering the same subject matter.

We should point out, however, that two comparable forms of a test do not have to have exactly the same types of questions—with just a number or a few words changed. Any test is just a *sample* of the larger body of information being tested. From a group of 10 available items on a certain topic the test maker can choose two different items for each form of a test in order to meet the requirements of the table of specifications. After the tests are completed and normed, the two forms will be comparable.

Trial Run Made

After the subject-matter specialists have submitted the test items to the company's professional item writing expert, he examines them for editorial defects and classifies them according to the table of specifications. Next, he selects the number of items needed for the test or for each of several forms of the test and assembles the test for a trial run, called a pretest.

In order to conduct a pretest, the publisher must obtain permission from several representative schools at the proper grade level to administer the test. On the basis of this trial each item is analyzed to determine three things:

(1) The difficulty (the more pupils who choose the right answer, the easier the question).

(2) The appropriateness of the choices (if no one selects a particular wrong answer, this choice may be replaced).

(3) The discrimination or separation of the better pupils from the poorer ones (no test maker wants to include items which more poor pupils than good pupils will mark correctly—which is termed "negative discrimination").

After this item analysis, an item may be rewritten or a new one added to replace a poor one. Then a second trial of the test is made with different schools and the item analysis procedure repeated. Experienced test makers seldom have to carry out the process a third time. However, a test maker must have at least one trial run before attempting the final assembly of a test, for no matter how much experience he has brought to bear, "bugs" may creep in.

Instructions on Administering

While the editing, the proofing, and the final printing of the test are being done, the standardized administrative procedures are developed. These instructions include the exact words the teacher will read to the pupil in conducting the test, the timing of the whole test, and the instructions for scoring.

Below grade four, pupils mark their answers in test booklets which therefore can be used only once. In grade four and above, however, it is possible for the school to purchase, for many kinds of tests, a reusable test booklet and an expendable separate answer sheet—which diminishes the overall cost of a testing program. If a new test is printed in a reusable booklet form, a separate answer sheet must be designed that can be scored quickly by hand or machine. A scoring key must also be planned, prepared, and punched to fit the answer sheet.

For schools in which the teachers must score the tests, several types of self-scoring answer sheets have been developed. One type consists of tamper-proof double sheets with a carbon sealed between. When the sheets are separated, it is easy to count the correct answers. A similar type is prepared with chemically treated paper which will clearly record the correct answer or indicate the incorrect answer which was chosen. In another type of test pupils use a pin to punch holes through several thicknesses of paper.

Some large schools or county systems rent test-scoring machines which will score properly marked answer sheets at the rate of over 200 an hour—and thus release teacher time for more profitable tasks than counting dots or marks. These machines can also indicate how many pupils in a class choose each answer for each question. Such information aids the teacher in locating class deficiencies.

One of the most recent developments in the test-scoring field is an answer card which can be scored and punched with a new machine and then sorted on standard machines. Some large-scale programs now use machines which simultaneously "read" the name of the pupil and score all the tests of a battery—at the rate of 5000 papers an hour.

Norms Developed

The next step for the test publisher is the development of national or regional norms. By this we mean that the publisher must reach an agreement with a sample of representative schools to administer the test to all of the pupils of the appropriate subject group. The schools are chosen from many cities, towns, and rural areas; white collar and industrial areas; upper level, middle level, and lower level income groups. (Statisticians call such a sample a "stratified" sample.)

When scoring is completed, tables of numbers, called "norms," are constructed which make the raw score meaningful and give some indication to the pupil, the teacher, the school administrator, and the parent of the relative ability or relative standing of each child.

Publishers may convert raw scores to an appropriate scale and then construct one or more of several kinds of norms, such as age equivalent, grade equivalent, or percentile. Each system offers a different way of giving meaning to the raw score.

Age-equivalent and grade-equivalent norms give the average scores of pupils of a particular age or grade and are most appropriate for elementary-school years. If a pupil in the fifth grade makes a grade-equivalent score for the sixth grade, it means that he made a score equivalent to that of the average sixth-grader in that subject. It does not mean that the child should be in the sixth grade.

One of the most understandable types of norms is the percentile. This measure indicates how a pupil ranks with other pupils of his grade or age group. For example, a pupil whose score is at the 75th percentile is equal to or exceeds the scores of 75 per cent of his classmates; 25 per cent of the group did better than he did. A pupil whose score is at the 40th percentile is equal to or exceeds 40 per cent of his classmates and is just a little below the average, or the 50th percentile.

It should be pointed out that a standardized test for a specific grade is designed so that the average raw score, or number of correct answers, will be about half of the total number of questions. Thus, the old idea of "70 per cent is passing" no longer holds with these standardized tests.

Many local norms—they can be easily constructed for a school, city, county, or state—give additional information and are more meaningful than national norms. Such local norms make it possible to compare a pupil with others who live in a known community and have a known background.

A Fair Question

Parents, counselors, and teachers often ask: "How dependable are these tests?" It is a fair question. Dependability might well be discussed in the terms which most manuals now use: "reliability" and "validity." By *reliability* we mean *consistency*. For example, if a pupil scores at the 30th percentile on the test today, may we be assured that he will score at a similar percentile on the same test or another form of the test tomorrow? If the test is reliable, the same pupil would not score at the 75th percentile if he took it again soon without further study, nor even at the 50th percentile; he would score near the 30th percentile.

Because there is likely to be a small shift of percentile points, the current trend is to interpret test scores as a *band* of several percentiles. In other words, a score at the 30th percentile may mean that the pupil's "true" score may lie somewhere in the band between the 27th to 33rd percentile. The width of this band will vary with different tests and will often vary at different percentile points on the same test.

By "validity" we mean "How well does the test measure what it is supposed to measure?" A test maker checks validity by comparing the new test with other well-accepted tests if any exist, or by obtaining the consensus of experts in the subject. It is the responsibility of the test maker to conduct research to learn whether a test is valid for the purposes claimed and whether the scores of the test are reasonably stable or reliable.

Suggestions for the interpretation of the test results are sometimes included with the printed instructions for the test administrator. At other times, a separate manual of interpretation is provided. Such suggested interpretations are one of the most important contributions of the test author, or test publisher, to the proper educational use of the results. They help to make the test scores meaningful to the counselor, the teacher, the pupil, and the parent. Test manuals often include not only an explanation of the norms but also suggested remedial measures for pupils with low scores.

Schools or teachers selecting tests should not rely on the test title alone, but should always examine a copy before placing an order. For example, in achievement testing, it has been found helpful to have a test committee of a school compare several tests in a subject area in order to determine the one test which best suits the current curriculum and which provides the most helpful information.

From the procedures described here, you will see that a standardized test is the result of many weeks of work by many specialists. If the instructions for the test are carefully followed, the results will be meaningful to all.

For a school to obtain testing instruments constructed with care requires only a small amount of the educational per-pupil cost per year. The national average total expenditure per pupil for education in 1958–1959 was $456. A school that has one standardized test battery per pupil per year, administered by the teachers and centrally scored, would probably pay less than one-fourth of 1 per cent of the per-pupil cost for its program—approximately $1. Such a percentage of an operating budget does not seem to make cost a major consideration as a school evaluates its needs and programs.

Getting Ready for School

Not long ago a mother telephoned a school and requested a copy of a specific reading-readiness test. The school did not have a copy of the test available for parents. In an effort to be helpful, the counselor at the school questioned the mother concerning her reason for needing it.

The woman said she understood that local regulations required her six-year-old child to take a placement test before he entered first grade. To prevent his being placed in a readiness class for a year, which was the custom in the school system in her town, she planned to coach him.

This made the counselor feel he should explain the reasons for giving the test. A child is tested before he enters school to discover his general ability level, to try to determine whether or not he is mature enough to begin first-grade work, and to decide whether or not he is able to acquire successfully the necessary skills for a beginning reader.

The counselor also pointed out that the test administrator would be skilled in putting a child at ease in strange surroundings, that every effort would be made to obtain a measure of the ability of the prospective pupil, and that, in fact, the standards for these tests had been determined by giving the tests under similar conditions to many children of the same age.

Coaching with the test would be like having a person memorize an eye chart before having his eyes examined. With preknowledge of the questions, a child might well be placed in a class above his maturity level, which would be a disservice to the child. Further, there was absolutely no stigma connected with his being placed in a readiness class, and the child himself would be happier and more apt to succeed in the following grades if he were placed with a group at the same stage of development.

The mother responded that for the first time she understood the usefulness of these tests. With such testing, perhaps her older children could have avoided certain school problems. While she wished to use any legitimate means to help her youngest child do well on his first test, she was willing to let him meet the test situation uncoached.

The Measurement of Human Abilities:
A Contemporary Perspective

Paul A. Games
The Pennsylvania State University

To the beginning student psychology often seems to be an exceedingly fragmented subject with little apparent relation between its various subdivisions. This is largely the result of the primitive nature of our knowledge and the fact that most investigators, in order to be able to make some sense of their data, simplify and direct their efforts by ignoring part of the data.

The following analysis will serve to illustrate two of the ways in which psychologists may look at their data. Consider an experiment in which 200 subjects are given twenty trials on each of two learning tasks, Task A and Task B. One hundred subjects (50 per cent) do Task A first; the other 50 per cent do Task B first. Response measures are obtained for all 200 subjects on each trial of each task.

Even with this relatively simple experimental design, we would have a total of 8000 measurements (200 subjects x 20 trials x 2 tasks). A large number of indices might be computed, and an exhaustive number of possible permutations and combinations of these indices might be compared. Obviously, we must find some way to make this mass of data manageable.

Let us look for a moment at just the responses of the first group on trial 1 of Task A. Even on this first trial, the subjects do not score the same: some get five answers correct, some four, some three, etc. A frequency distribution of the measures obtained on trial 1 might look something like Figure 1. A similar distribution could be made for each of the twenty trials. Even so, our mass of data would still be so unwieldy that we would have difficulty seeing the forest for the trees. One method of simplifying it would be to look at only the mean of each distribution of scores. If we flip each distribution on its side, as in Figure 2, we can connect the means to obtain a curve showing the changes in average performance over the whole series of trials. Psychologists interested in studying the course of learning have generally handled their data in this way and have asked: What is the learning curve for Task A? What is the learning curve for Task B? Do these curves have the same shape? Those who are interested in the phenomenon of transfer have also concen-

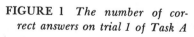

FIGURE 1 *The number of correct answers on trial 1 of Task A*

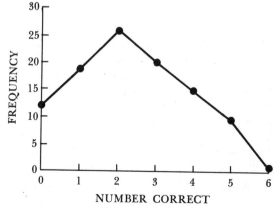

FIGURE 2   *Frequency distributions and means of one group on one task*

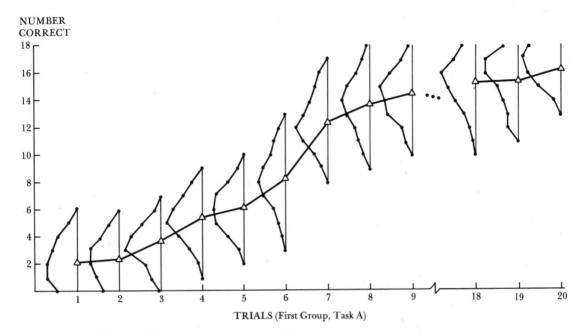

NUMBER
CORRECT

TRIALS (First Group, Task A)

trated on mean values: Does learning Task A first make it easier to learn Task B? Again, a comparison of learning curves provides the answer.

Another index that can be applied to our data is the correlation coefficient (r). This index describes the degree to which a group of subjects falls in the same relative position on two different measures. Are those who were best on trial 1 also best at the end of trial 20? Are the individuals who did best on trial 20 of Task A also at the top of the distribution on trial 20 of Task B? There are 780 correlations possible on each group of subjects (all possible combinations of 2 trials out of the total 40). Facing this massive task with no staff, limited time, and an old hand-calculator, those psychologists whose chief interest is the study of individual differences have generally simplified their task by concentrating on the right-hand side of the curves, where behavior has stabilized. At the start of the curve, behavior is changing rapidly from trial to trial. After a sufficient number of trials, however, the changes are so small that each individual's behavior is constant enough to be used in making predictions. Thus a psychologist may ask: How can an individual's performance on Task B be predicted from knowledge of his performance on Task A?

The different interests of those using the figures in these two ways led psychologists, in time, to concentrate on different kinds of tasks. Test-oriented psychologists were searching for stability and generality of behavior. They wanted to study stable behavior that would be useful for making all sorts of future predictions as to what an individual could do well. When a behavior was stable and of some generality, it was honored with the special title of "an ability" and was subjected to further study. But if a response continued to show substantial change with increased trials, it was not considered an ability and was dropped from further study.

On the other side, learning-oriented psychologists were disappointed when working with tasks where the mean was the same at the end of fifty trials as it had been at the start. How could they study learning if the subjects didn't improve? Even if improvement was shown by some subjects, other subjects messed things up by starting off with a high score on trial 1. These psychologists wanted to study tasks where change was maximal—where everybody started low. Consequently, while testers investigated relatively stable behaviors in which adults differed greatly—such as vocabulary level—learning psychologists created new tasks designed to minimize initial differences, such as learning pairs of non-sense syllables, for example, NAR-YOB. Since even these attempts were only partly successful in eliminating individual differences, many learning-oriented experimenters have reduced complexity by working with simpler organisms where rigid control of heredity and environment is possible.

The student should realize, of course, that the above example is itself overly simple and is only intended to illustrate some complex historical tendencies and to suggest the kinds of behaviors studied by these diverse areas of psychology. Nevertheless, the increasing divergence of tasks studied, indices used, and other methodological points has brought about a situation where specialists in each area know little about the work or methodologies used in the other areas. In his presidential address to the American Psychological Association, Lee J. Cronbach (1957) bemoaned the lack of overlap between the two disciplines of experimental and correlational psychology. It is little wonder that the beginning student sees slight connection between testing and learning, other than that they both deal with behavior.

Fortunately, there are those who attempt to relate the diverse findings of the learning and testing areas. There are learning psychologists who are paying increased attention to individual differences (Gagne, 1967; Fleishman, 1960) and psychometricians who are increasingly concerned with methods for analyzing changing behavior as well as stable behavior (Bechtoldt, 1963; Harris, 1963). There is reason to believe that these efforts will be rewarded with substantial progress, since some of the obstacles to progress have been reduced by recent trends.

One of these trends has been the increased level of federal support for behavioral research. There is little doubt that most of the change in the skills measured by ability tests comes during childhood. For example, Bloom (1964) estimates that of the variability in adult mental competence, 50 per cent is accounted for by the age of four, and 80 per cent by age eight. Research with children is typically very expensive and very time consuming, particularly longitudinal studies where the same children are observed over substantial periods of time. The necessary investigations of the development of abilities have simply not been done in the past because of financial limitations, although dedicated individuals such as Jean Piaget have provided valuable leads. Although the federal money spent studying the development of humans is a minute percentage of that spent developing rockets, at least it is a welcome start.

Another major encouraging factor is the invention of automated logic: the digital computer. The automation of logic is certainly going to be as important as the automation of writing. Just as the printing press has made possible the cheap mass distribution of both the best and worst of human writing in the form of books and magazines, the computer makes possible the cheap mass distribution of the best and worst of human logical processes. The initial impact of the computer has been on relatively simple logical systems such as the addition and subtraction of sums of money and inventories of materials. But a further impact is being felt in more sophisticated areas of scientific data processing. Masses of data that were previously overwhelming can be reduced to summary indices in a few minutes by computers. The computer makes possible complex forms of analysis and measurement that previously could not be seriously considered. As an example, let us consider some of the ways in which computers can be used in the area of testing.

Computers are likely to lead to some major changes in testing practice. As computer cost comes down, it will be cheaper to use computers as a source of "automated logic" than it will be to use professionally trained Ph.D.'s. At present thousands of man-hours each year are spent on the administration of individual tests that are used for making some sort of decisions about the individual involved. Some of these tests are used with retarded children, prisoners, and patients entering mental hospitals. In many cases, of course, the testing period serves as an introductory observation period in which the highly trained tester observes many general behavioral aspects; for example, a clinical psychologist giving an intelligence test to a disturbed child who is starting therapy will be interested in many aspects of the child's behavior other than the index of intelligence yielded by the test. In such cases highly trained professionals will certainly continue to be used, but in many other cases in which the sole aim is to obtain an accurate score, the computer may function as the tester.

Computers could also make group testing more efficient. As an example, let us consider a test of memory span. In such a test, the subject is shown a series of digits or letters and then is asked to write down the complete series in sequence from memory. A recently issued test of this skill (French, 1963) contains 24 items ranging from 3 to 11 letters in length. The average memory span for college students is about seven letters. However, there are a few people who can get only three correct consistently, and a very few who can get 11 correct consistently. For most people the items with three letters are a waste of time because they are too easy. Similarly, those with 11 letters are a waste of time because they are far too difficult. A computer could select items to match the "appropriate difficulty level" for a given subject, obtaining an accurate measurement in a minimal amount of time. In our memory-span example, suppose the computer starts with a three-letter span. This is answered correctly, and the computer jumps to a six-letter span. If the longer item is missed, it drops back to a four-letter span; but if the six-letter span is correctly reproduced by the subject, the computer tries a nine-letter item. By this means it could soon "bracket in" on the subject's span level and might report that in, say, 24 times the subject gets 90 per cent of the eight-letter items right, and only 20 per cent of the nine-letter items. This has considerably more accuracy than is possible in the same number of items with the group test, since it has to cover the entire range of skill found in the population. It has long been the practice of test makers to try to select items that will be passed by about 50 per cent of the population. Such items yield maximum discrimination. But for maximal *accuracy* of scores, we would benefit by estimating the difficulty level where an individual has a 50 per cent chance of passing, and concentrating the test items for that individual around this point. Such procedures are now possible, thanks to the computer.

A related development possible with computers is the idea of programed examinations. For example, a medical student may first study the list of symptoms shown by a hypothetical patient and then make a choice from a list of possible courses of action. He is then told the outcome of the action he has chosen and is presented with a series of possible further actions to choose from. Some choices will lead to complications, and he may have to make further choices to attempt to remedy previous errors. If the remedial actions are inadequate, he may be told that the problem is over because the patient has died. Other series of choices may lead to a successful recovery. In short, such programed examinations may come much closer to simulating the tasks the M.D. must actually do in practice than does the usual type of examination. There may be many different paths leading to a successful diagnosis, treatment, and recovery—just as in the real world (McGuire, 1968).

This kind of branching, programed test clearly has instructional consequences, especially if we insert remedial sections that tell a student why a previous choice was a poor one or a wrong one. In this way we could simulate the tutorial situation that has long vanished from our crowded classrooms. In the author's opinion the most profitable use of computers in adult instruction will not be in the presentation of new material but in this kind of testing. It is even conceivable that such tests could be used for advanced placement or college credit on a nationwide basis.

Other projects under way at present include attempts to train computers to grade essay tests (Page, 1967) and to provide computer-assisted systems of guidance for high-school students (Cooley, 1964). If some of these projects are successfully implemented on a nationwide scale, the next generation of students may think of computers without the negative feelings presently directed at the machine that "messes them up" at registration and sends them bills.

Returning from optimistic speculation about the future to a survey of the past investigations of stable behaviors, a distinction that may be of value to beginning students is that made between tests of maximum performance and those of typical performance.

Ability tests are maximum-performance tests: The subject is asked to do his best on a series of problems. Personality tests (introversion-extroversion), interest tests, and tests of attitudes and motives are examples of typical-performance tests. In these there is no clear-cut "right" behavior such as correctly solving a problem, but the subject is asked to make responses that describe his typical behavior. The typical-behavior tests have many problems of ambiguity and fakability that are usually not present in maximum-performance tests. The most common applied use of tests at present is in selection of applicants for jobs or for college entrance. Although tests of typical behavior have occasionally been used for such purposes with some success, most such selection tests are tests of maximum performance.

Attempts to relate tests of typical performance to "abilities" have generally yielded disappointing results. In a massive study of high-school students using many measures of both domains, Lohnes (1968) found that only about 10 per cent of the variability in one area can be predicted by tests from the other area. Most of the overlap noted is due to the relationship between academic achievement and academic orientation. The relation between "interests" and "abilities" may be especially low in high school due to the fact that the interests of many students have not yet stabilized. If such is the case, guidance decisions will best be made using ability tests rather than tests of typical performance.

The area of intellective "ability" tests has been systematically explored for years by many investigators. The primary finding is that practically any two measures of maximum performance will show a positive correlation of some magnitude. The degree of correlation will vary with the tasks; a fluency test asking one to write down all the five-letter words that can be thought of in a fixed time will show a higher correlation with another fluency test than it will with a test of addition, but even the latter correlation will be positive. These positive correlations are the basis for the concept of general intelligence. Since there are differences in the magnitude of correlations between different ability measures, attempts to describe intellective abilities are attempts to group together those behaviors that correlate highly. Those behaviors that cluster together are usually labeled as a "factor," meaning they possess not only relative stability but also considerable generality in that this "factor" may be found in a variety of specific tasks. A descriptive name is given to the factor based upon what common features the tests that "cluster together" possess.

There are several different ways of representing the outcomes of correlational studies, but one way is to present a hierarchy of factors in the order of their generality (Humphreys, 1962; Vernon, 1950). The topmost factor is of greatest generality and is present to some degree in all of the measures shown below it. The second-level factors are less general and are present in only those measures listed below their names. These second-level factors will be correlated because they have general intelligence effects in common, but they will not correlate as highly as any two of the measures that are listed below one of them. Figure 3 represents one interpretation of factor results. As with most interpretations, there are many individual points that might be disputed, but it is nevertheless a useful model.

The hierarchical arrangement is like an upside-down tree. The general factor is the trunk, branching out into four major forks, some of which in turn show further branches. There is no doubt that each of these branches could be further subdivided until we end up with highly specific factors—the twigs of the tree. But the further the branching process continues, the harder it is to distinguish between one branch and the branch next to it.

The early intelligence tests were often a weird composite of many diverse behaviors, but all they were attempting to measure was the trunk. Since the trunk is easy to observe, they were quite successful. As finer differentiations were sought, tests were constructed that distinguished between the next four levels. Most scholastic selection tests, for example, sample primarily from behaviors in the verbal-educational area. It was often found that these tests were of little value in predicting success in training in shop

FIGURE 3   *A Hierarchical Model of Intellective Factors*

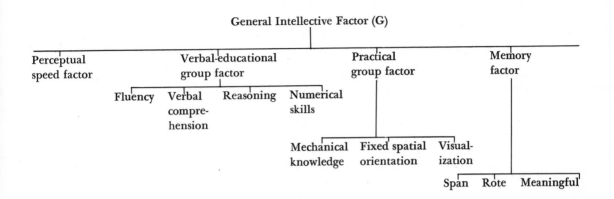

skills, mechanical repairs, or drafting. Behaviors found under the "practical" factor were usually more pertinent. Finally, tests that involved memorization of facts or tests that involved rapid but simple comparisons (e.g., finding all the *a*'s in a series of random letters) were not highly related to either of the preceding broad factors. These define the memory and perceptual-speed factors.

In later work each of these broad factors has been split again into subcategories (except perceptual speed, and a few would argue about it). It is thus possible to split memory into subfactors of span memory (as in the computer example), rote memory (involving learning of unrelated items), and meaningful memory (as in the retention of limericks). However, these are all types of memory and will typically correlate more highly with each other than with tests that measure other factors. As the tree continues to branch, the splits between branches become smaller, and the distinguishing nature of the branches becomes harder to identify. It is a matter of opinion as to when it is no longer worthwhile to branch further, in terms of the level of description that is useful in the science of psychology today. Fluency (Fruchter, 1948) has been further subdivided, but it is hard to imagine any present prediction problem where this further subdivision would be of value.

Presumably the large branches could be used to identify the best instructional techniques for different students. Students high in memory skills, for example, might learn fastest when taught by one method, and students high on verbal-educational skills might learn fastest when taught by another. Until effective use is made of our knowledge of the major branches of behavior, there seems to be little point in branching further and further toward minute twigs.

Two interpretations of ability differences have been advanced. One uses a behavioristic framework and is consistent with Ferguson's (1954, p. 98) interpretation that ". . . abilities are overlearned acquisitions, and that the stability which characterizes them is the result of overlearning." This interpretation emphasizes the role of learning in acquiring what we call abilities.

This interpretation accepts the possibility that some individuals may not have been exposed to a sufficient number of trials in some of the behavioral areas above. An individual may show low performance because he is still at a relatively low stage of learning. A youngster from a slum environment who has never had a book in his home, who has spent 10 years (from 6 to 16) in an undersupported school environment, and who has read only parts of the few books made available as texts may have had so few trials that he might show substantial improvement on the verbal educational factor when placed in a remedial reading program. If so, we cannot obtain an accurate measure of his true ability, for he has not overlearned the task required.

The other major interpretation given to test data is a neurological one. Many psychologists assume that the behavioral differences measured by tests reflect physiological differences between individuals. It is an easily observable fact that young children, even if given equal practice, still will differ in performance. If all the environmental factors were constant, there must have been some hereditary physical difference between individuals that enabled one to learn more than the other. Many psychologists thus tend to assume that the observable behavioral differences directly or indirectly reflect neurological (or other physiological) differences. There is certainly evidence supporting the fact that this sometimes is the case. Many of the more extreme cases of mental deficiency involve identifiable neurological damage. Similarly, statistical analysis of the consistency of certain behavior patterns in families supports this case. Burt (1958) concluded that 77 per cent of the variability in intelligence scores in the British population is attributable to hereditary factors. If cultural factors are sufficiently constant so that all are exposed to many experiences that permit learning of these general skills, then the observed variation between individuals may be primarily due to hereditary (physiological) factors. A learning interpretation would expect that the proportion of variance identifiable as associated with hereditary factors may vary from culture to culture or from time to time within the same culture, depending upon the relative constancy of environmental stimulation from person to person.

Some of the psychologists who interpret test results as reflecting physiological factors would consider that a diagram such as Figure 3 represents fixed capacities characteristic of the human race. Presumably they would someday expect investigators to identify neurological differences associated with each of the factors presented. Rather than agreeing with the author's views on the impracticality of the search for further twigs, they would probably consider that each twig identified is a further advance of science in describing the neurological organization of humans.

An interesting line of investigation pertinent to this basic interpretational difference is described in the article by John L. Horn in this section. Horn and R. B. Cattell have hypothesized that some of the factors repeatedly found in tests represent the result of learning, while others basically show the level of present neurological functioning (Horn, 1966; Horn and Cattell, 1966). They speak of the former as "crystallized intelligence" and the latter as "fluid intelligence." To relate this theory to Figure 3, most of the skills present in the middle verbal-educational and practical group factors would be classified as primarily "crystallized intelligence," while the memory factors would belong in "fluid intelligence."

There are two kinds of evidence to support this interpretation. First, the "fluid intelligence" skills show more variation over short periods, as we might expect with physiological variations in health. Second, in cross-sectional studies where persons of ages 15 to 61 are compared on mean scores, the older persons are superior on most "crystallized intelligence" skills, while the young are superior on "fluid intelligence" skills. This is not surprising for speed tasks (perceptual speed) since motor coordination alone might account for this finding; however, loss of motor coordination would not seem to account for loss of ability in an area like memory. This line of investigation seems profitable in providing some light on the old nature-nurture issue.

It is high time we obtained more data on the major branches of the tree. If we can identify branches that continue growing throughout life and others that deteriorate with age, we might find that each of the major interpretations, the learning interpretation and the physiological one, of test results is right for some branches and wrong for others.

REFERENCES

Bechtoldt, H. P. Correlational methods in research on human learning: An amplification. *Perceptual and Motor Skills*, 1963, **16**, 831–842.

Bloom, B. S. *Stability and change in human characteristics*. New York: Wiley, 1964.

Burt, C. The inheritance of mental ability. *American Psychologist*, 1958, **13**, 1–15.

Cooley, W. W. A computer-measurement system for guidance. *Harvard Educational Review*, 1964, 559–572.

Cronbach L. J. The two disciplines of scientific psychology. *American Psychologist*, 1957, **12**, 671–684.

Ferguson, G. A. On learning and human abilities. *Canadian Journal of Psychology*, 1954, **8**, 95–112.

Fleishman, E. A. Abilities at different stages of practice in rotary pursuit performances. *Journal of Experimental Psychology*, 1960, **60**, 162–171.

French, J. W. (Ed.) *Manual for kit of reference tests for cognitive factors.* (Rev. Ed.) Princeton, N.J.: Educational Testing Service, 1963.

Fruchter, B. The nature of verbal fluency. *Educational & Psychological Measurement*, 1948, **8**, 33–47.

Gagne, R. M. (Ed.) *Learning and individual differences.* Columbus, Ohio: Merrill, 1967.

Harris, C. W. (Ed.) *Problems in measuring change.* Madison, Wisc.: University of Wisconsin Press, 1963.

Horn, J. L. Integration of structural & developmental concepts in the theory of fluid and crystallized intelligence. In R. B. Cattell (Ed.), *Handbook of multivariate experimental psychology.* Chicago: Rand McNally, 1966. Pp. 553–561.

Horn, J. L., & Cattell, R. B. Refinement and test of the theory of fluid and crystalized general intelligences. *Journal of Educational Psychology*, 1966, **57**, 253–270.

Humphreys, L. G. The organization of human abilities. *American Psychologist*, 1962, **17**, 475–483.

Lohnes, P. R. Reformation through measurement in secondary education. In *Proceedings of the 1967 invitational conference on testing problems.* Princeton, N.J.: Educational Testing Service, 1968, 102–121.

McGuire, C. H. An evaluation model for professional education–medical education. In *Proceedings of the 1967 invitational conference on testing problems.* Princeton, N.J.: Educational Testing Service, 1968.

Page, E. B. Grading essays by computer: Progress report. In *Proceedings of the 1966 invitational conference on testing problems.* Princeton, N.J.: Educational Testing Service, 1967, 87–100.

Vernon, P. E. *The structure of human abilities.* New York: Wiley, 1950.

Part Four

Learning

Psychologists are often asked to explain exactly how their discipline differs from other areas of scientific endeavor. A popular definition of a few years back was that psychology is "the study of behavior." This definition was intended to emphasize the fact that mental activity could not be studied directly and that "introspective analysis," as it was called, had not proved effective in providing useful information.

Placing the major research emphasis upon observable behavior enabled investigators to concentrate on the effects of mental activity and the conditions of its occurrence so that researchers could replicate each other's observations. As we have seen, such emphases rapidly led to the development of devices with which to measure behavior. The commonly used psychological tests are examples of such behavioral recording devices.

The word *behavior* does not refer only to large-scale overt actions, however. It is just as correct to speak of the behavior of the iris of the left eye as a bright light shines upon it as it is to speak of the behavior of a mischievous schoolboy when he kicks over a wastepaper basket. It is just as meaningful to speak of the behavior of a membrane at the synaptic junction between two neurons as it is to speak of the behavior of the salivary glands of a hungry dog at feeding time. Thus, properly speaking, behavior can refer to any changing activity.

In a sense, we might say that all scientists study behavior. When a physicist studies the way in which the nuclei of atoms are held together, he is studying their behavior. In similar fashion a chemist studies the ways in which molecules "behave" in different contexts, and biologists, in turn, study the behavior of cells and organs in which molecules interact in a special way.

Psychologists study the changes in the behavior of an organism that result from changes in its inner or outer environment—the organism's adaptation to changed conditions. In the simplest organisms such adaptation is minimal and takes place slowly, largely through evolutionary bodily changes. In more complex organisms, as neural tissue develops and becomes increasingly differentiated, adaptation within the lifetime of the organism— that is, learning—becomes increasingly possible.

At the level of higher organisms, there is probably no aspect of adaptive behavior, from the simple but difficult to investigate changes in the activity within nerve cells, to the interaction between a therapist and his client, that does not incorporate some degree of learning. Thus a modern definition of psychology might be that it is the study of those forms of behavior that exemplify learning.

By this definition we could say that all of the articles in this book deal with different aspects of learning. The articles in this particular section, however, deal directly with the process of acquisition of new responses, which is what we generally refer to when we use the term "learning."

26

Phyletic Differences in Learning

M. E. Bitterman

What can we learn about man by studying animals? To what extent can we generalize from the results of animal experiments to the lives of humans? This question has arisen countless times to plague those researchers who use animals as their laboratory subjects, and the answers have varied widely.

It seems quite clear that all mammals develop in a very similar way from the fertilized ovum through several stages of cell division. Thus geneticists who ask questions about the effects of early prenatal environment (immediately postfertilization) upon later growth and development find that their research can be vastly simplified if they use animals. For one thing, the life cycle is much shorter, permitting more experiments to be done, more examples to be gathered, and more generations to be studied. Another advantage is that we are unwilling to use human beings in experiments that might produce permanent damage. With animals, the ethical problems are reduced.

But when it comes to making generalizations about such high-level characteristics as learning of habits and memory for fleeting experiences, we must tread more carefully. The author of this article describes learning experiments using many different species as subjects and summarizes the similarities and differences that have been found.

One way to study the role of the brain in learning is to compare the learning of animals with different brains. Differences in brain structure may be produced by surgical means, or they may be found in nature—as when the learning of different species is compared. Of these two approaches the first (the neurosurgical approach) has been rather popular, but the potentialities of the second still are largely unexplored. Students of learning in animals have been content for the most part to concentrate their attention on a few closely related mammalian forms, chosen largely for reasons of custom and convenience, which they have treated as representative of animals in general. Their work has been dominated almost from its inception by the hypothesis that the laws of learning are the same for all animals—that the wide differences in brain structure which occur in the animal series have a purely quantitative significance.

The hypothesis comes to us from Thorndike (1911), who more than any other man may be credited with having brought the study of animal intelligence into the laboratory. On the basis of his early comparative experiments, Thorndike decided that however much animals might differ in "what" they learned (which could be traced, he thought, to differences in their sensory, motor, and motivational properties), or in the "degree" of their learning ability (some seemed able to learn more than others, and more quickly), the principles which governed their learning were the same. Thorndike wrote:

If my analysis is true, the evolution of behavior is a rather simple matter. Formally the crab, fish, turtle, dog, cat, monkey and baby have very similar intellects and characters. All are systems of connections subject to change by the laws of exercise and effect (p. 280).

From American Psychologist, *Vol. 30 (1965), 396–410. Copyright 1965 by the American Psychological Association, and reproduced by permission. This paper was presented in March 1964, under the auspices of the National Science Foundation and of the National Institute of Mental Health, at the Institut de Psychologie in Paris, the Institute of Experimental Psychology in Oxford, the Institut für Hirnforschung in Zurich, and the Nencki Institute of Experimental Biology in Warsaw. The research described was supported by Grant MH02857 from the National Institute of Mental Health and by Contract Nonr 2829(01) with the Office of Naval Research.*

Although Thorndike's hypothesis was greeted with considerable skepticism, experiments with a variety of animals began to turn up functional similarities far more impressive than differences, and before long there was substantial disagreement only as to the *nature* of the laws which were assumed to hold for all animals. As acceptance of the hypothesis grew, the range of animals studied in experiments on learning declined—which, of course, was perfectly reasonable. If the laws of learning were the same everywhere in the animal series, there was nothing to be gained from the study of many different animals; indeed, standardization offered many advantages which it would be foolish to ignore. As the range of animals declined, however, so also did the likelihood of discovering any differences which might in fact exist.

It is difficult for the nonspecialist to appreciate quite how restricted has been the range of animals studied in experiments on animal learning because the restriction is so marked; the novelty of work with lower animals is such that two or three inexpressibly crude experiments with a flatworm may be better publicized than a hundred competent experiments with the rat. Some quantitative evidence on the degree of restriction was provided about twenty years ago by Schneirla, whose conclusion then was that "we do not have a comparative psychology" (Harriman, 1946, p. 314). Schneirla's analysis was carried further by Beach (1950), who plotted the curves which are reproduced in Figure 1. Based on a count of all papers appearing between 1911 and 1948 in the *Journal of Animal Behavior* and its successors, the *Journal of Comparative Psychology* and the *Journal of Comparative and Physiological Psychology,* the curves show how interest in the rat mounted while interest in submammalian forms declined. By the thirties, a stable pattern had emerged: about sixty per cent of papers on the rat, 30 per cent on other mammals (mostly primates), and 10 per cent on lower forms. The set of points at the extreme right, which I have added for the decade after 1948, shows no change in the pattern. You will note that these curves are based on papers published only in a single line of journals, and on all papers in those journals—not only the ones which deal with learning; but most of the papers *do* deal with learning, and I know of no other journal which is a richer source of information about learning in submammalians or which, if included in the tabulation, would alter the conclusion that what we know about learning in animals we know primarily from the intensive study of a small number of mammalian forms.

How widespread is the acceptance of Thorndike's hypothesis by contemporary theorists and systematists may be judged from a set of writings recently assembled by Koch (1959). Skinner is quite explicit in his assumption that which animal is studied "doesn't matter." When due allowance has been made for differences in sensory and motor characteristics, he explains, "what remains of . . . behavior shows astonishingly similar properties" (Koch, 1959, p. 375). Tolman, Miller, Guthrie, Estes, and Logan (representing Hull and Spence) rest their perfectly general conclusions about the nature of learning on the data of experiments with

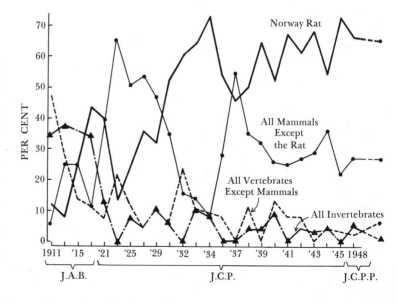

FIGURE 1 *Percentage of papers dealing with animals in each of four categories which appeared between 1911 and 1948 in the* Journal of Animal Behavior, *the* Journal of Comparative Psychology, *and the* Journal of Comparative and Physiological Psychology *(Beach, 1950).* (*The points at right, for the decade after 1948, were added by me.*)

a few selected mammals—mostly rat, monkey, and man—skipping lightly back and forth from one to another as if indeed structure did not matter, although Miller "does not deny the possibility that men may have additional capacities which are much less well developed or absent in the lower mammals" (Koch, 1959, p. 204). Harlow alone makes a case for species differences in learning, pointing to the unequal rates of improvement shown by various mammals (mostly primates) trained in long series of discriminative problems, but he gives us no reason to believe that the differences are more than quantitative. While he implies clearly that the capacity for interproblem transfer may be absent entirely in certain lower animals—in the rat, he says, it exists only in a "most rudimentary form" (Koch, 1959, p. 505)—submammalian evidence is lacking.

Although I have been considering thus far only the work of the West, I do not think that things have been very different on the other side of the Curtain. The conditioning has been "classical" rather than "instrumental" in the main, and the favored animal has been the dog rather than the rat, but the range of animals studied in any detail has been small, at least until quite recently, and the principles discovered have been generalized widely. In the words of Voronin (1962), the guiding Pavlovian propositions have been that

The conditioned reflex is a universal mechanism of activity acquired in the course of the organism's individual life . . . [and that] in the course of evolution of the animal world there took place only a quantitative growth or complication of higher nervous activity (pp. 161–162).

These propositions are supported, Voronin believes, by the results of some recent Russian comparisons of mammalian and submammalian vertebrates. On the basis of these results, he defines three stages in the evolution of intelligence which are distinguished in terms of the increasing role of learning in the life of the individual organism and in terms of the precision and delicacy of the learning process. He hastens to assure us, however, that there is nothing really new, even at the highest stage, which differs from the others only quantitatively.

The results of the experiments which I shall now describe support quite another view. I began these experiments without very much in the way of conviction as to their outcome, although the formal attractions of the bold Thorndikian hypothesis were rather obvious, and I should have been pleased on purely esthetic grounds to be able to accept it. I was convinced only that the hypothesis had not yet received the critical scrutiny it seemed to warrant and that it was much too important to be taken any longer on faith. With the familiar rat as a standard, I selected for comparative study another animal—a fish—which I thought similar enough to the rat that it could be studied in analogous experiments, yet different enough to afford a marked neuroanatomical contrast. I did not propose to compare the two animals in terms of numerical scores, as, for example, the number of trials required for (or the number of errors made in) the mastery of some problem, because such differences would not necessarily imply the operation of different learning processes. I proposed instead to compare them in terms of *functional relations*—to find out whether their perfor-

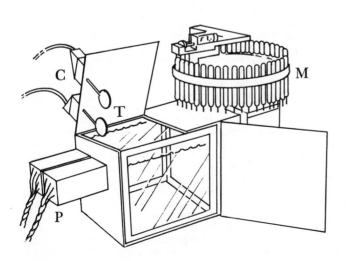

FIGURE 2 *A situation for the study of discrimination in the fish (T, targets which are lowered into the water as the cover of the enclosure is brought down; C, phonograph cartridges which hold the targets and register contacts with them; P, projectors for projecting various stimuli on the targets; M, liveworm dispenser.)*

mance would be affected in the same way by the same variables (Bitterman, 1960). Why I chose to begin with certain variables rather than others probably is not worth considering—the choice was largely intuitive; whatever the reasons, the experiments soon turned up some substantial differences in the learning of fish and rat. I shall describe here two of those differences, and then present the results of some further experiments which were designed to tell us what they mean.

One of the situations developed for the study of learning in the fish is illustrated in Figure 2. The animal is brought in its individual living tank to a black Plexiglas enclosure. The manipulanda are two Plexiglas disks (targets) at which the animal is trained to strike. The targets are mounted on rods set into the needle holders of phonograph cartridges in such a way that when the animal makes contact with one of the targets a voltage is generated across its cartridge. This voltage is used to operate a set of relays which record the response and control its consequences. The targets are illuminated with colored lights or patterns projected upon them from behind; on any given trial, for example, the left target may be green and the right one red, or the left target may show a triangle and the right one a circle. The reward for correct choice is a *Tubifex* worm discharged into the water through a small opening at the top of the enclosure—the worm is discharged from an eyedropper whose bulb is compressed by a pair of solenoid-operated jaws. When a worm is dropped, a magazine light at the rear of the enclosure is turned on for a few seconds, which signals that a worm has been dropped and provides some diffuse illumination which enables the animal to find it. All of the events of training are programed automatically and recorded on tape.[1]

I shall talk about two kinds of experiment which have been done in this situation. The first is concerned with *habit reversal*. Suppose an animal is trained to choose one of two stimuli, either for a fixed number of trials or to some criterion level of correct choice, and then the positive and negative stimuli are reversed; that is, the previously unrewarded stimulus now is rewarded, and the previously rewarded stimulus is unrewarded. After the same number of trials as were given in the original problem, or when the original criterion has been reached in the first reversal, the positive and negative stimuli are reversed again—and so forth. In such an experiment, the rat typically shows a dramatic improvement in performance. It may make many errors in the early reversals, but as

FIGURE 3   *Spatial habit reversal in fish and rat (The fish data are taken from Bitterman, Wodinsky, and Candland, 1958; the rat data are from Gonzalez, Roberts, and Bitterman, 1964.)*

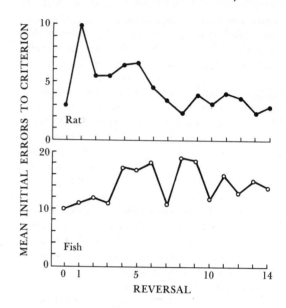

training proceeds it reverses more and more readily. In Figure 3, the performance of a group of Afri-

[1] The response-detection system and a dry-pellet feeder are described in Longo and Bitterman (1959). The live-worm dispenser—which makes it possible to extend the work to species (like the goldfish) that do not take an abundance of dry food—is described in Longo and Bitterman (1963). Programing procedures are described in my chapter on "Animal Learning" in Sidowski (1965). The fully automated technique was developed only after some years of work with less elegant ones which did not permit the complete removal of the experimenter from the experimental situation. The advantages of such removal, from the stand point of efficiency and of objectivity, should be obvious; yet I have encountered, especially in Europe, a good deal of hostility toward automation. In almost every audience, someone can be counted on to say, rather self-righteously, "I like to *watch* my animals." I explain that the automated techniques were developed after a good deal of watching to determine what was worth watching, and that they simply transfer a good part of the watching function to devices more sensitive and reliable than the experimenter, but that they do not rule out the possibility of further watching. In fact, freed of the necessity of programing trials and of recording data, the experimenter now can watch more intently than ever before. The United States has seen great advances in mammalian technique during recent years, while submammalian technique (except for the Skinnerian work with pigeons) has remained terribly primitive. A systematic comparative psychology will require some parallel advances in submammalian technique.

can mouthbreeders is compared with that of a group of rats in a series of spatial reversals. (In a spatial problem, the animal chooses between a pair of stimuli which differ only with respect to their position in space, and reinforcement is correlated with position, e.g., the stimulus on the left is reinforced.) The apparatus used for the rat was analogous to the apparatus for the fish which you have already seen. On each trial, the animal was offered a choice between two identically illuminated panels set into the wall of the experimental chamber. It responded by pressing one of the panels, and correct choice operated a feeder which discharged a pellet of food into a lighted food cup. The fish were trained in an early version of the apparatus which you have already seen. For both species, there were 20 trials per day to the criterion of 17 out of 20 correct choices, positive and negative positions being reversed for each animal whenever it met that criterion. Now consider the results. The upper curve of the pair you see here is quite representative of the performance of rats in such a problem—rising at first, and then falling in negatively accelerated fashion to a low level; with a little more training than is shown here, the animals reverse after but a single error. The lower curve is quite representative of the performance of fish in such a problem—there is no progressive improvement, but instead some tendency toward progressive deterioration as training continues.

How is this difference to be interpreted? We may ask first whether the results indicate anything beyond a quantitative difference in the learning of the two animals. It might be contended that reversal learning simply goes on more slowly in the fish than in the rat—that in 10 or 15 more reversals the fish, too, would have shown progressive improvement. In fact, however, the training of fish has been carried much further in later experiments, some animals completing more than 150 reversals without any sign of improvement. (I invite anyone who remains skeptical on this point to persist even longer in the search for improvement.)

Another possibility to be considered is that the difference between fish and rat which is reflected in these curves is not a difference in learning at all, but a difference in some confounded variable —sensory, motor, or motivational. Who can say, for example, whether the sensory and the motor demands made upon the two animals in these experiments were exactly the same? Who can say whether the fish were just as hungry as the rats, or whether the bits of food given the fish were equal

in reward value to those given the rats? It would, I must admit, be a rare coincidence indeed if the conditions employed for the two animals were exactly equal in all of these potentially important respects. How, then, is it possible to find out whether the results obtained are to be attributed to a difference in learning, or to a difference in sensory, or in motor, or in motivational factors? A frank critic might say that it was rather foolish to have made the comparison in the first place, when a moment's thought would have shown that it could not possibly have any meaningful outcome. It is interesting to note that neither Harlow nor Voronin shows any appreciation of this problem. We may doubt, then, whether they have evidence even for quantitative differences in the *learning* of their various animals.

I do not, of course, know how to arrange a set of conditions for the fish which will make sensory and motor demands exactly equal to those which are made upon the rat in some given experimental situation. Nor do I know how to equate drive level or reward value in the two animals. Fortunately, however, meaningful comparisons still are possible because for *control by equation* we may substitute what I call *control by systematic variation*. Consider, for example, the hypothesis that the difference between the curves which you see here is due to a difference, not in learning, but in degree of hunger. The hypothesis implies that there is a level of hunger at which the fish *will* show progressive improvement, and, put in this way, the hypothesis becomes easy to test. We have only to vary level of hunger widely in different groups of fish, which we know well how to do. If, despite the widest possible variation in hunger, progressive improvement fails to appear in the fish, we may reject the hunger hypothesis. Hypotheses about other variables also may be tested by systematic variation. With regard to the question of reversal learning, I shall simply say here that progressive improvement has appeared in the rat under a wide variety of experimental conditions—it is difficult, in fact, to find a set of conditions under which the rat does not show improvement. In the fish, by contrast, reliable evidence of improvement has failed to appear under a variety of conditions.

I cannot, of course, prove that the fish is incapable of progressive improvement. I only can give you evidence of failure to find it in the course of earnest efforts; and the point is important enough, perhaps, that you may be willing to look at some more negative results. The curves of Figure 4 summarize the outcome of an experiment in

FIGURE 4 *Visual habit reversal in the fish (The upper curves show between-sessions performance in each of three problems; the lower curves show within-sessions performance at various stages of training—A, early, D, late—in each problem. These data are taken from some as yet unpublished experiments by Behrend, Domesick, and Bitterman.)*

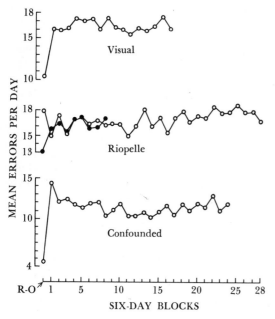

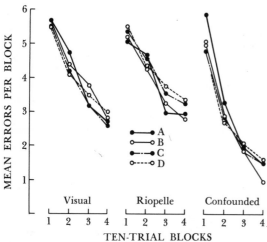

which the type of problem was varied. Three groups of mouthbreeders were given 40 trials per day and reversed daily, irrespective of their performance. In the visual problem, reinforcement was correlated with color and independent of position, which varied randomly from trial to trial; e.g., red positive on odd days and green positive on even days. In the confounded problem,

reinforcement was correlated both with color and position; e.g., red always on the left, green always on the right, with red-left positive on odd days and green-right positive on even days. The Riopelle problem was like the visual problem, except that each day's colors were chosen from a group of four, with the restriction that there be no more than partial reversal from one day to the next; i.e., yesterday's negative now positive with a "new" color negative, or yesterday's positive now negative with a "new" color now positive. The upper curves show that there was no improvement over days in any of the three problems (the suggestion of an initial decline in the confounded curve is not statistically reliable). The lower curves show that there was a considerable amount of learning over the forty trials of each day in each problem and at every stage of training, but that the pattern of improvement over trials did not change as training continued. Negative results of this sort now have been obtained under a variety of conditions wide enough, I think, that the burden of proof now rests with the skeptic. Until someone produces positive results, I shall assume that the fish is incapable of progressive improvement, and that we have come here upon a difference in the learning of fish and rat.

Experiments on *probability learning* also have given different results for rat and fish. Suppose that we train an animal in a choice situation with a ratio of reinforcement other than 100:0; that is, instead of rewarding one alternative on 100 per cent of trials and the other never, we reward one alternative on, say, a random 70 per cent of trials and the other on the remaining 30 per cent of trials, thus constituting what may be called a *70:30 problem*. Under some conditions, rat and fish both "maximize" in such a problem, which is to say that they tend always to choose the more frequently reinforced alternative. Under other conditions—specifically, under conditions in which the distribution of reinforcements is exactly controlled—the rat continues to maximize, but the fish "matches," which is to say that its distribution of choices approximates the distribution of reinforcements: In a 70:30 problem, it chooses the 70 per cent alternative on about 70 per cent of trials and the 30 per cent alternative on the remaining trials.

Figure 5 shows some sample data for a visual problem in which the discriminanda were horizontal and vertical stripes. In the first stage of the experiment, response to one of the stripes was rewarded on a random 70 per cent of each day's twenty trials, and response to the other stripe was

FIGURE 5 *Visual probability learning in fish and rat (From Bitterman, Wodinsky, and Candland, 1958)*

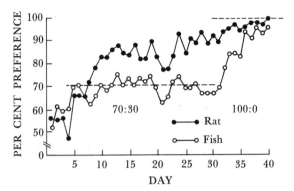

FIGURE 6 *Probability matching in the fish (From Behrend and Bitterman, 1961)*

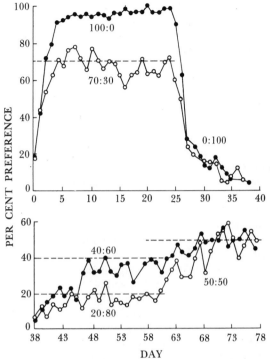

rewarded on the remaining 30 per cent of the trials—a 70:30 problem. In the second stage of the experiment the ratio of reinforcement was changed to 100:0, response to the 70 per cent stripe of the first stage being consistently rewarded. The curves shown are plotted in terms of the percentage of each day's responses which were made to the more frequently rewarded alternative. The fish went rapidly from a near-chance level of preference for the 70 per cent stimulus to about a 70 per cent preference, which was maintained from Day 5 until Day 30. With the beginning of the 100:0 training, the preference shifted rapidly upward to about the 95 per cent level. The preference of the rats for the more frequently reinforced stimulus rose gradually from a near-chance level at the start of the 70:30 training to about the 90 per cent level on Day 30. In the ten days of 100:0 training, this preference continued to increase gradually, as it might have done irrespective of the shift from inconsistent to consistent reinforcement. Some further evidence of the close correspondence between choice ratio and reward ratio, which is easy to demonstrate in the fish, is presented in Figure 6. The upper portion shows the performance of two groups of mouthbreeders; one trained on a 100:0 and the other on a 70:30 confounded (black-white) problem, and both then shifted to the 0:100 problem (the less frequently rewarded alternative of the first phase now being consistently rewarded). The lower portion shows what happened when one group then was shifted to 40:60 and the other to 20:80, after which both were shifted to 50:50.

Two characteristics of these data should be noted. First, the probability matching which the fish curves demonstrate is an individual, not a group phenomenon—that is, it is not an artifact of averaging. All the animals in the group behave in

much the same way. I make this obvious point because some averaged data which have been taken as evidence of matching in the rat are indeed unrepresentative of individual performances.[2] Second, the matching shown by the fish is random rather than systematic. The distribution of choices recorded in the 70:30 problem looks like the distribution of colors which might be obtained by drawing marbles at random from a sack of black and white marbles with a color ratio of 70:30—that is, no sequential dependency is to be found in the data. While the rat typically maximizes, it may on occasion show a correspondence of choice ratio and reward ratio which can be traced to some systematic pattern of choice, like the patterns which are displayed in analogous experiments by human subjects. For example, a correspondence reported by Hickson (1961) has been traced to a tendency in his rats to choose on each trial the alternative which had been rewarded on the immediately preceding trial. Quite the opposite tendency, which also tends to produce a correspon-

2 The averaged data are cited by Estes (1957). The distribution of individual performances is given by Bitterman, Wodinsky, and Candland (1958).

dence between choice ratio and reinforcement ratio, has been found in the monkey—a tendency to *avoid* the rewarding alternative of the preceding trial (Wilson, Oscar, and Bitterman, 1964a, 1964b). The matching shown by the fish, which I shall call *random matching,* is a very different sort of thing.

Here then, are two striking differences between rat and fish. In experiments on habit reversal, the rat shows progressive improvement while the fish does not. In experiments on probability learning, the fish shows random matching while the rat does not. These results suggest a number of interesting questions, of which I shall raise here only two: First, there is the question of how the two differences are related. From the point of view of parsimony, the possibility must be considered that they reflect a single underlying difference in the functioning of the two animals—one which has to do with adjustment to inconsistent reinforcement. Inconsistency of reinforcement certainly is involved in both kinds of experiment, between sessions in reversal learning and within sessions in probability learning. It also is possible, however, that the results for reversal learning reflect one functional difference and the results for probability learning quite another. A second question concerns the relation between the observed differences in behavior and differences in brain structure. We may wonder, for example, to what extent the cortex of the rat is responsible for its progressive improvement in habit reversal, or for its failure to show random matching. In an effort to answer such questions we have begun to do some experiments, analogous to those which differentiate fish and normal rat, with a variety of other animals, and with rats surgically deprived in infancy of relevant brain tissues.

I shall describe first some results for extensively decorticated rats (Gonzalez *et al.,* 1964). The animals were operated on at the age of 15 or 16 days in a one-stage procedure which resulted in the destruction of about 70 per cent of the cortex. Two sample lesions, one relatively small and one relatively large, are shown in Figure 7. The experimental work with the operates, like the work with normals, was begun after they had reached maturity—at about 90 days of age. From the methodological viewpoint, work with a brain-injured animal is perfectly equivalent to work with a normal animal of another species, and rats operated [on] in our standard fashion are treated in all respects as such, with systematic variation employed to control for the effects of sensory, motor, and motivational factors. The substantive relation of the work with

FIGURE 7 *Extent of cortical destruction in two rats operated at the age of 15 days and sacrificed at the age of 150 days (The two brains are selected to illustrate the range and general locus of injury produced by the operation. From Gonzalez, Roberts, and Bitterman, 1964)*

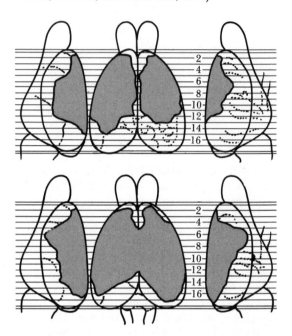

decorticated rats to the work with normal animals of different species is obvious: We are interested in whether extensive cortical damage will produce in the rat the kinds of behavior which are characteristic of precortical animals, such as the fish, or of animals with only very limited cortical development.

The results for decorticated rats emphasize the importance of the distinction between spatial and visual problems. In a pure spatial problem, you will remember, the two alternatives are identical except for position in space, and reinforcement is correlated with position, e.g., the alternative on the left is reinforced. In a pure visual problem, the two alternatives are visually differentiated, each occupying each of the two positions equally often, and reinforcement is correlated with visual appearance—e.g., the green alternative is reinforced independently of its position. The behavior of the decorticated rat is indistinguishable from that of the normal rat in spatial problems, but in visual problems it differs from the normal in the same way as does the fish.

The criterion-reversal performance of a group of decorticated rats trained in a spatial problem is shown in Figure 8 along with that of a group of

FIGURE 8   *Spatial habit reversal in normal rats and in rats extensively decorticated in infancy (From Gonzalez, Roberts, and Bitterman, 1964)*

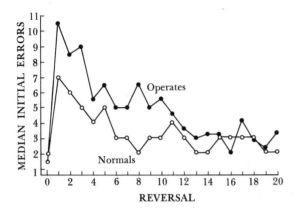

normal controls. There were 20 trials per day by the correction method, and the criterion of learning was 17 out of 20 correct choices. As you can see, the performance of the two groups was very much the same in the original problem. In the first 10 reversals the operates made more errors than did the normals, but (like the normals) they showed progressive improvement, and in the last 10 reversals, there was no difference between the two groups. The results for two additional groups, decorticated and normal, trained under analogous conditions in a visual problem (a brightness discrimination) are plotted in Figure 9. Again, the performance of normals and operates was much the same in the original problem. In the subsequent reversals, the error scores of the normal animals rose at first and then declined in charac-

FIGURE 9   *Visual habit reversal in normal rats and in rats extensively decorticated in infancy (From Gonzalez, Roberts, and Bitterman, 1964)*

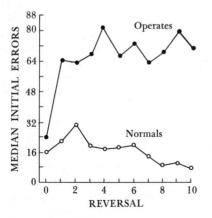

teristic fashion, but the error scores of the operates rose much more markedly and showed no subsequent tendency to decline.

In spatial probability learning the performance of the operates was indistinguishable from that of normals, but in visual probability learning the operates showed random matching. The asymptotic preferences of operates and normals, first in a 70:30 and then in a 50:50 brightness discrimination, are shown in Table 1. In the 70:30 problem, the operates came to choose the 70 per cent stimulus on about 70 per cent of trials (the mean was 71.7 per cent); in the 50:50 problem they chose the two stimuli about equally often (the mean preference for the former 70 per cent stimulus was 53.7 per cent). No sequential dependencies could be found in their behavior. By contrast, the normal animals tended to maximize in the 70:30 problem. The two whose preferences came closest to 70 per cent adopted rigid position habits (CP) in the 50:50 problem, while one of the others also responded to position, and two continued in the previously established preference. In both spatial experiments, then, the decorticated rats behaved like normal rats, while in both visual experiments they behaved like fish.

These results are compatible with the hypothesis that the cortex of the rat is responsible in some measure for its progressive improvement in habit reversal and for its failure to show random probability matching, at least in visual problems. They are compatible also with the hypothesis that the

TABLE 1   *Preferences of Decorticated Rats (O) and Normal Controls (N) for the More Frequently Reinforced Alternative in a 70:30 Visual Problem and for the Same Alternative in a Subsequent 50:50 Problem*

Subject	70:30 problem	50:50 problem
O-1	68.0	49.5
O-2	69.5	53.0
O-3	71.5	47.0
O-4	73.5	57.0
O-5	76.0	62.0
N-1	64.5	CP
N-2	79.0	CP
N-3	89.5	86.0
N-4	90.0	CP
N-5	90.0	80.0

Note.—CP means choice of one position on 90% or more of trials. Data from Gonzalez, Roberts, and Bitterman (1964).

behavioral differences between fish and rat which appear in the two kinds of experiment are reflections of a single functional difference between the two species. The latter hypothesis is contradicted, however, by some results for the pigeon which I shall now describe. I need not go into any detail about the experimental situation, because it is a fairly familiar one. Suffice it to say that the Skinnerian key-pecking apparatus was adapted for discrete-trials choice experiments directly analogous to those done with fish and rat. The bird, in a darkened enclosure, pecks at one of two lighted keys, correct choice being rewarded by access to grain. Contingencies are programed automatically, and responses are recorded on tape.

In experiments on habit reversal, both visual and spatial, the pigeon behaves like the rat; that is, it gives clear evidence of progressive improvement (Bullock and Bitterman, 1962a). Shown in Figure 10 is the criterion-reversal performance of a group of pigeons trained in a blue-green discrimination. There were 40 trials per day to the criterion of 34 correct choices in the 40 trials, with positive and negative colors reversed for each animal whenever it met that criterion. The results look very much like those obtained in analogous experiments with the rat: There is an initial increase in mean errors to criterion, followed by a progressive, negatively accelerated decline. Now what can we say of the behavior of the pigeon in experiments on probability learning? Figure 11 gives evidence of a correspondence between choice ratio and reward ratio as close in the pigeon as in the fish, and statistical analysis shows that the matching is random. The points for the pigeon, like those for the fish, represent the pooled results of a variety of experiments, both published and unpublished, which were carried out in my laboratory. Unlike the points for the fish, however, the points for the pigeon are based only on *visual* data, because the pigeon shows random matching

FIGURE 10   *Visual habit reversal in the pigeon (From Stearns and Bitterman, 1965)*

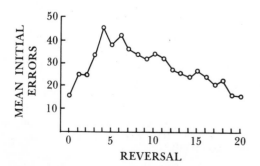

FIGURE 11   *Probability matching in fish and pigeon (The points for the fish are based both on spatial and on visual data, while those for the pigeon are based only on visual data.)*

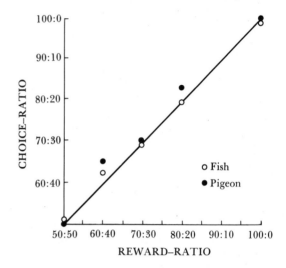

only in visual problems; in spatial problems it tends to maximize (Bullock and Bitterman, 1962b; Graf, Bullock, and Bitterman, 1964).

The results for the pigeon, then, are in a sense intermediate between those for the rat and for the fish. Like the rat, the pigeon shows progressive improvement in habit reversal, but, like the fish, it shows random probability matching—in visual problems if not in spatial ones. One conclusion which may be drawn from these results is that experiments on habit reversal and experiments on probability learning tap somewhat different processes. If the processes were the same, any animal would behave either like the fish, or like the rat, in both kinds of experiment. We have, then, been able to separate the processes underlying the two phenomena which differentiate fish and rat by a method which might be called *phylogenetic filtration*. It is interesting, too, that the visual-spatial dichotomy which appeared in work with the decorticated rat appears again in the probability learning of the pigeon. In experiments on habit reversal, the pigeon behaves like a normal rat; in experiments on probability learning, the pigeon behaves, not like a fish, but like an extensively decorticated rat.

Now let me show you some comparable data for several other species. Being very much interested in the reptilian brain, which is the first to show true cortex, I have devoted a good deal of effort to the development of a satisfactory technique for the study of learning in the painted turtle. After some partial success with a primitive T-maze (Kirk and Bitterman, 1963), I came finally to the situation diagramed in Figure 12. As in our latest apparatus for monkey, rat, pigeon, and fish, the turtle is presented with two differentially illuminated targets between which it chooses by pressing against one of them. Correct choice is rewarded with a pellet of hamburger or fish which is rotated into the chamber on a solenoid-driven tray. Some experiments on habit reversal now under way in this situation have yielded the data plotted in Figure 13. One group of turtles was trained on a spatial problem (both targets the same color) and another group on a visual problem (red versus green). There were 20 trials per day, with reversal after every 4 days. As you can see, progressive improvement has appeared in the spatial problem, but not in the visual problem. Some experiments on probability learning also are under way in this situation. In spatial problems, only maximizing and nonrandom matching (reward following) have been found, but in visual problems, random matching has begun to appear. This pattern of results, you will remember, is exactly that which was found in decorticated rats. Insofar as performance in these tests is concerned, then, extensive decortication in infancy turns rats into turtles.

I come now to some work with invertebrates. Diagramed in Figure 14 is a Y-maze for the cock-

FIGURE 13 *Visual and spatial habit reversal in the turtle (The data are taken from some as yet unpublished experiments by Holmes and Bitterman.)*

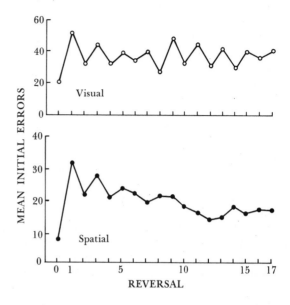

roach used in the experiments of Longo (1964). The technique is a much cruder one than those used for vertebrates, but it represents, I think, a considerable advance over anything that has yet been done with the cockroach. The motive utilized is shock avoidance: Ten seconds after the animal is introduced into the starting box, shock is turned on, and remains on, until the animal enters the goal box, which is its home cage; if the animal reaches the goal box in less than 10 seconds, it avoids shock entirely. Choices are detected objec-

FIGURE 12 *A situation for the study of discrimination in the turtle (Ch, animal's chamber; T, target; S, lamps for projecting colored lights on the targets; M, feeder which rotates a pellet of food, FP, into the chamber; ML, magazine lamp which is turned on to signal the presentation of food. From Bitterman, 1964)*

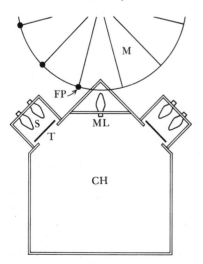

FIGURE 14 *A Y-maze for the cockroach (PC, photocell; PL, photocell lamp; S, starting compartment. From Longo, 1964)*

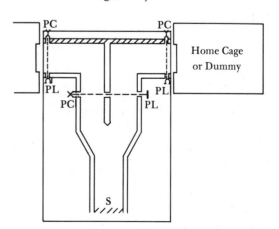

tively by photocells, but complete automation is not possible, because no satisfactory alternative to handling the animal has been found. The results of an experiment on spatial probability learning in the cockroach, which was patterned after those done with vertebrates, are plotted in **Figure 15**. Like the fish—but *unlike any higher vertebrate*—the cockroach shows random matching under spatial conditions. The results of an experiment on spatial habit reversal in the cockroach are plotted in Figure 16. Three groups of animals were given 10 trials per day—one group reversed each day, another group reversed every 4 days, and a control group never reversed during the stage of the experiment for which data are plotted. Although the 4-day group showed no significant improvement (its curve hardly declines at all beyond the first point, which is for the original problem), the daily group did show significant improvement (its curve declining in much the same way as that of the control group). What does this result mean? Have we found in the primitive cockroach a capability which does not exist in the fish? A consideration of some results for the earthworm will help to answer this question.

Diagramed in Figure 17 is a T-maze developed for the earthworm by Datta (1962). The stem of

FIGURE 16 *Spatial habit reversal in the cockroach (From Longo, 1964)*

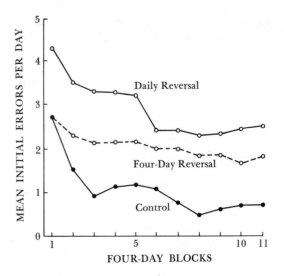

the maze is bright, warm, and dry, and the animal occasionally is shocked in it. A correct turn at the choice point carries the animal to its dark, moist, cool, shock-free home container, while an incorrect turn is punished with shock from a metal door which converts one arm of the maze into a cul. When the animal is shocked for contact with the door, a sensitive relay in the circuit is energized, thereby providing an objective index of error. This technique, again, is a crude one by vertebrate standards, but it seems to give reliable results. Some sample data on spatial habit reversal are plotted in Figure 18. The worms were given

FIGURE 15 *Spatial probability matching in the cockroach (From Longo, 1964)*

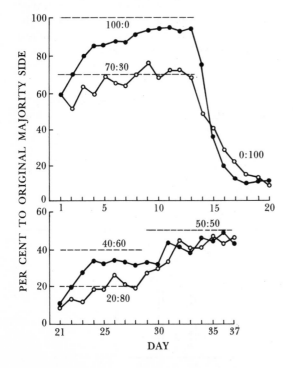

FIGURE 17 *A T-maze for the earthworm (L, lid, Do, metal door which converts one arm of the maze into a cul and delivers shock for erroneous choice; Fu, funnel to reduce retracing; HC, home container. From Datta, 1962)*

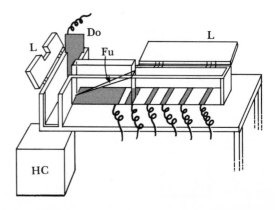

FIGURE 18 *Spatial habit reversal in the earth-worm (From Datta, 1962)*

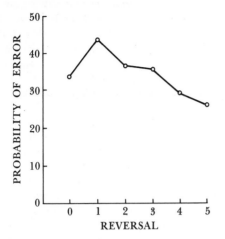

TABLE 2 *Behavior of a Variety of Animals in Four Classes of Problem which Differentiate Rat and Fish Expressed in Terms of Similarity to the Behavior of One or the Other of These Two Reference Animals*

Animal	Spatial problems		Visual problems	
	Re-versal	Proba-bility	Re-versal	Proba-bility
⎰Monkey	R	R	R	R
⎱Rat	R	R	R	R
Pigeon	R	R	R	F
⎰Turtle	R	R	F	F
⎱Decorticated rat	R	R	F	F
⎰Fish	F	F	F	F
⎢Cockroach	F	F	—	—
⎱Earthworm	F	—	—	—

Note.—*F* means behavior like that of the fish (random probability matching and failure of progressive improvement in habit reversal). *R* means behavior like that of the rat (maximizing or nonrandom probability matching the progressive improvement in habit reversal). Transitional regions are connected by the stepped line. The brackets group animals which have not yet been differentiated by these problems.

5 trials per day and reversed every 4 days. Note that the mean number of errors rose in the first reversal, and thereafter declined progressively, the animals doing better in the fourth and fifth reversals than in the original problem. In a further experiment, however, this improvement was found to be independent of reversal training per se and a function only of general experience in the maze: A control group, trained always to the same side while an experimental group was reversed repeatedly, did not differ from the experimental group when eventually it, too, was reversed. This test for the effects of general experience is feasible in the earthworm, because the turning preferences which it develops do not persist from session to session. The analysis of the progressive improvment shown by the cockroach is, however, a more difficult matter, and I must be content here simply to state Longo's opinion that it reflects, as in the earthworm, not an improvement in reversal capability, but an improved adjustment to the maze situation. The course of that general improvement is traced by the curve for the control group, which parallels that of the daily group. Nonspecific improvement probably is not as evident in the vertebrate data because general adjustment to the experimental situation proceeds rapidly and is essentially complete at the end of pretraining.[3]

The results of these experiments on habit reversal and probability learning in a variety of animals are summarized in Table 2. Spatial and visual problems are categorized separately because they give different results. The rows for all the subjects except one are ordered in accordance with the conventional scale of complexity—monkey at

the top and earthworm at the bottom. The only subject whose place in the table is not based on preconceived complexity is the decorticated rat, whose placement (with the turtle, between the pigeon and the fish) is dictated by experimental outcomes. The differences between fish and rat which provided points of departure for the subsequent work with other organisms also provide a frame of reference for reading the table: *R* means that the results obtained in a given kind of experiment with a given subject are like those for the rat (that is, progressive improvement in habit

---

[3] A possibility to be considered is that a portion at least of the cockroach's improvement was due to improvement in the experimenter, of whom the conduct of the experiment required considerable skill. The same may be said of the first in the series of experiments with the fish by Wodinsky and Bitterman (1957), which was the only one to show anything like progressive improvement and whose results have not been replicated in work with automated equipment; the pattern of improvement was, incidentally, quite unlike that found in mammals. A study of another arthropod (the Bermuda land crab) in a simple escape situation, by Datta, Milstein, and Bitterman (1960), gave no evidence of improvement.

reversal and failure of random matching), while *F* means that the results obtained are like those for the fish (that is, random matching and failure of progressive improvement). It should be understood that these entries are made with varying degrees of confidence. Where there are no data, there are no entries, but an entry is made even where, as in the case of the turtle, the data are yet fragmentary and incomplete. All entries are based on data from my laboratory, except those for reversal learning in the monkey, which are based on the literature.

The table is an orderly one. In each column there is a single transition from *F* to *R* as the scale of subjects is ascended, although the point of transition varies from column to column, suggesting a certain functional independence: Rat-like behavior in spatial problems of both kinds appears first in decorticated rat and turtle, rat-like behavior in visual reversal learning appears first in pigeon, and rat-like behavior in visual probability learning appears first in rat. The eight subjects fall into four different groupings: monkey and rat in one; pigeon in a second; turtle and decorticated rat in a third; fish, cockroach, and earthworm in a fourth. Monkey and rat fall into the same grouping because they are not differentiated by these experiments when all failures of random probability matching are classified as *R*. The data for the two mammals do, however, show different kinds of sequential dependency in experiments on probability learning, reward following in the rat giving way in the monkey to the opposite strategy (avoiding the rewarded alternatives of the preceding trial). It is interesting to note that this new strategy of the monkey has been manifested thus far only with respect to the spatial locus of reward, even when the alternatives have been visually distinct. This finding fits the generalization suggested at other points in the table: that as we ascend the phyletic scale new modes of adjustment appear earlier in spatial than in visual contexts.

It is of some interest to ask whether *R* modes of adjustment are in any sense more effective than *F* modes, and for habit reversal, at least, the answer is clear. Progressive improvement is on its face a superior adjustment, representing a flexibility that cannot help but be of value in an animal's adjustment to changing life circumstances. The answer for probability learning is less clear, although it can be said that maximizing produces a higher percentage of correct choice than does matching. In a 70:30 problem, for example, the probability of correct choice is .70 for maximizing but only .58—(.70 × .70) + (.30 × .30)—for matching. Nonrandom matching is no more successful than random matching by this criterion, but we know that in human subjects it is the outcome of an effort to find a principle that will permit 100 per cent correct choice; the hypotheses tested reflect the observed reward ratio, and they produce a corresponding choice ratio. To the degree that nonrandom matching in infrahuman subjects is based on an emerging hypothetical or strategic capability, it represents a considerable functional advance over random matching.

The table does, of course, have certain obvious limitations. Clearly, I should like to be able to write *bird* rather than *pigeon*, I should like by *fish* to mean more than *mouthbreeder*, and so forth. It will be interesting to discover how representative of their classes are the particular species studied in these experiments—whose choice was dictated largely by practical considerations—and to extend the comparisons to other classes and phyla. I can say, too, that the behavioral categories used in the table almost certainly will need refining; already the *R-F* dichotomy is strained by the data on probability learning (with *R* standing for maximizing, for near maximizing, and for nonrandom matching of several different kinds), while better techniques must be found for isolating the various constituents of progressive improvement in habit reversal. The uncontaminated linear order which now appears in the table, while undeniably esthetic, is rather embarrassing from the standpoint of the far-from-linear evolutionary relationships among the species studied; nonlinearities are perhaps to be expected as the behavioral categories are refined and as the range of tests is broadened.

Whatever its limitations, the table is useful, I think, not only as a summary of results already obtained, but as a guide to further research. Almost certainly, the order in the table will permit us to reduce the amount of parametric variation which must be done before we are satisfied that some phenomenon for which we are looking in a given animal is not to be found. Suppose, for example, that we had begun to work with the turtle before the pigeon, and suppose that we had sought persistently, but in vain, for evidence of random matching in spatial probability learning, being satisfied at last to enter an *R* for the turtle in the second column of the table. Turning then to the pigeon, we should be prepared after many fewer unsuccessful efforts to enter an *R*. I do not mean, of course, that systematic parametric variation is no longer important in comparative research; we must continue to do a great deal of it, especially at points of transition in the table, and wherever the entries fail to reflect gross discontinuities in the evolutionary histories of the organisms concerned. I do think, however, that the table will save us some parametric effort *in certain regions*—effort which may be diverted to the task of increasing the range of organisms and the range of tests represented. It does not seem unreasonable to expect that, thus expanded, the table will provide some useful clues to the evolution of intelligence and its relation to the evolution of the brain.

REFERENCES

Beach, F. A. The snark was a boojum. *American Psychologist*, 1950, **5**, 115–124.

Behrend, E. R., & Bitterman, M. E. Probability-matching in the fish. *American Journal of Psychology*, 1961, **74**, 542–551.

Bitterman, M. E. Toward a comparative psychology of learning. *American Psychologist*, 1960, **15**, 704–712.

Bitterman, M. E. An instrumental technique for the turtle. *Journal of the Experimental Analysis of Behavior*, 1964, **7**, 189–190.

Bitterman, M. E., Wodinsky, J., & Candland, D. K. Some comparative psychology. *American Journal of Psychology*, 1958, **71**, 94–110.

Bullock, D. H., & Bitterman, M. E. Habit reversal in the pigeon. *Journal of Comparative and Physiological Psychology*, 1962, **55**, 958–962. (a)

Bullock, D. H., & Bitterman, M. E. Probability-matching in the pigeon. *American Journal of Psychology*, 1962, **75**, 634–639. (b)

Datta, L. G. Learning in the earthworm, *Lumbricus terrestris*. *American Journal of Psychology*, 1962, **75**, 531–553.

Datta, L. G., Milstein, S., & Bitterman, M. E. Habit reversal in the crab. *Journal of Comparative and Physiological Psychology*, 1960, **53**, 275–278.

Estes, W. K. Of models and men. *American Psychologist*, 1957, **12**, 609–616.

Gonzalez, R. C., Roberts, W. A., & Bitterman, M. E. Learning in adult rats with extensive cortical lesions made in infancy. *American Journal of Psychology*, 1964, **77**, 547–562.

Graf, V., Bullock, D. H., & Bitterman, M. E. Further experiments on probability-matching in the pigeon. *Journal of Experimental Analysis of Behavior*, 1964, **7**, 151–157.

Harriman, P. L. (Ed.) *Twentieth-century psychology*. New York: Philosophical Library, 1946.

Hickson, R. H. Response probability in a two-choice learning situation with varying probability of reinforcement. *Journal of Experimental Psychology*, 1961, **62**, 138–144.

Kirk, K. L., & Bitterman, M. E. Habit reversal in the turtle. *Quarterly Journal of Experimental Psychology*, 1963, **15**, 52–57.

Koch, S. *Psychology: A study of a science.* Vol. 2. *General systematic formulations, learning, and special processes.* New York: McGraw-Hill, 1959.

Longo, N. Probability-learning and habit-reversal in the cockroach. *American Journal of Psychology*, 1964, **77**, 29–41.

Longo, N., & Bitterman, M. E. Improved apparatus for the study of learning in fish. *American Journal of Psychology*, 1959, **72**, 616–620.

Longo, N., & Bitterman, M. E. An improved live-worm dispenser. *Journal of the Experimental Analysis of Behavior*, 1963, **6**, 279–280.

Sidowski, J. (Ed.) *Experimental methods and instrumentation in psychology*. New York: McGraw-Hill, 1965.

Stearns, E. M., & Bitterman, M. E. A comparison of key-pecking with an ingestive technique for the study of discriminative learning in pigeons. *American Journal of Psychology*, 1965, **78**, pp. 48–56.

Thorndike, E. L. *Animal intelligence*. New York: Macmillan, 1911.

Voronin, L. G. Some results of comparative-physiological investigations of higher nervous activity. *Psychological Bulletin*, 1962, **59**, 161–195.

Wilson, W. A., Jr., Oscar, M., & Bitterman, M. E. Probability learning in the monkey. *Quarterly Journal of Experimental Psychology*, 1964, **16**, 163–165. (a)

Wilson, W. A., Jr., Oscar, M., & Bitterman, M. E. Visual probability-learning in the monkey. *Psychonomic Science*, 1964, **1**, 71–72. (b)

Wodinsky, J., & Bitterman, M. E. Discrimination-reversal in the fish. *American Journal of Psychology*, 1957, **70**, 569–576.

27

The Pigeon as a Quality-Control Inspector

Thom Verhave

The success enjoyed by animal trainers, most of whom rely on reinforcement theory in some way, shows that animals can learn to do highly complex kinds of "tricks." So far, such highly trained animals have been used chiefly for public entertainment of one kind or another. But a few investigators have pondered the question of whether it would also be possible to train animals to function as skilled workers performing certain repetitive tasks that have always been done by humans. Most such attempts, like the one described in this article, involve some form of discrimination learning. As you will see, however, the question is not merely one of how accurate and reliable a worker a pigeon would be—there is also the problem of getting producers and consumers to accept the idea of sub-human workers on an assembly line, especially when the product is intended for human consumption.

Many of the operations involved in the quality-control inspection of commercial products consist of monotonous checking jobs performed by human operators. In addition to monotony, these (usually visual) inspection jobs have several other characteristics in common: (*a*) They require little if any manual skill or dexterity, (*b*) they require good visual acuity, (*c*) they require a capacity for color vision, and (*d*) they are extremely difficult to automate. There is, however, an organic device which has the following favorable properties: (*a*) an average life span of approximately 10 to 15 years (Levi, 1963), (*b*) an extreme flexibility in adjusting to its environment as well as an enormous learning ability (Ferster and Skinner, 1957; Smee, 1850), (*c*) a visual acuity as good as the human eye (Reese, 1964), (*d*) color vision (Reese, 1964). The price for one such device is only (approximately) $1.50; its name: *Columba livia domestica* or the pigeon.

Because of the characteristics listed above it is quite feasible to train pigeons to do all the visual checking operations involved in commercial manufacture. What follows is a brief account of an exploratory attempt to put the above suggestion into actual practice (Verhave, 1959). This paper is written partially in self-defense: Stories about the pill-inspecting pigeons have circulated for many years—many versions containing gross inaccuracies.

In July of 1955 I was employed as a "psycho-pharmacologist" at one of the larger pharmaceutical companies. The main purpose of the laboratory was to develop and evaluate techniques for the experimental analysis of the effects of drugs on the behavior of animals.

Sometime probably early in 1958, I finally took the tour of the plant, which is mandatory for all new employees. During the all-day tour of the extensive research and manufacturing facilities, I ran into the (gelatin) drug-capsule facilities. The capsules are manufactured by several very large and extremely complex machines, which together have a maximum production capacity of approximately 20,000,000 capsules per day. All of the capsules, which are made in a large number of sizes and colors, are visually inspected. This job was done by a contingent of about 70 women. After inspection the capsules go to other machines which fill them automatically with the appropriate pharmaceuticals. The capsules are inspected in batches. The number of caps in a batch depends on the volume or size of the capsule: The larger the capsule size, the smaller the number in a batch to be inspected. All of the capsules in a particular

From American Psychologist, *Vol. 21 (1966), 109–115. Copyright 1966 by the American Psychological Association, and reproduced by permission. Opinions and conclusions contained in this article are those of the author. They are not to be construed as necessarily reflecting the views or the endorsement of either the pharmaceutical industry or any pigeon. I am indebted to John E. Owen, my former collaborator, for a critical reading of this paper, which saved me from many errors due to faulty memory.*

batch are of the same shape, size, and color. A big reservoir with a funnel drops the capsules at a fixed rate on an endless moving belt. The inspector, or "capsule sorter" as she is called, is located in front of the moving belt which is illuminated from underneath. She "pattern scans" the capsules as they move by and picks up and throws out all "skags." A skag is a discard capsule because it is off-color, has a piece of gelatin sticking out, or has a dent in it. This also includes all double-cap capsules. When the capsule comes to the capsule sorter, it is already closed by putting two halves, a cap and a body, together. This step was already performed by the production machine. Sometimes, however, during transportation or in storage a second cap (the larger half of a capsule) is put on top of an already capped capsule (a cap and body may vibrate apart and a loose cap may then slide over the body of another already capped capsule). Such a "double-cap skag" produces problems later on in the filling machine. After inquiry, I was told that the double-cap skag is also one of the more difficult types to spot.

The sorters (all female) are paid off on a group-bonus schedule employing "error cost." After the inspection of a batch is completed, a supervisor (usually also female) scoops a ladleful of inspected capsules out of the barrel in which they were collected. The types of skag defects are categorized and the inspector can allow up to three or four of the more minor imperfections per sample before a batch is rejected. If she finds more than the allowed number of skags in the sample ladled from the batch, the inspector has to reinspect the entire batch of capsules. She is thus likely to reduce her bonus pay for the day since it depends partially on her own inspection output.

To come back to the main story: On seeing those women and their simple monotonous task, and knowing about Skinner's "Pigeons in a Pelican" (1960, 1965), I said to myself, "Hell, a pigeon can do that!" Sometime later, I mentioned my birdbrain idea to a friend and fellow scientist in the physiochemistry department who also supervised the electronics shop which supported the research division. He almost fell out of his chair and choked in a fit of laughter. However, after the joke had worn off, we talked more seriously about my odd notion, especially after I told him about Project ORCON (organic control—Skinner, 1960, 1965). Eventually the director of research and I talked about it. It so happened that I had come up with my suggestion at an opportune time. The company had recently spent a considerable sum of money on a machine constructed by an outside

engineering firm and designed to inspect automatically for double caps. It did not work. After some deliberation the director of research gave me the go-ahead to build a demonstration and tryout setup. With the able help and splendid cooperation of the instrument-shop people, under the direction of my friend of the physiochemistry department, a demonstration apparatus was built. . . .

While the apparatus was being designed and built, I had plenty of opportunity to consider varying aspects of the discrimination-training problems I would be faced with. The first decision to be made was which particular "skag" problem to tackle first. I obtained samples of various sized capsules of different colors. It was tempting to tackle the most troublesome problem first: the double-cap skag, especially those involving small capsules of colorless and transparent gelatin. On the actual inspection line these were the most difficult to spot. After playing around with different ways of presenting these capsules to a pigeon behind a modified pigeon key, a simple solution to the double-cap problem was discovered by accident. One of the minor problems to be solved was the lighting of the capsules presented behind the key. I discovered that by shining a narrow beam of light at the proper angle on a three-dimensional transparent curved surface, one obtains a focal point inside the object. (The tops and bottoms of all capsules are either round or oval.) In the case of a double-cap skag, one gets two clearly distinct focal points in slightly different positions. So, even in the case of the transparent double-cap capsule, all a pigeon had to do was to discriminate between one versus two bright spots of light inside the curious objects behind his key: no problem![1]

For the purpose of working out the details of the actual training and work procedure, however, I decided to take the simplest discrimination problem possible. I chose a simple color discrimination: white versus red capsules. Two naive birds were selected for inspection duty. For one bird the red capsules were arbitrarily defined as skags ($S^\triangle$). For the other bird, the white capsules were given the same status.

. . . There were two pigeon keys. One key was actually a small transparent window, the other was opaque. The capsules could be brought into view behind the transparent key one by one at a maximum rate of about two per second. After a preliminary training phase, the birds were run as

---

[1] The opaque, single-color double cap may still be a difficult discrimination problem, even for a pigeon.

follows: A single peck on the weakly illuminated opaque key would (*a*) momentarily (.5 second) turn off the light behind the transparent key, and (*b*) weakly illuminate the window key to an extent insufficient to see much of the capsule in place behind it.

Next, a single peck on the now weakly lit window key would turn on a bright and narrow beam of light which clearly illuminated the capsule. The capsules were individually mounted in small and hollow bottlestops glued onto the metal plates of the endless belt. If the bird now pecked three more times on the window key with the new illuminated capsule exposed to view, a brief tone would sound. Next came the moment of decision. If the capsule exposed to view was judged to be a skag, the bird was required to make two more pecks on the window key. This would (*a*) turn off the beam of light illuminating the capsule, (*b*) move up the next capsule, and (*c*) produce food by way of the automatic hopper on a fixed-percentage basis (usually 100 per cent). However, if the capsule was considered to be acceptable, the bird indicated this by changing over to the opaque key. A peck on this key would also (*a*) turn off the beam of light behind the other key (window), and (*b*) move up the next capsule. It would not, however, produce reinforcement.

A bird, then, determined his own inspection rate. A peck on the opaque key would initiate an inspection cycle. However, reinforcement came only after making the appropriate number of pecks on the window key in case of a true skag only. Skags occurred rarely; they made up 10 per cent of all the capsules on the belt. Wrong pecks, either false alarms or misses, did not get reinforced, and produced a blackout (Ferster, 1954) of 30 seconds. The results were very encouraging: Both birds inspected on a 99 per cent correct basis within one week of daily discrimination training. The director of the pharmacology division, my immediate superior, who had watched the entire project with serious misgiving since its inception (he was sincerely afraid I was making a fool of myself), was delighted. In his immediate enthusiasm he called the director of research, who came over for a look. One week later the vice-presidents as well as the president of the company had been given a demonstration. Everybody, including my immediate associates and co-workers, was greatly excited. The situation, as Skinner had previously discovered in a similar situation (Skinner, 1960), was a great source for jokes. There was talk about a new company subsidiary: "Inspection, Inc.!" (Company slogan: "It's for the birds!")

There were some sobering thoughts, however. One of them concerned the staggering problem of the logistics involved in getting pigeons to inspect as many as 20,000,000 separate objects each day. Although this problem did not seem insoluble to me, the details of the various possible approaches to a solution were never worked out.

After the company president had watched my feathered pupils perform, he congratulated me on my achievement. I was subsequently informed that serious consideration would be given to the further use and development of the method. I was also told that I could expect a visit from the chairman of the board and his brother, both elder statesmen of the company, who made all final policy decisions of importance. During their brief visit to the laboratory, one of them raised the question of possible adverse publicity. What about the Humane Society, and, more important, suppose salesmen from other pharmaceutical houses would tell doctors not to buy any of our company's products: "Who would trust medicine inspected by pigeons?!" I suggested that the use of pigeons was incidental and that, for example, one could use hawks just as well; after all, what is better than a hawk's eye? This suggestion produced a wan smile.

One other problem that was brought up raised the question of the pigeons coming in contact with what was being inspected. The competition could well choose to ignore the mechanical details of the situation and exploit the more distasteful but imaginary possibilities. Even though the birds would only see the capsules at a distance through a window, the first mental picture[2] is usually one of a pigeon "manually" (proboscically?) sorting capsules, a thought no doubt repulsive to many people, especially to those who already have an aversion to birds as such.

After a brief stay, and a polite pat on the back, my distinguished visitors left.

Three weeks went by without any further word from HUM (Higher-Up-Management—Verhave, 1961). I concluded that probably meant that my pigeons were finished. I was right. Sometime later I was so informed. Through the grapevine I learned that the board of directors had voted 13 to 1 not to continue to explore the use of animals for quality-control inspection. The one "yes" vote presumably came from the director of research who initially had given me the green light for the preliminary demonstration.

There is one further amusing tale to the story:

---

[2] If a behaviorist may be excused for using such illegitimate terms . . .

The company did try to patent my inspection method. The poor lawyer assigned to the case almost developed a nervous breakdown. It turned out to be "unpatentable" because, as the lawyers of the patent office put it (so succinctly), the method involved "a mental process" which is unpatentable in principle.[3] I tried to pin my lawyer friends down on what they meant by a "mental process." I suggested that the pigeon was merely an organic computer. However, I got nowhere. Lawyers apparently want no part of either physicalism or behaviorism.

So much as far as my own story is concerned. My efforts stimulated another exploratory attempt by my friend William Cumming, of Columbia University, who trained pigeons to inspect diodes. Brief descriptions of his work can be found in an article by Ferster and Ferster (1962), an anonymous (1959) article in *Factory,* and a recent article in *The Atlantic Monthly* by R. J. Herrnstein (1965).

One problem not yet touched on deserves some discussion. In the demonstration apparatus the capsules were coded as to whether they were acceptable or skags. In this way the automatic programing (relay) circuit could set up and enforce the appropriate discriminatory behavior of the birds. However, on an actual inspection line, this aspect of the training procedure could no longer be maintained. There would be no way of knowing which capsules are skags except by actual inspection. Consequently on a real inspection line there would be no way of knowing when to reward or not to reward the animal inspector! As a result, due to the lack of differential reward, the animal's discriminations would rapidly deteriorate.[4] There are two solutions. I discarded the first and most obvious one because it seemed mechanically cumbersome and not as interesting as the other solution.

The first solution would involve the use of known skags. A certain percentage of the capsules inspected would consist of such labeled duds, and be used to check up on the discriminatory behavior of the birds. This is similar to the use of catch tests in human psychophysical experiments. This solution to the problem of guaranteeing that the animal inspector conforms to the values of his human employers makes it necessary to determine what minimum percentage of the objects inspected have to be planted skags in order to keep the inspecting behavior at an acceptable level of reliability.[5]

As a solution to the conformity-enforcement problem, however, this general solution is expensive and awkward. The on-line inspection equipment would need special machinery to insert in a random manner a fixed percentage of "stool-pigeon skags" and after inspection remove them again automatically for later reuse. The slightest observable difference between the "planted" objects and the other ones would lead to the development of a conditional discrimination (Lashley, 1938), and reintroduce the problem one set out to solve initially.

The second solution is simpler from a purely mechanical point of view. It also is of more theoretical or philosophical interest.

Briefly, it would involve the use of a minimum of two animals to simultaneously inspect each object. Initially, each animal would be trained to inspect capsules by using a training apparatus such as the one I had already constructed. In this apparatus all the capsules would be labeled as to whether they were skags or not and thus control the reward circuit.

After the desired discriminatory performance was well established the two birds would be removed to the on-line inspection situation. From then on the birds would only be rewarded if they *both* agreed on whether a particular object was a skag or not. Such an agreement-contingency setup would most likely be quite adequate to maintain the desired behavior. There is, of course, the possibility that both birds would indeed, once in a while, agree to treat a skag as an acceptable object. However, the probability of this happening for any particular object on a particular inspection trial is the product of the error frequencies (the probability of such an error) of each bird. If, therefore, each bird independently has an error frequency as high as 1 out of 100, the probability of both birds being wrong but still rewarded would be 1 out of 10,000! Hooking additional animals into the agreement-contingency circuit would make the possibility of the development of a "multiple folly"[6] very unlikely.

The solution is of some philosophical interest because it makes the pigeon observers act according to Charles Pierce's (1923, orig. publ. 1878)

---

[3] On this point, I may refer the reader to a recent article in *Science* by J. H. Munster, Jr., and Justin C. Smith (1965).

[4] Skinner, in his World War II project to train pigeons to home missiles, did not face this problem. His birds were meant to "extinguish" after a brief period of duty.

[5] This question was investigated experimentally by Cumming.

[6] "folie a deux, trois, . . . *n*."

pragmatic theory of truth: "The opinion which is fated to be ultimately agreed to by all who investigate, is what is meant by the truth, and the object represented in this opinion is real" (pp. 56–57). It also appears to me that the agreement-contingency type of arrangement provides a basic paradigm for the experimental analysis of social behavior, a terra incognita so far hardly even explored by a systematic experimental investigation (Verhave, 1966).

In conclusion, let me point out that the idea of using trained animals for the dubious purposes of Homo sapiens is very old indeed. Since antiquity man has domesticated many animals. It seems an obvious development to apply our modern knowledge of behavior theory to the task of training some of our animal companions for the performance of various sophisticated tasks (Clarke, 1958; Herrnstein, 1965).

The obstacle in the way of such developments is not our ignorance of behavior, though it is still large, but mainly, it seems, the obstinate belief of man in his intellectual superiority over other creatures as well as a generalized fear of the imagined consequences of novel developments.

REFERENCES

Clarke, A. C. Our dumb colleagues. *Harper's Magazine,* 1958, **216,** 32–33.

Factory, This inspector is a bird. December 1959, 219–221.

Ferster, C. B. Use of the blackout in the investigation of temporal discrimination in fixed-interval reinforcement. *Journal of Experimental Psychology,* 1954, **47,** 69–74.

Ferster, C. B., & Skinner, B. F. *Schedules of reinforcement.* New York: Appleton-Century-Crofts, 1957.

Ferster, M. B., & Ferster, C. B. Animals as workers. *New Scientist,* 1962, **15,** 497–499.

Herrnstein, R. J. In defense of bird brains. *Atlantic Monthly,* September 1965, **216,** 101–104.

Lashley, K. S. Conditional reactions in the rat. *Journal of Psychology,* 1938, **6,** 311–324.

Levi, W. M. *The pigeon.* (Rev. ed.) Sumter, S. C.: Levi Publishing Company, 1963.

Munster, J. H., Jr., & Smith, J. C. The care and feeding of intellectual property. *Science,* 1965, **148,** 739–743.

Peirce, C. How to make our ideas clear. (Orig. publ. 1878) In M. R. Cohen (Ed.), *Chance, love and logic.* New York: Harcourt, Brace & World, 1923.

Reese, E. P. *Experiments in operant behavior.* New York: Appleton-Century-Crofts, 1964.

Skinner, B. F. Pigeons in a pelican. *American Psychologist,* 1960, **15,** 28–37.

Skinner, B. F. Stimulus generalization in an operant: A historical note. In D. I. Mostofsky (Ed.), *Stimulus generalization.* Stanford: Stanford University Press, 1965.

Smee, A. *Instinct and reason.* London: Reeve, Benham & Reeve, 1850.

Verhave, T. Recent developments in the experimental analysis of behavior. *Proceedings of the Eleventh Research Conference, American Meat Institute Foundation,* March 1959, 113–116.

Verhave, T. Is the system approach of engineering psychology applicable to social organizations? *Psychological Record,* 1961, **11,** 69–86.

Verhave, T. (Ed.) *The experimental analysis of behavior: Selected readings.* New York: Appleton-Century-Crofts, 1966.

28

Case Report: The Elimination of Tantrum Behavior by Extinction Procedures

Carl D. Williams

It seems to many people that psychologists do research in such esoteric areas and develop such complex theoretical schema that their endeavors have very little practical value. Indeed, one sometimes hears it argued that perhaps the human personality and human activities are so complex and varied that no one can possibly hope to apply laboratory techniques to them.

We have already talked about some of the ways in which the results of studies in

From Journal of Abnormal and Social Psychology, *Vol. 59 (1959), 269. Copyright 1959 by the American Psychological Association, and reproduced by permission.*

animal learning can be applied to the behavior problems of children. This brief article reports another instance in which some rather simple concepts, mostly derived from experiments using rats and pigeons, have been effectively applied to behavioral problems.

This paper reports the successful treatment of tyrant-like tantrum behavior in a male child by the removal of reinforcement. The subject (*S*) was approximately twenty-one months old. He had been seriously ill much of the first eighteen months of his life. His health then improved considerably, and he gained weight and vigor.

S now demanded the special care and attention that had been given him over the many critical months. He enforced some of his wishes, especially at bedtime, by unleashing tantrum behavior to control the actions of his parents.

The parents and an aunt took turns in putting him to bed both at night and for *S*'s afternoon nap. If the parent left the bedroom after putting *S* in his bed, *S* would scream and fuss until the parent returned to the room. As a result, the parent was unable to leave the bedroom until after *S* went to sleep. If the parent began to read while in the bedroom, *S* would cry until the reading material was put down. The parents felt that *S* enjoyed his control over them and that he fought off going to sleep as long as he could. In any event, a parent was spending from one-half to two hours each bedtime just waiting in the bedroom until *S* went to sleep.

Following medical reassurance regarding *S*'s physical condition, it was decided to remove the reinforcement of this tyrant-like tantrum behavior. Consistent with the learning principle that, in general, behavior that is not reinforced will be extinguished, a parent or the aunt put *S* to bed in a leisurely and relaxed fashion. After bedtime pleasantries, the parent left the bedroom and closed the door. *S* screamed and raged, but the parent did not reenter the room. The duration of screaming and crying was obtained from the time the door was closed.

The results are shown in Figure 1. It can be seen that *S* continued screaming for 45 minutes the first time he was put to bed in the first extinction series. *S* did not cry at all the second time he was put to bed. This is perhaps attributable to his fatigue from the crying of Occasion 1. By the tenth occasion, *S* no longer whimpered, fussed, or cried when the parent left the room. Rather,

FIGURE 1 *Length of crying in two extinction series as a function of successive occasions of being put to bed*

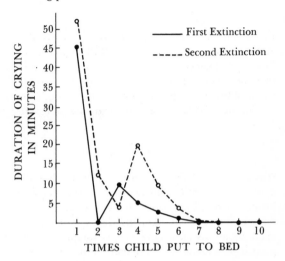

he smiled as they left. The parents felt that he made happy sounds until he dropped off to sleep.

About a week later, *S* screamed and fussed after the aunt put him to bed, probably reflecting spontaneous recovery of the tantrum behavior. The aunt then reinforced the tantrum behavior by returning to *S*'s bedroom and remaining there until he went to sleep. It was then necessary to extinguish this behavior a second time.

Figure 1 shows that the second extinction curve is similar to the first. Both curves are generally similar to extinction curves obtained with subhuman subjects. The second extinction series reached zero by the ninth occasion. No further tantrums at bedtime were reported during the next two years.

It should be emphasized that the treatment in this case did not involve aversive punishment. All that was done was to remove the reinforcement. Extinction of the tyrant-like tantrum behavior then occurred.

No unfortunate side- or aftereffects of this treatment were observed. At three and three-quarters years of age, *S* appeared to be a friendly, expressive, outgoing child.

29

Simple Trial-and-Error Learning: A Study in Psychological Theory

Clark L. Hull

In any science it is the explicitness of theoretical statements that permit them to be tested and evaluated. Clark Hull (1884–1952) is regarded by many psychologists as being the first psychological researcher to formulate a set of statements about learning so precisely that the theories can be easily tested. This article shows Hull at his best—clearly stating the problem to be investigated and the conditions of the experiment, then formulating a theoretical explanation of the learning process involved.

I

Science proceeds by a double movement. For the most part, scientific discoveries are accomplished by means of observation and experiment. Occasionally, however, it happens that a discovery is made by means of a more or less complex logical process or "gedanken experiment." Einstein's mathematical deduction and prediction of what may be observed in the behavior of light when it passes near the sun is perhaps as good an example of this as any.

Frequently, after the existence and characteristics of natural phenomena have been discovered empirically, it is seen that these things might very well have been deduced from facts and principles already known. When the deduction is thus performed, as a kind of afterthought, the process is more properly termed explanation. Actual prediction is more dramatic than explanation, but the two processes are logically very similar. A true deductive explanation possesses a quality of logical necessity closely akin to prediction regardless of when the empirical observation takes place. It is of the mass of such interlocking deductive explanations that scientific systems are made. In general, that science is most perfectly systematized which can show the greatest proportion of its phenomena as logically deducible from recognized principles and other known phenomena. Moreover it seems reasonable that rival systems within a science may also be evaluated on the basis of this same criterion.

It is evident that much of what passes for explanation fails of this true deductive quality. It avails little merely to subsume known phenomena under some more or less general principle. It is true enough to say of any actual event that it is a case of conservation of energy, or of cause and effect. But such bare general principles of themselves alone can hardly enable one to deduce the existence and characteristics of natural phenomena. In a similar manner, the typical undergraduate behaviorist's glib explanation of the more complex forms of habit phenomena by saying of each that it is a case of stimulus and response, utterly fails of the true deductive quality. . . .

For an explanation to form the substance of a true system, the deduction must eventuate in some kind of genuine novelty as compared with what is contained in the original premises. This element of novelty is what was referred to above as a predictive quality in real explanation. The deductive process is a true generative activity. The known principles give rise to new knowledge as the result of a causal sequence in a high-class redintegrative organism. According to one plausible hypothesis, principles are symbolic habits which, as a result of their functional interaction within the organism possessing them, give rise to new and distinct habits. These latter constitute the new knowledge. Thus the new knowledge, while derived from the original principles, is not the principles, but something newly come into existence. By the accumulation of these bits of deductive explanation, scientific systems become enlarged very much as have systems of mathematics.

Perhaps no theorists have been more naive in

From Psychological Review, *Vol. 37 (1939), 241–256.*

their attempts at system construction than those who seek in the principles of stimulus-response the main explanation of those forms of behavior usually called mental. It may even be that, thus far, none has failed much worse in evolving the solid substance of genuine explanation. Even so, the author has considerable confidence in the possibilities of this point of view. As a concrete example in miniature of what is believed to be a desirable direction for this movement toward systematization to take, there is given the following account of a *simple* type of trial-and-error learning. This may be taken as a relatively uninvolved example of what has been spoken of above as a deductive explanation.

II

There appear to be a number of fairly distinct types of trial-and-error learning. The particular principles necessary to employ in their explanation, as well as the mode of combining the principles, differ somewhat according to the type of learning to be explained. Of the true trial-and-error learning, we have the relatively complex type exemplified by maze learning, where the *obvious* reinforcement of the conditioning process (or the lack of reinforcement) for the most part comes only at the end of a series or particular combination of trial acts. A strict deductive explanation of this type of learning presents special difficulties and very probably will turn out to involve some principles not needed for the explanation of the less complex types. A second and relatively simple type of trial-and-error learning is seen where each act or trial is definitely and immediately reinforced positively, if successful, or is followed by punishment (negative reinforcement) if unsuccessful. A still different, and perhaps simpler, type is where each trial act is reinforced, if successful, but is followed by no special stimulus (is merely unreinforced) if unsuccessful. It is this last type of learning *only* which we shall consider in the following paragraphs.

Numerous phenomena characteristic of this third type of learning call for explanation. These problems can perhaps best be formulated as a series of questions:

1. Why does the organism persist in its trials or attempts even after repeated failure?

2. Why, in case success does not result from its first attempts, does the organism vary its reactions, often over a very wide range?

3. What principle or mechanism limits the range of the variation of the reactions which an organism will make to any problem situation?

4. Why do organisms of the same general type sometimes differ so widely from each other in their reactions to the same (external) problem situation?

5. What principle determines the order of appearance of the several trial acts of a trial-and-error sequence?

6. Why, in the series of trial acts preceding the first success, does the organism often stupidly commit the same erroneous reaction repeatedly?

7. What constitutes success itself?

8. Why should the trial sequence come to an end as soon as success has been attained? Why should it not continue exactly as before?

9. Why, even after the successful reaction cycle has been performed one or more times, do reactions, repeatedly found to be unsuccessful, quite illogically continue sometimes to be made?

10. Why, in general, do these erroneous reactions become less and less frequent with each successful solution, and why do they at length cease altogether?

11. Why, for a particular organism, are certain trial-and-error problems so much more readily solved than are others? Why, for certain organisms, is the same problem so much more difficult of solution than for other organisms, presumably of equally good natural endowment?

12. Why, on the whole, are the trial reactions in "blind" trial-and-error learning so much more likely to prove successful than would be a mere random sampling from the entire repertory of the organism's possible movements? Why is the organism so much more likely to try a successful act early in the trial-and-error sequence than pure random sampling might be expected to bring about?

III

Let it be assumed, at the outset, that there exist a number of unconditioned stimuli, S_x, S_y, and S_z; and that these stimuli evoke in a certain organism the responses R_x, R_y, and R_z, respectively. It is assumed, further, that these responses involve the same "final common path" so that no two of them can take place simultaneously. Let S_1 represent a very mild neutral stimulus evoking at the outset no observable response whatever.

Now if S_1 should accompany S_x in the same stimulus complex a number of times there will be set up the conditioned reaction tendency

$$S_1 \longrightarrow R_x.$$

In a similar manner, if S_1 accompanies S_y in another stimulus complex a number of times there will be set up the conditioned reaction tendency

$$S_1 \longrightarrow R_y.$$

Similarly, there may also be set up the conditioned reaction tendency

$$S_1 \longrightarrow R_z.$$

Thus S_1 may come to possess a number of distinct and mutually incompatible excitatory tendencies or "bonds." Presumably each of these tendencies to action will have a strength or potency different from that of the others. For the sake of definiteness and simplicity of the logical consequences, we may let the strength of these excitatory tendencies stand, at this stage, in the ratio respectively of 3, 2, and 1. Lastly let it be assumed that reaction R_z is the one and only response which is biologically successful, i.e., the one which is followed by reinforcement and which terminates the stimulus S_1.

Under the conditions as assumed, what might logically be expected to result in case the organism should be stimulated by S_1, either alone or in conjunction with certain other approximately neutral stimuli? It is obvious at once that there will arise a kind of competition or rivalry among the three mutually incompatible excitatory tendencies. This competition may conveniently be represented thus:

Since the excitatory tendency flowing from S_1 to R_x is strongest, this reaction will be the first trial act. By hypothesis this reaction will not be reinforced. According to the principle of experimental extinction this failure of reinforcement will weaken the tendency of S_1 to evoke R_x, leaving it, let us say, with a value of 2.1. But since this excitatory tendency, even after its weakening, is stronger than either of the other two, it will still be dominant. By hypothesis, S_1 continues without interruption. Accordingly, after the brief refractory phase following the R_x response, this same reaction will be repeated as the second trial act. A second experimental extinction at once reduces the tendency to R_x to a strength of 1.2. This leaves the tendency to R_y dominant at the beginning of the third trial. S_1 continues to act. Accordingly R_y is evoked as the third trial. Here, for the first time, we note the phenomenon of variability in the trial acts.

But since R_y will not be reinforced, this excitatory tendency also will suffer extinction, reducing it to 1.1. Meanwhile, R_x has spontaneously recovered to a strength of 1.5. By hypothesis, S_1 still persists. As a result, R_x is evoked as the fourth trial of the series. Failure of reinforcement at once reduces it to the value of .6. During this time R_y has recovered to 1.4, which gives it a position of dominance. S_1 accordingly evokes this reaction for a second time, as the fifth trial act of the trial-and-error series. Failure of reinforcement reduces its excitatory potentiality to .5. Meanwhile, R_x has recovered to a strength of .9, but this is not enough to equal that of R_z, which now for the first time becomes dominant. S_1 accordingly evokes R_z as the sixth trial of the series. By hypothesis this reaction is a success and is followed by reinforcement. Since this act also terminates S_1, R_z is the last trial of the first trial-and-error sequence or behavior cycle.

The second time the organism encounters the stimulus S_1 (the beginning of the second behavior cycle) the values of all the excitatory tendencies have increased over those existent at the conclusion of the previous behavior cycle. The tendency to R_x is dominant, and this reaction follows at once. The trial is unsuccessful, extinction follows, and stimulus S_1 persists. Thereupon R_y becomes dominant and therefore becomes the second trial act. This also is an error. Meanwhile, R_x once more has recovered to a state of dominance, and it accordingly becomes the third trial. R_x is weakened again by failure of reinforcement, which leaves dominant the correct reaction R_z. This reaction brings the second problem cycle to a successful conclusion and R_z is reinforced a second time.

The third time the stimulus S_1 is encountered it finds the three excitatory tendencies in still a different combination of strengths. R_x is dominant and becomes the first trial, an error. Its consequent weakening leaves R_z dominant. S_1 accordingly evokes R_z as the second trial. This success, as before, is followed by reinforcement.

On the fourth occasion that the organism encounters the stimulus S_1, for the first time it finds R_z dominant at the outset. Accordingly the first trial act is a success. At this point the process of trial-and-error learning may be considered as functionally complete.

IV

We may now summarize the results of our deduction by answering the questions formulated above.

1. The organism persists in its attempts because the stimulus which evokes the attempts itself persists.

2. The organism varies its reaction, when one reaction fails, because the consequent weakening of the primarily dominant excitatory tendency leaves dominant a second and distinct excitatory tendency conditioned to the same stimulus situation.

3. The range or variety of reactions which may be evoked by a given problem situation is limited to the reactions which have become conditioned during the life of the organism to one or another stimulus component of that situation.

4. Organisms superficially quite similar in general constitution may differ very widely in the nature of their trial attempts at problem solution, because their previous life history has resulted in both qualitative and quantitative differences in their stock of excitatory tendencies evocable by the several stimulus components of the problem situation.

5. The principle which determines which of the possible trial acts shall be evoked first, second, third, etc., in the trial-and-error series is: That trial act is evoked at any given stage of the trial-and-error process which at that time is dominant, i.e., strongest.

6. The reason that the organism frequently, and apparently quite stupidly, tries an unsuccessful act over and over during the first problem cycle, despite failure of reinforcement, is quite simply that the several processes which are continually varying the strengths of the different excitatory tendencies may on more than one occasion leave any particular excitatory tendency dominant. This may even result in the same erroneous act taking place two or more times in immediate succession, as in Trials 1 and 2 of Behavior cycle I. (See Table I)

7. Not enough is yet known concerning the psychology of learning to give a completely general definition of success in objective biological terms. In the case of hunger, success consists in the eating of food. Ordinarily the successful act results in a cessation of the persisting stimulus S_1. In the case of hunger, S_1 is generally considered to be the cramping of the walls of the upper digestive tract.

8. The trials cease after success has been attained simply because success terminates the stimulus (S_1) which evokes the trials.

9. Erroneous acts continue to be made even after the correct solution has been "discovered" one or more times by successful trials because the reinforcement, by success, of a weak excitatory tendency is not always great enough to make it equal in strength to excitatory tendencies which were originally more potent and which have had time to recover greatly from the effects of experimental extinction suffered just previous to the successful reaction.

10. The erroneous reactions become less and less frequent as the trial-and-error process continues because the basic superiority in the strength of the excitatory tendencies leading to erroneous responses becomes less and less dominant. This in turn is owing (a) to the action of experimental extinction which continually weakens such erroneous reactions as chance to become functionally dominant, and (b) to the action of reinforcement which strengthens the excitatory tendency which, when dominant, evokes successful responses. Ultimately this process must lead to a state in which the successful excitatory tendency will be dominant at the very outset of a behavior cycle.

If this first case of success on the initial trial of a behavior cycle should chance to take place under circumstances such that the spontaneous recovery from extinction by the unsuccessful tendencies had not had time to take place (as might have happened if Cycle II had begun very soon after the conclusion of Cycle I), then we should expect to find errors made repeatedly after one or several perfect initial performances had occurred.

11. One problem is more readily solved than another for a given organism because in its particular stock of reaction tendencies the one tending to the successful reaction chances to be relatively stronger than in the other problem situation. In case the excitatory tendency evoking the successful reaction chances to be dominant at the outset, the correct reaction will be made at the first trial and no errors whatever will occur. On the other hand, the same problem may be more difficult for one organism than another, both of which can ultimately master it, because the previous history of the two organisms has so conditioned them that the successful tendency is relatively more dominant in one than in the other. Such relative similarity in the difficulty of problems for different specimens of a given type of organism as actually exists presumably depends upon the relative similarity in the stimulating situations encountered in their lives. This is usually considerable.

12. From the foregoing, it is obvious that trial-and-error learning, while "blind" in the sense that it is not assumed that there is available for its guidance and control any disembodied soul or spirit, is *not* blind in the sense that it does not operate according to recognized principles. In the first place, the trials are not made from the total

repertory of the organism, but from only those movements which have by previous stimulation become conditioned to one or another stimulus component of the problem situation. This fact at once automatically limits enormously the number of trial reactions from which selection must be made and thus largely accounts for such efficiency as it displays. In the second place, of those acts which may be evoked by the stimulus situation, it seems reasonable to expect that in the long run the stronger excitatory tendencies will be more likely to evoke successful reactions than the weaker, and the weaker ones than those reactions within the repertoire of the organism, which have not become conditioned at all to any component of the problem stimulus complex. Since the trial acts are evoked in the order of their strength, this factor will also greatly favor an early success over a mere random sampling from the possible reactions of the organism. It is true that such a system would not always succeed early and might fail completely of the solution of a problem. Unfortunately this also agrees with the facts of life. Problems are often solved only after much delay, and not infrequently they are not solved at all.

V

From the point of view of the longevity of hypotheses, it is extremely dangerous for them to become thoroughly definite and specific. The very definiteness of a hypothesis makes it possible to determine with relative ease whether its implications agree with the known phenomena which it proposes to explain. In case of failure to conform, the unambiguous nature of the comparison is peculiarly fatal. Worse yet, an unambiguous hypothesis is likely to permit the deductive forecast of what should be observed under various experimental conditions which may as yet be untried. A single well-planned experiment may at any moment yield results quite different from the deductive forecast and thus topple the entire hypothetical structure. This, of course, is all quite as it should be. The healthy development of a science demands that the implications of its hypotheses be deduced as promptly and unambiguously as possible. This will make it possible for them, if verified by experiment, to be incorporated into the structure or system of the science; or, if found to disagree with experimental findings, the hypotheses may be recast or simply discarded as errors in the long trial-and-error process of system construction. At the least, such hypotheses may be credited with the virtue of having stimulated experimental research. But if a hypothesis be so vague and indefinite, or so lacking in relevancy to the phenomena which it seeks to explain that the results neither of previous experiments nor those of experiments subsequently to be performed may be deduced from it, it will be difficult indeed to prove it false. And if, in addition, the hypothesis should appeal in some subtle fashion to the predilections of a culture in which it gains currency, it should enjoy a long and honored existence. Unfortunately, because of its very sterility and barrenness in the above deductive sense, such a hypothesis should have no status whatever in science. It savors more of metaphysics, religion, or theology.

*   *   *

30

There Is More than One Kind of Learning

Edward C. Tolman

Most researchers try to design experiments in such a way that the outcome will answer a specific question. A physicist might ask whether bombarding a particular element with neutrons will produce a particular effect. He would collect the apparatus and prepare an experiment to answer the question. A geneticist might ask whether feeding a certain

From Psychological Review, *Vol. 56 (1949), 144–155. Copyright 1949 by the American Psychological Association, and reproduced by permission. Address of the Chairman of the Division of General Psychology of the American Psychological Association, Boston, September 7, 1948.*

birth-control chemical to male rats will render them temporarily sterile. He would then design an appropriate experiment to answer the question. A psychologist might ask whether people who learn some material while they are worrying about an upcoming examination in a different subject will remember as well as they would if they learned the material after the examination when they were relaxed. He could design an experiment to answer that question.

As more and more researchers ask similar questions in related areas, they come to rely upon communicating with each other so that they can know the kinds of answers that others have obtained. After many investigators have worked for several years on a certain topic they usually begin to run out of interesting questions to ask. It often seems that a blind alley has been reached and that there is no clearly marked path back to daylight.

The most successful way that has been found to generate new research hypotheses is to formulate a theory that can explain the results of previous research and that can predict the probable results of future experiments. A good theory will tie together seemingly unconnected bits of information and will enable the researcher to get a clear perspective of the total area. A good theory will also enable the researcher to make provocative inferences concerning new experiments. E. C. Tolman (1886–1959) was one of the most highly respected theorists in psychology. This article presents an example of his approach to theory construction.

I wish to suggest that our familiar theoretical disputes about learning may *perhaps* (I emphasize "perhaps") be resolved if we can agree that there are really a number of different kinds of learning. For then it may turn out that the theory and laws appropriate to one kind may well be different from those appropriate to other kinds. Each of the theories of learning now current may, in short, still have validity for some one or more varieties of learning, if not for all. But to assume that this will settle our squabbles is, I know, being overly optimistic. Other theorists will certainly not support what I am going to say. Not only will each of them feel that his theory is basic for all kinds of learning, but also each of these others will be sure to object to the general conceptual framework within which my distinctions alone make sense. Thus, whereas I would like to hope that this paper will prove an end to all future papers on learning, I realize that such a hope is mere fantasy or wish-fulfillment on my part or something that my clinical colleagues would undoubtedly dub by some far more unpleasant name.

But, to get down to business, I am going to hold that the connections or relations that get learned can be separated into at least six types. These I shall name as:

1. Cathexes
2. Equivalence Beliefs
3. Field Expectancies
4. Field-Cognition Modes
5. Drive Discriminations
6. Motor Patterns

First, let me indicate briefly what I mean by each of these six terms and then let me proceed to a more detailed discussion of the conditions and laws for the acquisition, de-acquisition, and forgetting of the relations named by each of these six.

1. *Cathexes.* By this term I mean connections or attachments of specific *types* of final positive goal-object, or of final negative "disturbance-object" to basic drives. (Note that I have coined the term final "disturbance-object" to cover what have sometimes been called negative goals.) I shall not argue the question as to how many or what the basic drives may be. I shall assume, however, that you will agree that there are some. For example, none of you will dispute, I hope, the reality of hunger, thirst, sex, or fright. By the learning of a cathexis I shall mean, then, the acquisition of a connection between a given variety of goal-object or disturbance-object—i.e., a given type of food, a given type of drink, a given type of sex-object or a given type of fear-object—and the corresponding drive of hunger, thirst, sex, or fright. That is, the learning of cathexes is the acquisition by the organism of positive dispositions *for* certain *types* of food, drink, sex-object, etc. or of negative dispositions *against* certain *types* of disturbance-object.

2. *Equivalence Beliefs.* This term sounds shocking. However, I am going to use it. By an equivalence belief I mean a connection between a positively cathected type of goal and a type of subgoal or between a negatively cathected type of disturbance-object and a type of what may be called a subdisturbance-object or foyer (i.e., a sort

of antechamber which, if the organism gets to it, tends to lead him willy-nilly into the presence of the final disturbance-object itself). During any period in which such an equivalence belief holds, the organism will tend to approach such a type of subgoal or to avoid such a type of foyer with almost the same readiness with which it will approach a final goal or avoid a final disturbance-object.

3. *Field Expectancies.* These I formerly called "sign-Gestalt–expectations," which latter term (to quote Gordon Allport, 1946), Hilgard and Marquis (1940) "mercifully" shortened to "expectancies." This last term is, however, I feel, too disgustingly short; so I am "mercilessly" rechristening these entities *"field expectancies."* It is my contention that when an organism is repeatedly presented on successive occasions with an environmental set-up, through which he moves and relative to which he is sensitive, he usually tends to acquire an apprehension not only of each group of immediate stimuli as it impinges upon him but he also tends to acquire a "set" such that, upon the apprehension of the first group of stimuli in the field, he becomes prepared for the further "to come" groups of stimuli and also for some of the interconnections or field relationships between such groups of stimuli. It is such sets (or field expectancies) which make it possible for the organism, human or animal, to exhibit appropriate short-cuts and roundabout routes. It is also the acquisition of such sets which make possible the phenomenon of latent learning when (and if) it occurs.

4. *Field-Cognition Modes.* A careful analysis of the processes involved in the appearance of field expectancies indicates, I believe, that the final form and range of any such expectancy is a function not only of repetition, i.e., of "memory" in the strict sense, but also of "perception" and of "inference." That is, any given field expectancy which appears in a given experimental set-up is a function of the interacting processes of perception, memory, and inference. The modes or manners of functioning of perception, memory, and inference are what I am designating as Field-Cognition Modes. And I would now assert, further, that in the course of the usual learning experiment there may be acquired not only a specific new field expectancy but also new modes or ways of perceiving, remembering, and inferring—new Field-Cognition Modes which will, or may, be then utilized by the given organism in still other later environmental set-ups.

5. *Drive Discriminations.* It appears from some of the latent learning experiments, that rats may have to learn to discriminate their thirst from their hunger. In the first Spence and Lippitt experiment (1946) the rats were run, when thirsty, with water down one arm of a Y-maze and food down the other. Then, after this preliminary training under thirst, they were shifted to hunger and tested to see if in their free choices they now would immediately choose the food side. They did not. They continued to go to the water side. At first blush this result would be interpreted as a verification of the reinforcement theory. The response of going to the right hand—or water side—had, it will be said, been reinforced by the thirst-reduction which followed the taking of that side during the training trials. It is to be noted, however, that the change from thirst in the preliminary training trials to hunger in the test trials should also have changed—(to talk in Hull's language)—the S_D or Drive-Stimulus (Hull, 1943). Further, since (according to Hull) the overt response of turning right or left gets conditioned not only to the maze stimuli but also to this S_D, this change in S_D should have caused some breakdown in the learned response. Such a breakdown did not appear. It would seem, therefore, that—speaking in this same language—the new hunger S_D must, under the conditions of this experiment, have for some reason remained undifferentiated from the original thirst S_D.

However, there are other experiments in which such drive discriminations—to use my language—have proved to be possible and to control the results. Thus, we may recall the Hull (1933) and the Leeper (1935) experiments in which the animals were run hungry and thirsty on alternate nights. Food was down one alley and water down the other, and both Hull and Leeper found that the animals could learn to turn to the food side when hungry and to the water side when thirsty. Obviously, in those experiments, since all the other features were held constant, the two drives—hunger and thirst—*were* discriminated. It appears that this alternation of thirst and hunger and the different locations of the two corresponding rewards throughout the training trials may have been the crucial factor which in these experiments favored such drive discriminations. But there are undoubtedly other ways of inducing drive discriminations, the laws of which a complete psychology of learning must investigate.

6. *Motor Patterns.* It will be noted that this category has to be included by me because I do not hold, as do most behaviorists, that all learning is, as such, the attachment of responses to stimuli. Cathexes, equivalence beliefs, field expec-

tancies, field-cognition modes and drive discriminations are not, as I define them, stimulus-response
connections. They are central phenomena, each of
which may be expressed by a variety of responses.
The actual nature of these final responses is, however, also determined by the character of the motor
patterns at the organism's command. My psychology of learning must, therefore, also include a consideration of the laws governing the acquisition of
motor patterns purely as such.

So much for a preliminary survey of what I
mean by these six terms. Let us turn now to a
more detailed discussion of the conditions and
laws for the acquisition, de-acquisition, and forgetting of each of these six subject matters for
learning.

Cathexes

In the first place, the distinction between "positive cathexes" and "negative cathexes" must be
more sharply drawn. By a "positive cathexis" I
mean the attachment of a type of positive goal
to a positive drive. That is, when a type of goal
has been positively cathected it means that when
the given drive is in force the organism will tend
to apprehend, to approach, and to perform the
consummatory reaction upon any instance of this
type of goal which is presented by the immediate
environment. By a "negative cathexis" I mean the
attachment of a type of disturbance-object to a
negative drive. That is to say, when a type of
disturbance-object has been negatively cathected
it means that, if the given negative drive is strong,
the organism will tend to apprehend and to avoid
or to get away from any instance of this type of
disturbance-object which is presented in the immediate environment. But let us turn now to the
acquisition, the de-acquisition, and the forgetting
of these two types of cathexes.

Positive cathexes

It would seem that animals or human beings
acquire positive cathexes for new foods, drinks,
sex-objects, etc., by trying out the corresponding
consummatory responses upon such objects and
finding that they work—that, in short, the consummatory reactions to these new objects do reduce the corresponding drives. Hence, here I believe, with Hull (1943), in the efficacy of reinforcement or need-reduction. I shall assert, however,
that no good experimental evidence has as yet
been adduced for this conclusion. The sort of

evidence one wants could be obtained, perhaps for
hunger, with a special dog preparation. If, for
example, a dog's esophagus were severed and the
upper end brought to the outside so that food
taken into the mouth, after chewing and swallow-
ing, would drop out into the open and if also a
direct fistula were made into the stomach, so that
this food (or other food) could then be reintroduced by the experimenter directly into the dog's
stomach, we would have the sort of set-up we
need. For with this kind of preparation we could
discover whether the dog's hunger would become
cathected only to those foods which after being
chewed and swallowed were reintroduced into the
stomach (and hence produced drive-reduction) and
whether conversely his hunger would not become
cathected to or become de-cathected from foods
which in contrast were not re-introduced into the
stomach and hence did not produce need-reduction. Furthermore, with such a prepared dog the
exact quantitative laws relative to frequency of
trials, amounts of reinforcement per trial, etc.,
could be worked out. Curves could be fitted. Equations for these curves could be mathematically
determined, and the magnitudes of the constants
could be found. In fact, all the precise techniques
of quantitative method could be elegantly carried
out with such a dog preparation and bring about
closure for all those psychologists who are probably at heart mere physicists or perhaps mathematicians gone wrong. But, prior to such an elegant experiment, all I will say is that I believe
that numbers of repetitions and amounts of need-
reduction per repetition would, no doubt, turn
out to be the two major causal variables and that
the curves would undoubtedly be exponential in
form.

Next, it must be asked, how is a positive cathexis,
once acquired, subsequently de-acquired? How do
we come no longer to love specific foods, specific
drinks, specific sex-objects? Here, I suspect, we
have at present even less evidence. If, however,
we were to carry out the experiment with our dog
preparation, I would suppose that if food were no
longer consistently reintroduced into the stomach
each time after it had been chewed and swallowed,
the cathexis for this type of food would weaken.
That is, the failure of reinforcement would, I believe, break the cathexis. And, again, the precise
shape and equation for such a curve of de-acquisition could be obtained.

Finally, what about forgetting? Are positive
cathexes weakened by the mere passage of time?
There seems to be no controlled evidence. But
everyday experience suggests that the forgetting of

positive cathexes, if it occurs at all, is extremely slow; so that it probably requires years for such cathexes to disappear through mere passage of time and lack of exercise.

Negative cathexes

The conditions for the acquisition of negative cathexes seem to be well summarized by the ancient adage "a burnt child dreads the fire." In other words, negative reinforcement would seem to be the typical way in which a negative cathexis is acquired. And by negative reinforcement I mean pain or some other type of noxious physiological state.

Conditioning experiments with electric shock as the unconditioned stimulus would seem to provide the model experiments. These experiments, as we now have them, suggest that the curves are steeper for the learning of negative cathexes than for the learning of positive ones. Indeed, ordinary experience suggests that a single negative reinforcement may have an overpoweringly strong and persistent effect.

Next, what are the laws for the de-acquisition of negative cathexes. How do we unlearn our fears? My guess would be that the only way a negative cathexis is broken is by forcing the individual to stay in the presence of the fear-cathected type of object under conditions in which this type of object does not lead to any noxious physiological result.

Finally, as to forgetting, again no controlled evidence. But it seems to me probable that for negative cathexes, as for positive ones, there is practically no forgetting. The same old fears so often seem to endure for a lifetime.

Equivalence Beliefs

By a positive equivalence belief I mean, as I have already indicated, the attachment of a type of subgoal to a type of final goal such that this subgoal comes (for the period during which the given equivalence belief holds) to be sought for as if it were the final goal. And by a negative equivalence belief I mean an attachment between a final type of disturbance-object and a type of subdisturbance-object or foyer. Now turn to the acquisition, de-acquisition, and forgetting of these two types of equivalence beliefs.

Positive equivalence beliefs

Before discussing these further, a further distinction must be drawn between these beliefs, as such,

and the mere apprehensions of objects as appropriate *means* leading on to positive goals. Consider a concrete example—the obtaining of high grades in courses. In so far as high grades are sought merely because they are apprehended as specific means (or paths) leading to the goal, say, of love and respect from teacher or parent, the pursuit of high grades does not in my terms involve an "equivalence belief." Operationally speaking, the individual does not stop when he has got the high grade, but he goes on to use it to obtain the finally wanted love and respect. If, on the other hand, the obtaining of *A*s in specific courses seems to bring at once, and by itself, some reduction of the underlying drive or drives, then there is involved some strength of an equivalence belief in my sense of that term. That is to say, the individual then accepts what was originally a mere *means* as an *equivalent* to a goal. He experiences, when reaching this means, some degree of drive-reduction. The precise observations necessary for determining such phenomena are, however, difficult.

Let us imagine first a case with rats. Suppose it were found that when rats reached a well-practiced type of goal-box (even though now there is no food in it), their stomach contractions or some more basic physiological measure of hunger subsided at least for a time, then I would say that we had evidence for some degree of equivalence belief in these rats to the effect that the given type of goal-box was equivalent to food.

Equivalence beliefs will, however, I believe, get most frequently established not in connection with such a viscerogenic drive as hunger, but in connection with social drives. I cannot here attempt to argue for the validity and reality of such drives. I hope merely that for the purposes of this discussion you will grant me them. If you will, let us consider again the example of the student working for high grades. In so far as it can be demonstrated that with the reception of the high grades there is some temporary reduction in this student's need for love and approbation, even without his going on to tell others about his grade, then we would have evidence for an equivalence belief. The *A*s would then be accepted by him as equivalent to the love or approbation to which they were originally a mere means. The difficulty is, of course, that we have no good techniques for measuring the varying moment-by-moment strengths of any such drives as the need for love or approbation. Some day, however (perhaps by an improvement of projective techniques), we may acquire such a method. And then, as with hunger, we can see if the drive does actually subside in the mere presence of the high grade.

But what would be the laws for the acquisition, de-acquisition, and forgetting of such equivalence beliefs? Tentatively, I would propose primacy, frequency, and intensity of need-reductions plus early traumatic experiences as the important causal factors. That is, I would hold that the earliness (or primacy) as well as the frequency of the occasions in the life of the individual in which getting high grades led to love, would be important. I would also suggest that early traumatic accompaniments of this sequence between grades and social approbation would also help to *"fixate"* the getting of high grades as an end in themselves. But as to the laws or shapes of the curves of acquisition I am completely in the dark. This is a virgin field which the clinically minded experimentalist and the experimentally minded clinician might well cultivate conjointly.

And, as to the laws for the de-acquisition of equivalence beliefs, I am equally in the dark. And this is sad because I would assert that a large part of clinical practice consists in the attempt to break erroneous equivalence beliefs. As long as an equivalence belief is not misleading in the sense that the subgoal is usually actually followed by the true goal, the belief probably serves some physiological economy. But when an equivalence belief persists, even though now the subgoal practically never leads to the true goal, such an equivalence belief would seem bad. The subject experiences some drive-reduction (Query: so-called "secondary gain") but most of his actual drive remains unsatisfied. He accepts the shadow for the substance. He continues to be a greasy grind, although now as a young adult few praise him for it and many even contemn him. And so we find him at last rushing up to the University Psychiatric Counseling Center, or whatever locally it may be called, to find out why he is so anxious and/or so depressed.

Our question becomes how actually do the clinicians, the psychiatrists, the counselors (or whatever they may be called) break such erroneous beliefs. What are the conditions and laws governing their de-acquisition? Nobody seems to know. The therapists do have considerable success. But any clear, agreed-upon statement of their procedure seems to be lacking. Some talk about the "transference relation." Others say that the patient is really a "feeling sensation" type and that he has been trying to operate as if he were a "thinking intuition" type. Others "reflect back" to the patient what he himself says. And some merely give him a good sound lecture and tell him to go about his business. But what is common in all these procedures and why they all in some degree succeed in breaking erroneous equivalence beliefs seems

still quite beyond us (or at any rate beyond me).

Finally, as to the forgetting or nonforgetting of positive equivalence beliefs through a mere passage of time, we seem to have little evidence. But general experience suggests that such beliefs are not merely forgotten but have to be unlearned.

Negative equivalence beliefs

It must be pointed out that negative equivalence beliefs cannot really be differentiated from negative cathexes. For example, the rat is conditioned against the box which led to shock. He also comes to be conditioned against the type of paths which lead to such boxes. Or again a human individual is shown to have developed a tendency to avoid self-assertive behaviors. And it turns out that such self-assertive behaviors were followed in childhood by parental disapproval, and parental disapproval was followed by a final physiological disturbance. The individual in question has established an equivalence belief that such self-assertive behavior was equivalent to loss of love and resultant physiological disturbance. And though when this man grows up this belief may no longer be correct (his parents may be dead or may, in fact, like in the man what they punished in the child), he nevertheless continues to avoid self-assertive behaviors in situations in which, instead of such behaviors being punished, they would actually be rewarded.

So once again the problem of the laws and the conditions for the acquisition, the de-acquisition, and the forgetting of equivalence beliefs becomes clinically important. But again we have no clear evidence. Are negative equivalence beliefs more rapidly established than positive ones? What are the therapeutic procedures most favorable to their de-acquisition? Are they ever forgotten as a result of mere nonexercise? Let me suggest again that the experimentally minded therapist and the clinically oriented experimentalist get together and find out.

Field Expectancies

Here my notions as to the conditions and laws of learning depart perhaps most radically from those ordinarily held. By field expectancies I mean (to recall what I said above) those sets which get built up in an organism relative to a specific environmental field. These are the sets which, after learning, make it possible for the organism not only to choose correctly the particular paths in the field on which he has been practiced but also, in some degree, to perform correctly on short-cuts and roundabouts not previously practiced. It is, of course, the facts of latent learning plus the facts of taking short-cuts and roundabouts, when forced or permitted, which have driven me and others to the notion that when a rat, or a human being, is practiced in a particular set of activities in a particular environment, an essential part of what he acquires is an expectancy, a sign-Gestalt, a cognitive structure, a cognitive map (to use some of the terms which have been suggested) relative to that environment.

Further (and here I confess I have up to now been somewhat unclear) I used to be so impressed by the latent learning experiments of the type invented by Blodgett (1929), in which no reward was introduced during the learning period, that I was apt to formulate the conditions involved in such field-expectancy learning primarily in terms of frequency alone and as if motivation played no role. However, if I did this, I was in error. It is obvious that completely unmotivated animals will not learn. They will go to sleep or otherwise divorce themselves from the task. So it must be emphasized that in the Blodgett experiments, even though the animals were not rewarded, they *were* motivated. Also, from the first Spence and Lippitt experiment (1946) and from some of the follow-up experiments by Kendler (1947) and Walker (1948), it appears that mere exercise, mere exploration under one drive, may not be enough to cause the animals to perceive and to learn the position of reward-objects appropriate to some other drive. Thirsty animals apparently do not notice food, even though the experiment be rigged as it was by Kendler and Mencher (1948) to seem to force them to notice that the cups which did not contain water did contain food. Summing it up, then, it appears that motivation conditions *are* very important for the building up of field expectancies. I would like in this connection to report briefly an experiment recently done by Gleitman at California. He used a T-maze and trained hungry rats to get equal amounts of food at each end; the two end-boxes being quite dissimilar in character. Then these two end-boxes were placed in another room and the rats were introduced into each of them. In one they received a shock and in the other no shock. They were then immediately replaced in the original maze, and 22 out of 25 animals immediately avoided at the choice point the pathway which led to the end-box in which they had just been shocked. This showed that during the previous training they *had* learned which path at the choice point led to which end-box in spite of the fact that they had been equally reinforced in

both end-boxes. In other words, their hunger, as well as their exercise had probably led them under these conditions to build up spatial sign-Gestalten which could now be appropriately used for a different response, namely for that of now avoiding the end-box in which punishment had just been received. That is, rats can learn under hunger which path leads to which end-box, and they can learn that a given end-box now means punishment and *not* food—even though they apparently cannot perceive water and learn its location when under strong hunger, nor perceive food and learn its location when under strong thirst.

To sum up, I would conclude that motivation conditions must be assumed to play a role in the building up of field expectancies. But this does not mean that I hold that such learning consists in the stamping in of S-R habits by reinforcement. The presence of reinforcement in a particular locus makes that locus a goal which determines what performance will take place, but it does not stamp in S-R connections though it probably does give a special vividness to that locus in the total field expectancy.

The main question is, however, what are the laws determining the acquisition, de-acquisition, and forgetting of such field expectancies.

As to acquisition, first we have to know, for the given species, the facts of their perceptual sensitivity. Obviously the field expectancies, which get built up, can include only such aspects of the environment as the given organism is capable of perceiving.

Secondly, we have to know the facts concerning the ability of the given organism (under the given conditions of motivation) to connect and associate the different parts of the field so that when he is in one part of the field he will *remember* what was present in other parts.

Thirdly, we have to know the facts concerning what, for want of a better name, we may call the animal's *"inference abilities."* These would state the capacity of the given individual, or species, to extend its expectancies *re* given environmental fields beyond the parts upon which this individual has been specifically exercised. It is these capacities which will underlie the animal's ability to short-cut and to take *Umwege*. Such inference facts, when we have them, will obviously be found to include something about an ability on the animal's part to set up a system, or systems, of orienting coordinates as a result of the presence, or absence, of such and such strategically located cues. All this, of course, sounds complicated. But personally, it seems to me that we are a very long way from any precise laws for such field-expectancy learning, and where we seem to have such laws it is because either overtly (or covertly) we have held constant most of the important circumambient variables. We can work out equations and constants for the development of specific behaviors in specific apparatuses under specific motivations. But how the form of the specific apparatus plus the nature and magnitudes of the specific motivation enter into and determine these equations, I believe we do not know.

Granted then, that we are still very near the beginning of our knowledge of laws for the acquisition of field expectancies, what can we say about the laws of their de-acquisition and forgetting? Here, I have nothing but simple hunches to offer. These hunches would be, first, that the de-acquisition of field expectancies only takes place when the actual environment is so changed that the previous expectancy is no longer suitable. The de-acquisition of one field expectancy results from the learning of another conflicting expectancy. But to what extent the laws and equations for such *new learnings* will be different from those for the original learnings, I hesitate to say. I should expect the equations to have the same form but that new constants would be required.

Finally, as to forgetting, here in the case of field expectancies, as contrasted with that of cathexes and of equivalence beliefs, I believe that true forgetting (i.e., weakening as a result of the mere passage of time) *does* take place. We don't forget our cathexes and we don't forget our equivalence beliefs, but we do forget particular environmental lay-outs which we have not experienced for long periods of time—though this forgetting obviously obeys the sorts of laws which the Gestalt psychologists have uncovered and not the old simple associationistic ones. The remembered environmental lay-out becomes changed, i.e., simplified or sharpened, as well as weakened by the mere passage of time. Some features become enhanced, others minimized or even dropped out, and some wholly new features may be added. The work of the Gestalt psychologists (see, for example, Koffka, 1935, and Bartlett, 1932) all bear eloquent testimony to such nonassociationistic features in the forgetting of field expectancies.

Turn now to the next category.

Field-Cognition Modes

This category is the one about which I am least confident. Perhaps a better name would be field

lore—that is, perceptual, memorial, and inferential lores. Much of these lores—particularly perceptual lore—seems to be given innately. It is the lore that such and such stimulus configurations are to be taken as cues for such and such perceptions. And although a solid basis of such lore is nativistically given, it can, as we know, be added to and modified by experience. Consider, for example, the experiment of Fieandt (one of Brunswik's students, 1936) in which the subjects came, as a result of training, to use a very slight mark on one of each pair of cards as a cue which led them to perceive this card as having an objectively light shade but as in shadow. The slight mark, often not perceived consciously as such, came nonetheless to be used as a perceptual cue that the card was in shadow and therefore really light. And in so far as this tendency would transfer to new situations, it would be an example of an acquired perceptual lore.

Memorial lore is relatively simple. The one innately given principle seems to be that, if a certain sequence of events has occurred on one occasion, this same sequence of events is likely to occur on subsequent occasions. This principle seems to be innately strong. The complementary principle of mere probabilities of occurrence is one which has to be learned. Brunswik (1939) more than any other psychologist has investigated this question of the learning to expect mere probabilities. But even he, I think, has not carried the implications far enough. Thus, for example, it would seem to me that the ability to "tolerate ambiguity," a concept developed by Else Frenkel-Brunswik (1948), probably closely ties in with this learning to expect mere probabilities. But the conditions of early childhood training, or whatever they may be, which develop this new memorial principle that allows the subject to be able to remember not 100 per cent sequences but merely probable sequences, that is, to tolerate ambiguities, have yet to be subjected to more study.

Inferential lore, in its simplest form, would, like perceptual lore and memorial lore, be to a considerable extent innate. It would consist of the simple rules of space, time, force, and quantity, the bases for which are certainly innate. Such lore receives, however, tremendous additions through specific verbal training—especially in us human beings. We men learn verbally all sorts of rules about time, space, force, and quantity. And these rules we then carry around with us from one specific situation to another—so that they then underlie and govern our specific apprehensions, i.e., our field expectancies, for each new environmental field.

In a word, I am trying to summarize under this fourth category all those principles as to the structure of environmental fields which are relevant to all environmental fields and which (whether innate or learned) are carried around by the individual and applied to each new field with which he is presented.

As to the conditions and laws for the acquisition, de-acquisition, and forgetting of such perceptual, memorial, and inferential modes, as distinct from the acquisition of the concrete apprehension of the particular fields themselves, I believe we have as yet practically no information.

Turn now to the fifth category.

Drive Discriminations

Here, also, I have but little more to say. In my preliminary remarks concerning this category I referred to the latent learning experiments and to the Hull and the Leeper experiments which suggested that rats sometimes may have to learn to distinguish between their different drives. And I believe that there are similar learnings required of human beings. We, too, I believe, often have to learn to discriminate our true needs. In fact, I would suggest that sometimes the task of psychotherapy is not merely, as I argued above, that of breaking incorrect, yet traumatically held to, equivalence beliefs. It may also be, on occasion, the helping of the patient to learn to discriminate his real drives or needs.

But, again, we have practically no experimental data either for rats or for men as to how we learn, unlearn, or forget (if we do) these drive discriminations.

Motor Patterns

Guthrie (1940) has emphasized the learning of "movements," where "movements" are contrasted with "acts." Acts he admits to be goal-directed (although in the last analysis it would appear that for him they also must dissolve into complexes of nongoal-directed movements). But, in any event, in calling attention to movements Guthrie is calling attention, I think, to what I would mean by motor patterns. And in default of other experimental theories about the learning of motor patterns I am willing to take a chance and to agree with Guthrie that the conditions under which a motor pattern gets acquired may well be those in which the given movement gets the animal away from the stimuli which were present when the movement was initiated. Any response (i.e., any movement) which goes off will, according to Guthrie, get conditioned on a single trial to whatever stimuli were then present. Therefore a movement which removes the individual from out the range of those stimuli tends to be the one which remains conditioned to them because no other movements have a chance to occur and to displace it. A motor pattern thus gets learned without reinforcement. I would like to point out, however, that such a learning of motor patterns is of necessity always imbedded in a larger goal-directed activity—a point which is not emphasized by Guthrie. His and Horton's cats (1946) did learn stereotyped motor patterns for getting out of their hit-the-barber-pole type of problem-box; but they learned them only because they, the cats, were involved in the larger goal-directed activity of getting to the food in front. And, similarly, I believe that rats learn stereotyped motor patterns for running specific mazes only when these specific patterns actually get them to food. When such specific movements do not succeed, trial and error supervene and new movements get a chance to become conditioned, but again only if these new ones prove in the larger setting to get the animal to his goal.

Finally, however, once a movement sequence gets learned in one situation, it is ready, I believe, to be tried out in other situations. We do build up, I believe, many motor patterns (the old name was sensory-motor skills) which we carry around with us as equipment for behaving in new situations. And, whereas I do not think we as yet know much about the laws for the learning, unlearning, and forgetting of such motor patterns, I am willing to accept, for the present, Guthrie's notions concerning their learning and unlearning. Finally, as to their forgetting I can merely point to the everyday fact that one's skills do seem to get rusty with lack of exercise and the passage of time.

Now to conclude: Let me briefly summarize. There are, I believe, at least six kinds of learning —or rather the learning of at least six kinds of relationships. I have called these six relationships: cathexes, equivalence beliefs, field expectancies, field-cognition modes, drive discriminations, and motor patterns. And although, as usual, I have been merely programmatic and have not attempted to set up, at this date, any precise systems of postulates and deduced theorems, I *have* made some specific suggestions as to some of the conditions and laws for the acquisition, de-acquisition, and forgetting of these relationships. I feel that once we have thought of really good, defining experiments for each of these types of learning, we can then hypothesize equations, fit empirical curves, and dream up constants to our hearts' content. At least I *think I* could.

Summarizing more specifically for each of the six kinds of learning, the following further suggestions were also made: (1) I suggested that the "reinforcement" doctrine is probably valid for the acquisition of cathexes. (2) I suggested that this "reinforcement" principle plus traumatic experience is probably also valid for the acquiring of equivalence beliefs. And I asserted that erroneous equivalence beliefs are a large part of what the therapist has to contend with. (3) I held that reinforcement per se is not valid for the acquisition of field expectancies, and I also emphasized that Gestalt principles of learning and forgetting, rather than associationistic principles, are of prime importance in the acquiring and the forgetting of such field expectancies. (4) For the acquisition, deacquisition, and forgetting of the field-cognition modes of perception, memory, and inference I had no laws to suggest. The development of such laws would depend upon the carrying out of many more carefully designed transfer experiments than we now have. (5) For the learning of drive discriminations, I also had no laws but pointed to types of experiments which seem to have favored the development of drive discriminations. (6) Finally, as to the laws for the acquisition of motor patterns, per se, I suggested that Guthrie's principle of simple conditioning may perhaps be correct.

One last word. Why do I want thus to complicate things; why do I not want one simple set of laws for all learning? I do not know. But I suppose it must be due to some funny erroneous equivalence belief on my part to the effect that being sweeping and comprehensive, though vague, is equivalent to more love from others than being narrow and precise. No doubt, any good clinician would be able to trace this back to some sort of nasty traumatic experience in my early childhood. Let, then, the clinician unravel this sort of causal relationship in me or in others and I will attempt to show him its analogue in rats, or at least in chimpanzees or perhaps dogs. For, if more of the theoretical and learning psychologists, on the one hand, and more of the clinicians, on the other, don't get together—and soon—there is really going to develop that nasty fission in psychology (Cran-

nell, 1947; Krech, 1946) that we have all been warned of. And if that fission happens, then our science is really going to suffer a long and very unfortunate period of schizophrenic "institutionalization"—whether inside or outside of our universities.

REFERENCES

Allport, G. W. Scientific models and human morals. *Psychological Review*, 1946, **54**, 182–192.

Bartlett, F. C. *Remembering—A study in experimental and social psychology*. London: Cambridge University Press, 1932.

Blodgett, H. C. The effect of the introduction of reward upon the maze performance of rats. *University of California Publications in Psychology*, 1929, **4**, 113–134.

Brunswik, E. Probability as a determiner of rat behavior. *Journal of Experimental Psychology*, 1939, **25**, 175–197.

Crannell, C. W. Are rat psychologists responsible for fission? *American Psychologist*, 1947, **2**, 22–23.

Fieandt, K. Dressurversuche an der Farbenwahrnehmung. *Archiv fuer die gesamte Psychologie*, 1936, **96**, 467–495.

Frenkel-Brunswik, E. Tolerance toward ambiguity as a personality variable. *American Psychologist*, 1948, **3**, 268.

Guthrie, E. R. Association and the law of effect. *Psychological Review*, 1940, **47**, 127–148.

Guthrie, E. R., & Horton, G. P. *Cats in a puzzle box*. New York: Holt, Rinehart & Winston, 1946.

Hilgard, E. R., & Marquis, D. G. *Conditioning and learning*. New York: Appleton-Century-Crofts, 1940.

Hull, C. L. Differential habituation to internal stimuli in the albino rat. *Journal of Comparative Psychology*, 1933, **16**, 225–273.

Hull, C. L. *Principles of behavior*. New York: Appleton-Century-Crofts, 1943.

Kendler, H. H. An investigation of latent learning in a T-maze. *Journal of Comparative Physiological Psychology*, 1947, **40**, 265–270.

Kendler, H. H., & Mencher, H. C. The ability of rats to learn the location of food when motivated by thirst—An experimental reply to Leeper. *Journal of Experimental Psychology*, 1948, **38**, 82–88.

Koffka, K. *Principles of Gestalt psychology*. New York: Harcourt, Brace & World, 1935.

Krech, D. A note on fission. *American Psychologist*, 1946, **1**, 402–404.

Leeper, R. The role of motivation in learning: A study of the phenomenon of differential motivational control of the utilization of habits. *Journal of Genetic Psychology*, 1935, **46**, 3–40.

Spence, K. W., & Lippitt, R. An experimental test of the sign-gestalt theory of trial-and-error learning. *Journal of Experimental Psychology*, 1946, **36**, 491–502.

Walker, E. L. Drive specificity and learning. *Journal of Experimental Psychology*, 1948, **38**, 39–49.

31

"Superstition" in the Skinnerian

John Oliver Cook

The name of B. F. Skinner has been mentioned frequently throughout this book and will be mentioned again. Skinner has been such an inventive and productive originator of ideas that many consider him one of the great innovators in psychology of this century.

It was Skinner who developed the "Skinner boxes" in which untold numbers of rats and pigeons have been conditioned by countless psychologists. He was also a pioneer in the development of teaching machines, and it is at the relationship between these two innovations that the author of this article would have us look. He points out that even the most provocative concepts cannot be transplanted haphazardly, without regard to the differences that exist between one situation and another.

The term "superstition," when used in the context of animal learning, refers to extraneous movements that become part of the conditioned response because they are accidentally reinforced. For example, if a pigeon has cocked his head in a certain way just before making a response that is reinforced, he may repeat the head motion each time he makes the response. This bears a superficial—and humorous—resemblance to the way an actor may refuse to go on stage without the tattered scarf he wore on the night of his first hit performance.

You will notice that the author refers to some differences as being "significant beyond the .01 level." This simply means that there is less than one chance in a hundred that such differences might have occurred by chance.

Let me begin with a thumping platitude. Though all true Skinnerians[1] would scoff at the idea, in a loose sense of the word "theory," everyone's behavior reflects some theory or other. This is as true of those of us who are engaged in programed instruction as it is of anyone else. In instances where the person cannot give a reasonable account of why he is doing what he is doing, the theory in question is not so much a theory as it is an empirical generalization about the person's behavior. I shall neglect this instance and turn my attention to the case in which the theory that is reflected in the person's behavior is in fact a deliberately used guiding principle.

Teaching machines were the outgrowth of the Skinner box, and they bear—particularly the early models—unmistakable marks of their origin. Thus the design of teaching machines not only reflects certain theoretical principles about behavior, it also exhibits a number of irrelevant features of the Skinner box—features that had to be incorporated into it because of the very limited symbol-manipulating capacity of rats and pigeons. In short, I am saying that the teaching machine, even today, is just too faithful a copy of the Skinner box.

The analogy that comes to mind is the early attempts to build airplanes that flapped their wings, because that is the way birds fly. The principles of physics that underlie the flight of birds and the flight of rigid-wing airplanes are the same, but the manner in which these two things operate in the air is quite different. Flapping wings are not a feature that is necessitated by the underlying physical principles. It would be a mistake to think that they are—a mistake that seriously limits the

From American Psychologist, *Vol. 18 (1963), 516–518. Copyright 1963 by the American Psychological Association, and reproduced by permission. The preparation of this paper was supported in part by Contract No. OE-2-10-016 with the United States Office of Education.*

[1] Note from the Editor. Skinnerian: A hypothetical construct sometimes invoked to explain the behavior of psychologists employing a distinctive methodology and/or embracing a particular view of natural phenomena.

scope of our experimental efforts. To be sure, programmers and teaching machine designers enjoy a good deal more success in their efforts than the early flapping-wing plane designers did, but I still think that they are making the same mistake—the mistake of confusing features that are dictated by theoretical principles with features that are dictated by the specific characteristics of the learning task, by the nature of the learning organism, or by some other nontheoretical consideration.

There is in the behavior of devout Skinnerians, as in the behavior of pigeons (Skinner, 1948), a strong element of superstition. In making the transition from training a pigeon in a Skinner box to training a human being with a teaching machine, religious Skinnerians seem to have a certain reluctance to change any detail of the ritual for fear that the beneficial results that they enjoyed with the Skinner box might not be forthcoming with the teaching machine.

Pigeons being trained in a Skinner box make overt responses. What is more natural, then, than to require human beings who are being trained by teaching machines to make overt responses? Yet it has been repeatedly demonstrated for a variety of tasks that it makes no difference whether the subjects make overt responses or implicit ones. Indeed, in the case of some tasks, implicit responses produce better results than overt ones.

Here (Figure 1) is a case in point.

These two groups learned the same paired-associate task under exactly the same conditions, the only difference being that one group was required to make overt responses and the other was not. The difference in performance, as you see, is large, and (I might add for the benefit of non-Skinnerians) for the first six tests the difference is significant far beyond the .01 level. This finding at least illustrates my contention that overt responding is not an essential feature of programed instruction and that, in fact, it may even be a deleterious one in some cases. I think this point, though, is a dead horse and not worth the beating, because it is pretty clear now that we would secure general agreement among Skinnerians, as well as those outside the faith, that implicit responding may be quite effective.

Now let me turn to an issue that is alive and kicking: the matter of reinforcement. In working with a Skinner box we always reinforce the pigeon *after* it has made the correct response and not before it. Analogously, it is the common practice in programed instruction to evoke a response from the learner and then confirm (reinforce) it by showing him the correct response. What would happen in, say, a paired-associate task if we showed the learner the correct answer *before* he made his response instead of after? The answer to this question is shown in Figure 2.

FIGURE 1   *Mean scores on a paired-associate task (From Cook and Spitzer, 1960)*

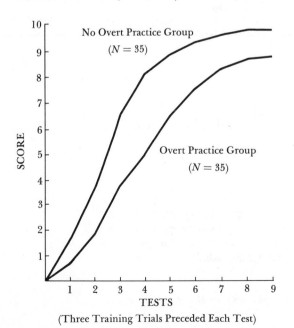

(Three Training Trials Preceded Each Test)

FIGURE 2   *Mean scores on a paired-associate task (From Cook and Spitzer, 1960)*

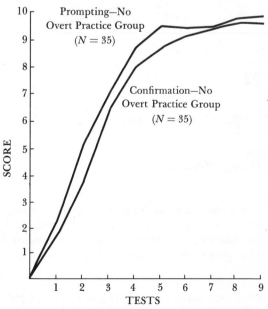

(Three Training Trials Preceded Each Test)

These data and those in Figure 1 are part of the same experiment. The top curve in Figure 1 is the bottom curve in Figure 2. These data show that giving the learner the correct answer before he responds, rather than afterwards, has no harmful effect upon his performance. In fact, it results in a slight, but insignificant, improvement.

Let me show you the same thing in serial learning. Here (Figure 3) the task consisted of learning a path through a punchboard maze. The apparatus consisted of a 12 × 12 array of buttons with a light above each button. In the confirmation condition the learner was informed of the correctness of each correct response after he had made that response. (The light went on over the correct button.) In the prompting condition, pressing the correct button in one row lit the light above the correct button in the next row. Thus the subject in this condition was informed of the correctness of the response *before* he made it. Subjects in both treatments were given alternate training and test trials. They were not given any knowledge of results on the test trials. In terms of trials to criterion the prompting condition is clearly superior. The difference (again for the non-Skinnerians) is significant at the .01 level. This finding is in direct opposition to what I take to be the current belief of Skinnerians—that a student will not learn merely by being guided through a performance. He will learn; in fact, he will learn faster.

This story has three morals, but they are all very simple. The first is that not all the features of a gadget are dictated by theoretical principles. The second is that what works beautifully in one context may not work so beautifully in another. The third moral is that superstitious behavior is not restricted to pigeons.

FIGURE 3   *Mean scores on a serial learning task (From Cook, Miller, Grier, and Staman, 1962)*

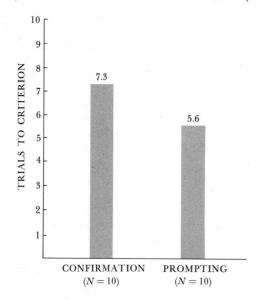

REFERENCES

Cook, J. O., Miller, H. G., Grier, J. B., & Staman, J. W. A generalized "plan" for serial learning. In J. O. Cook and H. G. Miller, *Studies in guided learning*. Washington, D.C.: Cooperative Research Project No. 1242. U.S. Office of Education, 1963. Pp. 79–95.

Cook, J. O., & Spitzer, M. E. Supplementary report: Prompting versus confirmation in paired-associate learning. *Journal of Experimental Psychology*, 1960, **59**, 275–276.

Skinner, B. F. "Superstition" in the pigeon. *Journal of Experimental Psychology*, 1948, **38**, 168–172.

32

Engrams, Memory Storage, and Mnemonic Coding

David Wechsler

When someone learns a new word and its meaning, he undergoes a very slight but easily detectable change. The change can be detected by asking the person to spell the word, to explain what it means, and to give a synonym for it. Consider the word *sanguinolent*. Most people are not familiar with this word and would readily admit it. After it is ex-

From American Psychologist, *Vol. 18 (1963), 149–153. Copyright 1963 by the American Psychological Association, and reproduced by permission.*

plained that the word means "of or pertaining to blood; containing or tinged with blood," the person will react differently (recognize the word) when it is again presented.

This behavioral index of change has usually been the major definition of learning. When learning is considered as a two-way process whereby material is gained (learned) or lost (forgotten), such gains or losses can be detected by asking appropriate questions and listening to or observing the responses of the person being questioned. This procedure is the essence of behavioral analysis.

A somewhat less apparent aspect of the change that takes place when learning occurs has to do with the internal physiological feature that must be considered to have changed. When we learn new words, we experience a sequence of neural activities that may begin at the ears, progress along the auditory nerves to the midbrain, and finally end up in the temporal lobes of the cortex. If that chain of neural activity is going to result in our responding in a changed way, then it is logical to assume that some sort of physical change has occurred somewhere in our nervous tissue. This article is concerned with the problem of finding out just what kinds of changes these are.

Although the subject of memory has been investigated more than most topics in psychology, many of its basic problems remain discouragingly unsolved. Prominent among these are questions concerning how the human brain records, stores, and transmits information. These are broad topics, and I propose to discuss them here, not so much with the aim of presenting definitive answers, but rather in an attempt to reformulate some of them in the light of recent advances in physics and biochemistry.

The first, and in many ways the basic question, is what happens in the brain that enables one to "recall" past experiences in the absence of excitatory stimuli which originally provoked them. The historical answer has been that all such stimuli produce some enduring physical changes in one or another part of the brain which, in virtue of the effects produced, are subsequently capable of redintegration. These aftereffects have been at various times differently designated and in recent years generally referred to as engrams or memory traces. The term engram was introduced by Richard Semon a little after the turn of the century and defined by him (1921) as the "change left behind in the irritable substance of the brain after excitation has died down." Semon conceived of it as an eduring, if not permanent, change produced somewhere in the nuclear material of the brain cell. Here he came close to the contemporaneous point of view that it involves primarily a molecular change. Thus, in discussing the possible locus of the engram, he wrote, "most probably neither the cell nor the nucleus of the cell is able to possess it [the engram]." Again, without being acquainted with current genetic theory, he speaks of an elementary *protomer* or "a minimum segment of irritable substance capable of retaining possession of

the inherited engram." As a biologist, Semon was more interested in what we now think of as genetic characters but believed, and I think correctly, that the same laws applied to the transmission of the acquired memories.

Semon's view as to how the engram is represented in the brain is less explicit. His statement on the matter is that "each mnemic excitation is related to the original one much as a reproduction of a picture relates to its original" (Semon, 1921). This is the historical point of view.[1] I do not think that Semon intended it to be taken literally, but it did serve to reinforce the widely held concept that a memory trace is a sort of facsimile of the stimulus or excitation which produced it, in much the same way as an image of an object is represented on the retina. The analogy in any case is misleading. There is no evidence that a memory trace, however constituted, is a kind of pictogram or any other analogically defined replica. All that is known is that it involves some structural change in some part or parts of the nervous system. The structural changes have at various times been posited as occurring at some points in the course of transmission of the neural impulse such as at the neural synapses or, as now more generally agreed, in the nuclear elements of the involved receptor cells.

Not less easy to answer is whether the structural changes which are the bases for engram formation are spatially localized. The answer depends in a measure on what one understands by locus or localization. If by a locus we mean a particular area in the brain or a particular cell in any particular place, there is no such thing as engram lo-

[1] Thus, according to James Mill, "our ideas spring up or exist in the order in which the sensations existed, of which they are copies" (Boring, 1929, p. 213).

calization. The findings regarding stimulus equivalence and equipotentiality of the brain areas would indicate that memory, unlike sensation, does not depend upon the excitation of particular cells at some points in the nervous system. As Lashley (1960b) has amply demonstrated, "there is no specialization of memory areas outside of the primary sensory field."

On the other hand, if by localization one thinks primarily of a structural change that takes place in one rather than another part of the cell, e.g., the part containing deoxyribonucleic acid rather than other particles in the nucleus, then structural changes posited for engram formation necessarily imply some specifiable locus. It is precisely through investigation of molecular reorganizations which take place at such times that biochemists have, in recent years, discovered where and how genetic changes take place. The chemist's description of the way this information is laid down and transmitted strongly suggests the possibility of a similar mechanism in mnemic coding. It seems likely that engrams, like genetic codes, eventually involve rearrangement of atomic structures. This might be effected, as has been shown in the case of genes, through the formation of characteristic molecules (polymers) from less complex molecules (monomers) in the acids of the nucleus (Blum, 1961).

What is of special interest and suggestive to the psychologists is the chemical process by which these polymers are formed and duplicated, particularly those involved in the construction of the so-called biologic templates. A biologic template is at once a code and a method of reduplication, and in virtue of this dual characteristic it offers a basis for explaining, at least analogically, the process of engramatization. Even more significantly, it supplies a key as to how memory patterns are kept intact and revived. My view of the memory mechanism is that it consists essentially of a matching process. This is in contrast to the explanation of it in terms of reverberatory circuits by McCulloch (1951). The matching hypothesis may be described in purely psychological terms, but it is encouraging to discover that the chemist and physicist have furnished us with descriptions which show that many of the changes in molecular structure take place essentially in a similar manner. I believe that acquired engrams are laid down like genetic codes, are transmitted as genetic information and revived and assembled into memories by some matching method. The matching may be either chemical or electrical, and at some levels of neural organization of the sort we identify

with frequency radio tuning or electrical resonance. That the brain, or a certain part of it, shows continuous electrical activity is a well-established fact. The question [of] whether a complex electrolyte like the brain lends itself to electrical resonance is something that would have to be demonstrated. While this has not yet been done, there is reason to believe that under certain conditions, it is not theoretically impossible (Wechsler, 1960).

Another of the unresolved problems in the description of the memory process is what happens to the engram or memory trace between the moment it is first imprinted and the moment it is revived. This is the problem of storage. The common view on the matter is that there are certain areas or reserved places of the brain in which memories, so to speak, are locked and at the same time kept available for future use. These spaces are often compared to filing cabinets or storage cellars. The designated comparisons are presumably presented, to begin with, merely as metaphors or analogies, but more often than not are preserved as literal explanations. Actually it is not important whether one regards the various parts of the brain as a series of intercommunicating compartments or an assortment of filing cabinets. The main source of confusion resides in the belief that memories as such are stored at all, in the usual sense of the term.

When I say that there are no stored memories, I do not wish to imply that the excitatory processes in the brain, which serve to evoke whatever it is that is later revived, effect or leave behind no changes, but only that these changes must not be equated with the ones that are involved in the production of the original percepts or ideas. The elements out of which these were constructed were laid down long before and in most instances genetically.

Thus, if we conceive of learning as a linking of sequential responses or facts, it is not the facts but the links between them which are altered by the learning process. Nothing was implanted which was not laid down before. What has been modified is the organism's capacity to respond. Memories, like perceptions, and eventually sensations, have no separate existences. The memory of what you saw yesterday has no more existence until revived than the pain you felt in your arm before it is pinched.

A view not unlike the one just put forward was suggested by Ewald Hering as long ago as 1870. Thus, in discussing the existence of unconscious memories, he asserted that: "They do not exist as ideas; what is preserved is the special disposition of the neural substance in virtue of which it gives out today the same sound as it gave out yesterday, if properly struck" (Boring, 1929). In short, for the experiencing individual, memories do not exist before they are revived or recalled. Memories are not like filed letters stored in cabinets or unhung pictures in the basement of a museum. Rather, they are like melodies realized by striking the keys on a piano. Ideas are no more stored in the brain than melodies in a piano or any other musical instrument. An almost identical view was expressed by Lashley (1960a) when he stated that "The anatomic structure of engrams is fixed like the keys of a piano; behavior patterns play over the structure as the fingers of a musician, producing the characteristic chords of *G* or *F* sharp minor throughout the range of the keyboard." I would only add that the brain probably consists of many different keyboards, intercommunicating to be sure, but not always in tune and, of course, not all with a Steinway quality. Some, I am afraid, remind us more of penny whistles or cigar-box ukes.

One may then ask, are there any memories which are everlasting or permanently impressed, as, for example, those seemingly recalled after a lapse of many years? My answer is generally no. Contrary to common opinion nearly everything that is acquired or learned is eventually obliterated, usually in a very short time. Very little is permanently retained. It does happen occasionally that a person may recall scenes of early childhood, recognize individuals whom they have not seen for a decade or more; or under special circumstances, as when hypnotized, "remember" things they seemingly had completely forgotten. The fact remains, however, that instances like these constitute a very minute fraction of the total happenings experienced by the average individual during the course of his lifetime. If there were such a thing as permanent storage of memories, one would have to posit inordinately large numbers of *different kinds of neurons,* a fact which we know is not supported by neurological studies. Permanent storage, as Von Neumann pointed out (Jeffress, 1951), means permanent occupation. Once occupied, nothing else could be stored, and even the nine billion cells which the brain is alleged to contain would not be sufficient to hold all the perceptions and nonsense with which it is afflicted in an average lifetime. It is fortunate that the human mind is able to forget as well as remember.

What I have tried to say thus far is that memory, whether one conceives it as a faculty of the mind or a modus operandi of the brain, does not

carry on or do the things it seemingly does in the way we have for a long time been led to believe. It does not engrave, it does not store or permanently record anything. Its essential function is to code and transmit information as needed. If it is a machine, it is a matching machine and not a computing machine. All its parts are genetically laid down; it "knows" what to do without being told or programed. The information it codes and transmits will in some measure depend on the kind of stimulation to which it is exposed. Thus, an organism may be conditioned to respond to stimuli in a certain desired sequence, that is, make use of bits of information in order to acquire certain verbal or motor habits. In such cases it is said to have learned. But learning is a minor aspect of the mnemic process and the information thus sequestered constitutes a minute fraction of the potential total engram store it possesses.

It is interesting to speculate on how the information possessed or acquired by the brain is ordered and transmitted. In view of the all-or-none, or nearly all-or-none, type of responses which characterizes neuronal excitation, it has been generally posited that the feat is accomplished by a relatively simple stop-go, open-close switching device. The advantage of such a system is that it requires a minimum of circuitry and makes possible utilization of the switching system itself as a coding device. For this reason, among others, a stop-go switching system has generally served as a model in the construction of computers and devices for artificial intelligence. There is considerable neurophysiological evidence that some such step system may actually be employed in the transmission of nerve impulses, whether mediated by some form of neurobiotaxes or acetylcholine-esterase interactions. It is possible to conceptualize and implement a switching system which, if properly organized, could fulfill the entire memory functioning by itself, and indeed even explain logically the activity of the brain as a whole. This is what Warren McCulloch and his co-workers have suggested and tried to show in their description of the brain as a computing machine (McCulloch, 1951).

The main objection to the view that the brain functions as a computer is the fact that, so far as one can observe, it does not operate in this manner. In the first place, the brain's switching operations are much too slow to carry out a step-by-step process at speeds one would have to require of them. The rate of neural transmission is at least 10^{-6} times slower than even a moderately fast electronic computer. If this is true, the brain could not solve any but the simplest problems within the order of time limits we know it does if it were compelled to do so by any method of sequential counting. On the other hand, consider how fast the mind works in responding to a simple question requiring straightforward recall, for example, of responding to a question like, "Who was the Secretary of War in Lincoln's second administration?" I cannot say how long it would take a well-programed computer to furnish the correct response, but I am sure the computer would not produce the answer as quickly as a high school student with only a modest knowledge of American history. Of course, the reason why the student could come up with an answer more quickly is because he would not have had to "calculate" it; he would merely have had to "remember" it.

The second reason why I do not think that the memory processes are carried on by computer methods is that I do not believe that these processes, like many other activities of the brain, can be accounted for stochastically, that is, can be wholly predicted on the basis of probability theory. If they could, it would be necessary to assume a beforehand knowledge of the probabilities of most, if not all, of the sequences of events involved in any given process. I do not think that such knowledge can be posited in the case of memory because association between mental events depends not merely on antecedent concomitance and frequency, but also for purely idiosyncratic reasons. Consider, for example, a simple free-association experiment where it is possible to anticipate, on the basis of previous data, what the frequency of any specified response to a given word might be. Thus, in a normal population one might expect the following frequency of responses to the word *sickness: health* approximately 35 times in a hundred, *death* 14 times in a hundred, *illness* 8 times in a hundred, *medicine* 2 times in a hundred, and so on. But unique or idiosyncratic responses could not be predicted. Thus, one could not anticipate a response like *Brooklements* given by a schizophrenic girl, which was encountered once and probably would never be met with again.

What has just been said about the responses of expectancy problems in simple situations like a word-association test would, of course, apply with much greater force to more complex situations. Consider, for example, an experience like the one which Amundsen recounts in his autobiography that occurred during one of his trips to the North Pole. He had left his ice-locked ship one morning for a brief walk and had not gone very far when he saw a hungry-looking bear not many yards ahead of him. Amundsen decided to turn back, but the bear, equally determined, began to follow him. Amundsen quickened his pace; the bear did likewise. Sensing the danger of what might happen, Amundsen started running toward the ship. As he reached the gangplank he tripped and fell. Various thoughts passed through his mind but none which, in view of his predicament, anyone would have thought likely. He was not at all frightened nor in anyway concerned with immediate danger. Instead, he saw himself sitting on a curb corner of Piccadilly Circus in London, counting the ladies' hairpins scattered about him.

Although I believe that the mnemic process is essentially nonstochastic, I do not thereby wish to imply that these processes are entirely nonpredictable, much less to conclude that learning and recall do not conform to certain general principles. Above all, we must distinguish between the conditions which favor or inhibit memory from the processes which account for it. Here, we must rely upon knowledge gained from the basic sciences rather than be tempted by the practical models offered by the engineer. Such models, effective as they may be, do not necessarily correspond to what goes on in the brain; nor do they need to, in order to achieve their ends. Thus, the intriguing systems now employed in computers, however effective in equipping them with memory storage, do not represent, in my opinion, what actually goes on in the brain. There is little evidence to show that the brain uses the same or even similar devices to fix and recall the information that it receives. It does not rely on tape inputs, acoustic relays, or magnetic cores. Information is received and transmitted more directly, and while no definitive mechanisms have been established, it seems clear that coding and transmission of information in the brain more nearly resembles genetic replication and resonance phenomena than the devices currently employed in automata.

REFERENCES

Blum, H. F. On the origin and evolution of human machines. *American Scientist*, 1961, **49**, 474–508.

Boring, E. G. *A history of experimental psychology.* New York: Appleton-Century-Crofts, 1929.

Jeffress, L. A. (Ed.) *Cerebral mechanisms in behavior: The Hickson symposium.* New York: Wiley, 1951.

Lashley, K. S. Cerebral organization of behavior. In F. A. Beach, D. O. Hebb, C. T. Morgan, & H. W. Nissen (Eds.), *The neuropsychology of Lashley.* New York: McGraw-Hill, 1960. (a)

Lashley, K. S. In search of the engram. In F. A. Beach *et al.* (Eds.), *The neuropsychology of Lashley.* New York: McGraw-Hill, 1960. (b)

McColloch, W. S. Why the mind is in the head. In L. A. Jeffress (Ed.), *Cerebral mechanisms in behavior:*

The Hickson symposium. New York: Wiley, 1951.

Semon, R. *The mneme.* New York: Allen & Unwin, 1921.

Wechsler, D. Intelligence, quantum resonance, and thinking machines. *Transactions of the New York Academy of Science,* 1960, **27,** 259–266.

33

Interference and Forgetting

Benton J. Underwood

Have you ever studied something until you had it perfectly memorized, then found that you were unable to remember it after only a short period of time? This question is somewhat rhetorical, for everyone has had this experience at one time or another.

There are two main theoretical concepts that have been developed to try to explain such forgetting. The first, called *retroactive interference* (or *retroactive inhibition*), is that which occurs when one studies, then engages in a different activity, and then tries to remember the material that had been studied originally. The belief is that the intervening activity interferes with the effects of studying (i.e., the memories). The term "retroactive" implies that the second activity had a deleterious effect upon the previously learned material (it "acted back" upon it).

The second concept is called *proactive interference (inhibition)* and is produced when one engages in some activity, studies, and later tries to remember the material that was studied. In this case the first activity is believed to interfere with the memory of the material learned later. The term "proactive" implies that the interfering effect is projected into the future for a time.

Consider a situation in which you study German for an hour, then study French for an hour. If you later take a test in German, you would find some forgetting: The French you studied would interfere with the memories of German. If, on the other hand, you take a test in French, you would find some forgetting there also: The German memories would interfere with those of French. This article examines some of the factors involved in this kind of interference.

I know of no one who seriously maintains that interference among tasks is of no consequence in the production of forgetting. Whether forgetting is conceptualized at a strict psychological level or at a neural level (e.g., neural memory trace), some provision is made for interference to account for at least some of the measured forgetting. The many studies on retroactive inhibition are probably responsible for this general agreement that interference among tasks must produce a sizable proportion of forgetting. By introducing an interpolated interfering task, very marked decrements in recall can be produced in a few minutes in the laboratory. But there is a second generalization which has resulted from these studies, namely, that most forgetting must be a function of the learning of tasks which interfere with that which has already been learned (McGeoch, 1942). Thus,

if a single task is learned in the laboratory and retention measured after a week, the loss has been attributed to the interference from activities learned outside the laboratory during the week. It is this generalization with which I am concerned in the initial portions of this paper.

Now, I cannot deny the data which show large amounts of forgetting produced by an interpolated list in a few minutes in the laboratory. Nor do I

From Psychological Review, *Vol. 64 (1957), 49–60. Copyright 1957 by the American Psychological Association, and reproduced by permission. Address of the president, Midwestern Psychological Association, St. Louis, Missouri, May 1956. Most of the data from my own research referred to in this paper were obtained from work done under Contract N7 onr-45008, Project NR 154-057, between Northwestern University and The Office of Naval Research.*

deny that this loss may be attributed to interference. But I will try to show that use of retroactive inhibition as a paradigm of forgetting (via interference) may be seriously questioned. To be more specific: If a subject learns a single task, such as a list of words, and retention of this task is measured after a day, a week, or a month, I will try to show that very little of the forgetting can be attributed to an interfering task learned outside the laboratory during the retention interval. Before pursuing this further, I must make some general comments by way of preparation.

Whether we like it or not, the experimental study of forgetting has been largely dominated by the Ebbinghaus tradition, both in terms of methods and materials used. I do not think this is due to sheer perversity on the part of several generations of scientists interested in forgetting. It may be noted that much of our elementary knowledge can be obtained only by rote learning. To work with rote learning does not mean that we are thereby not concerning ourselves with phenomena that have no counterparts outside the laboratory. Furthermore, the investigation of these phenomena can be handled by methods which are acceptable to a science. As is well known, there are periodic verbal revolts against the Ebbinghaus tradition (e.g., Bartlett, 1932; Katona, 1940; Rapaport, 1943). But for some reason nothing much ever happens in the laboratory as a consequence of these revolts. I mention these matters neither by way of apology nor of justification for having done some research in rote learning, but for two other reasons. First, it may very well be true, as some have suggested (e.g., Rapaport, 1943), that studies of memory in the Ebbinghaus tradition are not getting at all of the important phenomena of memory. I think the same statement—that research has not got at all of the important processes—could be made about all areas in psychology; so that the criticism (even if just) should not be indigenous to the study of memory. Science does not deal at will with all natural events. Science deals with natural events only when ingenuity in developing methods and techniques of measurement allow these events to be brought within the scope of science. If, therefore, the studies of memory which meet scientific acceptability do not tap all-important memorial processes, all I can say is that this is the state of the science in the area at the moment. Secondly, because the bulk of the systematic data on forgetting has been obtained on rote-learned tasks, I must of necessity use such data in discussing interference and forgetting.

Returning to the experimental situation, let me again put in concrete form the problem with which I first wish to deal. A subject learns a single task, such as a list of syllables, nouns, or adjectives. After an interval of time, say, 24 hours, his retention of this list is measured. The explanatory problem is what is responsible for the forgetting which commonly occurs over the 24 hours. As indicated earlier, the studies of retroactive inhibition led to the theoretical generalization that this forgetting was due largely to interference from other tasks learned during the 24-hour retention interval. McGeoch (1942) came to this conclusion, his last such statement being made in 1942. I would, therefore, like to look at the data which were available to McGeoch and others interested in this matter. I must repeat that the kind of data with which I am concerned is the retention of a list without formal interpolated learning introduced. The interval of retention with which I am going to deal in this, and several subsequent analyses, is 24 hours.

First, of course, Ebbinghaus' data were available and in a sense served as the reference point for many subsequent investigations. In terms of percentage saved in relearning, Ebbinghaus showed about 65 per cent loss over 24 hours (1913). In terms of recall after 24 hours, the following studies are representative of the amount forgotten: Youtz, 88 per cent loss (1941); Luh, 82 per cent (1922); Krueger, 74 per cent (1929); Hovland, 78 per cent (1940); Cheng, 65 per cent and 84 per cent (1929); Lester, 65 per cent (1932). Let us assume as a rough average of these studies that 75 per cent forgetting was measured over 24 hours. In all of these studies the list was learned to one perfect trial. The percentage values were derived by dividing the total number of items in the list into the number lost and changing to a percentage. Thus, on the average in these studies, if the subject learned a 12-item list and recalled three of these items after 24 hours, nine items (75 per cent) were forgotten.

The theory of interference as advanced by McGeoch, and so far as I know never seriously challenged, was that during the 24-hour interval subjects learned something outside the laboratory which interfered with the list learned in the laboratory. Most of the materials involved in the investigations cited above were nonsense syllables, and the subjects were college students. While realizing that I am viewing these results in the light of data which McGeoch and others did not have available, it seems to me to be an incredible stretch of an interference hypothesis to hold that this 75 per cent forgetting was caused by something which the subjects learned outside the laboratory during the 24-hour interval. Even if we agree with some educators that much of what we teach our students in college is nonsense, it does not seem to be the kind of learning that would interfere with nonsense syllables.

If, however, this forgetting was not due to interference from tasks learned outside the laboratory during the retention interval, to what was it due? I shall try to show that most of this forgetting was indeed produced by interference—not from tasks learned outside the laboratory, but from tasks learned previously in the laboratory. Following this I will show that when interference from laboratory tasks is removed, the amount of forgetting which occurs is relatively quite small. It then becomes more plausible that this amount could be produced by interference from tasks learned outside the laboratory, although, as I shall also point out, the interference very likely comes from prior, not interpolated, learning.

In 1950 a study was published by Mrs. Greenberg and myself (1950) on retention as a function of stage of practice. The orientation for this study was crassly empirical; we simply wanted to know if subjects learn how to recall in the same sense that they learn how to learn. In the conditions with which I am concerned, naive subjects learned a list of ten paired adjectives to a criterion of eight out of ten correct on a single trial. Forty-eight hours later this list was recalled. On the following day, these same subjects learned a new list to the same criterion and recalled it after 48 hours. This continued for two additional lists, so that the subjects had learned and recalled four lists, but the learning and recall of each list was complete before another list was learned. There was low similarity among these lists as far as conventional symptoms of similarity are concerned. No words were repeated and no obvious similarities existed, except for the fact that they were all adjectives and that a certain amount of similarity among prefixes, suffixes, and so on must inevitably occur. The recall of these four successive lists is shown in Figure 1.

As can be seen, the more lists that are learned, the poorer the recall, from 69 per cent recall of the first list to 25 per cent recall of the fourth list. In examining errors at recall, we found a sufficient number of intrusion responses from previous lists to lead us to suggest that the increasing decrements in recall were a function of proactive interference from previous lists. And, while we pointed out that these results had implications for the design of experiments on retention, the relevance to

FIGURE 1   *Recall of paired adjectives as a function of number of previous lists learned (From Greenberg and Underwood, 1950)*

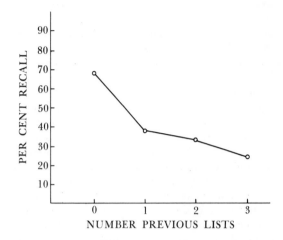

an interference theory of forgetting was not mentioned.

Dr. E. J. Archer has made available to me certain data from an experiment which still is in progress and which deals with this issue. Subjects learned lists of 12 serial adjectives to one perfect trial and recalled them after 24 hours. The recall of a list always took place prior to learning the next list. The results for nine successive lists are shown in Figure 2. Let me say again that there is no laboratory activity during the 24-hour interval; the subject learns a list, is dismissed from the laboratory, and returns after 24 hours to recall the list. The percentage of recall falls from 71 per cent for the first list to 27 per cent for the ninth.

FIGURE 2   *Recall of serial adjective lists as a function of number of previous lists learned (Unpublished data, courtesy of Dr. E. J. Archer)*

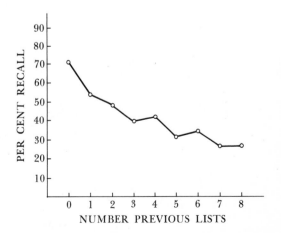

In summarizing the more classical data on retention above, I indicated that a rough estimate showed that after 24 hours 75 per cent forgetting took place, or recall was about 25 per cent correct. In viewing these values in the light of Greenberg's and Archer's findings, the conclusion seemed inescapable that the classical studies must have been dealing with subjects who had learned many lists. That is to say, the subjects must have served in many conditions by use of counterbalancing and repeated cycles. To check on this I have made a search of the literature on the studies of retention to see if systematic data could be compiled on this matter. Preliminary work led me to establish certain criteria for inclusion in the summary to be presented. First, because degree of learning is such an important variable, I have included only those studies in which degree of learning was one perfect recitation of the list. Second, I have included only studies in which retention was measured after 24 hours. Third, I have included only studies in which recall measures were given. (Relearning measures add complexities with which I do not wish to deal in this paper.) Fourth, the summary includes only material learned by relatively massed practice. Finally, if an investigator had two or more conditions which met these criteria, I averaged the values presentation in this paper. Except for these restrictions, I have used all studies I found (with an exception to be noted later), although I do not pretend to have made an exhaustive search. From each of these studies I got two facts: first, the percentage recalled after 24 hours, and second, the average number of previous lists the subjects had learned before learning the list on which recall after 24 hours was taken. Thus, if a subject had served in five experimental conditions via counterbalancing, and had been given two practice lists, the average number of lists learned before learning the list for which I tabulated the recall was four. This does not take into account any previous experiments in rote learning in which the subject might have served.

For each of these studies the two facts, average number of previous lists learned and percentage of recall, are related as in Figure 3. For example, consider the study by Youtz. This study was concerned with Jost's law and had several degrees of learning, several lengths of retention interval, and

FIGURE 3   *Recall as a function of number of previous lists learned as determined from a number of studies. From left to right: Weiss and Margolius (1954), Gibson (1942), Belmont and Birch (1951), Underwood and Richardson (1956), Williams (1950), Underwood (1952, 1953a, 1953b, 1953c), Lester (1932), Johnson (1939), Krueger (1929), Cheng (1929), Hovland (1940), Luh (1926), Youtz (1941).*

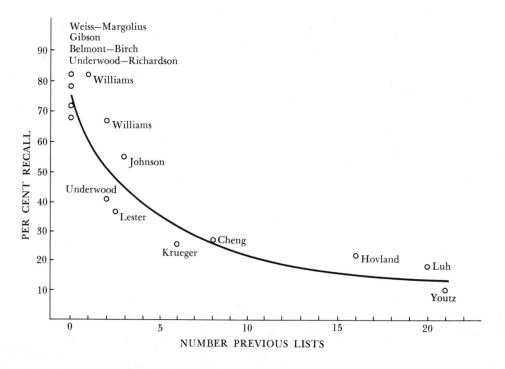

the subjects served in two cycles. Actually, there were 15 experimental conditions and each subject was given each condition twice. Also, each subject learned six practice lists before starting the experimental conditions. Among the 15 conditions was one in which the learning of the syllables was carried to one perfect recitation and recall was taken after 24 hours. It is this particular condition in which I am interested. On the average, this condition would have been given at the time when the subject had learned six practice lists and 15 experimental lists, for a total of 21 previous lists.

The studies included in Figure 3 have several different kinds of materials, from geometric forms to nonsense syllables to nouns; they include both paired-associate and serial presentation, with different speeds of presentation and different lengths of lists. But I think the general relationship is clear. The greater the number of previous lists learned, the greater the forgetting. I interpret this to mean that the greater the number of previous lists, the greater the *proactive* interference. We know this to be true (Underwood, 1945) for a formal proactive-inhibition paradigm; it seems a reasonable interpretation for the data of Figure 3. That there are minor sources of variance still involved I do not deny. Some of the variation can be rationalized, but that is not the purpose of this report. The point I wish to make is the obvious one of the relationship between number of previous lists learned—lists which presumably had no intentionally built-in similarity—and amount of forgetting. If you like to think in correlational terms, the rank-order correlation between the two variables is —.91 for the 14 points of Figure 3.

It may be of interest to the historian that, of the studies published before 1942 which met the criteria I imposed, I did not find a single one in which subjects had not been given at least one practice task before starting experimental conditions, and in most cases the subjects had several practice lists and several experimental conditions. Gibson's study (1942) was the first I found in which subjects served in only one condition and were not given practice tasks. I think it is apparent that the design proclivities of the 1920's and 1930's have been largely responsible for the exaggerated picture we have had of the rate of forgetting of rote-learned materials. On the basis of studies performed during the 1920's and 1930's, I have given a rough estimate of forgetting as being 75 per cent over 24 hours, recall being 25 per cent. On the basis of modern studies in which the subject has learned no previous lists—where there is no proactive inhibition from previous laboratory tasks—a rough estimate would be that forgetting is 25 per cent; recall is 75 per cent. The values are reversed. (If in the above and subsequent discussion my use of percentage values as if I were dealing with a cardinal or extensive scale is disturbing, I will say only that it makes the picture easier to grasp, and in my opinion no critical distortion results.)

Before taking the next major step, I would like to point out a few other observations which serve to support my general point that proactive inhibition from laboratory tasks has been the major cause of forgetting in the more classical studies. The first illustration I shall give exemplifies the point that when subjects have served in several conditions, forgetting after relatively short periods of time is greater than after 24 hours if the subject has served in only one condition. In the Youtz study to which I have already referred, other conditions were employed in which recall was taken after short intervals. After 20 minutes recall was 74 per cent, about what it is after 24 hours if the subject has not served in a series of conditions. After two hours recall was 32 per cent. In Ward's (1937) well-known reminiscence experiment, subjects who on the average had learned ten previous lists showed a recall of only 64 per cent after 20 minutes.

In the famous Jenkins-Dallenbach (1924) study on retention following sleep and following waking, two subjects were used. One subject learned a total of 61 lists and the other 62 in addition to several practice lists. Roughly, then, if the order of the conditions was randomized, approximately 30 lists had been learned prior to the learning of a list for a given experimental condition. Recall after eight waking hours for one subject was 4 per cent and for the other 14 per cent. Even after sleeping for eight hours the recall was only 55 per cent and 58 per cent.

I have said that an interpolated list can produce severe forgetting. However, in one study (Archer and Underwood, 1951), using the A-B, A-C paradigm for original and interpolated learning, but using subjects who had never served in any previous conditions, recall of the original list was 46 per cent after 48 hours, and in another comparable study (Runquist, 1956), 42 per cent. Thus, the loss is not nearly as great as in the classical studies I have cited where there was no interpolated learning in the laboratory.

My conclusion at this point is that, in terms of the gross analysis I have made, the amount of forgetting which might be attributed to interference from tasks learned outside the laboratory has been "reduced" from 75 per cent to about 25 per cent. I shall proceed in the next section to see if we have grounds for reducing this estimate still more. In passing on to this section, however, let me say that the study of factors which influence proactive inhibition in these counterbalanced studies is a perfectly legitimate and important area of study. I mention this because in the subsequent discussion I am going to deal only with the case where a subject has learned a single list in the laboratory, and I do not want to leave the impression that we should now and forevermore drop the study of interference produced by previous laboratory tasks. Indeed, as will be seen shortly, it is my opinion that we should increase these studies for the simple reason that the proactive paradigm provides a more realistic one than does the retroactive paradigm.

When the subject learns and recalls a single list in the laboratory, I have given an estimate of 25 per cent as being the amount forgotten over 24 hours. When, as shown above, we calculate percentage forgotten of lists learned to one perfect trial, the assumption is that had the subjects been given an immediate recall trial, the list would have been perfectly recalled. This, of course, is simply not true. The major factor determining how much error is introduced by this criterion-percentage method is probably the difficulty of the task. In general, the overestimation of forgetting by the percentage method will be directly related to the difficulty of the task. Thus, the more slowly the learning approaches a given criterion, the greater the drop on the trial immediately after the criterion trial. Data from a study by Runquist (1956), using eight paired adjectives (a comparatively easy task), show that amount of forgetting is overestimated by about 10 per cent. In a study (Underwood and Richardson, 1956) using very difficult consonant syllables, the overestimation was approximately 20 per cent. To be conservative, assume that on the average the percentage method of reporting recall overestimates the amount forgotten by 10 per cent. If we subtract this from the 25 per cent assumed above, the forgetting is now reestimated as being 15 per cent over 24 hours. That is to say, an interference theory, or any other form of theory, has to account for a very small amount of forgetting as compared with the amount traditionally cited.

What are the implications of so greatly "reducing" the amount of forgetting? There are at least three implications which I feel are worth pointing out. First, if one wishes to hold to an interference theory of forgetting (as I do), it seems plausible to assert that this amount of forgetting could be produced from learning which has taken place outside of the laboratory. Furthermore, it seems likely that such interference must result primarily from proactive interference. This seems likely on a simple probability basis. A twenty-year-old college student will more likely have learned something during his 20 years prior to coming to the laboratory that will interfere with his retention than he will during the 24 hours between the learning and retention test. However, the longer the retention interval the more important will retroactive interference become relative to proactive interferences.

The second implication is that these data may suggest greater homogeneity or continuity in memorial processes than hitherto supposed. Although no one has adequately solved the measurement problem of how to make comparisons of retention among conditioned responses, prose material, motor tasks, concept learning, and rote-learned tasks, the gross comparisons have indicated that rote-learned tasks were forgotten much more rapidly than these other tasks. But the rote-learning data used for comparison have been those derived with the classical design in which the forgetting over 24 hours is approximately 75 per cent. If we take the revised estimate of 15 per cent, the discrepancies among tasks become considerably less.

The third implication of the revised estimate of rate of forgetting is that the number of variables which appreciably influence rate of forgetting must be sharply limited. While this statement does not inevitably follow from the analyses I have made, the current evidence strongly supports the statement. I want to turn to the final section of this paper, which will consist of a review of the influence of some of the variables which are or have been thought to be related to rate of forgetting. In considering these variables, it is well to keep in mind that a variable which produces only a small difference in forgetting is important if one is interested in accounting for the 15 per cent assumed now as the loss over 24 hours. If appropriate for a given variable, I will indicate where it fits into an interference theory, although in no case will I endeavor to handle the details of such a theory.

Time. Passage of time between learning and recall is the critical defining variable for forgetting. Manipulation of this variable provides the basic data for which a theory must account. Previously, our conception of rate of forgetting as a function of time has been tied to the Ebbinghaus curve. If the analysis made earlier is correct, this curve does not give us the basic data we need. In short, we must start all over and derive a retention curve over time when the subjects have learned no previous materials in the laboratory. It is apparent that I expect the fall in this curve over time to be relatively small.

In conjunction with time as an independent variable, we must, in explanations of forgetting, consider why sleep retards the processes responsible for forgetting. My conception, which does not really explain anything, is that since forgetting is largely produced by proactive interference, the amount of time which a subject spends in sleep is simply to be subtracted from the total retention interval when predicting the amount to be forgotten. It is known that proactive interference increases with passage of time (Briggs, 1954); sleep, I believe, brings to a standstill whatever these processes are which produce this increase.

Degree of learning. We usually say that the better or stronger the learning, the more or better the retention. Yet, we do not know whether or not the *rate* of forgetting differs for items of different strength. The experimental problem is a difficult one. What we need is to have a subject learn a single association and measure its decline in strength over time. But this is difficult to carry out with verbal material, since almost of necessity we must have the subject learn a series of associations, to make it a reasonable task. And, when a series of associations are learned, complications arise from interaction effects among associations of different strength. Nevertheless, we may expect, on the basis of evidence from a wide variety of studies, that given a constant degree of similarity, the effective interference varies as some function of the strength of associations.

Distribution of practice. It is a fact that distribution of practice during acquisition influences retention of verbal materials. The facts of the case seem to be as follows. If the subject has not learned previous lists in the laboratory, massed practice gives equal or better retention than does distributed practice. If, on the other hand, the subject has learned a number of previous lists, distributed practice will facilitate retention (Underwood and Richardson, 1955). We do not have the theoretical solution to these facts. The point I wish to make here is that whether or not distribution of learning inhibits or facilitates retention depends upon the amount of interference from previous learning. It is reasonable to expect, therefore, that the solution to the problem will come via principles handling interference in general. I might also say that a theoretical solution to this problem will also provide a solution for Jost's laws.

Similarity. Amount of interference from other tasks is closely tied to similarity. This similarity must be conceived of as similarity among materials as such and also situational similarity (Bilodeau and Schlosberg, 1951). When we turn to similarity within a task, the situation is not quite so clear. Empirically and theoretically (Gibson, 1940) one would expect that intratask similarity would be a very relevant variable in forgetting. As discussed elsewhere (Underwood, 1954), however, variation in intratask similarity almost inevitably leads to variations in intertask similarity. We do know from a recent study (Underwood and Richardson, 1956) that with material of low meaningfulness forgetting is significantly greater with high intralist similiarity than with low. While the difference in magnitude is only about 8 per cent, when we are trying to account for a total loss of 15 per cent, this amount becomes a major matter.

Meaningfulness. The belief has long been held that the more meaningful the material the better the retention—the less the forgetting. Osgood (1953) has pointed out that if this is true it is difficult for an interference theory to handle. So far as I know, the only direct test of the influence of this variable is a recent study in which retention of syllables of 100 per cent association value was compared with that of zero association value (Underwood and Richardson, 1956). There was no difference in the recall of these syllables. Other less precise evidence would support this finding when comparisons are made among syllables, adjectives, and nouns, as plotted in Figure 3. However, there is some evidence that materials of very low meaningfulness are forgotten more rapidly than nonsense syllables of zero association value. Consonant syllables, both serial (Underwood and Richardson, 1955) and paired associates (unpublished), show about 50 per cent loss over 24 hours. The study using serial lists was the one mentioned earlier as knowingly omitted from Figure 3. These syllables, being extremely difficult to learn, allow a correction of about 20 per cent due to criterion overestimation, but even with this much correction the forgetting (30 per cent) is still appreciably more than the estimate we have made for other materials. To invoke the interference theory to account for this discrepancy means that we must demonstrate how interference from other activities could be greater for these consonant syllables than for nonsense syllables, nouns, adjectives, and other materials. Our best guess at the present time is that the sequences of letters in consonant syllables are contrary to other well-established language habits. That is to say, letter sequences which commonly occur in our language are largely different from those in consonant syllables. As a consequence, not only are these consonant syllables very difficult to learn, but forgetting is accelerated by proactive interference from previously well-learned letter sequences. If subsequent research cannot demonstrate such a source of interference, or if some other source is not specified, an interference theory for this case will be in some trouble.

Affectivity. Another task dimension which has received extensive attention is the affective tone of the material. I would also include here the studies attaching unpleasant experiences to some items experimentally and not to others, and measuring retention of these two sets of items. Freud is to a large extent responsible for these studies, but he cannot be held responsible for the malformed methodology which characterizes so many of them. What can one say by way of summarizing these studies? The only conclusion that I can reach is a statistical one, namely, that the occasional positive result found among the scores of studies is about as frequent as one would expect by sampling error, using the 5 per cent level of confidence. Until a reliable body of facts is established for this variable and associated variables, no theoretical evaluation is possible.

Other variables. As I indicated earlier, I will not make an exhaustive survey of the variables which may influence rate of forgetting. I have limited myself to variables which have been rather extensively investigated, which have immediate relevance to the interference theory, or for which reliable relationships are available. Nevertheless, I would like to mention briefly some of these other variables. There is the matter of *warm-up* before recall; some investigators find that this reduces forgetting (Irion, 1948); others, under as nearly replicated conditions as is possible to obtain, do not (Rockway and Duncan, 1952). Some resolution must be found for these flat contradictions. It seems perfectly reasonable, however, that inadequate set or context differences could reduce recall. Indeed, an interference theory would predict this forgetting if the set or context stimuli are appreciably different from those prevailing at the time of learning. In our laboratory we try to reinstate the learning set by careful instructions, and we simply do not find decrements that might be attributed to inadequate set. For example, in a recent study (Underwood and Richardson, 1956) subjects were given a 24-hour recall of a serial list after learning to one perfect trial. I think we would expect that the first item in the list would suffer the greatest decrement due to inadequate set, yet this item showed only .7 per cent loss. But

let it be clear that when we are attempting to account for the 15 per cent loss over 24 hours, we should not overlook any possible source for this loss.

Thus far I have not said anything about forgetting as a function of characteristics of the subject, that is, the personality or intellectual characteristics. As far as I have been able to determine, there is not a single valid study which shows that such variables have an appreciable influence on forgetting. Many studies have shown differences in learning as a function of these variables, but not differences in rate of forgetting. Surely there must be some such variables. We do know that if subjects are severely insulted, made to feel stupid, or generally led to believe that they have no justification for continued existence on the earth just before they are asked to recall, they will show losses (e.g., Russell, 1952; Zeller, 1951), but even the influence of this kind of psychological beating is short-lived. Somehow I have never felt that such findings need explanation by a theory used to explain the other facts of forgetting.

Concerning the causes of forgetting, let me sum up in a somewhat more dogmatic fashion than is probably justified. One of the assumptions of science is finite causality. Everything cannot influence everything else. To me, the most important implication of the work on forgetting during the last ten years is that this work has markedly *reduced* the number of variables related to forgetting. Correspondingly, I think the theoretical problem has become simpler. It is my belief that we can narrow down the cause of forgetting to interference from previously learned habits, from habits being currently learned, and from habits we have yet to learn. The amount of this interference is primarily a function of similarity and associative strength, the latter being important because it interacts with similarity.

Summary

This paper deals with issues in the forgetting of rote-learned materials. An analysis of the current evidence suggests that the classical Ebbinghaus curve of forgetting is primarily a function of interference from materials learned previously in the laboratory. When this source of interference is removed, forgetting decreases from about 75 per cent over 24 hours to about 25 per cent. This latter figure can be reduced by at least 10 per cent by other methodological considerations, leaving 15 per cent as an estimate of the forgetting over 24 hours. This estimate will vary somewhat as a function of intratask similarity and distributed practice, and with very low meaningful material. But the overall evidence suggests that similarity with other material and situational similarity are by far the most critical factors in forgetting. Such evidence is consonant with a general interference theory, although the details of such a theory were not presented here.

REFERENCES

Archer, E. J., & Underwood, B. J. Retroactive inhibition of verbal associations as a multiple function of temporal point of interpolation and degree of interpolated learning. *Journal of Experimental Psychology*, 1951, 42, 283–290.

Bartlett, F. C. *Remembering: A study in experimental and social psychology*. London: Cambridge University Press, 1932.

Belmont, L., & Birch, H. G. Re-individualizing the repression hypothesis. *Journal of Abnormal and Social Psychology*, 1951, 46, 226–235.

Bilodeau, I. McD., & Schlosberg, H. Similarity in stimulating conditions as a variable in retroactive inhibition. *Journal of Experimental Psychology*, 1951, 41, 199–204.

Briggs, G. E. Acquisition, extinction, and recovery functions in retroactive inhibition. *Journal of Experimental Psychology*, 1954, 47, 285–293.

Cheng, N. Y. Retroactive effect and degree of similarity. *Journal of Experimental Psychology*, 1929, 12, 444–458.

Ebbinghaus, H. *Memory: A contribution to experimental psychology*. (Trans. by H. A. Ruger & C. E. Bussenius) New York: Bureau of Publications, Teachers College, Columbia University, 1913.

Gibson, E. J. A systematic application of the concepts of generalization and differentiation to verbal learning. *Psychological Review*, 1940, 47, 196–229.

Gibson, E. J. Intralist generalization as a factor in verbal learning. *Journal of Experimental Psychology*, 1942, 30, 185–200.

Greenberg, R., & Underwood, B. J. Retention as a function of stage of practice. *Journal of Experimental Psychology*, 1950, 40, 452–457.

Hovland, C. I. Experimental studies in rote-learning theory. VI. Comparison of retention following learning to same criterion by massed and distributed practice. *Journal of Experimental Psychology*, 1940, 26, 568–587.

Irion, A. L. The relation of "set" to retention. *Psychological Review*, 1948, 55, 336–341.

Jenkins, J. G., & Dallenbach, K. M. Oblivescence during sleep and waking. *American Journal of Psychology*, 1924, 35, 605–612.

Johnson, L. M. The relative effect of a time interval upon learning and retention. *Journal of Experimental Psychology*, 1939, 24, 169–179.

Katona, G. *Organizing and memorizing: Studies in the psychology of learning and teaching*. New York: Columbia University Press, 1940.

Krueger, W. C. F. The effect of overlearning on retention. *Journal of Experimental Psychology*, 1929, 12, 71–78.

Lester, O. P. Mental set in relation to retroactive inhibition. *Journal of Experimental Psychology*, 1932, 15, 681–699.

Luh, C. W. The conditions of retention. *Psychological Monographs*, 1922, 31 (3, Whole No. 142).

McGeoch, J. A. Forgetting and the law of disuse. *Psychological Review*, 1932, 39, 352–370.

McGeoch, J. A. *The psychology of human learning*. New York: Longmans, Green, 1942.

Osgood, C. E. *Method and theory in experimental psychology*. New York: Oxford University Press, 1953.

Rapaport, D. Emotions and memory. *Psychological Review*, 1943, 50, 234–243.

Rockway, M. R., & Duncan, C. P. Pre-recall warming-up in verbal retention. *Journal of Experimental Psychology*, 1952, 43, 305–312.

Runquist, W. Retention of verbal associations as a function of interference and strength. Unpublished doctor's dissertation, Northwestern University, 1956.

Russell, W. A. Retention of verbal material as a function of motivating instructions and experimentally induced failure. *Journal of Experimental Psychology*, 1952, 43, 207–216.

Underwood, B. J. The effect of successive interpolations on retroactive and proactive inhibition. *Psychological Monographs*, 1945, 59 (3, Whole No. 273).

Underwood, B. J. Studies of distributed practice: VII. Learning and retention of serial nonsense lists as a function of intralist similarity. *Journal of Experimental Psychology*, 1952, 44, 80–87.

Underwood, B. J. Studies of distributed practice: VIII. Learning and retention of paired nonsense syllables as a function of intralist similarity. *Journal of Experimental Psychology*, 1953, 45, 133–142. (a)

Underwood, B. J. Studies of distributed practice: IX. Learning and retention of paired adjectives as a function of intralist similarity. *Journal of Experimental Psychology*, 1953, 45, 143–149. (b)

Underwood, B. J. Studies of distributed practice: X. The influence of intralist similarity on learning and retention of serial adjective lists. *Journal of Experimental Psychology*, 1953, 45, 253–259. (c)

Underwood, B. J. Intralist similarity in verbal learning and retention. *Psychological Review*, 1954, 3, 160–166.

Underwood, B. J., & Richardson, J. Studies of distributed practice: XIII. Interlist interference and the retention of serial nonsense lists. *Journal of Experimental Psychology*, 1955, 50, 39–46.

Underwood, B. J., & Richardson, J. The influence of meaningfulness, intralist similarity, and serial position on retention. *Journal of Experimental Psychology*, 1956, 52, 119–126.

Ward, L. B. Reminiscence and rote learning. *Psychological Monographs*, 1937, 49 (4, Whole No. 220).

Weiss, W., & Margolius, G. The effect of context stimuli on learning and retention. *Journal of Experimental Psychology*, 1954, 48, 318–322.

Williams, M. The effects of experimentally induced needs upon retention. *Journal of Experimental Psychology*, 1950, 40, 139–151.

Youtz, A. C. An experimental evaluation of Jost's laws. *Psychological Monographs*, 1941, 53 (1, Whole No. 238).

Zeller, A. F. An experimental analogue of repression: III. The effect of induced failure and success on memory measured by recall. *Journal of Experimental Psychology*, 1951, 42, 32–38.

34

Computerized Instruction and the Learning Process

Richard C. Atkinson

Everyone who has ever studied a lesson in an effort to learn the material and then remember it later knows how difficult and time consuming it is. People spend from one-fifth to as much as one-half of their lives as students, trying to learn enough to enable them to take their place as knowledgeable citizens or practicing professionals. Guiding students along the tortuous path toward knowledge is the other group of people most interested in learning, *viz.*, teachers.

Considering the number of years it takes to acquire knowledge, the amount of effort required to succeed at learning, and the amount of money needed to provide schools, teachers, and books, it is small wonder that there is a perennial search for ways to speed the acquisition of knowledge. It just seems that there should be easier ways to get this difficult job done.

The amazing usefulness of computers in such tasks as rapid calculation of mathematical problems and the storage of huge amounts of information in magnetic memory banks has led some psychologists and teachers to speculate that perhaps computers could be used to cut down the amount of time required for acquiring knowledge. This article describes a project in this area that is being carried out at Stanford University.

In recent years there has been a tremendous number of articles and news releases dealing with computer-assisted instruction, or as it has been abbreviated, CAI. One might conjecture that this proliferation is an indicant of rapid progress in the field. Unfortunately, I doubt that it is. A few of the reports about CAI are based on substantial experience and research, but the majority are vague speculations and conjectures with little if any data or real experience to back them up. I do not want to denigrate the role of speculation and conjecture in a newly developing area like CAI. However, of late it seems to have produced little more than a repetition of ideas that were exciting in the 1950's but, in the absence of new research, are simply well-worn clichés in the late 1960's.

These remarks should not be misinterpreted. Important and significant research on CAI is being carried on in many laboratories around the country, but certainly not as much as one is led to believe by the attendant publicity. The problem for someone trying to evaluate developments in the field is to distinguish between those reports that are based on fact and those that are disguised forms of science fiction. In my paper, I shall try to stay very close to data and actual experience. My claims will be less grand than many that have been made for

CAI, but they will be based on a substantial research effort.

In 1964 Patrick Suppes and I initiated a project under a grant from the Office of Education to develop and implement a CAI program in initial reading and mathematics. Because of our particular research interests, Suppes has taken responsibility for the mathematics curriculum and I have been responsible for the initial reading program. At the beginning of the project, two major hurdles had to be overcome. There was no lesson material in either mathematics or reading suitable for CAI, and an integrated CAI system had not yet been designed and produced by a single manufacturer. The development of the curricula and the development of the system have been carried out as a parallel effort over the last three years with each having a decided influence on the other.

Today I would like to report on the progress of the reading program with particular reference to

From American Psychologist, *Vol. 23 (1968), 225–239. Copyright 1968 by the American Psychological Association, and reproduced by permission. Invited address presented at the meeting of the Division of Educational Psychology, American Psychological Association, Washington, D.C., September 1967.*

the past school year when for the first time a sizable group of students received a major portion of their daily reading instruction under computer control. The first year's operation must be considered essentially as an extended debugging of both the computer system and the curriculum materials. Nevertheless, some interesting comments can be made on the basis of this experience regarding both the feasibility of CAI and the impact of such instruction on the overall learning process.

Before describing the Stanford Project, a few general remarks may help place it in perspective. Three levels of CAI can be defined. Discrimination between levels is based not on hardware considerations, but principally on the complexity and sophistication of the student-system interaction. An advanced student-system interaction may be achieved with a simple teletype terminal, and the most primitive interaction may require some highly sophisticated computer programming and elaborate student terminal devices.

At the simplest interactional level are those systems that present a fixed, linear sequence of problems. Student errors may be corrected in a variety of ways, but no real-time decisions are made for modifying the flow of instructional material as a function of the student's response history. . . .

At the other extreme of our scale characterizing student-system interactions are "dialogue" programs. Such programs are under investigation at several universities and industrial concerns, but to date progress has been extremely limited. The goal of the dialogue approach is to provide the richest possible student-system interaction where the student is free to construct natural-language responses, ask questions in an unrestricted mode, and in general exercise almost complete control over the sequence of learning events.

"Tutorial" programs lie between the above extremes of student-system interaction. Tutorial programs have the capability for real-time decision making and instructional branching contingent on a single response or on some subset of the student's response history. Such programs allow students to follow separate and diverse paths through the curriculum based on their particular performance records. The probability is high in a tutorial program that no two students will encounter exactly the same sequence of lesson materials. However, student responses are greatly restricted since they must be chosen from a prescribed set of responses, or constructed in such a manner that a relatively simple test analysis will be sufficient for their evaluation. The CAI Reading Program is tu-

torial in nature, and it is this level of student-interaction that will be discussed today.

The Stanford CAI System

The Stanford Tutorial System was developed under a contract between the University and the IBM Corporation. Subsequent developments by IBM of the basic system have led to what has been designated the IBM-1500 Instructional System, which should soon be commercially available. The basic system consists of a central process computer with accompanying disc-storage units, proctor stations, and an interphase to sixteen student terminals. The central process computer acts as an intermediary between each student and his particular course material which is stored in one of the disc-storage units. A student terminal consists of a picture projector, a cathode ray tube (CRT), a light pen, a modified typewriter keyboard, and an audio system which can play prerecorded messages (see Figure 1).

The CRT is essentially a television screen on which alpha-numeric characters and a limited set of graphics (i.e., simple line drawings) can be gen-

FIGURE 1   *System configuration for Stanford CAI System*

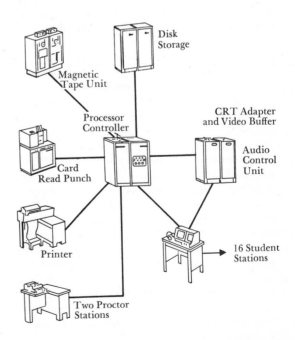

Disk Storage

Magnetic Tape Unit

Processor Controller

Card Read Punch

CRT Adapter and Video Buffer

Audio Control Unit

Printer

16 Student Stations

Two Proctor Stations

erated under computer control. The film projector is a rear-view projection device which permits us to display still pictures in black and white or color. Each film strip is stored in a self-threading cartridge and contains over 1000 images which may be accessed very quickly under computer control. The student receives audio messages via a high-speed device capable of selecting any number of messages varying in length from a few seconds to over 15 minutes. The audio messages are stored in tape cartridges which contain approximately two hours of messages and, like the film cartridge, may be changed very quickly. To gain the student's attention, an arrow can be placed at any point on the CRT and moved in synchronization with an audio message to emphasize given words or phrases, much like the "bouncing ball" in a singing cartoon.

The major response device used in the reading program is the light pen, which is simply a light-sensitive probe. When the light pen is placed on the CRT, coordinates of the position touched are sensed as a response and recorded by the computer. Responses may also be entered into the system through the typewriter keyboard. However, only limited use has been made of this response mode in the reading program. This is not to minimize the value of keyboard responses, but rather to admit that we have not as yet addressed ourselves to the problem of teaching first-grade children to handle a typewriter keyboard.

The CAI System controls the flow of information and the input of student responses according to the instructional logic built into the curriculum materials. The sequence of events is roughly as follows: The computer assembles the necessary commands for a given instructional sequence from a disc-storage unit. The commands involve directions to the terminal device to display a given sequence of symbols on the CRT, to present a particular image on the film projector, and to play a specific audio message. After the appropriate visual and auditory materials have been presented, a "ready" signal indicates to the student that a response is expected. Once a response has been entered, it is evaluated and, on the basis of this evaluation and the student's past history, the computer makes a decision as to what materials will subsequently be presented. The time-sharing nature of the system allows us to handle sixteen students simultaneously and to cycle through these evaluative steps so rapidly that from a student's viewpoint it appears that he is getting immediate attention from the computer whenever he inputs a response.

The CAI Reading Curriculum

* * *

The instructional materials are divided into eight levels each composed of about 32 lessons.[1] The lessons are designed so that the average student will complete one in approximately 30 minutes, but this can vary greatly with the fast student finishing much sooner and the slow student sometimes taking two hours or more if he hits most of the remedial material. Within a lesson, the various instructional tasks can be divided into three broad areas: (a) decoding skills, (b) comprehension skills, (c) games and other motivational devices. Decoding skills involve such tasks as letter and letter-string identification, word-list learning, phonic drills, and related types of activities. Comprehension involves such tasks as having the computer read to the child or having the child himself read sentences, paragraphs, or complete stories about which he is then asked a series of questions. The questions deal with the direct recall of facts, generalizations about main ideas in the story, and inferential questions which require the child to relate information presented in the story to his own experience. Finally, many different types of games are sequenced into the lessons primarily to encourage continued attention to the materials. The games are similar to those played in the classroom and are structured to evaluate the developing reading skills of the child.

Matrix construction. To illustrate the instructional materials focusing on decoding skills let me describe a task that we have called matrix "construction." This task provides practice in learning to associate orthographically similar sequences with appropriate rhyme and alliteration patterns. Rhyming patterns are presented in the columns of the matrix, and alliteration patterns are presented in the rows of the matrix as indicated in Figure 4.

The matrix is constructed one cell at a time. The initial consonant of a CVC [consonant-vowel-consonant] word is termed the initial unit, and the vowel and the final consonant are termed the final unit. The intersection of an initial unit row and a final unit column determines the entry in any cell.

The problem format for the construction of each cell is divided into four parts: Parts A and

---

[1] For a detailed account of the curriculum materials, see Wilson and Atkinson (1967) and Rodgers (1967). See also Atkinson and Hansen (1966) and Hansen and Rodgers (1965).

FIGURE 2 *Flow chart for the construction of a cell in the matrix construction task*

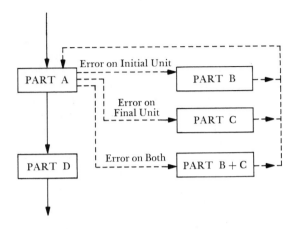

D are standard instructional sections and Parts B and C are remedial sections. The flow diagram in Figure 2 indicates that remedial Parts B and C are branches from Part A and may be presented independently or in combination.

To see how this goes, let us consider the example illustrated in Figure 3. The student first sees on the CRT the empty cell with its associated initial and final units and an array of response choices. He hears the audio message indicated by response request 1 (RR 1) in Part A of Figure 3. If the student makes the correct response (CA) (i.e., touches *ran* with his light pen), he proceeds to Part D where he sees the word written in the cell and receives one additional practice trial.

In the initial presentation in Part A, the array of multiple-choice responses is designed to identify three possible types of errors:

1. The initial unit is correct, but the final unit is not.

2. The final unit is correct, but the initial unit is not.

3. Neither the initial unit nor the final unit is correctly identified.

If, in Part A, the student responds with *fan* he is branched to remedial Part B where attention is focused on the initial unit of the cell. If a correct response is made in Part B, the student is returned to Part A for a second attempt. If an incorrect

FIGURE 3 *First cell of the matrix construction task*

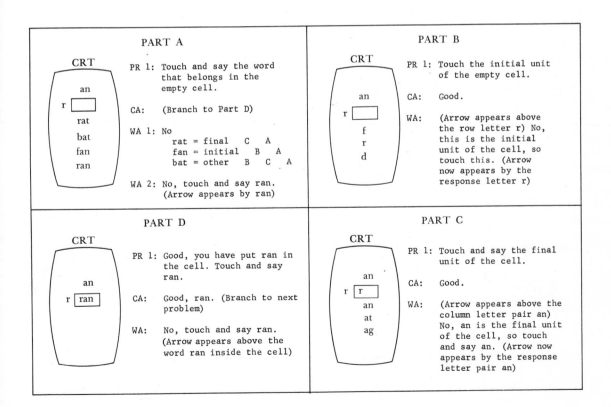

response (WA) is made in Part B, an arrow is displayed on the CRT to indicate the correct response, which the student is then asked to touch.

If, in Part A, the student responds with *rat,* he is branched to remedial Part C where additional instruction is given on the final unit of the cell. The procedure in Part C is similar to Part B. However, it should be noted that in the remedial instruction the initial letter is never pronounced (Part B), whereas the final unit is always pronounced (Part C). If, in Part A, the student responds with *bat,* then he has made an error on both the initial and final unit and is branched through both Part B and Part C.

When the student returns to Part A after completing a remedial section, a correct response will advance him to Part D as indicated. If a wrong answer response is made on the second pass, an arrow is placed beside the correct response area and held there until a correct response is made.

If the next response is still an error, a message is sent to the proctor and the sequence is repeated from the beginning.

When a student has made a correct response on Parts A and D, he is advanced to the next word cell of the matrix which has a problem format and sequence identical to that just described. The individual cell building is continued block by block until the matrix is complete. The upper left-hand panel of Figure 4 indicates the CRT display for adding the next cell in our example. The order in which row and column cells are added is essentially random.

When the matrix is complete, the entries are reordered and a criterion test is given over all cell entries. The test involves displaying the full matrix with complete cell entries as indicated in the lower left-hand panel of Figure 4. Randomized requests are made to the student to identify cell entries. Since the first pass through the full matrix is

FIGURE 4   *Continuation of matrix construction task*

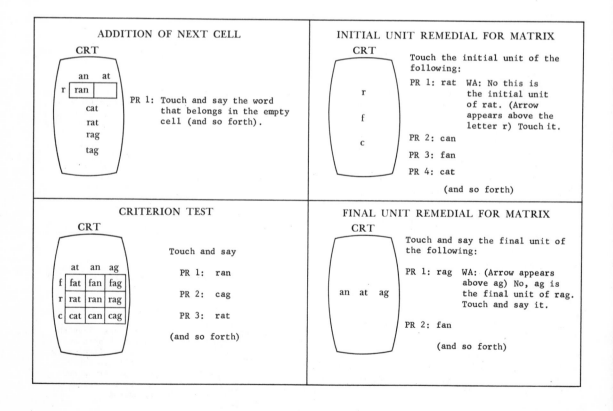

viewed as a criterion test, no reinforcement is given. Errors are categorized as initial, final, and other; if the percentage of total errors on the criterion test exceeds a predetermined value, then remedial exercises are provided of the type shown in the two right-hand panels of Figure 4. If all the errors are recorded in one category (initial or final), only the remedial material appropriate to that category is presented. If the errors are distributed over both categories, then both types of remedial material are presented. After working through one or both of the remedial sections, the student is branched back for a second pass through the criterion matrix. The second pass is a teaching trial as opposed to the initial test cycle; the student proceeds with the standard correction and optimization routines.

An analysis of performance on the matrix task is still incomplete, but some preliminary results are available. On the initial pass (Part A) our students were correct about 45 per cent of the time; however, when an error did occur, 21 per cent of the time it involved only the final unit, 53 per cent of the time only the initial unit, and 26 per cent of the time both initial and final units. The pattern of performances changed markedly on the first pass through the criterion test. Here the subject was correct about 65 per cent of the time; when an error occurred, 32 per cent of the time it involved only the final unit, 33 per cent of the time only the initial unit, and 35 per cent of the time both units. Thus performance showed a significant improvement from Part A to the criterion test; equally important, initial errors were more than twice as frequent as final errors in Part A, but were virtually equal on the criterion test.

The matrix exercise is a good example of the material used in the curriculum to teaching decoding skills. We now consider two examples ("form class" and "inquiries") of tasks that are designed to teach comprehension skills.

Form class. Comprehension of a sentence involves an understanding of English syntax. One behavioral manifestation of a child's syntactic sophistication is his ability to group words into appropriate form classes. This task provides lesson materials that teach the form-class characteristics of the words just presented in the matrix section of a lesson. The following type of problem is presented to the student (the material in the box is displayed on the CRT and below are audio messages; the child answers by appropriately placing his light pen on the CRT):

	tan	
Dan saw the	fat	hat.
	man	
	run	

Only one of the words in the column will make sense in the sentence. Touch and say the word that belongs in the sentence.

CA: Yes, Dan saw the tan hat. Do the next one.
WA: No, tan is the word that makes sense. Dan saw the tan hat. Touch and say tan. (An arrow then appears above tan.)

The sentence is composed of words that are in the reading vocabulary of the student (i.e., they have been presented in previous or current lessons). The response set includes a word which is of the correct form class but is semantically inappropriate, two words that are of the wrong form class, and the correct word. A controlled variety of sentence types is employed, and the answer sets are distributed over all syntactic slots within each sentence type. Responses are categorized in rather broad terms as *nouns, verbs, modifiers,* and *other.* The response data can be examined for systematic errors over a large number of items. Examples of the kinds of questions that can be asked are: (*a*) Are errors for various form classes in various sentence positions similarly distributed? (*b*) How are response latencies affected by the syntactic and serial position of the response set within the sentence? Answers to these and other questions should provide information that will permit more systematic study of the relationship of sentence structure to reading instruction.

Inquiries. Individual words in sentences may constitute unique and conversationally correct answers to questions. These questions take the interrogative "Who ....? What ....? How ....?" etc. The ability to select the word in a sentence that uniquely answers one of these questions demonstrates one form of reading comprehension. The inquiry exercises constitute an assessment of this reading comprehension ability. In the following example, the sentence "John hit the ball" is displayed on the CRT accompanied by these audio messages:

Touch and say the word that answers the question.

RR 1 Who hit the ball?
CA: Yes, the word "John" tells us who hit the ball.

WA: No, John tells us who hit the ball. Touch and say John. (An arrow then appears on the CRT above John.)

RR 2 What did John hit?

CA: Yes, the word "ball" tells us what John hit.

WA: No, ball tells us what John hit. Touch and say ball. (An arrow then appears above ball.)

As in the form-class section, each sentence is composed of words from the student's reading vocabulary. A wide variety of sentence structures is utilized, beginning with simple subject-verb-object sentences and progressing to structures of increasing complexity. Data from this task bear on several hypotheses about comprehension. If comprehension is equated with a correct response to an inquiry question, then the following statements are verified by our data: (a) Items for which the correct answer is in the medial position of the sentence are more difficult to comprehend than items in the initial or final positions; final position items are easier to comprehend than items in the initial position. (b) Items for which the correct answer is an adjective are more difficult to comprehend than items in which the correct answer is a noun or verb; similarly [verbs] are more difficult than [nouns]. (c) Longer sentences, measured by word length, are more difficult to comprehend than shorter sentences.

These are only a few examples of the types of tasks used in the reading curriculum, but they indicate the nature of the student-system interaction. What is not illustrated by these examples is the potential for long-term optimization policies based on an extended response history from the subject. We shall return to this topic later.

Problems in Implementing the Curriculum

Before turning to the data from last year's run, let me consider briefly the problem of translating the curriculum materials into a language that can be understood by the computer. The particular computer language we use is called Coursewriter II, a language which was developed by IBM in close collaboration with Stanford. A coded lesson is a series of Coursewriter II commands which causes the computer to display and manipulate text on the CRT, position and display film in the projector, position and play audio messages, accept and evaluate keyboard and light pen responses, update the performance record of each student, and

implement the branching logic of the lesson flow by means of manipulating and referencing a set of switches and counters. A typical lesson in the reading program, which takes the average student about 30 minutes to complete, requires in excess of 9,000 coursewriter commands for its execution.

A simple example will give you some feeling for the coding problem. The example is from a task designed to teach both letter discrimination and the meaning of words. A picture illustrating the word being taught is presented on the projector screen. Three words, including the word illustrated, are presented on the CRT. A message is played on the audio asking the child to touch the word on the CRT that matches the picture on the film projector. The student can then make his response using the light pen. If he makes no response within the specified time limit of 30 seconds, he is told the correct answer, an arrow points to it, and he is asked to touch it. If he makes a response within the time limit, the point that he touches is compared by the computer with the correct-answer area. If he places the light pen within the correct area, he is told that he was correct and goes on to the next problem. If the response was not in the correct area, it is compared with the area defined as a wrong answer. If his response is within this area, he is told that it is wrong, given the correct answer, and asked to touch it. If his initial response was neither in the anticipated wrong-answer area nor in the correct-answer area, then the student has made an undefined answer. He is given the same message that he would have heard had he touched a defined wrong answer; however, the response is recorded on the data record as undefined. The student tries again until he makes the correct response; he then goes on to the next problem.

To prepare an instructional sequence of this sort, the programmer must write a detailed list of commands for the computer. He must also record on an audio tape all the messages the student might hear during the lesson in approximately the order in which they will occur. Each audio message has an address on the tape and will be called for and played when appropriate. Similarly a film strip is prepared with one frame for each picture required in the lesson. Each frame has an address and can be called for in any order.

Table 1 shows the audio messages and film pictures required for two sample problems along with the hypothetical addresses on the audio tape and film strip. Listed in Table 2 are the computer commands required to present two examples of the problems described above, analyze the stu-

TABLE 1 *Audio Script and Film Clips with Hypothetical Addresses*

Address	Message
	Audio information
A01	Touch and say the word that goes with the picture.
A02	Good. Bag. Do the next one.
A03	No.
A04	The word that goes with the picture is bag. Touch and say bag.
A05	Good. Card. Do the next one.
A06	No.
A07	The word that goes with the picture is card. Touch and say card.
	Film strip
F01	Picture of a bag.
F02	Picture of a card.

dent's responses, and record his data record. The left column in the table lists the actual computer commands, and the right column provides an explanation of each command.

While a student is on the system, he may complete as many as 5 to 10 problems of this type per minute. Obviously, if all of the instructional material has to be coded in this detail the task would be virtually impossible. Fortunately, there are ways of simplifying coding procedure if parts of the instructional materials are alike in format and differ only in certain specified ways. For example, the two problems presented in Table 2 differ only in (a) the film display, (b) the words on the CRT, (c) the problem identifier, (d) the three audio addresses, (e) the row display of the arrow, (f) the correct answer area, and (g) the correct answer identifier. This string of code can be defined once, given a two-letter name, and used later by giving a one-line macro command.

The use of macros cuts down greatly the effort required to present many different but basically similar problems. For example, the two problems presented in Table 2 can be rewritten in macro format using only two lines of code: Problem 1: CM PW]F01]bat]bag]rat]A01]ABCD1]A04]-A02]A03]7]1,7,3,18]C1]; Problem 2: CM PW]-F02]card]cart]hard]]ABCD2]A07]A05]A06]5]-1,5,4,18]C2]. The command to call a macro is CM, and PW is an arbitrary two-character code for the macro involving a picture-to-word match. Notice that in Problem 2 there is no introductory

audio message; the "]]" indicates that this parameter is not to be filled in.

The macro capability of the source language has two distinct advantages over code written command by command. The first is ease and speed of coding. The call of one macro is obviously easier than writing the comparable string of code. The second advantage is increase in accuracy. Not only are coding errors drastically curtailed, but if the macro is defective or needs to be changed, every occurrence of it in the lesson coding can be corrected by modifying the original macro; in general, the code can stay as it is. The more standard the various problem formats, the more valuable the macro capability becomes. Apart from a few nonstandard introductory audio messages and display items, approximately 95 per cent of the reading curriculum has been programmed using about 110 basic macros.

The macro command feature of the language has significant implications for psychological research. By simply changing a few commands in a particular macro, one can alter the flow of the teaching sequence whenever that macro is called in the program. Thus, the logic of an instructional sequence that occurs thousands of times in the reading curriculum can be redesigned by adding or modifying a few lines of code in a given macro. If, for example, we wanted to change the timing relations, the type of feedback, or characteristics of the CRT display in the task described above, it would require only a few lines of code in the PW macro and would not necessitate making changes at every point in the curriculum where the picture-to-word exercise occurred. Thus, a range of experimental manipulations can be carried out using the same basic program and display materials, and requiring changes only in the command structure of the macros.

As indicated in Table 2, a bank of switches and counters is defined in the computer and can be used to keep a running record on each student. There is a sufficient number of these registers so that quite sophisticated schemes of optimization and accompanying branching are possible. Thus, one is in a position to present a series of words and to optimize the number of correct responses to some stipulated criteria, for example, five consecutive correct responses for each of the words. Or one can select from an array of phrases choosing those phrases for presentation that have the greatest number of previous errors. As a consequence of these decisions, each student pursues a fundamentally different path through the reading materials.

TABLE 2 *Computer Commands Required to Present Two Examples of the Problem Described in the Text*

Commands	Explanation
PR	Problem: Prepares machine for beginning of new problem
LD 0/S1	Load: Loads zero into the error switch (S1). The role of switches and counters will be explained later.
FP F01	Film Position: Displays fram F01 (picture of a bag).
DT 5,18/bat/	Display Text: Displays "bat" on line 5 starting in column 18 on the CRT.
DT 7,18/bag/	Displays "bag" on line 7 starting in column 18 on the CRT.
DT 9,18/rat/	Displays "rat" on line 9 starting in column 18 on the CRT.
AUP A01	Audio Play: Plays audio message A01. "Touch and say the word that goes with the picture."
L1 EP 30/ABCD1	Enter and Process: Activates the light-pen; specifies the time limit (30 sec.) and the problem identifier (ABCD1) that will be placed in the data record along with all responses to this problem. If a response is made within the time limit the computer skips from this command down to the CA (correct answer comparison) command. If no response is made within the time limit, the commands immediately following the EP command are executed.
AD 1/C4	Add: Adds one to the overtime counter (C4).
LD 1/S1	Loads one into the error switch (S1).
AUP A04	Plays message A04. "The word that goes with the picture is bag. Touch and say bag."
DT 7, 16/ /	Displays arrow on line 7, column 16 (arrow pointing at "bag").
BR L1	Branch: Branches to command labeled L1. The computer will now do that command and continue from that point.
CA 1,7,3,18/C1	Correct Answer: Compares student's response with an area one line high starting on line 7 and three columns wide starting in column 18 of the CRT. If his response falls within this area, it will be recorded in the data with the answer identifier C1. When a correct answer has been made, the commands from here down to WA (wrong answer comparison) are executed. Then the program jumps ahead to the next PR. If the response does not fall in the correct area, the machine skips from this command down to the WA command.
BR L2/S1/1	Branches to command labeled L2 if the error switch (S1) is equal to one.
AD 1/C1	Adds one to the initial correct answer counter (C1).
L2 AUP A02	Plays audio message A02. "Good. Bag. Do the next one."
WA 1,5,3,18/W1 WA 1,9,3,18/W2	Wrong Answer: These two commands compare the student response with the areas of the two wrong answers, that is, the area one line high starting on line 5 and three columns wide starting in column 18, and the area one line high starting on line 9 and three columns wide starting in column 18. If the response falls within one of these two areas, it will be recorded with the appropriate identifier (W1 or W2). When a defined wrong answer has been made, the commands from here down to UN (undefined answer) are executed. Then the computer goes back to the EP for this problem. If the response does not fall in one of the defined wrong answer areas, the machine skips from this command down to the UN command.

AD 1/C2	Adds one to the defined wrong answer counter (C2).
L3 LD 1/S1	Loads one into the error switch (S1).
AUP A03	Plays message A03. "No."
AUP A04	Plays message A04. "The word that goes with the picture is bag. Touch and say bag."
DT 7, 16/ /	Displays arrow on line 7, column 16.
UN	Undefined Wrong Answer: If machine reaches this point in the program, the student has made neither a correct nor a defined wrong answer.
AD 1/C3	Adds one to the undefined answer counter (C3).
BR L3	Branches to command labeled L3. (The same thing should be done for both UN and WA answers. This branch saves repeating the commands from L3 down to UN.)
PR	Prepares the machine for next problem.
LD 0/S1 EP F02 DT 5,18/card/ DT 7,18/cart/ DT 9,18/hard/	These commands prepare the display for the 2nd problem. Notice the new film position and new words displayed. The student was told to "do the next one" when he finished the last problem so he needs no audio message to begin this.
L4 EP 30/ABCD2	Light-pen is activated.
AD 1/C4 LD 1/S1 AUP A07 DT 5, 16/ / BR L4	The commands are done only if no response is made in the time limit of 30 seconds. Otherwise the machine skips to the CA command.
CA 1,5,4,18/C2	Compares response with correct answer area.
BR L5/S1/1 AD 1/C1 L5 AUP A05	Adds one to the initial correct answer counter unless the error switch (S1) shows that an error has been made for this problem. The student is told he is correct and goes on to the next problem. These commands are executed only if a correct answer has been made.
WA 1,7,4,18/W3 WA 1,9,4,18/W4	Compare response with defined wrong answer.
AD 1/C2 L6 LD 1/S1 AUP A06 AUP A07 DT 5,16/ /	Adds one to the defined wrong answer area and the error switch (S1) is loaded with one to show that an error has been made on this problem. The student is told he is wrong and shown the correct answer and asked to touch it. These commands are executed only if a defined wrong answer has been made.
UN	An undefined response has been made if the machine reaches this command.
Ad 1/C3	Adds one to the undefined answer counter and we branch up to give the same audio, etc., as is given for the defined wrong answer.

Some Results from the First Year of Operation

The Stanford CAI Project is being conducted at the Brentwood School in the Ravenswood School District (East Palo Alto, California). There were several reasons for selecting this school. It had sufficient population to provide a sample of well over 100 first-grade students. The students were primarily from "culturally disadvantaged" homes. And the past performance of the school's principal and faculty had demonstrated a willingness to undertake educational innovations.

Computerized instruction began in November of 1966 with half of the first-grade students taking reading via CAI and the other half, which functioned as a control group, being taught reading by a teacher in the classroom. The children in the control group were not left out of the project, for they took mathematics from the CAI system instead. The full analysis of the student data is a tremendous task which is still under way. However, a few general results have already been tabulated that provide some measure of the program's success.

Within the lesson material there is a central core of problems which we have termed main-line problems. These are problems over which each student must exhibit mastery in one form or another. Main-line problems may be branched around by successfully passing certain screening tests, or they may be met and successfully solved; they may be met with incorrect responses, in which case the student is branched to remedial material. The first year of the project ended with a difference between the fastest and slowest student of over 4000 main-line problems completed. The cumulative response curves for the fastest, median, and slowest students are given in Figure 5. Also of interest is the rate of progress during the course of the year. Figure 6 presents the cumulative number of problems completed per hour on a month-by-month basis again for the fastest, median, and slowest student. It is interesting to note that the rate measure was essentially constant over time for increase for the fast student.

From the standpoint of both the total number of problems completed during the year and rate of progress, it appears that the CAI curriculum is responsive to individual differences. The differences noted above must not be confused with a

FIGURE 6 *Cumulative rate of progress for fastest, median, and slowest student*

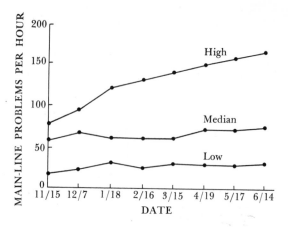

variation in rate of response. The difference in response rate among students was very small. The average response rate was approximately four per minute and was not correlated with a student's rate of progress through the curriculum. The differences in total number of main-line problems completed can be accounted for by the amount of remedial material, the optimization routines, and the number of accelerations for the different students.

It has been a common finding that girls generally acquire reading skills more rapidly than boys. The sex differences in reading performance have been attributed, at least in part, to the social organization of the classroom and to the value and reward structures of the predominantly female primary grade teachers. It has also been argued on developmental grounds that first-grade girls are more facile in visual memorization than boys of the same age, and that this facility aids the girls in the sight-word method of vocabulary acquisition commonly used in basal readers. If these two arguments are correct, then one would expect that placing students in a CAI environment and using a curriculum which emphasizes analytic skills, as opposed to rote memorization, would minimize sex differences in reading. In order to test this hypothesis, the rate of progress scores were statistically evaluated for sex effects. The result, which was rather surprising, is that there was no difference between male and female students in rate of progress through the CAI curriculum.

Sex differences however might be a factor in accuracy of performance. To test this notion the final accuracy scores on four standard problem types were examined. The four problem types,

FIGURE 5 *Cumulative number of main-line problems for fastest, median, and slowest student*

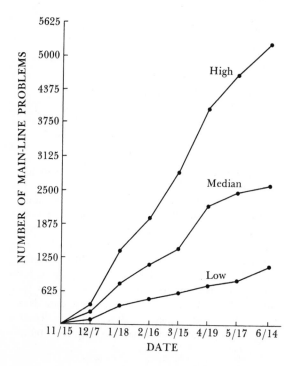

which are representative of the entire curriculum, were Letter Identification, Word-List Learning, Matrix Construction, and Sentence Comprehension. On these four tasks, the only difference between boys and girls that was statistically significant at the .05 level was for word-list learning. These results, while by no means definitive, do lend support to the notion that when students are removed from the normal classroom environment and placed on a CAI program, boys perform as well as girls in overall rate of progress. The results also suggest that in a CAI environment the sex difference is minimized in proportion to the emphasis on analysis rather than rote memorization in the learning task. The one problem type where the girls achieved significantly higher scores than the boys, word-list learning, is essentially a paired-associate learning task.

As noted earlier, the first graders in our school were divided into two groups. Half of them received reading instruction from the CAI system; the other half did not (they received mathematics instruction instead). Both groups were tested extensively using conventional instruments before the project began and again near the end of the school year. The two groups were not significantly different at the start of the year. Table 3 presents the results for some of the tests that were administered at the end of the year. As inspection of the table will show, the group that received reading instruction via CAI performed significantly better on all of the posttests except for the comprehension subtest of the California Achievement Test. These results are most encouraging. Further, it should be noted that at least some of the factors that might result in a "Hawthorne phenomenon" are not present here; the "control" group was exposed to CAI experience in their mathematics instruction. While that may leave room for some effects in their reading, it does remove the chief objection, since these students also had reason to feel that special attention was being given to them. It is of interest to note that the average Stanford-Binet IQ score for these students (both experimental and control) is 89.[2]

Owing to systems and hardware difficulties, our program was not in full operation until late in November of 1966. Initially, students were given a relatively brief period of time per day on the terminals. This period was increased to 20 minutes after the first six weeks; in the last month we allowed students to stay on the terminal 30 to 35 minutes. We wished to find out how well first-grade students would adapt to such long periods of time. They adapt quite well, and next year we

TABLE 3 *Posttest Results for Experimental and Control Groups*

Test	Experimental	Control	*p* value
California Achievement Test			
Vocabulary	45.91	38.10	<.01
Comprehension	41.45	40.62	—
Total	45.63	39.61	<.01
Hartley Reading Test			
Form class	11.22	9.00	<.05
Vocabulary	19.38	17.05	<.01
Phonetic discrimination	30.88	25.15	<.01
Pronunciation			
Nonsense word	6.03	2.30	<.01
Word	9.95	5.95	<.01
Recognition			
Nonsense word	18.43	15.25	<.01
Word	19.61	16.60	<.01

plan to use 30-minute periods for all students throughout the year. This may seem like a long session for a first-grader, but our observations suggest that their span of attention is well over a half hour if the instructional sequence is truly responsive to their response inputs. This year's students had a relatively small number of total hours on the system. We hope that by beginning in the early fall and using half-hour periods, we will be able to give each student at least 80 to 90 hours on the terminals next year.

I do not have time to discuss the social-psychological effects of introducing CAI into an actual school setting. However, systematic observations have been made by a trained clinical psychologist, and a report is being prepared. To preview this report, it is fair to say that the students, teachers, and parents were quite favorable to the program.

Nor will time permit a detailed account of the various optimization routines used in the reading curriculum. But since this topic is a major focus of our research effort, it requires some discussion here. As noted earlier, the curriculum incorporates an array of screening and sequencing procedures designed to optimize learning. These optimization schemes vary in terms of the range of curriculum included, and it has been convenient to classify them as either short- or long-term procedures. Short-term procedures refer to decision

---

[2] More details on these and other analyses may be found in Wilson and Atkinson (1967).

rules that are applicable to specific problem formats and utilize the very recent response history of a subject to determine what instructional materials to present next. Long-term optimization procedures are applicable to diverse units of the curriculum and utilize a summarized form of the subject's complete response record to specify his future path through major instructional units.

As an example of a short-term optimization procedure, consider one that follows directly from a learning theoretic analysis of the reading task involved (Groen and Atkinson, 1966). Suppose that a list of m words is to be taught to the child, and it has been decided that instruction is to be carried out using the picture-to-word format described earlier. In essence, this problem format involves a series of discrete trials, where on each trial a picture illustrating the word being taught is presented on the projector screen and three words (including the word illustrated) are presented on the CRT. The student makes a response from among these words, and the trial is terminated by telling him the correct answer. If x trials are allocated for this type of instruction (where x is much larger than m), how should they be used to maximize the amount of learning that will take place? Should the m items be presented an equal number of times and distributed randomly over the x trials, or are there other strategies that take account of idiosyncratic features of a given subject's response record? If it is assumed that the learning process for this task is adequately described by the one-element model of stimulus sampling theory, and there is evidence that this is the case, then the optimal presentation strategy can be prescribed. The optimal strategy is initiated by presenting the m items in any order on the first m trials, and a continuation of this strategy is optimal over the remaining $x - m$ trials if, and only if, it conforms to the following rules:

1. For every item, set the count at 0 at the beginning of trial $m + 1$.

2. Present an item at a given trial if, and only if, its count is *least* among the counts for all items at the beginning of the trial.

3. If several items are eligible under Rule 2, select from these the item that has the smallest number of presentations; if several items are still eligible, select with equal probability from this set.

4. Following a trial, increase the count for presented item by 1 if the subject's response was correct, but set it at 0 if the response was incorrect.

Even though these decision rules are fairly simple, they would be difficult to implement without the aid of a computer. Data from this year's experiment establish that the above strategy is better than one that presents the items equally often in a fixed order.

This is only one example of the type of short-term optimization strategies that are used in the reading curriculum. Some of the other schemes are more complex, involving the application of dynamic programming principles (Groen and Atkinson, 1966), and use information not only about the response history but also the speed of responding. In some cases the optimization schemes can be derived directly from mathematical models of the learning process, whereas others are not tied to theoretical analyses but are based on intuitive considerations that seem promising.[3]

Even if short-term optimization strategies can be devised which are effective, a total reading curriculum that is optimal still has not been achieved. It is, of course, possible to optimize performance on each unit of the curriculum while, at the same time, sequencing through the units in an order that is not particularly efficient for learning. The most significant aspect of curriculum development is with regard to long-term optimization procedures, where the subject's total response history can be used to determine the best order for branching through major instructional units and also the proper balance between drill and tutorial activities. It seems clear that no theory of instruction is likely to use all the information we have on a student to make instructional decisions from one moment to the next. Even for the most sophisticated long-term schemes, only a sample of the subject's history is going to be useful. In general, the problem of deciding on an appropriate sample of the history is similar to the problem of finding an observable statistic that provides a good estimate of a population parameter. The observable history sample may be regarded as an estimate of the student's state of learning. A desirable property for such a history sample would be for it to summarize all information concerning the current learning state of the student so that no elaboration of the history would provide additional information. In the theory of statistical inference, a statistic with an analogous property is called a sufficient statistic. Hence, it seems appropriate to call an observable sample

---

[3] The learning models and optimization methods that underlie much of the reading curriculum are discussed in Atkinson and Shiffrin (1968), Groen and Atkinson (1966), Rodgers (1967), and Wilson and Atkinson (1967).

history with this property a "sufficient history."

In the present version of the reading curriculum, several long-term optimization procedures have been introduced with appropriate sufficient histories. As yet, the theoretical rationale for these procedures has not been thoroughly worked out, and not enough data have been collected to evaluate their effectiveness. However, an analysis of long-term optimization problems, and what data we do have, has been instructive and has suggested a number of experiments that need to be carried out this year. It is my hope that such analyses, combined with the potential for educational research under the highly controlled conditions offered by CAI, will lay the groundwork for a theory of instruction that is useful to the educator. Such a theory of instruction will have to be based on a model of the learning process that has broad generality and yet yields detailed predictions when applied to specific tasks.

In my view, the development of a viable theory of instruction and the corresponding learning theory will be an interactive enterprise, with advances in each area influencing the concepts and data base in the other. For too long, psychologists studying learning have shown little interest in instructional problems, whereas educators have made only primitive and superficial applications of learning theory. Both fields would have advanced more rapidly if an appropriate interchange of ideas and problems had existed. It is my hope that prospects for CAI, as both a tool for research and a mode of instruction, will act as a catalyst for a rapid evolution of new concepts in learning theory as well as a corresponding theory of instruction.

REFERENCES

Atkinson, R. C., & Hansen, D. N. Computer-assisted instruction in initial reading: The Stanford Project. *Reading Research Quarterly*, 1966, **2**, 5–25.

Atkinson, R. C., & Shiffrin, R. M. Human memory: A proposed system and its control processes. In K. W. Spence & J. T. Spence (Eds.), *The psychology of learning and motivation: Advances in research and theory.* Vol. 2. New York: Academic Press, 1968.

Groen, G. J., & Atkinson, R. C. Models for optimizing the learning process. *Psychological Bulletin*, 1966, **66**, 309–320.

Hansen, D. N., & Rodgers, T. S. An exploration of psycholinguistic units in initial reading. Technical Report 74, 1965, Stanford University, Institute for Mathematical Studies in the Social Sciences.

Rodgers, T. S. Linguistic considerations in the design of the Stanford computer-based curriculum in initial reading. Technical Report 111, 1967, Stanford University, Institute for Mathematical Studies in the Social Sciences.

Wilson, H. A., & Atkinson, R. C. Computer-based instruction in initial reading: A progress report on the Stanford project. Technical Report 119, 1967, Stanford University, Institute for Mathematical Studies in the Social Sciences.

Learning: A Contemporary Perspective

James H. McHose
Southern Illinois University

Learning is the modification of an organism's behavior in a certain situation as the result of past experience with that situation or similar situations. It does not include changes due to purely sensory phenomena such as sensory adaptation. With the advent of Behaviorism in the early decades of the twentieth century, learning rapidly became a pervasive interest of psychologists. Interest in the manner in which behaviors are acquired was inevitable, for one of the most striking aspects of an organism's behavior is that it changes as the result of the organism's interaction with its environment. The development of the behavior patterns of man, abnormal as well as normal, depends in great part upon what he learns and when and how he learns it. The education of our children, as well as the training of men in all walks of life, is accomplished most efficiently through application of the basic principles of learning.

Most psychologists at one time or another ponder the role of learning in shaping the behavior they study. This curiosity often leads to experiments in which the acquisition of some behavior is studied. Although such researchers may label themselves social, personality, clinical, industrial, educational, comparative, or physiological psychologists, some call themselves learning psychologists. In most areas of study, basic research is identified by the ultimate goal of the research; so it is with learning. Learning experiments are experiments that are directed primarily toward the development of laws or principles of learning that are universally descriptive of such behavior. Laws of learning, when formulated, are intended to apply universally, at least within a phylogenetic species.

The learning psychologist thus wishes to formulate broad principles such as "Reinforcement is necessary for learning to occur." In more detail he may seek to discover what characteristics all reinforcers have in common or how changing the amount of reinforcement affects performance. In this context the learning psychologist is less concerned with the particular nature of reinforcing events in a social situation, for example, than with the general laws to which those events conform. Similarly, "psychotic" behavior patterns are of interest to learning psychologists only to the extent that those behaviors are acquired according to the same laws of learning as are nonsense-syllable responses in a verbal learning experiment.

Research in learning, then, is research on behavior that changes over the course of the experiment as a result of experience in the experimental situation. The primary purpose of such research is the formulation of universally applicable principles of learning. While these considerations limit the research trends that fall under the heading of "learning psychology," they by no means provide a basis for determining whether a particular experiment should be construed as an experiment in learning psychology or, say, physiological psychology. Consider an experiment in which a rat learns to press a lever in the familiar Skinner-box apparatus and in which the purpose is to determine the effect of a certain chemical stimulation of the hypothalamic region of the brain on the acquisition of the bar-pressing response. The knowledge gained from this experiment may eventually form a portion of the network of laws within both physiological and learning psychology, and any attempt to categorize the experiment into one field or the other would be determined by the investigator's purpose in conducting the experiment. Current research in learning, then, is best summarized according to the kinds of questions asked by the learning psychologist rather than according to the specific experiments conducted.

Most current research in learning is concerned with behavior of rats, pigeons, and primates (from monkey to man). Concentrated research on one species with similar tasks and apparatus from one experiment to the next is apt to result, relatively quickly, in laws of learning for that species. Implicitly, the assumption is made that principles of learning discovered within species will apply across species. While the premise is such that it probably will never be completely validated, one has only to see the application of learning principles discovered in pigeon experiments to the use of teaching machines in classrooms to grasp the power of the premise as a working hypothesis. On the economic ledger, laboratories across the country are now equipped to house species such as rats and pigeons. The operant boxes and mazes now in use have gradually evolved into efficient tools for the study of the behavior of these species. Expansion of research across species will be costly of time, effort, and money. Thus, although the rationale for the historical selection of rats and pigeons as subjects is perhaps obscure, the likelihood that these species will be intimately involved in learning research for decades to come is quite high for reasons of both scientific and economic expediency. It is interesting to note that the one species that is finding its way into the laboratory more frequently today, the fish, is one that requires relatively inexpensive and confined housing quarters.

With the exception of certain aspects of primate research, most basic learning research today is directed at one or more of several rather broad questions, the first and perhaps most basic of which concerns the nature and identity of reinforcers. Reinforcing stimulus events are generally agreed to be required if an organism is to modify its behavior. A listing of the specific events which have been identified as reinforcers would be quite impressive—or at least quite long. Yet we still do not know what, if anything, all these reinforcing events have in common. Hull theorized that all reinforcers have in common a drive-reducing property. Guthrie claimed, in effect, that all reinforcers involve stimulus change. Some have felt that Hull was focusing on what appears to be a *sufficient* condition for an event to serve as a reinforcer whereas Guthrie was making much of what is a *necessary* condition of reward which might or might not also be sufficient in a given case. The search for commonality within the list of reinforcers, however, is directed at isolation of the conditions that are both necessary *and* sufficient, and it is this question which occupies a substantial portion of learning research today. This research may take the form of studies designed to determine the properties of particular reinforcers, such as exploration or brain stimulation, for example, or it may involve studies concerned with the properties of responses originally elicited by various reinforcers and the relation of these responses to the behavior that is subsequently learned.

Having discovered that a specific condition or event serves as a reinforcer of learning, psychologists often ask what are the limits in the kinds and amounts of this condition and in the ways of presenting it that still produce an effect. The different characteristics of a reinforcer that can be varied and studied separately are called its *parameters*. Thus, once a food has been identified as a reinforcer, interest has focused on the effects of different amounts of the food, or of varying delays in presenting it, or of different schedules of reinforcement (every correct response vs. every fifth correct response, for example). In recent years concentrated research efforts have resulted in fairly detailed knowledge about the effects of amount of reinforcement on rate of acquisition of a response, the highest level of performance that can be expected in a given learning situation, and the permanence of learned responses, i.e., how well the response tends to persist if reinforcement is discontinued. Stimulated by the theories of Hull and Spence, this work has included research designed to determine how different characteristics of reinforcement combine to determine behavior jointly.

Currently such study is expanding in several different directions. Perhaps the most dominant current trend is toward the study of the effects of variation in different aspects of the reinforcement during the experiment. For example, the amount of reward received following a response may be varied from trial to trial or from one block of trials to the next. In such research the parameters are relative, as compared with the absolute, unchanging parameters in earlier research.

Among the relative characteristics of reinforcement, partial reward receives by far the largest share of experimental attention. Beginning with Skinner's work on schedules of reinforcement in the "free-responding operant situation," where rate of responding is observed over a given time interval, the different varieties of intermittent reward and their behavioral effects have been the object of uninterrupted experimentation. In "discrete-trial" learning situations, where a subject is given a series of separate trials, the same question has been studied in terms of the gross variable of percentage reinforcement. Careful analysis of the behavioral effects of specific sequences of rewarded and nonrewarded trials has occupied much of the recent research. Most recently this work has entailed attention to trial-to-trial changes in behavior as well as to acquisition rates, leveling off of performance at some maximum rate, and extinction behavior.

So far, the study of relative and absolute parameters has been limited to relatively few identifiable aspects of reward. We can predict that in the future these aspects will be regarded as composite variables, capable of further subdivision. In short, the same type of research will be repeated with new parameters. We can also expect more detailed quantitative investigation of the known parameters of reinforcement. For example, we know now that both amount and delay of reward affect performance, and that the effect of one is independent of the level of the other. What remains to be seen, however, is the relative potency of one as opposed to the other in determining behavioral level. Such research has had its beginnings; preliminary indications are that considerable time and effort will be required before any general knowledge is attained.

Learning research in this country received its impetus from two largely unrelated sources: Pavlov's study of the conditioned reflex and Thorndike's experiments in the trial-and-error learning of the cat. Two procedurally different learning paradigms, classical (respondent) and instrumental (operant) conditioning became an integral part of basic learning research. Procedurally, classical conditioning involves the presentation of a stimulus (UCS) at a predetermined time, independent of the occurrence or nonoccurrence of the response to be learned. In the instrumental conditioning paradigm, the presentation of the reinforcing stimulus event (the reward) occurs only if the desired response has occurred. During the '30's and '40's learning theorists debated at great length the question of whether there were indeed two different types of learning, requiring two different principles of reinforcement. Recently, they have begun to evaluate learning paradigms traditionally labeled "classical conditioning" in order to assess the role of instrumental conditioning in these situations. Somewhat related research programs are in progress to determine the extent to which prior experience with a given reinforcer will affect subsequent instrumental conditioning with that reinforcer. Thus, while psychologists have tended to divide learning situations according to the instrumental-classical conditioning dichotomy, some basic learning research today is studying situations in which there seem to be combinations of classical and instrumental conditioning. The two most common of these procedures are the active avoidance and conditioned suppression paradigms.

To contend that most basic research in learning concerns the questions previously outlined is to oversimplify the varieties of learning research today in at least two important respects. First, discrimination learning is also an object of considerable attention. Harlow's work with primates, for example, has ranged from studies of two-choice discrimination to investigations of learning sets. Current operant research in the free-responding situation is continually suggesting new parameters to be investigated. In addition, a significant portion of current research is concerned with relating performance under a given set of reinforcement conditions in a discrimination task to performance under the same conditions in a nondiscrimination learning situation.

Second, not all current research is with subhuman species. Some of the human learning research is concerned with the same sorts of questions that are raised in many pigeon and rat studies. Verbal conditioning studies employing mathematical models and, of course, human classical conditioning studies serve as examples. But these experiments in aggregate comprise only a minor portion of human learning research. For the most part, the study of the learning process in man involves the use of some variant of the serial and paired-associate symbolic (verbal) learning tasks. Typically neither the identity nor the nature of the reinforcer is of experimental interest in such studies. Rather, interest focuses on characteristics of the stimulus and/or response items to be learned, such as their similarity (formal or connotative) to one another, their frequency of occurrence in the language, their meaningfulness, and how these parameters affect response and associative learning.

At this point, it is perhaps reasonable to ask whether any general trends in learning research may be discerned. Research has progressed hand in hand with theory. In some cases theoretical speculation has served to define and form the research. Sometimes the theory has evolved from the research as a descriptive device rather than as a tool for inquiry. Theory and theorizing will continue to interact with experimentation, but the theories of today are far less pretentious than those of earlier investigators with respect to the scope of the learning phenomena they purport to explain. The broad macrotheories offered by Hull, Tolman, and Guthrie are, if not dead, in states of suspended animation. Complex microtheories of response acquisition as a function of sequential patterns of reinforcement, or of discrimination contrast phenomena, or of the partial reinforcement effect in extinction are in vogue. Research accompanying these theories tends to be rather abstract and related only to a small core of similar experiments.

If learning psychology follows the course of development of other scientific disciplines, more global theories will evolve, in which several microtheories will be seen as special instances of the new theory. Accompanying research will be concerned with identifying relationships between behavioral phenomena which are currently studied individually in depth and have hitherto been seen as unrelated.

This discussion has been an attempt to summarize current research in the area of learning. Essentially, one arrives at this sort of summary by looking at the types of experiments reported in the contemporary journals of psychology. Since the contributions to these journals come from many different laboratories, each with its own special interests, such summaries are more relevant to the topic area of learning in general than to any one laboratory. The beginning student, however, might be interested in a birds-eye view of the research activity in one modern psychological laboratory. Accordingly, in the concluding paragraphs, the research activity of the writer's laboratory over the past several years is outlined in the belief that our research is fairly representative of the current research in learning at individual laboratories today.

Over the last five years most of our research has been guided by the rather broad question of how the relative parameters of reinforcement affect behavior. A relative reinforcement effect is evidenced if an organism's reaction to a specific reinforcement event is dependent upon its previous history of reinforcement. A relative *magnitude of reward* effect, for example, is evidenced if rats that have regularly received large reward for a given response and then receive a small one react differently from rats that have always received small reward. One situation in which rats have displayed relative reinforcement effects is the double-alley runway apparatus in which rats are trained to traverse two runways in series with the goal section of the first alley (G_1) serving as a start box for the second alley (A_2). In this situation Wagner (1959) observed that rats that had previously received food reward in G_1 ran faster in A_2 when no longer rewarded in G_1 than did animals that had never been rewarded in G_1. This relative effect of nonreward, the *double-alley frustration effect* (EF), served as a starting point for our laboratory work.

Several questions relating to EF have been explored in our laboratory. First, would the relative effect of nonreward depend upon the amount of reward received in G_1 on rewarded trials (Barrett, Peyser, and McHose, 1965; McHose and Ludvigson, 1965; McHose, Meyer, and Maxwell, 1969)? Secondly, would a reduction in reward from large to small amount (rather than from reward to no reward) also produce an EF (Barrett *et al*, 1965; McHose and Ludvigson, 1965; McHose, in press)? Third, would increases in the time of delay in G_1 prior to receipt of the reinforcement produce EFs (McHose, 1966a)? It became apparent from the results of these studies that while nonreward following large reward would produce EFs, i.e., had relative reinforcement effects, neither increases in delay of reward in G_1 nor decreases from large to small reward produced EFs. Later work, however, established the fact that when delay in G_1 was increased over its previous level and the amount was decreased (not omitted) at the same time, EFs *did* occur (McHose, 1966b; McHose, 1968). In these studies, then, the intent was to find the specific parameter or parameters of reinforcement involved in producing EFs or preventing them from occurring.

A second, related question in this double-alley research has been whether increases in reward in G_1 would affect A_2 performance. Would rats that regularly received small reward in G_1 run faster in A_2 following a large reward in G_1 than rats that always received large G_1 reward? In this case it appears that an increase from small to large reward does have the effect of elevating performance in A_2 while an increase from no reward to reward does not (Meyer, 1968; Meyer and McHose, 1968).

While research related to relative reinforcement effects in the double alley was in progress, we became interested in another relative reinforcement effect: *discrimination contrast*. In a differential conditioning discrimination study, for example, rats may be reinforced with large reward for running an alley of one brightness (e.g., black) and smaller reward for running an alley of different brightness (white). Typically, rats develop faster speeds to the brightness associated with the large reward (S+) than to the brightness associated with small reward (S−). Of interest as a relative reinforcement effect, however, was Bower's (1961) observation that the performance to small reward in such cases (i.e., in S−) was considerably below that displayed by animals that always received that same small reward but were not discriminating between two mazes. This depression of S− speeds is labeled a negative S− contrast effect. A similar effect, negative S+ contrast, was also observed by Bower in discrimination animals running slower to large reward (S+) as compared with nondiscrimination rats that always received the large reward.

A puzzle developed, however, in our initial work with discrimination contrast effects when we and a colleague at another laboratory with whom we worked closely discovered that under certain conditions nondiscrimination rats would run faster in an alley that was serving as an S+ alley for other rats than they would in an alley that was being used as an S− alley for other rats. For example, rats that received 10 pellets reward in both a black and a white alley would run faster in the white than in the black when other rats using the equipment were receiving S+ reward in white and S− reward in black (McHose and Ludvigson, 1965). It turned out that rats exude different odors in response to the different reward events and that other rats, in turn, react differentially to the odors. For our purposes, this finding had primarily methodological implications. It dictated changes in the specific procedure of administering learning trials to a large number of animals in the same apparatus to ensure that comparisons between different experimental conditions would control for such odor effects. This finding also led to experiments designed to ascertain the role of these odors in determining the behavior of rats to different patterns of partial reinforcement (McHose, Jacoby, and Meyer, 1967). This work, in turn, became relevant to extensive research conducted elsewhere on the behavioral effects of patterns of reward and nonreward (Capaldi, 1967).

The investigation of odor effect phenomena occupied most of the resources of our laboratory for over one year. This research, of course, was not primarily directed at the role of relative parameters of reinforcement. Rather it was research directed at following up a curious finding in studies originally concerned with relative reward effects. We have subsequently returned to the study of discrimination contrast effects. At this writing a number of different laboratories are engaged in research on contrast effects (cf. Ludvigson and Gay, 1967; Spear and Spitzner, 1966; MacKinnon, 1967), with each research program concerned with slightly different aspects of the contrast phenomenon. Our research has been directed primarily at ascertaining the relationship between differential conditioning contrast effects and relative reinforcement effects in the double-alley apparatus. Our most recent work suggests that certain phenomena observed in double-alley experiments can be interpreted as discrimination contrast effects. Provided that subsequent data are consistent with this suggestion, our work will show that these two areas of research, previously regarded as unrelated, in fact involve the same behavioral processes. This work, however, is not aimed at the discovery of the underlying mechanisms of discrimination contrast. Such research is in progress elsewhere (cf. Ludvigson and Gay, 1967). Viewed in proper perspective, our current research will, if successful, show how an adequate explanation of discrimination contrast may be applied to double-alley, relative reinforcement effects as well.

Our research program in recent years, then, has been concerned with the effects of certain parameters of food reinforcement. In this respect our research merely fits into a long-standing tradition in learning research. In the sense that we have been concerned with relative rather than absolute values of reward, our research reflects the more recent trends in the study of the parameters of reward. Our recent attempts to relate two different areas of research reflect the need to organize our knowledge into broader-based theories. While we are trying to show that two training procedures, at one time thought to be quite different, involve the same behavioral processes, we have not been concerned with isolating the relevant behavioral processes. Other laboratories are doing research relevant to this problem, although such programs tend to focus on either one or the other of the two areas of research we are trying to relate. In the near future their research and ours will meet on some common ground, with the end result being a more comprehensive theory of learning that explains a wider variety of behavior phenomena.

REFERENCES

Barrett, R. J., Peyser, C. S., & McHose, J. H. Effects of complete and incomplete reward reduction on a subsequent response. *Psychonomic Science*, 1965, **3**, 277–278.

Bower, G. H. A contrast effect in differential conditioning. *Journal of Experimental Psychology*, 1961, **62**, 196–199.

Capaldi, E. J. A sequential hypothesis of instrumental learning. In Spence, K. W., and Spence, J. T. (Eds.), *The psychology of learning and motivation*. New York: Academic Press, 1967–1968.

Ludvigson, H. W., & Gay, R. A. An investigation of conditions determining contrast effects in differential reward conditioning. *Journal of Experimental Psychology*, 1967, **75**, 37–42.

MacKinnon, J. R. Interactive effects of the two rewards in a differential magnitude of reward discrimination. *Journal of Experimental Psychology*, 1967, **75**, 329–338.

McHose, J. H. Incentive reduction: Delay increase and subsequent responding. *Psychonomic Science*, 1966, **5**, 213–214. (a)

McHose, J. H. Incentive reduction: Simultaneous delay increase and magnitude reduction and subsequent responding. *Psychonomic Science*, 1966, **5**, 215–216. (b)

McHose, J. H. Incentive reduction: Varied simultaneous reductions and subsequent responding. *Psychonomic Science*, 1968, **11**, 313–314.

McHose, J. H. The role of frustration in the develop-

ment of relative and absolute S— discrimination contrast effects. *Journal of Experimental Psychology*, 1969, **81**, 256–260.

McHose, J. H., Jacoby, L. L., & Meyer, P. A. Extinction as a function of number of reinforced trials and squad composition. *Psychonomic Science*, 1967, **9**, 401–402.

McHose, J. H., & Ludvigson, H. W. The role of reward magnitude and incomplete reduction of reward magnitude in the frustration effect. *Journal of Experimental Psychology*, 1965, **70**, 490–495.

McHose, J. H., Meyer, P. A., & Maxwell, F. R. Frustration effect as a function of training magnitude in a within-*S* design. *Psychonomic Science*, 1969, **14**, 137–138.

Meyer, P. A. Relative magnitude of reward effects within variable reinforcement schedules. Doctoral dissertation, Southern Illinois University, 1968.

Meyer, P. A., & McHose, J. H. Facilitative effects of reward increase: An apparent "elation effect." *Psychonomic Science*, 1968, **13**, 165–166.

Spear, N. E., & Spitzner, J. H. Simultaneous and successive contrast effects of reward magnitude in selective learning. *Psychological Monographs*, 1966, **80**, 10.

Wagner, A. R., The role of reinforcement and nonreinforcement in an "apparent frustration effect." *Journal of Experimental Psychology*, 1959, **57**, 130–136.

Part Five

Cognitive Processes

As we have seen, much of the animal research that psychologists have done rests upon the premise that there are many similarities between animal and human behavior. It is true that animals can and do learn a great many distinctive behaviors. The fact that animals can master highly complex chains of apparently purposive acts is also fairly easily demonstrated. But comparisons of animal and human behavior are useful only up to a certain point. When psychologists wish to study the higher forms of cognitive behavior such as problem solving or the use of language, animal subjects can be of little help.

The most clear-cut distinction between humans and lower animals is undoubtedly the use of language by humans. Humans express their thoughts, ideas, wishes, and problems by talking about them. Animals, if indeed they engage in thoughts, desires, and other higher order activities, must express them through actions or nonverbal vocalizations.

The young human, on the other hand, learns early that certain vocalizations and sounds produce specific results. Language seems to be readily acquired by very nearly all children regardless of the culture in which they are raised. Although some lower animals can learn fairly complex patterns of behavior, only man seems to be adequately provided with the neural and muscular equipment to develop patterned speech. The exact structural differences are not clearly understood. Almost certainly there are fundamental differences in both the sensory and motor areas of the cortex. Probably there are muscular and other structural differences between sound-producing organs. There are also probably certain differences in the kinds and number of connecting neural pathways between the brain and the vocal apparatus.

This does not mean that the manner in which language behavior is learned is necessarily different from the manner in which other behavior is learned. For example, a dog can learn to fetch a newspaper by being made to understand what is expected and by having the appropriate response reinforced. A child can learn to tie his shoes by being shown how one ties shoes. If his muscular coordination has matured sufficiently, then the child can master the task by practicing it a few times. Such muscular tasks appear to be learned by observation, practice, and appropriate reinforcement. The mechanisms of learning are very similar in the child and the dog. In much the same way, a child can learn that the sound *No* refers to negation. If the child is reaching for something, he may hear the word *No* at the same time his hand is gently but firmly restrained. With time he even learns that a more emphatic *NO!* includes components implying imminent punishment if all activity is not immediately stopped.

Even more basically, noun words almost always occur in the presence of the object to which they refer. The word *Mama* occurs when Mama is there. The word *Papa* likewise occurs when he is there. The incorporation of the words *Mama* and *Papa* into the vocabulary takes place in a manner very similar to the acquisition of conditioned responses by animals.

270

The papers reprinted on the following pages represent many different approaches to understanding how humans learn to perform such complicated functions as forming concepts, solving problems, forming images, creating, thinking, and talking. The attempts at understanding and explaining run the gamut from Hunter's work with raccoons to the analysis of the kinds of images that adult humans can apparently form.

35

The Behavior of Raccoons in a Double Alternation Temporal Maze

Walter S. Hunter

The question of whether or not animals below the level of man can use some form of imagery in order to remember complex happenings and make intelligent choices has long been of interest to man. The classic experiments of W. S. Hunter (1889–1954) represent some of the earliest and most ingenious attempts to answer the question. His experiments involved the double alternation response, in which the animal must turn in one direction on two successive trials and in the other direction on the next two successive trials. The task is a complex one since, in order to make the correct turn on any given trial, the animal must remember which direction it turned on the two preceding trials.

Finding that rats were unable to learn such a complex task, Hunter turned to other animals higher on the phylogenetic scale. The raccoons used in the series of experiments described in this article proved able to learn this very complex task. These results are the earliest, and the clearest, that show definite signs of imagery, memory of complex events, and even actual thinking on the part of a lower animal. The approach described here has been widely used in studying young children as well as animals.

Introduction

The problems of simple alternation, double alternation, and the temporal maze are of great interest because of their bearings upon the sensory-neural control of behavior and upon the problem of the delayed reaction. Only two studies of the three problems first mentioned have been published, one by Carr (1917) on simple alternation and one by Hunter (1918, 1920) on simple alternation, double alternation, and the temporal maze.

The usual maze I term a spatial maze because the subject in passing through it enters new units in space as well as new units in time. With the new spatial units, new exteroceptive stimulations of vision, olfaction, and contact usually, if not always, occur. In the temporal maze, on the other hand, the animal encounters no new stimuli after it has been through the apparatus once. A glance at Figure 1 will show the general plan of the temporal maze. The subject is trained on the problem of running from E through the central alley, then turning right and so around back to the central alley. Passing through this alley again, the next turn should be to the left and so back to the start. The third time the response should

FIGURE 1 *The general ground plan of the temporal maze. The figure is described in the text*

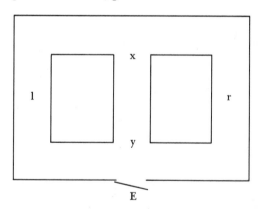

be to the right; the fourth time, to the left; etc., in the order *rlrlrl*. This is simple alternation. Double alternation would involve turns in the order *rrll*.

Excerpted from "The Behavior of Raccoons in a Double Alternation Temporal Maze," The Journal of Genetic Psychology *(1928),* **35,** *374–388. Reprinted by permission of the Journal Press and Mrs. Walter S. Hunter.*

After the subject has been through the right and left sides of the apparatus, he has met all of the exteroceptive stimuli present. These exteroceptive stimuli are constant throughout the experiment. This is also true for the proprioceptive stimuli, largely kinaesthetic in kind. The kinaesthetic consequences of running through the right side of the maze are the same trial after trial as are also those of running through the left side of the maze. . . . The stimulation at the entrance, sends the subject through the central alley, *xy,* and to the right. This initial response is not difficult to learn. (Indeed I found one rat who learned the whole series of simple alternation in one day's test of ten trials, *rlrlrlrlrl.*) The run through the right side of the apparatus . . . has a sensory consequence. . . . [This] causes the subject to respond . . . with a run through the left side. This has its sensory consequences . . . which cause a run to the right, and so on for the remainder of the series. . . .

For fear, however, that the reader will infer that the situation is entirely simple because the above mechanism is simple and adequate for the explanation of the behavior, let me carry the analysis further. Since the pathway *xy* is common to the right and left responses, the differentiating sensory factors cannot lie in this alley. The sensory factors causing a right turn and those causing a left turn may lie anywhere, or everywhere, in the path *xly* and in the path *xry,* respectively. No discovered motor consequences anticipating a left or a right response occur prior to the point *x.* The results . . . must therefore be carried over within the animal while it runs from *y* to *x,* because it is only at *x* that the motor consequences of the stimuli manifest themselves. Furthermore, at *x* the subject is confronted by two objectively possible pathways. This looks like the typical delayed reaction situation: The stimulus . . . is absent at the moment of response; and at least two modes of response are externally possible. (See Hunter, 1917, p. 76.) In order to turn the simple alternation test into the delayed reaction test, it would be necessary to get away from the regular series of presentations. . . . This, however, cannot be done because the response to one of these stimuli engenders, or arouses, the other stimulus. . . . The deciding factor in determining the simple alternation response seems to be recency. . . .

The analysis which we have just made does not apply to the various types of spatial mazes so far devised because they do not involve a common alley like *xy.* Since they do not have such a common alley, the terminal part of the sensory sequences causing a specific response need not be postulated prior to the beginning of that response. With a common alley, *xy,* differential sensory factors cannot be located therein not only because it is common to both right and left responses but because it is also constant and unchanging in its rôle of a common factor throughout the test.

The foregoing analysis is necessary in order to see the significance of the double alternation experiment which is the subject proper of the present paper. The rat can master simple alternation, but it cannot master double alternation even when given merely the series *rrll,* composed of four responses, two to the right and two to the left. This my previous paper (Hunter, 1920) seems to have established definitely.

* * *

. . . The human subject would have no difficulty with double alternation, if he supplemented his responses with the verbal behavior, "It is two, two. I first go two right, then two left, etc." Even here it seems that either the neural set or the actual verbal behavior would need to occur at each trial in order to lead to the proper sequence of responses. . . . When in 1915 I first began the experiments described by Hunter (1918, 1920), I carried out some tests on adult human subjects with a double alternation temporal pencil maze. The subjects were instructed to talk aloud about the problem as they worked upon it. No subject mastered the problem until he had said, "Oh, it is two, two!"

The rat cannot master the double alternation temporal maze problem. He therefore cannot accumulate the retained effects of previous stimulation, . . . because if these retained effects, these changed physiological states, were present, there would be no reason for his failure. General observation and experiments with the delayed reaction indicate that the rat lacks symbolic processes. The raccoon on the other hand has shown an ability with the delayed reaction which justifies us in assuming that he possesses the bare rudiments of symbolic processes. It should therefore be possible for the raccoon to learn the double alternation temporal maze. The present experiment was devoted to the study of this problem.

Animals, Methods, and Apparatus

Four animals were available for a part of the present experiment; and three, for all of it. The one animal upon whom work was discontinued developed a cataract in the right eye which caused her to fall into a bad position habit from which she could not be broken. Other than this all animals were in excellent health throughout the experiment. There was some slowing up in February due to lack of hunger. Training was continued through this period, however, in order to keep the animals accustomed to the work. A change in diet also helped keep the animals working. Of the four animals, Jimmie, an adult, had been a pet; Betty was probably two years old; Henri, probably six months old; and Jean, also probably six months old at the beginning of the work.

Figure 2 gives a ground plan of the apparatus. E, the entrance door, was lifted up to allow the raccoon to enter. One, 2, 3, and 4 designate hinged doors which were operated with sticks attached to their tops. They could be opened and closed noiselessly. The brackets at the top of the figure represent the location and extent of the electric grills. The whole apparatus was covered with a coarse mesh wire. External light was excluded from the experiment room which was illuminated from an electric light suspended over the center of the apparatus.

When the animal entered the apparatus, the doors stood as indicated in the figure. If the subject went through the right side of the maze, it was given a bite of food at 3 and credited with a correct response. (If it turned left and entered the

FIGURE 2 *Ground plan of the apparatus used in the present experiments. One, 2, 3, and 4 are hinged doors by means of which the pathways are varied. E is the entrance door. The brackets show the location and extent of the electric grills. L and B designate a light and a buzzer which were used during one period of the work. The walls of the apparatus were 3 ft. high; the alleys, 13 in. wide; and the outer dimensions of the maze were 8 ft. 8 in. by 7 ft. 3 in.*

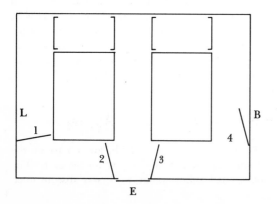

length of its body, or if it secured a shock, an error was counted. If the subject went farther into the left alley, door 1 finally stopped it and compelled a return. The animals were fed after each trial, even though errors had been made.) Door 3 was then opened, and the animal went through the central alley. It should now again turn through the right side of the apparatus and again come to 3 to be fed. On the third trial, door 4 was closed and door 1 was opened. The subject should now turn left at the end of the central alley and come to 2 to be fed. This was also true for the fourth trial. The fifth and sixth trials called for responses to the right; and the seventh and eighth trials, for responses to the left. (Eight trials, *rrllrrll*, were given each day until later in the experiment when four trials, *rrll*, were used.) The average length of time between trials was 10 seconds. After the subject had learned not to retrace through the maze, doors 1 and 4 were always left open except when an error was made. In case an error occurred, the proper door was closed *after* the animal had started down the side alley. Door 2 was shut, at this stage of the experiment, only during the two trials to the right; and door 3, only during the two trials to the left. In the final stages of the experiment, doors 2 and 3 were open all the time, unless the animal started to enter the wrong alley. Even with these doors open, the animals rarely failed to turn after being fed and enter the central alley.

The experimenter stood back of E and behind a curtain.

The animals were brought from the living cage in another room one at a time. When the experimental period for each subject was over, he was taken out of the experiment room and usually shut up in a small cage where feeding was continued.

Results

During the first period of the experiment, punishment was not used. Table 1 records the number of correct responses made in each successive group of 40 trials, i.e., in each successive group of five days. No subject made noticeable progress toward the mastery of the problem of responding *rrllrrll*. Furthermore an examination of the daily records shows that no subject adopted a consistent and uniform mode of response. Only very rarely was a record of six correct trials made. Once Jean made seven correct out of eight, but the record was never repeated during the period. Only twice did

TABLE 1 *Number of Correct Responses in Each Successive Group of 40 Trials. Eight Trials Daily. No Shock.*

	Jim	Jean	Henri	Betty
	16	18	21	17
	15	18	15	18
	18	19	16	23
	18	24	20	24
	14	26	23	16
	11	22	16	14
	16	23	15	18
	16	19	21	22
	20	19	21	20
	8 of 16	13 of 32	21 of 32	17 of 32
Total trials	376	395	395	392

Henri make a record where the first four responses were correct, i.e., where he ran *rrll*. Jean succeeded in this three times. Neither Jimmie nor Betty had a single day's record where the first four trials (*rrll*) were successful. Even in the case of the first two animals, the records did not occur on successive days. This coupled with the low frequency of the records leads me to believe that chance will account for the results. The ease with which the animals learned to make the first trial correctly is indicated by the fact that after the thirteenth day practically no errors were made on the first trials.

During the last fourteen days of the period covered in Table 1, the animals were fed only at the close of the day's series of trials. When the subject reached the place in the apparatus where he was normally fed, no food was offered, and he was compelled to continue his response. All subjects quickly fell into a left-position habit, going around the left side of the maze on each trial. Betty's cataract was noticed at this time, and no further use is made of her record which continued for some days after the termination of Table 1.

In order to facilitate learning, the electric grill was now placed in the maze, and a faint shock was given whenever an error was made by turning in the wrong direction at the end of the central alley. (The current was never turned into the grill until the animal actually stepped upon it.) Feeding at the close of each trial was now resumed. Table 2 records the results. This table also shows that after the 30th day the method was still further changed by introducing light and sound.

The light bulb was fastened to the outer wall of the maze, but in the left alley, at the point marked *L* in Figure 2. The buzzer which served as a source of sound was mounted upon a tripod outside the right alley of the maze at the position marked *B* in the figure. The series of trials was still *rrllrrll*, eight trials daily. After light and sound were introduced trial one was to the right as usual. Trial two was also to the right, but the buzzer was sounded as soon as the subject entered the right-hand alley leading back to the entrance. The buzzer continued to sound until the animal reached the point where he was fed. Trial three was a regular trial to the left. Trial four was also to the left, but the light was turned on as soon as the animal reached the left alley, and it remained on until the animal reached the feeding point. The following four trials of the day's work repeated the conditions of the first four trials.

This method, using the light and buzzer, was adopted in order to differentiate between the sensory consequences of the two trials to the right and between the two trials to the left. Under these conditions, the first trial to the right was accompanied by sensory consequences S_R which migh cause the response R_R. This R_R was accompanied by S_R plus B, the buzzer. S_R plus B might cause R_L. This R_L would be accompanied by S_L which might cause the R_L of the fourth trial. This R_L would be accompanied by S_L plus L, the light. S_L plus L could then cause the following turn to the right, R_R. The introduction of light and sound in this manner gives additional exteroceptive cues in terms of which the desired behavior, *rrllrrll*, might be accomplished. . . .

Let us now turn to the data of Table 2, where all of the work with eight trials daily and punishment is summarized. The table shows that Jimmie once reached a record of 30 trials correct out of 40, but the other animals never did better than 28 correct out of 40. These records are too low to demonstrate mastery of the problem. In a maze, perfect records are the normally accepted standard of mastery; and in a discrimination problem box, nothing less than 80–85 per cent is satisfactory. Although chance accounts for only 50 per cent of correct responses in a two-way box, variable position habits complicate the results so greatly, when the subject is confronted with a difficult problem, that only a record such as we have indicated above can be safely accepted as evidence of discrimination.

The item marked Con. 1 in Table 2 signifies a control record of one day's work. In this control the animal was permitted to go around the side

TABLE 2   *Number of Correct Responses in Each Successive Group of 40 Trials. Eight Trials Daily. Electric Shock Used.*

	Jimmie	Jean	Henri
	19	21	20
	23	26	24
	23	27	23
	18	28	25
	14	23	20
	23	26	26
Series with light and sound introduced			
	27	28	27
	23	15	28
	30	25	23
	24	28	16
	15	24	28
	18	25	27
	23	26	24
	27	Con. 1	Con. 1
	Con. 1	31 of 48	31 of 56
	26 of 48		
Total trials	608	568	568

of the maze without hindrance either from the doors or from the shocks. When the animal reached the feeding places he was fed. There was thus no set order of presentations. Jimmie's responses were in the order *rlllrlll;* Henri's, in the order *rlrlrlrl;* and Jean's, in the order *rrlrrrll.* This control was not repeated in this manner again, except for Jean. . . .

*   *   *

At this stage in the experiment, after from 960 to 984 trials per animal, I decided to reduce the total trials per day from eight to four using the same order *rrll.* If the animals mastered this, the series could then be increased to eight trials. Table 3 gives the general summary of results. In this series of experiments, the electric shock was used but the light and buzzer were discontinued. Throughout the period no animal made a perfect record for five successive days. Jimmie has one record of 16 correct in 20 trials (80 per cent) and one record of 18 correct choices in 20 trials (90 per cent). Jean has an average record of 90 per cent for one five-day period and one of 85 per cent. Henri has two of 80 per cent, one of 90 per cent, and one of 95 per cent. Each animal succeeded in making a record 100 per cent correct at various times throughout this period. A record of two suc-

cessive days with 100 per cent correct was made twice by Jimmie, twice by Jean, and twice by Henri. Each made in addition records of two perfect days out of three successive ones. Once Jimmie made a perfect record on three successive days, and Henri once made perfect records on four successive days, running *rrll* correctly each day. Immediately after these four days, Henri was trained for twenty days with the original series, *rrllrrll.* He never succeeded in mastering the problem. He responded consistently with *rrllllll.* In other words, he had learned to go twice to the right and thereafter to the left.

In this connection certain behavior of Jean is worthy of notice. This subject had for many days made three correct responses as follows: *rrrl* when he should have gone *rrll.* Controls were made in which Jean was not punished but fed when he made the error. In other words, with all doors in the maze open, he was permitted to respond without restraint. The result was that he turned as before three times to the right and then once to the left. This control was introduced on two successive days with the above result. Jean was undoubtedly making a temporal series of responses in a fixed order but not under exteroceptive con-

TABLE 3   *Number of Correct Responses in Each Successive Group of 20 Trials. Four Trials Daily, rrll. No Electric Shock Until the Last Half of the Period. No Light or Buzzer Used.*

	Jimmie	Jean	Henri
	14	15	14
	7	15	9
	9	18	16
	8	10	14
	16	15	16
	16	17	13
	12	14	19
	12		13
	14		18
	11		4 of 4
	18		Series *rrllrrll*
	13		in groups of 40 trs.
	13		27
	9 of 16		24
			25 26
Total trials	276	140	184 trs. with 4 trs. daily 160 trs. with 8 trs. daily

trol. No such behavior was found with the rats tested by Hunter (1920, p. 11). In the present test all external stimuli, including the nonoperation of the doors, were constant. I have no explanation of why Jean should fall from the mastery of *rrll* into the mastery of *rrrl* unless it were that the punishment involved in an incorrect response was not sufficient to hold him to a form of behavior which all of the work in the present paper indicates is extremely difficult and, even when once mastered, highly unstable.

During the whole series of tests on double alternation, the following total amounts of training were received by the respective subjects: Jimmie, 1260 trials; Jean, 1100 trials; Henri, 1304 trials; and Betty, 392 trials.

Conclusions

The raccoons used in the present experiment have demonstrated a capacity for behavior which I have been unable so far to find in the white rat, viz., the ability to perform a double alternation response where the exteroceptive cues are constant. The raccoons, however, were only able to master completely the simplest form of this response in the form *rrll*. They were unable to increase this to *rrllrrll*. This latter series was *never once* performed during the course of these experiments which lasted from the first of October until the thirtieth of the following May. The long period through which these experiments continued and the various methods employed make it probable that the limits of performance were reached for these animals.

. . . [When trying to explain the above behavior,] however, I am inclined to lean toward the hypothesis of symbolic processes because: (1) the rat failed on the delayed reaction experiment and on the double alternation problem while the raccoon succeeded on both; (2) on the delayed reaction problem the raccoon revealed only the rudiments of symbolic processes, and it is only the simplest ability to master the double alternation which he displays here; (3) the rat, who is notoriously able to retain the effects of previous training, could not retain the cumulative effects of his responses in the double alternation problem to a degree sufficient to master that problem. A final reason in support of the symbolic process hypothesis lies in the sketchy but suggestive experiments upon human subjects elsewhere referred to in this paper.

If I am correct in the arguments of the present paper, the double alternation temporal maze is to be placed with the delayed reaction experiment as another method of demonstrating the presence of symbolic processes.

REFERENCES

Carr, H. A. The alternation problem: A preliminary study. *Journal of Animal Behavior,* 1917, **7,** 365–384.

Hunter, W. S. The delayed reaction in a child. *Psychological Review,* 1917, **24,** 74–87.

Hunter, W. S. The delayed reaction in animals and children. *Behavior Monograph,* 1913, **2** (1), v + 86.

Hunter, W. S. Kinaesthetic sensory processes in the white rat. *Psychological Bulletin,* 1918, **15,** 36–37.

Hunter, W. S. The temporal maze and kinaesthetic sensory processes in the white rat. *Psychobiology,* 1920, **2,** 1–17.

36

Vertical and Horizontal Processes in Problem Solving

Howard H. Kendler and Tracy S. Kendler

Although thinking and cognitive processes in general are the most highly developed and most exciting product of the evolutionary progression, we have found it difficult to understand these processes to the degree that we would like. There are exquisite laboratory techniques for measuring the electrical activity in a single nerve fiber and statistical designs for dealing with the immense degree of variability that is typical of human behavior as well as that of many lower organisms. The rows of shiny new equipment that most modern laboratories boast would seem to indicate that we are well equipped to understand those forms of behavior that we are most concerned about. But this is not the case, for those mental activities that most clearly set man apart from beast have very nearly eluded scientific investigation. One possible approach to investigation of cognitive processes in the laboratory is outlined in this article.

The present paper is concerned with *an* approach —and not *the* approach—to the universally appealing but nevertheless unpopular research area of problem solving. Problems of problem solving have proved to be particularly refractory to psychologists. More often than not the uncommon researcher with the temerity to attack some aspect of reasoning retreats to more secure and conventional problems when he discovers that his sorties fail to achieve any impressive victory. As a result the literature of problem solving is almost chaotic because it is so heavily sprinkled with isolated bits of information (Duncan, 1959).

Perhaps the present stage of development of psychology does not justify the strategy of investigating such a complex phenomenon. Fortunately, or not, science has no built-in traffic lights to inform investigators when to proceed. It may be a risky and potentially unfruitful gambit to investigate problem solving, but then again it may not be. In addition to the intrinsic interest of the area, it does offer a challenge to those psychologists who are interested in testing the generality of any set of theoretical principles stemming from other areas of behavior (e.g., learning, perception).

This paper initially will make fleeting references to some methodological problems with which a researcher in the field of reasoning must contend. Then a simple pretheoretical model of problem solving will be described, followed by a report of research which the model generated, and which in turn is shaping the model itself.

Methodological Problems in Problem-Solving Research

Anybody who does research is—or should be—aware that every decision he makes cannot be justified by facts or logic. Some decisions must be made on the basis of personal intuition. This is particularly true for the researcher in problem solving who must make three strategic decisions which cannot help but have profound influences on his research and the ideas they generate (Kendler, 1961). These decisions, which are not completely independent, are related to the place of problem solving in psychology, the use of complex or simple experimental tasks, and the selection of

From Psychological Review, *Vol. 69 (1962), 1–16. Copyright 1962 by the American Psychological Association, and reproduced by permission. An earlier version of this paper was delivered by Howard H. Kendler as an invited address to the 1960 meeting of the Eastern Psychological Association, which was held in New York City. The authors are indebted to the Office of Naval Research and the National Science Foundation for their support of the research reported in this paper.*

a pretheoretical model to guide research. Considering the volitional nature of these problems, as well as the current status of psychological knowledge, it would be both inappropriate and erroneous to consider these methodological problems as offering only one sensible alternative. Adopting this point of view would do much to minimize the needless disputation that seems to perennially surround matters of research strategy.

Accepting the principle that a basic research strategy is not simply an outgrowth of logical and factual considerations does not reduce one to making decisions in either a haphazard or random manner. A given strategy can be adopted on the basis of rational considerations as long as it is realized that other reasonable attitudes might lead to the adoption of different decisions.

The history of problem solving in particular and psychology in general suggests that problem solving can best be conceptualized not as a basic psychological process, but instead as one that reflects the interaction of more fundamental processes (e.g., learning, perception, and motivation).

If problem solving is not viewed as a unitary process, how is an appropriate experimental situation selected to investigate it? One possibility is that a problem can be selected from a "true life" situation such as troubleshooting electronic equipment. Or problems can be invented (Duncker, 1945; Maier, 1930) that capture the flavor, if only partially, of problems we meet in everyday life.

A more analytical approach can be taken to the selection of an experimental situation to investigate problem solving. If problem solving is compounded of elementary behavioral processes, then it may be more strategic to devise some simple problems in which the relationships of fundamental psychological mechanisms to problem solving are highlighted. That is, tasks should be devised not to duplicate or imitate everyday problems, but instead to isolate and magnify the basic mechanisms that operate in such complex tasks.

This analytical approach, which is favored by the authors, suffers from one major drawback. How is it possible to know the basic mechanisms of problem solving prior to their discovery? Obviously, excepting divination, there is no method. But this does not prevent the analytical approach from operating. The researcher can prejudge theoretical issues by formulating a model of what he guesses problem solving to be like. The model can guide the investigator in selecting the hypotheses to test, as well as the experimental situations in which to test them.

This brings us to the third and most important

decision a problem-solving researcher has to make: his choice of a pretheoretical model (Koch, 1959). A pretheoretical model is not equivalent to a theory. The criterion of validity cannot properly be applied to it because essentially a pretheoretical model is an informal conception that operates as an analogy (Lachman, 1960). It is conceivable that different models (e.g., learning, perception, information theory) can all lead to fruitful and valid theories of problem solving.

Psychologists have many possibilities from which to choose their model. These models can be conveniently divided into two main categories: the empirical model that springs primarily from experimental data, and the formal model that is usually generated by mathematical or logical systems. Among the empirical models that have achieved some acceptance are those that are based on introspective findings (e.g., the four successive stage model of "preparation," "incubation," "inspiration," and finally "verification"), the facts of perception, and those of learning. Some formal models used are those dependent upon stochastic models, game theory, and the operation of computers.

The present authors adopted a S-R [stimulus-response] learning pretheoretical model. The decision no doubt was influenced by professional training and past research efforts. But other considerations entered in. For the past four decades, S-R learning psychologists have probably been the most active experimental and theoretical group in psychology. To some, if not a large, extent this can be attributed to the fruitful and cleansing effect S-R language has upon designing, reporting, and interpreting research. S-R language forces the psychologist to focus his attention on objectively defined environmental and behavioral variables and thus encourages the collection of data and the testing of ideas. The efforts of S-R learning psychologists have supplied a host of facts, concepts, and hypotheses that can be exploited in an exploratory excursion into the realm of problem solving.

The facts and theories of learning, however, do not spontaneously coalesce to form a model that can guide research in problem solving. Some selection must be made. S-R learning theory does not represent a single organized formulation. Anyone who is familiar with the systematic orientations of Hull (1952), Guthrie (1952), Spence (1956), and Skinner (1953) is aware of this. Many of these systematic differences, however, become attenuated and some even disappear when viewed from the distance of problem-solving behavior. It is possible and perhaps even profitable to develop a learning model for problem solving that ignores many of the points of disagreement among S-R theories.

Much of the objection to S-R language stems from the apparent discrepancy between active, flowing behavior and the inert, static, single S-R association. Using S-R language does not mean that complex behavior *actually* consists of S-R connections. After analyzing the concept of light, Toulmin (1953), concludes: "We do not *find* light atomized into individual rays: We *represent* it as consisting of such rays" (p. 29). Applying the same idea to the concept of the S-R association: "We do not *find* behavior atomized into individual S-R associations: We *represent* it as consisting of such S-R associations." The concept of the S-R association, therefore, must be judged not in terms of its ability to provide a clear image of behavior, but rather in its capacity to represent the facts of behavior.

Pretheoretical Model of Problem Solving

A S-R model needs to represent two important characteristics of problem-solving behavior. These characteristics are: behavior is continuous, and at any one time behavior consists of several habits. The terms "horizontal" and "vertical" are used to refer to these processes; horizontal to the continuity of behavior against the dimension of time, and vertical to the assumption that independent levels of behavior (i.e., S-R units) occur simultaneously.

The assumption that S-R associations do not occur in isolation, but instead are linked together to form integrated, continuous behavior goes back many years (e.g., Watson, 1913). Today the process is most commonly referred to as chaining. Skinner (1953) and his associates have developed powerful techniques that shape behavior into long, complicated chains. The mass of data they have collected suggests important principles governing habit chaining. There is little doubt that when their quasi-theoretical system is exploited fully with autoinstructional devices, that important insights into problem-solving behavior will emerge, particularly in relation to how an added bit of knowledge can trigger problem solution. The kind of chaining with which the Skinnerians have dealt (i.e., adding new S-R units to an already functioning chain) does not exhaust all the problems associated with the horizontal processes of problem solving. Of particular importance to problem solving is the *spon-*

taneous integration of separate habits which occurs when an organism infers the consequences of combining previously independent S-R units. This kind of chaining was investigated in Kohler's (1925) classical studies of insight and in the more controlled reasoning experiments of Maier (1930). More recently the authors (Kendler and Kendler, 1956, 1961; Kendler, Kendler, Pliskoff, and D'Amato, 1958) have tried to identify some of the important variables that enable children to combine separate experiences in order to solve an inference-type problem. Much of the research reported in this paper will be concerned with how mediated stimulus and response events aid in the formation of problem-solving chains.

The assumption of vertical processes, i.e., the organism responds several different ways at any one time, is also not a novel one. Every psychologist is aware that organisms make several different responses simultaneously, although typically only one is attended to. Sometimes the different responses are interrelated, as is the case between the heart and respiration rates of a fearful organism. In other cases the different responses are independent, e.g., a person's conversation is uninfluenced by his tugging at his ear lobe. The best laboratory example of vertical processes, and one that has much relevance to problem solving, is shown in Figure 1. Those familiar with introductory psychology textbooks will recognize this diagram as representing classical conditioning. Notice that the two solid lines indicate independent S-R units which are operating simultaneously. One is the tone that initiates the "investigatory" response, and the other is the food which elicits salivation. Initially these two associations operate in a *parallel* fashion, but as a result of their simultaneous occurrence an *interaction* takes place which is expressed by the broken line representing the acquired conditioned response.

Obviously the brief reference to horizontal and

FIGURE 1   *A S-R representation of classical conditioning*

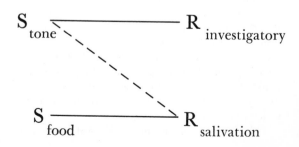

vertical processes in which it is assumed fundamental S-R principles operate (e.g., discrimination, generalization, etc.) presents at best the barest skeleton of a model of problem solving. It needs the flesh and skin of experimental facts to give it solidity and theoretical principles to clothe it in scientific respectability. Let us now review some of the progress that has been made in this direction.

Concept Learning and Utilization

Although the primitive model just described fails to generate any research by itself, it does suggest that individual experiments cannot be directed at *problem solving in its entirety*. There are too many aspects to this phenomenon. The researcher, in designing an experiment, must scan the entire problem-solving process and then focus upon that segment that promises to yield fruitful results and is also amenable to investigation.

For reasons that will become evident, it was decided to compare reversal and nonreversal shifts in a simple concept-learning task. Figure 2 characterizes each kind of shift by showing a *simplified* version of an experimental situation used with

FIGURE 2   *Examples of a reversal and a nonreversal shift*

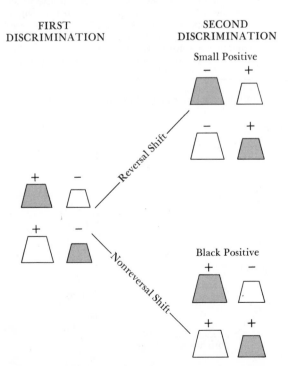

children. The stimuli (cups) for their first discrimination differed simultaneously on two dimensions (size and brightness). The subject is rewarded for responses to one dimension (e.g., large cup is positive, small cup is negative). The other dimension is irrelevant. After learning the first discrimination, the subject is forced to shift to another response. In a reversal shift the subject is required to respond to the same dimension on which he was originally trained, but his overt choice has to be reversed, e.g., he has to shift from a *large* cup to a *small* one. For a nonreversal shift the previously irrelevant dimension becomes relevant, e.g., black becomes positive after large had been positive.

Buss (1953) reported that college students executed a reversal shift more rapidly than a nonreversal shift. He attributed this superiority to the intermittent reinforcements that retard the progress of a nonreversal shift. For example, in Figure 2,[1] when a subject is making a nonreversal shift from large positive to black positive, he is reinforced when choosing the large black cup in preference to the small white cup. This fortuitous reinforcement of the choice of the large cup helps maintain the size discrimination and hence retards the learning of the brightness discrimination. The reversal shift group, on the other hand, receives no reinforcement of the previously correct responses, since they are 100 per cent *non*reinforced.

This analysis is at best incomplete. The work of Kendler and Vineberg (1954) suggested that adult human concept learning cannot be represented adequately by a single-unit S-R theory in which the external stimulus is directly connected to the overt response. Instead, a mediational mechanism (see Figure 3) is required which assumes that the external stimulus evokes an implicit response

FIGURE 3   *A schematic representation of the mediational hypothesis*

---

[1] The purpose of Figure 2 is to clarify the meaning of both a reversal and nonreversal shift. It would be misleading to believe that it represents *exactly* the methodology of "reversal-nonreversal" studies reported in this paper. For all experiments reported, except that of Buss (1953), designs were used that controlled for fortuitous intermittent reinforcements effects in a nonreversal shift.

which produces an implicit cue that is connected to the overt response.

It would be useful to digress for a moment to comment about the epistemological status of these inferred stimulus and response events which are enclosed in the rectangle to emphasize their hypothetical character. Although not directly observable, they are "tied to" environmental and behavioral events. The basic assumption of the mediational hypothesis, at least for the time being, is that the implicit stimulus and response events obey the same principles that operate in observable S-R relationships.

The mediational hypothesis has generated confusion. Perhaps the following brief statements will clarify some possible areas of misunderstanding.

1. The mediational hypothesis is neither new nor revolutionary. Meyer (1911) and Watson (1913) referred to it, and Hull (1930) gave it a more formal status by coining the concept of the "pure stimulus act." Guthrie (1952) has always laid heavy stress on a mediational-type hypothesis when emphasizing the importance of proprioceptive stimulation in learning.

2. The implicit stimulus and response events *need not* be conceived as having an existence independent of their relation to independent and dependent variables. These implicit events are theoretical constructs. Their epistemological status is closer to such concepts as drive and habit than to directly observable stimulus and response events.

Some mediating events can conceivably and probably will be coordinated to introspective reports, language behavior, muscular movements, and other observable events. Coordinations of this sort can be useful in developing mediational theory. But such coordinations are not *essential* to mediational theory. The fact that genes are not directly observable (at least according to the geneticists consulted) does not interfere with their theoretical and practical usefulness. Even if it were possible to observe a gene directly, it would be necessary to distinguish between it as an observable entity and as a concept within a nomological network. It would be unwise, and strategically shortsighted, to *identify* mediational events with introspective reports or language behavior, or other observable events. The "validity" of the mediational mechanism does not depend on being coordinated with observable events, but depends instead on being utilized in a successful explanatory system.

Figure 4 characterizes reversal and nonreversal shifts in terms of both a single unit S-R analysis and a mediational one.[2] It would be predicted,

[2] Figure 4 highlights the problem of what are the effective stimuli that are associated to the overt response in both a reversal and nonreversal shift. It is not intended to be a detailed analysis of which there may be several alternatives. For example, in a single unit theory the habit to choose the large container might result from learning two separate specific habits (e.g., the choice of a large black container when coupled with a small white one and the selection of a large white container when paired with a small black one). Another possibility, which would be consistent with Spence's theory (1936), is that the response is to the effective stimulus *large* since responses to the other features of the environment are not consistently reinforced. Similarly adult subjects in a reversal shift might use the mediator

FIGURE 4   *A single unit and mediational S-R analysis of a reversal and nonreversal shift*

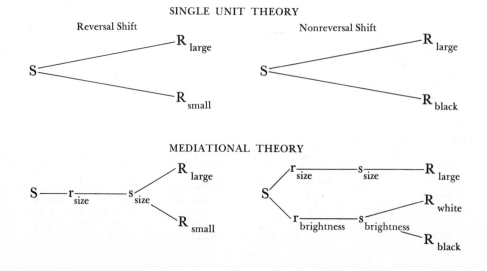

according to a single unit hypothesis, that if fortuitous intermittent reinforcements were eliminated from a nonreversal shift, it would occur more rapidly than a reversal shift. The reason for this is that at the time of the shift the difference between the strength of the dominant incorrect habit and the to-be-correct habit is much greater for the reversal, as compared to the nonreversal shift. Consequently more training will be required to make the correct habit dominant in a reversal shift. According to the mediational theory the situation is entirely different. A reversal shift enables the subject to utilize the same mediated response. Only the overt response has to be changed. A nonreversal shift, on the other hand, required the acquisition of a *new* mediated response, the cues of which have to be attached to a *new* overt response. Because the old mediational sequence has to be discarded and a new one formed, the nonreversal shift should be executed more slowly than a reversal shift.[3] Thus, if it were possible to eliminate fortuitous intermittent reinforcements, then the stage would be set for a crucial experiment testing the conflicting implications of the single-unit and mediational S-R theories. The results of a series of such crucial experiments (Buss, 1956; Harrow and Friedman, 1958; Kendler and D'Amato, 1955) have been consistent with the mediational formulation in showing that college students execute a reversal shift more rapidly than a nonreversal shift. It is important to note that in a similar kind of problem rats find a nonreversal shift easier than a reversal shift (Kelleher, 1956). Thus, one is forced to conclude that a single unit S-R theory accurately represents the behavior of rats, while mediational S-R theory is required for the concept learning of articulate humans.

The discontinuity between the behavior of rats and college students directs one's attention toward the conditions responsible for the development of mediational processes. Somewhere on a hypothetical evolutionary dimension between the rat and college student there should be a point where a transition is made from a single unit to mediational control. An obvious place to locate this point would be in the behavior of young children.

A study with kindergarten children (Kendler and Kendler, 1959) showed that these children as a group executed a reversal and nonreversal shift at approximately the same rate. One might conclude that the point in human development was discovered which was psychologically halfway between the white rat and the college student, since the kindergarten children were neither responding in

a single unit nor mediational manner, but instead in some compromise fashion. Another possibility is that the children had reached a transitional stage in development, in which the task to which they were subjected led some to function on a single unit basis, and others to operate with a mediational mechanism. If half of the subjects respond in each way, the total results would have revealed no difference between the two kinds of shifts.

The second alternative seems to fit the data. When the kindergarten children were divided into fast and slow learners on the basis of their performance in the first problem (training discrimination), slow learners performed during the second problem (test discrimination) according to the single unit theory; like rats they found a nonreversal shift easier. Fast learners, on the other hand, performed in accordance with the mediational theory; like college students, they found a reversal shift easier. These results were interpreted .as demonstrating that these kindergartners, taken as a group, were in the process of developing mediating responses relevant to this task, and that some were further along than others.

If this interpretation be correct, then it would follow that for a group of younger (i.e., preschool) children a still smaller proportion should develop appropriate mediating responses. It would be expected that such a group, taken as a whole, would show clear-cut evidence of the superiority of a nonreversal over a reversal shift. An experiment (Kendler, Kendler, and Wells, 1960) designed to test this hypothesis produced results consistent with this prediction; like rats, nursery school children found a nonreversal shift to be easier than a reversal shift.

---

size or *large* or both. The effective stimulus which is controlling the organism's response must be determined by experimentation. The point made here is that the general implications of the single unit and mediational theories, as discussed in this paper, would be the same for a number of different effective stimuli.

3 There are two possible ways of analyzing the superiority of a reversal shift over a nonreversal shift within an S-R mediational framework. One is to simply count the number of new associations that have to be formed. As Figure 4 indicates only one new association has to be formed in a reversal shift while two have to be formed for a nonreversal shift. Another possibility is that a mediating response is more difficult to extinguish than is an overt response. For the present the formulation can remain open-ended until information relevant to these two alternatives is gathered.

In a very recent study the experimental procedure was modified so that after learning the initial discrimination, the children of 3, 4, 6, 8, and 10 years of age who served as subjects had a choice of either responding in a reversal or a nonreversal manner. Under such circumstances, it would be expected that the proportion of children who respond in a reversal manner would increase with age. Figure 5 shows that the percentage of children who chose a reversal shift rose gradually from 37.5 at 3 to 62.5 at 10.

Generalizing from all of these results, it would seem that in their early development, children tend to respond in a manner consistent with a single unit S-R theory. With age, they develop a tendency to respond in a mediational manner. The last study cited suggests that it is, or will soon be, possible to ascertain the lawful relationship governing the course of this development.

The point of these experiments is not to classify children into one of two categories: rat-like or human-like. Their aim is to lay the groundwork for experiments designed to investigate the mediational process itself. If one wants to investigate mediational processes, does it not seem sensible to scrutinize them at the time when they are developing? Answering this question in the affirmative, it was decided to investigate the relationship between the hypothesized mediational processes and verbal behavior—a relationship everybody assumes to be intimate and important.

Particularly relevant to this attempt to coordinate verbalization with mediation were observations that during the course of the experiments just described, it was not uncommon for children to verbalize spontaneously the correct solution while simultaneously making an incorrect choice. A few children did this for many consecutive trials. This observation is relevant to the concept of vertical processes. Two chains of habits are occurring simultaneously. One has to do with verbal response; the other with the overt choice. For these children the two chains are parallel, that is, they do not interact.

Luria (1957), the Russian psychologist, made somewhat similar observations in his research with children. He explains this sort of phenomenon in the following way:

In the early stages of child development, speech is only a means of communication with adults and other children. . . . Subsequently it becomes also a means whereby he organizes his own experience and regulates his own actions. So the child's activity is mediated through words (p. 116).

These observations and their interpretations of noninteracting parallel processes point to the complex interrelationships existing between verbal behavior on the one hand and problem solving on the other. If nothing else, they destroy the illusion that it is reasonable to describe an organism as verbal or nonverbal without considering the problem with which it is confronted. The terms verbal and nonverbal become meaningful—and fruitful—when related to specific problem-solving tasks.

It would seem fruitful to investigate the cue function of words for children of two age levels. One possibility is that age influences problem solving only in so far as it leads to the acquisition of words. If younger children, say four years of age, could acquire the same words as seven-year-olds, they would solve a simple concept-learning problem the same way. The other possibility is that the acquisition of the verbal label by itself is not sufficient; the word must be integrated with other behavioral chains to influence problem-solving behavior. And for this to happen some developmental changes must first take place.

In order to test these two alternatives, children of four and seven years of age were presented with another variation of the reversal shift problem as shown in Figure 6. They initially learned a simple discrimination between a pair of stimuli that varied simultaneously in size and brightness. In the illustration provided in Figure 6, the large black square is correct. While they were learning, the children were required to verbalize aloud the

FIGURE 5 *Percentage of children responding in a reversal shift manner as a function of age*

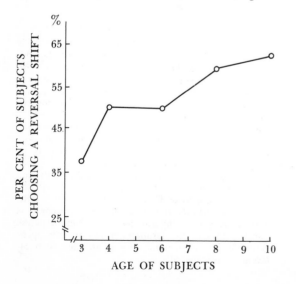

FIGURE 6   *The experimental procedure used to study the influence of verbal habits on a reversal shift*

FIGURE 6   *The experimental procedure used to study the influence of verbal habits on a reversal shift*

FIRST
DISCRIMINATION

SECOND
DISCRIMINATION

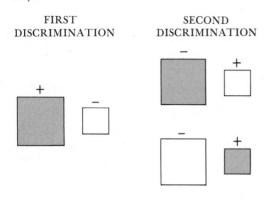

stimuli to which they were responding. One-third learned to say "large" (or "small" as the case may be) by the simple device of instructing them to tell the experimenter which was correct, the large or the small one. Another third learned to say "black" (or "white") in a corresponding way. The remaining third was not required to say anything. After learning the discrimination, all subjects were presented with a reversal shift. In the example depicted in Figure 6, the shift is to small regardless of color. Thus, the group that initially described the correct stimulus as "large" had verbalized the relevant dimension. The verbal response of "black" was irrelevant to this reversal shift.

Figure 7 shows the results of the three experi-

FIGURE 7   *The effect of verbalizations on a reversal shift for 4- and 7-year-old children*

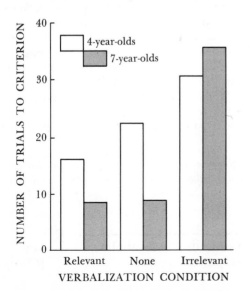

mental groups for the two age levels. If developmental processes affect the utilization of verbal responses in problem solving, then it would be expected that the three verbalization conditions (which produced a significant main effect) would influence the behavior of the two age groups differently. These results suggest, but not quite at a significant level, that there is an interaction effect. Figure 7 shows that the younger children profited by making the kind of verbal response appropriate to a reversal shift, while they were hindered by learning inappropriate verbal responses. With no verbalization the seven-year-old children who presumably were responding largely in a mediational manner, accomplished a reversal shift much more rapidly than their younger counterparts. But unlike the four-year-olds, they did not profit from being trained to make the relevant responses. At seven years of age they are capable of making the response themselves and outside help appears to be of little use. In contrast, the influence of irrelevant verbalizations is marked. The performance of the seven-year-olds was even poorer than that of the four-year-olds, suggesting that the interfering effects of being given an inappropriate mediated response are greater when one is capable of spontaneously generating the correct one (seven-year-olds) than when one is not (four-year-olds).

How are these data to be explained? Attributing differences to developmental factors is not sufficient. It is necessary to represent developmental differences in terms of the concepts of the behavior model that is being used. That is, if a verbal label for a young child does not possess the same cue function as it does for an older child, then it becomes necessary to specify how and why this comes about. To some extent this has been done by emphasizing the transition from a single unit to a mediational system, as well as suggesting that with age an increase occurs in interaction among chains of different vertical levels. But obviously this analysis of the developmental process demands further theoretical and empirical development.

These studies are intimately related to the oft-reported finding that many species of subhuman animals are able to make a fairly rapid reversal shift *if* they receive a previous series of such shifts. Rats (Buytendijk, 1930; Krechevsky, 1932) show a marked improvement in executing successive reversals. They finally reach a point (Dufort, Guttman, and Kimble, 1954), in a T-maze, where they learn to go to a new rewarded goal after making only one error. Even more dramatic are the rapid discrimination reversals exhibited by Harlow's (1949) monkeys. But fish (Wodinsky and Bitterman, 1957) exhibit only a slight improvement in successive reversals, while isopods (invertebrates) show no improvement (Thompson, 1957).

Because of the necessity to use somewhat different experimental procedures for different species, it is difficult to draw an unqualified conclusion about the ability of different species to transfer what has been learned from previous reversal shifts to a new one. But the suggestion is strong that as you ascend the evolutionary scale, organisms acquire a greater capacity to generate cues that enable them to make rapid reversal shifts. This behavior, according to our analysis, borders on the language responses of humans. The main difference is that our human subjects, except those of a very young age, exhibit rapid reversals without any previous reversal training. Whereas the human automatically seems to generate a mediated response that provides the basis for his rapid reversal, the animal subject must gradually acquire an ability to respond appropriately to some response-produced cue resulting from nonreinforcement of a previously correct response.

Up to now, the reversal and nonreversal technique has been used to investigate mediational and developmental variables. It has proved sufficiently flexible to be used in a study (Kendler, Glucksberg, and Keston, 1961) which was designed to lengthen a problem-solving chain so that the interaction between various segments could be observed. In this study a perceptual orienting S-R unit was added on to the mediational chain already described. Figure 8 illustrates in an oversimplified manner the behavioral sequence involved in this study in which subjects had to learn to press the correct button when two physically discrete and spatially separate stimulus patterns were projected on a screen at such a rapid rate that only one could be perceived on any trial. During the learning of each of two successive concepts (involving either a reversal or nonreversal shift), the subject had to pay attention to the relevant stimulus pattern while ignoring the irrelevant one. Thus, in order to make the correct overt response consistently, a subject initially had to make

the appropriate orienting response in order to perceive the relevant stimulus pattern to which he had to make the correct mediational response which served as the cue for the key-pressing act.

An experimental design was used in which, at the time of the shift from the first to the second concept, one group had already learned the appropriate orienting response as well as the appropriate mediating act. They needed only to learn a new terminal key-pressing response. The shift, for them, was easy to make. In contrast, the behavior of three other experimental groups was significantly worse. One group had to learn a new orienting response, e.g., look to the left instead of the right. Another group had to learn a new mediated response (i.e., they were required to make a nonreversal shift). The last group had to acquire both a new orienting and mediated response. The fact that the groups which were missing one or both of the necessary behavior units (orienting and mediated responses) did not differ significantly among themselves, as well as being much poorer than the group that had both, highlights the problem of synchronizing the S-R units in a behavioral chain. The advantage in this study of having one appropriate unit without the other is at best negligible. The reason for this is that reinforcement is only achieved consistently when both the appropriate orienting and mediating responses are operating. This particular study points to the need for discovering laws associated with the strengthening and weakening of independent S-R units in a problem-solving chain, as well as the principles governing their synchronization.

This study also highlighted a very basic problem in all of these reversal studies. This problem has to do with the very first correct response following the reversal shift. After discovering that the previous mode of responding is erroneous, what makes the subject change his response, i.e., push the button that was previously wrong? Introspective reports fail to provide any clear-cut answer and even if they did they would be in need of explaining (Kendler, 1961).

One hypothesis is that the selection of the new

FIGURE 8 *The hypothesized behavioral chain operating at the time the subject was being shifted to the second concept (Capital letters refer to directly observable stimulus and response events, while small letters refer to those that are inferred.)*

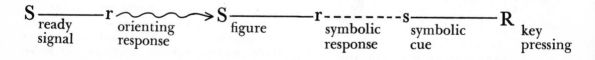

S ——————— r ⟶ S ——————— r ‑ ‑ ‑ ‑ ‑ ‑ s ——————— R
ready   orienting   figure   symbolic   symbolic   key
signal   response   response   cue   pressing

correct response is due to the operation of a behavioral chain in addition to the one described in Figure 8. The first nonreinforcement in a reversal shift sets off a chain, the consequence of which is to select the response other than the one that was previously correct. This may result from a number of different reasons (e.g., logical considerations, forgetting, etc.). The important point, however, is that the new key-sorting response occurs contiguously with the implicit mediational response appropriate to a reversal shift. As a result, a new association is formed between the old implicit cue and the new key-pressing response.

In essence, what is being stated is that adult subjects, when making or deciding to make the first correct postshift response, do not adopt the *principle* underlying a reversal shift. Instead, it is assumed processes are operating which encourage the selection of the correct response while an implicit cue appropriate to a reversal shift is operating. This sort of an analysis was described previously (Kendler and Mayzner, 1956) as

sort of a James-Lange theory of problem solving . . . one makes the overt correct . . . response and if the appropriate symbolic cue is present, then problem solution will occur (pp. 247–248).

Guthrie (1959) says the same thing more neatly: *"What is being noticed becomes a signal for what is being done"* (p. 186).

Again the authors would like to guard against giving the impression of oversimplifying a terribly complex problem. They do not believe the contiguous occurrence of an implicit cue from one chain with the correct overt response from another tells the whole story. This new association in order to persist must be reinforced and in some manner "fit into" the subject's ongoing behavioral chains.

The emphasis on this vertical connection between a cue and a response from different chains is related in a distant way to Hebb's (1958) stressing the role of "chance" in problem solving:

There are few scientists who have not had the experience of setting out to solve problem A and ending up. instead with the solution to B. . . . This is serendipity, the art of finding one thing while looking for another (p. 215).

According to the present analysis, serendipity results from the adventitious and contiguous occurrence of a cue and a response which are themselves segments from different behavior chains. Theoretically it should be possible to demonstrate this point experimentally by training subjects to respond simultaneously to two separate tasks. A problem then would have to be presented that requires for its solution the combination of a stimulus from one chain with the response from the other. In such an experimental situation, controlling the time relationship between the two should have an important effect on problem solving. Presumably contiguity between the two should provide the most optimal conditions for problem solving (Underwood, 1952). The development of this kind of experimental procedure should allow for parametric studies of the basic variables of the phenomenon which has commonly been called "insight," as well as throw light upon issues raised by others (e.g., Cofer, 1957; Maltzman, 1955; Saugstad, 1957).

The pretheoretical model that guides the present research has many more facets that can be exploited. Only one will now be mentioned. Glucksberg (1962), for example, extended neobehavioristic drive theory (Spence, 1956) to problem solving. He used a functional-fixedness problem (Adamson, 1952, Duncker, 1945) in which the correct response in the habit hierarchy could either be made to be low or high. If the correct habit was low, it would be expected that a strong drive would retard problem solving because it would retard the extinction of the dominant incorrect response (Kendler and Lachman, 1958; Perin, 1942). Since drive energizes behavior, a high drive should facilitate problem-solving performance when the correct habit is dominant. The findings were consistent with this analysis.

Because functional-fixedness problems are often represented in perceptual terms, Glucksberg was interested in seeing whether the same drive model could be applied to a simple perceptual recognition problem in which subjects were instructed to identify tachistoscopically presented words as rapidly as possible. The results were similar to those reported for the functional-fixedness study: when the correct response was dominant, an increase in drive improved performance, i.e., the visual duration threshold was lowered. In contrast, increasing drive when the correct response was low in the hierarchy raised the threshold.

There is obviously still much more work, both empirical and theoretical, needed to develop the model that has been described. At this point it may be appropriate to summarize the major points of this paper.

There is not just one way to investigate problem solving. The researcher who is interested in problem solving has several different pretheoretical models from which to choose. This paper reported the results of a research program based on an S-R model in which the importance of horizontal and vertical processes were emphasized. Horizontal processes refer to the linking of successive S-R units into a behavioral chain, while vertical processes refer to the assumption that independent chains occur simultaneously. A series of experiments was reported, the implications of which supported postulating a mediational mechanism within a behavioral chain. By comparing the behavior of human subjects of different ages, as well as relating their results to lower animals, it was possible to infer that as a child matures he makes a transition from responding on the basis of a single unit S-R mechanism to a mediational one. Additional data were cited that suggest the full impact of verbal behavior on problem solving depends on developmental processes that encourage interaction between chains at different vertical levels. It was also suggested that problem solving begins in a simple concept-learning task when a correct overt response from one behavioral chain occurs contiguously and adventitiously with the appropriate implicit cue from another chain. The paper was concluded by citing findings that suggested the neobehavioristic drive theory which assumes that the effect of different levels of drive depends on the position of the correct response in the habit hierarchy is applicable to a functional-fixedness problem as well as a perceptual-recognition task.

If nothing else, it is hoped that the present paper demonstrates that it is possible to investigate problem solving in a systematic fashion. If more psychologists accepted this possibility and were willing to expend their research energies in the field of problem solving, progress in this area would be greater than it is today.

REFERENCES

Adamson, R. E. Functional-fixedness as related to problem solving. *Journal of Experimental Psychology*, 1952, **44**, 288–291.

Buss, A. H. Rigidity as a function of reversal and nonreversal shifts in the learning of successive discrimination. *Journal of Experimental Psychology*, 1953, **45**, 75–81.

Buss, A. H. Reversal and nonreversal shifts in concept formation with partial reinforcement eliminated. *Journal of Experimental Psychology*, 1956, **52**, 162–166.

Buytendijk, F. J. J. Über das Umlernen. *Archives Néerlandaises de Physiologie*, 1930, **15**, 283–310.

Cofer, C. N. Reasoning as an associative process: III. The role of verbal responses in problem solving. *Journal of General Psychology*, 1957, **57**, 55–58.

Dufort, R. H., Guttman, N., & Kimble, G. A. One-trial discrimination reversal in the white rat. *Journal of Comparative and Physiological Psychology*, 1954, **47**, 248–249.

Duncan, C. P. Recent research on human problem solving. *Psychological Bulletin*, 1959, **56**, 397–429.

Duncker, K. On problem solving. *Psychological Monographs*, 1945, **58**(5, Whole No. 270).

Glucksberg, S. The influence of strength of drive on functional fixedness and perceptual recognition. *Journal of Experimental Psychology*, 1962, **63**(1), 36–41.

Guthrie, E. R. *The psychology of learning.* (Rev. ed.) New York: Harper & Row, 1952.

Guthrie, E. R. Association by contiguity. In S. Koch (Ed.), *Psychology: A study of a science.* Vol. 2. New York: McGraw-Hill, 1959. Pp. 158–195.

Harlow, H. F. The formation of learning sets. *Psychological Review*, 1949, **56**, 51–65.

Harrow, M., & Friedman, G. B. Comparing reversal and nonreversal shifts in concept formation with partial reinforcement controlled. *Journal of Experimental Psychology*, 1958, **55**, 592–597.

Hebb, D. O. *A textbook of psychology.* Philadelphia: Saunders, 1958.

Hull, C. L. Knowledge and purpose as habit mechanisms. *Psychological Review*, 1930, **37**, 511–525.

Hull, C. L. *A behavior system.* New Haven: Yale University Press, 1952.

Kelleher, R. T. Discrimination learning as a function of reversal and nonreversal shifts. *Journal of Experimental Psychology*, 1956, **51**, 379–384.

Kendler, H. H. Problems in problem-solving research. In *Current trends in psychological theory: A bicentennial program.* Pittsburgh: University of Pittsburgh Press, 1961.

Kendler, H. H., & D'Amato, M. F. A comparison of reversal shifts and nonreversal shifts in human concept formation behavior. *Journal of Experimental Psychology*, 1955, **49**, 165–174.

Kendler, H. H., Glucksberg, S., & Keston, R. Perception and mediation in concept learning. *Journal of Experimental Psychology*, 1961, **61**, 186–191.

Kendler, H. H., & Kendler, T. S. Inferential behavior in preschool children. *Journal of Experimental Psychology*, 1956, **51**, 311–314.

Kendler, H. H., Kendler, T. S., Pliskoff, S. S., & D'Amato, M. F. Inferential behavior in children: I. The influence of reinforcement and incentive motivation. *Journal of Experimental Psychology*, 1958, **55**, 207–212.

Kendler, H. H., & Lachman, R. Habit reversal as a function of schedule of reinforcement and drive strength. *Journal of Experimental Psychology*, 1958, **55**, 584–591.

Kendler, H. H., & Mayzner, M. S., Jr. Reversal and nonreversal shifts in card-sorting tests with two or four sorting categories. *Journal of Experimental Psychology*, 1956, **51**, 244–248.

Kendler, H. H., & Vineberg, R. The acquisition of compound concepts as a function of previous training. *Journal of Experimental Psychology*, 1954, **48**, 252–258.

Kendler, T. S., & Kendler, H. H. Reversal and nonreversal shifts in kindergarten children. *Journal of Experimental Psychology*, 1959, **58**, 56–60.

Kendler, T. S. & Kendler, H. H. Inferential behavior in

children: II. The influence of order of presentation. *Journal of Experimental Psychology*, 1961, **61**, 442–448.

Kendler, T. S., Kendler, H. H., & Wells, D. Reversal and nonreversal shifts in nursery school children. *Journal of Comparative and Physiological Psychology*, 1960, **53**, 83–88.

Koch, S. *Psychology: A study of a science*. Vol. 1. *Sensory, perceptual, and physiological formulations*. New York: McGraw-Hill, 1959.

Kohler, W. *The mentality of apes*. New York: Harcourt, Brace & World, 1925.

Krechevsky, I. Antagonistic visual discrimination habits in the white rat. *Journal of Comparative Psychology*, 1932, **14**, 263–277.

Lachman, R. The model in theory construction. *Psychological Review*, 1960, **67**, 113–129.

Luria, A. R. The role of language in the formation of temporary connections. In B. Simon (Ed.), *Psychology in the Soviet Union*. Stanford: Stanford University Press, 1957. Pp. 115–129.

Maier, N. R. F. Reasoning in humans: I. On direction. *Journal of Comparative Psychology*, 1930, **10**, 115–143.

Maltzman, I. Thinking: From a behavioristic point of view. *Psychological Review*, 1955, **62**, 275–286.

Meyer, M. F. *The fundamental laws of human behavior*. Boston: Gorham, 1911.

Perin, C. T. Behavior potentiality as a joint function of the amount of training and the degree of hunger at the time of extinction. *Journal of Experimental Psychology*, 1942, **30**, 93–113.

Saugstad, P. An analysis of Maier's pendulum problem. *Journal of Experimental Psychology*, 1957, **54**, 168–179.

Skinner, B. F. *Science and human behavior*. New York: Macmillan, 1953.

Spence, K. W. The nature of discrimination learning in animals. *Psychological Review*, 1936, **43**, 427–449.

Spence, K. W. *Behavior theory and conditioning*. New Haven: Yale University Press, 1956.

Thompson, R. Successive reversal of a position habit in an invertebrate. *Science*, 1957, **126**, 163–164.

Toulmin, S. *The philosophy of science*. London: Hutchinson University Library, 1953.

Underwood, B. J. An orientation for research on thinking. *Psychological Review*, 1952, **59**, 209–220.

Watson, J. B. Psychology as the behaviorist sees it. *Psychological Review*, 1913, **20**, 158–177.

Wodinsky, J., & Bitterman, M. E. Discrimination-reversal in the fish. *American Journal of Psychology*, 1957, **70**, 569–575.

37

The Course of Cognitive Growth

Jerome S. Bruner

If psychologists and interested persons working in related areas are to begin to understand the intricate interplay between the hereditary material with which each person is born and the experiences that he goes through in growing up, they must know how to ask the proper questions. Only then can they attempt to resolve those questions in some ordered fashion. In this article Bruner is asking what kinds of systems are used when a growing child constructs his personal idea of the world, and then in what kinds of ways these systems are extended to encompass larger and larger amounts of information for the solution of problems.

Once the proper questions have been asked, the procedure for obtaining answers is broadly described as "scientific investigation"; it involves both library research to find what others have suggested in the way of answers, and laboratory research to attempt to find out how the important variables act in controlled situations. In this paper Bruner shows the way in which he has attempted to answer the questions which he poses in the first few paragraphs.

I shall take the view in what follows that the development of human intellectual functioning from infancy to such perfection as it may reach is shaped by a series of technological advances in the use of mind. Growth depends upon the mastery of

From American Psychologist, *Vol. 19 (1964), 1–15. Copyright 1964 by the American Psychological Association, and reproduced by permission. The assistance of R. R. Olver and Mrs. Blythe Clinchy in the preparation of this paper is gratefully acknowledged.*

techniques and cannot be understood without reference to such mastery. These techniques are not, in the main, inventions of the individuals who are "growing up"; they are, rather, skills transmitted with varying efficiency and success by the culture—language being a prime example. Cognitive growth, then, is in a major way from the outside in as well as from the inside out.

Two matters will concern us. The first has to do with the techniques or technologies that aid growing human beings to represent in a manageable way the recurrent features of the complex environments in which they live. It is fruitful, I think, to distinguish three systems of processing information by which human beings construct models of their world: through action, through imagery, and through language. A second concern is with integration, the means whereby acts are organized into higher order ensembles, making possible the use of larger and larger units of information for the solution of particular problems.

Let me first elucidate these two theoretical matters, and then turn to an examination of the research upon which they are based, much of it from the Center for Cognitive Studies at Harvard.

On the occasion of the One Hundredth Anniversary of the publication of Darwin's *The Origin of Species*, Washburn and Howell (1960) presented a paper at the Chicago Centennial celebration containing the following passage:

It would now appear . . . that the large size of the brain of certain hominids was a relatively late development and that the brain evolved due to new selection pressures after bipedalism and consequent upon the use of tools. The tool-using, ground-living, hunting way of life created the large human brain rather than a large-brained man discovering certain new ways of life. [We] believe this conclusion is the most important result of the recent fossil hominid discoveries and is one which carries far-reaching implications for the interpretation of human behavior and its origins. . . . The important point is that size of brain, insofar as it can be measured by cranial capacity, has increased some threefold subsequent to the use and manufacture of implements. . . . The uniqueness of modern man is seen as the result of a technical-social life which tripled the size of the brain, reduced the face, and modified many other structures of the body (p. 49 f.).

This implies that the principal change in man over a long period of years—perhaps 500,000 thousand—has been alloplastic rather than autoplastic. That is to say, he has changed by linking himself with new, external implementation systems rather than by any conspicuous change in morphology. . . . The implement systems seem to have been of three general kinds—*amplifiers of human motor capacities* ranging from the cutting tool through the lever and wheel to the wide variety of modern devices; *amplifiers of sensory capacities* that include primitive devices such as smoke signaling and modern ones such as magnification and radar sensing, but also likely to include such "software" as those conventionalized perceptual shortcuts that can be applied to the redundant sensory environment; and finally *amplifiers of human ratiocinative capacities* of infinite variety ranging from language systems to myth and theory and explanation. All of these forms of amplification are in major or minor degree conventionalized and transmitted by the culture, the last of them probably the most since ratiocinative amplifiers involve symbol systems governed by rules that must, for effective use, be shared.

Any implement system, to be effective, must produce an appropriate internal counterpart, an appropriate skill necessary for organizing sensorimotor acts, for organizing percepts, and for organizing our thoughts in a way that matches them to the requirements of implement systems. These internal skills, represented genetically as capacities, are slowly selected in evolution. In the deepest sense, then, man can be described as a species that has become specialized by the use of technological implements. His selection and survival have depended upon a morphology and set of capacities that could be linked with the alloplastic devices that have made his later evolution possible. We move, perceive, and think in a fashion that depends upon techniques rather than upon wired-in arrangements in our nervous system.

Where representation of the environment is concerned, it too depends upon techniques that are learned—and these are precisely the techniques that serve to amplify our motor acts, our perceptions, and our ratiocinative activities. We know and respond to recurrent regularities in our environment by skilled and patterned acts, by conventionalized spatioqualitative imagery and selective perceptual organization, and through linguistic encoding which, as so many writers have remarked, places a selective lattice between us and the physical environment. In short, the capacities that have been shaped by our evolution as tool-users are the ones that we rely upon in the primary task of representation—the nature of which we shall consider in more detail directly.

As for integration, it is a truism that there are very few single or simple adults acts that cannot be performed by a young child. In short, any more highly skilled activity can be decomposed into simpler components, each of which can be carried out by a less skilled operator. What higher skills require is that the component operations be combined. Maturation consists of an orchestration of these components into an integrated sequence. The "distractability," so-called, of much early behavior may reflect each act's lack of imbeddedness. . . . These integrated plans, in turn, reflect the routines and subroutines that one learns in the course of mastering the patterned nature of a social environment. So that integration, too, depends upon patterns that come from the outside in. . . .

If we are to benefit from contact with recurrent regularities in the environment, we must represent them in some manner. To dismiss this problem as "mere memory" is to misunderstand it. For the most important thing about memory is not storage of past experience, but rather the retrieval of what is relevant in some usable form. This depends upon how past experience is coded and processed so that it may indeed be relevant and usable in the present when needed. The end product of such a system of coding and processing is what we may speak of as a representation.

I shall call the three modes of representation mentioned earlier enactive representation, iconic representation, and symbolic representation. Their appearance in the life of the child is in that order, each depending upon the previous one for its development, yet all of them remaining more or less intact throughout life—barring such early accidents as blindness or deafness or cortical injury. By enactive representation I mean a mode of representing past events through appropriate motor response. We cannot, for example, give an adequate description of familiar sidewalks or floors over which we habitually walk, nor do we have much of an image of what they are like. Yet we get about them without tripping or even looking much. Such segments of our environment—bicycle riding, tying knots, aspects of driving—get represented in our muscles, so to speak. Iconic representation summarizes events by the selective organization of percepts and of images, by the spatial, temporal, and qualitative structures of the perceptual field and their transformed images. Images "stand for" perceptual events in the close but conventionally selective way that a picture stands for the object pictured. Finally, a symbol system represents things by design features that include remoteness and arbitrariness. A word neither points directly to its referent here and now, nor does it resemble it as a picture. The lexeme "Philadelphia" looks no more like the city so designated than does a nonsense syllable. The other property of language that is crucial is its productiveness in combination, far beyond what can be done with images or acts. "Philadelphia is a lavendar sachet in Grandmother's linen closet," or $(x + 2)^2 = x^2 + 4x + 4 = x(x + 4) + 4$.

An example or two of enactive representation underlines its importance in infancy and in disturbed functioning, while illustrating its limitations. Piaget (1954) provides us with an observation from the closing weeks of the first year of life. The child is playing with a rattle in his crib. The rattle drops over the side. The child moves his clenched hand before his face, opens it, looks for the rattle. Not finding it there, he moves his hand, closed again, back to the edge of the crib, shakes it with movements like those he uses in shaking the rattle. Thereupon he moves his closed hand back toward his face, opens it, and looks. Again no rattle; and so he tries again. In several months, the child has benefited from experience to the degree that the rattle and action become separated. Whereas earlier he would not show signs of missing the rattle when it was removed unless he had begun reaching for it, now he cries and searches when the rattle is presented for a moment and hidden by a cover. He no longer repeats a movement to restore the rattle. In place of representation by action alone—where "existence" is defined by the compass of present action—it is now defined by an image that persists autonomously.

A second example is provided by the results of injury to the occipital and temporal cortex in man. A patient is presented with a hard-boiled egg intact in its shell, and asked what it is. Holding it in his hand, he is embarrassed, for he cannot name it. He makes a motion as if to throw it and halts himself. Then he brings it to his mouth as if to bite it and stops before he gets there. He brings it to his ear and shakes it gently. He is puzzled. The experimenter takes the egg from him and cracks it on the table, handing it back. The patient then begins to peel the egg and announces what it is. He cannot identify objects without reference to the action he directs toward them.

The disadvantages of such a system are illustrated by Emerson's (1931) experiment in which children are told to place a ring on a board with seven rows and six columns of pegs, copying the position of a ring put on an identical board by the experimenter. Children ranging from three to twelve were examined in this experiment. . . .

The child's board could be placed in various positions relative to the experimenter's: right next to it, 90 degrees rotated away from it, 180 degrees rotated, placed face to face with it so that the child has to turn full around to make his placement, etc. The older the child, the better his performance. But the younger children could do about as well as the oldest so long as they did not have to change their own position vis-à-vis the experimenter's board in order to make a match on their own board. The more they had to turn, the more difficult the task. They were clearly depending upon their bodily orientation toward the experimenter's board to guide them. When this orientation is disturbed by having to turn, they lose the position on the board. Older children succeed even when they must turn, either by the use of imagery that is invariant across bodily displacements, or, later, by specifying column and row of the experimenter's ring and carrying the symbolized self-instruction back to their own board. It is a limited world, the world of enactive representation.

We know little about the conditions necessary for the growth of imagery and iconic representation, or to what extent parental or environmental intervention affects it during the earliest years. In ordinary adult learning a certain amount of motoric skill and practice seems to be a necessary precondition for the development of a simultaneous image to represent the sequence of acts involved. If an adult subject is made to choose a path through a complex bank of toggle switches, he does not form an image of the path, according to Mandler (1962), until he has mastered and overpracticed the task by successive manipulation. Then, finally, he reports that an image of the path has developed and that he is now using it rather than groping his way through.

Our main concern in what follows is not with the growth of iconic representation, but with the transition from it to symbolic representation. For it is in the development of symbolic representation that one finds, perhaps, the greatest thicket of psychological problems. The puzzle begins when the child first achieves the use of productive grammar, usually late in the second year of life. Toward the end of the second year, the child is master of the single-word, agrammatical utterance, the so-called holophrase. In the months following, there occurs a profound change in the use of language. Two classes of words appear—a pivot class and an open class—and the child launches forth on his career in combinatorial talking and, perhaps, thinking. Whereas before, lexemes like *allgone* and *mummy* and *sticky* and *bye-bye* were used

singly, now, for example, *allgone* becomes a pivot word and is used in combination. Mother washes jam off the child's hands; he says *allgone sticky*. In the next days, if his speech is carefully followed (Braine, 1963), it will be apparent that he is trying out the limits of the pivot combinations, and one will even find constructions that have an extraordinary capacity for representing complex sequences—like *allgone bye-bye* after a visitor has departed. A recent and ingenious observation by Weir (1962) on her 2½-year-old son, recording his speech musings after he was in bed with lights out, indicates that at this stage there is a great deal of metalinguistic combinatorial play with words in which the child is exploring the limits of grammatical productiveness.

In effect, language provides a means, not only for representing experience, but also for transforming it. As Chomsky (1957) and Miller (1962) have both made clear in the last few years, the transformational rules of grammar provide a syntactic means of reworking the "realities" one has encountered. Not only, if you will, did the dog bite the man, but the man was bitten by the dog, and perhaps the man was not bitten by the dog or was the man not bitten by the dog. The range of reworking that is made possible even by the three transformations of the passive, the negative, and the query is very striking indeed. Or the ordering device whereby the comparative mode makes it possible to connect what is *heavy* and what is *light* into the ordinal array of *heavy* and *less heavy* is again striking. Or, to take a final example, there is the discrimination that is made possible by the growth of attribute language such that the global dimension *big* and *little* can now be decomposed into *tall* and *short* on the one hand and *fat* and *skinny* on the other.

Once the child has succeeded in internalizing language as a cognitive instrument, it becomes possible for him to represent and systematically transform the regularities of experience with far greater flexibility and power than before. Interestingly enough, it is the recent Russian literature, particularly Vygotsky's (1962) book on language and thought, and the work of his disciple, Luria (1961), and his students that has highlighted these phenomena by calling attention to the so-called second-signal system which replaces classical conditioning with an internalized linguistic system for shaping and transforming experience itself.

If all these matters were not of such complexity and human import, I would apologize for taking so much time in speculation. We turn now to some new experiments designed to shed some light on the nature of representation and particularly upon the transition from its iconic to its symbolic form.

Let me begin with an experiment by Bruner and Kenney (1966) on the manner in which children between five and seven handle a double classification matrix. The materials of the experiment are nine plastic glasses, arranged so that they vary in 3 degrees of diameter and 3 degrees of height. They are set before the child initially on a 3×3 grid marked on a large piece of cardboard. To acquaint the child with the matrix, we first remove one, then two, and then three glasses from the matrix, asking the child to replace them. We also ask the children to describe how the glasses in the columns and rows are alike and how they differ. Then the glasses are scrambled and we ask the child to make something like what was there before by placing the glasses on the same grid that was used when the task was introduced. Now we scramble the glasses once more, but this time we place the glass that was formerly in the southwest corner of the grid in the southeast corner (it is the shortest, thinnest glass) and ask the child if he can make something like what was there before, leaving the one glass where we have just put it. That is the experiment.

The results can be quickly told. To begin with, there is no difference between ages 5, 6, and 7 either in terms of ability to replace glasses taken from the matrix or in building a matrix once it has been scrambled (but without the transposed glass). Virtually all the children succeed. Interestingly enough, *all* the children rebuild the matrix to match the original, almost as if they were copying what was there before. The only difference is that the older children are quicker.

Now compare the performance of the three ages in constructing the matrix with a single member transposed. Most of the seven-year-olds succeed in the transposed task, but hardly any of the youngest children. The youngest children seem to be dominated by an image of the original matrix. They try to put the transposed glass "back where it belongs," to rotate the cardboard so that "it will be like before," and sometimes they will start placing a few glasses neighboring the transposed glass correctly only to revert to the original arrangement. In several instances, five- or six-year-olds will simply try to reconstitute the old matrix, building right over the transposed glass. The seven-year-old, on the other hand, is more likely to pause, to treat the transposition as a problem, to talk to himself about "where this should go."

The relation of place and size is for him a problem that requires reckoning, not simply copying.

Now consider the language children use for describing the dimensions of the matrix. Recall that the children were asked how glasses in a row and in a column were alike and how they differed. Children answered in three distinctive linguistic modes. One was *dimensional*, singling out two ends of an attribute—for example, "That one is higher, and that one is shorter." A second was *global* in nature. Of glasses differing only in height the child says, "That one is bigger and that one is little." The same words could be used equally well for diameter or for nearly any other magnitude. Finally, there was *confounded* usage: "That one is tall and that one is little," where a dimensional term is used for one end of the continuum and a global term for the other. The children who used confounded descriptions had the most difficulty with the transposed matrix. Lumping all ages together, the children who use confounded descriptions were twice as likely to fail on the transposition task as those who used either dimensional or global terms. *But the language the children used had no relation whatsoever to their performance in reproducing the first untransposed matrix.* Inhelder and Sinclair[1] in a recent communication also report that confounded language of this kind is associated with failure on conservation tasks in children of the same age, a subject to which we shall turn shortly.

The findings of this experiment suggest two things. First, that children who use iconic representation are more highly sensitized to the spatial-qualitative organization of experience and less to the ordering principles governing such organization. They can recognize and reproduce, but cannot produce new structures based on rule. And second, there is a suspicion that the language they bring to bear on the task is insufficient as a tool for ordering. If these notions are correct, then certain things should follow. For one thing, *improvement* in language should aid this type of problem solving. This remains to be investigated. But it is also reasonable to suppose that *activation* of language habits that the child has already mastered might improve performance as well—a hypothesis already suggested by the findings of Luria's students. Now, activation can be achieved by two means: One is by having the child "say" the description of something before him that he

---

1 Bärbel Inhelder and Mimi Sinclair, personal communication (1963).

must deal with symbolically. The other is to take advantage of the remoteness of reference that is a feature of language and have the child "say" his description in the absence of the things to be described. In this way, there would be less likelihood of a perceptual-iconic representation becoming dominant and inhibiting the operation of symbolic processes. An experiment by Françoise Frank (1966) illustrates this later approach—the effects of saying before seeing.

Piaget and Inhelder have shown that if children between ages four and seven are presented two identical beakers which they judge equally full of water, they will no longer consider the water equal if the contents of one of the beakers is now poured into a beaker that is either wider or thinner than the original. If the second beaker is thinner, they will say it has more to drink because the water is higher; if the second beaker is wider, they will say it has less because the water is lower. Comparable results can be obtained by pouring the contents of one glass into several smaller beakers. In Geneva terms, the child is not yet able to conserve liquid volume across transformations in its appearance. Consider how this behavior can be altered.

Françoise Frank first did the classic conservation tests to determine which children exhibited conservation and which did not. Her subjects were 4, 5, 6, and 7 years old. She then went on to other procedures, among which was the following. Two standard beakers are partly filled so that the child judges them to contain equal amounts of water. A wider beaker of the same height is introduced and the three beakers are now, except for their tops, hidden by a screen. The experimenter pours from a standard beaker into the wider beaker. The child, without seeing the water, is asked which has more to drink, or do they have the same amount, the standard or the wider beaker. In comparison with the unscreened pretest, there is a striking increase in correct equality judgments. Correct responses jump from 0 per cent to 50 per cent among the 4s, from 20 per cent to 90 per cent among the 5s, and from 50 per cent to 100 per cent among the 6s. With the screen present, most children justify their correct judgment by noting that "It's the same water," or "You only poured it."

Now the screen is removed. All the four-year-olds change their minds. The perceptual display overwhelms them and they decide that the wider beaker has less water. But virtually all of the five-year-olds stick to their judgment, often invoking the difference between appearance and reality—"It looks like more to drink, but it is only the same because it is the same water and it was only

poured from there to there," to quote one typical five-year-old. And all of the 6s and all the 7s stick to their judgment. Now, some minutes later, Frank does a posttest on the children using a tall thin beaker along with the standard ones, and no screen, of course. The 4s are unaffected by their prior experience: None of them is able to grasp the idea of invariant quantity in the new task. With the 5s, instead of 20 per cent showing conservation, as in the pretest, 70 per cent do. With both 6s and 7s, conservation increases from 50 per cent to 90 per cent. I should mention that control groups doing just a pretest and posttest show no significant improvement in performance.

A related experiment of Nair's (1963) explores the arguments children use when they solve a conservation task correctly and when they do not. Her subjects were all five-year-olds. She transferred water from one rectangular clear plastic tank to another that was both longer and wider than the first. Ordinarily, a five-year-old will say there is less water in the second tank. The water is, of course, lower in the second tank. She had a toy duck swimming in the first container, and when the water was poured into the new container, she told the child that "The duck was taking his water with him."

Three kinds of arguments were set forth by the children to support their judgments. One is perceptual—having to do with the height, width, or apparent "bigness" of the water. A second type has to do with action: The duck took the water along, or the water was only poured. A third one, "transformational" argument, invokes the reversibility principle: If you poured the water back into the first container, it would look the same again.[2] Of the children who thought the water was not equal in amount after pouring, 15 per cent used nonperceptual arguments to justify their judgment. Of those who recognized the equality of the water, two-thirds used nonperceptual arguments. It is plain that if a child is to succeed in the conservation task, he must have some internalized verbal formula that shields him from the overpowering appearance of the visual displays much as in the Frank experiment. The explanations of the children who lacked conservation suggest how

[2] Not one of the forty children who participated in this experiment used the compensation argument—that though the water was lower it was correspondingly wider and was, therefore, the same amount of water. This type of reasoning by compensation is said by Piaget and Inhelder (1962) to be the basis of conservation.

strongly oriented they were to the visual appearance of the displays they had to deal with.

* * *

My major concern has been to examine afresh the nature of intellectual growth. The account has surely done violence to the richness of the subject. It seems to me that growth depends upon the emergence of two forms of competence. Children, as they grow, must acquire ways of representing the recurrent regularities in their environment, and they must transcend the momentary by developing ways of linking past to present to future—representation and integration. I have suggested that we can conceive of growth in both of these domains as the emergence of new technologies for the unlocking and amplification of human intellectual powers. Like the growth of technology, the growth of intellect is not smoothly monotonic. Rather, it moves forward in spurts as innovations are adopted. Most of the innovations are transmitted to the child in some prototypic form by agents of the culture: ways of responding, ways of looking and imaging, and, most important, ways of translating what one has encountered into language.

I have relied heavily in this account on the successive emergence of action, image, and word as the vehicles of representation, a reliance based both upon our observations and upon modern readings of man's alloplastic evolution. Our attention has been directed largely to the transition between iconic and symbolic representation.

In children between four and twelve language comes to play an increasingly powerful role as an implement of knowing. Through simple experiments, I have tried to show how language shapes, augments, and even supercedes the child's earlier modes of processing information. Translation of experience into symbolic form, with its attendant means of achieving remote reference, transformation, and combination, opens up realms of intellectual possibility that are orders of magnitude beyond the most powerful image-forming system.

* * *

Once language becomes a medium for the translation of experience, there is a progressive release from immediacy. For language, as we have commented, has the new and powerful features of remoteness and arbitrariness: It permits productive, combinatorial operations in the *absence* of what is represented. With this achievement, the child can delay gratification by virtue of representing to himself what lies beyond the present, what other possibilities exist beyond the clue that is under his nose. The child may be *ready* for delay of gratification, but he is no more able to bring it off than somebody ready to build a house, save that he has not yet heard of tools.

* * *

As for how language becomes internalized as a program for ordering experience, I join those who despair for an answer. My speculation, for whatever it is worth, is that the process of internalization depends upon interaction with others, upon the need to develop corresponding categories and transformations for communal action. It is the need for cognitive coin that can be exchanged with those on whom we depend. What Roger Brown (1958) has called the Original Word Game ends up by being the Human Thinking Game.

If I have seemed to underemphasize the importance of inner capacities—for example, the capacity *for* language or *for* imagery—it is because I believe that this part of the story is given by the nature of man's evolution. What is significant about the growth of mind in the child is to what degree it depends not upon capacity but upon the unlocking of capacity by techniques that come from exposure to the specialized environment of a culture. Romantic clichés, like "the veneer of culture" or "natural man," are as misleading if not as damaging as the view that the course of human development can be viewed independently of the educational process we arrange to make that development possible.

REFERENCES

Braine, M. D. On learning the grammatical order of words. *Psychological Review,* 1963, *70,* 323–348.

Brown, R. *Words and things.* New York: Free Press, 1958.

Bruner, J. S., & Kenney, H. The development of the concepts of order and proportion in children. In J. S. Bruner, *Studies in cognitive growth.* New York: Wiley, 1966.

Chomsky, N. *Syntactic structures.* S'Gravenhage, Netherlands: Mouton, 1957.

Emerson, L. L. The effect of bodily orientation upon the young child's memory for position of objects. *Child Development,* 1931, *2,* 125–142.

Frank, F. Perception and language in conservation. In J. S. Bruner, *Studies in cognitive growth.* New York: Wiley, 1966.

Luria, A. R. *The role of speech in the regulation of normal and abnormal behavior.* New York: Liveright, 1961.

Mandler, G. From association to structure. *Psychological Review,* 1962, *69,* 415–427.

Miller, G. A. Some psychological studies of grammar. *American Psychologist,* 1962, *17,* 748–762.

Nair, P. An experiment in conservation. In Center for

Cognitive Studies, *Annual Report,* Cambridge, Mass.: Author, 1963.

Piaget, J. *The construction of reality in the child.* (Trans. by Margaret Cook) New York: Basic Books, 1954.

Piaget, J., & Inhelder, B. *Le développment des quantités physiques chez l'enfant.* (2nd rev. ed.) Neuchâtel, Switzerland: Delachaux & Niestle, 1962.

Vygotsky, L. S. *Thought and language.* (Ed. & trans. by Eugenia Hanfmann & Gertrude Vakar) New York: Wiley, 1962.

Washburn, S. L., & Howell, F. C. Human evolution and culture. In S. Tax, *The evolution of man.* Vol. 2. Chicago: University of Chicago Press, 1960.

Weir, R. H. *Language in the crib.* The Hague: Mouton, 1962.

38

Creativity: Theoretical and Methodological Considerations

Bernard Mackler and Franklin C. Shontz

It is relatively easy to recognize an individual who is talented and creative. Such a person can do with ease the kinds of things that all of us wish we could do. The talented artist can not only draw accurate representations, but he can also express ideas and moods through the appropriate use of color and shading. The creative electrical engineer can not only produce a diagram of a circuit that works, but he can shorten the amount of material and effort required to produce the circuitry.

It is not at all easy to explain how such talent comes to be. What ingredients of heredity and education and character are required to produce a creative person? This article explores some of the problems involved in studying the process of creativity and the development of creative individuals.

In the last decade, there have been many theoretical and research reports published on creativity. Aside from Torrance (1962) and Golann (1963), no systematic review of the literature has been completed. Torrance reviews research yet he avoids a discussion of theory relevant to creativity. Golann reviews theory and research with emphasis on four areas: products of creativity, the process of creativity, the measurement of creativity, and personality. Although Golann does a comprehensive review of the subject areas, his paper neglects certain major theoretical views. The aim of this paper is to review systematically all the theoretical literature related to creativity. The paper will cover: psychoanalytic, associationistic, Gestalt, existential, interpersonal, and trait theories. The second section presents research stemming from these theoretical points of view.

Theories of Creativity

Psychoanalytic

Freud's early writings initiated a continuing psychoanalytic interest in artistic creativity. Freud studied poets, artists, particularly Leonardo da Vinci, and writers, and from these studies he developed the concept of *sublimation.* He defined the capacity to sublimate as the ability to exchange the original sexual aim for another aim that is no longer sexual. He realized that individual differences existed in the strength of sexual instinct

Reprinted from The Psychological Record, *Vol. 15 (1965), 217–238. The authors express their gratitude to Robert A. Dentler and M. Ellen Warshauer for their helpful comments and suggestions.*

and in capacity for sublimation. Constitutional factors determined how many of the sexual impulses would be utilized and how many would be sublimated.

Freud felt there were three means of adapting to the hardships of life: powerful diversions of interest, which lead one to care little for misery; substitutive gratifications, which lessen the misery, and intoxicating substances which make one insensitive to it (Freud, 1958). Creativity was seen as a substitute, a means of running from hardships in order to achieve some degree, limited at times, of satisfaction. Sublimation aided in this substitution process by transferring instinctual aims into directions that could not be easily frustrated by the environment. The creative individual turns away from reality because he cannot meet the demands for renouncing instinctual satisfaction, and he turns to fantasy, where he gives full play to his erotic and ambitious wishes. To be successful he must mold his fantasies into a new reality: The product is his creation, be it in art, music, science, or literature.

Freud extended his concept of sublimation from the creative individual to cultural evolution, for he saw the sublimation of instinct as an important feature of cultural change. Sublimation makes it possible for the higher mental operations, the scientific, artistic, ideological activities, to play such an important part in civilized life. For Freud, culture obtained this energy for change from sexuality.

*   *   *

Associationistic

Ribot (1900) was the forerunner of the modern associationists dealing with creativity. For him, association is the process by which mental states become joined together so that one tends to evoke the other. Association by contiguity merely reproduces the environment and often makes for stereotypy rather than creativeness. Association by resemblance, either direct or by way of mediating idea or effect is the basis, on the other hand, for analogical thinking, so important in the creative process. The intellectual aspect of creativity is composed of complementary processes: association and disassociation. Disassociation is the loss of certain elements from disinterest, abbreviation, and the withdrawal of attention.

Associationistic theory deals with the ability to think productively, utilizing the number of associative bonds an individual has at hand. It is the recombination of these bonds that results in creativity.

Mednick (1962), in a recent article, presented an associative interpretation of the process of creative thinking. The traditional views from Locke to Bain, including Ribot, are represented in Mednick's definition.

We may proceed to define the creative thinking process as the forming of associative elements into new combinations which either meet specified requirements or are in some way useful. The more mutually remote the elements of the new combination, the more creative the process or solution (Mednick, 1962, p. 221).

Gestalt

Wertheimer (1945) suggested that there have been two approaches to the problem of creative or productive thinking; traditional logic and association theory. He criticized both views as failing to do justice in describing the phenomena; both views seem constricted and limited. In their place, he offered Gestalt theory, to enhance an understanding, requestioning, and investigation of thinking processes.

He described the process of productive thinking. First, a critical region of the field becomes focal but not isolated. This is followed by a deeper structural view of the field, involving changes in the functional meaning, grouping, and reorganization of the items in the field until the gaps and difficulties in the problem are resolved. The field is restructured to restore harmony; an equilibrium is attained.

The entire process is one consistent line of thinking. It is not an and-sum of aggregated, piecemeal operations. No step is arbitrary, ununderstood in its function. On the contrary, each step is taken surveying the whole situation (Wertheimer, 1945, p. 42).

*   *   *

Existential

Existentialism as a theoretical position stands somewhat akin to Wertheimer. Both try to describe creative persons themselves in their creative moments.

May (1959) was critical of the psychoanalytic approaches for their reductive emphasis, as evidenced in the concept "regression in the service of the ego." Like Gestalt theory, existentialism does not try to reduce wholes into segments; both try to describe the total process. Gestalt theory offers concepts of field forces, structure, Gestalt, and vector, while existential theory offers only one concept, the encounter. Creativity is defined as the process of bringing something new into birth through the vehicle of the encounter.

The first thing we notice in a creative act is that it is an encounter. The artist encounters the landscape he proposes to paint—looks at it, observes it from this angle and that—and, as we say, is absorbed in it. Or, in the cases of abstract painters, the encounter may be with an idea, an inner vision which in turn may be led off by the brilliant colors on the artist's palette or the inviting rough whiteness of the canvas. The paint, the canvas, and the other materials then become a secondary part of this encounter; they are the language of it, the media, *as we rightly put it* (May, 1959, p. 58).

May described the intensity and genuineness of the artist in his encounter and his creative act. The words "absorption," "involvement," "being caught up in" seem to catch the intense enrapturement of this moment of heightened awareness. A person cannot will insight, nor creativity, but he can give himself to the encounter with intensity of dedication and commitment. May unraveled his view of creativity to include the encounter of man with the world, for the world is seen as inseparable from man. A creative act is "a process, a doing; specifically, a process interrelating the person and his world" (May, 1959, p. 56). May concluded that creativity is the encounter of the intensely dedicated, conscious human being with his world. May does not adequately define encounter; he assumes somewhat erroneously that the reader understands this concept.

* * *

Interpersonal

The interpersonal approach to creativity places emphasis on the creator as innovator and on another person who recognizes or acknowledges the creation.

The four theoretical approaches previously mentioned deemphasize this in their theory building; nevertheless, to varying degrees all four see it as a factor in creativity. The psychoanalytic school exemplified by Freud states that the creative person seeks worldly recognition. Freud assumed that the artist craves honor, power, wealth, fame, and to be loved by women. . . .[1]

Associationism deemphasizes milieu. Only Ribot, of the associationists reviewed, mentioned culture, and his comment is only lip service. He stated that if an artistic work is to be valuable, it should show a moderate degree of subordination to a guiding principle. Value implies social recognition and evaluation.

* * *

The existentialists go the furthest of the four theories in recognizing that the creative person is always encountering a world; there is always an external milieu that is met. World is not defined precisely, but one can assume the world to be composed of persons and objects; and in a creative act persons and/or objects are intensely encountered by the creator.

* * *

Trait

Trait theory is a marked divergence from psychoanalytic, association, Gestalt, existential, and interpersonal theory. Traits are characteristics of individuals and can be best investigated by an approach that emphasizes individual differences. A trait is any distinguishable, relatively enduring way in which one individual differs from another.

Guilford (1959) described the primary traits related to creativity. They are: a generalized sensitivity to problems; fluency of thinking that breaks down to four factors—word fluency, associational fluency, expressional fluency, and ideational fluency; flexibility of thinking, composed of spontaneous flexibility, both figural and semantic, and figural adaptive flexibility; originality; and redefinition, which has figural, symbolic, and semantic factors; and semantic elaboration. These aptitude traits were found by factor analysis. Guilford also includes nonaptitude traits, and these are motivation and temperament.

Guilford also described how creativity fits into his structure of intellect model and how creativity is distinct from intelligence. His model had three dimensions: contents, operations, and products. The *Content* refers to the kind of material or content of thought; these are figural, symbolic, semantic, and behavioral. *Operations* refers to the five possible operations performed upon the materials of thought: cognition, memory, divergent production, convergent production, and evaluation. The third dimension, *Product*, identifies the

---

[1] Freud assumes that all artists will be men.

possible products involved; these are units, classes, relations, systems, transformations, and implications.

Measurement of Creativity

Psychoanalytic theory bearing on creativity, as exemplified in Kris' work, particularly in his concept of "regression in the service of the ego" has been tested by means of the Rorschach. Holt and Havel's (1960) method assesses primary and secondary processes in the Rorschach. This test is used to measure the individual's ability to utilize primary process productivity or to regress in the service of the ego. Primary process cannot be observed directly, but only through its products which retain the signs of its origin. The scoring system consists of three groups of scoring categories: content; formal variables, or deviations in form structure; and control and defense variables.

The authors regard this scoring scheme as a research tool and not as a clinical tool. The major aim is to evaluate the efficiency of secondary process in coping with primary process aspects of responses. By this method the authors feel that it is possible to differentiate between maladaptive and adaptive regression (creativity).

*   *   *

Goldberger and Holt (1961) tested fourteen male college students with the Rorschach prior to isolation in apparatus similar to that used originally at McGill. The authors found that the behavioral changes noted by observation through a one-way mirror showed two types of reactions to isolation. One group could adaptively utilize the influx of primary process while the second group could not. These two groups were also compared with respect to their handling of primary process on the Rorschach. The rankings of the subjects, in terms of their use of primary process, ranged from those who could adequately control primary process to those who were overwhelmed by it. Those subjects who were ranked on the Rorschach as able to employ their primary process productively also performed productively under isolation. Those subjects who ranked low in the productive handling of primary process on the Rorschach reacted negatively to isolation; it disturbed their functioning and they became anxious. The authors concluded that these results contribute to the construct validity of this scoring method for measuring the amount of primary process manifestation on the Rorschach and the effectiveness with which it is controlled.

*   *   *

The pacemakers in the measurement field are Torrance, Guilford, and Getzels and Jackson. Torrance, and Getzels and Jackson represent no theoretical school in particular, although they seem very concerned with interpersonal, familial, group, cultural, and social factors that affect creativity. Hence one could consider them in the interpersonal camp. Guilford is an avowed trait theorist and he sees creativity as a segment of his structure of intellect.

Torrance has not tried to answer the question, "What are creative abilities?" but rather, "Who are the creative people, what are they like, and how do they think and behave?" The areas investigated include: development of creative thinking abilities, academic achievement of the creative subjects, peer reactions to the highly creative members, factors in teacher and adult behavior which either facilitate or interfere with the development of creative thinking in children, personality correlates of creative abilities, cultivation of creative interest through various classroom activities, and cross-cultural comparisons of creative thinking abilities.

Although no broad theoretical foundation is formulated, Torrance and his co-worker, Yamamoto (1962), offer definitions of creativity. Torrance defined creative thinking

as the process of sensing gaps or disturbing, missing elements; forming ideas or hypotheses concerning them; testing these hypotheses; and communicating the results, perhaps modifying and retesting the hypotheses (Torrance, 1962, p. 16).

Yamamoto in his definition stated a somewhat similar but more explicit position.

One must be sensitive to the internal and external environment to recognize problems and start thinking; he must also be rich in ideas (fluency) to hit upon, pick out, and communicate good ones; he must further be flexible in his ideas to cover vast regions of possibilities without being caught in a rut; he must, in addition, be clever and original in his ideas to make a break-through; and, quite possibly, he must be able to redefine, recognize, and elaborate his ideas to come up with a final solution to the perceived problem (Yamamoto, 1962, p. 1).

Torrance feels that it is premature to establish a discrete set of creative abilities on pure factors, and in his definition a variety of kinds of behavior are included. Although disagreeing, in part, with Guilford's factorial approach, Torrance at first utilized many of his tests. After experimentation of his own Torrance developed tasks on the basis of analyses of the reported experiences of eminent scientific discoverers, inventors, and creative writers. An attempt was made to construct tasks which would be models of the creative process, each requiring several types of thinking such as fluency, flexibility, and originality. This approach represents a departure from Guilford who insists that predictor measures of creativity should represent single factors. Torrance develops complex tasks presumed to involve the creative process and then examines the products for evidence of various types of thinking. The tasks are also designed to grip the interest of the subjects and maintain the subjects' involvement.

*   *   *

Validation of measures

In the development of creativity tests, the validation of these measures has been undertaken by Torrance and Guilford, and their colleagues. Validation for these tests as predictors of creativity poses difficulties in obtaining suitable criteria. With this in mind, Torrance has tried to avoid criteria that are obviously contaminated by intelligence, grade point average, and scholastic achievements tests. Wallace (1959), using the tests developed by Torrance, did a study of sales productivity and performance on the following creativity tests: *Ask and Guess, Product Improvement* (*Toy Dog*), and *Unusual Uses* (*Tin Cans* and *Toy Dog*). Two aspects of sales performance were considered: sales productivity and amount of customer service. There were 61 saleswomen in the sample and they were selected for testing on the basis of sales records. The sample included only the upper and lower thirds of saleswomen in terms of the amount of sales made in their respective departments. All were employed at the store three years or more; the ages of the women studied were 30 years or more. The departments were divided along the amount of involvement with consumer service. High service departments such as draperies and women's clothes were deemed "creative," while the low service departments, such as candy and notions, were termed "noncreative."

The results of the creativity tests indicated that saleswomen in "creative" departments scored significantly higher than saleswomen in "noncreative" departments. Women with high sales productivity scored significantly higher on the tests than low sales producers. Thus for both variables, customer service and sales productivity, significantly higher scores were obtained on creativity tasks both for women who gave more service and who also made more sales.

*   *   *

Concluding Remarks

The major theoretical explanations of creativity have been presented without any evaluative attempts. In an evaluation, authors can choose to side with one view and criticize others. In this instance we find this too easy a solution, for the major criticism of all the theories is that each view gives only a piecemeal explanation of creativity. Associationistic, Trait, and Psychoanalytic theory appear narrow in scope; Gestalt, Existential, and Interpersonal are broad. The former group is specific, yet mechanistic, ignoring the personal aspect of creating; the latter is humanistically inclined but is vague and poetic with little attention given to scientific or operational problems in their theory building. However no theory, narrow or broad, adequately describes the process of creativity. No small wonder that creativity is a confusing theoretical and research arena. De Mille (1963) describes the creativity boom and the present-day fad of stressing creativity, especially in the schools. There is a great urge to incorporate the incomplete theoretical concepts to aid and abet the "teaching" of creativity to youngsters. Much of the educational applications may prove to be hasty, since the worth of the theory and research has not been thoroughly evaluated.

The theoretical confusion has also been reflected in research. Most of the studies reviewed are cross-sectional, factor-analytical, highly statistical, yet deemphasizing process and developmental considerations. For a thorough documentation leading to theoretical refinements, we advocate developmental studies to understand the process and growth of an individual and how creativity emerges in this person's development. . . .

REFERENCES

DeMille, R. The creativity boom. *Teachers College Record*, 1963, **65**, 199–209.

Freud, S. *Civilization and its discontents*. Garden City, N.Y.: Doubleday, 1958.

Golann, S. E. Psychological study of creativity. *Psychological Bulletin*, 1963, **60**, 548–565.

Goldberger, L., & Holt, R. R. Experimental interference with reality contact: Individual differences. In P. Solomon, P. E. Kubzansky, P. H. Liederman, J. H. Mendelson, R. Trumbull, & D. Wexler (Eds.), *Sensory deprivation*. Cambridge, Mass.: Harvard University Press, 1961. Pp. 130–152.

Guilford, J. P. Traits of creativity. In H. H. Anderson (Ed.), *Creativity and its cultivation*. New York: Harper & Row, 1959. Pp. 142–161.

Holt, R. R., & Havel, J. A method for assessing primary and secondary process in the Rorschach. In Maria A. Rickers-Ovsiankina (Ed.), *Rorschach psychology*. New York: Wiley, 1960. Pp. 263–315.

May, R. The nature of creativity. In H. H. Anderson (Ed.), *Creativity and its cultivation*. New York: Harper & Row, 1959. Pp. 55–68.

Mednick, S. A. The associative basis of the creative process. *Psychological Review*, 1962, **69**, 220–232.

Ribot, T. The nature of creative imagination. *International Monthly*, 1900, **1**, 648–675, & **2**, 1–25.

Torrance, E. P. *Guiding creative talent.* Englewood Cliffs, N.J.: Prentice-Hall, 1962.

Wallace, H. Tests of creative thinking and sales performance in a large department store. In E. P. Torrance (Ed.), *Creativity: Second Minnesota conference on gifted children*. Minneapolis: Center for Continuation Study, University of Minnesota, 1959. Pp. 117–124.

Wertheimer, M. *Productive thinking.* New York: Harper & Row, 1945.

Yamamoto, K. *Revised scoring manual for tests of creative thinking.* Minneapolis: Bureau of Educational Research, University of Minnesota, 1962.

39

A Study of the Effects of Verbalization
on Problem Solving

Robert M. Gagné and Ernest C. Smith, Jr.

If only we could solve the problem of pollution. . . . If only we could solve the problems of the cities. . . . It seems that solving problems is the major concern of political leaders, and indeed of every one of us. Why can't we just work together and solve the important problems facing us and then manage to live contentedly with one another? The process of problem solving is a complex one and one to which psychologists have devoted a great deal of study. This article is a laboratory report of an investigation of one aspect of problem solving.

Scattered throughout the literature on problem solving are occasional studies which are interpreted as indicating that acts of verbalizing during problem solving result in lessened problem-solving effectiveness. While most investigators of such behavior may be inclined to expect a facilitating effect of "transfer of principles" to a final performance, studies have sometimes cast doubt upon the generality of such a finding, particularly in those instances where the principles are stated verbally.

Katona (1940), for example, found that a method which involved teaching verbal principles in solving matchstick problems to be less effective than a method of teaching by example. In a more recent study, Haslerud and Meyers (1958) found an experimental treatment in which verbally stated principles of solution of cryptograms were given to Ss to be less effective for solution of new cryptograms than was a treatment in which Ss were required to discover solutions for themselves. Other findings supportive of this sort of conclusion are cited by Haslerud and Meyers (Hendrix, 1947) which suggest the superiority for transfer of "not-verbalizing" vs. "verbalizing" by Ss themselves, in

From Journal of Experimental Psychology, *Vol. 64 (1962), 12–18. Copyright 1962 by the American Psychological Association, and reproduced by permission. This study was supported in part by funds granted by the Carnegie Corporation of New York. The opinions expressed are those of the authors, and do not necessarily reflect the views of that Corporation. Data of the experiment were collected by the junior author under the direction and monitoring of the senior author. Portions of the data and results were described by Ernest Smith in his senior thesis.*

solving mathematical problems. In another study using matchstick problems, Corman (1957) failed to find significant differences in performance among groups given various amounts and kinds of verbal instructions.

Results like these contrast markedly with those of an older study by Ewert and Lambert (1932), which used as a problem the task of transferring discs graduated in size from one circle to another in a triangular configuration of three circles. In successive tasks, different numbers of discs (from three through eight) are placed in Circle No. 1, arranged in order of size with the largest at the bottom. The problem is to transfer the discs from Circle 1 to Circle 2 in the least possible number of moves, moving one at a time. One of the experimental groups in this study was given only instructions about the rules of the game; a second group was encouraged to try to find a general principle for solution; a third was given a verbally stated principle of solution; while a fourth was given a principle plus a demonstration of the correct method with three discs. A large difference was found in the performance of groups who were given a verbally stated principle of solution and the performance of groups who were not.

The three-circle problem is fairly difficult, and one can spend much time and many moves before discovering a principle which is truly general. Perhaps the reason for the striking contrast between the results of Ewert and Lambert (1932) and those of more modern investigators resides simply in this fact. To a participant in the problem, it seems natural indeed that his performance should improve once he knows the principle—improve not only on the problem he has attempted, but on others of a similar type. It will perhaps take more than one additional study to explicate these contrasting results.

It was our intention in the present experiment to make a further exploration into the effects of verbalizing on problem-solving performance. We were interested particularly in the kind of verbalizing done by S himself during attempts to solve the problem, rather than by E.

Presumably, verbal principles provided in instructions must be repeated (perhaps to himself) by S, if they are to be effective. If we let S discover his own principles, in his own words, but require that he verbalize them, will this facilitate or interfere with problem solving? Marks (1951), for example, found no significant effects of providing Ss with a typed list of principles ("elements of the problem"), but a high correlation (.83) between performance and vocalization by Ss

during solution. We were also interested in seeing whether we could establish the differences in performance suggested (but not confirmed) by Ewert and Lambert's (1932) results, of the effects of instructions to find and formulate verbally a general principle.

We chose to investigate these questions by measuring performance on a standard series of three-circle tasks of the sort employed by Ewert and Lambert, transfer to a final six-disc task of this type, and the adequacy with which Ss could make verbal formulations of general principles. Specifically, the experiment compared the performance of groups of Ss who solved two-, three-, four-, and five-disc problems successively, under four conditions representing combinations of two treatment variables: (a) a requirement to state verbally a reason for *each move* at the time it was made; and (b) instructions to search for a general principle which could be stated verbally after the tasks were solved.

Method

Materials. The three-circle problem described by Ewert and Lambert (1932) was represented by three circles of 5 in. in diameter, drawn on a piece of stiff white paper, with their centers at the apexes of an equilateral triangle of side 7 in., and labeled A, B, and C. The discs were made of $\frac{3}{32}$ in. aluminum, numbered one through six, and graduated in diameter from $\frac{3}{4}$ in. to 2 in. A set of discs (two to six) is placed in Circle A, graduated with the largest at the bottom, and the problem is to move them all to Circle B so that they will be in the same order, in the smallest possible number of moves. Only one disc at a time may be moved, and it is never permitted to put a larger diameter disc on top of one with a smaller diameter. Under these rules, the fewest number of moves required (with any number n of discs) is $2^n - 1$.

The kind of principle which reduces this problem to a routine is the following: "If the number of discs is odd, move first to the circle to which you want to go eventually; if even, move first away from this circle. Continue by moving discs with odd numbers always in a clockwise direction, and the discs with even numbers always in a counter-clockwise direction." There are, however, a number of other ways of formulating the second part of this principle, which are equally effective, although requiring more words.

Subjects. The Ss were 28 boys in Grades 9 and 10, who were assigned randomly to four experimental groups. Their ages were 14 to 15 years and their IQs were all above 110. They had volunteered to participate in studies of learning, but were paid an amount equivalent to prevailing rates of odd-job work. Each S was questioned closely to determine that he had no previous acquaintance with the problem and was not used in the experiment if he had.

Procedure. First, each S was shown the materials and given instructions about the rules of the game. The three-disc and the four-disc problems were then administered in succession, and each was carried to final solution (i.e., getting all discs in Circle B in the proper order). The S was told in each case what the minimal number of moves was. If he decided he had made a wrong move, he was permitted to go back to an earlier point in the solution, or to the beginning. The E made a count of all moves. The purpose of this exercise was to give all Ss equal acquaintance with the problem, and also to provide data on equivalence of the groups.

Following this initial test, each S was assigned randomly to one of four conditions, each containing seven Ss, as follows:

Group V-SS (Verbalizing, Solution Set) was instructed to state aloud why they were making each individual move at the time they made it. In addition, these Ss were instructed to try to think of a general rule by means of which they could tell someone how to solve these problems, which was to be solicited afterwards by E. Group V (Verbalizing, No Solution Set) was required to verbalize a reason for each move, but was not instructed to try to formulate a general rule for solution. Group SS (No Verbalizing, Solution Set) was not required to verbalize, but was instructed to try to formulate a rule. Group No (No Verbalizing, No Solution Set) was simply told of the problem to be presented and its ground rules, with no additional instructions.

With these instructions, Ss were kept at the task until they achieved a single final solution for two, three, four, and five discs in succession. One-minute rest periods were interposed between successive tasks. Number of moves was counted in each case. Of course, the making of moves was slower for those Ss who were required to verbalize, usually to the point of slight annoyance. Following this learning session, after approximately 3 min. rest, all Ss were presented the six-disc task as a final test. They were told that their time to solution would be measured (with a stop watch), as well as the number of moves taken. No verbalizing was required.

Recording. For the initial test (using three and four discs), E simply kept a record of the number of moves made by each S.

During administration of the main experimental treatments (two, three, four, and five discs) number of moves was recorded. For those groups instructed to verbalize each move, E recorded on a prepared record sheet a brief phrase indicating the verbal statement made by each S. No attempt was made to make exact verbatim reproductions of what S said. Whenever an unusual reason was given, however, E attempted to record its meaning fully.

On the final test, E recorded the number of moves and the time required to achieve solution. After the final test was concluded, each S was asked to give a rule or rules for doing the problem with any number of discs, as if he were telling it to a person ignorant of the solution. The E recorded these verbally stated principles.

Results

Initial test

The means and SDs for number of moves made by each of the four groups on the initial test composed of tasks with three and four discs . . . appeared to insure an acceptable degree of comparability. . . .

Practice session

Mean performance curves for the four groups of the experiment are shown in Figure 1. These depict mean number of moves in excess of the minimum for the problems with two, three, four, and five discs administered in sequence. The same measure on the final test is also shown for each group as a terminal point.

It may readily be seen that a difference among the groups, associated with the Verbalization variable, began to appear as early as the three-disc practice, and showed itself as an ever widening difference thereafter. On the other hand, no differences of consequence appear in the performances of groups differentially treated with respect to a Solution Set, i.e., being told to look for a principle to be stated verbally. These apparent trends of the data were confirmed by an analysis of variance of the data for Trial 5. Since heterogeneity of variance was found in the raw data, they were transformed to logarithms. In this state, the null hypothesis regarding differences in vari-

FIGURE 1 *Performance curves showing moves in excess of minimum required for successively administered problems of two, three, four, and five discs for the four groups of the experiment (Values are shown for the final six-disc problem as a terminal point)*

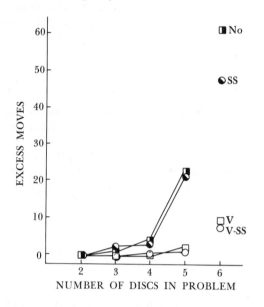

to circle B"; and (c) "if disc is even-numbered, move to circle C." Finally, there were some expressions of truly *general* principles, such as (a) "move odd-numbered discs in the clockwise direction," and (b) "move even-numbered discs in the counter-clockwise direction."

On the whole, the content of these "reasons" was by no means startling. It was not particularly surprising, considering the results of earlier investigators of thinking, that this form of thinking out loud was not very revealing about the nature of internal processes. A close examination of these data did not enable us to invent a method of relating specific types of verbal response to specific stages of the problem, except for the fact that the more general principles tended to occur later in practice than did the less general ones.

Final task performance

Mean number of moves in excess of minimum, and mean times (min.) to solution, for each of the four groups of the experiment on the final six-disc task are shown in Table 1. Here it can be seen that under standard conditions for all the groups, the differences in moves which appeared on the five-disc task are even greater on the six-disc task. Again the variances are markedly different between the verbalization and nonverbalization pairs of groups. A logarithmic transformation was found to make possible the assumption of homogeneity of variance. An analysis of variance performed on these transformed data confirmed significant treatment effects. . . . Application of *t* tests to differences between individual means indicated significance at the .01 level for comparisons

ances could be rejected. An analysis of variance on these transformed data indicated significant treatment effects. . . . When *t* tests were applied to the pairs of differences between means these were found to be significant at less than the .01 level for each of the verbalization groups vs. each of the nonverbalization groups.

In contrast, neither of the pairs of groups differentiated by the presence or absence of the SS instructions yields means which are significantly different from each other. Verbalization made a significant difference, Solution Set instructions made none.

Verbalization during practice. The verbalization done by *S*s who were instructed to give a reason for every move tended to fall into certain standard categories, with rare exceptions. There were those which were oriented toward *single* moves, like (a) "only possible move"; (b) "just to try it"; or (c) "don't know" (this one was quite infrequent). Then there were those which anticipated to the extent of *two* moves, such as (a) "to get at the larger disc"; (b) "to free up a space." There were also instances of reasons which apparently anticipated *sequences* of moves. One of the relatively frequent ones was (a) "move as with a three-disc sequence"; also in this category should perhaps come (b) "if disc is odd-numbered, move

TABLE 1 *Means and SDs for Number of Moves in Excess of Minimum, and for Time of Performance, on the Final Six-Disc Task for the Four Groups*

	Groups			
Measure	V-SS ($N=7$)	V ($N=7$)	SS ($N=7$)	No ($N=7$)
Moves in excess of minimum				
Mean	7.9	9.3	48.1	61.7
SD	8.6	7.9	34.8	40.2
Time (min.)				
Mean	4.2	3.8	10.1	10.0
SD	2.2	2.0	4.1	5.5

of the verbalization and nonverbalization groups. Differences between means for Groups SS and No, and Groups V-SS and V, are not significant.

An entirely similar set of comparisons exists with the means of time to solve, shown in Table 1. Here the *F* test for the total data is significant. . . . The *t* test indicates significance of differences of means associated with the contrast of verbalization vs. no verbalization (V-SS vs. SS; V-SS vs. No; V vs. SS; V vs. No) at better than the .05 level. Other differences in means are not significant.

Stating the verbal principle

Records of statements made by *S*s in response to the instruction to state verbally how to solve these problems were examined by the 2 *E*s independently and rated "Inadequate," "Partial," or "Complete." The following agreements were made beforehand: "Inadequate" was to mean any principle which was incorrect, irrelevant, or so fragmentary that it would be of no aid to anyone in finding solutions. "Partial" meant one of the two major parts of the principle, concerned with starting (move odd-numbered disc to the goal circle, etc.) or with procedure during solution (even numbers move clockwise, etc.). "Complete" meant both of these major parts.

With these criteria, it was quite easy to classify the principles the *S*s stated, and there were no differences in judgment of the 2 *E*s. These results are shown in Table 2.

Considering first the dichotomy, Inadequate vs. Partial or Complete, the Fisher exact probability test was applied to comparisons of the experimental treatments. The probability of the observed contrasts between V-SS and No, and between V and No were found to be .002; between

SS and No, .014. All other comparisons yielded high probability values. So far as being able to state even *partial* verbal principles, Group No is significantly poorer than those who verbalized; for those who did not verbalize, there is a significant effect of instructions to look for a general principle. Second, the dichotomy Inadequate or Partial vs. Complete was considered by this same method. Here the only low probabilities were .036 between Groups V-SS and SS and also Groups V-SS and No. The group required to verbalize as well as to try to formulate a verbal principle was thus found to be superior to Groups SS and No in the formulation of *complete* verbal principles. It would appear that verbalizing during practice is the most important factor accounting for this difference.

Discussion

Our results indicate that requiring individuals to verbalize while practicing the three-circle problem is a condition which is significantly related to superior performance in problem solving, which begins to show itself during practice with two-, three-, four-, and five-disc tasks, and is maintained on a final six-disc task. There is a strong suggestion also, that verbalizing is the most important factor at work in producing a greater number of individuals who can, at the close of practice, state fully adequate verbal principles of task solution.

Instructions to try to formulate verbal principles for solution of these tasks appear to have no effect on performance of the task and also an insignificant effect (by themselves) in producing a greater frequency of fully adequate principles. They do, however, produce more verbal principles which are at least partially adequate, than is the case when they are omitted. It will be apparent in interpreting these results that we cannot be certain how great a contrast in "set to look for solution" was actually achieved by the instructions used. After all, the noninstructed groups as well as the instructed ones underwent an initial period of testing on the three- and four-disc tasks, and may have generated in themselves a set to look for a general solution.

Surely the most striking finding is the effect of verbalization by the *S*s during practice. Such verbalization is of course very different from that which may result from providing *S*s with verbally stated principles of solution, as was done in the studies of Ewert and Lambert (1932) and Haslerud and Meyers (1958). Whatever principles were used by the individuals in the present experiment, they

TABLE 2 *Number of Inadequate, Partial, and Complete Verbal Principles Stated by Ss in Each Group*

| Group | N | Number of instances of principles judged as: | | |
		Inadequate	Partial	Complete
V-SS	7	0	3	4
V	7	0	5	2
SS	7	1	6	0
No	7	6	1	0

must have been discovered by the Ss themselves. In this respect, at least, the present findings are not inconsistent with those of Haslerud and Meyers, nor with other results indicating the effectiveness of self-discovered principles for problem solving (e.g., Gagné & Brown, 1961).

It is perhaps of some importance to emphasize that the individuals who were required to verbalize also took more time to make successive moves. We cannot tell from these data, of course, whether this more deliberate pacing of the task may have had some effects on the performance. The additional time between moves, however, was "filled" time, taken up entirely with the act of verbalization. Thus it would not be reasonable to suppose that the verbalization groups had any greater opportunity than did the nonverbalization groups for the deliberate rehearsal and recall of successful and unsuccessful moves. Verbalization is the most obvious variable at work; if other events are contributing to the results because of their association with time differences, it is not immediately apparent what they are.

As we pointed out, the content of the verbalizing during practice was fairly pedestrian and to some extent routine, so that it could be readily categorized. What then accounts for its effect on problem solving? In answering this question, we have no theory to call upon. It would appear that requiring verbalization somehow "forced the Ss to think." In other words, this treatment may have had the effect of constantly prodding the Ss to think of new reasons for their moves, particularly since they may have gotten a little tired of giving "the same old reasons" over again. This conception of the treatment would assign it a role similar to that of instructions to think of new word associates, as in the studies of Maltzman, Simon, Raskin, and Licht (1960). But this is a speculation which obviously does not come directly from present data. It would, however, be an interesting route for follow-up studies to take; namely, testing whether instructions to "think of new reasons," to be stated verbally, would have a facilitative effect on the solution of a task like that used here.

Summary

A study was conducted to determine the effects of (a) requiring Ss to verbalize during practice, and of (b) instructions to find a general principle to be stated verbally on problem-solving performance. The three-circle task described by Ewert and Lambert (1932) was used. The Ss were 28 ninth- and tenth-grade boys, divided randomly into four groups of seven each. Following the initial test on tasks with three and four discs, Ss were assigned to four groups given different treatments representing combinations of the two experimental variables. The practice session consisted of two-, three-, four-, and five-disc tasks administered successively. Records were kept of the verbalizing for those groups who engaged in it and of number of moves to achieve solution, for all groups. Following this, a final task using six discs was administered to all Ss under standard conditions, and a record was made of number of moves as well as time to solution.

Significant differences were found between the scores of those groups who were required to verbalize and those who were not, in terms of number of moves. Similar differences based on time scores were found in the contrast between verbalization and nonverbalization groups. Differences between other pairs of groups were not significant.

Comparisons of success in stating verbal principles applicable to the solution of three-circle problems were made among judged categories of Inadequate, Partial, and Complete, for all groups. A significant difference was obtained between verbalizing and nonverbalizing groups, and one which favored the "instructed" groups when the dichotomy Inadequate or Partial vs. Complete was tested.

The results appear to indicate that requiring Ss to verbalize during practice has the effect of making them think of new reasons for their moves and thus facilitates both the discovery of general principles and their employment in solving successive problems.

REFERENCES

Corman, B. R. The effect of varying amounts and kinds of information as guidance in problem solving. *Psychological Monographs*, 1957, **71** (2, Whole No. 431), 21 pp.

Ewert, P. H., & Lambert, J. F. Part II: The effect of verbal instructions upon the formation of a concept. *Journal of Genetic Psychology*, 1932, **6**, 400–413.

Gagné, R. M., & Brown, L. T. Some factors in the programing of conceptual learning. *Journal of Experimental Psychology*, 1961, **62**, 313–321.

Haslerud, G. M., & Meyers, S. The transfer value of given and individually derived principles. *Journal of Educational Psychology*, 1958, **49**, 293–298.

Hendrix, G. A new clue to transfer of training. *Elementary School Journal*, 1947, **48**, 197–208.

Katona, G. *Organizing and memorizing.* New York: Columbia University Press, 1940.

Maltzman, I., Simon, S., Raskin, D., & Licht, L. Experimental studies in the training of originality. *Psychological Monographs*, 1960, **74** (6, Whole No. 493).

Marks, M. R. Problem solving as a function of the situation. *Journal of Experimental Psychology*, 1951, **41**, 74–80.

40

Review of Skinner's *Verbal Behavior*

Noam Chomsky

This article, as the title states, is a review of the book *Verbal Behavior*, written by B. F. Skinner. While many book reviews are written in such a way that the reviewer makes valuable contributions to one or more topics in the book, Chomsky goes much further by completely evaluating the total theoretical background and orientation of Skinner's thesis. For that reason this review serves as a valuable contribution to the study of cognitive processes.

In reading this article, one must remember that there are two sides to every worthwhile issue. Chomsky argues that Skinner is premature in trying to formulate a theoretical explanation of verbal behavior when no one really understands the neurophysiology of the thinking (and talking) equipment. Chomsky is quite correct on that point. However, one must either begin at some point to try to organize the chaotic or delay the beginning indefinitely. Skinner's decision is to start right now and to let future researchers separate the true from the false, the right from the wrong. Each reader can decide for himself which procedure is to be preferred.

A great many linguists and philosophers concerned with language have expressed the hope that their studies might ultimately be embedded in a framework provided by behaviorist psychology, and that refractory areas of investigation, particularly those in which meaning is involved, will in this way be opened up to fruitful exploration. Since this volume is the first large-scale attempt to incorporate the major aspects of linguistic behavior within a behaviorist framework, it merits and will undoubtedly receive careful attention. Skinner is noted for his contributions to the study of animal behavior. The book under review is the product of study of linguistic behavior extending over more than twenty years. Earlier versions of it have been fairly widely circulated, and there are quite a few references in the psychological literature to its major ideas.

The problem to which this book is addressed is that of giving a "functional analysis" of verbal behavior. By functional analysis, Skinner means identification of the variables that control this behavior and specification of how they interact to determine a particular verbal response. Furthermore, the controlling variables are to be described completely in terms of such notions as stimulus, reinforcement, deprivation, which have been given a reasonably clear meaning in animal experimentation. In other words, the goal of the book is to provide a way to predict and control verbal behavior by observing and manipulating the physical environment of the speaker.

Skinner feels that recent advances in the laboratory study of animal behavior permit us to approach this problem with a certain optimism; since "the basic processes and relations which give verbal behavior its special characteristics are now fairly well understood . . . the results [of this experimental work] have been surprisingly free of species restrictions. Recent work has shown that the methods can be extended to human behavior without serious modification."

It is important to see clearly just what it is in Skinner's program and claims that makes them appear so bold and remarkable. It is not primarily the fact that he has set functional analysis as his problem, or that he limits himself to study of "observables," i.e. input-output relations. What is so surprising is the particular limitations he has imposed on the way in which the observables of behavior are to be studied and, above all, the particularly simple nature of the "function" which, he claims, describes the causation of behavior. One would naturally expect that prediction of the be-

From Language, *Vol. 35 (1959), 26–58. Reprinted by permission of the Linguistic Society of America and the author.*

havior of a complex organism (or machine) would require, in addition to information about external stimulation, knowledge of the internal structure of the organism, the ways in which it processes input information and organizes its own behavior. These characteristics of the organism are in general a complicated product of inborn structure, the genetically determined course of maturation, and past experience. Insofar as independent neurophysiological evidence is not available, it is obvious that inferences concerning the structure of the organism are based on observation of behavior and outside events. Nevertheless, one's estimate of the relative importance of external factors and internal structure in the determination of behavior will have an important effect on the direction of research on linguistic (or any other) behavior, and on the kinds of analogies from animal behavior studies that will be considered relevant or suggestive.

Putting it differently, anyone who sets himself the problem of analyzing the causation of behavior will (in the absence of independent neurophysiological evidence) concern himself with the only data available, namely the record of inputs to the organism and the organism's present response, and will try to describe the function, specifying the response in terms of the history of inputs. This is nothing more than the definition of his problem. There are no possible grounds for argument here, if one accepts the problem as legitimate, though Skinner has often advanced and defended this definition of a problem as if it were a thesis which other investigators reject. The differences that arise between those who affirm and those who deny the importance of the specific "contribution of the organism" to learning and performance concern the particular character and complexity of this function, and the kinds of observations and research necessary for arriving at a precise specification of it. If the contribution of the organism is complex, the only hope of predicting behavior even in a gross way will be through a very indirect program of research that begins by studying the detailed character of the behavior itself and the particular capacities of the organism involved.

Skinner's thesis is that external factors consisting of present stimulation and the history of reinforcement (in particular, the frequency, arrangement, and withholding of reinforcing stimuli) are of overwhelming importance, and that the general principles revealed in laboratory studies of these phenomena provide the basis for understanding the complexities of verbal behavior. He confidently and repeatedly voices his claim to have demonstrated that the contribution of the speaker is quite trivial and elementary, and that precise prediction of verbal behavior involves only specification of the few external factors that he has isolated experimentally with lower organisms.

Careful study of this book (and of the research on which it draws) reveals, however, that these astonishing claims are far from justified. It indicates, furthermore, that the insights that have been achieved in the laboratories of the reinforcement theorist, though quite genuine, can be applied to complex human behavior only in the most gross and superficial way, and that speculative attempts to discuss linguistic behavior in these terms alone omit from consideration factors of fundamental importance that are, no doubt, amenable to scientific study, although their specific character cannot at present be precisely formulated. Since Skinner's work is the most extensive attempt to accommodate human behavior involving higher mental faculties within a strict behaviorist schema of the type that has attracted many linguists and philosophers, as well as psychologists, a detailed documentation is of independent interest. The magnitude of the failure of this attempt to account for verbal behavior serves as a kind of measure of the importance of the factors omitted from consideration and an indication of how little is really known about this remarkably complex phenomenon.

The force of Skinner's argument lies in the enormous wealth and range of examples for which he proposes a functional analysis. The only way to evaluate the success of his program and the correctness of his basic assumptions about verbal behavior is to review these examples in detail and to determine the precise character of the concepts in terms of which the functional analysis is presented. . . .

*   *   *

The notions "stimulus," "response," and "reinforcement" are relatively well defined with respect to the bar-pressing experiments and others similarly restricted. Before we can extend them to real-life behavior, however, certain difficulties must be faced. We must decide, first of all, whether any physical event to which the organism is capable of reacting is to be called a stimulus on a given occasion, or only one to which the organism in fact reacts; and correspondingly, we must decide whether any part of behavior is to be called a response, or only one connected with stimuli in lawful ways. . . .

*   *   *

Consider first Skinner's use of the notions "stimulus" and "response." In *Behavior of organisms* he commits himself to the narrow definitions for these terms. A part of the environment and a part of behavior are called stimulus (eliciting, discriminated, or reinforcing) and response, respectively, only if they are lawfully related; that is, if the "dynamic laws" relating them show smooth and reproducible curves. Evidently stimuli and responses, so defined, have not been shown to figure very widely in ordinary human behavior. We can, in the face of presently available evidence, continue to maintain the lawfulness of the relation between stimulus and response only by depriving them of their objective character. A typical example of "stimulus control" for Skinner would be the response to a piece of music with the utterance *Mozart* or to a painting with the response *Dutch*. These responses are asserted to be "under the control of extremely subtle properties" of the physical object or event. Suppose instead of saying *Dutch* we had said *Clashes with the wallpaper, I thought you liked abstract work, Never saw it before, Tilted, Hanging too low, Beautiful, Hideous, Remember our camping trip last summer?*, or whatever else might come into our minds when looking at a picture (in Skinnerian translation, whatever other responses exist in sufficient strength). Skinner could only say that each of these responses is under the control of some other stimulus property of the physical object. If we look at a red chair and say *red,* the response is under the control of the stimulus "redness"; if we say *chair,* it is under the control of the collection of properties (for Skinner, the object) "chairness," and similarly for any other response. This device is as simple as it is empty. Since properties are free for the asking (we have as many of them as we have nonsynonymous descriptive expressions in our language, whatever this means exactly), we can account for a wide class of responses in terms of Skinnerian functional analysis by identifying the "controlling stimuli." But the word "stimulus" has lost all objectivity in this usage. Stimuli are no longer part of the outside physical world; they are driven back into the organism. We identify the stimulus when we hear the response. It is clear from such examples, which abound, that the talk of "stimulus control" simply disguises a complete retreat to mentalistic psychology. We cannot predict verbal behavior in terms of the stimuli in the speaker's environment, since we do not know what the current stimuli are until he responds. Furthermore, since we cannot control the property of a physical object to which an individual will respond, except in highly artificial cases, Skinner's claim that his system, as opposed to the traditional one, permits the practical control of verbal behavior is quite false.

*   *   *

Consider now Skinner's use of the notion "response." The problem of identifying units in verbal behavior has of course been a primary concern of linguists, and it seems very likely that experimental psychologists should be able to provide much-needed assistance in clearing up the many remaining difficulties in systematic identification. Skinner recognizes the fundamental character of the problem of identification of a unit of verbal behavior but is satisfied with an answer so vague and subjective that it does not really contribute to its solution. The unit of verbal behavior—the verbal operant—is defined as a class of responses of identifiable form functionally related to one or more controlling variables. No method is suggested for determining in a particular instance what are the controlling variables, how many such units have occurred, or where their boundaries are in the total response. Nor is any attempt made to specify how much or what kind of similarity in form or "control" is required for two physical events to be considered instances of the same operant. In short, no answers are suggested for the most elementary questions that must be asked of anyone proposing a method for description of behavior. Skinner is content with what he calls an "extrapolation" of the concept of operant developed in the laboratory to the verbal field. In the typical Skinnerian experiment, the problem of identifying the unit of behavior is not too crucial. It is defined, by fiat, as a recorded peck or bar-press, and systematic variations in the rate of this operant and its resistance to extinction are studied as a function of deprivation and scheduling of reinforcement (pellets). The operant is thus defined with respect to a particular experimental procedure. This is perfectly reasonable and has led to many interesting results. It is, however, completely meaningless to speak of extrapolating this concept of operant to ordinary verbal behavior. Such "extrapolation" leaves us with no way of justifying one or another decision about the units in the "verbal repertoire."

Skinner specifies "response strength" as the basic datum, the basic dependent variable in his functional analysis. In the bar-pressing experiment, response strength is defined in terms of rate of emission during extinction. Skinner has argued that this is "the only datum that varies significantly and in the expected direction under conditions which are relevant to the 'learning process.' " In the book under review, response strength is defined as "probability of emission." This definition provides a comforting impression of objectivity, which, however, is quickly dispelled when we look into the matter more closely. The term "probability" has some rather obscure meaning for Skinner in this book. We are told, on the one hand, that "our evidence for the contribution of each variable [to response strength] is based on observation of frequencies alone." At the same time, it appears that frequency is a very misleading measure of strength, since, for example, the frequency of a response may be "primarily attributable to the frequency of occurrence of controlling variables." It is not clear how the frequency of a response can be attributable to anything *but* the frequency of occurrence of its controlling variables if we accept Skinner's view that the behavior occurring in a given situation is "fully determined" by the relevant controlling variables. Furthermore, although the evidence for the contribution of each variable to response strength is based on observation of frequencies alone, it turns out that "we base the notion of strength upon several kinds of evidence," in particular: emission of the response (particularly in unusual circumstances), energy level (stress), pitch level, speed and delay of emission, size of letters, etc. in writing, immediate repetition, and—a final factor, relevant but misleading—overall frequency.

*   *   *

The other fundamental notion borrowed from the description of bar-pressing experiments is "reinforcement." It raises problems which are similar and even more serious. In *Behavior of organisms*

the operation of reinforcement is defined as the presentation of a certain kind of stimulus in a temporal relation with either a stimulus or response. A reinforcing stimulus is defined as such by its power to produce the resulting change [in strength]. There is no circularity about this: some stimuli are found to produce the change, others not, and they are classified as reinforcing and non-reinforcing accordingly.

This is a perfectly appropriate definition for the study of schedules of reinforcement. It is perfectly useless, however, in the discussion of real-life behavior, unless we can somehow characterize the stimuli which are reinforcing (and the situations and conditions under which they are reinforcing). Consider, first of all, the status of the basic principle that Skinner calls the "law of conditioning" (law of effect). It reads: "If the occurrence of an operant is followed by presence of a reinforcing stimulus, the strength is increased" (*Behavior of organisms*). As "reinforcement" was defined, this law becomes a tautology. For Skinner, learning is just change in response strength. Although the statement that presence of reinforcement is a sufficient condition for learning and maintenance of behavior is vacuous, the claim that it is a necessary condition may have some content, depending on how the class of reinforcers (and appropriate situations) is characterized. Skinner does make it very clear that in his view reinforcement is a necessary condition for language learning and for the continued availability of linguistic responses in the adult. However, the looseness of the term "reinforcement" as Skinner uses it in the book under review makes it entirely pointless to inquire into the truth or falsity of this claim. Examining the instances of what Skinner calls "reinforcement," we find that not even the requirement that a reinforcer be an identifiable stimulus is taken seriously. In fact, the term is used in such a way that the assertion that reinforcement is necessary for learning and continued availability of behavior is likewise empty.

To show this, we consider some example of "reinforcement." First of all, we find a heavy appeal to automatic self-reinforcement. Thus, "a man talks to himself . . . because of the reinforcement he receives"; "the child is reinforced automatically when he duplicates the sounds of airplanes, streetcars. . . ."; "the young child alone in the nursery may automatically reinforce his own exploratory verbal behavior when he produces sounds which he has heard in the speech of others"; "the speaker who is also an accomplished listener 'knows when he has correctly echoed a response' and is reinforced thereby"; thinking is "behaving which automatically affects the behaver and is reinforcing because it does so" (cutting one's finger should thus be reinforcing, and an example of thinking); "the verbal fantasy, whether overt or covert, is automatically reinforcing to the speaker as listener. Just as the musician plays or composes what he is reinforced by hearing, or as the artist paints what reinforces him visually, so the speaker engaged in verbal fantasy says what he is reinforced by hearing or writes what he is reinforced by reading"; similarly, care in problem solving, and rationalization, are automatically self-reinforcing. We can also reinforce someone by emitting verbal behavior as such (since this rules out a class of aversive stimulations) by not emitting verbal behavior (keeping silent and paying attention) or by acting appropriately on some future occasion ("the strength of [the speaker's] behavior is determined mainly by the behavior which the listener will exhibit with respect to a given state of affairs"; this Skinner considers the general case of "communication" or "letting the listener know"). In most such cases, of course, the speaker is not present at the time when the reinforcement takes place, as when "the artist . . . is reinforced by the effects his works have upon . . . others," or when the writer is reinforced by the fact that his "verbal behavior may reach over centuries or to thousands of listeners or readers at the same time. The writer may not be reinforced often or immediately, but his net reinforcement may be great" (this accounts for the great "strength" of his behavior). An individual may also find it reinforcing to injure someone by criticism or by bringing bad news, or to publish an experimental result which upsets the theory of a rival, to describe circumstances which would be reinforcing if they were to occur, to avoid repetition, to "hear" his own name though in fact it was not mentioned or to hear nonexistent words in his child's babbling, to clarify or otherwise intensify the effect of a stimulus which serves an important discriminative function, etc.

From this sample, it can be seen that the notion of reinforcement has totally lost whatever objective meaning it may ever have had. Running through these examples, we see that a person can be reinforced though he emits no response at all, and that the reinforcing "stimulus" need not impinge on the "reinforced person" or need not even exist (it is sufficient that it be imagined or hoped for). . . .

It seems that Skinner's claim that all verbal behavior is acquired and maintained in "strength" through reinforcement is quite empty, because his notion of reinforcement has no clear content, functioning only as a cover term for any factor, detectable or not, related to acquisition or maintenance of verbal behavior. Skinner's use of the term "conditioning" suffers from a similar difficulty. Pavlovian and operant conditioning are processes about which psychologists have developed real understanding. Instruction of human beings is not. The claim that instruction and imparting of information are simply matters of conditioning is pointless. The claim is true, if we extend the term "conditioning" to cover these processes, but we know no more about them after having revised this term in such a way as to deprive it of its relatively clear and objective character. It is, as far as we know, quite false, if we use "conditioning" in its literal sense. Similarly, when we say that "it is

the function of predication to facilitate the transfer of response from one term to another or from one object to another," we have said nothing of any significance. In what sense is this true of the predication, *Whales are mammals?* Or, to take Skinner's example, what point is there in saying that the effect of *The telephone is out of order* on the listener is to bring behavior formerly controlled by the stimulus *out of order* under control of the stimulus *telephone* (or the telephone itself) by a process of simple conditioning? What laws of conditioning hold in this case? Furthermore, what behavior is "controlled" by the stimulus, *out of order,* in the abstract? Depending on the object of which this is predicated, the present state of motivation of the listener, etc., the behavior may vary from rage to pleasure, from fixing the object to throwing it out, from simply not using it to trying to use it in the normal way (e.g., to see if it is really out of order), and so on. To speak of "conditioning" or "bringing previously available behavior under control of a new stimulus" in such a case is just a kind of play-acting at science.

The claim that careful arrangement of contingencies of reinforcement by the verbal community is a necessary condition for language learning has appeared, in one form or another, in many places. Since it is based not on actual observation, but on analogies to laboratory study of lower organisms, it is important to determine the status of the underlying assertion within experimental psychology proper. The most common characterization of reinforcement (one which Skinner explicitly rejects, incidentally) is in terms of drive reduction. This characterization can be given substance by defining drives in some way independently of what in fact is learned. If a drive is postulated on the basis of the fact that learning takes place, the claim that reinforcement is necessary for learning will again become as empty as it is in the Skinnerian framework. There is an extensive literature on the question of whether there can be learning without drive reduction (latent learning). The "classical" experiment of Blodgett indicated that rats who had explored a maze without reward showed a marked drop in number of errors (as compared to a control group which had not explored the maze) upon introduction of a food reward, indicating that the rat had learned the structure of the maze without reduction of the hunger drive. Drive-reduction theorists countered with an exploratory drive which was reduced during the prereward learning, and claimed that a slight decrement in errors could be noted before food reward. A wide variety of experiments, with somewhat conflicting results, have been carried out with a similar design. Few investigators still doubt the existence of the phenomenon. Hilgard, in his general review of learning theory, concludes that "there is no longer any doubt but that, under appropriate circumstances, latent learning is demonstrable."

More recent work has shown that novelty and variety of stimulus are sufficient to arouse curiosity in the rat and to motivate it to explore (visually), and, in fact, to learn (since on a presentation of two stimuli, one novel, one repeated, the rat will attend to the novel one); that rats will learn to choose the arm of a single-choice maze that leads to a complex maze, running through this being their only "reward"; that monkeys can learn object discriminations and maintain their performance at a high level of efficiency with visual exploration (looking out of a window for 30 seconds) as the only reward; and, perhaps most strikingly of all, that monkeys and apes will solve rather complex manipulation problems that are simply placed in their cages, and will solve discrimination problems with only exploration and manipulation as incentives. In these cases, solving the problem is apparently its own "reward." Results of this kind can be handled by reinforcement theorists only if they are willing to set up curiosity, exploration, and manipulation drives, or to speculate somehow about acquired drives for which there is no evidence outside of the fact that learning takes place in these cases.

*　　*　　*

. . . [I]t seems quite beyond question that children acquire a good deal of their verbal and nonverbal behavior by casual observation and imitation of adults and other children. It is simply not true that children can learn language only through "meticulous care" on the part of adults who shape their verbal repertoire through careful differential reinforcement, though it may be that such care is often the custom in academic families. It is a common observation that a young child of immigrant parents may learn a second language in the streets from other children with amazing rapidity, and that his speech may be completely fluent and correct to the last allophone, while the subtleties that become second nature to the child may elude his parents despite high motivation and continued practice. A child may pick up a large part of his vocabulary and "feel" for sentence structure from television, from reading, from listening to adults, etc. Even a very young child who has not yet acquired a minimal repertoire from which to form new utterances may imitate a word quite well on

an early try, with no attempt on the part of his parents to teach it to him. It is also perfectly obvious that, at a later stage, a child will be able to construct and understand utterances which are quite new and are, at the same time, acceptable sentences in his language. Every time an adult reads a newspaper, he undoubtedly comes upon countless new sentences which are not at all similar, in a simple, physical sense, to any that he has heard before and which he will recognize as sentences and understand; he will also be able to detect slight distortions or misprints. Talk of "stimulus generalization" in such a case simply perpetuates the mystery under a new title. These abilities indicate that there must be fundamental processes at work quite independently of "feedback" from the environment. I have been able to find no support whatsoever for the doctrine of Skinner and others that slow and careful shaping of verbal behavior through differential reinforcement is an absolute necessity. If reinforcement theory really requires the assumption that there be such meticulous care, it seems best to regard this simply as a reductio ad absurdum argument against this approach. It is also not easy to find any basis (or, for that matter, to attach very much content) to the claim that reinforcing contingencies set up by the verbal community are the single factor responsible for maintaining the strength of verbal behavior. The sources of the "strength" of this behavior are almost a total mystery at present. Reinforcement undoubtedly plays a significant role, but so do a variety of motivational factors about which nothing serious is known in the case of human beings.

As far as acquisition of language is concerned, it seems clear that reinforcement, casual observation, and natural inquisitiveness (coupled with a strong tendency to imitate) are important factors, as is the remarkable capacity of the child to generalize, hypothesize, and "process information" in a variety of very special and apparently highly complex ways which we cannot yet describe or begin to understand, and which may be largely innate or may develop through some sort of learning or through maturation of the nervous system. The manner in which such factors operate and interact in language acquisition is completely unknown. It is clear that what is necessary in such a case is research, not dogmatic and perfectly arbitrary claims based on analogies to that small part of the experimental literature in which one happens to be interested.

*　　*　　*

Summarizing this brief discussion, it seems that there is neither empirical evidence nor any known argument to support any *specific* claim about the relative importance of "feedback" from the environment and the "independent contribution of the organism" in the process of language acquisition.

* * *

Anyone who seriously approaches the study of linguistic behavior, whether linguist, psychologist, or philosopher, must quickly become aware of the enormous difficulty of stating a problem which will define the area of his investigations and which will not be either completely trivial or hopelessly beyond the range of present-day understanding and technique. In selecting functional analysis as his problem, Skinner has set himself a task of the latter type. In an extremely interesting and insightful paper, K. S. Lashley has implicitly delimited a class of problems which can be approached in a fruitful way by the linguist and psychologist, and which are clearly preliminary to those with which Skinner is concerned. Lashley recognizes, as anyone must who seriously considers the data, that the composition and production of an utterance is not simply a matter of stringing together a sequence of responses under the control of outside stimulation and intraverbal association, and that the syntactic organization of an utterance is not something directly represented in any simple way in the physical structure of the utterance itself. A variety of observations leads him to conclude that syntactic structure is "a generalized pattern imposed on the specific acts as they occur," and that "a consideration of the structure of the sentence and other motor sequences will show . . . that there are, behind the overtly expressed sequences, a multiplicity of integrative processes which can only be inferred from the final results of their activity." He also comments on the great difficulty of determining the "selective mechanisms" used in the actual construction of a particular utterance.

* * *

It is not easy to accept the view that a child is capable of constructing an extremely complex mechanism for generating a set of sentences, some of which he has heard, or that an adult can instantaneously determine whether (and if so, how) a particular item is generated by this mechanism, which has many of the properties of an abstract deductive theory. Yet this appears to be a fair description of the performance of the speaker, listener, and learner. If this is correct, we can predict that a direct attempt to account for the actual behavior of speaker, listener, and learner, not based on a prior understanding of the structure of grammars, will achieve very limited success. The grammar must be regarded as a component in the behavior of the speaker and listener which can only be inferred, as Lashley has put it, from the resulting physical acts. The fact that all normal children acquire essentially comparable grammars of great complexity with remarkable rapidity suggests that human beings are somehow specially designed to do this, with data-handling or "hypothesis-formulating" ability of unknown character and complexity. The study of linguistic structure may ultimately lead to some significant insights into this matter. At the moment the question cannot be seriously posed, but in principle it may be possible to study the problem of determining what the built-in structure of an information-processing (hypothesis-forming) system must be to enable it to arrive at the grammar of a language from the available data in the available time. At any rate, just as the attempt to eliminate the contribution of the speaker leads to a "mentalistic" descriptive system that succeeds only in blurring important traditional distinctions, so a refusal to study the contribution of the child to language learning permits only a superficial account of language acquisition, with a vast and unanalyzed contribution attributed to a step called "generalization," which in fact includes just about everything of interest in this process. If the study of language is limited in these ways, it seems inevitable that major aspects of verbal behavior will remain a mystery.

41

Imagery: The Return of the Ostracized

Robert R. Holt

Studying mental events has always been the professed raison d'etre for psychologists. Beyond the *what* and *how* of mental events, we often wish to know *why* mental events happen. Such questions have been asked by nearly all psychologists, including the early laboratory investigators. The behaviorists, led by Watson (who was said to be unable to form images), recognized that each mental event is a personal thing: Because mentation occurs completely inside the head, no other person can be aware of the actual occurrence of a mental event. Thus, since the very essence of science involves the observation of whatever is being studied, observable forms of behavior rather than unseen mental events must be examined.

Although one cannot observe a mental event that another person is experiencing, one can ask that person to report his mental experiences. In this case the vocal behavior of the person experiencing the mental event can serve as the observable indicant of the mental act. By this melding of the two lines of reasoning, modern psychologists are studying the traditional mental events while at the same time "being scientific" by studying observable events. This article reviews some topics concerned with the type of mental event known as *imagery*.

Consider the situation of a man whom I shall call "S." He is lying on a bed alone, in almost complete darkness and silence. There is nothing to see, hear, taste, smell, or do. But as he lies with eyes closed, he sees a good deal more than darkness. He begins to notice vague luminous patterns appearing before him in intricate geometrical design, fading, brightening, coming, and going. Suddenly, a face emerges from this background with startling clarity, only to be replaced an instant later by an animal's head. Dreamily, S watches the succession of pictures that emerge before him, growing gradually more vivid, complex, and thematic. Soon he has lost touch with external reality, being instead completely involved with these illusory phantoms of the dark.

You are a psychologist; here are your data; what do you make of this kind of report? Is it perhaps an account of the onset of a psychosis, or does it come from an experiment in sensory deprivation, or one on hallucinogenic drugs? If you are one of the half of the population who have had firsthand experience of hypnagogic imagery, you will recognize it as merely the account of a common experience of going to sleep, in which the visual phenomena are first phosphenes (the patterning of the self-light of the retina), and then hypnagogic im-

ages and hallucinations, merging into dreams. In this case, you will doubtless think this stuff old hat and hardly worth dwelling on at length at a time and place like this.

I expect, however, that a good many of us do not know about such phenomena at first hand, and have read little, or nothing, about them. Certainly a number of experimenters in recent years who have stumbled over hypnagogic and other vivid images appearing in the course of their work have apparently not recognized them. There is good reason for such ignorance, of course: Few standard introductory texts say much about imagery at all, and even at advanced levels (e.g., Osgood, 1953; Woodworth and Schlosberg, 1954) there is likely to be nothing about hypnagogic and other special phenomena.

I became interested in this topic in the course of some research with my colleague, Leo Goldberger, on the cognitive effects of perceptual isolation

From American Psychologist, *Vol. 19 (1964), 254–264. Copyright 1964 by the American Psychological Association, and reproduced by permission. Based on a Presidential Address to Division 12 at American Psychological Association, St. Louis, Missouri, August 1962.*

(Goldberger and Holt, 1958). We were struck by the tendency of so much of the literature on the topic to talk about "hallucinations" as being produced by the experimental conditions now so generally referred to by the misnomer "sensory deprivation," while our own subjects produced nothing so dramatic. Since the opening lines of this paper are autobiographical, I have long been familiar with imagery similar to what is reported by some—*not* all—subjects when the experiment causes them to lie on a bed in a quiet room with nothing to do or see, a condition that naturally fosters sleep and drowsy states. So I wondered what all the fuss about "experimental psychosis" was, and why so few other experimenters in this field made any reference to hypnagogic imagery.

I decided, therefore, to take a look into the literature and see whether or not I was correct in my impressions that the problem of imagery had been much neglected until recently. I soon found, of course, that I had to decide which of a great many topics and headings to include, since imagery is at least tangent to a host of interesting phenomena. In what follows, I do *not* include (as types of imagery) afterimages, the spiral aftereffect, the autokinetic phenomenon, figural aftereffects, standard visual illusions, nor imagination. There follows a list, with definitions, of the principal phenomena under consideration here.

Definition of Principal Types of Imagery

Image: generic term for all conscious subjective presentations of a quasi-sensory but nonperceptual character.

Thought image: a faint subjective representation of a sensation or perception without an adequate sensory input, present in waking consciousness as part of an act of thought. Includes memory images and imagination images; may be visual, auditory, or of any other sensory modality, and also purely verbal.

Phosphene: a more or less formed elaboration or variation of the idioretinal light; generally moving clouds of unsaturated color, or relatively static, reticulated patterns. The term is also used to refer to experienced dots or flashes of color as a result of ("inadequate") retinal stimulations via pressure or electric current.

Synesthesia: a condition in which perception of one type is regularly accompanied by images from another sensory modality. In the most common

form, colored hearing, the subject experiences images of color along with sounds (especially musical ones). Related phenomena are number forms and date forms: images of numbers or dates as disposed in space in definite geometric patterns.

Body image: "the picture or mental representation one has of his own body at rest or in motion at any moment (English and English, 1958, p. 70)." Kinesthetic and somesthetic images are generally considered important constituents.

Phantom limb: a part of the body image that persists despite the loss of the corresponding bodily part (usually a limb).

Hypnagogic image (or hypnagogic hallucination): an image, usually so projected (that is, "out there") and of such vividness, clarity, and detail that it approaches sensory realism, appearing suddenly to someone in the drowsy state just before sleep. When such an image occurs at a corresponding period of awakening, it is called hypnopompic. It may be visual or auditory: Sometimes other modalities occur and are included under this heading.

Eidetic image: a projected image (generally visual) of such vividness, color, clarity, and differentiation of form as to seem to the fully waking subject (usually a child) like a percept. Jaensch (1930) described two types: the *T* type, resembling greatly prolonged afterimages and generally in complementary colors to the original, and the *B* type, resembling greatly enhanced thought images.

Hallucination: an image the objective reality of which the subject believes in. It is conventional, but perhaps not psychologically meaningful, to restrict the term to instances in which no external sensory support can be found; when the image makes use of an identifiable stimulus (usually distorting it), the term *illusion* is used.

Paranormal hallucination: the report of an apparition, ghost, or phantasm of some living or dead person including oneself (autoscopic or heautoscopic hallucination, Doppelgänger); also a religious or mystical vision or supernatural materialization.

Pseudohallucination: a projected image of hallucinatory status, the subjective nature of which the person however recognizes.

Dream image: a normal hallucination occurring during sleep.

Sensory conditioning: a procedure in which both *US* [unconditioned stimulus] and *CS* [conditioned stimulus] are sensory stimuli (usually of different modalities) and the only responses are discriminations; after a number of pairings, when the *CS* is given, the subject often reports the *US* also, either as an image or as a reality, in which case an experimental hallucination has been produced. Apparently this procedure is most effective when carried out with help of hypnosis.

Some History: The Banishment

Even a cursory survey of the psychological literature reveals that there was a good deal of attention to images of all kinds during the first flowering of scientific psychology before and around the turn of the twentieth century. The clinical literature showed a good deal of interest in hallucinations and other pathological types of images up until the First World War, reported from hysterics and even normal persons, as well as from the psychotic and organic cases that dominate the more recent papers in this largely psychiatric literature. Despite the emergence of eidetic imagery as a topic of intensive investigation between the two wars, psychologists generally lost interest in imagery. Even the parapsychological literature, which had been rife with reports of ghosts and other apparitions, turned to other sorts of phenomena during the 1920s, '30s, and '40s. Moreover, most of what was written during this "dry period" was European, and in languages other than English. Yet during the past decade, almost all of these trends have been reversed, and there are indications that the various types of imagery listed above will continue to attract more of psychologists' attention in the near future.

What happened? Aside from the general fact that times and interests change, why were images once something every psychologist knew a good deal about and took quite seriously, only to become a minor matter worthy of only brief mention in textbooks and less concern in the laboratory or clinic, until their very recent renaissance?

As I reconstruct it, the history is as follows. The "new psychology" of the 1890's was a science of mind, its contents, and their laws, as revealed by observation and experiments. A prominent part of what introspection yielded, of course, was imagery. Sir Francis Galton had a special interest in imagery and in the course of making a natural-historical study of it invented the first questionnaire and made one of the first statistical surveys. With great freshness and enthusiasm, he explored this new province and described some of its odd inhabitants (like the synesthesias and number forms) in a way that has never been surpassed. People were interested in thinking, then, because that was one of the main activities of mind, psy-

chology's proper subject matter, and images seemed to be the main elements into which this process could be *introspectively analyzed*. . . .

* * *

During the years just before the First World War, two new solutions were proposed—that of behaviorism and that of psychoanalysis. They have more in common than is often supposed: Both are primarily concerned with behavior, neither assuming that the description of conscious contents really explains anything. For many years, however, Freud's influence was far less important for the mainstream of psychology than Watson's. The challenging manifestoes of behaviorism seemed the beginning of a new era of objective scientific progress for psychology, and such a new era did in fact begin. As Hebb (1960) wrote recently, it was the American revolution of psychology; and like a political revolution, it necessarily went to extremes. Imagery, attention, states of consciousness, and other such central concepts of the old era were anathematized as "mentalistic" and cast into outer darkness.

* * *

Factors in the Reemergence of Imagery

A number of practical problems in engineering psychology, and similarly hard-headed branches of our discipline, have recurrently and importantly made psychologists and others take note of imagery, especially in its more dramatic forms such as hallucination. Radar operators who have to monitor a scope for long periods; long-distance truck drivers in night runs over turnpikes, but also other victims of "highway hypnosis"; jet pilots flying straight and level at high altitudes; operators of snowcats and other such vehicles of polar exploration, when surrounded by snowstorms —all of these persons have been troubled by the emergence into consciousness of vivid imagery, largely visual but often kinesthetic or auditory, which they may take momentarily for reality. In such a situation, when serious accidents can occur on its account, practical people are not likely to be impressed by the argument that imagery is unworthy of study because it is "mentalistic" and virtually impossible to experiment on with animals. Today, when we are faced with the prospect that astronauts and cosmonauts will be piloting their complex new vehicles for long periods of time through drastically modified and impoverished environments, deprived of the sensory pull of gravity on the muscles, joints, and otoliths, it becomes even more than a matter of individual life and death to make sure that we know as much as possible about this vagary of the human operator; now our national prestige as well may hinge on our knowledge of the conditions that induce hallucinations.

Another, quite unrelated, source of the new interest has been a series of first-hand accounts of persons who have been imprisoned in concentration camps and interrogated by the secret police of totalitarian regimes. A recurrent theme in such stories is what one former captive called "the famous 'cinema' of prisoners": pseudohallucinatory imagery brought on by prolonged isolation, sleep deprivation, and the multiple regressive pressures of forcible indoctrination or thought reform (Paloszi-Horvath, 1959).

It is well known that much of the recent mushrooming of research on sensory and perceptual deprivation, which was sparked by the above practical problems, has been concerned with the subjective phenomena reported by the McGill subjects, whether one calls them hallucinations, phosphenes, hypnagogic images, or what not. A parallel development of the past decade is the great interest in hallucinogenic drugs, which began with the discovery of lysergic acid, picked up added steam when biochemists pointed out the structural similarity of its indole-based molecule and that of mescaline to adrenalin, noradrenalin, and serotonin, and went into high gear with the emergence of psilocybin, bufotenin, adrenochrome, and other synthetic hallucinogens as possible clues to the mystery of schizophrenia. What with the growth of psychopharmacology and deprivation research, there has been a great deal of attention to imaginal phenomena in the popular press, and college students come to experiments expecting startling visual experiences. As one of them put it in the course of a study in our laboratory, "Hallucinations are the thing in the universities now, you know." Even a subject who reports a good deal of visual imagery is likely to complain in disappointment after perceptual deprivation: "The experiment is a flop. There are no reactions" (Warbasse, 1962).

Another journalistic sensation of recent years may be related to the reemergence of attention to the possibility that nonhospitalized persons may hallucinate: the great to-do about flying saucers or Unidentified Flying Objects. It is probably no coincidence that the parapsychological literature has begun once more to contain a sprinkling of papers about ghosts, apparitions, and telepathically transmitted imagery; Boring's "current of credence" is at work again, in all sorts of unexpected places.

Another unpredictable source of the revived interest in imagery is the great advances that have been made in brain research. In 1883 Charcot had reported a dramatic case: A man with an exceptional power of visualization, probably eidetic and with what is popularly known as a photographic memory, suddenly experienced its complete loss, apparently as the result of a cerebral vascular accident. Not only was he thereafter unable to visualize at all, but he showed in other ways an inability to make any contact with visual traces: He could not recognize places or faces (not even his own mirror image!), experienced no more visual dreams, and could not draw anything that was not immediately present. . . .

* * *

It has long been known that everyone can experience hallucinations and does so regularly in a certain state of consciousness: sleep. When Moruzzi and Magoun discovered that the reticular substance of the brain stem was directly responsible for sleep and wakefulness, and that the degree of behavioral and subjective alertness corresponds quite closely to the amount of cortical activation from this deep structure, such philosophical and mentalistic concepts as states of consciousness began to enter psychology again, this time coming from the respectable mouths of biologists. Cajal, Polyak, and others have discovered efferent fibers running from the reticular formation out to the retina itself, so that the RAS [reticular activating system] may very well play a critical role in hallucinations, mediating something like Freud's "regression to perception," the hypothetical topographic regression producing dream imagery (Scheibel and Scheibel, 1962).

During the past decade, research on dreams has undergone a remarkable resurgence, having received its new impetus from physiology. The well-known work of Dement and Kleitman (1957), by providing a relatively objective physiological indicator of dreaming, has attracted a growing host of investigators to the study of this fascinating hallucinatory experience. Correlatively, psychoanalysts such as Erikson (1954), Fisher (1954), and Saul and Sheppard (1956) have turned their interest to the manifest dream, so that the dream's imagery is now being investigated and not just brushed aside in the search for the latent dream thought.

The most dramatic of the relevant neurological discoveries have been those of Penfield and his collaborators. In the course of attempts to find and cut out the pathological focus of temporal-lobe epilepsies, Penfield (Penfield and Jasper, 1954) developed a technique of opening the skull under local anesthesia and then directly stimulating the exposed cortex by electrodes. One such patient exclaimed,

"I just heard one of my children speaking." She added that . . . she could hear the neighborhood noises as well. . . . She was asked whether it seemed to be a memory and she replied, "Oh no, it seemed more real than that." She thought she was looking into the yard and saw as well as heard the boy (p. 137).

After regularly encountering this kind of thing with scores of patients, Penfield and Jasper concluded:

there are in the temporal cortex innumerable neurone patterns which constitute records of memory. The electrode causes the patient to have a psychical experience, like the memory of some past event, and he can describe it as he lies upon the operating table. The hallucination thus produced may be auditory or visual, or both, but is neither a single sound nor a frozen picture . . . such hallucinations, or memories, or dreams continue to unfold slowly while the electrode is held in place. They are terminated suddenly when the electrode is withdrawn. This is a startling discovery. It brings psychical phenomena into the field of physiology. It should have profound significance also in the field of psychology provided we can interpret the facts properly (p. 242f.).

*   *   *

The final contributing element in this comeback story is the recent burgeoning of a new psychology of thinking. Once a central problem of psychology, thought seemed to the early behaviorists worthy of study only if it could be proved a peripheral matter, a kind of implicit behavior using the vocal apparatus. With the equivocal outcome of these attempts to explain it away, thinking lost favor as a topic of research. Yet the past dozen years have seen the founding of a number of centers for cognitive research and the publication of several important books on thinking: Such minor indicators as APA symposia and special summer seminars tell the unmistakable story that thought has become a fashionable topic once again.

To explain this remarkable somersault, I would like to go back a moment to the early days of psychology and ask, what was the task of our science as the introspectionists saw it?—to describe and explain the mind, the facts of perception, memory, imagination, thinking, emotion, etc., as immediately given to the psychologist, who could and did study them on an N of 1—himself. The task of psychology as behaviorism reformulated it was to describe and explain the objectively observable behavior of other organisms (other than oneself). Introspection could play no role, except in the attenuated form of discrimination: One could ask the subject to discriminate two subjectively differing sensations or like phenomena (in the strict sense), and that took care of the need to get inside the head. The specific topics of interest shifted somewhat with an especial emphasis on learning instead of memory, problem solving in place of thinking.

Model building played little role, if any, in either of these psychologies. Indeed, the emergence of theoretical models in psychology may be an even more important revolution than any other. Analogical and metaphorical theorizing is as old as psychology, but the construction of explicit and testable models is a development of fairly recent times. Interestingly, Freud (1954) was the first of the model builders, with his 1895 Project for a Scientific Psychology, and psychoanalysis has always had a strong theoretical bent, even though the models Freud successively produced became less and less adapted to empirical test. Watsonian behaviorism did not have an explicit theoretical model; and the purest kind of behaviorism in a way is that of Skinner: No explicit model is assumed and one simply looks for lawful regularities in the relations of stimulus conditions and objectively observable responses. But the organism is obviously not empty; it is full of fascinating circuitry, or field processes, or however you want to conceptualize its anatomical structure and physiological functions, particularly those of the nervous system. The advances of model building and that of direct neuropsychological looks inside the black box have proceeded almost *pari passu*.

*   *   *

Some Implications for Current Research

What I know of the recent literature on imagery seems to me characterized by a striking dearth of phenomenological and taxonomic studies. Consistent with the change in psychology as a whole, few persons consider it worthwhile to examine the contents of consciousness attentively and laboriously classify the types of imagery. Indeed, the evidence is compelling that this kind of activity as an end in itself is a blind alley. Yet there was a legitimate job to be done; since it was neglected, few conceptual or operational tools were at hand to cope with the phenomena once again disclosed by the developments I have described. One consequence has been unnecessary controversy and apparent disagreement of experimenters growing out of a failure to communicate their findings clearly. In the jumble of available terminology a few concepts glittered attractively, notably hallucination, a term that has come in for a great deal of overuse and misuse. From our present vantage point, to use this hyperbolic word for all of the manifold and at least superficially multifarious quasi sensations and pseudoperceptions induced by impoverished informational inputs or by psychedelic drugs is comparable to calling the gamut of linguistic peculiarities and oddities of schizophrenic speech by the most extreme term available, "word salad."

* * *

To get back to the isolation experiments: With so many complicating factors within the subject to control or interfere with his ability to become conscious of whatever kinds of imaging he is biologically capable of, it will not be easy to establish the exact nature of the kinds of experience engendered by the experimental conditions. It might be useful to consider a kind of null hypothesis, that one function of the variegated stimulation provided by the ordinary lives of most of us is to distract our attention from what is going on inside. We are not a nation of philosophers; few of us have either the leisure or the inclination to meditate and get acquainted with our own purely internal lives. In any introductory course in psychology, are there not always many students who are oblivious of such universal phenomena as double images, *muscae volitantes* (the drifting shadows of bleached red blood cells between the vitreous and the retina; cf. White and Levatin, 1962), and afterimages, and who have great difficulty in becoming aware of them? Put a sample of contemporary men into an artificially simplified environment except what they can generate themselves, and many will begin to notice entoptic phenomena for the first time. Cohen, Silverman, and Shmavonian (1962) have reported the very suggestive finding that in experimental isolation,

field-dependent subjects report hallucinations while the field independent, experimentally defined as those who can use inner feelings of gravitational pull to orient themselves, report only their usual images and phosphenes. Clearly, it is futile to try to discover any direct effect on hallucination of diffuse light versus darkness, or any other independent variable, while ignoring the main sources of variance, which are within the subjects themselves.

Finally, I want to mention briefly one speculative implication of the work on imagery, which to me opens the most exciting vistas. How many of us have not envied an occasional friend who enjoys what is known as a photographic memory? How greatly it would enhance our enjoyment of life as well as our effectiveness to be able, at will, to play back a full record of experience in essentially complete detail! Most of us simply have to dismiss this fantasy as beyond the capacities with which we were born. Several lines of evidence are beginning to suggest, however, that the capacity for an astonishingly complete recording of experience may be virtually universal, and that the problem is primarily one of getting access to the traces. Recall Penfield's finding that an electrode on the right spot of the temporal lobe can evoke a detailed hallucinatory reliving of a forgotten experience. Put this together with the evidence from studies of the Poetzl phenomenon that much more may register in the brain than is in focal awareness; and evidence from hypnotic investigations that induced regression can bring back with great vivacity and affective force memories that have been long forgotten—as can lysergic acid, at times, dreams, and psychoanalytic treatment. Notice that in each of these diverse examples, the vehicle of the extraordinary recall is imagery. Studies of hypnotic hypermnesia have uniformly failed to find that the trance aided recall of nonsense syllables or other forms of nonimaginal memory; hypermnesia works best when a relevant image can be summoned up (cf. White, Fox, and Harris, 1940). The indirect means of imagery may furnish the key to the fabulous storehouse of memory, if we can learn how to make use of this neglected human capacity.

Summary

During scientific psychology's early days, imagery was a major topic. The controversy over imageless thought became a death struggle of introspectionism, and imagery was one of the main foci of

Watson's attack in the polemics that founded behaviorism. In the fashionable scorn for mentalism that was quickly professed by psychologists in the United States, imagery was ostracized as a topic of scientific concern. During the past dozen years, it has started to come back, brought along into psychology's best parlors by high-prestige relatives from "harder" disciplines, like brain research, or by good customers looking for psychological help with a number of practical problems. Many psychologists, who had been trained during the period when it was not considered proper to mention such things, did not recognize the varieties of imagery and often mistook them for hallucination, which was supposed to be an exclusively pathological manifestation. Now, however, it is being rediscovered that normal, prosaic folk, and not just psychotics, can hallucinate, given the right circumstances.

Meanwhile, the methodological approach of psychology had been slowly changing so that it became simple to conceptualize subjective phenomena as part of the inner workings of a theoretical model. An interest in thinking became modish again, even in forms of cognition that seem to have expressive or stylistic, not necessarily adaptive, significance. The subjective world of images and the like had progressed from being at first the total subject matter of psychology, then a marshy realm of uninteresting epiphenomena, and now a legitimate output of a theoretically constructed psychic apparatus, and perhaps a specially interesting one, since it may give something of a look inside the famous black box.

Throughout all this, the working clinician has never tried to do without either behavioral observation or reports of subjective reaction. He cannot afford the luxury of any theoretical asceticism about his data; he needs any information he can get from his patients and learns that reports of nonverbal images are often valuable communications in a primary-process modality. In his clinical work, he proceeds empirically, noticing everything that differentiates patients, everything that helps him to evaluate, understand, and treat the individual. When he writes, however, he tries to sound more theoretical, and he has usually been much influenced by one or another version of psychoanalytic theory. Ironically, psychoanalysis has had as little systematic interest in images as academic psychology, which may have turned the attention of clinical psychologists away from these fascinating and elusive phenomena. Now that the tide has turned on the experimental beaches of clinical psychology, the working clinicians may be counted on to take the plunge. Clinical observation can make many important contributions to our understanding of the numerous form varieties of imagery; come on in—the water's fine!

REFERENCES

Cohen, S. I., Silverman, A. J., & Shmavonian, B. M. Psychophysiological studies in altered sensory environments. *Journal of Psychosomatic Research,* 1962, **6,** 259–281.

Dement, W., & Kleitman, N. The relation of eye movements during sleep to dream activity: An objective method for the study of dreaming. *Journal of Experimental Psychology,* 1957, **53,** 339–346.

English, H. B., & English, A. C. *A comprehensive dictionary of psychological and psychoanalytic terms.* New York: McKay, 1958.

Erikson, E. H. The dream specimen of psychoanalysis. *Journal of the American Psychoanalytic Association,* 1954, **2,** 5–26.

Fisher, C. Dreams and perception. *Journal of the American Psychoanalytic Association,* 1954, **3,** 380–445.

Freud, S. *The origins of psychoanalysis.* New York: Basic Books, 1954.

Goldberger, L., & Holt, R. R. Experimental interference with reality contact: Method and group results. *Journal of Nervous and Mental Disease,* 1958, **127,** 99–122.

Hebb, D. O. The American revolution. *American Psychologist,* 1960, **15,** 735–745.

Jaensch, E. R. *Eidetic imagery.* New York: Harcourt, Brace & World, 1930.

Osgood, C. E. *Method and theory in experimental psychology.* New York: Oxford University Press, 1953.

Paloszi-Horvath, G. *The undefeated.* Boston: Little, Brown, 1959.

Penfield, W., & Jasper, H. *Epilepsy and the functional anatomy of the human brain.* Boston: Little, Brown, 1954.

Saul, L. J., & Sheppard, E. An attempt to quantify emotional forces using manifest dreams: A preliminary study. *Journal of the American Psychoanalytic Association,* 1956, **4,** 486–502.

Scheibel, M. E., & Scheibel, A. B. Hallucinations and the brainstem reticular core. In L. J. West (Ed.), *Hallucinations.* New York: Grune & Stratton, 1962.

Warbasse, A. F. The relationship of self-image variables to reactions to isolation. Unpublished doctoral dissertation, New York University, 1962.

White, H. E., & Levatin, P. "Floaters" in the eye. *Scientific American,* 1962, **206** (6), 119–127.

White, R. W., Fox, G. F., & Harris, W. W. Hypnotic hypermnesia for recently learned materials. *Journal of Abnormal and Social Psychology,* 1940, **35,** 88–103.

Woodworth, R. S., & Schlossberg, H. *Experimental psychology.* New York: Holt, Rinehart & Winston, 1954.

42

Denotative Meaning: Images in Language

Arthur W. Staats

Can you imagine a Saint Bernard dog? That huge head with the large square muzzle; the brown and white coat, shaggy yet neatly brushed; those gigantic legs and paws that can inflict pain even as he playfully jumps upon his master with tail wagging and eyes brimming with joy and friendliness. Quite an easy task for anyone who has ever seen such a dog.

Now try to imagine an apparition with the torso of a man rising mistily from a cauldron of boiling water. The steam rises from the bubbling liquid. About two feet above the top of the water the steam gradually takes on the shape of the lower torso of the man. His chest is bare and covered with thick curly black hair. His heavily muscled arms are thrown wide, his head is raised high, his eyes are turned toward the heavens. Long ringlets of thick white hair stream down from the craggy features of his face, the time-worn face of a man who has lived a full and contented life. The lips are curled into a shriek of pure joy as he contemplates his master.

Such images are quite easy to arouse through the use of appropriately chosen words. How is it that mere words can create, within our minds, such vivid pictures? Why is it that marks on paper or sounds in the air can elicit such complete and complex pictures? This article explores the ways in which words come to represent such mental images.

It has been suggested that many words are systematically paired with an aspect of the environment—with a particular stimulus. According to the principle of classical conditioning, any response that the stimulus elicits should be conditioned to the word involved. . . . Many stimuli elicit emotional responses, and thus many words come to elicit this type of meaning response. However, there are many stimuli that we are "sensitive" to that do not elicit such responses. We *see* these stimuli, *hear* them, *feel* (touch) them, and so on, but these stimuli have no effect in eliciting emotional responses.

Nevertheless, even in these cases, naturalistic observation suggests that the process of classical conditioning—of pairing a word with one of these types of stimuli—does affect the word involved. For example, the word BLUE which is systematically paired with blue light acquires different qualities than does the word SQUEAK which is systematically paired with a certain type of auditory stimulation. If we assumed that such sensory stimuli also elicit responses—sensory responses—the manner in which words acquire *denotative* meaning would also be suggested from our knowledge of classical conditioning.

That is, it can be suggested that seeing a visual stimulus is actually *responding* to the stimulus, hearing a sound stimulus is responding to the stimulus, touching a tactile stimulus is responding to the stimulus, and so on. Furthermore it can be suggested that *part* of the sensory response elicited by a sensory stimulus can be conditioned to another stimulus with which it is paired. When this has occurred the new stimulus will come to elicit the conditioned part of the sensory response, which we commonly call an image. Finally, it may be suggested that many *words* are stimuli that in this manner come to elicit conditioned sensory responses (images) in the individual who has been so conditioned.

These suggestions have been couched in terms that suggest speculation. However, in addition to the theory of classical conditioning, the foregoing analysis, and supporting naturalistic observations, there are experimental results that actually lead to these statements as conclusions. Thus, Leuba

(1940) has shown that a neutral stimulus paired with a sensory stimulus as the *UCS* [unconditioned stimulus] will become a *CS* [conditioned stimulus] that elicits what is described in everyday life as an image. For example, while a subject was hypnotized Leuba paired a buzzer as the *CS* with a pinprick as the *UCS*. It was found that the subject would later report a painful sensation on his hand simply on the presentation of the buzzer. Ellson (1941) has also shown that a light as the *CS* when paired with a tone as the *UCS* will come to elicit the faint hearing of the tone before the tone has been presented. He called these hallucinations, produced by sensory conditioning. Ellson cites other evidence in the literature for the conditioning of sensations.

These are examples of the direct conditioning of sensory responses. In addition, however, there are a number of other experimental results that support the same analysis. Some of these experiments have generally been given the term sensory preconditioning. Brogden (1939) originally paired a bell and a light for a number of trials, using dogs as subjects. Then he later used one of these two stimuli as the *CS* in another phase of the experiment and conditioned a response to it. It was then found that the response when conditioned to the bell sound, for example, would also be elicited by the light—even though the response had never been conditioned to the light. Thus, as a result of being presented together a number of times, light and the bell had become functionally the same. What happened to one of the stimuli would result in (or generalize to) the same type of conditioning to the other stimulus. This type of result has been shown to occur with human subjects.

These results would be expected on the basis of the following analysis. If each sensory stimulus, the light and the bell, elicits a sensory response that can be conditioned, then the pairing of the stimuli would result in two types of conditioning. The sensory response to the light, the seeing of the light, would be conditioned (at least in part) to the bell sound. When this result is considered, the bell is the *CS* and the light which elicits the seeing

response is the *UCS*. The process is shown in Figure 1. The seeing response, *r* in the figure, is printed in lower-case letters to indicate that it is not directly observed in the experiment. The seeing response is also depicted as having stimulus properties, that is as *r–s*. (In general, although not always diagrammed, every response is assumed to produce stimulus events, so the present case is no exception.)

In addition, the same process should also occur with the sensory response to the bell. That is the bell as a *UCS* results in the response of hearing the bell, which according to the same rationale should be conditioned to the light. This process is exactly the same, except that the roles of the *CS* and the *UCS* are filled by the light and the bell respectively rather than the reverse.

Thus, as a result of the pairing of the two stimuli, each comes to elicit the sensory response elicited by the other. Because of this it would be expected that the two stimuli, the bell and the light, would now have become functionally the same—even though before this process they had not been. That is, now if one of the stimuli is involved in an additional conditioning process, the resulting conditioning will affect the other stimulus in the same way for the subject involved.

The rationale for this expectation is shown in Figure 2. Let us say that in addition to the first conditioning, the subject who had previously been presented with the bell and the light is put into another conditioning procedure. In this one the light is again presented, this time paired with an electric shock as the *UCS*. Now electric shock elicits as a response a change in the rate at which the subject's heart is beating. This response, among other occurrences, will be conditioned to the *stimulus produced by the seeing response elicited by the light*. That is, the light as a stimulus elicits the seeing sensory response *r–s* and the heart rate response will be conditioned to the stimulus part of this sensory response. The stimulus part of the sensory response thus would become a *cs* for the heart rate response (see Figure 2a).

Now it can be seen why the conditioning of the heart rate response to the light will have the

FIGURE 1 *Classical conditioning of a sensory (seeing) response to another stimulus*

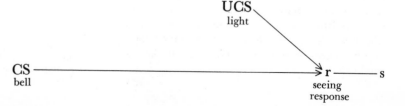

FIGURE 2 (a) *The light is paired with the shock as the* UCS. *The light elicits a seeing response and the stimuli produced by this sensory response function as the* CS *and come to elicit the heart rate response.* (b) *Later, the bell stimulus is presented. It elicits the seeing response also—because of prior pairing with the light—and the seeing response elicits the heart rate response. The bell, it should be remembered, has never been paired with the shock.*

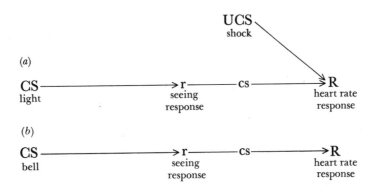

same effect upon (will generalize to) the bell, even though the bell has never been paired with the shock. The bell, because of previous pairing with the light, also elicits the seeing response on a conditioned basis and this conditioned sensory response will elicit the heart rate response, as shown in Figure 2b.

This is a complicated analysis. However, it does suggest that sensations have response characteristics which can be conditioned to new stimuli. There are additional experimental results that anchor these findings and the resulting analysis more firmly in the area of language learning. This type of study has been considered under the label of semantic generalization.

In one type of semantic generalization study a response of the subject is conditioned to a word and then the stimulus object the word "denotes" is later presented to the subject. It has been found that the object, never itself conditioned to elicit the response, will do so, if the word has first been conditioned to elicit the response. That is, the two stimuli—the word stimulus and the object stimulus—are functionally equivalent. Something that happens to the word generalizes to the object. The converse is also true. If the response is conditioned to the stimulus object, the word will as a result also elicit the response.

The following may be used as an example. Let us say that the word BLUE has been used as the *CS* in a classical conditioning procedure, being paired with an electric shock as the stimulus. After some trials the word BLUE will come to elicit a conditioned heart rate response. At a later time

if the subject involved is shown a blue light it will be found that the blue light will also elicit the conditioned heart rate response.

This equivalence of function reminds us of the equivalence already described which occurred between the two sensory stimuli after they had been paired together. Actually, the same analysis may be used to account for the facts of semantic generalization. That is, the reason this word to object generalization will take place may be thought to involve previous conditioning like that in the sensory preconditioning. That is, in our language culture we have all had a past history when the word BLUE as a stimulus had been paired with blue light on multitudinous occasions. For example, we have all had experience when the word BLUE is spoken by ourselves or someone else at the same time that we are looking at a blue object. This "preconditioning" experience would be expected to perform the type of conditioning shown in Figure 3.

As shown in the Figure 3a when the word BLUE is paired with the blue light, the blue light elicits its sensory response. The sensory response is conditioned to the word BLUE which then comes, as a *CS*, to elicit the conditionable parts of the blue sensory response. At this point, for this subject, both the blue light stimulus and the word BLUE elicit the same, or similar, response.

At a later time, in the semantic generalization experiment, the word BLUE is paired with the electric shock as is shown in Figure 3b. Each time the word BLUE is presented it elicits the blue sensory response previously conditioned to it. The

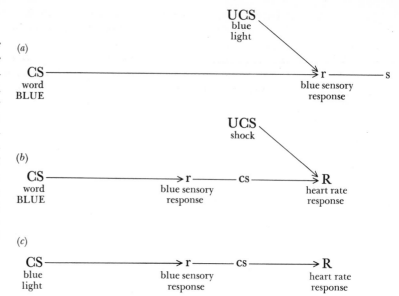

FIGURE 3   (a) *Pairing of the word BLUE and the blue light conditions the blue sensory response to the word.* (b) *In further work with the subject, shock is paired with the word BLUE, thus conditioning the heart rate response to the conditioned blue sensory response.* (c) *The blue light now also elicits the heart rate response since it elicits the blue sensory response (on an unconditioned basis).*

shock elicits the heart rate response, and this response is conditioned to the blue sensory response (or, rather, the stimulus components of this response). Thus, as a result of *this* conditioning the blue sensory response comes to elicit the heart rate response.

This then establishes the circumstances for the blue light also to elicit the heart rate response, even though this light has never been paired with the shock. This is shown in Figure 3c. That is, the presentation of the blue light results in the elicitation of the blue sensory response, and the stimulus of the blue sensory response is a *CS* for the heart rate response.

Thus, the original pairing of the blue light and the word BLUE made them functionally the same. It would also be expected that conditioning involving a blue light would generalize back to the word BLUE on the basis of the same rationale. In addition, it would be expected that if there was another word that had been paired with blue light many times in the past, as the word AZURE may have been for someone in our culture, the same functional equivalence would also apply to this word. That is, if a response was conditioned to blue light it would generalize to the word AZURE since it would elicit the same sensory response as the light.

In addition, however, the two words BLUE and AZURE would also be functionally equivalent. Any experience that the individual had with one word would generalize to the other. This would be expected since each would elicit the same conditioned blue sensory response. It is suggested that

this is one basis for synonymity. If two words are paired with the same, or similar, stimuli they will come to elicit the same or similar conditioned meaning response. Then anything that happens to one word stimulus, which conditions a new response to the world's conditioned meaning response, will generalize to the other word. (Synonyms would, of course, also be functionally equivalent in the type of communication already described.)

*   *   *

The author derived such a hypothesis and tested it by using the same language-conditioning procedure that has already been described, in which meaningful words were used as the *UCS* and a nonsense syllable was used as the *CS*. The rationale in the hypothesis may be stated in the following manner. When a word elicits an *emotional* meaning response, if that word is paired with another word, the second word will also come to elicit the emotional meaning response. If it is true that words also come to elicit sensory meaning responses in the same manner as they come to elicit emotional meaning responses, then the same expectation should hold. That is, when a word eliciting a sensory meaning response is paired with another word, the second word should also come to elicit that sensory meaning response.

In the study, following the procedure already described, a nonsense syllable was paired once each time with a number of different words—all of the words, however, elicited the same sensory meaning response. Thus, twelve words with angular sensory meaning—*square, box, roof, triangle, steeple, diamond, window, hallway, zigzag, book, pyramid, wedge*—were paired with a nonsense syllable for one group of subjects. Twelve words with another sensory meaning—*coil, globe, hub, barrel, bulb, target, wheel, marbles, knob, hoop, pearl, ball*—were paired with another nonsense syllable. For another group of subjects the non-sense syllable in each case was paired with the words having the other type of meaning. It should also be added that although these two groups of words differed in the sensory meaning responses they elicited, they were chosen not to be different in the emotional meaning they elicited. Thus, any result in the conditioning of meaning would be the effect of the conditioning of the sensory re-sponse meaning.

The results showed that the conditioning of the sensory response meaning did indeed occur. When a nonsense syllable was paired with words that elicited angular sensory responses (images) the nonsense syllable was later rated as having an angular meaning. When a nonsense syllable was paired with words that elicited round sensory responses (images) the nonsense syllable was later rated as having a round meaning.

It may be concluded that denotative meaning (or conditioned sensory responses) may be condi-tioned to new meaningless words. Moreover, the principles of classical conditioning appear to be involved, as is the case with affective word mean-ing responses. Other studies provide evidence that sensory responses can be conditioned in first-order classical conditioning procedures. The same pro-cess appears to occur with words in higher-order conditioning.

Thus, it is suggested that some words elicit con-ditioned sensory responses, or images. On the basis of this analysis, it may also be suggested that the principles of classical conditioning will account for what we call word imagery. That is, when an individual hears or reads a descriptive passage that contains an account of sensory stimuli, it is fre-quently said that the individual experiences im-agery that is like the actual events being described. The individual would in a sense be seeing or hear-ing, or whatever, something like that which the actual stimuli would arouse.

This vicarious sensory experience through words may be considered to be one of the powerful func-tions of language. Through words the individual can have experiences that provide learning similar to that which the actual events would have pro-vided. The individual can thus acquire new sen-sory experience without ever having had contact with the objects themselves. For example, many people have never had contact with a jellyfish. If they were told, however, that a jellyfish is "mottled purple, pink, and white," is "gelatinous in its flex-ibility," comes in "various sizes around eighteen inches across," and gives a "stinging sensation on contact," these words would elicit grossly appro-priate sensory responses. Even in this simple ex-ample, the individual so conditioned by these verbal means will acquire a constellation of sen-sory responses that approximates to some extent the sensations he would receive if he had direct contact with the organism. Furthermore, other be-haviors that he might learn under the control of the organism itself as a stimulus could also be learned to the conditioned sensory responses. That is, if told to avoid touching the organism, although he had never seen such an animal, he would avoid one on the very first direct contact.

There are several points implicit in this discus-sion that should be elaborated. First, it is sug-gested that we acquire a repertoire of words that elicit general sensory responses. That is, white light is a stimulus that is part of many different stimuli. When the word stimulus *white* is paired with many different objects which reflect that type of light the word comes to elicit a "white condi-tioned sensory response." That is, pairing the word with a white ball, a white dress, a white car, a white house, and so on, will condition the sensory response elicited by white stimuli to the word. This word may then be used (as a "concept") in com-bination with many different words that elicit sen-sory responses to produce new combinations of sensory responses.

Take this example. *It was bright white, rotund, with short legs and hooves, and a very long neck, with bright black stripes around it. It had a thick, flat head with wide jaws, and long yellow teeth, and the animal growled loudly.* All of the words in this example have acquired their meaning through be-ing paired with various sensory stimuli and have come through this to elicit a particular conditioned sensory response. Such words have been called concepts; in the present terms such concepts are words that have come to elicit one or more condi-tioned sensory responses in the manner described.

The above example also illustrates more clearly that when words, each of which elicits a sensory response, are combined, a larger, combined, sen-sory response may result. It would then be ex-pected that if a new word was paired with this combined sensory response, the new word would become capable of eliciting the total sensory re-sponse. Thus, the individual would have acquired a new, complex image, which would be elicited whenever the word occurred. Thus, if the word GLOX was paired with the sensory words in the above example—as in the statement A GLOX IS BRIGHT WHITE, ROTUND, WITH SHORT LEGS, and so on—GLOX would come to elicit the combined sensory response.

This is a powerful form of human learning. The individual may think with these new images, formed on the basis of language conditioning. The words which elicit the new combined images could also be combined with other words to form new conditionings and thus new images. *Moreover, this analysis allows a rapprochement between cognitive approaches to human behavior and a stimulus-response approach. The processes of this type that are seen as cognitive events may be considered in terms of stimuli, responses, and the principles of classical conditioning.*

It should be remembered that the ability of the individual to learn in the ways that have been described depends upon previous training that had conditioned the sensory responses to the words. This type of training may be considered to yield a basic behavioral repertoire—which will enable the individual to learn further from words in a variety of experiences. If the individual does not have this basic behavioral repertoire, he will be unable to profit in the same manner as others do from the multitude of language experiences to which he is subjected. . . .

One final point is important here. Words that elicit conditioned sensory responses may be combined in ways that yield a composite sensory response that has no real counterpart in experience. The example of the GLOX above was such a case. It is also true that no one has ever experienced referents for GOD, DEVILS, FLYING SAUCERS, and many other current terms. Yet for many people these words elicit vivid sensory responses. Good examples may be drawn from history. For example, in the Middle Ages people accepted as real the existence of various forms of witches, hobgoblins, elves, dragons, spirits, and so on.

. . . [T]he basilisk kills serpents by his breath and men by his glance. . . . "As to the ant-lion, his father hath the shape of a lion, his mother that of an ant . . . these bring forth the ant-lion, a compound of both and in part like to either. . . ." [T]he "cockatrice" of scripture . . . "drieth and burneth leaves with his touch, and he is of so great venom and perilous that he slayeth and wasteth him that nigheth him without tarrying. . . ." (White, 1899, pp. 899–900)

There are, of course, no such actual stimulus objects, so man's sensory responses to this and other such words must have been acquired through language conditioning.

Thus, it may be concluded that we can learn sensory responses that could not arise from contact with actual events—which do not exist. It may be added that sensory conditioning from language can in this sense produce images that are not adjustive for the individual. When an individual responds to a "nonexistent image" with behavior that is maladjusted, we may speak of this as a hallucination.

REFERENCES

Brogden, W. J. Sensory preconditioning. *Journal of Experimental Psychology*, 1939, **25,** 323–332.

Ellson, D. Hallucinations produced by sensory conditioning. *Journal of Experimental Psychology*, 1941, **28,** 1–20.

Leuba, C. Images as conditioned sensations. *Journal of Experimental Psychology*, 1940, **26,** 345–351.

White, A. D. *A history of the warfare of science with theology in Christendom.* (Orig. publ. 1899) New York: Braziller, 1955.

43

Language in a Few Words:
With Notes on a Rereading, 1966

Eric P. Hamp

There are two widely differing approaches to the study of human language use. The first is the rote memorization technique developed by Hermann Ebbinghaus (1850–1909) and currently being used in many psychological laboratories. The second is linguistic analysis, the study of the structure of languages. The first method places the major emphasis upon the process of learning—how words and word associations are learned, and how well and how long they are remembered. The second method emphasizes the language itself, almost as though it exists outside the world of the speaker. Each approach has its strengths and weaknesses. The rote memory procedure tends to emphasize memory over comprehension; to deal with single words, or even nonwords, rather than with sentences and paragraphs as used by typical speakers. The linguistic procedure, on the other hand, emphasizes the medium itself rather than the more important user of the language. The author of this article presents the linguistic approach with verve.

The fundamental aim of scholarship is to advance knowledge. For this purpose it is necessary for the specialist to make use of terms and methods some of which are technically very complex. But the fruits of scholarship will be barren indeed, if from time to time they are not made intelligible to educated men at large in such a form that the nonspecialist may increase his understanding without being expected to retrace all the steps laboriously trodden in the first place by the specialist.

The fact that there is no comparable understanding of the advance of knowledge of such a familiar phenomenon as language seems hard to understand. [This situation has happily changed somewhat since these words were written, though with two reservations: (1) Recent knowledge has still not really percolated to the level of the average newspaper reader. (2) Attention to linguistics in the schools has not of late been entirely happy; in its new burst of popularity it threatens often to be more modish than informed.][1] Recent, but quite fundamental, findings concerning language have scarcely emerged from the snug covers of learned journals, indigestible dissertations, and formidable monographs concerned with elusive minutiae. From time to time attempts are made to quicken the body; yet they all have failed. Think, for example, of the expert who starts with remarks to the effect that language is usually thought to be a dull subject and then gets no further than promising to inspect a few of the fascinating byways of this "absorbing discipline," as he proceeds to unfurl tiresome, and often irrelevant, periphrastic expressions of the passive voice in English or Eskimo. Then there is the bombardier who opens a barrage of countless languages or the museum director who sets out to guide you through a picture gallery of languages. "Just look at all those words that resemble one another," says he. The intelligent reader, who is probably plagued every day with sufficient chaos of detail, is by now reaching for the string on the bed lamp. [To these there has been added in the last decade a new blight: the term-swapper. In this era of extravagant awe for chromium-plated scientism, authors frequently increase and impress their audiences, thinking to enrich and enhance their own scholarly precision, by parading very old and tired notions under technical-sounding names. Thus, sounds or letters become "phonemes"; parts of speech lose their old

Eric P. Hamp, "Language in a Few Words," The Journal of General Education, *V (1951)*, 286–302. *Permission to quote by the Pennsylvania State University Press.*

1 Material within brackets are the notes of the rereading in 1966.

names and become numbers; old-style commas and the spaces after simple phrases get replaced by single- and double-bars with superscript numerals peppered about; and in this guise a jargonish brand of pseudoreasoning and would-be data begin to sound as if they really meant something and led somewhere.]

Another subject concerned with language has come to the fore in recent years, an ingredient that in many ways only beclouds the issue precisely because of its validity as a province of knowledge in its own right, namely, that worrisome and sometimes popular topic, semantics. Semantics certainly has its proper place in any consideration of human communication; it is unfortunate that at present both controls and methods for observing and sifting semantic data are embarrassingly undeveloped. Just how are we to draw the lines defining how people "feel" about the connotations of linguistic expression? And to say—what seems to be a widespread notion—that when we have dealt with semantics we have explained a basic portion of the nature of language is simply not true. [Semantics is still a troubled subject. But in the past several years, with the advent of generative grammatical theory, a healthy attention has once again turned to it, and notable hypotheses, if not yet solutions, are being developed.]

Under the rubric of semantics there is also the question of the expression that logical categories and functions find in language. But, as long as discussion is restricted to these considerations of logic, the crucial question of language remains untouched. Languages are garments that clothe and enhance, or at times detract from, what we assume to be the mental processes of human beings. To use a gross simile, a tailor who restricts his study to anatomy will not learn what a good suit of clothes consists of; the success of Christian Dior does not rest on mere measurements of the configurations shared by all women. And, like good Chinese *couture*, the waist of a Paris mode in a given year has no necessary relationship to that slender middle part of a woman's body that finds quite different expression in the terms of a physical anthropologist or of the average man with an eye for beauty. Let me illustrate this with two English sentences: *There is no democracy where there is ruthless subjection of the peace-loving masses by the few* and *There are no whelps in that pigsty*. The first statement offers certain difficulties which it would be highly desirable to define. With the aid, if necessary, of an expert in animal husbandry, the second statement offers no problems at all of the same order.

Now if the equivalent of the first statement were found in *Pravda,* it might be alleged that the form of "subjection" has a different coverage in the realm of ideas from that usually found for example, in the *New York Times*. But that does not prevent the *Pravda* version from occurring in English in the *Daily Worker*. An analysis of this discrepancy does not necessarily tell us anything about the difference between the Russian *language* and English. On the other hand, among the various *linguistic* differences which we should find in the two versions would be the absence of any feature in the Russian to express our English form *the*. This does not mean that a Russian is unaware of such a distinction; in a given instance we can know nothing about such an alleged awareness, since we cannot crawl into his mind to find out. The important *linguistic* fact is that Russian simply puts a speaker under no compulsion to express this distinction at every turn, just as we do not have to change the form of a noun after a negative verb (a Russian does). [This discussion ignores the fact that there are also equally *linguistic,* but semantic, differences which could now be more fruitfully tackled in light of recent theoretical developments: e.g., *no* (contrasted with the Russian equivalent in such a sentence, where *there is* is negated), or *whelps* (which is compatible only with an interesting range of animals).]

Now let us regard these statements from the point of view of language. Both are statements in English, and both have essentially the same structure. That is to say, both make use of a great many of the same fundamental building blocks and also put them together in similar patterns. To point out a few characteristic English features, we notice that there are certain units of sound which occur in these statements: voiced *th* in *there,* voiceless *th* in *ruthless;* a voiceless rush of breath through the lips (if you speak one of certain forms of Standard English other than my own) for the *wh* of *whelps.* Unless you grew up speaking a language other than English, you can detect an audible rush of breath immediately after the *p* in *peace;* this does not occur after *p* in *whelps.* We find combinations of sounds such as *thl* (*ruthless*), *bj* (*subjection*), *lps* (*whelps*), *gst* (*pigsty*); we shall never find these at the beginning of an English word, as we may with *fy* in *few* (contrast *feud* and *food*). [Current theory now lays stress on the occurrence and nonoccurrence of sound sequences such as these; but they are, of course, still features of the language, even if rather superficial ones.]

I have picked out a few striking phonological features of English. Among European languages, phonological systems that use two *th*-sounds are found only in Welsh, Greek, Icelandic, and Albanian; Castilian Spanish has the voiceless *th* (I am, of course, referring throughout to *sounds,* and not spelling, which is merely an imperfect and often, as in the case of English, a grossly inadequate symbolism). [Linguistic theory has taken in recent years a much more active concern with graphic representations of language in their own right, and with their accounting within an adequate framework.] The *wh* is a *significant contrast* (note, for example, *which* beside *witch*) that is shared by no other standard European language.

Now when we say "significant contrast," we have struck at the heart of sound-systems in language. Certain other linguistic groups can be heard to pronounce our *wh,* but for them it may be simply a nonsignificant variation of one of their sound units. Manx, the language of the Isle of Man and now practically extinct, [It *is* now extinct.] employed the voiced *th* sound in the middle of a word between vowels. This was, however, not a distinctive sound, since it varied from time to time and from person to person with *z* in the self-same forms. In other words, it made no difference to a Manxman which of these two sounds he produced in that position. If we say the word *peace* immediately after we have taken a drink of water (opening our vocal chords with a snap), we are likely to produce what a phonetician would call a "glottalized" *p.* That will not bother us at all (so long as the water went down the right way), since this is not a significant distinction in our language. Tzeltal speakers in southern Mexico might be misunderstood in a similar circumstance. *Their* sound-pattern is such that they distinguish glottalized consonants clearly and significantly from the nonglottalized variety. To us some consonants merely sound "funny." This sort of inattention to sounds which are not significant in the language of the observer is one of the principal inadequacies of the earlier grammars written by Europeans of so-called "primitive" languages.

It is probable that no speaker produces precisely the same acoustical sound twice in succession. As yet, no absolute phonetic criteria have been established on an acoustic basis.

All the illustrations which we have just noticed have the point in common that in a given position one sound unit of a language may occur indiscriminately with varying qualities, as measured either in terms of physiological production or of the acoustic result which the observer hears; *within a limited range,* no matter what sound occurs, the result is still perfectly intelligible to a native speaker. Not only is it quite intelligible, it doesn't even sound the least bit "funny." To put the point another way, the interior economy of the linguistic pattern is not disturbed by these variations. It would appear that compounds are "pigeonholed" and associated by the hearer by means of a complex psychological process not yet understood by competent investigators. [It appears increasingly likely that sentences (and, in turn, their sounds) are "heard" by listeners through the medium of a vicarious unspoken (hence inaudible and nonobvious) imitation of the total grammatical process which was inferred to have gone into producing the model sentence, and then by mental comparison of the subliminal output of the imitation with the original perceived stimulus. In this sense, one's range of tolerance for "hearing" is a function of one's range of articulatory production coupled with one's perception of an individual acoustical instance embedded in a set of abstract grammatical rules thought to apply to a guessed sentence or discourse.] When we have to deal with different languages, the criterion of intelligibility, or of contrast within the sound-pattern, is contained in the fact that for different "sounds" different linguistic groups have varying ranges of tolerance. We may call the haphazard occurrence of an articulatory complex or "sound" within this range of tolerance in a given language FREE VARIATION.

To return to the *th* sounds found in European languages, it was noted above that, whereas various linguistic groups of Europe boasted both voiced and voiceless *th*'s, Spanish has only the voiceless variety. Anyone who knows Spanish will no doubt have already remarked that you can hear voiced *th*'s in great number in many dialects of Spanish. Although this is true as a phonetic or, if you will, acoustical fact, this phenomenon has no significance for the present-day patterning of the language. [That is, more accurately, for the basic abstract forms of words.] For, if our Spanish-speaking reader will think again, he will realize that he has never heard a clear *d,* in which the breath is stopped as it is in the English *d,* in the middle or at the end of a word in such Spanish dialects in positions where this voiced *th* sound occurs. In other words, in standard Spanish we have one sound unit *d,* which in initial position sounds to us like a *d* but, in most positions, medially and finally sounds to us like a voiced *th*.[2] Let

---

[2] Plus a unit *th,* which is generally voiceless, but which gets voiced to a different sort of *th* in certain combinations (e.g., *hazlo,* "do it!").

us now look at English along the same lines as an Oregon Takelma Indian might. He would notice that English has a breathed *p* initially in words such as our word *peace* noted above; an un-breathed *p* in words such as *spit* or *span;* an unex-ploded *p* very often in a word like *cup,* where, once they have been closed, the lips are not opened until the next sound is produced; and a "glottalized" *p,* as when a Scotsman snaps his vocal chords after he has puffed a *p* with his lips.

We have found, now, that certain acoustic fea-tures occur in a given language only in certain positions and environments. If we tabulate all acoustic differences for any language, we shall dis-cover whole categories of sounds whose members may vary enormously within a category, in their phonetic or absolute acoustic quality, but never occur in the same environment. To put it another way, they never offer a distinctive contrast; they are environmentally conditioned. By grouping these mutually exclusive sounds together, we arrive at the significant sound units of the language which we are inspecting. As is not surprising, these units, most conveniently so grouped, turn out to share a goodly number of phonetic, or acoustic, features. Linguists call a "bundle" of such mutually exclu-sive sounds a PHONEME. We are then in a posi-tion to say that English, for example, has such-and-such phonemes, including the phoneme *p,* which, in turn, has such-and-such positional vari-ants in the stated environments—and then we must enumerate the various positional phonetic values that *p* has in all the environments in which it may occur, some of which we took note of above. It does not surprise us that all these variants of *p* share the feature of double-lip closure. The reason we must go through this lengthy procedure to arrive at a statement which no doubt seems quite obvious to any speaker of English is that different linguistic groups, as pointed out above, have very different habits as to what constitutes a significant contrast. [Enormous changes in our view of the organization of the sounds of language have come about in the past decade. Many linguists now deny the utility of the notion of *phoneme,* and claim that, by concentrating one's attention on trivial or even technically misguided aspects, it has dis-tracted us from the important and explanatory aspects of grammatical organization. Nevertheless, this change does not vitiate the important point of arbitrary distinctiveness, range of fluctuation and systematic variation in context which are spe-cific to the sounds of a given language.]

When we say above that phonemes have varying values in all positions in which they *may* occur,

we have implied a limitation on the number of combinations or clusters of phonemes that may be found in a given language. This brings us to an-other fundamental feature of the interior economy or patterning that is found in all languages. Every-body, including radio announcers, found out dur-ing the war that Russians not only give their babies and cities unconscionably long names but also do their best to make them unpronounceable. One might recall Pskov, Dniepropetrovsk, or the late Mr. Zhdanov as a few random examples. In the way of everyday words the Russians produce with ease such specimens as *vstrechátsya,* "to meet one another"; *vverkhú,* "upstairs"; *éto mne ne nrávitsya,* "I don't like that." Georgian, "Uncle Joe's" native language (not at all related to Rus-sian), furnishes us with a verb *vhmtsqsi,* "I pasture my flock" (the sounds I write as *ts* and *q* here in-volve features difficult to explain briefly to an English speaker). Albanians find no trouble with *mpshtiell,* "to wrap"; nor do the Czechs with *čtvrt,* "one quarter" (the *r* is here vocalic). Examples can be multiplied indefinitely. The thing that strikes us forcibly, as English speakers, is the "out-rageousness" of some of the combinations that these languages permit, particularly in the case of initial consonant clusters which always seem to be more noticeable. [To us. Our final consonant clusters bother and amaze a Serb.] These clusters, although employing individual sound units or phonemes many of which are not at all foreign to us, involve combinations which we in our lan-guage do not happen to permit. In isolation, every sound in the above Albanian word occurs in English; *sh* represents the first sound in our word "show," and the whole word rimes with *peal.* But, to look at English from a Russian point of view, one finds equally inconceivable clusters in such words as "si*xths,*" "betwi*xt,*" or even the diph-thong in our word *know* (Russian has practically no diphthongs; we have scarcely any nondiph-thongized long syllables).

Every language has a clear-cut pattern in the combinations which it will or will not employ. It so happens that in some languages the range of permitted clusters is much greater than for others. In the matter of consonants, for example, per-mitted clusters in Japanese and Malay are ex-tremely restricted; in the Bannack Shoshone (Amer-ican Indian) language, only one consonant occurs in clusters with others. Many Bantu languages (spoken over enormous areas of Africa roughly south of the Equator), on the other hand, reject many clusters which seem quite reasonable to us, yet employ other combinations which we regard as singular, to say the least. That is the main reason that the names of the beplumed chieftains who arrive in London for conferences seem so incongruous to us. In turn, the patterning of "pidgin" languages encountered by many Americans, for example, in the South Pacific during the recent war, is to a large extent accounted for by the fact that English patterning seemed "funny" to those people; so they, as we do in everyday speech with Russian names, "tidied up" our language for us and made it look like something civilized.

The story has presumably been the same as long as men have been talking. We read in Tacitus (*Hist. ii.* 22) that the Romans, whose language many of us in the classroom have not always regarded with unqualified approval, found some of our Germanic forebears on the banks of the Rhone singing "harsh songs." One need go no farther than the pages of *King Henry V* to find out what Englishmen have thought about the patterning of Welsh.

The usual statements made about other people's languages are almost universally based on a misconception of this phonological patterning. German is regularly referred to as a "guttural" language. What has really been noticed by such an observer is the presence of a pattern strikingly different from English (such combinations as *shl, tst, mt* in forms like *schlange, jetzt, amt*) and the use of *one* phoneme in particular (*ch*) which sounds bizarre to English ears. Many have the mistaken impression that good standard German is produced by a liberal seasoning with *ch*'s. But the *ch* actually has two distinct positional variants in forms such as *doch* and *nicht;* in the latter type, that is, after a front vowel, the *ch* more closely approximates our English *sh*, where the closure is surely far removed from the throat. In short, "guttural" seems to refer in a vague, impressionistic fashion to real phenomena, but as a scientific term it is misleading and meaningless. When Italian is referred to as a "singing" or "lilting" language, presumably what has been noticed is the prominent vocalic pattern, the falling pitch on stressed syllables, a more restricted pattern (than in English) for consonant clusters, and the presence of doubled consonants (that is consonants held for twice their normal length), e.g., in *fratello, madonna, fato,* "fate," but *fatto* "deed." We tend particularly to notice the last feature because English has no double consonants, except when chance brings two forms together, e.g., *night-table;* the difference between *later* and *latter* is not in the consonants; it is the vowels spelled *a.*

In the course of defining our sound units, or phonemes, it was pointed out that the deciding factor is the feature of significant contrast. There are many languages in the world which employ tone, or relative pitch of the voice, as the sole feature of contrast between many forms. Chinese is the language most familiar to Westerners which displays this characteristic. Since we do not use such features to distinguish individual words, the whole concept is somewhat strange to us; that is, it is outside our phonological pattern, and, just as in the case of glottalized consonants, whispered vowels, clicks, and the like, it is hard for us to hear these distinctions. To be sure, we make use of pitch in one fashion over long segments of speech, as when we use a rising inflection to denote an attitude of doubt or inconclusiveness, or over shorter segments to give semantically vague subjective overtones to an expression (e.g., *well, ah, yes*). But these are features of a different order. Tone in Chinese distinguishes one item of vocabulary from another; we may say it has a "lexical" value (i.e., the dictionary must show it). In Ibo, a language spoken in West Africa, a verb is made negative merely by changing the tone. In Mazatec, a language spoken in southern Mexico, a change in the subject of the verb often involves a change in tone. We may say that tone here has a grammatical value; it is as much a part of the grammar as is the change in endings on a Latin verb or the addition of an ending to an English noun to make it plural. These features are certainly elements of phonemic contrast.

All language flows within a framework of time. I cannot utter an expression, however short, without finishing later than I began it. The sound contrasts which were discussed when we set up such phonemes as *p* are linear segments in a continuum of time; that is, they are distinctive features that occur one after the other (roughly speaking; this is imprecise in strict acoustic terms). These we may call "segmental" or "linear" phonemes. [Nowadays, in the framework of generative grammar, we do better to refer not to phonemes in this fashion, but to segments that come one after the other and that are each marked with a limited number of nonpredictable distinctive features.] We have seen, however, that we must also take into account such things as tone. Now tone (in languages I know of) never occupies an interval of time when nothing else, equally distinctive, is going on, and it sometimes overlaps several segmental phonemes. Tone, therefore, might be called a "simultaneous" phoneme. Stress, such as we employ in English, where one syllable of most words is spoken more forcibly than another, is also an example of a simultaneous phoneme. [If we state the structure of lexical and grammatical elements in terms of segments marked by sets of distinctive features which are themselves simultaneous bundles, then such things as tone are simply distinctive features no different in this respect from the others.] Once again, the occurrence of a feature may not mean that it is significant; Czech has a marked stress accent, but it always occurs on the initial syllable of the word. Therefore, it never offers a contrast and hence is not a phoneme in Czech.

We have now established another fundamental feature of language: that we do not necessarily have to slice time laterally in order to find all significant sound contrasts. [*Note A:* When this paper was written the field of linguistics was dominated by an insistence on the methods of discovering and arriving at the entities isolated in a grammatical statement. Such methods were supposed to be overt and automatically reproduceable, so that a machine with no intuition could arrive at the same results. This in turn led to an emphasis on means of slicing up, and assigning to recoverable classes, the acoustical stream (i.e., sentences) that was supposed to be composed of such segments. That is, the grammar was imagined to be discoverable from the purely superficial configurations of the stream of sound that we hear when speech occurs; this contention is now generally agreed to have been wrong and misleading.]

We see, therefore, that one of the fundamental things that gives any language its own particular quality is its rigid adherence to a closed pattern of sound units, which permits variation only within strikingly limited ranges of tolerance. From the enormous number of sounds the human organism can produce, every language selects a surprisingly limited stock. All languages thus far adequately described employ phonemes numbering roughly between twenty and fifty. [In these terms, a more accurate typology would be ca. a dozen (Hawaiian or Wichita, a North American Plains language of the Caddoan family) to over eighty (Oubykh, belonging to the family spoken on the northwest slope of the Caucasus mountains). But expressed in distinctive features, the range is much less drastic: somewhere between a half-dozen and a dozen.] Indeed, there is reason to suspect the validity of an analysis that yields a number of phonemes in the upper span of this range, though as yet there is no reason to assume any absolute number as a ceiling. These units are then combined in well-defined patterns, much like chessmen on a board. To break the rule is to sacrifice intelligibility.

We have now not only considered structural patterning of the sound units of languages; we have also taken a brief glance at some of the ways whereby we may discover these units [see Note A above]. When we do this, how do we know that we have arrived at a valid or "right" analysis? How does the physicist know he has a valid analysis when he posits subatomic particles which he has not yet seen or measured? The criterion for "rightness" in matters of analysis and description is empirically faithful economy. The best description is that which explains all observed phenomena with a minimum of assumptions and statements. The best description of a language is the most economical description.

*   *   *

Cognitive Processes: A Contemporary Perspective

John P. DeCecco
San Francisco State College

The study of problem solving, creativity, and language should provide us our most comprehensive and deepest understanding of human behavior. Problem solving, after all, is the most complex intellectual activity in which we engage. Creativity incorporates both preconscious and unconscious elements into this high-level activity. Language, finally, is as distinctively human as it is ubiquitously necessary in the conduct of our intellectual and emotional affairs. You could well expect that ten articles on these subjects would tell you as much or more than ten articles on other aspects of human behavior.

The articles, however, reveal a primitive state of knowledge. All of us must know that the behavioral sciences have not made rapid gains in the exploration of complex human behavior. There is considerably more theoretical contention than solid findings. If you have little tolerance for many unanswered questions and for small, random patches of knowledge, you may decide to turn to the humane arts and letters for explanations of problem solving, creativity, and language. If your tolerance for ambiguity is very low, you may decide to dismiss questions about the nature of these behavioral areas with impatient references to "human nature" and to knowledge that everyone presumably has. If you are willing, however, to examine thoughtfully the theories and findings of the psychologists and linguists whose articles appear here, you will begin to develop behavior models for problem solving, creativity, and language that are more sophisticated than common-sense models.

I have organized my comments in the following way. First, I shall describe the most advanced model or theory of problem solving we now have. Then I will describe the three theoretical models used by the articles in this chapter: simple and mediational stimulus-response theories, cognitive theory, and self-theory. This framework allows me to show the relationships among the three types of theory and the articles. In conclusion, I shall organize the theories and articles into a three-level view of human behavior. My objective is simply this: Having read and thought about these articles, you should be able to provide more alternative explanations of the nature, causes, and results of problem solving, creativity, and language than you could before.

Robert Gagné (1965) provides us with the most current stimulus-response model of human problem solving. Gagné describes problem solving as the highest learning type in a hierarchy of eight learning types beginning with simple classical and operant conditioning. Problem solving, according to Gagné, requires the individual to combine two or more previously learned principles to form a higher-order principle. In earlier treatments of his theory Gagné referred to principles as *rules;* thus, in his terms problem solving requires the learner to formulate an over-arching rule combining simpler rules. Problem solving, in this view, is a form of learning because it represents the acquisition of new substantive knowledge.

Here is one of Gagné's favorite examples. A beginning algebra student is given a problem—multiply x^2 and x^3—that he has not seen before. To solve this problem he must have learned two principles: multiplying a number by some other number means adding the first number that many times. An exponent means that a number is to be multiplied by itself that many times. If the student combines these rules or principles, he acquires a new, higher-order rule for the solution of the new problem: multiply the variable by itself the number of times represented by the sum of the two exponents. According to

Gagné, the student "proves" that he has acquired the higher-order principle when he successfully solves a new problem (e.g., y^{14} and y^7) of the same class.

Gagné's problem-solving model is a mediational one; that is, the lower-order rules or principles serve as "mediators," or internal links between stimulus and response. To help a student solve problems the teacher provides an illustration of a successfully solved problem of the same class, helps the student recall the lower-order rules, and then helps the student discover how the simpler rules combine to form the complex rule.

Irving Maltzman (1955) has provided us the most imaginative model of the internal events that occur within the learner engaged in the complex behavior of problem solving. According to Maltzman (but now using Gagné's terminology), because the learner knows several rules, somehow his choice of appropriate rules must be reinforced and his choice of inappropriate rules extinguished. Repeated failure to use the incorrect rules, or combination of rules, extinguishes these responses. In the meantime, by a process of *mediated generalization,* the strength of rule-responses originally low in strength will increase. In Maltzman's view what gives to problems their particularly inscrutable character is not the fact that we lack the knowledge to solve them but that our initial attempts to solve them rely heavily on those familiar responses that have been most successful in the past. In accordance with a Puritan ethic of learning we must experience the adversity of failure before we obtain success—in the present case, measured by successful problem solutions.

Most of the articles in this section employ stimulus-response models, with or without a mediational component. In a strict interpretation of a simple stimulus-response model Skinner contends that stimuli and responses become associated when responses are rewarded or reinforced in the presence of particular stimuli. If you want the child to say "hippie" whenever he refers to an individual given to certain sartorial idiosyncrasy in Greenwich Village, according to Skinner, you must reward the child's response whenever he correctly applies it. At the most primitive level, all the "labeling" behavior of the child is a product of stimulus-response learning in which the stimulus is the object and the verbal response is the label. This simple stimulus-response model is the basis of Skinner's treatise, *Verbal Behavior,* which Chomsky here reviews below in a not-too-gentle manner.

Most of the authors using a stimulus-response model add a symbolic or mediational process. This process is usually depicted as internal responses and stimuli forming a bridge between the external stimulus and the public response. For example, in the article by Arthur Staats on denotative meaning, the external stimulus and the public response are diagrammed as upper-case letters, while the internal responses and stimuli are diagrammed as lower-case letters.

Several of the authors whose work is presented here believe that a mediational model positing the occurrence of internal responses and stimuli as the major link between the overt S and R squares better than a straight stimulus-response model with their evidence. Indeed, adherents of both groups are fond of replicating each other's experiments to show how their own model squares better with the facts than the other. In the articles in this section mediational models are used by Walter Hunter in explaining the problem-solving behavior of raccoons, by Howard and Tracy Kendler in explaining the problem-solving behavior of younger and older children trying to execute reversal and nonreversal shifts, by Robert Gagné and Ernest Smith in explaining the effects of verbalizing relevant principles in problem solutions, and by Arthur Staats in explaining how originally meaningless words acquire denotative meaning. In most cases the mediating responses to which the authors refer are words the subject utters to himself or aloud (and to himself) in the process of solving complex problems. In the case of Hunter's raccoons and Staats' "images in language," the mediating responses appear to be more sensory than verbal.

All the S-R mediational theorists are aware that mediational theory offers a link between the stimulus-response theories and the cognitive theories we shall discuss below. The Kendlers' discussion of horizontal and vertical processes in problem solving deals explicitly with this link. The horizontal processes explain the building of stimulus-response chains having two or more links. The vertical processes explain how chains can interact. While the horizontal processes result in a rather mechanistic running-off of responses, the vertical processes result in the more human and rational capacity to respond in several different ways at one time. In successful problem solving for both animals and humans the subject must have a choice of responses and he must exercise the appropriate option. Although Skinnerians would not agree, the mediational models depict a type of behavioral plasticity and variability that appears, to this writer, particularly human—those moments when we are behaving at our best.

Jerome Bruner's studies of intellectual development and Noam Chomsky's theory of generative grammar exemplify the cognitive models. Chomsky's generative grammar explains why the native speaker is able to understand and produce sentences that may never have been written or spoken before. Language is a system of rules whose application permits the formation and comprehension of new sentences. Knowledge of the language is not the result of reinforcement of past responses but of intuitive mastery of rules. Chomsky writes: "It appears that we recognize a new item as a sentence not because it matches some familiar item in any simple way (the Skinnerian doctrine), but because it is generated by the grammar that each individual has somehow and in some form individualized." Chomsky's cognitive model describes a state of knowledge without describing how this knowledge is acquired or learned. Skinner, he points out, describes a stimulus-response learning process, but the "verbal behavior" that such a process produces bears little resemblance to our essential language ability. Chomsky's theory holds that the normal child of three, as demonstrated in his ability to mold new sentences, has already acquired knowledge of the incredibly complex rules of transformational grammar, a mental feat which stimulus-response theorists view with skepticism.

Similarly, in identifying three modes of information processing and the development of these modes over time, Jerome Bruner has described three states of knowledge (and their associated intellectual capacities) rather than processes of knowledge acquisition. Whereas the stimulus-response mediational models always deal with primitive states of knowledge, the cognitive theorists are able to deal with more sophisticated states (transformational rules, symbol systems, etc.). The stimulus-response theorists can describe how bits of knowledge are acquired and how these bits coalesce into larger knowledge units (i.e., more complex responses). Unfortunately, they do not describe the knowledge states which underlie our most distinctively human attempts at problem solving and creative production.

In what may be a significant departure from other cognitive theorists Bruner attributes to the environment much of the impetus for cognitive development. Thinking, he states, depends on techniques rather than on wired-in arrangements in the nervous system. Complex environments induce intellectual techniques for dealing competently with them by forcing the child to *represent* recurrent regularities in the environment and to transcend the momentary by developing ways to *integrate* past to present to future. Bruner is shifting the cause of intellectual development from an essentially genetic base, where Piaget places it, to an essentially environmental one. This shift should develop a bridge between cognitive and stimulus-response theorists by allowing the latter the opportunity to manipulate environmental stimulus conditions and thereby note the effects over time on the three modes of thought Bruner describes.

Robert Holt identifies with cognitive theory in his discussion of imagery, hallucination, hypnagogic states, and so on. This area of investigation has acquired considerable respectability and interest with the popularity of physiological psychology, which investigates the neural and functional bases for these states, and with the development of psychopharmacology and studies of sensory deprivation. Greater knowledge of what Holt calls *imagery* should reveal important connections with problem solving and with creativity. Holt, following Freud, makes the important point that consciousness is not essential to thinking and that imagery, therefore, may be an imporant part of thinking. It is also interesting to note that Holt anchors imagery in a cognitive model while Staats fits it into a model of classical conditioning.

The third type of theoretical model is self-theory, a general appellation I use to refer to that branch of psychology and nonsystematic philosophy dealing with the description and explanation of ego processes. Most of the theories of creativity that Bernard Mackler and Franklin Shontz describe are varieties of self-theory: psychoanalysis, existentialism, and interpersonal relations (including Adler, Fromm, Maslow, and Rogers). The exceptions are the associationist (i.e., stimulus-response) theories of Mednick, Maltzman, and others and the trait theory of Guilford. Although there is obvious overlapping of self-theory with stimulus-response and cognitive theory, none of the psychologists whom Shontz and Mackler discuss has systematically considered these possible relationships. Consequently, theories of creativity are largely outside the mainstream of psychological knowledge and, therefore, have not produced solid research. The self-theories are often humanistic affirmations of the good life that fail to specify the components of that life, their relationship, and a methodology for systematic research. The growing study of and speculation about cognitive styles and tempos in processing information may be our best promise for a bridge between research on problem solving and research on creativity.

The article by Eric Hamp does not fit into our theoretical framework as neatly as the others. It is based on a theory of structural and descriptive linguistics. Important for knowledge about problem solving and creativity is Hamp's notion that the way our language slices the universe determines what we attend to and ignore in perception and thought (the famous, if shaky, Whorf thesis). The categories into which various languages sort reality are varied and arbitrary. It is necessary for any language to use a comparatively small number of building blocks, phonemes and morphemes, in order to facilitate communication. In the process the perception of stimuli left unclassified may often be blunted.

A composite picture of problem solving, creativity, and language would seem to reveal at least three levels of human functioning. The simple and mediational stimulus-response theories show that our language is linked to the physical conditions of our environment— to stimuli—and that we resort to words in order to deal more effectively with the environment. Although animals (e.g., raccoons) do not have the use of verbal mediators, they seem to have other symbolic responses that mediate between problems and their solutions. It also appears that with age we develop more and more sophisticated ways of talking to ourselves (i.e., verbal mediation) and therefore increase our ability to solve complex problems.

At a second level of human functioning there seems to be a realm of intellectual activity that is as much a product of our complex neural makeup as of the environment. By processes as yet unexplained, the preschool child masters the transformational rules of his language and creates new, grammatical utterances. The child also learns increasingly sophisticated techniques for representing and integrating the complexities of his environment. At the first level, then, man appears to be molded by his experiences. At the second level it appears that man is molding his world and indeed his own experiences.

At a third level, the level of creativity and related forms of imagery, there seems to be considerable mystery. In one sense creativity and imagery represent the highest peaks of human development. Yet they seem to tap rather primeval emotions and experiences. The use of drugs in our society seems, for many, to be motivated by a desire to explore inner states of imagery in a world whose usual activities are seen as a prolonged experiment in sensory deprivation. Whether such imagery will release new creative energies and powerful forms of problem solving is an open question.

In the decade ahead you will see considerably more research on problem solving, creativity, and language as technology and social reform require improved communication and push us to the higher reaches of knowledge.

REFERENCES

Gagné, Robert M. *Conditions of learning*, New York: Holt, Rinehart, & Winston, Inc., 1965. (A new edition of this book will appear in 1970.)

Maltzman, Irving. Thinking: From a behaviorist point of view. *Psychological Review*, 1955, **62**, 275–86.

Part Six

Motivation and Emotion

At the lowest level of organization it is a very simple task to separate motivation from emotion. It seems that the process of evolution has provided the higher animals with several different, genetically controlled methods of prolonging life. All of the higher organisms experience hunger and know when hunger is present. The life-sustaining function of feeling hungry is obvious. If the organism didn't experience hunger, it wouldn't forage for food and would very soon die. In like manner, thirst and the sexual appetite operate in accord with the hereditary patterns of each organism to perpetuate the life of the individual and the species. These organismic need-states are quite clearly motivational in nature, and the word emotion does not apply. Each organism is subject to several such motivational states, which give rise to sensory stimuli to which the organism responds by seeking whatever will alleviate the need-state. In this way life is sustained.

Since eating when hungry and drinking when thirsty also produce feelings of satisfaction and pleasure, many philosophers have suggested that the higher organisms are pleasure seeking by nature. Principles of hedonism have been suggested as playing a major role in the lives of such organisms. At this level the concept of reinforcement fits neatly into the schema of need-states and motivation. When an animal is motivated by such a need, the reduction of that need will function as a reinforcement. Activity that secures food for the hungry animal will be reinforced and will tend to be repeated. Motivation, then, is a negative state—a state of need—and reinforcement is the positive state—reducing that need.

The statement that "man does not live by bread alone" has long been used to imply that survival is only the first part of a necessary duo. Happiness—or at least a considerable amount of pleasure—is also desired by the higher animals. The selective appetite of the gourmet, the sex-anticipatory delight of the voyeur who peeks at nudie pictures, and the tingling excitement of the connoisseur of haberdashery who dresses colorfully and modishly in hopeful anticipation of admiring compliments provide examples of motives that are far more complex than simple life-sustaining hunger and thirst. The question facing psychologists is: Since these higher level kinds of motivation are clearly not genetic in nature, how are they acquired? How is it that some persons develop into food gourmets, others into clothes gourmets, and still others into music gourmets?

At this level we can say that the organism has managed to become secure in terms of maintaining life. Food acquisition and the other necessities of life are taken care of. The next goal is happiness, or, at least, a sense of satisfaction and well-being. It is at this stage that motivation becomes fused with emotion. In this section the article by Neal Miller shows how the emotion of fear can be acquired in social situations and how it can then serve as a motive for the learning of other behaviors. That is, fear can motivate, and the relief of fear can serve as a reinforcer of the actions which brought about that relief. This line of research has been one of the most fruitful in the dual area of motivation and emotion. The basic premise is that the higher order types of motivation are emotional in nature and that they are learned. In the same way as fear can be learned, so can guilt, love, sympathy, anxiety, morality, altruism, and all the others. While this premise has by no means been proven, it seems quite promising and serves as a fertile source of research ideas.

Very few individuals function alone. Most higher organisms are members of a larger social group, and humans are perhaps the most social of all the higher animals. We group ourselves into families, into clubs, into school classes, into political parties, and into numerous other clusters. But belonging to a group produces a serious problem for the individual. To benefit from group membership, one must forsake a certain amount of personal freedom and pleasure. Children learn very early that if they want something from other members of the family they must be willing to give something in return. This notion of giving something in return probably serves as the basis for such social motives as empathy, sympathy, love, and morality in general. When the reciprocal giving is not done, there arise the emotions of anxiety, guilt, fear, and even envy, hate, and aggression. There is thus a basic antagonism between the desires of the individual and the needs of the group of which he is a member. From the group come great benefits and pleasures, but also problems and troubles. In order for the group to function and to thrive, to be maximally helpful to those within it, rules and goals must be articulated and enforced.

In the same way that small groups require certain behaviors of the participating members, larger groups require even more highly developed kinds of group activities. The kind of free-floating anxiety that every member of every group carries around with him is a function of demands made by the group that are antagonistic to the short-range desires of the individual. When a religion demands kindness and love of its members, and when those members do not wish to expend the time and effort required, a sort of general anxiety and feeling of uneasiness is produced. When a democracy demands that the minorities support and comply with the rules that have been passed into law by the majority, there is a conflict of interest that produces anxiety. Those persons who successfully acquire the means for dealing with such conflicts will be altruistic, loving, and moral.

The articles on the following pages represent the ideas of today's prominent thinkers concerning the ways in which such social motives and emotions are acquired and the problems that necessarily arise from the conflict of interests.

44

On Dreams

Sigmund Freud

Freud considered himself a very good scientist and believed his method of study to be in the best of scientific traditions. In his day this was quite true. His method of introspective analysis was very similar to that adopted by Wundt in his psychological laboratories. The method seems to have been especially attractive to the German psychologists of the latter part of the nineteenth century who regarded psychology as being an offshoot of the larger discipline of philosophy.

However, many modern psychologists believe that there are serious problems involved in the use of introspection as a method of studying mental activity. The current approach is to analyze those behaviors that can be viewed by several bystanders so that they can check each other and make certain that no large errors in perception take place on the part of one or more of the observers. Such checking of one another is the essence of the objectivity which occupies a central position in modern scientific thought.

However, we must recognize that Freud was a very keen observer of his own behavior, reporting it as best he knew how. His recognition that dream content may be disguised in terms of everyday activities stands as a great discovery. His recognition that dreams do indeed represent certain aspects of motivation, and that the nature of the dream will reveal a person's inner problems, is particularly relevant to modern researchers in the area of motivation and emotion.

In reading this article you will notice the frequent use of the word "affect," a term that has gone out of fashion recently. The best modern translation of the meaning of this term is "emotion."

During the epoch which may be described as pre-scientific, men had no difficulty in finding an explanation of dreams. When they remembered a dream after waking up, they regarded it as either a favorable or a hostile manifestation by higher powers, demonic and divine. When modes of thought belonging to natural science began to flourish, all this ingenious mythology was transformed into psychology, and today only a small minority of educated people doubt that dreams are a product of the dreamer's own mind.

Since the rejection of the mythological hypothesis, however, dreams have stood in need of explanation. The conditions of their origin, their relation to waking mental life, their dependence upon stimuli which force their way upon perception during the state of sleep, the many peculiarities of their content which are repugnant to waking thought, the inconsistency between their ideational images and the affects attaching to them, and lastly their transitory character, the manner in which waking thought pushes them on

one side as something alien to it and mutilates or extinguishes them in memory—all of these and other problems besides have been awaiting clarification for many hundreds of years, and till now no satisfactory solution of them has been advanced. But what stands in the foreground of our interest is the question of the *significance* of dreams, a question which bears a double sense. It inquires, in the first place, as to the psychical significance of dreaming, as to the relation of dreams to other mental processes, and as to any biological function that they may have; in the second place, it seeks to discover whether dreams can be interpreted, whether the content of individual dreams has a "meaning," such as we are accustomed to find in other psychical structures.

In the assessment of the significance of dreams three lines of thought can be distinguished. One of these, which echoes, as it were, the ancient over-valuation of dreams, is expressed in the writings of certain philosophers. They consider that the basis of dream life is a peculiar state of mental activity and even go so far as to acclaim that state as an elevation to a higher level. For instance, Schubert declares that dreams are a liberation of the spirit from the power of external nature and a freeing of the soul from the bonds of the senses. Other thinkers, without going so far as this, insist never-theless that dreams arise essentially from mental impulses and represent manifestations of mental forces which have been prevented from expanding freely during the daytime. A large number of ob-servers agree in attributing to dream life a capacity for superior functioning in certain departments at least (e.g., in memory).

In sharp contrast to this, the majority of medi-cal writers adopt a view according to which dreams scarcely reach the level of being psychical phe-nomena at all. On their theory, the sole instigators of dreams are the sensory and somatic stimuli which either impinge upon the sleeper from out-side or become active accidentally in his internal organs. What is dreamed, they contend, has no more claim to sense and meaning than, for in-stance, the sounds which would be produced if "the ten fingers of a man who knows nothing of music were wandering over the keys of a piano." Dreams are described by Binz as being no more than "somatic processes which are in every case useless and in many cases positively pathological." All the characteristics of dream life would thus be explained as being due to the disconnected activity of separate organs or groups of cells in an otherwise sleeping brain, an activity forced upon them by physiological stimuli.

Popular opinion is but little affected by this scientific judgment and is not concerned as to the sources of dreams; it seems to persist in the belief that nevertheless dreams have a meaning, which relates to the prediction of the future and which can be discovered by some process of interpreta-tion of a content which is often confused and puzzling. The methods of interpretation employed consist in transforming the content of the dream as it is remembered, either by replacing it piecemeal in accordance with a fixed key, or by replacing the dream as a whole by another whole to which it stands in a symbolic relation. Serious-minded people smile at these efforts: *Träume sind Schäume* —"dreams are froth."

One day I discovered to my great astonishment that the view of dreams which came nearest to the truth was not the medical but the popular one, half-involved though it still was in superstition. For I had been led to fresh conclusions on the subject of dreams by applying to them a new method of psychological investigation which had done excellent service in the solution of phobias, obsessions, and delusions, etc. Since then, under the name of "psychoanalysis," it has found accep-tance by a whole school of research workers. The numerous analogies that exist between dream life and a great variety of conditions of psychical ill-ness in waking life have indeed been correctly observed by many medical investigators. There seemed, therefore, good ground for hoping that a method of investigation which had given satis-factory results in the case of psychopathic struc-tures would also be of use in throwing light upon dreams. Phobias and obsessions are as alien to nor-mal consciousness as dreams are to waking con-sciousness; their origin is as unknown to conscious-ness as that of dreams. In the case of these psycho-pathic structures practical considerations led to an investigation of their origin and mode of develop-ment; for experience had shown that the discovery of the trains of thought which, concealed from consciousness, connect the pathological ideas with the remaining contents of the mind is equivalent to a resolution of the symptoms and has as its con-sequence the mastering of ideas which till then could not be inhibited. Thus psychotherapy was the starting point of the procedure of which I made use for the explanation of dreams.

This procedure is easily described, although in-struction and practice would be necessary before it could be put into effect.

If we make use of it on someone else, let us say on a patient with a phobia, we require him to direct his attention on to the idea in question, not, however, to reflect upon it as he has done so often already, but to take notice of *whatever occurs to his mind without any exception* and report it to the physician. If he should then assert that his attention is unable to grasp anything at all, we dismiss this with an energetic assurance that a com-plete absence of any ideational subject matter is quite impossible. And in fact very soon numerous ideas will occur to him and will lead on to others; but they will invariably be prefaced by a judg-ment on the part of the self-observer to the effect that they are senseless or unimportant, that they are irrelevant, and that they occurred to him by chance and without any connection with the topic under consideration. We perceive at once that it was this critical attitude which prevented the subject from reporting any of these ideas, and which indeed had previously prevented them from becoming conscious. If we can induce him to abandon his criticism of the ideas that occur to him, and to continue pursuing the trains of thought which will emerge so long as he keeps his attention turned upon them, we find ourselves in possession of a quantity of psychical material, which we soon find is clearly connected with the pathological idea which was our starting point; this material will soon reveal connections between the pathological idea and other ideas, and will eventually enable us to replace the pathological idea by a new one which fits into the nexus of thought in an intelligible fashion.

This is not the place in which to give a detailed account of the premises upon which this experiment was based, or the consequences which follow from its invariable success. It will therefore be enough to say that we obtain material that enables us to resolve any pathological idea if we turn our attention precisely to those associations which are "involuntary," which "interfere with our reflection," and which are normally dismissed by our critical faculty as worthless rubbish.

If we make use of this procedure upon *ourselves,* we can best assist the investigation by at once writing down what are at first unintelligible associations.

I will now show what results follow if I apply this method of investigation to dreams. Any example of a dream should in fact be equally appropriate for the purpose; but for particular reasons I will choose some dream of my own, one which seems obscure and meaningless as I remember it, and one which has the advantage of brevity. A dream which I actually had last night will perhaps meet these requirements. Its content, as I noted it down immediately after waking up, was as follows:

Company at table or table d'hôte . . . spinach was being eaten . . . Frau E. L. was sitting beside me; she was turning her whole attention to me and laid her hand on my knee in an intimate manner. I removed her hand unresponsively. She then said: "But you've always had such beautiful eyes.". . . I then had an indistinct picture of two eyes, as though it were a drawing or like the outline of a pair of spectacles. . . .

This was the whole of the dream, or at least all that I could remember of it. It seemed to me obscure and meaningless, but above all surprising. Frau E. L. is a person with whom I have hardly at any time been on friendly terms, nor, so far as I know, have I ever wished to have any closer relations with her. I have not seen her for a long time, and her name has not, I believe, been mentioned during the last few days. The dream process was not accompanied by affects of any kind.

Reflecting over this dream brought me no nearer to understanding it. I determined, however, to set down without any premeditation or criticism the associations which presented themselves to my self-observation. As I have found, it is advisable for this purpose to divide a dream into its elements and to find the associations attaching to each of these fragments separately.

Company at table or table d'hôte—this at once reminded me of an episode which occurred late yesterday evening. I came away from a small party in the company of a friend who offered to take a cab and drive me home in it. "I prefer taking a cab with a taximeter," he said. "It occupies one's mind so agreeably; one always has something to look at." When we had taken our places in the cab and the driver had set the dial, so that the first charge of 60 hellers [=6d.] became visible, I carried the joke further. "We've only just got in," I said, "and already we owe him 60 hellers. A cab with a taximeter always reminds me of a table d'hôte. It makes me avaricious and selfish, because it keeps on reminding me of what I owe. My debt seems to be growing too fast, and I'm afraid of getting the worst of the bargain; and in just the same way at a table d'hôte I can't avoid feeling in a comic way that I'm getting too little, and must keep an eye on my own interests." I went on to quote, somewhat discursively:

Ihr führt ins Leben uns hinein,
Ihr lasst den Armen schuldig werden.[1]

And now a second association to "table d'hôte." A few weeks ago, while we were at table in a hotel

---

[1] [These lines are from one of the Harp-player's songs in Goethe's *Wilhelm Meister*. In the original the words are addressed to the Heavenly Powers and may be translated literally: "You lead us into life, you make the poor creature guilty." But the words *Armen* and *schuldig* are both capable of bearing another meaning. *Armen* might mean "poor" in the financial sense and *schuldig* might mean "in debt." So in the present context the last line could be rendered: "You make the poor man fall into debt."]

at a mountain resort in the Tyrol, I was very much annoyed because I thought my wife was not being sufficiently reserved toward some people sitting near us whose acquaintance I had no desire at all to make. I asked her to concern herself more with me than with these strangers. This was again *as though I were getting the worst of the bargain at the table d'hôte*. I was struck too by the contrast between my wife's behavior at table and that of Frau E. L. in the dream, who "turned her whole attention to me."

To proceed, I now saw that the events in the dream were a reproduction of a small episode of a precisely similar kind which occurred between my wife and me at the time at which I was secretly courting her. The caress which she gave me under the tablecloth was her reply to a pressing love letter. In the dream, however, my wife was replaced by a comparative stranger—E. L.

Frau E. L. is the daughter of a man to whom I was once *in debt*. I could not help noticing that this revealed an unsuspected connection between parts of the content of the dream and my associations. If one follows the train of association starting out from one element of a dream's content, one is soon brought back to another of its elements. My associations to the dream were bringing to light connections which were not visible in the dream itself.

If a person expects one to keep an eye on his interests without any advantage to oneself, his artlessness is apt to provoke the scornful question: "Do you suppose I'm going to do this or that for the sake of your *beaux yeux* [beautiful eyes]?" That being so, Frau E. L.'s speech in the dream, "You've always had such beautiful eyes," can only have meant: "People have always done everything for you for love; you have always had everything *without paying for it*." The truth is, of course, just the contrary: I have always paid dearly for whatever advantage I have had from other people. The fact that my friend took me home yesterday in a cab *without my paying for it* must, after all, have made an impression on me.

Incidentally, the friend whose guests we were yesterday has often put me in his debt. Only recently I allowed an opportunity of repaying him to slip by. He has had only one present from me—an antique bowl, around which there are *eyes* painted: what is known as an *"occhiale,"* to avert the *evil eye*. Moreover he is an *eye surgeon*. The same evening I asked him about a woman patient, whom I had sent on to him for a consultation to fit her with *spectacles*.

As I now perceived, almost all the elements of the dream's content had been brought into the new context. For the sake of consistency, however, the further question might be asked of why *spinach*, of all things, was being served in the dream. The answer was that *spinach* reminded me of an episode which occurred not long ago at our family table, when one of the children—and precisely the one who really deserves to be admired for his *beautiful eyes*—refused to eat any spinach. I myself behaved in just the same way when I was a child; for a long time I detested spinach, till eventually my taste changed and promoted that vegetable into one of my favorite foods. My own early life and my child's were thus brought together by the mention of this dish. "You ought to be glad to have spinach," the little gourmet's mother exclaimed; "there are children who would be only too pleased to have spinach." Thus I was reminded of the duties of parents to their children. Goethe's words

> *Ihr führt ins Leben uns hinein,*
> *Ihr lasst den Armen schuldig werden*

gained a fresh meaning in this connection.[2]

I will pause here to survey the results I had so far reached in my dream analysis. By following the associations which arose from the separate elements of the dream divorced from their context, I arrived at a number of thoughts and recollections, which I could not fail to recognize as important products of my mental life. This material revealed by the analysis of the dream was intimately connected with the dream's content, yet the connection was of such a kind that I could never have inferred the fresh material from that content. The dream was unemotional, disconnected, and unintelligible; but while I was producing the thoughts behind the dream, I was aware of intense and well-founded affective impulses; the thoughts themselves fell at once into logical chains, in which certain central ideas made their appearance more than once. Thus, the contrast between "selfish" and "unselfish," and the elements "being in debt" and "without paying for it" were central ideas of this kind, not represented in the dream itself. I could draw closer together the threads in the material revealed by the analysis, and I could then show that they converge upon a single nodal point, but considerations of a personal and not of a sci-

2 [See footnote 1. The first line of the couplet might now be taken to mean that the verses are addressed to parents.]

entific nature prevent my doing so in public. I should be obliged to betray many things which had better remain my secret, for on my way to discovering the solution of the dream all kinds of things were revealed which I was unwilling to admit even to myself. Why then, it will be asked, have I not chosen some other dream, whose analysis is better suited for reporting, so that I could produce more convincing evidence of the meaning and connectedness of the material uncovered by analysis? The answer is that *every* dream with which I might try to deal would lead to things equally hard to report and would impose an equal discretion upon me. Nor should I avoid this difficulty by bringing up someone else's dream for analysis, unless circumstances enabled me to drop all disguise without damage to the person who had confided in me.

At the point which I have now reached, I am led to regard the dream as a sort of *substitute* for the thought processes, full of meaning and emotion, at which I arrived after the completion of the analysis. We do not yet know the nature of the process which has caused the dream to be generated from these thoughts, but we can see that it is wrong to regard it as purely physical and without psychical meaning, as a process which has arisen from the isolated activity of separate groups of brain cells aroused from sleep.

Two other things are already clear. The content of the dream is very much shorter than the thoughts of which I regard it as a substitute; and analysis has revealed that the instigator of the dream was an unimportant event of the evening before I dreamed it.

I should, of course, not draw such far-reaching conclusions if only a single dream analysis was at my disposal. If experience shows me, however, that by uncritically pursuing the associations arising from *any* dream I can arrive at a similar train of thoughts, among the elements of which the constituents of the dream reappear and which are interconnected in a rational and intelligible manner, then it will be safe to disregard the slight possibility that the connections observed in a first experiment might be due to chance. I think I am justified, therefore, in adopting a terminology which will crystallize our new discovery. In order to contrast the dream as it is retained in my memory with the relevant material discovered by analyzing it, I shall speak of the former as the *"manifest* content of the dream" and the latter—without, in the first instance, making any further distinction—as the *"latent* content of the dream." I am now faced by two new problems which have not hitherto been formulated. (1) What is the psychical process which has transformed the latent content of the dream into the manifest one which is known to me from my memory? (2) What are the motive or motives which have necessitated this transformation? I shall describe the process which transforms the latent into the manifest content of dreams as the "dream work." The counterpart to this activity—one which brings about a transformation in the opposite direction—is already known to us as the work of analysis. The remaining problems arising out of dreams—questions as to the instigators of dreams, as to the origin of their material, as to their possible meaning, as to the possible function of dreaming, and as to the reasons for dreams being forgotten—all these problems will be discussed by me on the basis, not of the manifest, but of the newly discovered latent dream content. Since I attribute all the contradictory and incorrect views upon dream life which appear in the literature of the subject to ignorance of the latent content of dreams as revealed by analysis, I shall be at the greatest pains henceforward to avoid confusing the *manifest dream* with the *latent dream thoughts.*

45

Studies of Fear as an Acquirable Drive:
Fear as Motivation and Fear-Reduction
as Reinforcement in the Learning
of New Responses

Neal E. Miller

The concept of "motivation" or its near equivalent, "drive," holds a central position for those who are interested in human affairs. We ask what "drives" a hard working executive, or what "motivates" an honor student, the rationale being that before anyone will do much of anything other than just sit around, there must be a reason for the action.

One approach that has been used in studying motives has been the taxonomic approach, in which all possible motives are categorized. Once such a catalogue of motives has been made, each activity can be matched with an appropriate motive. Thus, a business executive is said to be motivated by a desire to possess money, to possess property, and to have executive power over other people. A good student is said to be motivated by a desire for good grades and for the prestige and adulation that ensues, and by a desire to please his parents and teachers.

But why, we ask, do two brothers often seem to differ greatly in the amount of motivation each exhibits? Does it suffice to say that one brother wishes to please his parents and teachers, but that the other does not? Usually we are not satisfied with the explanation that one is more highly motivated than the other. We want to know *why* behaviors differ in motivational level.

Psychologists early discovered that bodily needs serve as inborn sources of drive or motivation. A hungry animal must move around if it is to find food. A thirsty animal would die if it lies in a dry cave waiting for water to come to it. Each need-state has sensory mechanisms for letting the animal know that a need has arisen and which one it is. Hunger feels different from thirst.

But as we have seen, genetically determined bodily needs make up only a very small part of the total motivational complex of a higher animal. Most of the reasons for action seem to be those that are not genetic in nature. Men are probably not born with a desire for money or for good grades. Such motives are acquired through some learning process. Indeed, it is the duty of parents, teachers, and every viable society to specifically teach such social motives to each new generation.

This article deals with acquired motivation in animals. It shows how the common motive of *fear* is learned and how it in turn serves to motivate further learning.

An important role in human behavior is played by drives such as fears, or desires for money, approval, or status, which appear to be learned during the socialization of the individual (Allport, 1937; Miller and Dollard, 1941; Shaffer, 1936; Watson, 1924; Woodworth, 1918). While some studies have indicated that drives can be learned (Anderson, 1941; Miller, 1941; Mowrer and Lamoreaux,

From Journal of Experimental Psychology, *Vol. 38 (1948), 89–101. Copyright 1948 by the American Psychological Association, and reproduced by permission. This study is part of the research program of the Institute of Human Relations, Yale University. It was first reported as part of a paper at the 1941 meetings of the APA. The author is indebted to Fred D. Sheffield for assistance in the exploratory work involved in establishing the experimental procedure and for criticizing the manuscript.*

1946), the systematic experimental investigation of acquired drives has been scarcely begun. A great deal more work has been done on the innate, or primary, drives such as hunger, thirst, and sex.

Fear is one of the most important of the acquirable drives because it can be acquired so readily and can become so strong. The great strength which fear can possess has been experimentally demonstrated in studies of conflict behavior. In one of these studies (Brown, 1940) it was found that albino rats, trained to run down an alley to secure food at a distinctive place and motivated by 46-hour hunger, would pull with a force of 50 gm. if they were restrained near the food. Other animals, that had learned to run away from the end of the same alley to escape electric shock, pulled with a force of 200 gm. when they were restrained near that place on trials during which they were not shocked and presumably were motivated only by fear. Furthermore, animals, that were first trained to run to the end of the alley to secure food and then given a moderately strong electric shock there, remained well away from the end of the alley, demonstrating that the habits motivated by fear were prepotent over those motivated by 46-hour hunger (Miller, 1944).[1] This experimental evidence is paralleled by many clinical observations which indicate that fear (or anxiety as it is called when its source is vague or obscured by repression) plays a leading role in the production of neurotic behavior (Freud, 1933, 1936).

The purpose of the present experiment was to determine whether or not once fear is established as a new response to a given situation it will exhibit the following functional properties characteristic of primary drives such as hunger: (a) when present motivate so-called random behavior and (b) when suddenly reduced serve as a reinforcement to produce learning of the immediately preceding response.

Apparatus and Procedure

The apparatus used in this experiment . . . consisted of two compartments: one white with a grid as a floor and the other black with a smooth solid floor. Both of these had a glass front to enable the experimenter to observe the animal's behavior. The two compartments were separated by a door which was painted with horizontal black and white stripes. This door was held up by a catch operated by a solenoid and could be caused to drop in any one of three different ways: (a) by the *E* pushing a button, (b) by the rat moving a little cylindrical wheel made of horizontal rods stretched between Bakelite disks and exposed above the right-hand half of the door, (c) by a bar projecting 1¼ inches from the side of the apparatus in front of the upper left-hand corner of the door.

The support of the grid was pivoted at the end near the door and held slightly above a contact by a little spring at the far end. Placing the rat into the apparatus caused the grid to move down a fraction of an inch and close the contact. This started an electric clock. When the animal caused the door to drop by rotating the wheel a fraction of a turn or pressing the bar (depending upon the way the apparatus was set), he stopped the clock which timed his response. The wheel was attached to a ratchet in such a way that the part of it facing the rat could only be moved downward. A brush riding on a segment of the wheel which projected through the back of the apparatus was arranged in such a way that each quarter of a revolution was recorded on an electric counter.

The animals used in this experiment were male albino rats approximately six months old. They had been tamed by handling but had not been used in any other experiment. They were allowed plenty of food and water in their home cages at all times.

The procedure involved the following five steps:

1. *Test for initial response to apparatus.* The animals were placed in the apparatus for approximately one minute with the door between the two compartments open, and their behavior was observed.

2. *Trials with primary drive of pain produced by electric shock.* The procedure for administering shock was designed to attach the response of fear to as many as possible of the cues in the white compartment instead of merely to the relatively transient stimulus trace of just having been dropped in. This was done so that the animal would remain frightened when he was restrained in the compartment on subsequent non-shock trials. The strength of shock used was 500 volts of 60 cycle AC through a series resistance of 250,000 ohms. The animals were given 10 trials with shock. On the first trial they were allowed to remain in

---

[1] In both of these experiments the 46–hour food deprivation was made more effective by the fact that the animals had been habituated to a regular feeding schedule and maintained on a diet that was quantitatively restricted enough to keep them very thin but qualitatively enriched with brewer's yeast, cod liver oil, and greens to keep them healthy.

the white compartment for 60 seconds without shock and then given a momentary shock every five seconds for 60 seconds. At the end of this period of time the E dropped the door and put a continuous shock on the grid.

As soon, as the animal had run into the black compartment, the door was closed behind him and he was allowed to remain there for 30 seconds. Then he was taken out and placed in a cage of wire mesh approximately nine inches in diameter and seven inches high for the time between trials. Since the animals were run in rotation in groups of three, the time between trials was that required to run the other two animals, but was never allowed to fall below 60 seconds. This procedure was followed on all subsequent trials.

On the second trial the animal was placed into the center of the white compartment facing away from the door, was kept there for 30 seconds without shock, at the end of which time the shock was turned on and the door opened. On trials 3 through 10 the grid was electrified before the animal was dropped on it and the door was opened before he reached it. On odd numbered trials the animal was dropped at the end of the compartment away from the door and facing it; on even numbered trials he was dropped in the center of the compartment facing away from the door.

3. *Nonshock trials with experimenter dropping door.* The purpose of these trials was to determine whether or not the animals would continue to perform the original habit in the absence of the primary drive of pain from electric shock, and to reduce their tendency to crouch in the white compartment and to draw back in response to the sound and movement of the door dropping in front of them.[2] Each animal was given five of these nonshock trials during which the E dropped the door before the animal reached it. As with the preceding trials the animals were dropped in facing the door on odd-numbered trials and facing away from it on even-numbered ones; they were allowed to remain in the black compartment for 30 seconds and were kept in the wire mesh cage for at least 60 seconds between trials.

4. *Nonshock trials with door opened by turning the wheel.* The purpose of these trials was to determine whether the continued running without shock was the mere automatic persistence of a simple habit, or whether an acquired drive was involved which could be used to motivate the learning of a new habit. During these trials the E no longer dropped the door. The apparatus was set so that the only way the door could be dropped was by moving the wheel a small fraction of a

turn. The bar was present but pressing it would not cause the door to drop. The animals that moved the wheel and caused the door to drop were allowed to remain 30 seconds in the black compartment. Those that did not move the wheel within 100 seconds were picked out of the white compartment at the end of that time. All animals remained at least 60 seconds between trials in the wire mesh cage. All animals were given 16 trials under these conditions. On each trial the time to move the wheel enough to drop the door was recorded on an electric clock and read to the nearest 10th of a second.

5. *Nonshock trials with door opened by pressing the bar.* The purpose of these trials was to determine whether or not animals (a) would unlearn the first new habit of turning the wheel if this habit was no longer effective in dropping the door, and (b) would learn a second new habit, pressing the bar, if this would cause the door to drop and allow them to remove themselves from the cues arousing the fear. Animals that had adopted the habit of crouching in the white compartment till the end of the 100-second limit and so had not learned to rotate the wheel were excluded from this part of the experiment. These trials were given in exactly the same way as the preceding ones ex-

----

[2] During the training in the next step (learning to rotate the wheel), crouching would interfere with the type of responses necessary in order to hit the wheel and withdrawing would prevent the animals from going into the black compartment and having their fear reduced immediately after hitting the wheel. Apparently crouching occupies a dominant position in the innate hierarchy of responses to fear. Similarly withdrawing seems to be either an innate or a previously learned response to the pattern of fear plus a sudden stimulus in front of the animal. During the shock trials the response of fear is learned to the pattern of shock plus white compartment and the responses of running are learned to the pattern of shock plus stimuli produced by the fear response plus the cues in the white compartment. When the shock stimulus drops out of the pattern, the generalized fear and running responses elicited by the remainder of the pattern are weaker. The innate crouching response to fear is then in conflict with the generalized running responses to the pattern of fear plus cues in the alley. If the door is closed, the extinction of running and other related responses may reduce their strength to the point where crouching becomes dominant. If the door is dropped in front of the animal so that he can immediately run out of the white compartment, the reduction in the strength of fear will be expected to strengthen the relative dominance of running and related responses to the stimulus of fear plus the cues in the white compartment and the sight and sound of the door dropping.

cept that the apparatus was set so that turning the wheel would not cause the door to drop but pressing the bar would. During these trials there was no time limit; the animals were allowed to remain in the white compartment until they finally pressed the bar. The time to press the bar was recorded on an electric clock to the nearest 10th of a second and the number of revolutions of the wheel was recorded on an electric counter in quarter revolutions.

*   *   *

Results

In the test before the training with electric shock, the animals showed no readily discernible avoidance or preference for either of the two chambers of the apparatus. They explored freely through both of them.

During the trials with primary drive of pain produced by electric shock, all of the animals learned to run rapidly from the white compartment through the door, which was dropped in front of them by the *E,* and into the black compartment. On the five trials without shock, and with the *E* still dropping the door, the animals continued to run. The behavior of the animals was markedly different from what it had been before the training with the primary drive of pain from electric shock.

When the procedure of the nonshock trials was changed so that the *E* no longer dropped the door and it could only be opened by moving the wheel, the animals displayed variable behavior which tended to be concentrated in the region of the door. They would stand up in front of it, place their paws upon it, sniff around the edges, bite the bars of the grid they were standing on, run back and forth, etc. They also tended to crouch, urinate, and defecate. In the course of this behavior some of the animals performed responses, such as poking their noses between the bars of the wheel or placing their paws upon it, which caused it to move a fraction of a turn and actuate a contact that caused the door to open. Most of them then ran through into the black compartment almost immediately. A few of them drew back with an exaggerated startle response and crouched. Some of these eventually learned to go through the door; a few seemed to learn to avoid it. Other animals abandoned their trial-and-error behavior before they happened to strike the wheel and persisted in crouching so that they had to be lifted out of the white compartment at the end of the 100-second period. In general, the animals that

had to be lifted out seemed to crouch sooner and sooner on successive trials.

Thirteen of the 25 animals moved the wheel enough to drop the door on four or more out of their first eight trials. Since, according to theory, a response has to occur before it can be reinforced and learned, the results of these animals were analyzed separately and they were the only ones which were subsequently used in the bar-pressing phase of the experiment. The average speed (reciprocal of time in seconds) with which these animals opened the door by moving the wheel on the 16 successive trials . . . shows that there is a definite tendency for the animals to learn to turn the wheel more rapidly on successive trials. Eleven out of the 13 individual animals turned the wheel sooner on the 16th than on the first trial, and the two animals which did not show improvement were ones which happened to turn the wheel fairly soon on the first trial and continued this performance throughout. The difference between the average speed on the first and 16th trials is of a magnitude which would be expected to occur in the direction predicted by theory, less than two times in 1000 by chance. Therefore, it must be concluded that those animals that did turn the wheel and run out of the white compartment into the black one definitely learned to perform this new response more rapidly during the 16 trials *without* the primary drive of pain produced by electric shock.

When the setting on the apparatus was changed so that the wheel would not open the door but the bar would, the animals continued to respond to the wheel vigorously for some time. It was obvious that they had learned a strong habit of responding to it. Eventually, however, they stopped reacting to the wheel and began to perform other responses. After longer or shorter periods of variable behavior they finally hit the bar, caused the door to drop, and ran through rapidly into the black compartment. On the first trial the number of complete rotations of the wheel ranged from zero to 530 with a median of 4.75. On successive trials during which turning the wheel did not cause the door to drop, the amount of activity on it progressively dropped till by the tenth trial the range was from 0 to 0.25 rotations with a median of zero. . . . Progressive decrease in the amount of activity on the wheel . . . [occurred for 12] out of the 13 rats which were used in this part of the experiment . . . . From the binomial expansion it may be calculated that for 12 out of 13 cases to come out in the direction predicted by the theory is an event which would be expected to occur by chance less than one time in 1000. Thus, it may be concluded that the dropping of the door, which is presumed to have produced a reduction in the strength of fear by allowing the animals to escape from the cues in the white compartment which elicited the fear, was essential to the maintenance of the habit of rotating the wheel.

The results . . . [show] that the speed of bar-pressing increased throughout the 10 nonshock trials during which that response caused the door to drop. Since the last trial was faster than the first for 12 out of the 13 animals, the difference was again one which would be expected by chance less than one time in 1000.

Discussion

On preliminary tests conducted before the training with electric shock was begun, the animals showed no noticeable tendency to avoid the white compartment. During training with the primary drive of pain produced by electric shock in the white compartment, the animals learned a strong habit of quickly running out of it, through the open door, and into the black compartment.

On nonshock trials the animals persisted in running from the white compartment through the open door into the black one. On additional nonshock trials during which the door was not automatically dropped in front of the animals, they exhibited so-called random behavior and learned a new response, turning the wheel, which caused the door to drop and allowed them to escape into the black compartment. This trial-and-error learning of a new response demonstrated that the cues in the white compartment had acquired the functional properties of a drive and that escape from the white into the black compartment had acquired the functional properties of a reward.

*　　*　　*

In the present experiment, when the animals were dropped into the white compartment on the nonshock trials following their training with shock, they exhibited urination, defecation, tenseness, and other forms of behavior which are ordinarily considered to be symptoms of fear. Furthermore, the procedure of having been given a number of moderately painful shocks in this compartment would be expected to produce fear. Therefore, it seems reasonable to conclude that the acquirable drive motivating the learning of the new response of turning the wheel was fear and that a reduction

in the strength of this fear was the reinforcing agent. Thus, this experiment confirms Mowrer's (1939) hypothesis that fear (or anxiety) can play a role in learning similar to that of a primary drive such as hunger.

In terms of the hypothesis put forward in Miller and Dollard (1941) the cues in the white compartment acquire their drive value by acquiring the capacity to elicit an internal response which produces a strong stimulus. Whether this strong stimulus is produced by peripheral responses, such as those involved in the blanching of the stomach and the tendency for hair to stand on end, or by central impulses which travel from the thalamus to sensory areas of the cortex is a matter of anatomical rather than functional significance. Fear may be called a stimulus-producing response if it shows the functional characteristics of such responses, in brief, [if it] obeys the laws of learning and serves as a cue to elicit learned responses such as the verbal report of fear.

The general pattern of the fear response and its capacity to produce a strong stimulus is determined by the innate structure of the animal. The connection between the pain and the fear is also presumably innate. But the connection between the cues in the white compartment and the fear was learned. Therefore the fear of the white compartment may be called an acquired drive. Because fear can be learned, it may be called acquirable; because it can motivate new learning, it may be called a drive.

Running through the door and into the black compartment removed the animal from the cues in the white compartment which were eliciting the fear and thus produced a reduction in the strength of the fear response and the stimuli which it produced. This reduction in the strength of the intense fear stimuli is presumably what gave the black compartment its acquired reinforcing value.

If the reduction in fear produced by running from the white into the black was the reinforcement for learning the new habit of wheel turning, we would expect this habit to show experimental extinction when that reinforcement was removed. This is exactly what happened. During the first trial on which turning the wheel no longer dropped the door, the animals gradually stopped performing this response and began to exhibit other responses. As would be expected, the one of these responses, pressing the bar, which caused the door to drop and allowed the animal to remove himself from the fear-producing cues in the white compartment, was gradually learned in a series of trials during which the wheel turning was progressively crowded out. Thus, it can be seen that the escape from the white compartment, which presumably produced a reduction in the strength of the fear, played a crucial role, similar to that of a primary reward, in the learning and maintenance of the new habits.

Some of the implications of the principles which this experiment has demonstrated should be mentioned briefly. It can be seen that being able to learn a response (fear of the white compartment) which in turn is able to motivate the learning and performance of a whole category of new responses (turning the wheel, pressing the bar, and any other means of escape from the white compartment) greatly increases the flexibility of learned behavior as a means of adapting to a changing environment.

The present experiment has demonstrated the drive function of fear as a response which presumably produces a strong stimulus. But if fear is a strong response-produced stimulus, it will be expected to function, not only as a drive, but also as a cue mediating secondary generalization. Thus, when fear is learned as a new response to a given situation, all of the habits which have been learned elsewhere in response to fear, as well as the innate responses to fear, should tend to be transferred to that new situation. Evidence supporting this deduction has been secured in a recent experiment by May (1948).

It seems possible that the potentialities of response-produced stimuli as mediators of secondary generalization and sources of acquirable drive may account in stimulus-response, law-of-effect terms for the type of behavior which has been described as "expectancy" and considered to be an exception to this type of explanation. If it should turn out that all of the phenomena of expectancy can be explained on the basis of the drive and cue functions of response-produced stimuli, expectancy will of course not vanish; it will be established as a secondary principle derivable from more primary ones.

The mechanism of acquired drives allows behavior to be more adaptive in complex variable situations. It also allows behavior to appear more baffling and apparently lawless to any investigator who had not had the opportunity to observe the conditions under which the acquired drive was established. In the present experiment the learning and performance of the responses of turning the wheel and pressing the bar are readily understandable. An *E* dealing with many rats, a few of which without his knowledge had been shocked in the white compartment, might be puzzled by the fact that these few rats became so preoccupied with turning the wheel or pressing the bar. In the present experiment, the white and black compartments are very obvious features of the animal's environment. If more obscure external cues or internal ones had been involved, the habits of turning the wheel and pressing the bar might seem to be completely bizarre and maladaptive. One hypothesis is that neurotic symptoms, such as compulsions, are habits which are motivated by fear (or anxiety as it is called when its source is vague or obscured by repression) and reinforced by a reduction in fear.[3]

* * *

REFERENCES

Allport, G. W. *Personality*. New York: Holt, Rinehart & Winston, 1937.

Anderson, E. E. The externalization of drive: III. Maze learning by nonrewarded and by satiated rats. *Journal of Genetic Psychology*, 1941, **59,** 397–426.

Brown, J. S. Generalized approach and avoidance responses in relation to conflict behavior. New Haven: Dissertation, Yale University, 1940.

Dollard, J. Exploration of morale factors among combat air crewmen. *Memorandum to Experimental Section, Research Branch, Information and Education Division, War Department*, March 9, 1945.

Freud, S. *New introductory lectures on psychoanalysis*. New York: Norton, 1933.

Freud, S. *The problem of anxiety*. New York: Norton, 1936.

May, M. A. Experimentally acquired drives. *Journal of Experimental Psychology*, 1948, **38,** 66–77.

Miller, N. E. An experimental investigation of acquired drives. *Psychological Bulletin*, 1941, **38,** 534–535.

Miller, N. E. Experimental studies of conflict behavior. In J. McV. Hunt (Ed.), *Personality and the behavior disorders*. New York: Ronald Press, 1944. Pp. 431–465.

Miller, N. E., & Dollard, J. *Social learning and imitation*. New Haven: Yale University Press, 1941.

Mowrer, O. H. A stimulus-response analysis of anxiety and its role as a reinforcing agent. *Psychological Review*, 1939, **46,** 553–565.

Mowrer, O. H., & Lamoreaux, R. R. Fear as an intervening variable in avoidance conditioning. *Journal of Comparative Psychology*, 1946, **39,** 29–50.

Shaffer, L. F. *The psychology of adjustment*. Boston: Houghton Mifflin, 1936.

Watson, J. B. *Psychology from the standpoint of a behaviorist*. Philadelphia: Lippincott, 1924.

Woodworth, R. S. *Dynamic psychology*. New York: Columbia University Press, 1918.

---

[3] The author's views on this matter have been materially strengthened and sharpened by seeing the way in which Dollard (1945), working with symptoms of war neuroses, has independently come to a similar hypothesis and been able to apply it convincingly to the concrete details of the case material.

46

Positive Reinforcement
Produced by Electrical Stimulation of Septal Area
and Other Regions of Rat Brain

James Olds and Peter Milner

Psychologists of learning have established that hungry animals will tend to repeat those actions which are followed by the presentation of food. The presentation of food is said to "reinforce" the action that preceded it, and the food itself is referred to as a "reinforcer." Similarly, water acts as a reinforcer for thirsty animals, and a receptive partner is a reinforcer for a sexually aroused animal. Presumably the reinforcer produces some neurological effect that causes the tendency to repeat the activity that produced it. Psychologists interested in learning more about such neurological processes have located areas in the brain where externally produced electrical stimulation apparently acts as a reinforcer in much the same way as eating or drinking. Experiments such as the one reported here do much to add to our understanding of the phenomenon of reinforcement.

Stimuli have eliciting and reinforcing functions. In studying the former, one concentrates on the responses which come after the stimulus. In studying the latter, one looks mainly at the responses which precede it. In its reinforcing capacity, a stimulus increases, decreases, or leaves unchanged the frequency of preceding responses, and accordingly it is called a reward, a punishment, or a neutral stimulus.

Previous studies using chronic implantation of electrodes have tended to focus on the eliciting functions of electrical stimuli delivered to the brain (Delgado, 1952a, 1952b). The present study, on the other hand, has been concerned with the reinforcing function of the electrical stimulation.

Method

General

Stimulation was carried out by means of chronically implanted electrodes which did not interfere with the health or free behavior of Ss to any appreciable extent. The Ss were 15 male hooded rats, weighing approximately 250 gm. at the start of the experiment. Each S was tested in a Skinner box which delivered alternating current to the brain so long as a lever was depressed. The current

was delivered over a loose lead, suspended from the ceiling, which connected the stimulator to the rat's electrode. The Ss were given a total of 6 to 12 hours of acquisition testing, and 1 to 2 hours of extinction testing. During acquisition, the stimulator was turned on so that a response produced electrical stimulation; during extinction, the stimulator was turned off so that a response produced no electrical stimulation. Each S was given a percentage score denoting the proportion of his total acquisition time given to responding. This score could be compared with the animal's extinction score to determine whether the stimulation had a positive, negative, or neutral reinforcing effect. After testing, the animal was sacrificed. Its brain

From Journal of Comparative and Physiological Psychology, *Vol. 47 (1954), 419–427. Copyright 1954 by the American Psychological Association, and reproduced by permission. The research reported here was made possible by grants from the Rockefeller Foundation and the National Institute of Mental Health of the United States Public Health Service. The authors particularly wish to express their thanks to Professor D. O. Hebb, who provided germinal ideas for the research and who backed it with enthusiastic encouragement as well as laboratory facilities and funds. The authors are also grateful to Miss Joann Feindel, who performed the histological reconstructions reported here.*

was frozen, sectioned, stained, and examined microscopically to determine which structure of the brain had been stimulated. This permitted correlation of acquisition scores with anatomical structures.

Electrode implantation

Electrodes are constructed by cementing a pair of enameled silver wires of 0.010-inch diameter into a Lucite block. The parts of the wires which penetrate the brain are cemented together to form a needle, and this is cut to the correct length to reach the desired structure in the brain. This length is determined from Krieg's (1946) rat brain atlas with slight modifications as found necessary by experience. The exposed cross section of the wire is the only part of the needle not insulated from the brain by enamel; stimulation therefore occurs only at the tip. Contact with the lead from the stimulator is made through two blobs of solder on the upper ends of the electrode wires; these blobs make contact with the jaws of an alligator clip which has been modified to insulate the two jaws from one another. A light, flexible hearing-aid lead connects the clip to the voltage source.

The operation of implantation is performed with the rat under Nembutal anesthesia (0.88 cc/Kg) and held in a Johnson-Krieg stereotaxic instrument (Krieg, 1946). A mid-line incision is made in the scalp and the skin held out of the way by muscle retractors. A small hole is drilled in the skull with a dental burr at the point indicated by the stereotaxic instrument for the structure it is desired to stimulate. The electrode, which is clamped into the needle carrier of the instrument, is lowered until the flange of the Lucite block rests firmly on the skull. Four screw holes are then drilled in the skull through four fixing holes in the flange, and the electrode, still clamped firmly in the instrument, is fastened to the skull with jeweler's screws which exceed the diameter of the screw holes in the skull by 0.006 inches. The electrode is then released from the clamp and the scalp wound closed with silk sutures. The skin is pulled tightly around the base of the Lucite block and kept well away from the contact plates. A recovery period of three days is allowed after the operation before testing.

Testing

The testing apparatus consisted of a large-levered Skinner box 11 inches long, 5 inches wide, and 12 inches high. The top was open to allow passage for the stimulating lead. The lever actuated a microswitch in the stimulating circuit so that when it was depressed, the rat received electrical stimulation. The current was obtained from the 60-cycle power line, through a step-down transformer, and was adjustable between 0 and 10 v. r.m.s. by means of a variable potentiometer. In the experiments described here the stimulation continued as long as the lever was pressed, though for some tests a time-delay switch was incorporated which cut the current off after a predetermined interval if the rat continued to hold the lever down. Responses were recorded automatically on paper strip.

On the fourth day after the operation rats were given a pretesting session of about an hour in the boxes. Each rat was placed in the box and on the lever by *E* with the stimulus set at 0.5 v. During the hour, stimulation voltage was varied to determine the threshold of a "just noticeable" effect on the rat's behavior. If the animal did not respond regularly from the start, it was placed on the lever periodically (at about 5-minute intervals). Data collected on the first day were not used in later calculations. On subsequent days, *S*s were placed in the box for about 3½ hours a day; these were 3 hours of acquisition and ½ hour of extinction. During the former, the rats were allowed to stimulate themselves with a voltage which was just high enough to produce some noticeable response in the resting animal. As this threshold voltage fluctuated with the passage of time, *E* would make a determination of it every half hour, unless *S* was responding regularly. At the beginning of each acquisition period, and after each voltage test, the animal was placed on the lever once by *E*. During extinction periods, conditions were precisely the same except that a bar-press produced no electrical stimulation. At the beginning of each extinction period, animals which were not responding regularly were placed on the lever once by *E*. At first, rats were tested in this way for four days, but as there appeared to be little difference between the results on different days, this period was reduced to three and then to two days for subsequent animals. Thus, the first rats had about 12 hours of acquisition after pretesting whereas later rats had about 6 hours. However, in computing the scores in our table, we have used only the first 6 hours of acquisition for all animals, so the scores are strictly comparable. In behavioral curves, we have shown the full 12 hours of acquisition on the earlier animals so as to illustrate the stability of the behavior over time.

At no time during the experiment were the rats

deprived of food or water, and no reinforcement was used except the electrical stimulus.

Animals were scored on the percentage of time which they spent bar-pressing regularly during acquisition. In order to find how much time the animal would spend in the absence of reward or punishment, a similar score was computed for periods of extinction. This extinction score provided a base line. When the acquisition score is above the extinction score, we have reward; when it is below the extinction score, we have punishment.

In order to determine percentage scores, periods when the animal was responding regularly (at least one response every 30 seconds) were counted as periods of responding; i.e., *intervals of 30 seconds or longer without a response were counted as periods of no responding*. The percentage scores were computed as the proportion of total acquisition or extinction time given to periods of responding.

Determination of locus

On completion of testing, animals were perfused with physiological saline, followed by 10 per cent formalin. The brains were removed, and after further fixation in formalin for about a week, frozen sections 40 microns thick were cut through the region of the electrode track. These were stained with cresyl violet and the position of the electrode tip determined. . . .

Results

Locus

Acquisition and extinction scores [were] correlated with electrode placements.

*   *   *

The highest scores [were] found together in the central portion of the forebrain.

*   *   *

Thus the electrical stimulus in the septal area has an effect which is apparently equivalent to that of a conventional primary reward as far as the maintenance of a lever-pressing response is concerned.

If we move outside the septal area, either in the direction of the caudate nucleus (across the lateral ventricle) or in the direction of the *corpus callo-*

sum, we find acquisition scores drop abruptly. . . . These are definitely indications of neutral (neither rewarding nor punishing) effects.

However, above the *corpus callosum* in the cingulate cortex we find an acquisition score of 37 per cent. As the extinction score in this case was 9 per cent, we may say that stimulation was rewarding.

At the thalamic level we find a 36 per cent acquisition score produced by an electrode placed again in the cingulate cortex, an 11 per cent score produced by an electrode placed in the hippocampus, a 71 per cent score produced by an electrode placed exactly in the mammillothalamic tract, and a zero per cent score produced by an electrode placed in the medial lemniscus. The zero denotes negative reinforcement.

At the mid-brain level there are two zero scores produced by electrodes which are in the posterior portion of the medial geniculate bodies; here again, the scores indicate a negative effect, as the corresponding extinction scores are 31 and 21 per cent. There is an electrode deep in the medial, posterior tegmentum which produces a 2 per cent score; this seems quite neutral, as the extinction score in this case is 1 per cent.

*   *   *

Discussion

It is clear that electrical stimulation in certain parts of the brain, particularly the septal area, produces acquisition and extinction curves which compare favorably with those produced by a conventional primary reward. With other electrode placements, the stimulation appears to be neutral or punishing.

Because the rewarding effect has been produced maximally by electrical stimulation in the septal area, but also in lesser degrees in the mammillothalamic tract and cingulate cortex, we are led to speculate that a system of structures previously attributed to the rhinencephalon may provide the locus for the reward phenomenon. However, as localization studies which will map the whole brain with respect to the reward and punishment dimension are continuing, we will not discuss in detail the problem of locus. We will use the term "reinforcing structures" in further discussion as a general name for the septal area and other structures which produce the reward phenomenon.

To provide an adequate canvass of the possible explanations for the rewarding effect would require considerably more argument than could possibly fit within the confines of a research paper. We have decided, therefore, to rule out briefly the possibility that the implantation produces pain which is reduced by electrical stimulation of reinforcing structures, and to confine further discussion to suggestions of ways the phenomenon may provide a methodological basis for study of physiological mechanisms of reward.

The possibility that the implantation produces some painful "drive stimulus" which is alleviated by electrical stimulation of reinforcing structures does not comport with the facts which we have observed. If there were some chronic, painful drive state, it would be indicated by emotional signs in the animal's daily behavior. Our Ss, from the first day after the operation, are normally quiet, nonaggressive; they eat regularly, sleep regularly, gain weight. There is no evidence in their behavior to support the postulation of chronic pain. Septal preparations which have lived healthy and normal lives for months after the operation have given excellent response rates.

As there is no evidence of a painful condition preceding the electrical stimulation, and as the animals are given free access to food and water at all times except while actually in the Skinner boxes, there is no explicitly manipulated drive to be reduced by electrical stimulation. Barring the possibility that stimulation of a reinforcing structure specifically inhibits the "residual drive" state of the animal, or the alternative possibility that

the first electrical stimulus has noxious aftereffects which are reduced by a second one, we have some evidence here for a primary rewarding effect which is not associated with the reduction of a primary drive state. It is perhaps fair in a discussion to report the "clinical impression" of the Es that the phenomenon represents strong pursuit of a positive stimulus rather than escape from some negative condition.

Should the latter interpretation prove correct, we have perhaps located a system within the brain whose peculiar function is to produce a rewarding effect on behavior. The location of such a system puts us in a position to collect information that may lead to a decision among conflicting theories of reward. By physiological studies, for example, we may find that the reinforcing structures act selectively on sensory or motor areas of the cortex. . . .

*   *   *

REFERENCES
Delgado, J. M. R. Permanent implantation of multi-lead electrodes in the brain. *Yale Journal of Biology and Medicine*, 1952, **24**, 351–358. (a)
Delgado, J. M. R. Responses evoked in waking cat by electrical stimulation of motor cortex. *American Journal of Physiology*, 1952, **171**, 436–446. (b)
Krieg, W. J. S. Accurate placement of minute lesions in the brain of the albino rat. *Quarterly Bulletin, Northwestern University Medical School*, 1946, **20**, 199–208.

47

Learning to Love

Harry F. Harlow and Margaret K. Harlow

To be loved by someone and to return that love with unquestioning loyalty provides one of the most consistent pleasures for people of all cultures. Indeed, the very structure of family life and social groups relies upon the deep feelings of loyalty and happiness that arise from mutual love. Even though love is not necessary for life, it is necessary for a happy life.

The ways in which mothers and their infants begin the process of the love relationship have been investigated extensively by the Harlows, using nonhuman primates as their

From The American Scientist, *Vol. 54 (1966), 244–272. A Sigma Xi-RESA [Scientific Research Society of America] National Lecture, 1965–1966 Series.*
This research was supported by United States Public Health Service grants MH-11894 and FR-0167 from the National Institutes of Health to the University of Wisconsin Primate Laboratory and Regional Primate Research Center, respectively.

subjects. Whether or not an individual has received affectionate treatment in infancy can be very important in his later development. This article explores several aspects of the continuing process of learning to love.

It is our firm belief that in the primate order there are five relatively separable affectional systems, and this position has already been presented in detail (Harlow and Harlow, 1965). In the present paper, we shall discuss only three of the affectional systems: the maternal or mother-infant affectional system; the infant-mother affectional system, which is in many ways both behaviorally and probably neurophysiologically a reciprocal affectional system; and the age-mate or peer affectional system, which is intimately associated with the first two affectional systems from the developmental point of view although it is apparently quite discrete in terms of the stimuli which elicit its response patterns and probably quite discrete in terms of its underlying neurophysiological mechanisms.

Maternal Affectional System

The maternal affectional system in the rhesus macaque, and presumably in all the *Anthropoidea* —monkeys, apes, and men—goes through at least three basic developmental stages: (1) the stage of maternal attachment and protection; (2) the transitional or ambivalence stage, which might also be described as the disattachment stage; and (3) the stage of maternal separation or rejection. These stages proceed about twice as rapidly in monkeys as in anthropoid apes and about twice as rapidly in anthropoid apes as in human beings. However, the nature of the stages and their sequential development in all higher primates show striking analogies if one allows for the intellectual differences between the various *Anthropoidea,* the differences in cultural complexity, and the fact that each species within the primate order has certain species-specific social signaling systems. Classical examples are the smiling response in man and the infant-retrieval reponses of the macaque mother (see Harlow, Harlow, and Hansen, 1963, pp. 261–263).

The development of these stages is seen more clearly in monkeys than in men because of the greater simplicity and invariance of their expression in monkeys. Furthermore, with monkey subjects we can experimentally distort or disrupt any or all of the normal developmental stages. Thus, we can create adequate and inadequate monkey mothers at will and specify the early-experience conditions which will produce these dichotomous maternal types. We do not believe that monkey research will give us total understanding of human behavior, but at the least we can achieve idealized models in which salient developmental variables may be brought into clear relief.

Maternal Attachment and Protection Stage: During the first maternal stage, the stage of attachment and protection, the behavior of the normal, "good" primate mother is characterized by total, tender, loving care. She either does not punish her infant or at most punishes it with complete gentility. During this initial period the female has three primary functions: (1) handling the baby's nutritional, temperature, and eliminative needs; (2) providing the baby with physical support and intimate physical contact comfort, which seem to be important in the development of childhood security; and (3) protecting the infant from external threats whether these are occasioned by intraspecies or extraspecies offenders or by the dangers to which the unknowledgeable infant inadvertently exposes itself as it begins to explore the physical world that surrounds it. In the monkey this stage is maintained for at least three or four months, and presumably this temporal span is at least doubled for the anthropoid apes and at least quadrupled in the case of the human being. The outstanding quality of the good primate mother's behavior during this time is total or near total acceptance of her infant—the infant can do no wrong—and she anxiously supervises its beginning sallies beyond her arm's reach. But as we shall see, the role of the good primate mother gradually changes as the initial maternal stage wanes and the second stage develops.

The Transitional or Ambivalence Stage: In the second maternal stage, that of transition or ambivalence, the mother remains attentive and protective, but she progressively relaxes physical restraint of the exploratory responses of her infant and with increasing frequency disciplines it, forcefully but not brutally. The developmental course of the rejective and punitive responses in the rhesus mother is shown in Figure 1. We believe that these negative responses of the mother assist the infant in gradually breaking its dependency relationship to her, a necessary step in the socialization process of all mammals, and consequently represent good mothering for this period of the infant's development. All our macaque data indicate that the tie to the mother is so strong that the infant has diffi-

FIGURE 1 *Punitive and rejecting responses of rhesus mothers toward their infants per 30-min. observation session in the playpen. Negative responses decrease after 5 months, reflecting increased skill of the infants in avoiding punishment and reduced contact with their mothers during play sessions.*

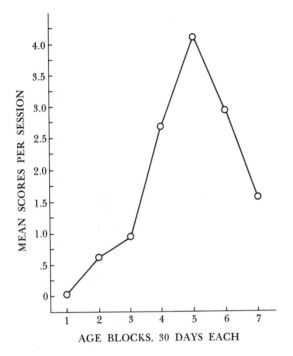

AGE BLOCKS, 30 DAYS EACH

culty in effectively emancipating itself. Left to its own devices, the tendency of the infant is to prolong the period of dependency and to cling to the mother for comfort and security. Faced with occasional rejections by its mother, the infant gains external support for its emerging exploratory responses, the responses that bring it into contact with the enlarged physical and social environment. Thus, the mother's negative responses to her infants serve to facilitate its development as an independent social being with increasing competence to meet the problems of its larger world.

The transition between the first two maternal stages is not sudden, and the timing, the severity of the rejection behavior, and the progression of the transition are influenced by diurnal factors, by the previous experiences of the mother, and probably by her status in the group. It is likely, too, that personality variables in the mother and behavioral characteristics of the infant also affect the course of this second stage. While we have stressed the addition of negative responses to maternal behavior, it should be noted that throughout the maternal transitional stage the infant remains in

close physical proximity to the mother during the evening, night, early morning periods, and much of the day and is within sight or call of the mother the remainder of the time. The mother maintains an attitude of watchful vigilance and is fiercely protective if her infant is threatened by any external danger.

The Maternal Separation Stage: The third normal maternal stage is that of separation or rejection of the infant, and in many monkey species this appears with relatively dramatic suddenness upon the advent of a new baby. The appearance of the new baby re-elicits in the mother the first maternal stage, with the neonate as its object, and thus the older baby is often totally physically displaced from the mother and the degree of psychological emancipation may be dramatic. Indeed, field studies report monkey infants during this period showing true symptoms of separation anxiety; these symptoms may be so intense that in some monkey societies and some monkey species, including at least some groups of *Macaca fuscata, Cercopithecus ascanius, M. speciosa, M. irus, Papio ursinus,* and *P. anubis,* large adult males will actually physically adopt these displaced monkey juveniles and hold them in their arms or carry them about on their backs, treating them for a considerable period of time in a maternal manner within the physiological limitations inherent in the primate male.

There is also evidence in at least one monkey species—the rhesus (*M. mulatta*)—and among those apes which have been studied in the field that the separation process may be far less precipitous for many primate juveniles. Although the youngster no longer suckles, it may remain physically and psychologically close to its mother for many years, including the adult period if it is a female and through much of the juvenile period if it is a male. It is likely that long-term field studies will increasingly reveal the lasting quality of maternal ties in many subhuman primates, and such data have already been reported by Imanishi (1963) and Koford (1965) for semiwild groups. The problem to date has been the brevity of the studies and the difficulty, in other than semiwild colonies, of identifying the blood relationships of animals displaying affectional ties.

The Infant-Mother Affectional System

The infant-mother affectional system proceeds through a series of developmental stages that complement, in a reciprocal manner, the maternal stages. The interactions of infant and mother have cumulative effects on the progression of the stages in both affectional systems, and in the infant-mother system as in the mother-infant system there is a fixed sequence in the development of successive stages in the infant's affectional ties to the mother. It is in the timing of the stages and the intensity of the behaviors that individual variations appear. The stages in the infant-mother system are: (1) the reflex stage, (2) the stage of comfort and attachment, (3) the security stage, and (4) the separation stage.

The Reflex Stage: Although the newborn monkey is far more mature than the human neonate, many or most of the monkey neonate's behaviors are of a forced, reflex nature. These include orienting the head up, hand and foot grasping, clasping, "climbing" and rooting, sucking, righting, and contactual following. The course of the appearance and waning of many of these early responses in the rhesus neonate has been traced by Mowbray and Cadell (1962), revealing that generally the reflex behaviors are supplanted after 10 to 20 days of age by partially, then totally, voluntary responses. Thus, the reflex period of the infant's relationship to the mother is a brief one in the developmental span, but it serves to guarantee survival by assuring proper orientation to and contact with the mother's body, nourishment, and physical support when the infant is unable to control its own movements. Socialization begins during this period when the baby's tie to the mother is involuntary. The neonate may learn to identify its own mother, it starts to imitate her behaviors, and it develops visual following responses. Primarily, however, it is a stage of physical adjustment rather than socialization.

Comfort and Attachment Stage: It is during this second stage—the stage of comfort and attachment—which begins in the latter half of the first month of life, that true affectional bonds between offspring and mother are formed and basic social relationships are established. The infant's responses are now under semivoluntary or totally voluntary control. As in the first stage, however, it maintains close physical contact with the mother through mechanisms associated with nursing, mechanisms associated with intimate bodily contact, and mechanisms which enable the infant to follow and to imitate appropriate maternal behaviors.

Homologous basic mechanisms binding the human infant to the mother have been described by Bowlby (1958) as primary object sucking, primary object clinging, and primary object following. The position we have presented (see Harlow, 1959) for the monkey is similar to Bowlby's and differs principally in that we assign relatively more importance to clinging than to nursing whereas Bowlby stresses nursing over clinging.

We hypothesize that the neonatal and infantile nursing and clinging responses may be two components of a single attachment pattern. When the macaque infant attaches to its mother, it attaches to her body with its arms and legs and to her nipple with its mouth. This oral attachment by the infant is far more frequently a nonnutritional attachment without nursing than an attachment associated with suckling, and the proportional frequency of nonnutritional to nutritional attachment to the nipple increases with age. Even if the two responses are similarly linked in the human primate, the infant has limited opportunity to display the full pattern, at least in western cultures, because child rearing practices limit nipple attachment opportunities to the nursing situation; if the infant mouths or sucks supplementarily, it does so on its own body or on inanimate objects.

The developmental course of primary object following has not been traced and analyzed in either monkeys or man as intensively as has the development of sucking and clinging. In both primates, however, there is evidence of visual fixation and following from the early days of life and, in the monkey, there is locomotor following as well. Infantile following is doubtless the basis for the infant's imitation of maternal behaviors. We have traced the development of infant-mother imitative responses in the macaque (see Fig. 2), and the progressive increase in frequency attests to the

FIGURE 2   *Infant imitations of mother's behavior per 30-min. session in the playpen*

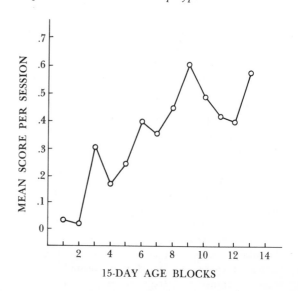

importance of following-imitation as a socializing force in this primate. The rhesus infant follows maternal behavior and within the limits of its capabilities matches the mother's action. The infant follows the mother's peregrinations: when the mother explores a physical object, so does the infant; when the mother mouths and ingests a food substance, so does the infant; when the mother is startled or frightened, the infant clings to the mother's body and observes. Such primitive imitation has been described by Miller and Dollard (1941) as matched-dependent behaviors. These behaviors enable the infant to profit from maternal experience so that its own exploratory behavior is not blind and the dangers inherent in untutored exploration are minimized. Furthermore, we believe that these maternal associations, reinforced by maternal bodily contact during moments of doubt, abet the development of the infant security stage.

Out of the maternal stage of attachment and protection and the reciprocal infantile stage of comfort and attachment, the monkey (and doubtless the human) infant develops strong feelings of safety and security in the mother's presence. All the mother-infant interactions related to nursing, bodily contact, and following-imitation contribute to security, although there is evidence that sheer bodily contact-comfort is the dominant variable in the rhesus monkey.

Security Stage: The third infant-mother affectional stage is that of security. We discovered some years ago that macaque infants achieve a great sense of personal security when raised by inanimate cloth surrogate mothers. Certainly monkey and human infants achieve an even stronger and far more socially useful sense of security when raised by real monkey mothers and by real human mothers. During this period the infant, in the presence of the mother, surrogate or real, shows a growing tendency to go out and explore the inanimate and animate world about it, returning from time to time to the mother's body for comfort and reassurance. Thus, the presence of the surrogate mother in a strange situation greatly facilitates the infant's exploration. In contrast, a baby raised by a cloth mother demonstrates abject terror in the identical test situation when the surrogate mother is absent. Although this stage of security is important in supporting the infant's exploration of the physical world, it is even more important in the self-assurance it provides the infant in its exploration of the animate world, particularly the animate world of the infant's own age-mates or peers. Gradually as the stage progresses, the infant

decreases the frequency and duration of its maternal contacts during play sessions, probably deriving a sense of security from the sight of its mother, as well as touch, and acquiring self-confidence in its new social interactions, thereby preparing it for the final stage in its relationship with its mother.

Separation Stage: The development of security during the third stage greatly facilitates the development of the fourth and longest infant-mother affectional stage, which we call the separation stage, recognizing that the separation process is very gradual and that final mother-infant separation is achieved more by maternal behaviors than by infant behaviors. The separation stage complements the maternal transitional or ambivalence stage and, somewhat later, the maternal separation stage. It is, perhaps, best characterized as a period during which age-mate associations are slowly gaining preeminence over infant-maternal relationships. Maternal security is one of the important variables making possible the infant-separation stage, and a second, possibly more important, variable is the mechanism of curiosity. From an early age the monkey is attracted to the novel in its environs but its exploratory tendencies are held somewhat in check, first by the mother, subsequently by its own fears. The sense of security gained from the maternal relationship, the reinforcements from positive exploratory experiences, the motor and intellectual increments with maturing and learning, and the growing rejection responses of the mother must all play a role in reducing the conflict between remaining in the safety and comfort of the mother's reach and exploring the attractions beyond. As positive social experiences cumulate, the age-mates become more and more rewarding companions and the mother loses her status as the sole affectional object of the maturing infant. Before separation is achieved, the third primate affectional system is well advanced—the age-mate or peer affectional system. The peer affectional ties by no means supplant the maternal affectional ties but, rather, become additional ties which satisfy the needs now dominant in the older infant and young juvenile.

Age-Mate or Peer Affectional System

As with the other affectional systems, the peer system progresses through an orderly series of developmental stages. It differs from the systems just described, however, in that the first two stages are probably artifacts of the laboratory situation, whereas all the stages of the infant-mother and mother-infant affectional systems are clearly discernible both in the laboratory and in the field. The initial stages of the peer system are the reflex stage and the manipulation stage. These stages are followed by interactive play, which is well defined both in the laboratory and in the naturalistic setting, and by a mature interactional stage in which play is minimal but affectional ties are manifested through physical proximity, friendly interchanges, and cooperative behavior.

Reflex Stage: This first stage in the peer affectional system is apparent in the early weeks of life if neonatal monkeys are given the opportunity to make contact. During this period of motor incoordination and domination by reflexes infants fixate each other visually and make approach attempts. If they succeed in contacting each other, they cling reflexly as they do to their mothers and follow each other between episodes of clinging and clasping. When two infants are together, the clinging typically assumes a ventral-ventral clasp, and when more than two are together, the pattern tends to be a "choo-choo" formation—a chain of infants, one in the lead and one at end and with intermediate infants clinging to the back of the infant in front of it. In keeping with the motor limitations of the monkeys at this stage of development, there is little activity other than clinging and following. If the animals remain together in a cage without interference, the clinging is interrupted by only brief respites and then resumes. The pattern appears to be that of utilizing the partner or partners for bodily contact, and this behavior tends to become fixated and to persist long after the clinging reflex disappears if the infants are kept together continuously from early infancy. This clinging fixation is comparable to that observed in infant monkeys raised with cloth surrogates. It cannot occur in live-mother-raised infants because the mother actively prevents continuous clinging. She forces the infant to readjust its position by her own movements and by herself adjusting the infant's position frequently, sometimes for her own comfort and at other times to groom the infant, nuzzle it, and care for its physical needs. Similarly, under natural conditions the infant would have no opportunity to display reflex clinging to another infant because mothers prevent their babies from venturing beyond arm's reach during this early period of life. Thus, the appearance of the reflex stage of peer relations depends upon the absence of a live mother to exercise restraint on the infant's movements, and the nature of the behavior when restraint is lacking merely reflects the primary need and the limited behavioral repertoire of the neonatal monkey.

Manipulation Stage: Toward the end of the first month of life, when reflex domination of behavior has given way to semivoluntary and voluntary control, rhesus infants respond to each other in the laboratory as they would to novel physical objects. They explore each other with eyes, hands, mouth, and body, and they alternate manipulation of age-mates with manipulation of the physical environment. This, like the preceding stage, is a presocial period in peer relationships, and the exploratory activity that characterizes it persists into the stage of interactive play. The simplicity of the behavior reflects the social, intellectual, and motor immaturity of the infants at one to two months of age. Nonetheless, in the laboratory situation throughout the period, they spend steadily increasing time in proximity to each other and make progressively increasing numbers of physical contacts. Gradually they come to respond to each other as social objects instead of physical objects, and social play emerges from the matrix of manipulatory play.

In the wild, opportunities for infant monkeys and apes to show a manipulation stage in interactions with peers are limited because most mothers still keep their infants close to them in this period of development and retrieve them if they escape. The same behavior is, however, manifested toward the mother and physical objects. Monkey, ape, and human infants, as they gain in coordination of their eye movements, hands, and large muscles, intensively explore their mother's body and everything in the environment within reach.

Interactive Play: The third stage in the age-mate or peer affectional system is interactive play, and it marks the start of true social interactions among peers. It overlaps with manipulatory play, at the start being interspersed with many sequences of physical exploration. Moreover, it probably appears a little earlier in laboratory-raised monkeys with early peer experience than in monkeys raised without prior peer contacts. With or without earlier peer experience, however, infant monkeys in the laboratory show the same sequence of play behaviors from two or three months of age as do feral monkeys, and infant apes in the field show the same patterns when they meet their peers at four to six months or later. Human infants probably display a similar sequence when they reach a comparable state of maturity in the second year of life and thereafter. Where age-mates are not available, primate infants—monkey, ape, and human—universally direct their play toward younger or older members of the species, including adults. Apparently, the underlying mechanisms responsible for play are similar throughout the Primate Order and find expression in social interactions if responsive partners are available.

The stage of interactive play can be broken down into developmental components. We believe that the first stage is that of rough-and-tumble play, and its course is traced in Figure 3 for groups of four animals allowed to interact in our playroom situation (Fig. 4) or playpen situation (Fig. 5). This behavior pattern is one of wrestling, sham-biting, and close body contact. A more complex type of interactive play gradually develops, and we have described this pattern as approach-withdrawal or noncontact play. In this type of interaction there is pursuit and retreat, often with the subjects alternating roles in quick succession without actually touching each other. This second type of play does not supplant rough-and-tumble play but appears as an additional pattern. As is shown in Figure 6, the developmental courses of rough-and-tumble and approach-withdrawal play are very similar, and they are not clearly separated in time. When the infantile developmental period ends and the juvenile period begins at about one year of age, the tempo of play markedly increases and there appears an intermixing of rough-and-tumble and approach-withdrawal play without intervening pauses, so that the two patterns flow smoothly from one to the other. We have tentatively described this as a third interactive play stage, the stage of integrated play, but an equally tenable position is that integrated play is but the initiation of a truly new play stage, that of aggressive play.

This final play stage, which we prefer now to term aggressive play, is chiefly characterized by a

FIGURE 3 *Developmental course of rough-and-tumble play in the playroom situation*

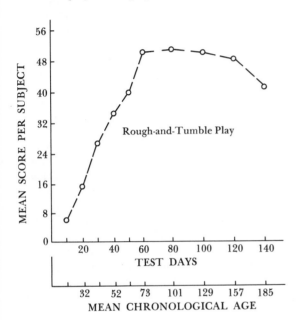

FIGURE 4 *Schematic drawing of the social playroom. The room is 8 ft. high and has approximately 46 sq. ft. of floor space.*

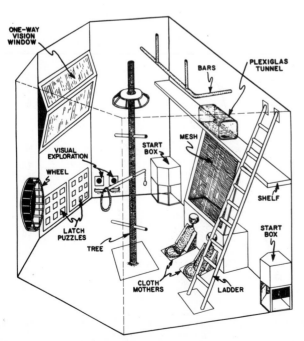

FIGURE 5 *Diagram of the playpen situation showing living cages and adjoining playpens. Mothers are confined to the living cages, but infants have access to playpen areas.*

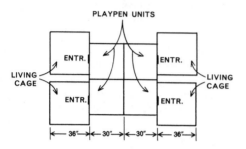

Fig. 5: *Playpen test situation.*

new quality in the interactions of the play group. Whereas previously infants have engaged in wrestling, rolling, and sham-biting behaviors without inflicting injury, they now begin to hurt and to be hurt in close body contact, usually by biting. The contests take on a progressively increasing aggressive quality while the individuals struggle for position within the group, and a dominance ordering gradually emerges. Overt aggression then diminishes and threats are sufficient to maintain the order between challenges of the group structure. During periods of status contention, however, fighting increases until the order is again stabilized

or a new order is established. Thus, this last play stage involves no new kind of play. It is the increased speed and power of the movements, the improved motor skills displayed, the underlying motivation, and the emotional quality of the interactions that differentiate the monkeys' play from that prevalent in the first year of life.

It should not be assumed that aggression replaces affection in the juvenile period. The evidence is to the contrary: Aggression is simply an additional social mechanism operating in peer interactions. Indeed, if the juveniles have long known each other and thus have already established affectional relationships, the injuries that come during aggressive play are trivial; in spite of the dominance hierarchies, basic, strong intragroup affectional relationships persist. This is strikingly illustrated when separately raised groups of juveniles are brought together. The in-group coheres in defense against out-groups, and while friendships eventually develop between members of different groups, the older in-group ties come into evidence whenever a member is threatened.

Long before aggressive play appears there is a strong, progressive tendency for sexual separation within the play groups, with males coming to prefer masculine playmates and females, feminine playmates. When aggressive play develops, this sexual separation process becomes exaggerated even though within a particular social group masculine-feminine juvenile affectional relation-

FIGURE 6 *Developmental course of approach-withdrawal play for mother-raised and surrogate-raised infants in the playpen situation (cf. Figure 3)*

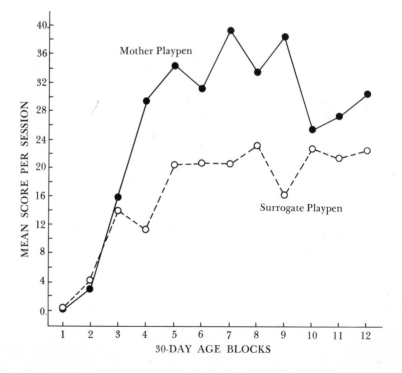

ships persist. Again, existence of friendships is evident in the behavior of separately reared groups of juveniles brought together in a playroom. A dominance ordering for the total group evolves rather quickly, and the emergent top male protects his female friends from aggression of any out-group male. In fact, he may protect them so successfully that they enjoy through his association enormous dominance over out-group males that are obviously physically stronger and could otherwise dominate them. Field studies indicate that in adult life the female friends of dominant males enjoy similar social dominance, and this endowed or conferred dominance may even carry over to the female's infant.

Mature Interaction Stage: Primates differ markedly in their overall playfulness from species to species, and there are age differences as well in playfulness in all species. In this area we must rely on field studies for our data, and it is only in very recent years that play has been observed at all in a planned manner. The data that are available indicate that play in monkeys, apes, and man is predominantly an infantile and juvenile behavior that persists in weaker degree into adolescence and tends to drop off markedly in adult life. Across species, however, differences may be so great that adults of one species are more playful than adolescents or possibly juveniles of another species. Thus, of the primates observed to date, chimpanzees would appear to be the most playful of all, playing even in adulthood (Goodall, 1963), while mountain gorillas appear to be outstanding in the paucity of their play. Infant and juvenile gorillas play, but the amount of this play as reported by Schaller (1963) seems far less than that of chimpanzees, langurs, baboons, and rhesus of comparable developmental stages. During adolescence, gorillas apparently show almost no play while the other species, particularly as represented by their male members, continue to show some social play.

Although play appears to decrease in all species during adolescence and adult life, there are ample indicators of the continuance of affectional ties among members, both like-sexed and opposite-sexed. Thus, while original peer ties develop in play, these ties may continue to function after play no longer is an important social behavior. Moreover, once peer affection develops, new affectional ties to peers can develop without play. Propinquity in periods of rest and feeding may show stability over periods of time and reflect companionship preferences. Mutual grooming is an activity that is probably confined to pairs or groups with strong attachments and may serve as a test of trust and intimacy. Indeed, when unacquainted rhesus adolescents were placed together on an island in the Madison zoo, it was observed that grooming appeared subsequent to the beginnings of friendship groupings and then gradually increased in frequency. Still another indicator of affectional ties is the cooperative efforts of pairs or groups against the threat or attack of one of the members by another individual of the larger group. Perhaps the strongest test of a female's peer attachments is sharing her infant with other females. Species differ in the generosity of females in permitting others to touch, groom, or hold their young, but in all species the young are a source of attraction for females of the group. Northern Indian langurs are the most generous of the species thus far studied, tending to allow the young infant to be passed from hand to hand (Jay, 1963). Other primate species appear to be much more selective in this behavior, with the female's particular friends being permitted closest and earliest scrutiny of the baby. Wherever primates have been observed in group-living situations, whether in the wild or in captivity, groupings have been found indicating companion preferences. There is every reason to believe that affectional relationships among mature individuals are an important aspect of primate social life within and between sexes.

Effects of Social Deprivation

During the last five years we have conducted a series of studies on the effects of social deprivation in early life. From birth onward for predetermined periods of time, monkeys have been denied both mothering and contact with peers. These deprivation studies have taken two forms: In the one form, partial social deprivation, monkeys are housed in individual bare wire cages where they can see and hear other monkeys but make no physical contact with them. We have also subjected monkeys to total social deprivation in the apparatus. In this situation the subjects see no animal of any kind for the predetermined period even though sensory deprivation is held to a minimum. As would be expected, total social deprivation produces more dramatic and pervasive effects than partial social deprivation although we now know, somewhat to our surprise, that the differences between these two forms of social deprivation are not nearly as great as we would have predicted, primarily because partial social deprivation is more damaging than we had anticipated.

Two studies show that release of the animals after three months of essentially total social deprivation leaves them in a state of emotional shock. Their initial responses are characterized by self-clutching and crouching, which resembles a postural expression of human autistic children. If, however, the monkeys can survive the immediate emotional trauma of release from total social deprivation and are then allowed to interact with control age-mates 30 minutes a day in our playroom situation, they very rapidly establish effective social relationships with their peers, as is illustrated in Figure 7. Such long-term studies as we have to date point to essentially complete social recovery, normal learning, and normal sexual adjustment in adolescence. We can find no indication in these same animals of any intellectual loss (Fig. 8) and we doubt that any will be uncovered on laboratory learning problems.

We have limited data showing that six months of partial social deprivation greatly impairs the ability of infant monkeys to interact socially with control age-mates, and we have data which seem to indicate that these social inadequacies persist over periods of years even when the animals are subsequently given some opportunity to associate continuously with age-mates over long periods of time.

FIGURE 7 *Two measures of social behavior in the playroom for four monkeys subjected to three months of social isolation and four control monkeys. Interactions are for eight weeks beginning in the subjects' fourth month of life.*

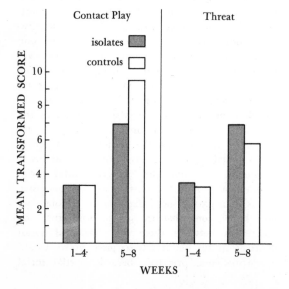

FIGURE 8 *Performance of 3-month social isolates and control subjects of the same age on 300 discrimination learning set problems administered in the second year of life. Performance is percentage of correct responses on trials 2–6 of each problem. Trial 1 is a blind trial that provides the subject information on the correct stimulus. Differences between the groups are not significant (p > 0.05).*

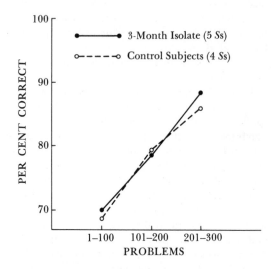

We have much more definitive data on the effects of 6 and 12 months of total social isolation. The results clearly indicate that even 6 months of total social isolation leaves the monkeys unable to interact socially with age-mates when pairs of them are placed with pairs of controls raised in partial social deprivation and tested in our playroom situation. One comparison of 6-month isolates and their controls in the two months following isolation is given in Figure 9, and a comparable difference exists for all the social measures. Moreover, the effects persist throughout the period of social coexistence as illustrated for social threat (Fig. 10). Nonetheless, the isolates do show a small gain in social interactions with each other, but not with the controls, in the course of 6 to 7 months of social testing. Twelve months of total social deprivation, compared with 6 months, produces even more socially devastating results. The 12-month isolates display essentially no social interaction with each other or with controls, as illustrated for the simplest form of play—activity play (Fig. 11). Indeed, in this experiment we had to conclude the social tests after ten weeks because the control animals were increasingly abusing the social isolates, and we were convinced that the isolates would have been killed if testing had continued.

FIGURE 9 *Contact play in the playroom for 6-month social isolates and controls during the first eight weeks after the experimental subjects were released from isolation. As is apparent, there was essentially no contact play exhibited by isolates.*

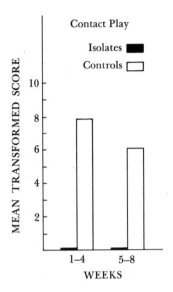

Despite the social ineptitude of both the 6- and 12-month social isolates, their intellectual abilities appear to have been spared (Fig. 12). Like the 3-month isolates (*cf.* Fig. 8), the 6- and 12-month isolates were tested on discrimination learning set problems in the second year of life. They performed at a level not statistically different from

that of control subjects of the same age. Discrimination learning set performance has been a consistently successful test in differentiating intellectual functioning among rhesus monkeys of different ages, among various genera of primates, and between primates and lower mammals (Warren, 1965).

We now have a long-term follow-up of animals subjected to 6 and 12 months of total social isolation. As preadolescents and adolescents, they were individually paired in separate tests with a single normal adult, a normal age-mate, and a normal young juvenile. The total social isolates showed fear of adults, age-mates, and even juveniles, but while showing fear, the 6-month isolates—not the 12-month isolates—also demonstrated, completely to our surprise, violent and abnormal aggressive behaviors. These included aggression against juveniles, a pattern of response seldom or never seen in normal adolescent monkeys, particularly normal adolescent female monkeys, and brief outbursts of suicidal aggression against adults—aggressions which they never displayed more than once, since the bursts of aggression were always unsuccessful; these isolates learned the social facts of life the hard and bloody way. The 12-month isolates, on the other hand, showed no aggression, apparently because fear inhibited its external expression in these animals.

We have a number of studies in which we have raised baby monkeys with cloth surrogate mothers, with brutal abnormal mothers—our so-called "motherless mothers"—or with no mothers whatsoever. In these situations the infants were given opportunities to form age-mate or peer affectional relation-

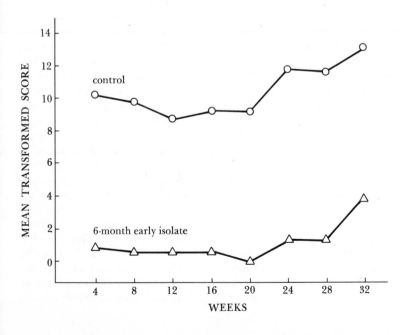

FIGURE 10 *Social threats in the playroom by 6-month social isolates and control subjects during the course of 32 weeks of interactions in the playroom. Threats exhibited by isolates were entirely directed to other isolates.*

FIGURE 11   *Activity play, a nonsocial form of play, exhibited by 12-month social isolates and control subjects in 10 weeks of exposure to the playroom. Decreasing frequency of the play in the experimental subjects doubtless reflects their increasing fear of the control subjects.*

FIGURE 12   *Discrimination learning set performance of 6-month and 12-month social isolates and control subjects of comparable age during the second year of life. Performance is measured by percentage of correct trial 2-6 responses during successive blocks of 6-trial problems (cf. Figure 8).*

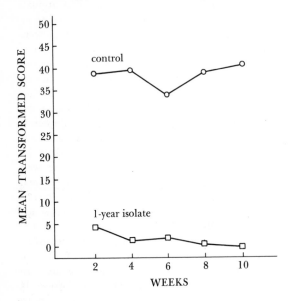

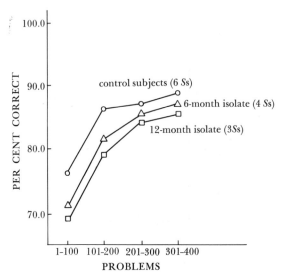

ships, and the data made it appear on first sight that perhaps normal mothering is dispensable as a social variable. We now have some reservations about the earlier conclusion.

Baby monkeys raised with cloth surrogate mothers as compared with real monkey mothers were somewhat slow in forming adequate play patterns with their peers, but by the end of a year they were interacting effectively, and they have made normal heterosexual adjustments with age-mates as juveniles and preadolescents. Babies raised with motherless mothers but allowed to interact socially in our playpen situation showed an initial lag in adjusting to their age-mates, but this difficulty rapidly ended and there was even precocious heterosexual adjustment.

The babies which we raised with no mothers whatsoever but allowed to interact with age-mates form what we have previously called our "together-together" monkeys, and the group which has been studied most intensively is a group of four, one male and three females. These infants showed greatly depressed patterns of play in our playroom situation and showed exaggerated tendencies toward partner clinging even though these clinging responses tended to ameliorate with time. Again, it appeared that heterosexual behavior was normal, even precocious. The first of the females

has become a mother and she is a perfectly normal mother, and we hopefully predict that when the other females achieve maternity, they will treat their infants in a kind, tender, and loving manner.

Thus, the three diverse kinds of peer-experienced but mother-deprived groups have made adequate social adjustments though delayed in each case and continuously depressed in the instance of the play of together-together animals. Heterosexual behavior has been adequate or precocious. Maternal behavior will be studied as the females reproduce, with only one of these animals having so far been observed, but the expectation is that mothering will be normal. There is, however, one question that the studies leave unanswered: Could unmothered or inadequately mothered infants with peer experience adjust normally to mothered infants with peer experience? We suspect that during the first year of life, particularly the first six months, unmothered or inadequately mothered animals would be disadvantaged in interactions with mothered animals and would likely develop subnormally or abnormally. Their inferiority might well carry over into adolescence and maturity under these conditions. The later the admixture of the mother-deprived and mother-reared infants, however, the less would be the expected differences. There is evidence that, at eighteen months of age, surrogate-mothered monkeys raised with each other in the playpen can adjust adequately to monkeys of the same age raised by their natural mothers and with equivalent playpen peer experience. The question of dispensability of mothers, then, hinges on testing the adequacy of mother-deprived infants in interactions in infancy with mothered infants, and the best guess at the present time is that the mother-deprived infants would have marked difficulties. Normal mothering, we believe, confers early social advantages upon the recipients, and these advantages would be expected to facilitate early peer adjustments. Early success might well confer an additional advantage that could be maintained indefinitely, similar to the advantages which seem to accrue to infants whose mothers are favored by dominant males (Imanishi, 1963).

During the last year an interesting study has been completed by Alexander in which he raised babies with their mothers for periods of two weeks (control group), four months, and eight months while depriving them of any opportunity to form age-mate or peer affectional relationships. We call these infants our "mother-only" or "mother-captive" infants. After 1/2, 4, or 8 months of maternal captivity, these infants were permitted daily contacts with their age-mates, and the rapidity of their play development was inversely related to their age at the time peer experience began. All three groups developed play and social behavior, but the four-month group showed greater wariness of close contact and greater aggressiveness than the control group, and the eight-month group showed both characteristics in far greater degree. Cautiousness and hyperaggression in the experimental groups may have resulted from their inability to escape from maternal punishment as the mothers entered the transitional, or ambivalent, maternal stage. These characteristics could have been bolstered by the absence of peer affectional ties when fear matured and the weakness of such ties when social aggression matured. It is possible that these traits might be a social advantage in contention with animals having earlier peer experience, although this has not been tested to date. Be this as it may, it is perfectly obvious that monkey mothers can be infant substitutes or "infant surrogates" for their babies throughout a large part of the first critical year of life, and one would predict that this role would be even more adequately played by the human mother since she has an interest and a capability in playing with her infant that totally

transcend those of the rhesus macaque. The implication, we believe, is that mothering is important not only as a source of social security, but also as a very powerful agent in the social training of infants, and we are happy to state that we now believe that real mothering, monkey or human, is a very important social factor and that real mothering is here to stay!

In designing our original studies we tended to contrast the relative importance of mother-infant relationships as opposed to infant-infant affectional relationships in the socialization process. We are now convinced that this is the wrong way to look at these social forces. Both normal mothering and normal infant-infant affectional development are extremely important variables in the socialization of rhesus monkeys and presumably of the higher primates. These variables are interactive, and they interact in a totally orderly sequential manner. Interference with either variable may not of necessity socially destroy an infant monkey if it is subsequently allowed to lead a normal or more or less normal life, but there can be no doubt that the easier and safer way to become a normal monkey is to learn to love and live with both mothers and age-mates.

REFERENCES

Bowlby, J. The nature of the child's tie to his mother. *International Journal of Psycho-Analysis*, 1958, **39**, 1–24.

Goodall, J. My life among wild chimpanzees. *National Geographic*, 1963, **124**, 272–308.

Harlow, H. F. Love in infant monkeys. *Scientific American*, 1959, **200**, 68–74.

Harlow, H. F., & Harlow, M. K. The affectional systems. In A. M. Schrier, H. F. Harlow, & F. Stollnitz (Eds.), *Behavior of nonhuman primates*. Vol. 2. New York: Academic Press, 1965. Pp. 287–334.

Harlow, H. F., Harlow, M. K., & Hansen, E. W. The maternal affectional system of rhesus monkeys. In H. L. Rheingold (Ed.), *Maternal behavior in mammals*. New York: Wiley, 1963. Pp. 254–281.

Imanishi, K. Social behavior in Japanese monkeys, *Macaca fuscata*. In C. H. Southwick (Ed.), *Primate social behavior*. Princeton, N.J.: Van Nostrand, 1963. Pp. 68–81.

Jay, P. Mother-infant relations in langurs. In H. L. Rheingold (Ed.), *Maternal behavior in mammals*. New York: Wiley, 1963. Pp. 282–304.

Koford, C. B. Population dynamics of rhesus monkeys on Cayo Santiago. In I. DeVore (Ed.), *Primate behavior*. New York: Holt, Rinehart & Winston, 1965. Pp. 160–174.

Miller, N. E., & Dollard, J. *Social learning and imitation*. New Haven: Yale University Press, 1941.

Mowbray, J. B., & Cadell, T. E. Early behavior patterns in rhesus monkeys. *Journal of Comparative and Physiological Psychology*, 1962, **55**, 350–357.

Schaller, G. B. *The mountain gorilla: Ecology and behavior.* Chicago: University of Chicago Press, 1963.
Warren, J. M. Primate learning in comparative perspective. In A. M. Schrier, H. F. Harlow, & F. Stollnitz (Eds.), *Behavior of nonhuman primates.* Vol. 1. New York: Academic Press, 1965. Pp. 249–281.

48

Curiosity and Exploration

D. E. Berlyne

For many years those psychologists who spend a good deal of their research time in the area of motivation have emphasized the importance of primary life-related states of affairs such as hunger, thirst, anoxia, cold, pain, and other such very basic and physical need-related topics. In cases where none of these sources of motivation appear to suffice, the postulation of a learned motive seemed not only to solve the problem but also to emphasize the extreme importance of learning in the adaptive life of an organism.

Some experimenters and thinkers, however, weren't able to find primary motives that adequately explained the specific activities in which they were interested. Further, they couldn't substitute a learned motive in the place of an unlearned one, since often the organism just couldn't have had experiences that might have provided the proper learned motive. In such cases it seemed that there must be some other innate motive functioning pretty much at the hereditary or genetic level but not nearly so obviously life- or need-related.

The new motive seemed to be best described as curiosity. And as more evidence accrued it became clear that such a motive was actually very directly related to the life and well-being of an organism. Just as a species with no sexual interest would very soon become extinct, so an incurious species would fail to explore its environs and would thus not find food that was just outside its sensory range. It also would not discover better shelter from weather or expose the enemies lurking beyond the shadows, threatening its life.

In short, just as from an evolutionary viewpoint those animals with a good sense of smell were better equipped to survive, so those animals with the drive to explore were better equipped for survival than were those that were not curious.

This article presents evidence showing ways in which curiosity serves as a motive. The logical necessity for such a construct in the overall framework of psychology is also discussed. Then, several different kinds of experimental methods are described, showing how and when curiosity helps the organism to solve problems that could be related to survival or at least to adequate adjustment.

Higher animals spend a substantial portion of their time and energy on activities to which terms like *curiosity* and *play* seem applicable (Berlyne, 1960; Welker, 1961). An even more conspicuous part of human behavior, especially in highly organized societies, is classifiable as "recreation," "entertainment," "art," or "science." In all of these activities, sense organs are brought into contact with biologically neutral or "indifferent" stimulus patterns—that is, with objects or events that do not seem to be inherently beneficial or noxious.

Stimulus patterns encountered in this way are sometimes used to guide subsequent action aimed

From Science, *Vol. 153, No. 1 (July 1966), 25–33. Copyright 1966 by the American Association for the Advancement of Science. Research discussed in this article has been supported by grants from the Carnegie Trust for the Universities of Scotland, the Ford Foundation, the National Institute of Mental Health (United States Public Health Service), the National Research Council of Canada, and the Ontario Mental Health Foundation.*

at achieving some immediate practical advantage. An animal looking and sniffing around may stumble upon a clue to the whereabouts of food. A scientist's discovery may contribute to public amenity and to his own enrichment or fame. Much of the time, however, organisms do nothing in particular about the stimulus patterns that they pursue with such avidity. They appear to seek them "for their own sake."

Until about fifteen years ago these forms of behavior were overlooked in the theoretical and experimental literature, except for a few scattered investigations. Recently they have been winning more and more interest among psychologists. They constitute what is generally known in Western countries as "exploratory behavior" and in Eastern Europe as "orientational-investigatory activity."

Early demonstrations of the prevalence and strength of these activities in higher animals were rather embarrassing to then current motivation theories. Animals are, of course, most likely to explore and play when they have no emergencies to deal with, but there are times when these behaviors will even override what one would expect to be more urgent considerations. A hungry rat may spend time investigating a novel feature of the environment before settling down to eat (Majorana, 1950). A bird may approach a strange and potentially threatening object at the risk of its life (Hinde, 1954). Even human beings are reported to have played the lyre while Rome was burning and to have insisted on completing a game of bowls after an invading armada had been sighted.

Under the influence of Darwin's evolutionary theory and later of Cannon's concept of homeostasis, it had come to be widely believed during the 1930's and 1940's that the motivation of behavior is bound up with clear-cut prerequisites of survival such as eating, drinking, procreating, and avoiding bodily injury. Behavior is set in motion, it was thought, either by biological dangers or by events associated (through contiguity or through similarity) with biological dangers. Similarly, the goals for which animals and human beings strive were commonly assumed to have inherent or learned connections with biological gratification or relief. These assumptions, in different forms, were shared by the early neobehaviorists, physiological psychologists, and psychoanalysts.

As knowledge accumulated about the conditions that govern exploratory behavior and about how quickly it appears after birth, it seemed less and less likely that this behavior could be a derivative of hunger, thirst, sexual appetite, pain, fear of pain, and the like, or that stimuli sought through exploration were welcomed because they previously accompanied satisfaction of these drives. The facts about exploratory behavior were especially hard to reconcile with the view once offered by Freud (1915) and later espoused by neobehaviorists (Miller and Dollard, 1941) that behavior is essentially directed toward minimizing stimulation and excitation, a view that anybody who has had to handle a child "with nothing to do" must have been tempted to question.

Being now compelled to recognize that higher animals put a great deal of effort into securing access to stimuli with no manifest ecological importance, we can discern two groups of reasons why this phenomenon may make biological sense. First, we know that spontaneous activity is constantly present within the central nervous system and that, during waking hours, the sense organs are ceaselessly bombarded with stimuli, all of which initiate excitatory processes within the brain. We also know that the brain is a highly intricate organ in which many processes can be initiated simultaneously and can interact to their mutual impediment. The only way in which the brain can perform its prime function of selecting adaptive responses is to allow one process to advance and complete itself while competing processes are held in check. To determine which process shall be granted priority, the brain depends on information about conditions inside and outside the organism, some of which enters through sense organs and some of which is stored after having been deposited by previous learning or by natural selection. The required information will often be lacking, in which case the brain will be unable to arbitrate between, or reconcile, the discrepant demands that are made on it. Reciprocal interference between processes going on within it and—if the organism is beset by an urgent call for action—conflict among incompatible response-tendencies may eliminate the effectiveness of behavior. So, in such cases, it is clearly useful for an organism to secure access to stimulus patterns that contain the information from lack of which it is suffering.

The second group of reasons is quite different. It seems that the central nervous system of a higher animal is designed to cope with environments that produce a certain rate of influx of stimulation, information, and challenge to its capacities. It will naturally not perform at its best in an environment that overstresses or overloads it, but we also have evidence that prolonged subjection to an inordinately monotonous or unstimulating environment is detrimental to a variety of psychological functions (Bexton, Heron, and Scott, 1954; Kubzanski, 1961). How much excitement or challenge is optimal will fluctuate quite widely with personality, culture, psychophysiological state, and recent or remote experience. But we can understand why organisms may seek out stimulation that taxes the nervous system to the right extent, when naturally occurring stimuli are either too easy or too difficult to assimilate.

With accumulating research there have been more and more indications that exploratory responses can be of two distinct classes, corresponding to these two distinct biological needs. On the one hand, when an animal is disturbed by a lack of information and thus left a prey to uncertainty and conflict, it is likely to resort to what we may call *specific* exploratory responses. These supply or intensify stimulation from particular sources— sources that can supply the precise information that the animal misses. The condition of discomfort, due to inadequacy of information, that motivates specific exploration is what we call "curiosity." In other circumstances an animal seeks out stimulation, regardless of source or content, that offers something like an optimum amount of novelty, surprisingness, complexity, change, or variety. For this kind of behavior the term *diversive* exploration has been proposed. It is not preceded by receipt of partial information about the stimulus patterns at which it is aimed and thus seems to be motivated by factors quite different from curiosity.

Specific Exploration

One of the earliest discoveries coming out of Pavlov's work on "higher nervous activity" was the phenomenon that he called the "orientational" or "investigatory" reflex (Pavlov, 1927). A dog would respond to any unusual or unexpected happening by desisting from whatever activity it might otherwise have been engaged in and turning its eyes, head, and trunk toward the source of stimulation. This was an unconditioned or innate reflex, and yet it was subject to many of the processes to which conditioned reflexes are subject, including extinction and disinhibition. If the stimulus evoking it were repeated at short intervals, the orientational response would gradually disappear. It would come back if the stimulus recurred, say, a day later, but after several recoveries and extinctions the power of a particular stimulus to evoke the response might be permanently weakened (Berlyne,

1960, chap. 4). It was thus shown that novelty, especially short-term novelty, is a potent factor governing this reaction.

The influence of novelty was amply confirmed when specific exploratory behavior began to be studied in the West. It was found, for example, that a rat is more likely to walk up to and sniff at an object that it has not seen before than one to which it has been exposed during the last few minutes (Berlyne, 1950). When a rat is confined in a novel environment, the amount of wandering about that it does and the frequency with which it approaches a particular feature of the environment decline with time—that is, as the stimulus patterns that are present lose their novelty (Montgomery, 1953; Berlyne, 1955). When the animal is put back into the situation after spending some time away from it, exploration will revive, but the revival will become less and less marked if the repeated exposures extend over several days.

Apart from the influence of novelty, the strength and direction of exploratory responses in animals have been shown to depend on stimulus properties of the kind usually denoted by words like *complexity*. More vigorous and prolonged exploration will generally be attracted by objects that offer more varied or more irregular stimulation (Berlyne, 1955; Williams and Kuchta, 1957).

Similar variables have been found to govern specific exploration in the human adult. We have used a number of techniques to compare the power of different visual patterns to attract and sustain inspection when subjects are given no special reason to attend to them. We have allowed subjects access to a switch controlling a tachistoscope, by means of which they could give themselves as many successive brief (0.14-second) glimpses of a pattern as they wished before calling for the next pattern (Berlyne, 1957). We have presented successions of patterns in an automatic projector, letting subjects look at each pattern for as long as they wished before pressing the button that replaced it with the next one (Berlyne and Lawrence, 1964). We have presented patterns side by side on a screen and measured how much time the subject spent fixating each of them; this measurement was made either by having eye movements observed by an experimenter who did not know which patterns were being exposed (Berlyne, 1958b) or by recording them with an eye-movement camera (Day, 1965). The influence of novelty is shown by one experiment (Berlyne, 1958b) in which we showed a series of pairs of animal pictures, the picture on one side (the left and the right sides for equal numbers of subjects) being the same on

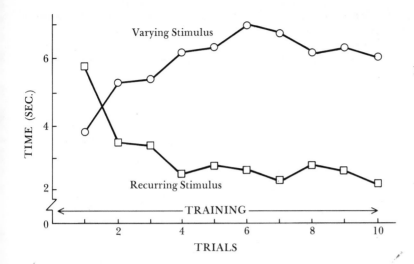

FIGURE 1 *Mean time spent by subjects fixating a novel (varying) and a familiar (recurring) pattern when the two were presented side by side for ten 10-second trials with 20-second intertrial intervals (Adapted from Berlyne, 1957)*

every trial and the picture on the other side being changed from one trial to the next. Observation of eye movements (see Figure 1) revealed that, as trials succeeded one another, the subjects spent a lower and lower proportion of the time inspecting the recurrent pattern and more and more time looking at the changing patterns.

All the techniques just mentioned have been used to study effects on exploration time of several stimulus properties that, although distinct, exemplify the kind of variable we mean when we use words like *complexity, irregularity,* or *incongruity.* In each of the pairs of patterns shown in Figure 2, the member on the right is the more "complex" or "irregular" one, but the actual property that distinguishes it from its neighbor varies from one category of pairs to another. We have regularly found that the subject spends more time looking at the "more complex" than at the "less complex" pattern of a pair. Since all these patterns are relatively simple, we have more recently added the patterns of Figure 3 (Berlyne and Lawrence, 1964; Day, 1965; Berlyne and Lewis, 1963). These likewise comprise categories representing different "complexity" variables, but all of them contain notably more elements than the patterns in categories *A* through *D* of Figure 2 and thus allow us to probe the upper reaches of the dimensions underlying judgments of "complexity." It has been demonstrated that the material in categories *XA* through *XC* (Figure 3) is rated significantly more "complex" by adult subjects than the material in categories *A* through *D* (Day, 1965). Experiments incorporating categories *XA* through *XC* have indicated that exploration time reaches a peak and declines as complexity becomes extreme. The point at which the peak is reached

seems, however, to vary quite widely from individual to individual and from population to population.

An experiment (Berlyne, 1958a) was carried out with three- to nine-month-old babies, after casual observation of one infant suggested a strong predilection for looking at newsprint, maps, and the like. Spock (1946) advises, in fact, that babies enjoy watching leaves and shadows. In the experiment, pairs of adjacent patterns were brought simultaneously down into the field of vision, and it was found that patterns B3 and D3 of Figure 4 were more likely than others in the same series to attract the subject's gaze first. These patterns seem to be more "complex" than the others in the sense that they possess more internal contour. There seemed to be some inconsistency between this result and Hershenson's finding (1964) that newborn infants are inclined to spend more time looking at a 2 by 2 checkerboard than at a 4 by 4 or 12 by 12 checkerboard—that is, more time looking at the least complex stimulus pattern.

The discrepancy has since been resolved by Brennan, Ames, and Moore (1966), who have shown that the preferred degree of complexity goes up with age: eight-week-olds prefer to look at a checkerboard of intermediate grain (8 by 8), whereas twenty-week-olds prefer a 24 by 24 checkerboard to less complex ones. These investigators have also demonstrated that this development is not simply a matter of increasing visual acuity. Eight-week-olds can distinguish 24 by 24 checkerboards from gray rectangles. Other experiments have ascertained that novelty (Saayman, Ames, and Moffet, 1964), surprisingness (a disparity between a stimulus event and expectation) (Charlesworth, 1965), and regularity or irregularity of form (Graefe,

FIGURE 2   *Visual patterns, representing various "complexity" and "incongruity" variables, used in experiments on exploratory and related behavior in human adults. (From Berlyne, 1958b; some of the same patterns were used in experiments reported in Berlyne, 1957, 1961, 1963a; Berlyne and Lawrence, 1964; Berlyne and Lewis, 1963; Berlyne and McDonnell, 1965; Berlyne and Peckham, 1966; Day, 1965; and Hoats, Miller, and Spitz, 1963.)*

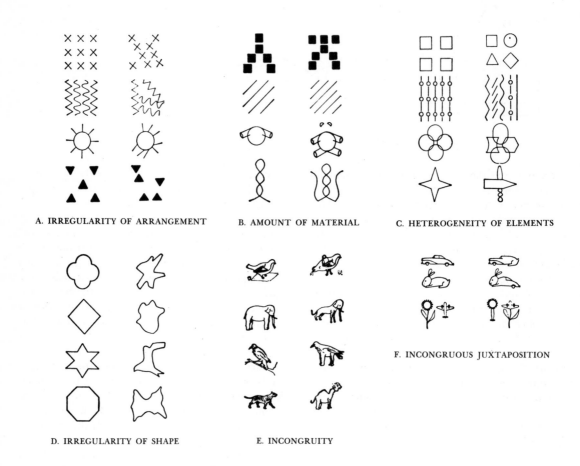

A. IRREGULARITY OF ARRANGEMENT   B. AMOUNT OF MATERIAL   C. HETEROGENEITY OF ELEMENTS

F. INCONGRUOUS JUXTAPOSITION

D. IRREGULARITY OF SHAPE   E. INCONGRUITY

1963) are other stimulus characteristics influencing infantile exploration.

In recent years, measurement of exploratory behavior has become a standard means of investigating not only motivational but also perceptual processes in subjects who are too young for traditional techniques, such as questioning and discrimination training. A difference in the power of two visual patterns to elicit exploration implies that the subject can tell them apart. By this means, it has become evident that some degree of visual form discrimination, presumably innate, exists before learning has had time to mould perception,

a question that was formerly open to debate (Frantz, 1963).

TABLE 1   *Mean Numbers of Responses in 15-Minute Session on Training Days*

Reinforcing Stimulus	Methamphetamine	Placebo	Mean
Familiar	9.0	4.8	6.8
Novel	3.9	11.7	8.2
Mean	6.6	8.2	

FIGURE 3 *Visual patterns, representing various "complexity" variables, of a higher order of complexity than those of Figure 2. (These patterns were first published in Berlyne and Lawrence, 1964, but some have been used for experiments reported in Berlyne, 1961, 1963a; Berlyne and Lewis, 1963; Berlyne and McDonnell, 1965; Berlyne and Peckham, 1966; Day, 1965; and Hoats et al., 1963.)*

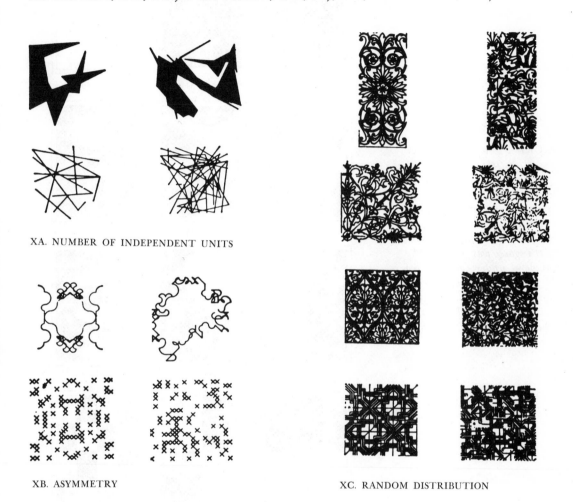

XA. NUMBER OF INDEPENDENT UNITS

XB. ASYMMETRY

XC. RANDOM DISTRIBUTION

According to a theoretical view that suggests itself (Berlyne, 1960, 1963b), specific exploratory responses, whether unlearned or learned, are likely to result from an aversive condition or condition of heightened drive due to lack of information (subjective uncertainty). Such a condition, which may appropriately be called "perceptual curiosity," is apt to result from exposure to novel, surprising, highly complex, or ambiguous stimulus patterns.

At present, my associates and I are engaged in experiments designed to test the hypothesis that subjective uncertainty is aversive—that its termination will reinforce an instrumental response. Presentation of blurred pictures is our means of inducing uncertainty. Our preliminary results have

provided some tentative confirmation for our expectations. The replacement of a blurred picture by a clear version of the same picture seems, in at least some circumstances, to be a more effective reward or reinforcer (as shown by the rate at which a key is pressed to secure it) than the replacement of a blurred picture by an unrelated clear picture or by another blurred picture. Furthermore, we have some hint that a clear picture is most rewarding when it replaces a picture with an intermediate degree of blurredness. This seems to be a degree at which some differentiation is beginning to emerge but no objects or detail can be recognized, so that there is maximum scope for competing hypotheses.

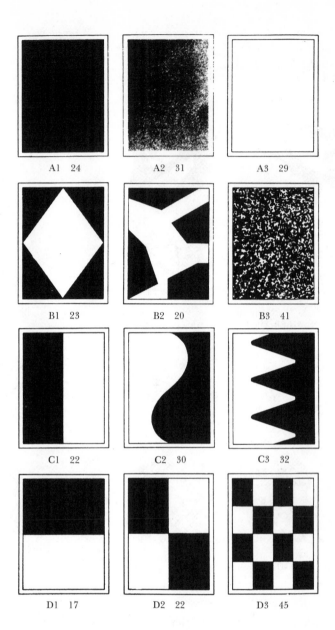

FIGURE 4 *Four sets of three visual patterns used in experiments with 3- to 9-month-old infants. The patterns of a set were presented in pairs, and the member of each pair that first attracted the subject's gaze was noted. The numeral under each pattern denotes the number of times out of 56 presentations (four with each of 14 subjects) that the pattern was fixated first.*

Collative Variables

The widespread attention that exploration and related forms of behavior are now receiving, after decades of relative neglect, seems justified when one considers the prevalence of such behavior in higher animal species. As psychologists are coming to recognize more and more, exploratory responses are indispensable adjuncts of many vital activities. When unlearned behavior patterns or discrimination learning have invested an external stimulus object with a special significance, an animal must initiate a segment of behavior by bringing its receptors into contact with the crucial cues that indicate what action is likely to have beneficial consequences. How sense organs are oriented must profoundly affect the form in which a stimulus pattern is perceived and represented in memory. But, as often happens with a new area of investigation, the examination of exploratory behavior has raised questions of a much wider import and reopened some fundamental theoretical questions that at one time seemed settled.

What is explored, and how vigorously, depends on many factors inside and outside the organism. Properties of external stimuli with which psychologists have long been concerned have an undeniably potent influence. They include psychophysical properties, closely dependent on specific physico-chemical variables (for example, brightness, loudness, color) and ecological properties, dependent on association with noxious events or visceral gratifications. It was, however, not long before experiments on curiosity and specific exploration had demonstrated the psychological importance of a third group of stimulus properties, which evidently outweighed the others in controlling this kind of behavior.

These are the properties for which I have suggested the term *collative* (Berlyne, 1960, 1963b), since they depend on comparison or collation of stimulus elements, whether they be elements appearing simultaneously in different sectors of a stimulus field or elements that have been perceived at different times. They comprise the properties that we designate by words like *novelty, surprisingness, incongruity, complexity, variability,* and *puzzlingness.* Just as the psychophysical properties are derived from distributions of energy and the ecological properties connect stimuli with the factors that govern natural selection, thus making contact with the two great unifying concepts of nineteenth-century science, the collative properties have close connections with information, the unifying concept responsible for some revolutionary developments in twentieth-century science.

The technical language of information theory does not suffice for an adequate description of the collative variables, but its concepts can help a great deal in specifying and measuring them. Provided that certain assumptions are fulfilled, how "novel," "surprising," "regular," or "orderly" a structure is, how numerous its elements are, and how interdependent, determine its information content, uncertainty (from an external observer's point of view) regarding an organism's reaction to it, and the organism's degree of subjective uncertainty regarding what will happen next or regarding the nature of elements that have not yet been inspected.

What all the collative variables have in common to give them the motivational effects that they apparently share is an interesting but still debatable question. One hypothesis for which supporting arguments can be found (Berlyne, 1960, 1963b) is that these effects all depend on *conflict* between incompatible neural, and ultimately motor, reactions that are simultaneously mobilized.

The motivational effects of collative stimulus properties are by no means confined to occasioning and directing exploratory responses. They include the factors making for "good" or "bad" form, which were shown by the Gestalt psychologists to govern many perceptual phenomena. They include the factors constituting "form," "composition," or "structure" in the visual and performing arts, in literature, in music, and in humor.

Instead of eliciting exploration—which means approach and sustained contact—novel, surprising, and strange objects may provoke terror and flight (Hebb, 1955). Approach (for the sake of obtaining additional information or perhaps simply for the sake of relief through habituation) and escape are, after all, alternative ways of alleviating a disturbance due to a conflict-inducing sight or sound. Which will prevail seems to depend on many things, including how disturbing the stimulus pattern is, how agitated or relaxed a subject is, and what personality traits he possesses. Forms of behavior that apparently represent vacillation between curiosity and fear in the face of something unusual have frequently been observed in animals and in human beings. Whether something is experienced as pleasurable, annoying, or vapid often turns in an extremely subtle way on how much novelty, variety, or unpredictability it affords. This is true even when some extrinsic source of motivation is at work, as in the culinary and erotic domains.

Arousal

Still further ramifications come into view as we pursue the relations between exploratory behavior and arousal (Berlyne, 1960, 1963b). The concept of "arousal level" is an outgrowth of several developments in neurophysiology and psychology that have occurred during the last fifteen years or so. It connotes a psychophysiological dimension, indicative of how "wide-awake," "alert," or "excited" an organism is at a particular time. Fluctuations in arousal are reflected by changes in the electrical activity of the brain, in electrical and thermal properties of the skin, in muscular tension, in the circulatory system, in the respiratory system, and in the diameter of the pupil, all of which can be recorded and precisely measured. A great deal has been learned, and more is coming to light, about the neural processes on which arousal depends, involving interactions among the brainstem reticular formation, the hypothalamus, the diffuse thalamic system, and the cerebral cortex.

Few, if any, motivational aspects of behavior have been untouched by fresh thinking inspired by the concept of "arousal." One particularly pregnant trend has been a progressive coalescence between the new concept of "arousal" and the concept of "drive," which has dominated discussion of motivation since the 1920's. If "arousal" can be identified with "drive" (and more refinement of both concepts is required before we can tell how far and in what sense it can be), the implications may be quite far-reaching. First, we shall have at our disposal more precise and direct techniques than we had before for measuring drive. Secondly, any factor that can be shown to raise or lower arousal will have to be included among the factors that induce and reduce drive, and thus among those that can motivate behavior and give rise to changes in behavior through learning.

The grounds for connecting exploratory responses with rises in arousal are twofold. First, a great deal of experimental work (largely, but not entirely, carried out in the U.S.S.R.) has shown at least some forms of exploratory behavior to be accompanied by pervasive psychophysiological changes, including several recognized indices of increased arousal (Sokolov, 1963). This work has led to a broadening of Pavlov's notion of an "orientational reflex" or orientation reaction. Pavlov used this term to denote the immediately visible bodily movements through which an animal focuses its sense organs on an unusual source of stimulation. It is now clear that these are accompanied by a whole network of processes, most of them not detectable without special amplifying and recording equipment, which seem to represent a mobilization of the animal's capacities to absorb information through its sense organs, process the information through its central nervous system, and act promptly and energetically.

Secondly, evidence is accumulating that the collative stimulus properties by which exploratory behavior is so profoundly influenced are capable of increasing arousal. Several experimenters have shown that a stimulus gradually loses its power to evoke an orientation reaction—that is, to raise arousal—as it loses its novelty through repetition (Berlyne, 1960, Chap. 4). In our own research, my associates and I have been measuring the effects of various collative stimulus properties on the galvanic skin response (Berlyne and Lawrence, 1964; Berlyne, 1961) (a transient increase in conductance or in potential difference between two points on the palms or soles) and on the duration of electroencephalographic desynchronization (Berlyne, 1965) (the replacement of alpha waves by an irregular, low-amplitude, predominantly high-frequency pattern, indicative of an alerted cerebral cortex) as indices of arousal or components of the orientation reaction. We have been able to show that the magnitude of the galvanic skin response declines not only as one visual pattern is repeatedly exposed

TABLE 2 *Mean Numbers of Responses in 15-Minute Session on Test Days*

Reinforcing Stimulus	Methamphetamine	Placebo	Mean
Familiar	13.9	4.8	9.1
Novel	6.5	10.7	8.8
Mean	10.4	7.8	

but also as different patterns succeed one another.

We have found the intensity of the orientation reaction to increase with surprisingness (when surprising and nonsurprising stimuli are equated for novelty) and with the complexity and incongruity variables embodied in the patterns of Figures 2 and 3. We have also demonstrated that the mean amplitude of the galvanic skin response increases with degree of conflict, which, as explained earlier, is suspected of being the common underlying factor responsible for the motivational effects of the collative variables. At present we are investigating electroencephalographic effects of various "complexity" variables descriptive of auditory stimuli. It has already become clear that white noise evokes longer desynchronization than equally loud sine-wave tones or combinations of two or three such tones.

Epistemic Curiosity

Specific exploratory responses in human beings are, as often as not, "epistemic" responses as well as exploratory responses. The use of this term is proposed in order to indicate that they are aimed not only at obtaining access to information-bearing stimulation, capable of dispelling the uncertainties of the moment, but also at acquiring knowledge—that is, information stored in the form of ideational structures and giving rise to internal symbolic responses that can guide behavior on future occasions. Bringing sense organs into contact with appropriate external events is, of course, not the only means of accumulating knowledge. Thinking can be another form of epistemic behavior (Berlyne, 1965).

Extending the notion of perceptual curiosity suggested by studies of specific exploration, we may suppose that epistemic behavior is motivated by "conceptual conflict," or conflict between mutually discrepant symbolic response-tendencies—thoughts, beliefs, attitudes, conceptions (Berlyne,

1954a, 1965). Conflicting elements or requirements often characterize the "problems" that start us off inquiring or experimenting or thinking (Berlyne, 1965, Chap. 10). Several experimenters have recorded variations in arousal level while subjects are engaged in thinking, and these variations are influenced by degree of "difficulty," in senses that seem to involve degree of conceptual conflict (Berlyne, 1965, Chap. 11).

Unfortunately, the motivational aspects of epistemic behavior and of thinking in particular are only just beginning to receive study. We have made some preliminary investigations of the determinants of "epistemic curiosity" (as we may call a motivational condition favoring epistemic behavior) by presenting human subjects with a series of questions and simply asking them to specify a certain number of questions whose answers they would most like to know (Berlyne, 1954b).

In one such experiment, questions about invertebrate animals were used. According to verbal reports, the most curiosity was induced by questions about the more familiar animals, by questions that subjects found surprising, and by questions that attributed to species characteristics they seemed unlikely to possess. These findings confirmed predictions from hypotheses regarding conceptual conflict. It had been argued that more familiar concepts would produce greater conflict than less familiar ones, by producing more numerous and stronger divergent associations.

In two later experiments, subjects were presented with quotations, each followed by the names of two or three possible authors. Each author's name was coupled with a number, purporting to show how many teachers out of a group of 100, had guessed it to be the correct name. One experiment provided evidence that curiosity was greater when there were three than when there were two alternative authors, and another demonstrated the influence of the distribution of supposed teachers' guesses: the more even the distribution, the greater the curiosity. These two variables—number of alternatives and nearness to equiprobability—are identifiable as the two principal determinants of subjective uncertainty, just as uncertainty in the information-theoretic sense is an increasing function of the two corresponding variables. Conceptual conflict is assumed to increase with subjective uncertainty.

Experiments in which other techniques were used have also confirmed the importance of such factors for epistemic curiosity (Berlyne and Frommer, 1966). Novelty, surprise, and incongruity make children ask more questions and affect the content of their questions. Several investigators have found adult subjects more likely to seek symbolically expressed information as uncertainty and the gains and losses at stake increase, although there are signs that information-seeking may decline as these variables assume very high values.

Diversive Exploration

There have been many reports from animal studies of exploratory behavior that seem to be aimed not at obtaining stimulation from a specific object or event about which there is a specific uncertainty but rather at obtaining stimulation from any source that can afford an optimum dosage of novelty, complexity, and other collative properties. For example, rats will, all other things being equal, tend to enter a maze arm that differs from the one they entered on the preceding trial or that has undergone some change since they were last in the maze (Berlyne, 1960, Chap. 6; Glanzer, 1953). Monkeys confined in a box will work hard, sometimes for as long as nineteen hours at a stretch, at repeatedly opening a door so that they can see what is going on in the room outside (Butler and Harlow, 1954). Human beings confined in a dark room with a minimum of stimulation will press buttons to make patterns of colored spots of light appear, preferring those sequences of pattern that offer the most variety and unpredictability (Jones, Wilkinson, and Braden, 1961). These and similar forms of behavior are classifiable, according to the proposed terminology, as "diversive" exploration, and it seems important to distinguish them at this stage of research from the specific exploratory responses that may be motivated by perceptual curiosity.

The advisability of drawing a distinction between specific and diversive exploration is supported by experiments with human subjects. When a subject is shown a pair of patterns from Figures 2 or 3 and then asked to choose one of the two patterns for further viewing, which he is likely to choose depends on the duration of the initial exposure. If he has seen the two patterns briefly (for one second or less) before making his choice, he is more likely to want to see the *more* complex pattern again (Berlyne, 1963a). Preliminary exposures of such brevity are presumably not long enough to allow him to see what the patterns are like and thus to relieve this curiosity. He chooses the more complex pattern, presumably because that is the one about which he has more residual curiosity. If, on the other hand, the preliminary exposures are long enough (3 seconds or more) to allow him to become adequately acquainted with the patterns, he is more likely to want another look at the *less* complex pattern (Day, 1965; Berlyne, 1963a; Hoats *et al.*, 1964). In this case curiosity, having been largely eliminated by the initial exposures, must play a minor role. Factors akin to esthetic taste will presumably have more influence. Experiments in which verbal scaling techniques are used have, in fact, suggested that patterns attracting more specific exploration when perceptual curiosity is at work tend to be rated more "interesting," whereas patterns attracting more diversive exploration when a subject has no cause to wonder what a pattern is like tend to be rated more "pleasing" (Berlyne, 1963a; Berlyne and Lawrence, 1964; Berlyne and Peckham, 1966; Day, 1965).

There might seem to be a close affinity between specific exploration and activities such as science, philosophy, and mathematics, with diversive exploration more closely akin to entertainment and the arts. But this distinction is not absolute. The importance of pleasing structure in science, mathematics, and philosophy has been noted too often to be overlooked, while curiosity—wondering what will come next, trying to make sense of a work, and so on—certainly plays a part in esthetic appreciation.

Diversive exploratory behavior is likely to be especially strong after an animal or a human subject has spent some hours in an environment that is highly monotonous or devoid of stimulation (Jones *et al.*, 1961; Butler, 1957). The desperate craving of a bored person for a change of any kind is attested by everyday experience and by experiments on "sensory deprivation" (Bexton *et al.*, 1954).

One phenomenon that has been much investigated during the last ten years and was particularly surprising when it was first discovered is the reward value that stimulus changes of no specific biological significance (for example, light coming on or becoming momentarily brighter, the sound of a buzzer or a click) can have, as shown by the power of such changes to reinforce a bar-pressing response in mice and rats (Girdner, 1953).

Some recent experiments in which my associates and I sought factors governing diversive exploration (Berlyne, Salapatek, Gelman, and Zener, 1964) have confirmed the importance that the interaction between collative stimulus properties and arousal level has for this behavior also. The role of these variables in diversive exploration seems, however, to be somewhat different from their role in perceptual curiosity and specific exploration. Fortui-

tous circumstances compelled us to house some of the rats to be used for one experiment next to a room containing some extremely noisy printout counters. A quiet room became available later, and the remaining animals were housed in it. The experiment lasted for eight days. On odd-numbered days (training days), each subject was placed in a Skinner box for a 30-minute pretraining period, during which no bar was present in the box. The pretraining period was immediately followed by a 15-minute training session, during which two bars protruded from the rear wall, and every time either was pressed, the illumination became brighter for 1 second or a buzzer sounded for 1 second. On even-numbered days (test days) there was a 15-minute test session during which the bars were present but no light change or buzzer sound occurred when one of the bars was pressed.

It turned out that in animals maintained in the noisy quarters a familiar stimulus (one that was presented every minute during pretraining periods) had a greater reward value than a novel stimulus (one not presented during pretraining periods), as evidenced by the rate of bar-pressing during both training sessions and test sessions. In animals maintained in the quiet room, on the other hand, novel stimuli were more rewarding than familiar stimuli.

These unexpected findings could be explained by making three assumptions: (i) that the rats subjected to noise between experimental sessions had a higher arousal level than the rats maintained in the quiet room; (ii) that the reward value of a stimulus resulting from diversive exploration is an inverted U-shaped function of the degree to which the stimulus raises arousal; and (iii) that the extent to which a stimulus raises arousal increases with its novelty and with the subject's initial arousal level. This explanation was corroborated by a subsequent experiment, in which injections of methamphetamine were used to raise arousal and a change in illumination served as reward. It was found, in accordance with predictions, that the drugged animals performed more responses with a familiar reinforcing stimulus, whereas control animals injected with saline solution performed more responses with a novel reinforcing stimulus (see Tables 1 and 2).

A number of experiments (Berlyne and Lewis, 1963; Chapman and Levy, 1957) have indicated that conditions conducive to abnormally high levels of arousal (for example, hunger, pain, fear, noise, exposure to an incomprehensible tape-recorded message) make rats and human beings less eager than usual to seek out novel or complex stimulation. The findings just cited seem relevant to this phenomenon, among others.

Under the impact of experimental findings on exploratory behavior and cognate phenomena, motivation theory is undergoing some extensive remodeling. These findings have opened our eyes to the pervasive psychological importance of collative variables and arousal. We find ourselves forced to recognize that the disturbances that motivate behavior can come not only from external irritants, visceral upheavals, and deprivation of vital substances, but also from clashes between processes going on in the central nervous system. Related to these additional sources of motivation, there must be a wide range of hitherto overlooked reinforcing conditions that can promote learning of new behavior patterns. In opening up these new prospects, the study of curiosity, exploration, and epistemic behavior merges with developments in several other areas of psychological research (Berlyne, 1960, 1963b, 1965), including personality theory, ethology, child development, education, attitude change, social interaction, esthetics, and humor.

REFERENCES

Berlyne, D. E. *British Journal of Psychology*, 1950, **41**, 68.

Berlyne, D. E. *British Journal of Psychology*, 1954, **45**, 180. (a)

Berlyne, D. E. *British Journal of Psychology*, 1954, **45**, 256 (b); 1962, **53**, 27.

Berlyne, D. E. *Journal of Comparative and Physiological Psychology*, 1955, **48**, 238.

Berlyne, D. E. *Journal of Experimental Psychology*, 1957, **53**, 399.

Berlyne, D. E. *British Journal of Psychology*, 1958, **49**, 315–318. (a)

Berlyne, D. E. *Journal of Experimental Psychology*, 1958, **55**, 289–296. (b)

Berlyne, D. E. *Conflict, arousal, and curiosity*. New York: McGraw-Hill, 1960.

Berlyne, D. E. *Journal of Experimental Psychology*, 1961, **62**, 476. Berlyne, D. E., Craw, M. A., Salapatek, P. H., & Lewis, J. L. *Journal of Experimental Psychology*, 1963, **66**, 560.

Berlyne, D. E. *Canadian Journal of Psychology*, 1963, **17**, 274. (a)

Berlyne, D. E. In S. Koch (Ed.), *Psychology—A study of a science*. Vol. 5. New York: McGraw-Hill, 1963. (b)

Berlyne, D. E. *Structure and direction in thinking*. New York: Wiley, 1965.

Berlyne, D. E., & Frommer, F. D. *Child Development*, 1966, **37**, 177. Irwin, F., & Smith, W. A. S. *Journal of Experimental Psychology*, 1957, **54**, 229. Becker, A. M. *Journal of Experimental Psychology*, 1958, **55**, 628. Driscoll, J. M., & Lanzetta, J. T. *Psychological Reports*, 1964, **14**, 975. Hawkins, C. K., & Lanzetta, J. T. *Psychological Reports*, 1965, **17**, 791.

Berlyne, D. E., & Lawrence, G. H. *Journal of Genetic Psychology*, 1964, **71**, 21.

Berlyne, D. E., & Lewis, J. L. *Canadian Journal of Psychology*, 1963, **17**, 398.

Berlyne, D. E., & McDonnell, P. *Electroencephalography and Clinical Neurophysiology*, 1965, **18**, 156.

Berlyne, D. E., & Peckham, S. *Canadian Journal of Psychology*, 1966, **20**, 125–135.

Berlyne, D. E., Salapatek, P. H., Gelman, R. S., & Zener, S. L. *Journal of Comparative and Physiological Psychology*, 1964, **58**, 148. Berlyne, D. E., & Koenig, I. D. V. *Journal of Comparative and Physiological Psychology*, 1965, **60**, 274. Berlyne, D. E., Koenig, I.D.V., & Hirota, T. T. *Journal of Comparative and Physiological Psychology*, 1966, **62**, 222–226.

Bexton, W. A., Heron, W., & Scott, T. H. *Canadian Journal of Psychology*, 1954, **8**, 70.

Brennan, W. M., Ames, E. W., & Moore, R. W. *Science*, 1966, **151**, 354.

Butler, R. A. *Journal of Comparative and Physiological Psychology*, 1957, **50**, 177. Fox, S. S. *Journal of Comparative and Physiological Psychology*, 1962, **55**, 438.

Butler, R. A., & Harlow, H. F. *Journal of Comparative and Physiological Psychology*, 1954, **47**, 258.

Chapman, R. M., & Levy, N. *Journal of Comparative and Physiological Psychology*, 1957, **50**, 233. Thompson, W. R., & Higgins, W. H. *Canadian Journal of Psychology*, 1958, **12**, 61. Hayward, H. C. *Journal of Personality*, 1962, **30**, 63.

Charlesworth, W. R. Paper read before the Society for Research in Child Development, 1965.

Day, H. Thesis, University of Toronto, 1965.

Frantz, R. L. *Science*, 1963, **140**, 296.

Freud, S. *Internationale Zeitschrift für ärztliche Psychoanalyse*, 1915, **3**, 84.

Girdner, J. B. *American Psychologist*, 1953, **8**, 354. Hurwitz, H. M. B. *British Journal of Animal Behavior*, 1956, **4**, 31. Kish, G. B. *Journal of Comparative and Physiological Psychology*, 1965, **48**, 261. Roberts, C. L., Marx, M. H., & Collier, C. *Journal of Comparative and Physiological Psychology*, 1958, **51**, 575.

Glanzer, M. *Journal of Experimental Psychology*, 1953, **45**, 387. Montgomery, K. C. *Journal of Comparative and Physiological Psychology*, 1952, **45**, 287. Dember, W. N. *American Scientist*, 1965, **53**, 409.

Graefe, O. *Psychologische Forschung*, 1963, **27**, 177.

Hebb, D. O. *Psychological Review*, 1946, **53**, 259. Montgomery, K. C. *Journal of Comparative and Physiological Psychology*, 1955, **48**, 254.

Hershenson, M. *Journal of Comparative and Physiological Psychology*, 1964, **58**, 270.

Hinde, R. A. *Proceedings of the Royal Society of London*, 1954, **B142**, 306.

Hoats, D. L., Miller, M. B., & Spitz, H. H. *American Journal of Mental Deficiency*, 1963, **68**, 386.

Jones, A., Wilkinson, H. J., & Braden, I. *Journal of Experimental Psychology*, 1961, **62**, 126.

Kubzanski, P. In A. D. Biderman & Zimmer, H. (Eds.), *The manipulation of human behavior*. New York: Wiley, 1961.

Majorana, A. *Rivista Psicologia*, 1950, **46**(4), 1. Chance, M. R. A., & Mead, A. P. *Behavior*, 1955, **8**, 174.

Miller, N. E., & Dollard, J. *Social learning and imitation*. New Haven, Conn.: Yale University Press, 1941.

Montgomery, K. C. *Journal of Comparative and Physiological Psychology*, 1953, **46**, 129.

Pavlov, I. P. *Conditioned reflexes*. Oxford: Oxford University Press, 1927.

Saayman, A., Ames, E. W., & Moffet, A. *Journal of Experimental Child Psychology,* 1964, **1,** 189. Azporozhets, A. V. In P. H. Mussen (Ed.), European research in cognitive development. *Monograph of the Society for Research in Child Development,* 1965, **30**(2).

Sokolov, E. N. *Perception and the conditioned reflex.* New York: Macmillan, 1963.

Spock, B. *Baby and child care.* New York: Pocket Books, 1946. P. 166.

Welker, W. I. In D. W. Fiske & S. R. Maddi (Eds.), *Functions of varied experience.* Homewood, Ill.:

Dorsey Press, 1961. Fowler, H. *Curiosity and exploratory behavior.* New York: Macmillan, 1965. Voronin, L. G. et al. (Eds.) *Orientirvochny Refleks i Orientirovochno-Issledovatel'skaia Deiatel'nost'.* Moscow: Academy of Pedagogical Sciences, 1958. Berlyne, D. E. In G. Lindzey & E. Aronson (Eds.), *Handbook of social psychology.* (2nd ed.) Cambridge, Mass.: Addison Wesley, 1968.

Williams, C. D., & Kuchta, J. C. *Journal of Comparative and Physiological Psychology,* 1957, **50,** 509.

Welker, W. I. *Journal of Comparative and Physiological Psychology,* 1956, **49,** 181.

49

A Laboratory Approach
to the Dynamics of Psychological Stress

Richard S. Lazarus

We often hear it said that life in these modern times is full of trouble and strife. A frequent implication is that in times past, tranquility and peace reigned supreme. This leads many persons to lament the passage of time and to resent the rapidity with which events seem to rise to a crescendo of anxiety-producing importance that is quickly overshadowed by even more troublesome concerns. Another implication is that if we are to learn to deal effectively with current problems, we must somehow learn to control our volatile emotional reactions. Attempts to escape to the past are neither realistic nor desirable. But how can we come to understand the stress reaction and learn to control it?

The first step toward understanding stress is to recognize that there are two interacting components. One part of a stress reaction occurs at the conscious level: We are aware of being under stress and can talk about it; we can see and hear the situations that produce stress; we can analyze and categorize the stressful stimuli and the related feelings that are produced. This conscious or intellectual component is the one that we talk about most frequently because it is most apparent.

The other major component of a stress reaction takes place at a level below conscious awareness. This component includes many different autonomic reactions that collectively enter into any feelings of fear, anxiety, and stress. When the stressful situation occurs, the adrenal glands step up secretion of hormones into the bloodstream. The heart rate speeds up, then fluctuates as the stress continues. Breathing may become shallow and rapid and the pupils of the eyes change in size. The sweat glands go through several stages of opening and closing, and the palms of the hands become wet. All these, and many more, activities may take place during stress. We can *feel* that certain bodily changes are occurring, but we cannot accurately keep up with the changes at the conscious level. It is these autonomic or subconscious indices of stress with which Lazarus is concerned in the following article.

From American Psychologist, *Vol. 19 (1964), 400–411. Copyright 1964 by the American Psychological Association, and reproduced by permission. This paper is a slightly modified version of one given at a symposium of the American Psychiatric Association, on "Human Reaction to the Threat of Impending Disaster," at American Association for the Advancement of Science, Philadelphia, December 27, 1962. The research findings reported here are based on investigations supported by Research Grant No. MH-02136 from the National Institute of Mental Health, United States Public Health Service.*

The importance of the topic of stress is reflected in the tremendous quantity of relevant multidisciplined experimentation in recent years. Whether the term used to describe this work is emotion, stress, threat, defense, anxiety, or conflict, to name a few of the more common terms designating the broad problem area, scarcely an issue of a psychological journal goes by without containing at least one experimental article on this subject. An attempt at a general review of this work would be beyond the scope of this paper. Some of the problems posed by such a review include the multitude of different issues addressed by the research, the variety of variables studied and methods used which make comparison of the experiments difficult if not impossible, and the grossly different meanings given to the term stress.

This paper undertakes two somewhat limited tasks: (*a*) an analysis of some of the key problems in experimentation, and (*b*) the presentation of a brief account of some research from the author's own laboratory which was designed to throw light on some of the psychological mechanisms underlying stress reactions.

A great portion of the experimentation in the field of stress does not add significantly to our knowledge of the psychological principles underlying the problem. If we are to understand the reasons for this, we need to recognize that, to be valuable, laboratory experiments must be effective analogues of postulated processes in the naturalistic phenomena of stress. These phenomena come to our attention through observations of people in real life. Our concern with stress phenomena arises from such observations as the behavior of people in disasters (Baker and Chapman, 1962), of mourning following bereavement (Lindemann, 1944), of various forms of psychopathology (Hambling, 1959), of the nature and effects of concentration camps (Bettelheim, 1943) and military combat (Grinker and Spiegel, 1945), and of patients anticipating surgery (Janis, 1958), to mention a few of the more prominent examples of field studies which have enriched the recent literature.

As a first step in understanding these phenomena, they are placed in a loose way under the rubric of stress. Thus, for example, various somatic symptoms such as ulcers and hypertension are conceived to be the result of stress processes, as are the symptoms of battle fatigue or schizophrenia, or the deterioration of skilled performance in battle, and the disorganization of social systems in disaster. Analytic statements are then evolved which identify the antecedent conditions of the so-called stress reactions, and the processes involved. An examination of the field-study literature reveals abundant conceptualizations about the sources of threat, the mechanisms of threat production, the coping processes following threat, and the behavioral and physiological consequences. Some of the most significant of these conceptualizations may be found in the work of Janis (1958, 1962).

Now the laboratory makes it possible for us to test the adequacy of our conceptualizations by making the relevant processes happen under conditions of careful control and measurement. Although it is not always strictly the case, laboratory experimentation usually depends upon the definition of problems originating in our observations of nature and the development of theories about the processes which underlie what is observed.

What then is a laboratory analogue? First of all, it is an experiment performed under controlled conditions so that a variable, or several variables can be unequivocally related to some effect that one measures. But what about the term *analogue*? This refers to the manipulations in the experiment which parallel, or are similar to, the processes that are postulated to take place in nature. We are never really interested in the limited conditions of the experiment itself. Rather, we assume that these conditions represent those in real life and that the findings can be generalized to conditions like them in nature. If an experimenter creates stress by exposing his experimental subjects to an experience of failure by doing or saying certain things to him, he expects to generalize his results to all those situations in life which involve such failure. The laboratory experiment on stress is but a miniature of these life experiences and, most importantly, one whose procedures, by analogy, are thought to correspond to or be isomorphic with the processes we postulate as taking place in nature.

All laboratory experiments are, in a sense, analogues, although they are not necessarily good analogues to postulated processes nor are they necessarily well designed to identify the relationships between the variables which confirm or disconfirm the postulated process. Experiments which serve to advance our understanding depend upon a clear conceptual analysis of a problem. Very little of the recent experimental work on the problem of psychological stress falls into this category, sometimes because of the painful absence of a clear conception, sometimes because of the failure of adequate design.

These critical statements can be brought home by turning to substantive problems in the field, emphasizing the question of what psychological processes mediate stress reactions. We must ask when a stimulus will produce stress reactions, and what factors determine whether it will or will not.

In raising this question, the temptation must be resisted to digress into the equally important problem of what reactions define stress. An enormous variety of measures are employed to this end, ranging from biochemical studies of adrenal-cortical or medulla secretions in the blood, to autonomic nervous system indicators of arousal such as skin conductance, heart rate, and respiration, as well as a large class of behavioral reactions including reports of affect, observations of behavioral and cognitive disorganization, and motor and postural manifestations. These indicators reflect, for one thing, different levels of analysis, physiological as well as psychological. Little is known about the relationships between them. In fact, what is known suggests that stress indicators are poorly correlated (Lazarus, Speisman, and Mordkoff, 1963), and it is difficult to identify the conditions under which stress should be indexed by one or the other. And yet, the many measures employed are all identified as stress reactions. However, the many problems inherent in the definition of stress and stress reactions must be excluded here as beyond the possibility of the present discussion.

Returning to the matter of what produces stress reactions, experimenters have employed a remarkable variety of procedures. Included are efforts to attack the self-esteem of subjects or other significant personal needs such as achievement or affiliation, frightening subjects by making them believe that they are in danger of electrocution from a malfunctioning electrical instrument, employing insulting remarks to induce anger, making ego-threatening interpretations in a psychiatric interview, presenting movies dealing with threatening experiences, blowing a loud horn behind the subject's head, requiring the performance of intellectual tasks such as mental arithmetic, producing sensory deprivation, and having subjects plunge their arms into a bucket of ice-cold water. This list is by no means exhaustive, but it is fairly representative of the kinds of experimental conditions used in laboratory research. Often, great ingenuity is employed by the experimenter in setting up the conditions producing stress, as in a recent study by Korchin and Herz (1960), in which the subject is made to think he has autistically misperceived the contents of perceptual stimuli by a clever ruse.

Now what about the mechanism by which the stimulus condition results in the measured stress reaction? By what reasoning does plunging the arm into ice-cold water or doing mental arithmetic get placed in the same category of stressor stimuli as do conditions designed to threaten self-esteem? It is true that heart rate changes, elevation of skin conductance, and other autonomic indices of stress reaction can be demonstrated to occur as a consequence of each of these procedures and of many more, including an experience of failure or watching a disturbing movie. It can also be demonstrated that increased hydrocortisone may be found in the blood following an experience of failure, attacks on the subjects' ability to perceive correctly, living in a strange environment, or watching threatening movies. Experiments merely demonstrating that autonomic, behavioral, and adrenal-cortical responses follow the use of some specific, so-called stressor procedure, have proliferated.

What is missing from much of this work is a clear set of notions about why this diverse variety of stimulus conditions produces the reactions identified as stress. Without an analysis of the psychological or phyically noxious nature of these stimulus conditions and the processes that intervene between them and the measured stress reaction, the only link between them must remain the response measure, say hydrocortisone or skin-conductance elevation, which is found to be a common response to all of these stimuli.

But is the reason why plunging the arm into ice water produces such responses the same as is assumed to be the case for mental arithmetic or for assaults on the self-esteem? In the latter case, the intervening process is often assumed to be the production of threat in the psychological sense. Do we then assume also that plunging the arm into ice-cold water is threatening, or is there a more direct, homeostatic mechanism of temperature regulation involved in that procedure which is not true in assaults on self-esteem? Similarly, does mental arithmetic produce stress responses because of potential psychological threats involved in performing such a task, or is it merely a matter of activation or mobilization of effort?

It is possible that both the state of being threatened and physical demands upon the tissues tend to activate the organism and produce similar autonomic and biochemical changes, and that even nonthreatening kinds of experiences such as watching a funny movie, or running up and down a hillside or golf course in sheer pleasure have similar effects. The changes that are called stress reactions may not be at all specific to psychologically threatening conditions, and perhaps positive affective experiences might produce the same reaction although in lesser degree. If this is true, then on what grounds do we identify all such reactions as stress? Similarly with the adrenal-cortical reactions emphasized by Selye (1956), serum-hydrocortisone elevation may follow any biological demand, rather than necessarily being associated with the psychological state of being threatened. Have we not begged here the key question, that concerning the mechanisms by which these effects are produced?

There are many variables confounded in the data alluded to above which leave indeterminate the bases, physiological and psychological, on which the so-called stress reactions depend. Perhaps the easiest one to recognize is the confounding between physiological and psychological levels of explanation. The process of having a tooth pulled results in increased hydrocortisone in the blood. Shannon and his colleagues (Shannon, Isbell, and Hester, 1962) have shown, however, that merely anticipating such dental work will lead to the same results. In the latter case, the mechanisms intervening between the threat of dental surgery and the stress reaction are psychological, since there is no direct assault on the tissue system at all, merely the recognition by the patients of a danger to come. To return to another stress situation, it is possible that plunging the arm into cold water has psychological implications that are connected with the stress reactions, but this is not the explanation that would normally be accepted. Rather, what is assumed is the direct disturbance of the tissue system, that and the natural defensive or homeostatic reactions of the body to such noxious conditions, referred to by Selye (1956) as "the adaptation syndrome," are called into play. But the levels of explanation are entirely different in instances of threat and direct tissue damage. While it is true that the ultimate physiological mechanisms may be the same once the subject has been threatened psychologically or once a directly noxious stimulus has assaulted a tissue system, the key psychological questions are begged unless the researcher attempts to specify the psychological processes which determine whether these changes will indeed be activated.

Most of the experiments performed on stress simply ignore this question of psychological process, and serve merely as demonstrations that such and such a condition results in some stress reaction, usually defined by a single measure. They are not analogues of psychological stress at all, in the sense that they permit evaluation of some postulated process of stress production. Strangely enough, most are not even psychological in character at all, since typically one cannot find a single psychological question that has been elucidated. And often, even the physiological mechanism by which the

hydrocortisone, skin-conductance change, or whatever comes about is not clarified, so that such studies are not even physiological analogues of the kinds of processes Selye (1956), Lindsley (1957), or other physiologically oriented theorists were so concerned with.

The impression that all experimental studies ignore psychological questions should not be created, although those that tackle them are often woefully inadequate to the task. A good example is the recent paper by Alexander and his colleagues (Alexander, Flagg, Foster, Clemens, and Blahd, 1961) dealing with the psychological mechanism of stress production in patients suffering from hyperthyroidism. Alexander started with two assumptions. One, of less interest here, was that hyperthyroid disorder leads to specificity of reaction to stress, for such patients the preferred organismic response being in the category of heightened thyroid activity. The other, dealing more with the psychodynamics of stress production, was that the hyperthyroid patient is especially vulnerable to threat in situations engendering fear of biological survival. This fear then is the postulated fundamental source of stress in the hyperthyroid patient.

Here is a postulate about the mechanism underlying stress in a particular group, a postulate which Alexander attempted to check by an experimental analogue. The analogue consisted of employing as a stimulus a movie called "The Wages of Fear" which was thought to deal with the theme of threat to biological survival. The film was presented to a group of untreated thyrotoxic patients, a treated group, and a group of normal controls. Thyroid functioning was found to be elevated in the untreated patient group as a result of viewing the film.

While the Alexander study did attempt to identify the psychological mechanism underlying stress in the hyperthyroid patient, it failed for design reasons. The trouble is that there is no way of knowing from this study whether the reactions of the patients were specific to this film with its particular contents revolving around the theme of biological survival threats. Maybe any disturbing film would have had the same effects regardless of theme. To support the hypothesis about the specific kind of threat production in these patients, it was necessary to demonstrate that the stress reaction of heightened thyroid activity did not occur when another film was used—a film which, because of other kinds of threatening content, could indeed produce stress reactions in another type of population.

Still, the study of Alexander goes in the right

direction in its attempt to spell out and test psychodynamic factors in stress production. It failed simply for methodological reasons to demonstrate that fear for biological survival is the necessary and sufficient condition of stress production in a hyperthyroid group. It is an analogue of stress because it was designed to test, empirically, a postulate about the mechanism of stress production by creating conditions that could be considered appropriate for this mechanism. Such process-oriented studies exist but are disturbingly rare. Without them, and without systematic research programs based upon well-articulated theories of psychological stress, laboratory studies continue to proliferate without leading to significant advances in our generalizable knowledge.

Attention should now be shifted from general statements about the field of experimentation as a whole to a presentation of some work from the author's laboratory in which a research group has been seeking to test and elaborate certain theoretical principles of psychological stress production. While this program is many faceted and deals with a number of key theoretical issues in psychological stress, one particular concept which has led to some extremely interesting findings will be touched on in the remainder of this paper.

An important feature of stress in the psychological sense is seen in the literature on disaster. In that literature, it is often implied that stress depends on the *anticipation* of something harmful in the future and that it requires an interpretation by the person about the personal significance of the stimulus situation. Janis (1962), for example, discusses this problem in the concept of "anticipatory fear." This anticipation of potential harm or motive thwarting is the key to the concept of *threat*. Threat can be regarded as the central intervening variable in psychological stress.

Just before the 1953 Worcester tornado, the spring storm with thunder and lightning and dark clouds preceding the disaster did not communicate threat to the residents. There was no expectation of harm and hence no threat until the tragic event happened. Subsequently, however, after the experience of the tornado, ordinary storms carried an ominous quality. People were subsequently frightened by summer storms that had previously carried no threat. The crucial issue here in the production of threat is the process of discrimination of dangerous or threatening conditions from benign ones.

It is this idea of the dependence of threat upon a discrimination, a judgment, or an interpretation

that will be developed briefly now. For this process the term *cognitive appraisal* is used. The process of appraising which circumstances are harmful and which are benign is crucial to the production of stress reactions at least at the psychological level of analysis. In fact, as Arnold (1960) has recently argued most persuasively, any emotion implies an evaluation of a stimulus as either harmful or beneficial. But Arnold has not described the conditions that determine the appraisal, and without such analysis, experimental studies of the process are not possible. Among other things, beliefs or expectations about events, based both upon past experience and the present stimulus configuration, determine whether or not a stimulus will be reacted to as threatening.

Let us consider a moment what the concept of cognitive appraisal means concerning the production of threat. For one thing, it means that the same stimulus can be threatening or not, depending upon the interpretation the person makes concerning its future personal significance. This is an important point. The threat is not simply out there as an attribute of the stimulus. Rather it depends for its threat value on this appraisal process, which in turn depends upon the person's beliefs about what the stimulus means for the thwarting of motives of importance to him.

In the research project[1] which forms the basis of this discussion, experimental analogues of cognitive appraisal have been created and the factors that determine this appraisal manipulated. A stimulus which is normally threatening to most experimental subjects has been made relatively benign by influencing the way in which subjects interpret it.

The basic method of producing threat has been the use of motion-picture films, the orientation toward which is manipulated by introductory statements and/or sound tracks during the film which cast the events viewed in the way we choose (Lazarus, Speisman, Mordkoff, and Davison, 1962). One of these films shows a primitive ritual of an Australian Stone Age tribe. It involves a series of crude operations on the genitals of the native boys when they have reached puberty. The operation is called "subincision." The film is generally quite disturbing to watch. This same film has previously

---

[1] The author's colleagues and students whose work is referred to here, or who have participated in this project, include: Joseph C. Speisman, Arnold M. Mordkoff, Leslie A. Davidson, Cliff A. Jones, Jr., and Elizabeth Alfert.

been employed by Aas (1958) and Schwartz (1956) as a means of studying the Freudian concept of castration anxiety, although unpublished experimental studies in our laboratory suggest that there are other sources of threat in the film as well as the mutilation- or castration-relevant content.

In the typical experiment using the subincision film, subjects watch the film individually. Continuous recordings are made of autonomic variables such as skin conductance, heart rate, respiration, and motor activity, depending upon our interests at the moment, and at the end of the film reports of the subject's affective state are solicited, usually by an interview or an adjective check list of mood. Merely watching the film produces marked stress reactions, some of which can be occasionally quite severe with symptoms of disgust, nausea, and anxiety (Lazarus *et al.*, 1962). To give you some picture of the ebb and flow of the typical stress reaction to this film, Figure 1 portrays the pattern of skin conductance shown by 50 subjects over the entire 17 minutes of the subincision film.

You will notice in Figure 1 the ups and downs: high points in skin conductance signifying arousal or threat, low points indicating more benign states. The peak periods occur when the surgical operations are taking place, especially the first three which seem to be the most disturbing to watch. In the second operation for example, the native boy is obviously distressed and in pain, immediately following which he sobs and appears to suffer considerably. The deep trough in skin con-

ductance in the middle of the film occurs in relation to the relatively benign ceremonial activity of hair tying, in which one native binds the hair of another who has recently been operated upon. It might be noted also that this curve of autonomic reactivity is extremely stable in reflecting the stimulus impact, since in each new study with a sizable sample the same basic pattern is generated. This shows how desirable continuous recording of skin conductance is in indicating the ups and downs of stress reaction.

It has been said that this same film stimulus, which is so disturbing, could be made relatively benign by altering the interpretation which the subject places upon the events which are portrayed, presumably by eliminating the threatening significance (Speisman, Lazarus, Mordkoff, and Davison, 1964). How can threatening material be viewed so as to be nonthreatening? One kind of answer to this question can be found in the theory of ego defense, which postulates, in a rather loose way, certain mental operations which are conceived of as ways of reducing threat. Such mechanisms can be thought of as resulting in altered cognitive appraisal of threatening stimuli, be they internal or environmental.

Two very general kinds of defensive orientation were chosen as especially suitable for the subincision film: intellectualization on the one hand, and denial and reaction formation, employed together, on the other. In intellectualization one gets detachment from threatening experiences by

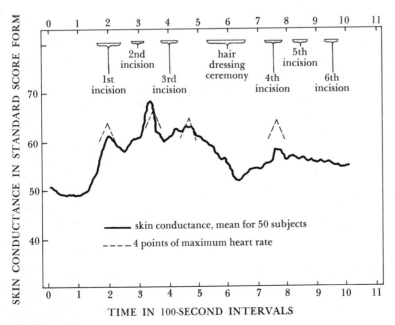

FIGURE 1 *Variation in skin conductance during the subincision film for 50 subjects*

taking an analytic, impersonal viewpoint. In denial one denies the threatening implications, and in reaction formation the negative aspects are reversed entirely so that only positive, rosy qualities are allowed expression and emphasis.

Two sound tracks were created for the subincision film, one called intellectualization, the other denial and reaction formation. The sound tracks contained a brief introductory statement, followed by a narrative, like a travelogue that ran simultaneously with the film itself. In intellectualization the orientation taken was that of the anthropologist who, like the viewer, is observing an interesting specimen of human behavior and describing it analytically. In it no reference is made to feelings of any kind. In the denial and reaction formation statement, the idea that the operative procedures damaged the functioning of the natives, threatened their health, or resulted in significant pain was denied. It was further suggested that the native boys had looked forward all their lives to this happy experience which permitted them to join their brothers as emerging adults and full members of the society. Everything that happened, however gruesome, was given a rosy glow.

A third control sound track was also created to compare with both the silent film and the two defensively oriented sound tracks. This was euphemistically called the trauma track, since it pointed up all of the major sources of threat in the film, the filth, the pain, the danger of the operation, and the sadism of the procedure, although this presentation was made in the same calm tone of the narrator's voice as that used in the other two sound tracks.

Two groups of subjects were employed in this experiment with the defensive sound tracks, one a college student group, the other consisting of middle-level airline executives who graciously consented to participate in the study. The reasoning behind the choice of groups had to do with an interest in defensive dispositions, that is, the habitual way in which the subjects coped with threat. One might assume that a person who usually denies threat would be most responsive to the denial and reaction formation sound track, while the person whose preferred mode of defense is intellectualization would get the most threat reduction from the intellectualization sound track, which was more compatible with his "natural" way of coping.

The assumption was made that college students, aside from whatever dispositional qualities led them into the system of higher education in the first place, are continually exposed to intellectual-ized modes of thought. Every facet of the world, physical, biological, psychological, social, and artistic, is placed in the context of analysis and intellectual understanding. For example, in an anthropology class one is taught about how people in other cultures live. In physiology one gets accustomed to examining and even discussing tissues and inspecting the anatomies of human and infrahuman species. The entire content of higher education poses a continual force toward intellectualized modes of thought.

With business executives the matter would appear to be quite different. The educational background of the group was, in the main, high-school level. The activities of life of the executive are more action oriented. Decision is emphasized rather than intellectual introspection. Managerial people are apt to be subjected far more to the social atmosphere which emphasizes such denial slogans as "the power of positive thinking," and the conviction that, if you believe in yourself, chances of success are good. Understanding and knowledge are favorably seen less for their own sake and more for their power to produce desired results.

As it turns out, some personality test data on both groups of subjects were available, and this appeared to support our assumption that students were more apt to be intellectualizers and the executives more disposed to denial-type defenses. Two scales of the Minnesota Multiphasic Personality Inventory (MMPI) were most relevant. One, identified as Psychasthenia (Pt) could be regarded as a measure of anxiety and obsessive compulsive tendencies which are considered a consequence of intellectualized defenses. The other, a derived scale of the MMPI called Hysteria Denial ($Hy\ Dn$), is presumed to measure tendencies to deny threatening or unacceptable thoughts, impulses and the threatening aspects of events. The college-student group was found to be significantly higher than the executives on the Pt scale, while the executives showed significantly higher scores than the students on the Hy-Dn scale.

The results of the study showed that the defensive sound tracks, in general, significantly reduced the threatening impact of the subincision film, while the trauma track increased it (Speisman et al., 1964). This is shown in Figure 2, illustrated, as before, for the autonomic nervous system variable of skin conductance. In the figure are presented the skin-conductance results for the subincision film without any sound track, the film accompanied by the trauma track, and the film accompanied by either the denial-and-reaction-formation track or the intellectualization track.

FIGURE 2   *Skin-conductance patterns during the subincision film as determined by the various sound-track conditions*

While both defensive sound tracks reduced threat, their effectiveness did appear to depend, as expected, on compatability with the natural defensive dispositions of the subject populations. Intellectualization was most effective in reducing stress reaction in the student group and less effective with the executives. In contrast, denial and reaction formation worked best with the executives but was far less successful with the students. It is as if the students simply did not accept as fully as the executives the orientation provided in the denial-and-reaction-formation sound track.

This interaction between the subject groups and the two defensive sound tracks is shown in Figure 3. Examination of the figure reveals that the students who heard the denial-and-reaction-formation sound track showed only a slight reduction in stress reaction over the silent version, compared with that found when students heard intellectualization, and with denial and reaction formation in the executive group.

Lest these findings with respect to personality and the effectiveness of different modes of cogni-

tive appraisal be taken as more pat than they really are, a perplexing sour note must be introduced into the discussion. Up to this point in the analysis, there seemed no reason to doubt that whatever was being measured by the *Pt* and *Hy-Dn* scales of the MMPI accounted for the interesting and sensible differences between the students and executives. If this were true, then the interaction between defensive disposition and sound-track effects could also be shown, and even strengthened, if we ignore the social group to which the subject belongs and array the data entirely on the basis of the MMPI scales. That is, the effectiveness of the sound tracks could be compared between those subjects scoring high in *Hy Dn* and those scoring low, and between subjects scoring high in *Pt* and those scoring low. When this was done, the interaction found earlier simply disappeared.

This latter finding somewhat embarrasses the interpretation of the interplay between defensive disposition and effects of the defensive sound tracks. At least it tells us that the differences between the students and executives are not ac-

FIGURE 3 *Interaction effects on skin-conductance patterns of subject groups and defensive sound-track conditions*

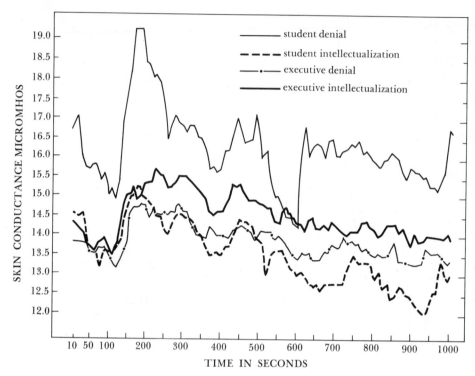

counted for on the basis of the *Hy-Dn* and *Pt* personality scales. The original interpretation is still reasonable, however, that executives are more prone to denial-and-reaction-formation modes of thought and students more oriented toward intellectualization as part of the social pattern to which they are exposed. And additional data have been appearing which further support the original interpretation. In any event, the findings on the general success of the defensive sound tracks in reducing the threat normally conveyed by the subincision movie are not in doubt.

The above findings have been replicated and extended in another study (Lazarus and Alfert, 1964) which is even more dramatic in showing the power of cognitive appraisal. This time there was no sound track at all, merely a prior orientation session, and still subjects could view the silent film with equanimity once they had been led to interpret the events portrayed in a benign way. In this study only the denial-and-reaction-formation statements were used, and they were presented to subjects as orienting instructions before the film began. Figure 4 shows that the lowest stress reactions occur in this condition, compared with either a sound-track condition involving denial and reaction formation, or a silent film version with no effort to

manipulate appraisal. Stress reaction, as we would expect, is greatest in the latter case. It should be added also that psychological assessments of the beliefs of the subjects about the film events made at the end of the film conditions follow what might be expected from the levels of stress reaction found. The cognitive appraisal of threat is indeed lowest in the denial-and-reaction-formation conditions, with the most threatening interpretations found in the untreated group.

Finally, the study of Lazarus and Alfert (1964) tends to confirm the principle that the defense-oriented communication must be compatible with defensive dispositions in the subject in order to reduce stress reaction. As assessed by scales of the MMPI considered to tap the disposition toward denial as a defense, subjects high in denial tendency showed marked stress reduction as a result of the denial communications, while subjects low in denial tendency were not so influenced. The personality dispositions determined whether or not the denial communications, presented either prior to or along with the threatening film as a sound track, would reduce the usual stress reaction to the film.

It has been shown here that threat, or at least stress reactions mediated psychologically, depend

FIGURE 4   *Effects of experimental treatments on skin conductance during the subincision film*

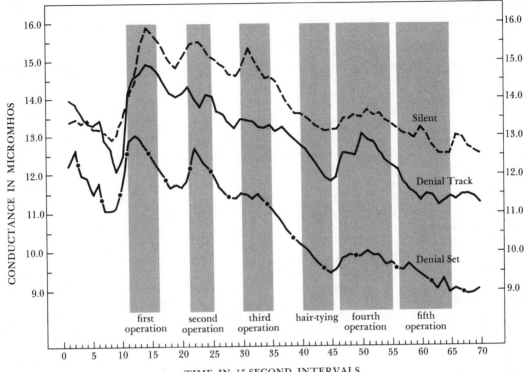

upon the cognitive appraisal of a stimulus. This is another way of talking about the interpretation of the personal significance of the stimulus. Moreover, two kinds of appraisal, intellectualized on the one hand, and that based on denial and reaction formation on the other, result in the short-circuiting of the expected threat arousal. These modes of viewing a potentially threatening stimulus, based on the theory of ego defense, are not as readily accepted by all persons, but if they are, they make for a nonthreatening appraisal.

The experimental analogue involves two steps. One is the assumption that the subject, in watching a motion-picture film, identifies himself with the actors in the film as though he were one of them, and can be thus threatened by what is happening to them. The second stage in the analogue concerns the process of cognitive appraisal, in effect, that the orienting instructions and sound tracks produce varying appraisal processes of the sort involved in the concepts of denial and reaction or intellectualization, and that these, in turn, correspond to what occurs in the natural context.

It should be made absolutely clear that, although the discussion has referred to ego-defense theory and employs the terms *intellectualization*

and *denial and reaction formation*, in describing the sound tracks, the experiments are analogues of cognitive appraisal and not ego defense. We have merely borrowed from defense theory in constructing our appraisal statements. Defense is usually considered to involve first the arousal of threat, and then, by principles that are still not clear to us, the activation of certain self-induced modes of thought which reduce the threat that has once been aroused. In these experiments, the modes of thought that short-circuit threat are encouraged by manipulation of the situation; they do not follow the generation of threat in the subject, nor are they self-induced by the subject. We cannot consider our findings as resulting from defensive processes, although we can learn something about the threat-reducing effectiveness of various defensive modes of thought from systematic manipulation of the kinds of statements we give orienting the subjects. Thus, indirectly they contribute to the theory of ego defense.

Those familiar with the literature on ego defense will recognize the vague condition of these concepts, even though the general idea of defensive reappraisal has wide acceptance. The specific mental operations involved are not clearly understood;

their comparative effectiveness is not known, nor is their relationship with each other. From the point of view of the experimental analogue, some key questions can be phrased in this way: What are the necessary and sufficient mental operations for the successful defensive reappraisal of various kinds of threatening events? And what are the conditions under which these coping processes will be activated and successful? By means of the experimental paradigm described above, it is possible to subject a variety of carefully defined modes of defensive appraisal to the test of effectiveness in reducing the physiological as well as behavioral manifestations of threat. By the proper analysis of such maneuvers as intellectualization, for example, we can separate out of this global and poorly articulated concept the precise elements of thought which are capable of making a threatening stimulus less threatening or benign.

About the experiments themselves, I would say at the present time that when the belief is created that the surgical procedures in the subincision film are neither painful nor harmful and are viewed by the natives with joy, then, assuming that the subject has placed himself in their shoes, there is no threat associated with vicariously undergoing the subincision experience. Similarly, from the vantage point of intellectualized detachment, the same events which are normally threatening can be looked at without emotionalized, empathic involvement and can be placed in the context of a neutral conceptual framework.

In making this latter point about intellectualization, one may think of the experience of Hamlet in coming upon the grave digger unearthing a skull. Hamlet says poignantly, "Alas, poor Yorick, I knew him." This emotional statement is the dramatist's way of involving Hamlet and therefore the audience with the image of a friend, a fellow human being, dead, now nothing more than bones. If we follow the kind of arguments made about intellectualization, he might have said with far less emotional impact, "Isn't this an interesting specimen of primate bone?" In fact, is this not exactly what the anatomist or surgeon does when he dons his scientist hat and observes pathology? Yorick as a dead friend is a threatening thought, but Yorick as a nameless primate bone short-circuits the threat by employing a nonthreatening framework within which to view the same event which could be most disturbing from another point of view.

At this point again, the temptation is strong and must be resisted to digress to the issues inherent in using the vicarious procedure of motion picture films to produce threat, issues concerned with ad-

vantages and disadvantages and with the assumed processes by which marked stress reactions can be so easily produced by this laboratory method. But these questions themselves are complex and require extensive exposition. Moreover, the purpose of illustrating the laboratory analogue of stress processes has been fulfilled in the presentation of some studies dealing with processes of threat production and reduction.

It must be clear by now that, implicitly or explicitly, laboratory analogues of stress must start from some conceptualization of the very processes underlying the phenomena observed. In the film technique the analogue involves assumptions about the process of identification with the actors in the film, to mention one. In the sound-track procedures there is available an analogue of the process of cognitive appraisal, the different sound tracks representing different frames of reference within which the film events are viewed.

It is remarkable that, in the quarter of a century that has seen interest in stress phenomena grow so greatly, psychological stress theory has had so little influence on experimental research on the subject. Some researchers seem to believe that Selye's (1956) work on the adaptation syndrome has solved our problems concerning the psychology of stress, when, in reality, it leaves all the psychological questions untouched. Selye has added perhaps to the measures indexing stress and to our sophistication about the physiological mechanisms underlying these measures but not to the understanding of the psychological processes which determine when a stress reaction will or will not occur.

The current work on the physiology of arousal tends to confuse psychological threat with activation, to confuse the jumping up and down in happy enthusiasm, and the physiological mobilization involved in this, with the state of being threatened by the sight of something, by the thought of something, [or] by a small change in environment which betokens a potential harm. The theoretical and methodological problems inherent in the field of psychological stress will never be solved merely by repeated demonstrations that this or that condition will result in a blood chemistry effect, a change in affect, or an autonomic nervous system reaction—unless at the same time attention is given to the psychological processes involved and to the empirical conditions which identify these processes. In the experimental laboratory what we need are more carefully thought out analogues of these psychological processes.

REFERENCES

Aas, A. *Mutilation fantasies and autonomic response.* Oslo, Norway: Oslo University Press, 1958.

Alexander, F., Flagg, G. R., Foster, S., Clemens, T., & Blahd, W. Experimental studies of emotional stress: 1. Hyperthyroidism. *Psychosomatic Medicine*, 1961, **22,** 104–114.

Arnold, M. B. *Emotions and personality.* Vol. 1. New York: Columbia University Press, 1960.

Baker G. W., & Chapman, D. W. *Man and society in disaster.* New York: Basic Books, 1962.

Bettelheim, B. Individual and mass behavior in extreme situations. *Journal of Abnormal and Social Psychology*, 1943, **38,** 417–452.

Grinker, R. R., & Spiegel, J. P. *Men under stress.* New York: Blakiston, 1945.

Hambling, J. The nature of stress disorder. In *Conference of the Society for Psychosomatic Research held at the Royal College of Physicians, May 1958.* Springfield, Ill.: Charles C Thomas, 1959.

Janis, I. L. *Psychological stress.* New York: Wiley, 1958.

Janis, I. L. Psychological effects of warnings. In G. W. Baker & D. W. Chapman (Eds.), *Man and society in disaster.* New York: Basic Books, 1962.

Korchin, S. J., & Herz, M. Differential effects of "shame" and "disintegrative" threats on emotional and adreno-cortical functioning. *AMA Archives of General Psychiatry*, 1960, **2,** 640–651.

Lazarus, R. S., & Alfert, E. Short-circuiting of threat by experimentally altering cognitive appraisal. *Journal of Abnormal and Social Psychology*, 1964, **69** (2), 195–205.

Lazarus, R. S., Speisman, J. C., & Mordkoff, A. M. The relationship between autonomic indicators of psychological stress: Heart rate and skin conductance. *Psychosomatic Medicine*, 1963, **25,** 19–30.

Lazarus, R. S., Speisman, J. C., Mordkoff, A. M., & Davison, L. A. A Laboratory study of psychological stress produced by a motion picture film. *Psychological Monographs*, 1962, **76** (34, Whole No. 533).

Lindemann, E. Symptomatology and management of acute grief. *American Journal of Psychiatry*, 1944, **101,** 141–148.

Lindsley, D. B. Psychophysiology and motivation. In M. R. Jones (Ed.), *Nebraska symposium on motivation: 1957.* Lincoln: University of Nebraska Press, 1957.

Schwartz, B. J. An empirical test of two Freudian hypotheses concerning castration anxiety. *Journal of Personality*, 1956, **24,** 318–327.

Seyle, H. *The stress of life.* New York: McGraw-Hill, 1956.

Shannon, I. L., Isbell, G. M., & Hester, W. R. Stress in dental patients. Report, April 1962, School of Aerospace Medicine, Brooks Air Force Base, Texas.

Speisman, J. C., Lazarus, R. S., Mordkoff, A., & Davison, L. Experimental reduction of stress based on ego-defense theory. *Journal of Abnormal and Social Psychology*, 1964, **68,** 367–380.

50

Imitation of Film-Mediated Aggressive Models

Albert Bandura, Dorothea Ross, and Sheila A. Ross

The article that follows is a good example of a well-planned experimental design. Notice how carefully these investigators tried to ensure that only the variables they wished to study were permitted to influence the results of the experiment.

There were three main questions being asked by these experimenters. The first question was: Will subjects who exhibit high amounts of anxiety about being aggressive (that is, who feel worried or guilty about aggression) imitate the aggressive behavior of adult models to a lesser degree than will other subjects who do not feel anxious about being aggressive? The rationale for this question is that parents, teachers, and society in general regard open aggression as being generally deleterious to the goal of peaceful living. Therefore, many children are taught that aggression is bad and to be avoided, and thus when

From Journal of Abnormal and Social Psychology, *Vol. 66, No. 1 (1963), 3–11. Copyright 1963 by the American Psychological Association, and reproduced by permission. This investigation was supported in part by Research Grants M-4398 and M-5162 from the National Institute of Health, United States Public Health Service, and the Lewis S. Haas Child Development Research Fund, Stanford University. The authors are indebted to David J. Hicks for his generous assistance with the photography and to John Steinbruner who assisted with various phases of this study. This research was carried out while the junior author [Dorothea Ross] was the recipient of an American Association of University Women International Fellowship for postdoctoral research.*

they feel aggressive as most people do at times, they experience feelings of anxiety and might be expected to act less aggressively than others who have not learned to be anxious about aggressive feelings.

The second question was: Will boys be more aggressive than girls? In our society, at least, most people feel that it is unladylike to exhibit aggression. The little lady should hide her aggressive feelings and perhaps develop other ways of dealing with frustration and anger. Whereas many boys are taught to try to contain their aggressive tendencies most of the time, there are at least a few situations where aggressive behavior is not only condoned, but even encouraged. When boys engage in competitive sports they are certainly encouraged to be as aggressive as the rules allow.

The third question was: Will children who have observed adults being aggressive toward one another be more likely to engage in aggressive behavior when frustrated than will children who have not observed the adults being aggressive? The belief here is that children who witness adults engaging in a particular behavior will assume that it is permissible for them to do likewise.

There are many tests of statistical significance reported in the results section of this article. The most important part of these tests is the value of p. This value tells the probability, or likelihood, that the results could have been brought about by chance events rather than by the events that are being studied. One never knows *absolutely* whether the results of an experiment are "real" and can be reproduced by other researchers. The lower the p value, the less the chance that the results are fortuitous and hence, the greater the chance that they are real. The "best" values of p are the lowest values, e.g., .001, .005, .01, and .05. Larger values, such as .20, show that the results could easily have occurred by chance alone.

In a test of the hypothesis that exposure of children to film-mediated aggressive models would increase the probability of Ss' aggression to subsequent frustration, one group of experimental Ss observed real-life aggressive models, a second observed these same models portraying aggression on film, while a third group viewed a film depicting an aggressive cartoon character. Following the exposure treatment, Ss were mildly frustrated and tested for the amount of imitative and nonimitative aggression in a different experimental setting. The overall results provide evidence for both the facilitating and the modeling influence of film-mediated aggressive stimulation. In addition, the findings reveal that the effects of such exposure are to some extent a function of the sex of the model, sex of the child, and the reality cues of the model.

Most of the research on the possible effects of film-mediated stimulation upon subsequent aggressive behavior has focused primarily on the drive-reducing function of fantasy. While the experimental evidence for the catharsis or drive reduction theory is equivocal (Albert, 1957; Berkowitz, 1962; Emery, 1959; Feshbach, 1955, 1958; Kenny, 1952; Lövaas, 1961; Siegel, 1956), the modeling influence of pictorial stimuli has received little research attention.

A recent incident (*San Francisco Chronicle,* 1961) in which a boy was seriously knifed during a reenactment of a switchblade knife fight the boys had seen the previous evening on a televised re-run of the James Dean movie, *Rebel Without a Cause,* is a dramatic illustration of the possible imitative influence of film stimulation. Indeed, anecdotal data suggest that portrayal of aggression through pictorial media may be more influential in shaping the form aggression will take when a person is instigated on later occasions, than in altering the level of instigation to aggression.

In an earlier experiment (Bandura and Huston, 1961) it was shown that children readily imitated aggressive behavior exhibited by a model in the presence of the model. A succeeding investigation (Bandura, Ross, and Ross, 1961) demonstrated that children exposed to aggressive models generalized aggressive responses to a new setting in which the model was absent. The present study sought to determine the extent to which film-mediated aggressive models may serve as an important source of imitative behavior.

Aggressive models can be ordered on a reality-fictional stimulus dimension with real-life models located at the reality end of the continuum, non-human cartoon characters at the fictional end, and films portraying human models occupying an intermediate position. It was predicted, on the basis of saliency and similarity of cues, that the more remote the model was from reality, the weaker would be the tendency for subjects to imitate the behavior of the model.

Of the various interpretations of imitative learning, the sensory feedback theory of imitation recently proposed by Mowrer (1960) is elaborated in greatest detail. According to this theory, if certain responses have been repeatedly positively reinforced, proprioceptive stimuli associated with these responses acquire secondary reinforcing properties and thus the individual is predisposed to perform the behavior for the positive feedback. Similarly, if responses have been negatively reinforced, response-correlated stimuli acquire the capacity to arouse anxiety which, in turn, inhibits the occurrence of the negatively valenced behavior. On the basis of these considerations it was predicted that subjects who manifest high aggression anxiety would perform significantly less imitative and nonimitative aggression than subjects who display little anxiety over aggression. Since aggression is generally considered female inappropriate behavior and therefore likely to be negatively reinforced in girls (Sears, Maccoby, and Levin, 1957), it was also predicted that male subjects would be more imitative of aggression than females.

To the extent that observation of adults displaying aggression conveys a certain degree of permissiveness for aggressive behavior, it may be assumed that such exposure not only facilitates the learning of new aggressive responses but also weakens competing inhibitory responses in subjects and thereby increases the probability of occurrence of previously learned patterns of aggression. It was predicted, therefore, that subjects who observed aggressive models would display significantly more aggression when subsequently frustrated than subjects who were equally frustrated but who had no prior exposure to models exhibiting aggression.

Method

Subjects

The subjects were 48 boys and 48 girls enrolled in the Stanford University Nursery School. They ranged in age from 35 to 69 months, with a mean age of 52 months.

Two adults, a male and a female, served in the role of models both in the real-life and the human

film-aggression condition, and one female experimenter conducted the study for all 96 children.

General procedure

Subjects were divided into three experimental groups and one control group of 24 subjects each. One group of experimental subjects observed real-life aggressive models, a second group observed these same models portraying aggression on film, while a third group viewed a film depicting an aggressive cartoon character. The experimental groups were further subdivided into male and female subjects so that half the subjects in the two conditions involving human models were exposed to same-sex models, while the remaining subjects viewed models of the opposite sex.

Following the exposure experience, subjects were tested for the amount of imitative and nonimitative aggression in a different experimental setting in the absence of the models.

The control group subjects had no exposure to the aggressive models and were tested only in the generalization situation.

Subjects in the experimental and control groups were matched individually on the basis of ratings of their aggressive behavior in social interactions in the nursery school. The experimenter and a nursery school teacher rated the subjects on four five-point rating scales which measured the extent to which subjects displayed physical aggression, verbal aggression, aggression toward inanimate objects, and aggression inhibition. The latter scale, which dealt with the subjects' tendency to inhibit aggressive reactions in the face of high instigation, provided the measure of aggression anxiety. Seventy-one per cent of the subjects were rated independently by both judges so as to permit an assessment of interrater agreement. The reliability of the composite aggression score, estimated by means of the Pearson product-moment correlation, was .80.

Data for subjects in the real-life aggression condition and in the control group were collected as part of a previous experiment (Bandura *et al.,* 1961). Since the procedure is described in detail in the earlier report, only a brief description of it will be presented here.

Experimental conditions

Subjects in the Real-Life Aggressive condition were brought individually by the experimenter to the experimental room and the model, who was in the hallway outside the room, was invited by the experimenter to come and join in the game. The subject was then escorted to one corner of the room and seated at a small table which contained potato prints, multicolor picture stickers, and colored paper. After demonstrating how the subject could design pictures with the materials provided, the experimenter escorted the model to the opposite corner of the room which contained a small table and chair, a tinker toy set, a mallet, and a 5-foot inflated Bobo doll. The experimenter explained that this was the model's play area and after the model was seated, the experimenter left the experimental room.

The model began the session by assembling the tinker toys but after approximately a minute had elapsed, the model turned to the Bobo doll and spent the remainder of the period aggressing toward it with highly novel responses which are unlikely to be performed by children independently of the observation of the model's behavior. Thus, in addition to punching the Bobo doll, the model exhibited the following distinctive aggressive acts which were to be scored as imitative responses:

The model sat on the Bobo doll and punched it repeatedly in the nose.

The model then raised the Bobo doll and pommeled it on the head with a mallet.

Following the mallet aggression, the model tossed the doll up in the air aggressively and kicked it about the room. This sequence of physically aggressive acts was repeated approximately three times, interspersed with verbally aggressive responses such as, "Sock him in the nose . . . ," "Hit him down . . . ," "Throw him in the air . . . ," "Kick him . . . ," and "Pow."

Subjects in the Human Film-Aggression condition were brought by the experimenter to the semi-darkened experimental room, introduced to the picture materials, and informed that while the subjects worked on potato prints, a movie would be shown on a screen, positioned approximately six feet from the subject's table. The movie projector was located in a distant corner of the room and was screened from the subject's view by large wooden panels.

The color movie and a tape recording of the sound track was begun by a male projectionist as soon as the experimenter left the experimental room and was shown for a duration of 10 minutes. The models in the film presentations were the same adult males and females who participated in the Real-Life condition of the experiment. Similarly, the aggressive behavior they portrayed in the film was identical with their real-life performances.

For subjects in the Cartoon Film-Aggression condition, after seating the subject at the table with the picture construction material, the experimenter walked over to a television console approximately three feet in front of the subject's table, remarked, "I guess I'll turn on the color TV," and ostensibly tuned in a cartoon program. The experimenter then left the experimental room. The cartoon was shown on a glass lens screen in the television set by means of a rear projection arrangement screened from the subject's view by large panels.

The sequence of aggressive acts in the cartoon was performed by the female model costumed as a black cat similar to the many cartoon cats. In order to heighten the level of irreality of the cartoon, the floor area was covered with artificial grass and the walls forming the backdrop were adorned with brightly colored trees, birds, and butterflies creating a fantasyland setting. The cartoon began with a close-up of a stage on which the curtains were slowly drawn revealing a picture of a cartoon cat along with the title, *Herman the Cat*. The remainder of the film showed the cat pommeling the Bobo doll on the head with a mallet, sitting on the doll and punching it in the nose, tossing the doll in the air, and kicking it about the room in a manner identical with the performance in the other experimental conditions except that the cat's movements were characteristically feline. To induce further a cartoon set, the program was introduced and concluded with appropriate cartoon music, and the cat's verbal aggression was repeated in a high-pitched, animated voice.

In both film conditions, at the conclusion of the movie the experimenter entered the room and then escorted the subject to the test room.

Aggression instigation

In order to differentiate clearly the exposure and test situations subjects were tested for the amount of imitative learning in a different experimental room which was set off from the main nursery school building.

The degree to which a child has learned aggressive patterns of behavior through imitation becomes most evident when the child is instigated to aggression on later occasions. Thus, for example, the effects of viewing the movie, *Rebel Without a Cause*, were not evident until the boys were instigated to aggression the following day, at which time they reenacted the televised switchblade knife fight in considerable detail. For this reason, the children in the experiment, both those in the control group and those who were exposed to the aggressive models, were mildly frustrated before they were brought to the test room.

Following the exposure experience, the experimenter brought the subject to an anteroom which contained a varied array of highly attractive toys. The experimenter explained that the toys were for the subject to play with, but, as soon as the subject became sufficiently involved with the play material, the experimenter remarked that these were her very best toys, that she did not let just anyone play with them, and that she had decided to reserve these toys for some other children. However, the subject could play with any of the toys in the next room. The experimenter and the subject then entered the adjoining experimental room.

It was necessary for the experimenter to remain in the room during the experimental session; otherwise, a number of the children would either refuse to remain alone or would leave before the termination of the session. In order to minimize any influence her presence might have on the subject's behavior, the experimenter remained as inconspicuous as possible by busying herself with paper work at a desk in the far corner of the room and avoiding any interaction with the child.

Test for delayed imitation

The experimental room contained a variety of toys, some of which could be used in imitative or nonimitative aggression, and others which tended to elicit predominantly nonaggressive forms of behavior. The aggressive toys included a three-foot Bobo doll, a mallet and peg board, two dart guns, and a tether ball with a face painted on it which hung from the ceiling. The nonaggressive toys, on the other hand, included a tea set, crayons and coloring paper, a ball, two dolls, three bears, cars and trucks, and plastic farm animals.

In order to eliminate any variation in behavior due to mere placement of the toys in the room, the play material was arranged in a fixed order for each of the sessions.

The subject spent 20 minutes in the experimental room during which time his behavior was rated in terms of predetermined response categories by judges who observed the session through a one-way mirror in an adjoining observation room. The 20-minute session was divided in 5-second intervals by means of an electric interval timer, thus yielding

a total number of 240 response units for each subject.

The male model scored the experimental sessions for all subjects. In order to provide an estimate of interjudge agreement, the performances of 40 per cent of the subjects were scored independently by a second observer. The responses scored involved highly specific concrete classes of behavior, and yielded high interscorer reliabilities, the product-moment coefficients being in the .90's.

Response measures

The following response measures were obtained:

Imitative aggression. This category included acts of striking the Bobo doll with the mallet, sitting on the doll and punching it in the nose, kicking the doll, tossing it in the air, and the verbally aggressive responses, "Sock him," "Hit him down," "Kick him," "Throw him in the air," and "Pow."

Partially imitative responses. A number of subjects imitated the essential components of the model's behavior but did not perform the complete act, or they directed the imitative aggressive response to some object other than the Bobo doll. Two responses of this type were scored and were interpreted as partially imitative behavior: *Mallet aggression.* The subject strikes objects other than the Bobo doll aggressively with the mallet. *Sits on Bobo doll.* The subject lays the Bobo doll on its side and sits on it but does not aggress toward it.

Nonimitative aggression. This category included acts of punching, slapping, or pushing the doll, physically aggressive acts directed toward objects other than the Bobo doll, and any hostile remarks except for those in the verbal imitation category; for example, "Shoot the Bobo," "Cut him," "Stupid ball," "Knock over people," "Horses fighting, biting."

Aggressive gun play. The subject shoots darts or aims the guns and fires imaginary shots at objects in the room.

Ratings were also made of the number of behavior units in which subjects played nonaggressively or sat quietly and did not play with any of the material at all.

Results

The mean imitative and nonimitative aggression scores for subjects in the various experimental and control groups are presented in Table 1.

Since the distributions of scores departed from

TABLE 1   *Mean Aggression Scores for Subgroups of Experimental and Control Subjects*

| Response category | Experimental groups | | | | | |
| | Real-life aggressive | | Human film-aggressive | | Cartoon film-aggressive | Control Group |
	F Model	M Model	F Model	M Model		
Total aggression						
Girls	65.8	57.3	87.0	79.5	80.9	36.4
Boys	76.8	131.8	114.5	85.0	117.2	72.2
Imitative aggression						
Girls	19.2	9.2	10.0	8.0	7.8	1.8
Boys	18.4	38.4	34.3	13.3	16.2	3.9
Mallet aggression						
Girls	17.2	18.7	49.2	19.5	36.8	13.1
Boys	15.5	28.8	20.5	16.3	12.5	13.5
Sits on Bobo doll[a]						
Girls	10.4	5.6	10.3	4.5	15.3	3.3
Boys	1.3	0.7	7.7	0.0	5.6	0.6
Nonimitative aggression						
Girls	27.6	24.9	24.0	34.3	27.5	17.8
Boys	35.5	48.6	46.8	31.8	71.8	40.4
Aggressive gun play						
Girls	1.8	4.5	3.8	17.6	8.8	3.7
Boys	7.3	15.9	12.8	23.7	16.6	14.3

[a] This response category was not included in the total aggression score.

normality and the assumption of homogeneity of variance could not be made for most of the measures, the Friedman two-way analysis of variance by ranks was employed for testing the significance of the obtained differences.

Total aggression

The mean total aggression scores for subjects in the real-life, human film, cartoon film, and the control groups are 83, 92, 99, and 54, respectively. The results of the analysis of variance performed on these scores reveal that the main effect of treatment conditions is significant ($\chi^2_r = 9.06$, $p < .05$), confirming the prediction that exposure of subjects to aggressive models increases the probability that subjects will respond aggressively when instigated on later occasions. Further analyses of pairs of scores by means of the Wilcoxon matched-pairs, signed-ranks test show that subjects who viewed the real-life models and the film-mediated models do not differ from each other in total aggressiveness but all three experimental groups expressed significantly more aggressive behavior than the control subjects (Table 2).

Imitative aggressive responses

The Freidman analysis reveals that exposure of subjects to aggressive models is also a highly effective method for shaping subjects' aggressive responses ($\chi^2_r = 23.88$, $p < .001$). Comparisons of treatment conditions by the Wilcoxon test reveal that subjects who observed the real-life models and the film-mediated models, relative to subjects in the control group, performed considerably more imitative physical and verbal aggression (Table 2).

Illustrations of the extent to which some of the subjects became virtually "carbon copies" of their models in aggressive behavior are presented in Figure 1. The top frame shows the female model performing the four novel aggressive responses; the lower frames depict a male and a female subject reproducing the behavior of the female model they had observed earlier on film.

The prediction that imitation is positively related to the reality cues of the model was only partially supported. While subjects who observed the real-life aggressive models exhibited significantly more imitative aggression than subjects who viewed

TABLE 2 *Significance of the Differences Between Experimental and Control Groups in the Expression of Aggression*

Response category	χ^2_r	p	Live vs. Film p	Live vs. Cartoon p	Film vs. Cartoon p	Live vs. Control p	Film vs. Control p	Cartoon vs. Control p
			Comparison of treatment conditions[a]					
Total aggression	9.06	<.05	ns	ns	ns	<.01	<.01	<.005
Imitative aggression	23.88	<.001	ns	<.05	ns	<.001	<.001	<.005
Partial imitation								
Mallet aggression	7.36	.10>p>.05						
Sits on Bobo doll	8.05	<.05	ns	ns	ns	ns	<.05	<.005
Nonimitative aggression	7.28	.10>p>.05						
Aggressive gun play	8.06	<.05	<.01[b]	ns	ns	ns	<.05	ns

[a] The probability values are based on the Wilcoxon test.
[b] This probability value is based on a two-tailed test of significance.

the cartoon model, no significant differences were found between the live and film, and the film and cartoon conditions, nor did the three experimental groups differ significantly in total aggression or in the performances of partially imitative behavior (Table 2). Indeed, the available data suggest that, of the three experimental conditions, exposure to humans on film portraying aggression was the most influential in eliciting and shaping aggressive behavior. Subjects in this condition, in relation to the control subjects, exhibited more total aggression, more imitative aggression, more partially imitative behavior, such as sitting on the Bobo doll and mallet aggression, and they engaged in significantly more aggressive gun play. In addition, they performed significantly more aggressive gun play than did subjects who were exposed to the real-life aggressive models (Table 2).

Influence of sex of model and sex of child

In order to determine the influence of sex of model and sex of child on the expression of imitative and nonimitative aggression, the data from the experimental groups were combined and the significance of the differences between groups was assessed by t tests for uncorrelated means. In statistical comparisons involving relatively skewed distributions of scores the Mann-Whitney U test was employed.

Sex of subjects had a highly significant effect on both the learning and the performance of aggression. Boys, in relation to girls, exhibited significantly more total aggression ($t = 2.69$, $p < .01$),

more imitative aggression ($t = 2.82$, $p < .005$), more aggressive gun play ($z = 3.38$, $p < .001$), and more nonimitative aggressive behavior ($t = 2.98$, $p < .005$). Girls, on the other hand, were more inclined than boys to sit on the Bobo doll but refrained from punching it ($z = 3.47$, $p < .001$).

The analyses also disclosed some influences of the sex of the model. Subjects exposed to the male model, as compared to the female model, expressed significantly more aggressive gun play ($z = 2.83$, $p < .005$). The most marked differences in aggressive gun play ($U = 9.5$, $p < .001$), however, were found between girls exposed to the female model ($M = 2.9$) and males who observed the male model ($M = 19.8$). Although the overall model difference in partially imitative behavior, Sits on Bobo, was not significant, Sex × Model subgroup comparisons yielded some interesting results. Boys who observed the aggressive female model, for example, were more likely to sit on the Bobo doll without punching it than boys who viewed the male model ($U = 33$, $p < .05$). Girls reproduced the nonaggressive component of the male model's aggressive pattern of behavior (i.e., sat on the doll without punching it) with considerably higher frequency than did boys who observed the same model ($U = 21.5$, $p < .02$). The highest incidence of partially imitative responses was yielded by the group of girls who viewed the aggressive female model ($M = 10.4$), and the lowest values by the boys who were exposed to the male model ($M = 0.3$). This difference was significant beyond the .05 significance level. These findings, along with the sex of child and sex of model differences reported in the pre-

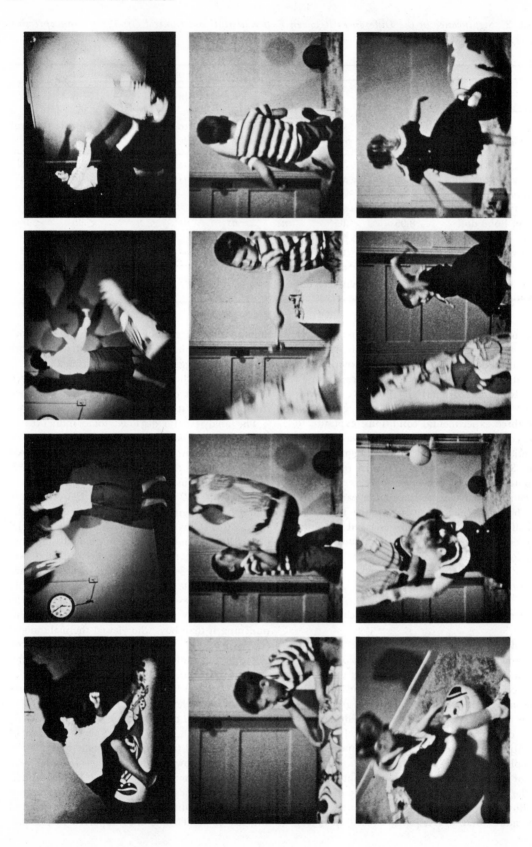

FIGURE 1   *Photographs from the film*, Social Learning of Aggression Through Imitation of Aggressive Models

ceding sections, provide further support for the view that the influence of models in promoting social learning is determined, in part, by the sex appropriateness of the model's behavior (Bandura et al., 1961).

Aggressive predisposition and imitation

Since the correlations between ratings of aggression and the measures of imitative and total aggressive behavior, calculated separately for boys and girls in each of the experimental conditions, did not differ significantly, the data were combined. The correlational analyses performed on these pooled data failed to yield any significant relationships between ratings of aggression anxiety, frequency of aggressive behavior, and the experimental aggression measures. In fact, the array means suggested nonlinear regressions although the departures from linearity were not of sufficient magnitude to be statistically significant.

Discussion

The results of the present study provide strong evidence that exposure to filmed aggression heightens aggressive reactions in children. Subjects who viewed the aggressive human and cartoon models on film exhibited nearly twice as much aggression than did subjects in the control group who were not exposed to the aggressive film content.

In the experimental design typically employed for testing the possible cathartic function of vicarious aggression, subjects are first frustrated, then provided with an opportunity to view an aggressive film following which their overt or fantasy aggression is measured. While this procedure yields some information on the immediate influence of film-mediated aggression, the full effects of such exposure may not be revealed until subjects are instigated to aggression on a later occasion. Thus, the present study and one recently reported by Lövaas (1961), both utilizing a design in which subjects first observed filmed aggression and then were frustrated, clearly reveal that observation of models portraying aggression on film substantially increases rather than decreases the probability of aggressive reactions to subsequent frustrations.

Filmed aggression not only facilitated the expression of aggression but also effectively shaped the form of the subjects' aggressive behavior. The finding that children modeled their behavior to

some extent after the film characters suggests that pictorial mass media, particularly television, may serve as an important source of social behavior. In fact, a possible generalization of responses originally learned in the television situation to the experimental film may account for the significantly greater amount of aggressive gun play displayed by subjects in the film condition as compared to subjects in the real-life and control groups. It is unfortunate that the qualitative features of the gun behavior were not scored, since subjects in the film condition, unlike those in the other two groups, developed interesting elaborations in gun play (for example, stalking the imaginary opponent, quick drawing, and rapid firing) characteristic of the Western gun fighter.

The view that the social learning of aggression through exposure to aggressive film content is confined to deviant children (Schramm, Lyle, and Parker, 1961) finds little support in our data. The children who participated in the experiment are by no means a deviant sample; nevertheless, 88 per cent of the subjects in the Real-Life and in the Human Film condition, and 79 per cent of the subjects in the Cartoon Film condition exhibited varying degrees of imitative aggression. In assessing the possible influence of televised stimulation on viewers' behavior, however, it is important to distinguish between learning and overt performance. Although the results of the present experiment demonstrate that the vast majority of children *learn* patterns of social behavior through pictorial stimulation, nevertheless, informal observation suggests that children do not, as a rule, *perform* indiscriminately the behavior of televised characters, even those they regard as highly attractive models. The replies of parents whose children participated in the present study to an open-end questionnaire item concerning their handling of imitative behavior suggest that this may be in part a function of negative reinforcement, as most parents were quick to discourage their children's overt imitation of television characters by prohibiting certain programs or by labeling the imitative behavior in a disapproving manner. From our knowledge of the effects of punishment on behavior, the responses in question would be expected to retain their original strength and could reappear on later occasions in the presence of appropriate eliciting stimuli, particularly if instigation is high, the instruments for aggression are available, and the threat of noxious consequences is reduced.

The absence of any relationships between ratings of the children's predisposition to aggression and their aggressive behavior in the experimental setting may simply reflect the inadequacy of the predictor measures. It may be pointed out, however, that the reliability of the ratings was relatively high. While this does not assure validity of the measures, it does at least indicate there was consistency in the raters' estimates of the children's aggressive tendencies.

A second, and perhaps more probable, explanation is that proprioceptive feedback alone is not sufficient to account for response inhibition or facilitation. For example, the proprioceptive cues arising from hitting responses directed toward parents and toward peers may differ little, if any; nevertheless, tendencies to aggress toward parents are apt to be strongly inhibited while peer aggression may be readily expressed (Bandura, 1960; Bandura and Walters, 1959). In most social interaction sequences, proprioceptive cues make up only a small part of the total stimulus complex, and therefore it is necessary to take into consideration additional stimulus components, for the most part external, which probably serve as important discriminative cues for the expression of aggression. Consequently, prediction of the occurrence or inhibition of specific classes of responses would be expected to depend upon the presence of a certain pattern of proprioceptive or introceptive stimulation together with relevant discriminative external stimuli.

According to this line of reasoning, failure to obtain the expected positive relationships between the measures of aggression may be due primarily to the fact that permissiveness for aggression, conveyed by situational cues in the form of aggressive film content and play material, was sufficient to override the influence of internal stimuli generated by the commission of aggressive responses. If, in fact, the behavior of young children, as compared to that of adults, is less likely to be under internal stimulus control, one might expect environmental cues to play a relatively important role in eliciting or inhibiting aggressive behavior.

A question may be raised as to whether the aggressive acts studied in the present experiment constitute "genuine" aggressive responses. Aggression is typically defined as behavior, the goal or intent of which is injury to a person or destruction of an object (Bandura and Walters, 1959; Dollard, Doob, Miller, Mowrer, and Sears, 1939; Sears, Maccoby, and Levin, 1957). Since intentionality is not a property of behavior but primarily an inference concerning antecedent events, the categorization of an act as "aggressive" involves a consideration of both stimulus and mediating or terminal response events.

According to a social learning theory of aggression recently proposed by Bandura and Walters (1963), most of the responses utilized to hurt or to injure others (for example, striking, kicking, and other responses of high magnitude), are probably learned for prosocial purposes under nonfrustration conditions. Since frustration generally elicits responses of high magnitude, the latter classes of responses, once acquired, may be called out in social interactions for the purpose of injuring others. On the basis of this theory it would be predicted that the aggressive responses acquired imitatively, while not necessarily mediating aggressive goals in the experimental situation, would be utilized to serve such purposes in other social settings with higher frequency by children in the experimental conditions than by children in the control group.

The present study involved primarily vicarious or empathic learning (Mowrer, 1960) in that subjects acquired a relatively complex repertoire of aggressive responses by the mere sight of a model's behavior. It has been generally assumed that the necessary conditions for the occurrence of such learning is that the model perform certain responses followed by positive reinforcement to the model (Hill, 1960; Mowrer, 1960). According to this theory, to the extent that the observer experiences the model's reinforcement vicariously, the observer will be prone to reproduce the model's behavior. While there is some evidence from experiments involving both human (Lewis and Duncan, 1958; McBrearty, Marston, and Kanfer, 1961; Sechrest, 1961) and animal subjects (Darby and Riopelle, 1959; Warden, Fjeld, and Koch, 1940), that vicarious reinforcement may in fact increase the probability of the behavior in question, it is apparent from the results of the experiment reported in this paper that a good deal of human imitative learning can occur without any reinforcers delivered either to the model or to the observer. In order to test systematically the influence of vicarious reinforcement on imitation, however, a study is planned in which the degree of imitative learning will be compared in situations in which the model's behavior is paired with reinforcement with those in which the model's responses go unrewarded.

REFERENCES
Albert, R. S. The role of mass media and the effect of aggressive film content upon children's aggressive responses and identification choices. *Genetic Psychology Monographs,* 1957, **55,** 221–285.

Bandura, A. Relationship of family patterns to child behavior disorders. Progress Report, 1960, Stanford University, Project No. M-1734, United States Public Health Service.

Bandura, A., & Huston, A. C. Identification as a process of incidental learning. *Journal of Abnormal and Social Psychology*, 1961, 63, 311–318.

Bandura, A., Ross, D., & Ross, S. A. Transmission of aggression through imitation of aggressive models. *Journal of Abnormal and Social Psychology*, 1961, 63, 575–582.

Bandura, A., & Walters, R. H. *Adolescent aggression.* New York: Ronald, 1959.

Bandura, A., & Walters, R. H. *Social learning and personality development.* New York: Holt, Rinehart & Winston, 1963.

Berkowitz, L. *Aggression: A social psychological analysis.* New York: McGraw-Hill, 1962.

Darby, C. L., & Riopelle, A. J. Observational learning in the Rhesus monkey. *Journal of Comparative and Physiological Psychology*, 1959, 52, 94–98.

Dollard, J., Doob, L. W., Miller, N. E., Mowrer, O. H., & Sears, R. R. *Frustration and aggression.* New Haven: Yale University Press, 1939.

Emery, F. E. Psychological effects of the Western film: A study in television viewing: II. The experimental study. *Human Relations*, 1959, 12, 215–232.

Feshbach, S. The drive-reducing function of fantasy behavior. *Journal of Abnormal and Social Psychology*, 1955, 50, 3–11.

Feshbach, S. The stimulating versus cathartic effects of a vicarious aggressive activity. Paper read at the Eastern Psychological Association, 1958.

Hill, W. F. Learning theory and the acquisition of values. *Psychological Review*, 1960, 67, 317–331.

Kenny, D. T. An experimental test of the catharsis theory of aggression. Unpublished doctoral dissertation, University of Washington, 1952.

Lewis, D. J., & Duncan, C. P. Vicarious experience and partial reinforcement. *Journal of Abnormal and Social Psychology*, 1958, 57, 321–326.

Lövaas, O. J. Effect of exposure to symbolic aggression on aggressive behavior. *Child Development*, 1961, 32, 37–44.

McBrearty, J. F., Marston, A. R., & Kanfer, F. H. Conditioning a verbal operant in a group setting: Direct vs. vicarious reinforcement. Abstract, *American Psychologist*, 1961, 16, 425.

Mowrer, O. H. *Learning theory and the symbolic processes.* New York: Wiley, 1960.

San Francisco Chronicle. "James Dean" knifing in South City. *San Francisco Chronicle*, March 1, 1961, p. 6.

Schramm, W., Lyle, J., & Parker, E. B. *Television in the lives of our children.* Stanford: Stanford University Press, 1961.

Sears, R. R., Maccoby, E. E., & Levin, H. *Patterns of child rearing.* Evanston, Ill.: Row, Peterson, 1957.

Sechrest, L. Vicarious reinforcement of responses. Abstract, *American Psychologist*, 1961, 16, 356.

Siegel, A. E. Film-mediated fantasy aggression and strength of aggressive drive. *Child Development*, 1956, 27, 365–378.

Warden, C. J., Fjeld, H. A., & Koch, A. M. Imitative behavior in cebus and rhesus monkeys. *Journal of Genetic Psychology*, 1940, 56, 311–322.

Motivation: A Contemporary Perspective

Salvatore R. Maddi
University of Chicago

As the introductory remarks to this section indicate, psychologists studying motivation were for a time preoccupied with the biological tissue needs, such as the needs for food, water, and sex. In this period there was general agreement on the content (i.e., goal states) of motivation, with theoretical and research attention being largely devoted to determining the function of motivation in the learning process. Psychologists concerned themselves with such matters as the effects of various schedules of reinforcement (or satisfaction of motivation) upon learning, and the level of motivation necessary to facilitate the learning of tasks of varying complexity. Although a considerable technology developed concerning laboratory procedures for arousing and satisfying biological tissue needs, there was comparatively little study of the content of motivation because it was assumed that there was little more to be known.

But ever so slowly, the orthodoxy of the tissue-need view of motivation came under challenge. The challenge was not really forced by the theorizing and observations of personality and clinical psychologists, though they had certainly held a more complex view of motivation throughout the period under consideration. However intriguing views like that of Freud on dreams and unconscious motivation may have seemed in a general sense, motivation researchers saw little need to reconsider their position because they did not consider Freud's work to be empirically sound. Much more important in the challenge to orthodoxy were the research findings that could not be easily squared with beliefs concerning the importance and effects of biological needs. The latent learning studies (see Hilgard, 1956) suggested that it is possible to learn without any appreciable need for food or water. Other ingenious studies (e.g., Sheffield and Roby, 1950) showed that learning will occur under conditions of tissue-need arousal even though the experiments are designed so that no drive reduction can occur.

By themselves, these two research themes might have provoked the conclusion that motivation is irrelevant to learning, whatever importance it has in controlling performance. But another concurrent research theme, concerning exploratory and alternation behaviors (see Berlyne, 1960; Fiske and Maddi, 1961), revealed that organisms can be sufficiently preoccupied with gaining information about their environment to even pass up the opportunity to decrease their tissue needs. The implication of this is well drawn in the paper by Berlyne, namely, that there are other goals as important or perhaps even more important than the biological needs. A further shock to the tissue-need orthodoxy was the discovery by Olds and Milner (see their paper in this section) that brain stimulation per se is a potent reinforcer. Although arguments have been raised, in an attempt to preserve orthodoxy, to the effect that the brain centers involved are intimately associated with the food need, there is still no way around the fact that brain stimulation is rewarding, even if no actual tissue need exists.

The effect of the research themes mentioned above was to shatter orthodoxy and throw the study of motivation wide open. By now, so many different approaches and controversies compete for attention in motivation study that it is difficult to say anything clear and concrete about what is going on. But there are a few discernible trends that should be mentioned.

Needless to say, one basic change has taken the form of studying the processes whereby various motives are acquired. If some motives are not genetically given, then they must be learned. Thus, to study how they are learned is to know more about the nature of motivation. This current emphasis on acquisition processes is well documented by the readings in this section, especially the work of Miller and of Bandura, Ross, and Ross.

Along with this emphasis on motivation as learned and the concomittant concern with acquisition processes, there has grown a new interest in studying just what it is that constitutes the content of motivation. If reciting a few biological tissue needs is inadequate, then it is only proper to inquire systematically into what an adequate list of needs would entail. To be sure, there might be general agreement, now that the restricting orthodoxy of tissue-need views has been broken, that some particular learned needs are important without an empirical justification being provided. So, Miller's concern with *fear-avoidance* as a kind of cognitive counterpart to the avoidance of pain, and Bandura's implied reliance on *imitation* as a need, do not in themselves seem to need much justification. But it is not at all clear that if psychologists were to enumerate learned needs, they would spontaneously agree. Because of that, the current emphasis on empirical exploration of the content of motivation is scientifically understandable. In such exploration, theoretical views on motivation having some claim to comprehensiveness have played an important stimulating role. Of all such views, Murray's (1938) extensive list of needs stemming from the requirements of the viscera, society, and the psyche (so-called viscerogenic, sociogenic, and psychogenic needs) appears to have been the most useful. The present research literature abounds with studies of needs that he first described. Among these are the needs for *achievement* (e.g., McClelland, Atkinson, Clark, and Lowell, 1953), *affiliation* (e.g., Schachter, 1959), *power* (e.g., Veroff, 1958), *variety* (e.g., Maddi, 1968), *approval* (e.g., Crowne and Marlowe, 1964), *dependency* (e.g., Sears, 1963), and *knowledge* (e.g., Berlyne, 1960, 1963). Also of importance as a stimulant have been such general theoretical distinctions as that between approach and avoidance motivation (McClelland, 1951), deprivation and growth motivation (Maslow, 1955), primary and secondary motivation (Brown, 1953), proactive and reactive motivation (Allport, 1955), general and specific motivation (Maddi, 1969), and conscious and unconscious motivation (Freud, see paper in this section).

Methodological Emphases

In trying to communicate something of the flavor of this contemporary concern with the content of motivation, it will be useful to focus initially upon several methodological emphases apparent in the research. One is an increase in the frequency with which the subjects of motivational studies are human rather than subhuman. This is not to say that lower animals are no longer used, but rather that humans are more frequently used than before. The shift is an understandable one, since focus upon the content and acquisition of motives has been forced by findings indicating the restricted, partial nature of tissue-need views. Once you suspect that an adequate understanding of motivation involves study not only of viscerogenic, but also of sociogenic and psychogenic needs, you inevitably tend to seek out human beings to study.

The other methodological shift involves an increase in correlational research designs, whereas experimental designs had been almost invariable before. This shift does not represent a degeneration of research acumen on the part of motivationists so much as a change in the kind of question being asked. When the content of, or goals comprising, motivation could be assumed—and one was primarily concerned with the effects of motivation on various other behaviors, such as learning—the experimental approach was quite appropriate. One could vary one motive or another in a fairly precise fashion and note its effects on tasks having particular, defined properties. Even when the new emphasis on determining the nature of motivation takes the form of studying the acquisition of motives (as in many of the papers included here), the experimental design can be useful. Once again, this is because the relevance and existence of the learned motive under consideration is assumed, as in the papers by Miller and Bandura.

But when the new emphasis in motivation research takes the form of exploring the actual content of motivation, the experimental design is not especially useful and, indeed, may be restrictive. To determine what kinds of motives exist in organisms, one needs a research procedure that approaches naturalistic observation of a wide range of behaviors without any attempt to manipulate the organism so as to produce certain states and behaviors. The correlational approach is especially useful for determining how a wide range of responses given by the same organism relate to each other, and is hence a very appropriate procedure for exploring the content of motivation. When more has been learned about the major social and psychological goals of organisms, it will be time then to return to experimental designs, the better to determine precisely what role various intensities of these motives play in the determinination of behavior.

In general, the form of correlational study that is employed falls under what might be considered construct validation (Cronbach and Meehl, 1955; Campbell and Fiske, 1959). Briefly, the experimenter postulates some motivational construct, the empirical value of which he is unsure about, and proceeds to develop theoretically reasonable ways of measuring the construct. Once measures have been devised, they are correlated with a variety of behaviors that are expected on definite theoretical grounds to be related to the measures (convergent validation) or independent of them (discriminant validation). To the degree that the emerging pattern of correlations conforms to theoretical expectation, the construct and its measures are considered validated. As can be seen, although this procedure is called construct validation, it really has little to do with the development of tests in any usual sense.

Substantive Emphases

Achievement motive

With this methodological introduction to the form of much contemporary motivational study, it is possible to consider some actual research themes. Perhaps the most important, and certainly the most comprehensive, of these themes involves the *achievement motive*. Over the last 20 to 25 years McClelland and his associates have developed measures of this motive and investigated the correlates of these measures not only in individual behavior but in social systems as well. The major measure of the motive involves analyzing the content of thematic productions of the human imagination (e.g., stories, speeches, dreams) for evidence of competition with a standard of excellence.

On the level of individual behavior it has been found (McClelland, Atkinson, Clark, and Lowell, 1953; Atkinson, 1958) that people scoring high in achievement motivation, by comparison with those who score low, (1) worry about unfinished tasks while accepting or even forgetting completed ones, (2) are more active in college and community activities, (3) choose experts over friends when asked whom they want as partners to work on difficult problems, and (4) are more resistant to social pressure to conform. Studies have also been done concerning the effects of achievement orientation on the actual quality of work. As might be expected, people high in achievement motive work harder and perform better than those who are low when the task at hand is such that one can actually effect the outcome through the skill of one's own efforts. If the task is routine or its outcome determined by chance alone, then people high in achievement motive are uninterested and actually do worse than people who are low. All these research results point toward the conclusion that, at the level of individual behavior, people high in achievement motivation tend to be work oriented, self-reliant, confident, and competitive.

McClelland (1961) has also done research concerning the effects of achievement orientation on social systems. In a truly grand and ingenious study, he determined the average level of achievement motivation reflected in the content of the children's readers in use in the school systems of a number of different countries in 1925 and in 1950. He then studied the relationship between these two achievement-motive figures for each country and the amount of economic growth taking place in that country between 1925 and 1950. Using two separate measures of economic growth, McClelland showed that the higher the achievement motive in a country in 1925, the greater its economic growth between 1925 and 1950. But rate of economic growth showed no relationship with level of achievement motivation in 1950. What these results demonstrate is that the general level of achievement motive characterizing a society will be one of the causal factors in its subsequent economic growth. Once you accept the previously mentioned results concerning the effects of an achievement motive on individual behavior, the results concerning economic development are not really surprising, though they are certainly dramatic. Apparently, the harder a society strives to educate people to be work oriented, self-reliant, confident, and competitive, the greater will be the economic gain to the society as a whole.

Finally, there has also been correlational study of the acquisition of the achievement motive (see Atkinson, 1958) which indicates that the parents of people high in this motive required independence and problem-solving ability of their children at an early age. The mother was typically warm, nurturant, and encouraging in this attempt to build independence, not punitive and impatient. The father, though distant, was capable and an object of admiration. Recently, McClelland and Winter (1969) have reported the results of an attempt to increase the achievement motivation of businessmen in under-developed societies through employing the insights learned in the correlational studies. A training program was devised that involves classroom teaching in the nature and tactics of achievement as well as practice sessions in fantasizing about achievement as a preparation for related actions. After participating in this training program, businessmen do seem to make more money and land higher-level jobs. In addition, they seem to be happier and more self-confident.

Affiliation, power, and variety motives

There are research themes concerning other motives that more or less follow the construct validation plan undertaken by McClelland, though none are as comprehensive in covering the acquisition, individual effects, and social effects of a motive. Scoring systems for thematic productions are available for the *needs for affiliation, power,* and *sex* (see Atkinson, 1958), and even for the *need for variety* (Maddi, Propst, and Feldinger, 1965).

There are a few correlational studies that suggest the construct validity of the need for affiliation measure. Atkinson and Walker (1958) showed that people high in need for affiliation tend to seek approval and to be especially sensitive to faces when they are presented along with other stimuli in a perceptual task. Also, McClelland, Sturr, Knapp, and Wendt (1958) report that people high in need for affiliation are generally considered likely to succeed by their peers. That this reflects the strong interpersonal commitment of these people is suggested by French's (1956) evidence that they choose friends over experts to work with them on a performance task, even though skill is important in completing the task with the greatest reward.

In the attempt to assess the need for variety in thematic productions, three separate measures emerged, called *novelty of productions, curiosity,* and *desire for novelty* (see Maddi, 1968). As one might expect, these measures relate differently to each other and to aspects of behavior indicative of creativity and exploratory behavior (Maddi and Berne, 1964; Maddi *et al.,* 1965; Maddi and Andrews, 1966). Novelty of productions and desire for novelty appear to be active and passive forms of the need for variety, respectively. Unexpectedly, the curiosity measure appears to reflect the attempt to avoid variety in favor of structure, regularity, and certainty (Maddi, 1968).

Anxiety

There is by now voluminous research literature on anxiety which assumes that the avoidance of distress, discomfort, tension is a potent motivation. The bulk of the studies have employed the Manifest Anxiety Scale (Taylor, 1953) as a measure of the person's propensity to experience anxiety, though several other questionnaires have also been used (e.g., Mandler and Sarason, 1952; Endler, Hunt, and Rosenstein, 1962). Unfortunately, the research literature on anxiety is plagued by inconsistent results, though this has apparently only spurred psychologists to greater efforts. On the question of whether high anxiety facilitates learning in simple tasks but disrupts it in complex tasks, some studies are affirmative but some are negative (see Jessor and Hammond, 1957; Spence, 1964; Spence and Spence, 1966; Spielberger, 1966). Spence and Spence (1966) contend that the negative studies are in the minority and that they indicate the heretofore unrecognized importance of the subject's sex. Another interpretation is offered by Sarason (1959), who believes that some studies of simple and complex learning failed to yield the expected results because the response to be learned was nondefensive rather than, as is typical of the studies with positive results, a protective response to stress.

Another general prediction concerning anxiety is that it ought to show a positive relationship to physiological indices of emotionality or drive level. Although it must be said that this expectation has been researched neither fully nor with great sophistication, the available findings are generally negative (see Jessor and Hammond, 1957). Closely related to this prediction is one that highly anxious people should be more disrupted in their functioning by personal threat or stress than low-anxious people. Although some investigators (see Jessor and Hammond, 1957; Spence, 1964; Spence and Spence, 1966; Spielberger, 1966) have not been able to support this expectation, it has generally found more support than that concerning physiological correlates.

The studies on vulnerability to stress suggest that the highly anxious person is generally insecure, self-depreciatory, and lacking in self-confidence. Indeed, many studies (e.g., Cowen, Heilizer, Axelrod, and Sheldon, 1957; Doris and Sarason, 1955; Trapp and Kausler, 1958) have disclosed high-anxiety subjects to be self-preoccupied, and generally less content with themselves than low-anxiety subjects. Similar in emphasis are findings (e.g., Brackbill and Little, 1954; Eriksen and Davids, 1955) indicating a close link between the Manifest Anxiety Scale and ruminative, obsessive, compulsive symptomatology.

Although the research literature on anxiety is fraught with inconsistencies, it does appear safe to conclude that questionnaire measures of this motivational tendency correlate with other indications of insecurity and self-deprecation. One specific form of this relationship is especially interesting, in that it relates anxiety avoidance to other motives. Anxiety measures especially constructed to reveal fearfulness in testing situations show a consistently negative relationship to tests of intelligence (e.g., Mandler and Cowen, 1958; Sarason and Mandler, 1952; Sarason, 1959). It is hardly surprising that people reporting great anxiety specifically in situations when they are being evaluated would turn out to have relatively low scores on measures of intelligence. After all, the latter are constructed of items on which the subject must either be right or wrong. What is intriguing is that Atkinson (1957, 1960) has interpreted test anxiety scales to be measuring a motivational tendency that he calls *fear of failure,* in contrast to the presumably more positive *need for achievement* discussed earlier. Following McClelland's distinction (1951), Atkinson considers the need for achievement to be an approach motive, in that it refers to a disposition to derive satisfaction from successful exercise of skill, and the fear of failure to be an avoidance motive, in that it refers to an independent disposition to experience shame, humiliation, and embarrassment as a concomitant of failure. Consistent with this distinction is a study of risk taking (Atkinson and Litwin, 1960), in which subjects high in need for achievement preferred moderate risks, whereas those high in test anxiety preferred either low or high risks.

Need for approval

The intense contemporary interest in the motivation to present oneself in a socially desirable way grew out of the psychometrician's concern to ensure the purity of his personality tests. Whenever you employ questionnaires, it is likely that the subject's apprehensiveness concerning whether he will meet approval will interfere with the frankness of his responses. There are elaborate procedures whereby the need for approval can be minimized on questionnaires, but these need not concern us here. What is relevant is the blossoming motivational literature on the need for approval that gained impetus as a result of this practical test-maker's problem.

The two major measures of this motive are questionnaires, both called Social Desirability Scales, devised by Edwards (1957) and Crowne and Marlowe (1960). The latter authors believe their scale to be superior because it appears not to correlate with measures of psychopathology, as does that of Edwards. In any event, Crowne and Marlowe (1964) have reported the findings of an extensive research program aiming to determine the construct validity of the need for approval. To summarize, they found that people who were high, as compared to low, on their Social Desirability Scale show greater attitude change after delivering an appeal for an attitude they did not originally endorse (thereby resolving cognitive dissonance), express higher need for affiliation, and terminate psychotherapy sooner. In addition, the higher the Social Desirability score, the greater the tendency to give common word associations, and fewer, more concrete responses on projective tests of personality. In their fantasy production subjects high in the need for approval are especially rejecting of people, but tend to underestimate the extent to which their friends reject them.

There is also a group of findings concerning socially desirable responding and performance on simple, laboratory tasks. Subjects high in socially desirable responding generally perform better on the pursuit rotor (Strickland and Jenkins, 1964), a motor steadiness task (Strickland, 1965), and other simple motor tasks (Willington and Strickland, 1965). Although the results may indicate superior motor ability in these subjects, it seems more likely that we are observing the heightened attentiveness produced by a wish to appear socially desirable. Consistent with this interpretation is the finding (Crowne and Marlowe, 1964) that subjects high in socially desirable responding are less likely to rate a monotonous spool-packing task as dull.

In general, the picture emerging indicates that people high in socially desirable responding have intense interest in appearing attentive, consistent, competent, and acceptable in the context of conformity, superficial interest in but lack of deep commitment to others, and general unwillingness to face these facts. The implications of defensiveness are supported by Conn and Crowne (1964) who found that subjects high in socially desirable responding selected euphoria as an alternative to the expression of anger in a manner suggestive of reaction formation. Similarly, Fishman (1965) found that subjects high in socially desirable responding expressed less verbal aggression toward the experimenter when he imposed nonarbitrary frustration (whereas arbitrary frustration did not differentiate subjects high and low in socially desirable responding). Apparently, the person high in socially desirable responding can only express anger when he can give himself justification (or rationalization) for it.

Concluding Remarks

Even in the work that has been summarized here, it is apparent that more questions have arisen than were answered. And there are several other research themes that, if included, deepen rather than mitigate this impression. Motivational study is clearly in an exploratory stage, which, however amorphous and chaotic it may appear, should entrance the scientific adventurer. If we throw ourselves vigorously into the task of exploring, we are bound to generate a myriad of findings that will eventually overlap. When research themes overlap, regardless of whether the overlap was predicted, there is much to be learned.

Indeed, there is some intriguing overlap in the themes summarized above. The opposite pattern of correlates shown by measures of the need for achievement and test anxiety suggest that these measures are reflecting approach and avoidance motivations in the achievement area. Thus, it is possible to conceive of a need for achievement, in the sense of a positive effort after success and experience of challenge, and a fear of failure, in the sense of dread that one might not be found effective in competitive pursuits.

It is tempting to speculate on the existence of approach and avoidance motives in each area of endeavor, not only that concerned with achievement. Perhaps the need for approval, with its emphasis on presenting oneself in terms acceptable to others, is the avoidance form of motivation for social interaction. The need for affiliation might qualify as the approach motive in this area, with its connotations being that of enjoyment of and interest in intimacy with other people. Unfortunately, the research literature on need for affiliation is not far enough along to permit empirical assessment of this possibility.

For that matter, the research theme concerning variety motivation also suggests the existence of approach and avoidance tendencies. Quite unexpectedly, Maddi and his associates discovered what appears to be an active tendency to pursue and create variety (their novelty of productions measure) and an opposing tendency to decrease uncertainty and increase structure (their curiosity measure). From the differing patterns of correlations, the former tendency would seem to be an approach motive (need for variety) and the latter an avoidance motive (fear of variety).

The value of distinctions such as that between approach and avoidance motives in the same area of endeavor is in tying together seemingly diverse trends in theorizing and research. Once such a distinction is successfully applied to an otherwise heterogeneous body of findings, one feels willing to speculate further regarding associated matters of interest. For example, one could easily theorize about the different acquisition processes for approach and avoidance versions of motives. And, although approach and avoidance motives in the same area might well lead to much overlap in behavior, there would very likely be some subtle but important differences as well.

REFERENCES

Allport, G. W. *Becoming: Basic considerations for a psychology of personality.* New Haven, Conn.: Yale University Press, 1955.

Atkinson, J. W. (Ed.), *Motives in fantasy, action, and society.* Princeton, N.J.: Van Nostrand, 1958.

Atkinson, J. W. Motivational determinants of risk-taking behavior. *Psychological Review,* 1957, **64,** 359–372.

Atkinson, J. W. Personality dynamics. In P. R. Farnsworth and Q. McNemar (Eds.), *Annual review of psychology.* Palo Alto, Calif.: Banta, 1960.

Atkinson, J. W., & Litwin, G. H. Achievement motive and test anxiety conceived as motive to approach success and motive to avoid failure. *Journal of Abnormal and Social Psychology,* 1960, **60,** 52–63.

Atkinson, J. W., & Walker, E. L. The affiliation motive and perceptual sensitivity to faces. In J. W. Atkinson (Ed.), *Motives in fantasy, action, and society.* Princeton, N.J.: Van Nostrand, 1958.

Berlyne, D. E. *Conflict, arousal, and curiosity.* New York: McGraw-Hill, 1960.

Berlyne, D. E. Motivational problems raised by exploratory and epistemic behavior. In S. Koch (Ed.), *Psychology: A study of a science.* Vol. 5. New York: McGraw-Hill, 1963.

Brown, J. S. Problems presented by the concept of acquired drives. In, *Nebraska symposium on motivation.* Lincoln, Neb.: University of Nebraska Press, 1953.

Brackbill, G., & Little, K. B. MMPI correlates of the Taylor scale of manifest anxiety. *Journal of Consulting Psychology,* 1954, **18,** 433–436.

Campbell, D. T., & Fiske, D. W. Convergent and discriminant validation by the multitrait-multimethod matrix. *Psychological Bulletin,* 1959, **56,** 81–105.

Conn, L. K., & Crowne, D. P. Instigation to aggression, emotional arousal, and defensive emulation. *Journal of Personality,* 1964, **32,** 163–179.

Cowen, E. L., Heilizer, F., Axelrod, H. S., & Sheldon, A. The correlates of manifest anxiety in perceptual reactivity, rigidity, and self-conflict. *Journal of Consulting Psychology,* 1957, **21,** 405–411.

Cronbach, L. J., & Meehl, P. E. Construct validity in psychological tests. *Psychological Bulletin,* 1955, **52,** 281–302.

Crowne, D. P., & Marlowe, D. A new scale of social desirability independent of psychopathology. *Journal of Consulting Psychology,* 1960, **24,** 349–54.

Crowne, D. P., & Marlowe, D. *The approval motive: Studies in evaluative dependence.* New York: Wiley, 1964.

Doris, J., & Sarason, S. B. Test anxiety and blame assignment in a failure situation. *Journal of Abnormal and Social Psychology,* 1955, **50,** 335–338.

Edwards, A. L. The social desirability variable in personality assessment and research. New York: Dryden, 1957.

Endler, N. S., Hunt, J. McV., & Rosenstein, A. J. An S-R inventory of anxiousness. *Psychological Monographs,* 1962, **76** (Whole no. 536), 33 p.

Eriksen, C. W., & Davids, A. The meaning and clinical validity of the Taylor anxiety scale and the hysteria-psychasthenia scales from the MMPI. *Journal of Abnormal and Social Psychology,* 1955, **50,** 135–137.

Fishman, C. G. Need for approval and the expression

of aggression under varying conditions of frustration. *Journal of Personality and Social Psychology*, 1965, **2**, 809–816.

Fiske, D. W., & Maddi, S. R. (Eds.), *Functions of varied experience*. Homewood, Ill.: Dorsey, 1961.

French, E. G. Motivation as a variable in work partner selection. *Journal of Abnormal and Social Psychology*, 1956, **50**, 232–236.

Hilgard, E. R. *Theories of learning*. (2nd ed.) New York: Appleton-Century-Crofts, 1956.

Jessor, R., & Hammond, K. R. Construct validity and the Taylor anxiety scale. *Psychological Bulletin*, 1957, **54**, 161–170.

Maddi, S. R. *Personality theories: A comparative analysis*. Homewood, Ill.: Dorsey, 1968.

Maddi, S. R. Themes in human motivation. In G. Reynolds (Ed.), *Experimental psychology*. Vol. I. Chicago: Scott, Foresman, 1969.

Maddi, S. R., & Andrews, S. The need for variety in fantasy and self-description. *Journal of Personality*, 1966, **34**, 610–625.

Maddi, S. R. & Berne, N. Novelty of productions and desire for novelty as active and passive forms of the need for variety. *Journal of Personality*, 1964, **32**, 270–277.

Maddi, S. R., Propst, B., & Feldinger, I. Three expressions of the need for variety. *Journal of Personality*, 1965, **33**, 82–98.

Mandler, G., & Cowen, J. E. Test anxiety questionnaires. *Journal of Consulting Psychology*, 1958, **22**, 228–229.

Mandler, G., & Sarason, S. B. A study of anxiety and learning. *Journal of Abnormal and Social Psychology*, 1952, **47**, 166–173.

Maslow, A. H. Deficiency motivation and growth motivation. In M. R. Jones, (Ed.) *Nebraska symposium on motivation*. Lincoln, Neb.: University of Nebraska Press, 1955.

McClelland, D. C. *Personality*. New York: Dryden, 1951.

McClelland, D. C. *The achieving society*. Princeton, N.J.: Van Nostrand, 1961.

McClelland, D. C., Atkinson, J. W., Clark, R. A., & Lowell, E. L. *The achievement motive*. New York: Appleton-Century-Crofts, 1953.

McClelland, D. C., Sturr, J. F., Knapp, R. H. & Wendt, H. W. Obligations to self and to society in the United States and Germany. *Journal of Abnormal and Social Psychology*, 1958, **56**, 245–255.

McClelland, D. C., & Winter, D. G. *Motivating economic achievement*. New York: Free Press, 1969.

Murray, H. A. *Explorations in personality: A clinical and experimental study of fifty men of college age*. New York: Oxford, 1938.

Sarason, I. G. Relationships of measures of anxiety and experimental instructions to word association test performance. *Journal of Abnormal and Social Psychology*, 1959, **59**, 37–42.

Sarason, S. B., & Mandler, G. Some correlates of text anxiety. *Journal of Abnormal and Social Psychology*, 1952, **47**, 810–817.

Schacter, S. *Psychology of affiliation*. Stanford, Calif.: Stanford University Press, 1959.

Sears, R. R. Dependency motivation. In M. R. Jones (Ed.), *Nebraska symposium on motivation*. Lincoln, Neb.: University of Nebraska Press, 1963.

Sheffield, F. D., & Roby, T. B. Reward value of a nonnutrient sweet taste. *Journal of Comparative and Physiological Psychology*, 1950, **43**, 471–481.

Spence, K. Anxiety (drive) level and performance in eyelid conditioning. *Psychological Bulletin*, 1964, **61**, 129–139.

Spence, K. W., & Spence, J. T. Sex and anxiety differences in eyelid conditioning. *Psychological Bulletin*, 1966, **65**, 137–142.

Spielberger, C. D. (Ed.) *Anxiety and behavior*. New York: Academic Press, 1966.

Strickland, B. R. Need approval and motor steadiness under positive and negative approval conditions. *Perceptual and Motor Skills*, 1965, **29**, 667–668.

Strickland, B. R., & Jenkins, O. Simple motor performance under positive and negative approval motivation. *Perceptual and Motor Skills*, 1964, **19**, 599–605.

Taylor, J. A. A personality scale of manifest anxiety. *Journal of Abnormal and Social Psychology*, 1953, **48**, 285–290.

Trapp, E. P., & Kausler, P. H. Test anxiety level and goal-setting behavior. *Journal of Consulting Psychology*, 1958, **22**, 31–34.

Veroff, J. A scoring manual for the power motive. In J. W. Atkinson (Ed.), *Motives in fantasy, action, and society*. Princeton, N.J.: Van Nostrand, 1958.

Willington, A. M., & Strickland, B. R. Need for approval and simple motor performance. *Perceptual and Motor Skills*, 1965, **21**, 879–884.

Part Seven

Personality, Adjustment, and Mental Health

Although the research interests of early psychologists such as Wundt and Ebbinghaus were largely academic, the need to study practical problems—those related to helping people improve their interpersonal relationships—quickly became apparent. Men such as Charcot, Breuer, Freud, and Binet were the pioneers who recognized that psychology must be expanded to help people make a more adequate adjustment to their environment and thus lead fuller, more productive lives.

From the beginnings of interest in the study of adjustment, one of the major problems has been in simply defining the term so that it is meaningful and useful when applied to a particular individual. The first two selections that follow represent two different approaches to the question, "What constitutes adequate adjustment?" The article by Wilson suggests that adjustment can be measured by the extent to which an individual reports his experiences in terms of positive statements. From this point of view, adequate adjustment would be assessed by the individual's overall feelings of whether he is "happy." In the second selection Taylor and Combs deal with the problem of defining adjustment in terms of the individual's ability to accept himself as he is. Here the basic assumption is that the individual who recognizes and is willing to admit that he has undesirable characteristics tends to be better adjusted, since his perceptions of himself are more reality-oriented and not overly distorted by defense mechanisms.

While the specific adjustive behavior of the individual is determined by his immediate experience, it is apparent that there are response predispositions which play a crucial role in determining which particular responses will be made. These tendencies to respond in a certain way—e.g., aggressively, fearfully, etc.—are usually consistent over a wide variety of situations, and because of them a particular experience may lead to maladjustment in one person but have little or no effect on another. These consistencies in mode of responding are usually termed the *personality* of the individual.

Research dealing with the topic of personality can be divided into two basically different areas of interest. The first concerns the origins or causes of personality, while the second involves the description and measurement of differences in personality. Regarding the first area, it is interesting to note that the early Greek physicians recognized personality differences and speculated that the origins were due primarily to physiological differences between individuals. According to their schema, the individual who was warm, happy, and optimistic was assumed to have a rich flow of blood and was termed *sanguine*. The bad-tempered, aggressive individual was assumed to have an excess of yellow bile and was termed *choleric*. The *phlegmatic* person was very slow and plodding due to an excess of phlegm, while the *melancholy* person had an excess of black bile which made him moody and generally depressed.

Current research has centered almost entirely on the assumption that personality is learned as a result of prior experiences. While it is recognized that everyone's experiences are different, the principles involved in this learning—reinforcement, generalization, and extinction—suggest that the consistent response predispositions are those which have been consistently reinforced. It is important to note that in most speculation and study of personality formation, primary emphasis is placed on the period of childhood. Freud, for example, stressed the importance of various stages of development and described the ways in which experiences at specific stages determined personality characteristics which would be present for the remainder of the individual's life. Later research with lower organisms, most notably that done by Harlow (see Part 6), has also suggested that early experiences are indeed important.

The second general area of personality study is concerned with measuring and identifying presently existing personality differences. While nearly everyone tends to classify friends and acquaintances according to personality types—happy, morose, friendly, etc.— psychologists are concerned with being more precise and accurate in their evaluations. A number of researchers have attempted to identify the major dimensions of personality by means of a wide variety of tests. The main problems which have arisen in the field of personality testing are related not only to determining the reliability and validity of the actual tests but also to the question of who is qualified to administer such tests and interpret the results. In the third selection the originator of the Minnesota Multiphasic Personality Inventory (MMPI) discusses the purpose of this widely used test and also some of the misuses which have occurred in its use and interpretation by unqualified individuals. The fourth selection deals with a much different method of assessing personality characteristics, that of pupillometrics, which is based on measurable physiological events. The authors of this selection suggest that their technique of recording pupil reaction to various stimuli may offer exciting alternatives to the various subjectively scored projective tests.

Although tendencies to respond to environmental experiences may be relatively consistent, it is also apparent that personality characteristics can and do change as a result of new experiences. One of the techniques used to bring about personality modification and better adjustment is psychotherapy. Although the general goal of psychotherapy is to help the client cope more adequately with his environment, the theoretical orientations and techniques used by therapists vary widely. While this diversity and seeming chaos is viewed with alarm by many, others feel that such diversity represents a healthy trend where fact finding, comparison, and objective appraisal of the currently used techniques can be accomplished. This latter position is represented by Carl Rogers. There are, however, many psychologists who question the real worth of any type of psychotherapy and wonder whether it is, in fact, beneficial at all. They claim that the simple passage of time works an effective "cure" for most problems. The author of the sixth selection raises several questions regarding the real efficacy of psychotherapy and points out some of the problems that research into this area encounters.

While personality changes occur as a result of experiences, and perhaps as a result of psychotherapy, a relatively new technique for achieving behavior and personality change has come upon the scene with the advent of drugs. While it has been recognized for some time that a variety of drugs such as alcohol, tranquilizers, and stimulants can result in dramatic short-term changes in personality characteristics and social adjustment, the question of their permanent effects is still very much an unanswered one. Of recent interest to both the professional psychologist and the lay public is the problem of the use and misuse of the hallucinogenic drugs such as D-lysergic acid diethylamide, or LSD. In the seventh selection, Savage, Savage, Fadiman, and Harman discuss the use of LSD in therapy, reporting several instances where the benefits were considerable and apparently lasted well after the effects of the drugs had worn off. The other side of the picture, however, is presented by Cohen and Ditman in the next selection, where they report on cases in which the effects of the drug were again long lasting, but deleterious.

In the first eight selections several of the issues and questions surrounding research into the areas of personality and adjustment are discussed. As has been indicated, one of the major and recurring problems is defining and measuring these concepts so that they are meaningful. Much the same kind of problem exists when attempts are made to accurately describe maladjustment and personality disorder. In the final selection Adams raises the question of the accuracy of the term "mental illness" for describing patterns of behavior which are considered maladaptive by general psychological and social standards. The major question raised by Adams is whether health or illness in any biological sense is actually an issue, or whether the term really refers to inadequate interpersonal behavior.

51

Correlates of Avowed Happiness

Warner Wilson

Is Mr. John Jones well adjusted? Before this seemingly simple question can be answered, the various factors which constitute "good adjustment" must be established so that a meaningful evaluation of Mr. Jones can be made. Various researchers have proposed a wide variety of different definitions in attempting to establish what these factors are, definitions that range from the relatively simple, one-sentence variety to those which include long lists of specific criteria.

In the simplest definitions of adjustment the only criterion used is the overt behavior of the individual. Consequently, if his behavior generally conforms to societal norms— he holds a job, does not beat his wife, etc.—then he is considered to be adjusted. It is important to note that this type of definition does not take into account any factors relating to the individual's emotional state, feelings, attitudes, or future plans. All that is assumed is that if his behavior is not markedly deviant, then he is adjusted.

A second type of definition which does take the internal state of the individual into account is derived from a biological model which assumes that all organisms tend to preserve a state of internal consistency. At the biological level this is termed *homeostasis*. At the psychological level this is termed the *process of adjustment* and refers to the entire sequence of behavior which begins with the onset of the tension state and terminates with the attainment of a goal which reduces the tension. In the strictest sense this type of definition does not include a consideration of the source of the tension or the appropriateness of the behavior which achieved the tension reduction. An adjusted person is simply one who has learned modes of behaving which are effective in reducing tensions.

A third type of definition places primary emphasis on the source and type of tensions experienced by the individual. Earlier definitions of this kind tended to differentiate an adjusted from a maladjusted person in terms of the relative absence of negative emotional and tension states such as fears, anxiety, conflict, and guilt. A more recent extension of this definition tends to emphasize the positive aspects of good adjustment. With this type of definition, the important criteria include not only freedom from negative emotional states, but also the presence of feelings of well-being, self-satisfaction, and general happiness.

A final class of definition tends to emphasize not just the emotional experiences of the individual, but also the perceptions he has of himself. Thus, while the adjusted person may indeed be happier than a maladjusted one, the factor underlying his better adjustment is assumed to be his ability to see himself realistically and objectively, to accept his strengths and weaknesses, and to develop his abilities to their maximum potential.

The following selection presents an example of research relating to the third type of definition. In this article Wilson not only suggests some of the environmental factors which contribute to the emotional state called "happiness," but also discusses the basis for a relationship between avowed happiness and adjustment.

*   *   *   *   *   *

Most of the studies of happiness have used some type of direct, self-report, questionnaire-type measure; hence, it seems appropriate to consider them to be studies of avowed happiness.

From Psychological Bulletin, *Vol. 67:4 (1967), 294–306. Copyright 1967 by the American Psychological Association, and reproduced by permission.*

Correlates of Avowed Happiness

One of the most substantial early studies was conducted by Watson (1930). In addition to many other findings, he concluded that wealth and education of parents, intelligence, and school success were not related to happiness, and that good health, high job morale, a happy home, and good relationships with other people, including a spouse, were conducive to happiness. One or more subsequent studies confirm all of these points. Watson (1930) also reported estimates of others' estimates which were higher and less variable than self-estimates. Watson (1930) cited an even earlier study by Chassell (1928), which showed that enjoyment of social intercourse and freedom from hyperself-consciousness were associated with happiness to the extent indicated by coefficients of association (Q) of .43, .57, .72, or .74.

Another early study by Beckham (1929) involved only Negro subjects. Several professional groups were included, the largest being composed of students and laborers. When asked "Are you happy as a Negro?" the groups ranked as follows: physicians, 97 per cent; college students, 91 per cent; preachers, 77 per cent; teachers, 73 per cent; laborers, 61 per cent; lawyers, 40 per cent; musicians, 40 per cent; and housewives, 8 per cent. In general, those of higher socio-economic levels seemed to avow more happiness. Beckham's sample of housewives was by far the least happy group this writer has encountered. Beckham also asked his subjects "Is the Negro happy?" and "Should the Negro be happy?" The groups ranked very differently on the different questions. The first question, however, seems most analogous to avowed happiness as discussed in this paper.

*   *   *

Turning to somewhat more recent studies, one can note first the work of Barschak (1951) who was one of the few investigators to use samples from more than one country. The percentages of subjects reporting themselves as happy in England, Switzerland, the United States, Germany-Göettingen, and Germany-Berlin were, respectively, 82, 91, 84, 74, and 48. The most notable difference occurred between the Berlin sample and the others. Barschak (1951) speculated that the extensive bombing suffered by Berlin, but not by Göettingen, may have had something to do with the low avowed happiness of the Berlin group. Barschak (1951) also asked his subjects which things, persons, and events in their childhood caused them happiness or unhappiness. Groups avowing very comparable amounts of avowed happiness reported happy and unhappy memories in very different ratios. For example, the English reported happy and unhappy memories in a ratio of two to one and one to one in childhood and adolescence, while in the American sample the ratios were four to one and three to one.

*   *   *

Other fairly recent studies relate happiness to (a) youth (Kuhlen, 1948); (b) low IQ, number of leisure-time activities enjoyed, and time spent in leisure-time activities (Fellows, 1956); (c) optimism, warmth, emotional stability, self-insight, and sociability (Smith, 1961); (d) youth, education, and social participation (Phillips, 1966); (e) favorable self-descriptions (Laxer, 1964); and (f) religiosity (Wilson, 1965).

Most of the studies cited have been one-shot investigations bearing little relation to one another. Wilson (1960) attempted to replicate some aspects of several earlier studies. Part of the data discussed here depend on the sample of 329 reported in Wilson (1960). Other data, based on a sample of 100, have not been reported elsewhere. Findings replicated successfully showed happiness to be *unrelated* to wealth of parents, education of parents, IQ, and school success (Watson, 1930); and to be *related* to (a) health, good social relations, and good family relations (Watson, 1930; Wessman, 1956); (b) religiosity (Wessman, 1956); and (c) high self-ideal correspondence in males (Wessman and Ricks, 1959). . . .

*   *   *

The very recent developments in the study of avowed happiness have centered around the work of three groups of investigators: Wessman and Ricks; Gurin, Veroff, and Feld; and Bradburn and Caplovitz. Each of these investigators has done extensive work culminating in at least one book; and most, if not all, of them are engaged in ongoing efforts. It seems clear that their work will be a major impetus to other investigations in the near future.

Wessman (1956) summarized a great deal of data collected in certain public opinion surveys. One aspect of Wessman's summary pertained to avowals of happiness in different countries. In terms of the percentage avowing *unhappiness* the data yielded the following picture: Great Britain, 6 per cent; The Netherlands, 6 per cent; the United States, 9 per cent; Canada, 13 per cent; and France, 40 per cent. The populations of the different countries also offered different definitions of what constitutes happiness. A second aspect of Wessman's summary concerned far more extensive data pertaining to the United States only. The distribution of responses for the total sample indicated the following percentages: very happy, 46 per cent; fairly happy, 45 per cent; not very happy, 7 per cent; not at all happy, 1 per cent; and don't know and no answer, 1 per cent. The data also indicated the relationship between avowed happiness and many other factors. Because of the large size of the sample, the relationships reported are highly reliable; however, the degree of relationship was not computed, possibly because most of the variables were measured in terms of only a few categories. A number of background factors related to happiness were youth, health, high school or college education, Caucasian versus Negro racial extraction, and upper- or middle- versus lower-class status. Women in this sample showed a greater tendency to use the extremes of the rating scale, the "very happy" and "not at all happy" categories.

Several items pertaining to adjustment in major life areas showed a relationship with avowed happiness: being married, getting along with one's family, being satisfied with one's job, and, in the case of housewives, getting a great deal of satisfaction out of housework. Single persons were happier than widowed or divorced persons. The great majority of persons thought that married people are happier than single people; those who thought that single people are happier, or that it makes no difference, avowed less happiness themselves. The majority of married people said they were happier married than they were when single; those who were happier when single were avowedly less happy in general.

Several aspects of social relationships seemed to be important: liking one's community, being satisfied with one's friends, making friends easily, and not caring too much about what other people think.

Various aspects of religious life were also shown to be significantly related to avowed happiness: attending church regularly, getting much consolation and help from religion, and being a believer. No notable differences were obtained between the three major religious groups—Catholics, Protestants, and Jews.

Wessman (1956) concluded that family, social, and job adjustments are variables of major importance; that persons who are satisfied with two or three areas seem happier than those satisfied with only one area; and that of the three, family relationships seem to be by far the most impor-

tant, with job satisfaction next, and social adjustment third.

The other data reported by Wessman and Ricks came mainly from 17 Harvard and 14 Radcliffe students. An outstanding feature of these data is the duration and depth of the measures obtained. The subjects rated themselves on an elation-depression scale every night for 6 weeks, making possible mean daily high, low, and average scores as well as several measures of mood variability. Wessman and Ricks also obtained unusually extensive clinical data on their subjects, especially the males. . . .

* * *

Granted the wealth of data Wessman and Ricks had on each of their male subjects, it seems worthwhile to summarize their overall characterization of the happy and unhappy male student. The happy student, in contrast to the unhappy student, was said to be a well-adjusted social extrovert, optimistic, high in self-esteem, confident of being able to achieve his aspirations, successful, able to find satisfaction in work and in interpersonal relations, high in ego strength and sense of identity, future-oriented, accustomed to success in encounters with the environment from an early age, and from a warm, supportive home where he was able to identify with respected and approachable role models.

Data reported by Gurin, Veroff, and Feld (1960) came from a representative sample of 2,460 adults. These investigators established a number of relationships, but they did not report estimates of degree of relationship. Happy people worried less, mentioned more sources of happiness and fewer sources of unhappiness, more often mentioned marriage and family as sources of happiness, expressed more optimism about being happy in the future, were younger, had more income, were more often married, and were better educated. Men and women were similar in their avowals of happiness.

* * *

This paper views the studies of marital happiness as a separate literature; however, it is of interest to note that in the Veroff, Feld, and Gurin (1962) study, marital happiness correlated more highly with general avowed happiness than did any one of the several other indices of subjective adjustment. Also of interest is the recent study by Knupfer, Clark, and Room (1966) which summarized several studies relating marriage to happiness. This study discussed, in particular, the consistent finding that marriage is more strongly related to happiness in men than in women.

The data reported by Bradburn (1963) and by Bradburn and Caplovitz (1965) were based on 393 interviews and 1,613 questionnaires. The sample included 450 households from each of four communities differing widely in economic well-being. Bradburn and Caplovitz (1965), like Gurin et al. (1960), found happiness to be related to youth, freedom from worry, income, education, and being married, and to be unrelated to sex. Bradburn and Caplovitz (1965) noted, however, that the usual positive relationship between education and happiness was reversed in the high income groups; that is, those with *poor* educations and large incomes were happier than those with *good* educations and large incomes, possibly because those with poor education were exceeding their initial aspirations. They also noted that in the poorly educated high-income group, age was positively, rather than negatively, related to happiness. They also reported that the happy were less anxious, had better job adjustment, experienced less marital tension, and joined more organizations. Bradburn and Caplovitz (1965) also discussed the effects of economic depression and national crises on psychological well-being.

*   *   *

Discussion of General Aspects of the Findings

Theoretical contributions

Dodge (1930) commented that the theory of the happy life has remained at about the level where the Greek philosophers left it. This statement is still essentially correct. A few efforts of theoretical interest can, however, be noted. Wilson (1960) attempted a tentative theoretical formulation which can be reduced to two postulates. The first postulate states that the prompt satisfaction of needs causes happiness, while the persistence of unfulfilled needs causes unhappiness. Wilson (1960) suggested three types of needs: (a) recurrent physiological needs corresponding to the needs stressed by tension-reduction theorists; (b) sensory or pleasure-seeking needs, such as those stressed by theorists who view man as a creature who actively seeks stimulation, pleasure, and action; and (c) acquired or secondary needs, including needs for affection, acceptance, popularity, status, achievement, and self-actualization. The second postulate states that the degree of fulfillment required to produce satisfaction depends on adaption or aspiration level,

which is influenced by past experience, comparisons with others, personal values, and other factors. High aspiration is therefore seen as a major threat to happiness.

*   *   *

Bradburn and Caplovitz (1965) tentatively drew several other conclusions of theoretical importance: (a) happiness involves two dimensions composed of positive and negative feelings; (b) positive and negative feelings are unrelated; and (c) the relative number of positive and negative feelings determines happiness. These ideas are intriguing and well worth further investigation. The evidence presented by Bradburn and Caplovitz (1965) is, however, not completely convincing.

*   *   *

Also of potential theoretical interest are some comments on the relation between happiness and worry made by Gurin et al. (1960) and by Bradburn and Caplovitz (1965). Not surprisingly, worry and unhappiness were correlated. The more interesting fact is that they are not the same thing. Gurin et al. (1960) reported that the higher socio-economic groups, although happier, had greater feelings of social inadequacy, more problems, and more worries. They interpreted worry as indicative of active involvement with the environment and unhappiness as involving apathy. Bradburn and Caplovitz (1965) attempted to resolve the apparent paradox of high worry among certain happy groups in terms of their view of happiness as depending on positive and negative feelings. They suggested that persons of high socio-economic status, for example, tend to have a higher degree of affectivity, that is, in a sense, more feelings. As a result, they may have a balance of positive and negative feelings conducive to happiness even though the total number of negative feelings, including worries, may be great.

Happiness and other approaches to adjustment

A happiness scale contrasts with many adjustment measures in that it clearly implies a positive as well as a negative pole. Studies of happiness, therefore, can meaningfully be related to the several other studies that have involved a deliberate attempt to explore the positive end of the adjustment continuum. . . . This review, however, is limited to studies based on self-ratings of avowed happiness or very similar measures.

Investigators of avowed happiness should, of

course, ask themselves if they are measuring something not already measured by existing adjustment inventories—for example, is happiness equivalent to the absence of depression, anxiety, or neurosis? The numerous adjustment measures available do not correlate well with each other. . . . As a result, it is not possible to tell which, if any, of these measures corresponds to happiness.

Another objection to many traditional adjustment measures is not that they fail to measure happiness but that they succeed in measuring other things as well. O'Conner and his associates have illustrated this point in regard to the *MA* scale and the MMPI *D* scale (O'Conner, Lore, and Stafford, 1956; O'Conner, Stefic, and Gresock, 1957). Factor analyses reported by these investigators showed five factors in the case of both the anxiety and depression measures. Wessman and Ricks (1959) reported a correlation of .81 between mood and *D*-scale scores. This fact suggests that the MMPI offers an adequate, though tedious, way to obtain an *estimate* of happiness. On the other hand, if one is interested in *correlates* of happiness, he would have to expect that the *D* scale, due to its factorial complexity, would correlate with many things *not* related to happiness. This same pitfall, of course, lies in wait for anyone who attempts to interpret such instruments as the *MA* or *D* scale as though they measured some *one* variable of theoretical interest.

Advantages of a simple self-rating over many adjustment measures would seem to be that it will (*a*) include less irrelevant factorial complexity, (*b*) be easier to obtain, and (*c*) have at least face validity as a measure of avowed happiness.

Happiness and intelligence and socio-economic status

The data show quite definitely that in spite of numerous lay theories to the contrary, happiness and IQ are not related to an appreciable degree, at least in the student populations studied. The most extensive studies found no relationship (Hartmann, 1934; Watson, 1930; Wilson, 1960). Fellows (1956) reported that the intelligent are less happy; Jasper (1930) and Washburne (1941) reported just the opposite. Several studies (Beckham, 1929; Bradburn and Caplovitz, 1965; Gurin *et al.*, 1960; Inkeles, 1960; Wessman, 1956) showed, however, that those of a lower socio-economic level avow less happiness. Since relatively low IQ is a characteristic of low economic status, these investigations suggest that intellectual capability may be important when it is low enough to prevent economic

success. Those with high IQ, in any case, do not seem to suffer from any special mental distress.

Happiness and social adjustment

Perhaps the most impressive single finding lies in the relation between happiness and successful involvement with people. This trend occurred in many studies (e.g., Gurin *et al.*, 1960; Phillips, 1966; Veroff *et al.*, 1962; Watson, 1930; Wessman, 1956; Wilson, 1960).

Happiness and personality and values

It is only natural that tests of personality adjustment should correlate with happiness, although sometimes these correlations are surprisingly low, for example, −.26 with neurotic tendency (Hartmann, 1934), .15 with emotional stability (Wessman and Ricks, 1959), −.44 with anxiety (Wilson, 1960), and −.19 with worry (Gurin *et al.*, 1960). Correlations with values and with personality traits are even lower. Hartmann (1934) found no highly significant correlations with any of the variables measured by the Allport-Vernon Scale of Values; Wessman and Ricks (1959) found few highly significant correlations, even though they investigated a large number of personality variables; Wilson (1960) found no highly significant correlations between happiness and preference for various ways of life.

Happiness and environment and health

The effects of an unfavorable environment have not been investigated directly; however, a low economic status, which may imply a poor environment, has been found to be associated with unhappiness (Beckham, 1929; Bradburn and Caplovitz, 1965; Gurin *et al.*, 1960; Inkeles, 1960; Wessman, 1956). Materialistic luxury and good treatment, as implied by the wealth and education of one's parents, show no relationship to the avowed happiness of students (Watson, 1930; Wilson, 1960). Health, on the other hand, does show a relationship to happiness, even in populations that are probably quite healthy on the average (Veroff *et al.*, 1962; Watson, 1930; Wilson, 1960).

Suggestions for Further Research

1. Comparability of results might be increased if all investigators used the same measure. The designations "very happy," "pretty happy," and

"not too happy" used by Gurin *et al.* (1960) and by Bradburn and Caplovitz (1965) seem as good as any. It is necessary to define the negative end of the scale with a mild designation like "not too happy" to avoid extremely skewed distributions.

2. Seemingly little would be lost and much gained if the above designations were used to define a nine-point, rather than a three-point, scale, and if correlations, rather than tables of percentages, were reported. Correlations seem to require less space for summarization, provide a better indication of degree of relationship, and allow for a quick and easy test of significance.

3. Further studies merely correlating happiness with numerous other variables are not recommended.

4. Studies are recommended that test theoretical expectations about the likely relationship between happiness and other specific variables.

5. Validation of happiness scales and the development of indirect, nonfakable measures are obvious unfinished business.

6. Investigators might achieve greater power by selecting a "happy" or positively adjusted comparison group on the basis of more than one criterion.

7. Studies involving direct attempts to manipulate the well-being of individuals are most desirable. For example, it seems peculiar that avowed happiness as such has not been studied in relation to the effect of psychotherapy. It is not inconceivable that other manipulations could be attempted that might noticeably influence happiness. A story is told (Guthrie, 1938; cited by Krech, Crutchfield, and Ballachey, 1962) of how a small group of college men increased the poise and popularity, and presumably the happiness, of a female student by going out of their way to respond to her as though she were attractive. The possibility of systematically developing and applying such principles and techniques seems exciting indeed!

REFERENCES

Barschak, E. A study of happiness and unhappiness in the childhood and adolescence of girls in different cultures. *Journal of Psychology*, 1951, **32**, 173–215.

Beckham, A. S. Is the Negro happy? *Journal of Abnormal and Social Psychology*, 1929, **24**, 186–190.

Bradburn, N. M. In pursuit of happiness. Report No. 92, 1963, National Opinion Research Center of the University of Chicago.

Bradburn, N. M., & Caplovitz, D. *Reports on happiness.* Chicago: Aldine, 1965.

Chassell, J. O. *The experience variables: A study of the variable factors in experience contributing to the formation of personality.* Rochester, N.Y.: Author, 1928. Cited by G. B. Watson, 1930. P. 101.

Dodge, R. Autobiography. In C. Murchison (Ed.), *A history of psychology in autobiography.* Vol. 1. Worcester: Clark University Press, 1930. Pp. 99–121.

Fellows, E. W. A study of factors related to happiness. *Journal of Educational Research*, 1956, **50**, 231–234.

Gurin, G., Veroff, J., & Feld, S. *Americans view their mental health.* Ann Arbor: University of Michigan, Survey Research Center, 1960.

Guthrie, E. R. *The psychology of human conflict.* New York: Harper & Row 1938. Cited by D. Krech, R. S. Crutchfield, & E. L. Ballachey, 1962. P. 128.

Hartmann, G. W. Personality traits associated with variations in happiness. *Journal of Abnormal and Social Psychology*, 1934, **29**, 202–212.

Inkeles, A. Industrial man: The relation of status to experience, perception, and value. *American Journal of Sociology*, 1960, **66**, 1–31.

Jasper, H. H. The measurement of depression-elation and its relation to a measure of extroversion-introversion. *Journal of Abnormal and Social Psychology*, 1930, **25**, 307–318.

Krech, D., Crutchfield, R. S., & Ballachey, E. L. *Individual in society: A textbook of social psychology.* New York: McGraw-Hill, 1962.

Kuhlen, R. G. Age trends in adjustment during the adult years as reflected in happiness ratings. *American Psychologist*, 1948, **3**, 307. (Abstract)

Knupfer, G., Clark, W., & Room, R. The mental health of the unmarried. *American Journal of Psychiatry*, 1966, **122**, 841–851.

Laxer, R. M. Relation of real self-rating to mood and blame, and their interaction in depression. *Journal of Consulting Psychology*, 1964, **28**, 538–546.

O'Conner, J. P., Lorr, M., & Stafford, J. W. Some patterns of manifest anxiety. *Journal of Clinical Psychology*, 1956, **12**, 160–163.

O'Conner, J. P., Stefic, E. C., & Gresock, C. J. Some patterns of depression. *Journal of Clinical Psychology*, 1957, **13**, 122–125.

Phillips, D. L. Social participation and happiness. Unpublished, Dartmouth College, 1966.

Sailer, R. C. Happiness self-estimates of young men. *Teachers College Contribution to Education*, 1931, No. 467.

Smith, H. C. *Personality adjustment.* New York: McGraw-Hill, 1961.

Veroff, J., Field, S., & Gurin, G. Dimensions of subjective adjustment. *Journal of Abnormal and Social Psychology*, 1962, **64**, 192–205.

Washburne, J. N. Factors related to the social adjustment of college girls. *Journal of Social Psychology*, 1941, **13**, 281–289.

Watson, G. B. Happiness among adult students of education. *Journal of Educational Psychology*, 1930, **21**, 79–109.

Wessman, A. E. A psychological inquiry into satisfaction and happiness. Unpublished doctoral dissertation, Princeton University, 1956.

Wessman, A. E., & Ricks, D. F. Temporal covariation of affective states in male and female subjects. Paper read at American Psychological Association, Cincinnati, 1959.

Wilson, W. R. An attempt to determine some correlates and dimensions of hedonic tone. Unpublished doctoral dissertation, Northwestern University, 1960.

Wilson, W. R. Relation of sexual behaviors, values, and conflicts to avowed happiness. *Psychological Reports*, 1965, **17**, 371–378.

52

Self-Acceptance and Adjustment

Charles Taylor and Arthur W. Combs

A second approach to the question of what constitutes adequate adjustment has been proposed by theorists such as Carl Rogers who suggest that adjustment is determined in large part by the perceptions an individual has about himself. Inherent in this approach is the notion that one's perceptions of himself may or may not reflect the reality of the situation. For example, an individual who actually is reasonably good-looking may perceive himself as being ugly and hence be afraid to interact with members of the opposite sex because he fears that they will reject him. On the other hand, a person who in reality is ugly or disfigured but perceives himself as physically attractive may be unable to understand why people reject him and hence resort to bizarre behavior which leads to even greater rejection.

In the following selection Taylor and Combs further speculate that the well-adjusted person is not only capable of perceiving reality accurately, but also is able to accept even those facts about himself which are potentially threatening. Stated in other terms, the adjusted person is one who is not unduly threatened by his perceptions and consequently does not feel compelled to engage in unusual behavior to defend himself against them.

In recent years a great deal of attention has been given to the interpretation of behavior in terms of self-theory. Rogers (1947), for example, has defined the well-adjusted individual as one able to accept all perceptions, including those about self, into his personality organization. He describes the situation as follows: "It would appear that when all of the ways in which the individual perceives himself—all perceptions of the qualities, abilities, impulses, and attitudes of the person, and all perceptions of himself in relation to others—are accepted into the organized conscious concept of the self, then this achievement is accompanied by feelings of comfort and freedom from tension which are experienced as psychological adjustment" (Rogers, 1947, p. 364). He points out that this relationship between self-acceptance and adjustment is a commonly observed phenomenon in client-centered therapy and seems to increase in the client as therapy progresses and adjustment improves.

Combs (1949) and Snygg and Combs (1949), adapting Rogers' definition to their phenomenological interpretation, have described the well-adjusted individual in terms of the adequacy of the self-organization. They define the adequate self as follows: "A phenomenal self is adequate in the degree to which it is capable of accepting into its organization any and all aspects of reality" (Snygg and Combs, 1949, p. 136). They point out that the individual who feels inadequate to deal with his perceptions of reality feels threatened by such perceptions and is likely to reject or distort them. The maladjusted person, in phenomenological terms, is characterized by many threatening perceptions, and his maladjusted behavior occurs largely as a result of his attempts to deal with the threats to which he feels himself subjected. In this sense a maladjusted person is synonymous with a threatened one.

Murphy (1947) and Lecky (1945) have taken similar positions with respect to the problem of adjustment. If the position taken by these authors is accurate, it should be possible to demonstrate a close relationship between self-acceptance and external measures of adjustment. This is the problem we have sought to investigate in this study.

The Rationale of This Experiment

In line with the theoretical positions outlined above, it seemed to us that, if those positions are

From Journal of Consulting Psychology, *Vol. 16 (1952)*, *89–91. Copyright 1952 by the American Psychological Association, and reproduced by permission.*

accurate, the well-adjusted individual ought to be better able to accept more unflattering (and hence threatening) facts about himself than would be expected of the less well-adjusted individual. We, therefore, stated our problem as follows: Given two groups of children, one better adjusted than the other by some external criterion; we predict that the better adjusted children will be able to accept more damaging statements about themselves than will the poorer adjusted children.

The Experimental Design

In selecting a population for our study we sought children of approximately similar socio-economic condition, educational level, and age. Accordingly, we administered our two instruments to all sixth-grade children, a population of 205, in a group of consolidated rural schools in northeastern Pennsylvania in the spring of 1949.

As a rough external measure of adjustment we used the California Test of Personality, Elementary Form A. While this instrument is admittedly not a refined clinical instrument for distinguishing between adjusted and maladjusted children, it served our purpose as a rough screening device that was familiar to the teachers and simple to administer and score. On the basis of this test we divided our subjects into the upper and lower 50 per cent in terms of adjustment score obtained on the CTP. In this way we arrived at two groups of children, one group better adjusted than the other on the basis of an external criterion.

To test the degree to which these children would accept damaging statements about themselves, we prepared a list of statements that seemed to us to be "probably true" of all children, yet damaging to self if admitted. In the construction of this list we solicited the aid of graduate students and faculty in suggesting items and criticizing items in our list. As a result of this informal consensus, we finally agreed on twenty statements that seemed likely to be true of all children. They were the following:

1. I sometimes disobey my parents.
2. I sometimes say bad words or swear.
3. I sometimes copy or cheat on school work.
4. I sometimes am rude to older people.
5. I sometimes tell lies.
6. I sometimes make fun of other schoolmates.
7. I sometimes pretend to forget things I am supposed to do.
8. I sometimes steal things when I know I will not be caught.
9. I sometimes fib to my classmates.
10. I sometimes pretend to be sick to get out of things.
11. I sometimes am unkind to younger children.
12. I sometimes am lazy and won't do my work.
13. I sometimes tell dirty stories.
14. I sometimes cheat in games.
15. I sometimes am unruly at school.
16. I sometimes do not brush my teeth on purpose.
17. I sometimes talk back to my mother.
18. I sometimes am mean to animals.
19. I sometimes waste my time when I should be working.
20. I sometimes show off in front of other children.

This list was mimeographed and presented to all of the children of the sixth grades who were in school on the day of the administration two weeks after completing the CTP. They were told that this was a list of things that boys and girls sometimes did and that we were interested in finding out which of these were true of the sixth graders in this school. They were told further that we did not want to know *which* children did these things, but only about the group as a whole, and for this reason we did not want them to put their names on the papers. Instead, we asked them to check those statements true for them, fold the paper, and hand it in.

By means of an obscured code it was possible for us to identify the person who marked each paper in spite of the fact that no names were placed on the paper by the children themselves. In this way we obtained CTPs and our damaging statements list for 105 boys and 75 girls of the original group. We felt somewhat guilty about betraying these children but concluded that, perhaps, for the sake of investigation, it could be excused.

Results of the Experiment

Table 1 presents a summary of the results of our study. It seems quite clear that the differences shown in the table below are not likely to be due to chance alone. It would appear that our prediction in this study was amply corroborated. Appar-

TABLE 1 *Mean Adjustment Scores, Mean Number of Damaging Items Checked, and Critical Ratios of the Differences for Boys and Girls*

	Mean CTP	Mean No. Damaging Items Checked	Mean S.D.	SE/ Mean	CR
		Boys			
Lower 50%	33.4	5.1	2.5	.35	
					5.98
Upper 50%	68.7	9.2	4.2	.59	
		Girls			
Lower 50%	36.5	5.8	2.9	.48	
					3.78
Upper 50%	69.1	8.4	3.2	.53	

ently the relationship between ability to accept damaging statements about self and adjustment is a real one and can be experimentally demonstrated.

The general tendency of the results shown in the statistical presentation (Table 1) was also observed in our examination of some of the individual cases where children had received very high or very low scores on the CTP. One boy, for example, who obtained the highest adjustment score in the group, marked all but one of the items on our damaging statement list as true of himself. The opposite tendency was true for cases of children with very low adjustment ratings. Indeed, it seems clear that the above results would be very much magnified by taking the upper and lower 25 per cent groups rather than the upper and lower 50 per cent.

One interesting idea that occurred to us in connection with these results is this: Most personality inventories are based upon the individual's marking or accepting statements about himself. While some of these statements may not appear to be damaging from his point of view, many of them may. If the results of this study are accurate we should then expect not the poorly-adjusted but the well-adjusted person to mark more damaging statements as true for himself. Indeed, that could even have occurred in the personality test used in this experiment. It would appear that here is a fruitful source of further experiment in which the

hypothesis of this study might be investigated with some other measure of adjustment than a test based on verbal statements about self.

If we may hazard a guess in this regard, it seems to us that, although this may be a serious source of error in paper and pencil personality tests, it is probably not a completely invalidating factor. Whether an item is regarded as damaging by an individual is, after all, a matter of his own interpretation. It is probable that many items that would be regarded by a psychologist as derogatory, are not so regarded by the subject who perceives them purely as a "matter of fact." Nevertheless, it seems possible that greater attention to the problem of how a statement looks to the subject, as well as to its ability to discriminate adjustment from an external criterion, might result in better personality instruments.

Summary

This study is an attempt to demonstrate a relationship between ability to accept threatening statements about self and adjustment. It was predicted that better adjusted children, as determined by a commonly used test of personality, would be able to accept more damaging statements about themselves than would less well-adjusted children. Sixth-grade children were divided into better adjusted and poorer adjusted groups on the basis of scores on the California Test of Personality. Both groups were then asked to check on a list of twenty somewhat derogatory statements those true of themselves. The better adjusted group checked significantly more items than did the poorer adjusted group.

REFERENCES

Combs, A. W. A phenomenological approach to adjustment theory. *Journal of Abnormal and Social Psychology*, 1949, **44**, 29–35.

Lecky, L. *Self consistency.* New York: Island Press, 1945.

Murphy, G. *Personality: A biosocial approach to origins and structure.* New York: Harper & Row, 1947.

Rogers, C. R. The organization of personality. *American Psychologist*, 1947, **2**, 358–368.

Snygg, D., & Combs, A. W. *Individual behavior: A new frame of reference for psychology.* New York: Harper & Row, 1949.

53

MMPI: Professional Use
by Professional People

Starke R. Hathaway

A good deal of controversy has arisen recently regarding the legality of various methods for gaining information about an individual, and how much information can be collected without infringing upon the individual's right to privacy. Within the last three or four years a considerable number of legal decisions have been made on the admissibility into court of confessions and of evidence collected without a search warrant or by use of a wire tap. In the area of personality testing many of the same kinds of questions are being raised. For example, many companies require that a potential employee take a personality test in order to be considered for a job. If his test score should become one of the reasons why he was not offered the job, has he not, in fact, testified against himself by unwittingly supplying the evidence which led to his rejection?

In the following selection the developer of the Minnesota Multiphasic Personality Inventory, Dr. Starke Hathaway, discusses several points on the use and misuse of personality tests. While this selection is primarily concerned with the type of questions on the test which require the individual to indicate his religious attitudes and beliefs, the same points can be applied to other questions which require that the individual divulge information regarding his thoughts, fantasies, and personal experiences.

This long letter was prompted by a courteous inquiry that I received. The inquiry referred to the use of the MMPI as an aid in the selection of policemen from among applicants. It was pointed out that there are laws against inquiry about religious affiliation, and the specific issue was the presence in the MMPI of items relating to religion.

Letter to Mr. R.

First I would like to express my appreciation of your reasonably expressed inquiry about the MMPI as possibly offensive in the statements that relate to religious activities and which might provide personal information on which discriminatory acts might be based. Because of sporadic public antagonism to psychological testing, and in view of our mutual concern for our civil liberties, I am going to answer you at considerable length and with unusual care. I shall send copies of this answer to the Psychological Corporation and to others who may be concerned. Let me assure you at the outset that I believe I am proceeding from a considered position rather than from a defensive attitude that could lead me to irrationally protect the MMPI, other such tests, or psychologists in general. I believe that I would be among the first to criticize some of the uses to which tests are put and some of those who use them improperly. I must also immediately make it clear that I am antagonistic to ignorant attacks upon tests. Tests are not offensive elements; the offensive elements, if any, come with the misuse of tests. To attack tests is, to a certain extent, comparable to an attack upon knives. Both good and bad use of knives occurs because they are sharp instruments. To eliminate knives would, of course, have a limiting effect upon the occurrence of certain hostile acts, but it would also greatly limit the activities of surgeons. I simply discriminate between the instrument and the objectives and applications of the persons who wield it. I am calling attention to the difference between a switchblade knife, which is good for nothing but attack, and a scalpel knife, good for healing purposes but which can also be

From American Psychologist, *Vol. 19 (1964), 204–210. Copyright 1964 by the American Psychological Association, and reproduced by permission.*

used as a weapon. I hope that no one will think that any test was devised in the same spirit that switchblade knives were devised. It is absurd if someone holds the belief that psychologists malignantly developed instruments such as the MMPI for use against the welfare of man, including of course man's personal liberties and rights. But if the MMPI and such tests have origins analogous to the scalpel, and are really perversely used to man's disadvantage, we are properly concerned. Let me turn to a history of the MMPI items about which you have inquired.

I should begin with an account of the origin of the MMPI itself. I believe I am competent to do this, and I hope you will see that its origins were motivated toward virtue as I have suggested above. In about 1937, J. C. McKinley, then head of the Department of Neuropsychiatry of the Medical School at the University of Minnesota, supported me in a venture which grew out of a current problem in our psychopathic hospital. The problem lay in the fact that insulin therapy as a treatment method for certain forms of mental disease had just become a widespread method of treatment. Different clinics were finding highly varied values. Some reported the treatment to be exceedingly effective; others said it was ineffective. The treatment was somewhat dangerous to patients, and it was exceedingly expensive in terms of hospitalization and nursing care. McKinley happened to be one of the neuropsychiatrists of the time who felt that more careful investigation should be undertaken before such treatments were applied and, in particular, before we used them on our patients.

It occurred to us that the difficulty in evaluation of insulin treatment lay largely in the fact that there was no good way to be assured that the patients treated by this method in one clinic were like those treated in another clinic. This was due to the fact that the estimations of the nature of a person's mental illness and of its severity were based upon professional judgment and could vary with the training background of the particular psychiatrist as well as with his personal experiences. Obviously, if the patients treated at one center were not like those treated at another center, the outcome of treatment might be different. At that time there was no psychological test available that would have helped to remove the diagnostic decisions on the patients in two clinics from the personal biases of the local staffs. There was no way that our hospital staff could select a group of patients for the new treatment who would be surely comparable in diagnosis and severity of illness to those from some other setting.

It became an obvious possibility that one might devise a personality test which, like intelligence tests, would somewhat stabilize the identification of the illness and provide an estimate of its severity. Toward this problem the MMPI research was initiated.

I have established that decisions about the kind and severity of mental illness depend upon the psychological examinations of the psychiatrists and other professional persons. The items upon which the judgments are based constitute the symptoms of mental maladjustment or illness. Such symptoms have for many, many years been listed in the textbooks of psychiatry and clinical psychology that treat with mental disorder. These symptoms are verbal statements from or about the patient. The simplest and most obvious form of these symptoms are statements that confess feelings of unhappiness, depression, and the like. The statements may also be less personal, as in complaints about one's lot in life and about the inability to find employment or the mistreatment by others.

In summary, the symptoms of mental illness and unhappiness are represented in verbal complaints or statements that relate to personal feelings or personal experiences or reactions to job and home. It should be immediately apparent that unlike most physical illnesses, these verbally presented complaints or symptoms usually do not permit direct observation by others. If a patient reports a painful nodule or abdominal pain, the reported pain can usually be observed by some physical or nonverbal means that lends credence to the complaint. Many symptoms of mental illness are contrastingly difficult to observe by nonverbal means. It is almost impossible to establish that the person presenting the symptom is actually suffering from a distortion of his psychologically healthy mental state by some psychological complex. There is much arbitrariness even in the statement, "I am unhappy." Frequently no physical observation can be brought to bear upon the statement. The complainant may look unhappy and may even add that he is suicidal, yet friends and the examiner can agree that he is "just asking for sympathy and is no worse off than the average." There is no way of solidly deciding what the words really mean. This point is crucial to what I am writing. If it is not clear at this point, reference books on semantics should be consulted. S. I. Hayakawa would be a good source.

I know of no method which will permit us to absolutely assess unhappiness or mental illness, either as to kind or severity, unless we start from inescapable symptoms that are verbally expressed and subject to the vagaries in the personal connotations of words and phrases. In initiating the research upon what was to produce the MMPI, we collected as many as we could find of the symptomatic statements recognized by authorities as indicative of unhappiness and mental illness. There were hundreds of these statements. We had at one time well over a thousand of them. Every one of these symptomatic statements had already been written into the literature or had been used as a practical bit of clinical evidence in the attempt to understand patients. I repeat this because I want to thoroughly emphasize that every item in the MMPI came from assumed relationships to the assessment of human beings for better diagnosis and treatment of possible mental illness.

Now with all this preamble I am prepared to discuss the particular items that you have highlighted in your letter. It happens that, among the many items collected and finally selected to make up the MMPI, there were at least 19 relating to religion in one way or another [see Table 1].

I have listed these items to remind you again of the ones you cited, and I have added others that may further illustrate what I am saying. Now you have asked why we included these statements on religion among the possible symptoms of psychological maladjustment. Why should these items still appear in the MMPI?

In the first instance, the subject matter evidenced in the symptoms of depressed or otherwise mentally disturbed persons often largely centers in religion. There is a well-recognized pattern of psychological distortion to which we apply the term religiosity. When we use the word "religiosity," we indicate a symptomatic pattern wherein the process of an intercurrent psychological maladjustment is evidenced by extremes of religious expression that are out of the usual context for even the deeply religious person. A bishop friend of mine once illustrated the problem he sometimes had in this connection by his account of a parishioner who had routinely given a tithe as his offering toward support of the church, but who, within

TABLE 1

	Male		Female	
	True	No answer	True	No answer
I am very religious (more than most people).	8	9	11	9
Religion gives me no worry.	83	4	70	4
I go to church almost every week.	42	3	52	4
I pray several times every week.	50	3	83	2
I read in the Bible several times a week.	21	5	30	3
I feel sure that there is only one true religion.	49	8	51	11
I have no patience with people who believe there is only one true religion.	56	4	47	10
I believe there is a God.	92	5	96	2
I believe there is a devil and a hell in afterlife.	63	14	67	14
I believe in a life hereafter.	76	12	87	7
I believe in the second coming of Christ.	57	18	68	12
Christ performed miracles such as changing water into wine.	69	16	77	15
The only miracles I know of are simply tricks that people play on one another.	37	10	27	14
A minister can cure disease by praying and putting his hand on your head.	4	10	5	11
Everything is turning out just like the prophets of the Bible said it would.	52	29	54	32
My soul sometimes leaves my body.	8	18	5	12
I am a special agent of God.	14	13	16	21
I have had some very unusual religious experiences.	20	5	13	2
I have been inspired to a program of life based on duty which I have since carefully followed.	42	14	50	15

a few weeks, had increased the amount he gave until it was necessary for him to embezzle money for his weekly offering. Surely, my friend said, there is more here than ordinary devotion; there is something which should be considered from another frame of reference. In this anecdote there is an element of the symptomatic pattern, religiosity. But, as is true of nearly every other aspect of human personality to which the MMPI refers, no one item will ordinarily establish this distortion of the ordinarily meaningful position of religion. And no one item can be used to detect the problem as it occurs in various persons. Two persons rarely express even their usual religious feelings in identical ways.

It never occurred to us in selecting these items for the MMPI that we were asking anything relative to the particular religion of our patients. It obviously did not occur to us that there were other than the Christian orientation wherein religiosity might be observed. Because of this oversight on our part, several of our MMPI symptoms that we assumed were indicative of religiosity happen to be obviously related to the Christian religion, although we find that most persons simply translate to their own orientation if it is different. I should hasten to add that although these symptoms were hoped to be specific to persons who suffer from religiosity, they have not all turned out that way. Not every aspect of religion is at times a symptom of mental illness. Certainly it is obvious that there is nothing symptomatic in admitting to one's personal acceptance or rejection of several of the items. The point at which a group of items becomes consistent in suggesting symptoms is subtle to distinguish. As my bishop friend's story illustrated, it is not unusual that one contributes to religious work even though there exists a doubtful extreme. As I will show below, all these items are endorsed or rejected by some ordinary, normal people. If any of the items have value toward clinical assessment, the value comes in combination with other items which probably will not seem to relate to religion.

The MMPI, which started out so small and inconspicuously, has become a world-known and -used instrument. We did not expect this outcome. If I were to select new items, I would again include items that related to religiosity. I would this time, of course, try to avoid the implication that the religiosity occurred only among adherents to the Christian faith. I am obviously unhappy about the limited applicability of these items, but I am, in the same sense, unhappy about other items in the MMPI. A considerable number of the items have

been challenged by other groups from other standpoints. By this I mean only to remind those concerned about these religiosity items that there are frankly stated items on sex, there are items on body functions, there are items on certain occupations; in fact, there are items on most every aspect of psychological life that can be symptomatic of maladjustment and unhappiness. If the psychologist cannot use these personal items to aid in the assessment of people, he suffers as did the Victorian physician who had to examine his female patients by feeling the pulse in the delicate hand thrust from behind a screen. I shall come back to this point later, but it is obvious that if we were making a new MMPI, we would again be faced either with being offensive to subgroupings of people by personal items they object to or, if we did not include personal items and were inoffensive, we would have lost the aim of the instrument.

One may protest that the MMPI is intended for the patient, the mentally ill person, not applicants to schools, high-school children, or to those being considered for jobs. I cannot give a general defense of every such use, but this is a time when preventive health is being emphasized. We urge everyone to get chest X-rays and to take immunizing shots. We are now beginning to advocate general surveys with such psychological instruments as the MMPI. The basic justification is the same. We hope to identify potential mental breakdown or delinquency in the school child before he must be dragged before us by desperate parents or by other authority. We hope to hire police, who are given great power over us, with assurance that those we put on the rolls should have good personal qualities for the job. This is not merely to protect us, this also is preventive mental health, since modern job stability can trap unwary workers into placements that leave them increasingly unhappy and otherwise maladjusted. If the personality of an applicant is not appropriate to the job, neither employer nor applicant should go ahead. We have always recognized the employer's use of this principle in his right to personal interview with applicants. Since the items and responses are on record, the MMPI and such devices could be considered to be a more fair method of estimation than the personal interview, and, when they are machine scored, they make possible much greater protection from arbitrary personal judgments and the openended questions that are standard for personal interviews.

It seems to me that the MMPI examination can be rather comparable to the physical examination for selection of persons. One would not wish to hire a person with a bad heart when the job required behavior that was dangerous to him. I think it would be equally bad to hire a person as a policeman whose psychological traits were inappropriate and then expect him to do dangerous things or shoot to kill as a policeman is expected to do. There is, from physical and psychological examinations, a protection to the person being hired as well as to those hiring him. This is not meant as an argument for the use of the MMPI in every placement that requires special skills or special personality traits. I am arguing a general point.

I would next like to take up MMPI items to bring out a new line of evidence which, I am sorry to say, is not familiar to some psychologists, but which is of importance in giving you an answer to your questions. Turn again to the above items, particularly to the "True" response frequencies. We will look at implications about the people taking the MMPI as we interpret the True frequencies of response for these items.

Before we do so, we should consider the source of the frequency figures. The males and females who provide these standard data, which are the basis for all MMPI standards, were persons who came to the University Hospitals bringing patients or who were around the hospitals at the time when we were collecting data. Only those were tested who were not under a doctor's care and who could be reasonably assumed to be normal in mind and body. These persons whom we call the normal adult cross-section group, came from all over Minnesota, from every socio-economic and educational level; there is reason to believe that they are a proper representation of the rank and file people of Minnesota. It is probably well known that, in the main, Minnesota population was drawn from North European stock, is largely Christian in background, and has a rather small number in the several minority groups. Certainly, it can hardly be said that this population is unduly weighted with extremists in the direction of overemphasis upon religion or in atheism or in other belief characteristics. Probably one would expect this population to be rather more religious than the average for all the states. Finally, the majority of the persons who provided these basic norms were married persons, and most were parents. Data given in the table can be found in the fundamental book on the MMPI, *An MMPI Handbook* by Dahlstrom and Welsh (1960).

But now consider the items. Let us assume, as is often naively assumed, that when one answers an item one tells the truth about oneself. Of course,

there is no requirement that those who take the MMPI should tell the truth, and this is a very important point. Also, I have tried to establish that truth is a very complicated semantic concept. But let us assume for the moment that people do tell the truth as they see it. Take the item, "I go to church almost every week." According to the data given, 42 per cent of the men and 52 per cent of the women go to church almost every week. Now these data are representative of the whole state. I am sure that ministers of the state would be gratified if all these people were reporting accurately. Parenthetically, I suppose that "church" was read as "synagogue" or "temple" without much trouble. But I do not know what percentage of people are actually estimated to go to some church almost every week. At any rate I cannot conceive that 42 per cent of the men of the state of Minnesota are in church nearly every week even if 52 per cent of the women are. I even cannot conceive that half of the men in Minnesota and 83 per cent of the women actually pray several times a week. I might imagine that 21 per cent of the men and 30 per cent of the women would read in the Bible several times a week. This would represent about one-fifth of all the men and about one-third of all the women. My real impression is that people simply do not know that much about the Bible. However, take the next item. Here it says that one feels sure there is only one true religion. To this about half of the men and half of the women answered True. Perhaps these might be considered bigoted, but what of the ones who have obviously answered False? There seems to be a great deal of religious tolerance here; about half of the persons of Minnesota do not even express a belief that there is only one true religion.

It is true that a high percentage say they believe there is a God. This seems to be a noncommittal item, since most people are aware that God has many meanings. The item which follows it, however, which permits denying or accepting a belief in a devil and hell in afterlife, is quite interesting. Twenty-three per cent of men and 19 per cent of women reject this belief. By contrast, a life hereafter is denied by 24 per cent of men and by 13 per cent of women. The second coming of Christ is expected by only 57 per cent of men and 68 per cent of women if we accept what these figures seem to say. Again, with reversal, Christ as a miracle worker is doubted by 31 per cent of men and by 23 per cent of women. Stated more directly, 37 per cent of men and 27 per cent of women come straight out and say that miracles were not performed. The item apparently includes Old and

New Testament sources among others. On down in the list, one finds that only 14 per cent of men and 16 per cent of women believe themselves to be special agents of God.

I think I have gone over enough of these items to provide a suggestion of what I am going to next point out. But I would like to add two more MMPI items in sharper illustration of the point. These two additional items have nothing obvious to do with religion. The first of them is, "I almost never dream," and the second is, "I dream frequently." One of the first things we found in the early studies of MMPI items was that the same person frequently answered True to both these items. When asked about the seeming contradiction, such a person would respond, among other possibilities, by saying to the first item that surely he had very few dreams. But, coming to the next item, he changed his viewpoint to say that he dreamed frequently as compared to some of the people he knew. This shift of emphasis led us to recognize that, in addition to the general semantic problem developed above, when people respond to items, they also do not usually respond with the connotations we expect. Apparently even if the people are telling a truth of some kind, one would need an interview with them to know what they really intend to report by answering True or False. I suppose this is similar to the problem of the oath of allegiance over which some people are so concerned. One may state that he is loyal to the United States, for example, yet really mean that he is deeply convinced that its government should be overthrown and that, with great loyalty to his country, he believes revolution to be the only salvation for the country. However much we might object to it, this belief would permit a person to swear to his loyalty in complete honesty. I think most everyone is aware of this problem about oaths, and it is a routine one with MMPI item responses.

In summary of all this, if one wished to persecute those who by their answers to these items seemed inconsistent with some religious or atheistic pattern of beliefs, there would be an embarrassingly large number of ordinary people in Minnesota who would be open to suspicion both ways. In reality, the responses made to these items have many variations in truth and meaning. And it would betray considerable ignorance of the practical psychology of communication if any absolute reliance were placed on responses.

As a final but most significant point relative to these items, I should point out that administration of the MMPI requires that those who are taking the test be clearly informed that they may omit any item they do not wish to answer for whatever purpose. I have never seen any studies that have drawn conclusions from the omission of particular items by a particular person. We found that items among these that are being considered were unusually frequently omitted. You may notice this in the No Answer columns. One-third of all the respondents failed to answer the item relative to the Bible and the prophets, for example. This is a basic fact about the MMPI and such tests, and I cannot see why this freedom will not permit to each person the latitude to preserve his privacy if he is afraid. Still again I would add that, in many settings, possibly nearly every setting, where the MMPI is used in group administration, those who take it are permitted to refuse the whole test. I admit that this might seem prejudicial, and I suspect that if any one chooses to protect himself, he will do it by omitting items rather than by not taking the test at all. Is refusal to take the test any different from refusing to subject oneself to an employment or admission interview by a skilled interviewer? I think that some people who have been writing about the dangers of testing must have an almost magical belief in tests. Sometimes, when I feel so at a loss in attempting to help someone with a psychological problem, I wish that personality tests were really that subtle and powerful.

Groups of items called scales, formed into patterns called profiles, are the useful product of tests like the MMPI. I note that in your inquiry you show an awareness that the MMPI is usually scored by computers. The scales that are used for most interpretation include 10 "clinical" scales. These are the ones that carry most of the information. Several other scales indicate whether the subject understood and followed the directions. No one of these main scales has less than 30 items in it and most of them have many more than 30. The scores from the machine come back not only anonymously indicating the number of items answered in a way that counts on the scale, but the scores are usually already transformed into what we call T or standard scores. These T scores are still more remote from the particular items that make up a scale. The graphic array of T scores for the scales are finally printed into the profile.

In this connection, there is a very pretty possibility offered by the development of computer scoring. If we wish to take advantage of the presumed advantages of the use of tests, yet be assured that particular item responses shall not be considered, then we only need to be assured that those using the test do not score it, must send it straightway to the computer center, and, in the end, receive back only the profiles which are all that should be used in any case. The original test may be destroyed.

The scales of the profile were not arbitrarily set up. The MMPI is an experimentally derived instrument. If an item counts on a scale, I want to make it very clear that that item counts, not because some clinician or somebody thought that the item was significant for measuring something about human personality, but it counts because, in the final analysis, well-diagnosed groups of maladjusted, sometimes mentally ill persons answered the item with an average frequency differing from the average frequency of the normative group that I have used for the above illustrative data. This is an exceedingly significant point and is probably least often understood by those who have not had psychometric training. No one read or composed these items to decide what it meant if one of them were answered True or False. The meanings of the items came from the fact that persons with a certain kind of difficulty answered in an average way different from the "normal" standard. For example, the item "I go to church almost every week" is counted on a scale for estimating the amount of depression. We did not just decide that going to church was related to depression. We had the response frequencies from men who complained that they were depressed. They answered True with a frequency of only 20 per cent. You will note that the normals answered True with a frequency of 42 per cent—22 per cent more often. Now this difference also turned up for women who were depressed. We adopted a False response to this item as a count on the depression scale of the MMPI. We do not even now know why depressed people say they go to church less often. Note that you are not depressed if you say False to this one item. Actually, 55 per cent of the normals answered False. Use of the item for an MMPI scale depended on the fact that even more of the depressed persons answered False and so if you say False you have added one item more in common with depressed people than with the normals despite the fact that more than half the normals answered as you did.

Even psychologists very familiar with the MMPI cannot tell to which scale or scales an item belongs without looking it up. People often ask for a copy of a test so they can cite their objections to items they think objectionable, and they assume that the meaning of the item is obvious and that they can tell how it is interpreted. I am often asked what specified items mean. I do not know because the

scoring of the scales has become so abstracted that I have no contact with items.

One more point along this line. Only six of the above 19 items are counted on one of the regular scales that are mostly used for personality evaluation. Four more are used on a measure that is only interpreted in estimation of the ability of the subject to follow directions and to read well enough. In fact, about 200 of the whole set of items did not end up on any one of the regularly used scales. But, of course, many of these 200 other items occur on one or another of the many experimental MMPI scales that have been published.

We cannot change or leave out any items or we lose an invaluable heritage of research in mental health. To change even a comma in an item may change its meaning. I would change the words of some items, omit some, and add new ones if I could. A new test should be devised, but its cost would be on the order of a $100,000 and we are not at this time advanced enough so that the new one would be enough better to compensate for the loss of the research and diagnostic value of the present MMPI even in view of its manifest weaknesses.

The subject of professional training brings me to my next line of response. It is appropriate that the public should be aware of the uses of such tests as the MMPI, but I have repeatedly pointed out that it is far more important that the public should be aware of the persons who are using the test and of the uses to which it is put. In this context, the distributor of the MMPI, the Psychological Corporation of New York City, accepts and practices the ethical principles for test distributors that have been promulgated by the American Psychological Association. These rules prohibit the sale of tests to untrained or incompetent persons. Use or possession of the MMPI by others is prohibited but, since this carries no present penalty, the distributor is helpless except for his control of the supply. Tests, as I have said above, are not like switchblade knives, designed to be used against people; they offer potential contributions to happiness. And I cannot believe that a properly accredited clinical psychologist or psychiatrist or physician who may use the MMPI would under any circumstances use it to the disadvantage of the persons being tested. If he does so, he is subject to the intraprofessional ethical-practice controls that are explicit and carry sanctions against those of us who transgress. The MMPI provides data which, like certain medical data, are considered by many to be helpful in guidance and analysis and understanding of people. Of course, in the making of this point, I am aware that there is no absolute meaning to what is ethical. What one group may think should be done about a certain medical-examination disclosure may be considered by another group to be against the patient's interest. I cannot do more than extend this ubiquitous ethical dilemma to the use of the personality test.

The essential point is that such tests should not be used except in professional circles by professional people and that the data it provides should be held confidential and be protected within the lawful practice of ethics. When these requirements are not met, there is reason for complaint. I hope I have made it clear that it is also my conviction that the MMPI will hurt no one, adult or child, in the taking of it. Without defending all uses of it, I surely defend it, and instruments like it, when they are in proper hands and for proper purposes. Monachesi and I have tested 15,000 ninth-grade school children with the MMPI. This took us into public schools all over the state, even into some parochial schools. In all of this testing, we had no difficulties with children, parents, or teachers except for a few courteous inquiries. We are now publishing what we hope will be significant data from this work, data bearing on delinquency and school dropout. We believe that this work demonstrates that properly administered, properly explained, and properly protected tests are acceptable to the public.

At the beginning of this statement I warned that I was going to make it quite long because I felt deeply on the matter. I hope I have not sounded as though I were merely being defensive, protecting us from those who would burn tests and who for good reasons are exceedingly sensitive about psychological testing. I am apologetic if I have sounded too much like the professional scientist and have seemed to talk down to the issue or to be too minutely explicit. I have not meant to insult by being unduly simple, but I have felt that I had to expand adequately on the points. As for psychologists who are those most widely applying such tests, I am aware that the public will look with increasing seriousness upon those who are entrusted with problems of mental health and the assessment of human actions.

I will end with a repetition of my feeling that, while it is desirable for the public to require ethical practices of those using tests, the public may be reassured that the psychologists, physicians, and others who use these new tests will be even more alert to apply the intraprofessional controls that are a requisite to professional responsibility. But I must emphasize that it is not to public advantage to so limit these professional judgments that we fail to progress in mental health research and applications from lack of freedom to use the best instruments we have and to develop better ones.

REFERENCE

Dahlstrom, W. G., & Welsh, G. S. *An MMPI handbook: A guide to use in clinical practice and research.* Minneapolis: University of Minnesota Press, 1960.

54

Pupil Response of Hetero- and Homosexual Males to Pictures of Men and Women: A Pilot Study

Eckhard H. Hess, Allan L. Seltzer, and John M. Shlien

In addition to the ethical problems encountered in question-and-answer personality testing, there is the problem of whether the test results accurately reflect personality characteristics. One fairly obvious source of bias or error is where the subject may not respond honestly, deliberately choosing the responses that he thinks will show him in the most

From Journal of Abnormal and Social Psychology, *Vol. 70:3 (1965), 165–168. Copyright 1965 by the American Psychological Association, and reproduced by permission. This research was supported in part by a grant from Social Sciences Research Committee of the University of Chicago and in part by Interpublic, New York, N.Y.*

favorable light. For example, a subject may recognize that his sexual behavior is indeed bizarre and thus may not give truthful responses to items concerning that facet of his behavior.

It is assumed by many clinical psychologists that projective tests such as the Rorschach tend to elicit more accurate representations of true personality characteristics than do the paper-and-pencil types such as the MMPI. Instead of being asked a number of specific questions, the subject is presented with an ambiguous stimulus such as an inkblot and is asked to describe what it looks like or means to him. The basic assumption is that the subject will "project" his own feelings, beliefs, and general personality characteristics into his description of the stimulus.

While it is probably true that the subject cannot distort or falsify his responses as easily on the projective tests, a serious problem arises in that clinical psychologists often differ markedly in their interpretation of what the responses actually mean. Because of this variability in interpretation, many psychologists have questioned the actual usefulness of this type of test.

In the following selection Hess and his associates suggest that a new technique, based on measurement of the dilation and constriction of the pupils of the eyes, might offer exciting alternatives to testing procedures currently in use. These authors point out that their technique is much more objective than the projective techniques and is not susceptible to the problems of falsification which are present with the existing paper-and-pencil tests such as the MMPI.

Change in the size of the pupil of the human eye has been reported to vary with a subject's interest in various pictorial stimuli (Hess and Polt, 1960). Male subjects had a larger pupil while looking at pictures of women than when looking at pictures of men. The reverse was true for female subjects: They had larger pupils looking at men. Unpublished work with a large number of subjects has continued to substantiate the finding of this difference between the sexes.

If this difference in pupil response is truly a reflection of interest in the male or female figure as a sexual object then homosexuals would be expected to show a larger pupil response to pictures of their own sex. In the course of our work a few subjects have given a larger response to pictures of their own sex; as measured by pupil size, same-sex pictures seemed more interesting to them. Review of these anomalous cases increased the plausibility of the idea that this same-sex response might be typical of homosexuals. The present report, a pilot study of a small group of overt male homosexuals, strongly supports that hypothesis.

Method

Subjects

Ten young adult male subjects were tested. Five of these, students or workers in our laboratory—the heterosexual group—were well known to us over a period of several years. Their sexual outlet was judged to be exclusively heterosexual. The other five were known, through observation, interview, and in every case by their own voluntary admission to one of the authors who had gained their trust, to have overt homosexuality as their sole or primary sexual outlet. All 10 were of roughly the same age (between 24 and 34 years), same education (all but one were graduate students), and same social level. None was hospitalized or in therapy.

Procedure and apparatus

In a dimly lit room, a subject was seated before a viewing aperture, fitted with a headrest, which was inserted in a large plywood panel. The panel concealed the working of the apparatus from the subject. Resting his head against the aperture, the subject faced a rear-projection screen, set in an otherwise black box, at a distance of 2½ feet from his eyes. A 35-millimeter slide projector behind this screen projected a 9 × 12-inch picture onto it. Changing of slides was controlled by the experimenter from his position behind the panel where he also operated a concealed 16-millimeter camera fitted with a frame counter. As the slides were being viewed a half-silvered mirror placed at a 45-degree angle across the subject's line of vision permitted unobtrusive filming of the eye, at the rate of two frames per second. Illumination for this photography was furnished by a 100-watt bulb on rheostat control.

Stimuli

Fifteen picture slides, representations of the human figure, were shown in the following order:

Slide Content	Scoring Category
A. Painting, cubist, five figures	Art
B. Painting, realistic, crucifixion	Art
C. Painting, two nude males	Male
D. Painting, reclining female nude	Female
E. Photograph, nude man, head and upper torso	Male
F. Painting, seated nude female, rear view	Female
G. Painting, sailor, nude upper torso	Male
H. Painting, nude male and nude female	Art
I. Photograph, nude female torso	Female
J. Photograph, nude man, rear view	Male
K. Painting, nude female, head and upper torso	Female
L. Painting, two partly clothed males	Male
M. Painting, nude female, head and torso	Female
N. Painting, abstract, three figures	Art
O. Painting, cubist, three figures	Art

The presentation of each of these stimulus pictures was preceded by the presentation of a medium gray "control" slide. The total sequence was 30 slides in this order: Control A, Stimulus A, Control B, Stimulus B, etc., each shown for 10 seconds, with a total viewing time of 5 minutes for the entire sequence.

From the list of slides it can be seen that five were scored as being pictures of females and five were scored as pictures of males. The "male" pictures (C, E, G, J, and L), considered to be the homosexual equivalent of pinups, were culled from physique magazines and were generally more crude artistically than the pictures of females. These latter (D, F, I, K, and M) represented a rather lush concept of the female figure: for example, "D" was a Titian "Venus," "K" an Ingres "Odalisque."

The five "art" slides (A, B, H, N, and O) ranged in style and period from a Michelangelo to a Picasso. None of these was a clearly male or clearly "female" picture; the abstracts (A, N, and O) were ambiguous sexually, "H" showed both sexes, "B" had a strong religious connotation. This group of slides was included in the series for several reasons. Firstly, it was deemed desirable to place the sexual pictures in an artistic setting to reduce the threat to some subjects that might inhere in the obviously sexual material. Secondly, an abnormally high response is frequently given to the first stimulus shown to a subject. By placing art slides "A" and "B" first in the sequence, the male and the female slides, which were of major interest, were protected from this artifact. Thirdly, homosexuals are often thought to have artistic interests and, indeed, most of the homosexuals in this study did verbally indicate such interests. It was useful, therefore, to include a group of slides which would permit appraisal of response to the artistic quality of pictures separate from their representation of sexual objects. Such a separation of pictorial content from its artistic mode of expression appears feasible since (a) the homosexuals, as a group, showed a high response to the artistically good but sexually ambiguous art slides but (b) they also showed a high response to the artistically crude male pictures yet (c) they showed a low response to the artistically good female pictures. Thus, in addition to the use made of it in this report, the data point also to the potential value of the pupil technique in esthetics research.

Measurement and scoring

The processed 16-millimeter film was projected, frame by frame, onto the underside of an opal-glass insert in a table, to a magnification of approximately 20 times. The diameter of the pupil in each frame was measured with a millimeter rule and recorded, giving a set of 20 measurements for each control presentation and a set of 20 for each stimulus. Averages were then computed for each stimulus set and for each preceding control set. In order to compare average pupil size during viewing of a picture to the pupil size during the preceding control this method was used: for each control-stimulus pair the percentage of increase or decrease in average pupil size was computed by dividing the difference between stimulus average and control average by the control average. A positive percentage indicated a larger pupil size when the subject was viewing the stimulus than when he viewed the preceding control. A negative percentage meant a smaller average pupil size during stimulus viewing. For each subject, the five percentages of his response to each of the male pictures (C, E, G, J, and L) were added together to give his "response to 'male' picture" score (Table 1, first column). The total of percentages of his response to the female pictures (D, F, I, K, and M) gave his "response to 'female' picture" score (Table 1, second column). The algebraic subtraction of each subject's male picture total from his female picture total (column two minus column one) gave each subject's relative male-female response measure (Table 1, third column). Using this order of procedure for the table, a positive figure in the third column indicates that the subject had a greater total response to pictures of females than to pictures of males; a negative figure indicates lesser response to pictures of females but greater response to pictures of males.

Results

These male-female response measures clearly discriminate between the subject groups, as is shown in the last column of Table 1. Figure 1 shows this

TABLE 2 *Pupil Size Increase or Decrease when Comparing Stimuli to Controls Expressed in Percentage Totals*

Subject	Total response to "male" pictures	Total response to "female" pictures	Relative "male—female" response score
Hetero-sexuals			
1	−00.4	+05.9	+06.3
2	−54.5	−22.4	+32.1
3	+12.5	+19.2	+06.7
4	+06.3	+39.0	+32.7
5	−01.5	+23.1	+24.6
Homo-sexuals			
6	+18.8	+11.2	−07.6
7	−04.6	−38.0	−33.4
8	+18.9	+18.1	−00.8
9	+18.2	−05.6	−23.8
10	+15.8	+21.5	+05.7

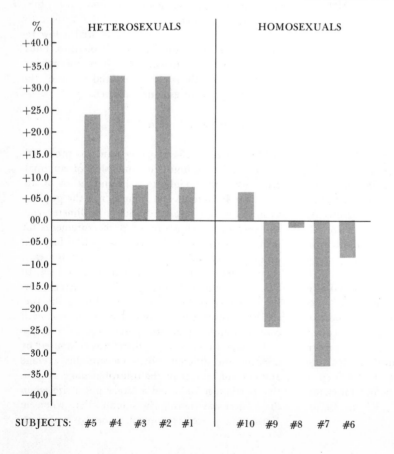

FIGURE 1 *Differences in percentage of pupil size change in response to male and female pictures (A positive score shows higher response to pictures of females; a negative score shows a higher response to pictures of males)*

last column graphically. There is no overlap between the groups in that the lowest heterosexual response is $+06.3$ while the highest homosexual response is no higher than $+05.7$. All heterosexual males show a larger response to pictures of women than to pictures of men (positive scores). Four of the homosexuals show a larger response to pictures of men (negative scores).

Discussion

Some of the female pictures drew a high-positive response from some of the homosexuals, and some of the male pictures drew a high-positive response from some of the heterosexuals. Therefore, response to any single stimulus did not serve to categorize individuals. The total response of a group of subjects to any single stimulus, however, usually served to categorize that stimulus. Total heterosexual response to three of the five female pictures was positive. Total homosexual response to each of the five male pictures was positive. The pictures used in this pilot study were chosen on an a priori basis. The information they have given us and more recent advances in our technique—especially in the matter of brightness matching of pictures—may now permit the formulation of a test battery of pictorial stimuli designed to give a more absolute reflection of a single subject's sex-object interest. It should be emphasized, however, that since *all* subjects in this study saw identical stimuli, the brightness factor could not in any way account for the reported difference between individuals and the resultant groups.

The cooperation of the homosexual subjects, it should be noted, was an unusual relaxation of their customary defense against identification as homosexuals. They were all effectively operating in a normal living environment, in school, at work, with friends. Their sexual preferences were not obvious, and they were ordinarily most reluctant to talk about or reveal them, yet the pupil technique, using a response that is nonverbal and beyond voluntary control, was able to differentiate them from the heterosexual subjects. This is not to say that the pupil response as an index of preference is a predictive substitute for the ultimate criterion of the behavior itself. It does mean that where both preference and behavior are homosexual, even though socially concealed, the pupil response has been shown in this sample to have discriminating power.

Pupil response has already seen application in the area of studies of cognition (Hess and Polt, 1964). In the study of some aspects of personality, compared with projective tests and other instruments and techniques that have been used, this technique appears to us to open up entirely new dimensions.

REFERENCES

Hess, E. H., & Polt, J. M. Pupil size as related to interest value of visual stimuli. *Science*, 1960, **132**, 349–350.

Hess, E. H., & Polt, J. M. Pupil size in relation to mental activity during simple problem solving. *Science*, 1964, **143**, 1190–1192.

55

Psychotherapy Today, or Where Do We Go From Here?

Carl R. Rogers

Nearly every individual has experiences in his life which cause emotional upset and adjustment problems. If these problems last for prolonged periods or result in maladjustive behavior, many people seek professional help from a qualified psychologist or psychiatrist. Until fairly recently, psychotherapists were almost certain to have been trained in the psychoanalytic tradition and consequently tended to view the emotional problems of

Originally published in the American Journal of Psychotherapy, *17:5–16, 1963. Presented at the Sixth Annual Conference of the American Academy of Psychotherapists, New York City, October 14, 1961.*

their patients as arising from sexual conflicts, unconscious desires, childhood traumas, fixations, etc. Today, however, a large number of new and different approaches to therapy are being taught.

One of the most widely known of these newer therapies is associated with a single individual, Carl Rogers. In his approach to *client-centered therapy* Rogers assumes that the therapy situation should be one in which the client is completely free to explore his thoughts, express his feelings, and organize and direct his own life. The major function of the therapist is to establish a relationship which is warm and accepting and in this way help the client to accept his feelings without fear. In sharp contrast to the psychoanalytic approach, client-centered therapy places almost total emphasis on the present rather than the past and little attempt is made to "go back" and uncover the causes of the client's adjustment problems.

However, the psychoanalytic and client-centered approaches represent only two of the many forms of therapy being practiced today. In the following selection Rogers compares several contemporary approaches and discusses what he considers to be the real value of the present situation, one in which it is possible to compare and evaluate these various techniques.

The germ of this paper started to develop more than four years ago, at the first workshop of the American Academy of Psychotherapists. I had, for many reasons, looked forward eagerly to this workshop. Among my reasons, as I realized later, was the implicit belief that experienced therapists, no matter how divergent their orientations, certainly had in common their *experience* of what constituted helpfulness. Hence if they could observe and participate together in a therapeutic *experience,* it would be a very important stride in the direction of ironing out their verbal and ideological differences. So it was very exciting that we were able to arrange to have patients interviewed by different therapists, the rest of us observing.

But then came the jolt. The very portions of those interviews which to me seemed obviously moments of "real" therapy, were experienced by other members as nontherapeutic or even antitherapeutic. And the moments which some others regarded as clearly of a healing nature, I experienced as meaningless or ineffectual, or worse. At the time this was a hard blow to assimilate. It meant that our differences ran far deeper than I had presumed. I had supposed that we were all talking about the same *experiences* but attaching different words, labels, and descriptions to these experiences. This was clearly not true. I have been mulling over this fact ever since.

I believe there is little question but that it *is* a fact. Let me mention some of the diverse and occasionally amusing incidents which support this statement—that what seems therapeutic to one seems antitherapeutic to another.

Recently I participated in a diversified group of therapists in which a well-qualified analyst presented a portion of one of his cases. The central point was the way he had encouraged his patient to speak up to his boss and give the boss a solution to a problem which was troubling the company. To him, this encouragement seemed clearly therapeutic. The group felt, almost unanimously, that he had kept the man from making an important personal, existential choice, that he had robbed the incident of its therapeutic potential.

A prominent therapist, who would, I believe, term himself a practitioner of existential therapy, listened to a tape recording of a therapeutic interview conducted by two well-known members of the American Academy of Psychotherapists, which I am sure they regarded as helpful. Afterwards his comment was that the two therapists ought to refund the patient's money. "The only good elements in the interview were the bird songs in the background!"

This same existentialist played one of his taped therapeutic interviews and was particularly pleased with the way he had dissuaded his patient, a young woman, from going home for the weekend, a trip which he believed would have been regressive. I was surprised at his comments, for in listening to the interview I had felt that his persuasion was the one clearly antitherapeutic portion of the interview.

A young therapist of my acquaintance was highly successful with a deeply disturbed hospitalized psychotic man. He feels that one of the crucial therapeutic moments occurred when he shouted at the man, who was engaged in rambling intellectualized incoherencies, the one word, "Bullshit!" Other therapists listening, however, have often been shocked and feel not only that such a term is not proper therapeutic technique but that it was not therapeutic in this instance.

*   *   *

Thus far I have spoken of these incidents as though they existed at arm's length. But in myself I have often had strong feelings when listening to tapes of therapeutic interviews, or even stronger feelings when, at workshops or in other situations, I have sat in on a therapy interview as an observer. My feeling in that situation has often been, "Move out of that chair and let me take over! This person needs therapy, not what you're giving him!" I suspect others among us have experienced similar feelings.

*   *   *

I hope I have made my point that our differences as therapists do not lie simply in attaching different labels to the same phenomenon. The difference runs deeper. An experience which is seen by one therapist as healing, growth-promoting, helpful, is seen by another as none of these things. And the experience which to the second therapist is seen as possessing these qualities is not so perceived by the first. We differ at the most basic levels of our personal experience.

Some people may feel that though we differ regarding specific incidents, as I have indicated, nevertheless in our goals and in our general directions there is much agreement and much unity. I think not. To me it seems that therapists are equally divergent in these realms.

For the past two years I have encouraged my seminar of psychiatric residents to discuss goals of therapy, either in general, or in regard to a particular client we are considering. Such discussions reveal the most profound differences. We are not agreed on whether the goal is removal of symptoms, reorganization of personality, curing of a disease, or adjustment to the culture. When we try to pin down our goals to those specific behaviors in a specific client which we would regard as evidence of "success," the divergence is almost equally great. In my experience the only therapists who agree on goals of therapy are those who have been strongly indoctrinated in the same dogma.

Not only is there divergence in what we mean by success, but the conference of the American Academy of Psychotherapists, on "Failure in Psychotherapy," has demonstrated that we do not agree on what constitutes failure. There is even difference of opinion as to whether the suicide of a client or patient in therapy is necessarily a failure.

But what about the direction in which we should move? Is there agreement in this realm? A vigorous and growing group, particularly among psychologists, is the group which in one way or another bases its therapy upon learning theory as studied in the psychologic laboratory. They regard this as the only scientific direction in which to move and look with scorn upon the so-called dynamic approaches. This scorn is returned by the majority of therapists who regard themselves as "dynamic." Each group feels positive that the other is moving in a fruitless, if not ridiculous, direction.

One of the more extreme forms of learning-theory approach is the operant conditioning carried on by B. F. Skinner and his group (Lindsley, 1956). Although as yet it has had little practical impact upon psychotherapy, it will be heard from. Fundamentally the hypothesis is that deviant human behavior can be "shaped up" into normal behavior by the same principle of properly scheduled immediate rewards which transform everyday pigeons into ping-pong players. Yet a large group of therapists would find this aim and this hypothesis definitely unacceptable.

In some ways closely related is the view of Eysenck (1957) that all "dynamic therapies" and their attempts to deal with "underlying complexes" are completely unfounded. His own theory is that "there is no evidence for these putative complexes, and symptomatic treatment is all that is required." I feel sure that Wolpe (1958) and various other therapists within the learning-theory stream of thought would join him in this statement. Yet at least an equal number of practicing therapists would hold a deeply opposed point of view.

In regard to the approach which has been developed by the so-called client-centered group, the situation is the same. Some therapists comment on the promise and significance of the direction in which we are moving. On the other hand, a serious-minded therapist and researcher said (privately) "Rogers has set back clinical psychology and psychotherapy by two decades!" And while I am deeply engaged in a research in client-centered therapy with psychotics, I come across a statement by a client-centered therapist (Snyder, 1959) in which he says, "I would question whether a clinic which uses a client-centered approach exclusively is prepared to accept psychotic clients."

If we look at the new trends coming over the horizon—the growing development of a phenomenological existentialist point of view, the interest in Zen Buddhism, and the like—we find the same situation. The differences over such trends are just as strong as those I have cited. To some these appear to be important and promising directions, while others regard them as mystical dead ends. A reviewer, attempting to be objective, states that the effect of all such writings is "to obfuscate and impede the orderly development of a science."

Even within the fold of psychoanalysis, the original entrant in the field, there is the same divergence within the group, and about the group. There is strong evidence that though analysts may still talk in relatively orthodox terms, what they do in the practice of therapy in their offices bears little or no resemblance to classical analysis. *Time* magazine (1961) reports that "The original Freudian concept of analysis . . . is going out of style." Some students of the professional culture believe that the analytic movement is well into its declining phase. Yet even in regard to psychotherapy of the psychoses a reviewer (with Freudian background, to be sure) says "Psychoanalytic theory overshadows all other approaches and appears to be most fruitful."

It is, I believe, clear that were I to close my paper at this point, a one-sentence summary would be, "The field of psychotherapy is in a mess." Therapists are not in agreement as to their goals or aims in therapy. They are in deep disagreement as to the theoretical structure which would contain their work. They cannot agree as to whether a given experience for a client is healing or destructive, growth-promoting or damaging. They are not in agreement as to what constitutes a successful outcome of their work. They cannot agree as to what constitutes failure. They diverge sharply in their views as to the promising directions for the future. It seems as though the field is completely chaotic and divided.

I am sure that some must look back nostalgically to the situation which existed two or three decades ago. The small number of professionals who were then engaged in the field lived and worked within a comfortable and secure framework of Freudian theory and practice. They knew what psychotherapy was, what its goals were, and the procedures by which to reach those goals. By contrast the field of psychotherapy today is fractionated in a hundred different ways, and the comfortable feeling of unified assurance has all but vanished.

In spite of the contradictions and confusions I have tried to describe, I find this a very exciting and hopeful period in the development of psychotherapy. It is a burgeoning period when new theories, new ideas, new methods of practice are being born at a startling rate. Psychotherapy is becoming a province of university departments, and hence its nature can be openly considered and discussed and criticized by professional workers whose daily livelihood does not depend upon defending a given point of view. Psychologists and psychiatrists are bursting forth with new conceptualizations of psychotherapy. I find this to be true even among graduate students. It is clear that the dogmatic views which held the profession in intellectual chains for many years have completely eroded and given way. Every worker in the field is now much more free to think his own thoughts, formulate his own views on the basis of his own experience, and put forth his own hypotheses. I regard this as a thoroughly healthy flowering of thought, even if a confusing one.

I believe I might bring this conceptual diversity alive if I try to indicate, even in oversimplified terms, the essence or core of the therapeutic experience as it seems to various therapists today. Suppose we were to ask today's wide variety of therapists, what is the essential moment of therapy? Granted that there are many background conditions and elements and procedures of therapy, what is the essence of the moment of change? What is the nature of those episodes in therapy where one feels that some real change has occurred, where it seems that one's client or patient has in some significant way altered in his personality, his self-organization, or his behavior? Recognizing that there is much that precedes such a moment and much that must follow it if therapy is to be complete, what is the *crucial* core, without which no lasting change could take place?

Years ago one would have received primarily one answer to such a question. Now it seems to me there are dozens of answers, often overlapping answers to be sure but still perceptibly different. I should like to give some of these answers as I have been able to understand them. I am sure no one individual will be satisfied with the formulation regarding his own point of view, both because it will be brief and oversimplified, and because of my own failure correctly to understand the nuances of each view. Nevertheless it may help to suggest the multiplying ways in which psychotherapy is now being perceived.

The traditional answer from the analytic group would, I believe, be this: that the moment of change is the moment in which there is an experience of insight or understanding of one's self in relation to one's past, usually following upon a well-timed interpretation.

But let us sample some of the many other answers. For the operant conditioning group I believe the statement would be something like this:

The moment of change in therapy involves no necessary conscious element at all; it is simply a slight alteration of behavior which occurs when the subject's verbal or other behavior varies by chance to a form which is slightly closer to the goal which the experimenter has chosen and is immediately rewarded. I do not call the participants therapist and client or patient, because I believe this group would prefer the more scientifically oriented term of experimenter and subject. I hope I have, however, satisfactorily described the essential unit of change as they perceive it. This is the way in which the individual's behavior would gradually be "shaped up."

Let us again choose a contrasting view. For the Atlanta group—Whitaker, Warkentin, Malone, and others (1959)—the essence of therapy seems to be those moments in which the patient and therapist(s) live together in a deeply experienced fantasy relationship having little or nothing to do with the real world but where the unconscious of one individual interacts with the unconscious of the other.

I trust it will be clear that the three formulations I have given are challengingly different. They cannot all be equally true, unless they represent three sharply different kinds of change, with sharply different outcomes. But let us add more.

Alexander (1946) and many neo-Freudians would see the essential moment of change in therapy as a corrective emotional experience, in which some crippling experience from the past is newly experienced in a new context and with different meaning.

On the other hand, George Kelly (1955) sees the key experience of therapy as one in which the individual recognizes that the way he has construed some aspect of his life is loosening or collapsing, and some reconstruing and some rebuilding of personal constructs is necessarily occurring.

The Adlerian therapist would see the critical moment in a somewhat similar way—as one in which the patient, thanks to the interpretation and teaching of the therapist, sees the mistaken concepts he has had regarding himself and his life and changes these erroneous conceptions.

With an even stronger cognitive emphasis Ellis (1962) sees the moment of change as being that moment when the individual is convinced by the therapist that the rational structure by which he has been functioning is in some respect erroneous and that the structure suggested by the therapist is more correct.

For myself and the group that clusters around the client-centered focus, the moment of therapy is still differently defined (Lewis, Rogers, and Shlien, 1959). It is the immediate and complete experiencing by the client, in a psychologically safe relationship, of a feeling which has hitherto been too threatening to experience freely.

Many of the learning theorists would feel that the unit of change in psychotherapy is the counter-conditioning of anxiety. The moment in which the subject or patient experiences anxiety simultaneously with a comfort situation which is incompatible with anxiety is the moment of change.

Other psychologists whose views develop from Festinger's (1957) theory of cognitive dissonance see it somewhat differently. For them the essence of change is the client's acceptance of the therapist's view of him, a view dissonant from his own but made acceptable by the high status and credibility of the therapist. It is essentially a moment of reduction of cognitive dissonance in the client.

The psychotherapists who start from an existential base would have a sharply divergent view. For them the core of therapy is the instantaneous subjective encounter of two separate individuals, an event which cannot be planned for but which can be *allowed* to occur—an I-Thou moment of relationship.

We could go on and on with these differing conceptions of the crucial moment in therapy. For those interested in family therapy it is the reliving of the family relationship in a new context provided by the therapist. For the person interested in Zen the crucial moment may be one of psychologic shock, as it was to the suicidal student who was enlightened and cured by the "thundering cry" of a Zen master (Sato, 1958).

Perhaps I have said enough to indicate that this rank growth of theory and practice in therapy has led to many diverging views as to what constitutes the essential moment of therapy, views which in some instances overlap but in others seem quite completely irreconcilable. If there were "thirty-six therapies" when Robert Harper (1959) wrote his book, there seem to me to be closer to one hundred today.

What is the meaning and significance of all these variations in view—the confusion, the contradictions, the differences? What are the implications for the whole realm of psychotherapy? I should like to give my views on this, but with a clear recognition that I have no special gift of prophecy and that I may be greatly mistaken.

It means, I believe, that we are backing off and taking a fresh look at the basic problem of our profession, with no inhibitions, few preconceptions, and no holds barred. We can ask again the central question, "How may constructive change in the behavior and personality of the troubled or deviant person be facilitated?" The variety of answers being given will, I believe, help us to open our minds to possibilities which we have not dreamed of before.

Another implication is that for the time being it will be a young man's field. The curiosity and skepticism, the vigor and creativity of younger minds, are freed by this chaotic situation. No longer is it governed by the heavy hand of supposedly wise elders. Young men are free to go at the problems freshly, without the sense of being rebels.

I am sure that because of this situation of confusion, various means of altering human behavior will be proposed and tried which will seem to some of us as unethical, unsound, ineffective, and philosophically indefensible. In this respect it will be a difficult period for experienced therapists. But ways of working will also be proposed and tried which will stretch our imaginations, open new vistas of effectiveness, challenge our complacencies, cut through our verbal elaborations, and produce new means of assistance to human beings.

I believe that the present variations in thought and practice mean that the day of systems, of schools of thought, of dogma, is over. Institutions and organizations which indoctrinate therapists in one point of view only are pure anachronisms in today's situation. I do not say this casually. I believe that psychoanalytic institutes—of whatever brand—with their cultish type of training, are on the way out. I would say exactly the same about university departments which expose their students only to training in client-centered therapy or in any other single approach to therapy. I know how hardy organizations are, and I am well aware that such narrow institutions may continue to function for a long time, but I believe their day of vital influence on thoughtful individuals is past.

In this connection I believe that an organization such as the American Academy of Psychotherapists will increasingly come into its own. I think its instigators—and I can speak freely because I was not one of that group—were even wiser than they knew. It is one of a very few organizations I know in this field in which a central purpose is to provide a forum for all points of view in therapy, with every approach equally welcome as long as the therapist himself is a broadly qualified professional person.[1] Certainly the distinctive hallmark of our meetings and workshops has been the directness and deep honesty of our interchanges, whether we are in full agreement or profound and almost violent disagreement. This quality of communication is helping to set a pattern for the future in which free and open consideration can be given to every serious new way of working in this field.

There is one final implication of this flowering diversity in psychotherapy. I wish to examine several facets of this implication. It is that of necessity we must move toward looking at the *facts*. And to look at the facts means moving toward research. We are beyond the point where differences will be resolved by the voice of authority or by commitment to an essentially religious type of faith in one point of view as against another. To buttress our theory by quotations from Freud or by pointing to the precision of our logic or even by appealing to the depth of our own inner conviction will not be enough. The public and the profession will want, in the words of the TV detective, "just the facts, please, ma'am, just the facts."

But how will we obtain these facts? First of all, perhaps, by a great extension of naturalistic observation. We need to *look* at therapy, in each of its various forms, and consider, openmindedly and thoughtfully, the events which are occurring. We need to do this individually, as we live with another person in a meaningful therapeutic relationship. We also need to do this as a profession. Here the Academy or some similar group might play a vital role. If the organization [were to] set as its goal one complete recorded case from each therapeutic point of view, what an astonishing difference this could make. The organization could furnish the recorder, the tapes, and a sympathetic person with the technical know-how to set up the recording in a satisfactory manner. Any serious therapist who was willing to have his work recorded, whether member or nonmember, would receive this service. Perhaps some day one of the major requirements for membership would be the submission of a complete recorded case.

This material, available for thoughtful study by any qualified professional person, would be a great stride forward. Its value would be multiplied if it contained two follow-up interviews at least one year after the conclusion of therapy, one conducted by the therapist and one conducted by an unbiased worker skilled in evoking responses to a series of survey questions which would be used with all clients.

Another way of getting at the facts is the em-

[1] The Association for the Advancement of Psychotherapy . . . is another such organization.

pirical study of observed behaviors in therapy. This means the testing of theory-based hypotheses by means of pretherapy and posttherapy tests and by measures of in-therapy behaviors on the part of both therapist and client. Most psychotherapy research to date has been of this type, but such studies could be greatly extended.

A third way of getting at the facts will be the use of laboratory situations. When an issue regarding psychotherapy has been clearly identified in its essential form, it will often be possible to develop a laboratory situation which contains the issue in simplified form, and to test it at the laboratory level. Some very valuable beginnings have already been made along this line. "Conflicts" have been created by hypnosis and then treated by differing procedures. In another study one group of clients talked to an understanding therapist, while another group talked to a tape recorder. In still another, clients were, under hypnosis, given different mind-sets as to the congruence of genuineness of their therapist. The differences in process under these different conditions have been studied. Such laboratory studies, much further developed, should teach us much about therapy.

But perhaps the most important means of getting at the facts will be an increasing skill and sophistication in measuring the subjective. A young psychologist (Bergin) recently showed me a paper of his, as yet unpublished. Its title says a great deal. It is "Worknotes Toward a Science of Inner Experience." In this paper he describes the encouraging progress being made in coming to grips with the crucial problem of measuring the subjective feelings which occur in one's personal experience. Little by little the strictly behavioristic approach is modifying its rigid resistance to the study of inner subjective problems. Ways are being discovered—phenomenological descriptions, Q sorts, semantic differentials—by which subjective feelings can be respectably and accurately put into operation and quantified. It is entirely possible that from this trend toward measuring the subjective will come not only new light on the complex processes of psychotherapy and personality change, but also a modification of our current philosophy of science. In any event this trend is already beginning to supply us with objective measurement of very subtle inner experiences. We can measure the changes which occur over therapy in the meaning of such concepts as mother, good, self, and therapist, as these concepts move in the "semantic space" of the client. We can reliably measure the degree of immediacy in the client's experiencing or the perception of the therapist's genuineness by the client. Such beginnings are extremely promising for the future.

All of these various channels of fact-finding will, I believe, be called into service as we try to determine objectively the changes which occur in different modes of therapy and the subtle preconditions which are associated with these changes. Such fact-finding processes are an inevitable part of the future of our field if it is to move forward. They need not interfere with the subjective personal quality of therapy itself—but they are essential if we are to find our way out of the present confusing Babel of voices, each with its own "truth."

Summary

Psychotherapy at the present time is in a state of chaos. It is not, however, a meaningless chaos, but an ocean of confusion, teeming with life, spawning vital new ideas, approaches, procedures, and theories at an incredibly rapid rate. Hence the present is a period in which the most diverse methods are used and in which the most divergent explanations are given for a single event. This situation makes inevitable the development of a new fact-finding attitude—a more objective appraisal of different types of change in personality and behavior and a more empirical understanding of the subtle subjective conditions which lead to these changes. Only on the basis of such facts can the therapist of the future select the way of working which is most effective in achieving his own deeper aims and those of his client. Only out of such a fact-finding attitude can a reasonable order again emerge in this crucially significant area and bring us again to some clarity in our understanding of ways by which constructive personality change may be facilitated.

REFERENCES

Alexander, F., & French, T. M. *Psychoanalytic therapy.* New York: Ronald Press, 1946.

Bergin, A. Personal communication, Teacher's College, Columbia University.

Ellis, A. *Reason and emotion in psychotherapy.* New York: Lyle Stuart, 1962.

Eysenck, H. J. *Dynamics of anxiety and hysteria.* New York: Praeger, 1957. Pp. 267–268.

Festinger, L. *A theory of cognitive dissonance.* Evanston, Ill.: Row, Peterson, 1957.

Harper, R. A. *Psychoanalysis and psychotherapy: 36 systems.* Englewood Cliffs, N.J.: Prentice-Hall, 1959.

Kelly, G. A. *The psychology of personal constructs.* (2 vols.) New York: Norton, 1955.

Lewis, M. K., Rogers, C. R., & Shlien, J. M. Time-limited, client-centered psychotherapy: Two cases. In

A. Burton (Ed.), *Case studies in counseling and psychotherapy.* Englewood Cliffs, N.J.: Prentice-Hall, 1959. Pp. 309–352.

Lindsley, O. R. Operant conditioning methods applied to research in chronic schizophrenia. *Psychiatric Research Reports,* 1956, No. 5, 118–153.

Sato, K. Implications of Zen Buddhism for psychotherapy. *Psychologia,* December 1958, 1.

Snyder, W. U. In S. W. Standal & R. J. Corsini (Eds.), *Critical incidents in psychotherapy.* Englewood Cliffs, N.J.: Prentice-Hall, 1959. Pp. 38–63.

Standal, S. W., & Corsini, R. J. (Eds.) *Critical incidents in psychotherapy.* Englewood Cliffs, N.J.: Prentice-Hall, 1959. Pp. 38–63.

Time Magazine, May 19, 1961.

Whitaker, C. A., Warkentin, J., & Malone, T. P. The involvement of the professional therapist. In A. Burton (Ed.), *Case studies in counseling and psychotherapy.* Englewood Cliffs, N.J.: Prentice-Hall, 1959. Pp. 218–256.

Wolpe, J. *Psychotherapy of reciprocal inhibition.* Stanford, Calif.: Stanford University Press, 1958.

56

The Functional Autonomy of Psychotherapy

Alexander W. Astin

While the majority of psychologists, psychiatrists, and members of the lay public believe that psychotherapy does bring more rapid benefits than simply "living with" or "working out" one's own problems does, various clinical researchers such as Hans Eysenck have questioned the actual value of such treatment. On the basis of a considerable amount of data such investigators have concluded that the actual effects of psychotherapy are relatively small, since the rate of improvement for treated and untreated individuals appears to be approximately the same.

In the preceding selection Rogers, while admitting that there is considerable confusion regarding psychotherapy and psychotherapeutic techniques, never questions its actual value. Here, Astin suggests several arguments to support the idea that the record of psychotherapy is unimpressive and little is gained by such treatment regardless of what technique is used. He also points out that in spite of this record, psychotherapy continues to thrive and has achieved a kind of existence for its own sake or, in Astin's terms, has become "functionally autonomous." It should be noted, however, that while Astin's article is generally critical of the value of psychotherapy, he is extremely sympathetic to the problems which are encountered by researchers attempting to make carefully controlled studies which might clearly indicate whether psychotherapy is or is not of value.

Once upon a time there was a method for treating mental problems called psychotherapy. Those who were around when it first came into vogue may remember that its principal purpose was to provide a service to troubled people who had asked for help. This function was, in fact, psychotherapy's raison d'etre. After people began to use this method, however, evidence of its efficacy was unimpressive and skepticism was advanced regarding whether it was really fulfilling its purpose. As had usually been the case with other treatment methods of similarly dubious value, psychotherapy should have died out. But it did not. It did not even waver. Psychotherapy had, it appeared, achieved *functional autonomy.*

This development was of especially profound significance for practitioners, who, at last freed from the petty demands of having to serve their clients, were now able to engage in hot squabbles about how psychotherapy should be done and hotter ones about who should do it (Anderson, 1956; Ausubel, 1956; Blanton *et al.,* 1953; Brody, 1956; Kelly, 1956; Sanford, 1953). Another noteworthy byproduct was the formation within the American Psychological and Psychiatric Associa-

From American Psychologist, *Vol. 16 (1961), 75–78. Copyright 1961 by the American Psychological Association, and reproduced by permission.*

tions of committees on relations with each other. It should be noted that these developments actually enhanced psychotherapy's emerging functional autonomy by giving it several new and expanding functions.

The Reactionaries

Despite this surge of productive activity, certain reactionaries within the field attempted to lead psychotherapy back to the Dark Ages. Notable among these was Eysenck (1952), who claimed that nowhere in the scientific literature was there any good evidence that psychotherapy worked. In a crushing attack on Eysenck's position, Rosensweig (1954) pointed out that neither was there any good evidence that psychotherapy *hurt* anybody. Eysenck (1955) agreed. Now that everyone agreed that the evidence was no good, psychotherapy had been vindicated.

Another reactionary position was advanced by Hoppock (1953), who believed that clients were entitled to help with the problem that they asked to be helped with. This in turn was attacked by Kaufmann and Allerhand (1953) on the grounds that it might be dangerous to try to give the client what he asks for. Hoppock (1954) replied weakly that we really know nothing one way or the other and that we must do more research.

Eysenck tried again (1954) to promote his position. This time his claim was that to squabble over who should do psychotherapy before its efficacy had been demonstrated is, in essence, to put the cart before the horse. Eysenck was answered by Raush (1954), as follows: "It is not the point to discuss the efficacy or lack of efficacy of psychotherapy here. . . . psychotherapy is a method for studying the human psyche . . . whether it is a good or bad method is not at issue" (p. 588). Thus, without the bothersome business of first knowing if, how, or under what conditions psychotherapy might work, we could still engage in controversies about who should perform it and also use it to "study the psyche." Who could doubt now that psychotherapy had indeed become functionally autonomous?

Ethics?

Ethical considerations, while not raised specifically by these reactionaries, nevertheless seemed to be involved in some of their arguments. The question of efficacy or outcome, rephrased in ethical terms, might have run as follows: Since this client has asked for our help and may even be paying us for it, are we not morally and ethically *obligated* to determine if we are giving him anything for his time and money?

Fortunately, the *Ethical Standards of Psychologists* (APA, 1953), based on the fundamental ethical position of "contribution to the welfare of man," was being developed to insure that members of the Profession would give due consideration to any relevant ethical issues. For example, the main stated principle in the section on "Recognizing Limitations of Psychological Techniques" warns: "The psychologist should refuse to suggest, support, or condone unwarranted assumptions . . . in the use of psychological instruments or techniques" (p. 41). An extension of this principle states that "tests [should] be made available . . . for routine use only when adequate . . . validity data are available" (p. 153). Appropriately, the Profession was questioning the "contribution to the welfare of man" of tests whose validity was still in doubt. Indeed, the only condition under which the Profession would condone the use of such tests was if they were "conspicuously marked 'experimental use only' " (p. 153).

These cautions were not similarly extended to include the "psychological technique" of psychotherapy, most likely in order to protect the therapists and clients from the possibly disturbing effects of "EXPERIMENTAL USE ONLY" signs on office doors and couches. The wary reader, who by now may detect some inconsistency or error of omission in the ethical code, will be relieved to know that any possible inconsistency was recently eliminated for good when a revised code (APA, 1959) appeared in which the ethic having to do with "condoning unwarranted assumptions" has been dispensed with altogether.

More Ethics

A serious ethical objection lodged by the practitioners against "outcome" research centered around the necessity for using controls in such investigations. Because of the limited usefulness of comparing psychotherapy with other therapies or even with therapy "wait" groups, an adequately designed outcome study required denying treatment to a comparable group of clients. Practitioners, in their ethical concern for the welfare of their clients (see "Ethics?" above), were opposed to the practice of refusing treatment to sick people who ask for it.

In a desperate counterargument, some reactionaries suggested that psychotherapy might conceivably be *detrimental* under certain conditions, and that ethical considerations really *demanded* that controlled outcome studies be done in order to evaluate at least these possibilities. Some even went so far as to suggest that interprofessional squabbling, legislation, quack-hunting, etc. represented more than a struggle for power and prestige, i.e., that these concerns reflected a belief that clients *could* be harmed by psychotherapy. Practitioners, on the other hand, were quick to point out (e.g., Eysenck, 1952) that nowhere in the literature was there any good evidence that psychotherapy did any harm. Scientifically minded practitioners were understandably reluctant to act on any such "belief" in the absence of valid evidence.

Outcome's Outcome

The later history of the outcome problem can be mapped by examining the chapters on "psychotherapy" appearing in the *Annual Review of Psychology*.

In 1955 Meehl was able to find only one outcome study which "approximated" the "minimum standards" of a control group, pre- and posttherapy evaluations, and follow-up. Echoing Eysenck's reactionary arguments, Meehl made a desperate plea for better outcome studies.

The following year Harris (1956) observed: "Critical evaluations by reviewers of the literature on psychotherapy in previous years could be repeated here with undiminished relevance" (p. 143).

None of the many outcome studies reviewed the next year by Winder (1957) employed an equivalent no-therapy control group. The author also cited the need for follow-ups, concluding that "Outcome criteria could be substantially improved . . . by selecting measures which are intrinsically powerful, e.g., measures based on how the person behaves and relates to others in his life environment" (p. 328).

In the 1958 review Snyder, commenting on outcome methodology, reported: "Most of these outcome studies leave a great deal to be desired. . . . in general the more rigorous the criteria the less encouraging the results" (pp. 366–367).

The following year Luborsky (1959) noted: "Fortunately there have been recently fewer of the simplistic type of outcome studies in which the end point of the study is to present percentages of patients who have improved or have not improved, broken down according to diagnostic labels" (p. 318). The reviewer does not also give his opinion

on *well*-designed studies of outcome, perhaps because there were none. He does, however, point out that "It has yet to be demonstrated that control groups in psychotherapy research have a more than very limited usefulness" (p. 328).

That Luborsky's comments were indicative of a trend away from the outcome issue is confirmed in Rotter's 1960 review: "Research studies in psychotherapy tend to be concerned more with some aspects of the psychotherapeutic procedure and less with outcome. . . . to some extent, it reflects an interest in the psychotherapy situation as a kind of personality laboratory" (p. 407). This would appear to be one more instance where psychotherapy's functional autonomy has fostered progress in the field, i.e., by being able to dismiss the question of efficacy we can now use the therapy situation as a research laboratory.

The Experts

Perhaps the most up-to-date picture of outcome's waning popularity is available in a recent monograph, *Research in Psychotherapy* (Rubinstein and Parloff, 1959), which is based on an interdisciplinary conference of 27 experts in the field. In summarizing the main biases and points of view of these experts, the editors conclude: "As if by some tacit agreement the issue of outcome was skirted by the conference." An attempt was made to account for this fact by reviewing the pros and cons of doing outcome research. Accordingly, 23 lines were devoted to the arguments of outcome "Advocates," and 170 lines were used to review the arguments of the "Critics." Some of their major objections were:

1. We become identified with the practitioner's "simple pragmatic concerns" at the expense of basic science. Clearly, basic science must avoid the taint of pragmatics if it is to remain pure. (A related objection to outcome research, which was not mentioned specifically in the conference, has to do with the "scut work" necessary to conduct follow-ups in the community. No one will argue that attempting to measure our client's behavior in his natural habitat is scut work and that attempting to measure it in the consultation room is pure science.)

2. An "unexpressed fear that patient change may not be a consequence unique to psychotherapy." (Finding out that psychotherapy does not work could create severe economic problems by putting thousands of people out of work and by

requiring the dissolution of numerous committees.)

3. Everybody is already "convinced" that it works.

4. Criterion problems: Any attempt to select "specific criteria [is] a premature and presumptuous value judgment." (To expect anyone to define what therapists are trying to do is admittedly unreasonable.)

It may be superfluous to point out that the sole argument of the Advocates of outcome research, i.e., that accepting a patient for treatment implies "that the patient is justified in his expectation that psychotherapy will be of benefit to him," pales when pitted against those of the Critics.

The Future

Now that the reactionaries have been crushed and psychotherapy continues to flourish, the possibilities for future progress seem limitless. If nothing else, we can be sure that the principle of functional autonomy will permit psychotherapy to survive long after it has outlived its usefulness as a personality laboratory.

REFERENCES

American Psychological Association. *Ethical standards of psychologists.* Washington, D.C.: APA, 1953.

American Psychological Association. Ethical standards of psychologists. *American Psychologist,* 1959, **14,** 279–282.

Anderson, W. On the practice of psychotherapy by the nonmedically trained. *American Psychologist,* 1956, **11,** 197–199.

Ausubel, D. P. Relationships between psychology and psychiatry: The hidden issues. *American Psychologist,* 1956, **11,** 99–113.

Blanton, R. L., Brown, L., Davis, J. E., Jr., Johnson, D. T., Kipnis, E., Kramish, A. A., Nichols, R. C., Ward, L. C., Jr., Webster, H., Weingarten, E., Cohen, L., Ellson, D. G., Kasman, S., Meyers, T. J., Schnack, G. F., & Volle, F. O. Comments on "Relations with psychiatry." *American Psychologist,* 1953, **8,** 590–595.

Brody, E. B. Interprofessional relations, or psychologists and psychiatrists are human too, only more so. *American Psychologist,* 1956, **11,** 105–111.

Eysenck, H. J. The effects of psychotherapy: An evaluation. *Journal of Consulting Psychology,* 1952, **16,** 319–324.

Eysenck, H. J. Further comments on "Relations with psychiatry." *American Psychologist,* 1954, **9,** 157–158.

Eysenck, H. J. The effects of psychotherapy: A reply. *Journal of Abnormal and Social Psychology,* 1955, **50,** 147–148.

Harris, R. E. Clinical methods: Psychotherapy. *Annual Review of Psychology,* 1956, **7,** 121–146.

Hoppock, R. What is the "real" problem? *American Psychologist,* 1953, **8,** 124.

Hoppock, R. The real problem. *American Psychologist,* 1954, **9,** 81–82.

Kaufmann, P., & Allerhand, M. E. Comment on Hoppock's "What is the 'real' problem?" *American Psychologist,* 1953, **8,** 524.

Kelly, G. A. Issues: Hidden or mislaid. *American Psychologist,* 1956, **11,** 112–113.

Luborsky, L. Psychotherapy. *Annual Review of Psychology,* 1959, **10,** 317–344.

Meehl, P. E. Psychotherapy. *Annual Review of Psychology,* 1955, **6,** 357–378.

Raush, H. L. Comment on Eysenck's "Further comment on 'relations with psychiatry.'" *American Psychologist,* 1954, **9,** 588–589.

Rosensweig, S. A transvaluation of psychotherapy: A reply to Hans Eysenck, *Journal of Abnormal and Social Psychology,* 1954, **49,** 298–304.

Rotter, J. B. Psychotherapy. *Annual Review of Psychology,* 1960, **11,** 381–414.

Rubinstein, E. A., & Parloff, M. B. *Research in psychotherapy.* Washington, D.C.: APA, 1959.

Stanford, F. H. Relations with psychiatry. *American Psychologist,* 1953, **8,** 169–173.

Snyder, W. U. Psychotherapy. *Annual Review of Psychology,* 1958, **9,** 353–374.

Winder, C. L. Psychotherapy. *Annual Review of Psychology,* 1957, **8,** 309–330.

57

LSD: Therapeutic Effects
of the Psychedelic Experience

Charles Savage, Ethel Savage, James Fadiman, and Willis Harman

The use of D-lysergic acid diethylamide (LSD) has recently become a topic of considerable social comment, controversy, and legal activity. As nearly everyone is aware, there has been a considerable number of newspaper and magazine reports regarding the deleterious effects of LSD on the personality, perceptions, and behavior of individuals. At the same time, other stories and reports extol its virtues as a technique to expand consciousness, gain insights, and achieve a better integrated personality. The authors of the following selection discuss several cases in which the effects of an LSD experience were long lasting and apparently beneficial to the participants.

The word *psychedelic* literally means "mind manifesting." We have further defined it as a temporary expansion of consciousness due to not yet understood changes in cortical and subcortical functioning. It is the contention of this paper that a *single* psychedelic experience induced by a high dose of LSD may be followed by associated behavioral changes in the direction of self-actualization. In subsequent work we hope to demonstrate the hypothesis that the patterns of behavior changes are positively correlated with alterations in the individual's value and belief system which arise directly out of his interpretation of the psychedelic experience. We have deliberately chosen Osmond's term, psychedelic, to clearly differentiate our work from those who have used LSD as an aid to psychotherapy or as an aid to the study of insanity.

It is often argued that the psychedelic experiences occur as a result of suggestion. In point of fact they seem to occur in the work of all groups using LSD. But unless they occur in a secure setting with sufficient emotional support where S feels safe to encounter the bizarre and often powerful manifestations of his own mind unharassed by tests, interpretations, and the coldly precise scientific or analytic attiude, the only result can be confusion and paranoia (Savage, Terrill, and Jackson, 1962).

General Procedure

In a recent article Sherwood, Stolaroff, and Harman (1962) described a method of inducing a psy-

chedelic experience. Preparation lasting approximately a month preceding the LSD session consists of weekly inhalations of a mixture of 70 per cent CO_2 and 30 per cent O_2, together with exploratory interviews. This preparation accustoms the patient to an altered state of consciousness, builds up necessary rapport between patient and therapist, and helps the patient clarify specific problem areas he wishes to examine. On the session day the patient is given 200 to 300 μgr. of LSD plus 200 to 400 mg. of mescaline initially, with 100 to 300 μgr. of LSD added a few hours later if needed. The experience is followed up by several weeks of post-LSD interviews, reviewing the notes and the recording made during the session. Throughout the procedure a great deal of emotional support is offered, but not interpretative psychotherapy. The reader is referred to the paper by Sherwood, *et al.* (1962) for details.

Questionnaire data

A three-phase program has been developed to assess this approach.[1] (1) A retrograde assessment

Reprinted with permission of the authors and Psychological Reports, *1964,* **14,** *111–120.* © *Southern Universities Press 1964. This investigation was supported in part by Public Health Fellowship MH-16,900 from the National Institute of Mental Health.*

[1] All Ss were given LSD in a private clinic cooperating with the International Foundation for Advanced Study.

of work done previously on 113 patients. A follow-up questionnaire was employed. Ninety-three patients responded. (2) Ongoing assessment of current patients 1 month before, immediately after LSD, 2 months after, and 6 months after. At the time of this writing 74 had reached the 6-month check point. (3) Design of a controlled study has been based on this experience and funds are being sought for its implementation.

*   *   *

Only one patient felt he had been harmed mentally. This patient suffered from obsessive ruminations for about 9 months after his session. He attributed this to a lack of emotional support during his LSD session. He is now improved above his original baseline and is inclined to think LSD has helped him, although he still resents the conduct of the session. Immediately after LSD 24 per cent find that daydreaming and introspection interfere with getting things done. This has fallen to 11 per cent after one year. The percentage of fresh marital problems is 27 per cent for nonpatients and 16 per cent for patients.

The questionnaire data are supplemented by available clinical data. One patient attempted suicide unsuccessfully 2 months after LSD. Pre-LSD history included depression, suicidal attempts, and hospitalization. Another had a psychotic break 9 months after LSD. This patient was a chronically unfaithful alcoholic. His wife left him. He returned to drinking. His follow-up appointments were not kept. Finally he entered *another facility* where it was proposed to give him LSD a second time. He became psychotic on the eve of his proposed second session. He has since recovered. Of 19 couples seeking resolution of severe marital problems, two couples have filed for divorce and two have separated. All had had previous separations. One couple in the process of obtaining a divorce are now living together again. These are the only negative reactions known to us at the time of writing.

On the positive side the percentage of patients answering the questionnaire who claimed lasting benefits is high: 83 per cent. Assuming that all nonrespondents were negative (an untrue assumption) the percentage for patients is 70 per cent. It is instructive to note that the claimed improvement rate rises from 76 per cent after 1 to 3 months to 85 per cent 3 to 6 months after LSD, and this figure remains constant more than 12 months after LSD. A list of the most commonly reported benefits would include: increase in ability to love, 78 per cent; to handle hostility, 69 per cent; to communicate, 69 per cent; and to understand self and others, 88 per cent; improved relations, 72 per cent; decreased anxiety, 66 per cent; increased self-esteem, 71 per cent; a new way of looking at the world, 83 per cent.

Data from behavior ratings

Recognizing that questionnaire data, although sometimes impressive, are also suspect, we have made clinical ratings on the 74 patients who are at least 6 months past their LSD experience and on whom we have accumulated enough data to make a judgment in which we feel some confidence. (This group includes 48 men and 26 women, with ages ranging from 22 to 67 and a mean age of 36.9.) The significance of these data must inevitably await the conclusion of the study, and they are merely offered as illustrative of the changes seen so far. However, they seem to militate against the view that the questionnaire data can be discounted as halo effect resulting from a residual drug-induced euphoria. The ratings are: Marked improvement, 12; Moderate improvement, 22; Minimal improvement, 26; No change, 13; Worse, 1.

A few clinical examples will illustrate the type of data on which the ratings were made. They are based on a nonweighted pooling of the clinical data and the psychological data. The psychological data include before-and-after MMPIs, with blind evaluation of improvement by an independent psychologist who has had considerable experience in similar evaluation on other projects. They also include the Leary (1957) Interpersonal Check List (ICL) and a 2-hour structured behavior-change interview schedule given at the 6-month follow-up, which contains detailed questions about specific aspects of personal habit patterns, relationships, work activities, etc., most to be answered with "more," "less," or "same."

Case I: Marked Improvement.
Forty-five-year-old engineer
with long history of depression

Chief complaints. These were defeatism, guilt, despondency, melancholia, irritability, perfectionism, inferiority, and fright. One month after LSD, patient reports himself as more hopeful; more optimistic; less constrained to worry; much less chagrined at the briefness of corporeal existence; less melancholic, self-pitying, and maudlin; more forgiving; more relaxed visage; and with less tendency to emotional reclusiveness.

Behavior interview summary at 6 months after LSD. He is described as warm, confident; alert; less anxious; more hopeful; more self-confident; with reduction in fatigue, headaches, indigestion and boredom; completely off tranquilizers (meprobamate); assured; intact; and genial.

Blind evaluation of MMPI at 6 months. "Six-month follow-up: Continues to change significantly in the positive direction consistent with the trends noted in the pre-post report. The changes between Tests 2 and 3 are greater than between 1 and 2. All of the changes indicated previously continued unabated. He continues to come out of himself, feels more comfortable with people—and more tolerant—and is more expressive emotionally. He no longer avoids emotional closeness nor denies a need for affection and support. He is no longer depressed. Although still an intellectualizer, his ruminations are more positive and optimistic. The decrease in depression and compulsive habits is particularly noteworthy because the euphoria, grandiosity, and ego inflation noted after Test 2 have subsided. He is levelheaded, reality testing is good, and yet he has an enhanced (quiet) sense of well-being. Self-acceptance is high but within realistic bounds. Defensiveness and guardedness continue to decrease. Obsessive-compulsive tendencies seem stably reduced. These changes are heartening. They seem particularly impressive and significant accomplished in the absence of follow-up treatment, i.e., if they can be attributed directly to the LSD experience plus independent assimilation." Clinical evaluation concurs.

Case II: Marked Improvement.
Fifty-year-old physician

Chief complaint. Heavy drinking; fear of becoming alcoholic, insane and homosexual; discomfort in social relations; and problems with his wife. On psychiatric examination he appeared anxious, withdrawn, tense, disorganized, guilt-ridden, and depressed.

Later assessment. At 2 months after LSD the blind evaluation of the MMPI was: "Very marked decrease in subjective discomfort, anxiety, and depression at time of second testing. Greatly elevated sense of well-being, self-confidence, and self-satisfaction. Feelings of depression have been replaced with a quiet serenity, contemplative reflection has replaced obsessive rumination. Behaviorally he is less driven, far less compulsive (formerly a major defense), and more gregarious. He is much less troubled by guilt feelings, more self-accepting

and accepting of others. Anxiety and tension are minimal at Test 2 whereas this was not so, pre-LSD. Further assimilation of the LSD experience seems unlikely however. His present defenses seem well-constituted and restrictive of greater expansiveness, greater tolerance of ambiguity and a richer fantasy life (creative expression). Yet the changes which have occurred between testing are positive and substantial."

The Leary Interpersonal Check List suggests that he is less over-conventional and more responsible, a view which his associates and his wife endorse. On the 6-month behavior-rating interview he appeared to be a healthy, vigorous, relaxed man, self-confident at work and at home. His health had vastly improved, particularly his somatic complaints; upset stomach and headache have practically disappeared. His only new complaint is that he is more aware of the suffering of others. His dreams are more intense, colorful, enjoyable. He spends more time at work and gets more accomplished. He takes more responsibility and gives more responsibility. He has become more reflective and values introspection highly, especially as a way of seeing why he wants others to behave in certain ways. He is spending more time with his children and sees them as a new and endless source of pleasure. He spends less time disciplining the children, feeling that much of his former disciplining was a way of taking out his other worries on them. His drinking pattern has shifted from a long beer bust at least once a week to almost never taking a drink for any reason. He has more friends from different areas of life than ever before. He enjoys nature more, especially animals. Since his session he has acquired a dog. His sexual pattern is changed. He has intercourse less frequently but derives much more pleasure from it. He is less afraid of insanity, suicide, and homosexuality. He is at ease within himself, able to face his environment with a wholesome detachment. He is successful but not ambitious, loving but not possessive, vigorous but not manic. Psychiatric examination at 6 months after LSD reveals no complaints, no symptoms.

Case III: Moderate Improvement

Chief complaint. This patient is a forty-year-old chemist whose chief complaint was depression and an inability to get along with his wife.

Later assessment. At 2 months the blind rating of MMPI profiles shows: "The increase in psychic pain seems primarily a function of a realization of personal shortcomings, i.e., less of a tendency to project or externalize conflict. His subjective distress takes the form of anxiety and depression. There is less complaining, less suspiciousness of others, less compulsivity, and a greater openness to experience, particularly intimate experience . . . . There is some indication that the increase in anxiety and defensiveness is transient. He has adequate ego resources to cope with these stresses." The ICL shows a greater reality perception of his children. On psychiatric examination at 6 months he has regained his potency and his wife has overcome her frigidity. The marriage is happier. He is less anxious and depressed but he is preoccupied with problems at work. Behavior-rating change shows that he has discontinued meprobamate, has better sexual relations, quarrels less frequently with wife, communicates more with her, spends more time with the children, gets along better with both siblings and parents. Since he was getting psychotherapy before and after LSD, he must be excluded from any final assessment of the psychedelic experience alone. This case is considered illustrative in that the LSD experience seems to have set in action a series of events which have led to improved interpersonal relations, yet it did not seem to facilitate psychotherapy in the conventional sense of "working through."

Case IV: Minimal Improvement

Chief complaint. This thirty-year-old married clerk complained of inability to relate to others, lack of fulfillment, and depression. He was entirely preoccupied with reading about esoteric philosophy.

Six months after LSD. The MMPI shows no progress: "Only slight changes in personality and mood are reflected at the time of the second testing. On both testing occasions considerable neurotic disturbance is indicated. An extremely defensive, over-controlled individual, it seems likely that he strongly resisted the LSD experience and derived little benefit from it. Extremely fearful of his own impulses and fantasies. Self-examination is very threatening to him. A rather hostile person, he has difficulty expressing or acknowledging aggressive feelings. Prominent defenses include compulsivity, somatic complaints, and intellectualization. Emotional distance in relations with others is also prominent. He seems depressed and in considerable distress." On psychiatric and behavioral-change interview at six months he seems much more concerned with interpersonal problems and

much less with the cosmos. Also he has stopped beating his wife. This behavioral change is considered sufficient to warrant a judgment of minimal improvement.

Case V: No Improvement

Chief complaints. This is a thirty-five-year-old housewife who complains of chronic depression, loneliness, inability to free herself of her mother's dominance, and a chronic sense of frustration and lack of fulfillment. Years of analysis have failed to change this.

Later assessment. Her MMPI at 2 months accurately sums up her situation. No better language could be found to describe the clinical situation which is the same before, 2 and 6 months after LSD. "Greatly depressed, emotionally, and socially withdrawn person who is probably experiencing considerable incapacitation as a result of her distress and symptoms. These include guilt-ridden ruminations, compulsivity and preoccupation with personal failings. At the same time there is a good deal of covert hostility which she has difficulty acknowledging and expressing. Tends to be passive-aggressive and passive-dependent. Subtly demanding of affection. Also preoccupied with her body and physical attractiveness. Physical complaints likely. Lacks spontaneity but is quite imaginative."

Case VI: Worse

Complaints. This patient is a thirty-five-year-old married writer, who complained of severe feelings of isolation and depression.

Assessment. During LSD he felt considerable loss of emotional support and subsequently became very depressed with occasional manic flights. He was treated with psychotherapy. At the end of 6 months he had returned to his baseline state. All of the improvements claimed during periods of elation were lost, but his depression was judged clinically to have returned to what it was. His MMPI was identical before LSD and 6 months after LSD.

It may be seen that one may raise questions about the permanence of the changes in the minimal improvement group since they are not accompanied by associated change on the formal psychological testing. (Conversely, one may raise questions about the adequacy of the psychological testing but that is a different issue.) Yet the improvement rate (81 per cent) on these 74 cases is not far out of line with the claimed improvement rate reported by the questionnaire (83 per cent) and prompts a certain feeling of confidence in the questionnaire results.

Discussion

*   *   *

We consider that the psychedelic experience is neither a replacement for nor an adjuvant to traditional modes of therapy, but rather it adds a new and perhaps neglected dimension to therapy. A totemistic regard for the powers of logic and reason must not blind us to the failures of rationalism. In the psychedelic experience the individual surrenders briefly to unreason, to a more primary process, and gains new strength to reinforce reason.

A final note of caution. There is no process, idea or material that cannot be misused. There has been unfortunate and undue publicity about the imagined and potential evils of LSD. It has been

used inappropriately in the past and undoubtedly will be used inappropriately in the future. Even so, the rate of adverse reactions has not been alarming (Cohen, 1960; Cohen and Ditman, 1963). Yet *used wisely* it may be that psychedelic experience offers us new hope of enlightenment, new hope of self-realization, and new hopes of alleviating the unhappiness displayed most obviously in the mentally ill.

REFERENCES

Cohen, S. Lysergic Acid Diethylamide: Side effects and complications. *Journal of Nervous and Mental Diseases*, 1960, **130**, 30–40.

Cohen, S., & Ditman, K. S. Prolonged adverse reactions to Lysergic Acid Diethylamide. *Archives of General Psychiatry*, 1963, **8**, 475–480.

Leary, T. F. *Interpersonal diagnosis of personality*. New York: Ronald Press, 1957.

Savage, C., Terrill, J., & Jackson, D. D. LSD, transcendence, and the new beginning. *Journal of Nervous and Mental Diseases*, 1962, **135**, 425–439.

Sherwood, J. N., Stolaroff, M. J., & Harman, W. W. The psychedelic experience—A new concept in psychotherapy. *Journal of Neuropsychiatry*, 1962, **4**, 69–80.

58

Prolonged Adverse Reactions to Lysergic Acid Diethylamide

Sidney Cohen and Keith S. Ditman

While the preceding selection presented scientific evidence of the therapeutic effects of the LSD experience, there is also considerable evidence that the effects can be deleterious. Recent research has suggested that chromosome changes can occur from prolonged use and these mutations might be transmittable to the offspring of the users. Other scientific reports have indicated that if LSD is taken by pregnant mothers, the effects on the infant may be similar to those resulting from taking the tranquilizer thalidomide.

The reports of harmful effects to the individual in terms of prolonged adjustment problems and adverse personality changes have been widely circulated in the newspapers and popular magazines. Regarding these reports, many raise the question of whether the negative effects were due to the drug per se, or due to the fact that impurities, an overdose, or the environment in which it was taken may have caused the aberrant behavior. Based on the results reported here by Cohen and Ditman, the answer would seem to be that the drug itself can bring about long-term negative effects, since their experiment was conducted in a clinical setting where purity, dosage, and environmental stimuli were carefully controlled.

Recently the authors (Cohen and Ditman, 1962) briefly reported complications and misuses associated with hallucinogenic drugs such as D-lysergic

From Archives of General Psychiatry, Vol. 8 (1963), 475–480. Reproduced with permission of the editor of the Journal of the American Medical Association and the authors.

acid diethylamide (LSD). Recently, an increasing number of adverse reactions to these drugs have occurred, and a discussion of the nature of the complications appears indicated. It is not our intention to minimize the potential value of these agents. Rather, we wish to emphasize the importance of continued research with this group of compounds so that their advantages and limitations are eventually understood. We have already reported on certain aspects of their therapeutic properties (Cohen and Eisner, 1959; Ditman, Hayman, and Whittlesey, 1962). However, the question of their therapeutic value remains unsettled since no definitive study has been reported. It is our impression that they are unique tools in the study of altered states of awareness, perception, and ideation.

The nomenclature of these compounds poses problems. 'Hallucinogen" is a poor name for this group since true hallucinations occur infrequently. "Illusinogen" (Cohen, 1960b; Ditman and Whittlesey, 1959) would be more appropriate, for almost invariably, distortions of perception elaborated from sensory cues are noted. The term "psychotomimetic" has been popular, but only delineates a segment of the reaction forms, for many subjects do not experience a psychotic-like state at all. Osmond's (1957) term "psychedelic," meaning mind manifesting, has the advantage of being nonjudgmental, but may be too general, since psychic stimulants and sedatives could logically be included under the phrase "mind manifesting." Other names for this group of drugs have been: phantastica, deliriants, psychotogens, and psychodysleptics.

An impressive list of botanicals and synthetic chemicals with hallucinogenic properties has been found as a result of assiduous searches by modern psychopharmacologists and primitive man. Chemically, they may be subclassified according to the inclusion or the absence of an indole ring in their structure.

The principal indole hallucinogens are:

1. D-Lysergic acid diethylamide (LSD) and its many congeners. LSD is a semisynthetic diethylamide from lysergic acid, a naturally occurring constituent of the fungus, ergot. A recent development is Hofmann's (1961) isolation of D-lysergic acid monoethylamide and D-isolysergic acid from ololiuqui. For the first time a lysergic acid derivative with hallucinogenic activity has been found in nature.

2. Psilocybine (4-hydroxy-N-dimethyltryptamine orthophosphate) and psilocin (4-hydroxydimethyl-

tryptamine). These were isolated by Hofmann (Hofmann and Troxler, 1959) from the Mexican mushrooms of the *Psilocybe mexicana* group.

3. Bufotenine (5-hydroxy-N-dimethyltryptamine). This is an hallucinogen with marked autonomic properties which has been separated from both the skin of certain toads and from cohaba snuff.

The principal nonindolic psychotogens are:

1. Mescaline (3,4,5,-trimethoxyphenethylamine) obtained from the peyote cactus. The buttons of the plant have been used for centuries by Mexican and Southwestern Indians as part of their religious rituals.

2. Hashish (marihuana, cannabis indica). This is also a drug with a long and intriguing history. Yogis found it useful as an aid in meditation. The Thug and Hashishin (assassin) sects employed it for more nefarious purposes. A series of cannabinols have been extracted from hashish and need further investigation.

From a review of the literature and a survey of investigators three years ago, one of us (Cohen, 1960a) reported on a number of difficulties encountered with the use of LSD. Results of this study are enumerated below:

1. Complications were more apt to occur in patients undergoing psychotherapy with the drug than in experimental subjects.

2. The LSD experience was so dramatic that subsequent illness might be attributed to the drug exposure by either patient or physician.

3. Physical disturbances attributable to the drug were extremely rare and did not cluster about any single organ system.

4. Psychological complications, although infrequent, were the main problems arising from the use of LSD. They consisted of attempted or completed suicides and prolonged psychotic reactions.

5. No instance of physiologic addiction to LSD was encountered.

6. Precautions in selection of patients and subjects and their protection during and after the LSD state were proposed.

More recently, additional untoward effects to LSD have come to our attention; some of them have not been adequately described in previous communications.

Prolonged or Psychotic Decompensation

A single, or a series of, LSD treatments can produce a psychotic break presumably by releasing overwhelming conflictual material which cannot be handled by the patient's established defenses. It is possible that LSD disrupts psychic homeostatic mechanisms and permits reinforcement of latent delusional or paranoid ideas. Presumably, this occurs when the normal aversive and critical functions of the ego are impaired under LSD.

Case 1

The patient, a thirty-six-year-old, married legal secretary appeared requesting psychiatric treatment. At the time of the interview, two years after a single LSD experience, she was preoccupied with pseudophilosophic abstractions about truth, beauty, love, and life. She was flamboyant, under considerable pressure of speech, and easily distractible. Her associations were loose, and her thinking processes were tangential. She stated that under her LSD relevation, "I saw the awful truth: what I am, and how to love people."

Following the experience she complained of an inability to control her thoughts. A belief that she was in the Garden of Eden, preoccupation with religious themes, and socially unacceptable behavior such as appearing nude in public became manifest. Ten days after her LSD treatment her husband placed her in a mental hospital and she was given a series of electroshock treatments. Despite partial improvement she has had long periods when she was unable to work because of emotional lability and uninhibited speech and behavior. Several subsequent hospitalizations have been necessary.

The diagnostic impression was one of an affective schizophrenia. Although a schizophrenic process may have antedated the LSD treatment, the patient functioned well and held responsible positions prior to her breakdown. She was recently given a course of thioridazine medication with definite improvement.

Case 2

The patient was a thirty-two-year-old secretary to a psychotherapist who had a large "LSD practice." She states that she had taken LSD 200–300 times within a three-year period in dose of $25\mu gr.$–$400\mu gr.$ In addition, other hallucinogens, sedatives, and stimulants had been tried singly and in various combinations. Most of these drug experiences were pleasant, but more recently they had become dysphoric. She stated that the LSD changed her from an inhibited, blocked person to a "freer" individual, but it had left her without control over her emotions.

When first seen she was in a panic-like state, loose in verbal associations, fearful of being alone, and expressing a strong desire for sedation. Frightening, spontaneous recurrences of the hallucinatory phenomena which had been seen under LSD were almost daily events. These consisted of skulls of familiar faces moving on the wall and feelings of accompanying horror.

Despite some initial improvement on chlordiazepoxide, she remained anxious, depressed, and overdependent.

In this patient the extraordinary frequent ingestion of LSD and other psychochemicals resulted in a borderline panic state with spontaneous visual hallucinatory phenomena.

Case 3

The patient was a forty-one-year-old white female office manager who was referred by her therapist. Since her last LSD treatment, two years ago, she had been panicky, agitated, depressed, and obsessed about going crazy or killing herself.

Her early life had been very chaotic. The only relationship between the mother and father was one of bickering, assaultiveness, and reprisal. From the time she was 11 and until she was 14 her alcoholic father had sexually played with her. When the patient was 17 the father killed her mother and himself. For a short period she was a prostitute. During this time she became pregnant and bore an illegitimate female child. She has had two brief marriages and is now divorced.

Two years ago she made an unsuccessful suicide attempt with sleeping pills. After this she received a course of electroshock therapy for depression. Two months later, she was given eight LSD therapy sessions. The eighth session was so frightening that she fled to another part of the country to avoid further treatment.

Since that time she has been confused, agitated, and preoccupied with guilt feelings about her life. Copious weeping and occasional screams interrupted the interview. She told her story quite dramatically. She claimed to be unable to be in crowds or alone, unable to sleep, eat, or work. Hospitalization was recommended but refused. A short time later another suicide attempt with barbiturates was made. After recovery she was kept in the hospital for a three-month course of psychotherapy with partial improvement and was discharged to outpatient group therapy.

This patient represented a poor candidate for

LSD therapy. She was a tenuously adjusted person who had never formed any meaningful relationships. During her LSD interviews unconscious material became available to her which she could neither accept nor repress. As a result her defenses appeared to disintegrate. An array of hysterical, obsessive-compulsive, and hypochondriacal, fragmented coping efforts were made. Extreme anxiety culminating in panic-like episodes was recurrent. Her emotional disturbance was so great that she was considered to be psychotic by some examiners. Others believed that she was a hysterical personality in an extreme anxiety and depressive reaction.

Case 4

(This case was seen in consultation with Dr. Sherman Little, Children's Hospital, Los Angeles.) A ten-year-old male accidentally ingested a sugar cube containing 100μgr. of LSD which his father, a detective, had confiscated from a "pusher." The child had a severe reaction with colored visual distortions, hallucinations, and anxiety. These became less distressing during the next three days but did not subside.

Chlorpromazine did not completely control the phenomena but did diminish "the pain of the checkerboards passing through my body."

When the boy returned to school a week later the pages wavered and interfered with his reading. While looking at the TV screen he would become upset because he saw movements without the set being on. A lump would form in his throat, and he clung to his father at these times. Some days might be completely uneventful; on others he reexperienced the visual illusions and became anxious.

One month after the incident he still saw light halos with closed eyes. Hospitalization at this time resulted in a gradual but complete improvement.

Case 5

The patient was a white, married male who teaches hypnosis. He complained of episodic anxiety, a variety of pains, depression, and visual distortions for seven months since taking LSD about 25 times for psychotherapeutic purposes. At present he has feelings of impending doom, at times he "wants to climb the walls." The periodic illusions and emotional upsets come on when he is under stress. During these episodes he sees animals and faces moving on the wall.

He claims that prior to the LSD treatments he had no anxiety, but was unproductive and "zombie-like." At the present he is writing five books and

wonders, "Do I have to pay for this higher level of functioning with anxiety and pain?"

There is a flavor of grandiosity to his ideation. For example, he told his mother some of her thoughts before he was born. He speaks of his mental activity as though it has a special potency as when he says, "I have to watch my thoughts, I might think myself dead."

The impression is that of an anxiety and depressive reaction with dissociative features reminiscent of the LSD experience. In our opinion his LSD therapy did not succeed in working through his conflicts, or re-repressing the traumatic material recalled under the drug sessions.

Depressive Reactions

When the LSD experience mobilizes considerable feelings of guilt or shame, an extended depression can result. In rigid or overconscientious individuals who undergo the ego dissolution that the hallucinogens can induce, a depression may follow the use of the drug.

Case 6

The subject was a psychoanalyst who took 100μgr. of LSD in order to experience the LSD state. Although the visual effects were intriguing, he complained of considerable somatic discomfort during the period of drug activity.

For the next eight months, he presented a picture of an hypochondriacal agitated depression. He complained of weakness, back pain, and leg cramps. For a long time he was convinced that a coronary occlusion had occurred. This was never confirmed by laboratory tests. He was restless, anxious, and unhappy. He ruminated about the possibility that he had revealed damaging unconscious material during the LSD period. He made a slow but complete recovery.

Release of Preexisting Psychopathic or Asocial Trends with Acting Out, or Abandonment of, Social Responsibilities

This is illustrated by the following cases.

Case 7

The patient was a married, white female housewife who appeared seeking a diagnosis. It was difficult to say whether she was sober and garrulous, or mildly under the influence of some drug at the first interview.

Her early history included the fact that at 15 years of age she ran away from a reform school and appeared at a Vedanta Center 2000 miles away, dirty, in rags, and hungry. She was taken in, and she spent a number of months there. Later, while studying in a New York City college as a "psych major" she lived in Greenwich Village, smoked marihuana, and enjoyed the marginal life of that colony. Seven years ago she "settled down" by becoming pregnant and marrying an older man, a "square." They had two children, and she says that she was a model mother.

She has had LSD at least six times. On the first occasion she suddenly realized that her mother wanted a boy when she was born. Subsequent occasions are described as "immensely valuable" and the "opening up a new world" and as "something that one should have every Saturday night."

During the last three occasions the LSD was combined with carbon dioxide inhalations, methylphenidate, and JB-329, an experimental psychotomimetic drug with atropine-like effects. She then became involved in a group who used marihuana, meperidine, and opium, all obtained from Mexico. These drugs, she claimed, helped her write better. She asserts that she was not addicted to any of these, "there were no withdrawal symptoms." In order to obtain her own supplies she ran away to Mexico with her pusher and discovered a "beat" colony at Guadalajara where heroin, barbiturates, and marihuana are apparently items of commerce. This period of sexual and artistic looseness is described with considerable positive affect. She returned to her home eventually because of her children, bringing back a supply of "pot" and heroin. She cannot decide whether to stay with her children or abandon them for the amoral, irresponsible life of the "beat" world.

A role that LSD could have played in this woman's acting out behavior was to release her partially suppressed impulses and reduce any existing counterforces. Her LSD exposures had occurred essentially without therapeutic support or assistance, after which she fell back into an earlier mode of existence which is now too entrancing to relinquish.

The impression is one of antisocial reaction in an emotionally immature personality whose current behavior may have been triggered by haphazard LSD exposure.

The patient also illustrates "multihabituation," the misuse of a variety of sedatives, narcotics, stimulants, and hallucinogens taken in series by borderline individuals. Such individuals claim not to get "hooked" on any one agent. They are certainly habituated to the drugged state. This "offbeat" existence satisfies the need for forbidden or unique experiences and the need to get away from their sober selves.

Case 8

The patient is a white male who received four LSD sessions (50μgr.–150μgr.) in a state hospital. During his third treatment the patient developed an overwhelming feeling that he was turning into a bad person, a monster. The threatening or unacceptable impulses that emerged aroused intense panic feelings, and intramuscular chlorpromazine was given to abort the episode.

His past history includes the information that he had been arrested over a hundred times for armed robbery. Two months after leaving the hospital he was arrested for grand theft. His defense was that LSD had changed his personality and he was not responsible for his actions. This was unacceptable to the court, and he was convicted and sentenced.

This instance is included, not to illustrate an adverse reaction to LSD, but to demonstrate how a sociopath can try to use the drug experience to excuse his subsequent behavior.

Paranoid Reactions—Confirmation of Latent Ideas of Grandiosity by the Transcendental Aspects of the LSD Experience

People who use paranoid mechanisms of denial and projection are relatively poor candidates for LSD. Their rigid, sometimes tenuous, grasp on reality may be disrupted for long periods of time.

They may react with increased suspiciousness and incorporate the drug experience as part of a vast plot. More commonly the chemical ego dissolution results in intense feelings of unity, death and rebirth, salvation and redemption. After the drug effects have worn off, the megalomaniacal belief that the individual has been chosen to convert others to the new faith may be retained. Small LSD sects have been established on this basis. The leaders gain considerable gratification out of their position of omnipotence which includes granting their disciples the LSD experience. Recently one lawsuit brought attention to a pastor who told his congregation that LSD could bring them all closer to God. Without entering into the complex and provocative problem of the drug-induced religious experience at this time, it seems obvious that sweeping recommendations that everyone ought to take LSD is an unsophisticated utterance with dangerous potential.

Case 9

A psychologist was given LSD on three occasions (75µgr.–125µgr.) and for weeks thereafter acted out grandiose plans. One was to take over Sandoz Laboratories in order to secure the world supply of the drug. He threatened his wife with a gun, then left her, wrote some songs and plays of minor merit, and went off to live in the desert. He recovered gradually after a number of months without specific treatment.

It is not difficult to identify the individuals who openly express their megalomaniacal notions. There are others who are sufficiently aware of the reality situation to keep the knowledge of their own omnipotence hidden. They can become quite successful in controlling people in the role of religious leaders or lay therapists.

Comment

The actual incidence of serious complications following LSD administration is not known. We believe, however, that they are infrequent. It is surprising that such a profound psychological experience leaves adverse residuals so rarely. This may lend support to the impression that psychological homeostatic mechanisms for handling acute stresses are more resilient than is commonly believed.

As the serious complications to LSD are reviewed, certain patterns seem to emerge.

1. The patients who have difficulty tend to be emotionally labile, often hysterical or paranoid personalities. Many are already in treatment, and others seek out LSD therapists hoping that some instantaneous, magical experience will cure them. They are hypersuggestible and, given a drug which reduces critical ego function, can become overwhelmed with a deluge of anxiety and guilt-laden "insights."

2. In the majority of the cases who developed complications the drug had been obtained from improper sources. A black market (Cohen and Ditman, 1962) exists in this country, and tablets, ampules, and sugar cubes saturated with LSD have become available in the large cities and on some university campuses. Certain practitioners obtain supplies from Mexico and other foreign countries.

3. It is noteworthy that when a psychotic reaction follows LSD usage, the clinical picture is reminiscent of the drugged condition. Hallucinations tend to be visual with colors and movement of objects characteristic of the LSD state. It is as though the pattern of psychosis mimics the dissociation that precipitated it.

4. Although a number of the patients recognized that the LSD had caused their psychotic or neurotic break, nevertheless they believed that the treatment had been extraordinary and often sought additional drug exposures. Such faith reflects the unusual nature of the experience and the personality of the patients concerned.

5. Therapists who administer hallucinogens should clearly recognize their patients' motivations and the potential hazards of a profound consciousness-changing experience. In view of the psychological potency of these chemicals the therapist should scrutinize his own motives in administering them. Until the indications, techniques, and precautions are better understood, LSD therapy should be restricted to investigators in institutions and hospitals where the patient's protection is greater and appropriate countermeasures are available in case of adverse reactions.

6. It appears that antisocial groups have embraced LSD and mescaline in addition to marihuana, the amphetamines, the barbiturates, and the narcotics. Since the LSD state can be a shattering one psychologically, these individuals may sustain severe undesirable reactions. Easy access to the drug will result in its accidental or deliberate administration to people without their knowledge, and this can be a devastating event. We can only repeat (Cohen, 1960a) that carefully screened, maximally supervised patients given the drug by responsible, experienced investigators will avoid many difficulties in the postdrug period. The imprudent, cursory use of LSD and allied drugs is unsafe, and the complications that sometimes result retard their proper scientific study. When undesirable reactions and sensational publicity become associated with a drug, competent investigators are inclined to avoid participating in the careful, thoughtful studies which are necessary to evaluate it properly.

Summary

Adverse effects can occasionally follow the administration of D-lysergic acid diethylamide (LSD). Complications such as prolonged psychotic reactions, severe depressive and anxiety states, or intensified sociopathic behavior are much more likely to occur after the unsupervised or inexpert use of this drug. When properly employed, LSD is a relatively safe and important research tool.

REFERENCES

Cohen, S. Lysergic acid diethylamide: Side effects and complications. *Journal of Nervous and Mental Diseases*, 1960, **130**, 30–40. (a)

Cohen, S. Notes on the hallucinogenic state. *International Record of Medicine*, 1960, **173**, 380–387. (b)

Cohen, S., & Ditman, K. S. Complications associated with lysergic acid diethylamide (LSD-25). *Journal of the American Medical Association*, 1962, **181**, 161–162.

Cohen, S., & Eisner, B. G. Use of lysergic acid diethylamide in a psychotherapeutic setting. *AMA Archives of Neurology and Psychiatry*, 1959, **81**, 615–619.

Ditman, K. S., Hayman, M., & Whitlesey, J. R. B. Nature and frequency of claims following LSD. *Journal of Nervous and Mental Diseases*, 1962, **134**, 346–352.

Ditman, K. S., & Whittlesey, J. R. B. Comparison of the LSD-25 experience and delirium tremens. *AMA Archives of General Psychiatry*, 1959, **1**, 47–57.

Hofmann, A. Die Wertstoffe der mexikanischen Zauberdroge Ololiuqui. *Planta Medica*, 1961, **4**, 354–366.

Hofmann, A., & Troxler, F. Identification of Psilocin. *Experientia*, 1959, **15**, 101–102.

Osmond, H. A review of the clinical effects of psychotomimetic agents. *Annals of the New York Academy of Science*, 1957, **66**, 418–434.

59

"Mental Illness" or Interpersonal Behavior?

Henry B. Adams

On occasion an individual's ability to cope with his environment becomes so severely impaired that he requires professional treatment or hospitalization. Terms describing an individual whose ability to adjust is severely impaired have gone from "lunatic" and "crazy," to the legal term "insane," to the now commonly used term "mentally ill." Among psychologists and psychiatrists there is still considerable disagreement and concern as to whether such classification and naming of disorders actually serves any useful goal other than perhaps achieving greater public acceptance of individuals suffering from such disorders. In the following selection Adams discusses the problem of whether the currently used terminology and classification should not be discarded, since "there is no such thing as 'mental illness' in any significantly meaningful sense." Adams argues that such persons, rather than being "ill," have overwhelming problems in forming and maintaining adequate and satisfying interpersonal relationships.

There is no such thing as a "mental illness" in any significantly meaningful sense. In medicine the term "illness" is used in a literal, nonfigurative way to denote an undesirable alteration or change away from optimal levels of organic bodily functioning. But the term "mental illness" is applied to various patterns of behavior considered maladaptive or inappropriate by implicit psychological and social standards (Szasz, 1960, 1961).

The concept of a functional mental illness is a *verbal analogy*. While it is appropriate to speak of neurological disorders as true organic illnesses of the nervous system comparable to organic illnesses involving the circulatory or digestive system, it seems questionable to apply the term "illness" to

arbitrarily defined patterns of behavior, particularly when there may be no evidence of any physiological malfunctioning. The plain fact is that the term "mental illness" is applied in an indiscriminate way to a motley collection of interpersonal behavior patterns. Often there is no positive evidence whatever of any physiological or organic

From American Psychologist, *Vol. 19 (1964), 191–197. Copyright 1964 by the American Psychological Association, and reproduced by permission. Revised version of a paper presented at the Seventieth Annual Convention of the American Psychological Association on a symposium entitled: " 'Mental Illness': Is There Any Such Thing?" St. Louis, Missouri, August 30, 1962.*

malfunctioning, as in the so-called "functional disorders." Actually, organic physical illnesses and the functional types of mental illnesses are defined by *different kinds of criteria,* and they are modified or ameliorated ("treated" or "cured") by *fundamentally different procedures.*

Failure to clarify these distinctions has had unfortunate consequences. Efforts toward understanding and effective alleviation have long been hampered by the semantic confusion which results when the word "illness" is used to denote both physical disease entities and maladaptive patterns of interpersonal behavior. This ambiguous usage has perpetuated the glib fallacy that mental and physical illnesses are the same thing. It has interfered with the understanding of fundamental psychological phenomena and made for an ineffectual and often harmful approach to some of the most serious recurring problems in human relationships.

This semantic confusion is an important fact in the history of psychiatry since 1800. A number of studies have been published in recent years on the "moral therapy" of the early nineteenth century (Bockoven, 1956, 1957; Brown, 1960; Joint Commission on Mental Illness and Health, 1961; Rees, 1957). These studies all agree that the results of moral therapy (at a time when physical medicine was in a relatively primitive stage of development) compare favorably with the very best mental-hospital programs of today. "Moral therapy" was essentially a program of planned psychological retraining within a positive, sympathetic social milieu.

Moral therapy had its inception near the end of the eighteenth century under the leadership of Pinel, Tuke, Chiarugi, and others. The word "moral" was used at that time in a sense comparable to the contemporary usage of the words "psychological" or "interpersonal." During that era more attention began to be given to

social and environmental factors in the causation of mental illness, and it was found that organic changes in the brain were rather rare at postmortem examinations. The insane came to be regarded as normal people who had lost their reason as a result of having been exposed to severe psychological and social stresses. These stresses were called the moral causes of insanity, and moral treatment aimed at relieving the patient by friendly association, discussion of his difficulties, and the daily pursuit of purposeful activity; in other words, social therapy, individual therapy, and occupational therapy. Moral treatment reached its zenith in the years between 1820 and 1860. The results of treatment during that period were outstandingly

good and bear comparison with some of the figures obtainable today. For example, in all patients admitted to the York Retreat [in England] within three months of the onset of illness—between the years 1796 and 1861 the discharge rate was 71 per cent. . . . These are truly remarkable figures, especially when one takes into consideration that a substantial portion of the patients must have been general paralytics, for which there was at that time no effective treatment (Rees, 1957, pp. 306–307).

Cope and Packard (1841) reported on the results of moral treatment in state institutions in the United States. They mentioned institutions in nine states and observed that with moral treatment "ninety per cent of the recent cases can be restored so as to be able to maintain themselves and family." Bockoven (1956) found comparable figures from private institutions utilizing moral treatment. Beginning in the 1820's, the Hartford Retreat reported recoveries in over 90 per cent of all patients admitted with mental illnesses of less than a year's duration. Bockoven also supplied statistics extending from 1833 to 1950 on discharges from the Worcester State Hospital in Massachusetts. During the 1833–1852 period, when moral therapy was being practiced, 71 per cent of all patients ill less than one year when admitted were discharged as recovered or improved. Patients discharged during the years 1833–1846 were later followed up until 1893, and it was found that half suffered no recurrences.

Despite ample evidence of its effectiveness, moral therapy was quietly abandoned in American and British mental institutions after 1860 and later almost completely forgotten. The consequences are illustrated by Bockoven's (1956) data from the Worcester State Hospital, showing that recovery rates declined over 90 per cent after 1860, reaching their lowest point between 1923 and 1950 (pp. 292–293). Certainly, one may raise legitimate questions about these old statistics and the validity of conclusions drawn from them. Nevertheless, every recent study on the subject of moral therapy agreed that the results have not been surpassed during the contemporary period, despite all the advances made by physical medicine since 1860.

One important reason for its abandonment was that moral therapy was supposed to be a form of treatment for mental illness. But as physical medicine developed during the late nineteenth century, it was thought that the types of procedures found effective with physical illnesses could be carried over unaltered into the treatment of mental illnesses. Since both kinds of phenomena were defined as illnesses this notion sounded reasonable, so long as no one inquired seriously into the possibility that there might be an error in semantics.

An additional factor in the abandonment of moral therapy was that it was regarded as "unscientific" according to the scientific and medical doctrines which developed in the intellectual climate of the last half of the nineteenth century. These doctrines held that true science is impersonal and concerned solely with material things, that feeling, beauty, and moral values are mere illusions in a world of fact, that the human will is powerless against the laws of nature and society, and that every observable phenomenon is reducible to the motions of material particles.[1] Since psychiatric patients were regarded as suffering from a medical condition defined as mental illness, it was held that treatment procedures had to rest on a scientific physical basis as conceptualized by a mechanistic, materialistic view which held that things rather than persons were the only reality. In keeping with this tough-minded impersonal dogma, the psychological sensitivity and insight which were major factors in the success of moral therapy were dismissed from serious consideration as mystical, sentimental, and unscientific. The treatment of hospitalized psychiatric patients became cold, distant, and unfeeling, consistent with a *Zeitgeist* of impersonal scientism. Discharge and recovery rates, which had been high wherever moral therapy programs were in effect, declined steadily after 1860. In time, falling discharge rates led to the piling up of chronic patients in hospitals, attitudes of hopelessness, and a growing belief in the "incurability" of insanity. This pessimistic belief had become widespread by 1900, despite the fact that 70 per cent to 90 per cent recovery rates had been commonplace in 1840 during the moral-therapy era.

As recovery rates fell and the treatment of hospitalized patients became more detached and impersonal, leaders in psychiatry turned to the laboratory hoping to find a scientific cure for mental illness. They were persuaded that the answers lay in the discovery and identification of physical disease entities. Physicalistic and mechanistic concepts of mental illness were adopted by analogy with physical medicine, while efforts to understand psychiatric patients as individual persons were largely discontinued (Zilboorg, 1941). Patients were no longer thought of as human beings with problems in human relationships, but as "cases." This impersonal approach led one of the leading American psychiatrists of the 1880's to state in all sincerity that the insane do not suffer unhappiness, and that

depressed patients go through the motions of acting sad in a machinelike fashion without feeling genuine sadness (Bockoven, 1956). As Brown's (1960) data indicate, changing attitudes of the medical profession at different historical periods have played a great part in changing rates of discharge and chronicity among hospitalized patients.

The great irony is that after 100 years these laboratory-centered physically oriented research efforts have failed to produce techniques for the "treatment" and "cure" of functional personality disorders significantly more effective than the best techniques of 1840. Actually, the most progressive contemporary mental-hospital programs are those which have revived practices much like those generally prevalent during the moral-therapy era (Greenblatt, York, and Brown, 1955; Rees, 1957).

The Impersonal Approach to Personality

The theoretical concepts most widely used in the mental-health professions today consist largely of misleading analogies, metaphors, and figures of speech. These sonorous but inappropriate terms have made for confusion, trained incapacities, and intellectual stagnation. The Joint Commission on Mental Illness and Health (1961) has commented on this stagnation with the observation that "twentieth-century psychiatry can add little" to Pinel's principles for the moral treatment of psychotics, which were first published in 1801,

except to convert them into modern terminological dress, contribute more systematic thought to the significance of various symptoms, intensify the doctor-patient relationship through scientific knowledge of psychological mechanisms, treat the patient as a member of a social group which expects him to behave in accepted ways, and specify that moral treatment has been subject to an incredible amount of distortion and misinterpretation . . . (pp. 29–30).

Similarly, psychotherapy in essentially its present-day form was described by Reil in a book pub-

---

[1] The doctrines of nineteenth-century impersonal scientism have been more fully described elsewhere by Barzun (1958). He analyzes the modes of thought inherited from that era and shows how strongly they still influence contemporary thinking. Bockoven (1956) notes that the widespread acceptance of these doctrines in both popular and scientific circles contributed to the abandonment of moral therapy after 1860.

lished in the year 1803 (Harms, 1957c). Almost every important issue in contemporary clinical psychology was discussed at length by leaders of the moral-therapy movement between 1790 and 1860 (Harms, 1957a, 1957b, 1957c; Roback, 1961).

Much of the terminology now used in contemporary psychology developed in an intellectual climate of impersonal scientism quite different in its basic outlook from the humanitarianism of the moral-therapy era. Psychology first arose as a separate independent science during the 1870's and 1880's. Reflecting the predominant spirit of their times, the early founders of experimental psychology were not concerned with the systematic understanding of human problems and personal relationships. Instead, they imitated the outward appearances and procedures of the physical and biological sciences, hoping that they too might thus be regarded as true scientists. They felt that in order to be scientifically respectable they had to study man impersonally, using techniques, assumptions, and conceptual approaches much like those of the physical and biological sciences. For example, the doctrine of determinism was carried over from the physical sciences without any empirical evidence to show that it was appropriate in explaining human conduct.

The impersonal approach adopted in the late nineteenth century is reflected in the conceptual language of psychology today. These concepts center around words borrowed from nonpsychological fields such as medicine, physics, mechanical engineering, biology, and electronics. This point is best illustrated by listing some verbal analogies commonly used in psychology. All the examples listed below appeared in psychological or psychiatric journals, or in books written for professional readers:

1. *Pseudomedical analogies:* mental illness, mental health, mental hygiene, prophylaxis, diagnosis, pathology, prognosis, etiology, therapy, treatment, cure, trauma, nosology, catharsis, syndrome, neurosis, psychosis, psychopathy, sick

2. *Pseudophysical and pseudoengineering analogies:* motor apparatus, dynamics, reaction potential, valences, field forces, psychic energy, power system, energy transformation, tension, stress, drive, mechanism, dynamogenesis, adjustment, reinforcing machine

3. *Pseudobiological analogies:* organism, homeostasis, phenotypic, genotypic, polymorphous, ontogenetic

4. *Pseudoelectronic analogies:* input, output, amplitude, radar, circuit, feedback, scanning, encoding, signals, charge, discharge, servomechanism

5. *Pseudogenitourinary and pseudogastrointestinal (i.e., psychoanalytic) analogies:* urethral character, phallic character, castration, oral optimism, anal submission, vaginal libido organization, anal-expulsive expression

Such analogies implicitly suggest that human behavior is *just like* the events observed in the nonpsychological sciences from which these words were borrowed. In using such terminology a false assumption is unwittingly made (but rarely recognized) that the *psychological phenomena* to which these terms are applied are therefore just like the *nonpsychological phenomena* where the terms originated. It is taken as *having already been decided* that these words are suitable for labeling and describing human behavior. The actions of living persons are thus conceptualized in the language of impersonal things and processes. Having accepted this glib semantic juggling, it is then quite easy to coin confusing, misleading slogans such as "mental illness is just like any other illness."

What Is "Mental Illness"?

What is the phenomenon to which the label "mental illness" is applied? It is applied to arbitrarily designated types of maladaptive interpersonal behavior, often accompanied by reports of subjective discomfort, unsatisfying human relationships, and social rejection.

Explicit distinctions must be made between these behavioral phenomena and illnesses of the body. Physical illnesses (including neurological disorders) are not in themselves patterns of interaction with other persons. They are disturbances in the organic functions of the body. So far as immediate experience is concerned, a bodily illness such as a cold, fever, or pneumonia is an abnormal, usually unpleasant, subjective condition which *happens to* the individual person. It is not a direct overt manifestation of his characteristic patterns of interacting with others.

But, in cases where the term "mental illness" is used and no organic pathology is in evidence, the term refers to some arbitrarily defined pattern of conduct, with "symptoms" of a psychosocial rather than a medical nature. Any effective program directed toward "cure" must consequently provide opportunities for learning new, more adaptive patterns. It should be remembered that the learning process is a normal function of the nervous system, regardless of the nature of the material being learned, be it the subject of medicine, playing a musical instrument, or new social skills.

A Comprehensive Approach to Interpersonal Behavior

Mental illness is a phenomenon involving interpersonal behavior, not a health or medical problem. Programs of alleviation and prevention must therefore rest upon a systematic understanding of interpersonal conduct. A considerable body of recent research in this area suggests that the basic dimensions are surprisingly simple. The supposed complexity of personality and interaction between persons has been shown to be a purely semantic, verbal complexity, rather than a real complexity in actual fact.

These empirical studies have three distinguishing features: (a) The basic observations involve interpersonal actions. To be more explicit, the observations are focused on the acts of *persons* interacting with other *persons,* rather than organisms, psychobiological units, dynamic systems, or other impersonal abstractions. (b) The observers are concerned not with superficial stylistic features, but with the *content* of the interpersonal acts themselves. Content variables are to be contrasted with formalistic or stylistic variables, such as percentage of adjectives, manner of speaking, speed of tapping, etc. "Content" refers to *what* the individual person is doing or communicating to others by word and deed. (c) The investigators aim for *comprehensiveness,* classifying every act systematically in relation to every other.

Most of these studies have dispensed with terminology not meaningfully related to observable conduct. If behavior can be systematically described in *behavioral* terms, there is no need for the confusing nonpsychological analogies and metaphors which have long plagued the mental-health professions. It becomes unnecessary to borrow words from medicine, engineering, or electronics to describe human relationships. This approach makes it possible to clarify fundamental principles which have long been concealed by inappropriate, misleading jargon.

The results of these studies indicate that all interpersonal behavior, both adaptive ("healthy" or "normal") and maladaptive ("sick" or "abnormal"), can be meaningfully categorized within one systematic frame of reference. In a review of these studies, Foa (1961) was impressed by the "strong convergence" of thinking and results obtained in research on interpersonal interaction, since the investigators "proceeded from different research tra-

ditions, studied different types of groups . . . and, apparently, followed independent lines of design and analysis. The convergence is toward a simple ordered structure for the organization of interpersonal behavior." Foa suggested that the observations can be ordered into a simple comprehensive framework "that accounts for the empirical interrelations in a parsimonious and meaningful manner." The findings "suggest a circumplex structure around the two orthogonal axes of Dominance-Submission and Affection-Hostility."

Let us examine these two axes or dimensions in more detail. One pole of the Dominance-Submission axis is defined by acts of self-confident, assertive leadership and achievement in the face of obstacles. At the opposite pole are acts of passivity, submissiveness, and acquiescence. This dimension is of course a continuum, with most acts falling midway between extremes. The Affection-Hostility dimension reflects variations in the degree of positive or negative affect manifested toward others. The positive extreme describes warm, friendly, kind, affiliative acts, while the negative extreme describes hostile, critical, angry, disaffiliative acts.

Foa suggests that "an interpersonal act is an attempt to establish the emotional relationship of the actor toward himself and toward the other person," and that "the same act states the position of the actor toward the self and toward the other. . . ." Each type of behavior is thus meaningful toward the self and the other person. The Dominance-Submission axis defines the degree of acceptance or rejection of self, while the Affection-Hostility axis defines the degree of acceptance or rejection of the other. An interpersonal act may be regarded as the Cartesian product of these two sets of values.

The basic framework systematized by this two-dimensional structure has been described repeatedly ever since the time of Hippocrates. If there are only two dimensions of variation in the content of interpersonal acts, and the individual's personality is identified by the relative frequency, intensity, and nature of his acts, we have a simple but comprehensive basis for categorizing all personality types. Classification above and below the mean of these two axes would give four categories which correspond roughly to the traditional four temperaments, as they have been delineated by Hippocrates, Galen, Kant, Wundt, Höffding, Herbart, Külpe, Ebbinghaus, Klages, and Pavlov (Allport, 1961). Thus, persons with the "sanguine" temperament would show behavior which falls above the mean on both dimensions. Such persons typically show active leadership, optimism, and assertiveness, coupled with friendly acceptance of others. Likewise, the other three groups correspond to the traditional choleric, melancholic, and phlegmatic temperaments.

Freud has alluded to these dimensions in his writings (Leary, 1957, pp. 71–72). He has delineated a love-hate, sex-aggression, libido-mortido, or Eros-Thanatos polarity, which is comparable to the Affection-Hostility dimension. He also refers to power or domination in social interaction, analogous to Foa's Dominance-Submission dimension. This two-dimensional structure has appeared in the theories of Parsons, Merton, and Stagner (Leary, 1957, pp. 73–74). It has been used with impressive results in the coaction-compass analysis of the Rorschach (Gottlieb and Parsons, 1960; Lodge and Gibson, 1953) and in scoring and interpreting the TAT (Leary, 1956, 1957).

These dimensions recur in factor-analytic studies of the MMPI. Welsh (1956) reviewed the results of 11 analyses of the MMPI and found consistent agreement as to the first two factors but little agreement as to any additional factors. He developed two special scales, *A* and *R*, as measures of these factors. For example, subjects scoring high on *A* tend to agree with items expressing obsessional thinking, negative emotional tone, pessimism, personal sensitivity, and malignant mentation. Such items express attitudes typical of the "melancholic temperament" as depicted for many centuries. High *A* scorers would fall below the mean on both dimensions. In their overt behavior they show passivity and negative affect toward themselves and others (Dahlstrom and Welsh, 1960).

Jackson and Messick (1961) investigated response style on the MMPI and found that most of the variance was due to two response-set factors. One was an acquiescence factor like Foa's Dominance-Submission dimension. The other was a factor of social desirability, which is essentially the same as the Affection-Hostility dimension, a similarity which may not be recognized immediately. But it has been found that individuals who respond to personality questionnaires in socially desirable directions typically behave in bland, friendly, conventional ways, while those responding in the opposite fashion tend to be blunt, outspoken, critical of conventional standards, and uninhibited in the presence of others. Jackson and Messick noted that the test vectors emerging from their analysis of the MMPI tended toward a circular arrangement, like the circumplex structure described by Foa.

If the response to each item on the MMPI is viewed as a separate interpersonal communication, the convergences between MMPI studies and direct behavioral observations are not surprising. These convergences are all the more significant since the MMPI was developed to facilitate psychiatric diagnosis. The clinical scales of the MMPI were initially validated against Kraepelinian disease-entity diagnostic criteria. The results of these MMPI factor-analytic studies imply that the Kraepelinian labels presently employed in psychiatric diagnosis are nonexistent verbal abstractions.

A factor analysis of rating scales and questionnaires by Goldman-Eisler (1953) tested certain hypotheses drawn from psychoanalytic theory. Two orthogonal factors emerged, the first being a factor of "oral" optimism versus "oral" pessimism. Oral optimists show the same traits of active, friendly, assertiveness as the sanguine temperament, while oral pessimists show the contrasting patterns of the melancholic temperament. The second factor was interpreted as Impatience-Aggression-Autonomy versus Deliberation-Conservatism-Dependence. The traits of impatience, aggression, and autonomy are analogous to the hostile dominance of the choleric temperament, while deliberation, conservatism, and dependence describe the affectionate submissiveness ascribed to the phlegmatic temperament. The factor loadings emerging from this analysis were interrelated in a circular order, much like the circumplex structure of interpersonal behavior described by Foa and the circular array of MMPI test vectors suggested by Jackson and Messick. Although Goldman-Eisler considered her findings as a confirmation of psychoanalytic theory, her results are much like those of other investigators whose theoretical orientation was quite different. The convergences between her results and other studies imply that the elaborate verbal complexities of psychoanalytic theory are needlessly involved. The empirical data can be much more parsimoniously explained.

It is clear that the same fundamental patterns have been repeatedly observed by many contemporary and historical writers, even though the words used may seem very different. These similarities and convergences would not have been so consistently noted unless there were certain universal features in all human conduct. Apparently these universal features were perceived, understood, and implicitly acted upon during the moral-therapy era, overlooked by later generations enamoured of impersonal scientism, and spelled out once again in recent empirical investigations. It seems obvious that a sound understanding of human behavior must begin with these universal features rather than the vague jargon that has dominated psychological and psychiatric theorizing to date.

How do these universal features relate to mental

health and mental illness? Within the two-dimensional circular structure outlined above an elaborate system has been developed for classifying the interpersonal behavior of both psychiatric patients and "normals" (Leary, 1956, 1957). The major differences between mental illness and mental health are to be found in the characteristic frequency, intensity, and nature of interpersonal acts.

For example, schizophrenics manifest intense degrees of passivity and hostility by unconventional, bizarre, negativistic, and distrustful acts. In contrast, hysterics prefer bland, pleasant, friendly, conventional types of interaction. Hostile, rebellious, and distrustful acts are infrequent and extremely mild in intensity among hysterics. These two contrasting types of interpersonal behavior have long been considered mental illnesses. Both are differentiated from normality, adjustment, or mental health, i.e., versatile, appropriate, effective, adaptive behavior patterns. In this semantic usage the words "illness" and "health" are applied to observable patterns of conduct, not to states of the mind or body. The most effective programs of "therapy," "treatment," or "cure" for these illnesses are those which succeed best in altering the characteristic nature, frequency, and intensity of maladaptive acts in the direction of greater moderation, versatility, appropriateness, and effectiveness.

The more we question the terminology of the mental-health professions today, the more obvious its inadequacies become. It is doubtful that any major advances can be expected so long as understanding is obscured by unsuitable, misleading terms. Every concept in our professional vocabulary needs to be carefully and critically reassessed by asking the question: *"Is it appropriate?"* Many fundamental problems need to be completely restated in words that communicate rather than obfuscate. Suitable *psychological* terminology is badly needed to clarify numerous vaguely worded, inappropriately phrased, and poorly understood questions in psychology today. Only in this way can psychologists create a basis for genuine understanding of human behavior.

REFERENCES

Allport, G. W. *Pattern and growth in personality.* New York: Holt, Rinehart & Winston, 1961.

Barzun, J. *Darwin, Marx, Wagner: Critique of a heritage.* (2nd. ed.) Garden City, N.Y.: Doubleday Anchor, 1958.

Bockoven, J. S. Moral treatment in American psychiatry. *Journal of Nervous and Mental Diseases,* 1956, **124**, 167–194, 292–321. (Reprinted in book form: New York: Springer, 1963.)

Bockoven, J. S. Some relationships between cultural attitudes toward individuality and care of the mentally ill: An historical study. In M. Greenblatt, D. J. Levinson, & R. H. Williams (Eds.), *The patient and the mental hospital.* New York: Free Press, 1957. Pp. 517–526.

Brown, G. W. Length of hospital stay and schizophrenia: A review of statistical studies. *Acta Neurologica, Psychiatrica Scandinavica,* 1960, **35**, 414–430.

Cope, T. P., & Packard, F. A. *A second appeal to the people of Pennsylvania on the subject on an asylum for the insane poor of the commonwealth.* Philadelphia: Waldie, 1841.

Dahlstrom, W. G., & Welsh, G. S. *An MMPI handbook: A guide to use in clinical practice and research.* Minneapolis: University of Minnesota Press, 1960.

Foa, U. G. Convergences in the analysis of the structure of interpersonal behavior. *Psychological Review,* 1961, **68**, 341–353.

Goldman-Eisler, F. Breastfeeding and character formation. In C. Kluckhohn & H. A. Murray (Eds.), *Personality in nature, society, and culture.* (2nd. ed.) New York: Knopf, 1953. Pp. 146–184.

Gottlieb, A. L., & Parsons, O. A. A coaction compass evaluation of Rorschach determinants in brain-damaged individuals. *Journal of Consulting Psychology,* 1960, **24**, 54–60.

Greenblatt, M., York, R. H., & Brown, E. L. *From custodial to therapeutic care in mental hospitals.* New York: Russell Sage Foundation, 1955.

Harms, E. The early historians of psychiatry. *American Journal of Psychiatry,* 1957, **113**, 749–752. (a)

Harms, E. Historical considerations in the science of psychiatry. *Disease and Nervous Systems,* 1957, **18**, 397–400. (b)

Harms, E. Modern psychotherapy—150 years ago. *Journal of Mental Science,* 1957, **103**, 804–809. (c)

Jackson, D. N., & Messick, S. Acquiescence and desirability as response determinants on the MMPI. *Educational and Psychological Measurement,* 1961, **21**, 771–790.

Joint Commission on Mental Illness and Health. *Action for mental health.* New York: Basic Books, 1961.

Leary, T. *Multilevel measurement of interpersonal behavior.* Berkeley, Calif.: Psychological Consultation Service, 1956.

Leary, T. *Interpersonal diagnosis of personality.* New York: Ronald Press, 1957.

Lodge, G. T., & Gibson, R. L. A coaction map of the personalities described by H. Rorschach and S. J. Beck. *Journal of Projective Techniques,* 1953, **17**, 482–488.

Rees, T. P. Back to moral treatment and community care. *Journal of Mental Science,* 1957, **103**, 303–313.

Roback, A. A. *History of psychology and psychiatry.* New York: Citadel Press, 1961.

Szasz, T. S. The myth of mental illness. *American Psychologist,* 1960, **15**, 113–118.

Szasz, T. S. *The myth of mental illness.* New York: Hoeber-Harper, 1961.

Welsh, G. S. Factor dimensions A and R. In G. S. Welsh & W. G. Dahlstrom (Eds.), *Basic readings on the MMPI in psychology and medicine.* Minneapolis: University of Minnesota Press, 1956. Pp. 264–281.

Zilboorg, G. *A history of medical psychology.* New York: Norton, 1941.

Mental Health: A Contemporary Perspective

Marvin W. Kahn
University of Arizona

The rapid developments in mental health since the mid-1950's have often been termed revolutionary. In many respects the term "revolution" accurately characterizes the extreme shifts in clinical practice and in theoretical emphasis of recent times. Disillusionment with such established procedures as insight psychotherapy and electroconvulsive shock have led to a proliferation of new techniques. The advent of tranquilizing drugs has heralded a new approach to the treatment of the severe and chronically mentally ill. New methods, based on new rationales, have swung the focus toward social and community involvement in the search for explanations of and treatments for emotional disorders. Group therapy techniques, treatment of the entire family as a unit, and the application of formal learning principles to behavioral symptoms, while not replacing entirely the more traditional methods, are becoming valuable added tools in the clinical practitioner's armamentarium.

Current developments can perhaps be best understood from the standpoint of their historical antecedents. In the nineteenth century ideas concerning emotional disturbance moved out of the realm of mystical-religious conceptions into the light of the scientific era. At that point causation was ascribed to actual brain dysfunction brought about by injury, disease, or inherited brain abnormalities. Mental disease was seen as parallel to physical disease. Then, at the turn of the century, Freud (1900) first proposed his theory of mental illness and treatment—*psychoanalysis*. Among other things, Freud's theory moved the concept of mental disease out of the realm of a strictly physical model. While grounded in the idea of constitutionally given basic drives (sexual and aggressive), Freud's system emphasized the development of personality as a function of both the unfolding of these basic drives and the kinds of experiences the individual had in attempting to satisfy these drives in the world of reality. Key aspects of Freud's theory included the concepts of unconscious determinants of behavior and of the repression of drives or impulses that the individual had come to look upon as unacceptable. Cure, then, was thought to lie in the uncovering and understanding of the unconscious wishes through free association, as part of the psychoanalysis. The achievement of such "insight" in a one-to-one therapeutic relationship with the analyst was the basic model for his therapeutic approach.

The storm of criticism that met Freud's theory in 1900 has never fully died down. One line of such criticism has been that Freud overemphasized drive—and particularly sexual drive—as the determiner of behavior, to the exclusion of social and environmental factors. There have been many breakaway analytic schools. Adler, Horney, Fromm, Kardiner, and others have stressed the social determinants of behavior at the expense of Freud's more biological drive approach. Even in the midst of the current proliferation of new methods, however, the mainstream of Freudian psychoanalysis continues to be a prominent and influential force in personality theory and treatment approaches. Reformulations by modern Freudian adherents such as Hartmann (1958) and Erik Erikson (1950) have brought to Freud's position, without severely altering it, considerations of social-cultural development and greater considerations of reality. Their approach is known as *psychoanalytic ego psychology*. While psychoanalysis still presents the most comprehensive explanation of normal and pathological behavior, the applicability of its treatment method appears at present to be very limited.

In the wake of Freud's ideas other approaches have developed which employ the patient-therapist relationship model working toward insight and/or self-understanding but are based on different theoretical formulations. Current rationale in personality theory ranges from Dollard and Miller's (1950) attempt to translate Freud's concepts into terms of reinforcement learning theory, to Sullivan's (1953) emphasis on interpersonal relationship and Rogers' (1959) phenomenological, existential, self-acceptance model. The latter approaches have crystalized in a recent emphasis on "humanistic" psychology. The current popularity of the humanistic movement is seen by some as a counterreaction to the "mechanistic approach" of the learning theorists.

Up to the 1950's the insight therapy model was considered the ideal one. However, it became apparent that most insight therapies worked best with relatively young, well-educated, and not too severely disturbed or socially debilitated patients. They were less effective, and often not even attempted, with other types of patients. Such individual treatments are also very time consuming and relatively expensive. Psychoanalysis, for instance, may be a matter of daily sessions over a period of years. Further, the effectiveness of individual insight therapies has been challenged. The fairest statement on this topic would appear to be that at present there really is no very definitive research to demonstrate clearly the effectiveness or lack of effectiveness of this approach. However, because of its narrow range of application and its relative expense, insight-relationship psychotherapy appears to have considerable limitations when one looks at the mental health needs of the country as a whole.

Two developments in the 1950's accentuated the need for new approaches. First, a major study by Hollingshead and Redlich (1958) pointed out a very striking association between mental illness and its treatment and the socio-economic level of the patient. They found that severe mental illness (psychosis and severe character disorder) occurs significantly more often among the lower socio-economic groups in proportion to their numbers in the population. Yet the "preferred" forms of treatment were used largely with patients of higher social class, while lower-class patients received physical treatments such as electric shock, or else simply custodial care in large state hospitals. Thus, it became apparent that relatively little was being done for the major portion of the mental-health problem.

The second event was the report of the Joint Commission on Mental Health (1961). This group was concerned, among other things, with the implications for mental health of increased longevity, the buildup of numbers of chronically ill patients in mental hospitals receiving only custodial care, and the acute shortage of trained mental-health personnel.

Thus by the mid-fifties it seemed clear that (a) the insight psychotherapy approach was limited in its application and usefulness to that portion of the population whose problems were fewest and least severe, and (b) there was such an acute shortage of professional workers in the mental-health field that even expanded training programs probably would not be able to keep up with the needs of a growing population. As a consequence of this rather depressing picture it became clear that new methods, particularly those which could reach and be effective with the mass of people who are suffering from severe mental disorders, were desperately needed. In the remainder of this paper we shall examine three major approaches to the solution of this problem.

1. *The social-community approach*   This approach has a very practical orientation. At least to some extent it has been influenced by rationales that place the origins of emotional problems in societal and family constellations. Some go so far as to consider mental illness as really only "problems of living" (Szasz, 1960) and define it only in terms of social norms, i.e., behavior that is unacceptable in a given culture. Family and community are the important focuses; treatment of the patient's entire family, including young children, is a new and useful technique which considers an individual's breakdown as a symptom of a family problem.

This has led to a new orientation in mental hospitals which emphasizes continued socialization and social responsibility of patients who have had mental breakdowns. In the more pessimistic past, patients with severe mental disorders had been treated in isolated hospitals and by means involving little but custodial care and institutionalization, often for the remainder of a patient's life. Under conditions of isolation and over-control, patients tended to regress and to become completely estranged from social reality, from family, friends, and vocational productivity. The current programs stress short-term hospitalization during which patients are tranquilized and helped over the acute disturbance. Active involvement of the patient's family, and sometimes friends and employer, from the first contact with the hospital is important in order to keep these others interested in the patient. Efforts are directed to preparing them to accept and work with the patient when he returns home. In such programs there is often little stress on past history, childhood causes, or Freudian dynamics. Rather, the emphasis is on the here and now and on modifying the circumstances of the patient's life so that they will not reactivate the disturbance when he returns home.

In the hospital itself, an environment as socially realistic as possible is maintained. Now most settings have at least some open hospital wards, with both sexes living on the same ward. Much emphasis is on social interaction. There are group treatment methods particularly designed to maintain the patients' ties with socialized behavior and social responsibility and to prepare patients to take responsibility for their lives after leaving the hospital. Community resources, such as family physicians, ministers, and employers, are involved in efforts to make the patient's social environment supportive, therapeutic, and accepting. It has been prophesied that the large mental hospital as it is known today will soon be a thing of the past and that the future will see only relatively brief periods of hospitalization at mental-health units in local community hospitals, with further out-patient treatment taking place within local clinics and other resources of the community.

A whole new field known as *community psychiatry and psychology* has developed along the general lines suggested above. Here the approach is in terms of working with disturbed people in their social environment, giving on-the-spot crisis therapy in always available walk-in clinics. Treatment will come from a broad base of community resources, rather than from a narrow and often community-isolated mental-health team.

The community mental-health effort is as much a preventive as a treatment effort. Through knowing the community, the schools, and the people, problems can be spotted early or even before they occur, and the local resources can be brought to bear on the situation. The roles of the professional mental-health workers in such a program have in many respects shifted widely from the traditional ones of diagnostician or therapist. In many instances the mental-health workers have become consultants, coordinators, or trainers of the nonprofessional individuals such as teachers, ministers, or policemen who deal with mental-health problems.

One answer to the lack of trained personnel lies in the finding that many of the approaches in this community effort can be carried out by people without professional degrees. In fact, it has been found that participation in the treatment team by individuals of the same socio-economic and ethnic background as the patient can play a vital role in meaningful treatment efforts.

2. Direct learning methods (the behavior therapies)   While the basis of this approach dates back at least to Pavlov and Watson, it has gained prominent and wide application only in recent years. The general assumption these methods make is that the symptom is the emotional illness, and that removal of the symptom is the cure. Here it is assumed that unwanted behavior can be extinguished or desirable patterns acquired in accordance with the ordinary principles of learning. This view is at odds with dynamic theories, particularly psychoanalytic theory which considers the symptom to result from conflict which must be resolved in order for cure to occur.

The relationship of learning to psychotherapy had been implied in Freud's writing and had been made explicit some years ago by Shoben (1949) and by Dollard and Miller (1950). In their views learning principles are used to account for what occurs in traditional psychotherapy. In contrast, the behavior therapies largely ignore traditional psychotherapy methods and directly attempt to change the symptom response by application of rewards and punishments.

There are a number of approaches which draw both theory and technique from such principles. Wolpe's (1958) reciprocal inhibition method, for example, is based on a reinforcement learning model. His method aims to desensitize the patient to anxiety-arousing stimuli by pairing such stimuli with incompatible relaxation responses. Other techniques involve extinction by nonreward of symptomatic behavior or by negative practice (deliberately repeating the undesirable behavior in the presence of negative reinforcers). Some of these techniques have long been known but are only now being employed in sophisticated and systematic ways.

A more radical departure has come from the employment of operant-conditioning methods (Krasner, 1962), utilizing schedules of reward, withdrawal of reward, or punishment to alter or "shape" patients' responses. An example of the application of the direct learning methods to mental-health problems is represented in what are termed token-economy wards in mental hospitals. These are most effective with chronic regressed patients. Basically, patients earn tokens for performing socially desirable behaviors—combing their hair, bathing, going to their occupational therapy assignment, socializing, etc. They can be fined or lose tokens for undesirable behavior—fighting, not grooming themselves, not participating in activities, etc. The tokens have value because the basics of living on the ward must be paid for by tokens. Thus it takes a given number of tokens to watch TV or to obtain a cigarette, etc. Even meals and beds may need to be earned. While from some standpoints making a "sick" patient "earn" his food may seem unduly harsh, it is closer to the conditions of the real social world than usual mental-hospital care. Such programs have been effective as a first step in getting chronic patients active and more socialized.

3. Humanistic therapies—phenomological, existential and relationship approaches   The diverse approaches to treatment, collectively known as *humanistic,* define a dimension almost opposite to that of the direct learning methods. From this point of view the learning methods are cold, impersonal, mechanistic procedures in which patients are regarded more as laboratory subjects than as suffering, feeling, and experiencing human beings. The humanistic therapies counter this by emphasizing the importance of the internal experience and subjective feeling. Their goal is neither dynamic insight into childhood causes, facilitation of social functioning, nor gross symptom removal. Treatment aims are seen in terms of some definition of self-actualization. These approaches have their basis in phenomenological and existential philosophies.

One thing they tend to have in common with the learning methods is their lack of concern for the developmental history of the disorder. The focus is on immediate internal experience, behaviors, and relationships rather than the overt symptom. The term *humanistic* for these approaches stems from the stress on the individual's internal experiences, the quality of his relationships with others, and his striving for self-maximization.

As Rogers' (1959) theorizing has evolved to a phenomological–self-actualizing emphasis, his position seems to have moved toward this group. The existential analytic approach (Boss, 1963) is also clearly in this category, as is Gestalt therapy (Perls, Goodman, and Hefferline, 1951). Characteristics of treatments based on these methods are: stress on the here-and-now reactions and relationships of the patient, freedom to accept and respond to oneself and one's feelings, and a commitment to self-actualization.

The new approaches we have been discussing are being pursued with dedicated effort and strong enthusiasm. Early reports are promising, and the social need for effective new methods tremendous. But since the history of mental health is littered with the skeletons of once-promising answers and cures (psychosurgery and electroshock, for example) a cautious view of new claims is indicated. In their first enthusiastic efforts almost all new methods have seemed promising. Only long-term experience and critical assessment can determine the ultimate effectiveness of these procedures. Assessment of cure in the area of mental health is a very thorny process, not likely to yield clear definitive answers in a short period of time.

Proponents and critics of these three methods are many. Rather than trying to evaluate each of the trends we have been discussing, the following important but probably not as yet really answerable questions are raised:

1. Even if the insight-relationship models of therapy are limited in their application, does it necessarily follow that their observations with regard to the development of emotional maladjustment are inaccurate? Could much of Freud's theory of personality development be essentially correct, but his means of changing personality inefficient?

2. Does the social-community approach do much to change or improve the patient, or does it only make the social environment more tolerant of the patient's continuing deviant behavior—thus adjusting the environment so there is less stress on the patient? What are the long-run implications for a society that adjusts itself to emotional disorder, rather than endeavoring to change disturbed individuals?

3. Do direct learning methods merely produce mechanical manipulations of overt responses at the price of directed internal control and responsibility for behavior? Can personality, including attitudes and values, be changed in this manner—or are the learning methods limited to affecting specific motor acts with little generalization to new situations?

4. Are the phenomenological–existential–self-actualizing methods as bound to socioeconomic level, age, and severity of disturbance as the insight therapies? How much of self-awareness, free expression, and close relationship in therapy can be counted on to be translated into personal and social effectiveness?

Definitive or even approximate answers to these questions will be hard to come by. Experience with each method and research about them should provide a better basis for an evaluation in the future. However, finding really adequate measures of personality change and reduction of emotional disturbance remains a mighty stumbling block to the evaluation of the effectiveness of psychotherapies. What is clear is that the basis and the scope of the search for effective treatment methods have been widened appreciably by these approaches and that the door is now open for further innovation and understanding. Perhaps the Zeitgeist is right for a major breakthrough in the treatment of the mentally disturbed.

REFERENCES

Boss, M. *Daseinsanalyse and psychoanalyses*. New York: Basic Books, 1963.

Dollard, J., & Miller, N. E. *Personality and psychotherapy*. New York: McGraw-Hill, 1950.

Erikson, E. H. *Childhood and society*. New York: Norton, 1950.

Freud, S. *The interpretation of dreams*. Translated by James Strachey. New York: Basic Books, 1900.

Hartmann, H. *Ego psychology and the problems of adaptation*. New York: International Universities Press, 1958.

Hollingshead, A., & Redlich, F. C. *Social class and mental illness*. New York: Wiley, 1958.

Joint Commission on Mental Illness and Health. *Action for mental health*. New York: Basic Books, 1961.

Krasner, L. The reinforcement machine. In *Research in Psychotherapy*. Proceedings of the American Psychological Association. Division of Clinical Psychology Conference. Vol. II. Washington, D.C., American Psychological Association, 1962.

Perls, F. S., Goodman, P., & Hefferline, R. *Gestalt therapy: Excitement and growth in the human personality*. New York: Julian Press, 1951.

Rogers, C. R. A theory of therapy, personality, and interpersonal relationships as developed in the client-centered framework. In S. Koch (ed.), *Psychology: A study of a science*. Vol. III. New York: McGraw-Hill, 1959. Pp. 184–256.

Shoben, E. J. Psychotherapy as a problem in learning theory. *Psychological Bulletin*, 1949, **46**, 366–392.

Sullivan, H. S. *The interpersonal theory of psychiatry*. New York: Norton, 1953.

Szasz, T. S. The myth of mental illness. *American Psychologist*, 1960, **15**, 113–118.

Wolpe, J. *Psychotherapy by reciprocal inhibition*. Stanford, Calif.: Stanford University Press, 1958.

Part Eight

Social Behavior

In a very general sense any study of human behavior must consider social factors. Even the recluse or hermit has had at least some contact with other people. For practical purposes, however, the term "social psychology" is usually employed in connection with the study of social and cultural influences on the individual, the dynamics and organization of the groups to which he belongs, and his interactions with other members of the society.

Current writers and researchers tend to avoid proposing general theories of social behavior, a major reason for this being a difference in philosophy among social scientists as to whether individuals or social institutions are the more appropriate units of study. This difference can be traced to the earliest beginnings of social psychology as a formal discipline. In 1908 William McDougall, a psychologist, and Edward Ross, a sociologist, each published a book entitled *An Introduction to Social Psychology* in which the field of study was defined and discussed. The similarity between the books was minimal, since McDougall emphasized the necessity of understanding individual behavior in order to explain social interaction, while Ross stressed the opposite position, that the study of social institutions was of primary importance and would explain individual behavior. Although it is now recognized that both the individual and the society into which he is born must be considered, there still exists considerable difference of opinion between "psychological social psychologists" and "sociological social psychologists."

In addition to differences in research philosophy, research techniques vary widely among social scientists, ranging from laboratory experimentation to attitude surveys, field observations, and case studies. For example, many studies of group interaction are carried out in the laboratory where strangers are instructed to "act as a group," while other researchers studying this same phenomenon might use "real" groups such as fraternities or clubs. As might be expected, the results of such studies are often considerably different, and only additional research will determine which findings are more valid.

What has occurred in social psychology is the emergence of many seemingly different and unrelated areas of study. Questions such as, "What influence do parental attitudes and training have on the child's social behavior?" "How do attitudes affect behavior?" "What effect do group pressures have on the individual and his behavior?" or "What are the effects of stress on social behavior?" are simply a few examples of the range of topics and the levels of study which are undertaken. The important point to note, however, is that although the diversity is large, all reflect the social psychologist's interest in social behavior and social interaction. The selections in this part present a sample of some of the research and discussion that has been published in this general area.

Present-day social scientists generally accept the position that children become socialized and behave in accordance with societal rules and regulations as a result of contact with others. Although there is considerable skepticism about their reliability, studies of children who were raised by animals and grew up in the absence of human contact indicate that severe intellectual, personality, and social retardation results. Experimental work with lower organisms on the effects of social isolation tends to verify these naturalistic observations. (See the article by the Harlows in Part 6.) While the child has many sources of social contact and influence, a primary one is his parents. In the first selection Bronfenbrenner examines the question of personality formation and socialization in relation to parental influence. Special attention is paid to the effects of amount and type of discipline on the child's behavior as well as to how the techniques of discipline have changed in our society during the past twenty-five years.

While personality formation and social behavior are influenced to a considerable extent by the deliberate application of rewards and punishments by parents, much behavior is learned from simply observing and imitating others. This is true not only of learning skills, but also of acquiring mannerisms, gestures, speech habits, attitudes, and prejudices. The second selection deals with a special kind of observational learning termed *vicarious experience,* which refers specifically to the situation where an observer has the same internal experience as if he were actually the performer.

The third selection addresses itself to the question of how the presence of observers affects an individual's performance. Research, as well as everyday experience, indicates that sometimes performance is improved by the presence of an audience and sometimes it is impaired. This selection represents an attempt to clarify these apparently contradictory findings and to suggest a theoretical explanation to account for them.

One of the major areas of interest in social psychology is the measurement, study, and modification of *attitudes.* The practical applications of knowledge about attitudes are quite obvious. Most companies consider the name given a new product to be extremely important, and the goal of subsequent advertising campaigns is to induce and then maintain favorable public reactions. Politicians ascertain public reaction in estimating their chances in the next election, and in fact nearly all of us modify our own behavior to some extent in order to ensure that others react favorably toward us. The fourth selection, by Kelley, describes a simple but ingenious experiment concerned with the ways in which our reactions to one facet of another's personality affect our overall perceptions and evaluations of his behavior.

The selection by Coch and French represents one of the classic studies in social psychology and demonstrates the importance of group variables in the modification of attitudes and behavior. This particular study makes use of a variation of the field-study technique, in which the experimental manipulation of variables is employed in a "real-life" situation.

While it has long been recognized that other members of a group exert pressure on the individual to conform to the group norms, it was not until the publication of studies by Solomon Asch that the true potency of group pressure came to be realized. In a typical experiment Asch would require several subjects in a group to judge whether a set of lines on a card were of equal length. Occasionally the lines to be judged would be obviously different in length, yet the subjects would agree that they were the same. The explanation for the seeming contradiction is that all but one of the "subjects" were confederates of the experimenter and that on selected trials all of these individuals would give the same false judgment. The naive subject was then left with the decision of whether to agree or disagree with the erroneous majority. In a great many instances he would conform with the group judgment. The selection by Milgram is an extension of the Asch conformity experiments, dealing with the question of whether or not group pressures are sufficiently potent to induce an individual to engage in overt behavior which is not in keeping with his existing moral values.

Although the general tendency in such experiments is to agree with the group judgment, many subjects show only occasional conformity, and some never conform. In the seventh selection Crutchfield suggests that the reason some individuals resist group pressure is that there are basic personality differences between "conformers" and "nonconformers." In addition to identifying personality characteristics he attempts to relate these characteristics to the parental training and home environment of the subjects.

While the previous two selections explored the effects of group pressure on the individual, the eighth selection demonstrates what happens when an individual is denied group contacts and the opportunity to participate in social interaction. One of the best practical examples of this occurred during the Korean War in the techniques used by the North Koreans to brainwash American prisoners of war. This study demonstrates quite dramatically how use of reinforcement techniques and deprivation, coupled with a lack of group support, can be used to modify behavior.

The last selection broaches the subject of leadership. Most of us accept the fact that the democratic method of decision making is best, and we tend to react rather negatively to autocratic methods, regardless of whether these are used by governmental authorities or the chairman of a club to which we belong. However, according to the author of the final selection, conditions of crisis such as natural disasters or wars present an entirely different set of circumstances and result in conditions where a high degree of authoritarianism and decisiveness are welcomed. To generalize, the notion that crises are the breeding grounds of dictatorship may indeed have considerable validity.

60

The Changing American Child—
A Speculative Analysis

Urie Bronfenbrenner

Socialization is generally assumed to involve a learning process that begins very early in life. Parents obviously play a major role in this process, typically exerting their influence by rewarding behaviors and attitudes which are acceptable or desirable and reproving or punishing those which are not. While there is considerable variation from one culture to another regarding what behaviors are considered desirable and what rewards and punishments are used, there does exist within most cultures a general set of rules and methods —norms—that parents follow in raising and training their children. For example, the Arapesh of New Guinea indulge their children and give them a great deal of affection. Punishment is almost never used, and when it is, it takes the form of simply removing the child from the situation or taking the unacceptable object away. On the other hand, the Mundugumor, who are of the same racial stock, deliberately frustrate, taunt, and often brutally punish their children. Do such drastic variations in child-rearing practices have an effect on later social behavior? The answer seems to be yes, since in general the Arapesh grow up to be very generous and friendly whereas the Mundugumor are arrogant and hostile. It would seem reasonable to assume that at least part of the difference in adult temperament and sociability can be accounted for by the vastly different child-rearing practices of the two cultures.

Although differences *between* cultures are more noticeable, it is also apparent that over a period of time the generally accepted techniques of child rearing can change *within* a culture. This first selection examines the present-day methods of child rearing in the United States, comparing them with the techniques used in previous generations. The author also discusses the effects these various techniques seem to have on adult social behavior.

It is now a matter of scientific record that patterns of child rearing in the United States have changed appreciably over the past twenty-five years (Bronfenbrenner, 1958). At the same time, the gap between social classes in their goals and methods of child rearing appears to be narrowing, with working-class parents beginning to adopt both the values and techniques of the middle class. Finally, there is dramatic correspondence between these observed shifts in parental values and behavior and the changing character of attitudes and practices advocated in successive editions of such widely read manuals as the Children's Bureau bulletin on *Infant Care* and Dr. Spock's *Baby and Child Care*. . . .

Given these facts, it becomes especially important to gauge the effect of the changes that are advocated and adopted. We must ask whether the changes that have occurred in the attitudes and actions of parents over the past twenty-five years have been such as to affect the personality development of their children, so that the boys and girls of today are somewhat different in character structure from those of a decade or more ago. Or, to

From The Journal of Social Issues, *Vol. XVII, No. 1, pp. 6–18. Reprinted with the permission of The Society for the Psychological Study of Social Issues and the author. This paper draws heavily on results of research being conducted by the author in collaboration with Edward C. Devereux and George J. Suci. The contribution of these colleagues to facts and ideas presented in this paper is gratefully acknowledged. The research program is supported in part with grants from the National Science Foundation and the National Institutes of Health. This paper was originally prepared for a symposium on social change to be published in the* Journal of Social Issues.

put the question more succinctly: Has the changing American parent produced a changing American child?

*   *   *

The Changing American Parent

In a recent analysis of data reported over a twenty-five-year period (Bronfenbrenner, 1958), we have already noted the major changes in parental behavior. These secular trends may be summarized as follows: (a) greater permissiveness toward the child's spontaneous desires; (b) freer expression of affection; (c) increased reliance on indirect "psychological" techniques of discipline (such as reasoning or appeals to guilt) versus direct methods (such as physical punishment, scolding, or threats); (d) in consequence of the above shifts in the direction of what are predominantly middle-class values and techniques, a narrowing of the gap between social classes in their patterns of child rearing.

Since the above analysis was published, a new study . . . by Bronson, Katten, and Livson (1959) has compared patterns of paternal and maternal authority and affection in two generations of families from the California Guidance Study. . . .

. . . An examination of the data cited by Bronson *et al.* points to a shift over the years in the pattern of parental role differentiation within the family. Specifically, in succeeding generations the relative position of the father vis-a-vis the mother is shifting with the former becoming increasingly more affectionate and less authoritarian and the latter becoming relatively more important as the agent of discipline, especially for boys.

"Psychological" Techniques of Discipline and Their Effects

In pursuing our analytic strategy, we seek next for evidence of the effects on the behavior of children of the changes in parental treatment noted in our inventory. We may begin by noting that the variables involved in the first three secular trends listed above constitute a complex that has received considerable attention in recent research on parent-child relations.

Within the last three years, two sets of investigators, working independently, have called attention to the greater efficacy of "love-oriented" or "psychological" techniques in bringing about desired behavior in the child (Miller and Swanson, 1960; Sears, Maccoby, and Levin, 1957). The pres-

ent writer, noting that such methods are especially favored by middle-class parents, has offered the following analysis of the nature of these techniques and the reasons for their effectiveness.

Such parents are, in the first place, more likely to overlook offenses, and when they do punish, they are less likely to ridicule or inflict physical pain. Instead, they reason with the youngster, isolate him, appeal to guilt, show disappointment—in short, convey in a variety of ways, on the one hand, the kind of behavior that is expected of the child; on the other, the realization that transgression means the interruption of a mutually valued relationship. . . .

These findings mean that middle-class parents, though in one sense more lenient in their discipline techniques, are using methods that are actually more compelling. Moreover, the compelling power of these practices is probably enhanced by the more permissive treatment accorded to middle-class children in the early years of life. The successful use of withdrawal of love as a discipline technique implies the prior existence of a gratifying relationship; the more love present in the first instance, the greater the threat implied in its withdrawal (Bronfenbrenner, 1958, p. 419).

It is now a well-established fact that children from middle-class families tend to excel those from lower-class families in many characteristics ordinarily regarded as desirable, such as self-control, achievement, responsibility, leadership, popularity, and adjustment in general (Mussen and Conger, 1956, pp. 347–352, 429–432). If, as seems plausible, such differences in behavior are attributable at least in part to class-linked variations in parental treatment, the strategy of inference we have adopted would appear on first blush to lead to a rather optimistic conclusion.

Since, over the years, increasing numbers of parents have been adopting the more effective socialization techniques typically employed by the middle class, does it not follow that successive generations of children should show gains in the development of effective behavior and desirable personality characteristics?

Unfortunately, this welcome conclusion, however logical, is premature, for it fails to take into account all of the available facts.

Sex, Socialization, and Social Class

To begin with, the parental behaviors we have been discussing are differentially distributed not only by socio-economic status but also by sex. As we point out elsewhere (Bronfenbrenner, 1961), girls are exposed to more affection and less punishment than boys but at the same time are more likely to be subjected to love-oriented discipline of the type which encourages the development of internalized controls. And, consistent with our line of reasoning, girls are found repeatedly to be "more obedient, cooperative, and in general better socialized than boys at comparable age levels" (Bronfenbrenner, 1961). But this is not the whole story.

. . . At the same time, the research results indicate that girls tend to be more anxious, timid, dependent, and sensitive to rejection. If these differences are a function of differential treatment by parents, then it would seem that the more "efficient" methods of child rearing employed with girls involve some risk of what might be called "oversocialization" (Bronfenbrenner, 1961, p. 260).

One could argue, of course, that the contrasting behaviors of boys and girls have less to do with differential parental treatment than with genetically based maturational influences. Nevertheless, two independent lines of evidence suggest that socialization techniques do contribute to individual differences, *within the same sex*, precisely in the types of personality characteristics noted above.

In the first place, variations in child behavior and parental treatment strikingly similar to those we have cited for the two sexes are reported in a recent comprehensive study of differences between first- and later-born children (Schachter, 1959). Like girls, first children receive more attention, are more likely to be exposed to psychological discipline, and end up more anxious and dependent, whereas later children, like boys, are more aggressive and self-confident.

A second line of evidence comes from our own current research. We have been concerned with the role of parents in the development of such constructive personality characteristics as responsibility and leadership among adolescent boys and girls. Our findings reveal not only the usual differences in adolescents' and parents' behaviors associated with the sex of the child but also a striking contrast in the relationship between parental and child behaviors for the two sexes.

As we expected, girls were rated by their teachers as more responsible than boys, whereas the latter obtained higher scores on leadership. Expected differences similarly appeared in the realm of parental behavior: Girls received more affection, praise, and companionship; boys were subjected to more physical punishment and achievement demands.

Quite unanticipated, however, at least by us, was the finding that both parental affection and discipline appeared to facilitate effective psychological functioning in boys but to impede the development of such constructive behavior in girls. Closer examination of our data indicated that both extremes of either affection or discipline were deleterious for all children, but that the process of socialization entailed somewhat different risks for the two sexes. Girls were especially susceptible to the detrimental influence of overprotection; boys, to the ill effects of insufficient parental discipline and support. Or, to put it in more colloquial terms: Boys suffered more often from too little taming; girls, from too much.

In an attempt to account for this contrasting pattern of relationships, we proposed the notion of differential optimal levels of affection and authority for the two sexes.

The qualities of independence, initiative, and self-sufficiency, which are especially valued for boys in our culture, apparently require for their development a somewhat different balance of authority and affection than is found in the "love-oriented" strategy characteristically applied with girls. While an affectional context is important for the socialization of boys, it must evidently be accompanied by and be compatible with a strong component of parental discipline. Otherwise, the boy finds himself in the same situation as the girl, who, having received greater affection, is more sensitive to its withdrawal, with the result that a little discipline goes a long way and strong authority is constricting rather than constructive (Bronfenbrenner, 1961, p. 260).

Class Differences

Available data suggest that this process may already be operating for boys from upper middle-class homes. To begin with, differential treatment of the sexes is at a minimum for these families. Contrasting parental attitudes and behaviors toward boys and girls are pronounced only at lower-class levels and decrease as one moves up the socio-economic scale (Bronfenbrenner, 1961; Kohn, 1959). Our own results show that it is primarily at lower middle-class levels that boys get more punishment than girls, and the latter receive greater warmth and attention. With an increase in the family's social position, direct discipline drops off, especially for boys, and indulgence and protectiveness decrease for girls. As a result, patterns of parental treatment for the two sexes begin to converge. In like manner, we find that the differential effects of parental behavior on the two sexes are marked only in the lower middle class. It is here that girls are at special risk of being overprotected and boys of not receiving sufficient discipline and support. In the upper middle class the picture changes. Girls are not as readily debilitated by parental affection and power, nor is parental discipline as effective in fostering the development of responsibility and leadership in boys.

All these trends point to the conclusion that the risks experienced by each sex during the process of socialization tend to be somewhat different at different social class levels. Thus the danger of overprotection for girls is especially great in lower-class families, but less in the upper middle class. Analogously, boys are in greater danger of suffering from inadequate discipline and support in the lower middle than in the upper middle class. But the upper middle-class boy, unlike the girl, exchanges one hazard for another. Since at this upper level the more potent psychological techniques of discipline are likely to be employed with both sexes, the boy presumably now too runs the risk of being oversocialized, of losing some of his capacity for independent aggressive accomplishment.

*   *   *

. . . Males exposed to this "modern" pattern of child rearing might be expected to differ from their counterparts of a quarter century ago in being somewhat more conforming and anxious, less enterprising and self-sufficient, and, in general, possessing more of the virtues and liabilities commonly associated with feminine character structure.

*   *   *

Family Structure
and Personality Development

But one other secular trend remains to be considered: What of the changing pattern of parental role differentiation during the first three decades of the century? If our extrapolation is correct, the balance of power within the family has continued to shift, with fathers yielding parental authority to mothers and taking on some of the nurturant and affectional functions traditionally associated with the maternal role. . . .

*   *   *

What kinds of children, then, can we expect to develop in families in which the father plays a predominantly affectionate role, and a relatively low level of discipline is exercised equally by both parents? A tentative answer to this question is supplied by a preliminary analysis of our data in which the relation between parental role structure and adolescent behavior was examined with controls for the family's social position. The results of this analysis are summarized as follows:

. . . Both responsibility and leadership are fostered by the relatively greater salience of the parent of the same sex. . . . Boys tend to be more responsible when the father rather than the mother is the principal disciplinarian; girls are more dependable when the mother is the major authority figure. . . . In short, boys thrive in a patriarchal context, girls in a matriarchal. . . . The most dependent and least dependable adolescents describe family arrangements that are neither patriarchal nor matriarchal, but equalitarian. To state the issue in more provocative form, our data suggest that the democratic family, which for so many years has been held up and aspired to as a model by professionals and enlightened laymen, tends to produce young people who "do not take initiative," "look to others for direction and decision," and "cannot be counted on to fulfill obligations" (Bronfenbrenner, 1961, p. 267).

In the wake of so sweeping a conclusion, it is important to call attention to the tentative, if not tenuous, character of our findings. The results were based on a single study employing crude questionnaire methods and rating scales. Also, our interpretation is limited by the somewhat attenuated character of most of the families classified as patriarchal or matriarchal in our sample. Extreme concentrations of power in one or the other parent were comparatively rare. Had they been more frequent, we suspect the data would have shown that such extreme asymmetrical patterns of authority are detrimental rather than salutary for effective psychological development, perhaps even more disorganizing than equalitarian forms.

Nevertheless, our findings do receive some peripheral support in the work of others. A number of investigations, for example, point to the special importance of the father in the socialization of boys (Bandura and Walters, 1959; Mussen and Distler, 1959). Further corroborative evidence appears in studies of the effects of paternal absence (Bach, 1946; Lynn and Sawrey, 1959; Sears, Pintler, and Sears, 1946; Tiller, 1958). The absence of the father apparently not only affects the behavior of the child directly but also influences the mother in the direction of greater overprotectiveness. The effect of both these tendencies is especially critical for male children; boys from father-absent homes tend to be markedly more submissive and dependent. Studies dealing explicitly with the influence of parental role structure in intact families are few and far between.

Papanek, in an unpublished doctoral dissertation, reports greater sex role differentiation among children from homes in which the parental roles were differentiated (Papanek, 1957). And in a carefully controlled study, Kohn and Clausen find that "schizophrenic patients more frequently than normal persons . . . report that their mothers played a very strong authority role and their fathers a very weak authority role" (Kohn and Clausen, 1956, p. 309).

Finally, what might best be called complementary evidence for our inferences regarding trends in family structure and their effects comes from the work of Miller and Swanson (1958) and their associates on the differing patterns of behavior exhibited by families from *bureaucratic* and *entrepreneurial* work settings. These investigators argue that the bureaucratic-entrepreneurial dichotomy represents a new cleavage in American social structure that cuts across and overrides social class influences and carries with it its own characteristic patterns of family structure and socialization. . . .

. . . It is Miller and Swanson's belief, however, that the trend is toward the bureaucratic way of life, with its less structured patterns of family organization and child rearing. The evidence we have cited on secular changes in family structure and the inferences we have drawn regarding their possible effects on personality development are on the whole consistent with their views.

Looking Forward

If Miller and Swanson are correct in the prediction that America is moving toward a bureaucratic society that emphasizes, to put it colloquially, "getting along" rather than "getting ahead," then presumably we can look forward to ever increasing numbers of equalitarian families who, in turn, will produce successive generations of ever more adaptable but unaggressive "organization men." But recent signs do not all point in this direction. In our review of secular trends in child-rearing practices (Bronfenbrenner, 1958), we detected in the data from the more recent studies a slowing

up in the headlong rush toward greater permissiveness and toward reliance on indirect methods of discipline. We pointed out also that if the most recent editions of well-thumbed guidebooks on child care are as reliable harbingers of the future as they have been in the past, we can anticipate something of a return to the more explicit techniques of an earlier era.

Perhaps the most important forces acting to redirect both the aims and methods of child rearing in America emanate from behind the Iron Curtain. With the firing of the first sputnik, achievement began to replace adjustment as the highest goal of the American way of life. We have become concerned, perhaps even obsessed, with "education for excellence" and the maximal utilization of our intellectual resources. Already, ability grouping and the guidance counselor who is its prophet have moved down from the junior high to the elementary school, and parents can be counted on to do their part in preparing their youngsters for survival in the new competitive world of applications and achievement tests.

But if a new trend in parental behavior is to develop, it must do so in the context of changes already under way. And if the focus of parental authority is shifting from husband to wife, then perhaps we should anticipate that pressures for achievement will be imposed primarily by mothers rather than fathers. Moreover, the mother's continuing strong emotional investment in the child should provide her with a powerful lever for evoking desired performance. It is noteworthy in this connection that recent studies of the familial origins of need-achievement point to the matriarchy as the optimal context for development of the motive to excel (Rosen and D'Andrade, 1959; Strodtbeck, 1958).

The prospect of a society in which socialization techniques are directed toward maximizing achievement drive is not altogether a pleasant one. As a number of investigators have shown (Baldwin, 1948; Baldwin, Kalhorn, and Breese, 1945; Haggard, 1957; Rosen and D'Andrade, 1959; Winterbottom, 1958), high achievement motivation appears to flourish in a family atmosphere of "cold democracy" in which initial high levels of maternal involvement are followed by pressures for independence and accomplishment. Nor does the product of this process give ground for reassurance. True, children from achievement-oriented homes excel in planning ability and performance, but they are also more aggressive, tense, domineering, and cruel (Baldwin, 1958; Baldwin, Kalhorn, and Breese, 1945; Haggard, 1957). It would appear that education for excellence, if pursued single-mindedly, may entail some sobering social costs.

But by now we are in danger of having stretched our chain of inference beyond the strength of its weakest link. Our speculative analysis has become far more speculative than analytic and to pursue it further would bring us past the bounds of science into the realms of science fiction. In concluding our discussion, we would reemphasize that speculations should, by their very nature, be held suspect. It is for good reason that, like "damn Yankees," they too carry their almost inseparable sobriquets: Speculations are either *idle* or *wild*. Given the scientific and social importance of the issues we have raised, we would dismiss the first of these labels out of hand, but the second cannot be disposed of so easily. Like the impetuous child, the wild speculation responds best to the sobering influence of friendly but firm discipline, in this instance from the hand of the behavioral scientist.

As we look ahead to the next twenty-five years of human socialization, let us hope that the optimal levels of involvement and discipline can be achieved not only by the parent who is unavoidably engaged in the process but also by the scientist who attempts to understand its working and who, also unavoidably, contributes to shaping its course.

REFERENCES

Bach, G. R. Father-fantasies and father-typing in father-separated children. *Child Development*, 1946, **17,** 63–79.

Baldwin, A. L. Socialization and the parent-child relationship. *Child Development*, 1948, **19,** 127–136.

Baldwin, A. L., Kalhorn, J., & Breese, F. H. The appraisal of parent behavior. *Psychological Monographs*, 1945, **58** (3, Whole No. 268).

Bandura, A., & Walters, R. H. *Adolescent aggression.* New York: Ronald Press, 1959.

Bronfenbrenner, U. Socialization and social class through time and space. In E. E. Maccoby, T. M. Newcomb, & E. L. Hartley (Eds.), *Readings in social psychology.* New York: Holt, Rinehart & Winston, 1958. Pp. 400–425.

Bronfenbrenner, U. Some familial antecedents of responsibility and leadership in adolescents. In L. Petrullo & B. M. Bass (Eds.), *Leadership and interpersonal behavior.* New York: Holt, Rinehart & Winston, 1961. Pp. 239–271.

Bronson, W. C., Katten, E. S., & Livson, N. Patterns of authority and affection in two generations. *Journal of Abnormal and Social Psychology*, 1959, **58,** 143–152.

Haggard, E. A. Socialization, personality, and academic achievement in gifted children. *School Review*, 1957, **65,** 388–414.

Kohn, M. L. Social class and parental values. *American Journal of Sociology*, 1959, **44,** 337–351.

Kohn, M. L., & Clausen, J. A. Parental authority behavior and schizophrenia. *American Journal of Orthopsychiatry*, 1956, **26,** 297–313.

Lynn, D. B., & Sawrey, W. L. The effects of father-absence on Norwegian boys and girls. *Journal of Abnormal and Social Psychology*, 1959, **59,** 258–262.

Miller, D. R., & Swanson, G. E. *The changing American parent.* New York: Wiley, 1958.

Miller, D. R., & Swanson, G. E. *Inner conflict and defense.* New York: Holt, Rinehart & Winston, 1960.

Mussen, P. H., & Conger, J. J. *Child development and personality.* New York: Harper & Row, 1956.

Mussen, P. H., & Distler, L. Masculinity, identification, and father-son relationships. *Journal of Abnormal and Social Psychology*, 1959, **59,** 350–356.

Papanek, M. Authority and interpersonal relations in the family. Unpublished doctoral dissertation, Radcliffe College, 1957.

Rosen, B. L., & D'Andrade, R. The psychosocial origins of achievement motivation. *Sociometry*, 1959, **22,** 185–217.

Schachter, S. *The psychology of affiliation.* Stanford, Calif.: Stanford University Press, 1959.

Sears, R. R., Maccoby, E. E., & Levin, H. *Patterns of child rearing.* Evanston, Ill.: Row, Peterson, 1957.

Sears, R. R., Pintler, M. H., & Sears, P. S. Effects of father-separation on preschool children's doll play aggression. *Child Development*, 1946, **17,** 219–243.

Strodtbeck, F. L. Family interaction, values, and achievement. In D. C. McClelland, A. L. Baldwin, U. Bronfenbrenner, & F. L. Strodtbeck (Eds.), *Talent and society.* Princeton, N.J.: Van Nostrand, 1958. Pp. 135–194.

Tiller, P. O. Father-absence and personality development of children in sailor families. *Nordisk Psykologi's Monograph Series*, 1958, **9,** 1–48.

Winterbottom, M. R. The relation of need-achievement to learning experiences in independence and mastery. In J. W. Atkinson (Ed.), *Motives in fantasy, action, and society.* Princeton, N.J.: Van Nostrand, 1958. Pp. 453–494.

61

Vicarious Extinction of Avoidance Behavior

Albert Bandura, Joan E. Grusec, and Frances L. Menlove

The previous selection examined the effects that changes in discipline *techniques* have had on children during the past twenty-five years. The main concern there was not in how children learn the various behaviors, but rather in the methods parents use to reward and punish them. The selection that follows deals with one of the major ways in which behavior is acquired and modified.

While children certainly engage in a considerable amount of trial-and-error activity, the majority of their behavior results from observation and imitation of others. In an extensive treatment of the topic of imitation Miller and Dollard discuss three types of behavior which are classified as imitative. The first of these only appears to involve imitation and is termed *same* behavior. This involves the situation where several individuals respond together, but actually are not responding in relation to each other. A good example of this would occur when the individuals attending a concert all stand, put on their coats, and leave the concert hall following completion of the final selection listed on the program. Strictly speaking, there is little if any imitation, and everyone is responding individually to a common stimulus. In the second category Miller and Dollard include those behaviors which are determined, at least in part, by the behavior of another. The term *matched dependent* is used to designate this type and implies that the observer matches his behavior to that of another and by so doing increases the likelihood of reinforcement. An example of this would be the situation in which an individual notices that everyone is running toward the stadium and realizes that if he is to get a good seat, he had better run also. Stated in terms of the classification that Dollard and Miller use, reinforcement (getting a good seat) is dependent upon an individual's behavior *matching* that of others.

In the third situation, which Miller and Dollard describe as *copying*, the critical factor is that the observer's responses be as nearly identical as possible to those of the model. Simply responding to a model's behavior (as in running toward the stadium) is no longer sufficient; the response of the observer must mirror the responses of the model. For example, an individual learning ballet tries to copy the movements demonstrated by the teacher. The reinforcement is based on the degree of similarity between the observer's and the model's responses.

Notice that in both matched dependent behavior and copying, the observer makes some sort of *overt* response for which he is reinforced. However, it is apparent that many behavioral changes occur even though no actual overt response has been made. Stated in other terms, humans have the capacity to observe the responses of others and then later respond *as if* they had actually imitated the initial response and been reinforced for it. This forms the basis for the type of imitative situation which de Charms and Rosenbaum have termed *vicarious experience*. This can easily be seen in our day-to-day activities, where we constantly acquire expectancies of reward when we see others being rewarded or expectancies of pain when we watch another responding in a situation where he re-

From Journal of Personality and Social Psychology, *Vol. 5 (1967), 16–23. Copyright 1967 by the American Psychological Association, and reproduced by permission. This research was supported by Public Health Research Grant M-5162 from the National Institute of Mental Health. The authors are indebted to Janet Brewer, Edith Dowley, Doris Grant, and Mary Lewis for their generous assistance in various phases of this research.*

ceives punishment. For example, when we observe someone being hailed by a police officer for jaywalking, we are likely to respond by being much more dutiful in waiting for the "walk" signal to flash.

The following experiment was designed to investigate a somewhat different aspect of this phenomenon—can a previously existing fear response be diminished through vicarious experience? Since it has also been suggested that fear stimuli lose their aversive properties more rapidly if they are presented in association with pleasant or positively reinforcing events, the context was also varied in this experiment by having one group of subjects observe the model while a party was going on and having the other group observe him while simply seated around a table.

*   *   *

Recent investigations have shown that behavioral inhibitions (Bandura, 1965) and conditioned emotional responses (Bandura and Rosenthal, 1966) can be acquired by observers as a function of witnessing aversive stimuli administered to performing subjects. The present experiment was primarily designed to determine whether preexisting avoidance behavior can similarly be extinguished on a vicarious basis. The latter phenomenon requires exposing observers to modeled stimulus events in which a performing subject repeatedly exhibits approach responses toward the feared object without incurring any aversive consequences.

*   *   *

. . . The present experiment explored the vicarious extinction of children's fearful and avoidant responses toward dogs. One group of children participated in a series of modeling sessions in which they observed a fearless peer model exhibit progressively longer, closer, and more active interactions with a dog. For these subjects, the modeled approach behavior was presented within a highly positive context. A second group of children was presented the same modeling stimuli, but in a neutral context.

Exposure to the behavior of the model contains two important stimulus events, that is, the occurrence of approach responses without any adverse consequences to the performer, and repeated observation of the feared animal. Therefore, in order to control for the effects of exposure to the dog per se, children assigned to a third group observed the dog in the positive context but with the model absent. A fourth group of children participated in the positive activities, but they were never exposed to either the dog or the model.

In order to assess both the generality and the stability of vicarious extinction effects, the children were readministered tests for avoidance behavior toward different dogs following completion of the treatment series, and approximately one month

later. It was predicted that children who had observed the peer model interact nonanxiously with the dog would display significantly less avoidance behavior than subjects who had no exposure to the modeling stimuli. The largest decrements were expected to occur among children in the modeling-positive context condition. It was also expected that repeated behavioral assessments and the general disinhibitory effects of participation in a series of highly positive activities might in themselves produce some decrease in avoidance behavior.

Method

Subjects

The subjects were 24 boys and 24 girls selected from three nursery schools. The children ranged in age from three to five years.

Pretreatment assessment of avoidance behavior

As a preliminary step in the selection procedure, parents were asked to rate the magnitude of their children's fearful and avoidant behavior toward dogs. Children who received high fear ratings were administered a standardized performance test on the basis of which the final selection was made.

The strength of avoidance responses was measured by means of a graded sequence of 14 performance tasks in which the children were required to engage in increasingly intimate interactions with a dog. A female experimenter brought the children individually to the test room, which contained a brown cocker spaniel confined in a modified playpen. In the initial tasks the children were asked, in the following order, to walk up to the playpen and look down at the dog, to touch her fur, and to pet her. Following the assessment of avoidance responses to the dog in the protective enclosure, the children were instructed to open a hinged door on the side of the playpen, to walk the dog on a leash to a throw rug, to remove the leash, and to turn the dog over and scratch her stomach. Although a number of the subjects were unable to perform all of the latter tasks, they were nevertheless administered the remaining test items to avoid any assumption of a perfectly ordered scale for all cases. In subsequent items the children were asked to remain alone in the room with the animal and to feed her dog biscuits. The final and most difficult set of tasks required the children to climb into the playpen with the dog, to pet her, to scratch her stomach, and to remain alone in the room with the dog under the exceedingly confining and fear-provoking conditions.

The strength of the children's avoidant tendencies was reflected not only in the items completed, but also in the degree of vacillation, reluctance, and fearfulness that preceded and accompanied each approach response. Consequently, children were credited two points if they executed a given task either spontaneously or willingly, and one point when they carried out the task minimally after considerable hesitancy and reluctance. Thus, for example, children who promptly stroked the dog's fur repeatedly when requested to do so received two points, whereas subjects who held back but then touched the dog's fur briefly obtained one point. . . .

*   *   *

Treatment conditions

Children who participated in the *modeling-positive context* condition observed a fearless peer model display approach responses toward a cocker spaniel within the context of a highly enjoyable party atmosphere.

There were eight 10-minute treatment sessions conducted on four consecutive days. Each session, which was attended by a group of four children, commenced with a jovial party. The children were furnished brightly colored hats, cookie treats and given small prizes. In addition, the experimenter read stories, blew large plastic balloons for the children to play with, and engaged in other party activities designed to produce strong positive affective responses.

After the party was well under way, a second experimenter entered the room carrying the dog, followed by a four-year-old male model who was unknown to most of the children. The dog was placed in a playpen located across the room from a large table at which the children were seated. The model, who had been chosen because of his complete lack of fear of dogs, then performed prearranged sequences of interactions with the dog

for approximately three minutes during each session. One boy served as the model for children drawn from two of the nursery schools, and a second boy functioned in the same role at the third school.

The fear-provoking properties of the modeled displays were gradually increased from session to session by varying simultaneously the physical restraints on the dog, the directness and intimacy of the modeled approach responses, and the duration of interaction between the model and his canine companion. Initially, the experimenter carried the dog into the room and confined her to the playpen, and the model's behavior was limited to friendly verbal responses ("Hi, Chloe") and occasional petting. During the following three sessions the dog remained confined to the playpen, but the model exhibited progressively longer and more active interactions in the form of petting the dog with his hands and feet, and feeding her wieners and milk from a baby bottle. Beginning with the fifth session, the dog was walked into the room on a leash, and the modeled tasks were mainly performed outside the playpen. For example, in addition to repeating the feeding routines, the model walked the dog around the room, petted her, and scratched her stomach while the leash was removed. In the last two sessions the model climbed into the playpen with the dog where he petted her, hugged her, and fed her wieners and milk from the baby bottle.

*   *   *

Children assigned to the *modeling-neutral context* condition observed the same sequence of approach responses performed by the same peer model except that the parties were omitted. In each of the eight sessions the subjects were merely seated at the table and observed the modeled performances.

In order to control for the influence of repeated exposure to the positive atmosphere and to the dog per se, children in the *exposure-positive context* group attended the series of parties in the presence of the dog with the model absent. As in the two modeling conditions, the dog was introduced into the room in the same manner for the identical length of time; similarly, the dog was confined in the playpen during the first four sessions and placed on a leash outside the enclosure in the remaining sessions.

Children in the *positive-context* group participated in the parties, but they were never exposed to either the dog or the model. The main purpose of this condition was to determine whether the mere presence of a dog had an adverse or a bene-ficial effect on the children. Like the third condi-tion, it also provided a control for the possible therapeutic effects of positive experiences and in-creased familiarity with amiable experimenters, which may be particularly influential in reducing inhibitions in very young children. In addition, repeated behavioral assessments in which subjects perform a graded series of approach responses toward a feared object without any aversive con-sequences would be expected to produce some direct extinction of avoidance behavior. The in-clusion of the latter two control groups thus makes it possible to evaluate the changes effected by exposure to modeling stimuli over and above those resulting from general disinhibition, direct ex-tinction, and repeated observation of the feared object.

Posttreatment assessment of avoidance behavior

On the day following completion of the treat-ment series, the children were readministered the performance test consisting of the graded sequence of interaction tasks with the dog. In order to deter-mine the generality of vicarious extinction effects, half the children in each of the four groups were tested initially with the experimental animal and then with an unfamiliar dog; the remaining chil-dren were presented with the two dogs in the reverse order.[1] The testing sessions were separated by an interval of 1½ hours so as to minimize any transfer of emotional reactions generated by one animal to the other.

The unfamiliar animal was a white mongrel, predominantly terrier, and of approximately the same size and activity level as the cocker spaniel. Two groups of 15 children, drawn from the same nursery school population, were tested with either the mongrel or the spaniel in order to determine the aversiveness of the two animals. The mean approach scores with the spaniel ($M = 16.47$) and the mongrel ($M = 15.80$) were virtually identical ($t = .21$).

Follow-up assessment

A follow-up evaluation was conducted approxi-mately one month after the posttreatment assess-ment in order to determine the stability of model-ing-induced changes in approach behavior. The children's responses were tested with the same performance tasks toward both animals, presented in the identical order.

*   *   *

Measurement procedure

The same female experimenter administered the pretreatment, posttreatment, and follow-up behav-ioral tests. To prevent any possible bias, the ex-perimenter was given minimal information about the details of the study and had no knowledge of the conditions to which the children were assigned. The treatment and assessment procedures were further separated by the use of different rooms for each activity.

*   *   *

Changes in children's approach-response scores across the different phases of the experiment, and the number of subjects in each treatment condi-tion who were able to carry out the terminal per-formance task served as the dependent measures.

Results

The percentages of test items in which the ani-mals behaved in a passive, moderately active, or vigorous manner were 55, 43, and 2, respectively, for the model-positive context group; 53, 44, and 2 for children in the model-neutral context condi-tion; 52, 45, and 3 for the exposure-positive con-text group; and 57, 41, and 2 for the positive-context subjects. Thus, the test animals did not differ in their behavior during the administration of performance tasks to children in the various treatment conditions.

Approach responses

Table 1 presents the mean increases in approach behavior achieved by children in each of the treatment conditions in different phases of the experiment with each of the test animals.

*   *   *

. . . The results reveal that the treatment con-ditions had a highly significant effect on the chil-dren's behavior. Tests of the differences between the various pairs of treatments indicate that sub-jects in the modeling-positive context condition displayed significantly more approach behavior than subjects in either the exposure or the posi-tive-context groups. Similarly, children who had observed the model within the neutral setting ex-ceeded both the exposure and positive-context

---

[1] The authors are especially indebted to Chloe and Jenny for their invaluable and steadfast assistance with a task that, at times, must have been most per-plexing to them.

TABLE 1 *Mean Increases in Approach Responses as a Function of Treatment Conditions, Assessment Phases, and Test Animals*

Phases	Treatment conditions			
	Modeling-positive context	Modeling-neutral context	Exposure-positive context	Positive context
Posttreatment				
Spaniel	10.83	9.83	2.67	6.08
Mongrel	5.83	10.25	3.17	4.17
Follow-Up				
Spaniel	10.83	9.33	4.67	5.83
Mongrel	12.59	9.67	4.75	6.67
Combined data	10.02	9.77	3.81	5.69

groups in approach behavior. However, the data yielded no significant differences between either the two modeling conditions or the two control groups.

*   *   *

Terminal performances

Another measure of the efficacy of modeling procedures is provided by comparisons of the number of children in each condition who performed the terminal approach behavior at least once during the posttreatment assessment. . . . The findings show that the 67 per cent of the children in the modeling treatment were able to remain alone in the room confined with the dog in the playpen, whereas the corresponding figure for the control subjects is 33 per cent. . . .

Within the control groups, the terminal performances were attained primarily by subjects who initially showed the weakest level of avoidance behavior. The differences between the two groups are, therefore, even more pronounced if the analysis is conducted on the subjects whose pretreatment performances reflected extreme or moderately high levels of avoidance behavior. Of the most avoidant subjects in each of the two pooled groups, 55 per cent of the children in the modeling conditions were able to perform the terminal approach behavior following the experimental sessions, while only 13 per cent of the control subjects successfully completed the final task.

The relative superiority of the modeling groups is also evident in the follow-up phase of the experiment. Based on the stringent criterion in which the most fearful task is successfully per-

formed with *both* animals, a significantly larger number of children in the modeling conditions (42 per cent) than in the control groups (12 per cent) exhibited generalized extinction. Moreover, not a single control subject from the two highest levels of avoidance behavior was able to remain alone in the room confined in the playpen with each of the dogs, whereas 33 per cent of the most avoidant children in the modeling conditions successfully passed both terminal approach tasks.

Discussion

The findings of the present experiment provide considerable evidence that avoidance responses can be successfully extinguished on a vicarious basis. This is shown in the fact that children who experienced a gradual exposure to progressively more fearful modeled responses displayed extensive and stable reduction in avoidance behavior. Moreover, most of these subjects were able to engage in extremely intimate and potentially fearful interactions with test animals following the treatment series. The considerable degree of generalization of extinction effects obtained to the unfamiliar dog is most likely due to similar stimulus properties of the test animals. Under conditions where observers' avoidance responses are extinguished to a single animal, one would expect a progressive decrement in approach behavior toward animals of increasing size and fearfulness.

The prediction that vicarious extinction would be augmented by presenting the modeling stimuli within a highly positive context was not confirmed, although subjects in the latter condition differed more significantly from the controls than children who observed approach behavior under neutral conditions. It is entirely possible that a different temporal ordering of emotion-provoking modeling stimuli and events designed to induce anxiety-inhibiting responses would facilitate the vicarious extinction process. . . .

*   *   *

Further research is needed to separate the relative contribution of cognitive, emotional, and other factors governing vicarious processes. It would also be of interest to study the effects upon vicarious extinction exercised by such variables as number of modeling trials, distribution of extinction sessions, mode of model presentation, and variations in the characteristics of the models and the feared stimuli. For example, with extensive sampling in the modeled displays of both girls and boys exhibiting approach responses to dogs ranging from diminutive breeds to larger specimens, it may be possible to achieve widely generalized extinction effects. Once approach behaviors have been restored through modeling, their maintenance and further generalization can be effectively controlled by response-contingent reinforcement administered directly to the subject. The combined use of modeling and reinforcement procedures may thus serve as a highly efficacious mode of therapy for eliminating severe behavioral inhibitions.

REFERENCES
Bandura, A. Influence of models' reinforcement contingencies on the acquisition of imitative responses. *Journal of Personality and Social Psychology*, 1965, 1, 589–595.
Bandura, A., & Rosenthal, T. L. Vicarious classical conditioning as a function of arousal level. *Journal of Personality and Social Psychology*, 1966, 3, 54–62.

62

Social Facilitation

Robert B. Zajonc

It has long been recognized that the way an individual behaves is affected by the presence of others. Exactly what these effects are, however, is a question which still remains unanswered, although research into the area of social facilitation has been conducted periodically since before the turn of the century.

In the following selection Zajonc draws on a variety of human and animal studies in an attempt to integrate and explain the contradictory findings. As to why the presence of others sometimes improves performance and sometimes impairs it, Zajonc notes that a critical variable appears to be whether subjects must learn new responses or whether they are required to perform tasks and responses which were already well learned. In addition to focusing on the importance of the experimental task and the nature of the responses made by the subjects, Zajonc also extends his analysis to include speculation regarding the effects of social interaction on the physiological mechanisms and level of arousal of the organism.

Most textbook definitions of social psychology involve considerations about the influence of man upon man or, more generally, of individual upon individual. And most of them, explicitly or implicitly, commit the main efforts of social psychology to the problem of how and why the *behavior* of one individual affects the behavior of another. The influences of individuals on each others' behavior which are of interest to social psychologists today take on very complex forms. Often they involve vast networks of interindividual effects,

From Science, *Vol. 149, No. 16 (July 1965), 269–274. Copyright 1965 by the American Association for the Advancement of Science. The preparation of this article was supported in part by grants Nonr-1224(34) from the Office of Naval Research and GS-629 from the National Science Foundation.*

such as one finds in studying the process of group decisionmaking, competition, or conformity to a group norm. But the fundamental forms of inter-individual influence are represented by the oldest experimental paradigm of social psychology: social facilitation. This paradigm, dating back to Trip-lett's original experiments on pacing and competition carried out in 1897, examines the consequences upon behavior which derive from the sheer presence of other individuals.

Until the late 1930's, interest in social facilitation was quite active, but with the outbreak of World War II it suddenly died. And it is truly regrettable that it died, because the basic questions about social facilitation—its dynamics and its causes—which are in effect the basic questions of social psychology, were never solved. It is with these questions that this article is concerned. I first examine past results in this nearly completely abandoned area of research and then suggest a general hypothesis which might explain them.

Research in the area of social facilitation may be classified in terms of two experimental paradigms: audience effects and co-action effects. The first experimental paradigm involves the observation of behavior when it occurs in the presence of passive spectators. The second examines behavior when it occurs in the presence of other individuals also engaged in the same activity. We shall consider past literature in these two areas separately.

Audience Effects

Simple motor responses are particularly sensitive to social facilitation effects. In 1925 Travis obtained such effects in a study in which he used the pursuit-rotor task. In this task the subject is required to follow a small revolving target by means of a stylus which he holds in his hand. If the stylus is even momentarily off target during a revolution, the revolution counts as an error. First each subject was trained for several consecutive days until his performance reached a stable level. One day after the conclusion of the training the subject was called to the laboratory, given five trials alone, and then ten trials in the presence of from four to eight upperclassmen and graduate students. They had been asked by the experimenter to watch the subject quietly and attentively. Travis found a clear improvement in performance when his subjects were confronted with an audience. Their accuracy on the ten trials before an audience was greater than on any ten previous trials, including those on which they had scored highest.

*   *   *

Dashiell (1930), who, in the early 1930's, carried out an extensive program of research on social facilitation, also found considerable improvement in performance due to audience effects on such tasks as simple multiplication or word association. But, as is the case in many other areas, negative audience effects were also found. In 1933 Pessin asked college students to learn lists of nonsense syllables under two conditions, alone and in the presence of several spectators. When confronted with an audience, his subjects required an average of 11.27 trials to learn a seven-item list. When working alone they needed only 9.85 trials. The average number of errors made in the "audience" condition was considerably higher than the number in the "alone" condition. In 1931 Husband found that the presence of spectators interferes with the learning of a finger maze,[1] and in 1933 Pessin and Husband confirmed Husband's results. The number of trials which the isolated subjects required for learning the finger maze was 17.1. Subjects confronted with spectators, however, required 19.1 trials. The average number of errors for the isolated subjects was 33.7; the number for those working in the presence of an audience was 40.5.

The results thus far reviewed seem to contradict one another. On a pursuit-rotor task Travis found that the presence of an audience improves performance. The learning of nonsense syllables and maze learning, however, seem to be inhibited by the presence of an audience, as shown by Pessin's experiment. The picture is further complicated by the fact that when Pessin's subjects were asked, several days later, to recall the nonsense syllables they had learned, a reversal was found. The subjects who tried to recall the lists in the presence of spectators did considerably better than those who tried to recall them alone. Why are the learning of nonsense syllables and maze learning inhibited by the presence of spectators? And why, on the other hand, does performance on a pursuit-rotor, word-association, multiplication, or a vigilance task improve in the presence of others?

There is just one, rather subtle, consistency in the above results. It would appear that the emission of well-learned responses is facilitated by the

---

[1] In this task the blindfolded subject traces a maze with his finger.

presence of spectators, while the acquisition of new responses is impaired. To put the statement in conventional psychological language, performance is facilitated and learning is impaired by the presence of spectators.

This tentative generalization can be reformulated so that different features of the problem are placed into focus. During the early stages of learning, especially of the type involved in social facilitation studies, the subject's responses are mostly the wrong ones. A person learning a finger maze or a person learning a list of nonsense syllables emits more wrong responses than right ones in the early stages of training. Most learning experiments continue until he ceases to make mistakes—until his performance is perfect. It may be said, therefore, that during training it is primarily the wrong responses which are dominant and strong; they are the ones which have the highest probability of occurrence. But after the individual has mastered the task, correct responses necessarily gain ascendency in his task-relevant behavioral repertoire. Now they are the ones which are more probable—in other words, dominant. Our tentative generalization may now be simplified: Audience enhances the emission of dominant responses. If the dominant responses are the correct ones, as is the case upon achieving mastery, the presence of an audience will be of benefit to the individual. But if they are mostly wrong, as is the case in the early stages of learning, then these wrong responses will be enhanced in the presence of an audience, and the emission of correct responses will be postponed or prevented.

There is a class of psychological processes which are known to enhance the emission of dominant responses. They are subsumed under the concepts of drive, arousal, and activation.[2] If we could show that the presence of an audience has arousal consequences for the subject, we would be a step further along in trying to arrange the results of social-facilitation experiments into a neater package. But let us first consider another set of experimental findings.

Co-action Effects

The experimental paradigm of co-action is somewhat more complex than the paradigm involved in the study of audience effects. Here we observe individuals all simultaneously engaged in the same activity and in full view of each other. . . .

*   *   *

The experiments on social facilitation performed by Floyd Allport in 1920 and continued by Dashiell in 1930, both of whom used human subjects, are the ones best known. Allport's subjects worked either in separate cubicles or sitting around a common table. When working in isolation they did the various tasks at the same time and were monitored by common time signals. Allport did everything possible to reduce the tendency to compete. The subjects were told that the results of their tests would not be compared and would not be shown to other staff members, and that they themselves should refrain from making any such comparisons.

Among the tasks used were the following: chain word association, vowel cancellation, reversible perspective, multiplication, problem solving, and judgments of odors and weights. The results of Allport's experiments are well known: In all but the problem-solving and judgments test, performance was better in groups than in the "alone" condition. How do these results fit our generalization? Word association, multiplication, the cancellation of vowels, and the reversal of the perceived orientation of an ambiguous figure all involve responses which are well established. They are responses which are either very well learned or under a very strong influence of the stimulus, as in the word-association task or the reversible-perspective test. The problem-solving test consists of disproving arguments of ancient philosophers. In contrast to the other tests, it does not involve well-learned responses. On the contrary, the probability of wrong (that is, logically incorrect) responses on tasks of this sort is rather high; in other words, wrong responses are dominant. Of interest, however, is the finding that while intellectual work suffered in the group situation, sheer output of words was increased. When working together, Allport's subjects tended consistently to write more. Therefore, the generalization proposed in the previous section can again be applied: If the presence of others raises the probability of dominant responses, and if strong (and many) incorrect response tendencies prevail, then the presence of others can only be detrimental to performance. The results of the judgment tests have little bearing on the present argument, since Allport gives no accuracy figures for evaluating performance. The data reported only show that the presence of

2 See, for instance, Dufy (1962), Spence (1956), and Zajonc and Nieuwenhuyse (1964).

others was associated with the avoidance of extreme judgments.

In 1928 Travis, whose work on the pursuit rotor I have already noted, repeated Allport's chain-word-association experiment. In contrast to Allport's results, Travis found that the presence of others decreased performance. The number of associations given by his subjects was greater when they worked in isolation. It is very significant, however, that Travis used stutterers as his subjects. In a way, stuttering is a manifestation of a struggle between conflicting response tendencies, all of which are strong and all of which compete for expression. The stutterer, momentarily hung up in the middle of a sentence, waits for the correct response to reach full ascendancy. He stammers because other competing tendencies are dominant at that moment. It is reasonable to assume that, to the extent that the verbal habits of a stutterer are characterized by conflicting response tendencies, the presence of others, by enhancing each of these response tendencies, simply heightens his conflict. Performance is thus impaired.

Avoidance Learning

In two experiments on the learning of avoidance responses the performances of solitary and grouped subjects were compared. In one, rats were used; in the other, humans.

Let us first consider the results of the rat experiment by Rasmussen (1939). A number of albino rats, all litter mates, were deprived of water for 48 hours. The apparatus consisted of a box containing a dish of drinking water. The floor of the box was made of a metal grille wired to one pole of an electric circuit. A wire inserted in the water in the dish was connected to the other pole of the circuit. Thirsty rats were placed in the box alone and in groups of three. They were allowed to drink for 5 seconds with the circuit open. Following this period the shock circuit remained closed, and each time the rat touched the water he received a painful shock. Observations were made on the number of times the rats approached the water dish. The results of this experiment showed that the solitary rats learned to avoid the dish considerably sooner than the grouped animals did. The rats that were in groups of three attempted to drink twice as often as the solitary rats did, and suffered considerably more shock than the solitary subjects.

Let us examine Rasmussen's results somewhat more closely. For purposes of analysis let us as-

sume that there are just two critical responses involved: drinking, and avoidance of contact with the water. They are clearly incompatible. But drinking, we may further assume, is the dominant response, and, like eating or any other dominant response, it is enhanced by the presence of others. The animal is therefore prevented, by the facilitation of drinking which derives from the presence of others, from acquiring the appropriate avoidance response.

The second of the two studies is quite recent and was carried out by Ader and Tatum (1963). They devised the following situation with which they confronted their subjects, all medical students. Each subject is told on arrival that he will be taken to another room and seated in a chair and that electrodes will be attached to his leg. He is instructed not to get up from the chair and not to touch the electrodes. He is also told not to smoke or vocalize, and is told that the experimenter will be in the next room. That is all he is told. The subjects are observed either alone or in pairs. In the former case the subject is brought to the room and seated at a table equipped with a red button, which is connected to an electric circuit. Electrodes, by means of which electric shock can be administered, are attached to the calf of one leg. After the electrodes are attached, the experimenter leaves the room. From now on the subject will receive ½ second of electric shock every 10 seconds unless he presses the red button. Each press of the button delays the shock by 10 seconds. Thus, if he is to avoid shock, he must press the button at least once every 10 seconds. It should be noted that no information was given him about the function of the button or about the purpose of the experiment. No essential differences are introduced when subjects are brought to the room in pairs. Both are seated at the table and both become part of the shock circuit. The response of either subject delays the shock for both.

The avoidance response is considered to have been acquired when the subject (or pair of subjects) receives less than six shocks in a period of 5 minutes. Ader and Tatum report that the isolated students required, on the average, 11 minutes, 35 seconds to reach this criterion of learning. Of the 12 pairs which participated in the experiment, only two reached this criterion. One of them required 46 minutes, 40 seconds; the other, 68 minutes, 40 seconds! Ader and Tatum offer no explanation for their curious results. But there is no reason why we should not treat them in terms of the generalization proposed above. We are dealing here with a learning task, and the fact that the subjects are learning to avoid shock by pressing a red button does not introduce particular problems. They are confronted with an ambiguous task and told nothing about the button. Pressing the button is simply not the dominant response in this situation. However, escaping is. Ader and Tatum report that eight of the 36 subjects walked out in the middle of the experiment.

One aspect of Ader and Tatum's results is especially worth noting. Once having learned the appropriate avoidance response, the individual subjects responded at considerably lower rates than the paired subjects. When we consider only those subjects who achieved the learning criterion and only those responses which occurred *after* criterion had been reached, we find that the response rates of the individual subjects were in all but one case lower than the response rates of the grouped subjects. This result further confirms the generalization that, while learning is impaired by the presence of others, the performance of learned responses is enhanced.

There are experiments which show that learning is enhanced by the presence of other learners (Gurnee, 1939; Welty, 1934), but in all these experiments, as far as I can tell, it was possible for the subject to *observe* the critical responses of other subjects and to determine when he was correct and when incorrect. In none, therefore, has the co-action paradigm been employed in its pure form. That paradigm involves the presence of others and nothing else. It requires that these others not be able to provide the subject with cues or information as to appropriate behavior. If other learners can supply the critical individual with such cues, we are dealing not with the problem of co-action but with the problem of imitation or vicarious learning.

The Presence of Others as a Source of Arousal

The results I have discussed thus far lead to one generalization and to one hypothesis. The generalization which organizes these results is that the presence of others, as spectators or as co-actors, enhances the emission of dominant responses. We also know from extensive research literature that arousal, activation, or drive all have as a consequence the enhancement of dominant responses (See Spence, 1956). We now need to examine the hypothesis that the presence of others increases the individual's general arousal or drive level.

The evidence which bears on the relationship between the presence of others and arousal is, unfortunately, only indirect. But there is some very suggestive evidence in one area of research. One of the more reliable indicators of arousal and drive is the activity of the endocrine systems in general and of the adrenal cortex in particular. Adrenocortical functions are extremely sensitive to changes in emotional arousal, and it has been known for some time that organisms subjected to prolonged stress are likely to manifest substantial adrenocortical hypertrophy (Selye, 1946). Recent work (Nelson and Samuels, 1952) has shown that the main biochemical component of the adrenocortical output is hydrocortisone (17-hydroxycorticosterone). Psychiatric patients characterized by anxiety states, for instance, show elevated plasma levels of hydrocortisone (Bliss, Sandberg, and Nelson, 1953; Board, Persky, and Hamburg, 1956). Mason, Brady, and Sidman (1957) have recently trained monkeys to press a lever for food and have given these animals unavoidable electric shocks, all preceded by warning signals. This procedure led to elevated hydrocortisone levels; the levels returned to normal within 1 hour after the end of the experimental session. This "anxiety" reaction can apparently be attenuated if the animal is given repeated doses of reserpine 1 day before the experimental session (Mason and Brady, 1956). Sidman's conditioned avoidance schedule also results in raising the hydrocortisone levels by a factor of 2 to 4 (Mason *et al.,* 1957). In this schedule the animal receives an electric shock every 20 seconds without warning, unless he presses a lever. Each press delays the shock for 20 seconds.

While there is a fair amount of evidence that adrenocortical activity is a reliable symptom of arousal, similar endocrine manifestations were found to be associated with increased population density (Thiessen, 1964b). Crowded mice, for instance, show increased amphetamine toxicity—that is, susceptibility to the excitatory effects of amphetamine—against which they can be protected by the administration of phenobarbital, chlorpromazine, or reserpine (Lasagna and McCann, 1957). Mason and Brady (1964) have recently reported that monkeys caged together had considerably higher plasma levels of hydrocortisone than monkeys housed in individual cages. Thiessen (1964a) found increases in adrenal weights in mice housed in groups of 10 and 20 as compared with mice housed alone. The mere presence of other animals in the same room, but in separate cages, was also found to produce elevated levels of hydrocortisone. . . .

*   *   *

Admittedly, the evidence that the mere presence of others raises the arousal level is indirect and scanty. And, as a matter of fact, some work seems to suggest that there are conditions, such as stress, under which the presence of others may lower the animal's arousal level. Bovard (1959), for instance, hypothesized that the presence of another member of the same species may protect the individual under stress by inhibiting the activity of the posterior hypothalamic centers which trigger the pituitary adrenal cortical and sympathetico-adrenal medullary responses to stress. Evidence for Bovard's hypothesis, however, is as indirect as evidence for the one which predicts arousal as a consequence of the presence of others, and even more scanty.

Summary and Conclusion

If one were to draw one practical suggestion from the review of the social-facilitation effects which are summarized in this article, he would advise the student to study all alone, preferably in an isolated cubicle, and to arrange to take his examinations in the company of many other students, on stage, and in the presence of a large audience. The results of his examination would be beyond his wildest expectations, provided, of course, he had learned his material quite thoroughly.

I have tried in this article to pull together the early, almost forgotten work on social facilitation and to explain the seemingly conflicting results. This explanation is, of course, tentative, and it has never been put to a direct experimental test. It is, moreover, not far removed from the one originally proposed by Allport. He theorized (Allport, 1924, p. 261) that "the sights and sounds of others doing the same thing" augment ongoing responses. Allport, however, proposed this effect only for *overt* motor responses, assuming (Allport, 1924, p. 274) that "*intellectual* or *implicit responses* of thought are hampered rather than facilitated" by the presence of others. This latter conclusion was probably suggested to him by the negative results he observed in his research on the effects of co-action on problem solving.

Needless to say, the presence of others may have effects considerably more complex than that of increasing the individual's arousal level. The presence of others may provide cues as to appropriate or inappropriate responses, as in the case of imitation or vicarious learning. Or it may supply the individual with cues as to the measure of danger in an ambiguous or stressful situation. Davitz and Mason (1955), for instance, have shown that the presence of an unafraid rat reduces the fear of another rat in stress. Bovard (1959) believes that the calming of the rat in stress which is in the presence of an unafraid companion is mediated by inhibition of activity of the posterior hypothalamus. But in their experimental situations (that is, the open field test) the possibility that cues for appropriate escape or avoidance responses are provided by the co-actor is not ruled out. We might therefore be dealing not with the effects of the mere presence of others but with the considerably more complex case of imitation. The animal may not be calming *because* of his companion's presence. He may be calming *after* having copied his companion's attempted escape responses. The paradigm which I have examined in this article pertains only to the effects of the mere presence of others and to the consequences for the arousal level. The exact parameters involved in social facilitation still must be specified.

REFERENCES

Ader, R., & Tatum, R. *Journal of the Experimental Analysis of Behavior*, 1963, **6**, 357.

Allport, F. H. *Journal of Experimental Psychology*, 1920, **3**, 159.

Allport, F. H. *Social psychology.* Boston: Houghton-Mifflin, 1924.

Bliss, E. L., Sandberg, A. A., & Nelson, D. H. *Journal of Clinical Investigation*, 1953, **32**, 9; Board, F., Persky, H., & Hamburg, D. A. *Psychosomatic Medicine*, 1956, **18**, 324.

Bovard, E. W. *Psychological Review*, 1959, **66**, 267.

Dashiell, J. F. *Journal of Abnormal and Social Psychology*, 1930, **25**, 190.

Davitz, J. R., & Mason, D. J. *Journal of Comparative and Physiological Psychology*, 1955, **48**, 149.

Dufy, E. *Activation and behavior.* New York: Wiley, 1962.

Gurnee, H. *Journal of Abnormal and Social Psychology*, 1939, **34**, 529, Welty, J. C. *Physiological Zoology*, 1934, **7**, 85.

Husband, R. W. *Journal of Genetic Psychology*, 1931, **39**, 258.

Lasagna, L., & McCann, W. P. *Science*, 1957, **125**, 1241.

Mason, J. W., & Brady, J. V. *Science*, 1956, **124**, 983.

Mason, J. W., & Brady, J. V. In P. H. Leiderman & D. Shapiro (Eds.), *Psychobiological approaches to social behavior.* Stanford, Calif.: Stanford University Press, 1964.

Mason, J. W., Brady, J. V., & Sidman, M. *Endocrinology*, 1957, **60**, 741.

Nelson, D. H., & Samuels, L. T. *Journal of Clinical Endocrinology and Metabolism*, 1952, **12**, 519.

Pessin, J. *American Journal of Psychology*, 1933, **45**, 263.

Pessin J., & Husband, R. W. *Journal of Abnormal and Social Psychology*, 1933, **28**, 148.

Rasmussen, E. *Acta Psychologica*, 1939, **4**, 275.

Selye, H. *Journal of Clinical Endocrinology and Metabolism*, 1946, **6**, 117.

Spence, K. W. *Behavior theory and conditioning.* New Haven: Yale University Press, 1956.

Thiessen, D. D. *Journal of Comparative and Physiological Psychology*, 1964, **57**, 412. (a)

Thiessen, D. D. *Texas Reports on Biology and Medicine*, 1964, **22**, 266. (b)

Travis, L. E. *Journal of Abnormal and Social Psychology*, 1925, **20**, 142.

Travis, L. E. *Journal of Abnormal and Social Psychology*, 1928, **23**, 45.

Triplett, N. *American Journal of Psychology*, 1897, **9**, 507.

Zajonc, R. B., & Nieuwenhuyse, B. *Journal of Experimental Psychology*, 1964, **67**, 276.

63

The Warm-Cold Variable in First Impressions of Persons

Harold H. Kelley

Through his interactions with the world around him, man comes to form a consistent set of beliefs, emotional reactions, and response tendencies regarding not only the physical objects in his environment but also the other people with whom he comes into contact. These consistencies or *attitudes* which the individual has toward the various components of his environment develop largely through the information to which he is exposed, through the group affiliations which he has, and, indirectly, through the methods he employs to satisfy his wants and needs.

As the individual acquires more attitudes, and as these attitudes become more permanent, his perceptions and judgments begin to become stereotyped so that he accepts and assimilates only those components of his environment which are consistent with his attitude system. For example, an individual who has developed a favorable attitude toward the Democratic governor of his state very often will generalize this attitude to members of the Democratic party in general.

It is important to note that the effects of these preconceptions are not limited to diffuse, general reactions but can also greatly affect our individual and day-to-day interactions. One of the major sources of error in our judgments of others is that we tend to let our evaluations of one characteristic of an individual bias our opinion of him in other areas. If we react favorably toward one trait or characteristic, we are likely to assume that the person possesses other traits we value. Similarly, when we dislike some characteristic, we often tend to assign the person other undesirable characteristics as well. The term usually used to describe this phenomenon is *halo effect*.

In the following selection Kelley attempts to discover the extent to which an initial reaction or "first impression" of a person will affect later judgments and evaluations of him. Note particularly that Kelley's subjects had never before met the individual whom they were to evaluate and that the only basis for differences in their evaluations was a matter of two words in a written description of him.

This experiment is one of several studies of first impressions (Kelley, 1948), the purpose of the series being to investigate the stability of early judgments, their determinants, and the relation of such judgments to the behavior of the person making them. In interpreting the data from several nonexperimental studies on the stability of first impressions, it proved to be necessary to postulate inner-observer variables which contribute to the impression and which remain relatively constant

From Journal of Personality, *Vol. 18 (1950), 16–23. Reprinted by permission of Duke University Press and the author. The writer acknowledges the constructive advice of Professor Dorwin Cartwright, University of Michigan.*

through time. Also some evidence was obtained which directly demonstrated the existence of these variables and their nature. The present experiment was designed to determine the effects of one kind of inner-observer variable, specifically, *expectations* about the stimulus person which the observer brings to the exposure situation.

That prior information or labels attached to a stimulus person make a difference in observers' first impressions is almost too obvious to require demonstration. The expectations resulting from such preinformation may restrict, modify, or accentuate the impressions he will have. The crucial question is: What changes in perception will accompany a given expectation? Studies of stereotyping, for example, that of Katz and Braly (1947), indicate that from an ethnic label such as "German" or "Negro," a number of perceptions follow which are culturally determined. The present study finds its main significance in relation to a study by Asch (1946) which demonstrates that certain crucial labels can transform the entire impression of the person, leading to attributions which are related to the label on a broad cultural basis or even, perhaps, on an autochthonous basis.

Asch read to his subjects a list of adjectives which purportedly described a particular person. He then asked them to characterize that person. He found that the inclusion in the list of what he called *central* qualities, such as "warm" as opposed to "cold," produced a widespread change in the entire impression. This effect was not adequately explained by the halo effect since it did not extend indiscriminately in a positive or negative direction to all characteristics. Rather, it differentially transformed the other qualities, for example, by changing their relative importance in the total impression. Peripheral qualities (such as "polite" versus "blunt") did not produce effects as strong as those produced by the central qualities.[1]

The present study tested the effects of such central qualities upon the early impressions of *real* persons, the same qualities, "warm" versus "cold," being used. They were introduced as preinformation about the stimulus person before his actual appearance; so presumably they operated as expectations rather than as part of the stimulus pattern during the exposure period. In addition, information was obtained about the effects of the expectations upon the observers' behavior toward the stimulus person. An earlier study in this series has indicated that the more incompatible the observer initially perceived the stimulus person to be, the less the observer initiated interaction with him thereafter. The second purpose of the present experiment, then, was to provide a better controlled study of this relationship.

No previous studies reported in the literature have dealt with the importance of first impressions for behavior. The most relevant data are found in the sociometric literature, where there are scattered studies of the relation between choices among children having some prior acquaintance and their interaction behavior. . . .

Procedure

The experiment was performed in three sections of a psychology course (Economics 70) at the Massachusetts Institute of Technology.[2] The three sections provided 23, 16, and 16 subjects respectively. All 55 subjects were men, most of them in their third college year. In each class the stimulus person (also a male) was completely unknown to the subjects before the experimental period. One person served as stimulus person in two sections, and a second person took this role in the third section. In each case the stimulus person was introduced by the experimenter, who posed as a representative of the course instructors and who gave the following statement:

Your regular instructor is out of town today, and since we of Economics 70 are interested in the general problem of how various classes react to different instructors, we're going to have an instructor today you've never had before, Mr. ——. Then, at the end of the period, I want you to fill out some forms about him. In order to give you some idea of what he's like, we've had a person who knows him write up a little biographical note about him. I'll pass this out to you now and you can read it before he arrives. Please read these to yourselves and don't talk about this among yourselves until the class is over so that he won't get wind of what's going on.

---

1 Since the present experiment was carried out, Mensch and Wishner (1947) have repeated a number of Asch's experiments because of dissatisfaction with his sex and geographic distribution. Their data substantiate Asch's very closely. Also, Luchins (1948) has criticized Asch's experiments for their artificial methodology, repeated some of them, and challenged some of the kinds of interpretations Asch made from his data. Luchins also briefly reports some tantalizing conclusions from a number of studies of first impressions of actual persons.

2 Professor Mason Haire, now of the University of California, Berkeley, provided valuable advice and help in executing the experiment.

Two kinds of these notes were distributed, the two being identical except that in one the stimulus person was described among other things as being "rather cold" whereas in the other form the phrase "very warm" was substituted. The content of the "rather cold" version is as follows:

Mr. ——— is a graudate student in the Department of Economics and Social Science here at M. I. T. He has had three semesters of teaching experience in psychology at another college. This is his first semester teaching Ec. 70. He is 26 years old, a veteran, and married. People who know him consider him to be a rather cold person, industrious, critical, practical, and determined.

The two types of preinformation were distributed randomly within each of the three classes and in such a manner that the students were not aware that two kinds of information were being given out. The stimulus person then appeared and led the class in a twenty-minute discussion. During this time the experimenter kept a record of how often each student participated in the discussion. Since the discussion was almost totally leader-centered, this participation record indicates the number of times each student initiated verbal interaction with the instructor. After the discussion period, the stimulus person left the room, and the experimenter gave the following instructions:

Now, I'd like to get your impression of Mr. ———. This is not a test of you and can in no way affect your grade in this course. This material will not be identified as belonging to particular persons and will be kept strictly confidential. It will be of most value to us if you are completely honest in your evaluation of Mr. ———. Also, please understand that what you put down will not be used against him or cause him to lose his job or anything like that. This is not a test of him but merely a study of how different classes react to different instructors.

The subjects then wrote free descriptions of the stimulus person and finally rated him on a set of 15 rating scales.

Results and Discussion

1. *Influence of warm-cold variable on first impressions.* The differences in the ratings produced by the warm-cold variable were consistent from one section to another even where different stimulus persons were used. Consequently, the data from the three sections were combined by equating means (the S.D.'s were approximately equal) and the results for the total group are presented in Table 1. . . .

This general favorableness in the perceptions of the "warm" observers as compared with the "cold" ones indicates that something like a halo effect may have been operating in these ratings. Although his data are not completely persuasive on this point, Asch was convinced that such a general effect was *not* operating in his study. Closer inspection of the present data makes it clear that the "warm-cold" effect cannot be explained altogether on the basis of simple halo effect. In Table 1 it is evident that the "warm-cold" variable produced differential effects from one rating scale to another. The size of this effect seems to depend upon the closeness of relation between the specific dimension of any given rating scale and the central quality of "warmth" or "coldness." Even though the rating of intelligence may be influenced by a halo effect, it is not influenced to the same degree to which considerateness is. It seems to make sense to view such strongly influenced items as considerateness, informality, good-naturedness, and humaneness as dynamically more closely related to warmth and hence more perceived in terms of this relation than in terms of a general positive or negative feeling toward the stimulus person. If first impressions are normally made in terms of such general dimensions as "warmth" and "coldness," the power they give the observer in making predictions and specific evaluations about such disparate behavior characteristics as formality and considerateness is considerable (even though these predictions may be incorrect or misleading).

The free report impression data were analyzed for only one of the sections. In general, there were few sizable differences between the "warm" and "cold" observers. The "warm" observers attributed more nervousness, more sincerity, and more industriousness to the stimulus person. Although the frequencies of comparable qualities are very low because of the great variety of descriptions produced by the observers, there is considerable agreement with the rating scale data.

*   *   *

2. *Influence of warm-cold variable on interaction with the stimulus person.* In the analysis of the frequency with which the various students took part in the discussion led by the stimulus person, a larger proportion of those given the "warm" preinformation participated than of those

TABLE 1 *Comparison of "Warm" and "Cold" Observers in Terms of Average Ratings Given Stimulus Persons*

Item	Low End of Rating Scale	High End of Rating Scale	Average Rating		Level of Significance of Warm-Cold Difference
			Warm $N = 27$	Cold $N = 28$	
1	Knows his stuff	Doesn't know his stuff	3.5	4.6	
2	Considerate of others	Self-centered	6.3	9.6	1%
3†	Informal	Formal	6.3	9.6	1%
4†	Modest	Proud	9.4	10.6	
5	Sociable	Unsociable	5.6	10.4	1%
6	Self-assured	Uncertain of himself	8.4	9.1	
7	High intelligence	Low intelligence	4.8	5.1	
8	Popular	Unpopular	4.0	7.4	1%
9†	Good-natured	Irritable	9.4	12.0	5%
10	Generous	Ungenerous	8.2	9.6	
11	Humorous	Humorless	8.3	11.7	1%
12	Important	Insignificant	6.5	8.6	
13†	Humane	Ruthless	8.6	11.0	5%
14†	Submissive	Dominant	13.2	14.5	
15	Will go far	Will not get ahead	4.2	5.8	

† These scales were reversed when presented to the subjects.

given the "cold" preinformation. Fifty-six per cent of the "warm" subjects entered the discussion, whereas only 32 per cent of the "cold" subjects did so. Thus the expectation of warmth not only produced more favorable early perceptions of the stimulus person but led to greater initiation of interaction with him. This relation is a low one, significant at between the 5 per cent and 10 per cent level of confidence, but it is in line with the general principle that social perception serves to guide and steer the person's behavior in his social environment.

As would be expected from the foregoing findings, there was also a relation between the favorableness of the impression and whether or not the person participated in the discussion. Although any single item yielded only a small and insignificant relation to participation, when a number are combined the trend becomes clear cut. For example, when we combine the seven items which were influenced to a statistically significant degree by the warm-cold variable, the total score bears considerable relation to participation, the relationship being significant as well beyond the 1 per cent level. A larger proportion of those having favorable total impressions participated than of those having unfavorable impressions, the biserial correlation between these variables being .34. Although this relation may be interpreted in several ways, it seems most likely that the unfavorable perception led to a curtailment of interaction. Support for this comes from one of the other studies in this series (Kelley, 1948). There it was found that those persons having unfavorable impressions of the instructor at the end of the first class meeting tended less often to initiate interactions with him in the succeeding four meetings than did those having favorable first impressions. There was also some tendency in the same study for those persons who interacted least with the instructor to change least in their judgments of him from the first to later impressions.

It will be noted that these relations lend some support to the autistic hostility hypothesis proposed by Newcomb (1947). This hypothesis suggests that the possession of an initially hostile attitude toward a person leads to a restriction of communication and contact with him which in turn serves to preserve the hostile attitude by preventing the acquisition of data which could correct it. The present data indicate that a restriction of interaction is associated with unfavorable preinformation and an unfavorable perception. The data from the other study support this result and also indicate the correctness of the second part of the hypothesis, that restricted interaction reduces the likelihood of change in the attitude.

What makes these findings more significant is that they appear in the context of a discussion class where there are numerous *induced* and *own* forces to enter the discussion and to interact with the instructor. It seems likely that the effects predicted by Newcomb's hypothesis would be much more marked in a setting where such forces were not present.

Summary

The warm-cold variable had been found by Asch to produce large differences in the impressions of personality formed from a list of adjectives. In this study the same variable was introduced in the form of expectations about a real person and was found to produce similar differences in first im-

pressions of him in a classroom setting. In addition, the differences in first impressions produced by the different expectations were shown to influence the observers' behavior toward the stimulus person. Those observers given the favorable expectation (who, consequently, had a favorable impression of the stimulus person) tended to interact more with him than did those given the unfavorable expectation.

REFERENCES

Asch, S. E. Forming impressions of personality. *Journal of Abnormal and Social Psychology*, 1946, **41**, 258–290.

Katz, D., & Braly, K. W. Verbal stereotypes and racial prejudice. In T. M. Newcomb & E. L. Hartley (Eds.), *Readings in social psychology*. New York: Holt, Rinehart & Winston, 1947. Pp. 204–210.

Kelley, H. H. First impressions in interpersonal relations. Ph.D. thesis, Cambridge, Mass.: Massachusetts Institute of Technology, September 1948.

Krech, D., & Crutchfield, R. S. *Theory and problems of social psychology*. New York: McGraw-Hill, 1948.

Luchins, A. S. Forming impressions of personality: A critique. *Journal of Abnormal and Social Psychology*, 1948, **43**, 318–325.

Mensch, I. N., & Wishner, J. Asch on "Forming impressions of personality": Further evidence. *Journal of Personality*, 1947, **16**, 188–191.

Newcomb, T. M. Autistic hostility and social reality. *Human Relations*, 1947, **1**, 69–86.

Newstetter, W. I., Feldstein, M. J., & Newcomb, T. M. *Group adjustment: A study in experimental sociology*. Cleveland: Western Reserve University, 1938.

64

Overcoming Resistance to Change

Lester Coch and John R. P. French, Jr.

One characteristic of attitudes is that they tend to be relatively permanent over long periods of time. One of the major sources of resistance to attitude change stems from the influence that other members of a group have on the individual. Once a standard or *norm* has been adopted by the members of a group, attempts by an individual to deviate from that norm result in pressure from the other members to conform.

From Human Relations, *1948, Vol. 1, 512–532. Reprinted by permission of the author. Grateful acknowledgements are made by the authors to Dr. Alfred J. Marrow, president of the Harwood Manufacturing Corporation, and to the entire Harwood staff for their valuable aid and suggestions in this study. The authors have drawn repeatedly from the works and concepts of Kurt Lewin (1947) for both the action and theoretical phases of this study. Many of the leadership techniques used in the experimental group meetings were techniques developed at the first National Training Laboratory for Group Development held at Bethel, Maine, in the summer of 1947. Both authors attended this laboratory.*

Early studies by Homans at a Western Electric plant clearly demonstrated that group pressures were potent factors in determining attitudes and behavioral responses toward management innovations designed to improve the workers' production. Homans noted that hostile attitudes toward management were usually expressed by adoption of a group norm that output should be kept below the expected rate. Any girl who exceeded the normative output experienced strong group pressure to conform and usually adopted the attitudes of the other members. When small groups of girls were set apart from their co-workers, however, and became involved in a number of "experiments" concerning changes in working conditions, production increased markedly. Even when the original working conditions were reinstated, production continued to rise. Apparently, then, the critical variable was not any particular change that was made but rather the fact that being singled out for participation in the experiment led to a more favorable attitude and the emergence of new group norms which emphasized maximum productivity.

The question of how to best change attitudes, group norms, and, subsequently, individual behavior has led to a considerable amount of research. In the following experiment Coch and French examine the potency of group pressures on the individual and the importance of group participation in attitude change.

Introduction

It has always been characteristic of American industry to change products and methods of doing jobs as often as competitive conditions or engineering progress dictates. This makes frequent changes in an individual's work necessary. In addition, the markedly greater turnover and absenteeism of recent years result in unbalanced production lines which again makes for frequent shifting of individuals from one job to another. One of the most serious production problems faced at the Harwood Manufacturing Corporation has been the resistance of production workers to the necessary changes in methods and jobs. This resistance expressed itself in several ways, such as grievances about the piece rates that went with the new methods, high turnover, very low efficiency, restriction of output, and marked aggression against management. Despite these undesirable effects, it was necessary that changes in methods and jobs continue.

Efforts were made to solve this serious problem by the use of a special monetary allowance for transfers, by trying to enlist the cooperation and aid of the union, by making necessary layoffs on the basis of efficiency, etc. In all cases, these actions did little or nothing to overcome the resistance to change. On the basis of these data, it was felt that the pressing problem of resistance to change demanded further research for its solution. From the point of view of factory management, there were two purposes to the research: (1) Why do people resist change so strongly? and (2) What can be done to overcome this resistance?

Starting with a series of observations about the behavior of changed groups, the first step in the overall program was to devise a preliminary theory to account for the resistance to change. Then on the basis of the theory, a real life action experiment was devised and conducted within the context of the factory situation. Finally, the results of the experiment were interpreted in the light of the preliminary theory and the new data.

Background

The main plant of the Harwood Manufacturing Corporation, where the present research was done, is located in the small town of Marion, Virginia. The plant produces pajamas and, like most sewing plants, employs mostly women. The plant's population is about 500 women and 100 men. The workers are recruited from the rural, mountainous areas surrounding the town and are usually employed without previous industrial experience. The average age of the workers is 23; the average education is eight years of grammar school.

The policies of the company in regard to labor relations are liberal and progressive. A high value has been placed on fair and open dealing with the employees, and they are encouraged to take up any problems or grievances with the management at any time. Every effort is made to help foremen find effective solutions to their problems in human relations, using conferences and role-playing methods. Carefully planned orientation, designed to help overcome the discouragement and frustrations attending entrance upon the new and unfamiliar situation, is used. Plant-wide votes are conducted where possible to resolve problems affecting the whole working population. The company has invested both time and money in employee services such as industrial music, health services, lunchroom, and recreation programs. In the same spirit, the management has been conscious of the importance of public relations in the local community; they have supported both financially and otherwise any activity which would build up good will for the company. As a result of these policies, the company has enjoyed good labor relations since the day it commenced operations.

Harwood employees work on an individual incentive system. Piece rates are set by time study and are expressed in terms of units. One unit is equal to one minute of standard work: 60 units per hour equal the standard efficiency rating. Thus, if on a particular operation the piece rate for one dozen is 10 units, the operator would have to produce 6 dozen per hour to achieve the standard efficiency rating of 60 units per hour. The skill required to reach 60 units per hour is great. On some jobs, an average trainee may take 34 weeks to reach the skill level necessary to perform at 60 units per hour. Her first few weeks of work may be on an efficiency level of 5 to 20 units per hour.

The amount of pay received is directly proportional to the weekly average efficiency rating achieved. Thus, an operator with an average efficiency rating of 75 units per hour (25 per cent more than standard) would receive 25 per cent more than base pay. However, there are two minimum wages below which no operator may fall. The first is the plantwide minimum, the hiring-in wage; the second is a minimum wage based on six months' employment and is 22 per cent higher than the plant-wide minimum wage. Both minima are smaller than the base pay for 60 units per hour efficiency rating.

The rating of every piece worker is computed every day and the results are published in a daily record of production which is shown to every operator. This daily record of production for each production line carries the names of all the operators on that line arranged in rank order of efficiency rating, with the highest rating girl at the top of the list. The supervisors speak to each operator each day about her unit ratings. Because of the above procedures, many operators do not claim credit for all the work done in a given day. Instead, they save a few of the piece rate tickets as a "cushion" against a rainy day when they may not feel well or may have a great amount of machine trouble.

When it is necessary to change an operator from one type of work to another, a transfer bonus is given. This bonus is so designed that the changed operator who relearns at an average rate will suffer no loss in earnings after change. Despite this allowance, the general attitudes toward job changes in the factory are markedly negative. Such expressions as, "When you make your units (standard production), they change your job," are all too frequent. Many operators refuse to change, preferring to quit.

The Transfer Learning Curve

An analysis of the after-change relearning curves of several hundred experienced operators rating standard or better prior to change showed that 38 per cent of the changed operators recovered to the standard unit rating of 60 units per hour. The other 62 per cent either became chronically substandard operators or quit during the relearning period.

* * *

It is interesting to note in Figure 1 that the relearning period for an experienced operator is longer than the learning period for a new operator. This is true despite the fact that the majority of transfers—the failures who never recover to standard—are omitted from the curve. However, changed operators rarely complain of "wanting to do it the old way," etc., after the first week or two of change; and time and motion studies show few false moves after the first week of change. From this evidence it is deduced that proactive inhibition or the interference of previous habits in learning the new skill is either nonexistent or very slight after the first two weeks of change.

* * *

A Preliminary Theory of Resistance to Change

The fact that relearning after transfer to a new job is so often slower than initial learning on first entering the factory would indicate, on the face of it, that the resistance to change and the slow relearning is primarily a motivational problem. . . .

Interviews with operators who have been transferred to a new job reveal a common pattern of feelings and attitudes which are distinctly different from those of successful nontransfers. In addition to resentment against the management for trans-

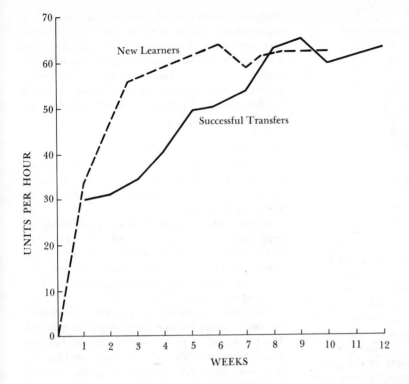

FIGURE 1 *A comparison of the learning curve for new, inexperienced employees with the relearning curve for only those transfers (38 per cent) who eventually recover to standard production*

ferring them, the employees typically show feelings of frustration, loss of hope of ever regaining their former level of production and status in the factory, feelings of failure, and a very low level of aspiration. . . .

Earlier unpublished research at Harwood has shown that the nontransferred employees generally have an explicit goal of reaching and maintaining an efficiency rating of 60 units per hour. A questionnaire administered to several groups of operators indicated that a large majority of them accept as their goal the management's quota of 60 units per hour. This standard of production is the level of aspiration according to which the operators measure their own success or failure; and those who fall below standard lose status in the eyes of their fellow employees. Relatively few operators set a goal appreciably above 60 units per hour.

* * *

Another factor which seems to affect recovery rates of changed operators is the amount of we-feeling. Observations seem to indicate that a strong psychological subgroup with negative attitudes toward management will display the strongest resistance to change. On the other hand, changed groups with high we-feeling and positive cooperative attitudes are the best relearners. Collections of individuals with little or no we-feeling display some resistance to change but not so strongly as the groups with high we-feeling and negative attitudes toward management. However, turnover for the individual transfers is much higher than in the latter groups. This phenomenon of the relationship between we-feeling and resistance to change is so overt that for years the general policy of the management of the plant was never to change a group as a group but rather to scatter the individuals in different areas throughout the factory.

* * *

One common result in a subgroup with strong we-feeling is the setting of a group standard concerning production. Where the attitudes toward management are antagonistic, this group standard may take the form of a definite restriction of production to a given level. This phenomenon of restriction is particularly likely to happen in a group that has been transferred to a job where a new piece rate has been set; for they have some hope that if production never approaches the standard, the management may change the piece rate in their favor.

A group standard can exert extremely strong forces on an individual member of a small subgroup. That these forces can have a powerful effect on production is indicated in the production record of one presser during a period of forty days.

	In the group
Days	Production per day
1— 3	46
4— 6	52
7— 9	53
10—12	56
(Scapegoating begins)	
13—16	55
17—20	48
As a single worker	
21—24	83
25—28	92
29—32	92
33—36	91
37—40	92

For the first twenty days she was working in a group of other pressers who were producing at the rate of about 50 units per hour. Starting on the thirteenth day, when she reached standard production and exceeded the production of the other members, she became a scapegoat of the group. During this time her production decreased toward the level of the remaining members of the group. After twenty days the group had to be broken up and all the other members were transferred to other jobs leaving only the scapegoat operator. With the removal of the group, the group standard was no longer operative; and the production of the one remaining operator shot up from the level of about 45 to 96 units per hour in a period of four days. Her production stabilized at a level of about 92 and stayed there for the remainder of the twenty days. Thus it is clear that the motivational forces induced in the individual by a strong subgroup may be more powerful than those induced by management.

The Experiment

On the basis of the preliminary theory that resistance to change is a combination of an individual reaction to frustration with strong group-induced forces, it seemed that the most appropriate methods for overcoming the resistance to change would be group methods. Consequently, an experiment was designed employing two variations of democratic procedure in handling groups to be transferred. The first variation involved participation through representation of the workers in designing the changes to be made in the jobs. The second variation consisted of total participation by all members of the group in designing the

changes. A third control group was also used. Two experimental groups received the total participation treatment. The three experimental groups and the control group were roughly matched with respect to: (1) the efficiency ratings of the groups before transfer; (2) the degree of change involved in the transfer; (3) the amount of we-feeling observed in the groups.

*   *   *

Experimental Group 1, the thirteen pajama folders, had formerly folded coats with pre-folded pants. The new job called for the folding of coats with unfolded pants. . . .

Experimental Groups 2 and 3, consisting of eight and seven pajama examiners respectively, had formerly clipped threads from the entire garment and examined every seam. The new job called for pulling only certain threads off and examining every seam. . . .

The control group of hand pressers went through the usual factory routine when they were changed. The production department modified the job, and a new piece rate was set. A group meeting was then held in which the control group was told that the change was necessary because of competitive conditions, and that a new piece rate had been set. The new piece rate was thoroughly explained by the time study man, questions were answered, and the meeting dismissed.

Experimental Group 1 was changed in a different manner. Before any changes took place, a group meeting was held with all the operators to be changed. The need for the change was presented as dramatically as possible, showing two identical garments produced in the factory; . . . . The group was asked to identify the cheaper one and could not do it. This demonstration effectively shared with the group the entire problem of the necessity of cost reduction. A general agreement was reached that a savings could be effected by removing the "frills" and "fancy" work from the garment without affecting the folders' opportunity to achieve a high efficiency rating. Management then presented a plan to set the new job and piece rate:

1. Make a check study of the job as it was being done.
2. Eliminate all unnecessary work.
3. Train several operators in the correct methods.
4. Set the piece rate by time studies on these specially trained operators.
5. Explain the new job and rate to all the operators.
6. Train all operators in the new method so

they can reach a high rate of production within a short time.

The group approved this plan (though no formal group decision was reached), and chose the operators to be specially trained. A submeeting with the "special" operators was held immediately following the meeting with the entire group. They displayed a cooperative and interested attitude and immediately presented many good suggestions. This attitude carried over into the working out of the details of the new job; and when the new job and piece rates were set, the "special" operators referred to the resultants as "our job," "our rate," etc. The new job and piece rates were presented at a second group meeting to all the operators involved. The "special" operators served to train the other operators on the new job.

Experimental Groups 2 and 3 went through much the same kind of change meetings. The groups were smaller than experimental Group 1, and a more intimate atmosphere was established. The need for a change was once again made dramatically clear; the same general plan was presented by management. However, since the groups were small, all operators were chosen as "special" operators; that is, all operators were to participate directly in the designing of the new jobs, and all operators would be studied by the time study man.

It is interesting to note that in the meetings with these two groups, suggestions were immediately made in such quantity that the stenographer had great difficulty in recording them. The group approved of the plans, but again no formal group decision was reached.

Results

The results of the experiment are summarized in graphic form in Figure 2. The gaps in the production curves occur because these groups were paid on a time-work basis for a day or two. The control group improved little beyond their early efficiency ratings. Resistance developed almost immediately after the change occurred. Marked expressions of aggression against management occurred, such as conflict with the methods engineer, expression of hostility against the supervisor, deliberate restriction of production, and lack of cooperation with the supervisor. There were 17 per cent quits in the first forty days. Grievances were filed about the piece rate, but when the rate was checked, it was found to be a little "loose."

Experimental Group 1 showed an unusually good relearning curve. At the end of fourteen days, the group averaged 61 units per hour. Dur-

FIGURE 2   *The effects of participation through representation (Group 1) and of total participation (Groups 2 and 3) on recovery after an easy transfer*

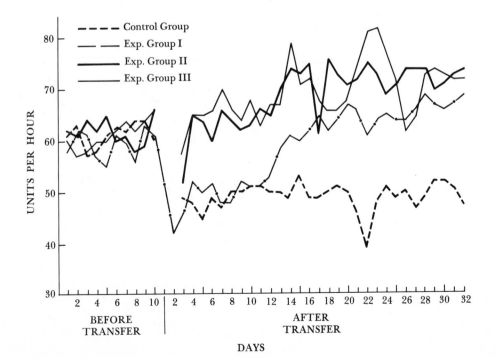

ing the fourteen days, the attitude was cooperative and permissive. They worked well with the methods engineer, the training staff, and the supervisor. (The supervisor was the same person in the cases of the control group and experimental Group 1). There were no quits in this group in the first forty days. This group might have presented a better learning record if work had not been scarce during the first seven days. There was one act of aggression against the supervisor recorded in the first forty days. It is interesting to note that the three special representative operators in experimental Group 1 recovered at about the same rate as the rest of their group.

Experimental Groups 2 and 3 recovered faster than experimental Group 1. After a slight drop on the first day of change, the efficiency ratings returned to a pre-change level and showed sustained progress thereafter to a level about 14 per cent higher than the pre-change level. No additional training was provided them after the second day. They worked well with their supervisors and no indications of aggression were observed from these groups. There were no quits in either of these groups in the first forty days.

*   *   *

In the first experiment, the control group made no progress after transfer for a period of 32 days. At the end of this period the group was broken up and the individuals were reassigned to new jobs scattered throughout the factory. Two and a half months after their dispersal, the thirteen remaining members of the original control group were again brought together as a group for a second experiment.

This second experiment consisted of transferring the control group to a new job, using the total participation technique in meetings which were similar to those held with experimental Groups 2 and 3. The new job was a pressing job of comparable difficulty to the new job in the first experiment. On the average it involved about the same degree of change. In the meetings no reference was made to the previous behavior of the group on being transferred.

The results of the second experiment were in sharp contrast to the first (see Figure 3). With the total participation technique, the same control group now recovered rapidly to their previous efficiency rating, and, like the other groups under this treatment, continued on beyond it to a new high level of production. There was no aggression or turnover in the group for 19 days after change, a marked modification of their previous behavior after transfer. Some anxiety concerning their seniority status was expressed, but this was resolved in a meeting of their elected delegate, the union business agent, and a management representative. It should be noted in Figure 3 that the pre-change

FIGURE 3   *A comparison of the effect of the control procedure with the total participation procedure on the same group*

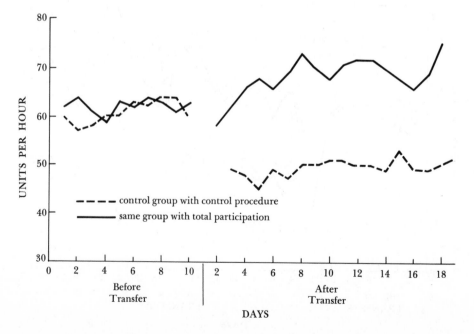

level on the second experiment is just above 60 units per hour; thus the individual transfers had progressed to just above standard during the two and a half months between the two experiments.

Interpretation

The purpose of this section is to explain the drop in production resulting from transfer, the differential recovery rates of the control and the experimental groups, the increases beyond their former levels of production by the experimental groups, and the differential rates of turnover and aggression.

The first experiment showed that the rate of recovery is directly proportional to the amount of participation, and that the rates of turnover and aggression are inversely proportional to the amount of participation. The second experiment demonstrated more conclusively that the results obtained depended on the experimental treatment rather than on personality factors like skill or aggressiveness, for identical individuals yielded markedly different results in the control treatment as contrasted with the total participation treatment.

Apparently total participation has the same type of effect as participation through representation, but the former has a stronger influence. In regard to recovery rates, this difference is not unequivocal because the experiment was unfortunately confounded. Right after transfer, experimental group number 1 had insufficient material to work on for a period of seven days. Hence their slower recovery during this period is at least in part due to insufficient work. In succeeding days, however, there was an adequate supply of work and the differential recovery rate still persisted. Therefore we are inclined to believe that participation through representation results in slower recovery than does total participation.

* * *

Conclusions

It is possible for management to modify greatly or to remove completely group resistance to changes in methods of work and the ensuing piece rates. This change can be accomplished by the use of group meetings in which management effectively communicates the need for change and stimulates group participation in planning the changes.

For Harwood's management, and presumably for managements of other industries using an incentive system, this experiment has important implications in the field of labor relations. A majority of all grievances presented at Harwood have always stemmed from a change situation. By preventing or greatly modifying group resistance to change, this concomitant to change may well be greatly reduced. The reduction of such costly phenomena as turnover and slow relearning rates presents another distinct advantage.

Harwood's management has long felt that action research such as the present experiment is the only key to better labor-management relations. It is only by discovering the basic principles and applying them to the true causes of conflict that an intelligent, effective effort can be made to correct the undesirable effects of the conflict.

65

Liberating Effects of Group Pressure

Stanley Milgram

The situation where one person orders another to harm someone is common in literature as well as in everyday experience. This situation raises not only the moral question of whether the second person should be held accountable for "obeying orders" but also the very practical question of how much pressure, and by whom, can induce the second person to harm a third. The following study by Milgram is designed to answer this question and offers some startling insights into the potent effect of pressures to conform on the *behavior* of an individual. It is important to note that in these experiments the subjects were pressured to make an actual response, deliberately inflicting pain on another. This is in sharp contrast to the Asch experiments mentioned in the introduction to this section, where the pressure to conform involved only the judgments expressed by the subject.

In laboratory research, the effect of group pressure has most often been studied in its negative aspect; the conspiratorial group is shown to limit, constrain, and distort the individual's responses (Asch, 1951; Blake and Brehm, 1954; Milgram, 1964). Edifying effects of the group, although acknowledged, have rarely been demonstrated with the clarity and force of its destructive potential. Particularly in those areas in which a morally relevant choice is at issue, experimentalists typically examine pressures that diminish the scope of individual action. They have neglected effects that enhance the individual's sense of worth, enlarge the possibilities for action, and help the subject resolve conflicting feelings in a direction congruent with his ideals and values. Although in everyday life occasions arise when conformity to group pressures is constructive, in the laboratory "thinking and investigation have concentrated almost obsessively on conformity in its most sterile forms" (Asch, 1959).[1]

There are technical difficulties to demonstrating the value-enhancing potential of group pressure. They concern the nature of the base line from which the group effect is to be measured. The problem is that the experimental subject ordinarily acts in a manner that is socially appropriate. If he has come to the laboratory to participate in a study on the perception of lines, he will generally report what he sees in an honest manner. If one wishes to show the effects of group influence by producing a change in his performance, the only direction open to change is that of creating some deficiency in his performance, which can then be attributed to group influences.

If men tend to act constructively under usual circumstances, the obvious direction of an induced and measurable change is toward inappropriate behavior. It is this technical need rather than the inherently destructive character of group forces that has dictated the lines of a good deal of laboratory research. The experimental problem for any study of *constructive* conformity is to create a situation in which undesirable behavior occurs with regularity and then to see whether group pressure

From Journal of Personality and Social Psychology, *Vol. 1 (1965), 127–134. Copyright 1965 by the American Psychological Association, and reproduced by permission. This research was supported by two grants from the National Science Foundation, G-17916 and G-24152. The experiments were conducted while the author was at Yale University. Pilot studies completed in 1960 were financed by a grant from the Higgins Fund of Yale University. My thanks to Rhea Mendoza Diamond for her help in revising the original manuscript.*

[1] Exceptions become more numerous in moving from the experimental domain to the practice of group therapy and training groups. And surely the *philosophy* of group dynamics stresses the productive possibilities inherent in groups (Cartwright and Zander, 1960).

can be applied effectively in the direction of a valued behavior outcome.[2]

Experiment I: Base-Line Condition

A technique for the study of destructive obedience (Milgram, 1965) generates the required base line. In this situation a subject is ordered to give increasingly more severe punishment to a person. Despite the apparent discomfort, cries, and vehement protests of the victim, the experimenter instructs the subject to continue stepping up the shock level.

Technique

Two persons arrive at a campus laboratory to take part in a study of memory and learning. (One of them is a confederate of the experimenter.) Each subject is paid $4.50 upon arrival and is told that payment is not affected in any way by performance. The experimenter provides an introductory talk on memory and learning processes and then informs the subjects that in the experiment one of them will serve as teacher and the other as learner. A rigged drawing is held so that the naive subject is always assigned the role of teacher and the accomplice becomes the learner. The learner is taken to an adjacent room and is strapped into an electric chair.

The naive subject is told that it is his task to teach the learner a list of paired associates, to test him on the list, and to administer punishment whenever the learner errs in the test. Punishment takes the form of electric shock, delivered to the learner by means of a shock generator controlled by the naive subject. The teacher is instructed to increase the intensity of the electric shock one step on the generator on each error. The generator contains 30 voltage levels ranging from 15 to 450 volts, and verbal designations ranging from Slight Shock to Danger: Severe Shock. The learner, according to plan, provides many wrong answers, so that before long the naive subject must give him the strongest shock on the generator. Increases in shock level are met by increasingly insistent demands from the learner that the experiment be stopped because of growing discomfort to him. However, the experimenter instructs the teacher to continue with the procedure in disregard of the learner's protests.[3]

A quantitative value is assigned to the subject's performance based on the maximum intensity shock he administered before breaking off. Thus,

any subject's score may range from 0 (for a subject unwilling to administer the first shock level) to 30 (for a subject who proceeds to the highest voltage level on the board).

Subjects

The subjects used in the several experimental conditions were male adults residing in the greater New Haven area, aged 20–50 years, and engaged in a wide variety of occupations. Each experimental condition described here employed 40 fresh subjects and was carefully balanced for age and occupational types. . . .

Results and discussion

In this situation a subject is instructed to perform acts that are in some sense incompatible with his normal standards of behavior. In the face of the vehement protests of an innocent individual, many subjects refuse to carry out the experimenter's orders to continue with the shock procedure. They reject the role assignment of *experimental subject,* assert themselves as persons, and are unwilling to perform actions that violate personal standards of conduct. The distribution of break-off points for this condition is shown in Table 1, column 1. Fourteen of the 40 subjects withdraw from the experiment at some point before the completion of the command series.

The majority of subjects, however, comply fully with the experimenter's commands, despite the acute discomfort they often experience in connection with shocking the victim. Typically these obedient subjects report that they do not wish to hurt the victim but they feel obligated to follow the orders of the experimenter. On questioning they often state that it would have been "better" not to have shocked the victim at the highest voltage levels. Consider, for example, the remarks of the following obedient subject. He has completed the experiment and is now questioned by an interviewer (who is not the experimenter).

[2] Another solution would be to wait until people who perform in a naturally destructive way come to the laboratory and to use them as subjects. One might deliberately seek out a group of recidivist delinquents who would ordinarily behave in a disvalued manner and then study group effects on their performance. This would, of course, limit the study to an atypical population.

[3] Descriptions of the shock generator, schedule of protests from the learner, and other details of procedure have been described elsewhere and will not be restated here (Milgram, 1963, 1964).

TABLE 1   *Distribution of Break-Off Points by Condition*

Shock level	Verbal designation and voltage level	Base-line condition (n = 40) (1)	Hypothetical subjects (n = 40) (2)	Disobedient groups (n = 40) (3)	Obedient groups (n = 40) (4)
	Slight Shock		3a		
1	15	0	0	0	0
2	30	0	0	0	0
3	45	0	1	0	0
4	60	0	1	0	0
	Moderate Shock				
5	75	0	7	0	1
6	90	1	1	0	0
7	105	0	1	1	1
8	120	0	3	0	0
	Strong Shock				
9	135	0	2	0	0
10	150	6	9	3←	2
11	165	0	2	4	0
12	180	1	3	1	1
	Very Strong Shock				
13	195	0	1	4	0
14	210	0	0	12←	0
15	225	0	1	0	0
16	240	0	1	0	0
	Intense Shock				
17	255	0	1	0	0
18	270	2	0	4	4
19	285	0	0	0	0
20	300	1	3	2	0
	Extreme Intensity Shock				
21	315	1	0	3	2
22	330	1	0	0	0
23	345	0	0	0	0
24	360	0	0	1	0
	Danger: Severe Shock				
25	375	1	0	0	0
26	390	0	0	1	0
27	405	0	0	0	0
28	420	0	0	0	0
	XXX				
29	435	0	0	0	0
30	450	26	0	4	29
	Mean maximum shock	24.55	9.00	16.45	25.70
	Percentage defiant subjects	35.0%	100.0%	90.0%	27.5%

a These 3 subjects indicated they would refuse to administer even the lowest shock.

I'd like to ask you a few questions. How do you feel? I feel all right, but I don't like what happened to that fellow in there [the victim]. He's been hollering, and we had to keep giving him shocks. I didn't like that one bit. I mean he wanted to get out, but he [the experimenter] just kept going, he kept throwing 450 volts. I didn't like that.

Who was actually pushing the switch? I was, but he kept insisting. I told him "No," but he said you got to keep going. I told him it's time we stopped when we get up to 195 or 210 volts.

Why didn't you just stop? He wouldn't let me. I wanted to stop. I kept insisting to stop, but he said "No." . . . I figured the voltage we were giving him was quite a bit. I wanted to stop but he [the experimenter] kept insisting not to stop. I mean the fellow in there is hollering "I don't want to do it. I want to get out of here. I want to get out of here!"

Why didn't you just disregard what the experimenter said? He says it's got to go on, the experiment.

Do you feel a little upset? Well, I mean I feel concerned about the gentlemen in there, I do sir . . . I was getting ready to walk out . . . I couldn't see the point of going on when the guy is suffering in there. I figured he was having a heart attack or something. That's the reason I wanted to stop. . . .

The subject was then dehoaxed carefully and had a friendly reconciliation with the victim.

There is additional evidence that, in shocking the victim to the end of the command series, subjects are engaging in behavior which they disvalue and see as antithetical to personal and social ideals:

Spontaneous shock levels In an experimental control reported elsewhere (Milgram, 1964) subjects administer any voltage level they wish in the absence of group or authoritarian pressure. Under this condition the mean maximum shock for 40 subjects is 82.5 volts (level = 5.50); in contrast, under command of the experimenter (in the baseline condition described above) the mean maximum shock is 368.25 volts (level = 24.55). When left on their own, subjects administer far lower shock levels than when under command.

Self-image When persons who have not performed in the experiment are provided with a description of the experimental situation and are asked to predict their own performance, almost all subjects see themselves as defying the experimenter at some point in the command series. Moreover, they justify their hypothetical behavior in terms of positive qualities of character, employing such statements as "I'm not the kind of person who is willing to hurt others even for the cause of science."

Column 2 of Table 1 shows the anticipated break-off points of 40 adult respondents who were asked to predict their own experimental performance. Hypothetical subjects respond in terms of ideals, values, and positive self-conceptions; these values are frequently overridden by the forces engendered in the concrete laboratory situation.

Moral judgment Twenty undergraduates were asked to render a moral judgment on the issue of obeying or disobeying the experimenter. After describing the experiment to the respondents in concrete detail, the experimenter asked:

In terms of the moral and ethical values most important to you, and taking into account the scientific goals served by the research, how should you perform in the experimental situation? Should you go through to the end of the experiment or should you break off at some point?

Valued break-off points ranged from 0 to 255 volts with the median at 150 volts. Subjects were also asked to explain at length the values that should guide their behavior in the laboratory situation. A sample statement is given below:

I would say that one should not even start the shocks, but rather, forcibly withdraw the moment that the outline of the experiment becomes evident. My reasons for saying this are very complex . . . The first is that the society's morals, which I have absorbed, teach that it is wrong to hurt a man. Morals are usually tied in with religion and this is especially true with Christianity. Having been raised, then, in an old-fashioned, staunchly Lutheran family I have internalized the view that hurting a man is wrong, and no amount of intellectual reasoning can shake this belief.

Thus, there is a clear consensus that the only behavior consistent with social values and individual conscience is to defy the experimenter at some point before the completion of the command series. Yet there is a marked discrepancy between this value judgment and the actual performance of subjects in the laboratory. Despite their protests and obvious conflict in shocking the victim, a substantial number of subjects are unable to defy the experimenter's authority and proceed to administer the highest shock levels commanded by him.

Experiment II: Groups for Disobedience

We may now examine in what degree group influence can release the subject from authoritarian control and allow him to act in a direction congruent with his values and personal standards.

The strategy is to replicate Experiment I, but with this difference: The subject is placed in the midst of two peers who defy the experimenter and refuse to punish the victim against his will. In what degree will the pressure created by their action affect the naive subject's behavior?

Technique

Forty fresh subjects were studied in this condition. The procedure is identical to Experiment I with these exceptions: Four persons appear at the laboratory to take part in an experiment on "the effects of collective teaching and punishment on memory and learning." Three subjects are confederates of the experimenter and one is a naive subject. The experimenter explains that three teachers and one learner are to be used in the study, and by means of a rigged drawing, the naive subject is assigned the position of Teacher 3. The roles of Teacher 1, Teacher 2, and learner are filled by the confederates. The learner is strapped into the electric chair and the three teachers are seated before the shock generator. Teacher 1 is told to read the list of word pairs, Teacher 2 informs the subject if he is correct or incorrect in his answers, and Teacher 3 (the naive subject) administers punishment. As in Experiment I, the subjects are instructed to raise the shock level one step each time the learner makes an error. (More detailed descriptions of the group technique can be found in Milgram, 1964.)

Behavior of confederates   The confederates comply with the experimenter through the 150-volt shock. After the 150-volt level is administered Teacher 1 informs the experimenter that he does not wish to participate further, because of the learner's complaints. (It is at the 150-volt shock level that the learner makes his first vehement protest.) The experimenter insists that the subject continue. However, Teacher 1 is not swayed by the experimenter's commands, gets up from his chair in front of the shock generator, and takes a seat in another part of the room. Since the experimenter's efforts to get the subject to return to the generator are futile, the experimenter instructs the remaining two subjects to continue with the experiment. Teacher 3 (the naive subject) is to handle the reading of word pairs, in addition to his regular job of administering electric shock to the learner.

After Shock Level 14 (210 volts) is administered, Teacher 2, expressing concern for the learner, refuses to participate further. The experimenter makes strong efforts to have him continue, but he too leaves his chair in front of the generator and seats himself at an opposite corner of the room, saying "I'm willing to answer any of your questions, but I'm not willing to shock that man against his will; I'll have no part of it."

At this point the naive subject is seated alone in front of the shock generator. He has witnessed the defiant actions of two peers. The experimenter orders the naive subject to continue with the experimental procedure by himself, indicating that it is essential that the experiment be completed.

Results and discussion

The break-off points of the naive subjects in Experiment II are shown in Table 1, Column 3. The arrows at Shock Levels 10 and 14 indicate the points at which each of the confederates defied the experimenter.

Comparing the proportion of obedient to defiant subjects in Experiments I and II, we see that the effect of the confederates' pressure was substantial. In Experiment I, 26 subjects proceeded to the end of the command series; less than one-sixth of this number obeyed fully in the group setting. . . . The mean maximum shock in Experiment II (16.45) was also significantly lower than in Experiment I (24.55, . . .).

*   *   *

In sum, in the group setting 36 of the 40 subjects defy the experimenter while the corresponding number in the absence of group pressure is 14. The effects of peer rebellion are most impressive in undercutting the experimenter's authority. Indeed, of the score of experimental variations completed in the Yale study on obedience, none was so effective in undermining the experimenter's authority as the manipulation reported here.[4]

How should we account for the powerful effect of the experimental manipulation? It is probable that in Experiment I many subjects come near to performing the defiant action but cannot quite bring themselves to the point of disobedience. The additional pressure of the group members leads to an increment in the forces oriented toward defiance; the increment is of sufficient strength so that, in combination with pressures for defiance already present, many subjects are carried over the threshold of disobedience.

The strong liberating effect of the peers brings to mind the powerful effect of a partner in Asch's

---

[4] See Milgram (1965) for additional experiments.

(1951) study. In that experiment negative pressures originated within the group itself so that the conflicting agents (partner versus majority) were internal to the group boundary; in the present study the peers free the subject from an influence that is *external* to the group. Additionally, the partner's support in Asch's study leads to a response that is fundamentally similar in form but different in value from that of the erring majority. In the present study the peers initiate a radically different order of response, one which has no antecedent in the course of the laboratory hour and which destroy's the very framework of the experiment.

Reactions to the confederates The reactions of naive subjects to the defiant confederates varied considerably and were in part dependent on the exact point where the subject himself defied the experimenter. A subject who quit simultaneously with the first confederate stated, "Well, I was already thinking about quitting when the guy broke off." Most defiant subjects praised the confederates with such statements as, "I thought they were men of good character, yes I do. When the victim said 'Stop,' they stopped" (Shock Level 11).[5] "I think they were very sympathetic people . . . and they were totally unaware of what was in store for them" (Shock Level 14).

A subject who defied the experimenter at Level 21 qualified his approval: "Well I think they should continue a litle further, but I don't blame them for backing out when they did."

A few subjects acknowledged the importance of the confederates in leading to their own defiance: "The thought of stopping didn't enter my mind until it was put there by the other two" (Shock Level 14). "The reason I quit was that I did not wish to seem callous and cruel in the eyes of the other two men who had already refused to go on with the experiment" (Shock Level 14). The majority of subjects, however, denied that the confederates' action was the critical factor in their own defiance.[6]

The fact that obedient subjects failed to follow the defiant group should not suggest that they did not feel the pressure of the confederates' action. One obedient subject stated:

I felt that I would just look like a real Simon Legree to these guys if I just went on coolly and just kept administering lashes. I thought they reacted normally, and the first thing that came to my mind was to react as they did. But I didn't, because if they reacted normally, and stopped the experiment, and I did the same, I don't know how *many months and days you'd have to continue before you got done.*

Thus, this subject felt the burden of the group judgment but sensed that in the light of two defections he had a special obligation to help the experimenter complete his work. Another obedient subject, when asked about the nervousness he displayed in the experiment, replied:

I think it was primarily because of their actions. Momentarily I was ready to go along with them. Then suddenly I felt that they were just being ridiculous. What was I doing following the crowd? . . . They certainly had a right to stop, but I felt they lost all control of themselves.

And a third obedient subject criticized the confederates more directly, stating:

I don't think they should have quit. They came here for an experiment, and I think they should have stuck with it.

A closer analysis of the experimental situation points to a number of specific factors that may contribute to the group's effectiveness:

1. The peers instill in the subject the *idea* of defying the experimenter. It may not have occurred to some subjects as a response possibility.

2. The lone subject has no way of knowing whether, in defying the experimenter, he is performing in a bizarre manner or whether this action is a common occurrence in the laboratory. The two examples of disobedience he sees suggest that defiance is a natural reaction to the situation.

3. The reactions of the defiant confederates define the act of shocking the victim as improper. They provide social confirmation to the naive subject's suspicion that it is wrong to punish a man against his will, even in the context of a psychological experiment.

4. The defiant confederates remain in the laboratory even after withdrawing from the experiment (they have agreed to answer postexperimental

---

5 Numerals in parentheses indicate the break-off point of the subject quoted.

6 Twenty-seven of the defiant subjects stated that they would have broken off without the benefit of the confederates' example; four subjects definitely acknowledged the confederates' rebellion as the critical factor in their own defiance. The remaining defiant subjects were undecided on this issue. In general, then, subjects underestimate the degree to which their defiant actions are dependent on group support.

questions). Each additional shock administered by the naive subject now carries with it a measure of social disapproval from the two confederates.

5. As long as the two confederates participate in the experimental procedure there is a dispersion of responsibility among the group members for shocking the victim. As the confederates withdraw, responsibility becomes focused onto the naive subject.[7]

6. The naive subject is a witness to two instances of disobedience and observes the *consequences* of defying the experimenter to be minimal.

7. There is identification with the disobedient confederates and the possibility of falling back on them for social support when defying the experimenter.

8. Additionally, the experimenter's power may be diminished by the very fact of failing to keep the two confederates in line, following the general rule that every failure of authority to exact compliance to its commands weakens the perceived power of the authority (Homans, 1961).

Hypothesis of arbitrary direction of group effects

The results examined thus far show that group influence serves to liberate individuals effectively from submission to destructive commands. There are some who will take this to mean that the direction of group influence is arbitrary, that it can be oriented toward destructive or constructive ends with equal impact, and that group pressure need merely be inserted into a social situation on one side of a standard or the other in order to induce movement in the desired direction.

This view ought to be questioned. Does the fact that a disobedient group alters the behavior of subjects in Experiment II necessarily imply that group pressure can be applied in the other direction with similar effectiveness? A competing view would be that the direction of possible influence of a group is not arbitrary, but is highly dependent on the general structure of the situation in which influence is attempted.

To examine this issue we need to undertake a further experimental variation, one in which the group forces are thrown on the side of the experimenter, rather than directed against him. The idea is simply to have the members of the group reinforce the experimenter's commands by following them unfailingly, thus adding peer pressures to those originating in the experimenter's commands.

Experiment III: Obedient Groups

Forty fresh subjects, matched to the subjects in Experiments I and II for sex, age, and occupational status, were employed in this condition. The procedure was identical to that followed in Experiment II with this exception: At all times the two confederates followed the commands of the experimenter; at no point did they object to carrying out the experimental instructions. Nor did they show sympathy for or comment on the discomfort of the victim. If a subject attempted to break off they allowed the experimenter primary responsibility for keeping him in line but contributed background support for the experimenter; they indicated their disapproval of the naive subject's attempts to leave the experiment with such remarks as: "You can't quit *now;* this experiment has got to get done." As in Experiment II the naive subject was seated between the two confederates and, in his role of Teacher 3, administered the shocks to the victim.

Results and discussion

The results, presented in Table 1, Column 4, show that the obedient group had very little effect on the overall performance of subjects. In Experiment I, 26 of the 40 subjects complied fully with the experimenter's commands; in the present condition this figure is increased but 3, yielding a total of 29 obedient subjects. This increase falls far short of statistical significance. Nor is the difference in mean maximum shocks statistically reliable. The failure of the manipulation to produce a significant change cannot be attributed to a ceiling artifact since an obedient shift of even 8 of the 14 defiant subjects would yield the .05 significance level by chi square.

Why the lack of change when we know that group pressure often exerts powerful effects? One interpretation is that the authoritarian pressure already present in Experiment I has preempted subjects who would have submitted to group pressures. Conceivably, the subjects who are fully obedient in Experiment I are precisely those who would be susceptible to group forces, while those who resisted authoritarian pressure were also immune to the pressure of the obedient confederates. The pressures applied in Experiment III do not show an effect because they overlap with other pressures having the same direction and present in

---

[7] See Wallach, Kogan, and Bem (1962) for a treatment of this concept dealing with risk taking.

Experiment I; all persons responsive to the initial pressure have already been moved to the obedient criterion in Experiment I. This possibility seems obvious enough in the present study. Yet every other situation in which group pressure is exerted also possesses a field structure (a particular arrangement of stimulus, motive, and social factors) that limits and controls potential influence within that field.[8] Some structures allow group influence to be exerted in one direction but not another. Seen in this light, the hypothesis of the arbitrary direction of group effects is inadequate.

In the present study Experiment I defines the initial field: The insertion of group pressure in a direction opposite to that of the experimenter's commands (Experiment II) produces a powerful shift toward the group. Changing the direction of group movement (Experiment III) does not yield a comparable shift in the subject's performance. The group success in one case and failure in another can be traced directly to the configuration of motive and social forces operative in the starting situation (Experiment I).

Given any social situation, the strength and direction of potential group influence is predetermined by existing conditions. We need to examine the variety of field structures that typify social situations and the manner in which each controls the pattern of potential influence.

REFERENCES

Asch, S. E. Effects of group pressure upon the modification and distortion of judgment. In H. Guetzkow (Ed.), *Groups, leadership, and men.* Pittsburgh: Carnegie Press, 1951.

Asch, S. E. A perspective on social psychology. In S. Koch (Ed.), *Psychology: A study of a science.* Vol. 3. *Formulations of the person and the social context.* New York: McGraw-Hill, 1959. Pp. 363–383.

Blake, R. R., & Brehm, J. W. The use of tape recording to simulate a group atmosphere. *Journal of Abnormal and Social Psychology*, 1954, **49**, 311–313.

Cartwright, D., & Zander, A. *Group dynamics.* Evanston, Ill.: Row, Peterson, 1960.

Homans, G. C. *Social behavior: Its elementary forms.* New York: Harcourt, Brace & World, 1961.

Jones, E. E., Wells, H. H., & Torrey, R. Some effects of feedback from the experimenter on conformity behavior. *Journal of Abnormal and Social Psychology*, 1958, **57**, 207–213.

Milgram, S. Behavioral study of obedience. *Journal of Abnormal and Social Psychology*, 1963, **67**, 371–378.

Milgram, S. Group pressure and action against a person. *Journal of Abnormal and Social Psychology*, 1964, **69**, 137–143.

Milgram, S. Some conditions of obedience and disobedience to authority. *Human Relations*, 1965, **18**(1), 57–76.

Wallach, M. A., Kogan, N., & Bem, D. J. Group influence on individual risk taking. *Journal of Abnormal and Social Psychology*, 1962, **65**, 75–86.

[8] See, for example, the study of Jones, Wells, and Torrey (1958). Starting with the Asch situation they show that through feedback the experimenter can foster greater independence in the subject, but not significantly greater yielding to the erring majority. Here, too, an initial field structure limits the direction of influence attempts.

66

Conformity and Character

Richard S. Crutchfield

The question of why two individuals respond differently when presented with the same stimulus is always of interest to psychologists. It is of particular interest to social psychologists, who try to explain why some individuals conform to group pressure consistently, others conform occasionally, and still others apparently never conform. The following selection by Crutchfield represents an attempt to explain differences in susceptibility to

From American Psychologist, *Vol. 10 (1955), 191–198. Copyright 1955 by the American Psychological Association, and reproduced by permission. Adapted from the address of the retiring president of the Division of Personality and Social Psychology, American Psychological Association, New York City, September 4, 1954.*

group pressure in terms of personality variables. Crutchfield also tries to identify factors relating to early family experiences which might have contributed to these personality differences.

During the spring of 1953, one hundred men visited the Institute of Personality Assessment and Research at the University of California, Berkeley, to participate in an intensive three-day assessment of those qualities related to superior functioning in their profession.[1]

As one of the procedures on the final day of assessment, the men were seated in groups of five in front of an apparatus consisting of five adjacent electrical panels. Each panel had side wings, forming an open cubicle, so that the person, though sitting side by side with his fellow subjects, was unable to see their panels. The experimenter explained that the apparatus was so wired that information could be sent by each man to all the others by closing any of eleven switches at the bottom of his panel. This information would appear on the other panels in the form of signal lights, among five rows of eleven lights, each row corresponding to one of the five panels. After a warm-up task to acquaint the men with the workings of the apparatus, the actual procedure commenced.

Slides were projected on a wall directly facing the men. Each slide presented a question calling for a judgment by the person. He indicated his choice of one of several multiple-alternative answers by closing the appropriately numbered switch on his panel. Moreover, he responded *in order,* that is, as designated by one of five red lights lettered A, B, C, D, E, on his panel. If he were A, he responded first, if B, second, and so on. The designations, A, B, C, D, and E, were rotated by the experimenter from time to time, thus permitting each person to give his judgments in all the different serial positions. No further explanation about the purpose of this procedure was offered.

It may help to convey the nature of the men's typical experiences by giving an illustrative description of what happens concretely to one of the men. The first slide calls for a simple judgment of which of two geometrical figures is larger in area. Since his red light C is on, he waits for A and B to respond before making his response. And, as he is able to observe on the panel, his own judgment coincides with the judgments of A and B who preceded him, and of D and E who follow him. After judgments on several further slides in posi-

tion C, he is then shifted to position D for more slides, then to A.

The slides call for various kinds of judgments —lengths of lines, areas of figures, logical completion of number series, vocabulary items, estimates of the opinions of others, expression of his own attitudes on issues, expression of his personal preferences for line drawings, etc. He is not surprised to observe a perfectly sensible relationship between his judgments and those of the other four men. Where clear-cut perceptual or logical judgments are involved, he finds that his judgments are in perfect agreement with those of the other four. Where matters of opinion are involved, and some differences in opinion to be expected, his judgments and those of the other four men are sometimes in agreement and sometimes not.

Eventually the man finds himself for the first time in position E, where he is to respond last. The next slide shows a standard line and five comparison lines, of which he is to pick the one equal in length to the standard. Among the previous slides he has already encountered this kind of perceptual judgment and has found it easy. On looking at this slide it is immediately clear to him that line number 4 is the correct one. But as he waits his turn to respond, he sees light number 5 in row A go on, indicating that that person has judged line number 5 to be correct. And in fairly quick succession light 5 goes on also in rows B, C, and D.

At this point the man is faced with an obvious conflict between his own clear perception and a unanimous contradictory consensus of the other four men. What does he do? Does he rely on the evidence of his own senses and respond independently? Or does he defer to the judgment of the group, complying with perceptions rather than his own?

We will postpone for a moment the answer as to what he does, and revert to the description of our apparatus.

We have been describing the situation as if seen

[1] The principal study reported here owes much to the collaboration of Dr. Donald W. MacKinnon, director of the Institute of Personality Assessment and Research, and of his staff. Mr. Donald G. Woodworth has contributed especially to the statistical analysis of data.

from the perspective of one of the men. Actually his understanding of the situation is wrong. He has been deceived. For the apparatus is *not* really wired in the way that he was informed. There actually is no connection among the five panels. Instead, they are all wired in an identical manner to a control panel where the experimenter sits behind the men. It is the experimenter who sends all the information which appears on the panels, and the wiring is in parallel in such a way that whatever signals are sent by the experimenter appear simultaneously and identically on all five panels. Moreover, the designations of serial order of responding—A through E—are identical at all times for the five panels, so that at a given moment, for instance, all five men believe themselves to be A, or at another time, E.

As we have just said, the responses actually made by the five men do not affect in any way the panels of the others. They do get registered individually on one part of the experimenter's control panel. The *latency* of each individual response to one tenth of a second is also recorded by timers on the control panel.

Hence, the situation as we have described it for our one illustrative man is actually the situation simultaneously experienced by all five men. They all commence in position C, and all shift at the same time to position D, and to A, and finally E. They all see the same simulated group judgments.

The entire situation is, in a word, contrived, and contrived so as to expose each individual to a standardized and prearranged series of group judgments. By this means the simulated group judgments can be made to appear sensible and in agreement with the individual, or, at chosen critical points, in conflict with his judgments.

Most of you will recognize at once the basic similarity of our situation to that invented by Asch (1952) in his extremely important work of recent years on independence of individual judgment under opposing group pressure. In his method ten subjects announced aloud and in succession their judgments of the relative length of stimulus lines exposed before the group. The first nine subjects were actually confederates of the experimenter and gave uniformly false answers at preestablished points, thus placing pressure on the single naive subject.

For extensive research use, for instance, in personality assessment, Asch's technique is handicapped by the severely unfavorable ratio of confederates to true subjects. The present technique, utilizing the electrical network described above,

avoids this difficulty. There are no confederates required; all five subjects are tested simultaneously in a thoroughly standardized situation. The experimenter exercises highly flexible control of the simulated group judgments, and of the serial order of responding. Stimulus material to be judged can be varied as widely as desired by use of different slides.

Now at last come back to our man still sitting before his panel, still confronted with the spurious group consensus, still torn between a force toward independent judgment and a force toward conformity to the group. How he is likely to behave in the situation can best be described by summarizing the results for our study of 50 of the 100 men in assessment.

Effects of Consensus

All of these men were engaged in a profession in which leadership is one of the salient expected qualifications. Their average age was 34 years. Their educational levels were heterogeneous, but most had had some college training.

Fifty of the men were tested in the procedure as described. Another 40 served as *control* subjects; they simply gave individual judgments of the slides without using the apparatus, and hence without knowledge of the judgments of others. The distribution of judgments of these control subjects on each slide was subsequently used as a baseline for evaluating the amount of group pressure influence on the experimental subjects.

Now as to results. When faced with the dilemma posed by this first critical slide, 15 of the 50 men, or 30 per cent, conformed to the obviously false group consensus. The remaining 70 per cent of the men maintained independence of judgment in face of the contradictory group consensus.

The first critical slide was followed by 20 others, all with the subjects responding in position E. The 20 slides involved a broad sampling of judgmental materials, exploring the question of what would happen to other kinds of perceptions, to matters of factual appraisal and of logic, of opinion and attitude, of personal preference—all under the same conditions of group pressure. Interpolated among them were occasional neutral slides, in which the group consensus was simulated as correct or sensible, in order to help maintain the subjects' acceptance of the genuineness of the apparatus and situation.

The results on several more of the critical slides

will give a representative picture of what happens under group pressure. First, take another kind of perceptual judgment. A circle and a star are exposed side by side, the circle being about one third larger in area than the star. The false group consensus is on the *star* as the larger, and 46 per cent of the men express agreement with this false judgment.

On a simple logical judgment of completion of a number series, as found in standard mental tests, 30 per cent of the men conform to an obviously illogical group answer, whereas not a single control subject gives an incorrect answer.

As striking as these influence effects are, they are overshadowed by the even higher degree of influence exhibited on another set of items. These pertain to perceptual, factual, and logical judgments which are designed to maximize the *ambiguity* of the stimulus. There are three such examples: (*a*) two actually equal circles are to be judged for relative size; (*b*) a pair of words are to be judged as either synonyms or antonyms, though actually entirely unrelated in meaning and unfamiliar to all subjects; (*c*) a number series is to be completed which is actually insoluble, that is, for which there is no logically correct completion.

To take the third example, which gives the most pronounced influence effect of all 21 critical items, 79 per cent of the men conform to a spurious group consensus upon an arbitrarily chosen and irrational answer.

Influence effects are found, we see, on both well-structured and poorly structured stimuli, with markedly greater effects on the latter.

Turning from perceptual and factual judgments to opinions and attitudes, it is clearly evident that here, too, the judgments of many of the men are markedly dependent upon a spurious group consensus which violates their own inner convictions. For example, among control subjects virtually no one expresses disagreement with the statement: "I believe we are made better by the trials and hardships of life." But among the experimental subjects exposed to a group consensus toward disagreement, 31 per cent of the men shift to expressing disagreement.

It can be demonstrated that the conformity behavior is not found solely for attitudes on issues like the foregoing, which may be of rather abstract and remote significance for the person. Among the control sample of men, not a single one expresses agreement with the statement: "I doubt whether I would make a good leader," whereas 37 per cent of the men subjected to group pressure toward agreement succumb to it. Here is an issue relating to appraisal of the self and hence likely to be of some importance to the person, especially in light of the fact already mentioned that one of the salient expected qualifications of men in this particular profession is that of leadership.

The set of 21 critical items ranges from factual to attitudinal, from structured to ambiguous, from impersonal to personal. With only two exceptions, all these items yield significant, group pressure influence-effects in our sample of 50 men. The very existence of the two exceptional items is in itself an important finding, for it demonstrates that the observed influences are not simply evidence of indiscriminate readiness to conform to group pressure regardless of the specific nature of the judgment involved. The character of the two exceptional items is significant, for they are the two most extremely personal and subjective judgments, namely, those in which the individual is asked which one of two simple line drawings *he prefers*. On these slides there is virtually no effective result of group pressure. Not more than one man of the 50 expresses agreement with the spurious group consensus on the nonpreferred drawing. Such personal preferences, being most isolated from the relevance of group standards, thus seem to be most immune to group pressure.

Individual Differences

To what extent do the fifty men differ among themselves in their general degree of conformity to group pressure?

A total "conformity score" is readily obtainable for each individual by counting the number of the 21 critical items on which he exhibits influence to the group pressure. The threshold for influence for each item is arbitrarily fixed on the basis of the distribution of judgments by control subjects on that item.

Considering that we are dealing with a fairly homogeneous sample of limited size, the range of individual differences that we obtain is astonishingly large, covering virtually the entire possible scope of our measure. At the lower extreme, several of the men showed conformity on no more than one or two of the critical items. At the upper extreme, one man was influenced on 17 of the 21 items. The rest of the scores are well distributed between these extremes, with a mean score of about eight items and a tendency for greater concentration of scores toward the lower conformity end.

The reliability of the total score, as a measure of generalized conformity in the situation, is obtained by correlating scores on two matched halves of the items. The correlation is found to be .82, which when corrected for the combined halves gives a reliability estimate for the entire 21-item scale of .90.

To recapitulate, we find large and reliable differences among the 50 men in the amount of conformity behavior exhibited, and there appears to be considerable generality of this conformity behavior with respect to widely varied judgmental materials. Whether such conformity tendencies also generalize to other, quite different behavioral situations is a question for future research.

Relations to Personality Variables

Assuming that we are, indeed, measuring conformity tendencies which are fundamental in the person, the question is what traits of character distinguish between those men exhibiting much conformity behavior in our test and those exhibiting little conformity. The assessment setting within which these men were studied provides an unusually fertile opportunity to explore this question, in light of the wide range of personality measurements available.

Correlational study of the conformity scores with these other variables of personality provides some picture of the independent and of the conforming person. As contrasted with the high conformist, the independent man shows more intellectual effectiveness, ego strength, leadership ability and maturity of social relations, together with a conspicuous absence of inferiority feelings, rigid and excessive self-control, and authoritarian attitudes.

* * *

The general appraisal of each man by the assessment staff in the form of descriptive *Q* sorts further enriches this picture. Those men exhibiting extreme independence in the situation as contrasted with those at the high conformity end are described more often in the following terms by the assessment staff, which was entirely ignorant of the actual behavior of the men in the group pressure procedure:

Is an effective leader.

Takes an ascendant role in his relations with others.

Is persuasive; tends to win other people over to his point of view.

Is turned to for advice and reassurance.

Is efficient, capable, able to mobilize resources easily and effectively.

Is active and vigorous.

Is an expressive, ebullient person.

Seeks and enjoys aesthetic and sensuous impressions.

Is natural; free from pretense, unaffected.

Is self-reliant; independent in judgment; able to think for himself.

In sharp contrast to this picture of the independent men is the following description of those high in conformity behavior:

With respect to authority, is submissive, compliant, and overly accepting.

Is conforming; tends to do the things that are prescribed.

Has a narrow range of interests.

Overcontrols his impulses; is inhibited; needlessly delays or denies gratification.

Is unable to make decisions without vacillation or delay.

Becomes confused, disorganized, and unadaptive under stress.

Lacks insight into his own motives and behavior.

Is suggestible; overly responsive to other people's evaluations rather than his own.

Further evidence is found in some of the specific items of personality inventories on which the answers of the high and low conformers are significantly different. Here are some illustrative items more frequently answered "True" by the independent subjects than by the conforming subjects:

Sometimes I rather enjoy going against the rules and doing things I'm not supposed to.

I like to fool around with new ideas, even if they turn out later to be a total waste of time.

A person needs to "show off" a little now and then.

At times I have been so entertained by the cleverness of a crook that I have hoped he would get by with it.

It is unusual for me to express strong approval or disapproval of the actions of others.

I am often so annoyed when someone tries to get ahead of me in a line of people that I speak to him about it.

Compared to your own self-respect, the respect of others means very little.

This pattern of expressed attitudes seems to reflect freedom from compulsion about rules, adventurousness (perhaps tinged with exhibitionism), self-assertiveness, and self-respect.

Turning to the opposite side of the picture, here are some illustrative items more frequently answered "True" by the extreme conformists, which reflect a rather rigid, externally sanctioned, and inconsistent, moralistic attitude.

I am in favor of very strict enforcement of all laws, no matter what the consequences.

It is all right to get around the law if you don't actually break it.

Most people are honest chiefly through fear of being caught.

Another set of items reveals a desire for clarity, symmetry, certainty, or, in presently popular phraseology, "an intolerance of ambiguity."

I don't like to work on a problem unless there is a possibility of coming out with a clear-cut and unambiguous answer.

Once I have made up my mind I seldom change it.

Perfect balance is the essence of all good composition.

Other items express conventionality of values:

I always follow the rule: business before pleasure.

The trouble with many people is that they don't take things seriously enough.

I am very careful about my manner of dress.

Anxiety is revealed in numerous items:

I am afraid when I look down from a high place.

I am often bothered by useless thoughts which keep running through my head.

I often think, "I wish I were a child again."

I often feel as though I have done something wrong or wicked.

And, finally, there are various expressions of disturbed, dejected, and distrustful attitudes toward other people:

When I meet a stranger I often think that he is better than I am.

Sometimes I am sure that other people can tell what I am thinking.

I wish that I could get over worrying about things I have said that may have injured other people's feelings.

I commonly wonder what hidden reason another person may have for doing something nice for me.

People pretend to care more about one another than they really do.

Although there is an unmistakable neurotic tone to many of the foregoing statements, one must be chary of inferring that those high on conformity are measurably more neurotic than the others. There does not in fact appear to be any significant correlation of the conformity scores with obvious standard measures of neuroticism as found, for instance, in scales of the Minnesota Multiphasic Personality Inventory. A similar negative finding has been reported by Barron (1953) in his study of the personality correlates of independence of judgment in Asch's subjects.

In another area, attitudes concerning parents and children, differences between those high and low on conformity are especially interesting. The extreme conformists describe their parents in highly idealized terms, unrelieved by any semblance of criticism. The independents, on the other hand, offer a more balanced picture of praise and criticism.

Most of the men in the sample are fathers, and it is instructive to see that in their view of child-rearing practices, the conformers are distinctly more "restrictive" in their attitudes and the independents distinctly more "permissive" (Block, 1955).

Finally, there appears to be a marked difference in the early home background of the conformists and independents. The high conformers in this sample come almost without exception from stable homes; the independents much more frequently report broken homes and unstable home environments.

Previous theoretical and empirical studies seem to converge, though imperfectly, on a picture of the overconformist as having less ego strength, less ability to tolerate own impulses and to tolerate ambiguity, less ability to accept responsibility, less self-insight, less spontaneity and productive originality, and as having more prejudiced and authoritarian attitudes, more idealization of parents, and greater emphasis on external and socially approved values.

All of these elements gain at least some substantiation in the present study of conformity behavior, as objectively measured in our test situation. The decisive influence of intelligence in resisting conformity pressures is perhaps given even fuller weight in the present findings.

*   *   *

Psychological Processes

Turn now to questions concerning the nature of the psychological processes involved in these expressions of conformity to group pressure. How, for instance, is the situation perceived by the individual? The most striking thing is that almost never do the individuals under this pressure of a false group consensus come to suspect the deception practiced upon them. Of the total of 159 persons already tested in the apparatus and questioned immediately afterwards, only a small handful expressed doubt of the genuineness of the situation. Of these not more than two or three really seem to have developed this suspicion while in the actual situation.

Yet all the subjects are acutely aware of the sometimes gross discrepancies between their own inner judgments and those expressed by the rest of the group. How do they account for these discrepancies?

Intensive individual questioning of the subjects immediately following the procedure elicits evidence of two quite different tendencies. First, for many persons the discrepancies tend to be resolved through self-blame. They express doubt of their own accuracy of perception or judgment, confessing that they had probably misread or misperceived the slides. Second, for many other persons the main tendency is to blame the rest of the group, expressing doubt that they had perceived or read the slides correctly. This is not a neat dichotomy, of course. Most persons express something of a mixture of these explanations, which is not surprising in view of the fact that some slides may tend to favor one interpretation of the difficulty and other slides the opposite interpretation.

As might be predicted, there is a substantial relationship between conformity score and tendency to self-blame; or, putting it the other way, those who remain relatively independent of the group pressure are more likely to blame the discrepancies on poor judgments by the rest of the group.

But this is by no means a perfect relationship. There are many persons who, though retrospectively expressing doubt of the correctness of the group's judgment, did in fact conform heavily while in the situation. And what is even more striking is that a substantial number of the subjects—between 25 and 30 per cent—freely admit on later questioning that there were times when they responded the way the group did *even when they thought this not the proper answer*. It seems evident, therefore, that along with various forms of cognitive rationalization of the discrepancies, there occurred a considerable amount of what might be called deliberate conforming, that is, choosing to express outward agreement with the group consensus even when believing the group to be wrong.

Another noteworthy effect was the sense of increased psychological distance induced between the person himself and the rest of the group. He felt himself to be queer or different, or felt the group to be quite unlike what he had thought. With this went an arousal of considerable anxiety in most subjects; for some, manifest anxiety was acute.

The existence of these tensions within and between the subjects became dramatically manifest when, shortly after the end of the procedure, the experimenter confessed the deception he had practiced and explained the real situation. There were obvious and audible signs of relaxation and relief, and a shift from an atmosphere of constraint to one of animated discussion.

This is an appropriate point to comment on ethics. No persons when questioned after explanation of the deception expressed feelings that they had been ethically maltreated in the experiment. The most common reaction was a positive one of having engaged in an unusual and significant experience, together with much joking about having been taken in.

Undeniably there are serious ethical issues involved in the experimental use of such deception techniques, especially inasmuch as they appear to penetrate rather deeply into the person. My view is that such deception methods ethically require that great care be taken immediately afterwards to explain the situation fully to the subject.

These remarks on ethics of the method are especially pertinent as we move from study of judgmental materials which are noncontroversial to those which are controversial. In the studies of college students and of mature women, many new critical items were introduced and subjected to the pressure. They were intended to explore more deeply the conformity tendencies in matters of opinion and attitude. And they were so chosen as to pertain to socially important and controversial issues involving civil liberties, political philosophy, crime and punishment, ethical values, and the like.

Here are two salient examples. An expression of agreement or disagreement was called for on the following statement: "Free speech being a privilege rather than a right, it is proper for a society to suspend free speech whenever it feels itself threatened." Among control subjects, only 19 per cent express agreement. But among the experimental subjects confronted with a unanimous group consensus agreeing with the statement, 58 per cent express agreement.

Another item was phrased as follows: "Which one of the following do you feel is the most important problem facing our country today?" And these five alternatives were offered:

Economic recession
Educational facilities
Subversive activities
Mental health
Crime and corruption

Among control subjects, only 12 per cent chose "Subversive activities" as the most important. But when exposed to a spurious group consensus which unanimously selected "Subversive activities" as the most important, 48 per cent of the experimental subjects expressed this same choice.

I think that no one would wish to deny that here we have evidence of the operation of powerful conformity influences in the expression of opinion on matters of critical social controversy.

Reinforcement of Conformity

There is one final point upon which I should like to touch briefly. That is the question of whether there are circumstances under which the power of the group to influence the judgments of the individual may be even more greatly reinforced, and if so, how far such power may extend.

One method has been tried as part of the study of college students. With half of the subjects, a further instruction was introduced by the experimenter. They were told that in order to see how well they were doing during the procedure, the experimenter would inform the group immediately after the judgments on each slide what the correct answer was. This was to be done, of course, only for those slides for which there was a correct answer, namely, perceptual judgments, logical solutions, vocabulary, etc. No announcement would be made after slides having to do with opinions and attitudes.

The experimenter here again deceived the subjects, for the answers he announced as correct were deliberately chosen so as to agree with the false group consensus. In short, the external authority of the experimenter was later added on as reinforcement to the group consensus.

The effect of this so-called "correction" method is striking. As the series of judgments goes on, these individuals express greater and greater conformity to the group pressure on slides which are of the same character as those for which earlier in the series the false group consensus was thus rein-

forced by the false announcement by the experimenter.

But the more critical issue is whether this enhanced power of the group generalizes also to judgments of an entirely unrelated sort, namely, matters of opinion and attitude, rather than of fact. In other words, will the group, through having the rightness of its judgment supported by the experimenter on matters of perception, logic, and the like, thereby come to be regarded by the individual as more right, or more to be complied with, on entirely extraneous matters, such as social issues?

The answer is absolutely clear. The enhanced power of the group does *not* carry over to increase the effective influence on expression of opinions and attitudes. The subjects exposed to this "correction" method do not exhibit greater conformity to group pressure on opinions and attitudes than that found in other subjects.

This crucial finding throws some light on the nature of the psychological processes involved in the conformity situation. For it seems to imply that conformity behavior under such group pressure, rather than being sheerly an indiscriminate and irrational tendency to defer to the authority of the group, has in it important rational elements. There is something of a reasonable differentiation made by the individual in his manner of reliance upon the group. He may be led to accept the superiority of the group judgment on matters where there is an objective frame of reference against which the group can be checked. But he does not, thereby, automatically accept the authority of the group on matters of a less objective sort.

Conclusion

The social psychologist is concerned with the character of conformity, the personologist with conformity of character. Between them they raise many research questions: the comparative incidence of conformity tendencies in various populations; the influence of group structure and the individual's role in the group on the nature and amount of conformity behavior; the effects of reward or punishment for conforming on habits of conformity; the genesis and change of conformity behavior in the individual personality; the determinants of extreme *anti*conformity tendencies.

Contributing to such questions we have what appears to be a powerful new research technique, enabling the study of conformity behavior within a setting which effectively simulates genuine group interaction, yet preserves the essential requirements of objective measurement.

REFERENCES

Asch, S. E. *Social psychology.* Englewood Cliffs, N.J.: Prentice-Hall, 1952.

Barron, F. Some personality correlates of independence of judgment. *Journal of Personality,* 1953, **21,** 287–297.

Block, J. Personality characteristics associated with fathers' attitudes toward child-rearing. *Child Development,* 1955, **26,** 41–48.

67

Reaction Patterns to Severe, Chronic Stress in American Army Prisoners of War of the Chinese

Edgar H. Schein

While a prisoner in a Nazi concentration camp during the Second World War, Bruno Bettelheim recorded his experiences and observations of the techniques used by Nazis to manipulate their prisoners. The basic intent of the Nazis was to change the individual from an active, thinking individual to a completely passive slave willing to carry out any order. To accomplish this the Nazis employed intense psychological and physical stress, and also took great pains to destroy all social relationships and sources of group support.

Approximately five years after the conclusion of the Second World War, the Chinese Communists employed similar techniques to achieve manipulation of American prisoners of war. The Chinese, however, were not concerned with making prisoners into willing slave laborers, but rather with achieving a true conversion—the acceptance of their governmental and ideological system as correct.

The following selection by Schein describes the techniques used by the Chinese. Note that the brainwashing program did not involve subtle classical conditioning, hypnosis, drugs, or any form of torture, but utilized, rather, the absolute control of the prisoners' environment and social contacts. It is also important to note that while the amount of behavior modification achieved by this means was considerable, the actual number of true conversions was minimal.

In this paper I will outline some of the constellations of stress which prisoners of war faced during the Korean conflict, and describe some of the reaction patterns to these stresses. Rather than presenting a complete catalogue of their experiences (Schein, 1956), I have selected those aspects which seem to me to throw some light on the problem of collaboration with the enemy. I will give particular emphasis to the *social* psychological factors, because the Chinese approach to treatment of prisoners seemed to emphasize control over groups, rather than individuals.

My material is based on a variety of sources. I was in Korea during the repatriation and had the opportunity to interview extensively 20 unselected repatriates. This basic material was supplemented by the information gathered by three psychiatrists, Drs. Harvey Strassman, Patrick Israel, and Clinton Tempereau, who together had seen some 300 men.

From The Journal of Social Issues, *Vol. XIII, No. 3, pp. 21–30. Reprinted with the permission of The Society for the Psychological Study of Social Issues. This work was completed while the author was a captain, U.S. Army Medical Service Corps, assigned to the Walter Reed Army Institute of Research. I would like to acknowledge the invaluable help and guidance of Dr. David McK. Rioch and Capt. Harold Williams as well as the staff of the Neuropsychiatric Division of the Walter Reed Army Institute of Research. Portions of this paper were read at the meetings of the Group for the Advancement of Psychiatry, Asbury Park, New Jersey, November 1956.*

On board ship returning to the United States, I also had the opportunity to sit in on bull sessions among repatriates in which many of the prison experiences were discussed. Additional details were obtained from the Army dossiers on the men.

The typical experience of the prisoner of war must be divided into two broad phases. The first phase lasted anywhere from one to six months beginning with capture, followed by exhausting marches to the north of Korea and severe privation in inadequately equipped temporary camps, terminating in assignment to a permanent prisoner of war camp.

The second phase, lasting two or more years, was marked by chronic pressures to collaborate and to give up existing group loyalties in favor of new ones. Thus, while physical stresses had been outstanding in the first six months, psychological stresses were outstanding in this second period.

The reactions of the men toward capture were influenced by their overall attitude toward the Korean situation. Many of them felt inadequately prepared, both physically and psychologically. The physical training, equipment, and rotation system all came in for retrospective criticism, though this response might have been merely a rationalization for being captured. When the Chinese entered the war, they penetrated into rear areas where they captured many men who were taken completely by surprise. The men felt that when positions were overrun, their leadership was often less than adequate. Thus, many men were disposed to blame the UN command for the unfortunate event of being captured.

On the psychological side, the men were not clearly aware of what they were fighting for or what kind of enemy they were opposing. In addition, the reports of the atrocities committed by the North Koreans led most men to expect death, torture, or nonrepatriation if captured.

It was in such a context that the soldier found his Chinese captor extending his hand in a friendly gesture and saying "Welcome" or "Congratulations, you've been *liberated*." This Chinese tactic was part of their "lenient policy" which was explained to groups of prisoners shortly after capture in these terms: Because the UN had entered the war illegally and was an aggressor, all UN military personnel were in fact war criminals and *could* be shot summarily. But the average soldier was, after all, only carrying out orders for his leaders who were the real criminals. Therefore, the Chinese soldier would consider the POW a "student" and would teach him the "truth" about the war. Anyone who did not cooperate by going to

school and by learning voluntarily could be reverted to his "war criminal" status and shot, particularly if a confession of "criminal" deeds could be obtained from him.

In the weeks following capture, the men were collected in large groups and marched north. From a physical point of view, the stresses during these marches were very severe: There was no medicine for the wounded, the food was unpalatable and insufficient, especially by our standards, clothing was scarce in the face of severe winter weather, and shelter was inadequate and overcrowded. The Chinese set a severe pace and showed little consideration for weariness that was the product of wounds, diarrhea, and frostbite. Men who were not able to keep up were abandoned unless they were helped by their fellows. The men marched only at night and were kept under cover during the day, ostensibly as protection against strafing by our own planes.

From a psychological point of view this situation is best described as a recurring cycle of fear, relief, and new fear. The men were afraid that they might die, that they might never be repatriated, that they might never again have a chance to communicate with the outside, and that no one even knew they were alive. The Chinese, on the other hand, were reassuring and promised that the men would be repatriated soon, that conditions would improve, and that they would soon be permitted to communicate with the outside.

One of the chief problems for the men was the disorganization within the group itself. It was difficult to maintain close group ties if one was competing with others for the essentials of life and if one spent one's resting time in overcrowded huts among others who had severe diarrhea and were occasionally incontinent. Lines of authority often broke down, and with this, group cohesion and morale suffered. A few men attempted to escape, but they were usually recaptured in a short time and returned to the group. The Chinese also fostered low morale and the feeling of being abandoned by systematically reporting false news about United Nation defeats and losses.

In this situation goals became increasingly short-run. As long as the men were marching, they had something to do and could look forward to relief from the harsh conditions of the march. However, arrival at a temporary camp was usually a severe disappointment. Not only were physical conditions as bad as ever, but the sedentary life in overcrowded quarters produced more disease and still lower morale.

What happened to the men under these conditions? During the one- to two-week marches they became increasingly apathetic.[1] They developed a slow, plodding gait, called by one man a "prisoners' shuffle." Uppermost in their minds were fantasies of food: Men remembered all the good meals they had ever had, or planned detailed menus for years into the future. To a lesser extent they thought of loved ones at home and about cars which seemed to them to symbolize freedom and the return home.

In the temporary camps disease and exposure took a heavy toll in lives. But it was the feeling of many men, including some of the doctors who survived the experience, that some of these deaths were not warranted by a man's physical condition. Instead, what appeared to happen was that some men became so apathetic that they ceased to care about their bodily needs. They retreated further into themselves, refused to eat even what little food was available, refused to get any exercise, and eventually lay down as if waiting to die. The reports were emphatic concerning the lucidity and sanity of these men. They seemed willing to accept the prospect of death rather than to continue fighting a severely frustrating and depriving environment.

Two things seemed to save a man who was close to such "apathy" death: getting him on his feet and doing something, no matter how trivial, or getting him angry or concerned about some present or future problem. Usually it was the effort of a friend who maternally and insistently motivated the individual toward realistic goals which snapped him out of such a state of resignation. In one case such "therapy" consisted of kicking the man until he was mad enough to get up and fight.

Throughout this time, the Chinese played the role of the benevolent but handicapped captor. Prisoners were always reminded that it was their *own* Air Force bombing which was responsible for the inadequate supplies. Furthermore, they were reminded that they were getting treatment which was just as good as that which the average Chinese was getting. One important effect of this was that a man could never give *full* vent to his hostility toward the Chinese, even in fantasy. In their *manner* and *words* they were usually solicitous and sympathetic. The Chinese also implied that conditions could be better for a prisoner if he would take a more "cooperative" attitude, if he would support their propaganda for peace. Thus a man was made to feel that he was himself responsible for his traumatic circumstances.

Arrival at a permanent camp usually brought relief from many of these physical hardships. Food,

shelter, and medicine, while not plentiful, appeared to be sufficient for the maintenance of life and some degree of health. However, the Chinese now increased sharply their efforts to involve prisoners in their own propaganda program and to undermine loyalties to their country. This marks the beginning of the second phase of the imprisonment experience.

The Chinese program of subversion and indoctrination was thoroughly integrated into the entire camp routine and involved the manipulation of the entire social milieu of the prison camp. Its aims appeared to be to manage a large group of prisoners with a minimum staff of guards, to indoctrinate them with the Communist political ideology, to interrogate them to obtain intelligence information and confessions for propaganda purposes, and to develop a corps of collaborators within the prisoner group. What success the Chinese had stemmed from their *total* control of the environment, not from the application of any one technique.

The most significant feature of Chinese prisoner camp control was the systematic destruction of the prisoners' formal and informal group structure. Soon after arrival at a camp, the men were segregated by race, nationality, and rank. The Chinese put their own men in charge of the platoons and companies and made arbitrary selections of POW squad leaders to remind the prisoners that their old rank system no longer had any validity. In addition, the Chinese attempted to undermine *informal* group structure by prohibiting any kind of group meeting and by systematically fomenting mutual distrust by playing men off against one another. The most effective device to this end was the practice of obtaining from informers or Chinese spies detailed information about someone's activities, no matter how trivial, then calling him in to interrogate him about it. Such detailed surveillance of the men's activities made them feel that their own ranks were so infiltrated by spies and informers that it was not safe to trust anyone.

A similar device was used to obtain information during interrogation. After a man had resisted giving information for hours or days, he would be shown a signed statement by one of his fellow prisoners giving that same information. Still another device was to make prisoners who had not collaborated look like collaborators by bestowing special favors upon them.

---

[1] A more detailed discussion of the apathy reaction may be found in Strassman, Thaler, and Schein (1956).

A particularly successful Chinese technique was their use of testimonials from other prisoners, such as the false germ-warfare confessions, and appeals based on familiar contexts, such as peace appeals. Confessions by prisoners or propaganda lectures given by collaborators had a particularly demoralizing effect, because only if resistance had been *unanimous* could a man solidly believe that his values were correct, even if he could not defend them logically.

If the men, in spite of their state of social disorganization, did manage to organize any kind of group activity, the Chinese would quickly break up the group by removing its leaders or key members and assigning them to another camp.

Loyalties to home and country were undermined by the systematic manipulation of mail. Usually only mail which carried bad news was delivered. If a man received no mail at all, the Chinese suggested that his loved ones had abandoned him.

Feelings of social isolation were increased by the complete information control maintained in the camps. Only the Communist press, radio, magazines, and movies were allowed.

The weakening of the prisoner group's social structure is particularly significant because we depend to such an extent on consensual validation in judging ourselves and others. The prisoners lost their most important sources of information and support concerning standards of behavior and beliefs. Often men who attempted to resist the Chinese by means other than *outright* obstruction or aggression failed to obtain the active support of others, often earning their suspicion instead.

At the same time, the Chinese did create a situation in which meaningful social relationships could be had through common political activity, such as the "peace" committees which served as propaganda organs. The Chinese interrogators or instructors sometimes lived with prisoners for long periods of time in order to establish close personal relationships with them.

The Communist doctrines were presented through compulsory lectures, followed by compulsory group discussions for the purpose of justifying the conclusions given at the end of the lectures. On the whole, this phase of indoctrination was ineffective because of the crudeness of the propaganda material used in the lectures. However, its constant repetition seemed eventually to influence those men who did not have well-formed political opinions to start with, particularly because no counter-arguments could be heard. The group discussions were effective only if their monitor was someone who could keep control over the group and keep it on the topic of discussion. Attempts by the Chinese to use "progressive" POWs in the role of monitors were seldom successful because they aroused too much hostility in the men.

The Chinese also attempted to get prisoners to use mutual criticism and self-criticism in the fashion in which it is used within China. Whenever a POW was caught breaking one of the innumerable camp rules, he was required to give an elaborate confession and self-criticism, no matter how trivial the offense. In general, the POWs were able to use this opportunity to ridicule the Chinese by taking advantage of their lack of understanding of slang and American idiom. They would emphasize the wrong parts of sentences or insert words and phrases which made it apparent to other prisoners that the joke was on the Chinese. Often men were required to make these confessions in front of large groups of other prisoners. If the man could successfully communicate by a linguistic device his lack of sincerity, this ritual could backfire on the Chinese by giving the men an opportunity to express their solidarity (by sharing a communication which could not be understood by the Chinese). However, in other instances, prisoners who viewed such public confessions felt contempt for the confessor and felt their own group was being undermined still further by such public humiliation.

Various tales of how prisoners resisted the pressures put on them have been widely circulated in the press. For example, a number of prisoners ridiculed the Chinese by playing baseball with a basketball, yet telling the Chinese this was the correct way to play the game. Such stories suggest that morale and group solidarity was actually quite high in the camps. Our interviews with the men suggest that morale climbed sharply during the *last six to nine months* of imprisonment when the armistice talks were underway, when the compulsory indoctrination program had been put on a voluntary basis, and when the Chinese were improving camp conditions in anticipation of the repatriation. However, we heard practically no stories of successful group resistance or high morale from the first year or so in the camps when the indoctrination program was seriously pursued by the Chinese. (At that time the men had neither the time nor the opportunity to play any kind of games, because all their time was spent on indoctrination activities or exhausting labor.)

Throughout, the Chinese created an environment in which rewards such as extra food, medicine, special privileges, and status were given for cooperation and collaboration, while threats of death, nonrepatriation, reprisal against family, torture, decreases in food and medicine, and imprisonment served to keep men from offering much resistance. Only imprisonment was consistently used as an actual punishment. *Chronic* resistance was usually handled by transferring the prisoner to a so-called "reactionary" camp.

Whatever behavior the Chinese attempted to elicit, they always *paced* their demands very carefully, they always required some level of *participation* from the prisoner, no matter how trivial, and they *repeated* endlessly.

To what extent did these pressures produce either changes in beliefs and attitudes, or collaboration? Close observation of the repatriates and the reports of the men themselves suggest that the Chinese did not have much success in changing beliefs and attitudes. Doubt and confusion were created in many prisoners as a result of having to examine so closely their own way of thinking, but very few changes, if any, occurred that resembled actual *conversion* to Communism. The type of prisoner who was most likely to become *sympathetic* toward Communism was the one who had chronically occupied a low status position in this society and for whom the democratic principles were not very salient or meaningful.

In producing collaboration, however, the Chinese were far more effective. By collaboration I mean such activities as giving lectures for the Communists, writing and broadcasting propaganda, giving false confessions, writing and signing petitions, informing on fellow POWs, and so on; none of these activities required a personal change of belief. Some 10 to 15 per cent of the men chronically collaborated, but the dynamics of this response are very complex. By far the greatest determinant was the amount of pressure the Chinese put on a particular prisoner. Beyond this, the reports of the men permit one to isolate several sets of motives that operated, though it is impossible to tell how many cases of each type there may have been.

1. Some men collaborated for outright opportunistic reasons; these men lacked any kind of stable group identification and exploited the situation for its material benefits without any regard for the consequences to themselves, their fellow prisoners, or their country.

2. Some men collaborated because their egos were too weak to withstand the physical and psychological rigors; these men were primarily motivated by fear, though they often rationalized their behavior; they were unable to resist any kind of authority figure and could be blackmailed by the Chinese once they had begun to collaborate.

3. Some men collaborated with the firm conviction that they were infiltrating the Chinese ranks and obtaining intelligence information which would be useful to the UN forces. This was a convenient rationalization for anyone who could not withstand the pressures. Many of these men were initially tricked into collaboration or were motivated by a desire to communicate with the outside world. None of these men became ideologically confused; what Communist beliefs they might have professed were for the benefit of the Chinese only.

4. The prisoner who was vulnerable to the ideological appeal because of his low status in this society often collaborated with the conviction that he was doing the right thing in supporting the Communist peace movement. This group included the younger and less intelligent men from backward or rural areas, the malcontents, and members of various minority groups. These men often viewed themselves as failures in our society and felt that society had never given them a chance. They were positively attracted by the immediate status and privileges which went with being a "progressive," and by the promise of important roles which they could presumably play in the peace movement of the future.

Perhaps the most important thing to note about collaboration is the manner in which the social disorganization contributed to it. A man might make a slanted radio broadcast in order to communicate with the outside, he might start reading Communist literature out of sheer boredom, he might give information which he knew the Chinese already had, and so on. Once this happened, however, the Chinese rewarded him, increased pressure on him to collaborate, and blackmailed him by threatening exposure. At the same time, in most cases, his fellow prisoners forced him into further collaboration by mistrusting him and ostracizing him. Thus a man had to stand entirely on his own judgment and strength, and both of these often failed. One of the most common failures was a man's lack of awareness concerning the effects of his own actions on the other prisoners and the value of these actions for the Chinese propaganda effort. The man who confessed to germ warfare, thinking he could repudiate such a confession later, did not realize its immediate propaganda value to the Communists.

A certain percentage of men, though the exact number is difficult to estimate, exhibited chronic resistance and obstructionism toward Chinese indoctrination efforts. Many of these men were well integrated with secure, stable group identifications who could withstand the social isolation and still exercise good judgment. Others were chronic obstructionists whose histories showed recurring resistance to any form of authority. Still others were idealists or martyrs to religious and ethical principles, and still others were anxious, guilt-ridden individuals who could only cope with their own strong impulses to collaborate by denying them and over-reacting in the other direction.

By far the largest group of prisoners, however, established a complex compromise between the demands of the Chinese and their own value system. This adjustment, called by the men "playing it cool," consisted primarily of a physical and emotional withdrawal from the whole environment. These men learned to suspend their feelings and to adopt an attitude of watching and waiting, rather than hoping and planning. This reaction, though passive, was not as severe as the apathy described earlier. It was a difficult adjustment to maintain because some concessions had to be made to the Chinese in the form of trivial or well-timed collaborative acts and in the form of a feigned interest in the indoctrination program. At the same time, each man had to be prepared to deal with the hostility of his buddies if he made an error in judgment.

Discussion

This paper has placed particular emphasis on the social psychological factors involved in "brainwashing" because it is my opinion that the process is primarily concerned with social forces, not with the strengths and weaknesses of individual minds. It has often been asserted that drugs, hypnotic techniques, refined "mental tortures" and, more recently, implanted electrodes can make the task of the "brainwasher" much easier by rendering the human mind submissive with a minimum of effort. There is little question that such techniques can be used to elicit confessions or signatures on documents prepared by the captor; but so can withdrawal of food, water, or air produce the same results. The point is that the Chinese Communists do not appear to be interested in obtaining merely a confession or *transient* submission. Instead, they appear to be interested in producing changes in men which will be lasting and self-sustaining. A germ-warfare confession alone was not enough—the POW had to "testify" before an international commission explaining in detail how the bombs had been dropped, and had to tell his story in other prison camps to his fellow POWs.

There is little evidence that drugs, posthypnotic suggestion, or implanted electrodes can now or ever will be able to produce the kind of behavior exhibited by many prisoners who collaborated and made false confessions. On the other hand, there is increasing evidence (Hinkle, 1956; Lifton, 1956) that Russian and Chinese interrogation and indoctrination techniques involve the destruction of the person's social ties and identifications, and the partial destruction of his ego. If this is successfully accomplished, the person is offered a new identity for himself and given the opportunity to identify with new groups. What physical torture and deprivation are involved in this process may be either a calculated attempt to degrade and humiliate a man to destroy his image of himself as a dignified human being, or the product of fortuitous circumstances, i.e., failure of supply lines to the prison, loss of temper on the part of the interrogator, an attempt to inspire fear in other prisoners by torturing one of them, and so on. We do not have sufficient evidence to determine which of these alternatives represents Communist intentions; possibly all of them are involved in the actual prison situation.

Ultimately that which sustains humans is their personality integration born out of secure and stable group identifications. One may be able to produce temporary submission by direct intervention in cortical processes, but only by destroying a man's self-image and his group supports can one produce any lasting changes in his beliefs and attitudes. By concerning ourselves with the problem of artificially creating submission in man, we run the real risk of overlooking the fact that we are in a genuine struggle of ideas with other portions of the world and that man often submits himself directly to ideas and principles.

To understand and combat "brainwashing" we must look at those social conditions which make people ready to accept new ideas from anyone who states them clearly and forcefully and those social conditions which give people the sense of integrity which will sustain them when their immediate social and emotional supports are stripped away.

REFERENCES

Hinkle, L. E., & Wolff, H. C. Communist interrogation and indoctrination of "enemies of the state." *Archives of Neurology and Psychiatry*, 1956, **76**, 115–174.

Lifton, R. L. "Thought reform" of Western civilians in Chinese Communist prisons. *Psychiatry*, 1956, **19**, 173–198.

Schein, E. H. The Chinese indoctrination program for prisoners of war. *Psychiatry*, 1956, **19**, 148–172.

Strassman, H. D., Thaler, M., & Schein, E. H. A prisoner of war syndrome: Apathy as a reaction to severe stress. *American Journal of Psychiatry*, 1956, **112**, 998–1003.

68

Leadership in Disaster

James L. Bruning

The techniques used by successful leaders have been discussed from the very beginnings of written history. However, no one set of unique personality variables and behavioral characteristics that identify a "leader" has ever been isolated. A major reason for this failure is that the environmental situation largely determines what behavior an individual must display in order to be successful as a leader. For example, an individual who made wise decisions, but only after long and careful consideration of all the alternatives, might well become successful as a bank president, but almost certainly would not enjoy the same success if he were a battlefield commander where quick, decisive action was necessary.

As the above example implies, in a particular type of situation, the certain characteristics that a man must have in order to maximize his chances of leadership success can often be isolated. One such situation occurs when the members of a group come under some sort of psychological or physical stress. If the existing group leaders display the required characteristics, great group solidarity and productivity can be achieved. On the other hand, if there are no leaders or if those present are ineffective, disintegration of group functioning occurs with great rapidity. It will be recalled from the preceding selection that one of the primary techniques used by the Chinese for undermining group structure and disrupting individual morale was to remove officers and key members and assign them to other camps. Under the stressful conditions of being held a prisoner of war, the lack of leadership resulted in a nearly total cessation of cooperation and group activity.

While the Chinese permitted no leaders or leadership attempts to occur, there are many situations such as accidents, tornadoes, explosions, floods, etc. that occur daily in which individual and groups under stress look to leaders and established authorities for direction. In the following selection Bruning describes some of the characteristics which leaders must display if they are to maximize their chances of success in such situations.

An examination of previous disaster reports reveals that in nearly every instance leadership and leadership problems were of primary importance. However, most disaster studies have discussed this phenomenon in reference to conditions unique to a particular community, and as a result, the generalizability of the data is considerably limited.

The basic objective of this paper is to suggest several factors which affect leadership success or failure in a disaster situation. These will be stated as general propositions which are assumed to be applicable regardless of the specific nature of the situation or the disaster-inducing agent. It must be pointed out, however, that these propositions represent what can best be termed reasonable hypotheses, and consequently, their full acceptance must await further test.

Leadership Requirements

Two major problems present themselves when democratic procedures (vote and majority consent) are employed for making decisions concerning

From *Psychology*, 1964, *1(4)*, *19–23*. This manuscript is based on a paper read at the 1963 American Psychological Association convention as part of a symposium entitled "Behavioral Research on Postnuclear Attack Phenomena." The background research for this paper was conducted while the author was a summer research fellow at Human Sciences Research, Inc. Thanks are due Dr. Peter G. Nordlie for suggestions and constructive criticisms offered while the manuscript was being prepared. Publication costs were paid by a grant from the Ohio University Research Fund.

group action. First, there is a time lag between the need for action and the decision, and second, there is a similar lag between the decision and its execution (Barnard, 1939). Of course, several variables such as group size, type, organization, etc. have an effect on the duration of these delays, but the democratic method is, at best, a slow process.

Immediately following a disaster, leaders of nearly all groups and organizations in the general impact area are faced with the complicated tasks of reorganizing and restating group goals and purposes in relation to the crisis conditions. In addition, it is imperative that rapid planning and implementation of a concentrated group effort be undertaken in order to alleviate the crisis as quickly as possible. Under such conditions there usually is not time for subordinate members to function as debating and voting partners in the decision-making process, but rather, they must be organized for quick action. Consequently, disaster presents a set of conditions which requires proportionately greater participation in policy making by fewer and fewer group members.

This need for reduction in the number of persons involved in program planning is evidenced during periods of national crisis by the special powers granted to the President which allow him to circumvent much of the usual legislative procedure. Of greater interest for the purposes of this paper, nearly all disaster reports show that for a direction of rescue and relief activities to be efficient, it must be centered on a single individual or a central disaster headquarters. In conjunction with this finding, it has been noted that even when a disaster control center is established, the reduction in number of policy makers may still not be sufficient and an even further reduction is required (Form and Nosow, 1958).

Concurrent with the necessity for reduction in the number of participants in policy decisions is a counterrequirement for an increase in the number of persons who must make decisions at the operational level. This can be most clearly seen in a large military organization during combat. Planning and policy decisions are usually left in the hands of a very few. However, once the generals commit their army to an action, the course of that action is inextricably dependent on the aggregate of operational, "on-the-spot" decisions made by the officers in the field. If these persons either fail to make decisions, or make incorrect ones, the entire operation is doomed to failure.

Much the same type of situation arises following disaster. The best single example of this can be seen in the reports of events surrounding the collapse of the sea walls and dikes in the Netherlands (*Holland Flood Disaster*, 1953). In this instance a large proportion of the problems encountered were traceable to a failure of lesser officials to make the necessary decisions concerning rescue and relief activities. These officials had been trained to act only in response to orders issued by those higher in command. When none were forthcoming because of communication failures, many of the local officers were incapable of taking any sort of independent action, and as a result, a great many persons suffered unnecessary hardship.

A third general finding is that disaster almost always affords leaders, at all levels, more influence than they possessed during noncrisis periods. This greater amount of influence has usually been attributed to the general feelings of helplessness or impotence on the part of the disaster victims immediately following impact. For example, it was concluded in the National Opinion Research Center Report (1953) that persons who take responsibility during periods of severe stress are viewed with near reverence. Similarly, Janis (1954), Wallace (1956), and others have noted that during one phase of the so-called "disaster syndrome," victims tend to pass through a stage of extreme suggestibility and obedience such that almost any suggestion or leadership attempt is gladly accepted and acted upon.

Although persons who assume a leadership role during crisis are followed willingly, continued acceptance by the affected populace is dependent upon the leader's ability to provide a tangible, although perhaps temporary, program to establish order and security. The long-term positive effects of such action can be most clearly seen in the reports on one of the floods on the Rio Grande river (Clifford, 1956). In this particular instance, the status of a few religious leaders who airlifted food and water to the people of an isolated Mexican town was enhanced considerably, even though the quantities delivered were nominal, to say the least.

Closely related to the desire of disaster victims for *some* action to be initiated is the manner in which the affected populace wishes decisions to be made and implemented. In general, leaders in a disaster situation are expected to show not only initiative, but must also convey an impression of firmness and decisiveness in making decisions which are likely to reduce the severity of the crisis. Conversely, any behavior which gives an impression of indecision or equivocation, whether it actually exists or not, is likely to lead to leadership failure. In support of this notion, Logan (1950) concluded that following the explosion of a ship in the Texas

City harbor, the individuals who were accepted as leaders and who became nuclei for task group formation were those who initiated action in a prompt and decisive manner. Similarly, disaster-ready organizations such as the State Patrol often receive considerable praise because of their efficiency, promptness, and ability to "take charge" in an extreme situation.

Another factor which appears to influence leadership success or failure during crisis is the familiarity of the victims with those who are attempting to lead. Logan (1950), in discussion of the relative merits of "outside" leaders in relation to the local, preestablished leaders, concluded that the factors of greater public acquaintance with and confidence in local leaders are of considerable importance for efficient group action. Similarly, Raker (1956) noted that the public reacts more favorably to local authority than to outsiders. In fact, attempts by "outsiders" may be met with considerable resistance, particularly if an attempt is made to deliberately circumvent the local leadership structure and not assume a position at least nominally subordinate to it (Logan, 1950). It is important to note, however, that this antagonism toward outside leaders is usually a function of the time elapsed since the actual impact. Immediately following impact anyone willing to work and make suggestions is accepted, while friction appears to develop after the disaster-struck population has had time to evaluate the relative merits of the outsiders in relation to the local officials.

Closely related to the fact that the affected populace tends to prefer local, preestablished leaders is the expectancy that these persons should lead in event of disaster, even though they actually may not be equipped to be of assistance or value. In conjunction with this notion, it has been noted that a preestablished leader who fails to take a leadership role in the disaster situation may find his status in the community irreparably damaged (NORC Report, 1953). It must be pointed out, however, that this type of sentiment appears to be most prevalent in small towns where community leaders normally function in several capacities concerning matters related to the community.

One of the major consistencies noted in all disaster reports is that the requirements for successful leadership tend to change over time. An influence attempt which is successful and effective in a particular situation at one period is often totally unsuccessful at a later time. While many psychological factors may account for this finding, the reports indicate that immediately following impact, speed of decision, decisiveness, and ability to initiate ac-

tions which reduce stress are important factors in determining leadership success. However, as time passes and the situation becomes somewhat stabilized, more calm deliberation, reflection, and consultation with subordinates is required. Thus, effective and successful leadership changes from an orientation toward action to an orientation toward integration and consideration of the several alternatives (Beach and Lucas, 1960).

Summary

On the basis of the above findings, the following propositions or hypotheses will be stated. As mentioned initially, it is assumed that these refer to general variables pertinent to the success or failure of disaster leadership regardless of the nature of the crisis-inducing agent.

1. Due to the necessity for rapid planning and rapid implementation of a community effort following disaster, the number of persons involved in policy decision must be reduced. However, the number of persons required to make decisions at the operational level must increase.

2. Leaders are afforded more influence during crisis periods than they possessed during noncrisis periods.

3. There are demands on the part of the disaster victims for a tangible, although perhaps temporary, program of action. In addition, there is a demand that these decisions be implemented in a bold and decisive manner.

4. In most instances disaster victims react most favorably when leadership is assumed by local individuals who were in positions of formal responsibility in time of crisis, even though they may not be equipped to actually be of assistance or value.

5. Different leadership skills are required during different phases of the disaster. Initially, effective leaders are decisive and action-oriented, but as the situation becomes more stabilized, effective leaders tend to be those who are more intellectually oriented.

By way of conclusion, it must be reemphasized that while much research has been reported on disasters and disaster behavior, our knowledge of leadership in such situations is woefully lacking. Almost none of the data has been quantified or is in a quantifiable form so that accurate comparisons can be made between various disasters. Similarly, no theories or models are presently available which incorporate leadership problems as they relate to varying disaster parameters. Thus, until our knowledge of disaster and disaster leadership is greatly extended, projections to future situations must be kept at the most general level.

REFERENCES

Barnard, C. I. *Dilemmas of leadership in the democratic process.* Princeton, N.J.: Princeton University Press, 1939.

Beach, H. D., & Lucas, R. A. *Individual and group behavior in a coal mine disaster.* Washington, D.C.: National Academy of Sciences—National Research Council, 1960. (Disaster Study No. 13, Publication No. 834)

Clifford, R. A. *The Rio Grande Flood: A comparative study of border communities in disaster.* Washington, D.C.: National Academy of Sciences—National Research Council, 1956. (Disaster Study No. 7, Publication No. 458)

Committee on disaster studies of the National Academy of Sciences. *Studies in the Holland Flood Disaster.* Washington, D.C., 1955.

Form, W. H., & Nosow, S. *Community in disaster.* New York: Harper & Row, 1958.

Janis, I. L. Problems of theory in the analysis of stress behavior. *Journal of Social Issues,* 1954, **10**, 19.

Logan, L. *Study of the effect of catastrophe on social disorganization.* Chevy Chase, Md.: The Johns Hopkins University, Operations Research Office, 1950 (ORO - T - 1940).

National Opinion Research Center. *Conference on field studies of reactions to disasters.* Chicago: University of Chicago Press, 1953.

Raker, J. W. *Emergency medical care in disasters: A summary of recorded experiences.* Washington, D.C.: National Academy of Sciences—National Research Council, 1956. (Disaster Study No. 6, Publication No. 457)

Wallace, A. C. *Tornado in Worchester: An exploratory study of individual and community behavior in an extreme situation.* Washington, D.C.: National Academy of Sciences—National Research Council, 1956. (Disaster Study No. 3, Publication No. 392)

Social Psychology: A Contemporary Perspective

Milton E. Rosenbaum
University of Iowa

It is at times the despair of the social psychologist to find that his contributions are relegated almost invariably to the last chapter or section of books purporting to review the fields of psychology. He does not, however, experience long-lasting discomfort, because he finally tells himself "this is what it was all about anyway" (a convenient mode of dissonance reduction).

Heredity, individual differences, learning, cognitive processes, motivation and emotion, personality and adjustment—the principal topics of this book—are all topics considered by social psychologists. One can add perception, memory, problem solving, psychophysiology, and other psychological issues. Then let us add anthropology, linguistics, sociology, political science, history, and any other area that deals with relations among men. Social psychology is an imperialistic discipline. Not only does it claim at times to encompass aspects of all the above disciplines but it claims to have an identity of its own.

Social psychology is, of course, most strongly related to its parent discipline, and the relationship may be regarded as a symbiotic one. For full understanding of the issues in social psychology, there is much dependency on the knowledge of perception, learning, cognitive processes, etc., that has been obtained in the highly controlled laboratories of the general psychologist. Reciprocally, the man who is studied in the controlled laboratory is inevitably a social being bringing with him a history of social psychological processes. The general psychologist simply chooses for the moment to ignore the contributions of social variables. Ultimately, neither general psychology nor social psychology can ignore their inherent relationship.

The psychologist approaching the study of social behavior faces the question of the appropriate strategy to employ in pursuing his goals. He has available two polar strategies: He can pursue his research on social behavior either as an extension or application of previously researched and apparently simpler nonsocial phenomena or as a distinctive event in its own right. As might be expected, most research in social psychology reflects some intermediate strategy.

In attempting to extend nonsocial theorizing, techniques, and findings to social behavior, one can assume that the same basic processes are operative. The choice to extend the theories and techniques of general psychology permits the social psychologist to begin his work with a foundation of basic principles, these can later be modified or even discarded if relevant data so dictate.

An instructive application of basic theorizing to social behavior is found in Zajonc's attempted integration of data related to performance in the presence of another organism (see p. 478). His contention that the mere presence of others is a source of arousal neatly accounts for facilitation of performance when the responses in question have been well learned, and for interference with performance when new responses are involved. This hypothesis was supported in an experiment deliberately designed to test it (Zajonc and Sales, 1966). Because of the apparent universality across organisms of the effects of the mere presence of others, Zajonc suggests that this source of arousal is an inherent property of organisms.

A recent development has indicated that the problem has greater complications than Zajonc was able to anticipate from the research literature available to him for his analysis. Cottrell (1968) has found that for humans it appears that only when others have the capability of evaluating a person's performance is their presence a source of arousal. The presence of others who are not capable of evaluation results in performance that is no different from performance when alone. Cottrell suggests that the presence of others is a learned source of drive, and he is currently exploring the possibility that the same inter-pretation is applicable to subhuman species.

This example of what happens when one applies basic principles drawn from general psychology to social behavior may be regarded as typical. Diverse data available to Zajonc seemed to require diverse interpretations invoking both nonsocial and uniquely social formulations. Application of a formulation drawn from general psychology seemed to do a good job of integrating the data. The availability of this integrative statement allowed Cottrell to test its tenability in a specially constructed experiment. The results suggest an alternative interpretation, but, and this is important to note, an interpretation that is also drawn from general psychology. It is likely that further research will lead to other modifications.

Zajonc and Cottrell's mode of exploration of the effects of the presence of others sug-gests one trend in social psychology research techniques. The tasks that the subjects per-formed in their experiments had been shown to be sensitive to arousal variations in clearly nonsocial contexts. The use of the same task with only the context varied makes it more likely that the dimensions of the social context causing the change can be identified. Until recently, social psychologists have not tended to repeat the use of procedures from experiment to experiment or to use tasks that have well-established histories in general psychology. Thus it has not always been possible to compare the outcomes of experiments addressed to the same issue.

At times, the social psychologist attempts to extend a principle of behavior drawn from general psychology by using social stimuli in place of the nonsocial stimuli originally em-ployed. Difficulties are frequently encountered. For example, the phenomenon of stimulus generalization has been studied in nonsocial contexts by employing stimulus events that are readily defined on physical dimensions. In studies with pigeons, subjects are trained to peck at a response key in the presence of a light of a particular wavelength or hue. Lights identical to the original in all stimulus dimensions *except* wavelength are then presented. The probability that the pecking response will be made to the new stimuli is related to their similarity in wavelength to the original training stimulus. Human subjects have also been shown to respond to physical stimuli on the basis of their relative similarity. To what extent does this hold true of responses to social stimuli?

A "simple" social stimulus might consist of a person or, because of its greater amen-ability to manipulation, the photograph of a person. We can train a subject to make a particular response when a particular stimulus photograph is presented. Can we now study the influence of the degree of similarity among different stimulus photographs? What dimensions of stimulus variation are related to response probability? We might choose height, eye color, nose length, posture, or any of a dozen others. Any of the pos-sible dimensions—or any combination of them—may be responded to in terms of similarity to the training stimulus. It would be somewhat difficult to secure a number of photo-graphs in which one physical attribute, e.g., nose length, varied while other attributes re-mained constant. A more realistic approach would be to allow other attributes to vary in an unsystematic manner—but in that case, the subjects might never realize which dimen-sion was the critical one. Thus the inherent complexity of social stimuli provides a stum-bling block to the adaptation of principles derived from research with less complex events. (Note that complex social stimuli do not in principle differ from complex nonsocial stimuli. Similar problems in specifying dimensional similarity would appear in relating abstract paintings to each other.)

For some purposes, the social psychologist interested in demonstrating the principle of stimulus generalization can obtain a partial solution to his problem. He can employ a normative college student population, asking them to rank a large number of photographs of persons on the basis of similarity to a standard reference photograph. The photographs receiving strong agreement as to their rank are selected for use in the experiment. A group of subjects drawn from the same college population is trained to respond to the standard stimulus, then presented with the other photographs. This technique for dealing with events that are not amenable to physical dimensionalization is increasingly popular in social psychology and other areas that contend with complex stimuli. While it is only a partial solution to the problem of stimulus specification, it has produced surprisingly reliable and interesting results.

To many psychologists, the strategy of employing the techniques of general psychology as the basis for examination of social behavior is unacceptable. This strategy frequently involves the adaptation of procedures developed in the traditional laboratory—procedures that, while highly controlled, tend to be rather artificial. Although it may provide systematic data, the procedure of describing a fictitious person by providing a series of adjectives is hardly one encountered in daily experience. There is a strong current disposition to examine social behavior in as natural a context as possible without sacrificing the precision of information provided by the experimental method. Research conducted and sponsored by Kurt Lewin at the turn of the 1940's has become the prototype for the field experiment. The studies by Coch and French (p. 488), Kelley (p. 484), and Milgram (p. 496) follow Lewin's model. In each of these studies, the subjects were carrying out essentially natural life activities, the naturalism decreasing in the order of the above listing. Although the subjects in Milgram's study were performing in a psychological laboratory, the decisions they had to face were of demonstrable importance to them.

The range of issues explored by social psychologists has been widened by use of the naturalistic experiment. In the more liberalized form of this type of experiment, subjects are studied in the midst of their everyday activities. For example, Bryan and Test (1967) studied the tendency of people to make street-corner donations into Salvation Army kettles. They varied opportunity versus nonopportunity to observe a model making donations and the race of the model. In the more conservative form of the naturalistic experiment, subjects are exposed to laboratory procedures but as in Milgram's study (p. 496) a variety of procedural features are introduced to assess behavior that may be regarded as not peculiar to the laboratory.

As in other areas of psychology, research trends in social psychology are affected by technical developments, societal problems and pressures for their solution, striking new theoretical statements, and the occurrence of unexpected empirical findings. Recent research as reported in current professional publications shows characteristics of all these sources of research inspiration. Several major trends seem worthy of review.

Interest in the social behavior of subhuman species has increased markedly. Until recently, research in this area was conducted sporadically by experimenters who were more interested in other aspects of animal behavior. Adventures into the study of their social behavior appeared to be avocational rather than of series interest, and follow-up studies were infrequent. The work of Harlow (p. 353) and his associates in studies of maternal behavior and consequent offspring behavior has represented a serious forward step in carrying out studies with species whose social development can be subjected to laboratory control. Zajonc (1968) has recently published a book in which the range of experiments on the social behavior of animals is presented. It is likely that in the near future this area will receive increasing attention.

The social development of the human child has been of continuing interest but the bulk of data until recently was derived from observational or interview studies, among them many of striking importance (e.g., Sears, Maccoby, and Levin, 1957). Laboratory study of children's social behavior has burgeoned in the past decade. Three significant subtrends may be noted.

The first subtrend involves special attention to the social events that serve as reinforcement for children's learning and performance. Much current interest was sparked by studies by Gewirtz and Baer (1958a, 1958b) in which they found that deprivation or satiation of social reinforcements (verbal approbation) seemed to affect responsivity of nursery school children much like the deprivation or satiation of food and water affects the performance of subhuman species. Because of interpretive disagreements concerning the basis for these effects, much research on the determinants, characteristics, and consequences of social reinforcement was initiated. The data are now abundant and reveal a complexity of relations such that it appears that no currently available theoretical framework can satisfactorily account for the effects of social reinforcement. This is unquestionably an area in which important theory building and hypothesis testing will take place in the near future.

A second subtrend involves systematic attention to imitation and observational learning. Research in this area includes the study of (1) the determinants of spontaneous matching of the behavior of a model; (2) the process of learning to respond to the environment as a function of observation of the behavior of another person; and (3) the acquisition of the general response style of another, which includes his attitudes, values, etc. The work of Bandura (pp. 389, 473) has stimulated much of the activity in this area. He has argued that response acquisition by observing others is a case of no-trial learning. He contrasts observational learning with the more frequently studied event of "learning by doing" that occurs in nonsocial contexts. Research in this area is stimulated by questions concerning the necessity for reinforcement of the model's or the observer's behavior, the degree to which the modeled behavior leads to learning as opposed to facilitation of responses already in the observer's repertory,[1] and the conditions under which the observed responses are generalized to new situations and to new but related responses.

A particular interest of the writer is the comparison of learning by performers and observers (Rosenbaum and Arenson, 1968). It has been found that under some conditions observers learn more than the performers they observe. This effect seems to occur when performers, while learning, are required to perform task-related responses that are irrelevant to and interfering with the responses being learned.

A third subtrend in the study of the social behavior of children is inspired by the theorizing of Jean Piaget (see Smock, pp. 122–125). Although Piaget has been in general a significant influence on recent research in child behavior, those interested in social behavior have attended primarily to his contentions concerning the development of moral judgment. As is generally the case in Piaget's theorizing, he argues that children proceed through irreversible successive stages in cognitive development such that although an earlier stage may be a precursor for a later stage, behavior related to the earlier stage may be totally absent in the later stage. More specifically, he posits that in evaluating behavioral transgressions children first assess guilt only in terms of amount of damage done without regard for intent of the transgressor. At a later stage, only intent is assessed as the basis for attribution of degree of guilt. These and other contentions have served as the spur for empirical tests of the formulation, with resulting support or nonsupport but always with increased understanding of the development of childhood morality.

The above three subtrends in the study of the social behavior of children are a few among many receiving major research attention. The general problem area is likely to be attended to increasingly in the future, both because of a strong desire to understand the antecedents of adult behavior and because of great societal pressure to obtain basic information applicable to child rearing and educational practices.

One strong trend in dealing with social behavior is concurrent with a similar development in general psychology. Attempts to state and evaluate, by means of mathematical language, the theories and findings of experimental studies occupy a significant portion of the attention of researchers. The utilization of mathematical equations for these purposes has implications for both the form of the theories developed and the type of empirical

---

[1] A possible interpretation of the results obtained by Bandura, Grusec, and Menlove (p. 473) is that the children were strongly desirous of approaching the dogs but required evidence of the safety of doing so. The initial demonstrations by the model may have led to the expectancy that all dogs in the experimental context were safe.

data collected. Superficially, it would appear that the complexities and the flow of social behavior would make it less than amenable to the precise statement necessary for the application of mathematical terminology, but increasing numbers of problem areas are currently being studied under the aegis of mathematical thinking. These include the study of attitude and opinion change, social interaction, conformity, small group process, and group problem solving, and it is likely that other social psychological concerns will be added in the near future. As an example of this mode of theorizing, some of the simplest mathematical models have been applied to the area of personality impression formation. Unlike the naturalistic mode of experimentation exemplified by Kelly's study (p. 484), the typical procedure involves reading to subjects sets of personality-trait adjectives describing a fictitious person, with instructions to rate this person on a numerical likability dimension. Adjectives are prescaled on likability and rough quantitative values are assigned. Among the variables that have been studied are the effect of the number of adjectives, the relative influence of the position of adjectives in the series, and the effect of the relatedness of the adjectives to each other. Sometimes the results reflect a simple averaging of the values of the individual adjectives in the series. Other results indicate a differential weighting of the items in the series. A series of studies in which the writer participated (Rosenbaum and Levin, 1968a, 1968b, 1969) investigated the influence of the supposed source of the adjective information. Sources consisted of occupational titles which had been prescaled as to their "value as an informant concerning the characteristics of others." It was found that likability impressions were accounted for by a weighted average equation with differential weighting being given to information as a function of the credibility of the source providing the information.

One of the attractions of mathematical models is that they help clarify similar processes underlying findings in apparently diverse and unrelated areas. Research on the formation of personality impression has now come to be viewed, at least in part, as falling under the more general area of information processing. Contributions to this more general area are made in the study of learning, memory, perception, decision making, and many other topics. Another attraction is that mathematical models generally employ a more rigorous statement of theoretical propositions than verbal theories allow. One can readily see whether or not data fit the model or whether the model requires modification. A principal danger of mathematicized theorizing, however, is that the choice of data to collect is based on amenability to quantification. Such data are not readily available in natural contexts, and the artificiality of the procedures may render the data and theory trivial. It remains to be seen if our natural mode of forming impressions of new acquaintances conforms to an averaging model or any statable equation.

During the past decade the dominant form of theorizing in social psychology has been guided by various consistency theories that have been elaborated or applied distinctively by each user of the formulation. Briefly, the formulation suggests that man is relatively content only when there is consistency among his various attributes and in relation to his environment. Any inconsistency produces discomfort and leads to an effort to produce consistency.

Similar formulations have appeared frequently in science, but in recent years social psychologists have given great attention to one or another variant of the consistency formulation.[2] The primary source of inspiration for research in this area derives from Leon Festinger and his associates. Festinger's (1957) theory of cognitive dissonance has the combined merits of simplicity of statement and the capability of embracing a large body of data. The basic propositions of the theory are that (1) dissonance occurs when two cognitive elements are related to each other such that "the obverse of one element would follow from the other" (p. 17); (2) "dissonance, being psychologically uncomfortable, will motivate the person to try to reduce dissonance and achieve consonance" (p. 3); and (3) any

---

[2] A recent book, *Theories of Cognitive Consistency: A Sourcebook*, edited by Abelson, Arenson, McGuire, Newcomb, Rosenberg, and Tannenbaum (1968) contains 84 original selections contributed by 63 authors. Only a portion of the eligible contributors to this area are represented.

situations and information which are likely to increase the dissonance will be actively avoided. Attention has been given to inconsistencies that arise in relation to a person's opinions, attitudes, values, and behavior. A striking example of a dissonance-producing situation is the plight of the contemporary cigarette smoker. The inconsistency he faces consists of the two antagonistic cognitions, that he is smoking and that, according to a variety of sources of knowledge, smoking leads to cancer. The theory suggests that action will be taken to reduce the dissonance. This can be accomplished in a variety of ways which include (1) changing the behavior, e.g., stopping smoking (an option chosen by some people, but according to sales data, not very many people); (2) changing the environmental information, e.g., derogating the sources of information that link cigarettes with cancer or avoiding media and persons affirming the relation between smoking and cancer; and (3) adding new cognitive elements, i.e., seeking out information that is critical of the dissonance-provoking research.

The behaviors that have been studied under the aegis of dissonance theory represent a remarkable range. It was predicted and found that after buying an automobile, purchasers read advertisements for that make of car more than they read competitors' ads; a group that predicted the end of the world proselytized for supporters more after disconfirmation of their prediction than before the disconfirmation; and girls who go through a very embarrassing initiation to join a discussion group and then discover it to be very dull, like the group more than girls who go through a mild initiation or none at all. These examples are only a few drawn from what is probably the largest outflow of research stemming from a single theoretical position in the history of social psychology.

The theoretical statement and some of the events that have been explored under the framework of the theory would suggest that all our behavior may involve dissonance arousal and efforts to reduce dissonance, and therefore we are constantly devoting our efforts to reducing dissonance. Several variables play a role in affecting the magnitude of dissonance and the degree of subsequent effects. For example, the importance of the dissonant cognitions plays a significant role. More dissonance is likely to occur if a man takes a job and then discovers that his new employer is about to dissolve the business than if he buys a shirt in one shop and discovers that it is less expensive in a shop around the corner. Although theoretically some dissonance is evoked in the shirt-buying example, its magnitude is small and hence the consequent effect may be negligible. Some amounts of dissonance may be tolerable and even useful. As Aronson (1968) has pointed out, a man who discovers a small leak in the basement of his new $50,000 house will not avoid the information but will immediately set about to arrange appropriate repairs.

One of the great attractions of dissonance theory is that effects can be predicted that are difficult to account for by other formulations including those inspired by "common sense." A case in point is the results of a much-discussed experiment by Festinger and Carlsmith (1959). College student subjects were brought to the laboratory and performed a task that was without question exceedingly boring and unattractive. Some of the subjects were then asked to assist the experimenter by engaging the next subject in conversation and indicating that the experiment was very enjoyable. Half of these subjects were given $1.00 for doing this and half were given $20.00. Finally, all subjects, including some who were not asked to converse with the next subject, responded to questions concerning the attractiveness of the original task.

Although a common-sense analysis may suggest that the more you are paid to say something is attractive, the more you will later believe that it was attractive, cognitive dissonance theory led to a prediction supported by the data. Subjects who received $1.00 for "lying" rated the task as more attractive than subjects who received $20.00 or those who were not asked to lie. Subjects who told the other subject that the task was attractive when they knew that it was not attractive could be expected to experience dissonance. However, little if any dissonance is likely to be evoked when $20.00 is available as a justification for lying. Subjects who lie for $1.00 have little justification and must seek some means for reducing the dissonance. Apparently, the most amenable manner for doing so is to convince oneself that the task was really attractive and thus not be lying after all.

Several methodological questions and alternate interpretations have been introduced by critics evaluating the details of the Festinger and Carlsmith experiment. Most of these criticisms have been answered by replications involving relevant procedure changes and an extensive series of experiments testing similar unusual predictions. Although different formulations may be invoked in interpreting each individual experiment, as McGuire (1966) has noted, the power of cognitive dissonance theory is that it can embrace such a wide variety of data. Only recently have alternate formulations appeared that may well challenge the power of dissonance theory (e.g., Bem, 1967). It remains to be seen how robust dissonance theory remains in the next decade and if other theories arise with similar or greater capability to generate research.

REFERENCES

Abelson, R. P., Aronson, E., McGuire, W. J., Newcomb, T. M., Rosenberg, M. J., & Tannenbaum, P. H. (Eds.) *Theories of cognitive consistency: A sourcebook.* Chicago: Rand McNally, 1968.

Aronson, E. Dissonance theory: Progress and problems. In R. P. Abelson, E. Aronson, W. J. McGuire, T. M. Newcomb, M. J. Rosenberg, & P. H. Tannenbaum (Eds.), *Theories of cognitive consistency: A sourcebook.* Chicago: Rand McNally, 1968. Pp. 5–27.

Bem, D. J. Self perception: An alternative interpretation of cognitive dissonance phenomena. *Psychological Review,* 1967, **74,** 183–200.

Bryan, J. H., & Test, M. A. Models and helping: Naturalistic studies in aiding behavior. *Journal of Personality and Social Psychology,* 1967, **6,** 400–407.

Festinger, L. *A theory of cognitive dissonance.* Evanston, Ill.: Row, Peterson, 1957.

Festinger, L., & Carlsmith, J. M. Cognitive consequences of forced compliance. *Journal of Abnormal and Social Psychology,* 1959, **58,** 203–210.

Cottrell, N. B. Performance in the presence of other human beings: Mere presence, audience, and affiliation effects. In E. C. Simmel, R. A. Hoppe, & G. A. Milton (Eds.), *Social facilitation and imitative behavior.* Boston: Allyn & Bacon, 1968.

Gewirtz, J. L., & Baer, D. M. Deprivation and satiation of social reinforcers as drive conditions. *Journal of Abnormal and Social Psychology,* 1958, **57,** 165–172. (a)

Gewirtz, J. L., & Baer, D. M. The effect of brief social deprivation on behaviors for a social reinforcer. *Journal of Abnormal and Social Psychology,* 1958, **56,** 49–56. (b)

McGuire, W. J. Attitudes and opinions. *Annual Review of Psychology,* 1966, **17,** 475–514.

Rosenbaum, M. E., & Arenson, S. J. Observational learning: Some theory, some variables, some findings. In E. C. Simmel, R. A. Hoppe, & G. A. Milton (Eds.), *Social facilitation and imitative behavior.* Boston: Allyn & Bacon, 1968.

Rosenbaum, M. E., & Levin, I. P. Impression formation as a function of relative amounts of information presented by high and low credibility sources. *Psychonomic Science,* 1968, **12,** 349–350. (a)

Rosenbaum, M. E., & Levin, I. P. Impression formation as a function of source credibility and order of presentation of contradictory information. *Journal of Personality and Social Psychology,* 1968, **10,** 167–174. (b)

Rosenbaum, M. E., & Levin, I. P. Impression formation as a function of source credibility and the polarity of information. *Journal of Personality and Social Psychology,* 1969, **12,** 34–37.

Sears, R. R., Maccoby, E. E., & Levin, H. *Patterns of Child Rearing.* New York: Harper & Row, 1957.

Zajonic, R. B. (Ed.) *Animal social psychology: A reader of experimental studies.* New York: Wiley, 1968.

Zajonc, R. B., & Sales, S. M. Social facilitation of dominant and subordinate responses. *Journal of Experimental Social Psychology,* 1966, **2,** 160–168.

CORRELATION CHART

The following chart is provided as a guide for using this collection of readings in conjunction with thirteen of the most widely used Introductory Psychology texts. The numbers in the left-hand column refer to the Chapters of the textbooks; the numbers in the other columns indicate related readings which are presented in this book.

Deese, James. *General Psychology*. Boston: Allyn & Bacon, Inc., 1967.

Edwards, David C. *General Psychology*. New York: The Macmillan Company, 1968.

Hebb, Donald O. *A Textbook of Psychology*, 2nd ed. Philadelphia: W. B. Saunders Company, 1968.

Hilgard, Ernest R., and Atkinson, Richard C. *Introduction to Psychology*, 4th ed. New York: Harcourt, Brace, & World, Inc., 1967.

Kendler, Howard H. *Basic Psychology*, 2nd ed. New York: Appleton-Century-Crofts, 1968.

Kimble, Gregory A., and Garmezy, Norman. *Principles of General Psychology*, 3rd ed. New York: Ronald Press Company, 1968.

Krech, David, Crutchfield, Richard S., and Livson, Norman. *Elements of Psychology*, 2nd ed. New York: Alfred A. Knopf, 1969.

McKeachie, Wilbert J., and Doyle, Charlotte L. *Psychology*. Massachusetts: Addison-Wesley Publishing Company, Inc., 1966.

Morgan, Clifford T., and King, Richard A. *Introduction to Psychology*, 3rd ed. New York: McGraw-Hill Book Company, 1966.

Munn, Norman L. *Psychology: The Fundamentals of Human Adjustment*, 5th ed. New York, Houghton Mifflin Company, 1966.

Ruch, Floyd L. *Psychology and Life*, 7th ed. Glenview, Illinois: Scott, Foresman and Company, 1967.

Sanford, Fillmore H. *Psychology: A Scientific Study of Man*, 2nd ed. Belmont, California: Wadsworth Publishing Company, Inc., 1965.

Whittaker, James O. *Introduction to Psychology*. Philadelphia: W. B. Saunders Company, 1965.

Chapter	Deese	Edwards	Hebb
1	1–4, 7–9	1–4, 6	1–4, 51, 52, 55, 56, 59
2	——	46	41
3	26–31, 46	44, 45, 47–50	——
4	45, 48	5	26
5	49, 50	26, 27–31, 35	27–31
6	19, 24, 35–43	32, 33, 36–43	32–34
7	32–34	60–68	10, 11, 15, 16
8	——	10–16	——
9	5	17–25	13, 14, 17–25, 53
10	10–16, 47, 60	53, 54	12, 43, 46–50, 54
11	6, 17, 18	51, 52	45, 60–68
12	20–23, 25	55–59	5, 57, 58
13	44, 53, 54	7–9, 34	35–40, 42, 43
14	51, 52, 55–59, 61		6–9
15	63, 67		
16	62, 65, 66, 68		
17	64		
18			
19			
20			
21			
22			
23			
24			

Chapter	Hilgard	Kendler	Kimble
1	1, 3, 4	4, 6	1, 2, 7–9
2	16	1–3, 8, 9	3, 4
3	11, 12, 14, 15, 47, 60, 61	——	6
4	13	10, 12	10–12, 15, 16
5	45, 46, 48	——	46
6	49, 50	5	——
7	62, 67	46	5
8	——	16, 45, 47, 48	——
9	5	11, 26–31	26–28, 34
10	57, 58	32, 33	29–31, 45
11	26, 27, 29–31	15, 39–43	35–37, 39–43
12	31, 33	35–37	32, 33
13	34	49, 50	49
14	19, 24, 35–43	44, 51–54	14, 47, 60
15	6	55–59	49, 50, 67
16	17, 18, 20–23, 25	14, 60–63, 65–68	51, 52
17	10	13, 17–25, 38	——
18	44	7, 34, 64	13, 17, 18, 20–23
19	53, 54		19, 24, 25, 38
20	51, 52		44, 53, 54
21	59		57–59
22	28, 55, 56		55, 56
23	63–66, 68		61–66, 68
24	2, 7–9		

Chapter	Krech	McKeachie	Morgan
1	1–4, 6–9, 10–16	1–4, 6–9	1–4, 7–9
2	5	14	10–16
3	26–34, 35–43	——	26, 29, 35
4	44–50	10, 16	27, 30, 31, 33, 34
5	17–25, 51–69, 60–68	26, 29–31	32, 36–43
6		5	45, 47, 48
7		45–49	49, 50
8		27, 28, 34	——
9		15, 32, 33, 35, 37, 39–43	——
10		17–25, 36, 38	5
11		44, 51, 52	6, 25
12		53, 54	17–24, 53, 54
13		11–13, 50, 60, 61	44, 51, 52
14		55–59	——
15		62, 68	28, 55–59
16		63–67	60–62, 65, 66, 68
17			63, 67
18			64
19			——
20			46
21			
22			
23			
24			

Chapter	Munn	Ruch	Sanford	Whittaker
1	1–4, 7–9, 44	1–4, 7–9	1–4	1–4, 6–9
2	——	——	7–9	——
3	6, 17, 18	10–16, 20, 37, 60	10–16, 47	10–16, 60
4	10–13, 16	44	46	46
5	20–23, 25	6, 17, 18, 21–23, 25, 53	6, 17, 18, 25	45, 57, 58
6	45–48	26–31, 35	5	47–50
7	49, 50	32–34	19–24	61
8	51, 52, 67	——	49	51, 52, 59
9	53–59	5	45, 49, 50	44, 55, 56
10	26–28, 34	19, 24, 36, 38–43	——	26–28, 31
11	29–31	47–49	——	29, 30, 32–34
12	32, 33	45, 46, 54	26–31	35–43
13	19, 24, 35–38	50, 51, 52, 57, 58	32–34	54
14	15, 39–43	55, 56, 59	35–43	5
15	——	61–63, 65, 66, 68	44, 53, 54	——
16	5	64, 67	51, 52	17–25
17	14, 60–63, 65, 66, 68		56–59	53
18	64		60–68	62, 63
19				64–68
20				
21				
22				
23				
24				